LITERATURE The Human Experience

Second Edition

LiTERATURE The Human Experience

Second Edition

RICHARD ABCARIAN AND MARVIN KLOTZ, EDITORS

California State University, Northridge

St. Martin's Press   New York

Library of Congress Catalog Card Number: 77-86004
Copyright © 1978 by St. Martin's Press, Inc.
All Rights Reserved.
Manufactured in the United States of America.
098
fedcba
For information, write: St. Martin's Press, Inc.,
175 Fifth Avenue, New York, N. Y. 10010
ISBN: 0-312-48790-8

ACKNOWLEDGMENTS

ABC/DUNHILL MUSIC, INC.: "The Royal Scam," written by W. Becker/D. Fagen, Copyright © 1976 by ABC/Dunhill Music, Inc. Used by permission only. All rights reserved.

ANTIOCH REVIEW: "Advice to My Son" by J. Peter Meinke. From *Antioch Review*, Vol. XXV, 1965, p. 374. Reprinted by permission of the publisher.

ATHENEUM PUBLISHERS, INC.: "The Dover Bitch" from *The Hard Hours* by Anthony Hecht. Copyright © 1959, 1967 by Anthony E. Hecht. Reprinted by permission of Atheneum Publishers.

RICHARD W. BARON PUBLISHING CO., INC.: "After the Rain" from *Ain't No Ambulances for No Nigguhs Tonight* by Stanley Crouch. Copyright © 1972 by Stanley Crouch. Reprinted by permission of the Richard W. Baron Publishing Co., Inc.

BROADSIDE PRESS: "Dreams" by Nikki Giovanni from *Black Judgement,* Copyright © 1968 by Nikki Giovanni. Reprinted by permission of Broadside Press.

JONATHAN CAPE LTD.: "Naming of Parts" and "Judging Distances" from *A Map of Verona* by Henry Reed. Reprinted by permission of Jonathan Cape Ltd.

CHAPPELL MUSIC CO.: "Do What You Want, Be What You Are" by Daryl Hall and John Oates. Copyright © 1976 by Unichappell Music, Inc. and Hot-Cha Music Co. International Copyright Secured. All rights reserved. Used by permission.

CHATTO AND WINDUS LTD.: "On a Squirrel Crossing the Road in Autumn, in New England" from *Collected Poems 1930–1976* by Richard Eberhart. Reprinted by permission of Richard Eberhart and Chatto and Windus Ltd.

"The Last Laugh" and "Dulce et Decorum Est" from *The Collected Poems of Wilfred Owen* edited by C. Day Lewis, together with the early version of "Last Words" by Wilfred Owen. Reprinted by permission of the Owen Estate and Chatto and Windus Ltd.

CONTINENTAL TOTAL MEDIA PROJECT, INC.: "Suzanne," words and music by Leonard Cohen. Published by Continental Total Media Project Inc., 515 Madison Ave., New York, N. Y. 10022. Reprinted by permission of the publisher.

THOMAS Y. CROWELL COMPANY, INC.: "The Man Who Lived Underground" from *Eight Men* by Richard Wright. Copyright 1944 by L. B. Fischer Publishing Corp. Reprinted by permission of Thomas Y. Crowell Company, Inc.

CURTIS BROWN LTD.: "To Room Nineteen" by Doris Lessing. Reprinted by permission of Curtis Brown Ltd., London, on behalf of Doris Lessing.

JOAN DAVES: "My Oedipus Complex" by Frank O'Connor from *The Stories of Frank O'Connor*. Reprinted by permission of Joan Daves. Copyright ‹ 1950 by Frank O'Connor.

CATHERINE DAVIS: "After a Time" by Catherine Davis. Reprinted by permission of the author.

J. M. DENT & SONS LTD.: "Everyman" (Anonymous) edited by A. C. Cawley from *Everyman, and Medieval Miracle Plays*, Everyman's Library series. Reprinted by permission of J. M. Dent & Sons Ltd., Publishers.

The Secret Sharer by Joseph Conrad. Reprinted by permission of J. M. Dent & Sons, Ltd. and the Trustees of the Joseph Conrad Estate.

"Fern Hill" and "Do Not Go Gentle into That Good Night" from *Collected Poems* by Dylan Thomas. Reprinted by permission of J. M. Dent & Sons Ltd. and the Trustees for the Copyrights of the late Dylan Thomas.

THE DIAL PRESS: "Going to Meet the Man," excerpted from the book *Going To Meet the Man* by James Baldwin. Copyright ‹ 1948, 1951, 1957, 1958, 1960, 1965 by James Baldwin. Reprinted by permission of The Dial Press.

DODD, MEAD & COMPANY, INC.: "We Wear the Mask" by Paul Laurence Dunbar. Reprinted by permission of Dodd, Mead & Company, Inc. from *The Complete Poems of Paul Laurence Dunbar*.

DOUBLEDAY & COMPANY, INC.: "First Confession" from *Nude Descending a Staircase* by X. J. Kennedy. Copyright 1951 by X. J. Kennedy. Reprinted by permission of Doubleday & Company, Inc.

"Dolor," copyright 1943 Modern Poetry Association, Inc. and "Elegy for Jane," copyright 1950 by Theodore Roethke from the book *The Collected Poems of Theodore Roethke*. Reprinted by permission of Doubleday & Company, Inc.

"Between the World and Me" from *White Man, Listen!* by Richard Wright. Copyright ‹ 1957 by Richard Wright. Reprinted by permission of Doubleday & Company, Inc.

ALAN DUGAN: "Love Song: I and Thou" by Alan Dugan. Copyright ‹ 1961 by Alan Dugan. Originally published in *Poems, 1961* by Yale University Press. Reprinted by permission of the author.

E. P. DUTTON & CO., INC.: "Everyman" (Anonymous) from the book *Everyman and Medieval Miracle Plays*. Edited and with an Introduction by A. C. Cawley. Published by E. P. Dutton & Co., Inc, in a paperback edition and used with their permission.

"In a Spring Still Not Written Of" from the book *Views from a Ferris Wheel* by Robert Wallace. Published by E. P. Dutton & Co., Inc. and used with their permission.

"People" from the book *Selected Poems* by Yevgeny Yevtushenko. Translated by Robin Milner-Gulland and Peter Levi. Copyright ‹ 1962 by Robin Milner-Gulland and Peter Levi. Published by E. P. Dutton & Co., Inc. and used with their permission.

HARLAN ELLISON: " 'Repent, Harlequin!' Said the Ticktockman" by Harlan Ellison. Copyright ‹ 1965 by Galaxy Publishing Corporation. All rights reassigned, 1966, to the Author. Reprinted by permission of the Author and the Author's agent, Robert P. Mills, Ltd.

EYRE METHUEN LTD.: *The Dumb Waiter* by Harold Pinter. Reprinted by permission of the publishers, Eyre Methuen. Copyright ‹ 1959 and 1960.

FABER AND FABER LTD.: "In Memory of W. B. Yeats," "That Night When Joy Began" (from *Five Songs*), and "The Unknown Citizen" by W. H. Auden. Reprinted by permission of Faber and Faber Ltd. from *Collected Poems* by W. H. Auden edited by Edward Mendelson. "Musée des Beaux Arts" by W. H. Auden. Reprinted by permission of Faber and Faber Ltd. from *Collected Shorter Poems* by W. H. Auden.

"The Love Song of J. Alfred Prufrock" by T. S. Eliot. Reprinted by permission of Faber and Faber Ltd. from *Collected Poems 1909–1962* by T. S. Eliot.

"Innocence" by Thom Gunn. Reprinted by permission of Faber and Faber Ltd. from *My Sad Captains* by Thom Gunn.

"Relic" by Ted Hughes. Reprinted by permission of Faber and Faber Ltd. from *Lupercal* by Ted Hughes.

FARRAR, STRAUS & GIROUX, INC.: "The Sandman" by Donald Barthelme. Reprinted with the permission of Farrar, Straus & Giroux, Inc. from *Sadness* by Donald Barthelme. Copyright ⊂ 1970, 1971, 1972 by Donald Barthelme.

"Innocence" from *My Sad Captains* by Thom Gunn. Reprinted with the permission of Farrar, Straus & Giroux, Inc. from *Moly and My Sad Captains* by Thom Gunn. Copyright ⊂ 1961, 1971, 1973 by Thom Gunn.

"The Lottery" by Shirley Jackson. From *The Lottery* by Shirley Jackson. Copyright 1948, 1949 by Shirley Jackson, copyright renewed ⊂ 1976 by Laurence Hyman, Barry Hyman, Mrs. Sarah Webster, and Mrs. Joanne Schnurer. "The Lottery" appeared originally in *The New Yorker*.

"Losses" from *The Complete Poems* by Randall Jarrell. Copyright 1948 by Randall Jarrell, renewed copyright ⊂ 1975 by Mary von Schrader Jarrell. "Death of the Ball Turret Gunner" from *The Complete Poems* by Randall Jarrell. Copyright 1945 by Randall Jarrell, renewed copyright ⊂ 1972 by Mrs. Randall Jarrell.

"Idiots First" by Bernard Malamud. Reprinted with the permission of Farrar, Straus & Giroux, Inc. from *Idiots First* by Bernard Malamud. Copyright ⊂ 1961, 1963 by Bernard Malamud.

JUDY GRAHN: "The Marilyn Monroe Poem" from *Edward the Dyke and Other Poems* ⊂ 1971 by Judy Grahn. Published by The Women's Press Collective, 5251 Broadway, Oakland, Calif. 94618.

GROVE PRESS, INC.: "Unwanted" from *Stand Up Friend With Me* by Edward Field. Reprinted by permission of Grove Press, Inc. Copyright ⊂ 1963 by Edward Field.

The Lesson by Eugene Ionesco. Reprinted by permission of Grove Press, Inc. Copyright ⊂ 1958 by Grove Press, Inc.

The Dumb Waiter by Harold Pinter. Reprinted by permission of Grove Press, Inc. Copyright ⊂ 1960 by Harold Pinter.

HARCOURT BRACE JOVANOVICH, INC.: "next to of course god america i" and "nobody loses all the time" by E. E. Cummings, copyright 1926 by Horace Liveright; renewed 1954 by E. E. Cummings. Reprinted from *Complete Poems 1913–1962* by E. E. Cummings by permission of Harcourt Brace Jovanovich, Inc. "if everything happens that can't be done," copyright 1944 by E. E. Cummings; renewed 1972 by Nancy Andrews. Reprinted from *Complete Poems 1913–1962* by E. E. Cummings by permission of Harcourt Brace Jovanovich, Inc. "the Cambridge ladies who live in furnished souls," copyright 1923, 1951 by E. E. Cummings. Reprinted from *Complete Poems 1913–1962* by E. E. Cummings by permission of Harcourt Brace Jovanovich, Inc.

"The Love Song of J. Alfred Prufrock" from *Collected Poems 1909–1962* by T. S. Eliot, copyright 1936 by Harcourt Brace Jovanovich, Inc.; copyright ⊂ 1963, 1964 by T. S. Eliot. Reprinted by permission of Harcourt Brace Jovanovich, Inc.

Molière's *The Misanthrope* translated by Richard Wilbur, copyright ⊂ 1954, 1955 by Richard Wilbur. Reprinted by permission of Harcourt Brace Jovanovich, Inc. CAUTION: Professionals and amateurs are hereby warned that this translation, being fully protected under the copyright laws of the United States, the British Empire, including the Dominion of Canada, and all other countries which are signatories to the Universal Copyright Convention and the International Copyright Union, is subject to royalty. All rights, including professional, amateur, motion picture, recitation, lecturing, public reading, radio broadcasting, and television, are strictly reserved. Particular emphasis is laid on the questions of readings, permission for which must be secured from the author's agent in writing. Inquiries on professional rights (except for amateur rights) should be addressed to Mr. Gilbert Parker, Curtis Brown, Ltd., 575 Madison Avenue, New York, N. Y. 10022. The amateur acting rights are controlled by the Dramatists Play Service, 440 Park Avenue South, New York, N. Y. 10016. No amateur performance of the play may be given without obtaining in advance the written permission of the Dramatists Play Service, Inc., and paying the requisite fee.

"Good Country People" by Flannery O'Connor. From *A Good Man Is Hard To Find and Other Stories*, copyright 1955 by Flannery O'Connor. Reprinted by permission of Harcourt Brace Jovanovich, Inc.

"The Jilting of Granny Weatherall" by Katherine Anne Porter. Copyright 1930, 1958 by Katherine Anne Porter. Reprinted from her volume *Flowering Judas and Other Stories* by permission of Harcourt Brace Jovanovich, Inc.

Antigone by Sophocles: An English Version by Dudley Fitts and Robert Fitzgerald, copyright 1939 by Harcourt Brace Jovanovich, Inc.; copyright 1967 by Dudley Fitts and Robert Fitzgerald. Reprinted by permission of the publisher. CAUTION: All rights, including professional, amateur, motion picture, recitation, lecturing, public reading, radio broadcasting, and television are strictly reserved. Inquiries on all rights should be addressed to Harcourt Brace Jovanovich, Inc., 757 Third Avenue, New York, N. Y. 10017.

"The Pardon" by Richard Wilbur. Copyright 1948, 1949, 1950 by Richard Wilbur. Reprinted from his volume *Ceremony and Other Poems* by permission of Harcourt Brace Jovanovich, Inc.

HARPER & ROW, PUBLISHERS, INC.: "The Accident Has Occurred" from *Power Politics* by Margaret Atwood. Copyright ‹ 1971 by Margaret Atwood. Reprinted by permission of Harper & Row, Publishers, Inc.

From *The World of Gwendolyn Brooks* (1971) by Gwendolyn Brooks: "The Sundays of Satin-Legs Smith," Copyright 1945 by Gwendolyn Brooks Blakely; "Life for My Child Is Simple," Copyright 1949 by Gwendolyn Brooks Blakely. "First Fight, Then Fiddle" from *Selected Poems* (1963) by Gwendolyn Brooks, Copyright 1949 by Gwendolyn Brooks Blakely. Reprinted by permission of Harper & Row, Publishers, Inc.

"Incident" from *On These I Stand* by Countee Cullen. Copyright 1925 by Harper & Row, Publishers, Inc.; renewed 1953 by Ida M. Cullen. Reprinted by permission of Harper & Row, Publishers, Inc.

"Relic" from *Selected Poems* (1974) by Ted Hughes. Copyright ‹ 1958 by Ted Hughes. Reprinted by permission of Harper & Row, Publishers, Inc.

"Will" from *The Privilege* by Maxine Kumin. Copyright ‹ 1962 by Maxine Kumin. Reprinted by permission of Harper & Row, Publishers, Inc.

"Daddy" from *Ariel* (1966) by Sylvia Plath. Copyright ‹ 1963 by Ted Hughes. Reprinted by permission of Harper & Row, Publishers, Inc.

"Simplicity" from *Adventures of the Letter I* by Louis Simpson. Copyright ‹ 1968 by Louis Simpson. Reprinted by permission of Harper & Row, Publishers, Inc.

HARVARD UNIVERSITY PRESS: Poems # 465, "I Heard a Fly Buzz," # 1509, "Mine Enemy Is Growing Old," # 341, "After Great Pain," # 435, "Much Madness," # 280, "I Felt a Funeral," # 923, "How the Waters Closed," # 288, "I'm Nobody," # 401, "What Soft—Cherubic Creatures," and # 1624, "Apparently with No Surprise" by Emily Dickinson. Reprinted by permission of the publishers and the Trustees of Amherst College from *The Poems of Emily Dickinson,* edited by Thomas H. Johnson, Cambridge, Mass.: The Belknap Press of Harvard University Press, Copyright ‹ 1951, 1955 by the President and Fellows of Harvard College.

HOLT, RINEHART AND WINSTON, INC.: "After Apple Picking," "Birches," "Provide, Provide," "Out, Out—," "The Silken Tent," "Fire and Ice," "Departmental," and "Design" by Robert Frost. From *The Poetry of Robert Frost* edited by Edward Connery Lathem. Copyright 1923, ‹ 1969 by Holt, Rinehart and Winston. Copyright 1936, 1942, 1951 by Robert Frost. Copyright ‹ 1964, 1970 by Lesley Frost Ballantine. Reprinted by permission of Holt, Rinehart and Winston, Publishers.

"Terence, This Is Stupid Stuff," "When I Was One-and-Twenty," and "To An Athlete Dying Young" by A. E. Housman. From "A Shropshire Lad"—Authorized Edition—from *The Collected Poems of A. E. Housman.* Copyright ‹ 1967, 1968 by Robert E. Symons. Reprinted by permission of Holt, Rinehart and Winston, Publishers.

HOUGHTON MIFFLIN COMPANY: "Patterns" from *The Complete Poetical Works of Amy Lowell.* Copyright 1955 by Houghton Mifflin Company. Reprinted by permission of Houghton Mifflin Company.

"The Farmer's Wife" by Anne Sexton from *To Bedlam and Part Way Back.* Copyright ‹ 1960 by Anne Sexton. Reprinted by permission of Houghton Mifflin Company.

OLWYN HUGHES: "Daddy" from *Ariel* by Sylvia Plath, published by Faber and Faber, London. Copyright Ted Hughes, 1965.

THE MARVELL PRESS: "Poetry of Departures" by Philip Larkin is reprinted from *The Less Deceived* by permission of The Marvell Press, England.

McCLELLAND AND STEWART LIMITED: "The Bull Calf" from *Collected Poems* by Irving Layton. Reprinted by permission of The Canadian Publishers, McClelland and Stewart Limited, Toronto.

ROBERT MEZEY: "My Mother" by Robert Mezey. From *The Door Standing Open* published by Houghton Mifflin Company and *White Blossoms* published by Cummington Press. Reprinted by permission of the author.

NEW DIRECTIONS PUBLISHING CORP.: "In Goya's Greatest Scenes" from Lawrence Ferlinghetti, *A Coney Island of the Mind*. Copyright © 1958 by Lawrence Ferlinghetti. Reprinted by permission of New Directions Publishing Corporation.

"The Ache of Marriage" from Denise Levertov, *O Taste and See*. Copyright © 1964 by Denise Levertov Goodman. Reprinted by permission of New Directions Publishing Corporation.

"Patriotism," translated by Geoffrey W. Sargent, from Yukio Mishima, *Death in Midsummer and Other Stories*. Copyright © 1966 by New Directions Publishing Corporation. Reprinted by permission of New Directions Publishing Corporation.

"The Last Laugh," "Last Words," and "Dulce et Decorum Est" from Wilfred Owen, *Collected Poems*. Copyright Chatto and Windus Ltd. 1946, © 1963. Reprinted by permission of New Directions Publishing Corporation.

"A Virginal" from Ezra Pound, *Personae*. Copyright 1926 by Ezra Pound. Reprinted by permission of New Directions Publishing Corporation.

"Fern Hill" and "Do Not Go Gentle into That Good Night" by Dylan Thomas. From *The Poems of Dylan Thomas*. Copyright 1946 by New Directions Publishing Corporation, copyright 1952 by Dylan Thomas. Reprinted by permission of New Directions Publishing Corporation.

"Tract" from William Carlos Williams, *Collected Earlier Poems*. Copyright 1938 by New Directions Publishing Corporation. Reprinted by permission of New Directions Publishing Corporation.

W. W. NORTON & COMPANY, INC.: "The Middle-aged" and "Living in Sin" by Adrienne Rich. Reprinted from *Poems, Selected and New, 1950–1974*, by Adrienne Rich. By permission of W. W. Norton & Company, Inc.

HAROLD OBER ASSOCIATES, INC.: "I Want To Know Why" by Sherwood Anderson from *The Triumph of the Egg*. Reprinted by permission of Harold Ober Associates Incorporated. Copyright 1921 by B. W. Huebsch, Inc. Renewed 1948 by Eleanor C. Anderson.

"Same in Blues" by Langston Hughes from *Montage of a Dream Deferred*. Reprinted by permission of Harold Ober Associates Incorporated. Copyright 1951 by Langston Hughes.

OXFORD UNIVERSITY PRESS (ENGLAND): "Spring and Fall: To a Young Child" and "Thou Art Indeed Just, Lord" by Gerard M. Hopkins, published by Oxford University Press.

"The Death of Ivan Ilych" from *Ivan Ilych, Hadji Murad and Other Stories* by Leo Tolstoy, translated by Louise and Aylmer Maude and published by Oxford University Press.

OXFORD UNIVERSITY PRESS, INC.: "On a Squirrel Crossing the Road in Autumn" by Richard Eberhart. From *Collected Poems 1930–1976* by Richard Eberhart. Reprinted by permission of Oxford University Press, Inc.

RANDOM HOUSE, INC.: "The Unknown Citizen," Copyright 1940 and renewed 1968 by W. H. Auden; Stanza II from "Five Songs" (previously titled "That Night When Joy Began"), Copyright 1937 and renewed 1965 by W. H. Auden; "Musée des Beaux Arts," Copyright 1940 and renewed 1968 by W. H. Auden; "In Memory of W. B. Yeats," Copyright 1940 and renewed 1968 by W. H. Auden. All reprinted from *Collected Poems* by W. H. Auden, by permission of Random House, Inc.

"Dry September" by William Faulkner. Copyright 1930 and renewed 1958 by William Faulkner.

Reprinted from *Selected Short Stories* of William Faulkner by permission of Random House, Inc.

"Hurt Hawks" by Robinson Jeffers. Reprinted from *Selected Poems* by Robinson Jeffers, by permission of Random House, Inc.

"The Conscientious Objector" by Karl Shapiro. Copyright 1947 by Karl Shapiro. Reprinted from *Selected Poems* by Karl Shapiro, by permission of Random House, Inc.

ROCKY MOUNTAIN NATIONAL PARK MUSIC CO.: "My Father Always Promised" by Judy Collins. Copyright 1968 Rocky Mountain National Park Music Co., Inc. All Rights Reserved. Used by permission.

SCHOCKEN BOOKS INC.: "The Metamorphosis" by Franz Kafka. Reprinted by permission of Schocken Books Inc. from *The Penal Colony* by Franz Kafka. Copyright 1948 by Schocken Books Inc. Copyright renewed 1975 by Schocken Books Inc.

SCORPION PRESS: "Five Ways To Kill a Man" by Edwin Brock from *With Love from Judas*. Reprinted by permission of Scorpion Press.

CHARLES SCRIBNER'S SONS: "Speaking of Poetry" by John Peale Bishop is reprinted with the permission of Charles Scribner's Sons from *The Collected Poems of John Peale Bishop*. Copyright 1933 Charles Scribner's Sons.

"A Marriage" by Robert Creeley is reprinted with the permission of Charles Scribner's Sons from *For Love*. Copyright 1962 Robert Creeley.

"The Short Happy Life of Francis Macomber" is reprinted by permission of Charles Scribner's Sons from *The Short Stories of Ernest Hemingway* by Ernest Hemingway. Copyright 1936 Ernest Hemingway.

"Richard Cory" and "Miniver Cheevy" by Edwin Arlington Robinson. "Richard Cory" from *The Children of the Night* and "Miniver Cheevy" from *Town Down the River* are reprinted with the permission of Charles Scribner's Sons. Copyright 1907 Charles Scribner's Sons.

PAUL SIMON: "The Dangling Conversation" by Paul Simon. 1966 Paul Simon. Used by Permission.

SIMON & SCHUSTER, INC.: *The Seventh Seal* by Ingmar Bergman from *Four Screen Plays of Ingmar Bergman*. Copyright 1960 by Ingmar Bergman. Reprinted by permission of Simon & Schuster, Inc.

"To Room Nineteen" from *A Man and Two Women* by Doris Lessing. Copyright 1958, 1962, 1963 by Doris Lessing. Reprinted by permission of Simon & Schuster, Inc.

SIQUOMB PUBLISHING CORP.: "The Circle Game" by Joni Mitchell. 1966 Siquomb Publishing Corp. Used by permission. All Rights Reserved.

THE SOCIETY OF AUTHORS: "When I Was One-and-Twenty," "To An Athlete Dying Young," and "Terence, This Is Stupid Stuff" by A. E. Housman. Reprinted by permission of The Society of Authors as the literary representative of the Estate of A. E. Housman and Jonathan Cape Ltd., publishers of A. E. Housman's *Collected Poems*.

MAY SWENSON: "Women" by May Swenson is used by permission of the author as it appears in *Iconographs*, copyright 1970 by May Swenson, published by Charles Scribner's Sons, New York.

MRS. JAMES THURBER: "The Greatest Man in the World" by James Thurber. Copyright 1935 James Thurber. Copyright 1963 Helen W. Thurber and Rosemary Thurber Sauers. From *The Middle Aged Man on the Flying Trapeze*, published by Harper & Row. Originally printed in *The New Yorker*.

TWAYNE PUBLISHERS: "If We Must Die" by Claude McKay from *Selected Poems of Claude McKay*. Reprinted with the permission of Twayne Publishers, A Division of G. K. Hall & Co., Boston.

(NOTE: Acknowledgments and picture credits continue on pages 1179–1180.)

PREFACE

The wide acceptance of the first edition of *Literature: The Human Experience* has made it possible for us to prepare this second edition in the light of comments and suggestions from many of our fellow teachers who have used the book in their classes. As a result, this edition, we believe, realizes much more fully the principles that have guided us from the beginning. Before mentioning specific revisions, we should perhaps say something about those underlying principles and about the structure of the book, which remains the same as before.

The short stories, poems, and plays represent literary traditions ranging from 400 B.C. to the present and reflect widely diverse cultures. In choosing the selections we have been governed by a belief that the first task of an introductory anthology of literature is to engage the reader's interest, to make the experience of literature an immediate and exciting one. A corollary of that belief is our conviction that a genuine interest in literary history or the formal analysis of literature arises out of the experience of being engaged by particular works. Thus, we have selected works not primarily because they illustrate critical definitions or lend themselves to a particular approach but because we find them exciting and believe that students will, too.

The arrangement of the works in four thematic groups provides opportunities to explore diverse attitudes toward the same powerful human tendencies and experiences and to contrast formal treatments as well. Within each thematic section, the works are arranged by genre—fiction, poetry, drama—chronologically. Each section is introduced by a short essay that examines some of the issues embodied in the works that follow. These essays are deliberately polemical, and, no doubt, readers will sometimes take exception to them. This is all to the good, for we believe that our proper mission as editors is to provide the groundwork for discussion and debate, not to promulgate "truths" for the edification of students.

It may be worthwhile to say a word about the questions—rarely more than two or three—that we have placed after about half of the stories, many of the poems, and all of the plays. We believe that too often students are prevented from responding to a work as fully as they might because they are immediately asked questions that require them to confront formal problems. But our students have convinced us that certain kinds of questions can be helpful by opening works that might otherwise prove difficult. The questions in this book are intended to serve this purpose. At the end of each of the four thematic sections we have provided a number of general questions, each alluding to several works in the section. We have found these questions especially useful as starting points for student writing.

The first appendix, "The Poet and His Craft," presents three poems in both early draft and published versions. A student who compares the two versions of each poem will, we think, gain some insight into the ways in which poems are created.

Although the emphasis throughout this book is on the values of literature as a means to enjoyment and to a better understanding of our own humanity, it is of course true that the fullest appreciation of literary achievement requires a certain facility in formal matters and some acquaintance with literary history as well. The essays "Reading Fiction," "Reading Poetry," and "Reading Drama" acquaint readers with some formal concepts and historical considerations that are basic to the study of the major genres of literary art. The essay on drama also includes a discussion of some of the less obvious differences between live performance and film art.

In another essay, "Three Critical Approaches: Formalist, Sociological, Psychoanalytic," we develop, for one story and one poem, three critical readings that emphasize different aspects of the works and reflect the diversity of response that may occur when readers bring different expectations and attitudes to literature. Seeing that a variety of critical approaches may all illuminate a work and complement one another helps to free students, we believe, from a timid acquiescence to some "correct" received view and enables them to respond to literature more honestly and openly.

"Writing About Literature," an essay we have added in this new edition, offers students specific and practical suggestions for approaching their own writing assignments and includes sample student essays on a story and a poem. At the end of the essay we include a brief discussion of the mechanics of manuscript form.

The "Glossary of Literary Terms" contains brief excerpts to illustrate the definitions presented there and also makes specific reference to selections in the anthology. We have also provided a list of sources of recordings and films of many of the selections.

The literary works themselves are of course the main thing. In the second edition we have retained the stories, poems, and plays that we and our fellow teachers across the country have found most valuable; replaced a few selections that we discovered were seldom assigned and a number of others for which more exciting alternatives were suggested; and included some additional works in each genre for the sake of diversity or balance. Specifically, nine of the stories, sixty-seven of the poems, and six of the plays in this edition are new.

We agreed with many users of the first edition that the anthology should offer a wider selection of plays. In addition to *Antigone,* we have have included *Oedipus Rex* for those who prefer it as an example of classical tragedy or who might wish to expose students to the two greatest plays of the Sophocles trilogy. We also agreed that there should be more examples of recent plays, and so we have added Eugene O'Neill's *Desire Under the Elms*, Tennessee Williams' *The Glass Menagerie*, Harold Pinter's *The Dumb Waiter*, and Eugène Ionesco's *The Lesson*. Among the short stories and poems new to the second edition are works by Ernest Hemingway, Flannery O'Connor, Shirley Jackson, Donald Barthelme, Doris Lessing, Kate Chopin, Adrienne Rich, Helen Sorrells, Louis Simpson, Nikki Giovanni, Anne Sexton, Richard Eberhart, Sylvia Plath, and Margaret Atwood.

We would like to acknowledge our debt to our colleagues William Anderson, Robert apRoberts, Wallace Graves, Arthur Lane, Ivy Trent, and Richard Vogler for their valuable comments and criticism. None of them, of course, is to blame for our blunders.

Finally, we wish to thank the many people at St. Martin's Press for their substantial help in preparing this edition, particularly Tom Broadbent, Peter Phelps, and Nancy Perry.

Richard Abcarian
Marvin Klotz

CONTENTS

Innocence and Experience   4

POETRY 401

POETRY

DRAMA

The Presence of Death

FICTION

POETRY

Appendices 1083

alternate table of contents
(arranged by genre)

FICTION

POETRY

DRAMA

innocence and experience

Snake Charmer, Henri Rousseau

iNNOCENCE ANd EXPERiENCE

Man strives to give order and meaning to his life, to reduce the mystery and unpredictability that constantly threaten him. Life is infinitely more complex and surprising than we imagine, and the categories we establish to give it order and meaning are, for the most part, "momentary stays against confusion." At any time, the equilibrium of our lives, the comfortable image of ourselves and the world around us, may be disrupted suddenly by something new, forcing us into painful reevaluation. These disruptions create pain, anxiety, terror but also wisdom and awareness.

The works in this section deal generally with the movement of a central character from moral simplicities and certainties into a more complex and problematic world. Though these works frequently issue in awareness, even wisdom, their central figures rarely act decisively; the protagonist is more often a passive figure who learns the difference between the ideal world he imagines and the injurious real world. If he survives the ordeal (and he doesn't always, emotionally or physically), he will doubtless be a better human—better able to wrest some satisfaction from a bleak and threatening world. It is no accident that so many of the works here deal with the passage from childhood to adulthood, for childhood is a time of simplicities and certainties that must give way to the complexities and uncertainties of adult life.

Almost universally, innocence is associated with childhood and youth, as experience is with age. We teach the young about an ideal world, without explaining that it has not yet been and may never be achieved. As innocents, they are terribly vulnerable to falsehood, to intrusive sexuality, to the machinations of the wicked who, despite all the moral tales, often do triumph. We know, if we have not already forgotten what the innocence of childhood celebrates, that time and experience will disabuse them.

But the terms *innocence* and *experience* range widely in meaning, and that range is reflected here. Innocence may be defined almost biologically, as illustrated by the sexual innocence of the young boy in Sherwood Anderson's "I Want to Know Why." Innocence may be social—the innocence of Robin in Nathaniel Hawthorne's "My Kinsman, Major Molineux" or the young boy in Frank O'Connor's "My Oedipus Complex." Or innocence may be seen as the child's ignorance of his own mortality, as in Gerard Manley Hopkins' "Spring and Fall" and Dylan Thomas' "Fern Hill."

Innocence almost always reflects a foolishness based on ignorance; sometimes, as well, it is the occasion for arrogance. The narrator of Joseph Conrad's "The Secret Sharer," at the beginning of his account, asserts confidently that "the sea was not likely to keep any special surprises expressly for my discomfiture" and explains that he is attracted to the sea because of its "great security" and "the singleness of its purpose." The events of the story markedly change his attitudes about himself and the moral universe in which he operates. In such works as Sophocles' *Oedipus Rex* and Robert Browning's "My Last Duchess," one discovers the tragic and violent consequences of an innocence that is blind. And in Eugène Ionesco's *The Lesson,* the confident, but innocent, young pupil is victimized by an unimaginable aspect of aged experience.

The contrast between what we thought in our youth and what we have come to know, painfully, as adults stands as an emblem of the passage from innocence to experience. Yet, all of us remain, to one degree or another, innocent throughout life, since we never, except with death, stop learning from experience. Looked at in this way, experience is the ceaseless assault life makes upon our innocence, moving us to a greater wisdom about ourselves and the world around us.

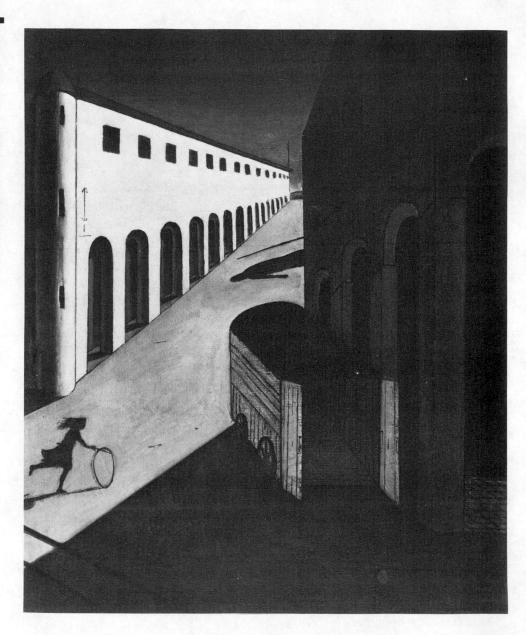

FICTION

My Kinsman, Major Molineux*

NATHANIEL HAWTHORNE   [1804–1864]

AFTER the kings of Great Britain had assumed the right of appointing the colonial governors, the measures of the latter seldom met with the ready and generous approbation which had been paid to those of their predecessors, under the original charters. The people looked with most jealous scrutiny to the exercise of power which did not emanate from themselves, and they usually rewarded their rulers with slender gratitude for the compliances by which, in softening their instructions from beyond the sea, they had incurred the reprehension of those who gave them. The annals of Massachusetts Bay will inform us, that of six governors in the space of about forty years from the surrender of the old charter, under James II., two were imprisoned by a popular insurrection; a third, as Hutchinson inclines to believe, was driven from the province by the whizzing of a musket-ball; a fourth, in the opinion of the same historian, was hastened to his grave by continual bickerings with the House of Representatives; and the remaining two, as well as their successors, till the Revolution, were favored with few and brief intervals of peaceful sway. The inferior members of the court party, in times of high political excitement, led scarcely a more desirable life. These remarks may serve as a preface to the following adventures, which chanced upon a summer night, not far from a hundred years ago. The reader, in order to avoid a long and dry detail of colonial affairs, is requested to dispense with an account of the train of circumstances that had caused much temporary inflammation of the popular mind.

It was near nine o'clock of a moonlight evening, when a boat crossed the ferry with a single passenger, who had obtained his conveyance at that unusual hour by the promise of an extra fare. While he stood on the landing-place, searching in either pocket for the means of fulfilling his agreement, the ferryman lifted a lantern, by the aid of which, and the newly risen moon, he took a very accurate survey of the stranger's figure. He was a youth of

---

* This story is considered in detail in the essay "Three Critical Approaches: Formalist, Sociological, Psychoanalytic" at the end of the book.

barely eighteen years, evidently country-bred, and now, as it should seem, upon his first visit to town. He was clad in a coarse gray coat, well worn, but in excellent repair; his under garments were durably constructed of leather, and fitted tight to a pair of serviceable and well-shaped limbs; his stockings of blue yarn were the incontrovertible work of a mother or a sister; and on his head was a three-cornered hat, which in its better days had perhaps sheltered the graver brow of the lad's father. Under his left arm was a heavy cudgel formed of an oak sapling, and retaining a part of the hardened root; and his equipment was completed by a wallet, not so abundantly stocked as to incommode the vigorous shoulders on which it hung. Brown, curly hair, well-shaped features, and bright, cheerful eyes were nature's gifts, and worth all that art could have done for his adornment.

The youth, one of whose names was Robin, finally drew from his pocket the half of a little province bill of five shillings, which, in the depreciation in that sort of currency, did but satisfy the ferryman's demand, with the surplus of a sexangular piece of parchment, valued at three pence. He then walked forward into the town, with as light a step as if his day's journey had not already exceeded thirty miles, and with as eager an eye as if he were entering London city, instead of the little metropolis of a New England colony. Before Robin had proceeded far, however, it occurred to him that he knew not whither to direct his steps; so he paused, and looked up and down the narrow street, scrutinizing the small and mean wooden buildings that were scattered on either side.

"This low hovel cannot be my kinsman's dwelling," thought he, "nor yonder old house, where the moonlight enters at the broken casement; and truly I see none hereabouts that might be worthy of him. It would have been wise to inquire my way of the ferryman, and doubtless he would have gone with me, and earned a shilling from the Major for his pains. But the next man I meet will do as well."

He resumed his walk, and was glad to perceive that the street now became wider, and the houses more respectable in their appearance. He soon discerned a figure moving on moderately in advance, and hastened his steps to overtake it. As Robin drew nigh, he saw that the passenger was a man in years, with a full periwig of gray hair, a wide-skirted coat of dark cloth, and silk stockings rolled above his knees. He carried a long and polished cane, which he struck down perpendicularly before him at every step; and at regular intervals he uttered two successive hems, of a peculiarly solemn and sepulchral intonation. Having made these observations, Robin laid hold of the skirt of the old man's coat, just when the light from the open door and windows of a barber's shop fell upon both their figures.

"Good evening to you, honored sir," said he, making a low bow, and still retaining his hold of the skirt. "I pray you tell me whereabouts is the dwelling of my kinsman, Major Molineux."

The youth's question was uttered very loudly; and one of the barbers, whose razor was descending on a well-soaped chin, and another who was dressing a Ramillies wig, left their occupations, and came to the door. The citizen, in the mean time, turned a long-favored countenance upon Robin, and answered him in a tone of excessive anger and annoyance. His two sepulchral hems, however, broke into the very centre of his rebuke, with most singular effect, like a thought of the cold grave obtruding among wrathful passions.

"Let go my garment, fellow! I tell you, I know not the man you speak of. What! I have authority, I have—hem, hem—authority; and if this be the respect you show for your betters, your feet shall be brought acquainted with the stocks by daylight, tomorrow morning!"

Robin released the old man's skirt, and hastened away, pursued by an ill-mannered roar of laughter from the barber's shop. He was at first considerably surprised by the result of his question, but, being a shrewd youth, soon thought himself able to account for the mystery.

"This is some country representative," was his conclusion, "who has never seen the inside of my kinsman's door, and lacks the breeding to answer a stranger civilly. The man is old, or verily—I might be tempted to turn back and smite him on the nose. Ah, Robin, Robin! even the barber's boys laugh at you for choosing such a guide! You will be wiser in time, friend Robin."

He now became entangled in a succession of crooked and narrow streets, which crossed each other, and meandered at no great distance from the water-side. The smell of tar was obvious to his nostrils, the masts of vessels pierced the moonlight above the tops of the buildings, and the numerous signs, which Robin paused to read, informed him that he was near the centre of business. But the streets were empty, the shops were closed, and lights were visible only in the second stories of a few dwelling-houses. At length, on the corner of a narrow lane, through which he was passing, he beheld the broad countenance of a British hero swinging before the door of an inn, whence proceeded the voices of many guests. The casement of one of the lower windows was thrown back, and a very thin curtain permitted Robin to distinguish a party at supper, round a well-furnished table. The fragrance of the good cheer steamed forth into the outer air, and the youth could not fail to recollect that the last remnant of his travelling stock of provision had yielded to his morning appetite, and that noon had found and left him dinnerless.

"Oh, that a parchment three-penny might give me a right to sit down at yonder table!" said Robin, with a sigh. "But the Major will make me welcome to the best of his victuals; so I will even step boldly in, and inquire my way to his dwelling."

He entered the tavern, and was guided by the murmur of voices and the fumes of tobacco to the public-room. It was a long and low apartment, with oaken walls, grown dark in the continual smoke, and a floor which was thickly sanded, but of no immaculate purity. A number of persons—the larger part of whom appeared to be mariners, or in some way connected with the sea—occupied the wooden benches, or leather-bottomed chairs, conversing on various matters, and occasionally lending their attention to some topic of general interest. Three or four little groups were draining as many bowls of punch, which the West India trade had long since made a familiar drink in the colony. Others, who had the appearance of men who lived by regular and laborious handicraft, preferred the insulated bliss of an unshared potation, and became more taciturn under its influence. Nearly all, in short, evinced a predilection for the Good Creature in some of its various shapes, for this is a vice to which, as Fast Day sermons of a hundred years ago will testify, we have a long hereditary claim. The only guests to whom Robin's sympathies inclined him were two or three sheepish countrymen, who were using the inn somewhat after the fashion of a Turkish caravansary; they had gotten themselves into the darkest corner of the room, and heedless of the Nicotian atmosphere, were supping on the bread of their own ovens, and the bacon cured in their own chimney-smoke. But though Robin felt a sort of brotherhood with these strangers, his eyes were attracted from them to a person who stood near the door, holding whispered conversation with a group of ill-dressed associates. His features were separately striking almost to grotesqueness, and the whole face left a deep impression on the memory. The forehead bulged out into a double prominence, with a vale between; the nose came boldly forth in an irregular curve, and its bridge was of more than a finger's breadth; the eyebrows were deep and shaggy, and the eyes glowed beneath them like fire in a cave.

While Robin deliberated of whom to inquire respecting his kinsman's dwelling, he was accosted by the innkeeper, a little man in a stained white apron, who had come to pay his professional welcome to the stranger. Being in the second generation from a French Protestant, he seemed to have inherited the courtesy of his parent nation; but no variety of circumstances was ever known to change his voice from the one shrill note in which he now addressed Robin.

"From the country, I presume, sir?" said he, with a profound bow. "Beg leave to congratulate you on your arrival, and trust you intend a long stay with us. Fine town here, sir, beautiful buildings, and much that may interest a stranger. May I hope for the honor of your commands in respect to supper?"

"The man sees a family likeness! the rogue has guessed that I am related to the Major!" thought Robin, who had hitherto experienced little superfluous civility.

All eyes were now turned on the country lad, standing at the door, in his worn three-cornered hat, gray coat, leather breeches, and blue yarn stockings, leaning on an oaken cudgel, and bearing a wallet on his back.

Robin replied to the courteous innkeeper, with such an assumption of confidence as befitted the Major's relative. "My honest friend," he said, "I shall make it a point to patronize your house on some occasion, when"—here he could not help lowering his voice—"when I may have more than a parchment three-pence in my pocket. My present business," continued he, speaking with lofty confidence, "is merely to inquire my way to the dwelling of my kinsman, Major Molineux."

There was a sudden and general movement in the room, which Robin interpreted as expressing the eagerness of each individual to become his guide. But the innkeeper turned his eyes to a written paper on the wall, which he read, or seemed to read, with occasional recurrences to the young man's figure.

"What have we here?" said he, breaking his speech into little dry fragments. " 'Left the house of the subscriber, bounden servant, Hezekiah Mudge, —had on, when he went away, gray coat, leather breeches, master's third-best hat. One pound currency reward to whosoever shall lodge him in any jail of the providence.' Better trudge, boy; better trudge!"

Robin had begun to draw his hand towards the lighter end of the oak cudgel, but a strange hostility in every countenance induced him to relinquish his purpose of breaking the courteous innkeeper's head. As he turned to leave the room, he encountered a sneering glance from the bold-featured personage whom he had before noticed, and no sooner was he beyond the door, than he heard a general laugh, in which the innkeeper's voice might be distinguished, like the dropping of small stones into a kettle.

"Now, is it not strange," thought Robin, with his usual shrewdness,— "is it not strange that the confession of an empty pocket should outweigh the name of my kinsman, Major Molineux? Oh, if I had one of those grinning rascals in the woods, where I and my oak sapling grew up together, I would teach him that my arm is heavy though my purse be light!"

On turning the corner of the narrow lane, Robin found himself in a spacious street, with an unbroken line of lofty houses on each side, and a steepled building at the upper end, whence the ringing of a bell announced the hour of nine. The light of the moon, and the lamps from the numerous shop-windows, discovered people promenading on the pavement, and amongst them Robin had hoped to recognize his hitherto inscrutable relative. The result of his former inquiries made him unwilling to hazard another, in a scene of such publicity, and he determined to walk slowly and silently up the street, thrusting his face close to that of every elderly gentleman, in search of the Major's lineaments. In his progress, Robin encountered many gay and gallant figures. Embroidered garments of showy colors, enormous periwigs, gold-laced hats, and silver-hilted swords glided past him and dazzled his optics. Travelled youths, imitators of the European fine gentlemen of the period, trod jauntily along, half dancing to the fashionable tunes which they hummed, and making poor Robin ashamed of his quiet and natural gait. At length, after many pauses to examine the gorgeous display of goods in the shop-windows, and after suffering some rebukes for the impertinence of his scrutiny into people's faces, the Major's kinsman found himself near the steepled building, still unsuccessful in his search. As yet, however, he had seen only one side of the thronged street; so Robin crossed, and continued the same sort of inquisition down the opposite pavement, with stronger hopes than the philosopher seeking an honest man, but with no better fortune. He had arrived about midway towards the lower end, from which his course began, when he overheard the approach of some one who struck down a cane on the flag-stones at every step, uttering at regular intervals, two sepulchral hems.

"Mercy on us!" quoth Robin, recognizing the sound.

Turning a corner, which chanced to be close at his right hand, he hastened to pursue his researches in some other part of the town. His patience now was wearing low, and he seemed to feel more fatigue from his rambles since he crossed the ferry, than from his journey of several days on the other side. Hunger also pleaded loudly within him, and Robin began to balance the propriety of demanding, violently, and with lifted cudgel, the necessary guidance from the first solitary passenger whom he should meet. While a resolution to this effect was gaining strength, he entered a street of mean appearance, on either side of which a row of ill-built houses was straggling towards the harbor. The moonlight fell upon no passenger along the whole extent, but in the third domicile which Robin passed there was a half-opened door, and his keen glance detected a woman's garment within.

"My luck may be better here," said he to himself.

Accordingly, he approached the door, and beheld it shut closer as he did so; yet an open space remained, sufficing for the fair occupant to observe the stranger, without a corresponding display on her part. All that Robin could discern was a strip of scarlet petticoat, and the occasional sparkle of an eye, as if the moonbeams were trembling on some bright thing.

"Pretty mistress," for I may call her so with a good conscience, thought the shrewd youth, since I know nothing to the contrary,—"my sweet pretty mistress, will you be kind enough to tell me whereabouts I must seek the dwelling of my kinsman, Major Molineux?"

Robin's voice was plaintive and winning, and the female, seeing nothing to be shunned in the handsome country youth, thrust open the door, and came forth into the moonlight. She was a dainty little figure, with a white neck, round arms, and a slender waist, at the extremity of which her scarlet petticoat jutted out over a hoop, as if she were standing in a balloon. Moreover, her face was oval and pretty, her hair dark beneath the little cap, and her bright eyes possessed a sly freedom, which triumphed over those of Robin.

"Major Molineux dwells here," said this fair woman.

Now, her voice was the sweetest Robin had heard that night, yet he could not help doubting whether that sweet voice spoke Gospel truth. He looked up and down the mean street, and then surveyed the house before which they stood. It was a small, dark edifice of two stories, the second of which projected over the lower floor, and the front apartment had the aspect of a shop for petty commodities.

"Now, truly, I am in luck," replied Robin, cunningly, "and so indeed is my kinsman, the Major, in having so pretty a housekeeper. But I prithee trouble him to step to the door; I will deliver him a message from his friends in the country, and then go back to my lodgings at the inn."

"Nay, the Major has been abed this hour or more," said the lady of the scarlet petticoat; "and it would be to little purpose to disturb him to-night, seeing his evening draught was of the strongest. But he is a kind-hearted man, and it would be as much as my life's worth to let a kinsman of his turn away from the door. You are the good old gentleman's very picture, and I could swear that was his rainy-weather hat. Also he has garments very much resembling those leather small-clothes. But come in, I pray, for I bid you hearty welcome in his name."

So saying, the fair and hospitable dame took our hero by the hand; and the touch was light, and the force was gentleness, and though Robin read in her eyes what he did not hear in her words, yet the slender-waisted woman in the scarlet petticoat proved stronger than the athletic country youth. She had drawn his half-willing footsteps nearly to the threshold, when the opening of a door in the neighborhood startled the Major's housekeeper, and, leaving the Major's kinsman, she vanished speedily into her own domicile. A heavy yawn preceded the appearance of a man, who, like the Moonshine of Pyramus and Thisbe,[1] carried a lantern, needlessly aiding his sister luminary in the heavens. As he walked sleepily up the street, he turned his broad, dull face on Robin, and displayed a long staff, spiked at the end.

"Home, vagabond, home!" said the watchman, in accents that seemed to fall asleep as soon as they were uttered. "Home, or we'll set you in the stocks by peep of day!"

"This is the second hint of the kind," thought Robin. "I wish they would end my difficulties, by setting me there to-night."

Nevertheless, the youth felt an instinctive antipathy towards the guardian of midnight order, which at first prevented him from asking his usual question. But just when the man was about to vanish behind the corner, Robin resolved not to lose the opportunity, and shouted lustily after him,—

"I say, friend! will you guide me to the house of my kinsman, Major Molineux?"

The watchman made no reply, but turned the corner and was gone; yet Robin seemed to hear the sound of drowsy laughter stealing along the solitary street. At that moment, also, a pleasant titter saluted him from the open window above his head; he looked up, and caught the sparkle of a saucy eye; a round arm beckoned to him, and next he heard light footsteps descending the staircase within. But Robin, being of the household of a New England clergyman, was a good youth, as well as a shrewd one; so he resisted temptation, and fled away.

He now roamed desperately, and at random, through the town, almost ready to believe that a spell was on him, like that by which a wizard of his country had once kept three pursuers wandering, a whole winter night,

---

1. In Shakespeare's *A Midsummer Night's Dream*, Act V, Scene 1, the moon is represented by a man carrying a lantern in the comic performance of the tragic love story of Pyramus and Thisbe.

within twenty paces of the cottage which they sought. The streets lay before him, strange and desolate, and the lights were extinguished in almost every house. Twice, however, little parties of men, among whom Robin distinguished individuals in outlandish attire, came hurrying along; but, though on both occasions, they paused to address him, such intercourse did not at all enlighten his perplexity. They did but utter a few words in some language of which Robin knew nothing, and perceiving his inability to answer, bestowed a curse upon him in plain English and hastened away. Finally, the lad determined to knock at the door of every mansion that might appear worthy to be occupied by his kinsman, trusting that perseverance would overcome the fatality that had hitherto thwarted him. Firm in this resolve, he was passing beneath the walls of a church, which formed the corner of two streets, when, as he turned into the shade of its steeple, he encountered a bulky stranger, muffled in a cloak. The man was proceeding with the speed of earnest business, but Robin planted himself full before him, holding the oak cudgel with both hands across his body as a bar to further passage.

"Halt, honest man, and answer me a question," said he, very resolutely. "Tell me, this instant, whereabouts is the dwelling of my kinsman, Major Molineux!"

"Keep your tongue between your teeth, fool, and let me pass!" said a deep, gruff voice, which Robin partly remembered. "Let me pass, or I'll strike you to the earth!"

"No, no, neighbor!" cried Robin, flourishing his cudgel, and then thrusting its larger end close to the man's muffled face. "No, no, I'm not the fool you take me for, nor do you pass till I have an answer to my question. Whereabouts is the dwelling of my kinsman, Major Molineux?"

The stranger, instead of attempting to force his passage, stepped back into the moonlight, unmuffled his face, and stared full into that of Robin.

"Watch here an hour, and Major Molineux will pass by," said he.

Robin gazed with dismay and astonishment on the unprecedented physiognomy of the speaker. The forehead with its double prominence, the broad hooked nose, the shaggy eyebrows, and fiery eyes were those which he had noticed at the inn, but the man's complexion had undergone a singular, or, more properly, a twofold change. One side of the face blazed an intense red, while the other was black as midnight, the division line being in the broad bridge of the nose; and a mouth which seemed to extend from ear to ear was black or red, in contrast to the color of the cheek. The effect was as if two individual devils, a fiend of fire and a fiend of darkness, had united themselves to form this infernal visage. The stranger grinned in Robin's face, muffled his party-colored features, and was out of sight in a moment.

"Strange things we travellers see!" ejaculated Robin.

He seated himself, however, upon the steps of the church-door, resolving to wait the appointed time for his kinsman. A few moments were consumed in philosophical speculations upon the species of man who had just left him; but having settled this point shrewdly, rationally, and satisfactorily, he was compelled to look elsewhere for his amusement. And first he threw his eyes along the street. It was of more respectable appearance than most of those into which he had wandered; and the moon, creating, like the imaginative power, a beautiful strangeness in familiar objects, gave something of romance to a scene that might not have possessed it in the light of day. The irregular and often quaint architecture of the houses, some of whose roofs were broken into numerous little peaks, while others ascended, steep and narrow, into a single point, and others again were square; the pure snow-white of some of their complexions, the aged darkness of others, and the thousand sparklings, reflected from bright substances in the walls of many; these matters engaged Robin's attention for a while, and then began to grow wearisome. Next he endeavored to define the forms of distant objects, starting away, with almost ghostly indistinctness, just as his eye appeared to grasp them; and finally he took a minute survey of an edifice which stood on the opposite side of the street, directly in front of the church-door, where he was stationed. It was a large, square mansion, distinguished from its neighbors by a balcony, which rested on tall pillars, and by an elaborate Gothic window, communicating therewith.

"Perhaps this is the very house I have been seeking," thought Robin.

Then he strove to speed away the time, by listening to a murmur which swept continually along the street, yet was scarcely audible, except to an unaccustomed ear like his; it was a low, dull, dreamy sound, compounded of many noises, each of which was at too great a distance to be separately heard. Robin marvelled at this snore of a sleeping town, and marvelled more whenever its continuity was broken by now and then a distant shout, apparently loud where it originated. But altogether it was a sleep-inspiring sound, and, to shake off its drowsy influence, Robin arose, and climbed a window-frame, that he might view the interior of the church. There the moonbeams came trembling in, and fell down upon the deserted pews, and extended along the quiet aisles. A fainter yet more awful radiance was hovering around the pulpit, and one solitary ray had dared to rest upon the open page of the great Bible. Had nature, in that deep hour, become a worshipper in the house which man had builded? Or was that heavenly light the visible sanctity of the place,—visible because no earthly and impure feet were within the walls? The scene made Robin's heart shiver with a sensation of loneliness stronger than he had ever felt in the remotest depths of his native woods; so he turned away and sat down again before the door. There were graves around the church, and now an uneasy thought obtruded into Robin's breast. What if the object of his search, which had been so often and so strangely thwarted, were all the time mouldering in his shroud? What if his kinsman should glide through yonder gate, and nod and smile to him in dimly passing by?

"Oh that any breathing thing were here with me!" said Robin.

Recalling his thoughts from this uncomfortable track, he sent them over forest, hill, and stream, and attempted to imagine how that evening of ambiguity and weariness had been spent by his father's household. He pictured them assembled at the door, beneath the tree, the great old tree, which had been spared for its huge twisted trunk and venerable shade, when a thousand leafy brethren fell. There, at the going down of the summer sun, it was his father's custom to perform domestic worship, that the neighbors might come and join with him like brothers of the family, and that the wayfaring man might pause to drink at that fountain, and keep his heart pure by freshening the memory of home. Robin distinguished the seat of every individual of the little audience; he saw the good man in the midst, holding the Scriptures in the golden light that fell from the western clouds; he beheld him close the book and all rise up to pray. He heard the old thanksgivings for daily mercies, the old supplications for their continuance, to which he had so often listened in weariness, but which were now among his dear remembrances. He perceived the slight inequality of his father's voice when he came to speak of the absent one; he noted how his mother turned her face to the broad and knotted trunk; how his elder brother scorned, because the beard was rough upon his upper lip, to permit his features to be moved; how the younger sister drew down a low hanging branch before her eyes; and how the little one of all, whose sports had hitherto broken the decorum of the scene, understood the prayer for her playmate, and burst into clamorous grief. Then he saw them go in at the door; and when Robin would have entered also, the latch tinkled into its place, and he was excluded from his home.

"Am I here, or there?" cried Robin, starting; for all at once, when his thoughts had become visible and audible in a dream, the long, wide, solitary street shone out before him.

He aroused himself, and endeavored to fix his attention steadily upon the large edifice which he had surveyed before. But still his mind kept vibrating between fancy and reality; by turns, the pillars of the balcony lengthened into the tall, bare stems of pines, dwindled down to human figures, settled again into their true shape and size, and then commenced a new succession of changes. For a single moment, when he deemed himself awake, he could have sworn that a visage—one which he seemed to remember, yet could not absolutely name as his kinsman's—was looking towards him from the Gothic window. A deeper sleep wrestled with and nearly overcame him, but fled at the sound of footsteps along the opposite pavement. Robin rubbed his eyes, discerned a man passing at the foot of the balcony, and addressed him in a loud, peevish, and lamentable cry.

"Hallo, friend! must I wait here all night for my kinsman, Major Molineux?"

The sleeping echoes awoke, and answered the voice; and the passenger, barely able to discern a figure sitting in the oblique shade of the steeple, traversed the street to obtain a nearer view. He was himself a gentleman in his prime, of open, intelligent, cheerful, and altogether prepossessing countenance. Perceiving a country youth, apparently homeless and without friends, he accosted him in a tone of real kindness, which had become strange to Robin's ears.

"Well, my good lad, why are you sitting here?" inquired he. "Can I be of service to you in any way?"

"I am afraid not, sir," replied Robin, despondingly; "yet I shall take it kindly, if you'll answer me a single question. I've been searching, half the night, for one Major Molineux; now, sir, is there really such a person in these parts, or am I dreaming?"

"Major Molineux! The name is not altogether strange to me," said the gentleman, smiling. "Have you any objection to telling me the nature of your business with him?"

Then Robin briefly related that his father was a clergyman, settled on a small salary, at a long distance back in the country, and that he and Major Molineux were brothers' children. The Major, having inherited riches, and acquired civil and military rank, had visited his cousin, in great pomp, a year or two before; had manifested much interest in Robin and an elder brother, and, being childless himself, had thrown out hints respecting the future establishment of one of them in life. The elder brother was destined to succeed to the farm which his father cultivated in the interval of sacred duties; it was therefore determined that Robin should profit by his kinsman's generous intentions, especially as he seemed to be rather the favorite, and was thought to possess other necessary endowments.

"For I have the name of being a shrewd youth," observed Robin, in this part of his story.

"I doubt not you deserve it," replied his new friend, good-naturedly; "but pray proceed."

"Well, sir, being nearly eighteen years old, and well grown, as you see," continued Robin, drawing himself up to his full height, "I thought it high time to begin in the world. So my mother and sister put me in handsome trim, and my father gave me half the remnant of his last year's salary, and five days ago I started for this place, to pay the Major a visit. But, would you believe it, sir! I crossed the ferry a little after dark, and have yet found nobody that would show me the way to his dwelling; only, an hour or two since, I was told to wait here, and Major Molineux would pass by."

"Can you describe the man who told you this?" inquired the gentleman.

"Oh, he was a very ill-favored fellow, sir," replied Robin, "with two great bumps on his forehead, a hook nose, fiery eyes; and, what struck me as the strangest, his face was of two different colors. Do you happen to know such a man, sir?"

"Not intimately," answered the stranger, "but I chanced to meet him a little time previous to your stopping me. I believe you may trust his word, and that the Major will very shortly pass through this street. In the mean time, as I have a singular curiosity to witness your meeting, I will sit down here upon the steps and bear you company."

He seated himself accordingly, and soon engaged his companion in animated discourse. It was but of brief continuance, however, for a noise of shouting, which had long been remotely audible, drew so much nearer that Robin inquired its cause.

"What may be the meaning of this uproar?" asked he. "Truly, if your town be always as noisy, I shall find little sleep while I am an inhabitant."

"Why, indeed, friend Robin, there do appear to be three or four riotous fellows abroad to-night," replied the gentleman. "You must not expect all the stillness of your native woods here in our streets. But the watch will shortly be at the heels of these lads and"—

"Ay, and set them in the stocks by peep of day," interrupted Robin, recollecting his own encounter with the drowsy lantern-bearer. "But, dear sir, if I may trust my ears, an army of watchmen would never make head against such a multitude of rioters. There were at least a thousand voices went up to make that one shout.'

"May not a man have several voices, Robin, as well as two complexions?" said his friend.

"Perhaps a man may; but Heaven forbid that a woman should!" responded the shrewd youth, thinking of the seductive tones of the Major's housekeeper.

The sounds of a trumpet in some neighboring street now became so evident and continual, that Robin's curiosity was strongly excited. In addition to the shouts, he heard frequent bursts from many instruments of discord, and a wild and confused laughter filled up the intervals. Robin rose from the steps, and looked wistfully towards a point whither people seemed to be hastening.

"Surely some prodigious merry-making is going on," exclaimed he. "I have laughed very little since I left home, sir, and should be sorry to lose an opportunity. Shall we step round the corner by that darkish house, and take our share of the fun?"

"Sit down again, sit down, good Robin," replied the gentleman, laying his hand on the skirt of the gray coat. "You forget that we must wait here for your kinsman; and there is reason to believe that he will pass by, in the course of a very few moments."

The near approach of the uproar had now disturbed the neighborhood; windows flew open on all sides; and many heads, in the attire of the pillow, and confused by sleep suddenly broken, were protruded to the gaze of whoever had leisure to observe them. Eager voices hailed each other from house to house, all demanding the explanation, which not a soul could give. Half-dressed men hurried towards the unknown commotion, stumbling as they went over the stone steps that thrust themselves into the narrow footwalk. The shouts, the laughter, and the tuneless bray, the antipodes of music, came onwards with increasing din, till scattered individuals, and then denser bodies, began to appear round a corner at the distance of a hundred yards.

"Will you recognize your kinsman, if he passes in this crowd?" inquired the gentleman.

"Indeed, I can't warrant it, sir; but I'll take my stand here, and keep a bright lookout," answered Robin, descending to the outer edge of the pavement.

A mighty stream of people now emptied into the street, and came rolling slowly towards the church. A single horseman wheeled the corner in the midst of them, and close behind him came a band of fearful wind-instruments, sending forth a fresher discord now that no intervening buildings kept it from the ear. Then a redder light disturbed the moonbeams, and a dense multitude of torches shone along the street, concealing, by their glare, whatever object they illuminated. The single horseman, clad in a military dress, and bearing a drawn sword, rode onward as the leader, and, by his fierce and variegated countenance, appeared like war personified; the red of one cheek was an emblem of fire and sword; the blackness of the other betokened the mourning that attends them. In his train were wild figures in the Indian dress, and many fantastic shapes without a model, giving the whole march a visionary air, as if a dream had broken forth from some feverish brain, and were sweeping visibly through the midnight streets. A mass of people, inactive, except as applauding spectators, hemmed the procession in; and several women ran along the sidewalk, piercing the confusion of heavier sounds with their shrill voices of mirth or terror.

"The double-faced fellow has his eye upon me," muttered Robin, with an indefinite but an uncomfortable idea that he was himself to bear a part in the pageantry.

The leader turned himself in the saddle, and fixed his glance full upon the country youth, as the steed went slowly by. When Robin had freed his eyes from those fiery ones, the musicians were passing before him, and the torches were close at hand; but the unsteady brightness of the latter formed a veil which he could not penetrate. The rattling of wheels over the stones sometimes found its way to his ear, and confused traces of a human form appeared at intervals, and then melted into the vivid light. A moment more, and the leader thundered a command to halt: the trumpets vomited a horrid breath, and then held their peace; the shouts and laughter of the people died away, and there remained only a universal hum, allied to silence. Right before Robin's eyes was an uncovered cart. There the torches blazed the brightest, there the moon shone out like day, and there, in tar-and-feathery dignity, sat his kinsman, Major Molineux!

He was an elderly man, of large and majestic person, and strong, square features betokening a steady soul; but steady as it was, his enemies had found means to shake it. His face was pale as death, and far more ghastly; the broad forehead was contracted in his agony, so that his eyebrows formed one grizzled line; his eyes were red and wild, and the foam hung white upon his quivering lip. His whole frame was agitated by a quick and continual tremor, which his pride strove to quell, even in those circumstances of overwhelming humiliation. But perhaps the bitterest pang of all was when his eyes met those of Robin; for he evidently knew him on the instant, as the youth stood witnessing the foul disgrace of a head grown gray in honor.

They stared at each other in silence, and Robin's knees shook, and his hair bristled, with a mixture of pity and terror. Soon, however, a bewildering excitement began to seize upon his mind; the preceding adventures of the night, the unexpected appearance of the crowd, the torches, the confused din and the hush that followed, the spectre of his kinsman reviled by that great multitude,—all this, and, more than all, a perception of tremendous ridicule in the whole scene, affected him with a sort of mental inebriety. At that moment a voice of sluggish merriment saluted Robin's ears; he turned instinctively, and just behind the corner of the church stood the lantern-bearer, rubbing his eyes, and drowsily enjoying the lad's amazement. Then he heard a peal of laughter like the ringing of silvery bells; a woman twitched his arm, a saucy eye met his, and he saw the lady of the scarlet petticoat. A sharp, dry cachinnation appealed to his memory, and standing on tiptoe in the crowd, with his white apron over his head, he beheld the courteous little innkeeper. And lastly, there sailed over the heads of the multitude a great, broad laugh, broken in the midst by two sepulchral hems; thus, "Haw, haw, haw,—hem, hem,—haw, haw, haw, haw!"

The sound proceeded from the balcony of the opposite edifice, and thither Robin turned his eyes. In front of the Gothic window stood the old citizen, wrapped in a wide gown, his gray periwig exchanged for a nightcap, which was thrust back from his forehead, and his silk stockings hanging about his legs. He supported himself on his polished cane in a fit of convulsive merriment, which manifested itself on his solemn old features like a funny inscription on a tombstone. Then Robin seemed to hear the voices of the barbers, of the guests of the inn, and of all who had made sport of him that night. The contagion was spreading among the multitude, when all at once, it seized upon Robin, and he sent forth a shout of laughter that echoed through the street,—every man shook his sides, every man emptied his lungs, but Robin's shout was the loudest there. The cloud-spirits peeped from their silvery islands, as the congregated mirth went roaring up the sky! The Man in the Moon heard the far bellow. "Oho," quoth he, "the old earth is frolicsome to-night!"

When there was a momentary calm in that tempestuous sea of sound, the leader gave the sign, the procession resumed its march. On they went, like fiends that throng in mockery around some dead potentate, mighty no more, but majestic still in his agony. On they went, in counterfeited pomp, in senseless uproar, in frenzied merriment, trampling all on an old man's heart. On swept the tumult, and left a silent street behind.

•　•　•　•　•　•

"Well, Robin, are you dreaming?" inquired the gentleman, laying his hand on the youth's shoulder.

Robin started, and withdrew his arm from the stone post to which he had instinctively clung, as the living stream rolled by him. His cheek was somewhat pale, and his eye not quite as lively as in the earlier part of the evening.

"Will you be kind enough to show me the way to the ferry?" said he, after a moment's pause.

"You have, then, adopted a new subject of inquiry?" observed his companion, with a smile.

"Why, yes, sir," replied Robin, rather dryly. "Thanks to you, and to my other friends, I have at last met my kinsman, and he will scarce desire to see my face again. I begin to grow weary of a town life, sir. Will you show me the way to the ferry?"

"No, my good friend Robin,—not to-night, at least," said the gentleman. "Some few days hence, if you wish it, I will speed you on your journey. Or, if you prefer to remain with us, perhaps, as you are a shrewd youth, you may rise in the world without the help of your kinsman, Major Molineux."

The Secret Sharer

JOSEPH CONRAD [1857–1924]

I

ON my right hand there were lines of fishing stakes resembling a mysterious system of half-submerged bamboo fences, incomprehensible in its division of the domain of tropical fishes, and crazy of aspect as if abandoned forever by some nomad tribe of fishermen now gone to the other end of the ocean; for there was no sign of human habitation as far as the eye could reach. To the left a group of barren islets, suggesting ruins of stone walls, towers, and blockhouses, had its foundations set in a blue sea that itself looked solid, so still and stable did it lie below my feet; even the track of light from the westering sun shone smoothly, without that animated glitter which tells of an imperceptible ripple. And when I turned my head to take a parting glance at the tug which had just left us anchored outside the bar, I saw the straight line of the flat shore joined to the stable sea, edge to edge, with a perfect and unmarked closeness, in one leveled floor half brown, half blue under the enormous dome of the sky. Corresponding in their insignificance to the islets of the sea, two small clumps of trees, one on each side of the only fault in the impeccable joint, marked the mouth of the river Meinam we had just left on the first preparatory stage of our homeward journey; and, far back on the inland level, a larger and loftier mass, the grove surrounding the great Paknam pagoda, was the only thing on which the eye could rest from the vain task of exploring the monotonous sweep of the horizon. Here and there gleams as of a few scattered pieces of silver marked the windings of the great river; and on the nearest of them, just within the bar, the tug steaming right into the land become lost to my sight, hull and funnel and masts, as though the impassive earth had swallowed her up without an effort, without a tremor. My eye followed the light cloud of her smoke, now here, now there, above the plain, according to the devious curves of the stream, but always fainter and farther away, till I lost it at last behind the miter-shaped hill of the great pagoda. And then I was left alone with my ship, anchored at the head of the Gulf of Siam.

She floated at the starting point of a long journey, very still in an immense stillness, the shadows of her spars flung far to the eastward by the setting sun. At that moment I was alone on her decks. There was not a sound in her—and around us nothing moved, nothing lived, not a canoe on the water, not a bird in the air, not a cloud in the sky. In this breathless pause at the threshold of a long passage we seemed to be measuring our fitness for a long and arduous enterprise, the appointed task of both our existences to be carried out, far from all human eyes, with only sky and sea for spectators and for judges.

There must have been some glare in the air to interfere with one's sight, because it was only just before the sun left us that my roaming eyes made out beyond the highest ridge of the principal islet of the group something which did away with the solemnity of perfect solitude. The tide of darkness flowed on swiftly; and with tropical suddenness a swarm of stars came out above the shadowy earth, while I lingered yet, my hand resting lightly on my ship's rail as if on the shoulder of a trusted friend. But, with all that multitude of celestial bodies staring down at one, the comfort of quiet communion with her was gone for good. And there were also disturbing sounds by this time—voices, footsteps forward; the steward flitted along the main deck, a busily ministering spirit; a hand bell tinkled urgently under the poop deck. . . .

I found my two officers waiting for me near the supper table, in the lighted cuddy. We sat down at once, and as I helped the chief mate, I said:

"Are you aware that there is a ship anchored inside the islands? I saw her mastheads above the ridge as the sun went down."

He raised sharply his simple face, overcharged by a terrible growth of whisker, and emitted his usual ejaculations: "Bless my soul, sir! You don't say so!"

My second mate was a sound-cheeked, silent young man, grave beyond his years, I thought; but as our eyes happened to meet I detected a slight quiver on his lips. I looked down at once. It was not my part to encourage sneering on board my ship. It must be said, too, that I knew very little of my officers. In consequence of certain events of no particular significance, except to myself, I had been appointed to the command only a fortnight before. Neither did I know much of the hands forward. All these people had been together for eighteen months or so, and my position was that of the only stranger on board. I mention this because it has some bearing on what is to follow. But what I felt most was my being a stranger to the ship; and if truth must be told, I was somewhat of a stranger to myself. The youngest man on board (barring the second mate), and untried as yet by a position of the fullest responsibility, I was willing to take the adequacy of the others for granted. They had simply to be equal to their tasks: but I wondered how far I should turn out faithful to that ideal conception of one's own personality every man sets up for himself secretly.

Meantime the chief mate, with an almost visible effect of collaboration on the part of his round eyes and frightful whiskers, was trying to evolve a theory of the anchored ship. His dominant trait was to take all things into earnest consideration. He was of a painstaking turn of mind. As he used to say, he "liked to account to himself" for practically everything that came in his way, down to a miserable scorpion he had found in his cabin a week before. The why and the wherefore of that scorpion—how it got on board and came to select his room rather than the pantry (which was a dark place and more what a scorpion would be partial to), and how on earth it managed to drown itself in the inkwell of his writing desk—had exercised him infinitely. The ship within the islands was much more easily accounted for; and just as we were about to rise from the table he made his pronouncement. She was, he doubted not, a ship from home lately arrived. Probably she drew too much water to cross the bar except at the top of spring tides. Therefore she went into that natural harbor to wait for a few days in preference to remaining in an open roadstead.

"That's so," confirmed the second mate, suddenly, in his slightly hoarse voice. "She draws over twenty feet. She's the Liverpool ship *Sephora* with a cargo of coal. Hundred and twenty-three days from Cardiff."

We looked at him in surprise.

"The tugboat skipper told me when he came on board for your letters, sir," explained the young man. "He expects to take her up the river the day after tomorrow."

After thus overwhelming us with the extent of his information he slipped out of the cabin. The mate observed regretfully that he "could not account for that young fellow's whims." What prevented him telling us all about it at once, he wanted to know.

I detained him as he was making a move. For the last two days the crew had had plenty of hard work, and the night before they had very little sleep. I felt painfully that I—a stranger—was doing something unusual when I directed him to let all hands turn in without setting an anchor watch. I proposed to keep on deck myself till one o'clock or thereabouts. I would get the second mate to relieve me at that hour.

"He will turn out the cook and the steward at four," I concluded, "and then give you a call. Of course at the lightest sign of any sort of wind we'll have the hands up and make a start at once."

He concealed his astonishment. "Very well, sir." Outside the cuddy he put his head in the second mate's door to inform him of my unheard-of caprice to take a five hours' anchor watch on myself. I heard the other raise his voice incredulously: "What? The captain himself?" Then a few more murmurs, a door closed, then another. A few moments later I went on deck.

My strangeness, which had made me sleepless, had prompted that unconventional arrangement, as if I had expected in those solitary hours of the night to get on terms with the ship of which I knew nothing, manned by men of whom I knew very little more. Fast alongside a wharf, littered like any ship in port with a tangle of unrelated things, invaded by unrelated shore people, I had hardly seen her yet properly. Now, as she lay cleared for sea, the stretch of her main deck seemed to me very fine under the stars. Very fine, very roomy for her size, and very inviting. I descended the poop and paced the waist, my mind picturing to myself the coming passage through the Malay Archipelago, down the Indian Ocean, and up the Atlantic. All its phases were familiar enough to me, every characteristic, all the alternatives which were likely to face me on the high seas—everything! ... except the novel responsibility of command. But I took heart from the reasonable thought that the ship was like other ships, the men like other men, and that the sea was not likely to keep any special surprises expressly for my discomfiture.

Arrived at that comforting conclusion, I bethought myself of a cigar and went below to get it. All was still down there. Everybody at the after end of the ship was sleeping profoundly. I came out again on the quarter-deck, agreeably at ease in my sleeping suit on that warm breathless night, barefooted, a glowing cigar in my teeth, and, going forward, I was met by the profound silence of the fore end of the ship. Only as I passed the door of the forecastle I heard a deep, quiet, trustful sigh of some sleeper inside. And suddenly I rejoiced in the great security of the sea as compared with the unrest of the land, in my choice of that untempted life presenting no disquieting problems, invested with an elementary moral beauty by the absolute straightforwardness of its appeal and by the singleness of its purpose.

The riding light in the fore-rigging burned with a clear, untroubled, as if symbolic, flame, confident and bright in the mysterious shades of the night. Passing on my way aft along the other side of the ship, I observed that the rope side ladder, put over, no doubt, for the master of the tug when he came to fetch away our letters, had not been hauled in as it should have been. I became annoyed at this, for exactitude in small matters is the very soul of discipline. Then I reflected that I had myself peremptorily dismissed my officers from duty, and by my own act had prevented the anchor watch being formally set and things properly attended to. I asked myself whether it was wise ever to interfere with the established routine of duties even from the kindest of motives. My action might have made me appear eccentric. Goodness only knew how that absurdly whiskered mate would "account" for my conduct, and what the whole ship thought of that informality of their new captain. I was vexed with myself.

Not from compunction certainly, but, as it were mechanically, I proceeded to get the ladder in myself. Now a side ladder of that sort is a light affair and comes in easily, yet my vigorous tug, which should have brought it flying on board, merely recoiled upon my body in a totally unexpected jerk. What the devil! . . . I was so astounded by the immovableness of that ladder that I remained stock-still, trying to account for it to myself like that imbecile mate of mine. In the end, of course, I put my head over the rail.

The side of the ship made an opaque belt of shadow on the darkling glassy shimmer of the sea. But I saw at once something elongated and pale floating very close to the ladder. Before I could form a guess a faint flash of phosphorescent light, which seemed to issue suddenly from the naked body of a man, flickered in the sleeping water with the elusive, silent play of summer lightning in a night sky. With a gasp I saw revealed to my stare a pair of feet, the long legs, a broad livid back immersed right up to the neck in a greenish cadaverous glow. One hand, awash, clutched the bottom rung of the ladder. He was complete but for the head. A headless corpse! The cigar dropped out of my gaping mouth with a tiny plop and a short hiss quite audible in the absolute stillness of all things under heaven. At that I suppose he raised up his face, a dimly pale oval in the shadow of the ship's side. But even then I could only barely make out down there the shape of his black-haired head. However, it was enough for the horrid, frost-bound sensation which had gripped me about the chest to pass off. The moment of vain exclamations was past, too. I only climbed on the spare spar and leaned over the rail as far as I could, to bring my eyes nearer to that mystery floating alongside.

As he hung by the ladder, like a resting swimmer, the sea lightning played about his limbs at every stir; and he appeared in it ghastly, silvery, fishlike. He remained as mute as a fish, too. He made no motion to get out of the water, either. It was inconceivable that he should not attempt to come on board, and strangely troubling to suspect that perhaps he did not want to. And my first words were prompted by just that troubled incertitude.

"What's the matter?" I asked in my ordinary tone, speaking down to the face upturned exactly under mine.

"Cramp," it answered, no louder. Then slightly anxious, "I say, no need to call anyone."

"I was not going to," I said.

"Are you alone on deck?"

"Yes."

I had somehow the impression that he was on the point of letting go the ladder to swim away beyond my ken—mysterious as he came. But, for the moment, this being appearing as if he had risen from the bottom of the sea (it was certainly the nearest land to the ship) wanted only to know the time. I told him. And he, down there, tentatively:

"I suppose your captain's turned in?"

"I am sure he isn't," I said.

He seemed to struggle with himself, for I heard something like the low, bitter murmur of doubt. "What's the good?" His next words came out with a hesitating effort.

"Look here, my man. Could you call him out quietly?"

I thought the time had come to declare myself.

"*I* am the captain."

I heard a "By Jove!" whispered at the level of the water. The phosphorescence flashed in the swirl of the water all about his limbs, his other hand seized the ladder.

"My name's Leggatt."

The voice was calm and resolute. A good voice. The self-possession of that man had somehow induced a corresponding state in myself. It was very quietly that I remarked:

"You must be a good swimmer."

"Yes. I've been in the water practically since nine o'clock. The question for me now is whether I am to let go this ladder and go on swimming till I sink from exhaustion, or—to come on board here."

I felt this was no mere formula of desperate speech, but a real alternative in the view of a strong soul. I should have gathered from this that he was young; indeed, it is only the young who are ever confronted by such clear issues. But at this time it was pure intuition on my part. A mysterious communication was established already between us two—in the face of that silent darkened tropical sea. I was young, too; young enough to make no comment. The man in the water began suddenly to climb up the ladder, and I hastened away from the rail to fetch some clothes.

Before entering the cabin I stood still, listening in the lobby at the foot of the stairs. A faint snore came through the closed door of the chief mate's room. The second mate's door was on the hook, but the darkness in there was absolutely soundless. He, too, was young and could sleep like a stone. Remained the steward, but he was not likely to wake up before he was called. I got a sleeping suit out of my room and, coming back on deck, saw the naked man from the sea sitting on the main hatch, glimmering white in the darkness, his elbows on his knees and his head in his hands. In a moment he had concealed his damp body in a sleeping suit of the same gray-stripe pattern as the one I was wearing and followed me like my double on the poop. Together we moved right aft, barefooted, silent.

"What is it?" I asked in a deadened voice, taking the lighted lamp out of the binnacle, and raising it to his face.

"An ugly business."

He had rather regular features; a good mouth; light eyes under somewhat heavy, dark eyebrows; a smooth, square forehead; no growth on his cheeks; a small, brown mustache, and a well-shaped, round chin. His expression was concentrated, meditative, under the inspecting light of the lamp I held up to his face; such as a man thinking hard in solitude might wear. My sleeping suit was just right for his size. A well-knit young fellow of twenty-five at most. He caught his lower lip with the edge of white, even teeth.

"Yes," I said, replacing the lamp in the binnacle. The warm, heavy tropical night closed upon his head again.

"There's a ship over there," he murmured.

"Yes, I know. The *Sephora*. Did you know of us?"

"Hadn't the slightest idea. I am the mate of her—" He paused and corrected himself. "I should say I *was*."

"Aha! Something wrong?"

"Yes. Very wrong indeed. I've killed a man."

"What do you mean? Just now?"

"No, on the passage. Weeks ago. Thirty-nine south. When I say a man—"

"Fit of temper," I suggested, confidently.

The shadowy, dark head, like mine, seemed to nod imperceptibly above the ghostly gray of my sleeping suit. It was, in the night, as though I had been faced by my own reflection in the depths of a somber and immense mirror.

"A pretty thing to have to own up to for a Conway boy," murmured my double, distinctly.

"You're a Conway boy?"

"I am," he said, as if startled. Then, slowly . . . "Perhaps you too—"

It was so; but being a couple of years older I had left before he joined. After a quick interchange of dates a silence fell; and I thought suddenly of my absurd mate with his terrific whiskers and the "Bless my soul—you don't say so" type of intellect. My double gave me an inkling of his thoughts by saying:

"My father's a parson in Norfolk. Do you see me before a judge and jury on that charge? For myself I can't see the necessity. There are fellows that an angel from heaven—And I am not that. He was one of those creatures that are just simmering all the time with a silly sort of wickedness. Miserable devils that have no business to live at all. He wouldn't do his duty and wouldn't let anybody else do theirs. But what's the good of talking! You know well enough the sort of ill-conditioned snarling cur—"

He appealed to me as if our experiences had been as identical as our clothes. And I knew well enough the pestiferous danger of such a character where there are no means of legal repression. And I knew well enough also that my double there was no homicidal ruffian. I did not think of asking him for details, and he told me the story roughly in brusque, disconnected sentences. I needed no more. I saw it all going on as though I were myself inside that other sleeping suit.

"It happened while we were setting a reefed foresail, at dusk. Reefed foresail! You understand the sort of weather. The only sail we had left to keep the ship running; so you may guess what it had been like for days. Anxious sort of job, that. He gave me some of his cursed insolence at the sheet. I tell you I was overdone with this terrific weather that seemed to have no end to it. Terrific, I tell you—and a deep ship. I believe the fellow himself was half crazed with funk. It was no time for gentlemanly reproof, so I turned round and felled him like an ox. He up and at me. We closed just as an awful sea made for the ship. All hands saw it coming and took to the rigging, but I had him by the throat, and went on shaking him like a rat, the men above us yelling, 'Look out! look out!' Then a crash as if the sky had fallen on my head. They say that for over ten minutes hardly anything was to be seen of the ship—just the three masts and a bit of the forecastle head and of the poop all awash driving along in a smother of foam. It was a miracle that they found us, jammed together behind the forebits. It's clear that I meant business, because I was holding him by the throat still when they picked us up. He was black in the face. It was too much for them. It seems they rushed us aft together, gripped as we were, screaming 'Murder!' like a lot of lunatics, and broke into the cuddy. And the ship running for her life, touch and go all the time, any minute her last in a sea fit to turn your hair gray only a-looking at it. I understand that the skipper, too, started raving like the rest of them. The man had been deprived of sleep for more than a week, and to have this sprung on him at the height of a furious gale nearly drove him out of his mind. I wonder they didn't fling me overboard after getting the carcass of their precious shipmate out of my fingers. They had rather a job to separate us, I've been told. A sufficiently fierce story to make an old judge and a respectable jury sit up a bit. The first thing I heard when I came to myself was the maddening howling of that endless gale, and on that the voice of the old man. He was hanging on to my bunk, staring into my face out of his sou'wester.

" 'Mr. Leggatt, you have killed a man. You can act no longer as chief mate of this ship.' "

His care to subdue his voice made it sound monotonous. He rested a hand on the end of the skylight to steady himself with, and all that time did not stir a limb, so far as I could see. "Nice little tale for a quiet tea party," he concluded in the same tone.

One of my hands, too, rested on the end of the skylight; neither did I stir a limb, so far as I knew. We stood less than a foot from each other. It occurred to me that if old "Bless my soul—you don't say so" were to put his head up the companion and catch sight of us, he would think he was seeing double, or imagine himself come upon a scene of weird witchcraft; the strange captain having a quiet confabulation by the wheel with his own gray ghost. I became very much concerned to prevent anything of the sort. I heard the other's soothing undertone.

"My father's a parson in Norfolk," it said. Evidently he had forgotten he had told me this important fact before. Truly a nice little tale.

"You had better slip down into my stateroom now," I said, moving off stealthily. My double followed my movements; our bare feet made no sound; I let him in, closed the door with care, and, after giving a call to the second mate, returned on deck for my relief.

"Not much sign of any wind yet," I remarked when he approached.

"No, sir. Not much," he assented, sleepily, in his hoarse voice, with just enough deference, no more, and barely suppressing a yawn.

"Well, that's all you have to look out for. You have got your orders."

"Yes, sir."

I paced a turn or two on the poop and saw him take up his position face forward with his elbow in the rat-lines of the mizzen-rigging before I went below. The mate's faint snoring was still going on peacefully. The cuddy lamp was burning over the table on which stood a vase with flowers, a polite attention from the ships' provision merchant—the last flowers we should see for the next three months at the very least. Two bunches of bananas hung from the beam symmetrically, one on each side of the rudder casing. Everything was as before in the ship—except that two of her captain's sleeping suits were simultaneously in use, one motionless in the cuddy, the other keeping very still in the captain's stateroom.

It must be explained here that my cabin had the form of the capital letter L, the door being within the angle and opening into the short part of the letter. A couch was to the left, the bed-place to the right; my writing desk and the chronometers' table faced the door. But anyone opening it, unless he stepped right inside, had no view of what I call the long (or vertical) part of the letter. It contained some lockers surmounted by a bookcase; and a few clothes, a thick jacket or two, caps, oilskin coat, and such like, hung on hooks. There was at the bottom of that part a door opening into my bathroom, which could be entered also directly from the saloon. But that way was never used.

The mysterious arrival had discovered the advantage of this particular shape. Entering my room, lighted strongly by a big bulkhead lamp swung on gimbals above my writing desk, I did not see him anywhere till he stepped out quietly from behind the coats hung in the recessed part.

"I heard somebody moving about, and went in there at once," he whispered.

I, too, spoke under my breath.

"Nobody is likely to come in here without knocking and getting permission."

He nodded. His face was thin and the sunburn faded, as though he had been ill. And no wonder. He had been, I heard presently, kept under arrest in his cabin for nearly seven weeks. But there was nothing sickly in his eyes or in his expression. He was not a bit like me, really; yet, as we stood leaning over my bed-place, whispering side by side, with our dark heads together and our backs to the door, anybody bold enough to open it stealthily would have been treated to the uncanny sight of a double captain busy talking in whispers with his other self.

"But all this doesn't tell me how you came to hang on to our side ladder," I inquired, in the hardly audible murmurs we used, after he had told me something more of the proceedings on board the *Sephora* once the bad weather was over.

"When we sighted Java Head I had had time to think all those matters out several times over. I had six weeks of doing nothing else, and with only an hour or so every evening for a tramp on the quarter-deck."

He whispered, his arms folded on the side of my bed-place, staring through the open port. And I could imagine perfectly the manner of this thinking out—a stubborn if not a steadfast operation; something of which I should have been perfectly incapable.

"I reckoned it would be dark before we closed with the land," he continued, so low that I had to strain my hearing, near as we were to each other, shoulder touching shoulder almost. "So I asked to speak to the old man. He always seemed very sick when he came to see me—as if he could not look me in the face. You know, that foresail saved the ship. She was too deep to have run long under bare poles. And it was I that managed to set it for him. Anyway, he came. When I had him in my cabin—he stood by the door looking at me as if I had the halter around my neck already—I asked him right away to leave my cabin door unlocked at night while the ship was going through Sunda Straits. There would be the Java coast within two or three miles, off Angier Point. I wanted nothing more. I've had a prize for swimming my second year in the Conway."

"I can believe it," I breathed out.

"God only knows why they locked me in every night. To see some of their faces you'd have thought they were afraid I'd go about at night strangling people. Am I a murdering brute? Do I look it? By Jove! if I had been he wouldn't have trusted himself like that into my room. You'll say I might have chucked him aside and bolted out, there and then—it was dark already. Well, no. And for the same reason I wouldn't think of trying to smash the door. There would have been a rush to stop me at the noise, and I did not mean to get into a confounded scrimmage. Somebody else might have got killed—for I would not have broken out only to get chucked back, and I did not want any more of that work. He refused, looking more sick than ever. He was afraid of the men, and also of that old second mate of his who had been sailing with him for years—a gray-headed old humbug; and his steward, too, had been with him devil knows how long—seventeen years or more—a dogmatic sort of loafer who hated me like poison, just because I was the chief mate. No chief mate ever made more than one voyage in the *Sephora*, you know. Those two old chaps ran the ship. Devil only knows what the skipper wasn't afraid of (all his nerve went to pieces altogether in that hellish spell of bad weather we had)—of what the law would do to him—of his wife, perhaps. Oh, yes! she's on board. Though I don't think she would have meddled. She would have been only too glad to have me out of the ship in any way. The 'brand of Cain' business, don't you see. That's all right. I was ready enough to go off wandering on the face of the earth—and that was price enough to pay for an Abel of that sort. Anyhow, he wouldn't listen to me. 'This thing must take its course. I represent the law here.' He was shaking life a leaf. 'So you won't?' 'No!' 'Then I hope you will be able to sleep on that,' I said, and turned my back on him. 'I wonder that *you* can,' cries he, and locks the door.

"Well, after that, I couldn't. Not very well. That was three weeks ago. We have had a slow passage through the Java Sea; drifted about Carimata for ten days. When we anchored here they thought, I suppose, it was all right. The nearest land (and that's five miles) is the ship's destination; the consul would soon set about catching me; and there would have been no object in bolting to these islets there. I don't suppose there's a drop of water on them. I don't know how it was, but tonight that steward, after bringing me my supper, went out to let me eat it, and left the door unlocked. And I ate it—all there was, too. After I had finished I strolled out on the quarter-deck. I don't know that I meant to do anything. A breath of fresh air was all I wanted, I believe. Then a sudden temptation came over me. I kicked off my slippers and was in the water before I had made up my mind fairly. Somebody heard the splash and they raised an awful hullabaloo. 'He's gone! Lower the boats! He's committed suicide! No, he's swimming.' Certainly I was swimming. It's not so easy for a swimmer like me to commit suicide by drowning. I landed on the nearest islet before the boat left the ship's side. I heard them pulling about in the dark, hailing, and so on, but after a bit they gave up. Everything quieted down and the anchorage became as still as death. I sat down on a stone and began to think. I felt certain they would start searching for me at daylight. There was no place to hide on those stony things—and if there had been, what would have been the good? But now I was clear of that ship, I was not going back. So after a while I took off all my clothes, tied them up in a bundle with a stone inside, and dropped them in the deep water on the outer side of the islet. That was suicide enough for me. Let them think what they liked, but I didn't mean to drown myself. I meant to swim till I sank—but that's not the same thing. I struck out for another of these little islands, and it was from that one that I first saw your riding light. Something to swim for. I went on easily, and on the way I came upon a flat rock a foot or two above water. In the daytime, I dare say, you might make it out with a glass from your poop. I scrambled up on it and rested myself for a bit. Then I made another start. That last spell must have been over a mile."

His whisper was getting fainter and fainter, and all the time he stared straight out through the porthole, in which there was not even a star to be seen. I had not interrupted him. There was something that made comment impossible in his narrative, or perhaps in himself; a sort of feeling, a quality, which I can't find a name for. And when he ceased, all I found was a futile whisper: "So you swam for our light?"

"Yes—straight for it. It was something to swim for. I couldn't see any stars low down because the coast was in the way, and I couldn't see the land, either. The water was like glass. One might have been swimming in a confounded thousand-feet deep cistern with no place for scrambling out anywhere; but what I didn't like was the notion of swimming round and round like a crazed bullock before I gave out; and as I didn't mean to go back ... No. Do you see me being hauled back, stark naked, off one of these little islands by the scruff of the neck and fighting like a wild beast? Somebody would have got killed for certain, and I did not want any of that. So I went on. Then your ladder—"

"Why didn't you hail the ship?" I asked, a little louder.

He touched my shoulder lightly. Lazy footsteps came right over our heads and stopped. The second mate had crossed from the other side of the poop and might have been hanging over the rail, for all we knew.

"He couldn't hear us talking—could he?" My double breathed into my very ear, anxiously.

His anxiety was an answer, a sufficient answer, to the question I had put to him. An answer containing all the difficulty of that situation. I closed the porthole quietly, to make sure. A louder word might have been overheard.

"Who's that?" he whispered then.

"My second mate. But I don't know much more of the fellow than you do."

And I told him a little about myself. I had been appointed to take charge while I least expected anything of the sort, not quite a fortnight ago. I didn't know either the ship or the people. Hadn't had the time in port to look about me or size anybody up. And as to the crew, all they knew was that

I was appointed to take the ship home. For the rest, I was almost as much of a stranger on board as himself, I said. And at the moment I felt it most acutely. I felt that it would take very little to make me a suspect person in the eyes of the ship's company.

He had turned about meantime; and we, the two strangers in the ship, faced each other in identical attitudes.

"Your ladder—" he murmured, after a silence. "Who'd have thought of finding a ladder hanging over at night in a ship anchored out here! I felt just then a very unpleasant faintness. After the life I've been leading for nine weeks, anybody would have got out of condition. I wasn't capable of swimming round as far as your rudder chains. And, lo and behold! there was a ladder to get hold of. After I gripped it I said to myself, 'What's the good?' When I saw a man's head looking over I thought I would swim away presently and leave him shouting—in whatever language it was. I didn't mind being looked at. I—I liked it. And then you speaking to me so quietly—as if you had expected me—made me hold on a little longer. It had been a confounded lonely time—I don't mean while swimming. I was glad to talk a little to somebody that didn't belong to the *Sephora*. As to asking for the captain, that was a mere impulse. It could have been no use, with all the ship knowing about me and the other people pretty certain to be round here in the morning. I don't know—I wanted to be seen, to talk with somebody, before I went on. I don't know what I would have said. . . . 'Fine night, isn't it?' or something of the sort."

"Do you think they will be round here presently?" I asked with some incredulity.

"Quite likely," he said, faintly.

He looked extremely haggard all of a sudden. His head rolled on his shoulders.

'H'm. We shall see then. Meantime get into that bed," I whispered. "Want help? There."

It was a rather high bed-place with a set of drawers underneath. This amazing swimmer really needed the lift I gave him by seizing his leg. He tumbled in, rolled over on his back, and flung one arm across his eyes. And then, with his face nearly hidden, he must have looked exactly as I used to look in that bed. I gazed upon my other self for a while before drawing across carefully the two green serge curtains which ran on a brass rod. I thought for a moment of pinning them together for greater safety, but I sat down on the couch, and once there I felt unwilling to rise and hunt for a pin. I would do it in a moment. I was extremely tired, in a peculiarly intimate way, by the strain of stealthiness, by the effort of whispering and the general secrecy of this excitement. It was three o'clock by now and I had been on my feet since nine, but I was not sleepy; I could not have gone to sleep. I sat there, fagged out, looking at the curtains, trying to clear my mind of the confused sensation of being in two places at once, and greatly bothered by an exasperating knocking in my head. It was a relief to discover suddenly that it was not in my head at all, but on the outside of the door. Before I could collect myself the words "Come in" were out of my mouth, and the steward entered with a tray, bringing in my morning coffee. I had slept, after all, and I was so frightened that I shouted, "This way! I am here, steward," as though he had been miles away. He put down the tray on the table next the couch and only then said, very quietly, "I can see you are here, sir." I felt him give me a keen look, but I dared not meet his eyes just then. He must have wondered why I had drawn the curtains of my bed before going to sleep on the couch. He went out, hooking the door open as usual.

I heard the crew washing decks above me. I knew I would have been told at once if there had been any wind. Calm, I thought, and I was doubly vexed. Indeed, I felt dual more than ever. The steward reappeared suddenly in the doorway. I jumped up from the couch so quickly that he gave a start.

"What do you want here?"

Close your port, sir—they are washing decks."

"It is closed," I said, reddening.

"Very well, sir." But he did not move from the doorway and returned my stare in an extraordinary, equivocal manner for a time. Then his eyes wavered, all his expression changed, and in a voice unusually gentle, almost coaxingly:

"May I come in to take the empty cup away, sir?"

"Of course!" I turned my back on him while he popped in and out. Then I unhooked and closed the door and even pushed the bolt. This sort of thing could not go on very long. The cabin was as hot as an oven, too. I took a peep at my double, and discovered that he had not moved, his arm was still over his eyes; but his chest heaved; his hair was wet; his chin glistened with perspiration. I reached over him and opened the port.

"I must show myself on deck," I reflected.

Of course, theoretically, I could do what I liked, with no one to say nay to me within the whole circle of the horizon; but to lock my cabin door and take the key away I did not dare. Directly I put my head out of the companion I saw the group of my two officers, the second mate barefooted, the chief mate in long india-rubber boots, near the break of the poop, and the steward halfway down the poop ladder talking to them eagerly. He happened to catch sight of me and dived, the second ran down on the main deck shouting some order or other, and the chief mate came to meet me, touching his cap.

There was a sort of curiosity in his eye that I did not like. I don't know whether the steward had told them that I was "queer" only, or downright drunk, but I know the man meant to have a good look at me. I watched him coming with a smile which, as he got into point-blank range, took effect and froze his very whiskers. I did not give him time to open his lips.

"Square the yards by lifts and braces before the hands go to breakfast."

It was the first particular order I had given on board that ship; and I stayed on deck to see it executed, too. I had felt the need of asserting myself without loss of time. That sneering young cub got taken down a peg or two on that occasion, and I also seized the opportunity of having a good look at the face of every foremast man as they filed past me to go to the after braces. At breakfast time, eating nothing myself, I presided with such frigid dignity that the two mates were only too glad to escape from the cabin as soon as decency permitted; and all the time the dual working of my mind distracted me almost to the point of insanity. I was constantly watching myself, my secret self, as dependent on my actions as my own personality, sleeping in that bed, behind that door which faced me as I sat at the head of the table. It was very much like being mad, only it was worse because one was aware of it.

I had to shake him for a solid minute, but when at last he opened his eyes it was in the full possession of his senses, with an inquiring look.

"All's well so far," I whispered. "Now you must vanish into the bath-room."

He did so, as noiseless as a ghost, and I then rang for the steward, and facing him boldly, directed him to tidy up my stateroom while I was having my bath— "and be quick about it." As my tone admitted of no excuses, he said, "Yes, sir," and ran off to fetch his dustpan and brushes. I took a bath and did most of my dressing, splashing, and whistling softly for the steward's edification, while the secret sharer of my life stood drawn up bolt upright in that little space, his face looking very sunken in daylight, his eyelids lowered under the stern, dark line of his eyebrows drawn together by a slight frown.

When I left him there to go back to my room the steward was finished dusting. I sent for the mate and engaged him in some insignificant conversation. It was, as it were, trifling with the terrific character of whiskers; but my object was to give him an opportunity for a good look at my cabin. And then I could at last shut, with a clear conscience, the door of my stateroom and get my double back into the recessed part. There was nothing else for it. He had to sit still on a small folding stool, half smothered by the heavy coats hanging there. We listened to the steward going into the bathroom out of the saloon, filling the water bottles there, scrubbing the bath, setting things to rights, whisk, bang, clatter—out again into the saloon—turn the key—click. Such was my scheme for keeping my second self invisible. Nothing better could be contrived under the circumstances. And there we sat; I at my writing desk ready to appear busy with some papers, he behind me, out of sight of the door. It would not have been prudent to talk in daytime; and I could not have stood the excitement of that queer sense of whispering to myself. Now and then, glancing over my shoulder, I saw him far back there, sitting rigidly on the low stool, his bare feet close together, his arms folded, his head hanging on his breast—and perfectly still. Anybody would have taken him for me.

I was fascinated by it myself. Every moment I had to glance over my shoulder. I was looking at him when a voice outside the door said:

"Beg pardon, sir."

"Well!" . . . I kept my eyes on him, and so, when the voice outside the door announced, "There's a ship's boat coming our way, sir," I saw him give a start—the first movement he had made for hours. But he did not raise his bowed head.

"All right. Get the ladder over."

I hesitated. Should I whisper something to him? But what? His immobility seemed to have been never disturbed. What could I tell him he did not know already? . . . Finally I went on deck.

II

THE skipper of the *Sephora* had a thin red whisker all round his face, and the sort of complexion that goes with hair of that color; also the particular, rather smeary shade of blue in the eyes. He was not exactly a showy figure; his shoulders were high, his stature but middling—one leg slightly more bandy than the other. He shook hands, looking vaguely around. A spiritless tenacity was his main characteristic, I judged. I behaved with a politeness which seemed to disconcert him. Perhaps he was shy. He mumbled to me as if he were ashamed of what he was saying; gave his name (it was something like Archbold—but at this distance of years I hardly am sure), his ship's name, and a few other particulars of that sort, in the manner of a criminal making a reluctant and doleful confession. He had had terrible weather on the passage out—terrible—terrible—wife aboard, too.

By this time we were seated in the cabin and the steward brought in a tray with a bottle and glasses. "Thanks! No." Never took liquor. Would have some water, though. He drank two tumblerfuls. Terrible thirsty work. Ever since daylight had been exploring the islands round his ship.

"What was that for—fun?" I asked, with an appearance of polite interest.

"No!" He sighed. "Painful duty."

As he persisted in his mumbling and I wanted my double to hear every word, I hit upon the notion of informing him that I regretted to say I was hard of hearing.

"Such a young man, too!" he nodded, keeping his smeary blue, unintelligent eyes fastened upon me. What was the cause of it—some disease? he inquired, without the least sympathy and as if he thought that, if so, I'd got no more than I deserved.

"Yes; disease," I admitted in a cheerful tone which seemed to shock him. But my point was gained, because he had to raise his voice to give me his tale. It is not worth while to record that version. It was just over two months since all this had happened, and he had thought so much about it that he seemed completely muddled as to its bearings, but still immensely impressed.

"What would you think of such a thing happening on board your own ship? I've had the *Sephora* for these fifteen years. I am a well-known shipmaster."

He was densely distressed—and perhaps I should have sympathized with him if I had been able to detach my mental vision from the unsuspected sharer of my cabin as though he were my second self. There he was on the other side of the bulkhead, four or five feet from us, no more, as we sat in the saloon. I looked politely at Captain Archbold (if that was his name), but it was the other I saw, in a gray sleeping suit, seated on a low stool, his bare feet close together, his arms folded, and every word said between us falling into the ears of his dark head bowed on his chest.

"I have been at sea now, man and boy, for seven-and-thirty years, and I've never heard of such a thing happening in an English ship. And that it should be my ship. Wife on board, too."

I was hardly listening to him.

"Don't you think," I said, "that the heavy sea which, you told me, came aboard just then might have killed the man? I have seen the sheer weight of a sea kill a man very neatly, by simply breaking his neck."

"Good God!" he uttered, impressively, fixing his smeary blue eyes on me. "The sea! No man killed by the sea ever looked like that." He seemed positively scandalized at my suggestion. And as I gazed at him, certainly not prepared for anything original on his part, he advanced his head close to mine and thrust his tongue out at me so suddenly that I couldn't help starting back.

After scoring over my calmness in this graphic way he nodded wisely. If I had seen the sight, he assured me, I would never forget it as long as I lived. The weather was too bad to give the corpse a proper sea burial. So next day at dawn they took it up on the poop, covering its face with a bit of bunting; he read a short prayer, and then, just as it was, in its oilskins and long boots, they launched it amongst those mountainous seas that seemed ready every moment to swallow up the ship herself and the terrified lives on board of her.

"That reefed foresail saved you," I threw in.

"Under God—it did," he exclaimed fervently. "It was by a special mercy, I firmly believe, that it stood some of those hurricane squalls."

"It was the setting of that sail which—" I began.

"God's own hand in it," he interrupted me. "Nothing less could have done it. I don't mind telling you that I hardly dared give the order. It seemed impossible that we could touch anything without losing it, and then our last hope would have been gone."

The terror of that gale was on him yet. I let him go on for a bit, then said, casually—as if returning to a minor subject:

"You were very anxious to give up your mate to the shore people, I believe?"

He was. To the law. His obscure tenacity on that point had in it something incomprehensible and a little awful; something, as it were, mystical, quite apart from his anxiety that he should not be suspected of "countenancing any doings of that sort." Seven-and-thirty virtuous years at sea, of which over twenty of immaculate command, and the last fifteen in the *Sephora*, seemed to have laid him under some pitiless obligation.

"And you know," he went on, groping shamefacedly amongst his feelings, "I did not engage that young fellow. His people had some interest with my owners. I was in a way forced to take him on. He looked very smart, very gentlemanly, and all that. But do you know—I never liked him, somehow. I am a plain man. You see, he wasn't exactly the sort for the chief mate of a ship like the *Sephora*."

I had become so connected in thoughts and impressions with the secret sharer of my cabin that I felt as if I, personally, were being given to understand that I, too, was not the sort that would have done for the chief mate of a ship like the *Sephora*. I had no doubt of it in my mind.

"Not at all the style of man. You understand," he insisted, superfluously, looking hard at me.

I smiled urbanely. He seemed at a loss for a while.

"I suppose I must report a suicide."

"Beg pardon?"

"Sui-cide! That's what I'll have to write to my owners directly I get in."

"Unless you manage to recover him before tomorrow," I assented, dispassionately. . . . "I mean, alive."

He mumbled something which I really did not catch, and I turned my ear to him in a puzzled manner. He fairly bawled:

"The land—I say, the mainland is at least seven miles off my anchorage."

"About that."

My lack of excitement, of curiosity, of surprise, of any sort of pronounced interest, began to arouse his distrust. But except for the felicitous pretense of deafness I had not tried to pretend anything. I had felt utterly incapable of playing the part of ignorance properly, and therefore was afraid to try. It is also certain that he had brought some ready-made suspicions with him, and that he viewed my politeness as a strange and unnatural phenomenon. And yet how else could I have received him? Not heartily! That was impossible for psychological reasons, which I need not state here. My only object was to keep off his inquiries. Surlily? Yes, but surliness might have provoked a point-blank question. From its novelty to him and from its nature, punctilious courtesy was the manner best calculated to restrain the man. But there was the danger of his breaking through my defense bluntly. I could not, I think, have met him by a direct lie, also for psychological (not moral) reasons. If he had only known how afraid I was of his putting my feeling of identity with the other to the test! But, strangely enough—(I thought of it only afterward)—I believe that he was not a little disconcerted by the reverse side of that weird situation, by something in me that reminded him of the man he was seeking—suggested a mysterious similitude to the young fellow he had distrusted and disliked from the first.

However that might have been, the silence was not very prolonged. He took another oblique step.

"I reckon I had no more than a two-mile pull to your ship. Not a bit more."

"And quite enough, too, in this awful heat," I said.

Another pause full of mistrust followed. Necessity, they say, is mother of invention, but fear, too, is not barren of ingenious suggestions. And I was afraid he would ask me point-blank for news of my other self.

"Nice little saloon, isn't it?" I remarked, as if noticing for the first time the way his eyes roamed from one closed door to the other. "And very well fitted out, too. Here, for instance," I continued reaching over the back of my seat negligently and flinging the door open, "is my bathroom."

He made an eager movement, but hardly gave it a glance. I got up, shut the door of the bathroom, and invited him to have a look round, as if I were very proud of my accommodation. He had to rise and be shown round, but he went through the business without any raptures whatever.

"And now we'll have a look at my stateroom," I declared, in a voice as loud as I dared to make it, crossing the cabin to the starboard side with purposely heavy steps.

He followed me in and gazed around. My intelligent double had vanished. I played my part.

"Very convenient—isn't it?"

"Very nice. Very comf . . ." He didn't finish, and went out brusquely as if to escape from some unrighteous wiles of mine. But it was not to be. I had been too frightened not to feel vengeful; I felt I had him on the run, and I meant to keep him on the run. My polite insistence must have had something menacing in it, because he gave in suddenly. And I did not let him off a single item; mate's room, pantry, storerooms, the very sail locker which was also under the poop—he had to look into them all. When at last I showed him out on the quarter-deck he drew a long, spiritless sigh, and mumbled dismally that he must really be going back to his ship now. I desired my mate, who had joined us, to see to the captain's boat.

The man of whiskers gave a blast on the whistle which he used to wear hanging round his neck, and yelled, "*Sephora* away!" My double down there in my cabin must have heard, and certainly could not feel more relieved than I. Four fellows came running out from somewhere forward and went over the side, while my own men, appearing on deck too, lined the rail. I escorted my visitor to the gangway ceremoniously, and nearly overdid it. He was a tenacious beast. On the very ladder he lingered, and in that unique, guiltily conscientious manner of sticking to the point:

"I say . . . you . . . you don't think that—"

I covered his voice loudly:

"Certainly not. . . . I am delighted. Good-by."

I had an idea of what he meant to say, and just saved myself by the privilege of defective hearing. He was too shaken generally to insist, but my mate, close witness of that parting, looked mystified and his face took on a thoughtful cast. As I did not want to appear as if I wished to avoid all communication with my officers, he had the opportunity to address me.

"Seems a very nice man. His boat's crew told our chaps a very extraordinary story, if what I am told by the steward is true. I suppose you had it from the captain, sir?"

"Yes. I had a story from the captain."

"A very horrible affair—isn't it, sir?"

"It is."

"Beats all these tales we hear about murders in Yankee ships."

"I don't think it beats them. I don't think it resembles them in the least."

"Bless my soul—you don't say so! But of course I've no acquaintance whatever with American ships, not I, so I couldn't go against your knowledge. It's horrible enough for me. . . . But the queerest part is that these fellows seemed to have some idea the man was hidden aboard here. They had really. Did you ever hear of such a thing?"

"Preposterous—isn't it?"

We were walking to and fro athwart the quarter-deck. No one of the crew forward could be seen (the day was Sunday), and the mate pursued:

"There was some little dispute about it. Our chaps took offense. 'As if we would harbor a thing like that,' they said. 'Wouldn't you like to look for him in our coal hole?' Quite a tiff. But they made it up in the end. I suppose he did drown himself. Don't you, sir?"

"I don't suppose anything."

"You have no doubt in the matter, sir?"

"None whatever."

I left him suddenly. I felt I was producing a bad impression, but with my double down there it was most trying to be on deck. And it was almost as trying to be below. Altogether a nerve-trying situation. But on the whole I felt less torn in two when I was with him. There was no one in the whole ship whom I dared take into my confidence. Since the hands had got to know his story, it would have been impossible to pass him off for anyone else, and an accidental discovery was to be dreaded now more than ever. . . .

The steward being engaged in laying the table for dinner, we could talk only with our eyes when I first went down. Later in the afternoon we had a cautious try at whispering. The Sunday quietness of the ship was against us; the stillness of air and water around her was against us; the elements, the men were against us—everything was against us in our secret partnership; time itself—for this could not go on forever. The very trust in Providence was, I suppose, denied to his guilt. Shall I confess that this thought cast me down very much? And as to the chapter of accidents which counts for so much in the book of success, I could only hope that it was closed. For what favorable accident could be expected?

"Did you hear everything?" were my first words as soon as we took up our position side by side, leaning over my bed-place.

He had. And the proof of it was his earnest whisper, "The man told you he hardly dared to give the order."

I understood the reference to be to that saving foresail.

"Yes. He was afraid of it being lost in the setting."

"I assure you he never gave the order. He may think he did, but he never gave it. He stood there with me on the break of the poop after the maintopsail blew away, and whimpered about our last hope—positively whimpered about it and nothing else—and the night coming on! To hear one's skipper go on like that in such weather was enough to drive any fellow out of his mind. It worked me up into a sort of desperation. I just took it into my hands and went away from him, boiling, and—But what's the use telling you? *You* know!... Do you think that if I had not been pretty fierce with them I should have got the men to do anything? Not it! The bosun perhaps? Perhaps! It wasn't a heavy sea—it was a sea gone mad! I suppose the end of the world will be something like that; and a man may have the heart to see it coming once and be done with it—but to have to face it day after day—I don't blame anybody. I was precious little better than the rest. Only—I was an officer of that old coal-wagon, anyhow—"

"I quite understand," I conveyed that sincere assurance into his ear. He was out of breath with whispering; I could hear him pant slightly. It was all very simple. The same strung-up force which had given twenty-four men a chance, at least, for their lives, had, in a sort of recoil, crushed an unworthy mutinous existence.

But I had no leisure to weigh the merits of the matter—footsteps in the saloon, a heavy knock. "There's enough wind to get under way with, sir." Here was the call of a new claim upon my thoughts and even upon my feelings.

"Turn the hands up," I cried through the door. "I'll be on deck directly."

I was going out to make the acquaintance of my ship. Before I left the cabin our eyes met—the eyes of the only two strangers on board. I pointed to the recessed part where the little campstool awaited him and laid my finger on my lips. He made a gesture—somewhat vague—a little mysterious, accompanied by a faint smile, as if of regret.

This is not the place to enlarge upon the sensations of a man who feels for the first time a ship move under his feet to his own independent word. In my case they were not unalloyed. I was not wholly alone with my command; for there was that stranger in my cabin. Or rather, I was not completely and wholly with her. Part of me was absent. That mental feeling of being in two places at once affected me physically as if the mood of secrecy had penetrated my very soul. Before an hour had elapsed since the ship had begun to move, having occasion to ask the mate (he stood by my side) to take a compass bearing of the Pagoda, I caught myself reaching up to his ear in whispers. I say I caught myself, but enough had escaped to startle the man. I can't describe it otherwise than by saying that he shied. A grave, preoccupied manner, as though he were in possession of some perplexing intelligence, did not leave him henceforth. A little later I moved away from the rail to look at the compass with such a stealthy gait that the helmsman noticed it—and I could not help noticing the unusual roundness of his eyes. These are trifling instances, though it's to no commander's advantage to be suspected of ludicrous eccentricities. But I was also more seriously affected. There are to a seaman certain words, gestures, that should in given conditions come as naturally, as instinctively as the winking of a menaced eye. A certain order should spring on to his lips without thinking; a certain sign should get itself made, so to speak, without reflection. But all unconscious alertness had abandoned me. I had to make an effort of will to recall myself back (from the cabin) to the conditions of the moment. I felt that I was appearing an irresolute commander to those people who were watching me more or less critically.

And, besides, there were the scares. On the second day out, for instance, coming off the deck in the afternoon (I had straw slippers on my bare feet) I stopped at the open pantry door and spoke to the steward. He was doing something there with his back to me. At the sound of my voice he nearly jumped out of his skin, as the saying is, and incidentally broke a cup.

"What on earth's the matter with you?" I asked, astonished.

He was extremely confused. "Beg your pardon, sir. I made sure you were in your cabin."

"You see I wasn't."

"No, sir. I could have sworn I had heard you moving in there not a moment ago. It's most extraordinary . . . very sorry, sir."

I passed on with an inward shudder. I was so identified with my secret double that I did not even mention the fact in those scanty, fearful whispers we exchanged. I suppose he had made some slight noise of some kind or other. It would have been miraculous if he hadn't at one time or another. And yet, haggard as he appeared, he looked always perfectly self-controlled, more than calm—almost invulnerable. On my suggestion he remained almost entirely in the bathroom, which, upon the whole, was the safest place. There could be really no shadow of an excuse for anyone ever wanting to go in there, once the steward had done with it. It was a very tiny place. Sometimes he reclined on the floor, his legs bent, his head sustained on one elbow. At others I would find him on the campstool, sitting in his gray sleeping suit and with his cropped dark hair like a patient, unmoved convict. At night I would smuggle him into my bed-place, and we would whisper together, with the regular footfalls of the officer of the watch passing and repassing over our heads. It was an infinitely miserable time. It was lucky that some tins of fine preserves were stowed in a locker in my stateroom; hard bread I could always get hold of; and so he lived on stewed chicken, paté de foie gras, asparagus, cooked oysters, sardines—on all sorts of abominable sham delicacies out of tins. My early morning coffee he always drank; and it was all I dared do for him in that respect.

Every day there was the horrible maneuvering to go through so that my room and then the bathroom should be done in the usual way. I came to hate the sight of the steward, to abhor the voice of that harmless man. I felt that it was he who would bring on the disaster of discovery. It hung like a sword over our heads.

The fourth day out, I think (we were working down the east side of the Gulf of Siam, tack for tack, in light winds and smooth water)—the fourth day, I say, of this miserable juggling with the unavoidable, as we sat at our evening meal, that man, whose slightest movement I dreaded, after putting down the dishes ran up on deck busily. This could not be dangerous. Presently he came down again; and then it appeared that he had remembered a coat of mine which I had thrown over a rail to dry after having been wetted in a shower which had passed over the ship in the afternoon. Sitting stolidly at the head of the table I became terrified at the sight of the garment on his arm. Of course he made for my door. There was no time to lose.

"Steward," I thundered. My nerves were so shaken that I could not govern my voice and conceal my agitation. This was the sort of thing that made my terrifically whiskered mate tap his forehead with his forefinger. I had detected him using that gesture while talking on deck with a confidential air to the carpenter. It was too far to hear a word, but I had no doubt that this pantomime could only refer to the strange new captain.

"Yes, sir," the pale-faced steward turned resignedly to me. It was this maddening course of being shouted at, checked without rhyme or reason, arbitrarily chased out of my cabin, suddenly called into it, sent flying out of his pantry on incomprehensible errands, that accounted for the growing wretchedness of his expression.

"Where are you going with that coat?"

"To your room, sir."

"Is there another shower coming?"

"I'm sure I don't know, sir. Shall I go up again and see, sir?"

"No! never mind."

My object was attained, as of course my other self in there would have heard everything that passed. During this interlude my two officers never raised their eyes off their respective plates; but the lip of that confounded cub, the second mate, quivered visibly.

I expected the steward to hook my coat on and come out at once. He was very slow about it; but I dominated my nervousness sufficiently not to shout after him. Suddenly I became aware (it could be heard plainly enough) that the fellow for some reason or other was opening the door of the bathroom. It was the end. The place was literally not big enough to swing a cat in. My voice died in my throat and I went stony all over. I expected to hear a yell of surprise and terror, and made a movement, but had not the strength to get on my legs. Everything remained still. Had my second self taken the poor wretch by the throat? I don't know what I would have done next moment if I had not seen the steward come out of my room, close the door, and then stand quietly by the sideboard.

Saved, I thought. But, no! Lost! Gone! He was gone!

I laid my knife and fork down and leaned back in my chair. My head swam. After a while, when sufficiently recovered to speak in a steady voice, I instructed my mate to put the ship round at eight o'clock himself.

"I won't come on deck," I went on. "I think I'll turn in, and unless the wind shifts I don't want to be disturbed before midnight. I feel a bit seedy."

"You did look middling bad a little while ago," the chief mate remarked without showing any great concern.

They both went out, and I stared at the steward clearing the table. There was nothing to be read on that wretched man's face. But why did he avoid my eyes I asked myself. Then I thought I should like to hear the sound of his voice.

"Steward!"

"Sir!" Startled as usual.

"Where did you hang up that coat?"

"In the bathroom, sir." The usual anxious tone. "It's not quite dry yet, sir."

For some time longer I sat in the cuddy. Had my double vanished as he had come? But of his coming there was an explanation, whereas his disappearance would be inexplicable.... I went slowly into my dark room, shut the door, lighted the lamp, and for a time dared not turn round. When at last I did I saw him standing bolt upright in the narrow recessed part. It would not be true to say I had a shock, but an irresistible doubt of his bodily existence flitted through my mind. Can it be, I asked myself, that he is not visible to other eyes than mine? It was like being haunted. Motionless, with a grave face, he raised his hands slightly at me in a gesture which meant clearly, "Heavens! what a narrow escape!" Narrow indeed. I think I had come creeping quietly as near insanity as any man who has not actually gone over the border. That gesture restrained me, so to speak.

The mate with the terrific whiskers was now putting the ship on the other tack. In the moment of profound silence which follows upon the hands going to their stations I heard on the poop his raised voice: "Hard alee!" and the distant shout of the order repeated on the maindeck. The sails, in that light breeze, made but a faint fluttering noise. It ceased. The ship was coming round slowly; I held my breath in the renewed stillness of expectation; one wouldn't have thought that there was a single living soul on her decks. A sudden brisk shout, "Mainsail haul!" broke the spell, and in the noisy cries and rush overhead of the men running away with the main brace we two, down in my cabin, came together in our usual position by the bed-place.

He did not wait for my question. "I heard him fumbling here and just managed to squat myself down in the bath," he whispered to me. "The fellow only opened the door and put his arm in to hang the coat up. All the same—"

"I never thought of that," I whispered back, even more appalled than before at the closeness of the shave, and marveling at that something unyielding in his character which was carrying him through so finely. There was no agitation in his whisper. Whoever was being driven distracted, it was not he. He was sane. And the proof of his sanity was continued when he took up the whispering again.

"It would never do for me to come to life again."

It was something that a ghost might have said. But what he was alluding to was his old captain's reluctant admission of the theory of suicide. It would obviously serve his turn—if I had understood at all the view which seemed to govern the unalterable purpose of his action.

"You must maroon me as soon as ever you can get amongst these islands off the Cambodje shore," he went on.

"Maroon you! We are not living in a boy's adventure tale," I protested. His scornful whispering took me up.

"We aren't indeed! There's nothing of a boy's tale in this. But there's nothing else for it. I want no more. You don't suppose I am afraid of what can be done to me? Prison or gallows or whatever they may please. But you don't see me coming back to explain such things to an old fellow in a wig and twelve respectable tradesmen, do you? What can they know whether I am guilty or not—or of *what* I am guilty, either? That's my affair. What does the Bible say? 'Driven off the face of the earth.' Very well. I am off the face of the earth now. As I came at night so I shall go."

"Impossible!" I murmured. "You can't."

"Can't? . . . Not naked like a soul on the Day of Judgment. I shall freeze on to this sleeping suit. The Last Day is not yet—and . . . you have understood thoroughly. Didn't you?"

I felt suddenly ashamed of myself. I may say truly that I understood—and my hesitation in letting that man swim away from my ship's side had been a mere sham sentiment, a sort of cowardice.

"It can't be done now till next night," I breathed out. "The ship is on the offshore tack and the wind may fail us."

"As long as I know that you understand," he whispered. "But of course you do. It's a great satisfaction to have got somebody to understand. You seem to have been there on purpose." And in the same whisper, as if we two whenever we talked had to say things to each other which were not fit for the world to hear, he added, "It's very wonderful."

We remained side by side talking in our secret way—but sometimes silent or just exchanging a whispered word or two at long intervals. And as usual he stared through the port. A breath of wind came now and again into our faces. The ship might have been moored in dock, so gently and on an even keel she slipped through the water, that did not murmur even at our passage, shadowy and silent like a phantom sea.

At midnight I went on deck, and to my mate's great surprise put the ship round on the other tack. His terrible whiskers flitted round me in silent criticism. I certainly should not have done it if it had been only a question of getting out of that sleepy gulf as quickly as possible. I believe he told the second mate, who relieved him, that it was a great want of judgment. The other only yawned. That intolerable cub shuffled about so sleepily and lolled against the rails in such a slack, improper fashion that I came down on him sharply.

"Aren't you properly awake yet?"

"Yes, sir! I am awake."

"Well, then, be good enough to hold yourself as if you were. And keep a lookout. If there's any current we'll be closing with some islands before daylight."

The east side of the gulf is fringed with islands, some solitary, others in groups. On the blue background of the high coast they seem to float on silvery patches of calm water, arid and gray, or dark green and rounded like clumps of evergreen bushes, with the larger ones, a mile or two long, show-ing the outlines of ridges, ribs of gray rock under the dark mantle of matted leafage. Unknown to trade, to travel, almost to geography, the manner of life they harbor is an unsolved secret. There must be villages—settlements of fishermen at least—on the largest of them, and some communication with the world is probably kept up by native craft. But all forenoon, as we headed for them, fanned along by the faintest of breezes, I saw no sign of man or canoe in the field of the telescope I kept on pointing at the scattered group.

At noon I gave no orders for a change of course, and the mate's whiskers became much concerned and seemed to be offering themselves unduly to my notice. At last I said:

"I am going to stand right in. Quite in—as far as I can take her."

The stare of extreme surprise imparted an air of ferocity also to his eyes, and he looked truly terrific for a moment.

"We're not doing well in the middle of the gulf," I continued, casually. "I am going to look for the land breezes tonight."

"Bless my soul! Do you mean, sir, in the dark amongst the lot of all them islands and reefs and shoals?"

"Well—if there are any regular land breezes at all on this coast one must get close inshore to find them, mustn't one?"

"Bless my soul!" he exclaimed again under his breath. All that after-noon he wore a dreamy, contemplative appearance which in him was a mark of perplexity. After dinner I went into my stateroom as if I meant to take some rest. There we two bent our dark heads over a half-unrolled chart lying on my bed.

"There," I said. "It's got to be Koh-ring. I've been looking at it ever since sunrise. It has got two hills and a low point. It must be inhabited. And on the coast opposite there is what looks like the mouth of a biggish river—with some town, no doubt, not far up. It's the best chance for you that I can see.

"Anything. Koh-ring let it be."

He looked thoughtfully at the chart as if surveying chances and dis-tances from a lofty height—and following with his eyes his own figure wan-dering on the blank land of Cochin China, and then passing off that piece of paper clean out of sight into uncharted regions. And it was as if the ship had two captains to plan her course for her. I had been so worried and restless running up and down that I had not had the patience to dress that day. I had remained in my sleeping suit, with straw slippers and a soft floppy hat. The closeness of the heat in the gulf had been most oppressive, and the crew were used to see me wandering in that airy attire.

"She will clear the south point as she heads now," I whispered into his ear. "Goodness only knows when, though, but certainly after dark. I'll edge her in to half a mile, as far as I may be able to judge in the dark—"

"Be careful," he murmured, warningly—and I realized suddenly that all my future, the only future for which I was fit, would perhaps go irretrievably to pieces in any mishap to my first command.

I could not stop a moment longer in the room. I motioned him to get out of sight and made my way on the poop. That unplayful cub had the watch. I walked up and down for a while thinking things out, then beckoned him over.

"Send a couple of hands to open the two quarter-deck ports," I said, mildly.

He actually had the impudence, or else so forgot himself in his wonder at such an incomprehensible order, as to repeat:

"Open the quarter-deck ports! What for, sir?"

"The only reason you need concern yourself about is because I tell you to do so. Have them open wide and fastened properly."

He reddened and went off, but I believe made some jeering remark to the carpenter as to the sensible practice of ventilating a ship's quarter-deck. I know he popped into the mate's cabin to impart the fact to him because the whiskers came on deck, as it were by chance, and stole glances at me from below—for signs of lunacy or drunkenness, I suppose.

A little before supper, feeling more restless than ever, I rejoined, for a moment, my second self. And to find him sitting so quietly was surprising, like something against nature, inhuman.

I developed my plan in a hurried whisper.

"I shall stand in as close as I dare and then put her round. I shall presently find means to smuggle you out of here into the sail locker, which communicates with the lobby. But there is an opening, a sort of square for hauling the sails out, which gives straight on the quarter-deck and which is never closed in fine weather, so as to give air to the sails. When the ship's way is deadened in stays and all the hands are aft at the main braces you shall have a clear road to slip out and get overboard through the open quarter-deck port. I've had them both fastened up. Use a rope's end to lower yourself into the water so as to avoid a splash—you know. It could be heard and cause some beastly complication."

He kept silent for a while, then whispered, "I understand."

"I won't be there to see you go," I began with an effort. "The rest . . . I only hope I have understood, too."

"You have. From first to last," and for the first time there seemed to be a faltering, something strained in his whisper. He caught hold of my arm, but the ringing of the supper bell made me start. He didn't, though; he only released his grip.

After supper I didn't come below again till well past eight o'clock. The faint, steady breeze was loaded with dew; and the wet, darkened sails held all there was of propelling power in it. The night, clear and starry, sparkled darkly, and the opaque, lightless patches shifting slowly against the low stars were the drifting islets. On the port bow there was a big one more distant and shadowily imposing by the great space of sky it eclipsed.

On opening the door I had a back view of my very own self looking at a chart. He had come out of the recess and was standing near the table.

"Quite dark enough," I whispered.

He stepped back and leaned against my bed with a level, quiet glance.

I sat on the couch. We had nothing to say to each other. Over our heads the officer of the watch moved here and there. Then I heard him move quickly. I knew what that meant. He was making for the companion; and presently his voice was outside my door.

"We are drawing in pretty fast, sir. Land looks rather close."

"Very well," I answered. "I am coming on deck directly."

I waited till he was gone out of the cuddy, then rose. My double moved too. The time had come to exchange our last whispers, for neither of us was ever to hear each other's natural voice.

"Look here!" I opened a drawer and took out three sovereigns. "Take this, anyhow. I've got six and I'd give you the lot, only I must keep a little money to buy some fruit and vegetables for the crew from native boats as we go through Sunda Straits."

He shook his head.

"Take it," I urged him, whispering desperately. "No one can tell what—"

He smiled and slapped meaningly the only pocket of the sleeping jacket. It was not safe, certainly. But I produced a large old silk handkerchief of mine, and tying the three pieces of gold in a corner, pressed it on him. He was touched, I suppose, because he took it at last and tied it quickly round his waist under the jacket, on his bare skin.

Our eyes met; several seconds elapsed, till, our glances still mingled, I extended my hand and turned the lamp out. Then I passed through the cuddy, leaving the door of my room wide open. . . . "Steward!"

He was still lingering in the pantry in the greatness of his zeal, giving a rub-up to a plated cruet stand the last thing before going to bed. Being careful not to wake up the mate, whose room was opposite, I spoke in an undertone.

He looked round anxiously. "Sir!"

"Can you get me a little hot water from the galley?"

"I am afraid, sir, the galley fire's been out for some time now."

"Go and see."

He fled up the stairs.

"Now," I whispered, loudly, into the saloon—too loudly, perhaps, but I was afraid I couldn't make a sound. He was by my side in an instant—the double captain slipped past the stairs—through the tiny dark passage . . . a sliding door. We were in the sail locker, scrambling on our knees over the sails. A sudden thought struck me. I saw myself wandering barefooted, bareheaded, the sun beating on my dark poll. I snatched off my floppy hat and tried hurriedly in the dark to ram it on my other self. He dodged and fended off silently. I wonder what he thought had come to me before he understood and suddenly desisted. Our hands met gropingly, lingered united in a steady, motionless clasp for a second. . . . No word was breathed by either of us when they separated.

I was standing quietly by the pantry door when the steward returned.

"Sorry, sir. Kettle barely warm. Shall I light the spirit lamp?"

"Never mind."

I came out on deck slowly. It was now a matter of conscience to shave the land as close as possible—for now he must go overboard whenever the ship was put in stays. Must! There could be no going back for him. After a moment I walked over to leeward and my heart flew into my mouth at the nearness of the land on the bow. Under any other circumstances I would not have held on a minute longer. The second mate had followed me anxiously.

I looked on till I felt I could command my voice.

"She will weather," I said then in a quiet tone.

"Are you going to try that, sir?" he stammered out incredulously.

I took no notice of him and raised my tone just enough to be heard by the helmsman.

"Keep her good full."

"Good full, sir."

The wind fanned my cheek, the sails slept, the world was silent. The strain of watching the dark loom of the land grow bigger and denser was too much for me. I had shut my eyes—because the ship must go closer. She must! The stillness was intolerable. Were we standing still?

When I opened my eyes the second view started my heart with a thump. The black southern hill of Koh-ring seemed to hang right over the ship like a towering fragment of the everlasting night. On that enormous mass of blackness there was not a gleam to be seen, not a sound to be heard. It was gliding irresistibly toward us and yet seemed already within reach of the hand. I saw the vague figures of the watch grouped in the waist, gazing in awed silence.

"Are you going on, sir?" inquired an unsteady voice at my elbow.

I ignored it. I had to go on.

"Keep her full. Don't check her way. That won't do now," I said warningly.

"I can't see the sails very well," the helmsman answered me, in strange, quavering tones.

Was she close enough? Already she was, I won't say in the shadow of the land, but in the very blackness of it, already swallowed up as it were, gone too close to be recalled, gone from me altogether.

"Give the mate a call," I said to the young man who stood at my elbow still as death. "And turn all hands up."

My tone had a borrowed loudness reverberated from the height of the land. Several voices cried out together: "We are all on deck, sir."

Then stillness again, with the great shadow gliding closer, towering higher, without a light, without a sound. Such a hush had fallen on the ship that she might have been a bark of the dead floating in slowly under the very gate of Erebus.

"My God! Where are we?"

It was the mate moaning at my elbow. He was thunderstruck, and as it were deprived of the moral support of his whiskers. He clapped his hands and absolutely cried out, "Lost!"

"Be quiet," I said sternly.

He lowered his tone, but I saw the shadowy gesture of his despair. "What are we doing here?"

"Looking for the land wind."

He made as if to tear his hair, and addressed me recklessly.

"She will never get out. You have done it, sir. I knew it'd end in something like this. She will never weather, and you are too close now to stay. She'll drift ashore before she's round. O my God!"

I caught his arm as he was raising it to batter his poor devoted head, and shook it violently.

"She's ashore already," he wailed, trying to tear himself away.

"Is she? . . . Keep good full there!"

"Good full, sir," cried the helmsman in a frightened, thin, childlike voice.

I hadn't let go the mate's arm and went on shaking it. "Ready about, do you hear? You go forward"—shake—"and stop there"—shake—"and hold your noise"—shake—"and see these head sheets properly overhauled" —shake, shake—shake.

And all the time I dared not look toward the land lest my heart should fail me. I released my grip at last and he ran forward as if fleeing for dear life.

I wondered what my double there in the sail locker thought of this commotion. He was able to hear everything—and perhaps he was able to understand why, on my conscience, it had to be thus close—no less. My first order "Hard alee!" re-echoed ominously under the towering shadow of Koh-ring as if I had shouted in a mountain gorge. And then I watched the land intently. In that smooth water and light wind it was impossible to feel the ship coming-to. No! I could not feel her. And my second self was making now ready to slip out and lower himself overboard. Perhaps he was gone already . . . ?

The great black mass brooding over our very mastheads began to pivot away from the ship's side silently. And now I forgot the secret stranger ready to depart, and remembered only that I was a total stranger to the ship. I did not know her. Would she do it? How was she to be handled?

I swung the mainyard and waited helplessly. She was perhaps stopped, and her very fate hung in the balance, with the black mass of Koh-ring like the gate of the everlasting night towering over her taffrail. What would she do now? Had she way on her yet? I stepped to the side swiftly, and on the shadowy water I could see nothing except a faint phosphorescent flash revealing the glassy smoothness of the sleeping surface. It was impossible to tell—and I had not learned yet the feel of my ship. Was she moving? What I needed was something easily seen, a piece of paper, which I could throw overboard and watch. I had nothing on me. To run down for it I didn't dare. There was no time. All at once my strained, yearning stare distinguished a white object floating within a yard of the ship's side. White on the black water. A phosphorescent flash passed under it. What was that thing? . . . I recognized my own floppy hat. It must have fallen off his head . . . and he didn't bother. Now I had what I wanted—the saving mark for my eyes. But I hardly thought of my other self, now gone from the ship, to be hidden forever from all friendly faces, to be a fugitive and a vagabond on the earth, with no brand of the curse on his sane forehead to stay a slaying hand ... too proud to explain.

And I watched the hat—the expression of my sudden pity for his mere flesh. It had been meant to save his homeless head from the dangers of the sun. And now—behold—it was saving the ship, by serving me for a mark to help out the ignorance of my strangeness. Ha! It was drifting forward, warning me just in time that the ship had gathered sternway.

"Shift the helm," I said in a low voice to the seaman standing still like a statue.

The man's eyes glistened wildly in the binnacle light as he jumped round to the other side and spun round the wheel.

I walked to the break of the poop. On the overshadowed deck all hands stood by the forebraces waiting for my order. The stars ahead seemed to be gliding from right to left. And all was so still in the world that I heard the quiet remark "She's round," passed in a tone of intense relief between two seamen.

"Let go and haul."

The foreyards ran round with a great noise, amidst cheery cries. And now the frightful whiskers made themselves heard giving various orders. Already the ship was drawing ahead. And I was alone with her. Nothing! no one in the world should stand now between us, throwing a shadow on the way of silent knowledge and mute affection, the perfect communion of a seaman with his first command.

Walking to the taffrail, I was in time to make out, on the very edge of a darkness thrown by a towering black mass like the very gateway of Erebus—yes, I was in time to catch an evanescent glimpse of my white hat left behind to mark the spot where the secret sharer of my cabin and of my thoughts, as though he were my second self, had lowered himself into the water to take his punishment: a free man, a proud swimmer striking out for a new destiny.

Questions

1. "And suddenly I rejoiced in the great security of the sea as compared with the unrest of the land, in my choice of that untempted life presenting no disquieting problems, invested with an elementary moral beauty by the absolute straightforwardness of its appeal and by the singleness of its purpose" (p. 25). Do the events of the story justify these early musings of the captain? Explain. Who in the story might represent elementary morality? Can that elementary morality be described as "beautiful"? Why or why not?   2. When the frightened mate cries out that the ship will founder, the captain catches his arm. "I hadn't let go the mate's arm and went on shaking it. 'Ready about, do you hear? You go forward'—shake—'and stop there'—shake—'and hold your noise'—shake—'and see these head sheets properly overhauled'—shake, shake—shake" (p. 50). What is the significance of the captain's behavior?   3. Why does the captain sail closer to the land than is necessary to ensure Leggatt's escape?   4. If the captain is "innocent" at the outset, in what way is he "experienced" at the conclusion?

The Bride Comes to Yellow Sky

STEPHEN CRANE [1871–1900]

I

THE great Pullman was whirling onward with such dignity of motion that a glance from the window seemed simply to prove that the plains of Texas were pouring eastward. Vast flats of green grass, dull-hued spaces of mesquit and cactus, little groups of frame houses, woods of light and tender trees, all were sweeping into the east, sweeping over the horizon, a precipice.

A newly married pair had boarded this coach at San Antonio. The man's face was reddened from many days in the wind and sun, and a direct result of his new black clothes was that his brick-coloured hands were constantly performing in a most conscious fashion. From time to time he looked down respectfully at his attire. He sat with a hand on each knee, like a man waiting in a barber's shop. The glances he devoted to other passengers were furtive and shy.

The bride was not pretty, nor was she very young. She wore a dress of blue cashmere, with small reservations of velvet here and there, and with steel buttons abounding. She continually twisted her head to regard her puff sleeves, very stiff, straight, and high. They embarrassed her. It was quite apparent that she had cooked, and that she expected to cook, dutifully. The blushes caused by the careless scrutiny of some passengers as she had entered the car were strange to see upon this plain, under-class countenance, which was drawn in placid, almost emotionless lines.

They were evidently very happy. "Ever been in a parlour-car before?" he asked, smiling with delight.

"No," she answered; "I never was. It's fine, ain't it?"

"Great! And then after a while we'll go forward to the diner, and get a big lay-out. Finest meal in the world. Charge a dollar."

"Oh, do they?" cried the bride. "Charge a dollar? Why, that's too much —for us—ain't it, Jack?"

"Not this trip, anyhow," he answered bravely. "We're going to go the whole thing."

Later he explained to her about the trains. "You see, it's a thousand miles from one end of Texas to the other; and this train runs right across it, and never stops but four times." He had the pride of an owner. He pointed out to her the dazzling fittings of the coach; and in truth her eyes opened wider as she contemplated the sea-green figured velvet, the shining brass, silver, and glass, the wood that gleamed as darkly brilliant as the surface of a pool of oil.

At one end a bronze figure sturdily held a support for a separated chamber, and at convenient places on the ceiling were frescos in olive and silver.

To the minds of the pair, their surroundings reflected the glory of their marriage that morning in San Antonio; this was the environment of their new estate; and the man's face in particular beamed with an elation that made him appear ridiculous to the negro porter. This individual at times surveyed them from afar with an amused and superior grin. On other occasions he bullied them with skill in ways that did not make it exactly plain to them that they were being bullied. He subtly used all the manners of the most unconquerable kind of snobbery. He oppressed them; but of this oppression they had small knowledge, and they speedily forgot that infrequently a number of travellers covered them with stares of derisive enjoyment. Historically there was supposed to be something infinitely humorous in their situation.

"We are due in Yellow Sky at 3:42," he said, looking tenderly into her eyes.

"Oh, are we?" she said, as if she had not been aware of it. To evince surprise at her husband's statement was part of her wifely amiability. She took from a pocket a little silver watch; and as she held it before her, and stared at it with a frown of attention, the new husband's face shone.

"I bought it in San Anton' from a friend of mine," he told her gleefully.

"It's seventeen minutes past twelve," she said, looking up at him with a kind of shy and clumsy coquetry. A passenger, noting this play, grew excessively sardonic, and winked at himself in one of the numerous mirrors.

At last they went to the dining-car. Two rows of negro waiters, in glowing white suits, surveyed their entrance with the interest, and also the equanimity, of men who had been forewarned. The pair fell to the lot of a waiter who happened to feel pleasure in steering them through their meal. He viewed them with the manner of a fatherly pilot, his countenance radiant with benevolence. The patronage, entwined with the ordinary deference, was not plain to them. And yet, as they returned to their coach, they showed in their faces a sense of escape.

To the left, miles down a long purple slope, was a little ribbon of mist where moved the keening Rio Grande. The train was approaching it at an angle, and the apex was Yellow Sky. Presently it was apparent that, as the distance from Yellow Sky grew shorter, the husband became commensurately restless. His brick-red hands were more insistent in their prominence. Occasionally he was even rather absent-minded and far-away when the bride leaned forward and addressed him.

As a matter of truth, Jack Potter was beginning to find the shadow of a deed weigh upon him like a leaden slab. He, the town marshal of Yellow Sky, a man known, liked, and feared in his corner, a prominent person, had gone to San Antonio to meet a girl he believed he loved, and there, after the usual prayers, had actually induced her to marry him, without consulting Yellow Sky for any part of the transaction. He was now bringing his bride before an innocent and unsuspecting community.

Of course people in Yellow Sky married as it pleased them, in accordance with a general custom; but such was Potter's thought of his duty to his friends, or of their idea of his duty, or of an unspoken form which does not control men in these matters, that he felt he was heinous. He had committed an extraordinary crime. Face to face with this girl in San Antonio, and spurred by his sharp impulse, he had gone headlong over all the social hedges. At San Antonio he was like a man hidden in the dark. A knife to sever any friendly duty, any form, was easy to his hand in that remote city. But the hour of Yellow Sky—the hour of daylight—was approaching.

He knew full well that his marriage was an important thing to his town. It could only be exceeded by the burning of the new hotel. His friends could not forgive him. Frequently he had reflected on the advisability of telling them by telegraph, but a new cowardice had been upon him. He feared to do it. And now the train was hurrying him toward a scene of amazement, glee, and reproach. He glanced out of the window at the line of haze swinging slowly in toward the train.

Yellow Sky had a kind of brass band, which played painfully, to the delight of the populace. He laughed without heart as he thought of it. If the citizens could dream of his prospective arrival with his bride, they would parade the band at the station and escort them, amid cheers and laughing congratulations, to his adobe home.

He resolved that he would use all the devices of speed and plainscraft in making the journey from the station to his house. Once within that safe citadel, he could issue some sort of vocal bulletin, and then not go among the citizens until they had time to wear off a little of their enthusiasm.

The bride looked anxiously at him. "What's worrying you, Jack?"

He laughed again. "I'm not worrying, girl; I'm only thinking of Yellow Sky."

She flushed in comprehension.

A sense of mutual guilt invaded their minds and developed a finer tenderness. They looked at each other with eyes softly aglow. But Potter often laughed the same nervous laugh; the flush upon the bride's face seemed quite permanent.

The traitor to the feelings of Yellow Sky narrowly watched the speeding landscape. "We're nearly there," he said.

Presently the porter came and announced the proximity of Potter's home. He held a brush in his hand, and, with all his airy superiority gone, he brushed Potter's new clothes as the latter slowly turned this way and that way. Potter fumbled out a coin and gave it to the porter, as he had seen others do. It was a heavy and muscle-bound business, as that of a man shoeing his first horse.

The porter took their bag, and as the train began to slow they moved forward to the hooded platform of the car. Presently the two engines and their string of coaches rushed into the station of Yellow Sky.

"They have to take water here," said Potter, from a constricted throat and in mournful cadence, as one announcing death. Before the train stopped his eye had swept the length of the platform, and he was glad and astonished to see there was none upon it but the station-agent, who, with a slightly hurried and anxious air, was walking toward the water-tanks. When the train had halted, the porter alighted first, and placed in position a little temporary step.

"Come on, girl," said Potter, hoarsely. As he helped her down they each laughed on a false note. He took the bag from the negro, and bade his wife cling to his arm. As they slunk rapidly away, his hang-dog glance perceived that they were unloading the two trunks, and also that the station-agent, far ahead near the baggage-car, had turned and was running toward him, making gestures. He laughed, and groaned as he laughed, when he noted the first effect of his marital bliss upon Yellow Sky. He gripped his wife's arm firmly to his side, and they fled. Behind them the porter stood, chuckling fatuously.

II

THE California express on the Southern Railway was due at Yellow Sky in twenty-one minutes. There were six men at the bar of the Weary Gentleman saloon. One was a drummer who talked a great deal and rapidly; three were Texans who did not care to talk at that time; and two were Mexican sheepherders, who did not talk as a general practice in the Weary Gentleman saloon. The barkeeper's dog lay on the board walk that crossed in front of the door. His head was on his paws, and he glanced drowsily here and there with the constant vigilance of a dog that is kicked on occasion. Across the sandy street were some vivid green grass-plots, so wonderful in appearance, amid the sands that burned near them in a blazing sun, that they caused a doubt in the mind. They exactly resembled the grass mats used to represent lawns on the stage. At the cooler end of the railway station, a man without a coat sat in a tilted chair and smoked his pipe. The fresh-cut bank of the Rio Grande circled near the town, and there could be seen beyond it a great plum-coloured plain of mesquit.

Save for the busy drummer and his companions in the saloon, Yellow Sky was dozing. The new-comer leaned gracefully upon the bar, and recited many tales with the confidence of a bard who has come upon a new field.

"—and at the moment that the old man fell downstairs with the bureau in his arms, the old woman was coming up with two scuttles of coal, and of course—"

The drummer's tale was interrupted by a young man who suddenly appeared in the open door. He cried: "Scratchy Wilson's drunk, and has turned loose with both hands." The two Mexicans at once set down their glasses and faded out of the rear entrance of the saloon.

The drummer, innocent and jocular, answered: "All right, old man. S'pose he has? Come in and have a drink, anyhow."

But the information had made such a obvious cleft in every skull in the room that the drummer was obliged to see its importance. All had become instantly solemn. "Say," said he, mystified, "what is this?" His three companions made the introductory gesture of eloquent speech; but the young man at the door forestalled them.

"It means, my friend," he answered, as he came into the saloon, "that for the next two hours this town won't be a health resort."

The barkeeper went to the door, and locked and barred it; reaching out of the window, he pulled in heavy wooden shutters, and barred them. Immediately a solemn, chapel-like gloom was upon the place. The drummer was looking from one to another.

"But say," he cried, "what is this, anyhow? You don't mean there is going to be a gun-fight?"

"Don't know whether there'll be a fight or not," answered one man, grimly; "but there'll be some shootin'—some good shootin'."

The young man who had warned them waved his hand. "Oh, there'll be a fight fast enough, if any one wants it. Anybody can get a fight out there in the street. There's a fight just waiting."

The drummer seemed to be swayed between the interest of a foreigner and a perception of personal danger.

"What did you say his name was?" he asked.

"Scratchy Wilson," they answered in chorus.

"And will he kill anybody? What are you going to do? Does this happen often? Does he rampage around like this once a week or so? Can he break in that door?"

"No; he can't break down that door," replied the barkeeper. "He's tried it three times. But when he comes you'd better lay down on the floor, stranger. He's dead sure to shoot at it, and a bullet may come through."

Thereafter the drummer kept a strict eye upon the door. The time had not yet been called for him to hug the floor, but, as a minor precaution, he sidled near to the wall. "Will he kill anybody?" he said again.

The men laughed low and scornfully at the question.

"He's out to shoot, and he's out for trouble. Don't see any good in experimentin' with him."

"But what do you do in a case like this? What do you do?"

A man responded: "Why, he and Jack Potter—"

"But," in chorus the other men interrupted, "Jack Potter's in San Anton'."

"Well, who is he? What's he got to do with it?"

"Oh, he's the town marshal. He goes out and fights Scratchy when he gets on one of these tears."

"Wow!" said the drummer, mopping his brow. "Nice job he's got."

The voices had toned away to mere whisperings. The drummer wished to ask further questions, which were born of an increasing anxiety and bewilderment; but when he attempted them, the men merely looked at him in irritation and motioned him to remain silent. A tense waiting hush was upon them. In the deep shadows of the room their eyes shone as they listened for sounds from the street. One man made three gestures at the barkeeper; and the latter, moving like a ghost, handed him a glass and a bottle. The man poured a full glass of whisky, and set down the bottle noiselessly. He gulped the whisky in a swallow, and turned again toward the door in immovable silence. The drummer saw that the barkeeper, without a sound, had taken a Winchester from beneath the bar. Later he saw this individual beckoning to him, so he tiptoed across the room.

"You better come with me back of the bar."

"No, thanks," said the drummer, perspiring; "I'd rather be where I can make a break for the back door."

Whereupon the man of bottles made a kindly but peremptory gesture. The drummer obeyed it, and, finding himself seated on a box with his head below the level of the bar, balm was laid upon his soul at sight of various zinc and copper fittings that bore a resemblance to armour-plate. The barkeeper took a seat comfortably upon an adjacent box.

"You see," he whispered, "this here Scratchy Wilson is a wonder with a gun—a perfect wonder; and when he goes on the war-trail, we hunt our holes —naturally. He's about the last one of the old gang that used to hang out along the river here. He's a terror when he's drunk. When he's sober he's all right— kind of simple—wouldn't hurt a fly—nicest fellow in town. But when he's drunk—whoo!"

There were periods of stillness. "I wish Jack Potter was back from San Anton'," said the barkeeper. "He shot Wilson up once—in the leg—and he would sail in and pull out the kinks in this thing."

Presently they heard from a distance the sound of a shot, followed by three wild yowls. It instantly removed a bond from the men in the darkened saloon. There was a shuffling of feet. They looked at each other. "Here he comes," they said.

III

A man in a maroon-coloured flannel shirt, which had been pur-chased for purposes of decoration, and made principally by some Jewish women on the East Side of New York, rounded a corner and walked into the middle of the main street of Yellow Sky. In either hand the man held a long, heavy, blue-black revolver. Often he yelled, and these cries rang through a semblance of a deserted village, shrilly flying over the roofs in a volume that seemed to have no relation to the ordinary vocal strength of a man. It was as if the surrounding stillness formed the arch of a tomb over him. These cries of ferocious challenge rang against walls of silence. And his boots had red tops with gilded imprints, of the kind beloved in winter by little sledding boys on the hillsides of New England.

The man's face flamed in a rage begot of whisky. His eyes, rolling, and yet keen for ambush, hunted the still doorways and windows. He walked with the creeping movement of the midnight cat. As it occurred to him, he roared menacing information. The long revolvers in his hands were as easy as straws; they were moved with an electric swiftness. The little fingers of each hand played sometimes in a musician's way. Plain from the low collar of the shirt, the cords of his neck straightened and sank, straightened and sank, as passion moved him. The only sounds were his terrible invitations. The calm adobes preserved their demeanour at the passing of this small thing in the middle of the street.

There was no offer of fight—no offer of fight. The man called to the sky. There were no attractions. He bellowed and fumed and swayed his revolvers here and everywhere.

The dog of the barkeeper of the Weary Gentleman saloon had not appreciated the advance of events. He yet lay dozing in front of his master's door. At sight of the dog, the man paused and raised his revolver humorously. At sight of the man, the dog sprang up and walked diagonally away, with a sullen head, and growling. The man yelled, and the dog broke into a gallop. As it was about to enter an alley, there was a loud noise, a whistling, and something spat the ground directly before it. The dog screamed, and, wheeling in terror, galloped headlong in a new direction. Again there was a noise, a whistling, and sand was kicked viciously before it. Fear-stricken, the dog turned and flurried like an animal in a pen. The man stood laughing, his weapons at his hips.

Ultimately the man was attracted by the closed door of the Weary Gentleman saloon. He went to it and, hammering with a revolver, demanded drink.

The door remaining imperturbable, he picked a bit of paper from the walk, and nailed it to the framework with a knife. He then turned his back contemptuously upon this popular resort and, walking to the opposite side of the street and spinning there on his heel quickly and lithely, fired at the bit of paper. He missed it by a half-inch. He swore at himself, and went away. Later he comfortably fusilladed the windows of his most intimate friend. The man was playing with this town; it was a toy for him.

But still there was no offer of fight. The name of Jack Potter, his ancient antagonist, entered his mind, and he concluded that it would be a glad thing if he should go to Potter's house, and by bombardment induce him to come out and fight. He moved in the direction of his desire, chanting Apache scalp-music.

When he arrived at it, Potter's house presented the same still front as had the other adobes. Taking up a strategic position, the man howled a challenge. But this house regarded him as might a great stone god. It gave no sign. After a decent wait, the man howled further challenges, mingling with them wonderful epithets.

Presently there came the spectacle of a man churning himself into deepest rage over the immobility of a house. He fumed at it as the winter wind attacks a prairie cabin in the North. To the distance there should have gone the sound of a tumult like the fighting of two hundred Mexicans. As necessity bade him, he paused for breath or to reload his revolvers.

IV

POTTER and his bride walked sheepishly and with speed. Sometimes they laughed together shamefacedly and low.

"Next corner, dear," he said finally.

They put forth the efforts of a pair walking bowed against a strong wind. Potter was about to raise a finger to point the first appearance of the new home when, as they circled the corner, they came face to face with a man in a maroon-coloured shirt, who was feverishly pushing cartridges into a large revolver. Upon the instant the man dropped his revolver to the ground and, like lightning, whipped another from its holster. The second weapon was aimed at the bridegroom's chest.

There was a silence. Potter's mouth seemed to be merely a grave for his tongue. He exhibited an instinct to at once loosen his arm from the woman's grip, and he dropped the bag to the sand. As for the bride, her face had gone as yellow as old cloth. She was a slave to hideous rites, gazing at the apparitional snake.

The two men faced each other at a distance of three paces. He of the revolver smiled with a new and quiet ferocity.

"Tried to sneak up on me," he said. "Tried to sneak up on me!" His eyes grew more baleful. As Potter made a slight movement, the man thrust his revolver venomously forward. "No; don't you do it, Jack Potter. Don't you move a finger toward a gun just yet. Don't you move an eyelash. The time has come for me to settle with you, and I'm goin' to do it my own way, and loaf along with no interferin'. So if you don't want a gun bent on you, just mind what I tell you."

Potter looked at his enemy. "I ain't got a gun on me, Scratchy," he said. "Honest, I ain't." He was stiffening and steadying, but yet somewhere at the back of his mind a vision of the Pullman floated: the sea-green figured velvet, the shining brass, silver, and glass, the wood that gleamed as darkly brilliant as the surface of a pool of oil—all the glory of the marriage, the environment of the new estate. "You know I fight when it comes to fighting, Scratchy Wilson; but I ain't got a gun on me. You'll have to do all the shootin' yourself."

His enemy's face went livid. He stepped forward, and lashed his weapon to and fro before Potter's chest. "Don't you tell me you ain't got no gun on you, you whelp. Don't tell me no lie like that. There ain't a man in Texas ever seen you without no gun. Don't take me for no kid." His eyes blazed with light, and his throat worked like a pump.

"I ain't takin' you for no kid," answered Potter. His heels had not moved an inch backward. "I'm takin' you for a damn fool. I tell you I ain't got a gun, and I ain't. If you're goin' to shoot me up, you better begin now; you'll never get a chance like this again."

So much enforced reasoning had told on Wilson's rage; he was calmer. "If you ain't got a gun, why ain't you got a gun?" he sneered. "Been to Sunday-school?"

"I ain't got a gun because I've just come from San Anton' with my wife. I'm married," said Potter. "And if I'd thought there was going to be any ga-loots like you prowling around when I brought my wife home, I'd had a gun, and don't you forget it."

"Married!" said Scratchy, not at all comprehending.

"Yes, married. I'm married," said Potter, distinctly.

"Married?" said Scratchy. Seemingly for the first time, he saw the drooping, drowning woman at the other man's side. "No!" he said. He was like a creature allowed a glimpse of another world. He moved a pace back-ward, and his arm, with the revolver, dropped to his side. "Is this the lady?" he asked.

"Yes; this is the lady," answered Potter.

There was another period of silence.

"Well," said Wilson at last, slowly, "I s'pose it's all off now."

"It's all off if you say so, Scratchy. You know I didn't make the trouble." Potter lifted his valise.

"Well, I 'low it's off, Jack," said Wilson. He was looking at the ground. "Married!" He was not a student of chivalry; it was merely that in the presence of this foreign condition he was a simple child of the earlier plains. He picked up his starboard revolver, and, placing both weapons in their holsters, he went away. His feet made funnel-shaped tracks in the heavy sand.

Questions

1. *Scratchy is described in the final paragraph as "a simple child of the earlier plains." In the context of the story what does this mean? Was Potter ever a simple child of the earlier plains?* 2. *Early in the story we read that ". . . Jack Potter was beginning to find the shadow of a deed weigh upon him like a leaden slab. He, the town marshal of Yellow Sky, a man known, liked, and feared in his corner, a prominent person, had gone to San Antonio to meet a girl he believed he loved, and there, after the usual prayers, had actually induced her to marry him, without consulting Yellow Sky for any part of the transaction. He was now bringing his bride before an innocent and unsuspecting com-munity." Jack Potter, like any man, has a right to marry. How do you account for his feel-ings as described in this passage?* 3. *How would you characterize Scratchy's behavior? How does it relate to the "myth of the West" preserved in films and western novels? How does the description of Scratchy's shirt at the beginning of part III affect that view of the West?* 4. *A "drummer" is a traveling salesman. What effect does his presence have on the "myth of the West"?* 5. *Why is Scratchy disconsolate at the end?*

I Want to Know Why

SHERWOOD ANDERSON [1876–1941]

WE got up at four in the morning, that first day in the east. On the evening before we had climbed off a freight train at the edge of town, and with the true instinct of Kentucky boys had found our way across town and to the race track and the stables at once. Then we knew we were all right. Hanley Turner right away found a nigger we knew. It was Bildad Johnson who in the winter works at Ed Becker's livery barn in our home town, Beckersville. Bildad is a good cook as almost all our niggers are and of course he, like everyone in our part of Kentucky who is anyone at all, likes the horses. In the spring Bildad begins to scratch around. A nigger from our country can flatter and wheedle anyone into letting him do most anything he wants. Bildad wheedles the stable men and the trainers from the horse farms in our country around Lexington. The trainers come into town in the evening to stand around and talk and maybe get into a poker game. Bildad gets in with them. He is always doing little favors and telling about things to eat, chicken browned in a pan, and how is the best way to cook sweet potatoes and corn bread. It makes your mouth water to hear him.

When the racing season comes on and the horses go to the races and there is all the talk on the streets in the evenings about the new colts, and everyone says when they are going over to Lexington or to the spring meeting at Churchill Downs or to Latonia, and the horsemen that have been down to New Orleans or maybe at the winter meeting at Havana in Cuba come home to spend a week before they start out again, at such a time when everything talked about in Beckersville is just horses and nothing else and the outfits start out and horse racing is in every breath of air you breathe, Bildad shows up with a job as cook for some outfit. Often when I think about it, his always going all season to the races and working in the livery barn in the winter where horses are and where men like to come and talk about horses, I wish I was a nigger. It's a foolish thing to say, but that's the way I am about being around horses, just crazy. I can't help it.

Well, I must tell you about what we did and let you in on what I'm talking about. Four of us boys from Beckersville, all whites and sons of men who live in Beckersville regular, made up our minds we were going to the races, not just to Lexington or Louisville, I don't mean, but to the big eastern track we were always hearing our Beckersville men talk about, to Saratoga. We were all pretty young then. I was just turned fifteen and I was the oldest of the four. It was my scheme. I admit that and I talked the others into trying it. There was Hanley Turner and Henry Rieback and Tom Tumberton and myself. I had thirty-seven dollars I had earned during the winter working nights and Saturdays in Enoch Myer's grocery. Henry Rieback had eleven dollars and the others, Hanley and Tom, had only a dollar or two each. We fixed it all up and laid low until the Kentucky spring meetings were over and some of our men, the sportiest ones, the ones we envied the most, had cut out—then we cut out too.

I won't tell you the trouble we had beating our way on freights and all. We went through Cleveland and Buffalo and other cities and saw Niagara Falls. We bought things there, souvenirs and spoons and cards and shells with pictures of the falls on them for our sisters and mothers, but thought we had better not send any of the things home. We didn't want to put the folks on our trail and maybe be nabbed.

We got into Saratoga as I said at night and went to the track. Bildad fed us up. He showed us a place to sleep in hay over a shed and promised to keep still. Niggers are all right about things like that. They won't squeal on you. Often a white man you might meet, when you had run away from home like that, might appear to be all right and give you a quarter or a half-dollar or something, and then go right and give you away. White men will do that, but not a nigger. You can trust them. They are squarer with kids. I don't know why.

At the Saratoga meeting that year there were a lot of men from home. Dave Williams and Arthur Mulford and Jerry Myers and others. Then there was a lot from Louisville and Lexington Henry Rieback knew but I didn't. They were professional gamblers and Henry Rieback's father is one too. He is what is called a sheet writer and goes away most of the year to tracks. In the winter when he is home in Beckersville he don't stay there much but goes away to cities and deals faro. He is a nice man and generous, is always sending Henry presents, a bicycle and a gold watch and a boy scout suit of clothes and things like that.

My own father is a lawyer. He's all right, but don't make much money and can't buy me things and anyway I'm getting so old now I don't expect it. He never said nothing to me against Henry, but Hanley Turner and Tom Tumberton's fathers did. They said to their boys that money so come by is no good and they didn't want their boys brought up to hear gamblers' talk and be thinking about such things and maybe embrace them.

That's all right and I guess the men know what they are talking about, but I don't see what it's got to do with Henry or with horses either. That's what I'm writing this story about. I'm puzzled. I'm getting to be a man and want to think straight and be O.K., and there's something I saw at the race meeting at the eastern track I can't figure out.

I can't help it, I'm crazy about thoroughbred horses. I've always been that way. When I was ten years old and saw I was growing to be big and couldn't be a rider I was so sorry I nearly died. Harry Hellinfinger in Beckersville, whose father is Postmaster, is grown up and too lazy to work, but liked to stand around in the street and get up jokes on boys like sending them to a hardware store for a gimlet to bore square holes and other jokes like that. He played one on me. He told me that if I would eat a half a cigar I would be stunted and not grow any more and maybe could be a rider. I did it. When father wasn't looking I took a cigar out of his pocket and gagged it down some way. It made me awful sick and the doctor had to be sent for, and then it did no good. I kept right on growing. It was a joke. When I told what I had done and why most fathers would have whipped me but mine didn't.

Well, I didn't get stunted and didn't die. It serves Harry Hellinfinger right. Then I made up my mind I would like to be a stable boy, but had to give that up too. Mostly niggers do that work and I knew father wouldn't let me go into it. No use to ask him.

If you've never been crazy about thoroughbreds it's because you've never been around where they are much and don't know any better. They're beautiful. There isn't anything so lovely and clean and full of spunk and honest and everything as some race horses. On the big horse farms that are all around our town Beckersville there are tracks and the horses run in the early morning. More than a thousand times I've got out of bed before daylight and walked two or three miles to the tracks. Mother wouldn't of let me go but father always says, "Let him alone." So I got some bread out of the bread box and some butter and jam, gobbled it and lit out.

At the tracks you sit on the fence with men, whites and niggers, and they chew tobacco and talk, and then the colts are brought out. It's early and the grass is covered with shiny dew and in another field a man is plowing and they are frying things in a shed where the track niggers sleep, and you know how a nigger can giggle and laugh and say things that make you laugh. A white man can't do it and some niggers can't but a track nigger can every time.

And so the colts are brought out and some are just galloped by stable boys, but almost every morning on a big track owned by a rich man who lives maybe in New York, there are always, nearly every morning, a few colts and some of the old race horses and geldings and mares that are cut loose.

It brings a lump up into my throat when a horse runs. I don't mean all horses but some. I can pick them nearly every time. It's in my blood like in the blood of race track niggers and trainers. Even when they just go slob-jogging along with a little nigger on their backs I can tell a winner. If my throat hurts and it's hard for me to swallow, that's him. He'll run like Sam Hill when you let him out. If he don't win every time it'll be a wonder and because they've got him in a pocket behind another or he was pulled or got off bad at the post or something. If I wanted to be a gambler like Henry Rieback's father I could get rich. I know I could and Henry says so, too. All I would have to do is to wait 'til that hurt comes when I see a horse and then bet every cent. That's what I could do if I wanted to be a gambler, but I don't.

When you're at the tracks in the morning—not the race tracks but the training tracks around Beckersville—you don't see a horse the kind I've been talking about, very often, but it's nice anyway. Any thoroughbred, that is sired right and out of a good mare and trained by a man that knows how, can run. If he couldn't what would he be there for and not pulling a plow?

Well, out of the stables they come and the boys are on their backs and it's lovely to be there. You hunch down on top of the fence and itch inside you. Over in the sheds the niggers giggle and sing. Bacon is being fried and coffee made. Everything smells lovely. Nothing smells better than coffee and manure and horses and niggers and bacon frying and pipes being smoked out of doors on a morning like that. It just gets you, that's what it does.

But about Saratoga. We was there six days and not a soul from home seen us and everything came off just as we wanted it to, fine weather and horses and races and all. We beat our way home and Bildad gave us a basket with fried chicken and bread and other eatables in, and I had eighteen dollars when we got back to Beckersville. Mother jawed and cried but Pop didn't say much. I told everything we done except one thing. I did and saw that alone. That's what I'm writing about. It got me upset. I think about it at night. Here it is.

At Saratoga we laid up nights in the hay in the shed Bildad had showed us and ate with the niggers early and at night when the race people had all gone away. The men from home stayed mostly in the grandstand and betting field, and didn't come out around the places where the horses are kept except to the paddocks just before a race when the horses are saddled. At Saratoga they don't have paddocks under an open shed as at Lexington and Churchill Downs and other tracks down in our country, but saddle the horses right out in an open place under trees on a lawn as smooth and nice as Banker Bohon's front yard here in Beckersville. It's lovely. The horses are sweaty and nervous and shine and the men come out and smoke cigars and look at them and the trainers are there and the owners, and your heart thumps so you can hardly breathe.

Then the bugle blows for post and the boys that ride come running out with their silk clothes on and you run to get a place by the fence with the niggers.

I always am wanting to be a trainer or owner, and at the risk of being seen and caught and sent home I went to the paddocks before every race. The other boys didn't but I did.

We got to Saratoga on a Friday and on Wednesday the next week the big Mullford Handicap was to be run. Middlestride was in it and Sunstreak. The weather was fine and the track fast. I couldn't sleep the night before.

What had happened was that both these horses are the kind it makes my throat hurt to see. Middlestride is long and looks awkward and is a gelding. He belongs to Joe Thompson, a little owner from home who only has a half-dozen horses. The Mullford Handicap is for a mile and Middlestride can't untrack fast. He goes away slow and is always way back at the half, then he begins to run and if the race is a mile and a quarter he'll just eat up everything and get there.

Sunstreak is different. He is a stallion and nervous and belongs on the biggest farm we've got in our country, the Van Riddle place that belongs to Mr. Van Riddle of New York. Sunstreak is like a girl you think about sometimes but never see. He is hard all over and lovely too. When you look at his head you want to kiss him. He is trained by Jerry Tillford who knows me and has been good to me lots of times, lets me walk into a horse's stall to look at him close and other things. There isn't anything as sweet as that horse. He stands at the post quiet and not letting on, but he is just burning up inside. Then when the barrier goes up he is off like his name, Sunstreak. It makes you ache to see him. It hurts you. He just lays down and runs like a bird dog. There can't anything I ever see run like him except Middlestride when he gets untracked and stretches himself.

Gee! I ached to see that race and those two horses run, ached and dreaded it too. I didn't want to see either of our horses beaten. We had never sent a pair like that to the races before. Old men in Beckersville said so and the niggers said so. It was a fact.

Before the race I went over to the paddocks to see. I looked a last look at Middlestride, who isn't such a much standing in a paddock that way, then I went to see Sunstreak.

It was his day. I knew when I see him. I forgot all about being seen myself and walked right up. All the men from Beckersville were there and no one noticed me except Jerry Tillford. He saw me and something happened. I'll tell you about that.

I was standing looking at that horse and aching. In some way, I can't tell how, I knew just how Sunstreak felt inside. He was quiet and letting the niggers rub his legs and Mr. Van Riddle himself put the saddle on, but he was just a raging torrent inside. He was like the water in the river at Niagara Falls just before it goes plunk down. That horse wasn't thinking about running. He don't have to think about that. He was just thinking about holding himself back 'til the time for the running came. I knew that. I could just in a way see right inside him. He was going to do some awful running and I knew it. He wasn't bragging or letting on much or prancing or making a fuss, but just waiting. I knew it and Jerry Tillford his trainer knew. I looked up and then that man and I looked into each other's eyes. Something happened to me. I guess I loved the man as much as I did the horse because he knew what I knew. Seemed to me there wasn't anything in the world but that man and the horse and me. I cried and Jerry Tillford had a shine in his eyes. Then I came away to the fence to wait for the race. The horse was better than me, more steadier, and now I know better than Jerry. He was the quietest and he had to do the running.

Sunstreak ran first of course and he busted the world's record for a mile. I've seen that if I never see anything more. Everything came out just as I expected. Middlestride got left at the post and was way back and closed up to be second, just as I knew he would. He'll get a world's record too some day. They can't skin the Beckersville country on horses.

I watched the race calm because I knew what would happen. I was sure.

Hanley Turner and Henry Rieback and Tom Tumberton were all more excited than me.

A funny thing had happened to me. I was thinking about Jerry Tillford the trainer and how happy he was all through the race. I liked him that afternoon even more than I ever liked my own father. I almost forgot the horses thinking that way about him. It was because of what I had seen in his eyes as he stood in the paddocks beside Sunstreak before the race started. I knew he had been watching and working with Sunstreak since the horse was a baby colt, had taught him to run and be patient and when to let himself out and not to quit, never. I knew that for him it was like a mother seeing her child do something brave or wonderful. It was the first time I ever felt for a man like that.

After the race that night I cut out from Tom and Hanley and Henry. I wanted to be by myself and I wanted to be near Jerry Tillford if I could work it. Here is what happened.

The track in Saratoga is near the edge of town. It is all polished up and trees around, the evergreen kind, and grass and everything painted and nice. If you go past the track you get to a hard road made of asphalt for automobiles, and if you go along this for a few miles there is a road turns off to a little rummy-looking farm house set in a yard.

That night after the race I went along that road because I had seen Jerry and some other men go that way in an automobile. I didn't expect to find them. I walked for a ways and then sat down by a fence to think. It was the direction they went in. I wanted to be as near Jerry as I could. I felt close to him. Pretty soon I went up the side road—I don't know why—and came to the rummy farm house. I was just lonesome to see Jerry, like wanting to see your father at night when you are a young kid. Just then an automobile came along and turned in. Jerry was in it and Henry Rieback's father, and Arthur Bedford from home, and Dave Williams and two other men I didn't know. They got out of the car and went into the house, all but Henry Rieback's father who quarreled with them and said he wouldn't go. It was only about nine o'clock, but they were all drunk and the rummy-looking farm house was a place for bad women to stay in. That's what it was. I crept up along a fence and looked through a window and saw.

It's what give me the fantods. I can't make it out. The women in the house were all ugly mean-looking women, not nice to look at or be near. They were homely too, except one who was tall and looked a little like the gelding Middlestride, but not clean like him, but with a hard ugly mouth. She had red hair. I saw everything plain. I got up by an old rose bush by an open window and looked. The women had on loose dresses and sat around in chairs. The men came in and some sat on the women's laps. The place smelled rotten and there was rotten talk, the kind a kid hears around a livery stable in a town like Beckersville in the winter but don't ever expect to hear talked when there are women around. It was rotten. A nigger wouldn't go into such a place.

I looked at Jerry Tillford. I've told you how I had been feeling about him on account of his knowing what was going on inside of Sunstreak in the minute before he went to the post for the race in which he made a world's record.

Jerry bragged in that bad woman house as I know Sunstreak wouldn't never have bragged. He said that he made that horse, that it was him that won the race and made the record. He lied and bragged like a fool. I never heard such silly talk.

And then, what do you suppose he did! He looked at the woman in there, the one that was lean and hard-mouthed and looked a little like the gelding Middlestride, but not clean like him, and his eyes began to shine just as they did when he looked at me and at Sunstreak in the paddocks at the track in the afternoon. I stood there by the window—gee!—but I wished I hadn't gone away from the tracks, but had stayed with the boys and the niggers and the horses. The tall rotten-looking woman was between us just as Sunstreak was in the paddocks in the afternoon.

Then, all of a sudden, I began to hate that man. I wanted to scream and rush in the room and kill him. I never had such a feeling before. I was so mad clean through that I cried and my fists were doubled up so my finger nails cut my hands.

And Jerry's eyes kept shining and he waved back and forth, and then he went and kissed that woman and I crept away and went back to the tracks and to bed and didn't sleep hardly any, and then next day I got the other kids to start home with me and never told them anything I seen.

I been thinking about it ever since. I can't make it out. Spring has come again and I'm nearly sixteen and go to the tracks mornings same as always, and I see Sunstreak and Middlestride and a new colt named Strident I'll bet will lay them all out, but no one thinks so but me and two or three niggers.

But things are different. At the tracks the air don't taste as good or smell as good. It's because a man like Jerry Tillford, who knows what he does, could see a horse like Sunstreak run, and kiss a woman like that the same day. I can't make it out. Darn him, what did he want to do like that for? I keep thinking about it and it spoils looking at horses and smelling things and hearing niggers laugh and everything. Sometimes I'm so mad about it I want to fight someone. It gives me the fantods. What did he do it for? I want to know why.

Araby*

JAMES JOYCE [1882–1941]

Nᴏʀᴛʜ Richmond Street, being blind, was a quiet street except at the hour when the Christian Brothers' School set the boys free. An uninhabited house of two storeys stood at the blind end, detached from its neighbours in a square ground. The other houses of the street, conscious of decent lives within them, gazed at one another with brown imperturbable faces.

The former tenant of our house, a priest, had died in the back drawing-room. Air, musty from having been long enclosed, hung in all the rooms, and the waste room behind the kitchen was littered with old useless papers. Among these I found a few paper-covered books, the pages of which were curled and damp: *The Abbot*, by Walter Scott, *The Devout Communicant* and *The Memoirs of Vidocq*. I liked the last best because its leaves were yellow. The wild garden behind the house contained a central apple-tree and a few straggling bushes under one of which I found the late tenant's rusty bicycle-pump. He had been a very charitable priest; in his will he had left all his money to institutions and the furniture of his house to his sister.

When the short days of winter came dusk fell before we had well eaten our dinners. When we met in the street the houses had grown sombre. The space of sky above us was the colour of ever-changing violet and towards it the lamps of the street lifted their feeble lanterns. The cold air stung us and we played till our bodies glowed. Our shouts echoed in the silent street. The career of our play brought us through the dark muddy lanes behind the houses where we ran the gauntlet of the rough tribes from the cottages, to the back doors of the dark dripping gardens where odours arose from the ashpits, to the dark odorous stables where a coachman smoothed and combed the horse or shook music from the buckled harness. When we returned to the street light from the kitchen windows had filled the areas. If my uncle was seen turning the corner we hid in the shadow until we had seen him safely housed. Or if Mangan's sister came out on the doorstep to call her brother in to his tea we watched her from our shadow peer up and down the street. We waited to see whether she would remain or go in and, if she remained, we left our shadow and walked up to Mangan's steps resignedly. She was waiting for us, her figure defined by the light from the half-opened door. Her brother always teased her before he obeyed and I stood by the railings looking at her. Her dress swung as she moved her body and the soft rope of her hair tossed from side to side.

---

*This story is considered in the essay "Reading Fiction" at the end of the book.

Every morning I lay on the floor in the front parlour watching her door. The blind was pulled down to within an inch of the sash so that I could not be seen. When she came out on the doorstep my heart leaped. I ran to the hall, seized my books and followed her. I kept her brown figure always in my eye and, when we came near the point at which our ways diverged, I quickened my pace and passed her. This happened morning after morning. I had never spoken to her, except for a few casual words, and yet her name was like a summons to all my foolish blood.

Her image accompanied me even in places the most hostile to romance. On Saturday evenings when my aunt went marketing I had to go to carry some of the parcels. We walked through the flaring streets, jostled by drunken men and bargaining women, amid the curses of labourers, the shrill litanies of shop-boys who stood on guard by the barrels of pigs' cheeks, the nasal chanting of street-singers, who sang a *come-all-you*[1] about O'Donovan Rossa, or a ballad about the troubles in our native land. These noises converged in a single sensation of life for me: I imagined that I bore my chalice safely through a throng of foes. Her name sprang to my lips at moments in strange prayers and praises which I myself did not understand. My eyes were often full of tears (I could not tell why) and at times a flood from my heart seemed to pour itself out into my bosom. I thought little of the future. I did not know whether I would ever speak to her or not or, if I spoke to her, how I could tell her of my confused adoration. But my body was like a harp and her words and gestures were like fingers running upon the wires.

One evening I went into the back drawing-room in which the priest had died. It was a dark rainy evening and there was no sound in the house. Through one of the broken panes I heard the rain impinge upon the earth, the fine incessant needles of water playing in the sodden beds. Some distant lamp or lighted window gleamed below me. I was thankful that I could see so little. All my senses seemed to desire to veil themselves and, feeling that I was about to slip from them, I pressed the palms of my hands together until they trembled, murmuring: "*O love! O love!*" many times.

At last she spoke to me. When she addressed the first words to me I was so confused that I did not know what to answer. She asked me was I going to *Araby*. I forgot whether I answered yes or no. It would be a splendid bazaar, she said she would love to go.

"And why can't you?" I asked.

While she spoke she turned a silver bracelet round and round her wrist. She could not go, she said, because there would be a retreat that week in her convent. Her brother and two other boys were fighting for their caps and I was alone at the railings. She held one of the spikes, bowing her head towards me. The light from the lamp opposite our door caught the white curve of her neck, lit up her hair that rested there and, falling, lit up the hand

---

1. A street ballad beginning with these words. This one is about Jeremiah Donovan, a nineteenth-century Irish nationalist popularly known as O'Donovan Rossa.

upon the railing. It fell over one side of her dress and caught the white border of a petticoat, just visible as she stood at ease.

"It's well for you," she said.

"If I go," I said, "I will bring you something."

What innumerable follies laid waste my waking and sleeping thoughts after that evening! I wished to annihilate the tedious intervening days. I chafed against the work of school. At night in my bedroom and by day in the classroom her image came between me and the page I strove to read. The syllables of the word *Araby* were called to me through the silence in which my soul luxuriated and cast an Eastern enchantment over me. I asked for leave to go to the bazaar on Saturday night. My aunt was surprised and hoped it was not some Freemason affair. I answered few questions in class. I watched my master's face pass from amiability to sternness; he hoped I was not beginning to idle. I could not call my wandering thoughts together. I had hardly any patience with the serious work of life which, now that it stood between me and my desire, seemed to me child's play, ugly monotonous child's play.

On Saturday morning I reminded my uncle that I wished to go to the bazaar in the evening. He was fussing at the hallstand, looking for the hat-brush, and answered me curtly:

"Yes, boy, I know."

As he was in the hall I could not go into the front parlour and lie at the window. I left the house in bad humour and walked slowly towards the school. The air was pitilessly raw and already my heart misgave me.

When I came home to dinner my uncle had not yet been home. Still it was early. I sat staring at the clock for some time and, when its ticking began to irritate me, I left the room. I mounted the staircase and gained the upper part of the house. The high cold empty gloomy rooms liberated me and I went from room to room singing. From the front window I saw my companions playing below in the street. Their cries reached me weakened and indistinct and, leaning my forehead against the cool glass, I looked over at the dark house where she lived. I may have stood there for an hour, seeing nothing but the brown-clad figure cast by my imagination, touched discreetly by the lamplight at the curved neck, at the hand upon the railings and at the border below the dress.

When I came downstairs again I found Mrs. Mercer sitting at the fire. She was an old garrulous woman, a pawnbroker's widow, who collected used stamps for some pious purpose. I had to endure the gossip of the tea-table. The meal was prolonged beyond an hour and still my uncle did not come. Mrs. Mercer stood up to go: she was sorry she couldn't wait any longer, but it was after eight o'clock and she did not like to be out late, as the night air was bad for her. When she had gone I began to walk up and down the room, clenching my fists. My aunt said:

"I'm afraid you may put off your bazaar for this night of Our Lord."

At nine o'clock I heard my uncle's latchkey in the halldoor. I heard him talking to himself and heard the hallstand rocking when it had received the weight of his overcoat. I could interpret these signs. When he was midway through his dinner I asked him to give me the money to go to the bazaar. He had forgotten.

"The people are in bed and after their first sleep now," he said.

I did not smile. My aunt said to him energetically:

"Can't you give him the money and let him go? You've kept him late enough as it is."

My uncle said he was very sorry he had forgotten. He said he believed in the old saying: "All work and no play makes Jack a dull boy." He asked me where I was going and, when I had told him a second time he asked me did I know *The Arab's Farewell to his Steed.* When I left the kitchen he was about to recite the opening lines of the piece to my aunt.

I held a florin tightly in my hand as I strode down Buckingham Street towards the station. The sight of the streets thronged with buyers and glaring with gas recalled to me the purpose of my journey. I took my seat in a third-class carriage of a deserted train. After an intolerable delay the train moved out of the station slowly. It crept onward among ruinous houses and over the twinkling river. At Westland Row Station a crowd of people pressed to the carriage doors; but the porters moved them back, saying that it was a special train for the bazaar. I remained alone in the bare carriage. In a few minutes the train drew up beside an improvised wooden platform. I passed out on to the road and saw by the lighted dial of a clock that it was ten minutes to ten. In front of me was a large building which displayed the magical name.

I could not find any sixpenny entrance and, fearing that the bazaar would be closed, I passed in quickly through a turnstile, handing a shilling to a weary-looking man. I found myself in a big hall girdled at half its height by a gallery. Nearly all the stalls were closed and the greater part of the hall was in darkness. I recognised a silence like that which pervades a church after a service. I walked into the centre of the bazaar timidly. A few people were gathered about the stalls which were still open. Before a curtain, over which the words *Café Chantant* were written in coloured lamps, two men were counting money on a salver. I listened to the fall of the coins.

Remembering with difficulty why I had come I went over to one of the stalls and examined porcelain vases and flowered tea-sets. At the door of the stall a young lady was talking and laughing with two young gentlemen. I remarked their English accents and listened vaguely to their conversation.

"O, I never said such a thing!"

"O, but you did!"

"O, but I didn't!"

"Didn't she say that?"

"Yes. I heard her."

"O, there's a . . . fib!"

Observing me the young lady came over and asked me did I wish to buy anything. The tone of her voice was not encouraging; she seemed to have spoken to me out of a sense of duty. I looked humbly at the great jars that stood like eastern guards at either side of the dark entrance to the stall and murmured:

"No, thank you."

The young lady changed the position of one of the vases and went back to the two young men. They began to talk of the same subject. Once or twice the young lady glanced at me over her shoulder.

I lingered before her stall, though I knew my stay was useless, to make my interest in her wares seem the more real. Then I turned away slowly and walked down the middle of the bazaar. I allowed the two pennies to fall against the sixpence in my pocket. I heard a voice call from one end of the gallery that the light was out. The upper part of the hall was now completely dark.

Gazing up into the darkness I saw myself as a creature driven and derided by vanity; and my eyes burned with anguish and anger.

The Short Happy Life of Francis Macomber

ERNEST HEMINGWAY [1898–1961]

IT was now lunch time and they were all sitting under the double green fly of the dining tent pretending that nothing had happened.

"Will you have lime juice or lemon squash?" Macomber asked.

"I'll have a gimlet," Robert Wilson told him.

"I'll have a gimlet too. I need something," Macomber's wife said.

"I suppose it's the thing to do," Macomber agreed. "Tell him to make three gimlets."

The mess boy had started them already, lifting the bottles out of the canvas cooling bags that sweated wet in the wind that blew through the trees that shaded the tents.

"What had I ought to give them?" Macomber asked.

"A quid would be plenty," Wilson told him. "You don't want to spoil them."

"Will the headman distribute it?"

"Absolutely."

Francis Macomber had, half an hour before, been carried to his tent from the edge of the camp in triumph on the arms and shoulders of the cook, the personal boys, the skinner and the porters. The gun-bearers had taken no part in the demonstration. When the native boys put him down at the door of his tent, he had shaken all their hands, received their congratulations, and then gone into the tent and sat on the bed until his wife came in. She did not speak to him when she came in and he left the tent at once to wash his face and hands in the portable wash basin outside and go over to the dining tent to sit in a comfortable canvas chair in the breeze and the shade.

"You've got your lion," Robert Wilson said to him, "and a damned fine one too."

Mrs. Macomber looked at Wilson quickly. She was an extremely handsome and well-kept woman of the beauty and social position which had, five years before, commanded five thousand dollars as the price of endorsing, with photographs, a beauty product which she had never used. She had been married to Francis Macomber for eleven years.

"He is a good lion, isn't he?" Macomber said. His wife looked at him now. She looked at both these men as though she had never seen them before.

One, Wilson, the white hunter, she knew she had never truly seen before. He was about middle height with sandy hair, a stubby mustache, a very red face and extremely cold blue eyes with faint white wrinkles at the corners that grooved merrily when he smiled. He smiled at her now and she looked away from his face at the way his shoulders sloped in the loose tunic he wore with the four big cartridges held in loops where the left breast pocket should have been, at his big brown hands, his old slacks, his very dirty boots and back to his red face again. She noticed where the baked red of his face stopped in a white line that marked the circle left by his Stetson hat that hung now from one of the pegs of the tent pole.

"Well, here's to the lion," Robert Wilson said. He smiled at her again and, not smiling, she looked curiously at her husband.

Francis Macomber was very tall, very well built if you did not mind that length of bone, dark, his hair cropped like an oarsman, rather thin-lipped, and was considered handsome. He was dressed in the same sort of safari clothes that Wilson wore except that his were new, he was thirty-five years old, kept himself very fit, was good at court games, had a number of big-game fishing records, and had just shown himself, very publicly, to be a coward.

"Here's to the lion," he said. "I can't ever thank you for what you did."

Margaret, his wife, looked away from him and back to Wilson.

"Let's not talk about the lion," she said.

Wilson looked over at her without smiling and now she smiled at him.

"It's been a very strange day," she said. "Hadn't you ought to put your hat on even under the canvas at noon? You told me that, you know."

"Might put it on," said Wilson.

"You know you have a very red face, Mr. Wilson," she told him and smiled again.

"Drink," said Wilson.

"I don't think so," she said. "Francis drinks a great deal, but his face is never red."

"It's red today," Macomber tried a joke.

"No," said Margaret. "It's mine that's red today. But Mr. Wilson's is always red."

"Must be racial," said Wilson. "I say, you wouldn't like to drop my beauty as a topic, would you?"

"I've just started on it."

"Let's chuck it," said Wilson.

"Conversation is going to be so difficult," Margaret said.

"Don't be silly, Margot," her husband said.

"No difficulty," Wilson said. "Got a damn fine lion."

Margot looked at them both and they both saw that she was going to cry. Wilson had seen it coming for a long time and he dreaded it. Macomber was past dreading it.

"I wish it hadn't happened. Oh, I wish it hadn't happened," she said and started for her tent. She made no noise of crying but they could see that her shoulders were shaking under the rose-colored, sun-proofed shirt she wore.

"Women upset," said Wilson to the tall man. "Amounts to nothing. Strain on the nerves and one thing'n another."

"No," said Macomber. "I suppose that I rate that for the rest of my life now."

"Nonsense. Let's have a spot of the giant killer," said Wilson. "Forget the whole thing. Nothing to it anyway."

"We might try," said Macomber. "I won't forget what you did for me though."

"Nothing," said Wilson. "All nonsense."

So they sat there in the shade where the camp was pitched under some wide-topped acacia trees with a boulder-strewn cliff behind them, and a stretch of grass that ran to the bank of a boulder-filled stream in front with forest beyond it, and drank their just-cool lime drinks and avoided one another's eyes while the boys set the table for lunch. Wilson could tell that the boys all knew about it now and when he saw Macomber's personal boy looking curiously at his master while he was putting dishes on the table he snapped at him in Swahili. The boy turned away with his face blank.

"What were you telling him?" Macomber asked.

"Nothing. Told him to look alive or I'd see he got about fifteen of the best."

"What's that? Lashes?"

"It's quite illegal," Wilson said. "You're supposed to fine them."

"Do you still have them whipped?"

"Oh, yes. They could raise a row if they chose to complain. But they don't. They prefer it to the fines."

"How strange!" said Macomber.

"Not strange, really," Wilson said. "Which would you rather do? Take a good birching or lose your pay?"

Then he felt embarrassed at asking it and before Macomber could answer he went on, "We all take a beating every day, you know, one way or another."

This was no better. "Good God," he thought. "I am a diplomat, aren't I?"

"Yes, we take a beating," said Macomber, still not looking at him. "I'm awfully sorry about that lion business. It doesn't have to go any further, does it? I mean no one will hear about it, will they?"

"You mean will I tell it at the Mathaiga Club?" Wilson looked at him now coldly. He had not expected this. So he's a bloody four-letter man as well as a bloody coward, he thought. I rather liked him too until today. But how is one to know about an American?

"No," said Wilson. "I'm a professional hunter. We never talk about our clients. You can be quite easy on that. It's supposed to be bad form to ask us not to talk though."

He had decided now that to break would be much easier. He would eat, then, by himself and could read a book with his meals. They would eat by themselves. He would see them through the safari on a very formal basis— what was it the French called it? Distinguished consideration—and it would be a damn sight easier than having to go through this emotional trash. He'd insult him and make a good clean break. Then he could read a book with his meals and he'd still be drinking their whisky. That was the phase for it when a safari went bad. You ran into another white hunter and you asked, "How is everything going?" and he answered, "Oh, I'm still drinking their whisky," and you knew everything had gone to pot.

"I'm sorry," Macomber said and looked at him with his American face that would stay adolescent until it became middle-aged, and Wilson noted his crew-cropped hair, fine eyes only faintly shifty, good nose, thin lips and hand-some jaw. "I'm sorry I didn't realize that. There are lots of things I don't know."

So what could he do, Wilson thought. He was all ready to break it off quickly and neatly and here the beggar was apologizing after he had just insulted him. He made one more attempt. "Don't worry about me talking," he said. "I have a living to make. You know in Africa no woman ever misses her lion and no white man ever bolts."

"I bolted like a rabbit," Macomber said.

Now what in hell were you going to do about a man who talked like that, Wilson wondered.

Wilson looked at Macomber with his flat, blue, machine-gunner's eyes and the other smiled back at him. He had a pleasant smile if you did not notice how his eyes showed when he was hurt.

"Maybe I can fix it up on buffalo," he said. "We're after them next, aren't we?"

"In the morning if you like," Wilson told him. Perhaps he had been wrong. This was certainly the way to take it. You most certainly could not tell a damned thing about an American. He was all for Macomber again. If you could forget the morning. But, of course, you couldn't. The morning had been about as bad as they come.

"Here comes the Memsahib," he said. She was walking over from her tent looking refreshed and cheerful and quite lovely. She had a very perfect oval face, so perfect that you expected her to be stupid. But she wasn't stupid, Wilson thought, no, not stupid.

"How is the beautiful red-faced Mr. Wilson? Are you feeling better, Francis, my pearl?"

"Oh, much," said Macomber.

"I've dropped the whole thing," she said, sitting down at the table. "What importance is there to whether Francis is any good at killing lions? That's not his trade. That's Mr. Wilson's trade. Mr. Wilson is really very impressive killing anything. You do kill anything, don't you?"

"Oh, anything," said Wilson. "Simply anything." They are, he thought, the hardest in the world; the hardest, the cruelest, the most predatory and the most attractive and their men have softened or gone to pieces nervously as they have hardened. Or is it that they pick men they can handle? They can't know that much at the age they marry, he thought. He was grateful that he had gone through his education on American women before now because this was a very attractive one.

"We're going after buff in the morning," he told her.

"I'm coming," she said.

"No, you're not."

"Oh, yes, I am. Mayn't I, Francis?"

"Why not stay in camp?"

"Not for anything," she said. "I wouldn't miss something like today for anything."

When she left, Wilson was thinking, when she went off to cry, she seemed a hell of a fine woman. She seemed to understand, to realize, to be hurt for him and for herself and to know how things really stood. She is away for twenty minutes and now she is back, simply enamelled in that American female cruelty. They are the damnedest women. Really the damnedest.

"We'll put on another show for you tomorrow," Francis Macomber said.

"You're not coming," Wilson said.

"You're very mistaken," she told him. "And I want so to see you perform again. You were lovely this morning. That is if blowing things' heads off is lovely."

"Here's the lunch," said Wilson. "You're very merry, aren't you?"

"Why not? I didn't come out here to be dull."

"Well, it hasn't been dull," Wilson said. He could see the boulders in the river and the high bank beyond with the trees and he remembered the morning.

"Oh, no," she said. "It's been charming. And tomorrow. You don't know how I look forward to tomorrow."

"That's eland he's offering you," Wilson said.

"They're the big cowy things that jump like hares, aren't they?"

"I suppose that describes them," Wilson said.

"It's very good meat," Macomber said.

"Did you shoot it, Francis?" she asked.

"Yes."

"They're not dangerous, are they?"

"Only if they fall on you," Wilson told her.

"I'm so glad."

"Why not let up on the bitchery just a little, Margot," Macomber said, cutting the eland steak and putting some mashed potato, gravy and carrot on the down-turned fork that tined through the piece of meat.

"I suppose I could," she said, "since you put it so prettily."

"Tonight we'll have champagne for the lion," Wilson said. "It's a bit too hot at noon."

"Oh, the lion," Margot said. "I'd forgotten the lion!"

So, Robert Wilson thought to himself, she *is* giving him a ride, isn't she? Or do you suppose that's her idea of putting up a good show? How should a woman act when she discovers her husband is a bloody coward? She's damn cruel but they're all cruel. They govern, of course, and to govern one has to be cruel sometimes. Still, I've seen enough of their damn terrorism.

"Have some more eland," he said to her politely.

That afternoon, late, Wilson and Macomber went out in the motor car with the native driver and the two gun-bearers. Mrs. Macomber stayed in the camp. It was too hot to go out, she said, and she was going with them in the early morning. As they drove off Wilson saw her standing under the big tree, looking pretty rather than beautiful in her faintly rosy khaki, her dark hair drawn back off her forehead and gathered in a knot low on her neck, her face as fresh, he thought, as though she were in England. She waved to them as the car went off through the swale of high grass and curved around through the trees into the small hills of orchard bush.

In the orchard bush they found a herd of impala, and leaving the car they stalked one old ram with long, wide-spread horns and Macomber killed it with a very creditable shot that knocked the buck down at a good two hundred yards and sent the herd off bounding wildly and leaping over one another's backs in long, leg-drawn-up leaps as unbelievable and as floating as those one makes sometimes in dreams.

"That was a good shot," Wilson said. "They're a small target."

"Is it a worth-while head?" Macomber asked.

"It's excellent," Wilson told him. "You shoot like that and you'll have no trouble."

"Do you think we'll find buffalo tomorrow?"

"There's a good chance of it. They feed out early in the morning and with luck we may catch them in the open."

"I'd like to clear away that lion business," Macomber said. "It's not very pleasant to have your wife see you do something like that."

I should think it would be even more unpleasant to do it, Wilson thought, wife or no wife, or to talk about it having done it. But he said, "I wouldn't think about that any more. Any one could be upset by his first lion. That's all over."

But that night after dinner and a whisky and soda by the fire before going to bed, as Francis Macomber lay on his cot with the mosquito bar over him and listened to the night noises it was not all over. It was neither all over nor was it beginning. It was there exactly as it happened with some parts of it indelibly emphasized and he was miserably ashamed at it. But more than shame he felt cold, hollow fear in him. The fear was still there like a cold slimy hollow in all the emptiness where once his confidence had been and it made him feel sick. It was still there with him now.

It had started the night before when he had wakened and heard the lion roaring somewhere up along the river. It was a deep sound and at the end there were sort of coughing grunts that made him seem just outside the tent, and when Francis Macomber woke in the night to hear it he was afraid. He could hear his wife breathing quietly, asleep. There was no one to tell he was afraid, nor to be afraid with him, and, lying alone, he did not know the Somali proverb that says a brave man is always frightened three times by a lion; when he first sees his track, when he first hears him roar and when he first confronts him. Then while they were eating breakfast by lantern light out in the dining tent, before the sun was up, the lion roared again and Francis thought he was just at the edge of camp.

"Sounds like an old-timer," Robert Wilson said, looking up from his kippers and coffee. "Listen to him cough."

"Is he very close?"

"A mile or so up the stream."

"Will we see him?"

"We'll have a look."

"Does his roaring carry that far? It sounds as though he were right in camp."

"Carries a hell of a long way," said Robert Wilson. "It's strange the way it carries. Hope he's a shootable cat. The boys said there was a very big one about here."

"If I get a shot, where should I hit him," Macomber asked, "to stop him?"

"In the shoulders," Wilson said. "In the neck if you can make it. Shoot for bone. Break him down."

"I hope I can place it properly," Macomber said.

"You shoot very well," Wilson told him. "Take your time. Make sure of him. The first one in is the one that counts."

"What range will it be?"

"Can't tell. Lion has something to say about that. Don't shoot unless it's close enough so you can make sure."

"At under a hundred yards?" Macomber asked.

Wilson looked at him quickly.

"Hundred's about right. Might have to take him a bit under. Shouldn't chance a shot at much over that. A hundred's a decent range. You can hit him wherever you want at that. Here comes the Memsahib."

"Good morning," she said. "Are we going after that lion?"

"As soon as you deal with your breakfast," Wilson said. "How are you feeling?"

"Marvellous," she said. "I'm very excited."

"I'll just go and see that everything is ready," Wilson went off. As he left the lion roared again.

"Noisy beggar," Wilson said. "We'll put a stop to that."

"What's the matter, Francis?" his wife asked him.

"Nothing," Macomber said.

"Yes, there is," she said. "What are you upset about?"

"Nothing," he said.

"Tell me," she looked at him. "Don't you feel well?"

"It's that damned roaring," he said. "It's been going on all night, you know."

"Why didn't you wake me," she said. "I'd love to have heard it."

"I've got to kill the damned thing," Macomber said, miserably.

"Well, that's what you're out here for, isn't it?"

"Yes. But I'm nervous. Hearing the thing roar gets on my nerves."

"Well then, as Wilson said, kill him and stop his roaring."

"Yes, darling," said Francis Macomber. "It sounds easy, doesn't it?"

"You're not afraid, are you?"

"Of course not. But I'm nervous from hearing him roar all night."

"You'll kill him marvellously," she said. "I know you will. I'm awfully anxious to see it."

"Finish your breakfast and we'll be starting."

"It's not light yet," she said. "This is a ridiculous hour."

Just then the lion roared in a deep-chested moaning, suddenly guttural, ascending vibration that seemed to shake the air and ended in a sigh and a heavy, deep-chested grunt.

"He sounds almost here," Macomber's wife said.

"My God," said Macomber. "I hate that damned noise."

"It's very impressive."

"Impressive. It's frightful."

Robert Wilson came up then carrying his short, ugly, shockingly big-bored .505 Gibbs and grinning.

"Come on," he said. "Your gun-bearer has your Springfield and the big gun. Everything's in the car. Have you solids?"

"Yes."

"I'm ready," Mrs. Macomber said.

"Must make him stop that racket," Wilson said. "You get in front. The Memsahib can sit back here with me."

They climbed into the motor car and, in the gray first daylight, moved off up the river through the trees. Macomber opened the breech of his rifle and saw he had metal-cased bullets, shut the bolt and put the rifle on safety. He saw his hand was trembling. He felt in his pocket for more cartridges and moved his fingers over the cartridges in the loops of his tunic front. He turned back to where Wilson sat in the rear seat of the doorless, box-bodied motor car beside his wife, them both grinning with excitement, and Wilson leaned forward and whispered,

"See the birds dropping. Means the old boy has left his kill."

On the far bank of the stream Macomber could see, above the trees, vultures circling and plummeting down.

"Chances are he'll come to drink along here," Wilson whispered. "Before he goes to lay up. Keep an eye out."

They were driving slowly along the high bank of the stream which here cut deeply to its boulder-filled bed, and they wound in and out through big trees as they drove. Macomber was watching the opposite bank when he felt Wilson take hold of his arm. The car stopped.

"There he is," he heard the whisper. "Ahead and to the right. Get out and take him. He's a marvellous lion."

Macomber saw the lion now. He was standing almost broadside, his great head up and turned toward them. The early morning breeze that blew toward them was just stirring his dark mane, and the lion looked huge, silhouetted on the rise of bank in the gray morning light, his shoulders heavy, his barrel of a body bulking smoothly.

"How far is he?" asked Macomber, raising his rifle.

"About seventy-five. Get out and take him."

"Why not shoot from where I am?"

"You don't shoot them from cars," he heard Wilson saying in his ear. "Get out. He's not going to stay there all day."

Macomber stepped out of the curved opening at the side of the front seat, onto the step and down onto the ground. The lion still stood looking majestically and coolly toward this object that his eyes only showed in silhouette, bulking like some super-rhino. There was no man smell carried toward him and he watched the object, moving his great head a little from side to side. Then watching the object, not afraid, but hesitating before going down the bank to drink with such a thing opposite him, he saw a man figure detach itself from it and he turned his heavy head and swung away toward the cover of the trees as he heard a cracking crash and felt the slam of a .30–06 220-grain solid bullet that bit his flank and ripped in sudden hot scalding nausea through his stomach. He trotted, heavy, big-footed, swinging wounded full-bellied, through the trees toward the tall grass and cover, and the crash came again to go past him ripping the air apart. Then it crashed again and he felt the blow as it hit his lower ribs and ripped on through, blood sudden hot and frothy in his mouth, and he galloped toward the high grass where he could crouch and not be seen and make them bring the crashing thing close enough so he could make a rush and get the man that held it.

Macomber had not thought how the lion felt as he got out of the car. He only knew his hands were shaking and as he walked away from the car it was almost impossible for him to make his legs move. They were stiff in the thighs, but he could feel the muscles fluttering. He raised the rifle, sighted on the junction of the lion's head and shoulders and pulled the trigger. Nothing happened though he pulled until he thought his finger would break. Then he knew he had the safety on and as he lowered the rifle to move the safety over he moved another frozen pace forward, and the lion seeing his silhouette now clear of the silhouette of the car, turned and started off at a trot, and, as Macomber fired, he heard a whunk that meant that the bullet was home; but the lion kept on going. Macomber shot again and every one saw the bullet throw a spout of dirt beyond the trotting lion. He shot again, remembering to lower his aim, and they all heard the bullet hit, and the lion went into a gallop and was in the tall grass before he had the bolt pushed forward.

Macomber stood there feeling sick at his stomach, his hands that held the Springfield still cocked, shaking, and his wife and Robert Wilson were standing by him. Beside him too were the two gun-bearers chattering in Wakamba.

"I hit him," Macomber said. "I hit him twice."

"You gut-shot him and you hit him somewhere forward," Wilson said without enthusiasm. The gun-bearers looked very grave. They were silent now.

"You may have killed him," Wilson went on. "We'll have to wait a while before we go in to find out."

"What do you mean?"

"Let him get sick before we follow him up."

"Oh," said Macomber.

"He's a hell of a fine lion," Wilson said cheerfully. "He's gotten into a bad place though."

"Why is it bad?"

"Can't see him until you're on him."

"Oh," said Macomber.

"Come on," said Wilson. "The Memsahib can stay here in the car. We'll go to have a look at the blood spoor."

"Stay here, Margot," Macomber said to his wife. His mouth was very dry and it was hard for him to talk.

"Why?" she asked.

"Wilson says to."

"We're going to have a look," Wilson said. "You stay here. You can see even better from here."

"All right."

Wilson spoke in Swahili to the driver. He nodded and said, "Yes, Bwana."

Then they went down the steep bank and across the stream, climbing over and around the boulders and up the other bank, pulling up by some projecting roots, and along it until they found where the lion had been trotting when Macomber first shot. There was dark blood on the short grass that the gun-bearers pointed out with grass stems, and that ran away behind the river bank trees.

"What do we do?" asked Macomber.

"Not much choice." said Wilson. "We can't bring the car over. Bank's too steep. We'll let him stiffen up a bit and then you and I'll go in and have a look for him."

"Can't we set the grass on fire?" Macomber asked.

"Too green."

"Can't we send beaters?"

Wilson looked at him appraisingly. "Of course we can," he said. "But it's just a touch murderous. You see we know the lion's wounded. You can drive an unwounded lion—he'll move on ahead of a noise—but a wounded lion's going to charge. You can't see him until you're right on him. He'll make himself perfectly flat in cover you wouldn't think would hide a hare. You can't very well send boys in there to that sort of a show. Somebody bound to get mauled."

"What about the gun-bearers?"

"Oh, they'll go with us. It's their *shauri*. You see, they signed on for it. They don't look too happy though, do they?"

"I don't want to go in there," said Macomber. It was out before he knew he'd said it.

"Neither do I," said Wilson very cheerily. "Really no choice though." Then as an afterthought, he glanced at Macomber and saw suddenly how he was trembling and the pitiful look on his face.

"You don't have to go in, of course," he said. "That's what I'm hired for, you know. That's why I'm so expensive."

"You mean you'd go in by yourself? Why not leave him there?"

Robert Wilson, whose entire occupation had been with the lion and the problem he presented, and who had not been thinking about Macomber except to note that he was rather windy, suddenly felt as though he had opened the wrong door in a hotel and seen something shameful.

"What do you mean?"

"Why not just leave him?"

"You mean pretend to ourselves he hasn't been hit?"

"No. Just drop it."

"It isn't done."

"Why not?"

"For one thing, he's certain to be suffering. For another, some one else might run onto him."

"I see."

"But you don't have to have anything to do with it."

"I'd like to," Macomber said. "I'm just scared, you know."

"I'll go ahead when we go in," Wilson said, "with Kongoni tracking. You keep behind me and a little to one side. Chances are we'll hear him growl. If we see him we'll both shoot. Don't worry about anything. I'll keep you backed up. As a matter of fact, you know, perhaps you'd better not go. It might be much better. Why don't you go over and join the Memsahib while I just get it over with?"

"No, I want to go."

"All right," said Wilson. "But don't go in if you don't want to. This is my *shauri* now, you know."

"I want to go," said Macomber.

They sat under a tree and smoked.

"Want to go back and speak to the Memsahib while we're waiting?" Wilson asked.

"No."

"I'll just step back and tell her to be patient."

"Good," said Macomber. He sat there, sweating under his arms, his mouth dry, his stomach hollow feeling, wanting to find courage to tell Wilson to go on and finish off the lion without him. He could not know that Wilson was furious because he had not noticed the state he was in earlier and sent him back to his wife. While he sat there Wilson came up. "I have your big gun," he said. "Take it. We've given him time, I think. Come on."

Macomber took the big gun and Wilson said:

"Keep behind me and about five yards to the right and do exactly as I tell you." Then he spoke in Swahili to the two gun-bearers who looked the picture of gloom.

"Let's go," he said.

"Could I have a drink of water?" Macomber asked. Wilson spoke to the older gun-bearer, who wore a canteen on his belt, and the man unbuckled it, unscrewed the top and handed it to Macomber, who took it noticing how heavy it seemed and how hairy and shoddy the felt covering was in his hand. He raised it to drink and looked ahead at the high grass with the flat-topped trees behind it. A breeze was blowing toward them and the grass rippled gently in the wind. He looked at the gun-bearer and he could see the gun-bearer was suffering too with fear.

Thirty-five yards into the grass the big lion lay flattened out along the ground. His ears were back and his only movement was a slight twitching up and down of his long, black-tufted tail. He had turned at bay as soon as he had reached this cover and he was sick with the wound through his full belly, and weakening with the wound through his lungs that brought a thin foamy red to his mouth each time he breathed. His flanks were wet and hot and flies were on the little openings the solid bullets had made in his tawny hide, and his big yellow eyes, narrowed with hate, looked straight ahead, only blinking when the pain came as he breathed, and his claws dug in the soft baked earth. All of him, pain, sickness, hatred and all of his remaining strength, was tightening into an absolute concentration for a rush. He could hear the men talking and he waited, gathering all of himself into this preparation for a charge as soon as the men would come into the grass. As he heard their voices his tail stiffened to twitch up and down, and, as they came into the edge of the grass, he made a coughing grunt and charged.

Kongoni, the old gun-bearer, in the lead watching the blood spoor, Wilson watching the grass for any movement, his big gun ready, the second gun-bearer looking ahead and listening, Macomber close to Wilson, his rifle cocked, they had just moved into the grass when Macomber heard the blood-choked coughing grunt, and saw the swishing rush in the grass. The next thing he knew he was running; running wildly, in panic in the open, running toward the stream.

He heard the *ca-ra-wong!* of Wilson's big rifle, and again in a second crashing *carawong!* and turning saw the lion, horrible-looking now, with half his head seeming to be gone, crawling toward Wilson in the edge of the tall grass while the red-faced man worked the bolt on the short ugly rifle and aimed carefully as another blasting *carawong!* came from the muzzle, and the crawling, heavy, yellow bulk of the lion stiffened and the huge, mutilated head slid forward and Macomber, standing by himself in the clearing where he had run, holding a loaded rifle, while two black men and a white man looked back at him in contempt, knew the lion was dead. He came toward Wilson, his tallness all seeming a naked reproach, and Wilson looked at him and said:

"Want to take pictures?"

"No," he said.

That was all any one had said until they reached the motor car. Then Wilson had said:

"Hell of a fine lion. Boys will skin him out. We might as well stay here in the shade."

Macomber's wife had not looked at him nor he at her and he had sat by her in the back seat with Wilson sitting in the front seat. Once he had reached over and taken his wife's hand without looking at her and she had removed her hand from his. Looking across the stream to where the gun-bearers were skinning out the lion he could see that she had been able to see the whole thing. While they sat there his wife had reached forward and put her hand on Wilson's shoulder. He turned and she had leaned forward over the low seat and kissed him on the mouth.

"Oh, I say," said Wilson, going redder than his natural baked color.

"Mr. Robert Wilson," she said. "The beautiful red-faced Mr. Robert Wilson."

Then she sat down beside Macomber again and looked away across the stream to where the lion lay, with uplifted, white-muscled, tendon-marked naked forearms, and white bloating belly, as the black men fleshed away the skin. Finally the gun-bearers brought the skin over, wet and heavy, and climbed in behind with it, rolling it up before they got in, and the motor car started. No one had said anything more until they were back in camp.

That was the story of the lion. Macomber did not know how the lion had felt before he started his rush, nor during it when the unbelievable smash of the .505 with a muzzle velocity of two tons had hit him in the mouth, nor what kept him coming after that, when the second ripping crash had smashed his hind quarters and he had come crawling on toward the crashing, blasting thing that had destroyed him. Wilson knew something about it and only expressed it by saying, "Damned fine lion," but Macomber did not know how Wilson felt about things either. He did not know how his wife felt except that she was through with him.

His wife had been through with him before but it never lasted. He was very wealthy, and would be much wealthier, and he knew she would not leave him ever now. That was one of the few things that he really knew. He knew about that, about motor cycles—that was earliest—about motor cars, about duck-shooting, about fishing, trout, salmon and big-sea, about sex in books, many books, too many books, about all court games, about dogs, not much about horses, about hanging on to his money, about most of the other things his world dealt in, and about his wife not leaving him. His wife had been a great beauty and she was still a great beauty in Africa, but she was not a great enough beauty any more at home to be able to leave him and better herself and she knew it and he knew it. She had missed the chance to leave him and he knew it. If he had been better with women she would probably have started to worry about him getting another new, beautiful wife; but she knew too much about him to worry about him either. Also, he had always had a great tolerance which seemed the nicest thing about him if it were not the most sinister.

All in all they were known as a comparatively happily married couple, one of those whose disruption is often rumored but never occurs, and as the society columnist put it, they were adding more than a spice of *adventure* to their much envied and ever-enduring *Romance* by a *Safari* in what was known as *Darkest Africa* until the Martin Johnsons lighted it on so many silver screens where they were pursuing *Old Simba* the lion, the buffalo, *Tembo* the elephant and as well collecting specimens for the Museum of Natural History. This same columnist had reported them *on the verge* at least three times in the past and they had been. But they always made it up. They had a sound basis of union. Margot was too beautiful for Macomber to divorce her and Macomber had too much money for Margot ever to leave him.

It was now about three o'clock in the morning and Francis Macomber, who had been asleep a little while after he had stopped thinking about the lion, wakened and then slept again, woke suddenly, frightened in a dream of the bloody-headed lion standing over him, and listening while his heart pounded, he realized that his wife was not in the other cot in the tent. He lay awake with that knowledge for two hours.

At the end of that time his wife came into the tent, lifted her mosquito bar and crawled cozily into bed.

"Where have you been?" Macomber asked in the darkness.

"Hello," she said. "Are you awake?"

"Where have you been?"

"I just went out to get a breath of air."

"You did, like hell."

"What do you want me to say, darling?"

"Where have you been?"

"Out to get a breath of air."

"That's a new name for it. You *are* a bitch."

"Well, you're a coward."

"All right," he said. "What of it?"

"Nothing as far as I'm concerned. But please let's not talk, darling, because I'm very sleepy."

"You think that I'll take anything."

"I know you will, sweet."

"Well, I won't."

"Please, darling, let's not talk. I'm so very sleepy."

"There wasn't going to be any of that. You promised there wouldn't be."

"Well, there is now," she said sweetly.

"You said if we made this trip that there would be none of that. You promised."

"Yes, darling. That's the way I meant it to be. But the trip was spoiled yesterday. We don't have to talk about it, do we?"

"You don't wait long when you have an advantage, do you?"

"Please let's not talk. I'm so sleepy, darling."

"I'm going to talk."

"Don't mind me then, because I'm going to sleep." And she did.

At breakfast they were all three at the table before daylight and Francis Macomber found that, of all the many men that he had hated, he hated Robert Wilson the most.

"Sleep well?" Wilson asked in his throaty voice, filling a pipe.

"Did you?"

"Topping," the white hunter told him.

You bastard, thought Macomber, you insolent bastard.

So she woke him when she came in, Wilson thought, looking at them both with his flat, cold eyes. Well, why doesn't he keep his wife where she belongs? What does he think I am, a bloody plaster saint? Let him keep her where she belongs. It's his own fault.

"Do you think we'll find buffalo?" Margot asked, pushing away a dish of apricots.

"Chance of it," Wilson said and smiled at her. "Why don't you stay in camp?"

"Not for anything," she told him.

"Why not order her to stay in camp?" Wilson said to Macomber.

"You order her," said Macomber coldly.

"Let's not have any ordering, nor," turning to Macomber, "any silliness, Francis," Margot said quite pleasantly.

"Are you ready to start?" Macomber asked.

"Any time," Wilson told him. "Do you want the Memsahib to go?"

"Does it make any difference whether I do or not?"

The hell with it, thought Robert Wilson. The utter complete hell with it. So this is what it's going to be like. Well, this is what it's going to be like, then.

"Makes no difference," he said.

"You're sure you wouldn't like to stay in camp with her yourself and let me go out and hunt the buffalo?" Macomber asked.

"Can't do that," said Wilson. "Wouldn't talk rot if I were you."

"I'm not talking rot. I'm disgusted."

"Bad word, disgusted."

"Francis, will you please try to speak sensibly?" his wife said.

"I speak too damned sensibly," Macomber said. "Did you ever eat such filthy food?"

"Something wrong with the food?" asked Wilson quietly.

"No more than with everything else."

"I'd pull yourself together, laddybuck," Wilson said very quietly. "There's a boy waits at table that understands a little English."

"The hell with him."

Wilson stood up and puffing on his pipe strolled away, speaking a few words in Swahili to one of the gun-bearers who was standing waiting for him. Macomber and his wife sat on at the table. He was staring at his coffee cup.

"If you make a scene I'll leave you, darling," Margot said quietly.

"No, you won't."

"You can try it and see."

"You won't leave me."

"No," she said. "I won't leave you and you'll behave yourself."

"Behave myself? That's a way to talk. Behave myself."

"Yes. Behave yourself."

"Why don't *you* try behaving?"

"I've tried it so long. So very long."

"I hate that red-faced swine," Macomber said. "I loathe the sight of him."

"He's really *very* nice."

"Oh, *shut up,*" Macomber almost shouted. Just then the car came up and stopped in front of the dining tent and the driver and the two gun-bearers got out. Wilson walked over and looked at the husband and wife sitting there at the table.

"Going shooting?" he asked.

"Yes," said Macomber, standing up. "Yes."

"Better bring a woolly. It will be cool in the car." Wilson said.

"I'll get my leather jacket," Margot said.

"The boy has it," Wilson told her. He climbed into the front with the driver and Francis Macomber and his wife sat, not speaking, in the back seat.

Hope the silly beggar doesn't take a notion to blow the back of my head off, Wilson thought to himself. Women *are* a nuisance on safari.

The car was grinding down to cross the river at a pebbly ford in the gray daylight and then climbed, angling up the steep bank, where Wilson had ordered a way shovelled out the day before so they could reach the parklike wooded rolling country on the far side.

It was a good morning, Wilson thought. There was a heavy dew and as the wheels went through the grass and low bushes he could smell the odor of the crushed fronds. It was an odor like verbena and he liked this early morning smell of the dew, the crushed bracken and the look of the tree trunks showing black through the early morning mist, as the car made its way through the untracked, parklike country. He had put the two in the back seat out of his mind now and was thinking about buffalo. The buffalo that he was after stayed in the daytime in a thick swamp where it was impossible to get a shot, but in the night they fed out into an open stretch of country and if he could come between them and their swamp with the car, Macomber would have a good chance at them in the open. He did not want to hunt buff with Macomber in thick cover. He did not want to hunt buff or anything else with Macomber at all, but he was a professional hunter and he had hunted with some rare ones in his time. If they got buff today there would only be rhino to come and the poor man would have gone through his dangerous game and things might pick up. He'd have nothing more to do with the woman and Macomber would get over that too. He must have gone through plenty of that before by the look of things. Poor beggar. He must have a way of getting over it. Well, it was the poor sod's own bloody fault.

He, Robert Wilson, carried a double size cot on safari to accommodate any windfalls he might receive. He had hunted for a certain clientele, the international, fast, sporting set, where the women did not feel they were getting their money's worth unless they had shared that cot with the white hunter. He despised them when he was away from them although he liked some of them well enough at the time, but he made his living by them; and their standards were his standards as long as they were hiring him.

They were his standards in all except the shooting. He had his own standards about the killing and they could live up to them or get some one else to hunt them. He knew, too, that they all respected him for this. This Macomber was an odd one though. Damned if he wasn't. Now the wife. Well, the wife. Yes, the wife. Hm, the wife. Well he'd dropped all that. He looked around at them. Macomber sat grim and furious. Margot smiled at him. She looked younger today, more innocent and fresher and not so professionally beautiful. What's in her heart God knows, Wilson thought. She hadn't talked much last night. At that it was a pleasure to see her.

The motor car climbed up a slight rise and went on through the trees and then out into a grassy prairie-like opening and kept in the shelter of the trees along the edge, the driver going slowly and Wilson looking carefully out across the prairie and all along its far side. He stopped the car and studied the opening with his field glasses. Then he motioned to the driver to go on and the car moved slowly along, the driver avoiding wart-hog holes and driving around the mud castles ants had built. Then, looking across the opening, Wilson suddenly turned and said,

"By God, there they are!"

And looking where he pointed, while the car jumped forward and Wilson spoke in rapid Swahili to the driver, Macomber saw three huge, black animals looking almost cylindrical in their long heaviness, like big black tank cars, moving at a gallop across the far edge of the open prairie. They moved at a stiff-necked, stiff bodied gallop and he could see the upswept wide black horns on their heads as they galloped heads out; the heads not moving.

"They're three old bulls," Wilson said. "We'll cut them off before they get to the swamp."

The car was going a wild forty-five miles an hour across the open and as Macomber watched, the buffalo got bigger and bigger until he could see the gray, hairless, scabby look of one huge bull and how his neck was a part of his shoulders and the shiny black of his horns as he galloped a little behind the others that were strung out in that steady plunging gait; and then, the car swaying as though it had just jumped a road, they drew up close and he could see the plunging hugeness of the bull, and the dust in his sparsely haired hide, the wide boss of horn and his outstretched, wide-nostrilled muzzle, and he was raising his rifle when Wilson shouted, "Not from the car, you fool!" and he had no fear, only hatred of Wilson, while the brakes clamped on and the car skidded, plowing sideways to an almost stop and Wilson was out on one side and he on the other, stumbling as his feet hit the still speeding-by of the earth, and then he was shooting at the bull as he moved away, hearing the bullets whunk into him, emptying his rifle at him as he moved steadily away, finally remembering to get his shots forward into the shoulder, and as he fumbled to re-load, he saw the bull was down. Down on his knees, his big head tossing, and seeing the other two still galloping he shot at the leader and hit him. He shot again and missed and he heard the *carawonging* roar as Wilson shot and saw the leading bull slide forward onto his nose.

"Get that other," Wilson said. "Now you're shooting!"

But the other bull was moving steadily at the same gallop and he missed, throwing a spout of dirt, and Wilson missed and the dust rose in a cloud and Wilson shouted, "Come on. He's too far!" and grabbed his arm and they were in the car again, Macomber and Wilson hanging on the sides and rocketing swayingly over the uneven ground, drawing up on the steady, plunging, heavy-necked, straight-moving gallop of the bull.

They were behind him and Macomber was filling his rifle, dropping shells onto the ground, jamming it, clearing the jam, then they were almost up with the bull when Wilson yelled "Stop," and the car skidded so that it almost swung over and Macomber fell forward onto his feet, slammed his bolt forward and fired as far forward as he could aim into the galloping, rounded black back, aimed and shot again, then again, then again, and the bullets, all of them hitting, had no effect on the buffalo that he could see. Then Wilson shot, the roar deafening him, and he could see the bull stagger. Macomber shot again, aiming carefully, and down he came, onto his knees.

"All right," Wilson said. "Nice work. That's the three."

Macomber felt a drunken elation.

"How many times did you shoot?" he asked.

"Just three," Wilson said. "You killed the first bull. The biggest one. I helped you finish the other two. Afraid they might have got into cover. You had them killed. I was just mopping up a little. You shot damn well."

"Let's go to the car," said Macomber. "I want a drink."

"Got to finish off that buff first," Wilson told him. The buffalo was on his knees and he jerked his head furiously and bellowed in pig-eyed, roaring rage as they came toward him.

"Watch he doesn't get up," Wilson said. Then, "Get a little broadside and take him in the neck just behind the ear."

Macomber aimed carefully at the center of the huge, jerking, rage-driven neck and shot. At the shot the head dropped forward.

"That does it," said Wilson. "Got the spine. They're a hell of a looking thing, aren't they?"

"Let's get the drink," said Macomber. In his life he had never felt so good.

In the car Macomber's wife sat very white faced. "You were marvellous, darling," she said to Macomber. "What a ride."

"Was it rough?" Wilson asked.

"It was frightful. I've never been more frightened in my life."

"Let's all have a drink," Macomber said.

"By all means," said Wilson. "Give it to the Memsahib." She drank the neat whisky from the flask and shuddered a little when she swallowed. She handed the flask to Macomber who handed it to Wilson.

"It was frightfully exciting," she said. "It's given me a dreadful headache. I didn't know you were allowed to shoot them from cars though."

"No one shot from cars," said Wilson coldly.

"I mean chase them from cars."

"Wouldn't ordinarily," Wilson said. "Seemed sporting enough to me though while we were doing it. Taking more chance driving that way across the plain full of holes and one thing and another than hunting on foot. Buffalo could have charged us each time we shot if he liked. Gave him every chance. Wouldn't mention it to any one though. It's illegal if that's what you mean."

"It seemed very unfair to me," Margot said, "chasing those big helpless things in a motor car."

"Did it?" said Wilson.

"What would happen if they heard about it in Nairobi?"

"I'd lose my licence for one thing. Other unpleasantnesses," Wilson said, taking a drink from the flask. "I'd be out of business."

"Really?"

"Yes, really."

"Well," said Macomber, and he smiled for the first time all day. "Now she has something on you."

"You have such a pretty way of putting things, Francis," Margot Macomber said. Wilson looked at them both. If a four-letter man marries a five-letter woman, he was thinking, what number of letters would their children be? What he said was, "We lost a gun-bearer. Did you notice it?"

"My God, no," Macomber said.

"Here he comes," Wilson said. "He's all right. He must have fallen off when we left the first bull."

Approaching them was the middle-aged gun-bearer, limping along in his knitted cap, khaki tunic, shorts and rubber sandals, gloomy-faced and disgusted looking. As he came up he called out to Wilson in Swahili and they all saw the change in the white hunter's face.

"What does he say?" asked Margot.

"He says the first bull got up and went into the bush," Wilson said with no expression in his voice.

"Oh," said Macomber blankly.

"Then it's going to be just like the lion," said Margot, full of anticipation.

"It's not going to be a damned bit like the lion," Wilson told her. "Did you want another drink, Macomber?"

"Thanks, yes," Macomber said. He expected the feeling he had had about the lion to come back but it did not. For the first time in his life he really felt wholly without fear. Instead of fear he had a feeling of definite elation.

"We'll go and have a look at the second bull," Wilson said. "I'll tell the driver to put the car in the shade."

"What are you going to do?" asked Margaret Macomber.

"Take a look at the buff," Wilson said.

"I'll come."

"Come along."

The three of them walked over to where the second buffalo bulked blackly in the open, head forward on the grass, the massive horns swung wide.

"He's a very good head," Wilson said. "That's close to a fifty-inch spread."

Macomber was looking at him with delight.

"He's hateful looking," said Margot. "Can't we go into the shade?"

"Of course," Wilson said. "Look," he said to Macomber, and pointed. "See that patch of bush?"

"Yes."

"That's where the first bull went in. The gun-bearer said when he fell off the bull was down. He was watching us helling along and the other two buff galloping. When he looked up there was the bull up and looking at him. Gun-bearer ran like hell and the bull went off slowly into that bush."

"Can we go in after him now?" asked Macomber eagerly.

Wilson looked at him appraisingly. Damned if this isn't a strange one, he thought. Yesterday he's scared sick and today he's a ruddy fire eater.

"No, we'll give him a while."

"Let's please go into the shade," Margot said. Her face was white and she looked ill.

They made their way to the car where it stood under a single, wide-spreading tree and all climbed in.

"Chances are he's dead in there," Wilson remarked. "After a little we'll have a look."

Macomber felt a wild unreasonable happiness that he had never known before.

"By God, that was a chase," he said. "I've never felt any such feeling. Wasn't it marvellous, Margot?"

"I hated it."

"Why?"

"I hated it," she said bitterly. "I loathed it."

"You know I don't think I'd ever be afraid of anything again," Macomber said to Wilson. "Something happened in me after we first saw the buff and started after him. Like a dam bursting. It was pure excitement."

"Cleans out your liver," said Wilson. "Damn funny things happen to people."

Macomber's face was shining. "You know something did happen to me," he said. "I feel absolutely different."

His wife said nothing and eyed him strangely. She was sitting far back in the seat and Macomber was sitting forward talking to Wilson who turned sideways talking over the back of the front seat.

"You know, I'd like to try another lion," Macomber said. "I'm really not afraid of them now. After all, what can they do to you?"

"That's it," said Wilson. "Worst one can do is kill you. How does it go? Shakespeare. Damned good. See if I can remember. Oh, damned good. Used to quote it to myself at one time. Let's see. 'By my troth, I care not; a man can die but once; we owe God a death and let it go which way it will he that dies this year is quit for the next.' Damned fine, eh?"

He was very embarrassed, having brought out this thing he had lived by, but he had seen men come of age before and it always moved him. It was not a matter of their twenty-first birthday.

It had taken a strange chance of hunting, a sudden precipitation into action without opportunity for worrying beforehand, to bring this about with Macomber, but regardless of how it had happened it had most certainly happened. Look at the beggar now, Wilson thought. It's that some of them stay little boys so long, Wilson thought. Sometimes all their lives. Their figures stay boyish when they're fifty. The great American boy-men. Damned strange people. But he liked this Macomber now. Damned strange fellow. Probably meant the end of cuckoldry too. Well, that would be a damned good thing. Damned good thing. Beggar had probably been afraid all his life. Don't know what started it. But over now. Hadn't had time to be afraid with the buff. That and being angry too. Motor car too. Motor cars made it familiar. Be a damn fire eater now. He'd seen it in the war work the same way. More of a change than any loss of virginity. Fear gone like an operation. Something else grew in its place. Main thing a man had. Made him into a man. Women knew it too. No bloody fear.

From the far corner of the seat Margaret Macomber looked at the two of them. There was no change in Wilson. She saw Wilson as she had seen him the day before when she had first realized what his great talent was. But she saw the change in Francis Macomber now.

ERNEST HEMINGWAY   93

"Do you have that feeling of happiness about what's going to happen?" Macomber asked, still exploring his new wealth.

"You're not supposed to mention it," Wilson said, looking in the other's face. "Much more fashionable to say you're scared. Mind you, you'll be scared too, plenty of times."

"But you *have* a feeling of happiness about action to come?"

"Yes," said Wilson. "There's that. Doesn't do to talk too much about all this. Talk the whole thing away. No pleasure in anything if you mouth it up too much."

"You're both talking rot," said Margot. "Just because you've chased some helpless animals in a motor car you talk like heroes."

"Sorry," said Wilson. "I have been gassing too much." She's worried about it already, he thought.

"If you don't know what we're talking about why not keep out of it?" Macomber asked his wife.

"You've gotten awfully brave, awfully suddenly," his wife said contemptuously, but her contempt was not secure. She was very afraid of something.

Macomber laughed, a very natural hearty laugh. "You know I *have*," he said. "I really have."

"Isn't it sort of late?" Margot said bitterly. Because she had done the best she could for many years back and the way they were together now was no one person's fault.

"Not for me," said Macomber.

Margot said nothing but sat back in the corner of the seat.

"Do you think we've given him time enough?" Macomber asked Wilson cheerfully.

"We might have a look," Wilson said. "Have you any solids left?"

"The gun-bearer has some."

Wilson called in Swahili and the older gun-bearer, who was skinning out one of the heads, straightened up, pulled a box of solids out of his pocket and brought them over to Macomber, who filled his magazine and put the remaining shells in his pocket.

"You might as well shoot the Springfield," Wilson said. "You're used to it. We'll leave the Mannlicher in the car with the Memsahib. Your gun-bearer can carry your heavy gun. I've this damned cannon. Now let me tell you about them." He had saved this until the last because he did not want to worry Macomber. "When a buff comes he comes with his head high and thrust straight out. The boss of the horns covers any sort of a brain shot. The only shot is straight into the nose. The only other shot is into his chest or, if you're to one side, into the neck or the shoulders. After they've been hit once they take a hell of a lot of killing. Don't try anything fancy. Take the easiest shot there is. They've finished skinning out that head now. Should we get started?"

He called to the gun-bearers, who came up wiping their hands, and the older one got into the back.

"I'll only take Kongoni," Wilson said. "The other can watch to keep the birds away."

As the car moved slowly across the open space toward the island of brushy trees that ran in a tongue of foliage along a dry water course that cut the open swale, Macomber felt his heart pounding and his mouth was dry again, but it was excitement, not fear.

"Here's where he went in," Wilson said. Then to the gun-bearer in Swahili, "Take the blood spoor."

The car was parallel to the patch of bush. Macomber, Wilson and the gun-bearer got down. Macomber, looking back, saw his wife, with the rifle by her side, looking at him. He waved to her and she did not wave back.

The brush was very thick ahead and the ground was dry. The middle-aged gun-bearer was sweating heavily and Wilson had his hat down over his eyes and his red neck showed just ahead of Macomber. Suddenly the gun-bearer said something in Swahili to Wilson and ran forward.

"He's dead in there," Wilson said. "Good work," and he turned to grip Macomber's hand and as they shook hands, grinning at each other, the gun-bearer shouted wildly and they saw him coming out of the bush sideways, fast as a crab, and the bull coming, nose out, mouth tight closed, blood dripping, massive head straight out, coming in a charge, his little pig eyes bloodshot as he looked at them. Wilson, who was ahead, was kneeling shooting, and Macomber, as he fired, unhearing his shot in the roaring of Wilson's gun, saw fragments like slate burst from the huge boss of the horns, and the head jerked, he shot again at the wide nostrils and saw the horns jolt again and fragments fly, and he did not see Wilson now and, aiming carefully, shot again with the buffalo's huge bulk almost on him and his rifle almost level with the on-coming head, nose out, and he could see the little wicked eyes and the head started to lower and he felt a sudden white-hot blinding flash explode inside his head and that was all he ever felt.

Wilson had ducked to one side to get in a shoulder shot. Macomber had stood solid and shot for the nose, shooting a touch high each time and hitting the heavy horns, splintering and chipping them like hitting a slate roof, and Mrs. Macomber, in the car, had shot at the buffalo with the 6.5 Mannlicher as it seemed about to gore Macomber and had hit her husband about two inches up and a little to one side of the base of his skull.

Francis Macomber lay now, face down, not two yards from where the buffalo lay on his side and his wife knelt over him with Wilson beside her.

"I wouldn't turn him over," Wilson said.

The woman was crying hysterically.

"I'd get back in the car," Wilson said. "Where's the rifle?"

She shook her head, her face contorted. The gun-bearer picked up the rifle.

"Leave it as it is," said Wilson. Then, "Go get Abdulla so that he may witness the manner of the accident."

He knelt down, took a handkerchief from his pocket, and spread it over Francis Macomber's crew-cropped head where it lay. The blood sank into the dry, loose earth.

Wilson stood up and saw the buffalo on his side, his legs out, his thinly-haired belly crawling with ticks. "Hell of a good bull," his brain registered automatically. "A good fifty inches, or better. Better." He called to the driver and told him to spread a blanket over the body and stay by it. Then he walked over to the motor car where the woman sat crying in the corner.

"That was a pretty thing to do," he said in a toneless voice. "He *would* have left you too."

"Stop it," she said.

"Of course it's an accident," he said. "I know that."

"Stop it," she said.

"Don't worry," he said. "There will be a certain amount of unpleasantness but I will have some photographs taken that will be very useful at the inquest. There's the testimony of the gun-bearers and the driver too. You're perfectly all right."

"Stop it," she said.

"There's a hell of a lot to be done," he said. "And I'll have to send a truck off to the lake to wireless for a plane to take the three of us into Nairobi. Why didn't you poison him? That's what they do in England."

"Stop it. Stop it. Stop it," the woman cried.

Wilson looked at her with his flat blue eyes.

"I'm through now," he said. "I was a little angry. I'd begun to like your husband."

"Oh, please stop it," she said. "Please, please stop it."

"That's better," Wilson said. "Please is much better. Now I'll stop."

Questions

1. *Although we frequently enter the consciousness of Wilson and occasionally enter the consciousness of Francis (at one point we even enter the consciousness of the wounded lion), we are never told what Margot is thinking. Why?* **2.** *Does Margot deliberately kill her husband? Explain.* **3.** *What accounts for the change in the relationship between Margot and Francis? Why does Wilson assume she has deliberately killed him?* **4.** *Explain the title of the story.*

My Oedipus Complex

FRANK O'CONNOR [1903–1966]

FATHER was in the army all through the war—the first war, I mean—so, up to the age of five, I never saw much of him, and what I saw did not worry me. Sometimes I woke and there was a big figure in khaki peering down at me in the candlelight. Sometimes in the early morning I heard the slamming of the front door and the clatter of nailed boots down the cobbles of the lane. These were Father's entrances and exits. Like Santa Claus he came and went mysteriously.

In fact, I rather liked his visits, though it was an uncomfortable squeeze between Mother and him when I got into the big bed in the early morning. He smoked, which gave him a pleasant musty smell, and shaved, an operation of astounding interest. Each time he left a trail of souvenirs—model tanks and Gurkha knives with handles made of bullet cases, and German helmets and cap badges and button-sticks, and all sorts of military equipment—carefully stowed away in a long box on top of the wardrobe, in case they ever came in handy. There was a bit of the magpie about Father; he expected everything to come in handy. When his back was turned, Mother let me get a chair and rummage through his treasures. She didn't seem to think so highly of them as he did.

The war was the most peaceful period of my life. The window of my attic faced southeast. My mother had curtained it, but that had small effect. I always woke with the first light and, with all the responsibilities of the previous day melted, feeling myself rather like the sun, ready to illumine and rejoice. Life never seemed so simple and clear and full of possibilities as then. I put my feet out from under the clothes—I called them Mrs. Left and Mrs. Right—and invented dramatic situations for them in which they discussed the problems of the day. At least Mrs. Right did; she was very demonstrative, but I hadn't the same control of Mrs. Left, so she mostly contented herself with nodding agreement.

They discussed what Mother and I should do during the day, what Santa Claus should give a fellow for Christmas, and what steps should be taken to brighten the home. There was that little matter of the baby, for instance. Mother and I could never agree about that. Ours was the only house in the terrace without a new baby, and Mother said we couldn't afford one till Father came back from the war because they cost seventeen and six. That showed how simple she was. The Geneys up the road had a baby, and everyone knew they couldn't afford seventeen and six. It was probably a cheap baby, and Mother wanted something really good, but I felt she was too exclusive. The Geneys' baby would have done us fine.

Having settled my plans for the day, I got up, put a chair under the attic window, and lifted the frame high enough to stick out my head. The window overlooked the front gardens of the terrace behind ours, and beyond these it looked over a deep valley to the tall, red-brick houses terraced up the opposite hillside, which were all still in shadow, while those at our side of the valley were all lit up, though with long strange shadows that made them seem unfamiliar; rigid and painted.

After that I went into Mother's room and climbed into the big bed. She woke and I began to tell her of my schemes. By this time, though I never seem to have noticed it, I was petrified in my nightshirt, and I thawed as I talked until, the last frost melted, I fell asleep beside her and woke again only when I heard her below in the kitchen, making the breakfast.

After breakfast we went into town; heard Mass at St. Augustine's and said a prayer for Father, and did the shopping. If the afternoon was fine we either went for a walk in the country or a visit to Mother's great friend in the convent, Mother St. Dominic. Mother had them all praying for Father, and every night, going to bed, I asked God to send him back safe from the war to us. Little, indeed, did I know what I was praying for!

One morning, I got into the big bed, and there, sure enough, was Father in his usual Santa Claus manner, but later, instead of uniform, he put on his best blue suit, and Mother was as pleased as anything. I saw nothing to be pleased about, because, out of uniform, Father was altogether less interesting, but she only beamed, and explained that our prayers had been answered, and off we went to Mass to thank God for having brought Father safely home.

The irony of it! That very day when he came in to dinner he took off his boots and put on his slippers, donned the dirty old cap he wore about the house to save him from colds, crossed his legs, and began to talk gravely to Mother, who looked anxious. Naturally, I disliked her looking anxious, because it destroyed her good looks, so I interrupted him.

"Just a moment, Larry!" she said gently.

This was only what she said when we had boring visitors, so I attached no importance to it and went on talking.

"Do be quiet, Larry!" she said impatiently. "Don't you hear me talking to Daddy?"

This was the first time I had heard those ominous words, "talking to Daddy," and I couldn't help feeling that if this was how God answered prayers, he couldn't listen to them very attentively.

"Why are you talking to Daddy?" I asked with as great a show of indifference as I could muster.

"Because Daddy and I have business to discuss. Now, don't interrupt again!"

In the afternoon, at Mother's request, Father took me for a walk. This time we went into town instead of out to the country, and I thought at first, in my usual optimistic way, that it might be an improvement. It was nothing of the sort. Father and I had quite different notions of a walk in town. He had no proper interest in trams, ships, and horses, and the only thing that seemed to divert him was talking to fellows as old as himself. When I wanted to stop he simply went on, dragging me behind him by the hand; when he wanted to stop I had no alternative but to do the same. I noticed that it seemed to be a sign that he wanted to stop for a long time whenever he leaned against a wall. The second time I saw him do it I got wild. He seemed to be settling himself forever. I pulled him by the coat and trousers, but, unlike Mother who, if you were too persistent, got into a wax and said: "Larry, if you don't behave yourself, I'll give you a good slap," Father had an extraordinary capacity for amiable inattention. I sized him up and wondered would I cry, but he seemed to be too remote to be annoyed even by that. Really, it was like going for a walk with a mountain! He either ignored the wrenching and pummeling entirely, or else glanced down with a grin of amusement from his peak. I had never met anyone so absorbed in himself as he seemed.

At teatime, "talking to Daddy" began again, complicated this time by the fact that he had an evening paper, and every few minutes he put it down and told Mother something new out of it. I felt this was foul play. Man for man, I was prepared to compete with him any time for Mother's attention, but when he had it all made up for him by other people it left me no chance. Several times I tried to change the subject without success.

"You must be quiet while Daddy is reading, Larry," Mother said impatiently.

It was clear that she either genuinely liked talking to Father better than talking to me, or else that he had some terrible hold on her which made her afraid to admit the truth.

"Mummy," I said that night when she was tucking me up, "do you think if I prayed hard God would send Daddy back to the war?"

She seemed to think about that for a moment.

"No, dear," she said with a smile. "I don't think he would."

"Why wouldn't he, Mummy?"

"Because there isn't a war any longer, dear."

"But, Mummy, couldn't God make another war, if he liked?"

"He wouldn't like to, dear. It's not God who makes wars, but bad people."

"Oh!" I said.

I was disappointed about that. I began to think that God wasn't quite what he was cracked up to be.

Next morning I woke at my usual hour, feeling like a bottle of champagne. I put out my feet and invented a long conversation in which Mrs. Right talked of the trouble she had with her own father till she put him in the Home. I didn't quite know what the Home was but it sounded the right place for Father. Then I got my chair and stuck my head out of the attic window. Dawn was just breaking, with a guilty air that made me feel I had caught it in the act. My head bursting with stories and schemes, I stumbled in next door, and in the half-darkness scrambled into the big bed. There was no room at

Mother's side so I had to get between her and Father. For the time being I had forgotten about him, and for several minutes I sat bolt upright, racking my brains to know what I could do with him. He was taking up more than his fair share of the bed, and I couldn't get comfortable, so I gave him several kicks that made him grunt and stretch. He made room all right, though. Mother waked and felt for me. I settled back comfortably in the warmth of the bed with my thumb in my mouth.

"Mummy!" I hummed, loudly and contentedly.

"Sssh! dear," she whispered. "Don't wake Daddy!"

This was a new development, which threatened to be even more serious than "talking to Daddy." Life without my early-morning conferences was unthinkable.

"Why?" I asked severely.

"Because poor Daddy is tired."

This seemed to me a quite inadequate reason, and I was sickened by the sentimentality of her "poor Daddy." I never liked that sort of gush; it always struck me as insincere.

"Oh!" I said lightly. Then in my most winning tone: "Do you know where I want to go with you today, Mummy?"

"No, dear," she sighed.

"I want to go down the Glen and fish for thornybacks with my new net, and then I want to go out to the Fox and Hounds, and—"

"Don't-wake-Daddy!" she hissed angrily, clapping her hand across my mouth.

But it was too late. He was awake, or nearly so. He grunted and reached for the matches. Then he stared incredulously at his watch.

"Like a cup of tea, dear?" asked Mother in a meek, hushed voice I had never heard her use before. It sounded almost as though she were afraid.

"Tea?" he exclaimed indignantly. "Do you know what the time is?"

"And after that I want to go up the Rathcooney Road," I said loudly, afraid I'd forget something in all those interruptions.

"Go to sleep at once, Larry!" she said sharply.

I began to snivel. I couldn't concentrate, the way that pair went on, and smothering my early-morning schemes was like burying a family from the cradle.

Father said nothing, but lit his pipe and sucked it, looking out into the shadows without minding Mother or me. I knew he was mad. Every time I made a remark Mother hushed me irritably. I was mortified. I felt it wasn't fair; there was even something sinister in it. Every time I had pointed out to her the waste of making two beds when we could both sleep in one, she had told me it was healthier like that, and now here was this man, this stranger, sleeping with her without the least regard for her health!

He got up early and made tea, but though he brought Mother a cup he brought none for me.

"Mummy," I shouted, "I want a cup of tea, too."

"Yes, dear," she said patiently. "You can drink from Mummy's saucer."

That settled it. Either Father or I would have to leave the house. I didn't want to drink from Mother's saucer; I wanted to be treated as an equal in my own home, so, just to spite her, I drank it all and left none for her. She took that quietly, too.

But that night when she was putting me to bed she said gently: "Larry, I want you to promise me something."

"What is it?" I asked.

"Not to come in and disturb poor Daddy in the morning. Promise?"

"Poor Daddy" again! I was becoming suspicious of everything involving that quite impossible man.

"Why?" I asked.

"Because poor Daddy is worried and tired and he doesn't sleep well."

"Why doesn't he, Mummy?"

"Well, you know, don't you, that while he was at the war Mummy got the pennies from the Post Office?"

"From Miss MacCarthy?"

"That's right. But now, you see, Miss MacCarthy hasn't any more pennies, so Daddy must go out and find us some. You know what would happen if he couldn't?"

"No," I said, "tell us."

"Well, I think we might have to go out and beg for them like the poor old woman on Fridays. We wouldn't like that, would we?"

"No," I agreed. "We wouldn't."

"So you'll promise not to come in and wake him?"

"Promise."

Mind you, I meant that. I knew pennies were a serious matter, and I was all against having to go out and beg like the old woman on Fridays. Mother laid out all my toys in a complete ring round the bed so that, whatever way I got out, I was bound to fall over one of them.

When I woke I remembered my promise all right. I got up and sat on the floor and played—for hours, it seemed to me. Then I got my chair and looked out the attic window for more hours. I wished it was time for Father to wake; I wished someone would make me a cup of tea. I didn't feel in the least like the sun; instead, I was bored and so very, very cold! I simply longed for the warmth and depth of the big featherbed.

At last I could stand it no longer. I went into the next room. As there was still no room at Mother's side I climbed over her and she woke with a start.

"Larry," she whispered, gripping my arm very tightly, "what did you promise?"

"But I did, Mummy," I wailed, caught in the very act. "I was quiet for ever so long."

"Oh, dear, and you're perished!" she said sadly, feeling me all over. "Now, if I let you stay will you promise not to talk?"

"But I want to talk, Mummy," I wailed.

"That has nothing to do with it," she said with a firmness that was new to me. "Daddy wants to sleep. Now, do you understand that?"

I understood it only too well. I wanted to talk, he wanted to sleep—whose house was it, anyway?

"Mummy," I said with equal firmness, "I think it would be healthier for Daddy to sleep in his own bed."

That seemed to stagger her, because she said nothing for a while.

"Now, once for all," she went on, "you're to be perfectly quiet or go back to your own bed. Which is it to be?"

The injustice of it got me down. I had convicted her out of her own mouth of inconsistency and unreasonableness, and she hadn't even attempted to reply. Full of spite, I gave Father a kick, which she didn't notice but which made him grunt and open his eyes in alarm.

"What time is it?" he asked in a panic-stricken voice, not looking at Mother but the door, as if he saw someone there.

"It's early yet," she replied soothingly. "It's only the child. Go to sleep again. . . . Now, Larry," she added, getting out of bed, "you've wakened Daddy and you must go back."

This time, for all her quiet air, I knew she meant it, and knew that my principal rights and privileges were as good as lost unless I asserted them at once. As she lifted me, I gave a screech, enough to wake the dead, not to mind Father. He groaned.

"That damn child! Doesn't he ever sleep?"

"It's only a habit, dear," she said quietly, though I could see she was vexed.

"Well, it's time he got out of it," shouted Father, beginning to heave in the bed. He suddenly gathered all the bedclothes about him, turned to the wall, and then looked back over his shoulder with nothing showing only two small, spiteful, dark eyes. The man looked very wicked.

To open the bedroom door, Mother had to let me down, and I broke free and dashed for the farthest corner, screeching. Father sat bolt upright in bed.

"Shut up, you little puppy!" he said in a choking voice.

I was so astonished that I stopped screeching. Never, never had anyone spoken to me in that tone before. I looked at him incredulously and saw his face convulsed with rage. It was only then that I fully realized how God had codded me, listening to my prayers for the safe return of this monster.

"Shut up, you!" I bawled, beside myself.

"What's that you said?" shouted Father, making a wild leap out of bed.

"Mick, Mick!" cried Mother. "Don't you see the child isn't used to you?"

"I see he's better fed than taught," snarled Father, waving his arms wildly. "He wants his bottom smacked."

All his previous shouting was as nothing to these obscene words referring to my person. They really made my blood boil.

"Smack your own!" I screamed hysterically. "Smack your own! Shut up! Shut up!"

At this he lost his patience and let fly at me. He did it with the lack of conviction you'd expect of a man under Mother's horrified eyes, and it ended up as a mere tap, but the sheer indignity of being struck at all by a stranger, a total stranger who had cajoled his way back from the war into our big bed as a result of my innocent intercession, made me completely dotty. I shrieked and shrieked, and danced in my bare feet, and Father, looking awkward and hairy in nothing but a short grey army shirt, glared down at me like a mountain out for murder. I think it must have been then that I realized he was jealous too. And there stood Mother in her nightdress, looking as if her heart was broken between us. I hoped she felt as she looked. It seemed to me that she deserved it all.

From that morning out my life was a hell. Father and I were enemies, open and avowed. We conducted a series of skirmishes against one another, he trying to steal my time with Mother and I his. When she was sitting on my bed, telling me a story, he took to looking for some pair of old boots which he alleged he had left behind him at the beginning of the war. While he talked to Mother I played loudly with my toys to show my total lack of concern. He created a terrible scene one evening when he came in from work and found me at his box, playing with his regimental badges, Gurkha knives and button-sticks. Mother got up and took the box from me.

"You mustn't play with Daddy's toys unless he lets you, Larry," she said severely. "Daddy doesn't play with yours."

For some reason Father looked at her as if she had struck him and then turned away with a scowl.

"Those are not toys," he growled, taking down the box again to see had I lifted anything. "Some of those curios are very rare and valuable."

But as time went on I saw more and more how he managed to alienate Mother and me. What made it worse was that I couldn't grasp his method or see what attraction he had for Mother. In every possible way he was less winning than I. He had a common accent and made noises at his tea. I thought for a while that it might be the newspapers she was interested in, so I made up bits of news of my own to read to her. Then I thought it might be the smoking, which I personally thought attractive, and took his pipes and went round the house dribbling into them till he caught me. I even made noises at my tea, but Mother only told me I was disgusting. It all seemed to hinge round that unhealthy habit of sleeping together, so I made a point of dropping into their bedroom and nosing round, talking to myself, so that they wouldn't know I was watching them, but they were never up to anything that I could see. In the end it beat me. It seemed to depend on being grown-up and giving people rings, and I realized I'd have to wait.

But at the same time I wanted him to see that I was only waiting, not giving up the fight. One evening when he was being particularly obnoxious, chattering away well above my head, I let him have it.

"Mummy," I said, "do you know what I'm going to do when I grow up?"

"No, dear," she replied. "What?"

"I'm going to marry you," I said quietly.

Father gave a great guffaw out of him, but he didn't take me in. I knew it must only be pretense. And Mother, in spite of everything, was pleased. I felt she was probably relieved to know that one day Father's hold on her would be broken.

"Won't that be nice?" she said with a smile.

"It'll be very nice," I said confidently. "Because we're going to have lots and lots of babies."

"That's right, dear," she said placidly. "I think we'll have one soon, and then you'll have plenty of company."

I was no end pleased about that because it showed that in spite of the way she gave in to Father she still considered my wishes. Besides, it would put the Geneys in their place.

It didn't turn out like that, though. To begin with, she was very pre-occupied—I supposed about where she would get the seventeen and six—and though Father took to staying out late in the evenings it did me no particular good. She stopped taking me for walks, became as touchy as blazes, and smacked me for nothing at all. Sometimes I wished I'd never mentioned the confounded baby—I seemed to have a genius for bringing calamity on myself.

And calamity it was! Sonny arrived in the most appalling hullabaloo—even that much he couldn't do without a fuss—and from the first moment I disliked him. He was a difficult child—so far as I was concerned he was always difficult—and demanded far too much attention. Mother was simply silly about him, and couldn't see when he was only showing off. As company he was worse than useless. He slept all day, and I had to go round the house on tiptoe to avoid waking him. It wasn't any longer a question of not waking Father. The slogan now was "Don't-wake-Sonny!" I couldn't understand why the child wouldn't sleep at the proper time, so whenever Mother's back was turned I woke him. Sometimes to keep him awake I pinched him as well. Mother caught me at it one day and gave me a most unmerciful flaking.

One evening, when Father was coming from work, I was playing trains in the front garden. I let on not to notice him; instead, I pretended to be talking to myself, and said in a loud voice: "If another bloody baby comes into this house, I'm going out."

Father stopped dead and looked at me over his shoulder.

"What's that you said?" he asked sternly.

"I was only talking to myself," I replied, trying to conceal my panic. "It's private."

He turned and went in without a word. Mind you, I intended it as a solemn warning, but its effect was quite different. Father started being quite nice to me. I could understand that, of course. Mother was quite sickening about Sonny. Even at mealtimes she'd get up and gawk at him in the cradle with an idiotic smile, and tell Father to do the same. He was always polite about it, but he looked so puzzled you could see he didn't know what she was talking about. He complained of the way Sonny cried at night, but she only got cross and said that Sonny never cried except when there was something up with him—which was a flaming lie, because Sonny never had anything up with him, and only cried for attention. It was really painful to see how simple-minded she was. Father wasn't attractive, but he had a fine intelligence. He saw through Sonny, and now he knew that I saw through him as well.

One night I woke with a start. There was someone beside me in the bed. For one wild moment I felt sure it must be Mother, having come to her senses and left Father for good, but then I heard Sonny in convulsions in the next room, and Mother saying: "There! There! There!" and I knew it wasn't she. It was Father. He was lying beside me, wide awake, breathing hard and apparently as mad as hell.

After a while it came to me what he was mad about. It was his turn now. After turning me out of the big bed, he had been turned out himself. Mother had no consideration now for anyone but that poisonous pup, Sonny. I couldn't help feeling sorry for Father. I had been through it all myself, and even at that age I was magnanimous. I began to stroke him down and say: "There! There!" He wasn't exactly responsive.

"Aren't you asleep either?" he snarled.

"Ah, come on and put your arm around us, can't you?" I said, and he did, in a sort of way. Gingerly, I suppose, is how you'd describe it. He was very bony but better than nothing.

At Christmas he went out of his way to buy me a really nice model railway.

Questions

1. *Is the story narrated from the point of view of a young child or a mature man?* 2. *Note that the narrator's most ardent wishes—for the return of his father and for a new baby in the house—are granted. What are the consequences for him?* 3. *What specific details in the story contribute to the appropriateness of its title?* 4. *With whom does the reader sympathize? How does the author control those sympathies?*

Good Country People

FLANNERY O'CONNOR [1925–1964]

Besides the neutral expression that she wore when she was alone, Mrs. Freeman had two others, forward and reverse, that she used for all her human dealings. Her forward expression was steady and driving like the advance of a heavy truck. Her eyes never swerved to left or right but turned as the story turned as if they followed a yellow line down the center of it. She seldom used the other expression because it was not often necessary for her to retract a statement, but when she did, her face came to a complete stop, there was an almost imperceptible movement of her black eyes, during which they seemed to be receding, and then the observer would see that Mrs. Freeman, though she might stand there as real as several grain sacks thrown on top of each other, was no longer there in spirit. As for getting anything across to her when this was the case, Mrs. Hopewell had given it up. She might talk her head off. Mrs. Freeman could never be brought to admit herself wrong on any point. She would stand there and if she could be brought to say anything, it was something like, "Well, I wouldn't of said it was and I wouldn't of said it wasn't," or letting her gaze range over the top kitchen shelf where there was an assortment of dusty bottles, she might remark, "I see you ain't ate many of them figs you put up last summer."

They carried on their most important business in the kitchen at breakfast. Every morning Mrs. Hopewell got up at seven o'clock and lit her gas heater and Joy's. Joy was her daughter, a large blonde girl who had an artificial leg. Mrs. Hopewell thought of her as a child though she was thirty-two years old and highly educated. Joy would get up while her mother was eating and lumber into the bathroom and slam the door, and before long, Mrs. Freeman would arrive at the back door. Joy would hear her mother call, "Come on in," and then they would talk for a while in low voices that were indistinguishable in the bathroom. By the time Joy came in, they had usually finished the weather report and were on one or the other of Mrs. Freeman's daughters, Glynese or Carramae. Joy called them Glycerin and Caramel. Glynese, a redhead, was eighteen and had many admirers; Carramae, a blonde, was only fifteen but already married and pregnant. She could not keep anything on her stomach. Every morning Mrs. Freeman told Mrs. Hopewell how many times she had vomited since the last report.

Mrs. Hopewell liked to tell people that Glynese and Carramae were two of the finest girls she knew and that Mrs. Freeman was a *lady* and that she was never ashamed to take her anywhere or introduce her to anybody they might meet. Then she would tell how she had happened to hire the Freemans in the first place and how they were a godsend to her and how she had had them four years. The reason for her keeping them so long was that they were not trash. They were good country people. She had telephoned the man whose name they had given as a reference and he had told her that Mr. Freeman was a good farmer but that his wife was the nosiest woman ever to walk the earth. "She's got to be into everything," the man said. "If she don't get there before the dust settles, you can bet she's dead, that's all. She'll want to know all your business. I can stand him real good," he had said, "but me nor my wife neither could have stood that woman one more minute on this place." That had put Mrs. Hopewell off for a few days.

She had hired them in the end because there were no other applicants but she had made up her mind beforehand exactly how she would handle the woman. Since she was the type who had to be into everything, then, Mrs. Hopewell had decided, she would not only let her be into everything, she would see to it that she was into everything—she would give her the responsibility of everything, she would put her in charge. Mrs. Hopewell had no bad qualities of her own but she was able to use other people's in such a constructive way that she never felt the lack. She had hired the Freemans and she had kept them four years.

Nothing is perfect. This was one of Mrs. Hopewell's favorite sayings. Another was: that is life! And still another, the most important, was: well, other people have their opinions too. She would make these statements, usually at the table, in a tone of gentle insistence as if no one held them but her, and the large hulking Joy, whose constant outrage had obliterated every expression from her face, would stare just a little to the side of her, her eyes icy blue, with the look of someone who has achieved blindness by an act of will and means to keep it.

When Mrs. Hopewell said to Mrs. Freeman that life was like that, Mrs. Freeman would say, "I always said so myself." Nothing had been arrived at by anyone that had not first been arrived at by her. She was quicker than Mr. Freeman. When Mrs. Hopewell said to her after they had been on the place a while, "You know, you're the wheel behind the wheel," and winked, Mrs. Freeman had said, "I know it. I've always been quick. It's some that are quicker than others."

"Everybody is different," Mrs. Hopewell said.

"Yes, most people is," Mrs. Freeman said.

"It takes all kinds to make the world."

"I always said it did myself."

The girl was used to this kind of dialogue for breakfast and more of it for dinner; sometimes they had it for supper too. When they had no guest they ate in the kitchen because that was easier. Mrs. Freeman always managed to arrive at some point during the meal and to watch them finish it. She would stand in the doorway if it were summer but in the winter she would stand with one elbow on top of the refrigerator and look down on them, or she would stand by the gas heater, lifting the back of her skirt slightly. Occasionally she would stand against the wall and roll her head from side to side. At no time was she in any hurry to leave. All this was very trying on Mrs. Hopewell but she was a woman of great patience. She realized that nothing is perfect and that in the Freemans she had good country people and that if, in this day and age, you get good country people, you had better hang onto them.

She had had plenty of experience with trash. Before the Freemans she had averaged one tenant family a year. The wives of these farmers were not the kind you would want to be around you for very long. Mrs. Hopewell, who had divorced her husband long ago, needed someone to walk over the fields with her; and when Joy had to be impressed for these services, her remarks were usually so ugly and her face so glum that Mrs. Hopewell would say, "If you can't come pleasantly, I don't want you at all," to which the girl, standing square and rigid-shouldered with her neck thrust slightly forward, would reply, "If you want me, here I am—LIKE I AM."

Mrs. Hopewell excused this attitude because of the leg (which had been shot off in a hunting accident when Joy was ten). It was hard for Mrs. Hopewell to realize that her child was thirty-two now and that for more than twenty years she had had only one leg. She thought of her still as a child because it tore her heart to think instead of the poor stout girl in her thirties who had never danced a step or had any *normal* good times. Her name was really Joy but as soon as she was twenty-one and away from home, she had had it legally changed. Mrs. Hopewell was certain that she had thought and thought until she had hit upon the ugliest name in any language. Then she had gone and had the beautiful name, Joy, changed without telling her mother until after she had done it. Her legal name was Hulga.

When Mrs. Hopewell thought the name, Hulga, she thought of the broad blank hull of a battleship. She would not use it. She continued to call her Joy to which the girl responded but in a purely mechanical way.

Hulga had learned to tolerate Mrs. Freeman who saved her from taking walks with her mother. Even Glynese and Carramae were useful when they occupied attention that might otherwise have been directed at her. At first she had thought she could not stand Mrs. Freeman for she had found that it was not possible to be rude to her. Mrs. Freeman would take on strange resentments and for days together she would be sullen but the source of her displeasure was always obscure; a direct attack, a positive leer, blatant ugliness to her face—these never touched her. And without warning one day, she began calling her Hulga.

She did not call her that in front of Mrs. Hopewell who would have been incensed but when she and the girl happened to be out of the house together, she would say something and add the name Hulga to the end of it, and the big spectacled Joy-Hulga would scowl and redden as if her privacy had been intruded upon. She considered the name her personal affair. She had arrived at it first purely on the basis of its ugly sound and then the full genius of its fitness had struck her. She had a vision of the name working like the ugly sweating Vulcan who stayed in the furnace and to whom, presumably, the goddess had to come when called. She saw it as the name of her highest creative act. One of her major triumphs was that her mother had not been able to turn her dust into Joy, but the greater one was that she had been able to turn it herself into Hulga. However, Mrs. Freeman's relish for using the name only irritated her. It was as if Mrs. Freeman's beady steel-pointed eyes had penetrated far enough behind her face to reach some secret fact. Something about her seemed to fascinate Mrs. Freeman and then one day Hulga realized that it was the artificial leg. Mrs. Freeman had a special fondness for the details of secret infections, hidden deformities, assaults upon children. Of diseases, she preferred the lingering or incurable. Hulga had heard Mrs. Hopewell give her the details of the hunting accident, how the leg had been literally blasted off, how she had never lost consciousness. Mrs. Freeman could listen to it any time as if it had happened an hour ago.

When Hulga stumped into the kitchen in the morning (she could walk without making the awful noise but she made it—Mrs. Hopewell was certain—because it was ugly-sounding), she glanced at them and did not speak. Mrs. Hopewell would be in her red kimono with her hair tied around her head in rags. She would be sitting at the table, finishing her breakfast and Mrs. Freeman would be hanging by her elbow outward from the refrigerator, looking down at the table. Hulga always put her eggs on the stove to boil and then stood over them with her arms folded, and Mrs. Hopewell would look at her—a kind of indirect gaze divided between her and Mrs. Freeman—and would think that if she would only keep herself up a little, she wouldn't be so bad looking. There was nothing wrong with her face that a pleasant expression wouldn't help. Mrs. Hopewell said that people who looked on the bright side of things would be beautiful even if they were not.

Whenever she looked at Joy this way, she could not help but feel that it would have been better if the child had not taken the Ph.D. It had certainly not brought her out any and now that she had it, there was no more excuse for her to go to school again. Mrs. Hopewell thought it was nice for girls to go to school to have a good time but Joy had "gone through." Anyhow, she would not have been strong enough to go again. The doctors had told Mrs. Hopewell that with the best of care, Joy might see forty-five. She had a weak heart. Joy had made it plain that if it had not been for this condition, she would be far from these red hills and good country people. She would be in a university lecturing to people who knew what she was talking about. And Mrs. Hopewell could very well picture her there, looking like a scarecrow and lecturing to more of the same. Here she went about all day in a six-year-old skirt and a yellow sweat shirt with a faded cowboy on a horse embossed on it. She thought this was funny; Mrs. Hopewell thought it was idiotic and showed simply that she was still a child. She was brilliant but she didn't have a grain of sense. It seemed to Mrs. Hopewell that every year she grew less like other people and more like herself—bloated, rude, and squint-eyed. And she said such strange things! To her own mother she had said—without warning, without excuse, standing up in the middle of a meal with her face purple and her mouth half full—"Woman! do you ever look inside? Do you ever look inside and see what you are *not?* God!" she had cried sinking down again and staring at her plate, "Malebranche was right: we are not our own light. We are not our own light!" Mrs. Hopewell had no idea to this day what brought that on. She had only made the remark, hoping Joy would take it in, that a smile never hurt anyone.

The girl had taken the Ph.D. in philosophy and this left Mrs. Hopewell at a complete loss. You could say, "My daughter is a nurse," or "My daughter is a school teacher," or even, "My daughter is a chemical engineer." You could not say, "My daughter is a philosopher." That was something that had ended with the Greeks and Romans. All day Joy sat on her neck in a deep chair, reading. Sometimes she went for walks but she didn't like dogs or cats or birds or flowers or nature or nice young men. She looked at nice young men as if she could smell their stupidity.

One day Mrs. Hopewell had picked up one of the books the girl had just put down and opening it at random, she read, "Science, on the other hand, has to assert its soberness and seriousness afresh and declare that it is concerned solely with what-is. Nothing—how can it be for science anything but a horror and a phantasm? If science is right, then one thing stands firm: science wishes to know nothing of nothing. Such is after all the strictly scientific approach to Nothing. We know it by wishing to know nothing of Nothing." These words had been underlined with a blue pencil and they worked on Mrs. Hopewell like some evil incantation in gibberish. She shut the book quickly and went out of the room as if she were having a chill.

This morning when the girl came in, Mrs. Freeman was on Carramae. "She thrown up four times after supper," she said, "and was up twict in the night after three o'clock. Yesterday she didn't do nothing but ramble in the bureau drawer. All she did. Stand up there and see what she could run up on."

"She's got to eat," Mrs. Hopewell muttered, sipping her coffee, while she watched Joy's back at the stove. She was wondering what the child had said to the Bible salesman. She could not imagine what kind of a conversation she could possibly have had with him.

He was a tall gaunt hatless youth who had called yesterday to sell them a Bible. He had appeared at the door, carrying a large black suitcase that weighted him so heavily on one side that he had to brace himself against the door facing. He seemed on the point of collapse but he said in a cheerful voice, "Good morning, Mrs. Cedars!" and set the suitcase down on the mat. He was not a bad-looking young man though he had on a bright blue suit and yellow socks that were not pulled up far enough. He had prominent face bones and a streak of sticky-looking brown hair falling across his forehead.

"I'm Mrs. Hopewell," she said.

"Oh!" he said, pretending to look puzzled but with his eyes sparkling, "I saw it said 'The Cedars,' on the mailbox so I thought you was Mrs. Cedars!" and he burst out in a pleasant laugh. He picked up the satchel and under cover of a pant, he fell forward into her hall. It was rather as if the suitcase had moved first, jerking him after it. "Mrs. Hopewell!" he said and grabbed her hand. "I hope you are well!" and he laughed again and then all at once his face sobered completely. He paused and gave her a straight earnest look and said, "Lady, I've come to speak of serious things."

"Well, come in," she muttered, none too pleased because her dinner was almost ready. He came into the parlor and sat down on the edge of a straight chair and put the suitcase between his feet and glanced around the room as if he were sizing her up by it. Her silver gleamed on the two sideboards; she decided he had never been in a room as elegant as this.

"Mrs. Hopewell," he began, using her name in a way that sounded almost intimate, "I know you believe in Chrustian service."

"Well yes," she murmured.

"I know," he said and paused, looking very wise with his head cocked on one side, "that you're a good woman. Friends have told me."

Mrs. Hopewell never liked to be taken for a fool. "What are you selling?" she asked.

"Bibles," the young man said and his eye raced around the room before he added, "I see you have no family Bible in your parlor, I see that is the one lack you got!"

Mrs. Hopewell could not say, "My daughter is an atheist and won't let me keep the Bible in the parlor." She said, stiffening slightly, "I keep my Bible by my bedside." This was not the truth. It was in the attic somewhere.

"Lady," he said, "the word of God ought to be in the parlor."

"Well, I think that's a matter of taste," she began. "I think . . ."

"Lady," he said, "for a Chrustian, the word of God ought to be in every room in the house besides in his heart. I know you're a Chrustian because I can see it in every line of your face."

She stood up and said, "Well, young man, I don't want to buy a Bible and I smell my dinner burning."

He didn't get up. He began to twist his hands and looking down at them, he said softly, "Well lady, I'll tell you the truth—not many people want to buy one nowadays and besides, I know I'm real simple. I don't know how to say a thing but to say it. I'm just a country boy." He glanced up into her unfriendly face. "People like you don't like to fool with country people like me!"

"Why!" she cried, "good country people are the salt of the earth! Besides, we all have different ways of doing, it takes all kinds to make the world go 'round. That's life!"

"You said a mouthful," he said.

"Why, I think there aren't enough good country people in the world!" she said, stirred. "I think that's what's wrong with it!"

His face had brightened. "I didn't inraduce myself," he said. "I'm Manley Pointer from out in the country around Willohobie, not even from a place, just from near a place."

"You wait a minute," she said. "I have to see about my dinner." She went out to the kitchen and found Joy standing near the door where she had been listening.

"Get rid of the salt of the earth," she said, "and let's eat."

Mrs. Hopewell gave her a pained look and turned the heat down under the vegetables. "*I* can't be rude to anybody," she murmured and went back into the parlor.

He had opened the suitcase and was sitting with a Bible on each knee.

"You might as well put those up," she told him. "I don't want one."

"I appreciate your honesty," he said. "You don't see any more real honest people unless you go way out in the country."

"I know," she said, "real genuine folks!" Through the crack in the door she heard a groan.

"I guess a lot of boys come telling you they're working their way through college," he said, "but I'm not going to tell you that. Somehow," he said, "I don't want to go to college. I want to devote my life to Chrustian service. See," he said, lowering his voice, "I got this heart condition. I may not live long. When you know it's something wrong with you and you may not live long, well then, lady . . ." He paused, with his mouth open, and stared at her.

He and Joy had the same condition! She knew that her eyes were filling with tears but she collected herself quickly and murmured, "Won't you stay for dinner? We'd love to have you!" and was sorry the instant she heard herself say it.

"Yes mam," he said in an abashed voice, "I would sher love to do that!"

Joy had given him one look on being introduced to him and then throughout the meal had not glanced at him again. He had addressed several remarks to her, which she had pretended not to hear. Mrs. Hopewell could not understand deliberate rudeness, although she lived with it, and she felt she had always to overflow with hospitality to make up for Joy's lack of courtesy. She urged him to talk about himself and he did. He said he was the seventh child of twelve and that his father had been crushed under a tree when he himself was eight year old. He had been crushed very badly, in fact, almost cut in two and was practically not recognizable. His mother had got along the best she could by hard working and she had always seen that her children went to Sunday School and that they read the Bible every evening. He was now nineteen year old and he had been selling Bibles for four months. In that time he had sold seventy-seven Bibles and had the promise of two more sales. He wanted to become a missionary because he thought that was the way you could do most for people. "He who losest his life shall find it," he said simply and he was so sincere, so genuine and earnest that Mrs. Hopewell would not for the world have smiled. He prevented his peas from sliding onto the table by blocking them with a piece of bread which he later cleaned his plate with. She could see Joy observing sidewise how he handled his knife and fork and she saw too that every few minutes, the boy would dart a keen appraising glance at the girl as if he were trying to attract her attention.

After dinner Joy cleared the dishes off the table and disappeared and

Mrs. Hopewell was left to talk with him. He told her again about his childhood and his father's accident and about various things that had happened to him. Every five minutes or so she would stifle a yawn. He sat for two hours until finally she told him she must go because she had an appointment in town. He packed his Bibles and thanked her and prepared to leave, but in the doorway he stopped and wrung her hand and said that not on any of his trips had he met a lady as nice as her and he asked if he could come again. She had said she would always be happy to see him.

Joy had been standing in the road, apparently looking at something in the distance, when he came down the steps toward her, bent to the side with his heavy valise. He stopped where she was standing and confronted her directly. Mrs. Hopewell could not hear what he said but she trembled to think what Joy would say to him. She could see that after a minute Joy said something and that then the boy began to speak again, making an excited gesture with his free hand. After a minute Joy said something else at which the boy began to speak once more. Then to her amazement, Mrs. Hopewell saw the two of them walk off together, toward the gate. Joy had walked all the way to the gate with him and Mrs. Hopewell could not imagine what they had said to each other, and she had not yet dared to ask.

Mrs. Freeman was insisting upon her attention. She had moved from the refrigerator to the heater so that Mrs. Hopewell had to turn and face her in order to seem to be listening. "Glynese gone out with Harvey Hill again last night," she said. "She had this sty."

"Hill," Mrs. Hopewell said absently, "is that the one who works in the garage?"

"Nome, he's the one that goes to chiropracter school," Mrs. Freeman said. "She had this sty. Been had it two days. So she says when he brought her in the other night he says, 'Lemme get rid of that sty for you,' and she says, 'How?' and he says, 'You just lay yourself down acrost the seat of that car and I'll show you.' So she done it and he popped her neck. Kept on a-popping it several times until she made him quit. This morning," Mrs. Freeman said, "she ain't got no sty. She ain't got no traces of a sty."

"I never heard of that before," Mrs. Hopewell said.

"He ast her to marry him before the Ordinary," Mrs. Freeman went on, "and she told him she wasn't going to be married in no *office*."

"Well, Glynese is a fine girl," Mrs. Hopewell said, "Glynese and Carramae are both fine girls."

"Carramae said when her and Lyman was married Lyman said it sure felt sacred to him. She said he said he wouldn't take five hundred dollars for being married by a preacher."

"How much would he take?" the girl asked from the stove.

"He said he wouldn't take five hundred dollars," Mrs. Freeman repeated.

"Well we all have work to do," Mrs. Hopewell said.

"Lyman said it just felt more sacred to him," Mrs. Freeman said. "The doctor wants Carramae to eat prunes. Says instead of medicine. Says them cramps is coming from pressure. You know where I think it is?"

"She'll be better in a few weeks," Mrs. Hopewell said.

"In the tube," Mrs. Freeman said. "Else she wouldn't be as sick as she is."

Hulga had cracked her two eggs into a saucer and was bringing them to the table along with a cup of coffee that she had filled too full. She sat down carefully and began to eat, meaning to keep Mrs. Freeman there by questions if for any reason she showed an inclination to leave. She could perceive her mother's eye on her. The first roundabout question would be about the Bible salesman and she did not wish to bring it on. "How did he pop her neck?" she asked.

Mrs. Freeman went into a description of how he had popped her neck. She said he owned a '55 Mercury but that Glynese said she would rather marry a man with only a '36 Plymouth who would be married by a preacher. The girl asked what if he had a '32 Plymouth and Mrs. Freeman said what Glynese had said was a '36 Plymouth.

Mrs. Hopewell said there were not many girls with Glynese's common sense. She said what she admired in those girls was their common sense. She said that reminded her that they had a nice visitor yesterday, a young man selling Bibles. "Lord," she said, "he bored me to death but he was so sincere and genuine I couldn't be rude to him. He was just good country people, you know," she said, "—just the salt of the earth."

"I seen him walk up," Mrs. Freeman said, "and then later—I seen him walk off," and Hulga could feel the slight shift in her voice, the slight insinuation, that he had not walked off alone, had he? Her face remained expressionless but the color rose into her neck and she seemed to swallow it down with the next spoonful of egg. Mrs. Freeman was looking at her as if they had a secret together.

"Well, it takes all kinds of people to make the world go 'round," Mrs. Hopewell said. "It's very good we aren't all alike."

"Some people are more alike than others," Mrs. Freeman said.

Hulga got up and stumped, with about twice the noise that was necessary, into her room and locked the door. She was to meet the Bible salesman at ten o'clock at the gate. She had thought about it half the night. She had started thinking of it as a great joke and then she had begun to see profound implications in it. She had lain in bed imagining dialogues for them that were insane on the surface but that reached below to depths that no Bible salesman would be aware of. Their conversation yesterday had been of this kind.

He had stopped in front of her and had simply stood there. His face was bony and sweaty and bright, with a little pointed nose in the center of it, and his look was different from what it had been at the dinner table. He was gazing at her with open curiosity, with fascination, like a child watching a new fantastic animal at the zoo, and he was breathing as if he had run a great distance to reach her. His gaze seemed somehow familiar but she could not think where she had been regarded with it before. For almost a minute he didn't say anything. Then on what seemed an insuck of breath, he whispered, "You ever ate a chicken that was two days old?"

The girl looked at him stonily. He might have just put this question up for consideration at the meeting of a philosophical association. "Yes," she presently replied as if she had considered it from all angles.

"It must have been mighty small!" he said triumphantly and shook all over with little nervous giggles, getting very red in the face, and subsiding finally into his gaze of complete admiration, while the girl's expression remained exactly the same.

"How old are you?" he asked softly.

She waited some time before she answered. Then in a flat voice she said, "Seventeen."

His smiles came in succession like waves breaking on the surface of a little lake. "I see you got a wooden leg," he said. "I think you're real brave. I think you're real sweet."

The girl stood blank and solid and silent.

"Walk to the gate with me," he said. "You're a brave sweet little thing and I liked you the minute I seen you walk in the door."

Hulga began to move forward.

"What's your name?" he asked, smiling down on the top of her head.

"Hulga," she said.

"Hulga," he murmured, "Hulga. Hulga. I never heard of anybody name Hulga before. You're shy, aren't you, Hulga?" he asked.

She nodded, watching his large red hand on the handle of the giant valise.

"I like girls that wear glasses," he said. "I think a lot. I'm not like these people that a serious thought don't ever enter their heads. It's because I may die."

"I may die too," she said suddenly and looked up at him. His eyes were very small and brown, glittering feverishly.

"Listen," he said, "don't you think some people was meant to meet on account of what all they got in common and all? Like they both think serious thoughts and all?" He shifted the valise to his other hand so that the hand nearest her was free. He caught hold of her elbow and shook it a little. "I don't work on Saturday," he said. "I like to walk in the woods and see what Mother Nature is wearing. O'er the hills and far away. Pic-nics and things. Couldn't we go on a pic-nic tomorrow? Say yes, Hulga," he said and gave her a dying look as if he felt his insides about to drop out of him. He had even seemed to sway slightly toward her.

During the night she had imagined that she seduced him. She imagined that the two of them walked on the place until they came to the storage barn beyond the two back fields and there, she imagined, that things came to such a pass that she very easily seduced him and that then, of course, she had to reckon with his remorse. True genius can get an idea across even to an inferior mind. She imagined that she took his remorse in hand and changed it into a deeper understanding of life. She took all his shame away and turned it into something useful.

She set off for the gate at exactly ten o'clock, escaping without drawing Mrs. Hopewell's attention. She didn't take anything to eat, forgetting that food is usually taken on a picnic. She wore a pair of slacks and a dirty white shirt, and as an afterthought, she had put some Vapex on the collar of it since she did not own any perfume. When she reached the gate no one was there.

She looked up and down the empty highway and had the furious feeling that she had been tricked, that he had only meant to make her walk to the gate after the idea of him. Then suddenly he stood up, very tall, from behind a bush on the opposite embankment. Smiling, he lifted his hat which was new and wide-brimmed. He had not worn it yesterday and she wondered if he had bought it for the occasion. It was toast-colored with a red and white band around it and was slightly too large for him. He stepped from behind the bush still carrying the black valise. He had on the same suit and the same yellow socks sucked down in his shoes from walking. He crossed the highway and said, "I knew you'd come!"

The girl wondered acidly how he had known this. She pointed to the valise and asked, "Why did you bring your Bibles?"

He took her elbow, smiling down on her as if he could not stop. "You can never tell when you'll need the word of God, Hulga," he said. She had a moment in which she doubted that this was actually happening and then they began to climb the embankment. They went down into the pasture toward the woods. The boy walked lightly by her side, bouncing on his toes. The valise did not seem to be heavy today; he even swung it. They crossed half the pasture without saying anything and then, putting his hand easily on the small of her back, he asked softly, "Where does your wooden leg join on?"

She turned an ugly red and glared at him and for an instant the boy looked abashed. "I didn't mean you no harm," he said. "I only meant you're so brave and all. I guess God takes care of you."

"No," she said, looking forward and walking fast, "I don't even believe in God."

At this he stopped and whistled. "No!" he exclaimed as if he were too astonished to say anything else.

She walked on and in a second he was bouncing at her side, fanning with his hat. "That's very unusual for a girl," he remarked, watching her out of the corner of his eye. When they reached the edge of the wood, he put his hand on her back again and drew her against him without a word and kissed her heavily.

The kiss, which had more pressure than feeling behind it, produced that extra surge of adrenalin in the girl that enables one to carry a packed trunk out of a burning house, but in her, the power went at once to the brain. Even before he released her, her mind, clear and detached and ironic anyway, was regarding him from a great distance, with amusement but with pity. She had never been kissed before and she was pleased to discover that it was an unexceptional experience and all a matter of the mind's control. Some people might enjoy drain water if they were told it was vodka. When the boy, looking expectant but uncertain, pushed her gently away, she turned and walked on, saying nothing as if such business, for her, were common enough.

He came along panting at her side, trying to help her when he saw a root that she might trip over. He caught and held back the long swaying blades of thorn vine until she had passed beyond them. She led the way and he came breathing heavily behind her. Then they came out on a sunlit hillside, sloping softly into another one a little smaller. Beyond, they could see the rusted top of the old barn where the extra hay was stored.

The hill was sprinkled with small pink weeds. "Then you ain't saved?" he asked suddenly, stopping.

The girl smiled. It was the first time she had smiled at him at all. "In my economy," she said, "I'm saved and you are damned but I told you I didn't believe in God."

Nothing seemed to destroy the boy's look of admiration. He gazed at her now as if the fantastic animal at the zoo had put its paw through the bars and given him a loving poke. She thought he looked as if he wanted to kiss her again and she walked on before he had the chance.

"Ain't there somewheres we can sit down sometime?" he murmured, his voice softening toward the end of the sentence.

"In that barn," she said.

They made for it rapidly as if it might slide away like a train. It was a large two-story barn, cool and dark inside. The boy pointed up the ladder that led into the loft and said, "It's too bad we can't go up there."

"Why can't we?" she asked.

"Yer leg," he said reverently.

The girl gave him a contemptuous look and putting both hands on the ladder, she climbed it while he stood below, apparently awestruck. She pulled herself expertly through the opening and then looked down at him and said, "Well, come on if you're coming," and he began to climb the ladder, awkwardly bringing the suitcase with him.

"We won't need the Bible," she observed.

"You never can tell," he said, panting. After he had got into the loft, he was a few seconds catching his breath. She had sat down in a pile of straw. A wide sheath of sunlight, filled with dust particles, slanted over her. She lay back against a bale, her face turned away, looking out the front opening of the barn where hay was thrown from a wagon into the loft. The two pink-speckled hillsides lay back against a dark ridge of woods. The sky was cloudless and cold blue. The boy dropped down by her side and put one arm under her and the other over her and began methodically kissing her face, making little noises like a fish. He did not remove his hat but it was pushed far enough back not to interfere. When her glasses got in his way, he took them off of her and slipped them into his pocket.

The girl at first did not return any of the kisses but presently she began to and after she had put several on his cheek, she reached his lips and remained there, kissing him again and again as if she were trying to draw all the breath out of him. His breath was clear and sweet like a child's and the kisses were sticky like a child's. He mumbled about loving her and about knowing when he first seen her that he loved her, but the mumbling was like the sleepy fretting of a child being put to sleep by his mother. Her mind, throughout this, never stopped or lost itself for a second to her feelings. "You ain't said you loved me none," he whispered finally, pulling back from her. "You got to say that."

She looked away from him off into the hollow sky and then down at a black ridge and then down farther into what appeared to be two green swelling lakes. She didn't realize he had taken her glasses but this landscape could not seem exceptional to her for she seldom paid any close attention to her surroundings.

"You got to say it," he repeated. "You got to say you love me."

She was always careful how she committed herself. "In a sense," she began, "if you use the word loosely, you might say that. But it's not a word I use. I don't have illusions. I'm one of those people who see *through* to nothing."

The boy was frowning. "You got to say it. I said it and you got to say it," he said.

The girl looked at him almost tenderly. "You poor baby," she murmured. "It's just as well you don't understand," and she pulled him by the neck, face-down, against her. "We are all damned," she said, "but some of us have taken off our blindfolds and see that there's nothing to see. It's a kind of salvation."

The boy's astonished eyes looked blankly through the ends of her hair. "Okay," he almost whined, "but do you love me or don'tcher?"

"Yes," she said and added, "in a sense. But I must tell you something. There mustn't be anything dishonest between us." She lifted his head and looked him in the eye. "I am thirty years old," she said. "I have a number of degrees."

The boy's look was irritated but dogged. "I don't care," he said. "I don't care a thing about what all you done. I just want to know if you love me or don'tcher?" and he caught her to him and wildly planted her face with kisses until she said, "Yes, yes."

"Okay then," he said, letting her go. "Prove it."

She smiled, looking dreamily out on the shifty landscape. She had seduced him without even making up her mind to try. "How?" she asked, feeling that he should be delayed a little.

He leaned over and put his lips to her ear. "Show me where your wooden leg joins on," he whispered.

The girl uttered a sharp little cry and her face instantly drained of color.

The obscenity of the suggestion was not what shocked her. As a child she had sometimes been subject to feelings of shame but education had removed the last traces of that as a good surgeon scrapes for cancer; she would no more have felt it over what he was asking than she would have believed in his Bible. But she was as sensitive about the artificial leg as a peacock about his tail. No one ever touched it but her. She took care of it as someone else would his soul, in private and almost with her own eyes turned away. "No," she said.

"I known it," he muttered, sitting up. "You're just playing me for a sucker."

"Oh no no!" she cried. "It joins on at the knee. Only at the knee. Why do you want to see it?"

The boy gave her a long penetrating look. "Because," he said, "it's what makes you different. You ain't like anybody else."

She sat staring at him. There was nothing about her face or her round freezing-blue eyes to indicate that this had moved her; but she felt as if her heart had stopped and left her mind to pump her blood. She decided that for the first time in her life she was face to face with real innocence. This boy, with an instinct that came from beyond wisdom, had touched the truth about her. When after a minute, she said in a hoarse high voice, "All right," it was like surrendering to him completely. It was like losing her own life and finding it again, miraculously, in his.

Very gently he began to roll the slack leg up. The artificial limb, in a white sock and brown flat shoe, was bound in a heavy material like canvas and ended in an ugly jointure where it was attached to the stump. The boy's face and his voice were entirely reverent as he uncovered it and said, "Now show me how to take it off and on."

She took it off for him and put it back on again and then he took it off himself, handling it as tenderly as if it were a real one. "See!" he said with a delighted child's face. "Now I can do it myself!"

"Put it back on," she said. She was thinking that she would run away with him and that every night he would take the leg off and every morning put it back on again. "Put it back on," she said.

"Not yet," he murmured, setting it on its foot out of her reach. "Leave it off for a while. You got me instead."

She gave a little cry of alarm but he pushed her down and began to kiss her again. Without the leg she felt entirely dependent on him. Her brain seemed to have stopped thinking altogether and to be about some other function that it was not very good at. Different expressions raced back and forth over her face. Every now and then the boy, his eyes like two steel spikes, would glance behind him where the leg stood. Finally she pushed him off and said, "Put it back on me now."

"Wait," he said. He leaned the other way and pulled the valise toward him and opened it. It had a pale blue spotted lining and there were only two Bibles in it. He took one of these out and opened the cover of it. It was hollow and contained a pocket flask of whiskey, a pack of cards, and a small blue box with printing on it. He laid these out in front of her one at a time in an evenly-spaced row, like one presenting offerings at the shrine of a goddess. He put the blue box in her hand. THIS PRODUCT TO BE USED ONLY FOR THE PREVENTION OF DISEASE, she read, and dropped it. The boy was unscrewing the top of the flask. He stopped and pointed, with a smile, to the deck of cards. It was not an ordinary deck but one with an obscene picture on the back of each card. "Take a swig," he said, offering her the bottle first. He held it in front of her, but like one mesmerized, she did not move.

Her voice when she spoke had an almost pleading sound. "Aren't you," she murmured, "aren't you just good country people?"

The boy cocked his head. He looked as if he were just beginning to understand that she might be trying to insult him. "Yeah," he said, curling his lip slightly, "but it ain't held me back none. I'm as good as you any day in the week."

"Give me my leg," she said.

He pushed it farther away with his foot. "Come on now, let's begin to have us a good time," he said coaxingly. "We ain't got to know one another good yet."

"Give me my leg!" she screamed and tried to lunge for it but he pushed her down easily.

"What's the matter with you all of a sudden?" he asked, frowning as he screwed the top on the flask and put it quickly back inside the Bible. "You just a while ago said you didn't believe in nothing. I thought you was some girl!"

Her face was almost purple. "You're a Christian!" she hissed. "You're a fine Christian! You're just like them all—say one thing and do another. You're a perfect Christian, you're . . ."

The boy's mouth was set angrily. "I hope you don't think," he said in a lofty indignant tone, "that I believe in that crap! I may sell Bibles but I know which end is up and I wasn't born yesterday and I know where I'm going!"

"Give me my leg!" she screeched. He jumped up so quickly that she barely saw him sweep the cards and the blue box back into the Bible and throw the Bible into the valise. She saw him grab the leg and then she saw it for an instant slanted forlornly across the inside of the suitcase with a Bible at either side of its opposite ends. He slammed the lid shut and snatched up the valise and swung it down the hole and then stepped through himself.

When all of him had passed but his head, he turned and regarded her with a look that no longer had any admiration in it. "I've gotten a lot of interesting things," he said. "One time I got a woman's glass eye this way. And you needn't to think you'll catch me because Pointer ain't really my name. I use a different name at every house I call at and don't stay nowhere long. And I'll tell you another thing, Hulga," he said, using the name as if he didn't think much of it, "you ain't so smart. I been believing in nothing ever since I was born!" and then the toast-colored hat disappeared down the hole and the girl was left, sitting on the straw in the dusty sunlight. When she turned her churning face toward the opening, she saw his blue figure struggling success-fully over the green speckled lake.

Mrs. Hopewell and Mrs. Freeman, who were in the back pasture, dig-ging up onions, saw him emerge a little later from the woods and head across the meadow toward the highway. "Why, that looks like that nice dull young man that tried to sell me a Bible yesterday," Mrs. Hopewell said, squinting. "He must have been selling them to the Negroes back in there. He was so simple," she said, "but I guess the world would be better off if we were all that simple."

Mrs. Freeman's gaze drove forward and just touched him before he disappeared under the hill. Then she returned her attention to the evil-smelling onion shoot she was lifting from the ground. "Some can't be that simple," she said. "I know I never could."

Questions

1. Why does Joy feel that changing her name to Hulga is "her highest creative act"? 2. Does this story have any heroes in the conventional sense? Are any of its characters admirable? Explain. 3. In what ways do Mrs. Freeman's descriptions of her daughters Glynese and Carramae contribute to the theme of the story? 4. Does Hulga's experience with Manley Pointer confirm her cynical philosophy of "nothing"?

innocence and experience

POETRY

The Chimney Sweeper

WILLIAM BLAKE [1757–1827]

When my mother died I was very young,
And my Father sold me while yet my tongue
Could scarcely cry " 'weep! 'weep! 'weep! 'weep!"
So your chimneys I sweep, and in soot I sleep.

There's little Tom Dacre, who cried when his head,
That curled like a lamb's back, was shaved; so I said,
"Hush, Tom! never mind it, for when your head's bare
You know that the soot cannot spoil your white hair."

And so he was quiet and that very night
As Tom was a-sleeping, he had such a sight!   10
That thousands of sweepers, Dick, Joe, Ned, and Jack,
Were all of them locked up in coffins of black.

And by came an Angel who had a bright key,
And he opened the coffins and set them all free;
Then down a green plain leaping, laughing, they run,
And wash in a river, and shine in the Sun.

Then naked and white, all their bags left behind,
They rise upon clouds and sport in the wind;
And the Angel told Tom, if he'd be a good boy,
He'd have God for his father, and never want joy.   20

And so Tom awoke; and we rose in the dark,
And got with our bags and our brushes to work.
Though the morning was cold, Tom was happy and warm;
So if all do their duty they need not fear harm.

The Garden of Love

WILLIAM BLAKE [1757–1827]

I went to the Garden of Love,
And saw what I never had seen:
A Chapel was built in the midst,
Where I used to play on the green.

And the gates of this Chapel were shut,
And "Thou shalt not" writ over the door;
So I turn'd to the Garden of Love,
That so many sweet flowers bore,

And I saw it was filled with graves,
And tomb-stones where flowers should be: 10
And Priests in black gowns were walking their rounds,
And binding with briars my joys & desires.

1. What meanings does the word "love" have in this poem? 2. What is Blake's judgment on established religion? 3. Explain the meaning of "Chapel" (l. 3) and of "briars" (l. 12).

The Tyger

WILLIAM BLAKE [1757–1827]

Tyger! Tyger! burning bright
In the forests of the night,
What immortal hand or eye
Could frame thy fearful symmetry?

In what distant deeps or skies
Burnt the fire of thine eyes?
On what wings dare he aspire?
What the hand, dare seize the fire?

And what shoulder, & what art,
Could twist the sinews of thy heart?   10
And when thy heart began to beat,
What dread hand? & what dread feet?

What the hammer? what the chain?
In what furnace was thy brain?
What the anvil? what dread grasp
Dare its deadly terrors clasp?

When the stars threw down their spears,
And water'd heaven with their tears,
Did he smile his work to see?
Did he who made the Lamb make thee?   20

Tyger! Tyger! burning bright
In the forests of the night,
What immortal hand or eye
Dare frame thy fearful symmetry?

To a Mouse

ON TURNING HER UP IN HER NEST WITH THE PLOUGH,
NOVEMBER, 1785

ROBERT BURNS   [1759–1796]

Wee, sleekit,° cow'rin, tim'rous beastie,	*sleek*
O, what a panic's in thy breastie!	
Thou need na start awa sae hasty,	
Wi' bickering° brattle!°	*hurried/scamper*
I wad be laith to rin an' chase thee,	
Wi' murd'ring pattle!°	*plowstaff*

I'm truly sorry man's dominion
Has broken Nature's social union,
An' justifies that ill opinion
      Which makes thee startle   10
At me, thy poor earth-born companion,
      An' fellow-mortal!

I doubt na, whiles,° but thou may thieve;	*sometimes*
What then? poor beastie, thou maun° live!	*must*
A daimen° icker° in a thrave°	*occasional/corn-ear/shock*
'S a sma' request:	
I'll get a blessin wi' the lave,°	*rest*
And never miss't!	

Thy wee bit housie, too, in ruin!
Its silly wa's the win's are strewin!
An' naething, now, to big° a new ane,
        O' foggage° green!
An' bleak December's winds ensuin,
        Baith snell° an' keen!

Thou saw the fields laid bare and waste,
An' weary winter comin fast,
An' cozie here, beneath the blast,
        Thou thought to dwell,
Till crash! the cruel coulter° past
        Out thro' thy cell.

That wee bit heap o' leaves an' stibble
Has cost thee mony a weary nibble!
Now thou's turned out, for a' thy trouble,
        But° house or hald,
To thole° the winter's sleety dribble,
        An' cranreuch° cauld!

But, Mousie, thou art no thy lane°
In proving foresight may be vain:
The best laid schemes o' mice an' men
        Gang° aft a-gley.°
An' lea'e us nought but grief an' pain
        For promised joy.

Still thou art blest, compared wi' me!
The present only toucheth thee:
But och! I backward cast my e'e
        On prospects drear!
An' forward, tho' I canna see,
        I guess an' fear!

20
build
mosses

bitter

plowshare
30

without
endure
hoarfrost

not alone

39
go / awry

Lines[1]

COMPOSED A FEW MILES ABOVE TINTERN ABBEY
ON REVISITING THE BANKS OF THE WYE
DURING A TOUR. JULY 13, 1798

WILLIAM WORDSWORTH   [1770–1850]

Five years have passed;[2] five summers, with the length
Of five long winters! and again I hear
These waters, rolling from their mountain-springs
With a soft inland murmur. Once again
Do I behold these steep and lofty cliffs,
That on a wild secluded scene impress
Thoughts of more deep seclusion; and connect
The landscape with the quiet of the sky.
The day is come when I again repose
Here, under this dark sycamore, and view   10
These plots of cottage ground, these orchard tufts,
Which at this season, with their unripe fruits,
Are clad in one green hue, and lose themselves
'Mid groves and copses. Once again I see
These hedgerows, hardly hedgerows, little lines
Of sportive wood run wild; these pastoral farms,
Green to the very door; and wreaths of smoke
Sent up, in silence, from among the trees!
With some uncertain notice, as might seem
Of vagrant dwellers in the houseless woods,   20
Or of some Hermit's cave, where by his fire
The Hermit sits alone.

                These beauteous forms,
Through a long absence, have not been to me
As is a landscape to a blind man's eye;
But oft, in lonely rooms, and 'mid the din
Of towns and cities, I have owed to them,
In hours of weariness, sensations sweet,
Felt in the blood, and felt along the heart;
And passing even into my purer mind,
With tranquil restoration—feelings too   30
Of unremembered pleasure; such, perhaps,
As have no slight or trivial influence
On that best portion of a good man's life,

---

1.   Wordsworth wrote this poem during a four- or five-day walking tour through the Wye valley with his sister Dorothy.
2.   The poet had visited the region on a solitary walking tour in August of 1793 when he was twenty-three years old.

His little, nameless, unremembered, acts
Of kindness and of love. Nor less, I trust,
To them I may have owed another gift,
Of aspect more sublime; that blessed mood,
In which the burthen of the mystery,
In which the heavy and the weary weight
Of all this unintelligible world,   40
Is lightened—that serene and blessed mood,
In which the affections gently lead us on—
Until, the breath of this corporeal frame
And even the motion of our human blood
Almost suspended, we are laid asleep
In body, and become a living soul;
While with an eye made quiet by the power
Of harmony, and the deep power of joy,
We see into the life of things.

                                            If this
Be but a vain belief, yet, oh! how oft—   50
In darkness and amid the many shapes
Of joyless daylight; when the fretful stir
Unprofitable, and the fever of the world,
Have hung upon the beatings of my heart—
How oft, in spirit, have I turned to thee,
O sylvan Wye! thou wanderer through the woods,
How often has my spirit turned to thee!

    And now, with gleams of half-extinguished thought
With many recognitions dim and faint,
And somewhat of a sad perplexity,   60
The picture of the mind revives again;
While here I stand, not only with the sense
Of present pleasure, but with pleasing thoughts
That in this moment there is life and food
For future years. And so I dare to hope,
Though changed, no doubt, from what I was when first
I came among these hills; when like a roe
I bounded o'er the mountains, by the sides
Of the deep rivers, and the lonely streams,
Wherever nature led—more like a man   70
Flying from something that he dreads than one
Who sought the thing he loved. For nature then
(The coarser pleasures of my boyish days,
And their glad animal movements all gone by)
To me was all in all.—I cannot paint
What then I was. The sounding cataract
Haunted me like a passion; the tall rock,
The mountain, and the deep and gloomy wood,
Their colors and their forms, were then to me
An appetite; a feeling and a love,   80

That had no need of a remoter charm,
By thought supplied, nor any interest
Unborrowed from the eye.—That time is past,
And all its aching joys are now no more,
And all its dizzy raptures. Not for this
Faint[3] I, nor mourn nor murmur; other gifts
Have followed; for such loss, I would believe,
Abundant recompense. For I have learned
To look on nature, not as in the hour
Of thoughtless youth; but hearing oftentimes   90
The still, sad music of humanity,
Nor harsh nor grating, though of ample power
To chasten and subdue. And I have felt
A presence that disturbs me with the joy
Of elevated thoughts; a sense sublime
Of something far more deeply interfused,
Whose dwelling is the light of setting suns,
And the round ocean and the living air,
And the blue sky, and in the mind of man:
A motion and a spirit, that impels   100
All thinking things, all objects of all thought,
And rolls through all things. Therefore am I still
A lover of the meadows and the woods,
And mountains; and of all that we behold
From this green earth; of all the mighty world
Of eye, and ear—both what they half create,
And what perceive; well pleased to recognize
In nature and the language of the sense
The anchor of my purest thoughts, the nurse,
The guide, the guardian of my heart, and soul   110
Of all my moral being.

                    Nor perchance,
If I were not thus taught, should I the more
Suffer my genial spirits to decay:
For thou art with me here upon the banks
Of this fair river; thou my dearest Friend,[4]
My dear, dear Friend; and in thy voice I catch
The language of my former heart, and read
My former pleasures in the shooting lights
Of thy wild eyes. Oh! yet a little while
May I behold in thee what I was once,   120
My dear, dear Sister! and this prayer I make,
Knowing that Nature never did betray
The heart that loved her; 'tis her privilege,
Through all the years of this our life, to lead

---

3.   Lose heart.
4.   The poet addresses his sister Dorothy.

From joy to joy: for she can so inform
The mind that is within us, so impress
With quietness and beauty, and so feed
With lofty thoughts, that neither evil tongues,
Rash judgments, nor the sneers of selfish men,
Nor greetings where no kindness is, nor all   130
The dreary intercourse of daily life,
Shall e'er prevail against us, or disturb
Our cheerful faith, that all which we behold
Is full of blessings. Therefore let the moon
Shine on thee in thy solitary walk;
And let the misty mountain winds be free
To blow against thee: and, in after years,
When these wild ecstasies shall be matured
Into a sober pleasure; when thy mind
Shall be a mansion for all lovely forms,   140
Thy memory be as a dwelling place
For all sweet sounds and harmonies; oh! then,
If solitude, or fear, or pain, or grief
Should be thy portion, with what healing thoughts
Of tender joy wilt thou remember me,
And these my exhortations! Nor, perchance—
If I should be where I no more can hear
Thy voice, nor catch from thy wild eyes these gleams
Of past existence⁵—wilt thou then forget
That on the banks of this delightful stream   150
We stood together; and that I, so long
A worshiper of Nature, hither came
Unwearied in that service; rather say
With warmer love—oh! with far deeper zeal
Of holier love. Nor wilt thou then forget,
That after many wanderings, many years
Of absence, these steep woods and lofty cliffs,
And this green pastoral landscape, were to me
More dear, both for themselves and for thy sake!

1. *In this poem the poet distinguishes between two important periods in his life: the first is described in lines 65–83, and the second is described in lines 83–111. How does he characterize these two periods?* **2.** *The poem describes a visit to a familiar scene of the poet's youth and includes a meditation upon the changes that have occurred. Are the changes in the poet, the scene itself, or both?*

---

5. I.e., the poet's past experience. Note lines 116–119.

On First Looking into Chapman's Homer[1]

JOHN KEATS [1795–1821]

Much have I travelled in the realms of gold,
And many goodly states and kingdoms seen:
Round many western islands have I been
Which bards in fealty to Apollo[2] hold.
Oft of one wide expanse had I been told
That deep-browed Homer ruled as his demesne;°   *realm*
Yet did I never breathe its pure serene°   *clear air*
Till I heard Chapman speak out loud and bold:
Then felt I like some watcher of the skies
When a new planet swims into his ken;   10
Or like stout Cortez[3] when with eagle eyes
He stared at the Pacific—and all his men
Looked at each other with a wild surmise—
Silent, upon a peak in Darien.

My Last Duchess

ROBERT BROWNING   [1812–1889]

FERRARA

That's my last Duchess painted on the wall,
Looking as if she were alive. I call
That piece a wonder, now: Frà Pandolf's[4] hands
Worked busily a day, and there she stands.
Will't please you sit and look at her? I said
"Frà Pandolf" by design, for never read
Strangers like you that pictured countenance,
The depth and passion of its earnest glance,
But to myself they turned (since none puts by
The curtain I have drawn for you, but I)   10

---

1. George Chapman published translations of *The Iliad* (1611) and *The Odyssey* (1616).
2. The god of poetry.
3. Keats mistakenly attributes the discovery of the Pacific Ocean by Europeans to Hernando Cortez (1485–1547), the Spanish conqueror of Mexico. Vasco Nuñez de Balboa (1475–1517) first saw the Pacific from a mountain located in eastern Panama.

---

4. Fra Pandolf and Claus of Innsbruck (mentioned in the last line) are fictitious artists.

And seemed as they would ask me, if they durst,
How such a glance came there; so, not the first
Are you to turn and ask thus. Sir, 'twas not
Her husband's presence only, called that spot
Of joy into the Duchess' cheek: perhaps
Frà Pandolf chanced to say "Her mantle laps
"Over my lady's wrist too much," or "Paint
"Must never hope to reproduce the faint
"Half-flush that dies along her throat": such stuff
Was courtesy, she thought, and cause enough   20
For calling up that spot of joy. She had
A heart—how shall I say?—too soon made glad,
Too easily impressed; she liked whate'er
She looked on, and her looks went everywhere.
Sir, 'twas all one! My favor at her breast,
The dropping of the daylight in the West,
The bough of cherries some officious fool
Broke in the orchard for her, the white mule
She rode with round the terrace—all and each
Would draw from her alike the approving speech,   30
Or blush, at least. She thanked men—good! but thanked
Somehow—I know not how—as if she ranked
My gift of a nine-hundred-years-old name
With anybody's gift. Who'd stoop to blame
This sort of trifling? Even had you skill
In speech—which I have not—to make your will
Quite clear to such an one, and say, "Just this
"Or that in you disgusts me; here you miss,
"Or there exceed the mark"—and if she let
Herself be lessoned so, nor plainly set
Her wits to yours, forsooth, and made excuse,   40
—E'en then would be some stooping; and I choose
Never to stoop. Oh sir, she smiled, no doubt,
Whene'er I passed her; but who passed without
Much the same smile? This grew; I gave commands;
Then all smiles stopped together. There she stands
As if alive. Will't please you rise? We'll meet
The company below, then. I repeat,
The Count your master's known munificence
Is ample warrant that no just pretense   50
Of mine for dowry will be disallowed;
Though his fair daughter's self, as I avowed
At starting, is my object. Nay, we'll go
Together down, sir. Notice Neptune, though,
Taming a sea-horse, thought a rarity,
Which Claus of Innsbruck cast in bronze for me!

1. To whom is the duke speaking and what is the occasion? 2. Is the duke an admir-

able character? Do you share his judgment of his last duchess? Explain. **3.** Contrast the duke's moral and aesthetic sensibility. **4.** Note that this poem employs the same prevailing meter and rhyme scheme as Pope's "An Essay on Man" (p. 402), but that the effect is very different. Can you suggest why?

Out of the Cradle Endlessly Rocking

WALT WHITMAN [1819–1892]

Out of the cradle endlessly rocking,
Out of the mocking-bird's throat, the musical shuttle,
Out of the Ninth-month¹ midnight,
Over the sterile sands and the fields beyond, where the child leaving his bed
    wander'd alone, bareheaded, barefoot,
Down from the shower'd halo,
Up from the mystic play of shadows twining and twisting as if they were alive,
Out from the patches of briers and blackberries,
From the memories of the bird that chanted to me,
From your memories sad brother, from the fitful risings and fallings I heard,
From under that yellow half-moon late-risen and swollen as if with tears,   10
From those beginning notes of yearning and love there in the mist,
From the thousand responses of my heart never to cease,
From the myriad thence-arous'd words,
From the word stronger and more delicious than any,
From such as now they start the scene revisiting,
As a flock, twittering, rising, or overhead passing,
Borne hither, ere all eludes me, hurriedly,
A man, yet by these tears a little boy again,
Throwing myself on the sand, confronting the waves,
I, chanter of pains and joys, uniter of here and hereafter,   20
Taking all hints to use them, but swiftly leaping beyond them,
A reminiscence sing.

Once Paumanok,²
When the lilac-scent was in the air and Fifth-month grass was growing,
Up this seashore in some briers,
Two feather'd guests from Alabama, two together,
And their nest, and four light-green eggs spotted with brown,
And every day the he-bird to and fro near at hand,
And every day the she-bird crouch'd on her nest, silent, with bright eyes,

---

1. Quaker designation for September.
2. Paumanok is the Indian name of Long Island, where the poet was born and grew up.

And every day I, a curious boy, never too close, never disturbing them,   *30*
Cautiously peering, absorbing, translating.

Shine! shine! shine!
Pour down your warmth, great sun!
While we bask, we two together.

Two together!
Winds blow south, or winds blow north,
Day come white, or night come black,
Home, or rivers and mountains from home,
Singing all time, minding no time,
While we two keep together.   *40*

Till of a sudden,
May-be kill'd, unknown to her mate,
One forenoon the she-bird crouch'd not on the nest,
Nor return'd that afternoon, nor the next,
Nor ever appear'd again.

And thenceforward all summer in the sound of the sea,
And at night under the full of the moon in calmer weather,
Over the hoarse surging of the sea,
Or flitting from brier to brier by day,
I saw, I heard at intervals the remaining one, the he-bird,   *50*
The solitary guest from Alabama.

Blow! blow! blow!
Blow up sea-winds along Paumanok's shore;
I wait and I wait till you blow my mate to me.

Yes, when the stars glisten'd,
All night long on the prong of a moss-scallop'd stake,
Down almost amid the slapping waves,
Sat the lone singer wonderful causing tears.

He call'd on his mate,
He pour'd forth the meanings which I of all men know.   *60*

Yes my brother I know,
The rest might not, but I have treasur'd every note,
For more than once dimly down to the beach gliding,
Silent, avoiding the moonbeams, blending myself with the shadows,
Recalling now the obscure shapes, the echoes, the sounds and sights after
     their sorts,
The white arms out in the breakers tirelessly tossing,
I, with bare feet, a child, the wind wafting my hair,
Listen'd long and long.

Listen'd to keep, to sing, now translating the notes,
Following you my brother.   70

Soothe! soothe! soothe!
Close on its wave soothes the wave behind,
And again another behind embracing and lapping, every one close,
But my love soothes not me, not me.

Low hangs the moon, it rose late,
It is lagging—O I think it is heavy with love, with love.

O madly the sea pushes upon the land,
With love, with love.

O night! do I not see my love fluttering out among the breakers?
What is that little black thing I see there in the white?   80

Loud! loud! loud!
Loud I call to you, my love!

High and clear I shoot my voice over the waves,
Surely you must know who is here, is here,
You must know who I am, my love.

Low-hanging moon!
What is that dusky spot in your brown yellow?
O it is the shape, the shape of my mate!
O moon do not keep her from me any longer.

Land! land! O land!   90
Whichever way I turn, O I think you could give me my mate back again if you
     only would,
For I am almost sure I see her dimly whichever way I look.

O rising stars!
Perhaps the one I want so much will rise, will rise with some of you.

O throat! O trembling throat!
Sound clearer through the atmosphere!
Pierce the woods, the earth,
Somewhere listening to catch you must be the one I want.

Shake out carols!
Solitary here, the night's carols!   100
Carols of lonesome love! death's carols!
Carols under that lagging, yellow, waning moon!

O under that moon where she droops almost down into the sea!
O reckless despairing carols.

But soft! sink low!
Soft! let me just murmur,
And do you wait a moment you husky-nois'd sea,
For somewhere I believe I heard my mate responding to me,
So faint, I must be still, be still to listen,
But not altogether still, for then she might not come immediately to me.   110

Hither my love!
Here I am! here!
With this just-sustain'd note I announce myself to you,
This gentle call is for you my love, for you.

Do not be decoy'd elsewhere,
That is the whistle of the wind, it is not my voice,
That is the fluttering, the fluttering of the spray,
Those are the shadows of leaves.

O darkness! O in vain!
O I am very sick and sorrowful.   120

O brown halo in the sky near the moon, drooping upon the sea!
O troubled reflection in the sea!
O throat! O throbbing heart!
And I singing uselessly, uselessly all the night.

O past! O happy life! O songs of joy!
In the air, in the woods, over fields,
Loved! loved! loved! loved! loved!
But my mate no more, no more with me!
We two together no more.

The aria sinking,   130
All else continuing, the stars shining,
The winds blowing, the notes of the bird continuous echoing,
With angry moans the fierce old mother incessantly moaning,
On the sands of Paumanok's shore gray and rustling,
The yellow half-moon enlarged, sagging down, drooping, the face of the sea
     almost touching,
The boy ecstatic, with his bare feet the waves, with his hair the atmosphere
     dallying,
The love in the heart long pent, now loose, now at last tumultuously bursting,
The aria's meaning, the ears, the soul, swiftly depositing,
The strange tears down the cheeks coursing,
The colloquy there, the trio, each uttering,   140
The undertone, the savage old mother incessantly crying,

To the boy's soul's questions sullenly timing, some drown'd secret hissing,
To the outsetting bard.

Demon or bird! (said the boy's soul,)
Is it indeed toward your mate you sing? or is it really to me?
For I, that was a child, my tongue's use sleeping, now I have heard you,
Now in a moment I know what I am for, I awake,
And already a thousand singers, a thousand songs, clearer, louder and more
    sorrowful than yours,
A thousand warbling echoes have started to life within me, never to die.

O you singer solitary, singing by yourself, projecting me,   150
O solitary me listening, never more shall I cease perpetuating you,
Never more shall I escape, never more the reverberations,
Never more the cries of unsatisfied love be absent from me,
Never again leave me to be the peaceful child I was before what there in the
    night,
By the sea under the yellow and sagging moon,
The messenger there arous'd, the fire, the sweet hell within,
The unknown want, the destiny of me.

O give me the clew! (it lurks in the night here somewhere,)
O if I am to have so much, let me have more!

A word then, (for I will conquer it,)   160
The word final, superior to all,
Subtle, sent up—what is it?—I listen;
Are you whispering it, and have been all the time, you sea-waves?
Is that it from your liquid rims and wet sands?

Whereto answering, the sea,
Delaying not, hurrying not,
Whisper'd me through the night, and very plainly before daybreak,
Lisp'd to me the low and delicious word death,
And again death, death, death, death,
Hissing melodious, neither like the bird nor like my arous'd child's heart,   170
But edging near as privately for me rustling at my feet,
Creeping thence steadily up to my ears and laving me softly all over,
Death, death, death, death, death.

Which I do not forget,
But fuse the song of my dusky demon and brother,
That he sang to me in the moonlight on Paumanok's gray beach,
With the thousand responsive songs at random,
My own songs awaked from that hour,
And with them the key, the word up from the waves,
The word of the sweetest song and all songs,   180

That strong and delicious word which, creeping to my feet,
(Or like some old crone rocking the cradle, swathed in sweet garments, bend-
ing aside,)
The sea whisper'd me.

1. In this poem Whitman reminisces about an event that proved crucial to him. What was the event? What awareness did it generate in the young boy? 2. In what way does the young boy emulate the bird? (See ll. 114–157.) 3. This poem utilizes neither rhyme nor metrical regularity. What poetic devices and patterns distinguish it from prose?

I Felt a Funeral, in My Brain

EMILY DICKINSON [1830–1886]

I felt a Funeral, in my Brain,
And Mourners to and fro
Kept treading—treading—till it seemed
That Sense was breaking through—

And when they all were seated,
A Service, like a Drum—
Kept beating—beating—till I thought
My Mind was going numb—

And then I heard them lift a Box
And creak across my Soul
With those same Boots of Lead, again,   10
Then Space—began to toll,

As all the Heavens were a Bell,
And Being, but an Ear,
And I, and Silence, some strange Race
Wrecked, solitary, here—

And then a Plank in Reason, broke,
And I dropped down, and down—
And hit a World, at every plunge,
And Finished knowing—then—   20

The Ruined Maid

THOMAS HARDY [1840–1928]

"O'Melia, my dear, this does everything crown!
Who could have supposed I should meet you in Town?
And whence such fair garments, such prosperi-ty?"
"O didn't you know I'd been ruined?" said she.

"You left us in tatters, without shoes or socks,
Tired of digging potatoes, and spudding up docks;°   *digging herbs*
And now you've gay bracelets and bright feathers three!"
"Yes: that's how we dress when we're ruined," said she.

"At home in the barton° you said 'thee' and 'thou,'   *farmyard*
And 'thik onn,' and 'theäs oon,' and 't'other; but now   10
Your talking quite fits 'ee for high compa-ny!"
"Some polish is gained with one's ruin," said she.

"Your hands were like paws then, your face blue and bleak
But now I'm bewitched by your delicate cheek,
And your little gloves fit as on any la-dy!"
"We never do work when we're ruined," said she.

"You used to call home-life a hag-ridden dream,
And you'd sigh, and you'd sock; but at present you seem
To know not of megrims° or melancho-ly!"   *sick headaches*
"True. One's pretty lively when ruined," said she.   20

"I wish I had feathers, a fine sweeping gown,
And a delicate face, and could strut about Town!"
"My dear—a raw country girl, such as you be,
Cannot quite expect that. You ain't ruined," said she.

Hap

THOMAS HARDY [1840–1928]

If but some vengeful god would call to me
From up the sky, and laugh: "Thou suffering thing,
Know that thy sorrow is my ecstasy,
That thy love's loss is my hate's profiting!"

Then would I bear it, clench myself, and die,
Steeled by the sense of ire unmerited;
Half-eased in that a Powerfuller than I
Had willed and meted me the tears I shed.

But not so. How arrives it joy lies slain,
And why unblooms the best hope ever sown?   10
—Crass Casualty° obstructs the sun and rain,   *chance*
And dicing Time for gladness casts a moan. . . .
These purblind Doomsters¹ had as readily strown
Blisses about my pilgrimage as pain.

Spring and Fall

TO A YOUNG CHILD

GERARD MANLEY HOPKINS   [1844–1889]

Márgarét, áre you gríeving
Over Goldengrove unleaving?°   *losing leaves*
Leáves, líke the things of man, you
With your fresh thoughts care for, can you?
Áh! ás the heart grows older
It will come to such sights colder
By and by, nor spare a sigh
Though worlds of wanwood leafmeal² lie;
And yet you wíll weep and know why.
Now no matter, child, the name: 10
Sórrow's spríngs are the same.
Nor mouth had, no nor mind, expressed
What heart heard of, ghost° guessed: *soul*
It ís the blight man was born for,
It is Margaret you mourn for.

1. *In this poem Margaret grieves over the passing of spring and the coming of fall. What does the coming of fall symbolize?*   **2.** *Why, when Margaret grows older, will she not sigh over the coming of fall?*   **3.** *What are "Sorrow's springs" (l. 11)?*

---

1.   Those who decide one's fate.

---

2.   Pale woods littered with mouldering leaves.

When I Was
One-and-Twenty

A. E. HOUSMAN [1859–1936]

When I was one-and-twenty
    I heard a wise man say,
"Give crowns and pounds and guineas
    But not your heart away;
Give pearls away and rubies
    But keep your fancy free."
But I was one-and-twenty,
    No use to talk to me.

When I was one-and-twenty
    I heard him say again,   10
"The heart out of the bosom
    Was never given in vain;
'Tis paid with sighs a plenty
    And sold for endless rue."
And I am two-and-twenty,
    And oh, 'tis true, 'tis true.

Terence, This Is
Stupid Stuff[1]

A. E. HOUSMAN [1859–1936]

    "Terence, this is stupid stuff:
You eat your victuals fast enough;
There can't be much amiss, 'tis clear,
To see the rate you drink your beer.
But oh, good Lord, the verse you make,

---

1. Housman originally titled the volume in which this poem appeared *The Poems of Terence Hearsay*. Terence was a Roman satiric playwright.

It gives a chap the bellyache.
The cow, the old cow, she is dead;
It sleeps well, the hornéd head:
We poor lads, 'tis our turn now
To hear such tunes as killed the cow.   10
Pretty friendship 'tis to rhyme
Your friends to death before their time
Moping melancholy mad:
Come, pipe a tune to dance to, lad."

    Why, if 'tis dancing you would be,
There's brisker pipes than poetry.
Say, for what were hopyards meant,
Or why was Burton built on Trent?[2]
Oh many a peer of England brews
Livelier liquor than the Muse,   20
And malt does more than Milton can
To justify God's ways to man.[3]
Ale, man, ale's the stuff to drink
For fellows whom it hurts to think:
Look into the pewter pot
To see the world as the world's not.
And faith, 'tis pleasant till 'tis past:
The mischief is that 'twill not last.
Oh I have been to Ludlow fair
And left my necktie God knows where,   30
And carried halfway home, or near,
Pints and quarts of Ludlow beer:
Then the world seemed none so bad,
And I myself a sterling lad;
And down in lovely muck I've lain,
Happy till I woke again.
Then I saw the morning sky.
Heigho, the tale was all a lie;
The world, it was the old world yet,
I was I, my things were wet,   40
And nothing now remained to do
But begin the game anew.

    Therefore, since the world has still
Much good, but much less good than ill,
And while the sun and moon endure
Luck's a chance, but trouble's sure,
I'd face it as a wise man would,

---

2.   The river Trent provides water for the town's brewing industry.
3.   In the invocation to *Paradise Lost,* Milton declares that his epic will "justify the ways of God to men."

And train for ill and not for good.
'Tis true the stuff I bring for sale
Is not so brisk a brew as ale: 50
Out of a stem that scored the hand
I wrung it in a weary land.
But take it: if the smack is sour,
The better for the embittered hour;
It should do good to heart and head
When your soul is in my soul's stead;
And I will friend you, if I may,
In the dark and cloudy day.

    There was a king reigned in the East:
There, when kings will sit to feast,   60
They get their fill before they think
With poisoned meat and poisoned drink.
He gathered all that springs to birth
From the many-venomed earth;
First a little, thence to more,
He sampled all her killing store;
And easy, smiling, seasoned sound,
Sate the king when healths went round.
They put arsenic in his meat
And stared aghast to watch him eat;   70
They poured strychnine in his cup
And shook to see him drink it up:
They shook, they stared as white's their shirt:
Them it was their poison hurt.
—I tell the tale that I heard told.
Mithridates, he died old.[4]

1. *What does the speaker of the first fourteen lines object to in Terence's poetry?* 2. *What is Terence's response to the criticism of his verse? What function of true poetry is implied by his comparison of bad poetry with liquor?* 3. *How does the story of Mithridates (ll. 59–76) illustrate the theme of the poem?*

---

4. Mithridates, the King of Pontus (in Asia Minor) reputedly immunized himself against poisons by administering to himself gradually increasing doses.

Leda and the Swan[1]

WILLIAM BUTLER YEATS [1865–1939]

A sudden blow: the great wings beating still
Above the staggering girl, her thighs caressed
By the dark webs, her nape caught in his bill;
He holds her helpless breast upon his breast.

How can those terrified vague fingers push
The feathered glory from her loosening thighs?
And how can body, laid in that white rush,
But feel the strange heart beating where it lies?

A shudder in the loins engenders there
The broken wall, the burning roof and tower   10
And Agamemnon dead.
               Being so caught up,
So mastered by the brute blood of the air,
Did she put on his knowledge with his power
Before the indifferent beak could let her drop?

Lapis Lazuli[2]

(FOR HARRY CLIFTON)

WILLIAM BUTLER YEATS [1865–1939]

I have heard that hysterical women say
They are sick of the palette and fiddle-bow,
Of poets that are always gay,
For everybody knows or else should know
That if nothing drastic is done
Aeroplane and Zeppelin will come out,

---

1. In Greek myth, Zeus, in the form of a swan, rapes Leda. As a consequence, Helen and Cly-temnestra are born. Each sister marries the king of a city-state; Helen marries Menelaus and Cly-temnestra marries Agamemnon. Helen, the most beautiful woman on earth, elopes with Paris, a prince of Troy, an act that precipitates the Trojan War in which Agamemnon commands the combined Greek armies. The war ends with the destruction of Troy. Agamemnon, when he returns to his home, is murdered by his unfaithful wife.

---

2. An azure blue, semiprecious stone, often carved in bas relief.

Pitch like King Billy[3] bomb-balls in
Until the town lie beaten flat.

All perform their tragic play,
There struts Hamlet, there is Lear,   10
That's Ophelia, that Cordelia;
Yet they, should the last scene be there,
The great stage curtain about to drop,
If worthy their prominent part in the play,
Do not break up their lines to weep.
They know that Hamlet and Lear are gay;
Gaiety transfiguring all that dread.
All men have aimed at, found and lost;
Black out; Heaven blazing into the head:
Tragedy wrought to its uttermost.   20
Though Hamlet rambles and Lear rages,
And all the drop-scenes drop at once
Upon a hundred thousand stages,
It cannot grow by an inch or an ounce.

On their own feet they came, or on shipboard,
Camelback, horseback, ass-back, mule-back,
Old civilizations put to the sword.
Then they and their wisdom went to rack:
No handiwork of Callimachus,[4]   30
Who handled marble as if it were bronze,
Made draperies that seemed to rise
When sea-wind swept the corner, stands;
His long lamp-chimney shaped like the stem
Of a slender palm, stood but a day;
All things fall and are built again,
And those that build them again are gay.

Two Chinamen, behind them a third,
Are carved in lapis lazuli,
Over them flies a long-legged bird,
A symbol of longevity;
The third, doubtless a serving-man,   40
Carries a musical instrument.

Every discoloration of the stone,
Every accidental crack or dent,
Seems a water-course or an avalanche,
Or lofty slope where it still snows
Though doubtless plum or cherry-branch

---

3. William III, the Protestant king of England, defeated the forces of the deposed Catholic king, James II, on July 1, 1690, at the Battle of Boyne. Ever since, William III has been a prototypical villain in Catholic Ireland.
4. A fifth-century B.C. Greek sculptor.

Sweetens the little half-way house
Those Chinamen climb towards, and I
Delight to imagine them seated there;   50
There, on the mountain and the sky,
On all the tragic scene they stare.
One asks for mournful melodies;
Accomplished fingers begin to play.
Their eyes mid many wrinkles, their eyes,
Their ancient, glittering eyes, are gay.

1. What do "palette" and "fiddle-bow" refer to (l. 2)? Why are the women hysterical?
2. What "cannot grow by an inch or an ounce" (l. 24)? Since they are central to great
tragedies, how do you interpret the paradoxical "Hamlet and Lear are gay" (l. 16)? In
what way does the third stanza suggest answers to these questions? **3.** This poem was
published on the eve of World War II. What function is served by its movement from
the present to Shakespearean England, to classical Greece, and finally to ancient China?

Birches

ROBERT FROST   [1874–1963]

When I see birches bend to left and right
Across the lines of straighter darker trees,
I like to think some boy's been swinging them.
But swinging doesn't bend them down to stay.
Ice-storms do that. Often you must have seen them
Loaded with ice a sunny winter morning
After a rain. They click upon themselves
As the breeze rises, and turn many-colored
As the stir cracks and crazes their enamel.
Soon the sun's warmth makes them shed crystal shells   10
Shattering and avalanching on the snow-crust—
Such heaps of broken glass to sweep away
You'd think the inner dome of heaven had fallen.
They are dragged to the withered bracken by the load,
And they seem not to break; though once they are bowed
So low for long, they never right themselves:
You may see their trunks arching in the woods
Years afterwards, trailing their leaves on the ground
Like girls on hands and knees that throw their hair
Before them over their heads to dry in the sun.   20
But I was going to say when Truth broke in
With all her matter-of-fact about the ice-storm
I should prefer to have some boy bend them
As he went out and in to fetch the cows—
Some boy too far from town to learn baseball,
Whose only play was what he found himself,

Summer or winter, and could play alone.
One by one he subdued his father's trees
By riding them down over and over again
Until he took the stiffness out of them,   30
And not one but hung limp, not one was left
For him to conquer. He learned all there was
To learn about not launching out too soon
And so not carrying the tree away
Clear to the ground. He always kept his poise
To the top branches, climbing carefully
With the same pains you use to fill a cup
Up to the brim, and even above the brim.
Then he flung outward, feet first, with a swish,
Kicking his way down through the air to the ground.   40
So was I once myself a swinger of birches.
And so I dream of going back to be.
It's when I'm weary of considerations,
And life is too much like a pathless wood
Where your face burns and tickles with the cobwebs
Broken across it, and one eye is weeping
From a twig's having lashed across it open.
I'd like to get away from earth awhile
And then come back to it and begin over.
May no fate willfully misunderstand me   50
And half grant what I wish and snatch me away
Not to return. Earth's the right place for love:
I don't know where it's likely to go better.
I'd like to go by climbing a birch tree,
And climb black branches up a snow-white trunk
Toward heaven, till the tree could bear no more,
But dipped its top and set me down again.
That would be good both going and coming back.
One could do worse than be a swinger of birches.

Provide, Provide

ROBERT FROST [1874–1963]

The witch that came (the withered hag)
To wash the steps with pail and rag,
Was once the beauty Abishag,[1]

---

1. "Now King David was old and advanced in years; and although they covered him with clothes, he could not get warm. Therefore his servants said to him, 'Let a young maiden be sought for my lord the king, and let her wait upon the king, and be his nurse; let her lie in your bosom, that my lord the king may be warm.' So they sought for a beautiful maiden throughout all the territory of Israel, and found Abishag, the Shunammite, and brought her to the king. The maiden was very beautiful. . . ."— I Kings 1:1–4.

The picture pride of Hollywood.
Too many fall from great and good
For you to doubt the likelihood.

Die early and avoid the fate.
Or if predestined to die late,
Make up your mind to die in state.

Make the whole stock exchange your own!   10
If need be occupy a throne,
Where nobody can call *you* crone.

Some have relied on what they knew;
Others on being simply true.
What worked for them might work for you.

No memory of having starred
Atones for later disregard,
Or keeps the end from being hard.

Better to go down dignified
With boughten friendship at your side   20
Than none at all. Provide, provide!

Peter Quince at the Clavier[1]

WALLACE STEVENS [1879–1955]

1
Just as my fingers on these keys
Make music, so the selfsame sounds
On my spirit make a music, too.

Music is feeling, then, not sound;
And thus it is that what I feel,
Here in this room, desiring you,

---

1. A clavier is a keyboard instrument. The title is probably a whimsical reference to Peter Quince of Shakespeare's *A Midsummer Night's Dream*, who directs the mechanics' production of the "most cruel death of Pyramus and Thisby" to be performed at the king's wedding festival. One of the actors, Bottom, advises the director, "First, good Peter Quince, say what the play treats on, then read the names of the actors, and so grow on to a point." Peter Quince, here a musician, seems to follow that advice.

Thinking of your blue-shadowed silk,
Is music. It is like the strain
Waked in the elders by Susanna.[2]

Of a green evening, clear and warm,   10
She bathed in her still garden, while
The red-eyed elders watching, felt

The basses of their beings throb
In witching chords, and their thin blood
Pulse pizzicati of Hosanna.[3]

2
In the green water, clear and warm,
Susanna lay.
She searched
The touch of springs,
And found   20
Concealed imaginings.
She sighed,
For so much melody.

Upon the bank, she stood
In the cool
Of spent emotions.
She felt, among the leaves,
The dew
Of old devotions.

She walked upon the grass,   30
Still quavering.
The winds were like her maids,
On timid feet,
Fetching her woven scarves,
Yet wavering.

A breath upon her hand
Muted the night.
She turned—
A cymbal crashed,
And roaring horns.   40

3
Soon, with a noise like tambourines,
Came her attendant Byzantines.[4]

---

2. The Old Testament Apocrypha includes the story of Susanna, who is saved by the wisdom of
Daniel from a death sentence for adultery based on the perjured testimony of the "elders."
3. Pizzicati notes are produced by plucking the strings rather than bowing. Hosanna is a cry of accla-
mation and adoration.
4. From Byzantium (now Istanbul). The attendants are slaves.

They wondered why Susanna cried
Against the elders by her side;

And as they whispered, the refrain
Was like a willow swept by rain.

Anon, their lamps' uplifted flame
Revealed Susanna and her shame.

And then, the simpering Byzantines
Fled, with a noise like tambourines.   50

4
Beauty is momentary in the mind—
The fitful tracing of a portal;
But in the flesh it is immortal.

The body dies; the body's beauty lives.
So evenings die, in their green going,
A wave, interminably flowing.
So gardens die, their meek breath scenting
The cowl of winter, done repenting.
So maidens die, to the auroral
Celebration of a maiden's choral.   60

Susanna's music touched the bawdy strings
Of those white elders; but, escaping,
Left only Death's ironic scraping.
Now, in its immortality, it plays
On the clear viol of her memory,
And makes a constant sacrament of praise.

1. Trace the relationship of the narrative in lines 10–50 to lines 1–9 and to section IV.   **2.**
Is the statement contained in lines 51–54 self-contradictory? Explain.   **3.** This poem is
famous for its sound patterns. What are the dominating consonant and vowel sounds in
lines 1–11? What sounds dominate lines 12–15? Can you suggest some formal reasons
for the change?

Speaking of Poetry

JOHN PEALE BISHOP   [1892–1944]

The ceremony must be found
That will wed Desdemona to the huge Moor.[1]

                       It is not enough—
To win the approval of the Senator
Or to outwit his disapproval; honest Iago
Can manage that: it is not enough. For then,
Though she may pant again in his black arms
(His weight resilient as a Barbary stallion's)
She will be found
When the ambassadors of the Venetian state arrive   10
Again smothered. These things have not been changed,
Not in three hundred years

                 (Tupping° is still tupping   *copulating*
Though that particular word is obsolete.
Naturally, the ritual would not be in Latin.)

For though Othello had his blood from kings
His ancestry was barbarous, his ways African,
His speech uncouth. It must be remembered
That though he valued an embroidery—
Three mulberries proper on a silk like silver—   20
It was not for the subtlety of the stitches,
But for the magic in it. Whereas, Desdemona
Once contrived to imitate in needlework
Her father's shield, and plucked it out
Three times, to begin again, each time
With diminished colors. This is a small point
But indicative.

               Desdemona was small and fair,
Delicate as a grasshopper
At the tag-end of summer: a Venetian   30
To her noble finger-tips.

             O, it is not enough
That they should meet, naked, at dead of night
In a small inn on a dark canal. Procurers
Less expert than Iago can arrange as much.

---

1.   This poem is based on Shakespeare's *Othello* (p. 655).

The ceremony must be found

Traditional, with all its symbols
Ancient as the metaphors in dreams;
Strange, with never before heard music; continuous
Until the torches deaden at the bedroom door.   40

1. What fundamental difference separates the nature of Othello from the nature of Desdemona?   **2.** Is it possible that "the ceremony" to wed them exists? If not, why not? If so, of what would it consist?   **3.** What does Bishop see as the major theme of Shakespeare's Othello? Do you agree with his reading of the play?

Incident

COUNTEE CULLEN   [1903–1946]

Once riding in old Baltimore,
    Heart-filled, head-filled with glee,
I saw a Baltimorean
    Keep looking straight at me.

Now I was eight and very small,
    And he was no whit bigger,
And so I smiled, but he poked out
    His tongue and called me, "Nigger."

I saw the whole of Baltimore
    From May until December: 10
Of all the things that happened there
    That's all that I remember.

Fern Hill

DYLAN THOMAS   [1914–1953]

Now as I was young and easy under the apple boughs
About the lilting house and happy as the grass was green,
    The night above the dingle° starry,   *small wooded valley*
        Time let me hail and climb

Golden in the heydays of his eyes,
And honored among wagons I was prince of the apple towns
And once below a time I lordly had the trees and leaves
        Trail with daisies and barley
    Down the rivers of the windfall light.

And as I was green and carefree, famous among the barns   10
About the happy yard and singing as the farm was home,
    In the sun that is young once only,
            Time let me play and be
    Golden in the mercy of his means,
And green and golden I was huntsman and herdsman, the calves
Sang to my horn, the foxes on the hills barked clear and cold,
        And the sabbath rang slowly
    In the pebbles of the holy streams.

All the sun long it was running, it was lovely, the hay
Fields high as the house, the tunes from the chimneys, it was air   20
    And playing, lovely and watery
    And fire green as grass.
    And nightly under the simple stars
As I rode to sleep the owls were bearing the farm away,
All the moon long I heard, blessed among stables, the nightjars[1]
    Flying with the ricks, and the horses
        Flashing into the dark.

And then to awake, and the farm, like a wanderer white
With the dew, come back, the cock on his shoulder: it was all
    Shining, it was Adam and maiden,   30
        The sky gathered again
    And the sun grew round that very day.
So it must have been after the birth of the simple light
In the first, spinning place, the spellbound horses walking warm
    Out of the whinnying green stable
        On to the fields of praise.

And honored among foxes and pheasants by the gay house
Under the new made clouds and happy as the heart was long,
    In the sun born over and over,
        I ran my heedless ways,   40
    My wishes raced through the house high hay
And nothing I cared, at my sky blue trades, that time allows
In all his tuneful turning so few and such morning songs
    Before the children green and golden
        Follow him out of grace,

---

1. Nightjars are harsh-sounding nocturnal birds.

Nothing I cared, in the lamb white days, that time would take me
Up to the swallow thronged loft by the shadow of my hand,
   In the moon that is always rising,
      Nor that riding to sleep
   I should hear him fly with the high fields   50
And wake to the farm forever fled from the childless land.
Oh as I was young and easy in the mercy of his means,
      Time held me green and dying
   Though I sang in my chains like the sea.

*1. Lines 17–18, 25, 30–36, and 45–46 incorporate religious language and biblical allu-
sion. What function do they serve? 2. What emotional impact does the color imagery
in the poem provide? 3. Trace the behavior of "time" in the poem. 4. Fairy tales often begin with the words "once upon a time." Why does Thomas alter that formula in
line 7? 5. Explain the paradox in line 53.*

With My Back

DAVID IGNATOW [b. 1914]

With my back to the insane world
of the next room I look into my poetry
for the gentleness in making do
with the known facts. On his side
of the wall sits a young man
spilling fear from his mouth.
I read in my poetry that fear teaches
me to love and that love also
is the beginning of fear
so that I find myself upon a cutting edge.   10
He in the room next door is bloody,
I look in my poetry for what to do
to help and read I must remain
absolutely still. He must be allowed
to think he is alone and that the world
waits on him for decision.

Curiosity

ALASTAIR REID [b. 1926]

may have killed the cat; more likely
the cat was just unlucky, or else curious
to see what death was like, having no cause
to go on licking paws, or fathering
litter on litter of kittens, predictably.

Nevertheless, to be curious
is dangerous enough. To distrust
what is always said, what seems,
to ask odd questions, interfere in dreams,
leave home, smell rats, have hunches   10
does not endear him to those doggy circles
where well-smelt baskets, suitable wives, good lunches
are the order of things, and where prevails
much wagging of incurious heads and tails.

Face it. Curiosity
will not cause him to die—
only lack of it will.
Never to want to see
the other side of the hill,
or that improbable country   20
where living is an idyll
(although a probable hell)
would kill us all.
Only the curious
have, if they live, a tale
worth telling at all.

Dogs say he loves too much, is irresponsible,
is changeable, marries too many wives,
deserts his children, chills all dinner tables
with tales of his nine lives.   30
Well, he is lucky. Let him be
nine-lived and contradictory,
curious enough to change, prepared to pay
the cat price, which is to die
and die again and again,
each time with no less pain.
A cat minority of one
is all that can be counted on
to tell the truth. And what he has to tell
on each return from hell   40
is this: that dying is what the living do,

that dying is what the loving do,
and that dead dogs are those who do not know
that hell is where, to live, they have to go.

April Inventory

W. D. SNODGRASS   [b. 1926]

The green catalpa tree has turned
All white; the cherry blooms once more.
In one whole year I haven't learned
A blessed thing they pay you for.
The blossoms snow down in my hair;
The trees and I will soon be bare.

The trees have more than I to spare.
The sleek, expensive girls I teach,
Younger and pinker every year,
Bloom gradually out of reach.   10
The pear tree lets its petals drop
Like dandruff on a tabletop.

The girls have grown so young by now
I have to nudge myself to stare.
This year they smile and mind me how
My teeth are falling with my hair.
In thirty years I may not get
Younger, shrewder, or out of debt.

The tenth time, just a year ago,
I made myself a little list   20
Of all the things I'd ought to know;
Then told my parents, analyst,
And everyone who's trusted me
I'd be substantial, presently.

I haven't read one book about
A book or memorized one plot.
Or found a mind I didn't doubt.
I learned one date. And then forgot.
And one by one the solid scholars
Get the degrees, the jobs, the dollars.   30

And smile above their starchy collars.
I taught my classes Whitehead's notions;
One lovely girl, a song of Mahler's.

Lacking a source-book or promotions,
I showed one child the colors of
A luna moth and how to love.

I taught myself to name my name,
To bark back, loosen love and crying;
To ease my woman so she came,
To ease an old man who was dying.   40
I have not learned how often I
Can win, can love, but choose to die.

I have not learned there is a lie
Love shall be blonder, slimmer, younger;
That my equivocating eye
Loves only by my body's hunger;
That I have poems, true to feel,
Or that the lovely world is real.

While scholars speak authority
And wear their ulcers on their sleeves,   50
My eyes in spectacles shall see
These trees procure and spend their leaves.
There is a value underneath
The gold and silver in my teeth.

Though trees turn bare and girls turn wives,
We shall afford our costly seasons;
There is a gentleness survives
That will outspeak and has its reasons.
There is a loveliness exists,
Preserves us. Not for specialists.   60

1. What do the words "I have not learned" (ll. 41, 43) mean in the context of the poem?
2. In what way does the tone of the first four stanzas differ from the tone of the last two?
3. What is the meaning of "specialists" in the last line?   4. What is the speaker's conception of teaching?

Innocence

FOR TONY WHITE

THOM GUNN [b. 1929]

He ran the course and as he ran he grew,
And smelt his fragrance in the field. Already,
Running he knew the most he ever knew,
The egotism of a healthy body.

Ran into manhood, ignorant of the past:
Culture of guilt and guilt's vague heritage,

Self-pity and the soul; what he possessed
Was rich, potential, like the bud's tipped rage.

The Corps developed, it was plain to see,
Courage, endurance, loyalty and skill
To a morale firm as morality,
Hardening him to an instrument, until

The finitude of virtues that were there
Bodied within the swarthy uniform
A compact innocence, child-like and clear,
No doubt could penetrate, no act could harm.

When he stood near the Russian partisan
Being burned alive, he therefore could behold
The ribs wear gently through the darkening skin
And sicken only at the Northern cold,

Could watch the fat burn with a violet flame
And feel disgusted only at the smell,
And judge that all pain finishes the same
As melting quietly by his boots it fell.

First Confession

X. J. KENNEDY [b. 1929]

Blood thudded in my ears. I scuffed,
    Steps stubborn, to the telltale booth
Beyond whose curtained portal coughed
    The robed repositor of truth.

The slat shot back. The universe
    Bowed down his cratered dome to hear
Enumerated my each curse,
    The sip snitched from my old man's beer,

My sloth pride envy lechery,
    The dime held back from Peter's Pence
With which I'd bribed my girl to pee
    That I might spy her instruments.

Hovering scale-pans when I'd done
    Settled their balance slow as silt
While in the restless dark I burned
    Bright as a brimstone in my guilt

Until as one feeds birds he doled
     Seven Our Fathers and a Hail
Which I to double-scrub my soul
     Intoned twice at the altar rail   *20*

Where Sunday in seraphic light
     I knelt, as full of grace as most,
And stuck my tongue out at the priest:
     A fresh roost for the Holy Ghost.

The Middle-aged

ADRIENNE RICH [b. 1929]

Their faces, safe as an interior
Of Holland tiles and Oriental carpet,
Where the fruit-bowl, always filled, stood in a light
Of placid afternoon—their voices' measure,
Their figures moving in the Sunday garden
To lay the tea outdoors or trim the borders,
Afflicted, haunted us. For to be young
Was always to live in other peoples' houses
Whose peace, if we sought it, had been made by others,
Was ours at second-hand and not for long.   *10*
The custom of the house, not ours, the sun
Fading the silver-blue Fortuny¹ curtains,
The reminiscence of a Christmas party
Of fourteen years ago—all memory,
Signs of possession and of being possessed,
We tasted, tense with envy. They were so kind,
Would have given us anything; the bowl of fruit
Was filled for us, there was a room upstairs
We must call ours: but twenty years of living
They could not give. Nor did they ever speak   *20*
Of the coarse stain on that polished balustrade,
The crack in the study window, or the letters
Locked in a drawer and the key destroyed.
All to be understood by us, returning
Late, in our own time—how that peace was made,
Upon what terms, with how much left unsaid.

---

1.   Elegant fabric based on Moorish tile designs.

Advice to My Son

J. PETER MEINKE [b. 1932]

The trick is, to live your days
as if each one may be your last
(for they go fast, and young men lose their lives
in strange and unimaginable ways)
but at the same time, plan long range
(for they go slow: if you survive
the shattered windshield and the bursting shell
you will arrive
at our approximation here below
of heaven or hell).   10

To be specific, between the peony and the rose
plant squash and spinach, turnips and tomatoes;
beauty is nectar
and nectar, in a desert, saves—
but the stomach craves stronger sustenance
than the honied vine.
Therefore, marry a pretty girl
after seeing her mother;
show your soul to one man,
work with another;   20
and always serve bread with your wine.

But, son,
always serve wine.

1. The advice of the first stanza seems contradictory. In what ways does the second stanza attempt to resolve the contradiction or explain "The trick" (l. 1)? What do the various plants and the bread and wine symbolize? 2. Explain how the advice of lines 17–21 is logically related to the preceding lines. 3. What do the final two lines tell the reader about the speaker?

In a Spring Still Not Written Of

ROBERT WALLACE [b. 1932]

This morning
with a class of girls outdoors, I saw
how frail poems are
in a world burning up with flowers,
in which, overhead,

the great elms
—green, and tall—
stood carrying leaves in their arms.

The girls listened equally
to my drone, reading, and to the bees'   10
ricocheting
among them for the blossom on the bone,
or gazed off at a distant mower's
astronomies of green
and clover, flashing,
threshing in the new, untarnished sunlight.

And all the while, dwindling,
tinier, the voices—Yeats, Marvell, Donne—
sank drowning
in a spring still not written of,   20
as only the sky
clear above the brick bell-tower
—blue, and white—
was shifting toward the hour.

Calm, indifferent, cross-legged
or on elbows half-lying in the grass—
how should the great dead
tell them of dying?
They will come to time for poems at last,
when they have found they are no more   30
the beautiful and young
all poems are for.

1. *Explain the paradox developed in this poem.* **2.** *What is the speaker's attitude toward the "class of girls" he is teaching? Toward his job as a teacher?* **3.** *Explain the meaning of the title.* **4.** *Explain the various meanings of "drone" (l. 10).*

Suzanne

LEONARD COHEN [b. 1934]

Suzanne takes you down
to her place near the river,
you can hear the boats go by
you can stay the night beside her.
And you know that she's half crazy
but that's why you want to be there
and she feeds you tea and oranges
that come all the way from China.
Just when you mean to tell her

that you have no gifts to give her,
she gets you on her wave-length
and she lets the river answer
that you've always been her lover.
    And you want to travel with her,
    you want to travel blind
    and you know that she can trust you
    because you've touched her perfect body
    with your mind.

Jesus was a sailor
when he walked upon the water
and he spent a long time watching
from a lonely wooden tower
and when he knew for certain
only drowning men could see him
he said All men will be sailors then
until the sea shall free them,
but he himself was broken
long before the sky would open,
forsaken, almost human,
he sank beneath your wisdom like a stone.
    And you want to travel with him,
    you want to travel blind
    and you think maybe you'll trust him
    because he touched your perfect body
    with his mind.

Suzanne takes your hand
and she leads you to the river,
she is wearing rags and feathers
from Salvation Army counters.
The sun pours down like honey
on our lady of the harbour
as she shows you where to look
among the garbage and the flowers,
there are heroes in the seaweed
there are children in the morning,
they are leaning out for love
they will lean that way forever
while Suzanne she holds the mirror.
    And you want to travel with her
    and you want to travel blind
    and you're sure that she can find you
    because she's touched her perfect body
    with her mind.

1. In what ways is Suzanne associated with Jesus? What is the significance of that association? **2.** What statement does the poem make about the ancient distinction between body and mind? Does the poem assert the superiority of one over the other? **3.** Why is Suzanne described as "wearing rags and feathers" (l. 38)? Compare this with "the garbage and the flowers" (l. 43). What do these rather surprising contrasts suggest about the nature of Suzanne and the values she embodies?

My Mother

ROBERT MEZEY [b. 1935]

My mother writes from Trenton,
a comedian to the bone
but underneath, serious
and all heart. "Honey," she says,
"be a mensch[1] and Mary too,
its no good to worry, you
are doing the best you can
your Dad and everyone
thinks you turned out very well
as long as you pay your bills   10
nobody can say a word
you can tell them to drop dead
so save a dollar it can't
hurt—remember Frank you went
to highschool with? he still lives
with his wife's mother, his wife
works while he writes his books and
did he ever sell a one
the four kids run around naked
36 and he's never had,   20
you'll forgive my expression
even a pot to piss in
or a window to throw it,
such a smart boy he couldn't
read the footprints on the wall
honey you think you know all
the answers you dont, please try
to put some money away
believe me it wouldn't hurt
artist shmartist life's too short   30
for that kind of, forgive me,
horseshit, I know what you want
better than you, all that counts
is to make a good living
and the best of everything,
as Sholem Aleichem said
he was a great writer did
you ever read his books dear,
you should make what he makes a year
anyway he says some place   40
Poverty is no disgrace
but its no honor either
that's what I say,
        love,
           Mother"

---

1. Man, in the sense of "human being."

My Father

JUDY COLLINS [b. 1939]

My father always promised us
    that we would live in France,
We'd go boating on the Seine
    and I would learn to dance.
We lived in Ohio then
    he worked in the mines,
On his streams like boats we knew
    we'd sail, in time.

All my sisters soon were gone
    to Denver and Cheyenne,   10
Marrying their grownup dreams,
    the lilacs and the man.
I stayed behind the youngest still,
    only danced alone,
The colors of my father's dreams
    faded without a sigh.

And I live in Paris now,
    my children dance and dream
Hearing the ways of a miner's life
    in words they've never seen.   20
I sail my memories afar
    like boats across the Seine,
And watch the Paris sun
    set in my father's eyes again.

My father always promised us
    that we would live in France,
We'd go boating on the Seine
    and I would learn to dance.
We lived in Ohio then
    he worked in the mines,   30
On his streams like boats we knew
    we'd sail, in time

Dangling Conversation

PAUL SIMON [b. 1942]

It's a still-life water color
Of a now late afternoon
As the sun shines through the curtain lace
And shadows wash the room.

And we sit and drink our coffee
Cast in our indifference
Like shells upon a shore
You can hear the ocean roar.

In the dangling conversation
And the superficial sighs   10
The borders of our lives.

And you read your Emily Dickinson
And I my Robert Frost
As we note our place with bookmarkers
That measure what we've lost.

Like a poem poorly written
We are verses out of rhythm
Couplets out of rhyme
In syncopated time.

And the dangling conversation   20
And the superficial sighs
Are the borders of our lives.

Yes, we speak the things that matter
With words that must be said
Can analysis be worthwhile?
Is the theatre really dead?

And now the room is softly faded
And I only kiss your shadow
I cannot feel your hand
You're a stranger now unto me.   30

Lost in the dangling conversation
And the superficial sighs
In the borders of our lives.

The Circle Game

JONI MITCHELL [b. 1943]

Yesterday a child came out to wonder,
Caught a dragon fly inside a jar.
Fearful when the sky was full of thunder,
And tearful at the falling of a star.

Chorus:
And the seasons, they go 'round and 'round,
And the painted ponies go up and down.
We're captive on the carousel of time.
We can't return, we can only look behind
From where we came, and go 'round
And 'round and 'round in the circle game.   10

Then the child moved ten times
'Round the seasons,
Skated over ten clear frozen streams,
Words like, when you're older
Must appease him, and promises of
Someday make his dreams.
Chorus

Sixteen springs and sixteen summers
Gone now, cartwheels turn to car wheels
Thru the town, and they tell him,
Take your time, it won't be long now,   20
Till you drag your feet to
Slow the circles down.
Chorus

So the years spin by,
And now the boy is twenty.
Dreams have lost some grandeur
Coming true. There'll be new dreams,
Maybe better dreams, and plenty
Before the last revolving year is through.
Chorus

The Royal Scam[1]

WALTER BECKER [b. 1950] and DONALD FAGEN [b. 1948]

And they wandered in from the city
Of St. John[2] without a dime,
Wearing coats that shine both red and green
Colors from their sunny island.
From their boats of iron they looked upon
The promised land where surely life was sweet.
On the rising tide to New York City
Did they ride into the street.
See the glory of the Royal Scam.

They are hounded down to the bottom   10
Of a bad town amid the ruins
Where they learn to fear an angry race
Of fallen kings, their dark companions,
While the memory of their southern sky
Was clouded by the savage winter.
Every patron saint hung on the wall
Shared the room with twenty sinners.
See the glory of the Royal Scam

By the blackened wall he does it all;
He thinks he's died and gone to heaven.   20
Now the tale is told by the old man.
Back home he reads the letter—
How they are paid in gold just to babble
In the back room all night and waste the time.
And they wandered in from the city
Of St. John without a dime.
See the glory of the Royal Scam.

---

1. A scam is a scheme to defraud.
2. I.e., San Juan, Puerto Rico.

innocence and experience

DRAMA

Oedipus Rex*

SOPHOCLES [496?–406 B.C.]

PERSONS REPRESENTED

Oedipus	Messenger
A Priest	Shepherd of Laïos
Creon	Second Messenger
Teiresias	Chorus of Theban Elders
Iocastê	

SCENE. *Before the palace of Oedipus, King of Thebes. A central door and two lateral doors open onto a platform which runs the length of the facade. On the platform, right and left, are altars; and three steps lead down into the "orchestra," or chorus-ground. At the beginning of the action these steps are crowded by suppliants who have brought branches and chaplets of olive leaves and who lie in various attitudes of despair. Oedipus enters.*

Prologue

Oedipus.   My children, generations of the living
          In the line of Kadmos,¹ nursed at his ancient hearth:
          Why have you strewn yourselves before these altars
          In supplication, with your boughs and garlands?
          The breath of incense rises from the city
          With a sound of prayer and lamentation.

                                                  Children,
          I would not have you speak through messengers,
          And therefore I have come myself to hear you—

---

*An English version by Dudley Fitts and Robert Fitzgerald.
1.   The legendary founder of Thebes.

I, Oedipus, who bear the famous name
[*To a Priest.*] You, there, since you are eldest in the company,   10
Speak for them all, tell me what preys upon you,
Whether you come in dread, or crave some blessing:
Tell me, and never doubt that I will help you
In every way I can; I should be heartless
Were I not moved to find you suppliant here.

Priest.   Great Oedipus, O powerful King of Thebes!
You see how all the ages of our people
Cling to your altar steps: here are boys
Who can barely stand alone, and here are priests
By weight of age, as I am a priest of God,   20
And young men chosen from those yet unmarried;
As for the others, all that multitude,
They wait with olive chaplets in the squares,
At the two shrines of Pallas,[2] and where Apollo[3]
Speaks in the glowing embers.
                           Your own eyes
Must tell you: Thebes is in her extremity
And can not lift her head from the surge of death.
A rust consumes the buds and fruits of the earth;
The herds are sick; children die unborn,
And labor is vain. The god of plague and pyre   30
Raids like detestable lightning through the city,
And all the house of Kadmos is laid waste,
All emptied, and all darkened: Death alone
Battens upon the misery of Thebes.

You are not one of the immortal gods, we know;
Yet we have come to you to make our prayer
As to the man of all men best in adversity
And wisest in the ways of God. You saved us
From the Sphinx,[4] that flinty singer, and the tribute
We paid to her so long; yet you were never   40
Better informed than we, nor could we teach you:
It was some god breathed in you to set us free.

Therefore, O mighty King, we turn to you:

---

2. Athena, goddess of wisdom.
3. God of sunlight, medicine, and prophecy.

4.   A winged monster, with a woman's head and breasts and a lion's body, that destroyed those who
failed to answer her riddle: "What walks on four feet in the morning, two at noon, and three in the
evening?" When the young Oedipus correctly answered, "Man" ("three" alluding to a cane in old
age), the Sphinx killed herself, and the plague ended.

Find us our safety, find us a remedy,
Whether by counsel of the gods or men.
A king of wisdom tested in the past
Can act in a time of troubles, and act well.
Noblest of men, restore
Life to your city! Think how all men call you
Liberator for your triumph long ago;   50
Ah, when your years of kingship are remembered,
Let them not say *We rose, but later fell*—
Keep the State from going down in the storm!
Once, years ago, with happy augury,
You brought us fortune; be the same again!
No man questions your power to rule the land:
But rule over men, not over a dead city!
Ships are only hulls, citadels are nothing,
When no life moves in the empty passageways.

Oedipus.   Poor children! You may be sure I know   60
All that you longed for in your coming here.
I know that you are deathly sick; and yet,
Sick as you are, not one is as sick as I.
Each of you suffers in himself alone
His anguish, not another's; but my spirit
Groans for the city, for myself, for you.

I was not sleeping, you are not waking me.
No, I have been in tears for a long while
And in my restless thought walked many ways.
In all my search, I found one helpful course,   70
And that I have taken: I have sent Creon,
Son of Menoikeus, brother of the Queen,
To Delphi, Apollo's place of revelation,
To learn there, if he can,
What act or pledge of mine may save the city.
I have counted the days, and now, this very day,
I am troubled, for he has overstayed his time.
What is he doing? He has been gone too long.
Yet whenever he comes back, I should do ill
To scant whatever hint the god may give.   80

Priest.   It is a timely promise. At this instant
They tell me Creon is here.

Oedipus.   O Lord Apollo!
May his news be fair as his face is radiant!

Priest.   It could not be otherwise: he is crowned with bay,
The chaplet is thick with berries.

Oedipus.   We shall soon know;
  He is near enough to hear us now.

[*Enter Creon.*]

                  O Prince:
  Brother: son of Menoikeus:
  What answer do you bring us from the god?
Creon. It is favorable. I can tell you, great afflictions
  Will turn out well, if they are taken well.   90
Oedipus. What was the oracle? These vague words
  Leave me still hanging between hope and fear.
Creon. Is it your pleasure to hear me with all these
  Gathered around us? I am prepared to speak,
  But should we not go in?
Oedipus.   Let them all hear it.
  It is for them I suffer, more than for myself.
Creon. Then I will tell you what I heard at Delphi.

  In plain words
  The god commands us to expel from the land of Thebes
  An old defilement that it seems we shelter.   100
  It is a deathly thing, beyond expiation.
  We must not let it feed upon us longer.
Oedipus. What defilement? How shall we rid ourselves of it?
Creon. By exile or death, blood for blood. It was
  Murder that brought the plague-wind on the city.
Oedipus. Murder of whom? Surely the god has named him?
Creon. My lord: long ago Laïos was our king,
  Before you came to govern us.
Oedipus.   I know;
  I learned of him from others; I never saw him.
Creon. He was murdered; and Apollo commands us now   110
  To take revenge upon whoever killed him.
Oedipus. Upon whom? Where are they? Where shall we find a clue
  To solve that crime, after so many years?
Creon. Here in this land, he said.
                      If we make enquiry,
  We may touch things that otherwise escape us.
Oedipus. Tell me: Was Laïos murdered in his house,
  Or in the fields, or in some foreign country?
Creon. He said he planned to make a pilgrimage.
  He did not come home again.
Oedipus.   And was there no one,
  No witness, no companion, to tell what happened?   120

Creon.   They were all killed but one, and he got away
So frightened that he could remember one thing only.
Oedipus.   What was that one thing? One may be the key
To everything, if we resolve to use it.
Creon.   He said that a band of highwaymen attacked them,
Outnumbered them, and overwhelmed the King.
Oedipus.   Strange, that a highwayman should be so daring—
Unless some faction here bribed him to do it.
Creon.   We thought of that. But after Laïos' death
New troubles arose and we had no avenger.   130
Oedipus.   What troubles could prevent your hunting down the killers?
Creon.   The riddling Sphinx's song
Made us deaf to all mysteries but her own.
Oedipus.   Then once more I must bring what is dark to light.
It is most fitting that Apollo shows,
As you do, this compunction for the dead.
You shall see how I stand by you, as I should,
To avenge the city and the city's god,
And not as though it were for some distant friend,
But for my own sake, to be rid of evil.   140
Whoever killed King Laïos might—who knows?—
Decide at any moment to kill me as well.
By avenging the murdered king I protect myself.
Come, then, my children: leave the altar steps,
Lift up your olive boughs!
                              One of you go
And summon the people of Kadmos to gather here.
I will do all that I can; you may tell them that.

[*Exit a page.*]

So, with the help of God,
We shall be saved—or else indeed we are lost.
Priest.   Let us rise, children. It was for this we came,   150
And now the King has promised it himself.
Phoibos[5] has sent us an oracle; may he descend
Himself to save us and drive out the plague.

[*Exeunt Oedipus and Creon into the palace by the central door. The Priest and the suppliants disperse R and L. After a short pause the Chorus enters the orchestra.*]

---

5.   Phoebus Apollo, god of the sun.

Párodos[6]

Chorus. What is God singing in his profound   [Strophe 1]
    Delphi of gold and shadow?
    What oracle for Thebes, the sunwhipped city?
    Fear unjoints me, the roots of my heart tremble.
    Now I remember, O Healer, your power, and wonder;
    Will you send doom like a sudden cloud, or weave it
    Like nightfall of the past?
    Speak, speak to us, issue of holy sound:
    Dearest to our expectancy: be tender!

    Let me pray to Athenê, the immortal daughter of Zeus,   [Antistrophe 1]
    And to Artemis her sister   11
    Who keeps her famous throne in the market ring,
    And to Apollo, bowman at the far butts of heaven—

    O gods, descend! Like three streams leap against
    The fires of our grief, the fires of darkness;
    Be swift to bring us rest!

    As in the old time from the brilliant house
    Of air you stepped to save us, come again!

    Now our afflictions have no end,   [Strophe 2]
    Now all our stricken host lies down   20
    And no man fights off death with his mind;

    The noble plowland bears no grain,
    And groaning mothers can not bear—

    See, how our lives like birds take wing,
    Like sparks that fly when a fire soars,
    To the shore of the god of evening.

    The plague burns on, it is pitiless,   [Antistrophe 2]
    Though pallid children laden with death
    Lie unwept in the stony ways,

    And old gray women by every path   30
    Flock to the strand about the altars

---

6. The *Párodos* is the ode sung by the Chorus as it entered the theater and moved down the aisles to the playing area. The *strophe*, in Greek tragedy, is the unit of verse the Chorus chanted as it moved to the left in a dance rhythm. The Chorus sang the *antistrophe* as it moved to the right and the *epode* while standing still.

There to strike their breasts and cry
Worship of Phoibos in wailing prayers:
Be kind, God's golden child!

There are no swords in this attack by fire,   [Strophe 3]
No shields, but we are ringed with cries.
Send the besieger plunging from our homes
Into the vast sea-room of the Atlantic
Or into the waves that foam eastward of Thrace—
For the day ravages what the night spares—   40

Destroy our enemy, lord of the thunder!
Let him be riven by lightning from heaven!

Phoibus Apollo, stretch the sun's bowstring,   [Antistrophe 3]
That golden cord, until it sing for us,
Flashing arrows in heaven!
                              Artemis, Huntress
Race with flaring lights upon our mountains!

O scarlet god, O golden-banded brow,
O Theban Bacchos in a storm of Maenads,[7]

[Enter Oedipus, C.]

Whirl upon Death, that all the Undying hate!
Come with blinding cressets, come in joy!   50

Scene 1

Oedipus. Is this your prayer? It may be answered. Come,
    Listen to me, act as the crisis demands,
    And you shall have relief from all these evils.

    Until now I was a stranger to this tale,
    As I had been a stranger to the crime.
    Could I track down the murderer without a clue?
    But now, friends,
    As one who became a citizen after the murder,
    I make this proclamation to all Thebans:
    If any man knows by whose hand Laïos, son of Labdakos,   10
    Met his death, I direct that man to tell me everything,

---

7. Bacchos is the god of wine and revelry, hence scarlet-faced. The Maenads were Bacchos' female attendants.

No matter what he fears for having so long withheld it.
Let it stand as promised that no further trouble
Will come to him, but he may leave the land in safety.

Moreover: If anyone knows the murderer to be foreign,
Let him not keep silent: he shall have his reward from me.
However, if he does conceal it; if any man
Fearing for his friend or for himself disobeys this edict,
Hear what I propose to do:

I solemnly forbid the people of this country,   20
Where power and throne are mine, ever to receive that man
Or speak to him, no matter who he is, or let him
Join in sacrifice, lustration, or in prayer.
I decree that he be driven from every house,
Being, as he is, corruption itself to us: the Delphic
Voice of Zeus has pronounced this revelation.
Thus I associate myself with the oracle
And take the side of the murdered king.

As for the criminal, I pray to God—
Whether it be a lurking thief, or one of a number—   30
I pray that that man's life be consumed in evil and wretchedness.
And as for me, this curse applies no less
If it should turn out that the culprit is my guest here,
Sharing my hearth.
                         You have heard the penalty.
I lay it on you now to attend to this
For my sake, for Apollo's, for the sick
Sterile city that heaven has abandoned.
Suppose the oracle had given you no command:
Should this defilement go uncleansed for ever?
You should have found the murderer: your king,   40
A noble king, had been destroyed!
                         Now I,
Having the power that he held before me,
Having his bed, begetting children there
Upon his wife, as he would have, had he lived—
Their son would have been my children's brother,
If Laïos had had luck in fatherhood!
(But surely ill luck rushed upon his reign)—
I say I take the son's part, just as though
I were his son, to press the fight for him
And see it won! I'll find the hand that brought   50
Death to Labdakos' and Polydoros' child,

Heir of Kadmos's and Agenor's line.
And as for those who fail me,
May the gods deny them the fruit of the earth,
Fruit of the womb, and may they rot utterly!
Let them be wretched as we are wretched, and worse!

For you, for loyal Thebans, and for all
Who find my actions right, I pray the favor
Of justice, and of all the immortal gods.

Choragos.[8]   Since I am under oath, my lord, I swear   60
I did not do the murder. I can not name
The murderer. Might not the oracle
That has ordained the search tell where to find him?

Oedipus.   An honest question. But no man in the world
Can make the gods do more than the gods will.

Choragos.   There is one last expedient—

Oedipus.   Tell me what it is.
Though it seem slight, you must not hold it back.

Choragos.   A lord clairvoyant to the lord Apollo,
As we all know, is the skilled Teiresias.
One might learn much about this from him, Oedipus.   70

Oedipus.   I am not wasting time:
Creon spoke of this, and I have sent for him—
Twice, in fact; it is strange that he is not here.

Choragos.   The other matter—that old report—seems useless.

Oedipus.   Tell me. I am interested in all reports.

Choragos.   The King was said to have been killed by highwaymen.

Oedipus.   I know. But we have no witnesses to that.

Choragos.   If the killer can feel a particle of dread,
Your curse will bring him out of hiding!

Oedipus.   No.
The man who dared that act will fear no curse.   80

[*Enter the blind seer Teiresias, led by a page.*]

Choragos.   But there is one man who may detect the criminal.
This is Teiresias, this is the holy prophet
In whom, alone of all men, truth was born.

Oedipus.   Teiresias: seer: student of mysteries,
Of all that's taught and all that no man tells,
Secrets of Heaven and secrets of the earth:
Blind though you are, you know the city lies
Sick with plague; and from this plague, my lord,

---

8.   Choragos is the leader of the Chorus.

We find that you alone can guard or save us.

Possibly you did not hear the messengers?   90
Apollo, when we sent to him,
Sent us back word that this great pestilence
Would lift, but only if we established clearly
The identity of those who murdered Laïos.
They must be killed or exiled.
                              Can you use
Birdflight or any art of divination
To purify yourself, and Thebes, and me
From this contagion? We are in your hands.
There is no fairer duty
Than that of helping others in distress.   100

Teiresias.   How dreadful knowledge of the truth can be
When there's no help in truth! I knew this well,
But did not act on it: else I should not have come.

Oedipus.   What is troubling you? Why are your eyes so cold?

Teiresias.   Let me go home. Bear your own fate, and I'll
Bear mine. It is better so: trust what I say.

Oedipus.   What you say is ungracious and unhelpful
To your native country. Do not refuse to speak.

Teiresias.   When it comes to speech, your own is neither temperate
Nor opportune. I wish to be more prudent.   110

Oedipus.   In God's name, we all beg you—

Teiresias.   You are all ignorant.
No; I will never tell you what I know.
Now it is my misery; then, it would be yours.

Oedipus.   What! You do know something, and will not tell us?
You would betray us all and wreck the State?

Teiresias.   I do not intend to torture myself, or you.
Why persist in asking? You will not persuade me.

Oedipus.   What a wicked old man you are! You'd try a stone's
Patience! Out with it! Have you no feeling at all?

Teiresias.   You call me unfeeling. If you could only see   120
The nature of your own feelings . . .

Oedipus.   Why,
Who would not feel as I do? Who could endure
Your arrogance toward the city?

Teiresias.   What does it matter!
Whether I speak or not, it is bound to come.

Oedipus.   Then, if "it" is bound to come, you are bound to tell me.

Teiresias.   No, I will not go on. Rage as you please.

Oedipus.   Rage? Why not!

And I'll tell you what I think:
You planned it, you had it done, you all but
Killed him with your own hands: if you had eyes,
I'd say the crime was yours, and yours alone.   130

Teiresias.   So? I charge you, then,
Abide by the proclamation you have made:
From this day forth
Never speak again to these men or to me;
You yourself are the pollution of this country.

Oedipus.   You dare say that! Can you possibly think you have
Some way of going free, after such insolence?

Teiresias.   I have gone free. It is the truth sustains me.

Oedipus.   Who taught you shamelessness? It was not your craft.

Teiresias.   You did. You made me speak. I did not want to.   140

Oedipus.   Speak what? Let me hear it again more clearly.

Teiresias.   Was it not clear before? Are you tempting me?

Oedipus.   I did not understand it. Say it again.

Teiresias.   I say that you are the murderer whom you seek.

Oedipus.   Now twice you have spat out infamy! You'll pay for it!

Teiresias.   Would you care for more? Do you wish to be really angry?

Oedipus.   Say what you will. Whatever you say is worthless.

Telresias.   I say you live in hideous shame with those
Most dear to you. You can not see the evil.

Oedipus.   It seems you can go on mouthing like this for ever.   150

Teiresias.   I can, if there is power in truth.

Oedipus.   There is:
But not for you, not for you,
You sightless, witless, senseless, mad old man!

Teiresias.   You are the madman. There is no one here
Who will not curse you soon, as you curse me.

Oedipus.   You child of endless night! You can not hurt me
Or any other man who sees the sun.

Teiresias.   True: it is not from me your fate will come.
That lies within Apollo's competence,
As it is his concern.

Oedipus.   Tell me: 160
Are you speaking for Creon or for yourself?

Teiresias.   Creon is no threat. You weave your own doom.

Oedipus.   Wealth, power, craft of statesmanship!
Kingly position, everywhere admired!
What savage envy is stored up against these,
If Creon, whom I trusted, Creon my friend,
For this great office which the city once
Put in my hands unsought—if for this power

Creon desires in secret to destroy me!

He has brought this decrepit fortune-teller, this   170
Collector of dirty pennies, this prophet fraud—
Why, he is no more clairvoyant than I am!
                              Tell us:
Has your mystic mummery ever approached the truth?
When that hellcat the Sphinx was performing here,
What help were you to these people?
Her magic was not for the first man who came along:
It demanded a real exorcist. Your birds—
What good were they? or the gods, for the matter of that?
But I came by,
Oedipus, the simple man, who knows nothing—   180
I thought it out for myself, no birds helped me!
And this is the man you think you can destroy,
That you may be close to Creon when he's king!
Well, you and your friend Creon, it seems to me,
Will suffer most. If you were not an old man,
You would have paid already for your plot.

Choragos.   We can not see that his words or yours
Have been spoken except in anger, Oedipus,
And of anger we have no need. How can God's will
Be accomplished best? That is what most concerns us.   190

Teiresias.   You are a king. But where argument's concerned
I am your man, as much a king as you.
I am not your servant, but Apollo's.
I have no need of Creon to speak for me.

Listen to me. You mock my blindness, do you?
But I say that you, with both your eyes, are blind:
You can not see the wretchedness of your life,
Nor in whose house you live, no, nor with whom.
Who are your father and mother? Can you tell me?
You do not even know the blind wrongs   200
That you have done them, on earth and in the world below.
But the double lash of your parents' curse will whip you
Out of this land some day, with only night
Upon your precious eyes.
Your cries then—where will they not be heard?
What fastness of Kithairon⁹ will not echo them?
And that bridal-descant of yours—you'll know it then,

---

9. A mountain range near Thebes where the infant Oedipus was left to die.

The song they sang when you came here to Thebes
And found your misguided berthing.
All this, and more, that you can not guess at now,   *210*
Will bring you to yourself among your children.

Be angry, then. Curse Creon. Curse my words.
I tell you, no man that walks upon the earth
Shall be rooted out more horribly than you.

Oedipus. Am I to bear this from him?—Damnation
Take you! Out of this place! Out of my sight!

Teiresias. I would not have come at all if you had not asked me.

Oedipus. Could I have told that you'd talk nonsense, that
You'd come here to make a fool of yourself, and of me?

Teiresias. A fool? Your parents thought me sane enough.   *220*

Oedipus. My parents again!—Wait: who were my parents?

Teiresias. This day will give you a father, and break your heart.

Oedipus. Your infantile riddles! Your damned abracadabra!

Teiresias. You were a great man once at solving riddles.

Oedipus. Mock me with that if you like; you will find it true.

Teiresias. It was true enough. It brought about your ruin.

Oedipus. But if it saved this town?

Teiresias [*to the page*].   Boy, give me your hand.

Oedipus. Yes, boy; lead him away.
                              —While you are here
We can do nothing. Go; leave us in peace.

Teiresias. I will go when I have said what I have to say.   *230*
How can you hurt me? And I tell you again:
The man you have been looking for all this time,
The damned man, the murderer of Laïos,
That man is in Thebes. To your mind he is foreignborn,
But it will soon be shown that he is a Theban,
A revelation that will fail to please.
                              A blind man,
Who has his eyes now; a penniless man, who is rich now;
And he will go tapping the strange earth with his staff;
To the children with whom he lives now he will be
Brother and father—the very same; to her   *240*
Who bore him, son and husband—the very same
Who came to his father's bed, wet with his father's blood.

Enough. Go think that over.
If later you find error in what I have said,
You may say that I have no skill in prophecy.

[*Exit Teiresias, led by his page. Oedipus goes into the palace.*]

Ode I

Chorus.   The Delphic stone of prophecies   [*Strophe 1*]
    Remembers ancient regicide
    And a still bloody hand.
    That killer's hour of flight has come.
    He must be stronger than riderless
    Coursers of untiring wind,
    For the son of Zeus[10] armed with his father's thunder
    Leaps in lightning after him;
    And the Furies follow him, the sad Furies.[11]

    Holy Parnassos' peak of snow   [*Antistrophe 1*]
    Flashes and blinds that secret man,   11
    That all shall hunt him down:
    Though he may roam the forest shade
    Like a bull gone wild from pasture
    To rage through glooms of stone.
    Doom comes down on him; flight will not avail him;
    For the world's heart calls him desolate,
    And the immortal Furies follow, for ever follow.

    But now a wilder thing is heard   [*Strophe 2*]
    From the old man skilled at hearing Fate in the wingbeat of a bird.   20
    Bewildered as a blown bird, my soul hovers and can not find
    Foothold in this debate, or any reason or rest of mind.
    But no man ever brought—none can bring
    Proof of strife between Thebes' royal house,
    Labdakos' line, and the son of Polybos;[12]
    And never until now has any man brought word
    Of Laïos' dark death staining Oedipus the King.

    Divine Zeus and Apollo hold   [*Antistrophe 2*]
    Perfect intelligence alone of all tales ever told;
    And well though this diviner works, he works in his own night;   30
    No man can judge that rough unknown or trust in second sight,
    For wisdom changes hands among the wise.
    Shall I believe my great lord criminal
    At a raging word that a blind old man let fall?
    I saw him, when the carrion woman faced him of old,
    Prove his heroic mind! These evil words are lies.

---

10.   I.e., Apollo (see note 3).
11.   The goddesses of divine vengeance.
12.   Labdakos was an early king of Thebes and an ancestor of Oedipus. Oedipus is mistakenly referred to as the son of Polybus.

Scene II

Creon. Men of Thebes:
I am told that heavy accusations
Have been brought against me by King Oedipus.

I am not the kind of man to bear this tamely.

If in these present difficulties
He holds me accountable for any harm to him
Through anything I have said or done—why, then,
I do not value life in this dishonor.
It is not as though this rumor touched upon
Some private indiscretion. The matter is grave.   10
The fact is that I am being called disloyal
To the State, to my fellow citizens, to my friends.
Choragos. He may have spoken in anger, not from his mind.
Creon. But did you not hear him say I was the one
Who seduced the old prophet into lying?
Choragos. The thing was said; I do not know how seriously.
Creon. But you were watching him! Were his eyes steady?
Did he look like a man in his right mind?
Choragos.   I do not know.
I can not judge the behavior of great men.
But here is the King himself.

[*Enter Oedipus.*]

Oedipus.   So you dared come back.   20
Why? How brazen of you to come to my house,
You murderer!
                 Do you think I do not know
That you plotted to kill me, plotted to steal my throne?
Tell me, in God's name: am I coward, a fool,
That you should dream you could accomplish this?
A fool who could not see your slippery game?
A coward, not to fight back when I saw it?
You are the fool, Creon, are you not? hoping
Without support or friends to get a throne?
Thrones may be won or bought: you could do neither.   30
Creon. Now listen to me. You have talked; let me talk, too.
You can not judge unless you know the facts.
Oedipus. You speak well: there is one fact; but I find it hard
To learn from the deadliest enemy I have.
Creon. That above all I must dispute with you.
Oedipus. That above all I will not hear you deny.

Creon. If you think there is anything good in being stubborn
    Against all reason, then I say you are wrong.
Oedipus. If you think a man can sin against his own kind
    And not be punished for it, I say you are mad.   40
Creon. I agree. But tell me: what have I done to you?
Oedipus. You advised me to send for that wizard, did you not?
Creon. I did. I should do it again.
Oedipus.   Very well. Now tell me:
    How long has it been since Laïos—
Creon.   What of Laïos?
Oedipus. Since he vanished in that onset by the road?
Creon. It was long ago, a long time.
Oedipus.   And this prophet,
    Was he practicing here then?
Creon.   He was; and with honor, as now.
Oedipus. Did he speak of me at that time?
Creon.   He never did;
    At least, not when I was present.
Oedipus.   But . . . the enquiry?
    I suppose you held one?
Creon.   We did, but we learned nothing.   50
Oedipus. Why did the prophet not speak against me then?
Creon. I do not know; and I am the kind of man
    Who holds his tongue when he has no facts to go on.
Oedipus. There's one fact that you know, and you could tell it.
Creon. What fact is that? If I know it, you shall have it.
Oedipus. If he were not involved with you, he could not say
    That is was I who murdered Laïos.
Creon. If he says that, you are the one that knows it!—
    But now it is my turn to question you.
Oedipus. Put your questions. I am no murderer.   60
Creon. First then: You married my sister?
Oedipus.   I married your sister.
Creon. And you rule the kingdom equally with her?
Oedipus. Everything that she wants she has from me.
Creon. And I am the third, equal to both of you?
Oedipus. That is why I call you a bad friend.
Creon. No. Reason it out, as I have done.
    Think of this first. Would any sane man prefer
    Power, with all a king's anxieties,
    To that same power and the grace of sleep?
    Certainly not I.   70
    I have never longed for the king's power—only his rights.
    Would any wise man differ from me in this?
    As matters stand, I have my way in everything

With your consent, and no responsibilities.
If I were king, I should be a slave to policy.

How could I desire a scepter more
Than what is now mine—untroubled influence?
No, I have not gone mad; I need no honors,
Except those with the perquisites I have now.
I am welcome everywhere; every man salutes me,   *80*
And those who want your favor seek my ear,
Since I know how to manage what they ask.
Should I exchange this ease for that anxiety?
Besides, no sober mind is treasonable.
I hate anarchy
And never would deal with any man who likes it.

Test what I have said. Go to the priestess
At Delphi, ask if I quoted her correctly.
And as for this other thing: if I am found   *90*
Guilty of treason with Teiresias,
Then sentence me to death! You have my word
It is a sentence I should cast my vote for—
But not without evidence!
               You do wrong
When you take good men for bad, bad men for good.
A true friend thrown aside—why, life itself
Is not more precious!
              In time you will know this well:
For time, and time alone, will show the just man,
Though scoundrels are discovered in a day.
Choragos.   This is well said, and a prudent man would ponder it.
Judgments too quickly formed are dangerous.   *100*
Oedipus.   But is he not quick in his duplicity?
And shall I not be quick to parry him?
Would you have me stand still, hold my peace, and let
This man win everything, through my inaction?
Creon.   And you want—what is it, then? To banish me?
Oedipus.   No, not exile. It is your death I want,
So that all the world may see what treason means.
Creon.   You will persist, then? You will not believe me?
Oedipus.   How can I believe you?
Creon.   Then you are a fool.
Oedipus.   To save myself?
Creon.   In justice, think of me.   *110*
Oedipus.   You are evil incarnate.
Creon.   But suppose that you are wrong?

Oedipus. Still I must rule.

Creon. But not if you rule badly.

Oedipus. O city, city!

Creon. It is my city, too!

Choragos. Now, my lords, be still. I see the Queen,
Iocastê, coming from her palace chambers;
And it is time she came, for the sake of you both.
This dreadful quarrel can be resolved through her.

[Enter Iocastê.]

Iocastê. Poor foolish men, what wicked din is this?
With Thebes sick to death, is it not shameful
That you should rake some private quarrel up?   120
[To Oedipus.] Come into the house.

                   —And you, Creon, go now:
Let us have no more of this tumult over nothing.

Creon. Nothing? No, sister: what your husband plans for me
Is one of two great evils: exile or death.

Oedipus. He is right.

                 Why, woman I have caught him squarely
Plotting against my life.

Creon.   No! Let me die
Accurst if ever I have wished you harm!

Iocastê. Ah, believe it, Oedipus!
In the name of the gods, respect this oath of his
For my sake, for the sake of these people here!   130

Choragos. Open your mind to her my lord. Be ruled by her,   *[Strophe 1]*
I beg you!

Oedipus. What would you have me do?

Choragos. Respect Creon's word. He has never spoken like a fool,
And now he has sworn an oath.

Oedipus.   You know what you ask?

Choragos.   I do.

Oedipus.   Speak on, then.

Choragos. A friend so sworn should not be baited so,
In blind malice, and without final proof.

Oedipus. You are aware, I hope, that what you say
Means death for me, or exile at the least.

Choragos. No, I swear by Helios,[13] first in Heaven!   *[Strophe 2]*
May I die friendless and accurst,   140
The worst of deaths, if ever I meant that!

---

13. The sun god.

It is the withering fields
    That hurt my sick heart:
     Must we bear all these ills,
      And now your bad blood as well?

Oedipus. Then let him go. And let me die, if I must,
   Or be driven by him in shame from the land of Thebes.
   It is your unhappiness, and not his talk,
   That touches me.
        As for him—
   Wherever he is, I will hate him as long as I live.   150

Creon. Ugly in yielding, as you were ugly in rage!
   Natures like yours chiefly torment themselves.

Oedipus. Can you not go? Can you not leave me?

Creon.   I can.
   You do not know me; but the city knows me,
   And in its eyes I am just, if not in yours.

[*Exit Creon.*]

Choragos. Lady Iocastê, did you not ask the King to go   [*Antistrophe 1*]
   to his chambers?

Iocastê. First tell me what has happened.

Choragos. There was suspicion without evidence; yet it rankled
   As even false charges will.

Iocastê.   On both sides?

Choragos.   On both.

Iocastê.   But what was said?

Choragos. Oh let it rest, let it be done with!   160
   Have we not suffered enough?

Oedipus. You see to what your decency has brought you:
   You have made difficulties where my heart saw none.

Choragos. Oedipus, it is not once only I have told you—   [*Antistrophe 2*]
     You must know I should count myself unwise
   To the point of madness, should I now forsake you—
     You, under whose hand,
      In the storm of another time,
     Our dear land sailed out free.
      But now stand fast at the helm!   170

Iocastê. In God's name, Oedipus, inform your wife as well:
   Why are you so set in this hard anger?

Oedipus. I will tell you, for none of these men deserves
   My confidence as you do. It is Creon's work,
   His treachery, his plotting against me.

Iocastê. Go on, if you can make this clear to me.

Oedipus. He charges me with the murder of Laïos.

Iocastê.   Has he some knowledge? Or does he speak from hearsay?
Oedipus.   He would not commit himself to such a charge,
   But he has brought in that damnable soothsayer   *180*
   To tell his story.
Iocastê.   Set your mind at rest.
   If it is a question of soothsayers, I tell you
   That you will find no man whose craft gives knowledge
   Of the unknowable.
                  Here is my proof:

   An oracle was reported to Laïos once
   (I will not say from Phoibos himself, but from
   His appointed ministers, at any rate)
   That his doom would be death at the hands of his own son—
   His son, born of his flesh and of mine!

   Now, you remember the story: Laïos was killed   *190*
   By marauding strangers where three highways meet;
   But his child had not been three days in this world
   Before the King had pierced the baby's ankles
   And left him to die on a lonely mountainside.

   Thus, Apollo never caused that child
   To kill his father, and it was not Laïos' fate
   To die at the hands of his son, as he had feared.
   This is what prophets and prophecies are worth!
   Have no dread of them.
                  It is God himself
   Who can show us what he wills, in his own way.   *200*
Oedipus.   How strange a shadowy memory crossed my mind,
   Just now while you were speaking; it chilled my heart.
Iocastê.   What do you mean? What memory do you speak of?
Oedipus.   If I understand you, Laïos was killed
   At a place where three roads meet.
Iocastê.   So it was said;
   We have no later story.
Oedipus.   Where did it happen?
Iocastê.   Phokis, it is called: at a place where the Theban Way
   Divides into the roads towards Delphi and Daulia.
Oedipus.   When?
Iocastê.   We had the news not long before you came
   And proved the right to your succession here.   *210*
Oedipus.   Ah, what net has God been weaving for me?
Iocastê.   Oedipus! Why does this trouble you?
Oedipus.   Do not ask me yet.

First, tell me how Laïos looked, and tell me
How old he was.

Iocastê.   He was tall, his hair just touched
With white; his form was not unlike your own.

Oedipus.   I think that I myself may be accurst
By my own ignorant edict.

Iocastê.   You speak strangely.
It makes me tremble to look at you, my King.

Oedipus.   I am not sure that the blind man can not see.
But I should know better if you were to tell me—   220

Iocastê.   Anything—though I dread to hear you ask it.

Oedipus.   Was the King lightly escorted, or did he ride
With a large company, as a ruler should?

Iocastê.   There were five men with him in all: one was a herald;
And a single chariot, which he was driving.

Oedipus.   Alas, that makes it plain enough!

                                        But who—
Who told you how it happened?

Iocastê.   A household servant,
The only one to escape.

Oedipus.   And is he still
A servant of ours?

Iocastê.   No; for when he came back at last
And found you enthroned in the place of the dead king,   230
He came to me, touched my hand with his, and begged
That I would send him away to the frontier district
Where only the shepherds go—
As far away from the city as I could send him.
I granted his prayer; for although the man was a slave,
He had earned more than this favor at my hands.

Oedipus.   Can he be called back quickly?

Iocastê.   Easily.
But why?

Oedipus.   I have taken too much upon myself
Without enquiry; therefore I wish to consult him.

Iocastê.   Then he shall come.

                        But am I not one also   240
To whom you might confide these fears of yours?

Oedipus.   That is your right; it will not be denied you,
Now least of all; for I have reached a pitch
Of wild foreboding. Is there anyone
To whom I should sooner speak?
Polybos of Corinth is my father.
My mother is a Dorian: Meropê.
I grew up chief among the men of Corinth

Until a strange thing happened—
Not worth my passion, it may be, but strange.   250

At a feast, a drunken man maundering in his cups
Cries out that I am not my father's son!

I contained myself that night, though I felt anger
And a sinking heart. The next day I visited
My father and mother, and questioned them. They stormed,
Calling it all the slanderous rant of a fool;
And this relieved me. Yet the suspicion
Remained always aching in my mind;
I knew there was talk; I could not rest;
And finally, saying nothing to my parents,   260
I went to the shrine at Delphi.
The god dismissed my question without reply;
He spoke of other things.
                              Some were clear,
Full of wretchedness, dreadful, unbearable:
As, that I should lie with my own mother, breed
Children from whom all men would turn their eyes;
And that I should be my father's murderer.

I heard all this, and fled. And from that day
Corinth to me was only in the stars
Descending in that quarter of the sky,   270
As I wandered farther and farther on my way
To a land where I should never see the evil
Sung by the oracle. And I came to this country
Where, so you say, King Laïos was killed.

I will tell you all that happened there, my lady.

There were three highways
Coming together at a place I passed;
And there a herald came towards me, and a chariot
Drawn by horses, with a man such as you describe
Seated in it. The groom leading the horses   280
Forced me off the road at his lord's command;
But as this charioteer lurched over towards me
I struck him in my rage. The old man saw me
And brought his double goad down upon my head
As I came abreast.
                      He was paid back, and more!
Swinging my club in this right hand I knocked him

Out of his car, and he rolled on the ground.
I killed him.

I killed them all.
Now if that stranger and Laïos were—kin,
Where is a man more miserable than I?   290
More hated by the gods? Citizen and alien alike
Must never shelter me or speak to me—
I must be shunned by all.
                              And I myself
Pronounced this malediction upon myself!

Think of it: I have touched you with these hands,
These hands that killed your husband. What defilement!

Am I all evil, then? It must be so,
Since I must flee from Thebes, yet never again
See my own countrymen, my own country,
For fear of joining my mother in marriage   300
And killing Polybos, my father.
                              Ah,
If I was created so, born to this fate,
Who could deny the savagery of God?

O holy majesty of heavenly powers!
May I never see that day! Never!
Rather let me vanish from the race of men
Than know the abomination destined me!
Choragos.   We too, my lord, have felt dismay at this.
          But there is hope: you have yet to hear the shepherd.
Oedipus.   Indeed, I fear no other hope is left me.   310
Iocastê.   What do you hope from him when he comes?
Oedipus.   This much:
          If his account of the murder tallies with yours,
          Then I am cleared.
Iocastê.   What was it that I said
          Of such importance?
Oedipus.   Why, "marauders," you said,
          Killed the King, according to this man's story.
          If he maintains that still, if there were several,
          Clearly the guilt is not mine: I was alone.
          But if he says one man, singlehanded, did it,
          Then the evidence all points to me.
Iocastê.   You may be sure that he said there were several;   320
          And can he call back that story now? He can not.

The whole city heard it as plainly as I.
But suppose he alters some detail of it:
He can not ever show that Laïos' death
Fulfilled the oracle: for Apollo said
My child was doomed to kill him; and my child—
Poor baby!—it was my child that died first.

No. From now on, where oracles are concerned,
I would not waste a second thought on any.
Oedipus.   You may be right.
                                    But come: let someone go   *330*
For the shepherd at once. This matter must be settled.
Iocastê.   I will send for him.
I would not wish to cross you in anything,
And surely not in this.—Let us go in.

[*Exeunt into the palace.*]

Ode II

Chorus.   Let me be reverent in the ways of right,   [*Strophe 1*]
Lowly the paths I journey on;
Let all my words and actions keep
The laws of the pure universe
From highest Heaven handed down.
For Heaven is their bright nurse,
Those generations of the realms of light;
Ah, never of mortal kind were they begot,
Nor are they slaves of memory, lost in sleep:
Their Father is greater than Time, and ages not.   *10*

The tyrant is a child of Pride   [*Antistrophe 1*]
Who drinks from his great sickening cup
Recklessness and vanity,
Until from his high crest headlong
He plummets to the dust of hope.
That strong man is not strong.
But let no fair ambition be denied;
May God protect the wrestler for the State
In government, in comely policy,
Who will fear God, and on His ordinance wait.   *20*

Haughtiness and the high hand of disdain   [*Strophe 2*]
Tempt and outrage God's holy law;
And any mortal who dares hold

No immortal Power in awe
Will be caught up in a net of pain:
The price for which his levity is sold.
Let each man take due earnings, then,
And keep his hands from holy things,
And from blasphemy stand apart—
Else the crackling blast of heaven   30
Blows on his head, and on his desperate heart;
Though fools will honor impious men,
In their cities no tragic poet sings.

Shall we lose faith in Delphi's obscurities,   [Antistrophe 2]
We who have heard the world's core
Discredited, and the sacred wood
Of Zeus at Elis praised no more?
The deeds and the strange prophecies
Must make a pattern yet to be understood.
Zeus, if indeed you are lord of all,   40
Throned in light over night and day,
Mirror this in your endless mind:
Our masters call the oracle
Words on the wind, and the Delphic vision blind!
Their hearts no longer know Apollo,
And reverence for the gods has died away.

Scene III

[Enter Iocastê.]

Iocastê.   Princes of Thebes, it has occurred to me
To visit the altars of the gods, bearing
These branches as a suppliant, and this incense.
Our King is not himself: his noble soul
Is overwrought with fantasies of dread,
Else he would consider
The new prophecies in the light of the old.
He will listen to any voice that speaks disaster,
And my advice goes for nothing.

[She approaches the altar, R.]

                              To you, then, Apollo,
Lycean lord, since you are nearest, I turn in prayer.   10
Receive these offerings, and grant us deliverance
From defilement. Our hearts are heavy with fear
When we see our leader distracted, as helpless sailors

Are terrified by the confusion of their helmsman.

[*Enter Messenger.*]

Messenger.   Friends, no doubt you can direct me:
Where shall I find the house of Oedipus,
Or, better still, where is the King himself?
Choragos.   It is this very place, stranger; he is inside.
This is his wife and mother of his children.
Messenger.   I wish her happiness in a happy house,   20
Blest in all the fulfillment of her marriage.
Iocastê.   I wish as much for you: your courtesy
Deserves a like good fortune. But now, tell me:
Why have you come? What have you to say to us?
Messenger.   Good news, my lady, for your house and your husband.
Iocastê.   What news? Who sent you here?
Messenger.   I am from Corinth.
The news I bring ought to mean joy for you,
Though it may be you will find some grief in it.
Iocastê.   What is it? How can it touch us in both ways?
Messenger.   The people of Corinth, they say,   30
Intend to call Oedipus to be their king.
Iocastê.   But old Polybos—is he not reigning still?
Messenger.   No. Death holds him in his sepulchre.
Iocastê.   What are you saying? Polybos is dead?
Messenger.   If I am not telling the truth, may I die myself.
Iocastê [*to a maidservant*]. Go in, go quickly; tell this to your master.

O riddlers of God's will, where are you now!
This was the man whom Oedipus, long ago,
Feared so, fled so, in dread of destroying him—
But it was another fate by which he died.   40

[*Enter Oedipus, C.*]

Oedipus.   Dearest Iocastê, why have you sent for me?
Iocastê.   Listen to what this man says, and then tell me
What has become of the solemn prophecies.
Oedipus.   Who is this man? What is his news for me?
Iocastê.   He has come from Corinth to announce your father's death!
Oedipus.   Is it true, stranger? Tell me in your own words.
Messenger.   I can not say it more clearly: the King is dead.
Oedipus.   Was it by treason? Or by an attack of illness?
Messenger.   A little thing brings old men to their rest.
Oedipus.   It was sickness, then?
Messenger.   Yes, and his many years.   50
Oedipus.   Ah!

Why should a man respect the Pythian hearth,[14] or
Give heed to the birds that jangle above his head?
They prophesied that I should kill Polybos,
Kill my own father; but he is dead and buried,
And I am here—I never touched him, never,
Unless he died of grief for my departure,
And thus, in a sense, through me. No. Polybos
Has packed the oracles off with him underground.
They are empty words.

Iocastê.   Had I not told you so?   60
Oedipus.   You had; it was my faint heart that betrayed me.
Iocastê.   From now on never think of those things again.
Oedipus.   And yet—must I not fear my mother's bed?
Iocastê.   Why should anyone in this world be afraid,
Since Fate rules us and nothing can be foreseen?
A man should live only for the present day.

Have no more fear of sleeping with your mother:
How many men, in dreams, have lain with their mothers!
No reasonable man is troubled by such things.
Oedipus.   That is true; only—   70
If only my mother were not still alive!
But she is alive. I can not help my dread.
Iocastê.   Yet this news of your father's death is wonderful.
Oedipus.   Wonderful. But I fear the living woman.
Messenger.   Tell me, who is this woman that you fear?
Oedipus.   It is Meropê, man; the wife of King Polybos.
Messenger.   Meropê? Why should you be afraid of her?
Oedipus.   An oracle of the gods, a dreadful saying.
Messenger.   Can you tell me about it or are you sworn to silence?
Oedipus.   I can tell you, and I will.   80
Apollo said through his prophet that I was the man
Who should marry his own mother, shed his father's blood
With his own hands. And so, for all these years
I have kept clear of Corinth, and no harm has come—
Though it would have been sweet to see my parents again.

Messenger.   And is this the fear that drove you out of Corinth?
Oedipus.   Would you have me kill my father?
Messenger.   As for that
You must be reassured by the news I gave you.
Oedipus.   If you could reassure me, I would reward you.
Messenger.   I had that in mind, I will confess: I thought   90

---

14. Delphi, where Apollo spoke through an oracle.

I could count on you when you returned to Corinth.

Oedipus.   No: I will never go near my parents again.

Messenger.   Ah, son, you still do not know what you are doing—

Oedipus.   What do you mean? In the name of God tell me!

Messenger.   —If these are your reasons for not going home.

Oedipus.   I tell you, I fear the oracle may come true.

Messenger.   And guilt may come upon you through your parents?

Oedipus.   That is the dread that is always in my heart.

Messenger.   Can you not see that all your fears are groundless?

Oedipus.   How can you say that? They are my parents, surely?   100

Messenger.   Polybos was not your father.

Oedipus.   Not my father?

Messenger.   No more your father than the man speaking to you.

Oedipus.   But you are nothing to me!

Messenger.   Neither was he.

Oedipus.   Then why did he call me son?

Messenger.   I will tell you:
Long ago he had you from my hands, as a gift.

Oedipus.   Then how could he love me so, if I was not his?

Messenger.   He had no children, and his heart turned to you.

Oedipus.   What of you? Did you buy me? Did you find me by chance?

Messenger.   I came upon you in the crooked pass of Kithairon.

Oedipus.   And what were you doing there?

Messenger.   Tending my flocks   110

Oedipus.   A wandering shepherd?

Messenger.   But your savior, son, that day.

Oedipus.   From what did you save me?

Messenger.   Your ankles should tell you that.

Oedipus.   Ah, stranger, why do you speak of that childhood pain?

Messenger.   I cut the bonds that tied your ankles together.

Oedipus.   I have had the mark as long as I can remember.

Messenger.   That was why you were given the name you bear.[15]

Oedipus.   God! Was it my father or my mother who did it?
Tell me!

Messenger.   I do not know. The man who gave you to me
Can tell you better than I.   120

Oedipus.   It was not you that found me, but another?

Messenger.   It was another shepherd gave you to me.

Oedipus.   Who was he? Can you tell me who he was?

Messenger.   I think he was said to be one of Laïos' people.

Oedipus.   You mean the Laïos who was king here years ago?

Messenger.   Yes; King Laïos; and the man was one of his herdsmen.

Oedipus.   Is he still alive? Can I see him?

---

15. Oedipus literally means "swollen-foot."

Messenger. These men here
 Know best about such things.
Oedipus. Does anyone here
 Know this shepherd that he is talking about?
 Have you seen him in the fields, or in the town? 130
 If you have, tell me. It is time things were made plain.
Choragos. I think the man he means is that same shepherd
 You have already asked to see. Iocastê perhaps
 Could tell you something.
Oedipus. Do you know anything
 About him, Lady? Is he the man we have summoned?
 Is that the man this shepherd means?
Iocastê. Why think of him?
 Forget this herdsman. Forget it all.
 This talk is a waste of time.
Oedipus. How can you say that?
 When the clues to my true birth are in my hands?
Iocastê. For God's love, let us have no more questioning! 140
 Is your life nothing to you?
 My own is pain enough for me to bear.
Oedipus. You need not worry. Suppose my mother a slave,
 And born of slaves: no baseness can touch you.
Iocastê. Listen to me, I beg you: do not do this thing!
Oedipus. I will not listen; the truth must be made known.
Iocastê. Everything that I say is for your own good!
Oedipus. My own good
 Snaps my patience, then; I want none of it.
Iocastê. You are fatally wrong! May you never learn who you are!
Oedipus. Go, one of you, and bring the shepherd here. 150
 Let us leave this woman to brag of her royal name.
Iocastê. Ah, miserable!
 That is the only word I have for you now.
 That is the only word I can ever have.

[*Exit into the palace.*]

Choragos. Why has she left us, Oedipus? Why has she gone
 In such a passion of sorrow? I fear this silence:
 Something dreadful may come of it.
Oedipus. Let it come!
 However base my birth, I must know about it.
 The Queen, like a woman, is perhaps ashamed
 To think of my low origin. But I 160
 Am a child of Luck; I can not be dishonored.
 Luck is my mother; the passing months, my brothers,
 Have seen me rich and poor.

If this is so,
How could I wish that I were someone else?
How could I not be glad to know my birth?

Ode III

Chorus. If ever the coming time were known   [*Strophe*]
To my heart's pondering,
Kithairon, now by Heaven I see the torches
At the festival of the next full moon,
And see the dance, and hear the choir sing
A grace to your gentle shade:
Mountain where Oedipus was found,
O mountain guard of a noble race!
May the god who heals us lend his aid,
And let that glory come to pass   10
For our king's cradling-ground.

Of the nymphs that flower beyond the years,   [*Antistrophe*]
Who bore you, royal child,
To Pan of the hills or the timberline Apollo,
Cold in delight where the upland clears,
Or Hermês for whom Kyllenê's heights are piled?[16]
Or flushed as evening cloud,
Great Dionysos, roamer of mountains,
He—was it he who found you there,
And caught you up in his own proud   20
Arms from the sweet god-ravisher
Who laughed by the Muses' fountains?

Scene IV

Oedipus. Sirs: though I do not know the man,
I think I see him coming, this shepherd we want:
He is old, like our friend here, and the men
Bringing him seem to be servants of my house.
But you can tell, if you have ever seen him.

[*Enter Shepherd escorted by servants.*]

Choragos. I know him, he was Laïos' man. You can trust him.
Oedipus. Tell me first, you from Corinth: is this the shepherd

---

16. Hermês, the herald of the Olympian gods, was born on the mountain of Kyllenê.

We were discussing?

Messenger. This is the very man.

Oedipus [to Shepherd]. Come here. No, look at me. You must answer
Everything I ask. You belonged to Laïos? 10

Shepherd. Yes: born his slave, brought up in his house.

Oedipus. Tell me: what kind of work did you do for him?

Shepherd. I was a shepherd of his, most of my life.

Oedipus. Where mainly did you go for pasturage?

Shepherd. Sometimes Kithairon, sometimes the hills near-by.

Oedipus. Do you remember ever seeing this man out there?

Shepherd. What would he be doing there? This man?

Oedipus. This man standing here. Have you ever seen him before?

Shepherd. No. At least, not to my recollection.

Messenger. And that is not strange, my lord. But I'll refresh 20
His memory: he must remember when we two
Spent three whole seasons together, March to September,
On Kithairon or thereabouts. He had two flocks;
I had one. Each autumn I'd drive mine home
And he would go back with his to Laïos' sheepfold.—
Is this not true, just as I have described it?

Shepherd. True, yes; but it was all so long ago.

Messenger. Well, then: do you remember, back in those days
That you gave me a baby boy to bring up as my own?

Shepherd. What if I did? What are you trying to say? 30

Messenger. King Oedipus was once that little child.

Shepherd. Damn you, hold your tongue!

Oedipus. No more of that!
It is your tongue needs watching, not this man's.

Shepherd. My King, my Master, what is it I have done wrong?

Oedipus. You have not answered his question about the boy.

Shepherd. He does not know . . . He is only making trouble . . .

Oedipus. Come, speak plainly, or it will go hard with you.

Shepherd. In God's name, do not torture an old man!

Oedipus. Come here, one of you; bind his arms behind him.

Shepherd. Unhappy king! What more do you wish to learn? 40

Oedipus. Did you give this man the child he speaks of?

Shepherd. I did.
And I would to God I had died that very day.

Oedipus. You will die now unless you speak the truth.

Shepherd. Yet if I speak the truth, I am worse than dead.

Oedipus. Very well; since you insist on delaying—

Shepherd. No! I have told you already that I gave him the boy.

Oedipus. Where did you get him? From your house? From somewhere
else?

Shepherd. Not from mine, no. A man gave him to me.

Oedipus. Is that man here? Do you know whose slave he was?

Shepherd. For God's love, my King, do not ask me any more!   50

Oedipus. You are a dead man if I have to ask you again.

Shepherd. Then . . . Then the child was from the palace of Laïos.

Oedipus. A slave child? or a child of his own line?

Shepherd. Ah, I am on the brink of dreadful speech!

Oedipus. And I of dreadful hearing. Yet I must hear.

Shepherd. If you must be told, then . . .

                                 They said it was Laïos' child,

But it is your wife who can tell you about that.

Oedipus. My wife!—Did she give it to you?

Shepherd.   My lord, she did.

Oedipus. Do you know why?

Shepherd.   I was told to get rid of it.

Oedipus. An unspeakable mother!

Shepherd.   There had been prophecies . . .   60

Oedipus. Tell me.

Shepherd.   It was said that the boy would kill his own father.

Oedipus. Then why did you give him over to this old man?

Shepherd. I pitied the baby, my King,

And I thought that this man would take him far away

To his own country.

                 He saved him—but for what a fate!

For if you are what this man says you are,

No man living is more wretched than Oedipus.

Oedipus. Ah God!

It was true!

         All the prophecies!

               —Now,

O Light, may I look on you for the last time!   70

I, Oedipus,

Oedipus, damned in his birth, in his marriage damned,

Damned in the blood he shed with his own hand!

[*He rushes into the palace.*]

Ode IV

Chorus. Alas for the seed of men.   [*Strophe 1*]

     What measure shall I give these generations

     That breathe on the void and are void

     And exist and do not exist?

     Who bears more weight of joy

Than mass of sunlight shifting in images,
Or who shall make his thought stay on
That down time drifts away?

Your splendor is all fallen.

O naked brow of wrath and tears,   10
O change of Oedipus!
I who saw your days call no man blest—
Your great days like ghósts góne.

That mind was a strong bow.   [Antistrophe 1]

Deep, how deep you drew it then, hard archer,
At a dim fearful range,
And brought dear glory down!

You overcame the stranger—
The virgin with her hooking lion claws—
And though death sang, stood like a tower   20
To make pale Thebes take heart.

Fortress against our sorrow!

Divine king, giver of laws,
Majestic Oedipus!
No prince in Thebes had ever such renown,
No prince won such grace of power.

And now of all men ever known   [Strophe 2]
Most pitiful is this man's story:
His fortunes are most changed, his state
Fallen to a low slave's   30
Ground under bitter fate.

O Oedipus, most royal one!
The great door that expelled you to the light
Gave at night—ah, gave night to your glory:
As to the father, to the fathering son.

All understood too late.

How could that queen whom Laïos won,
The garden that he harrowed at his height,
Be silent when that act was done?

But all eyes fail before time's eye,   [Antistrophe 2]
All actions come to justice there   41
Though never willed, though far down the deep past,
Your bed, your dread sirings,
Are brought to book at last.
Child by Laïos doomed to die,
Then doomed to lose that fortunate little death,
Would God you never took breath in this air
That with my wailing lips I take to cry:

For I weep the world's outcast.

I was blind, and now I can tell why: 50
Asleep, for you had given ease of breath
To Thebes, while the false years went by.

Exodos

[*Enter, from the palace, Second Messenger.*]

Second Messenger.   Elders of Thebes, most honored in this land,
    What horrors are yours to see and hear, what weight
    Of sorrow to be endured, if, true to your birth,
    You venerate the line of Labdakos!
    I think neither Istros nor Phasis, those great rivers,
    Could purify this place of the corruption
    It shelters now, or soon must bring to light—
    Evil not done unconsciously, but willed.

    The greatest griefs are those we cause ourselves.
Choragos.   Surely, friend, we have grief enough already;   10
    What new sorrow do you mean?
Second Messenger.   The Queen is dead.
Choragos.   Iocastê? Dead? But at whose hand?
Second Messenger.   Her own.
    The full horror of what happened you can not know,
    For you did not see it; but I, who did, will tell you
    As clearly as I can how she met her death.

    When she had left us,
    In passionate silence, passing through the court,
    She ran to her apartment in the house,
    Her hair clutched by the fingers of both hands.

She closed the doors behind her; then, by that bed   20
Where long ago the fatal son was conceived—
The son who should bring about his father's death—
We heard her call upon Laïos, dead so many years,
And heard her wail for the double fruit of her marriage,
A husband by her husband, children by her child.

Exactly how she died I do not know:
For Oedipus burst in moaning and would not let us
Keep vigil to the end: it was by him
As he stormed about the room that our eyes were caught.
From one to another of us he went, begging a sword,   30
Cursing the wife who was not his wife, the mother
Whose womb had carried his own children and himself.
I do not know: it was none of us aided him,
But surely one of the gods was in control!
For with a dreadful cry
He hurled his weight, as though wrenched out of himself,
At the twin doors: the bolts gave, and he rushed in.
And there we saw her hanging, her body swaying
From the cruel cord she had noosed about her neck.
A great sob broke from him, heartbreaking to hear,   40
As he loosed the rope and lowered her to the ground.

I would blot out from my mind what happened next!
For the King ripped from her gown the golden brooches
That were her ornament, and raised them, and plunged them down
Straight into his own eyeballs, crying, "No more,
No more shall you look on the misery about me,
The horrors of my own doing! Too long have you known
The faces of those whom I should never have seen,
Too long been blind to those for whom I was searching!
From this hour, go in darkness!" And as he spoke,   50
He struck at his eyes—not once, but many times;
And the blood spattered his beard,
Bursting from his ruined sockets like red hail.

So from the unhappiness of two this evil has sprung,
A curse on the man and woman alike. The old
Happiness of the house of Labdakos
Was happiness enough: where is it today?
It is all wailing and ruin, disgrace, death—all
The misery of mankind that has a name—
And it is wholly and for ever theirs.   60
Choragos.   Is he in agony still? Is there no rest for him?

Second Messenger.   He is calling for someone to lead him to the gates
So that all the children of Kadmos may look upon
His father's murderer, his mother's—no,
I can not say it!
                    And then he will leave Thebes,
Self-exiled, in order that the curse
Which he himself pronounced may depart from the house.
He is weak, and there is none to lead him,
So terrible is his suffering.
                    But you will see:
Look, the doors are opening; in a moment   70
You will see a thing that would crush a heart of stone.

[*The central door is opened; Oedipus, blinded, is led in.*]

Choragos.   Dreadful indeed for men to see.
Never have my own eyes
Looked on a sight so full of fear.

Oedipus!
What madness came upon you, what daemon
Leaped on your life with heavier
Punishment than a mortal man can bear?
No: I can not even
Look at you, poor ruined one.   80
And I would speak, question, ponder,
If I were able. No.
You make me shudder.
Oedipus.   God. God.
Is there a sorrow greater?
Where shall I find harbor in this world?
My voice is hurled far on a dark wind.
What has God done to me?
Choragos.   Too terrible to think of, or to see.

Oedipus.   O cloud of night,   [*Strophe 1*]
Never to be turned away: night coming on,   91
I can not tell how: night like a shroud!

My fair winds brought me here.
                    Oh God. Again
The pain of the spikes where I had sight,
The flooding pain
Of memory, never to be gouged out.
Choragos.   This is not strange.
You suffer it all twice over, remorse in pain,

Pain in remorse.

Oedipus. Ah dear friend   [*Antistrophe 1*]
    Are you faithful even yet, you alone?   101
    Are you still standing near me, will you stay here,
    Patient, to care for the blind?
                       The blind man!
    Yet even blind I know who it is attends me,
    By the voice's tone—
    Though my new darkness hide the comforter.
Choragos. Oh fearful act!
    What god was it drove you to rake black
    Night across your eyes?

Oedipus. Apollo. Apollo. Dear   [*Strophe 2*]
    Children, the god was Apollo.   111
    He brought my sick, sick fate upon me.
    But the blinding hand was my own!
    How could I bear to see
    When all my sight was horror everywhere?
Choragos. Everywhere; that is true.
Oedipus. And now what is left?
    Images? Love? A greeting even,
    Sweet to the senses? Is there anything?
    Ah no, friends: lead me away.   120
    Lead me away from Thebes.
                  Lead the great wreck
    And hell of Oedipus, whom the gods hate.
Choragos. Your fate is clear, you are not blind to that.
    Would God you had never found it out!

Oedipus. Death take the man who unbound   [*Antistrophe 2*]
    My feet on that hillside
    And delivered me from death to life! What life?
    If only I had died,
    This weight of monstrous doom
    Could not have dragged me and my darlings down.   130
Choragos. I would have wished the same.
Oedipus. Oh never to have come here
    With my father's blood upon me! Never
    To have been the man they call his mother's husband!
    Oh accurst! Oh child of evil,
    To have entered that wretched bed—
                   the selfsame one!
    More primal than sin itself, this fell to me.

Choragos.   I do not know how I can answer you.
You were better dead than alive and blind.

Oedipus.   Do not counsel me any more. This punishment   *140*
That I have laid upon myself is just.
If I had eyes,
I do not know how I could bear the sight
Of my father, when I came to the house of Death,
Or my mother: for I have sinned against them both
So vilely that I could not make my peace
By strangling my own life.
                    Or do you think my children,
Born as they were born, would be sweet to my eyes?
Ah never, never! Nor this town with its high walls,
Nor the holy images of the gods.
                For I,   *150*
Thrice miserable!—Oedipus, noblest of all the line
Of Kadmos, have condemned myself to enjoy
These things no more, by my own malediction
Expelling that man whom the gods declared
To be a defilement in the house of Laïos.
After exposing the rankness of my own guilt,
How could I look men frankly in the eyes?
No, I swear it,
If I could have stifled my hearing at its source,
I would have done it and made all this body   *160*
A tight cell of misery, blank to light and sound:
So I should have been safe in a dark agony
Beyond all recollection.
                Ah Kithairon!
Why did you shelter me? When I was cast upon you,
Why did I not die? Then I should never
Have shown the world my execrable birth.

Ah Polybos! Corinth, city that I believed
The ancient seat of my ancestors: how fair
I seemed, your child! And all the while this evil
Was cancerous within me!
                For I am sick   *170*
In my daily life, sick in my origin.

O three roads, dark ravine, woodland and way
Where three roads met: you, drinking my father's blood,
My own blood, spilled by my own hand: can you remember
The unspeakable things I did there, and the things
I went on from there to do?

O marriage, marriage!
The act that engendered me, and again the act
Performed by the son in the same bed—
                                        Ah, the net
Of incest, mingling fathers, brothers, sons,
With brides, wives, mothers; the last evil   180
That can be known by men: no tongue can say
How evil!
            No. For the love of God, conceal me
Somewhere far from Thebes; or kill me; or hurl me
Into the sea, away from men's eyes for ever.

Come, lead me. You need not fear to touch me.
Of all men, I alone can bear this guilt.

[*Enter Creon.*]

Choragos.   We are not the ones to decide; but Creon here
    May fitly judge of what you ask. He only
    Is left to protect the city in your place.
Oedipus.   Alas, how can I speak to him? What right have I   190
    To beg his courtesy whom I have deeply wronged?
Creon.   I have not come to mock you, Oedipus,
    Or to reproach you, either.
    [*To attendants.*]   —You, standing there:
    If you have lost all respect for man's dignity,
    At least respect the flame of Lord Helios:
    Do not allow this pollution to show itself
    Openly here, an affront to the earth
    And Heaven's rain and the light of day. No, take him
    Into the house as quickly as you can.
    For it is proper   200
    That only the close kindred see his grief.
Oedipus.   I pray you in God's name, since your courtesy
    Ignores my dark expectation, visiting
    With mercy this man of all men most execrable:
    Give me what I ask—for your good, not for mine.
Creon.   And what is it that you would have me do?
Oedipus.   Drive me out of this country as quickly as may be
    To a place where no human voice can ever greet me.
Creon.   I should have done that before now—only,
    God's will had not been wholly revealed to me.   210
Oedipus.   But his command is plain: the parricide
    Must be destroyed. I am that evil man.
Creon.   That is the sense of it, yes; but as things are,
    We had best discover clearly what is to be done.

Oedipus.   You would learn more about a man like me?
Creon.   You are ready now to listen to the god.
Oedipus.   I will listen. But it is to you
    That I must turn for help. I beg you, hear me.

    The woman in there—
    Give her whatever funeral you think proper: 220
    She is your sister.
                   —But let me go, Creon!
    Let me purge my father's Thebes of the pollution
    Of my living here, and go out to the wild hills,
    To Kithairon, that has won such fame with me,
    The tomb my mother and father appointed for me,
    And let me die there, as they willed I should.
    And yet I know
    Death will not ever come to me through sickness
    Or in any natural way: I have been preserved
    For some unthinkable fate. But let that be.   230
    As for my sons, you need not care for them.
    They are men, they will find some way to live.
    But my poor daughters, who have shared my table,
    Who never before have been parted from their father—
    Take care of them, Creon; do this for me.
    And will you let me touch them with my hands
    A last time, and let us weep together?
    Be kind, my lord,
    Great prince, be kind!
                   Could I but touch them,
    They would be mine again, as when I had my eyes.   240

[*Enter Antigone and Ismene, attended.*]

    Ah, God!
    Is it my dearest children I hear weeping?
    Has Creon pitied me and sent my daughters?
Creon.   Yes, Oedipus: I knew that they were dear to you
    In the old days, and know you must love them still.
Oedipus.   May God bless you for this—and be a friendlier
    Guardian to you than he has been to me!

    Children, where are you?
    Come quickly to my hands: they are your brother's—
    Hands that have brought your father's once clear eyes   250
    To this way of seeing—
                Ah dearest ones,
    I had neither sight nor knowledge then, your father

By the woman who was the source of his own life!
And I weep for you—having no strength to see you—,
I weep for you when I think of the bitterness
That men will visit upon you all your lives.
What homes, what festivals can you attend
Without being forced to depart again in tears?
And when you come to marriageable age,
Where is the man, my daughters, who would dare   *260*
Risk the bane that lies on all my children?
Is there any evil wanting? Your father killed
His father; sowed the womb of her who bore him;
Engendered you at the fount of his own existence!
That is what they will say of you.

                          Then, whom

Can you ever marry? There are no bridegrooms for you,
And your lives must wither away in sterile dreaming.
O Creon, son of Menoikeus!
You are the only father my daughters have,
Since we, their parents, are both of us gone for ever.   *270*
They are your own blood: you will not let them
Fall into beggary and loneliness;
You will keep them from the miseries that are mine!
Take pity on them; see, they are only children,
Friendless except for you. Promise me this,
Great Prince, and give me your hand in token of it.

[*Creon clasps his right hand.*]

Children:
I could say much, if you could understand me,
But as it is, I have only this prayer for you:
Live where you can, be as happy as you can—   *280*
Happier, please God, than God has made your father!
Creon.   Enough. You have wept enough. Now go within.
Oedipus.   I must; but it is hard.
Creon.   Time eases all things.
Oedipus.   But you must promise—
Creon.   Say what you desire.
Oedipus.   Send me from Thebes!
Creon.   God grant that I may!
Oedipus.   But since God hates me . . .
Creon.   No, he will grant your wish.
Oedipus.   You promise?
Creon.   I can not speak beyond my knowledge.
Oedipus.   Then lead me in.

Creon.   Come now, and leave your children.

Oedipus. No! Do not take them from me!

Creon.   Think no longer

That you are in command here, but rather think   *290*

How, when you were, you served your own destruction.

[*Exeunt into the house all but the Chorus; the Choragos chants directly to the audience.*]

Choragos.   Men of Thebes: look upon Oedipus.

This is the king who solved the famous riddle
And towered up, most powerful of men.
No mortal eyes but looked on him with envy,
Yet in the end ruin swept over him.
Let every man in mankind's frailty
Consider his last day; and let none
Presume on his good fortune until he find
Life, at his death, a memory without pain.   *300*

Questions

1. *Could Oedipus have avoided the tragic outcome of this drama? What characteristics of Sophocles' world view are suggested by your answer? Is man's behavior in that world governed by free will or is his behavior determined? In view of your answers to the preceding questions, of what is Oedipus guilty?* **2.** *How does the Prologue establish the mood and theme of the play? What aspects of Oedipus' character are revealed there?* **3.** *The play embodies a pattern of figurative and literal allusions to darkness and light, to vision and blindness. How does that figurative language function and what relationship does it bear to Oedipus' self-inflicted punishment?* **4.** *Sophocles' audience knew the Oedipus story as you, for instance, know the story of the crucifixion. In the absence of suspense, what literary devices serve to hold the audience's attention?* **5.** *To what extent and in what ways does the chorus contribute to the dramatic development and tension of the play?*

The Glass Menagerie

TENNESSEE WILLIAMS [b. 1911]

CHARACTERS

Amanda Wingfield, the mother. A little woman of great but confused vitality clinging frantically to another time and place. Her characterization must be carefully created, not copied from type. She is not paranoiac, but her life is paranoia. There is much to admire in Amanda, and as much to love and pity as there is to laugh at. Certainly she has endurance and a kind of heroism, and though her foolishness makes her unwittingly cruel at times, there is tenderness in her slight person.

Laura Wingfield, her daughter. Amanda, having failed to establish contact with reality, continues to live vitally in her illusions, but Laura's situation is even graver. A childhood illness has left her crippled, one leg slightly shorter than the other, and held in a brace. This defect need not be more than suggested on the stage. Stemming from this, Laura's separation increases till she is like a piece of her own glass collection, too exquisitely fragile to move from the shelf.

Tom Wingfield, her son. And the narrator of the play. A poet with a job in a warehouse. His nature is not remorseless, but to escape from a trap he has to act without pity.

Jim O'Connor, the gentleman caller. A nice, ordinary, young man.

Scene. An alley in St. Louis.

Time. Now and the Past.

Scene I

The Wingfield apartment is in the rear of the building, one of those vast hive-like conglomerations of cellular living-units that flower as warty growths in overcrowded urban centers of lower middle-class population and are symptomatic of the impulse of this largest and fundamentally enslaved section of American society to avoid fluidity and differentiation and to exist and function as one interfused mass of automatism.

The apartment faces an alley and is entered by a fire-escape, a structure whose name is a touch of accidental poetic truth, for all of these huge buildings are always burning with the slow and implacable fires of human desperation. The fire-escape is included in the set—that is, the landing of it and steps descending from it.

The scene is memory and is therefore nonrealistic. Memory takes a lot of poetic license. It omits some details; others are exaggerated, according to the emotional value of the articles it touches, for memory is seated predominantly in the heart. The interior is therefore rather dim and poetic.

At the rise of the curtain, the audience is faced with the dark, grim rear wall of the Wingfield tenement. This building, which runs parallel to the footlights, is flanked on both sides by dark, narrow alleys which run into murky canyons of tangled clotheslines, garbage cans and the sinister latticework of neighboring fire-escapes. It is up and down these side alleys that exterior entrances and exits are made, during the play. At the end of Tom's opening commentary, the dark tenement wall slowly reveals (by means of a transparency) the interior of the ground floor Wingfield apartment.

Downstage is the living room, which also serves as a sleeping room for Laura, the sofa unfolding to make her bed. Upstage, center, and divided by a wide arch or second proscenium with transparent faded portieres (or second curtain), is the dining room. In an old-fashioned what-not in the living room are seen scores of transparent glass animals. A blown-up photograph of the father hangs on the wall of the living room, facing the audience, to the left of the archway. It is the face of a very handsome young man in a doughboy's First World War cap. He is gallantly smiling, ineluctably smiling, as if to say, "I will be smiling forever."

The audience hears and sees the opening scene in the dining room through both the transparent fourth wall of the building and the transparent gauze portieres of the dining-room arch. It is during this revealing scene that the fourth wall slowly ascends, out of sight. This transparent exterior wall is not brought down again until the very end of the play, during Tom's final speech.

The narrator is an undisguised convention of the play. He takes whatever license with dramatic convention as is convenient to his purposes.

Tom enters dressed as a merchant sailor from alley, stage left, and strolls across the front of the stage to the fire-escape. There he stops and lights a cigarette. He addresses the audience.

Tom. Yes, I have tricks in my pocket, I have things up my sleeve. But I am the opposite of a stage magician. He gives you illusion that has the appearance of truth. I give you truth in the pleasant disguise of illusion. To begin with, I turn back time. I reverse it to that quaint period, the thirties, when the huge middle class of America was matriculating in a school for the blind. Their eyes had failed them, or they had failed their eyes, and so they were having their fingers pressed forcibly down on the fiery Braille alphabet of a dissolving economy. In Spain there was revolution. Here there was only shouting and confusion. In Spain there was Guernica. Here there were disturbances of labor, sometimes pretty violent, in otherwise peaceful cities such as Chicago, Cleveland, Saint Louis. . . . This is the social background of the play.

Music.

The play is memory. Being a memory play, it is dimly lighted, it is sentimental, it is not realistic. In memory everything seems to happen to music.
That explains the fiddle in the wings. I am the narrator of the play, and also
a character in it. The other characters are my mother, Amanda, my sister,
Laura, and a gentleman caller who appears in the final scenes. He is the
most realistic character in the play, being an emissary from a world of
reality that we were somehow set apart from. But since I have a poet's
weakness for symbols, I am using this character also as a symbol; he is the
long delayed but always expected something that we live for. There is a
fifth character in the play who doesn't appear except in this larger-than-
life photograph over the mantel. This is our father who left us a long time
ago. He was a telephone man who fell in love with long distances; he gave
up his job with the telephone company and skipped the light fantastic out
of town . . . The last we heard of him was a picture post-card from
Mazatlan, on the Pacific coast of Mexico, containing a message of two
words—"Hello—Good-bye!" and an address. I think the rest of the play
will explain itself. . . .

Amanda's voice becomes audible through the portieres.

(Legend on Screen: "Où Sont Les Neiges.")

He divides the portieres and enters the upstage area.
   *Amanda and Laura are seated at a drop-leaf table. Eating is indicated by
gestures without food or utensils. Amanda faces the audience. Tom and Laura
are seated in profile.*
   *The interior has lit up softly and through the scrim we see Amanda and
Laura seated at the table in the upstage area.*

Amanda *(calling).*   Tom?
Tom.   Yes, Mother.
Amanda.   We can't say grace until you come to the table!
Tom.   Coming, Mother. *(He bows slightly and withdraws, reappearing a few
   moments later in his place at the table.)*
Amanda *(to her son).*   Honey, don't *push* with your *fingers.* If you have to
   push with something, the thing to push with is a crust of bread. And
   chew—chew! Animals have sections in their stomachs which enable them
   to digest food without mastication, but human beings are supposed to
   chew their food before they swallow it down. Eat food leisurely, son, and
   really enjoy it. A well-cooked meal has lots of delicate flavors that have to
   be held in the mouth for appreciation. So chew your food and give your
   salivary glands a chance to function!

Tom deliberately lays his imaginary fork down and pushes his chair back from the table.

Tom.   I haven't enjoyed one bite of this dinner because of your constant directions on how to eat it. It's you that makes me rush through meals with your hawk-like attention to every bite I take. Sickening—spoils my appetite—all this discussion of animals' secretion—salivary glands—mastication!

Amanda *(lightly).*   Temperament like a Metropolitan star! *(He rises and crosses downstage.)* You're not excused from the table.

Tom.   I am getting a cigarette.

Amanda.   You smoke too much.

Laura rises.

Laura.   I'll bring in the blanc mange.

He remains standing with his cigarette by the portieres during the following.

Amanda *(rising).*   No, sister, no, sister—you be the lady this time and I'll be the darky.

Laura.   I'm already up.

Amanda.   Resume your seat, little sister—I want you to stay fresh and pretty—for gentlemen callers!

Laura.   I'm not expecting any gentlemen callers.

Amanda *(crossing out to kitchenette. Airily).*   Sometimes they come when they are least expected! Why, I remember one Sunday afternoon in Blue Mountain—*(Enters kitchenette.)*

Tom.   I know what's coming!

Laura.   Yes. But let her tell it.

Tom.   Again?

Laura.   She loves to tell it.

Amanda returns with bowl of dessert.

Amanda.   One Sunday afternoon in Blue Mountain—your mother received—seventeen!—gentlemen callers! Why, sometimes there weren't chairs enough to accommodate them all. We had to send the nigger over to bring in folding chairs from the parish house.

Tom *(remaining at portieres).*   How did you entertain those gentlemen callers?

Amanda.   I understood the art of conversation!

Tom.   I bet you could talk.

Amanda.   Girls in those days *knew* how to talk, I can tell you.

Tom.   Yes?

(Image on Screen: Amanda As A Girl On A Porch Greeting Callers.)

Amanda.   They knew how to entertain their gentlemen callers. It wasn't enough for a girl to be possessed of a pretty face and a graceful figure—although I wasn't slighted in either respect. She also needed to have a nimble wit and a tongue to meet all occasions.

Tom. What did you talk about?

Amanda. Things of importance going on in the world! Never anything coarse or common or vulgar. (*She addresses Tom as though he were seated in the vacant chair at the table though he remains by portieres. He plays this scene as though he held the book.*) My callers were gentlemen—all! Among my callers were some of the most prominent young planters of the Mississippi Delta—planters and sons of planters!

Tom motions for music and a spot of light on Amanda. Her eyes lift, her face glows, her voice becomes rich and elegiac.

(Legend on Screen: "Où Sont Les Neiges.")

There was young Champ Laughlin who later became vice-president of the Delta Planters Bank. Hadley Stevenson who was drowned in Moon Lake and left his widow one hundred and fifty thousand in Government bonds. There were the Cutrere brothers, Wesley and Bates. Bates was one of my bright particular beaux! He got in a quarrel with that wild Wainright boy. They shot it out on the floor of Moon Lake Casino. Bates was shot through the stomach. Died in the ambulance on his way to Memphis. His widow was also well-provided for, came into eight or ten thousand acres, that's all. She married him on the rebound—never loved her—carried my picture on him the night he died! And there was that boy that every girl in the Delta had set her cap for! That beautiful, brilliant young Fitzhugh boy from Green County!

Tom. What did he leave his widow?

Amanda. He never married! Gracious, you talk as though all of my old admirers had turned up their toes to the daisies!

Tom. Isn't this the first you mentioned that still survives?

Amanda. That Fitzhugh boy went North and made a fortune—came to be known as the Wolf of Wall Street! He had the Midas touch, whatever he touched turned to gold! And I could have been Mrs. Duncan J. Fitzhugh, mind you! But—I picked your *father*!

Laura (*rising*). Mother, let me clear the table.

Amanda. No dear, you go in front and study your typewriter chart. Or practice your shorthand a little. Stay fresh and pretty!—It's almost time for our gentlemen callers to start arriving. (*She flounces girlishly toward the kitchenette.*) How many do you suppose we're going to entertain this afternoon?

Tom throws down the paper and jumps up with a groan.

Laura (*alone in the dining room*). I don't believe we're going to receive any, Mother.

Amanda (*reappearing, airily*).   What? No one—not one? You must be joking! (*Laura nervously echoes her laugh. She slips in a fugitive manner through the half-open portieres and draws them gently behind her. A shaft of very clear light is thrown on her face against the faded tapestry of the curtains.*) (*Music: "The Glass Menagerie" under faintly.*) (*Lightly.*) Not one gentleman caller? It can't be true! There must be a flood, there must have been a tornado!

Laura.   It isn't a flood, it's not a tornado, Mother. I'm just not popular like you were in Blue Mountain. . . . (*Tom utters another groan. Laura glances at him with a faint, apologetic smile. Her voice catching a little*). Mother's afraid I'm going to be an old maid.

The scene dims out with "Glass Menagerie" music.

Scene II

"Laura, Haven't You Ever Liked Some Boy?"

On the dark stage the screen is lighted with the image of blue roses.
   Gradually Laura's figure becomes apparent and the screen goes out.
   The music subsides.
   Laura is seated in the delicate ivory chair at the small clawfoot table.
   She wears a dress of soft violet material for a kimono—her hair tied back from her forehead with a ribbon.
   She is washing and polishing her collection of glass.
   Amanda appears on the fire-escape steps. At the sound of her ascent, Laura catches her breath, thrusts the bowl of ornaments away and seats herself stiffly before the diagram of the typewriter keyboard as though it held her spellbound. Something has happened to Amanda. It is written in her face as she climbs to the landing: a look that is grim and hopeless and a little absurd.
   She has on one of those cheap or imitation velvety-looking cloth coats with imitation fur collar. Her hat is five or six years old, one of those dreadful cloche hats that were worn in the late twenties, and she is clasping an enormous black patent-leather pocketbook with nickel clasp and initials. This is her full-dress outfit, the one she usually wears to the D.A.R.
   Before entering she looks through the door.
   She purses her lips, opens her eyes wide, rolls them upward and shakes her head.
   Then she slowly lets herself in the door. Seeing her mother's expression Laura touches her lips with a nervous gesture.

Laura.   Hello, Mother, I was—(*She makes a nervous gesture toward the chart on the wall. Amanda leans against the shut door and stares at Laura with a martyred look.*)

Amanda. Deception? Deception? *(She slowly removes her hat and gloves, continuing the swift suffering stare. She lets the hat and gloves fall on the floor—a bit of acting.)*

Laura *(shakily.)* How was the D.A.R. meeting? *(Amanda slowly opens her purse and removes a dainty white handkerchief which she shakes out delicately and delicately touches to her lips and nostrils.)* Didn't you go to the D.A.R. meeting, Mother?

Amanda *(faintly, almost inaudibly)*—No.—No. *(Then more forcibly.)* I did not have the strength—to go to the D.A.R. In fact, I did not have the courage! I wanted to find a hole in the ground and hide myself in it forever! *(She crosses slowly to the wall and removes the diagram of the typewriter keyboard. She holds it in front of her for a second, staring at it sweetly and sorrowfully—then bites her lips and tears it in two pieces.)*

Laura *(faintly).* Why did you do that, Mother? *(Amanda repeats the same procedure with the chart of the Gregg Alphabet.)* Why are you—

Amanda. Why? Why? How old are you, Laura?

Laura. Mother, you know my age.

Amanda. I thought that you were an adult; it seems that I was mistaken. *(She crosses slowly to the sofa and sinks down and stares at Laura.)*

Laura. Please don't stare at me, Mother.

Amanda closes her eyes and lowers her head. Count ten.

Amanda. What are we going to do, what is going to become of us, what is the future?

Count ten.

Laura. Has something happened, Mother? *(Amanda draws a long breath and takes out the handkerchief again. Dabbing process.)* Mother, has—something happened?

Amanda. I'll be all right in a minute. I'm just bewildered—*(count five)*—by life. . . .

Laura. Mother, I wish that you would tell me what's happened.

Amanda. As you know, I was supposed to be inducted into my office at the D.A.R. this afternoon. **(Image on Screen: A Swarm of Typewriters.)** But I stopped off at Rubicam's Business College to speak to your teachers about your having a cold and ask them what progress they thought you were making down there.

Laura. Oh. . . .

Amanda. I went to the typing instructor and introduced myself as your mother. She didn't know who you were. Wingfield, she said. We don't have any such student enrolled at the school! I assured her she did, that you had been going to classes since early in January. "I wonder," she said, "if you could be talking about that terribly shy little girl who dropped out of school after only a few days' attendance?" "No," I said, "Laura, my daughter, has been going to school every day for the past six weeks!"

"Excuse me," she said. She took the attendance book out and there was your name, unmistakably printed, and all the dates you were absent until they decided that you had dropped out of school. I still said, "No, there must have been some mistake! There must have been some mix-up in the records!" And she said, "No—I remember her perfectly now. Her hand shook so that she couldn't hit the right keys! The first time we gave a speed-test, she broke down completely—was sick at the stomach and almost had to be carried into the wash-room! After that morning she never showed up any more. We phoned the house but never got any answer"—while I was working at Famous and Barr, I suppose, demonstrating those—Oh! I felt so weak I could barely keep on my feet. I had to sit down while they got me a glass of water! Fifty dollars' tuition, all of our plans—my hopes and ambitions for you—just gone up the spout, just gone up the spout like that. *(Laura draws a long breath and gets awkwardly to her feet. She crosses to the victrola and winds it up.)* What are you doing?

Laura.   Oh! *(She releases the handle and returns to her seat.)*

Amanda.   Laura, where have you been going when you've gone out pretending that you were going to business college?

Laura.   I've just been going out walking.

Amanda.   That's not true.

Laura.   It is. I just went walking.

Amanda.   Walking? Walking? In winter? Deliberately courting pneumonia in that light coat? Where did you walk to, Laura?

Laura.   It was the lesser of two evils, Mother. **(Image on Screen: Winter Scene In Park.)** I couldn't go back up. I—threw up—on the floor!

Amanda.   From half past seven till after five every day you mean to tell me you walked around in the park, because you wanted to make me think that you were still going to Rubicam's Business College?

Laura.   It wasn't as bad as it sounds. I went inside places to get warmed up.

Amanda.   Inside where?

Laura.   I went in the art museum and the bird-houses at the Zoo. I visited the penguins every day! Sometimes I did without lunch and went to the movies. Lately I've been spending most of my afternoons in the Jewel-box, that big glass house where they raise the tropical flowers.

Amanda.   You did all this to deceive me, just for the deception? *(Laura looks down.)* Why?

Laura.   Mother, when you're disappointed, you get that awful suffering look on your face, like the picture of Jesus' mother in the museum!

Amanda.   Hush!

Laura.   I couldn't face it.

Pause. A whisper of strings.

(Legend on Screen: "The Crust of Humility.")

Amanda *(hopelessly fingering the huge pocketbook).*   So what are we going to do the rest of our lives? Stay home and watch the parades go by? Amuse ourselves with the glass menagerie, darling? Eternally play those worn-out phonograph records your father left as a painful reminder of him? We won't have a business career—we've given that up because it gave us nervous indigestion! *(Laughs wearily.)* What is there left but dependency all our lives? I know so well what becomes of unmarried women who aren't prepared to occupy a position. I've seen such pitiful cases in the South—barely tolerated spinsters living upon the grudging patronage of sister's husband or brother's wife!—stuck away in some little mouse-trap of a room—encouraged by one in-law to visit another—little birdlike women without any nest—eating the crust of humility all their life! Is that the future that we've mapped out for ourselves? I swear it's the only alternative I can think of! It isn't a very pleasant alternative, is it? Of course—some girls *do marry. (Laura twists her hands nervously.)* Haven't you ever liked some boy?

Laura.   Yes. I liked one once. *(Rises.)* I came across his picture a while ago.

Amanda *(with some interest).*   He gave you his picture?

Laura.   No, it's in the year-book.

Amanda *(disappointed).*   Oh—a high-school boy.

(Image on Screen: Jim As A High-School Hero Bearing A Silver Cup.)

Laura.   Yes. His name was Jim. *(Laura lifts the heavy annual from the clawfoot table.)* Here he is in *The Pirates of Penzance.*

Amanda *(absently).*   The what?

Laura.   The operetta the senior class put on. He had a wonderful voice and we sat across the aisle from each other Mondays, Wednesdays and Fridays in the Aud. Here he is with the silver cup for debating! See his grin?

Amanda *(absently).*   He must have had a jolly disposition.

Laura.   He used to call me—Blue Roses.

(Image on Screen: Blue Roses.)

Amanda.   Why did he call you such a name as that?

Laura.   When I had that attack of pleurosis—he asked me what was the matter when I came back. I said pleurosis—he thought that I said Blue Roses! So that's what he always called me after that. Whenever he saw me, he'd holler, "Hello, Blue Roses!" I didn't care for the girl that he went out with. Emily Meisenbach. Emily was the best-dressed girl at Soldan. She never struck me, though, as being sincere . . . It says in the Personal Section—they're engaged. That's—six years ago! They must be married by now.

Amanda.   Girls that aren't cut out for business careers usually wind up married to some nice man. *(Gets up with a spark of revival.)* Sister, that's what you'll do!

Laura utters a startled, doubtful laugh. She reaches quickly for a piece of glass.

Laura. But, Mother—

Amanda. Yes? *(Crossing to photograph.)*

Laura *(in a tone of frightened apology).* I'm—crippled!

Amanda. Nonsense! Laura, I've told you never, never to use that word. Why, you're not crippled, you just have a little defect—hardly noticeable, even! When people have some slight disadvantage like that, they cultivate other things to make up for it—develop charm—and vivacity—and—*charm!* That's all you have to do! *(She turns again to the photograph.)* One thing your father had *plenty of*—was charm!

Tom motions to the fiddle in the wings. The scene fades out with music.

Scene III

(Legend on Screen: "After The Fiasco—")

Tom speaks from the fire-escape landing.

Tom. After the fiasco at Rubicam's Business College, the idea of getting a gentleman caller for Laura began to play a more important part in Mother's calculations. It became an obsession. Like some archetype of the universal unconscious, the image of the gentleman caller haunted our small apartment.... **(Image on Screen: Young Man At Door With Flowers.)** An evening at home rarely passed without some allusion to this image, this spectre, this hope.... Even when he wasn't mentioned, his presence hung in Mother's preoccupied look and in my sister's frightened, apologetic manner—hung like a sentence passed upon the Wingfields! Mother was a woman of action as well as words. She began to take logical steps in the planned direction. Late that winter and in the early spring—realizing that extra money would be needed to properly feather the nest and plume the bird—she conducted a vigorous campaign on the telephone, roping in subscribers to one of those magazines for matrons called *The Home-maker's Companion,* the type of journal that features the serialized sublimations of ladies of letters who think in terms of delicate cup-like breasts, slim, tapering waists, rich, creamy thighs, eyes like wood-smoke in autumn, fingers that soothe and caress like strains of music, bodies as powerful as Etruscan sculpture.

(Image on Screen: Glamor Magazine Cover.)

Amanda enters with phone on long extension cord. She is spotted in the dim stage.

Amanda. Ida Scott? This is Amanda Wingfield! We *missed* you at the D.A.R.

last Monday! I said to myself: She's probably suffering with that sinus condition! How is that sinus condition? Horrors! Heaven have mercy!— You're a Christian martyr, yes, that's what you are, a Christian martyr! Well, I just now happened to notice that your subscription to the *Companion's* about to expire! Yes, it expires with the next issue, honey!—just when that wonderful new serial by Bessie Mae Hopper is getting off to such an exciting start. Oh, honey, it's something that you can't miss! You remember how *Gone With the Wind* took everybody by storm? You simply couldn't go out if you hadn't read it. All everybody *talked* was Scarlett O'Hara. Well, this is a book that critics already compare to *Gone With the Wind*. It's the *Gone With the Wind* of the post–World War generation!—What?—Burning?—Oh, honey, don't let them burn, go take a look in the oven and I'll hold the wire! Heavens—I think she's hung up!

Dim out.

(Legend on Screen: "You Think I'm In Love With Continental Shoemakers?")

Before the stage is lighted, the violent voices of Tom and Amanda are heard. They are quarreling behind the portieres. In front of them stands Laura with clenched hands and panicky expression.
   A clear pool of light on her figure throughout this scene.

Tom.   What in Christ's name am I—
Amanda *(shrilly).*   Don't you use that—
Tom.   Supposed to do!
Amanda.   Expression! Not in my—
Tom.   Ohhh!
Amanda.   Presence! Have you gone out of your senses?
Tom.   I have, that's true, *driven* out!
Amanda.   What is the matter with you, you—big—big—IDIOT!
Tom.   Look—I've got *no thing,* no single thing—
Amanda.   Lower your voice!
Tom.   In my life here that I can call my OWN! Everything is—
Amanda.   Stop that shouting!
Tom.   Yesterday you confiscated my books! You had the nerve to—
Amanda.   I took that horrible novel back to the library—yes! That hideous book by that insane Mr. Lawrence. *(Tom laughs wildly.)* I cannot control the output of diseased minds or people who cater to them—*(Tom laughs still more wildly.)* BUT I WON'T ALLOW SUCH FILTH BROUGHT INTO MY HOUSE! No, no, no, no, no!
Tom.   House, house! Who pays rent on it, who makes a slave of himself to—
Amanda *(fairly screeching).*   Don't you DARE to—
Tom.   No, no, I mustn't say things! *I've* got to just—

Amanda. Let me tell you—

Tom. I don't want to hear any more! *(He tears the portieres open. The up- stage area is lit with a turgid smoky red glow.)*

Amanda's hair is in metal curlers and she wears a very old bathrobe, much too large for her slight figure, a relic of the faithless Mr. Wingfield.

An upright typewriter and a wild disarray of manuscripts are on the drop- leaf table. The quarrel was probably precipitated by Amanda's interruption of his creative labor. A chair lying overthrown on the floor.

Their gesticulating shadows are cast on the ceiling by the fiery glow.

Amanda. You *will* hear more, you—

Tom. No, I won't hear more, I'm going out!

Amanda. You come right back in—

Tom. Out, out, out! Because I'm—

Amanda. Come back here, Tom Wingfield! I'm not through talking to you!

Tom. Oh, go—

Laura *(desperately).* Tom!

Amanda. You're going to listen, and no more insolence from you! I'm at the end of my patience! *(He comes back toward her.)*

Tom. What do you think I'm at? Aren't I supposed to have any patience to reach the end of, Mother? I know, I know. It seems unimportant to you, what I'm *doing*—what I *want* to do—having a little *difference* between them! You don't think that—

Amanda. I think you've been doing things that you're ashamed of. That's why you act like this. I don't believe that you go every night to the movies. Nobody goes to the movies night after night. Nobody in their right minds goes to the movies as often as you pretend to. People don't go to the movies at nearly midnight, and movies don't let out at two A.M. Come in stumbling. Muttering to yourself like a maniac! You get three hours sleep and then go to work. Oh, I can picture the way you're doing down there. Moping, doping, because you're in no condition.

Tom *(wildly).* No, I'm in no condition!

Amanda. What right have you got to jeopardize your job? Jeopardize the se- curity of us all? How do you think we'd manage if you were—

Tom. Listen! You think I'm crazy *about* the *warehouse? (He bends fiercely toward her slight figure.)* You think I'm in love with the Continental Shoe- makers? You think I want to spend fifty-five *years* down there in that— *celotex interior!* with—*fluorescent—tubes!* Look! I'd rather somebody picked up a crowbar and battered out my brains—than go back mornings! I *go!* Every time you come in yelling that God damn *"Rise and Shine!"* *"Rise and Shine!"* I say to myself *"How lucky dead people are!"* But I get up. I *go!* For sixty-five dollars a month I give up all that I dream of doing and being *ever!* And you say self—*self's* all I ever think of. Why, listen, if self is what I thought of, Mother, I'd be where he is—GONE! *(Pointing to father's picture.)* As far as the system of transportation reaches! *(He starts past her. She grabs his arm.)* Don't grab at me, Mother!

Amanda. Where are you going?

Tom. I'm going to the *movies!*

Amanda. I don't believe that lie!

Tom *(crouching toward her, overtowering her tiny figure. She backs away, gasping).* I'm going to opium dens! Yes, opium dens, dens of vice and criminals' hang-outs, Mother. I've joined the Hogan gang, I'm a hired assassin, I carry a tommy-gun in a violin case! I run a string of cat-houses in the Valley! They call me Killer, Killer Wingfield, I'm leading a double-life, a simple, honest warehouse worker by day, by night a dynamic *czar* of the *underworld, Mother.* I go to gambling casinos, I spin away fortunes on the roulette table! I wear a patch over one eye and a false mustache, sometimes I put on green whiskers. On those occasions they call me—*El Diablo!* Oh, I could tell you things to make you sleepless! My enemies plan to dynamite this place. They're going to blow us all sky-high some night! I'll be glad, very happy, and so will you! You'll go up, up on a broomstick, over Blue Mountain with seventeen gentlemen callers! You ugly—babbling old—*witch.* . . . *(He goes through a series of violent, clumsy movements, seizing his overcoat, lunging to the door, pulling it fiercely open. The women watch him, aghast. His arm catches in the sleeve of the coat as he struggles to pull it on. For a moment he is pinioned by the bulky garment. With an outraged groan he tears the coat off again, splitting the shoulders of it, and hurls it across the room. It strikes against the shelf of Laura's glass collection, there is a tinkle of shattering glass. Laura cries out as if wounded.)*

Music: "The Glass Menagerie."

Laura *(shrilly).* My glass!—menagerie. . . . *(She covers her face and turns away.)*

But Amanda is still stunned and stupefied by the "ugly witch" so that she barely notices this occurrence. Now she recovers her speech.

Amanda *(in an awful voice).* I won't speak to you—until you apologize! *(She crosses through portieres and draws them together behind her. Tom is left with Laura. Laura clings weakly to the mantel with her face averted. Tom stares at her stupidly for a moment. Then he crosses to shelf. Drops awkwardly to his knees to collect the fallen glass, glancing at Laura as if he would speak but couldn't.)*

"The Glass Menagerie" music steals in as the scene dims out.

Scene IV

The interior is dark. Faint light in the alley.

A deep-voiced bell in a church is tolling the hour of five as the scene commences.

Tom appears at the top of the alley. After each solemn boom of the bell in the tower, he shakes a little noise-maker or rattle as if to express the tiny spasm of man in contrast to the sustained power and dignity of the Almighty. This and the unsteadiness of his advance make it evident that he has been drinking.

As he climbs the few steps to the fire-escape landing light steals up inside. Laura appears in night-dress, observing Tom's empty bed in the front room.

Tom fishes in his pockets for the door-key, removing a motley assortment of articles in the search, including a perfect shower of movie-ticket stubs and an empty bottle. At last he finds the key, but just as he is about to insert it, it slips from his fingers. He strikes a match and crouches below the door.

Tom *(bitterly).* One crack—and it falls through!

Laura opens the door.

Laura. Tom! Tom, what are you doing?
Tom. Looking for a door-key.
Laura. Where have you been all this time?
Tom. I have been to the movies.
Laura. All this time at the movies?
Tom. There was a very long program. There was a Garbo picture and a Mickey Mouse and a travelogue and a newsreel and a preview of coming attractions. And there was an organ solo and a collection for the milk-fund—simultaneously—which ended up in a terrible fight between a fat lady and an usher!
Laura *(innocently).* Did you have to stay through everything?
Tom. Of course! And, oh, I forgot! There was a big stage show! The headliner on this stage show was Malvolio the Magician. He performed wonderful tricks, many of them, such as pouring water back and forth between pitchers. First it turned to wine and then it turned to beer and then it turned to whiskey. I know it was whiskey it finally turned into because he needed somebody to come up out of the audience to help him, and I came up—both shows! It was Kentucky Straight Bourbon. A very generous fellow, he gave souvenirs. *(He pulls from his back pocket a shimmering rainbow-colored scarf.)* He gave me this. This is his magic scarf. You can have it, Laura. You wave it over a canary cage and you get a bowl of gold-fish. You wave it over the gold-fish bowl and they fly away canaries. . . . But the wonderfullest trick of all was the coffin trick. We nailed him into a coffin and he got out of the coffin without removing one nail.

(He has come inside). There is a trick that would come in handy for me—get me out of this 2 by 4 situation! *(Flops onto bed and starts removing shoes.)*

Laura. Tom—Shhh!

Tom. What're you shushing me for?

Laura. You'll wake up Mother.

Tom. Goody, goody! Pay'er back for all those "Rise an' Shines." *(Lies down, groaning.)* You know it don't take much intelligence to get yourself into a nailed-up coffin, Laura. But who in hell ever got himself out of one without removing one nail?

As if in answer, the father's grinning photograph lights up. Scene dims out.

Immediately following: The church bell is heard striking six. At the sixth stroke the alarm clock goes off in Amanda's room, and after a few moments we hear her calling: "Rise and Shine! Rise and Shine! Laura, go tell your brother to rise and shine!"

Tom *(sitting up slowly).* I'll rise—but I won't shine.

The light increases.

Amanda. Laura, tell your brother his coffee is ready.

Laura slips into front room.

Laura. Tom! it's nearly seven. Don't make Mother nervous. *(He stares at her stupidly. Beseechingly.)* Tom, speak to Mother this morning. Make up with her, apologize, speak to her!

Tom. She won't to me. It's her that started not speaking.

Laura. If you just say you're sorry she'll start speaking.

Tom. Her not speaking—is that such a tragedy?

Laura. Please—please!

Amanda *(calling from kitchenette).* Laura, are you going to do what I asked you to do, or do I have to get dressed and go out myself?

Laura. Going, going—soon as I get on my coat! *(She pulls on a shapeless felt hat with nervous, jerky movement, pleadingly glancing at Tom. Rushes awkwardly for coat. The coat is one of Amanda's, inaccurately made-over, the sleeves too short for Laura.)* Butter and what else?

Amanda *(entering upstage).* Just butter. Tell them to charge it.

Laura. Mother, they make such faces when I do that.

Amanda. Sticks and stones may break our bones, but the expression on Mr. Garfinkel's face won't harm us! Tell your brother his coffee is getting cold.

Laura *(at door).* Do what I asked you, will you, will you, Tom?

He looks sullenly away.

Amanda. Laura, go now or just don't go at all!

Laura *(rushing out).* Going—going! *(A second later she cries out. Tom* springs up and crosses to the door. Amanda rushes anxiously in. Tom opens the door.)

Tom. Laura?

Laura. I'm all right. I slipped, but I'm all right.

Amanda *(peering anxiously after her).*   If anyone breaks a leg on those fire-escape steps, the landlord ought to be sued for every cent he possesses! *(She shuts door. Remembers she isn't speaking and returns to other room.)*

As Tom enters listlessly for his coffee, she turns her back to him and stands rigidly facing the window on the gloomy gray vault of the areaway. Its light on her face with its aged but childish features is cruelly sharp, satirical as a Daumier print.

Music under: "Ave Maria."

Tom glances sheepishly but sullenly at her averted figure and slumps at the table. The coffee is scalding hot; he sips it and gasps and spits it back in the cup. At his gasp, Amanda catches her breath and half turns. Then catches herself and turns back to window.

Tom blows on his coffee, glancing sidewise at his mother. She clears her throat. Tom clears his. He starts to rise. Sinks back down again, scratches his head, clears his throat again. Amanda coughs. Tom raises his cup in both hands to blow on it, his eyes staring over the rim of it at his mother for several moments. Then he slowly sets the cup down and awkwardly and hesitantly rises from the chair.

Tom *(hoarsely).*   Mother. I—I apologize. Mother. *(Amanda draws a quick, shuddering breath. Her face works grotesquely. She breaks into childlike tears.)* I'm sorry for what I said, for everything that I said, I didn't mean it.

Amanda *(sobbingly).*   My devotion has made me a witch and so I make myself hateful to my children!

Tom. No, you *don't.*

Amanda. I worry so much, don't sleep, it makes me nervous!

Tom *(gently).*   I understand that.

Amanda. I've had to put up a solitary battle all these years. But you're my right-hand bower! Don't fall down, don't fail!

Tom *(gently).*   I try, Mother.

Amanda *(with great enthusiasm).*   Try and you will SUCCEED! *(The notion makes her breathless.)* Why, you—you're just *full* of natural endowments! Both of my children—they're *unusual* children! Don't you think I know it? I'm so—*proud!* Happy and—feel I've—so much to be thankful for but—Promise me one thing, son!

Tom. What, Mother?

Amanda. Promise, son, you'll—never be a drunkard!

Tom *(turns to her grinning).*   I will never be a drunkard, Mother.

Amanda. That's what frightened me so, that you'd be drinking! Eat a bowl of Purina!

Tom. Just coffee, Mother.

Amanda. Shredded wheat biscuit?

Tom. No. No, Mother, just coffee.

Amanda. You can't put in a day's work on an empty stomach. You've got ten minutes—don't gulp! Drinking too-hot liquids makes cancer of the stomach. . . . Put cream in.

Tom. No, thank you.

Amanda. To cool it.

Tom. No! No, thank you, I want it black.

Amanda. I know, but it's not good for you. We have to do all that we can to build ourselves up. In these trying times we live in, all that we have to cling to is—each other. . . . That's why it's so important to—Tom, I—I sent out your sister so I could discuss something with you. If you hadn't spoken I would have spoken to you. *(Sits down.)*

Tom *(gently).* What is it, Mother, that you want to discuss?

Amanda. Laura!

Tom puts his cup down slowly.

(Legend on Screen: "Laura.")

Music: "The Glass Menagerie."

Tom. —Oh.—Laura . . .

Amanda *(touching his sleeve).* You know how Laura is. So quiet but—still water runs deep! She notices things and I think she—broods about them. *(Tom looks up.)* A few days ago I came in and she was crying.

Tom. What about?

Amanda. You.

Tom. Me?

Amanda. She has an idea that you're not happy here.

Tom. What gave her that idea?

Amanda. What gives her any idea? However, you do act strangely. I—I'm not criticizing, understand *that!* I know your ambitions do not lie in the warehouse, that like everybody in the whole wide world—you've had to—make sacrifices, but—Tom—Tom—life's not easy, it calls for—Spartan endurance! There's so many things in my heart that I cannot describe to you! I've never told you but I—*loved* your father. . . .

Tom *(gently).* I know that, Mother.

Amanda. And you—when I see you taking after his ways! Staying out late—and—well, you *had* been drinking the night you were in that—terrifying condition! Laura says that you hate the apartment and that you go out nights to get away from it! Is that true, Tom?

Tom. No. You say there's so much in your heart that you can't describe to me. That's true of me, too. There's so much in my heart that I can't describe to *you!* So let's respect each other's—

Amanda. But, why—*why,* Tom—are you always so *restless?* Where do you go to, nights?

Tom. I—go to the movies.

Amanda. Why do you go to the movies so much, Tom?

Tom. I go to the movies because—I like adventure. Adventure is something I don't have much of at work, so I go to the movies.

Amanda. But, Tom, you go to the movies *entirely* too *much!*

Tom. I like a lot of adventure.

Amanda looks baffled, then hurt. As the familiar inquisition resumes he becomes hard and impatient again. Amanda slips back into her querulous attitude toward him.

(Image on Screen: Sailing Vessel With Jolly Roger.)

Amanda. Most young men find adventure in their careers.

Tom. Then most young men are not employed in a warehouse.

Amanda. The world is full of young men employed in warehouses and offices and factories.

Tom. Do all of them find adventure in their careers?

Amanda. They do or they do without it! Not everybody has a craze for adventure.

Tom. Man is by instinct a lover, a hunter, a fighter, and none of those instincts are given much play at the warehouse!

Amanda. Man is by instinct! Don't quote instinct to me! Instinct is something that people have got away from! It belongs to animals! Christian adults don't want it!

Tom. What do Christian adults want, then, Mother?

Amanda. Superior things! Things of the mind and the spirit! Only animals have to satisfy instincts! Surely your aims are somewhat higher than theirs! Than monkeys—pigs—

Tom. I reckon they're not.

Amanda. You're joking. However, that isn't what I wanted to discuss.

Tom *(rising).* I haven't much time.

Amanda *(pushing his shoulders).* Sit down.

Tom. You want me to punch in red at the warehouse, Mother?

Amanda. You have five minutes. I want to talk about Laura.

(Legend on Screen: "Plans And Provisions.")

Tom. All right! What about Laura?

Amanda. We have to be making plans and provisions for her. She's older than you, two years, and nothing has happened. She just drifts along doing nothing. It frightens me terribly how she just drifts along.

Tom. I guess she's the type that people call home girls.

Amanda. There's no such type, and if there is, it's a pity! That is unless the home is hers, with a husband!

Tom. What?

Amanda. Oh, I can see the handwriting on the wall as plain as I see the nose in front of my face! It's terrifying! More and more you remind me of your father! He was out all hours without explanation—Then *left! Goodbye!* And me with the bag to hold. I saw that letter you got from the Merchant Marine. I know what you're dreaming of. I'm not standing here blindfolded. Very well, then. Then *do* it! But not till there's somebody to take your place.

Tom. What do you mean?

Amanda. I mean that as soon as Laura has got somebody to take care of her, married, a home of her own, independent—why, then you'll be free to go wherever you please, on land, on sea, whichever way the wind blows! But until that time you've got to look out for your sister. I don't say me because I'm old and don't matter! I say for your sister because she's young and dependent. I put her in business college—a dismal failure! Frightened her so it made her sick to her stomach. I took her over to the Young People's League at the church. Another fiasco. She spoke to nobody, nobody spoke to her. Now all she does is fool with those pieces of glass and play those worn-out records. What kind of a life is that for a girl to lead!

Tom. What can I do about it?

Amanda. Overcome selfishness! Self, self, self is all that you ever think of! *(Tom springs up and crosses to get his coat. It is ugly and bulky. He pulls on a cap with earmuffs.)* Where is your muffler? Put your wool muffler on! *(He snatches it angrily from the closet and tosses it around his neck and pulls both ends tight.)* Tom! I haven't said what I had in mind to ask you.

Tom. I'm too late to—

Amanda *(catching his arms—very importunately. Then shyly).* Down at the warehouse, aren't there some—nice young men?

Tom. No!

Amanda. There *must* be—some . . .

Tom. Mother—*(Gesture.)*

Amanda. Find out one that's clean-living—doesn't drink and—ask him out for sister!

Tom. What?

Amanda. For *sister!* To *meet!* Get *acquainted!*

Tom *(stamping to door).* Oh, my go-osh!

Amanda. Will you? *(He opens door. Imploringly.)* Will you? *(He starts down.)* Will you? *Will* you, dear?

Tom *(calling back).* YES!

Amanda closes the door hesitantly and with a troubled but faintly hopeful expression.

(Image on Screen: Glamor Magazine Cover.)

Spot Amanda at phone.

Amanda. Ella Cartwright? This is Amanda Wingfield! How are you, honey? How is that kidney condition! *(Count five.)* Horrors! *(Count five.)* You're a Christian martyr, yes, honey, that's what you are, a Christian martyr! Well, I just happened to notice in my little red book that your subscription to the *Companion* has just run out! I knew that you wouldn't want to miss out on the wonderful serial starting in this new issue. It's by Bessie Mae Hopper, the first thing she's written since *Honeymoon for Three*. Wasn't that a strange and interesting story? Well, this one is even lovelier, I believe. It has a sophisticated society background. It's all about the horsey set on Long Island!

Fade out.

Scene V

(Legend on Screen: "Annunciation.") *Fade with music.*

It is early dusk of a spring evening. Supper has just been finished in the Wingfield apartment. Amanda and Laura in light colored dresses are removing dishes from the table, in the upstage area, which is shadowy, their movements formalized almost as a dance or ritual, their moving forms as pale and silent as moths.

Tom, in white shirt and trousers, rises from the table and crosses toward the fire-escape.

Amanda *(as he passes her).* Son, will you do me a favor?
Tom. What?
Amanda. Comb your hair! You look so pretty when your hair is combed! *(Tom slouches on sofa with evening paper. Enormous caption "Franco Triumphs.")* There is only one respect in which I would like you to emulate your father.
Tom. What respect is that?
Amanda. The care he always took of his appearance. He never allowed himself to look untidy. *(He throws down the paper and crosses to fire-escape.)* Where are you going?

Tom. I'm going out to smoke.

Amanda. You smoke too much. A pack a day at fifteen cents a pack. How much would that amount to in a month? Thirty times fifteen is how much, Tom? Figure it out and you will be astounded at what you could save. Enough to give you a night-school course in accounting at Washington U! Just think what a wonderful thing that would be for you, son!

Tom is unmoved by the thought.

Tom. I'd rather smoke. *(He steps out on landing, letting the screen door slam.)*

Amanda *(sharply).* I know! That's the tragedy of it. . . . *(Alone, she turns to look at her husband's picture.)*

Dance music: "All the World Is Waiting for the Sunrise!"

Tom *(to the audience).* Across the alley from us was the Paradise Dance Hall. On evenings in spring the windows and doors were open and the music came outdoors. Sometimes the lights were turned out except for a large glass sphere that hung from the ceiling. It would turn slowly about and filter the dusk with delicate rainbow colors. Then the orchestra played a waltz or a tango, something that had a slow and sensuous rhythm. Couples would come outside, to the relative privacy of the alley. You could see them kissing behind ash-pits and telephone poles. This was the compensation for lives that passed like mine, without any change or adventure. Adventure and change were imminent in this year. They were waiting around the corner for all these kids. Suspended in the midst over Berchtesgaden, caught in the folds of Chamberlain's umbrella—In Spain there was Guernica! But here there was only hot swing music and liquor, dance halls, bars, and movies, and sex that hung in the gloom like a chandelier and flooded the world with brief, deceptive rainbows. . . . All the world was waiting for bombardments!

Amanda turns from the picture and comes outside.

Amanda *(sighing).* A fire-escape landings' a poor excuse for a porch. *(She spreads a newspaper on a step and sits down, gracefully and demurely as if she were settling into a swing on a Mississippi veranda.)* What are you looking at?

Tom. The moon.

Amanda. Is there a moon this evening?

Tom. It's rising over Garfinkel's Delicatessen.

Amanda. So it is! A little silver slipper of a moon. Have you made a wish on it yet?

Tom. Um-hum.

Amanda. What did you wish for?

Tom. That's a secret.

Amanda. A secret, huh? Well, I won't tell mine either. I will be just as mysterious as you.

Tom. I bet I can guess what yours is.

Amanda. Is my head so transparent?

Tom. You're not a sphinx.

Amanda. No, I don't have secrets. I'll tell you what I wished for on the moon. Success and happiness for my precious children! I wish for that whenever there's a moon, and when there isn't a moon, I wish for it, too.

Tom. I thought perhaps you wished for a gentleman caller.

Amanda. Why do you say that?

Tom. Don't you remember asking me to fetch one?

Amanda. I remember suggesting that it would be nice for your sister if you brought home some nice young man from the warehouse. I think I've made that suggestion more than once.

Tom. Yes, you have made it repeatedly.

Amanda. Well?

Tom. We are going to have one.

Amanda. *What?*

Tom. A gentleman caller!

The annunciation is celebrated with music. Amanda rises.

(Image on Screen: Caller With Bouquet.)

Amanda. You mean you have asked some nice young man to come over?

Tom. Yep. I've asked him to dinner.

Amanda. You really did?

Tom. I did!

Amanda. You did, and did he—*accept?*

Tom. He did!

Amanda. Well, well—well, well! That's—lovely!

Tom. I thought that you would be pleased.

Amanda. It's definite, then?

Tom. Very definite.

Amanda. Soon?

Tom. Very soon.

Amanda. For heaven's sake, stop putting on and tell me some things, will you?

Tom. What things do you want me to tell you?

Amanda. *Naturally* I would like to know when he's *coming!*

Tom. He's coming tomorrow.

Amanda. *Tomorrow?*

Tom. Yep. Tomorrow.

Amanda. But, Tom!

Tom.   Yes, Mother?

Amanda.   Tomorrow gives me no time!

Tom.   Time for what?

Amanda.   Preparations! Why didn't you phone me at once, as soon as you asked him, the minute that he accepted? Then, don't you see, I could have been getting ready!

Tom.   You don't have to make any fuss.

Amanda.   Oh, Tom, Tom, Tom, of course I have to make a fuss! I want things nice, not sloppy! Not thrown together. I'll certainly have to do some fast thinking, won't I?

Tom.   I don't see why you have to think at all.

Amanda.   You just don't know. We can't have a gentleman caller in a pig-sty! All my wedding silver has to be polished, the monogrammed table linen ought to be laundered! The windows have to be washed and fresh curtains put up. And how about clothes? We have to *wear* something, don't we?

Tom.   Mother, this boy is no one to make a fuss over!

Amanda.   Do you realize he's the first young man we've introduced to your sister? It's terrible, dreadful, disgraceful that poor little sister has never received a single gentleman caller! Tom, come inside! *(She opens the screen door.)*

Tom.   What for?

Amanda.   I want to ask you some things.

Tom.   If you're going to make such a fuss, I'll call it off, I'll tell him not to come.

Amanda.   You certainly won't do anything of the kind. Nothing offends people worse than broken engagements. It simply means I'll have to work like a Turk! We won't be brilliant, but we'll pass inspection. Come on inside. *(Tom follows, groaning.)* Sit down.

Tom.   Any particular place you would like me to sit?

Amanda.   Thank heavens I've got that new sofa! I'm also making payments on a floor lamp I'll have sent out! And put the chintz covers on, they'll brighten things up! Of course I'd hoped to have these walls re-papered. . . . What is the young man's name?

Tom.   His name is O'Connor.

Amanda.   That, of course, means fish—tomorrow is Friday! I'll have that salmon loaf—with Durkee's dressing! What does he do? He works at the warehouse?

Tom.   Of course! How else would I—

Amanda.   Tom, he—doesn't drink?

Tom.   Why do you ask me that?

Amanda.   Your father *did!*

Tom.   Don't get started on that!

Amanda.   He *does* drink, then?

Tom. Not that I know of!

Amanda. Make sure, be certain! The last thing I want for my daughter's a boy who drinks!

Tom. Aren't you being a little premature? Mr. O'Connor has not yet appeared on the scene!

Amanda. But will tomorrow. To meet your sister, and what do I know about his character? Nothing! Old maids are better off than wives of drunkards!

Tom. Oh, my God!

Amanda. Be still!

Tom (*leaning forward to whisper*).   Lots of fellows meet girls whom they don't marry!

Amanda. Oh, talk sensibly, Tom—and don't be sarcastic! (*She has gotten a hairbrush.*)

Tom. What are you doing?

Amanda. I'm brushing that cow-lick down! What is this young man's position at the warehouse?

Tom (*submitting grimly to the brush and the interrogation*).   This young man's position is that of a shipping clerk, Mother.

Amanda. Sounds to me like a fairly responsible job, the sort of a job *you* would be in if you just had more *get-up*. What is his salary? Have you got any idea?

Tom. I would judge it to be approximately eighty-five dollars a month.

Amanda. Well—not princely, but—

Tom. Twenty more than I make.

Amanda. Yes, how well I know! But for a family man, eighty-five dollars a month is not much more than you can just get by on. . . .

Tom. Yes, but Mr. O'Connor is not a family man.

Amanda. He might be, mightn't he? Some time in the future?

Tom. I see. Plans and provisions.

Amanda. You are the only young man that I know of who ignores the fact that the future becomes the present, the present the past, and the past turns into everlasting regret if you don't plan for it!

Tom. I will think that over and see what I can make of it.

Amanda. Don't be supercilious with your mother! Tell me some more about this—what do you call him?

Tom. James D. O'Connor. The D. is for Delaney.

Amanda. Irish on *both* sides! *Gracious!* And doesn't drink?

Tom. Shall I call him up and ask him right this minute?

Amanda. The only way to find out about those things is to make discreet inquiries at the proper moment. When I was a girl in Blue Mountain and it was suspected that a young man drank, the girl whose attentions he had been receiving, if any girl *was,* would sometimes speak to the minister of his church, or rather her father would if her father was living, and sort of feel him out on the young man's character. That is the way such things are discreetly handled to keep a young woman from making a tragic mistake!

Tom. Then how did you happen to make a tragic mistake?

Amanda. That innocent look of your father's had everyone fooled! He *smiled*—the world was *enchanted!* No girl can do worse than put herself at the mercy of a handsome appearance! I hope that Mr. O'Connor is not too good-looking.

Tom. No, he's not too good-looking. He's covered with freckles and hasn't too much of a nose.

Amanda. He's not right-down homely, though?

Tom. Not right-down homely. Just medium homely, I'd say.

Amanda. Character's what to look for in a man.

Tom. That's what I've always said, Mother.

Amanda. You've never said anything of the kind and I suspect you would never give it a thought.

Tom. Don't be suspicious of me.

Amanda. At least I hope he's the type that's up and coming.

Tom. I think he really goes in for self-improvement.

Amanda. What reason have you to think so?

Tom. He goes to night school.

Amanda *(beaming).* Splendid! What does he do, I mean study?

Tom. Radio engineering and public speaking!

Amanda. Then he has visions of being advanced in the world! Any young man who studies public speaking is aiming to have an executive job some day! And radio engineering? A thing for the future! Both of these facts are very illuminating. Those are the sort of things that a mother should know concerning any young man who comes to call on her daughter. Seriously or—not.

Tom. One little warning. He doesn't know about Laura. I didn't let on that we had dark ulterior motives. I just said, why don't you come have dinner with us? He said okay and that was the whole conversation.

Amanda. I bet it was! You're eloquent as an oyster. However, he'll know about Laura when he gets here. When he sees how lovely and sweet and pretty she is, he'll thank his lucky stars he was asked to dinner.

Tom. Mother, you mustn't expect too much of Laura.

Amanda. What do you mean?

Tom. Laura seems all those things to you and me because she's ours and we love her. We don't even notice she's crippled any more.

Amanda. Don't say crippled! You know that I never allow that word to be used!

Tom. But face facts, Mother. She is and—that's not all—

Amanda. What do you mean "not all"?

Tom. Laura is very different from other girls.

Amanda. I think the difference is all to her advantage.

Tom. Not quite all—in the eyes of others—strangers—she's terribly shy and lives in a world of her own and those things make her seem a little peculiar to people outside the house.

Amanda. Don't say peculiar.

Tom. Face the facts. She is.

The dance-hall music changes to a tango that has a minor and somewhat ominous tone.

Amanda. In what way is she peculiar—may I ask?

Tom *(gently).* She lives in a world of her own—a world of—little glass ornaments, Mother. . . . *(Gets up. Amanda remains holding brush, looking at him, troubled.)* She plays old phonograph records and—that's about all— *(He glances at himself in the mirror and crosses to door.)*

Amanda *(sharply).* Where are you going?

Tom. I'm going to the movies. *(Out screen door.)*

Amanda. Not to the movies, every night to the movies! *(Follows quickly to screen door.)* I don't believe you always go to the movies! *(He is gone. Amanda looks worriedly after him for a moment. Then vitality and optimism return and she turns from the door. Crossing to portieres.)* Laura! Laura! *(Laura answers from kitchenette.)*

Laura. Yes, Mother.

Amanda. Let those dishes go and come in front! *(Laura appears with dish towel. Gaily.)* Laura, come here and make a wish on the moon!

Laura *(entering).* Moon—moon?

Amanda. A little silver slipper of a moon. Look over your left shoulder, Laura, and make a wish! *(Laura looks faintly puzzled as if called out of sleep. Amanda seizes her shoulders and turns her at an angle by the door.)* Now! Now, darling, *wish!*

(Image on Screen: The Moon.)

Laura. What shall I wish for, Mother?

Amanda *(her voice trembling and her eyes suddenly filling with tears).* Happiness! Good Fortune!

The violin rises and the stage dims out.

Scene VI

(Image on Screen: High School Hero.)

Tom. And so the following evening I brought Jim home to dinner. I had known Jim slightly in high school. In high school Jim was a hero. He had tremendous Irish good nature and vitality with the scrubbed and polished look of white chinaware. He seemed to move in a continual spotlight. He was a star in basketball, captain of the debating club, president of the senior class and the glee club and he sang the male lead in the annual light operas. He was always running or bounding, never just walking. He seemed always at the point of defeating the law of gravity. He was shooting with such velocity through his adolescence that you would logically expect him to arrive at nothing short of the White House by the time he was thirty. But Jim apparently ran into more interference after his graduation from Soldan. His speed had definitely slowed. Six years after he left high school he was holding a job that wasn't much better than mine.

(Image on Screen: Clerk.)

He was the only one at the warehouse with whom I was on friendly terms. I was valuable to him as someone who could remember his former glory, who had seen him win basketball games and the silver cup in debating. He knew of my secret practice of retiring to a cabinet of the washroom to work on poems when business was slack in the warehouse. He called me Shakespeare. And while the other boys in the warehouse regarded me with suspicious hostility, Jim took a humorous attitude toward me. Gradually his attitude affected the others, their hostility wore off and they also began to smile at me as people smile at an oddly fashioned dog who trots across their path at some distance.

I knew that Jim and Laura had known each other at Soldan, and I had heard Laura speak admiringly of his voice. I didn't know if Jim remembered her or not. In high school Laura had been as unobtrusive as Jim had been astonishing. If he did remember Laura, it was not as my sister, for when I asked him to dinner, he grinned and said, "You know, Shakespeare, I never thought of you as having folks!"

He was about to discover that I did. . . .

Light up stage.

(Legend on Screen: "The Accent Of A Coming Foot.")

Friday evening. It is about five o'clock of a late spring evening which comes "scattering poems in the sky."

A delicate lemony light is in the Wingfield apartment.

Amanda has worked like a Turk in preparation for the gentleman caller. The results are astonishing. The new floor lamp with its rose-silk shade is in place, a colored paper lantern conceals the broken light fixture in the ceiling, new billowing white curtains are at the windows, chintz covers are on chairs and sofa, a pair of new sofa pillows make their initial appearance.

Open boxes and tissue paper are scattered on the floor.

Laura stands in the middle with lifted arms while Amanda crouches before her, adjusting the hem of the new dress, devout and ritualistic. The dress is colored and designed by memory. The arrangement of Laura's hair is changed;

it is softer and more becoming. A fragile, unearthly prettiness has come out in Laura: she is like a piece of translucent glass touched by light, given a momentary radiance, not actual, not lasting.

Amanda *(impatiently).*   Why are you trembling?

Laura.   Mother, you've made me so nervous!

Amanda.   How have I made you nervous?

Laura.   By all this fuss! You make it seem so important!

Amanda.   I don't understand you, Laura. You couldn't be satisfied with just sitting home, and yet whenever I try to arrange something for you, you seem to resist it. *(She gets up.)* Now take a look at yourself. No, wait! Wait just a moment—I have an idea!

Laura.   What is it now?

Amanda produces two powder puffs which she wraps in handkerchiefs and stuffs in Laura's bosom.

Laura.   Mother, what are you doing?

Amanda.   They call them "Gay Deceivers"!

Laura.   I won't wear them!

Amanda.   You will!

Laura.   Why should I?

Amanda.   Because, to be painfully honest, your chest is flat.

Laura.   You make it seem like we were setting a trap.

Amanda.   All pretty girls are a trap, a pretty trap, and men expect them to be. **(Legend on Screen: "A Pretty Trap.")** Now look at yourself, young lady. This is the prettiest you will ever be! I've got to fix myself now! You're going to be surprised by your mother's appearance! *(She crosses through portieres, humming gaily.)*

Laura moves slowly to the long mirror and stares solemnly at herself.

A wind blows the white curtains inward in a slow, graceful motion and with a faint, sorrowful sighing.

Amanda *(off stage).*   It isn't dark enough yet. *(She turns slowly before the mirror with a troubled look.)*

(Legend on Screen: "This Is My Sister: Celebrate Her With Strings!")

Music.

Amanda *(laughing, off).*   I'm going to show you something. I'm going to make a spectacular appearance!

Laura.   What is it, mother?

Amanda.   Possess your soul in patience—you will see! Something I've resurrected from that old trunk! Styles haven't changed so terribly much after all. . . . *(She parts the portieres.)* Now just look at your mother! *(She wears a girlish frock of yellowed voile with a blue silk sash. She carries a bunch of jonquils—the legend of her youth is nearly revived. Feverishly.)* This is the dress in which I led the cotillion. Won the cakewalk twice at Sunset Hill, wore one spring to the Governor's ball in Jackson! See how I sashayed around the ballroom, Laura? *(She raises her skirt and does a mincing step around the room.)* I wore it on Sundays for my gentlemen callers! I had it on the day I met your father—I had malaria fever all that spring. The change of climate from East Tennessee to the Delta—weakened re-sistance—I had a little temperature all the time—not enough to be serious—just enough to make me restless and giddy! Invitations poured in—parties all over the Delta!—"Stay in bed," said Mother, "you have fever!"—but I just wouldn't.—I took quinine but kept on going, going!—Evenings, dances!—Afternoons, long, long rides! Picnics—lovely!—So lovely, that country in May.—All lacy with dogwood, literally flooded with jonquils!—That was the spring I had the craze for jonquils. Jonquils be-came an absolute obsession. Mother said, "Honey, there's no more room for jonquils." And still I kept bringing in more jonquils. Whenever, wherever I saw them, I'd say "Stop! Stop! I see jonquils!" I made the young men help me gather the jonquils! It was a joke, Amanda and her jonquils! Finally there were no more vases to hold them, every available space was filled with jonquils. No vases to hold them? All right, I'll hold them myself! And then I—*(She stops in front of the picture.) (Music)* met your father! Malaria fever and jonquils and then—this—boy. . . . *(She switches on the rose-colored lamp.)* I hope they get here before it starts to rain. *(She crosses upstage and places the jonquils in bowl on table.)* I gave your brother a little extra change so he and Mr. O'Connor could take the service car home.

Laura *(with altered look).*   What did you say his name was?
Amanda.   O'Connor.
Laura.   What is his first name?
Amanda.   I don't remember. Oh, yes, I do. It was—Jim!

Laura sways slightly and catches hold of a chair.

(Legend on Screen: "Not Jim!")

Laura *(faintly).*   Not—Jim!
Amanda.   Yes, that was it, it was Jim! I've never known a Jim that wasn't nice!

Music: ominous.

Laura.   Are you sure his name is Jim O'Connor?

Amanda.   Yes. Why?

Laura.   Is he the one that Tom used to know in high school?

Amanda.   He didn't say so. I think he just got to know him at the warehouse.

Laura.   There was a Jim O'Connor we both knew in high school—*(Then, with effort.)* If that is the one that Tom is bringing to dinner—you'll have to excuse me, I won't come to the table.

Amanda.   What sort of nonsense is this?

Laura.   You asked me once if I'd ever liked a boy. Don't you remember I showed you this boy's picture?

Amanda.   You mean the boy you showed me in the year book?

Laura.   Yes, that boy.

Amanda.   Laura, Laura, were you in love with that boy?

Laura.   I don't know, Mother. All I know is I couldn't sit at the table if it was him!

Amanda.   It won't be him! It isn't the least bit likely. But whether it is or not, you will come to the table. You will not be excused.

Laura.   I'll have to be, Mother.

Amanda.   I don't intend to humor your silliness, Laura. I've had too much from you and your brother, both! So just sit down and compose yourself till they come. Tom has forgotten his key so you'll have to let them in, when they arrive.

Laura *(panicky).*   Oh, Mother—you answer the door!

Amanda *(lightly).*   I'll be in the kitchen—busy!

Laura.   Oh, Mother, please answer the door, don't make me do it!

Amanda *(crossing into kitchenette).*   I've got to fix the dressing for the salmon. Fuss, fuss—silliness!—over a gentleman caller!

Door swings shut. Laura is left alone.

(Legend on Screen: "Terror!")

She utters a low moan and turns off the lamp—sits stiffly on the edge of the sofa, knotting her fingers together.

(Legend on Screen: "The Opening Of A Door!")

Tom and Jim appear on the fire-escape steps and climb to landing. Hearing their approach, Laura rises with a panicky gesture. She retreats to the portieres.
   The doorbell. Laura catches her breath and touches her throat. Low drums.

Amanda *(calling).*   Laura, sweetheart! The door!

Laura stares at it without moving.

Jim.   I think we just beat the rain.

Tom. Uh-huh. (*He rings again, nervously. Jim whistles and fishes for a cigarette.*)

Amanda (*very, very gaily*). Laura, that is your brother and Mr. O'Connor! Will you let them in, darling?

Laura crosses toward kitchenette door.

Laura (*breathlessly*). Mother—you go to the door!

Amanda steps out of kitchenette and stares furiously at Laura. She points imperiously at the door.

Laura. Please, please!

Amanda (*in a fierce whisper*). What is the matter with you, you silly thing?

Laura (*desperately*). Please, you answer it, *please!*

Amanda. I told you I wasn't going to humor you, Laura. Why have you chosen this moment to lose your mind?

Laura. Please, please, please, you go!

Amanda. You'll have to go to the door because I can't!

Laura (*despairingly*). I can't either!

Amanda. Why?

Laura. I'm *sick!*

Amanda. I'm sick, too—of your nonsense! Why can't you and your brother be normal people? Fantastic whims and behavior! (*Tom gives a long ring.*) Preposterous goings on! Can you give me one reason—(*Calls out lyrically.*) COMING! JUST ONE SECOND!—why should you be afraid to open a door? Now you answer it, Laura!

Laura. Oh, oh, oh . . . (*She returns through the portieres. Darts to the victrola and winds it frantically and turns it on.*)

Amanda. Laura Wingfield, you march right to that door!

Laura. Yes—yes, Mother!

A faraway, scratchy rendition of "Dardanella" softens the air and gives her strength to move through it. She slips to the door and draws it cautiously open. Tom enters with the caller, Jim O'Connor.

Tom. Laura, this is Jim. Jim this is my sister, Laura.

Jim (*stepping inside*). I didn't know that Shakespeare had a sister!

Laura (*retreating stiff and trembling from the door*). How—how do you do?

Jim (*heartily extending his hand*). Okay!

Laura touches it hesitantly with hers.

Jim. Your hand's *cold,* Laura!

Laura. Yes, well—I've been playing the victrola. . . .

Jim. Must have been playing classical music on it! You ought to play a little hot swing music to warm you up!

Laura. Excuse me—I haven't finished playing the victrola. . . .

She turns awkwardly and hurries into the front room. She pauses a second by the victrola. Then catches her breath and darts through the portieres like a frightened deer.

Jim *(grinning).* What was the matter?

Tom. Oh—with Laura? Laura is—terribly shy.

Jim. Shy, huh? It's unusual to meet a shy girl nowadays. I don't believe you ever mentioned you had a sister.

Tom. Well, now you know. I have one. Here is the *Post Dispatch.* You want a piece of it?

Jim. Uh-huh.

Tom. What piece? The comics?

Jim. Sports! *(Glances at it.)* Ole Dizzy Dean is on his bad behavior.

Tom *(uninterested).* Yeah? *(Lights cigarette and crosses back to fire-escape door.)*

Jim. Where are *you* going?

Tom. I'm going out on the terrace.

Jim *(goes after him).* You know, Shakespeare—I'm going to sell you a bill of goods!

Tom. What goods?

Jim. A course I'm taking.

Tom. Huh?

Jim. In public speaking! You and me, we're not the warehouse type.

Tom. Thanks—that's good news. But what has public speaking got to do with it?

Jim. It fits you for—executive positions!

Tom. Awww.

Jim. I tell you it's done a helluva lot for me.

(Image on Screen: Executive At Desk.)

Tom. In what respect?

Jim. In every! Ask yourself what is the difference between you an' me and men in the office down front? Brains?—No!—Ability?—No! Then what? Just one little thing—

Tom. What is that one little thing?

Jim. Primarily it amounts to—social poise! Being able to square up to people and hold your own on any social level!

Amanda *(off stage).* Tom?

Tom. Yes, Mother?

Amanda. Is that you and Mr. O'Connor?

Tom. Yes, Mother.

Amanda. Well, you just make yourselves comfortable in there.

Tom. Yes, Mother.

Amanda. Ask Mr. O'Connor if he would like to wash his hands.

Jim. Aw—no—no—thank you—I took care of that at the warehouse. Tom—

Tom. Yes?

Jim. Mr. Mendoza was speaking to me about you.

Tom. Favorably?

Jim. What do you think?

Tom. Well—

Jim. You're going to be out of a job if you don't wake up.

Tom. I am waking up—

Jim. You show no signs.

Tom. The signs are interior.

(Image on Screen: The Sailing Vessel With Jolly Roger Again.)

Tom. I'm planning to change. *(He leans over the rail speaking with quiet exhilaration. The incandescent marquees and signs of the first-run movie houses light his face from across the alley. He looks like a voyager.)* I'm right at the point of committing myself to a future that doesn't include the warehouse and Mr. Mendoza or even a night-school course in public speaking.

Jim. What are you gassing about?

Tom. I'm tired of the movies.

Jim. Movies!

Tom. Yes, movies! Look at them—*(A wave toward the marvels of Grand Avenue.)* All of those glamorous people—having adventures—hogging it all, gobbling the whole thing up! You know what happens? People go to the *movies* instead of *moving!* Hollywood characters are supposed to have all the adventures for everybody in America, while everybody in America sits in a dark room and watches them have them! Yes, until there's a war. That's when adventure becomes available to the masses! *Everyone's* dish, not only Gable's! Then the people in the dark room come out of the dark room to have some adventures themselves—Goody, goody—It's our turn now, to go to the South Sea Island—to make a safari—to be exotic, far-off—But I'm not patient. I don't want to wait till then. I'm tired of the *movies* and I am *about* to *move!*

Jim *(incredulously).* Move?

Tom. Yes.

Jim. When?

Tom. Soon!

Jim. Where? Where?

Theme three: Music seems to answer the question, while Tom thinks it over. He searches among his pockets.

Tom. I'm starting to boil inside. I know I seem dreamy, but inside—well, I'm boiling! Whenever I pick up a shoe, I shudder a little thinking how short life is and what I am doing!—Whatever that means. I know it doesn't mean shoes—except as something to wear on a traveler's feet! *(Finds paper.)* Look—

Jim. What?

Tom. I'm a member.

Jim *(reading).* The Union of Merchant Seamen.

Tom. I paid my dues this month, instead of the light bill.

Jim. You will regret it when they turn the lights off.

Tom. I won't be here.

Jim. How about your mother?

Tom. I'm like my father. The bastard son of a bastard! See how he grins? And he's been absent going on sixteen years!

Jim. You're just talking, you drip. How does your mother feel about it?

Tom. Shhh—Here comes Mother! Mother is not acquainted with my plans!

Amanda *(enters portieres).* Where are you all?

Tom. On the terrace, Mother.

They start inside. She advances to them. Tom is distinctly shocked at her appearance. Even Jim blinks a little. He is making his first contact with girlish Southern vivacity and in spite of the night-school course in public speaking is somewhat thrown off the beam by the unexpected outlay of social charm.

Certain responses are attempted by Jim but are swept aside by Amanda's gay laughter and chatter. Tom is embarrassed but after the first shock Jim reacts very warmly. Grins and chuckles, is altogether won over.

(Image on Screen: Amanda As A Girl.)

Amanda *(coyly smiling, shaking her girlish ringlets).* Well, well, well, so this is Mr. O'Connor. Introductions entirely unnecessary. I've heard so much about you from my boy. I finally said to him, Tom—good gracious!—why don't you bring this paragon to supper? I'd like to meet this nice young man at the warehouse!—Instead of just hearing him sing your praises so much! I don't know why my son is so stand-offish—that's not Southern behavior! Let's sit down and—I think we could stand a little more air in here! Tom, leave the door open. I felt a nice fresh breeze a moment ago. Where has it gone? Mmm, so warm already! And not quite summer, even. We're going to burn up when summer really gets started. However, we're having—we're having a very light supper. I think light things are better fo' this time of year. The same as light clothes are. Light clothes an' light food are what warm weather calls fo'. You know our blood gets so thick during th' winter—it takes a while fo' us to *adjust* ou'selves!—when the season changes . . . It's come so quick this year. I wasn't prepared. All of a sudden—heavens! Already summer!—I ran to the trunk an' pulled out this light dress—Terribly old! Historical almost! But feels so good—so good an' co-ol, y'know. . . .

Tom. Mother—

Amanda. Yes, honey?

Tom. How about—supper?

Amanda. Honey, you go ask Sister if supper is ready! You know that Sister is in full charge of supper! Tell her you hungry boys are waiting for it. *(To Jim.)* Have you met Laura?

Jim. She—

Amanda. Let you in? Oh, good, you've met already! It's rare for a girl as sweet an' pretty as Laura to be domestic! But Laura is, thank heavens, not only pretty but also very domestic. I'm not at all. I never was a bit. I never could make a thing but angel-food cake. Well, in the South we had so many servants. Gone, gone, gone. All vestiges of gracious living! Gone completely! I wasn't prepared for what the future brought me. All of my gentlemen callers were sons of planters and so of course I assumed that I would be married to one and raise my family on a large piece of land with plenty of servants. But man proposes—and woman accepts the proposal!—To vary that old, old saying a little bit—I married no planter! I married a man who worked for the telephone company!—that gallantly smiling gentleman over there! *(Points to the picture.)* A telephone man who—fell in love with long-distance!—Now he travels and I don't even know where!—But what am I going on for about my—tribulations? Tell me yours—I hope you don't have any! Tom?

Tom *(returning).* Yes, Mother?

Amanda. Is supper nearly ready?

Tom. It looks to me like supper is on the table.

Amanda. Let me look—*(She rises prettily and looks through portieres.)* Oh, lovely—But where is Sister?

Tom. Laura is not feeling well and she says that she thinks she'd better not come to the table.

Amanda. What?—Nonsense!—Laura? Oh, Laura!

Laura *(off stage, faintly).* Yes, Mother.

Amanda. You really must come to the table. We won't be seated until you come to the table! Come in, Mr. O'Connor. You sit over there and I'll— Laura? Laura Wingfield! You're keeping us waiting, honey! We can't say grace until you come to the table!

The back door is pushed weakly open and Laura comes in. She is obviously quite faint, her lips trembling, her eyes wide and staring. She moves unsteadily toward the table.

(Legend on Screen: "Terror!")

Outside a summer storm is coming on abruptly. The white curtains billow in-

ward at the windows and there is a sorrowful murmur and deep blue dusk. Laura suddenly stumbles—She catches at a chair with a faint moan.

Tom.   Laura!

Amanda.   Laura! *(There is a clap of thunder.)* **(Legend on Screen: "Ah!")** *(Despairingly.)* Why, Laura, you are sick, darling! Tom, help your sister into the living room, dear! Sit in the living room, Laura—rest on the sofa. Well! *(To the gentleman caller.)* Standing over the hot stove made her ill!—I told her that it was just too warm this evening, but—*(Tom comes back in. Laura is on the sofa.)* Is Laura all right now?

Tom.   Yes.

Amanda.   What *is* that? Rain? A nice cool rain has come up! *(She gives the gentleman caller a frightened look.)* I think we may—have grace—now . . . *(Tom looks at her stupidly.)* Tom, honey—you say grace!

Tom.   Oh . . . "For these and all thy mercies—" *(They bow their heads, Amanda stealing a nervous glance at Jim. In the living room Laura, stretched on the sofa, clenches her hand to her lips, to hold back a shuddering sob.)* God's Holy Name be praised—

The scene dims out.

Scene VII

(A Souvenir.)

Half an hour later. Dinner is just being finished in the upstage area which is concealed by the drawn portieres.

As the curtain rises Laura is still huddled upon the sofa, her feet drawn under her, her head resting on a pale blue pillow, her eyes wide and mysteriously watchful. The new floor lamp with its shade of rose-colored silk gives a soft, becoming light to her face, bringing out the fragile, unearthly prettiness which usually escapes attention. There is a steady murmur of rain, but it is slackening and stops soon after the scene begins; the air outside becomes pale and luminous as the moon breaks out.

A moment after the curtain rises, the lights in both rooms flicker and go out.

Jim.   Hey, there, Mr. Light Bulb!

Amanda laughs nervously.

(Legend on Screen: "Suspension Of A Public Service.")

Amanda.   Where was Moses when the lights went out? Ha-ha. Do you know the answer to that one, Mr. O'Connor?

Jim.   No, Ma'am, what's the answer?

Amanda. In the dark! *(Jim laughs appreciatively.)* Everybody sit still. I'll light the candles. Isn't it lucky we have them on the table? Where's a match? Which of you gentlemen can provide a match?

Jim. Here.

Amanda. Thank you, sir.

Jim. Not at all, Ma'am!

Amanda. I guess the fuse has burnt out. Mr. O'Connor, can you tell a burnt-out fuse? I know I can't and Tom is a total loss when it comes to mechanics. *(Sound: getting up: voices recede a little to kitchenette.)* Oh, be careful you don't bump into something. We don't want our gentleman caller to break his neck. Now wouldn't that be a fine howdy-do?

Jim. Ha-ha! Where is the fuse-box?

Amanda. Right here next to the stove. Can you see anything?

Jim. Just a minute.

Amanda. Isn't electricity a mysterious thing? Wasn't it Benjamin Franklin who tied a key to a kite? We live in such a mysterious universe, don't we? Some people say that science clears up all the mysteries for us. In my opinion it only creates more! Have you found it yet?

Jim. No, Ma'am. All these fuses look okay to me.

Amanda. Tom!

Tom. Yes, Mother?

Amanda. That light bill I gave you several days ago. The one I told you we got the notices about?

Tom. Oh.—Yeah.

(Legend on Screen: "Ha!")

Amanda. You didn't neglect to pay it by any chance?

Tom. Why, I—

Amanda. Didn't! I might have known it!

Jim. Shakespeare probably wrote a poem on that light bill, Mrs. Wingfield.

Amanda. I might have known better than to trust him with it! There's such a high price for negligence in this world!

Jim. Maybe the poem will win a ten-dollar prize.

Amanda. We'll just have to spend the remainder of the evening in the nineteenth century, before Mr. Edison made the Mazda lamp!

Jim. Candlelight is my favorite kind of light.

Amanda. That shows you're romantic! But that's no excuse for Tom. Well, we got through dinner. Very considerate of them to let us get through dinner before they plunged us into everlasting darkness, wasn't it, Mr. O'Connor?

Jim. Ha-ha!

Amanda. Tom, as a penalty for your carelessness you can help me with the dishes.

Jim. Let me give you a hand.

Amanda. Indeed you will not!

Jim. I ought to be good for something.

Amanda. Good for something? *(Her tone is rhapsodic.)* You? Why, Mr. O'Connor, nobody, *nobody's* given me this much entertainment in years—as you have!

Jim. Aw, now, Mrs. Wingfield!

Amanda. I'm not exaggerating, not one bit! But Sister is all by her lonesome. You go keep her company in the parlor! I'll give you this lovely old candelabrum that used to be on the altar at the church of the Heavenly Rest. It was melted a little out of shape when the church burnt down. Lightning struck it one spring. Gypsy Jones was holding a revival at the time and he intimated that the church was destroyed because the Episcopalians gave card parties.

Jim. Ha-ha.

Amanda. And how about coaxing Sister to drink a little wine? I think it would be good for her! Can you carry both at once?

Jim. Sure. I'm Superman!

Amanda. Now, Thomas, get into this apron!

The door of kitchenette swings closed on Amanda's gay laughter; the flickering light approaches the portieres.

Laura sits up nervously as he enters. Her speech at first is low and breathless from the almost intolerable strain of being alone with a stranger.

(Legend on Screen: "I Don't Suppose You Remember Me At All!")

In her first speeches in this scene, before Jim's warmth overcomes her paralyzing shyness, Laura's voice is thin and breathless as though she has run up a steep flight of stairs.

Jim's attitude is gently humorous. In playing this scene it should be stressed that while the incident is apparently unimportant, it is to Laura the climax of her secret life.

Jim. Hello, there, Laura.

Laura *(faintly).* Hello. *(She clears her throat.)*

Jim. How are you feeling now? Better?

Laura. Yes. Yes, thank you.

Jim. This is for you. A little dandelion wine. *(He extends it toward her with extravagant gallantry.)*

Laura. Thank you.

Jim. Drink it—but don't get drunk! *(He laughs heartily. Laura takes the glass uncertainly; laughs shyly.)* Where shall I set the candles?

Laura. Oh—oh, anywhere . . .

Jim. How about here on the floor? Any objections?

Laura. No.

Jim. I'll spread a newspaper under to catch the drippings. I like to sit on the floor. Mind if I do?

Laura. Oh, no.

Jim. Give me a pillow?

Laura. What?

Jim. A pillow!

Laura. Oh . . . *(Hands him one quickly.)*

Jim. How about you? Don't you like to sit on the floor?

Laura. Oh—yes.

Jim. Why don't you, then?

Laura. I—will.

Jim. Take a pillow! *(Laura does. Sits on the other side of the candelabrum. Jim crosses his legs and smiles engagingly at her.)* I can't hardly see you sitting way over there.

Laura. I can—see you.

Jim. I know, but that's not fair, I'm in the limelight. *(Laura moves her pillow closer.)* Good! Now I can see you! Comfortable?

Laura. Yes.

Jim. So am I. Comfortable as a cow. Will you have some gum?

Laura. No, thank you.

Jim. I think that I will indulge, with your permission. *(Musingly unwraps it and holds it up.)* Think of the fortune made by the guy that invented the first piece of chewing gum. Amazing, huh? The Wrigley Building is one of the sights of Chicago—I saw it summer before last when I went up to the Century of Progress. Did you take in the Century of Progress?

Laura. No, I didn't.

Jim. Well, it was quite a wonderful exposition. What impressed me most was the Hall of Science. Gives you an idea of what the future will be in America, even more wonderful than the present time is! *(Pause. Smiling at her.)* Your brother tells me you're shy. Is that right, Laura?

Laura. I—don't know.

Jim. I judge you to be an old-fashioned type of girl. Well, I think that's a pretty good type to be. Hope you don't think I'm being too personal—do you?

Laura *(hastily, out of embarrassment).* I believe I will take a piece of gum, if you—don't mind. *(Clearing her throat.)* Mr. O'Connor, have you—kept up with your singing?

Jim. Singing? Me?

Laura. Yes. I remember what a beautiful voice you had.

Jim. When did you hear me sing?

Voice offstage in the pause.

Voice *(offstage).*
    O blow, ye winds, heigh-ho,

A-roving I will go!
I'm off to my love
With a boxing glove—
Ten thousand miles away!

Jim. You say you've heard me sing?

Laura. Oh, yes! Yes, very often . . . I—don't suppose you remember me—at all?

Jim (*smiling doubtfully*). You know I have an idea I've seen you before. I had that idea soon as you opened the door. It seemed almost like I was about to remember your name. But the name that I started to call you—wasn't a name! And so I stopped myself before I said it.

Laura. Wasn't it—Blue Roses?

Jim (*springs up, grinning*). Blue Roses! My gosh, yes—Blue Roses! That's what I had on my tongue when you opened the door! Isn't it funny what tricks your memory plays? I didn't connect you with the high school somehow or other. But that's where it was; it was high school. I didn't even know you were Shakespeare's sister! Gosh, I'm sorry.

Laura. I didn't expect you to. You—barely knew me!

Jim. But we did have a speaking acquaintance, huh?

Laura. Yes, we—spoke to each other.

Jim. When did you recognize me?

Laura. Oh, right away!

Jim. Soon as I came in the door?

Laura. When I heard your name I thought it was probably you. I knew that Tom used to know you a little in high school. So when you came in the door—Well, then I was—sure.

Jim. Why didn't you *say* something, then?

Laura (*breathlessly*). I didn't know what to say, I was—too surprised!

Jim. For goodness' sakes! You know, this sure is funny!

Laura. Yes! Yes, isn't it, though . . .

Jim. Didn't we have a class in something together?

Laura. Yes, we did.

Jim. What class was that?

Laura. It was—singing—Chorus!

Jim. Aw!

Laura. I sat across the aisle from you in the Aud.

Jim. Aw.

Laura. Mondays, Wednesdays and Fridays.

Jim. Now I remember—you always came in late.

Laura. Yes, it was so hard for me, getting upstairs. I had that brace on my leg—it clumped so loud!

Jim. I never heard any clumping.

Laura (*wincing at the recollection*). To me it sounded like—thunder!

Jim. Well, well, well. I never even noticed.

Laura. And everybody was seated before I came in. I had to walk in front of all those people. My seat was in the back row. I had to go clumping all the way up the aisle with everyone watching!

Jim. You shouldn't have been self-conscious.

Laura. I know, but I was. It was always such a relief when the singing started.

Jim. Aw, yes, I've placed you now! I used to call you Blue Roses. How was it that I got started calling you that?

Laura. I was out of school a little while with pleurosis. When I came back you asked me what was the matter. I said I had pleurosis—you thought I said Blue Roses. That's what you always called me after that!

Jim. I hope you didn't mind.

Laura. Oh, no—I liked it. You see, I wasn't acquainted with many—people. . . .

Jim. As I remember you sort of stuck by yourself.

Laura. I—I—never had much luck at—making friends.

Jim. I don't see why you wouldn't.

Laura. Well, I—started out badly.

Jim. You mean being—

Laura. Yes, it sort of—stood between me—

Jim. You shouldn't have let it!

Laura. I know, but it did, and—

Jim. You were shy with people!

Laura. I tried not to be but never could—

Jim. Overcome it?

Laura. No, I—I never could!

Jim. I guess being shy is something you have to work out of kind of gradually.

Laura (*sorrowfully*). Yes—I guess it—

Jim. Takes time!

Laura. Yes—

Jim. People are not so dreadful when you know them. That's what you have to remember! And everybody has problems, not just you, but practically everybody has got some problems. You think of yourself as having the only problems, as being the only one who is disappointed. But just look around you and you will see lots of people as disappointed as you are. For instance, I hoped when I was going to high school that I would be further along at this time, six years later, than I am now—You remember that wonderful write-up I had in *The Torch?*

Laura. Yes! (*She rises and crosses to table.*)

Jim. It said I was bound to succeed in anything I went into! (*Laura returns with the annual.*) Holy Jeez! *The Torch!* (*He accepts it reverently. They smile across it with mutual wonder. Laura crouches beside him and they begin to turn through it. Laura's shyness is dissolving in his warmth.*)

Laura. Here you are in *Pirates of Penzance!*

Jim (*wistfully*). I sang the baritone lead in that operetta.

Laura (*rapidly*). So—beautifully!

Jim *(protesting).*   Aw—

Laura.   Yes, yes—beautifully—beautifully!

Jim.   You heard me?

Laura.   All three times!

Jim.   No!

Laura.   Yes!

Jim.   All three performances?

Laura *(looking down).*   Yes.

Jim.   Why?

Laura.   I—wanted to ask you to—autograph my program.

Jim.   Why didn't you ask me to?

Laura.   You were always surrounded by your own friends so much that I never had a chance to.

Jim.   You should have just—

Laura.   Well, I—thought you might think I was—

Jim.   Thought I might think you was—what?

Laura.   Oh—

Jim *(with reflective relish).*   I was beleaguered by females in those days.

Laura.   You were terribly popular!

Jim.   Yeah—

Laura.   You had such a—friendly way—

Jim.   I was spoiled in high school.

Laura.   Everybody—liked you!

Jim.   Including you?

Laura.   I—yes, I—I did, too—*(She gently closes the book in her lap.)*

Jim.   Well, well, well!—Give me that program, Laura. *(She hands it to him. He signs it with a flourish.)* There you are—better late than never!

Laura.   Oh, I—what a—surprise!

Jim.   My signature isn't worth very much right now. But some day—maybe—it will increase in value! Being disappointed is one thing and being discouraged is something else. I am disappointed but I'm not discouraged. I'm twenty-three years old. How old are you?

Laura.   I'll be twenty-four in June.

Jim.   That's not old age!

Laura.   No, but—

Jim.   You finished high school?

Laura *(with difficulty).*   I didn't go back.

Jim.   You mean you dropped out?

Laura.   I made bad grades in my final examinations. *(She rises and replaces the book and the program. Her voice strained.)* How is—Emily Meisenbach getting along?

Jim.   Oh, that kraut-head!

Laura.   Why do you call her that?

Jim.   That's what she was.

Laura.   You're not still—going with her?

Jim. I never see her.

Laura. It said in the Personal Section that you were—engaged!

Jim. I know, but I wasn't impressed by that—propaganda!

Laura. It wasn't—the truth?

Jim. Only in Emily's optimistic opinion!

Laura. Oh—

(Legend on Screen: "What Have You Done Since High School?")

Jim lights a cigarette and leans indolently back on his elbows smiling at Laura with a warmth and charm which light her inwardly with altar candles. She remains by the table and turns in her hands a piece of glass to cover her tumult.

Jim *(after several reflective puffs on a cigarette).* What have you done since high school? *(She seems not to hear him.)* Huh? *(Laura looks up.)* I said what have you done since high school, Laura?

Laura. Nothing much.

Jim. You must have been doing something these six long years.

Laura. Yes.

Jim. Well, then, such as what?

Laura. I took a business course at business college—

Jim. How did that work out?

Laura. Well, not very—well—I had to drop out, it gave me—indigestion—

Jim laughs gently.

Jim. What are you doing now?

Laura. I don't do anything—much. Oh, please don't think I sit around doing nothing! My glass collection takes up a good deal of my time. Glass is something you have to take good care of.

Jim. What did you say—about glass?

Laura. Collection I said—I have one—*(She clears her throat and turns away again, acutely shy).*

Jim *(abruptly).* You know what I judge to be the trouble with you? Inferiority complex! Know what that is? That's what they call it when someone low-rates himself! I understand it because I had it, too. Although my case was not so aggravated as yours seems to be. I had it until I took up public speaking, developed my voice, and learned that I had an aptitude for science. Before that time I never thought of myself as being outstanding in any way whatsoever! Now I've never made a regular study of it, but I have a friend who says I can analyze people better than doctors that make a profession of it. I don't claim that to be necessarily true, but I can sure guess a person's psychology, Laura! *(Takes out his gum.)* Excuse me, Laura. I always take it out when the flavor is gone. I'll use this scrap of paper to wrap it in. I know how it is to get it stuck on a shoe. Yep—that's what I judge to be your principal trouble. A lack of confidence in yourself as a person. You don't have the proper amount of faith in yourself. I'm basing that fact on a number of your remarks and also on certain observations I've made. For instance that clumping you thought was so awful in high school. You say that you even dreaded to walk into class. You see what you did? You dropped out of school, you gave up an education because of a clump, which as far as I know was practically non-existent! A little physical defect is what you have. Hardly noticeable even! Magnified thousands of times by imagination! You know what my strong advice to you is? Think of yourself as *superior* in some way!

Laura. In what way would I think?

Jim. Why, man alive, Laura! Just look about you a little. What do you see? A world full of common people! All of 'em born and all of 'em going to die! Which of them has one-tenth of your good points! Or mine! Or anyone else's, as far as that goes—Gosh! Everybody excels in some one thing. Some in many! *(Unconsciously glances at himself in the mirror.)* All you've got to do is discover in *what!* Take me, for instance. *(He adjusts his tie at the mirror).* My interest happens to lie in electro-dynamics. I'm taking a course in radio engineering at night school, Laura, on top of a fairly responsible job at the warehouse. I'm taking that course and studying public speaking.

Laura. Ohhhh.

Jim. Because I believe in the future of television! *(Turning back to her.)* I wish to be ready to go up right along with it. Therefore I'm planning to get in on the ground floor. In fact, I've already made the right connections and all that remains is for the industry itself to get under way! Full steam—*(His eyes are starry.)* Knowledge—Zzzzzp! Money—Zzzzzzp!—Power! That's the cycle democracy is built on! *(His attitude is convincingly dynamic. Laura stares at him, even her shyness eclipsed in her absolute wonder. He suddenly grins.)* I guess you think I think a lot of myself!

Laura. No—o-o-o, I—

Jim. Now how about you? Isn't there something you take more interest in than anything else?

Laura. Well, I do—as I said—have my—glass collection—

A peal of girlish laughter from the kitchen.

Jim. I'm not right sure I know what you're talking about. What kind of glass is it?

Laura. Little articles of it, they're ornaments mostly! Most of them are little animals made out of glass, the tiniest little animals in the world. Mother calls them a glass menagerie! Here's an example of one, if you'd like to see it! This one is one of the oldest. It's nearly thirteen. *(He stretches out his hand.)* *(Music: "The Glass Menagerie.")* Oh, be careful—if you breathe, it breaks!

Jim. I'd better not take it. I'm pretty clumsy with things.

Laura. Go on, I trust you with him! *(Places it in his palm.)* There now—you're holding him gently! Hold him over the light, he loves the light! You see how the light shines through him?

Jim. It sure does shine!

Laura. I shouldn't be partial, but he is my favorite one.

Jim. What kind of a thing is this one supposed to be?

Laura. Haven't you noticed the single horn on his forehead?

Jim. A unicorn, huh?

Laura. Mmm-hmmm!

Jim. Unicorns, aren't they extinct in the modern world?

Laura. I know!

Jim. Poor little fellow, he must feel sort of lonesome.

Laura *(smiling).* Well, if he does he doesn't complain about it. He stays on a shelf with some horses that don't have horns and all of them seem to get along nicely together.

Jim. How do you know?

Laura *(lightly).* I haven't heard any arguments among them!

Jim *(grinning).* No arguments, huh? Well, that's a pretty good sign! Where shall I set him?

Laura. Put him on the table. They all like a change of scenery once in a while!

Jim *(stretching).* Well, well, well, well—Look how big my shadow is when I stretch!

Laura. Oh, oh, yes—it stretches across the ceiling!

Jim *(crossing to door).* I think it's stopped raining. *(Opens fire-escape door.)* Where does the music come from?

Laura. From the Paradise Dance Hall across the alley.

Jim. How about cutting the rug a little, Miss Wingfield?

Laura. Oh, I—

Jim. Or is your program filled up? Let me have a look at it. *(Grasps imaginary card.)* Why, every dance is taken! I'll just have to scratch some out. *(Waltz music: "La Golondrina.")* Ahhh, a waltz! *(He executes some sweeping turns by himself, then holds his arms toward Laura.)*

Laura *(breathlessly).* I—can't dance!

Jim. There you go, that inferiority stuff!

Laura. I've never danced in my life!

Jim. Come on, try!

Laura. Oh, but I'd step on you!

Jim. I'm not made out of glass.

Laura. How—how—how do we start?

Jim. Just leave it to me. You hold your arms out a little.

Laura. Like this?

Jim. A little bit higher. Right. Now don't tighten up, that's the main thing about it—relax.

Laura *(laughing breathlessly).* It's hard not to.

Jim. Okay.

Laura. I'm afraid you can't budge me.

Jim. What do you bet I can't? *(He swings her into motion.)*

Laura. Goodness, yes, you can!

Jim. Let yourself go, now, Laura, just let yourself go.

Laura. I'm—

Jim. Come on!

Laura. Trying!

Jim. Not so stiff—Easy does it!

Laura. I know but I'm—

Jim. Loosen th' backbone! There now, that's a lot better.

Laura. Am I?

Jim. Lots, lots better! *(He moves her about the room in a clumsy waltz.)*

Laura. Oh, my!

Jim. Ha-ha!

Laura. Goodness, yes you can!

Jim. Ha-ha-ha! *(They suddenly bump into the table. Jim stops.)* What did we hit on?

Laura. Table.

Jim. Did something fall off it? I think—

Laura. Yes.

Jim. I hope that it wasn't the little glass horse with the horn!

Laura. Yes.

Jim. Aw, aw, aw. Is it broken?

Laura. Now it is just like all the other horses.

Jim. It's lost its—

Laura. Horn! It doesn't matter. Maybe it's a blessing in disguise.

Jim. You'll never forgive me. I bet that that was your favorite piece of glass.

Laura. I don't have favorites much. It's no tragedy, Freckles. Glass breaks so easily. No matter how careful you are. The traffic jars the shelves and things fall off them.

Jim. Still I'm awfully sorry that I was the cause.

Laura *(smiling).* I'll just imagine he had an operation. The horn was removed to make him feel less—freakish! *(They both laugh.)* Now he will feel more at home with the other horses, the ones that don't have horns . . .

Jim. Ha-ha, that's very funny! *(Suddenly serious.)* I'm glad to see that you have a sense of humor. You know—you're—well—very different! Surprisingly different from anyone else I know! *(His voice becomes soft and hesitant with a genuine feeling.)* Do you mind me telling you that? *(Laura is abashed beyond speech.)* You make me feel sort of—I don't know how to put it! I'm usually pretty good at expressing things, but—This is something that I don't know how to say! *(Laura touches her throat and clears it—turns the broken unicorn in her hands.)* *(Even softer.)* Has anyone ever told you that you were pretty? *(Pause: music.)* *(Laura looks up slowly, with wonder, and shakes her head.)* Well, you are! In a very different way from anyone else. And all the nicer, because of the difference, too. *(His voice* *becomes low and husky. Laura turns away, nearly faint with the novelty of her emotions.)* I wish that you were my sister. I'd teach you to have some confidence in yourself. The different people are not like other people, but being different is nothing to be ashamed of. Because other people are not such wonderful people. They're one hundred times one thousand. You're one times one! They walk all over the earth. You just stay here. They're common as—weeds, but—you—well, you're—*Blue Roses!*

(Image on Screen: Blue Roses.)

Music changes.

Laura.   But blue is wrong for—roses . . .
Jim.   It's right for you—You're—pretty!
Laura.   In what respect am I pretty?
Jim.   In all respects—believe me! Your eyes—your hair—are pretty! Your hands are pretty! *(He catches hold of her hand.)* You think I'm making this up because I'm invited to dinner and have to be nice. Oh, I could do that! I could put on an act for you, Laura, and say lots of things without being very sincere. But this time I am. I'm talking to you sincerely. I happened to notice you had this inferiority complex that keeps you from feeling comfortable with people. Somebody needs to build your confidence up and make you proud instead of shy and turning away and—blushing—Somebody ought to—Ought to—*kiss you, Laura! (His hand slips slowly up her arm to her shoulder.) (Music swells tumultuously.) (He suddenly turns her about and kisses her on the lips. When he releases her Laura sinks on the sofa with a bright, dazed look. Jim backs away and fishes in his pocket for a cigarette.)* **(Legend on Screen: "Souvenir.")** Stumble-john! *(He lights the cigarette, avoiding her look. There is a peal of girlish laughter from Amanda in the kitchen. Laura slowly raises and opens her hand. It still contains the little broken glass animal. She looks at it with a tender, bewildered expression.)* Stumble-john! I shouldn't have done that—That was way off the beam. You don't smoke, do you? *(She looks up, smiling, not hearing the question. He sits beside her a little gingerly. She looks at him speechlessly—waiting. He coughs decorously and moves a little farther aside as he considers the situation and senses her feelings, dimly, with perturbation. Gently.)* Would you—care for a—mint? *(She doesn't seem to hear him but her look grows brighter even.)* Peppermint—Life Saver? My pocket's a regular drug store—wherever I go . . . *(He pops a mint in his mouth. Then gulps and decides to make a clean breast of it. He speaks slowly and gingerly.)* Laura, you know, if I had a sister like you, I'd do the same thing as Tom. I'd bring out fellows—introduce her to them. The right type of boys of a type to—appreciate her. Only—well—he made a mistake about me. Maybe I've got no call to be saying this. That may not have been the idea in having me over. But what if it was? There's nothing

wrong about that. The only trouble is that in my case—I'm not in a situation to—do the right thing. I can't take down your number and say I'll phone. I can't call up next week and—ask for a date. I thought I had better explain the situation in case you misunderstood it and—I hurt your feelings. . . . *(Pause. Slowly, very slowly, Laura's look changes, her eyes returning slowly from his to the ornament in her palm.)*

Amanda utters another gay laugh in the kitchen.

Laura *(faintly).*   You—won't—call again?
Jim.   No, Laura, I can't. *(He rises from the sofa.)* As I was just explaining, I've—got strings on me, Laura, I've—been going steady! I go out all the time with a girl named Betty. She's a home-girl like you, and Catholic, and Irish, and in a great many ways we—get along fine. I met her last summer on a moonlight boat trip up the river to Alton, on the *Majestic.* Well—right away from the start it was—love! **(Legend on Screen: Love!)** *(Laura sways slightly forward and grips the arm of the sofa. He fails to notice, now enrapt in his own comfortable being.)* Being in love has made a new man of me! *(Leaning stiffly forward, clutching the arm of the sofa, Laura struggles visibly with her storm. But Jim is oblivious, she is a long way off.)* The power of love is really pretty tremendous! Love is something that—changes the whole world, Laura! *(The storm abates a little and Laura leans back. He notices her again.)* It happened that Betty's aunt took sick, she got a wire and had to go to Centralia. So Tom—when he asked me to dinner—I naturally just accepted the invitation, not knowing that you—that he—that I—*(He stops awkwardly.)* Huh—I'm a stumble-john! *(He flops back on the sofa. The holy candles in the altar of Laura's face have been snuffed out! There is a look of almost infinite desolation. Jim glances at her uneasily.)* I wish that you would—say something. *(She bites her lip which was trembling and then bravely smiles. She opens her hand again on the broken glass ornament. Then she gently takes his hand and raises it level with her own. She carefully places the unicorn in the palm of his hand, then pushes his fingers closed upon it.)* What are you—doing that for? You want me to have him?—Laura? *(She nods.)* What for?
Laura.   A—souvenir . . .

She rises unsteadily and crouches beside the victrola to wind it up.

(Legend on Screen: "Things Have A Way Of Turning Out So Badly.")

(Or Image: "Gentleman Caller Waving Good-bye!—Gaily.")

At this moment Amanda rushes brightly back in the front room. She bears a pitcher of fruit punch in an old-fashioned cut-glass pitcher and a plate of macaroons. The plate has a gold border and poppies painted on it.

Amanda. Well, well, well! Isn't the air delightful after the shower? I've made you children a little liquid refreshment. *(Turns gaily to the gentleman caller.)* Jim, do you know that song about lemonade?

"Lemonade, lemonade
Made in the shade and stirred with a spade—
Good enough for any old maid!"

Jim *(uneasily).* Ha-ha! No—I never heard it.

Amanda. Why, Laura! You look so serious!

Jim. We were having a serious conversation.

Amanda. Good! Now you're better acquainted!

Jim *(uncertainly).* Ha-ha! Yes.

Amanda. You modern young people are much more serious-minded than my generation. I was so gay as a girl!

Jim. You haven't changed, Mrs. Wingfield.

Amanda. Tonight I'm rejuvenated! The gaiety of the occasion, Mr. O'Connor! *(She tosses her head with a peal of laughter. Spills lemonade.)* Oooo! I'm baptizing myself!

Jim. Here—let me—

Amanda *(setting the pitcher down).* There now. I discovered we had some maraschino cherries. I dumped them in, juice and all!

Jim. You shouldn't have gone to that trouble, Mrs. Wingfield.

Amanda. Trouble, trouble? Why it was loads of fun! Didn't you hear me cutting up in the kitchen? I bet your ears were burning! I told Tom how outdone with him I was for keeping you to himself so long a time! He should have brought you over much, much sooner! Well, now that you've found your way, I want you to be a very frequent caller! Not just occasional but all the time. Oh, we're going to have a lot of gay times together! I see them coming! Mmm, just breathe that air! So fresh, and the moon's so pretty! I'll skip back out—I know where my place is when young folks are having a—serious conversation!

Jim. Oh, don't go out. Mrs. Wingfield. The fact of the matter is I've got to be going.

Amanda. Going, now? You're joking! Why, it's only the shank of the evening, Mr. O'Connor!

Jim. Well, you know how it is.

Amanda. You mean you're a young workingman and have to keep workingmen's hours. We'll let you off early tonight. But only on the condition that next time you stay later. What's the best night for you? Isn't Saturday night the best night for you workingmen?

Jim. I have a couple of time-clocks to punch, Mrs. Wingfield. One at morning, another one at night!

Amanda. My, but you *are* ambitious! You work at night, too?

Jim. No, Ma'am, not work but—Betty! *(He crosses deliberately to pick up his* *hat. The band at the Paradise Dance Hall goes into a tender waltz.)*

Amanda. Betty? Betty? Who's—Betty! *(There is an ominous cracking sound in the sky.)*

Jim. Oh, just a girl. The girl I go steady with! *(He smiles charmingly. The sky falls.)*

(Legend on Screen: "The Sky Falls.")

Amanda *(a long-drawn exhalation).* Ohhhh . . . Is it a serious romance, Mr. O'Connor?

Jim. We're going to be married the second Sunday in June.

Amanda. Ohhhh—how nice! Tom didn't mention that you were engaged to be married.

Jim. The cat's not out of the bag at the warehouse yet. You know how they are. They call you Romeo and stuff like that. *(He stops at the oval mirror to put on his hat. He carefully shapes the brim and the crown to give a discreetly dashing effect.)* It's been a wonderful evening, Mrs. Wingfield. I guess this is what they mean by Southern hospitality.

Amanda. It really wasn't anything at all.

Jim. I hope it don't seem like I'm rushing off. But I promised Betty I'd pick her up at the Wabash depot, an' by the time I get my jalopy down there her train'll be in. Some women are pretty upset if you keep 'em waiting.

Amanda. Yes, I know—The tyranny of women! *(Extends her hand.)* Goodbye, Mr. O'Connor. I wish you luck—and happiness—and success! All three of them, and so does Laura!—Don't you, Laura?

Laura. Yes!

Jim *(taking her hand).* Goodbye, Laura. I'm certainly going to treasure that souvenir. And don't you forget the good advice I gave you. *(Raises his voice to a cheery shout.)* So long, Shakespeare! Thanks again, ladies— Good night!

He grins and ducks jauntily out.
    Still bravely grimacing, Amanda closes the door on the gentleman caller. Then she turns back to the room with a puzzled expression. She and Laura don't dare to face each other. Laura crouches beside the victrola to wind it.

Amanda *(faintly).* Things have a way of turning out so badly. I don't believe that I would play the victrola. Well, well—well—Our gentleman caller was engaged to be married! Tom!

Tom *(from back).* Yes, Mother?

Amanda. Come in here a minute. I want to tell you something awfully funny.

Tom *(enters with macaroon and a glass of the lemonade).* Has the gentleman caller gotten away already?

Amanda. The gentleman caller has made an early departure. What a wonderful joke you played on us!

Tom.   How do you mean?

Amanda.   You didn't mention that he was engaged to be married.

Tom.   Jim? Engaged?

Amanda.   That's what he just informed us.

Tom.   I'll be jiggered! I didn't know about that.

Amanda.   That seems very peculiar.

Tom.   What's peculiar about it?

Amanda.   Didn't you call him your best friend down at the warehouse?

Tom.   He is, but how did I know?

Amanda.   It seems extremely peculiar that you wouldn't know your best friend was going to be married!

Tom.   The warehouse is where I work, not where I know things about people!

Amanda.   You don't know things anywhere! You live in a dream; you manufacture illusions! *(He crosses to door.)* Where are you going?

Tom.   I'm going to the movies.

Amanda.   That's right, now that you've had us make such fools of ourselves. The effort, the preparations, all the expense! The new floor lamp, the rug, the clothes for Laura! All for what? To entertain some other girl's fiancé! Go to the movies, go! Don't think about us, a mother deserted, an unmarried sister who's crippled and has no job! Don't let anything interfere with your selfish pleasure! Just go, go, go—to the movies!

Tom.   All right, I will! The more you shout about my selfishness to me the quicker I'll go, and I won't go to the movies!

Amanda.   Go, then! Then go to the moon—you selfish dreamer!

Tom smashes his glass on the floor. He plunges out on the fire-escape, slamming the door. Laura screams.

Dance-hall music up. Tom goes to the rail and grips it desperately, lifting his face in the chill white moonlight penetrating the narrow abyss of the alley.

(Legend on Screen: "And So Good-bye. . .")

Tom's closing speech is timed with the interior pantomime. The interior scene is played as though viewed through soundproof glass. Amanda appears to be making a comforting speech to Laura who is huddled upon the sofa. Now that we cannot hear the mother's speech, her silliness is gone and she has dignity and tragic beauty. Laura's dark hair hides her face until at the end of the speech she lifts it to smile at her mother. Amanda's gestures are slow and graceful, almost dancelike, as she comforts her daughter. At the end of her speech she glances a moment at the father's picture—then withdraws through the portieres. At close of Tom's speech, Laura blows out the candles, ending the play.

Tom.   I didn't go to the moon, I went much further—for time is the longest distance between two places—Not long after that I was fired for writing a poem on the lid of a shoe-box. I left Saint Louis. I descended the steps of this fire-escape for a last time and followed, from then on, in my father's footsteps, attempting to find in motion what was lost in space—I traveled around a great deal. The cities swept about me like dead leaves, leaves that were brightly colored but torn away from the branches. I would have stopped, but I was pursued by something. It always came upon me unawares, taking me altogether by surprise. Perhaps it was a familiar bit of music. Perhaps it was only a piece of transparent glass—Perhaps I am walking along a street at night, in some strange city, before I have found companions. I pass the lighted window of a shop where perfume is sold. The window is filled with pieces of colored glass, tiny transparent bottles in delicate colors, like bits of a shattered rainbow. Then all at once my sister touches my shoulder. I turn around and look into her eyes . . . Oh, Laura, Laura, I tried to leave you behind me, but I am more faithful than I intended to be! I reach for a cigarette, I cross the street, I run into the movies or a bar, I buy a drink, I speak to the nearest stranger—anything that can blow your candles out! *(Laura bends over the candles.)*—for nowadays the world is lit by lightning! Blow out your candles, Laura—and so goodbye . . .

She blows the candles out. The scene dissolves.

PRODUCTION NOTES

Being a "memory play," *The Glass Menagerie* can be presented with unusual freedom of convention. Because of its considerably delicate or tenuous material, atmospheric touches and subtleties of direction play a particularly important part. Expressionism and all other unconventional techniques in drama have only one valid aim, and that is a closer approach to truth. When a play employs unconventional techniques, it is not, or certainly shouldn't be, trying to escape its responsibility of dealing with reality, or interpreting experience, but is actually or should be attempting to find a closer approach, a more penetrating and vivid expression of things as they are. The straight realistic play with its genuine frigidaire and authentic ice-cubes, its characters that speak exactly as its audience speaks, corresponds to the academic landscape and has the same virtue of a photographic likeness. Everyone should know nowadays the unimportance of the photographic in art: that truth, life, or reality is an organic thing which the poetic imagination can represent or suggest, in essence, only through transformation, through changing into other forms than those which were merely present in appearance.

These remarks are not meant as comments only on this particular play. They have to do with a conception of a new, plastic theater which must take the place of the exhausted theater of realistic conventions if the theater is to resume vitality as a part of our culture.

The Screen Device

There is *only one important difference between the original and acting version of the play* and that is the *omission* in the latter of the device which I tentatively included in my *original* script. This device was the use of a screen on which were projected magic-lantern slides bearing images or titles. I do not regret the omission of this device from the . . . Broadway production. The extraordinary power of Miss Taylor's performance made it suitable to have the utmost simplicity in the physical production. But I think it may be interesting to some readers to see how this device was conceived. So I am putting it into the published manuscript. These images and legends, projected from behind, were cast on a section of wall between the front-room and dining-room areas, which should be indistinguishable from the rest when not in use.

The purpose of this will probably be apparent. It is to give accent to certain values in each scene. Each scene contains a particular point (or several) which is structurally the most important. In an episodic play, such as this, the basic structure or narrative line may be obscured from the audience; the effect may seem fragmentary rather than architectural. This may not be the fault of the play so much as a lack of attention in the audience. The legend or image upon the screen will strengthen the effect of what is merely allusion in the writing and allow the primary point to be made more simply and lightly than if the entire responsibility were on the spoken lines. Aside from this structural value, I think the screen will have a definite emotional appeal, less definable but just as important. An imaginative producer or director may invent many other uses for this device than those indicated in the present script. In fact the possibilities of the device seem much larger to me than the instance of this play can possibly utilize.

The Music

Another extra-literary accent in this play is provided by the use of music. A single recurring tune, "The Glass Menagerie," is used to give emotional emphasis to suitable passages. This tune is like circus music, not when you are on the grounds or in the immediate vicinity of the parade, but when you are at some distance and very likely thinking of something else. It seems under those circumstances to continue almost interminably and it weaves in and out of your preoccupied consciousness; then it is the lightest, most delicate music in the world and perhaps the saddest. It expresses the surface vivacity of life with the underlying strain of immutable and inexpressible sorrow. When you look at a piece of delicately spun glass you think of two things: how beautiful it is and how easily it can be broken. Both of those ideas should be woven into the recurring tune, which dips in and out of the play as if it were carried on a wind that changes. It serves as a thread of connection and allusion between the narrator with his separate point in time and space and the subject of his story. Between each episode it returns as reference to the emotion, nostalgia, which is the first condition of the play. It is primarily Laura's music and therefore comes out most clearly when the play focuses upon her and the lovely fragility of glass which is her image.

The Lighting

The lighting in the play is not realistic. In keeping with the atmosphere of memory, the stage is dim. Shafts of light are focused on selected areas or actors, sometimes in contradistinction to what is the apparent center. For instance, in the quarrel scene between Tom and Amanda, in which Laura has no active part, the clearest pool of light is on her figure. This is also true of the supper scene. The light upon Laura should be distinct from the others, having a peculiar pristine clarity such as light used in early religious portraits of female saints or madonnas. A certain correspondence to light in religious paintings, such as El Greco's, where the figures are radiant in atmosphere that is relatively dusky, could be effectively used throughout the play. (It will also permit a more effective use of the screen.) A free, imaginative use of light can be of enormous value in giving a mobile, plastic quality to plays of a more or less static nature.

Questions

1. *Who is the central character in the play?* **2.** *What does the glass menagerie symbolize? Specifically, what does the unicorn symbolize? Why does Laura give the unicorn, after its horn has broken off, to Jim?* **3.** *In his address to the audience that begins the play, Tom tells the audience that Jim "is the most realistic character in the play . . . an emissary from a world of reality that we were somehow set apart from." What is the world of reality Jim represents?* **4.** *Are we meant to admire Amanda for holding together her family under very difficult circumstances or to condemn her for her destructive illusions? In this connection, explain the statement in the final stage direction: "Now that we cannot hear the mother's speech, her silliness is gone and she has dignity and tragic beauty."* **5.** *Although she has refused to accept the characterization from Tom, in her final words Amanda refers to Laura as "crippled." Why?* **6.** *In his opening address, Tom sketches in "the social background of the play." Why?* **7.** *Is Tom's escape as complete as his father's seems to have been? Explain.* **8.** *Are the magic lantern slides an effective device? Explain.*

The Lesson*

EUGÈNE IONESCO [b. 1912]

CHARACTERS

The Professor, *aged 50 to 60*
The Young Pupil, *aged 18*
The Maid, *aged 45 to 50*

SCENE. *The office of the old professor, which also serves as a dining room. To the left, a door opens onto the apartment stairs; upstage, to the right, another door opens onto a corridor of the apartment. Upstage, a little left of center, a window, not very large, with plain curtains; on the outside sill of the window are ordinary potted plants. The low buildings with red roofs of a small town can be seen in the distance. The sky is grayish-blue. On the right stands a provincial buffet. The table doubles as a desk, it stands at stage center. There are three chairs around the table, and two more stand on each side of the window. Light-colored wallpaper, some shelves with books.*

(When the curtain rises the stage is empty, and it remains so for a few moments. Then we hear the doorbell ring.)

Voice of the Maid *(from the corridor).* Yes. I'm coming.

(The Maid comes in, after having run down the stairs. She is stout, aged 45 to 50, red-faced, and wears a peasant woman's cap. She rushes in, slamming the door to the right behind her, and dries her hands on her apron as she runs toward the door on the left. Meanwhile we hear the doorbell ring again.)

Maid. Just a moment, I'm coming.

(She opens the door. A Young Pupil, aged 18, enters. She is wearing a gray student's smock, a small white collar, and carries a student's satchel under her arm.)

Maid. Good morning, miss.
Pupil. Good morning, madam. Is the Professor at home?
Maid. Have you come for the lesson?

---

*Translated by Donald M. Allen.

Pupil. Yes, I have.

Maid. He's expecting you. Sit down for a moment. I'll tell him you're here.

Pupil. Thank you.

(She seats herself near the table, facing the audience; the hall door is to her left; her back is to the other door, through which the Maid hurriedly exits, calling.)

Maid. Professor, come down please, your pupil is here.

Voice of the Professor *(rather reedy).*   Thank you. I'm coming . . . in just a
    moment . . .

(The Maid exits; the Pupil draws in her legs, holds her satchel on her lap, and waits demurely. She casts a glance or two around the room, at the furniture, at the ceiling too. Then she takes a notebook out of her satchel, leafs through it, and stops to look at a page for a moment as though reviewing a lesson, as though taking a last look at her homework. She seems to be a well-brought-up girl, polite, but lively, gay, dynamic; a fresh smile is on her lips. During the course of the play she progressively loses the lively rhythm of her movement and her carriage, she becomes withdrawn. From gay and smiling she becomes progressively sad and morose; from very lively at the beginning, she becomes more and more fatigued and somnolent. Towards the end of the play her face must clearly express a nervous depression; her way of speaking shows the effects of this, her tongue becomes thick, words come to her memory with difficulty and emerge from her mouth with as much difficulty; she comes to have a manner vaguely paralyzed, the beginning of aphasia. Firm and determined at the beginning, so much so as to appear to be almost aggressive, she becomes more and more passive, until she is almost a mute and inert object, seemingly inanimate in the Professor's hands, to such an extent that when he makes his final gesture, she no longer reacts. Insensible, her reflexes deadened, only her eyes in an expressionless face will show inexpressible astonishment and fear. The transition from one manner to the other must of course be made imperceptibly.

The Professor enters. He is a little old man with a little white beard. He wears pince-nez, a black skull cap, a long black schoolmaster's coat, trousers and shoes of black, detachable white collar, a black tie. Excessively polite, very timid, his voice deadened by his timidity, very proper, very much the teacher. He rubs his hands together constantly; occasionally a lewd gleam comes into his eyes and is quickly repressed.

During the course of the play his timidity will disappear progressively, imperceptibly; and the lewd gleams in his eyes will become a steady devouring flame in the end. From a manner that is inoffensive at the start, the Professor becomes more and more sure of himself, more and more nervous, aggressive, dominating, until he is able to do as he pleases with the Pupil, who has become, in his hands, a pitiful creature. Of course, the voice of the

Professor must change too, from thin and reedy, to stronger and stronger, until at the end it is extremely powerful, ringing, sonorous, while the Pupil's voice changes from the very clear and ringing tones that she has at the beginning of the play until it is almost inaudible. In these first scenes the Professor might stammer very slightly.)

Professor. Good morning, young lady. You . . . I expect that you . . . that you are the new pupil?

Pupil *(turns quickly with a lively and self-assured manner; she gets up, goes towards the Professor, and gives him her hand).* Yes, Professor. Good morning, Professor. As you see, I'm on time. I didn't want to be late.

Professor. That's fine, miss. Thank you, you didn't really need to hurry. I am very sorry to have kept you waiting . . . I was just finishing up . . . well . . . I'm sorry . . . You will excuse me, won't you? . . .

Pupil. Oh, certainly, Professor. It doesn't matter at all, Professor.

Professor. Please excuse me . . . Did you have any trouble finding the house?

Pupil. No . . . Not at all. I just asked the way. Everybody knows you around here.

Professor. For thirty years I've lived in this town. You've not been here for long? How do you find it?

Pupil. It's all right. The town is attractive and even agreeable, there's a nice park, a boarding school, a bishop, nice shops and streets . . .

Professor. That's very true, young lady. And yet, I'd just as soon live somewhere else. In Paris, or at least Bordeaux.

Pupil. Do you like Bordeaux?

Professor. I don't know. I've never seen it.

Pupil. But you know Paris?

Professor. No, I don't know it either, young lady, but if you'll permit me, can you tell me, Paris is the capital city of . . . miss?

Pupil *(searching her memory for a moment, then, happily guessing).* Paris is the capital city of . . . France?

Professor. Yes, young lady, bravo, that's very good, that's perfect. My congratulations. You have your French geography at your finger tips. You know your chief cities.

Pupil. Oh! I don't know them all yet, Professor, it's not quite that easy, I have trouble learning them.

Professor. Oh! it will come . . . you mustn't give up . . . young lady . . . I beg your pardon . . . have patience . . . little by little . . . You will see, it will come in time . . . What a nice day it is today . . . or rather, not so nice . . . Oh! but then yes it is nice. In short, it's not too bad a day, that's the main thing . . . ahem . . . ahem . . . it's not raining and it's not snowing either.

Pupil. That would be most unusual, for it's summer now.

Professor. Excuse me, miss, I was just going to say so . . . but as you will learn, one must be ready for anything.

Pupil. I guess so, Professor.

Professor. We can't be sure of anything, young lady, in this world.

Pupil. The snow falls in the winter. Winter is one of the four seasons. The other three are . . . uh . . . spr . . .

Professor. Yes?

Pupil. . . . ing, and then summer . . . and . . . uh . . .

Professor. It begins like "automobile," miss.

Pupil. Ah, yes, autumn . . .

Professor. That's right, miss. That's a good answer, that's perfect. I am convinced that you will be a good pupil. You will make real progress. You are intelligent, you seem to me to be well informed, and you've a good memory.

Pupil. I know my seasons, don't I, Professor?

Professor. Yes, indeed, miss . . . or almost. But it will come in time. In any case, you're coming along. Soon you'll know all the seasons, with your eyes closed. Just as I do.

Pupil. It's hard.

Professor. Oh, no. All it takes is a little effort, a little good will, miss. You will see. It will come, you may be sure of that.

Pupil. Oh, I do hope so, Professor. I have a great thirst for knowledge. My parents also want me to get an education. They want me to specialize. They consider a little general culture, even if it is solid, is no longer enough, in these times.

Professor. Your parents, miss, are perfectly right. You must go on with your studies. Forgive me for saying so, but it is very necessary. Our contemporary life has become most complex.

Pupil. And so very complicated too . . . My parents are fairly rich, I'm lucky. They can help me in my work, help me in my very advanced studies.

Professor. And you wish to qualify for . . . ?

Pupil. Just as soon as possible, for the first doctor's orals. They're in three week's time.

Professor. You already have your high school diploma, if you'll pardon the question?

Pupil. Yes, Professor, I have my science diploma and my arts diploma, too.

Professor. Ah, you're very far advanced, even perhaps too advanced for your age. And which doctorate do you wish to qualify for? In the physical sciences or in moral philosophy?

Pupil. My parents are very much hoping—if you think it will be possible in such a short time—they very much hope that I can qualify for the total doctorate.

Professor. The total doctorate? . . . You have great courage, young lady, I congratulate you sincerely. We will try, miss, to do our best. In any case, you already know quite a bit, and at so young an age too.

Pupil. Oh, Professor.

Professor. Then, if you'll permit me, pardon me, please, I do think that we ought to get to work. We have scarcely any time to lose.

Pupil. Oh, but certainly, Professor, I want to. I beg you to.

Professor. Then, may I ask you to sit down . . . there . . . Will you permit me, miss, that is if you have no objections, to sit down opposite you?

Pupil. Oh, of course, Professor, please do.

Professor. Thank you very much, miss. *(They sit down facing each other at the table, their profiles to the audience.)* There we are. Now have you brought your books and notebooks?

Pupil *(taking notebooks and books out of her satchel).* Yes, Professor. Certainly, I have brought all that we'll need.

Professor. Perfect, miss. This is perfect. Now, if this doesn't bore you . . . shall we begin?

Pupil. Yes, indeed, Professor, I am at your disposal.

Professor. At my disposal? *(A gleam comes into his eyes and is quickly extinguished; he begins to make a gesture that he suppresses at once.)* Oh miss, it is I who am at *your* disposal. I am only your humble servant.

Pupil. Oh, Professor . . .

Professor. If you will . . . now . . . we . . . we . . . I . . . I will begin by making a brief examination of your knowledge, past and present, so that we may chart our future course . . . Good. How is your perception of plurality?

Pupil. It's rather vague . . . confused.

Professor. Good. We shall see.

(He rubs his hands together. The Maid enters, and this appears to irritate the Professor. She goes to the buffet and looks for something, lingering.)

Professor. Now, miss would you like to do a little arithmetic, that is if you want to . . .

Pupil. Oh, yes, Professor. Certainly, I ask nothing better.

Professor. It is rather a new science, a modern science, properly speaking, It is more a method than a science . . . And it is also a therapy. *(To the Maid:)* Have you finished, Marie?

Maid. Yes, Professor, I've found the plate. I'm just going . . .

Professor. Hurry up then. Please go along to the kitchen, if you will.

Maid. Yes, Professor, I'm going. *(She starts to go out.)* Excuse me, Professor, but take care, I urge you to remain calm.

Professor. You're being ridiculous, Marie. Now, don't worry.

Maid. That's what you always say.

Professor. I will not stand for your insinuations. I know perfectly well how to comport myself. I am old enough for that.

Maid. Precisely, Professor. You will do better not to start the young lady on arithmetic. Arithmetic is tiring, exhausting.

Professor. Not at my age. And anyhow, what business is it of yours? This is my concern. And I know what I'm doing. This is not your department.

Maid. Very well, Professor. But you can't say that I didn't warn you.

Professor. Marie, I can get along without your advice.

Maid. As you wish, Professor. *(She exits.)*

Professor. Miss, I hope you'll pardon this absurd interruption . . . Excuse this woman . . . She is always afraid that I'll tire myself. She fusses over my health.

Pupil. Oh, that's quite all right, Professor. It shows that she's very devoted. She loves you very much. Good servants are rare.

Professor. She exaggerates. Her fears are stupid. But let's return to our arithmetical knitting.

Pupil. I'm following you, Professor.

Professor *(wittily).* Without leaving your seat!

Pupil *(appreciating his joke).* Like you, Professor.

Professor. Good. Let us arithmetize a little now.

Pupil. Yes, gladly, Professor.

Professor. It wouldn't be too tiresome for you to tell me . . .

Pupil. Not at all, Professor, go on.

Professor. How much are one and one?

Pupil. One and one make two.

Professor *(marveling at the Pupil's knowledge).* Oh, but that's very good. You appear to me to be well along in your studies. You should easily achieve the total doctorate, miss.

Pupil. I'm so glad. Especially to have someone like you tell me this.

Professor. Let's push on: how much are two and one?

Pupil. Three.

Professor. Three and one?

Pupil. Four.

Professor. Four and one?

Pupil. Five.

Professor. Five and one?

Pupil. Six.

Professor. Six and one?

Pupil. Seven.

Professor. Seven and one?

Pupil. Eight.

Professor. Seven and one?

Pupil. Eight again.

Professor. Very well answered. Seven and one?

Pupil. Eight once more.

Professor. Perfect. Excellent. Seven and one?

Pupil. Eight again. And sometimes nine.

Professor. Magnificent. You are magnificent. You are exquisite. I congratulate you warmly, miss. There's scarcely any point in going on. At addition you are a past master. Now, let's look at subtraction. Tell me, if you are not exhausted, how many are four minus three?

Pupil. Four minus three? . . . Four minus three?

Professor. Yes. I mean to say: subtract three from four.

Pupil. That makes . . . seven?

Professor. I am sorry but I'm obliged to contradict you. Four minus three does not make seven. You are confused: four plus three makes seven, four minus three does not make seven . . . This is not addition anymore, we must subtract now.

Pupil (*trying to understand*). Yes . . . yes . . .

Professor. Four minus three makes . . . How many? . . . How many?

Pupil. Four?

Professor. No, miss, that's not it.

Pupil. Three, then.

Professor. Not that either, miss . . . Pardon, I'm sorry . . . I ought to say, that's not it . . . excuse me.

Pupil. Four minus three . . . Four minus three . . . Four minus three? . . . But now doesn't that make ten?

Professor. Oh, certainly not, miss. It's not a matter of guessing, you've got to think it out. Let's try to deduce it together. Would you like to count?

Pupil. Yes, Professor. One . . . two . . . uh . . .

Professor. You know how to count? How far can you count up to?

Pupil. I can count to . . . to infinity.

Professor. That's not possible, miss.

Pupil. Well then, let's say to sixteen.

Professor. That is enough. One must know one's limits. Count then, If you will, please.

Pupil. One . . . two . . . and after two, comes three . . . then four . . .

Professor. Stop there, miss. Which number is larger? Three or four?

Pupil. Uh . . . three or four? Which is the larger? The larger of three or four? In what sense larger?

Professor. Some numbers are smaller and others are larger. In the larger numbers there are more units than in the smaller . . .

Pupil. Than in the small numbers?

Professor. Unless the small ones have smaller units. If they are very small, then there might be more units in the small numbers than in the large . . . if it is a question of other units . . .

Pupil. In that case, the small numbers can be larger than the large numbers?

Professor. Let's not go into that. That would take us much too far. You must realize simply that more than numbers are involved here . . . there are also magnitudes, totals, there are groups, there are heaps, heaps of such things as plums, trucks, geese, prune pits, etc. To facilitate our work, let's merely suppose that we have only equal numbers, then the bigger numbers will be those that have the most units.

Pupil. The one that has the most is the biggest? Ah, I understand, Professor, you are identifying quality with quantity.

Professor. That is too theoretical, miss, too theoretical. You needn't concern yourself with that. Let us take an example and reason from a definite case. Let's leave the general conclusions for later. We have the number four and the number three, and each has always the same number of units. Which number will be larger, the smaller or the larger?

Pupil. Excuse me, Professor . . . What do you mean by the larger number? Is it the one that is not so small as the other?

Professor. That's it, miss, perfect. You have understood me very well.

Pupil. Then, it is four.

Professor. What is four—larger or smaller than three?

Pupil. Smaller . . . no, larger.

Professor. Excellent answer. How many units are there between three and four? . . . Or between four and three, if you prefer?

Pupil. There aren't any units, Professor, between three and four. Four comes immediately after three; there is nothing at all between three and four!

Professor. I haven't made myself very well understood. No doubt, it is my fault. I've not been sufficiently clear.

Pupil. No, Professor, it's my fault.

Professor. Look here. Here are three matches. And here is another one, that makes four. Now watch carefully—we have four matches. I take one away, now how many are left?

(We don't see the matches, nor any of the objects that are mentioned. The Professor gets up from the table, writes on the imaginary blackboard with an imaginary piece of chalk, etc.)

Pupil. Five. If three and one make four, four and one make five.

Professor. That's not it. That's not it at all. You always have a tendency to add. But one must be able to subtract too. It's not enough to integrate, you must also disintegrate. That's the way life is. That's philosophy. That's science. That's progress, civilization.

Pupil. Yes, Professor.

Professor. Let's return to our matches. I have four of them. You see, there are really four. I take one away, and there remain only . . .

Pupil. I don't know, Professor.

Professor. Come now, think. It's not easy, I admit. Nevertheless, you've had enough training to make the intellectual effort required to arrive at an understanding. So?

Pupil. I can't get it, Professor. I don't know, Professor.

Professor. Let us take a simpler example. If you had two noses, and I pulled one of them off . . . how many would you have left?

Pupil. None.

Professor. What do you mean, none?

Pupil. Yes, it's because you haven't pulled off any, that's why I have one now. If you had pulled it off, I wouldn't have it anymore.

Professor. You've not understood my example. Suppose that you have only one ear.

Pupil. Yes, and then?

Professor. If I gave you another one, how many would you have then?

Pupil. Two.

Professor. Good. And if I gave you still another ear. How many would you have then?

Pupil. Three ears.

Professor. Now, I take one away . . . and there remain . . . how many ears?

Pupil. Two.

Professor. Good. I take away still another one, how many do you have left?

Pupil. Two.

Professor. No. You have two, I take one away, I eat one up, then how many do you have left?

Pupil. Two.

Professor. I eat one of them . . . one.

Pupil. Two.

Professor. One.

Pupil. Two.

Professor. One!

Pupil. Two!

Professor. One!!!

Pupil. Two!!!

Professor. One!!!

Pupil. Two!!!

Professor. One!!!

Pupil. Two!!!

Professor. No. No. That's not right. The example is not . . . it's not convincing. Listen to me.

Pupil. Yes, Professor.

Professor. You've got . . . you've got . . . you've got . . .

Pupil. Ten fingers!

Professor. If you wish. Perfect. Good. You have then ten fingers.

Pupil. Yes, Professor.

Professor. How many would you have if you had only five of them?

Pupil. Ten, Professor.

Professor. That's not right!

Pupil. But it is, Professor.

Professor. I tell you it's not!

Pupil. You just told me that I had ten . . .

Professor. I also said, immediately afterwards, that you had five!

Pupil. I don't have five, I've got ten!

Professor. Let's try another approach . . . for purposes of subtraction let's limit ourselves to the numbers from one to five . . . Wait now, miss, you'll soon see. I'm going to make you understand.

(The Professor begins to write on the imaginary blackboard. He moves it closer to the Pupil, who turns around in order to see it.)

Professor. Look here, miss . . . *(He pretends to draw a stick on the blackboard and the number 1 below the stick; then two sticks and the number 2 below, then three sticks and the number 3 below, then four sticks with the number 4 below.)* You see . . .

Pupil. Yes, Professor.

Professor. These are sticks, miss, sticks. This is one stick, these are two sticks, and three sticks, then four sticks, then five sticks. One stick, two sticks, three sticks, four and five sticks, these are numbers. When we count the sticks, each stick is a unit, miss . . . What have I just said?

Pupil. "A unit, miss! What have I just said?"

Professor. Or a figure! Or a number! One, two, three, four, five, these are the elements of numeration, miss.

Pupil *(hesitant).* Yes, Professor. The elements, figures, which are sticks, units and numbers . . .

Professor. At the same time . . . that's to say, in short—the whole of arithmetic is there.

Pupil. Yes, Professor. Good, Professor. Thanks, Professor.

Professor. Now, count, if you will please, using these elements . . . add and subtract . . .

Pupil *(as though trying to impress them on her memory).* Sticks are really figures and numbers are units?

Professor. Hmm . . . so to speak. And then?

Pupil. One could subtract two units from three units, but can one subtract two twos from three threes? And two figures from four numbers? And three numbers from one unit?

Professor. No, miss.

Pupil. Why, Professor?

Professor. Because, miss.

Pupil. Because why, Professor? Since one is the same as the other?

Professor. That's the way it is, miss. It can't be explained. This is only comprehensible through internal mathematical reasoning. Either you have it or you don't.

Pupil. So much the worse for me.

Professor. Listen to me, miss, if you don't achieve a profound understanding of these principles, these arithmetical archetypes, you will never be able to perform correctly the functions of a polytechnician. Still less will you be able to teach a course in a polytechnical school . . . or the primary grades. I realize that this is not easy, it is very, very abstract . . . obviously . . . but unless you can comprehend the primary elements, how do you expect to be able to calculate mentally—and this is the least of the things that even an ordinary engineer must be able to do—how much, for example, are three billion seven hundred fifty-five million nine hundred ninety-eight thousand two hundred fifty-one, multiplied by five billion one hundred sixty-two million three hundred and three thousand five hundred and eight?

Pupil *(very quickly).* That makes nineteen quintillion three hundred ninety quadrillion two trillion eight hundred forty-four billion two hundred nineteen million one hundred sixty-four thousand five hundred and eight . . .

Professor *(astonished).* No. I don't think so. That must make nineteen quintillion three hundred ninety quadrillion two trillion eight hundred forty-four billion two hundred nineteen million one hundred sixty-four thousand five hundred and nine . . .

Pupil. . . . No . . . five hundred and eight . . .

Professor *(more and more astonished, calculating mentally).* Yes . . . you are right . . . the result is indeed . . . *(He mumbles unintelligibly:)* . . . quintillion, quadrillion, trillion, billion, million . . . *(Clearly:)* one hundred sixty-four thousand five hundred and eight . . . *(Stupefied:)* But how did you know that, if you don't know the principles of arithmetical reasoning?

Pupil. It's easy. Not being able to rely on my reasoning. I've memorized all the products of all possible multiplications.

Professor. That's pretty good . . . However, permit me to confess to you that that doesn't satisfy me, miss, and I do not congratulate you: in mathematics and in arithmetic especially, the thing that counts—for in arithmetic it is always necessary to count—the thing that counts is, above all, understanding . . . It is by mathematical reasoning, simultaneously inductive and deductive, that you ought to arrive at this result—as well as at any other result. Mathematics is the sworn enemy of memory, which is excellent otherwise, but disastrous, arithmetically speaking! . . . That's why I'm not happy with this . . . this won't do, not at all . . .

Pupil *(desolated).* No, Professor.

Professor. Let's leave it for the moment. Let's go on to another exercise . . .

Pupil. Yes, Professor.

Maid *(entering).* Hmm, hmm, Professor . . .

Professor *(who doesn't hear her).* It is unfortunate, miss, that you aren't further along in specialized mathematics . . .

Maid *(taking him by the sleeve).* Professor! Professor!

Professor. I fear that you will not be able to qualify for the total doctor's orals . . .

Pupil. Yes, Professor, it's too bad!

Professor. Unless you . . . *(To the Maid:)* Let me be, Marie . . . Look here, why are you bothering me? Go back to the kitchen! To your pots and pans! Go away! Go away! *(To the Pupil:)* We will try to prepare you at least for the partial doctorate . . .

Maid. Professor! . . . Professor! . . . *(She pulls his sleeve.)*

Professor *(to the Maid).* Now leave me alone! Let me be! What's the meaning of this? . . . *(To the Pupil:)* I must therefore teach you, if you really do insist on attempting the partial doctorate . . .

Pupil. Yes, Professor.

Professor. . . . The elements of linguistics and of comparative philology . . .

Maid. No, Professor, no! . . . You mustn't do that! . . . '

Professor. Marie, you're going too far!

Maid. Professor, especially not philology, philology leads to calamity . . .

Pupil *(astonished)*. To calamity? *(Smiling, a little stupidly.)* That's hard to believe.

Professor *(to the Maid)*. That's enough now! Get out of here!

Maid. All right, Professor, all right. But you can't say that I didn't warn you! Philology leads to calamity!

Professor. I'm an adult, Marie!

Pupil. Yes, Professor.

Maid. As you wish. *(She exits.)*

Professor. Let's continue, miss.

Pupil. Yes, Professor.

Professor. I want you to listen now with the greatest possible attention to a lecture I have prepared . . .

Pupil. Yes, Professor!

Professor. . . . Thanks to which, in fifteen minutes' time, you will be able to acquire the fundamental principles of the linguistic and comparative philology of the neo-Spanish languages.

Pupil. Yes, Professor, oh good! *(She claps her hands.)*

Professor *(with authority)*. Quiet! What do you mean by that?

Pupil. I'm sorry, Professor. *(Slowly, she replaces her hands on the table.)*

Professor. Quiet! *(He gets up, walks up and down the room, his hands behind his back; from time to time he stops at stage center or near the Pupil, and underlines his words with a gesture of his hand; he orates, but without being too emotional. The Pupil follows him with her eyes, occasionally with some difficulty, for she has to turn her head far around; once or twice, not more, she turns around completely.)* And now, miss, Spanish is truly the mother tongue which gave birth to all the neo-Spanish languages, of which Spanish, Latin, Italian, our own French, Portuguese, Romanian, Sardinian or Sardanapalian, Spanish and neo-Spanish—and also, in certain of its aspects, Turkish which is otherwise very close to Greek, which is only logical, since it is a fact that Turkey is a neighbor of Greece and Greece is even closer to Turkey than you are to me—this is only one more illustration of the very important linguistic law which states that geography and philology are twin sisters . . . You may take notes, miss.

Pupil *(in a dull voice)*. Yes, Professor!

Professor. That which distinguishes the neo-Spanish languages from each other and their idioms from the other linguistic groups, such as the group of languages called Austrian and neo-Austrian or Hapsburgian, as well as the Esperanto, Helvetian, Monacan, Swiss, Andorran, Basque, and jai alai groups, and also the groups of diplomatic and technical languages—that which distinguishes them, I repeat, is their striking resemblance which makes it so hard to distinguish them from each other—I'm speaking of the neo-Spanish languages which one is able to distinguish from each other,

however, only thanks to their distinctive characteristics, absolutely indis-
putable proofs of their extraordinary resemblance, which renders indis-
putable their common origin, and which, at the same time, differentiates
them profoundly—through the continuation of the distinctive traits which
I've just cited.

Pupil. Oooh! Ye-e-e-s-s-s, Professor!

Professor. But let's not linger over generalities . . .

Pupil *(regretfully, but won over).* Oh, Professor . . .

Professor. This appears to interest you. All the better, all the better . . .

Pupil. Oh, yes, Professor . . .

Professor. Don't worry, miss. We will come back to it later . . . That is if we
come back to it at all. Who can say?

Pupil *(enchanted in spite of everything).* Oh, yes, Professor.

Professor. Every tongue—you must know this, miss, and remember it *until
the hour of your death* . . .

Pupil. Oh! yes, Professor, until the hour of my death . . . Yes, Professor . . .

Professor. . . . And this, too, is a fundamental principle, every tongue is at
bottom nothing but language, which necessarily implies that it is composed of sounds, or . . .

Pupil. Phonemes . . .

Professor. Just what I was going to say. Don't parade your knowledge. You'd
do better to listen.

Pupil. All right, Professor. Yes, Professor.

Professor. The sounds, miss, must be seized on the wing as they fly so that
they'll not fall on deaf ears. As a result, when you set out to articulate, it is
recommended, insofar as possible, that you lift up your neck and chin
very high, and rise up on the tips of your toes, you see, this way . . .

Pupil. Yes, Professor.

Professor. Keep quiet. Remain seated, don't interrupt me . . . And project the
sounds very loudly with all the force of your lungs in conjunction with that
of your vocal cords. Like this, look: "Butterfly," "Eureka," "Trafalgar,"
"Papaya." This way, the sounds become filled with a warm air that is
lighter than the surrounding air so that they can fly without danger of
falling on deaf ears, which are veritable voids, tombs of sonorities. If you
utter several sounds at an accelerated speed, they will automatically cling
to each other, constituting thus syllables, words, even sentences, that is to
say groupings of various importance, purely irrational assemblages of
sounds, denuded of all sense, but for that very reason the more capable of
maintaining themselves without danger at a high altitude in the air. By
themselves, words charged with significance will fall, weighted down by
their meaning, and in the end they always collapse, fall . . .

Pupil. . . . On deaf ears.

Professor. That's it, but don't interrupt . . . and into the worst confusion . . .
Or else burst like balloons. Therefore, miss . . . *(The Pupil suddenly appears to be unwell.)* What's the matter?

Pupil. I've got a toothache, Professor.

Professor. That's not important. We're not going to stop for anything so trivial. Let us go on . . .

Pupil *(appearing to be in more and more pain).* Yes, Professor.

Professor. I draw your attention in passing to the consonants that change their nature in combinations. In this case *f* becomes *v*, *d* becomes *t*, *g* becomes *k*, and vice versa, as in these examples that I will cite for you: "That's all right," "hens and chickens," "Welsh rabbit," "lots of nothing," "not at all."[1]

Pupil. I've got a toothache.

Professor. Let's continue.

Pupil. Yes.

Professor. To resume: it takes years and years to learn to pronounce. Thanks to science, we can achieve this in a few minutes. In order to project words, sounds and all the rest, you must realize that it is necessary to pitilessly expel air from the lungs, and make it pass delicately, caressingly, over the vocal cords, which, like harps or leaves in the wind, will suddenly shake, agitate, vibrate, vibrate, vibrate or uvulate, or fricate or jostle against each other, or sibilate, sibilate, placing everything in movement, the uvula, the tongue, the palate, the teeth . . .

Pupil. I have a toothache.

Professor. . . . And the lips . . . Finally the words come out through the nose, the mouth, the ears, the pores, drawing along with them all the organs that we have named, torn up by the roots, in a powerful, majestic flight, which is none other than what is called, improperly, the voice, whether modulated in singing or transformed into a terrible symphonic storm with a whole procession . . . of garlands of all kinds of flowers, of sonorous artifices: labials, dentals, occlusives, palatals, and others, some caressing, some bitter or violent.

Pupil. Yes, Professor, I've got a toothache.

Professor. Let's go on, go on. As for the neo-Spanish languages, they are closely related, so closely to each other, that they can be considered as true second cousins. Moreover, they have the same mother: Spanishe, with a mute *e*. That is why it is so difficult to distinguish them from one another. That is why it is so useful to pronounce carefully, and to avoid errors in pronunciation. Pronunciation itself is worth a whole language. A bad pronunciation can get you into trouble. In this connection, permit me, parenthetically, to share a personal experience with you. *(Slight pause. The Professor goes over his memories for a moment; his features mellow, but he recovers at once.)* I was very young, little more than a child. It was during my military service. I had a friend in the regiment, a vicomte, who suffered from a rather serious defect in his pronunciation: he

---

1. All to be heavily elided. [Translator's note.]

could not pronounce the letter f. Instead of f, *he said* f. Thus, instead of "Birds of a feather flock together," he said: "Birds of a feather flock together." He pronounced filly instead of filly, Firmin instead of Firmin, French bean instead of French bean, go frig yourself instead of go frig yourself, farrago instead of farrago, fee fi fo fum instead of fee fi fo fum, Philip instead of Philip, fictory instead of fictory, February instead of February, March-April instead of March-April, Gerard de Nerval and not as is correct—Gerard de Nerval, Mirabeau instead of Mirabeau, etc., instead of etc., and thus instead of etc., instead of etc., and thus and so forth. However, he managed to conceal his fault so effectively that, thanks to the hats he wore, no one ever noticed it.

Pupil. Yes, I've got a toothache.

Professor *(abruptly changing his tone, his voice hardening).*   Let's go on. We'll first consider the points of similarity in order the better to apprehend, later on, that which distinguishes all these languages from each other. The differences can scarcely be recognized by people who are not aware of them. Thus, all the words of all the languages . . .

Pupil. Uh, yes? . . . I've got a toothache.

Professor. Let's continue . . . are always the same, just as all the suffixes, all the prefixes, all the terminations, all the roots . . .

Pupil. Are the roots of words square?

Professor. Square or cube. That depends.

Pupil. I've got a toothache.

Professor. Let's go on. Thus, to give you an example which is little more than an illustration, take the word "front" . . .

Pupil. How do you want me to take it?

Professor. However you wish, so long as you take it, but above all do not interrupt.

Pupil. I've got a toothache.

Professor. Let's continue . . . I said: Let's continue. Take now the word "front." Have you taken it?

Pupil. Yes, yes, I've got it. My teeth, my teeth . . .

Professor. The word "front" is the root of "frontispiece." It is also to be found in "affronted." "Ispiece" is the suffix, and "af" the prefix. They are so called because they do not change. They don't want to.

Pupil. I've got a toothache.

Professor. Let's go on. *(Rapidly:)* These prefixes are of Spanish origin. I hope you noticed that, did you?

Pupil. Oh, how my tooth aches.

Professor. Let's continue. You've surely also noticed that they've not changed in French. And now, young lady, nothing has succeeded in changing them in Latin either, nor in Italian, nor in Portuguese, nor in Sardanapalian, nor in Sardanapali, nor in Romanian, nor in neo-Spanish, nor in Spanish, nor even in the Oriental: front, frontispiece, affronted, always the same word, invariably with the same root, the same suffix, the same prefix, in all the languages I have named. And it is always the same for all words.

Pupil. In all languages, these words mean the same thing? I've got a toothache.

Professor. Absolutely. Moreover, it's more a notion than a word. In any case, you have always the same signification, the same composition, the same sound structure, not only for this word, but for all conceivable words, in all languages. For one single notion is expressed by one and the same word, and its synonyms, in all countries. Forget about your teeth.

Pupil. I've got a toothache. Yes, yes, yes.

Professor. Good, let's go on. I tell you, let's go on . . . How would you say, for example, in French: the roses of my grandmother are as yellow as my grandfather who was Asiatic?

Pupil. My teeth ache, ache, ache.

Professor. Let's go on, let's go on, go ahead and answer, anyway.

Pupil. In French?

Professor. In French.

Pupil. Uhh . . . I should say in French: the roses of my grandmother are . . . ?

Professor. As yellow as my grandfather who was Asiatic . . .

Pupil. Oh well, one would say, in French, I believe, the roses . . . of my . . . how do you say "grandmother" in French?

Professor. In French? Grandmother.

Pupil. The roses of my grandmother are as yellow—in French is it "yellow"?

Professor. Yes, of course!

Pupil. Are as yellow as my grandfather when he got angry.

Professor. No . . . who was A . . .

Pupil. . . . siatic . . . I've got a toothache.

Professor. That's it.

Pupil. I've got a tooth . . .

Professor. Ache . . . so what . . . let's continue! And now translate the same sentence into Spanish, then into neo-Spanish . . .

Pupil. In Spanish . . . this would be: the roses of my grandmother are as yellow as my grandfather who was Asiatic.

Professor. No. That's wrong.

Pupil. And in neo-Spanish: the roses of my grandmother are as yellow as my grandfather who was Asiatic.

Professor. That's wrong. That's wrong. That's wrong. You have inverted it, you've confused Spanish with neo-Spanish, and neo-Spanish with Spanish . . . Oh . . . no . . . it's the other way around . . .

Pupil. I've got a toothache. You're getting mixed up.

Professor. You're the one who is mixing me up. Pay attention and take notes. I will say the sentence to you in Spanish, then in neo-Spanish, and finally, in Latin. You will repeat after me. Pay attention, for the resemblances are great. In fact, they are identical resemblances. Listen, follow carefully . . .

Pupil. I've got a tooth . . .

Professor. . . . Ache.

Pupil. Let us go on . . . Ah! . . .

Professor. . . . In Spanish: the roses of my grandmother are as yellow as my grandfather who was Asiatic; in Latin: the roses of my grandmother are as yellow as my grandfather who was Asiatic. Do you detect the differences? Translate this into . . . Romanian.

Pupil. The . . . how do you say "roses" in Romanian?

Professor. But "roses," what else?

Pupil. It's not "roses"? Oh, how my tooth aches!

Professor. Certainly not, certainly not, since "roses" is a translation in Oriental of the French word "roses," in Spanish "roses," do you get it? In Sardanapali, "roses" . . .

Pupil. Excuse me, Professor, but . . . Oh, my toothache! . . . I don't get the difference.

Professor. But it's so simple! So simple! It's a matter of having a certain experience, a technical experience and practice in these diverse languages, which are so diverse in spite of the fact that they present wholly identical characteristics. I'm going to try to give you a key . . .

Pupil. Toothache . . .

Professor. That which differentiates these languages, is neither the words, which are absolutely the same, nor the structure of the sentence which is everywhere the same, nor the intonation, which does not offer any differences, nor the rhythm of the language . . . that which differentiates them . . . are you listening?

Pupil. I've got a toothache.

Professor. Are you listening to me, young lady? Aah! We're going to lose our temper.

Pupil. You're bothering me, Professor. I've got a toothache.

Professor. Son of a cocker spaniel! Listen to me!

Pupil. Oh well . . . yes . . . yes . . . go on . . .

Professor. That which distinguishes them from each other, on the one hand, and from their mother, Spanishe with its mute *e,* on the other hand . . . is . . .

Pupil *(grimacing).* Is what?

Professor. Is an intangible thing. Something intangible that one is able to perceive only after very long study, with a great deal of trouble and after the broadest experience . . .

Pupil. Ah?

Professor. Yes, young lady. I cannot give you any rule. One must have a feeling for it, and well, that's it. But in order to have it, one must study, study, and then study some more.

Pupil. Toothache.

Professor. All the same, there are some specific cases where words differ from one language to another . . . but we cannot base our knowledge on these cases, which are, so to speak, exceptional.

Pupil. Oh, yes? . . . Oh, Professor, I've got a toothache.

Professor. Don't interrupt! Don't make me lose my temper! I can't answer for what I'll do. I was saying, then . . . Ah, yes, the exceptional cases, the so-called easily distinguished . . . or facilely distinguished . . . or conveniently . . . if you prefer . . . I repeat, if you prefer, for I see that you're not listening to me . . .

Pupil. I've got a toothache.

Professor. I say then: in certain expressions in current usage, certain words differ totally from one language to another, so much so that the language employed is, in this case, considerably easier to identify. I'll give you an example: the neo-Spanish expression, famous in Madrid: "My country is the new Spain," becomes in Italian: "My country is . . .

Pupil. The new Spain.

Professor. No! "My country is Italy." Tell me now, by simple deduction, how do you say "Italy" in French?

Pupil. I've got a toothache.

Professor. But it's so easy: for the word "Italy," in French we have the word "France," which is an exact translation of it. My country is France. And "France" in Oriental: "Orient!" My country is the Orient. And "Orient" in Portuguese: "Portugal!" The Oriental expression: My country is the Orient is translated then in the same fashion into Portuguese: My country is Portugal! And so on . . .

Pupil. Oh, no more, no more. My teeth . . .

Professor. Ache! ache! ache! . . . I'm going to pull them out, I will! One more example. The word "capital"—it takes on, according to the language one speaks, a different meaning. That is to say that when a Spaniard says: "I reside in the capital," the word "capital" does not mean at all the same thing that a Portuguese means when he says: "I reside in the capital." All the more so in the case of a Frenchman, a neo-Spaniard, a Romanian, a Latin, a Sardanapali . . . Whenever you hear it, young lady—young lady, I'm saying this for you! Pooh! Whenever you hear the expression: "I reside in the capital," you will immediately and easily know whether this is Spanish or Spanish, neo-Spanish, French, Oriental, Romanian, or Latin, for it is enough to know which metropolis is referred to by the person who pronounces the sentence . . . at the very moment he pronounces it . . . But these are almost the only precise examples that I can give you . . .

Pupil. Oh dear! My teeth . . .

Professor. Silence! Or I'll bash in your skull!

Pupil. Just try to! Skulldugger!

(The Professor seizes her wrist and twists it.)

Pupil. Oww!

Professor. Keep quiet now! Not a word!

Pupil *(whimpering).* Toothache . . .

Professor. One thing that is the most . . . how shall I say it? . . . the most paradoxical . . . yes . . . that's the word . . . the most paradoxical thing, is that a lot of people who are completely illiterate speak these different languages . . . do you understand? What did I just say?

Pupil. . . . "Speak these different languages! What did I just say?"

Professor. You were lucky that time! . . . The common people speak a Spanish full of neo-Spanish words that they are entirely unaware of, all the while believing that they are speaking Latin . . . or they speak Latin, full of Oriental words, all the while believing that they're speaking Romanian . . . or Spanish, full of neo-Spanish, all the while believing that they're speaking Sardanapali, or Spanish . . . Do you understand?

Pupil. Yes! yes! yes! yes! What more do you want . . . ?

Professor. No insolence, my pet, or you'll be sorry . . . *(In a rage:)* But the worst of all, young lady, is that certain people, for example, in a Latin that they suppose is Spanish, say: "Both my kidneys are of the same kidney," in addressing themselves to a Frenchman who does not know a word of Spanish, but the latter understands it as if it were his own language. For that matter he thinks it is his own language. And the Frenchman will reply, in French: "Me too, sir, mine are too," and this will be perfectly comprehensible to a Spaniard, who will feel certain that the reply is in pure Spanish and that Spanish is being spoken . . . when, in reality, it was neither Spanish nor French, but Latin in the neo-Spanish dialect . . . Sit still, young lady, don't fidget, stop tapping your feet . . .

Pupil. I've got a toothache.

Professor. How do you account for the fact that, in speaking without knowing which language they speak, or even while each of them believes that he is speaking another, the common people understand each other at all?

Pupil. I wonder.

Professor. It is simply one of the inexplicable curiosities of the vulgar empiricism of the common people—not to be confused with experience!—a paradox, a non-sense, one of the aberrations of human nature, it is purely and simply instinct—to put it in a nutshell . . . That's what is involved here.

Pupil. Hah! hah!

Professor. Instead of staring at the flies while I'm going to all this trouble . . . you would do much better to try to be more attentive . . . it is not I who is going to qualify for the partial doctor's orals . . . I passed mine a long time ago . . . and I've won my total doctorate, too . . . and my supertotal diploma . . . Don't you realize that what I'm saying is for your own good?

Pupil. Toothache!

Professor. Ill-mannered . . . It can't go on like this, it won't do, it won't do, it won't do . . .

Pupil. I'm . . . listening . . . to you . . .

Professor. Ahah! In order to learn to distinguish all the different languages, as I've told you, there is nothing better than practice . . . Let's take them up in order. I am going to try to teach you all the translations of the word "knife."

Pupil. Well, all right . . . if you want . . .

Professor *(calling the Maid).* Marie! Marie! She's not there . . . Marie! Marie! . . . Marie, where are you? *(He opens the door on the right.)* Marie! . . . *(He exits.)*

(The Pupil remains alone several minutes, staring into space, wearing a stupefied expression.)

Professor *(offstage, in a shrill voice).* Marie! What are you up to? Why don't you come! When I call you, you must come! *(He reenters, followed by the Maid.)* It is I who gives the orders, do you hear? *(He points at the Pupil:)* She doesn't understand anything, that girl. She doesn't understand!

Maid. Don't get into such a state, sir, you know where it'll end! You're going to go too far, you're going to go too far.

Professor. I'll be able to stop in time.

Maid. That's what you always say. I only wish I could see it.

Pupil. I've got a toothache.

Maid. You see, it's starting, that's the symptom!

Professor. What symptom? Explain yourself? What do you mean?

Pupil *(in a spiritless voice).* Yes, what do you mean? I've got a toothache.

Maid. The final symptom! The chief symptom!

Professor. Stupid! stupid! stupid! *(The Maid starts to exit.)* Don't go away like that! I called you to help me find the Spanish, neo-Spanish, Portuguese, French, Oriental, Romanian, Sardanapali, Latin and Spanish knives.

Maid *(severely).* Don't ask me. *(She exits.)*

Professor *(makes a gesture as though to protest, then refrains, a little helpless. Suddenly, he remembers).* Ah! *(He goes quickly to the drawer where he finds a big knife, invisible or real according to the preference of the director. He seizes it and brandishes it happily.)* Here is one, young lady, here is a knife. It's too bad that we only have this one, but we're going to try to make it serve for all the languages, anyway! It will be enough if you will pronounce the word "knife" in all the languages, while looking at the object, very closely, fixedly, and imagining that it is in the language that you are speaking.

Pupil. I've got a toothache.

Professor *(almost singing, chanting).* Now, say "kni," like "kni," "fe," like "fe" . . . And look, look, look at it, watch it . . .

Pupil. What is this one in? French, Italian or Spanish?

Professor. That doesn't matter now . . . That's not your concern. Say: "kni."

Pupil. "Kni."

Professor. . . . "fe" . . . Look. *(He brandishes the knife under the Pupil's eyes.)*

Pupil. "fe" . . .

Professor. Again . . . Look at it.

Pupil. Oh, no! My God! I've had enough. And besides, I've got a toothache, my feet hurt me, I've got a headache.

Professor *(abruptly)*. Knife . . . look . . . knife . . . look . . . knife . . . look . . .

Pupil. You're giving me an earache, too. Oh, your voice! It's so piercing!

Professor. Say: knife . . . kni . . . fe . . .

Pupil. No! My ears hurt, I hurt all over . . .

Professor. I'm going to tear them off, your ears, that's what I'm going to do to you, and then they won't hurt you anymore, my pet.

Pupil. Oh . . . you're hurting me, oh, you're hurting me . . .

Professor. Look, come on, quickly, repeat after me: "kni" . . .

Pupil. Oh, since you insist . . . knife . . . knife . . . *(In a lucid moment, ironically:)* Is that neo-Spanish . . .?

Professor. If you like, yes, it's neo-Spanish, but hurry up . . . we haven't got time . . . And then, what do you mean by that insidious question? What are you up to?

Pupil *(becoming more and more exhausted, weeping, desperate, at the same time both exasperated and in a trance).* Ah!

Professor. Repeat, watch. *(He imitates a cuckoo:)* Knife, knife . . . knife, knife . . . knife, knife . . . knife, knife . . .

Pupil. Oh, my head . . . aches . . . *(With her hand she caressingly touches the parts of her body as she names them:)* . . . My eyes . . .

Professor *(like a cuckoo).* Knife, knife . . . knife, knife . . .

(They are both standing. The Professor still brandishes his invisible knife, nearly beside himself, as he circles around her in a sort of scalp dance, but it is important that this not be exaggerated and that his dance steps be only suggested. The Pupil stands facing the audience, then recoils in the direction of the window, sickly, languid, victimized.)

Professor. Repeat, repeat: knife . . . knife . . . knife . . .

Pupil. I've got a pain . . . my throat, neck . . . oh, my shoulders . . . my breast . . . knife . . .

Professor. Knife . . . knife . . . knife . . .

Pupil. My hips . . . knife . . . my thighs . . . kni . . .

Professor. Pronounce it carefully . . . knife . . . knife . . .

Pupil. Knife . . . my throat . . .

Professor. Knife . . . knife . . .

Pupil. Knife . . . my shoulders . . . my arms, my breast, my hips . . . knife . . . knife . . .

Professor. That's right . . . Now, you're pronouncing it well . . .

Pupil. Knife . . . my breast . . . my stomach . . .

Professor (*changing his voice*).   Pay attention . . . don't break my window . . . the knife kills . . .

Pupil (*in a weak voice*).   Yes, yes . . . the knife kills?

Professor (*striking the Pupil with a very spectacular blow of the knife*).   Aaah! That'll teach you!

(*The Pupil also cries "Aaah!" then falls, flopping in an immodest position onto a chair which, as though by chance, is near the window. The murderer and his victim shout "Aaah!" at the same moment. After the first blow of the knife, the Pupil flops onto the chair, her legs spread wide and hanging over both sides of the chair. The Professor remains standing in front of her, his back to the audience. After the first blow, he strikes her dead with a second slash of the knife, from bottom to top. After that blow a noticeable convulsion shakes his whole body.*)

Professor (*winded, mumbling*).   Bitch . . . Oh, that's good, that does me good . . . Ah! Ah! I'm exhausted . . . I can scarcely breathe . . . Aah! (*He breathes with difficulty; he falls—fortunately a chair is there; he mops his brow, mumbles some incomprehensible words; his breathing becomes normal. He gets up, looks at the knife in his hand, looks at the young girl, then as though he were waking up, in a panic:*) What have I done! What's going to happen to me now! What's going to happen! Oh! dear! Oh dear, I'm in trouble! Young lady, young lady, get up! (*He is agitated, still holding onto the invisible knife, which he doesn't know what to do with.*) Come now, young lady, the lesson is over . . . you may go . . . you can pay another time . . . Oh! she is dead . . . dea-ead . . . And by my knife . . . She is dea-ead . . . It's terrible. (*He calls the Maid:*) Marie! Marie! My good Marie, come here! Ah! ah! (*The door on the right opens a little and the Maid appears.*) No . . . don't come in . . . I made a mistake . . . I don't need you, Marie . . . I don't need you anymore . . . do you understand? . . .

(*The Maid enters wearing a stern expression, without saying a word. She sees the corpse.*)

Professor (*in a voice less and less assured*).   I don't need you, Marie . . .

Maid (*sarcastic*).   Then, you're satisfied with your pupil, she's profited by your lesson?

Professor (*holding the knife behind his back*).   Yes, the lesson is finished . . . but . . . she . . . she's still there . . . she doesn't want to leave . . .

Maid (*very harshly*).   Is that a fact? . . .

Professor (*trembling*).   It wasn't I . . . it wasn't I . . . Marie . . . No . . . I assure you . . . it wasn't I, my little Marie . . .

Maid.   And who was it? Who was it then? Me?

Professor.   I don't know . . . maybe . . .

Maid. Or the cat?

Professor. That's possible . . . I don't know . . .

Maid. And today makes it the fortieth time! . . . And every day it's the same thing! Every day! You should be ashamed, at your age . . . and you're going to make yourself sick! You won't have any pupils left. That will serve you right.

Professor (*irritated*). It wasn't my fault! She didn't want to learn! She was disobedient! She was a bad pupil! She didn't want to learn!

Maid. Liar! . . .

Professor (*craftily approaching the Maid, holding the knife behind his back*). It's none of your business! (*He tries to strike her with a blow of the knife; the Maid seizes his wrist in mid-gesture and twists it; the Professor lets the knife fall to the floor*): . . . I'm sorry!

Maid (*gives him two loud, strong slaps; the Professor falls onto the floor, on his prat; he sobs*). Little murderer! bastard! You're disgusting! You wanted to do that to me? I'm not one of your pupils, not me! (*She pulls him up by the collar, picks up his skullcap and puts it on his head; he's afraid she'll slap him again and holds his arm up to protect his face, like a child.*) Put the knife back where it belongs, go on! (*The Professor goes and puts it back in the drawer of the buffet, then comes back to her.*) Now didn't I warn you, just a little while ago: arithmetic leads to philology, and philology leads to crime . . .

Professor. You said "to calamity"!

Maid. It's the same thing.

Professor. I didn't understand you. I thought that "calamity" was a city and that you meant that philology leads to the city of Calamity . . .

Maid. Liar! Old fox! An intellectual like you is not going to make a mistake in the meanings of words. Don't try to pull the wool over my eyes.

Professor (*sobbing*). I didn't kill her on purpose!

Maid. Are you sorry at least?

Professor. Oh, yes, Marie, I swear it to you!

Maid. I can't help feeling sorry for you! Ah! you're a good boy in spite of everything! I'll try to fix this. But don't start it again . . . It could give you a heart attack . . .

Professor. Yes, Marie! What are we going to do, now?

Maid. We're going to bury her . . . along with the thirty-nine others . . . that will make forty coffins . . . I'll call the undertakers and my lover, Father Auguste . . . I'll order the wreaths . . .

Professor. Yes, Marie, thank you very much.

Maid. Well, that's that. And perhaps it won't be necessary to call Auguste, since you yourself are something of a priest at times, if one can believe the gossip.

Professor. In any case, don't spend too much on the wreaths. She didn't pay for her lesson.

Maid. Don't worry . . . The least you can do is cover her up with her smock, she's not decent that way. And then we'll carry her out . . .

Professor. Yes, Marie, yes. *(He covers up the body.)* There's a chance that we'll get pinched . . . with forty coffins . . . Don't you think . . . people will be surprised . . . Suppose they ask us what's inside them?

Maid. Don't worry so much. We'll say that they're empty. And besides, people won't ask questions, they're used to it.

Professor. Even so . . .

Maid *(she takes out an armband with an insignia, perhaps the Nazi swastika).* Wait, if you're afraid, wear this, then you won't have anything more to be afraid of. *(She puts the armband around his arm.)* . . . That's good politics.

Professor. Thanks, my little Marie. With this, I won't need to worry . . . You're a good girl, Marie . . . very loyal . . .

Maid. That's enough. Come on, sir. Are you all right?

Professor. Yes, my little Marie. *(The Maid and the Professor take the body of the young girl, one by the shoulders, the other by the legs, and move towards the door on the right.)* Be careful. We don't want to hurt her. *(They exit.)*

(The stage remains empty for several moments. We hear the doorbell ring at the left.)

Voice of the Maid. Just a moment, I'm coming!

(She appears as she was at the beginning of the play, and goes towards the door. The doorbell rings again.)

Maid *(aside).* She's certainly in a hurry, this one! *(Aloud:)* Just a moment! *(She goes to the door on the left, and opens it.)* Good morning, miss! You are the new pupil? You have come for the lesson? The Professor is expecting you. I'll go tell him that you've come. He'll be right down. Come in, miss, come in!

Questions

1. *Discuss* **The Lesson** *in terms of Ionesco's assertion that "the true nature of things, truth itself, can be revealed to us only by fantasy, which is more realistic than all the realisms." In what sense is* **The Lesson** *a fantasy? Is it a fantasy from the very beginning?* **2.** *Ionesco asserts that "humor is the only possibility we possess of detaching ourselves . . . from our tragicomic human condition, the malaise of being. To become conscious of what is horrifying and to laugh at it is to become master of that which is horrifying. . . ." Does the play lend support to this view?* **3.** *What significance is there in the fact that the Pupil can add and multiply but is unable to subtract? In this connection, consider the Professor's statement that "one must be able to subtract too. It's not enough to in-*

tegrate, you must also disintegrate. That's the way life is. That's philosophy. That's science. That's progress, civilization." **4.** What is the significance of the Pupil's toothache that eventually spreads over her entire body? **5.** Ionesco's stage direction at the end of the play suggests that the armband that the Maid hands to the Professor might have the insignia of the Nazi swastika. Why would the swastika be appropriate? Would some other symbol be equally appropriate? **6.** In another stage direction, Ionesco states that the director may or may not choose to have the Professor wield a real knife. How will the choice affect the audience response to the play? If you were director, would you choose a real or imaginary knife? Explain.

iNNOCENCE ANd EXPERIENCE
QUESTIONS FOR FURTHER ANALYSIS

1. What support do the works in this section provide for Thomas Gray's well-known observation that "where ignorance is bliss,/'Tis folly to be wise?"

2. In such poems as Robert Burns' "To a Mouse," William Wordsworth's "Lines Composed a Few Miles Above Tintern Abbey," Robert Frost's "Birches," and Joni Mitchell's "The Circle Game," growing up is seen as a growing away from a kind of truth and reality; in other poems, such as Walt Whitman's "Out of the Cradle Endlessly Rocking," Gerard Manley Hopkins' "Spring and Fall," Dylan Thomas' "Fern Hill," and Robert Wallace's "In a Spring Still Not Written Of," growing up is seen as growing into truth and reality. Do these two groups of poems embody contradictory and mutually exclusive conceptions of childhood? Explain.

3. Consider the meaning of innocence in "The Short Happy Life of Francis Macomber" and "The Bride Comes to Yellow Sky." What are the sources of innocence in these works? What are the effects?

4. An eighteenth-century novelist wrote: "O Innocence, how glorious and happy a portion art thou to the breast that possesses thee! Thou fearest neither the eyes nor the tongues of men. Truth, the most powerful of all things, is thy strongest friend; and the brighter the light is in which thou art displayed, the more it discovers thy transcendent beauties." Which works in this section support this assessment of innocence? Which works contradict it? How would you characterize the relationship between "truth" and "innocence" in the fiction and the drama presented here?

5. A certain arrogance is associated with the innocence of Oedipus in Sophocles' *Oedipus Rex* and the young pupil in Ionesco's *The Lesson*. On what is the arrogance based? Is that arrogance finally destroyed in either case? How?

6. Robin in Hawthorne's "My Kinsman, Major Molineux" and the captain in Conrad's "The Secret Sharer" also exhibit a certain arrogance. On what is their arrogance based, and how is it modified?

7. Which poems in this section depend largely on irony for their force? Can you suggest why irony is a particularly useful device in literature that portrays innocence and experience?

8. Is the passage from innocence to experience a loss or a gain or both? Explain.

conformity and rebellion

Quadrille at the Moulin Rouge, Henri de Toulouse-Lautrec

CONFORMITY AND REBELLION

Although the works in this section, like those in "Innocence and Experience," may also feature a violation of innocence, the events are usually based on the clash between two well-articulated positions; the rebel, on principle, confronts and struggles with established authority. Central in these works is the sense of tremendous external forces—the state, the church, tradition—which can be obeyed only at the expense of conscience and humanity. At the most general level, these works confront a dilemma older than Antigone's Thebes: the very organizations men establish to protect and nurture the individual demand—on pain of economic ruin, social ostracism, even death, spiritual or physical—that he violate his most deeply cherished beliefs. When the individual refuses such a demand, he translates his awareness of a hostile social order into action against it and precipitates a crisis. In *Antigone,* the issue is drawn with utter clarity: Antigone must obey either the state (Creon) or the gods. In *A Doll's House,* Nora Helmer finally realizes that dehumanization is too high a price to pay for social stability.

Many of the works in this section, particularly the poems, do not treat the theme of conformity and rebellion quite so explicitly and dramatically. Some, like "Eleanor Rigby," describe a world devoid of human communion and community without directly accounting for it; others, like W. H. Auden's "The Unknown Citizen," tell us that the price exacted for total conformity to the industrial superstate is spiritual death. In "Easter 1916," William Butler Yeats meditates upon the awesome meaning of the lives and deaths of political·

revolutionaries, and in "Harlem," Langston Hughes warns that an inflexible and constricting social order will generate explosion.

Two basic modes, then, inform the literary treatment of conformity and rebellion. While in many of the works, the individual is caught up in a crisis that forces him into rebellion, in other works, especially the poems, the focus may be on the individual's failure to move from awareness into action, as in Amy Lowell's "Patterns." Indeed, the portraits of Auden's unknown citizen and of E. E. Cummings' Cambridge ladies affirm the necessity for rebellion by rendering so effectively the hollow life of mindless conformity.

However diverse in treatment and technique, all the works in this section are about individuals trapped by complex sets of external forces that regulate and define their lives. The social being, man, sometimes submits to these forces, but it is always an uneasy submission, for their purpose is to curb and control him. He may recognize that he must be controlled for some larger good; yet he is aware that established social power is often abusive. The tendency of power, at its best, is to act as a conserving force that brakes the disruptive impulse to abandon and destroy old ways and ideas. At its worst, power is self-serving. The individual must constantly judge which tendency power is enhancing. And since the power of the individual is negligible beside that of frequently abusive social forces, it is not surprising that many artists since the advent of the great nation-states have found a fundamental human dignity in the resistance of the individual to organized society. One of man's ancient and profound recognitions, after all, is that the impulse of a Creon is always to make unknown citizens of us all.

conformity and rebellion

The Shriek, 1896 by Edvard Munch

FICTION

The Metamorphosis*

FRANZ KAFKA [1883–1924]

I

AS Gregor Samsa awoke one morning from uneasy dreams he found himself transformed in his bed into a gigantic insect. He was lying on his hard, as it were armor-plated, back and when he lifted his head a little he could see his dome-like brown belly divided into stiff arched segments on top of which the bed quilt could hardly keep in position and was about to slide off completely. His numerous legs, which were pitifully thin compared to the rest of his bulk, waved helplessly before his eyes.

What has happened to me? he thought. It was no dream. His room, a regular human bedroom, only rather too small, lay quiet between the four familiar walls. Above the table on which a collection of cloth samples was unpacked and spread out—Samsa was a commercial traveler—hung the picture which he had recently cut out of an illustrated magazine and put into a pretty gilt frame. It showed a lady, with a fur cap on and a fur stole, sitting upright and holding out to the spectator a huge fur muff into which the whole of her forearm had vanished!

Gregor's eyes turned next to the window, and the overcast sky—one could hear rain drops beating on the window gutter—made him quite melancholy. What about sleeping a little longer and forgetting all this nonsense, he thought, but it could not be done, for he was accustomed to sleep on his right side and in his present condition he could not turn himself over. However violently he forced himself towards his right side he always rolled on to his back again. He tried it at least a hundred times, shutting his eyes to keep from seeing his struggling legs, and only desisted when he began to feel in his side a faint dull ache he had never experienced before.

Oh God, he thought, what an exhausting job I've picked on! Traveling about day in, day out. It's much more irritating work than doing the actual business in the office, and on top of that there's the trouble of constant

---

*Translated by Willa and Edwin Muir.

traveling, of worrying about train connections, the bed and irregular meals, casual acquaintances that are always new and never become intimate friends. The devil take it all! He felt a slight itching up on his belly; slowly pushed himself on his back nearer to the top of the bed so that he could lift his head more easily; identified the itching place which was surrounded by many small white spots the nature of which he could not understand and made to touch it with a leg, but drew the leg back immediately, for the contact made a cold shiver run through him.

He slid down again into his former position. This getting up early, he thought, makes one quite stupid. A man needs his sleep. Other commercials live like harem women. For instance, when I come back to the hotel of a morning to write up the orders I've got, these others are only sitting down to breakfast. Let me just try that with my chief; I'd be sacked on the spot. Anyhow, that might be quite a good thing for me, who can tell? If I didn't have to hold my hand because of my parents I'd have given notice long ago, I'd have gone to the chief and told him exactly what I think of him. That would knock him endways from his desk! It's a queer way of doing, too, this sitting on high at a desk and talking down to employees, especially when they have to come quite near because the chief is hard of hearing. Well, there's still hope; once I've saved enough money to pay back my parents' debts to him—that should take another five or six years—I'll do it without fail. I'll cut myself completely loose then. For the moment, though, I'd better get up, since my train goes at five.

He looked at the alarm clock ticking on the chest. Heavenly Father! he thought. It was half-past six o'clock and the hands were quietly moving on, it was even past the half-hour, it was getting on toward a quarter to seven. Had the alarm clock not gone off? From the bed one could see that it had been properly set for four o'clock; of course it must have gone off. Yes, but was it possible to sleep quietly through that ear-splitting noise? Well, he had not slept quietly, yet apparently all the more soundly for that. But what was he to do now? The next train went at seven o'clock; to catch that he would need to hurry like mad and his samples weren't even packed up, and he himself wasn't feeling particularly fresh and active. And even if he did catch the train he wouldn't avoid a row with the chief, since the firm's porter would have been waiting for the five o'clock train and would have long since reported his failure to turn up. The porter was a creature of the chief's, spineless and stupid. Well, supposing he were to say he was sick? But that would be most unpleasant and would look suspicious, since during his five years' employment he had not been ill once. The chief himself would be sure to come with the sick-insurance doctor, would reproach his parents with their son's laziness and would cut all excuses short by referring to the insurance doctor, who of course regarded all mankind as perfectly healthy malingerers. And would he be so far wrong on this occasion? Gregor really felt quite well, apart from a drowsiness that was utterly superfluous after such a long sleep, and he was even unusually hungry.

As all this was running through his mind at top speed without his being able to decide to leave his bed—the alarm clock had just struck a quarter to seven—there came a cautious tap at the door behind the head of his bed. "Gregor," said a voice—it was his mother's—"it's a quarter to seven. Hadn't you a train to catch?" That gentle voice! Gregor had a shock as he heard his own voice answering hers, unmistakably his own voice, it was true, but with a persistent horrible twittering squeak behind it like an undertone, that left the words in their clear shape only for the first moment and then rose up reverberating round them to destroy their sense, so that one could not be sure one had heard them rightly. Gregor wanted to answer at length and explain everything, but in the circumstances he confined himself to saying: "Yes, yes, thank you, Mother, I'm getting up now." The wooden door between them must have kept the change in his voice from being noticeable outside, for his mother contented herself with this statement and shuffled away. Yet this brief exchange of words had made the other members of the family aware that Gregor was still in the house, as they had not expected, and at one of the side doors his father was already knocking, gently, yet with his fist. "Gregor, Gregor," he called, "what's the matter with you?" And after a little while he called again in a deeper voice: "Gregor! Gregor!" At the other side door his sister was saying in a low, plaintive tone: "Gregor? Aren't you well? Are you needing anything?" He answered them both at once: "I'm just ready," and did his best to make his voice sound as normal as possible by enunciating the words very clearly and leaving long pauses between them. So his father went back to his breakfast, but his sister whispered: "Gregor, open the door, do." However, he was not thinking of opening the door, and felt thankful for the prudent habit he had acquired in traveling of locking all doors during the night, even at home.

His immediate intention was to get up quietly without being disturbed, to put on his clothes and above all eat his breakfast, and only then to consider what else was to be done, since in bed, he was well aware, his meditations would come to no sensible conclusion. He remembered that often enough in bed he had felt small aches and pains, probably caused by awkward postures, which had proved purely imaginary once he got up, and he looked forward eagerly to seeing this morning's delusions gradually fall away. That the change in his voice was nothing but the precursor of a severe chill, a standing ailment of commercial travelers, he had not the least possible doubt.

To get rid of the quilt was quite easy; he had only to inflate himself a little and it fell off by itself. But the next move was difficult, especially because he was so uncommonly broad. He would have needed arms and hands to hoist himself up; instead he had only the numerous little legs which never stopped waving in all directions and which he could not control in the least. When he tried to bend one of them it was the first to stretch itself straight; and did he succeed at last in making it do what he wanted, all the other legs meanwhile waved the more wildly in a high degree of unpleasant agitation. "But what's the use of lying idle in bed," said Gregor to himself.

He thought that he might get out of bed with the lower part of his body first, but this lower part, which he had not yet seen and of which he could form no clear conception, proved too difficult to move; it shifted so slowly; and when finally, almost wild with annoyance, he gathered his forces together and thrust out recklessly, he had miscalculated the direction and bumped heavily against the lower end of the bed, and the stinging pain he felt informed him that precisely this lower part of his body was at the moment probably the most sensitive.

So he tried to get the top part of himself out first, and cautiously moved his head towards the edge of the bed. That proved easy enough, and despite its breadth and mass the bulk of his body at last slowly followed the movement of his head. Still, when he finally got his head free over the edge of the bed he felt too scared to go on advancing, for after all if he let himself fall in this way it would take a miracle to keep his head from being injured. And at all costs he must not lose consciousness now, precisely now; he would rather stay in bed.

But when after a repetition of the same efforts he lay in his former position again, sighing, and watched his little legs struggling against each other more wildly than ever, if that were possible, and saw no way of bringing any order into this arbitrary confusion, he told himself again that it was impossible to stay in bed and that the most sensible course was to risk everything for the smallest hope of getting away from it. At the same time he did not forget meanwhile to remind himself that cool reflection, the coolest possible, was much better than desperate resolves. In such moments he focused his eyes as sharply as possible on the window, but, unfortunately, the prospect of the morning fog, which muffled even the other side of the narrow street, brought him little encouragement and comfort. "Seven o'clock already," he said to himself when the alarm clock chimed again, "seven o'clock already and still such a thick fog." And for a little while he lay quiet, breathing lightly, as if perhaps expecting such complete repose to restore all things to their real and normal condition.

But then he said to himself: "Before it strikes a quarter past seven I must be quite out of this bed, without fail. Anyhow, by that time someone will have come from the office to ask for me, since it opens before seven." And he set himself to rocking his whole body at once in a regular rhythm, with the idea of swinging it out of the bed. If he tipped himself out in that way he could keep his head from injury by lifting it at an acute angle when he fell. His back seemed to be hard and was not likely to suffer from a fall on the carpet. His biggest worry was the loud crash he would not be able to help making, which would probably cause anxiety, if not terror, behind all the doors. Still, he must take the risk.

When he was already half out of the bed—the new method was more a game than an effort, for he needed only to hitch himself across by rocking to and fro—it struck him how simple it would be if he could get help. Two strong people—he thought of his father and the servant girl—would be amply sufficient; they would only have to thrust their arms under his convex back, lever him out of the bed, bend down with their burden and then be patient enough to let him turn himself right over on to the floor, where it was to be hoped his legs would then find their proper function. Well, ignoring the fact that the doors were all locked, ought he really to call for help? In spite of his misery he could not suppress a smile at the very idea of it.

He had got so far that he could barely keep his equilibrium when he rocked himself strongly, and he would have to nerve himself very soon for the final decision since in five minutes' time it would be a quarter past seven—when the front door bell rang. "That's someone from the office," he said to himself, and grew almost rigid, while his little legs only jigged about all the faster. For a moment everything stayed quiet. "They're not going to open the door," said Gregor to himself, catching at some kind of irrational hope. But then of course the servant girl went as usual to the door with her heavy tread and opened it. Gregor needed only to hear the first good morning of the visitor to know immediately who it was—the chief clerk himself. What a fate, to be condemned to work for a firm where the smallest omission at once gave rise to the gravest suspicion! Were all employees in a body nothing but scoundrels, was there not among them one single loyal devoted man who, had he wasted only an hour or so of the firm's time in a morning, was so tormented by conscience as to be driven out of his mind and actually incapable of leaving his bed? Wouldn't it really have been sufficient to send an apprentice to inquire—if any inquiry were necessary at all—did the chief clerk himself have to come and thus indicate to the entire family, an innocent family, that this suspicious circumstance could be investigated by no one less versed in affairs than himself? And more through the agitation caused by these reflections than through any act of will Gregor swung himself out of bed with all his strength. There was a loud thump, but it was not really a crash. His fall was broken to some extent by the carpet, his back, too, was less stiff than he thought, and so there was merely a dull thud, not so very startling. Only he had not lifted his head carefully enough and had hit it; he turned it and rubbed it on the carpet in pain and irritation.

"That was something falling down in there," said the chief clerk in the next room to the left. Gregor tried to suppose to himself that something like what had happened to him today might some day happen to the chief clerk; one really could not deny that it was possible. But as if in brusque reply to this supposition the chief clerk took a couple of firm steps in the next-door room and his patent leather boots creaked. From the right-hand room his sister was whispering to inform him of the situation: "Gregor, the chief clerk's here." "I know," muttered Gregor to himself; but he didn't dare to make his voice loud enough for his sister to hear it.

"Gregor," said his father now from the left-hand room, "the chief clerk has come and wants to know why you didn't catch the early train. We don't know what to say to him. Besides, he wants to talk to you in person. So open the door, please. He will be good enough to excuse the untidiness of your room." "Good morning, Mr. Samsa," the chief clerk was calling amiably meanwhile. "He's not well," said his mother to the visitor, while his father was still speaking through the door, "he's not well, sir, believe me. What else would make him miss a train! The boy thinks about nothing but his work. It makes me almost cross the way he never goes out in the evenings; he's been here the last eight days and has stayed at home every single evening. He just sits there quietly at the table reading a newspaper or looking through railway timetables. The only amusement he gets is doing fretwork. For instance, he spent two or three evenings cutting out a little picture frame; you would be surprised to see how pretty it is; it's hanging in his room; you'll see it in a minute when Gregor opens the door. I must say I'm glad you've come, sir; we should never have got him to unlock the door by ourselves; he's so obstinate; and I'm sure he's unwell, though he wouldn't have it to be so this morning." "I'm just coming," said Gregor slowly and carefully, not moving an inch for fear of losing one word of the conversation. "I can't think of any other explanation, madam," said the chief clerk, "I hope it's nothing serious. Although on the other hand I must say that we men of business—fortunately or unfortunately—very often simply have to ignore any slight indisposition, since business must be attended to." "Well, can the chief clerk come in now?" asked Gregor's father impatiently, again knocking on the door. "No," said Gregor. In the left-hand room a painful silence followed this refusal, in the right-hand room his sister began to sob.

Why didn't his sister join the others? She was probably newly out of bed and hadn't even begun to put on her clothes yet. Well, why was she crying? Because he wouldn't get up and let the chief clerk in, because he was in danger of losing his job, and because the chief would begin dunning his parents again for the old debts? Surely these were things one didn't need to worry about for the present. Gregor was still at home and not in the least thinking of deserting the family. At the moment, true, he was lying on the carpet and no one who knew the condition he was in could seriously expect him to admit the chief clerk. But for such a small discourtesy, which could plausibly be explained away somehow later on, Gregor could hardly be dismissed on the spot. And it seemed to Gregor that it would be much more sensible to leave him in peace for the present than to trouble him with tears and entreaties. Still, of course, their uncertainty bewildered them all and excused their behavior.

"Mr. Samsa," the chief clerk called now in a louder voice, "what's the matter with you? Here you are, barricading yourself in your room, giving only 'yes' and 'no' for answers, causing your parents a lot of unnecessary trouble and neglecting—I mention this only in passing—neglecting your business duties in an incredible fashion. I am speaking here in the name of your parents and of your chief, and I beg you quite seriously to give me an immediate and precise explanation. You amaze me, you amaze me. I thought you were a quiet, dependable person, and now all at once you seem bent on making a disgraceful exhibition of yourself. The chief did hint to me early this morning a possible explanation for your disappearance—with reference to the cash payments that were entrusted to you recently—but I almost pledged my solemn word of honor that this could not be so. But now that I see how incredibly obstinate you are, I no longer have the slightest desire to take your part at all. And your position in the firm is not so unassailable. I came with the intention of telling you all this in private, but since you are wasting my time so needlessly I don't see why your parents shouldn't hear it too. For some time past your work has been most unsatisfactory; this is not the season of the year for a business boom, of course, we admit that, but a season of the year for doing no business at all, that does not exist, Mr. Samsa, must not exist."

"But, sir," cried Gregor, beside himself and in his agitation forgetting everything else, "I'm just going to open the door this very minute. A slight illness, an attack of giddiness, has kept me from getting up. I'm still lying in bed. But I feel all right again. I'm getting out of bed now. Just give me a moment or two longer! I'm not quite so well as I thought. But I'm all right, really. How a thing like that can suddenly strike one down! Only last night I was quite well, my parents can tell you, or rather I did have a slight presentiment. I must have showed some sign of it. Why didn't I report it at the office! But one always thinks that an indisposition can be got over without staying in the house. Oh sir, do spare my parents! All that you're reproaching me with now has no foundation; no one has ever said a word to me about it. Perhaps you haven't looked at the last orders I sent in. Anyhow, I can still catch the eight o'clock train, I'm much the better for my few hours' rest. Don't let me detain you here, sir; I'll be attending to business very soon, and do be good enough to tell the chief so and to make my excuses to him!"

And while all this was tumbling out pell-mell and Gregor hardly knew what he was saying, he had reached the chest quite easily, perhaps because of the practice he had had in bed, and was now trying to lever himself upright by means of it. He meant actually to open the door, actually to show himself and speak to the chief clerk; he was eager to find out what the others, after all their insistence, would say at the sight of him. If they were horrified then the responsibility was no longer his and he could stay quiet. But if they took it calmly, then he had no reason either to be upset, and could really get to the station for the eight o'clock train if he hurried. At first he slipped down a few times from the polished surface of the chest, but at length with a last heave he stood upright; he paid no more attention to the pains in the lower part of his body, however they smarted. Then he let himself fall against the back of a nearby chair, and clung with his little legs to the edges of it. That brought him into control of himself again and he stopped speaking, for now he could listen to what the chief clerk was saying.

"Did you understand a word of it?" the chief clerk was asking; "surely he can't be trying to make fools of us?" "Oh dear," cried his mother, in tears, "perhaps he's terribly ill and we're tormenting him. Grete! Grete!" she called out then. "Yes, Mother?" called his sister from the other side. They were calling to each other across Gregor's room. "You must go this minute for the doctor. Gregor is ill. Go for the doctor, quick. Did you hear how he was speaking?" "That was no human voice," said the chief clerk in a voice noticeably low beside the shrillness of the mother's. "Anna! Anna!" his father was calling through the hall to the kitchen, clapping his hands, "get a locksmith at once!" And the two girls were already running through the hall with a swish of skirts—how could his sister have got dressed so quickly?—and were tearing the front door open. There was no sound of its closing again; they had evidently left it open, as one does in houses where some great misfortune has happened.

But Gregor was now much calmer. The words he uttered were no longer understandable, apparently, although they seemed clear enough to him, even clearer than before, perhaps because his ear had grown accustomed to the sound of them. Yet at any rate people now believed that something was wrong with him, and were ready to help him. The positive certainty with which these first measures had been taken comforted him. He felt himself drawn once more into the human circle and hoped for great and remarkable results from both the doctor and the locksmith, without really distinguishing precisely between them. To make his voice as clear as possible for the decisive conversation that was now imminent he coughed a little, as quietly as he could, of course, since this noise too might not sound like a human cough for all he was able to judge. In the next room meanwhile there was complete silence. Perhaps his parents were sitting at the table with the chief clerk, whispering, perhaps they were all leaning against the door and listening.

Slowly Gregor pushed the chair towards the door, then let go of it, caught hold of the door for support—the soles at the end of his little legs were somewhat sticky—and rested against it for a moment after his efforts. Then he set himself to turning the key in the lock with his mouth. It seemed, unhappily, that he hadn't really any teeth—what could he grip the key with?—but on the other hand his jaws were certainly very strong; with their help he did manage to set the key in motion, heedless of the fact that he was undoubtedly damaging them somewhere, since a brown fluid issued from his mouth, flowed over the key and dripped on the floor. "Just listen to that," said the chief clerk next door; "he's turning the key." That was a great encouragement to Gregor; but they should all have shouted encouragement to him, his father and mother too: "Go on, Gregor," they should have called out, "keep going, hold on to that key!" And in the belief that they were all following his efforts intently, he clenched his jaws recklessly on the key with all the force at his command. As the turning of the key progressed he circled round the lock, holding on now only with his mouth, pushing on the key, as required, or pulling it down again with all the weight of his body. The louder click of the finally yielding lock literally quickened Gregor. With a deep breath of relief he said to himself: "So I didn't need the locksmith," and laid his head on the handle to open the door wide.

Since he had to pull the door towards him, he was still invisible when it was really wide open. He had to edge himself slowly round the near half of the double door, and to do it very carefully if he was not to fall plump upon his back just on the threshold. He was still carrying out this difficult manoeuvre, with no time to observe anything else, when he heard the chief clerk utter a loud "Oh!"—it sounded like a gust of wind—and now he could see the man, standing as he was nearest to the door, clapping one hand before his open mouth and slowly backing away as if driven by some invisible steady pressure. His mother—in spite of the chief clerk's being there her hair was still undone and sticking up in all directions—first clasped her hands and looked at his father, then took two steps towards Gregor and fell on the floor among her outspread skirts, her face quite hidden on her breast. His father knotted his fist with a fierce expression on his face as if he meant to knock Gregor back into his room, then looked uncertainly round the living room, covered his eyes with his hands and wept till his great chest heaved.

Gregor did not go now into the living room, but leaned against the inside of the firmly shut wing of the door, so that only half his body was visible and his head above it bending sideways to look at the others. The light had meanwhile strengthened; on the other side of the street one could see clearly a section of the endlessly long, dark gray building opposite—it was a hospital—abruptly punctuated by its row of regular windows; the rain was still falling, but only in large singly discernible and literally singly splashing drops. The breakfast dishes were set out on the table lavishly, for breakfast was the most important meal of the day to Gregor's father, who lingered it out for hours over various newspapers. Right opposite Gregor on the wall hung a photograph of himself on military service, as a lieutenant, hand on sword, a carefree smile on his face, inviting one to respect his uniform and military bearing. The door leading to the hall was open, and one could see that the front door stood open too, showing the landing beyond and the beginning of the stairs going down.

"Well," said Gregor, knowing perfectly that he was the only one who had retained any composure, "I'll put my clothes on at once, pack up my samples and start off. Will you only let me go? You see, sir, I'm not obstinate, and I'm willing to work; traveling is a hard life, but I couldn't live without it. Where are you going, sir? To the office? Yes? Will you give a true account of all this? One can be temporarily incapacitated, but that's just the moment for remembering former services and bearing in mind that later on, when the incapacity has been got over, one will certainly work with all the more industry and concentration. I'm loyally bound to serve the chief, you know that very well. Besides, I have to provide for my parents and my sister. I'm in great difficulties, but I'll get out of them again. Don't make things any worse for me than they are. Stand up for me in the firm. Travelers are not popular there, I know. People think they earn sacks of money and just have a good time. A prejudice there's no particular reason for revising. But you, sir, have a more comprehensive view of affairs than the rest of the staff, yes, let me tell you in confidence, a more comprehensive view than the chief himself, who, being the owner, lets his judgment easily be swayed against one of his employees. And you know very well that the traveler, who is never seen in the office almost the whole year round, can so easily fall a victim to gossip and ill luck and unfounded complaints, which he mostly knows nothing about, except when he comes back exhausted from his rounds, and only then suffers in person from their evil consequences, which he can no longer trace back to the original causes. Sir, sir, don't go away without a word to me to show that you think me in the right at least to some extent!''

But at Gregor's very first words the chief clerk had already backed away and only stared at him with parted lips over one twitching shoulder. And while Gregor was speaking he did not stand still one moment but stole away towards the door, without taking his eyes off Gregor, yet only an inch at a time, as if obeying some secret injunction to leave the room. He was already at the hall, and the suddenness with which he took his last step out of the living room would have made one believe he had burned the sole of his foot. Once in the hall he stretched his right arm before him towards the staircase, as if some supernatural power were waiting there to deliver him.

Gregor perceived that the chief clerk must on no account be allowed to go away in this frame of mind if his position in the firm were not to be endangered to the utmost. His parents did not understand this so well; they had convinced themselves in the course of years that Gregor was settled for life in this firm, and besides they were so occupied with their immediate troubles that all foresight had forsaken them. Yet Gregor had this foresight. The chief clerk must be detained, soothed, persuaded and finally won over; the whole future of Gregor and his family depended on it! If only his sister had been there! She was intelligent; she had begun to cry while Gregor was still lying quietly on his back. And no doubt the chief clerk, so partial to ladies, would have been guided by her; she would have shut the door of the flat and in the hall talked him out of his horror. But she was not there, and Gregor would have to handle the situation himself. And without remembering that he was still unaware what powers of movement he possessed, without even remembering that his words in all possibility, indeed in all likelihood, would again be unintelligible, he let go the wing of the door, pushed himself through the opening, started to walk towards the chief clerk, who was already ridiculously clinging with both hands to the railing on the landing; but immediately, as he was feeling for a support, he fell down with a little cry upon all his numerous legs. Hardly was he down when he experienced for the first time this morning a sense of physical comfort; his legs had firm ground under them; they were completely obedient, as he noted with joy; they even strove to carry him forward in whatever direction he chose; and he was inclined to believe that a final relief from all his sufferings was at hand. But in the same moment as he found himself on the floor, rocking with suppressed eagerness to move, not far from his mother, indeed just in front of her, she, who had seemed so completely crushed, sprang all at once to her feet, her arms and fingers outspread, cried: ''Help, for God's sake, help!'' bent her head down as if to see Gregor better, yet on the contrary kept backing senselessly away; had quite forgotten that the laden table stood behind her; sat upon it hastily, as if in absence of mind, when she bumped into it; and seemed altogether unaware that the big coffee pot beside her was upset and pouring coffee in a flood over the carpet.

"Mother, Mother," said Gregor in a low voice, and looked up at her. The chief clerk, for the moment, had quite slipped from his mind; instead, he could not resist snapping his jaws together at the sight of the streaming coffee. That made his mother scream again, she fled from the table and fell into the arms of his father, who hastened to catch her. But Gregor had now no time to spare for his parents; the chief clerk was already on the stairs; with his chin on the banisters he was taking one last backward look. Gregor made a spring, to be as sure as possible of overtaking him; the chief clerk must have divined his intention, for he leaped down several steps and vanished; he was still yelling "Ugh!" and it echoed through the whole staircase.

Unfortunately, the flight of the chief clerk seemed completely to upset Gregor's father, who had remained relatively calm until now, for instead of running after the man himself, or at least not hindering Gregor in his pursuit, he seized in his right hand the walking stick which the chief clerk had left behind on a chair, together with a hat and greatcoat, snatched in his left hand a large newspaper from the table and began stamping his feet and flourishing the stick and the newspaper to drive Gregor back into his room. No entreaty of Gregor's availed, indeed no entreaty was even understood; however humbly he bent his head his father only stamped on the floor the more loudly. Behind his father his mother had torn open a window, despite the cold weather, and was leaning far out of it with her face in her hands. A strong draught set in from the street to the staircase, the window curtain blew in, the newspapers on the table fluttered, stray pages whisked over the floor. Pitilessly Gregor's father drove him back, hissing and crying "Shoo!" like a savage. But Gregor was quite unpracticed in walking backwards, it really was a slow business. If he only had a chance to turn round he could get back to his room at once, but he was afraid of exasperating his father by the slowness of such a rotation and at any moment the stick in his father's hand might hit him a fatal blow on the back or on the head. In the end, however, nothing else was left for him to do since to his horror he observed that in moving backwards he could not even control the direction he took; and so, keeping an anxious eye on his father all the time over his shoulder, he began to turn round as quickly as he could, which was in reality very slowly. Perhaps his father noted his good intentions, for he did not interfere except every now and then to help him in the manoeuvre from a distance with the point of the stick. If only he would have stopped making that unbearable hissing noise! It made Gregor quite lose his head. He had turned almost completely round when the hissing noise so distracted him that he even turned a little the wrong way again. But when at last his head was fortunately right in front of the doorway, it appeared that his body was too broad simply to get through the opening. His father, of course, in his present mood was far from thinking of such a thing as opening the other half of the door, to let Gregor have enough space. He had merely the fixed idea of driving Gregor back into his room as quickly as possible. He would never have suffered Gregor to make the circumstantial preparations for standing up on end and perhaps slipping his way through the door. Maybe he was now making more noise than ever to urge Gregor forward, as if no obstacle impeded him; to Gregor, anyhow, the noise in his rear sounded no longer like the voice of one single father; this was really no joke, and Gregor thrust himself—come what might—into the doorway. One side of his body rose up, he was tilted at an angle in the doorway, his flank was quite bruised, horrid blotches stained the white door, soon he was stuck fast and, left to himself, could not have moved at all, his legs on one side fluttered trembling in the air, those on the other were crushed painfully to the floor—when from behind his father gave him a strong push which was literally a deliverance and he flew far into the room, bleeding freely. The door was slammed behind him with the stick, and then at last there was silence.

II

NOT until it was twilight did Gregor awake out of a deep sleep, more like a swoon than a sleep. He would certainly have waked up of his own accord not much later, for he felt himself sufficiently rested and well-slept, but it seemed to him as if a fleeting step and a cautious shutting of the door leading into the hall had aroused him. The electric lights in the street cast a pale sheen here and there on the ceiling and the upper surfaces of the furniture, but down below, where he lay, it was dark. Slowly, awkwardly trying out his feelers, which he now first learned to appreciate, he pushed his way to the door to see what had been happening there. His left side felt like one single long, unpleasantly tense scar, and he had actually to limp on his two rows of legs. One little leg, moreover, had been severely damaged in the course of that morning's events—it was almost a miracle that only one had been damaged—and trailed uselessly behind him.

He had reached the door before he discovered what had really drawn him to it: the smell of food. For there stood a basin filled with fresh milk in which floated little sops of white bread. He could almost have laughed with joy, since he was now still hungrier than in the morning, and he dipped his head almost over the eyes straight into the milk. But soon in disappointment he withdrew it again; not only did he find it difficult to feed because of his tender left side—and he could only feed with the palpitating collaboration of his whole body—he did not like the milk either, although milk had been his favorite drink and that was certainly why his sister had set it there for him, indeed it was almost with repulsion that he turned away from the basin and crawled back to the middle of the room.

He could see through the crack of the door that the gas was turned on in the living room, but while usually at this time his father made a habit of reading the afternoon newspaper in a loud voice to his mother and occasionally to his sister as well, not a sound was now to be heard. Well, perhaps his father had recently given up this habit of reading aloud, which his sister had mentioned so often in conversation and in her letters. But there was the same silence all around, although the flat was certainly not empty of occupants. "What a quiet life our family has been leading," said Gregor to himself, and as he sat there motionless staring into the darkness he felt great pride in the fact that he had been able to provide such a life for his parents and sister in such a fine flat. But what if all the quiet, the comfort, the contentment were now to end in horror? To keep himself from being lost in such thoughts Gregor took refuge in movement and crawled up and down the room.

Once during the long evening one of the side doors was opened a little and quickly shut again, later the other side door too; someone had apparently wanted to come in and then thought better of it. Gregor now stationed himself immediately before the living room door, determined to persuade any hesitating visitor to come in or at least to discover who it might be; but the door was not opened again and he waited in vain. In the early morning, when the doors were locked, they had all wanted to come in, now that he had opened one door and the other had apparently been opened during the day, no one came in and even the keys were on the other side of the doors.

It was late at night before the gas went out in the living room, and Gregor could easily tell that his parents and his sister had all stayed awake until then, for he could clearly hear the three of them stealing away on tiptoe. No one was likely to visit him, not until the morning, that was certain; so he had plenty of time to meditate at his leisure on how he was to arrange his life afresh. But the lofty, empty room in which he had to lie flat on the floor filled him with an apprehension he could not account for, since it had been his very own room for the past five years—and with a half-unconscious action, not without a slight feeling of shame, he scuttled under the sofa, where he felt comfortable at once, although his back was a little cramped and he could not lift his head up, and his only regret was that his body was too broad to get the whole of it under the sofa.

He stayed there all night, spending the time partly in a light slumber, from which his hunger kept waking him up with a start, and partly in worrying and sketching vague hopes, which all led to the same conclusion, that he must lie low for the present and, by exercising patience and the utmost consideration, help the family to bear the inconvenience he was bound to cause them in his present condition.

Very early in the morning, it was still almost night, Gregor had the chance to test the strength of his new resolutions, for his sister, nearly fully dressed, opened the door from the hall and peered in. She did not see him at once, yet when she caught sight of him under the sofa—well, he had to be somewhere, he couldn't have flown away, could he?—she was so startled that without being able to help it she slammed the door shut again. But as if regretting her behavior she opened the door again immediately and came in on tiptoe, as if she were visiting an invalid or even a stranger. Gregor had pushed his head forward to the very edge of the sofa and watched her. Would she notice that he had left the milk standing, and not for lack of hunger, and would she bring in some other kind of food more to his taste? If she did not do it of her own accord, he would rather starve than draw her attention to the fact, although he felt a wild impulse to dart out from under the sofa, throw himself at her feet and beg her for something to eat. But his sister at once noticed, with surprise, that the basin was still full, except for a little milk that had been spilt all around it, she lifted it immediately, not with her bare hands, true, but with a cloth and carried it away. Gregor was wildly curious to know what she would bring instead, and made various speculations about it. Yet what she actually did next, in the goodness of her heart, he could never have guessed at. To find out what he liked she brought him a whole selection of food, all set out on an old newspaper. There were old, half-decayed vegetables, bones from last night's supper covered with a white sauce that had thickened; some raisins and almonds; a piece of cheese that Gregor would have called uneatable two days ago; a dry roll of bread, a buttered roll, and a roll both buttered and salted. Besides all that, she set down again the same basin, into which she had poured some water, and which was apparently to be reserved for his exclusive use. And with fine tact, knowing that Gregor would not eat in her presence, she withdrew quickly and even turned the key, to let him understand that he could take his ease as much as he liked. Gregor's legs all whizzed towards the food. His wounds must have healed completely, moreover, for he felt no disability, which amazed him and made him reflect how more than a month ago he had cut one finger a little with a knife and had still suffered pain from the wound only the day before yesterday. Am I less sensitive now? he thought, and sucked greedily at the cheese, which above all the other edibles attracted him at once and strongly. One after another and with tears of satisfaction in his eyes he quickly devoured the cheese, the vegetables and the sauce; the fresh food, on the other hand, had no charms for him, he could not even stand the smell of it and actually dragged away to some little distance the things he could eat. He had long finished his meal and was only lying lazily on the same spot when his sister turned the key slowly as a sign for him to retreat. That roused him at once, although he was nearly asleep, and he hurried under the sofa again. But it took considerable self-control for him to stay under the sofa, even for the short time his sister was in the room, since the large meal had swollen his body somewhat and he was so cramped he could hardly breathe. Slight attacks of breathlessness afflicted him and his eyes were starting a little out of his head as he watched his unsuspecting sister sweeping together with a broom not only the remains of what he had eaten but even the things he had not touched, as if these were now of no use to anyone, and hastily shoveling it all into a bucket, which she covered with a wooden lid and carried away. Hardly had she turned her back when Gregor came from under the sofa and stretched and puffed himself out.

In this manner Gregor was fed, once in the early morning while his parents and the servant girl were still asleep, and a second time after they had all had their midday dinner, for then his parents took a short nap and the servant girl could be sent out on some errand or other by his sister. Not that they would have wanted him to starve, of course, but perhaps they could not have borne to know more about his feeding than from hearsay, perhaps too his sister wanted to spare them such little anxieties wherever possible, since they had quite enough to bear as it was.

Under what pretext the doctor and the locksmith had been got rid of on that first morning Gregor could not discover, for since what he said was not understood by the others it never struck any of them, not even his sister, that he could understand what they said, and so whenever his sister came into his room he had to content himself with hearing her utter only a sigh now and then and an occasional appeal to the saints. Later on, when she had got a little used to the situation—of course she could never get completely used to it—she sometimes threw out a remark which was kindly meant or could be so interpreted. "Well, he liked his dinner today," she would say when Gregor had made a good clearance of his food; and when he had not eaten, which gradually happened more and more often, she would say almost sadly: "Everything's been left standing again."

But although Gregor could get no news directly, he overheard a lot from the neighboring rooms, and as soon as voices were audible, he would run to the door of the room concerned and press his whole body against it. In the first few days especially there was no conversation that did not refer to him somehow, even if only indirectly. For two whole days there were family consultations at every mealtime about what should be done; but also between meals the same subject was discussed, for there were always at least two members of the family at home, since no one wanted to be alone in the flat and to leave it quite empty was unthinkable. And on the very first of these days the household cook—it was not quite clear what and how much she knew of the situation—went down on her knees to his mother and begged leave to go, and when she departed, a quarter of an hour later, gave thanks for her dismissal with tears in her eyes as if for the greatest benefit that could have been conferred on her, and without any prompting swore a solemn oath that she would never say a single word to anyone about what had happened.

Now Gregor's sister had to cook too, helping her mother; true, the cooking did not amount to much, for they ate scarcely anything. Gregor was always hearing one of the family vainly urging another to eat and getting no answer but: "Thanks, I've had all I want," or something similar. Perhaps they drank nothing either. Time and again his sister kept asking his father if he wouldn't like some beer and offered kindly to go and fetch it herself, and when he made no answer suggested that she could ask the concierge to fetch it, so that he need feel no sense of obligation, but then a round "No" came from his father and no more was said about it.

In the course of that very first day Gregor's father explained the family's financial position and prospects to both his mother and his sister. Now and then he rose from the table to get some voucher or memorandum out of the small safe he had rescued from the collapse of his business five years earlier.

One could hear him opening the complicated lock and rustling papers out and shutting it again. This statement made by his father was the first cheerful information Gregor had heard since his imprisonment. He had been of the opinion that nothing at all was left over from his father's business, at least his father had never said anything to the contrary, and of course he had not asked him directly. At that time Gregor's sole desire was to do his utmost to help the family to forget as soon as possible the catastrophe which had overwhelmed the business and thrown them all into a state of complete despair. And so he had set to work with unusual ardor and almost overnight had become a commercial traveler instead of a little clerk, with of course much greater chances of earning money, and his success was immediately translated into good round coin which he could lay on the table for his amazed and happy family. These had been fine times, and they had never recurred, at least not with the same sense of glory, although later on Gregor had earned so much money that he was able to meet the expenses of the whole household and did so. They had simply got used to it, both the family and Gregor; the money was gratefully accepted and gladly given, but there was no special uprush of warm feeling. With his sister alone had he remained intimate, and it was a secret plan of his that she, who loved music, unlike himself, and could play movingly on the violin, should be sent next year to study at the Conservatorium, despite the great expense that would entail, which must be made up in some other way. During his brief visits home the Conservatorium was often mentioned in the talks he had with his sister, but always merely as a beautiful dream which could never come true, and his parents discouraged even these innocent references to it; yet Gregor had made up his mind firmly about it and meant to announce the fact with due solemnity on Christmas Day.

Such were the thoughts, completely futile in his present condition, that went through his head as he stood clinging upright to the door and listening. Sometimes out of sheer weariness he had to give up listening and let his head fall negligently against the door, but he always had to pull himself together again at once, for even the slight sound his head made was audible next door and brought all conversation to a stop. "What can he be doing now?" his father would say after a while, obviously turning towards the door, and only then would the interrupted conversation gradually be set going again.

Gregor was now informed as amply as he could wish—for his father tended to repeat himself in his explanations, partly because it was a long time since he had handled such matters and partly because his mother could not always grasp things at once—that a certain amount of investments, a very small amount it was true, had survived the wreck of their fortunes and had even increased a little because the dividends had not been touched meanwhile. And besides that, the money Gregor brought home every month—he had kept only a few dollars for himself—had never been quite used up and now amounted to a small capital sum. Behind the door Gregor nodded his head eagerly, rejoiced at this evidence of unexpected thrift and foresight. True, he could really have paid off some more of his father's debts to the chief with his extra money, and so brought much nearer the day on which he could quit his job, but doubtless it was better the way his father had arranged it.

Yet this capital was by no means sufficient to let the family live on the interest of it; for one year, perhaps, or at the most two, they could live on the principal, that was all. It was simply a sum that ought not to be touched and should be kept for a rainy day; money for living expenses would have to be earned. Now his father was still hale enough but an old man, and he had done no work for the past five years and could not be expected to do much; during these five years, the first years of leisure in his laborious though unsuccessful life, he had grown rather fat and become sluggish. And Gregor's old mother, how was she to earn a living with her asthma, which troubled her even when she walked through the flat and kept her lying on a sofa every other day panting for breath beside an open window? And was his sister to earn her bread, she who was still a child of seventeen and whose life hitherto had been so pleasant, consisting as it did in dressing herself nicely, sleeping long, helping in the housekeeping, going out to a few modest entertainments and above all playing the violin? At first whenever the need for earning money was mentioned Gregor let go his hold on the door and threw himself down on the cool leather sofa beside it, he felt so hot with shame and grief.

Often he just lay there the long nights through without sleeping at all, scrabbling for hours on the leather. Or he nerved himself to the great effort of pushing an armchair to the window, then crawled up over the window sill and, braced against the chair, leaned against the window panes, obviously in some recollection of the sense of freedom that looking out of a window always used to give him. For in reality day by day things that were even a little way off were growing dimmer to his sight; the hospital across the street, which he used to execrate for being all too often before his eyes, was now quite beyond his range of vision, and if he had not known that he lived In Charlotte Street, a quiet street but still a city street, he might have believed that his window gave on a desert waste where gray sky and gray land blended indistinguishably into each other. His quick-witted sister only needed to observe twice that the armchair stood by the window; after that whenever she had tidied the room she always pushed the chair back to the same place at the window and even left the inner casements open.

If he could have spoken to her and thanked her for all she had to do for him, he could have borne her ministrations better; as it was, they oppressed him. She certainly tried to make as light as possible of whatever was disagreeable in her task, and as time went on she succeeded, of course, more and more, but time brought more enlightenment to Gregor too. The very way she came in distressed him. Hardly was she in the room when she rushed to the window, without even taking time to shut the door, careful as she was usually to shield the sight of Gregor's room from the others, and as if she were almost suffocating tore the casements open with hasty fingers, standing then in the open draught for a while even in the bitterest cold and drawing deep breaths. This noisy scurry of hers upset Gregor twice a day; he would crouch trembling under the sofa all the time, knowing quite well that she would certainly have spared him such a disturbance had she found it at all possible to stay in his presence without opening the window.

On one occasion, about a month after Gregor's metamorphosis, when there was surely no reason for her to be still startled at his appearance, she came a little earlier than usual and found him gazing out of the window, quite motionless, and thus well placed to look like a bogey. Gregor would not have been surprised had she not come in at all, for she could not immediately open the window while he was there, but not only did she retreat, she jumped back as if in alarm and banged the door shut; a stranger might well have thought that he had been lying in wait for her there meaning to bite her. Of course he hid himself under the sofa at once, but he had to wait until midday before she came again, and she seemed more ill at ease than usual. This made him realize how repulsive the sight of him still was to her, and that it was bound to go on being repulsive, and what an effort it must cost her not to run away even from the sight of the small portion of his body that stuck out from under the sofa. In order to spare her that, therefore, one day he carried a sheet on his back to the sofa—it cost him four hours' labor—and arranged it there in such a way as to hide him completely, so that even if she were to bend down she could not see him. Had she considered the sheet unnecessary, she would certainly have stripped it off the sofa again, for it was clear enough that this curtaining and confining of himself was not likely to conduce to Gregor's comfort, but she left it where it was, and Gregor even fancied that he caught a thankful glance from her eye when he lifted the sheet carefully a very little with his head to see how she was taking the new arrangement.

For the first fortnight his parents could not bring themselves to the point of entering his room, and he often heard them expressing their appreciation of his sister's activities, whereas formerly they had frequently scolded her for being as they thought a somewhat useless daughter. But now, both of them often waited outside the door, his father and his mother, while his sister tidied his room, and as soon as she came out she had to tell them exactly how things were in the room, what Gregor had eaten, how he had conducted himself this time and whether there was not perhaps some slight improvement in his condition. His mother, moreover, began relatively soon to want to visit him, but his father and sister dissuaded her at first with arguments which Gregor listened to very attentively and altogether approved. Later, however, she had to be held back by main force, and when she cried out: "Do let me in to Gregor, he is my unfortunate son! Can't you understand that I must go to him?" Gregor thought that it might be well to have her come in, not every day, of course, but perhaps once a week; she understood things, after all, much better than his sister, who was only a child despite the efforts she was making and had perhaps taken on so difficult a task merely out of childish thoughtlessness.

Gregor's desire to see his mother was soon fulfilled. During the daytime he did not want to show himself at the window, out of consideration for his parents, but he could not crawl very far around the few square yards of floor space he had, nor could he bear lying quietly at rest all during the night, while he was fast losing any interest he had ever taken in food, so that for mere recreation he had formed the habit of crawling crisscross over the walls and ceiling. He especially enjoyed hanging suspended from the ceiling; it was much better than lying on the floor. One could breathe more freely; one's body swung and rocked lightly; and in the almost blissful absorption induced by this suspension it could happen to his own surprise that he let go and fell plump on the floor. Yet he now had his body much better under control than formerly, and even such a big fall did him no harm. His sister at once remarked the new distraction Gregor had found for himself—he left traces behind him of the sticky stuff on his soles wherever he crawled—and she got the idea in her head of giving him as wide a field as possible to crawl in and of removing the pieces of furniture that hindered him, above all the chest of drawers and the writing desk. But that was more than she could manage all by herself; she did not dare ask her father to help her; and as for the servant girl, a young creature of sixteen who had had the courage to stay on after the cook's departure, she could not be asked to help, for she had begged as an especial favor that she might keep the kitchen door locked and open it only on a definite summons; so there was nothing left but to apply to her mother at an hour when her father was out. And the old lady did come, with exclamations of joyful eagerness, which, however, died away at the door of Gregor's room. Gregor's sister, of course, went in first, to see that everything was in order before letting his mother enter. In great haste Gregor pulled the sheet lower and rucked it more in folds so that it really looked as if it had been thrown accidentally over the sofa. And this time he did not peer out from under it; he renounced the pleasure of seeing his mother on this occasion and was only glad that she had come at all. "Come in, he's out of sight," said his sister, obviously leading her mother in by the hand. Gregor could now hear the two women struggling to shift the heavy old chest from its place, and his sister claiming the greater part of the labor for herself, without listening to the admonitions of her mother who feared she might overstrain herself. It took a long time. After at least a quarter of an hour's tugging his mother objected that the chest had better be left where it was, for in the first place it was too heavy and could never be got out before his father came home, and standing in the middle of the room like that it would only hamper Gregor's movements, while in the second place it was not at all certain that removing the furniture would be doing a service to Gregor. She was inclined to think to the contrary; the sight of the naked walls made her own heart heavy, and why shouldn't Gregor have the same feeling, considering that he had been used to his furniture for so long and might feel forlorn without it. "And doesn't it look," she concluded in a low voice—in fact she had been almost whispering all the time as if to avoid letting Gregor, whose exact whereabouts she did not know, hear even the tones of her voice, for she was convinced that he could not understand her words—"doesn't it look as if we were showing him, by taking away his furniture, that we have given up hope of his ever getting better and are just leaving him coldly to himself? I think it would be best to keep his room exactly as it has always been, so that when he comes back to us he will find everything unchanged and be able all the more easily to forget what has happened in between."

On hearing these words from his mother Gregor realized that the lack of all direct human speech for the past two months together with the monotony of family life must have confused his mind, otherwise he could not account for the fact that he had quite earnestly looked forward to having his room emptied of furnishing. Did he really want his warm room, so comfortably fitted with old family furniture, to be turned into a naked den in which he would certainly be able to crawl unhampered in all directions but at the price of shedding simultaneously all recollection of his human background? He had indeed been so near the brink of forgetfulness that only the voice of his mother, which he had not heard for so long, had drawn him back from it. Nothing should be taken out of his room; everything must stay as it was; he could not dispense with the good influence of the furniture on his state of mind; and even if the furniture did hamper him in his senseless crawling round and round, that was no drawback but a great advantage.

Unfortunately his sister was of the contrary opinion; she had grown accustomed, and not without reason, to consider herself an expert in Gregor's affairs as against her parents, and so her mother's advice was now enough to make her determined on the removal not only of the chest and the writing desk, which had been her first intention, but of all the furniture except the indispensable sofa. This determination was not, of course, merely the outcome of childish recalcitrance and of the self-confidence she had recently developed so unexpectedly and at such cost; she had in fact perceived that Gregor needed a lot of space to crawl about in, while on the other hand he never used the furniture at all, so far as could be seen. Another factor might have been also the enthusiastic temperament of an adolescent girl, which seeks to indulge itself on every opportunity and which now tempted Grete to exaggerate the horror of her brother's circumstances in order that she might do all the more for him. In a room where Gregor lorded it all alone over empty walls no one save herself was likely ever to set foot.

And so she was not to be moved from her resolve by her mother who seemed moreover to be ill at ease in Gregor's room and therefore unsure of herself, was soon reduced to silence and helped her daughter as best she could to push the chest outside. Now, Gregor could do without the chest, if need be, but the writing desk he must retain. As soon as the two women had got the chest out of his room, groaning as they pushed it, Gregor stuck his head out from under the sofa to see how he might intervene as kindly and cautiously as possible. But as bad luck would have it, his mother was the first to return, leaving Grete clasping the chest in the room next door where she was trying to shift it all by herself, without of course moving it from the spot. His mother however was not accustomed to the sight of him, it might sicken her and so in alarm Gregor backed quickly to the other end of the sofa, yet could not prevent the sheet from swaying a little in front. That was enough to put her on the alert. She paused, stood still for a moment and then went back to Grete.

Although Gregor kept reassuring himself that nothing out of the way was happening, but only a few bits of furniture were being changed round, he soon had to admit that all this trotting to and fro of the two women, their little ejaculations and the scraping of furniture along the floor affected him like a vast disturbance coming from all sides at once, and however much he tucked in his head and legs and cowered to the very floor he was bound to confess that he would not be able to stand it for long. They were clearing his room out; taking away everything he loved; the chest in which he kept his fret saw and other tools was already dragged off; they were now loosening the writing desk which had almost sunk into the floor, the desk at which he had done all his homework when he was at the commercial academy, at the grammar school before that, and yes, even at the primary school—he had no more time to waste in weighing the good intentions of the two women, whose existence he had by now almost forgotten, for they were so exhausted that they were laboring in silence and nothing could be heard but the heavy scuffling of their feet.

And so he rushed out—the women were just leaning against the writing desk in the next room to give themselves a breather—and four times changed his direction, since he really did not know what to rescue first, then on the wall opposite, which was already otherwise cleared, he was struck by the picture of the lady muffled in so much fur and quickly crawled up to it and pressed himself to the glass, which was a good surface to hold on to and comforted his hot belly. This picture at least, which was entirely hidden beneath him, was going to be removed by nobody. He turned his head towards the door of the living room so as to observe the women when they came back.

They had not allowed themselves much of a rest and were already coming; Grete had twined her arm round her mother and was almost supporting her. "Well, what shall we take now?" said Grete, looking round. Her eyes met Gregor's from the wall. She kept her composure, presumably because of her mother, bent her head down to her mother, to keep her from looking up, and said, although in a fluttering, unpremeditated voice: "Come, hadn't we better go back to the living room for a moment?" Her intentions were clear enough to Gregor, she wanted to bestow her mother in safety and then chase him down from the wall. Well, just let her try it! He clung to his picture and would not give it up. He would rather fly in Grete's face.

But Grete's words had succeeded in disquieting her mother, who took a step to one side, caught sight of the huge brown mass on the flowered wallpaper, and before she was really conscious that what she saw was Gregor screamed in a loud, hoarse voice: "Oh God, oh God!" fell with outspread arms over the sofa as if giving up and did not move. "Gregor!" cried his sister, shaking her fist and glaring at him. This was the first time she had directly addressed him since his metamorphosis. She ran into the next room for some aromatic essence with which to rouse her mother from her fainting fit. Gregor wanted to help too—there was still time to rescue the picture—but he was stuck fast to the glass and had to tear himself loose; he then ran after his sister into the next room as if he could advise her, as he used to do; but then had to stand helplessly behind her; she meanwhile searched among various small bottles and when she turned round started in alarm at the sight of him; one bottle fell on the floor and broke; a splinter of glass cut Gregor's face and some kind of corrosive medicine splashed him; without pausing a moment longer Grete gathered up all the bottles she could carry and ran to her mother with them; she banged the door shut with her foot. Gregor was now cut off from his mother, who was perhaps nearly dying because of him; he dared not open the door for fear of frightening away his sister, who had to stay with her mother; there was nothing he could do but wait; and harassed by self-reproach and worry he began now to crawl to and fro, over everything, walls, furniture and ceiling, and finally in his despair, when the whole room seemed to be reeling round him, fell down on to the middle of the big table.

A little while elapsed, Gregor was still lying there feebly and all around was quiet, perhaps that was a good omen. Then the doorbell rang. The servant girl was of course locked in her kitchen, and Grete would have to open the door. It was his father. "What's been happening?" were his first words; Grete's face must have told him everything. Grete answered in a muffled voice, apparently hiding her head on his breast: "Mother has been fainting, but she's better now. Gregor's broken loose." "Just what I expected," said his father, "just what I've been telling you, but you women would never listen." It was clear to Gregor that his father had taken the worst interpretation of Grete's all too brief statement and was assuming that Gregor had been guilty of some violent act. Therefore Gregor must now try to propitiate his father, since he had neither time nor means for an explanation. And so he fled to the door of his own room and crouched against it, to let his father see as soon as he came in from the hall that his son had the good intention of getting back into his room immediately and that it was not necessary to drive him there, but that if only the door were opened he would disappear at once.

Yet his father was not in the mood to perceive such fine distinctions. "Ah!" he cried as soon as he appeared, in a tone which sounded at once angry and exultant. Gregor drew his head back from the door and lifted it to look at his father. Truly, this was not the father he had imagined to himself; admittedly he had been too absorbed of late in his new recreation of crawling over the ceiling to take the same interest as before in what was happening elsewhere in the flat, and he ought really to be prepared for some changes. And yet, and yet, could that be his father? The man who used to lie wearily sunk in bed whenever Gregor set out on a business journey; who welcomed him back of an evening lying in a long chair in a dressing gown; who could not really rise to his feet but only lifted his arms in greeting, and on the rare occasions when he did go out with his family, on one or two Sundays a year and on high holidays, walked between Gregor and his mother, who were slow walkers anyhow, even more slowly than they did, muffled in his old greatcoat, shuffling laboriously forward with the help of his crook-handled stick which he set down most cautiously at every step and, whenever he wanted to say anything, nearly always came to a full stop and gathered his escort around him? Now he was standing there in fine shape; dressed in a smart blue uniform with gold buttons, such as bank messengers wear; his strong double chin bulged over the stiff high collar of his jacket; from under his bushy eyebrows his black eyes darted fresh and penetrating glances; his one-time tangled white hair had been combed flat on either side of a shining and carefully exact parting. He pitched his cap, which bore a gold monogram, probably the badge of some bank, in a wide sweep across the whole room on to a sofa and with the tail-ends of his jacket thrown back, his hands in his trouser pockets, advanced with a grim visage towards Gregor. Likely enough he did not himself know what he meant to do; at any rate he lifted his feet uncommonly high, and Gregor was dumbfounded at the enormous size of his shoe soles. But Gregor could not risk standing up to him, aware as he had been from the very first day of his new life that his father believed only the severest measures suitable for dealing with him. And so he ran before his father, stopping when he stopped and scuttling forward again when his father made any kind of move. In this way they circled the room several times without anything decisive happening, indeed the whole operation did not even look like a pursuit because it was carried out so slowly. And so Gregor did not leave the floor, for he feared that his father might take as a piece of peculiar wickedness any excursion of his over the walls or the ceiling. All the same, he could not stay this course much longer, for while his father took one step he had to carry out a whole series of movements. He was already beginning to feel breathless, just as in his former life his lungs had not been very dependable. As he was staggering along, trying to concentrate his energy on running, hardly keeping his eyes open; in his dazed state never even thinking of any other escape than simply going forward; and having almost forgotten that the walls were free to him, which in this room were well provided with finely carved pieces of furniture full of knobs and crevices— suddenly something lightly flung landed close behind him and rolled before him. It was an apple; a second apple followed immediately; Gregor came to a stop in alarm; there was no point in running on, for his father was determined to bombard him. He had filled his pockets with fruit from the dish on the sideboard and was now shying apple after apple, without taking particularly good aim for the moment. The small red apples rolled about the floor as if magnetized and cannoned into each other. An apple thrown without much force grazed Gregor's back and glanced off harmlessly. But another following immediately landed right on his back and sank in; Gregor wanted to drag himself forward, as if this startling, incredible pain could be left behind him; but he felt as if nailed to the spot and flattened himself out in a complete derangement of all his senses. With his last conscious look he saw the door of his room being torn open and his mother rushing out ahead of his screaming sister, in her underbodice, for her daughter had loosened her clothing to let her breathe more freely and recover from her swoon, he saw his mother rushing towards his father, leaving one after another behind her on the floor loosened petticoats, stumbling over her petticoats straight to his father and embracing him, in complete union with him—but here Gregor's sight began to fail—with her hands clasped round his father's neck as she begged for her son's life.

III

THE serious injury done to Gregor, which disabled him for more than a month—the apple went on sticking in his body as a visible reminder, since no one ventured to remove it—seemed to have made even his father recollect that Gregor was a member of the family, despite his present unfortunate and repulsive shape, and ought not to be treated as an enemy, that, on the contrary, family duty required the suppression of disgust and the exercise of patience, nothing but patience.

And although his injury had impaired, probably for ever, his power of movement, and for the time being it took him long, long minutes to creep across his room like an old invalid—there was no question now of crawling up the wall—yet in his own opinion he was sufficiently compensated for this worsening of his condition by the fact that towards evening the living-room door, which he used to watch intently for an hour or two beforehand, was always thrown open, so that lying in the darkness of his room, invisible to the family, he could see them all at the lamp-lit table and listen to their talk, by general consent as it were, very different from his earlier eavesdropping.

True, their intercourse lacked the lively character of former times, which he had always called to mind with a certain wistfulness in the small hotel bedrooms where he had been wont to throw himself down, tired out, on damp bedding. They were now mostly very silent. Soon after supper his father would fall asleep in his armchair; his mother and sister would admonish each other to be silent; his mother, bending low over the lamp, stitched at fine sewing for an underwear firm; his sister, who had taken a job as a salesgirl, was learning shorthand and French in the evenings on the chance of bettering herself. Sometimes his father woke up, and as if quite unaware that he had been sleeping said to his mother: "What a lot of sewing you're doing today!" and at once fell asleep again, while the two women exchanged a tired smile.

With a kind of mulishness his father persisted in keeping his uniform on even in the house; his dressing gown hung uselessly on its peg and he slept fully dressed where he sat, as if he were ready for service at any moment and even here only at the beck and call of his superior. As a result, his uniform, which was not brand-new to start with, began to look dirty, despite all the loving care of the mother and sister to keep it clean, and Gregor often spent whole evenings gazing at the many greasy spots on the garment, gleaming with gold buttons always in a high state of polish, in which the old man sat sleeping in extreme discomfort and yet quite peacefully.

As soon as the clock struck ten his mother tried to rouse his father with gentle words and to persuade him after that to get into bed, for sitting there he could not have a proper sleep and that was what he needed most, since he had to go to duty at six. But with the mulishness that had obsessed him since he became a bank messenger he always insisted on staying longer at the table, although he regularly fell asleep again and in the end only with the greatest trouble could be got out of his armchair and into his bed. However insistently Gregor's mother and sister kept urging him with gentle reminders, he would go on slowly shaking his head for a quarter of an hour, keeping his eyes shut, and refuse to get to his feet. The mother plucked at his sleeve, whispering endearments in his ear, the sister left her lessons to come to her mother's help, but Gregor's father was not to be caught. He would only sink down deeper in his chair. Not until the two women hoisted him up by the armpits did he open his eyes and look at them both, one after the other, usually with the remark: "This is a life. This is the peace and quiet of my old age." And leaning on the two of them he would heave himself up, with difficulty, as if he were a great burden to himself, suffer them to lead him as far as the door and then wave them off and go on alone, while the mother abandoned her needlework and the sister her pen in order to run after him and help him farther.

Who could find time, in this overworked and tired-out family, to bother about Gregor more than was absolutely needful? The household was reduced more and more; the servant girl was turned off; a gigantic bony charwoman with white hair flying round her head came in morning and evening to do the rough work; everything else was done by Gregor's mother, as well as great piles of sewing. Even various family ornaments, which his mother and sister used to wear with pride at parties and celebrations, had to be sold, as Gregor discovered of an evening from hearing them all discuss the prices obtained. But what they lamented most was the fact that they could not leave the flat which was much too big for their present circumstances, because they could not think of any way to shift Gregor. Yet Gregor saw well enough that consideration for him was not the main difficulty preventing the removal, for they could have easily shifted him in some suitable box with a few air holes in it; what really kept them from moving into another flat was rather their own complete hopelessness and the belief that they had been singled out for a misfortune such as had never happened to any of their relations or acquaintances. They fulfilled to the uttermost all that the world demands of poor people, the father fetched breakfast for the small clerks in the bank, the mother devoted her energy to making underwear for strangers, the sister trotted to and fro behind the counter at the behest of customers, but more than this they had not the strength to do. And the wound in Gregor's back began to nag at him afresh when his mother and sister, after getting his father into bed, came back again, left their work lying, drew close to each other and sat cheek by cheek; when his mother, pointing towards his room, said: "Shut that door now, Grete," and he was left again in darkness, while next door the women mingled their tears or perhaps sat dry-eyed staring at the table.

Gregor hardly slept at all by night or by day. He was often haunted by the idea that next time the door opened he would take the family's affairs in hand again just as he used to do; once more, after this long interval, there appeared in his thoughts the figures of the chief and the chief clerk, the commercial travelers and the apprentices, the porter who was so dull-witted, two or three friends in other firms, a chambermaid in one of the rural hotels, a sweet and fleeting memory, a cashier in a milliner's shop, whom he had wooed earnestly but too slowly—they all appeared, together with strangers or people he had quite forgotten, but instead of helping him and his family they were one and all unapproachable and he was glad when they vanished. At other times he would not be in the mood to bother about his family, he was only filled with rage at the way they were neglecting him, and although he had no clear idea of what he might care to eat he would make plans for getting into the larder to take the food that was after all his due, even if he were not hungry. His sister no longer took thought to bring him what might especially please him, but in the morning and at noon before she went to business hurriedly pushed into his room with her foot any food that was available, and in the evening cleared it out again with one sweep of the broom, heedless of whether it had been merely tasted, or—as most frequently happened—left untouched. The cleaning of his room, which she now did always in the evenings, could not have been more hastily done. Streaks of dirt stretched along the walls, here and there lay balls of dust and filth. At first Gregor used to station himself in some particularly filthy corner when his sister arrived, in order to reproach her with it, so to speak. But he could have sat there for weeks without getting her to make any improvements; she could see the dirt as well as he did, but she had simply made up her mind to leave it alone. And yet, with a touchiness that was new to her, which seemed anyhow to have infected the whole family, she jealously guarded her claim to be the sole caretaker of Gregor's room. His mother once subjected his room to a thorough cleaning, which was achieved only by means of several buckets of water—all this dampness of course upset Gregor too and he lay widespread, sulky and motionless on the sofa—but she was well punished for it. Hardly had his sister noticed the changed aspect of his room that evening than she rushed in high dudgeon into the living room and, despite the imploringly raised hands of her mother, burst into a storm of weeping, while her parents—her father had of course been startled out of his chair—looked on at first in helpless amazement; then they too began to go into action; the father reproached the mother on his right for not having left the cleaning of Gregor's room to his sister; shrieked at the sister on his left that never again was she to be allowed to clean Gregor's room; while the mother tried to pull the father into his bedroom, since he was beyond himself with agitation; the sister, shaken with sobs, then beat upon the table with her small fists; and Gregor hissed loudly with rage because not one of them thought of shutting the door to spare him such a spectacle and so much noise.

Still, even if the sister, exhausted by her daily work, had grown tired of looking after Gregor as she did formerly, there was no need for his mother's intervention or for Gregor's being neglected at all. The charwoman was there. This old widow, whose strong bony frame had enabled her to survive the worst a long life could offer, by no means recoiled from Gregor. Without being in the least curious she had once by chance opened the door of his room and at the sight of Gregor, who, taken by surprise, began to rush to and fro although no one was chasing him, merely stood there with her arms folded. From that time she never failed to open his door a little for a moment, morning and evening, to have a look at him. At first she even used to call him to her, with words which apparently she took to be friendly, such as: "Come along, then, you old dung beetle!" or "Look at the old dung beetle, then!" To such allocutions Gregor made no answer, but stayed motionless where he was as if the door had never been opened. Instead of being allowed to disturb him so senselessly whenever the whim took her, she should rather have been ordered to clean out his room daily, that charwoman! Once, early in the morning—heavy rain was lashing on the windowpanes, perhaps a sign that spring was on the way—Gregor was so exasperated when she began addressing him again that he ran for her, as if to attack her, although slowly and feebly enough. But the charwoman instead of showing fright merely lifted high a chair that happened to be beside the door, and as she stood there with her mouth wide open it was clear that she meant to shut it only when she brought the chair down on Gregor's back. "So you're not coming any nearer?" she asked, as Gregor turned away again, and quietly put the chair back into the corner.

Gregor was now eating hardly anything. Only when he happened to pass the food laid out for him did he take a bit of something in his mouth as a pastime, kept it there for an hour at a time and usually spat it out again. At first he thought it was chagrin over the state of his room that prevented him from eating, yet he soon got used to the various changes in his room. It had become a habit in the family to push into his room things there was no room for elsewhere, and there were plenty of these now, since one of the rooms had been let to three lodgers. These serious gentlemen—all three of them with full beards, as Gregor once observed through a crack in the door—had a passion for order, not only in their own room but, since they were now members of the household, in all its arrangements, especially in the kitchen. Superfluous, not to say dirty, objects they could not bear. Besides, they had brought with them most of the furnishings they needed. For this reason many things could be dispensed with that it was no use trying to sell but that should not be thrown away either. All of them found their way into Gregor's room. The ash can likewise and the kitchen garbage can. Anything that was not needed for the moment was simply flung into Gregor's room by the charwoman, who did everything in a hurry; fortunately Gregor usually saw only the object, whatever it was, and the hand that held it. Perhaps she intended to take the things away again as time and opportunity offered, or to collect them until she could throw them all out in a heap, but in fact they just lay wherever she happened to throw them, except when Gregor pushed his way through the junk heap and shifted it somewhat, at first out of necessity, because he had not room enough to crawl, but later with increasing enjoyment, although after such excursions, being sad and weary to death, he would lie motionless for hours. And since the lodgers often ate their supper at home in the common living room, the living-room door stayed shut many an evening, yet Gregor reconciled himself quite easily to the shutting of the door, for often enough on evenings when it was opened he had disregarded it entirely and lain in the darkest corner of his room, quite unnoticed by the family. But on one occasion the charwoman left the door open a little and it stayed ajar even when the lodgers came in for supper and the lamp was lit. They set themselves at the top end of the table where formerly Gregor and his father and mother had eaten their meals, unfolded their napkins and took knife and fork in hand. At once his mother appeared in the doorway with a dish of meat and close behind her his sister with a dish of potatoes piled high. The food steamed with a thick vapor. The lodgers bent over the food set before them as if to scrutinize it before eating, in fact the man in the middle, who seemed to pass for an authority with the other two, cut a piece of meat as it lay on the dish, obviously to discover if it were tender or should be sent back to the kitchen. He showed satisfaction, and Gregor's mother and sister, who had been watching anxiously, breathed freely and began to smile.

The family itself took its meals in the kitchen. None the less, Gregor's father came into the living room before going into the kitchen and with one prolonged bow, cap in hand, made a round of the table. The lodgers all stood up and murmured something in their beards. When they were alone again they ate their food in almost complete silence. It seemed remarkable to Gregor that among the various noises coming from the table he could always distinguish the sound of their masticating teeth, as if this were a sign to Gregor that one needed teeth in order to eat, and that with toothless jaws even of the finest make one could do nothing. "I'm hungry enough," said Gregor sadly to himself, "but not for that kind of food. How these lodgers are stuffing themselves, and here am I dying of starvation!"

On that very evening—during the whole of his time there Gregor could not remember ever having heard the violin—the sound of violin playing came from the kitchen. The lodgers had already finished their supper, the one in the middle had brought out a newspaper and given the other two a page apiece, and now they were leaning back at ease reading and smoking. When the violin began to play they pricked up their ears, got to their feet, and went on tiptoe to the hall door where they stood huddled together. Their movements must have been heard in the kitchen, for Gregor's father called out: "Is the violin-playing disturbing you gentlemen? It can be stopped at once." "On the contrary," said the middle lodger, "could not Fräulein Samsa come and play in this room, beside us, where it is much more convenient and comfortable?"

"Oh certainly," cried Gregor's father, as if he were the violin-player. The lodgers came back into the living room and waited. Presently Gregor's father arrived with the music stand, his mother carrying the music and his sister with the violin. His sister quietly made everything ready to start playing; his parents, who had never let rooms before and so had an exaggerated idea of the courtesy due to lodgers, did not venture to sit down on their own chairs; his father leaned against the door, the right hand thrust between two buttons of his livery coat, which was formally buttoned up; but his mother was offered a chair by one of the lodgers and, since she left the chair just where he had happened to put it, sat down in a corner to one side.

Gregor's sister began to play; the father and mother, from either side, intently watched the movements of her hands. Gregor, attracted by the playing, ventured to move forward a little until his head was actually inside the living room. He felt hardly any surprise at his growing lack of consideration for the others; there had been a time when he prided himself on being considerate. And yet just on this occasion he had more reason than ever to hide himself, since owing to the amount of dust which lay thick in his room and rose into the air at the slightest movement, he too was covered with dust; fluff and hair and remnants of food trailed with him, caught on his back and along his sides; his indifference to everything was much too great for him to turn on his back and scrape himself clean on the carpet, as once he had done several times a day. And in spite of his condition, no shame deterred him from advancing a little over the spotless floor of the living room.

To be sure, no one was aware of him. The family was entirely absorbed in the violin-playing; the lodgers, however, who first of all had stationed themselves, hands in pockets, much too close behind the music stand so that they could all have read the music, which must have bothered his sister, had soon retreated to the window, half-whispering with downbent heads, and stayed there while his father turned an anxious eye on them. Indeed, they were making it more than obvious that they had been disappointed in their expectation of hearing good or enjoyable violin-playing, that they had had more than enough of the performance and only out of courtesy suffered a continued disturbance of their peace. From the way they all kept blowing the smoke of their cigars high in the air through nose and mouth one could divine their irritation. And yet Gregor's sister was playing so beautifully. Her face leaned sideways, intently and sadly her eyes followed the notes of music. Gregor crawled a little farther forward and lowered his head to the ground so that it might be possible for his eyes to meet hers. Was he an animal, that music had such an effect upon him? He felt as if the way were opening before him to the unknown nourishment he craved. He was determined to push forward till he reached his sister, to pull at her skirt and so let her know that she was to come into his room with her violin, for no one here appreciated her playing as he would appreciate it. He would never let her out of his room, at least, not so long as he lived; his frightful appearance would become, for the first time, useful to him; he would watch all the doors of his room at once and spit at intruders; but his sister should need no constraint, she should stay with him of her own free will; she should sit beside him on the sofa, bend down her ear to him and hear him confide that he had had the firm intention of sending her to the Conservatorium, and that, but for his mishap, last Christmas—surely Christmas was long past?—he would have announced it to everybody without allowing a single objection. After this confession his sister would be so touched that she would burst into tears, and Gregor would then raise himself to her shoulder and kiss her on the neck, which, now that she went to business, she kept free of any ribbon or collar.

"Mr. Samsa!" cried the middle lodger, to Gregor's father, and pointed, without wasting any more words, at Gregor, now working himself slowly forwards. The violin fell silent, the middle lodger first smiled to his friends with a shake of the head and then looked at Gregor again. Instead of driving Gregor out, his father seemed to think it more needful to begin by soothing down the lodgers, although they were not at all agitated and apparently found Gregor more entertaining than the violin-playing. He hurried towards them and, spreading out his arms, tried to urge them back into their own room and at the same time to block their view of Gregor. They now began to be really a little angry, one could not tell whether because of the old man's behavior or because it had just dawned on them that all unwittingly they had such a neighbor as Gregor next door. They demanded explanations of his father, they waved their arms like him, tugged uneasily at their beards, and only with reluctance backed towards their room. Meanwhile Gregor's sister, who stood there as if lost when her playing was so abruptly broken off, came to life again, pulled herself together all at once after standing for a while holding violin and bow in nervelessly hanging hands and staring at her music, pushed her violin into the lap of her mother, who was still sitting in her chair fighting asthmatically for breath, and ran into the lodgers' room to which they were now being shepherded by her father rather more quickly than before. One could see the pillows and blankets on the beds flying under her accustomed fingers and being laid in order. Before the lodgers had actually reached their room she had finished making the beds and slipped out.

The old man seemed once more to be so possessed by his mulish self-assertiveness that he was forgetting all the respect he should show to his lodgers. He kept driving them on and driving them on until in the very door of the bedroom the middle lodger stamped his foot loudly on the floor and so brought him to a halt. "I beg to announce," said the lodger, lifting one hand and looking also at Gregor's mother and sister, "that because of the disgusting conditions prevailing in this household and family"—here he spat on the floor with emphatic brevity—"I give you notice on the spot. Naturally I won't pay you a penny for the days I have lived here, on the contrary I shall consider bringing an action for damages against you, based on claims—believe me— that will be easily susceptible of proof." He ceased and stared straight in front of him, as if he expected something. In fact his two friends at once rushed into the breach with these words: "And we too give notice on the spot." On that he seized the door-handle and shut the door with a slam.

Gregor's father, groping with his hands, staggered forward and fell into his chair; it looked as if he were stretching himself there for his ordinary evening nap, but the marked jerkings of his head, which was as if uncontrollable, showed that he was far from asleep. Gregor had simply stayed quietly all the time on the spot where the lodgers had espied him. Disappointment at the failure of his plan, perhaps also the weakness arising from extreme hunger, made it impossible for him to move. He feared, with a fair degree of certainty, that at any moment the general tension would discharge itself in a combined attack upon him, and he lay waiting. He did not react even to the noise made by the violin as it fell off his mother's lap from under her trembling fingers and gave out a resonant note.

"My dear parents," said his sister, slapping her hand on the table by way of introduction, "things can't go on like this. Perhaps you don't realize that, but I do. I won't utter my brother's name in the presence of this creature, and so all I say is: we must try to get rid of it. We've tried to look after it and to put up with it as far as is humanly possible, and I don't think anyone could reproach us in the slightest."

"She is more than right," said Gregor's father to himself. His mother, who was still choking for lack of breath, began to cough hollowly into her hand with a wild look in her eyes.

His sister rushed over to her and held her forehead. His father's thoughts seemed to have lost their vagueness at Grete's words, he sat more upright, fingering his service cap that lay among the plates still lying on the table from the lodgers' supper, and from time to time looked at the still form of Gregor.

"We must try to get rid of it," his sister now said explicitly to her father, since her mother was coughing too much to hear a word, "it will be the death of both of you, I can see that coming. When one has to work as hard as we do, all of us, one can't stand this continual torment at home on top of it. At least I can't stand it any longer." And she burst into such a passion of sobbing that her tears dropped on her mother's face, where she wiped them off mechanically.

"My dear," said the old man sympathetically, and with evident understanding, "but what can we do?"

Gregor's sister merely shrugged her shoulders to indicate the feeling of helplessness that had now overmastered her during her weeping fit, in contrast to her former confidence.

"If he could understand us," said her father, half questioningly; Grete, still sobbing, vehemently waved a hand to show how unthinkable that was.

"If he could understand us," repeated the old man, shutting his eyes to consider his daughter's conviction that understanding was impossible, "then perhaps we might come to some agreement with him. But as it is—"

"He must go," cried Gregor's sister, "that's the only solution, Father.

You must just try to get rid of the idea that this is Gregor. The fact that we've believed it for so long is the root of all our trouble. But how can it be Gregor? If this were Gregor, he would have realized long ago that human beings can't live with such a creature, and he'd have gone away on his own accord. Then we wouldn't have any brother, but we'd be able to go on living and keep his memory in honor. As it is, this creature persecutes us, drives away our lodgers, obviously wants the whole apartment to himself and would have us all sleep in the gutter. Just look, Father," she shrieked all at once, "he's at it again!" And in an access of panic that was quite incomprehensible to Gregor she even quitted her mother, literally thrusting the chair from her as if she would rather sacrifice her mother than stay so near to Gregor, and rushed behind her father, who also rose up, being simply upset by her agitation, and half-spread his arms out as if to protect her.

Yet Gregor had not the slightest intention of frightening anyone, far less his sister. He had only begun to turn round in order to crawl back to his room, but it was certainly a startling operation to watch, since because of his disabled condition he could not execute the difficult turning movements except by lifting his head and then bracing it against the floor over and over again. He paused and looked round. His good intentions seemed to have been recognized; the alarm had only been momentary. Now they were all watching him in melancholy silence. His mother lay in her chair, her legs stiffly outstretched and pressed together, her eyes almost closing for sheer weariness; his father and his sister were sitting beside each other, his sister's arm around the old man's neck.

Perhaps I can go on turning round now, thought Gregor, and began his labors again. He could not stop himself from panting with the effort, and had to pause now and then to take breath. Nor did anyone harass him, he was left entirely to himself. When he had completed the turn-round he began at once to crawl straight back. He was amazed at the distance separating him from his room and could not understand how in his weak state he had managed to accomplish the same journey so recently, almost without remarking it. Intent on crawling as fast as possible, he barely noticed that not a single word, not an ejaculation from his family, interfered with his progress. Only when he was already in the doorway did he turn his head round, not completely, for his neck muscles were getting stiff, but enough to see that nothing had changed behind him except that his sister had risen to her feet. His last glance fell on his mother, who was not quite overcome by sleep.

Hardly was he well inside his room when the door was hastily pushed shut, bolted and locked. The sudden noise in his rear startled him so much that his little legs gave beneath him. It was his sister who had shown such haste. She had been standing ready waiting and had made a light spring forward. Gregor had not even heard her coming, and she cried "At last!" to her parents as she turned the key in the lock.

"And what now?" said Gregor to himself, looking round in the darkness. Soon he made the discovery that he was now unable to stir a limb. This did not surprise him, rather it seemed unnatural that he should ever actually have been able to move on these feeble little legs. Otherwise he felt relatively comfortable. True, his whole body was aching, but it seemed that the pain was gradually growing less and would finally pass away. The rotting apple in his back and the inflamed area around it, all covered with soft dust, already hardly troubled him. He thought of his family with tenderness and love. The decision that he must disappear was one that he held to even more strongly than his sister, if that were possible. In this state of vacant and peaceful meditation he remained until the tower clock struck three in the morning. The first broadening of light in the world outside the window entered his consciousness once more. Then his head sank to the floor of its own accord and from his nostrils came the last faint flicker of his breath.

When the charwoman arrived early in the morning—what between her strength and her impatience she slammed all the doors so loudly, never mind how often she had been begged not to do so, that no one in the whole apartment could enjoy any quiet sleep after her arrival—she noticed nothing unusual as she took her customary peep into Gregor's room. She thought he was lying motionless on purpose, pretending to be in the sulks; she credited him with every kind of intelligence. Since she happened to have the long-handled broom in her hand she tried to tickle him up with it from the doorway. When that too produced no reaction she felt provoked and poked at him a little harder, and only when she had pushed him along the floor without meeting any resistance was her attention aroused. It did not take her long to establish the truth of the matter, and her eyes widened, she let out a whistle, yet did not waste much time over it but tore open the door of the Samsas' bedroom and yelled into the darkness at the top of her voice: "Just look at this, it's dead; it's lying here dead and done for!"

Mr. and Mrs. Samsa started up in their double bed and before they realized the nature of the charwoman's announcement had some difficulty in overcoming the shock of it. But then they got out of bed quickly, one on either side, Mr. Samsa throwing a blanket over his shoulders, Mrs. Samsa in nothing but her nightgown; in this array they entered Gregor's room. Meanwhile the door of the living room opened, too, where Grete had been sleeping since the advent of the lodgers; she was completely dressed as if she had not been to bed, which seemed to be confirmed also by the paleness of her face. "Dead?" said Mrs. Samsa, looking questioningly at the charwoman, although she could have investigated for herself, and the fact was obvious enough without investigation. "I should say so," said the charwoman, proving her words by pushing Gregor's corpse a long way to one side with her broomstick. Mrs. Samsa made a movement as if to stop her, but checked it. "Well," said Mr. Samsa, "now thanks be to God." He crossed himself, and the three women followed his example. Grete, whose eyes never left the corpse, said: "Just see how thin he was. It's such a long time since he's eaten anything. The food came out again just as it went in." Indeed, Gregor's body was completely flat and dry, as could only now be seen when it was no longer supported by the legs and nothing prevented one from looking closely at it.

"Come in beside us, Grete, for a little while," said Mrs. Samsa with a tremulous smile, and Grete, not without looking back at the corpse, followed her parents into their bedroom. The charwoman shut the door and opened the window wide. Although it was so early in the morning a certain softness was perceptible in the fresh air. After all, it was already the end of March.

The three lodgers emerged from their room and were surprised to see no breakfast; they had been forgotten. "Where's our breakfast?" said the middle lodger peevishly to the charwoman. But she put her finger to her lips and hastily, without a word, indicated by gestures that they should go into Gregor's room. They did so and stood, their hands in the pockets of their somewhat shabby coats, around Gregor's corpse in the room where it was now fully light.

At that the door of the Samsas' bedroom opened and Mr. Samsa appeared in his uniform, his wife on one arm, his daughter on the other. They all looked a little as if they had been crying; from time to time Grete hid her face on her father's arm.

"Leave my house at once!" said Mr. Samsa, and pointed to the door without disengaging himself from the women. "What do you mean by that?" said the middle lodger, taken somewhat aback, with a feeble smile. The two others put their hands behind them and kept rubbing them together, as if in gleeful expectation of a fine set-to in which they were bound to come off the winners. "I mean just what I say," answered Mr. Samsa, and advanced in a straight line with his two companions towards the lodger. He stood his ground at first quietly, looking at the floor as if his thoughts were taking a new pattern in his head. "Then let us go, by all means," he said and looked up at Mr. Samsa as if in a sudden access of humility he were expecting some renewed sanction for this decision. Mr. Samsa merely nodded briefly once or twice with meaning eyes. Upon that the lodger really did go with long strides into the hall, his two friends had been listening and had quite stopped rubbing their hands for some moments and now went scuttling after him as if afraid that Mr. Samsa might get into the hall before them and cut them off from their leader. In the hall they all three took their hats from the rack, their sticks from the umbrella stand, bowed in silence and quitted the apartment. With a suspiciousness which proved quite unfounded Mr. Samsa and the two women followed them out to the landing; leaning over the banister they watched the three figures slowly but surely going down the long stairs, vanishing from sight at a certain turn of the staircase on every floor and coming into view again after a moment or so; the more they dwindled, the more the Samsa family's interest in them dwindled, and when a butcher's boy met them and passed them on the stairs coming up proudly with a tray on his head, Mr. Samsa and the two women soon left the landing and as if a burden had been lifted from them went back into their apartment.

They decided to spend this day in resting and going for a stroll; they had not only deserved such a respite from work, but absolutely needed it. And so they sat down at the table and wrote three notes of excuse, Mr. Samsa to his board of management, Mrs. Samsa to her employer and Grete to the head of her firm. While they were writing, the charwoman came in to say that she was going now, since her morning's work was finished. At first they only nodded without looking up, but as she kept hovering there they eyed her irritably. "Well?" said Mr. Samsa. The charwoman stood grinning in the doorway as if she had good news to impart to the family but meant not to say a word unless properly questioned. The small ostrich feather standing upright on her hat, which had annoyed Mr. Samsa ever since she was engaged, was waving gaily in all directions. "Well, what is it then?" asked Mrs. Samsa, who obtained more respect from the charwoman than the others. "Oh," said the charwoman, giggling so amiably that she could not at once continue, "just this, you don't need to bother about how to get rid of the thing next door. It's been seen to already." Mrs. Samsa and Grete bent over their letters again, as if preoccupied; Mr. Samsa, who perceived that she was eager to begin describing it all in detail, stopped her with a decisive hand. But since she was not allowed to tell her story, she remembered the great hurry she was in, being obviously deeply huffed: "Bye, everybody," she said, whirling off violently, and departed with a frightful slamming of doors.

"She'll be given notice tonight," said Mr. Samsa, but neither from his wife nor his daughter did he get any answer, for the charwoman seemed to have shattered again the composure they had barely achieved. They rose, went to the window and stayed there, clasping each other tight. Mr. Samsa turned in his chair to look at them and quietly observed them for a little. Then he called out: "Come along, now, do. Let bygones be bygones. And you might have some consideration for me." The two of them complied at once, hastened to him, caressed him and quickly finished their letters.

Then they all three left the apartment together, which was more than they had done for months, and went by tram into the open country outside the town. The tram, in which they were the only passengers, was filled with warm sunshine. Leaning comfortably back in their seats they canvassed their prospects for the future, and it appeared on closer inspection that these were not at all bad, for the jobs they had got, which so far they had never really discussed with each other, were all three admirable and likely to lead to better things later on. The greatest immediate improvement in their condition would of course arise from moving to another house; they wanted to take a smaller and cheaper but also better situated and more easily run apartment than the one they had, which Gregor had selected. While they were thus conversing, it struck both Mr. and Mrs. Samsa, almost at the same moment, as they became aware of their daughter's increasing vivacity, that in spite of all the sorrow of recent times, which had made her cheeks pale, she had bloomed into a pretty girl with a good figure. They grew quieter and half unconsciously exchanged glances of complete agreement, having come to the conclusion that it would soon be time to find a good husband for her. And it was like a confirmation of their new dreams and excellent intentions that at the end of their journey their daughter sprang to her feet first and stretched her young body.

Questions

1. *In what way does the opening sentence establish the tone of the story?* **2.** *Why is it appropriate that Gregor is transformed into an insect rather than some other creature?* **3.** *Is there anything to suggest that Gregor is responsible for what happens to him?* **4.** *What function do the lodgers serve?* **5.** *What do the different reactions of Gregor's father, mother, and sister tell us about the Samsa family? Why does his sister finally turn against him?*

The Greatest Man in the World

JAMES THURBER   [1894–1961]

Looking back on it now, from the vantage point of 1950, one can only marvel that it hadn't happened long before it did. The United States of America had been, ever since Kitty Hawk, blindly constructing the elaborate petard by which, sooner or later, it must be hoist. It was inevitable that some day there would come roaring out of the skies a national hero of insufficient intelligence, background, and character successfully to endure the mounting orgies of glory prepared for aviators who stayed up a long time or flew a great distance. Both Lindbergh and Byrd, fortunately for national decorum and international amity, had been gentlemen; so had our other famous aviators. They wore their laurels gracefully, withstood the awful weather of publicity, married excellent women, usually of fine family, and quietly retired to private life and the enjoyment of their varying fortunes. No untoward incidents, on a worldwide scale, marred the perfection of their conduct on the perilous heights of fame. The exception to the rule was, however, bound to occur and it did, in July, 1937, when Jack ("Pal") Smurch, erstwhile mechanics' helper in a small garage in Westfield, Iowa, flew a second-hand, single-motored Bresthaven Dragon-Fly III monoplane all the way around the world, without stopping.

Never before in the history of aviation had such a flight as Smurch's ever been dreamed of. No one had even taken seriously the weird floating auxiliary gas tanks, invention of the mad New Hampshire professor of astronomy, Dr. Charles Lewis Gresham, upon which Smurch placed full reliance. When the garage worker, a slightly built, surly, unprepossessing young man of twenty-two appeared at Roosevelt Field in early July, 1937, slowly chewing a great quid of scrap tobacco, and announced "Nobody ain't seen no flyin' yet," the newspapers touched briefly and satirically upon his projected twenty-five-thousand-mile flight. Aeronautical and automotive experts dismissed the idea curtly, implying that it was a hoax, a publicity stunt. The rusty, battered, second-hand plane wouldn't go. The Gresham auxiliary tanks wouldn't work. It was simply a cheap joke.

Smurch, however, after calling on a girl in Brooklyn who worked in the flap-folding department of a large paper-box factory, a girl whom he later described as his "sweet patootie," climbed nonchalantly into his ridiculous plane at dawn of the memorable seventh of July, 1937, spat a curve of tobacco juice into the still air, and took off, carrying with him only a gallon of bootleg gin and six pounds of salami.

When the garage boy thundered out over the ocean the papers were forced to record, in all seriousness, that a mad, unknown young man—his name was variously misspelled—had actually set out upon a preposterous attempt to span the world in a rickety, one-engined contraption, trusting to the long-distance refueling device of a crazy schoolmaster. When, nine days later, without having stopped once, the tiny plane appeared above San Francisco Bay, headed for New York, spluttering and choking, to be sure, but still magnificently and miraculously aloft, the headlines, which long since had crowded everything else off the front page—even the shooting of the Governor of Illinois by the Vileti gang—swelled to unprecedented size, and the news stories began to run to twenty-five and thirty columns. It was noticeable, however, that the accounts of the epoch-making flight touched rather lightly upon the aviator himself. This was not because facts about the hero as a man were too meagre, but because they were too complete.

Reporters, who had been rushed out to Iowa when Smurch's plane was first sighted over the little French coast town of Serly-le-Mar, to dig up the story of the great man's life, had promptly discovered that the story of his life could not be printed. His mother, a sullen short-order cook in a shack restaurant on the edge of a tourists' camping ground near Westfield, met all enquiries as to her son with an angry, "Ah, the hell with him; I hope he drowns." His father appeared to be in jail somewhere for stealing spotlights and laprobes from tourists' automobiles; his younger brother, a weak-minded lad, had but recently escaped from the Preston, Iowa Reformatory and was already wanted in several Western towns for the theft of money-order blanks from post offices. These alarming discoveries were still piling up at the very time that Pal Smurch, the greatest hero of the twentieth century, blear-eyed, dead for sleep, half-starved, was piloting his crazy junk-heap high above the region in which the lamentable story of his private life was being unearthed, headed for New York under greater glory than any man of his time had ever known.

The necessity for printing some account in the papers of the young man's career and personality had led to a remarkable predicament. It was of course impossible to reveal the facts, for a tremendous popular feeling in favor of the young hero had sprung up, like a grass fire, when he was halfway across Europe on his flight around the globe. He was, therefore, described as a modest chap, taciturn, blond, popular with his friends, popular with girls. The only available snapshot of Smurch, taken at the wheel of a phony automobile in a cheap photo studio at an amusement park, was touched up so that the little vulgarian looked quite handsome. His twisted leer was smoothed into a pleasant smile. The truth was, in this way, kept from the youth's ecstatic compatriots; they did not dream that the Smurch family was despised and feared by its neighbors in the obscure Iowa town, nor that the hero himself, because of numerous unsavory exploits, had come to be regarded in Westfield as a nuisance and a menace. He had, the reporters discovered, once knifed the principal of his high school—not mortally, to be sure, but he had knifed him; and on another occasion, surprised in the act of stealing an altar-cloth from a church, he had bashed the sacristan over the head with a pot of Easter lilies; for each of these offences he had served a sentence in the reformatory.

Inwardly, the authorities, both in New York and in Washington, prayed that an understanding Providence might, however awful such a thing seemed, bring disaster to the rusty, battered plane and its illustrious pilot, whose unheard-of flight had aroused the civilized world to hosannas of hysterical praise. The authorities were convinced that the character of the renowned aviator was such that the limelight of adulation was bound to reveal him to all the world, as a congenital hooligan mentally and morally unequipped to cope with his own prodigious fame. "I trust," said the Secretary of State, at one of many secret Cabinet meetings called to consider the national dilemma, "I trust that his mother's prayer will be answered," by which he referred to Mrs. Emma Smurch's wish that her son might be drowned. It was, however, too late for that—Smurch had leaped the Atlantic and then the Pacific as if they were millponds. At three minutes after two o'clock on the afternoon of 17 July, 1937, the garage boy brought his idiotic plane into Roosevelt Field for a perfect three-point landing.

It had, of course, been out of the question to arrange a modest little reception for the greatest flier in the history of the world. He was received at Roosevelt Field with such elaborate and pretentious ceremonies as rocked the world. Fortunately, however, the worn and spent hero promptly swooned, had to be removed bodily from his plane, and was spirited from the field without having opened his mouth once. Thus he did not jeopardize the dignity of this first reception, a reception illumined by the presence of the Secretaries of War and the Navy, Mayor Michael J. Moriarity of New York, the Premier of Canada, Governors Fanniman, Groves, McFeely, and Critchfield, and a brilliant array of European diplomats. Smurch did not, in fact, come to in time to take part in the gigantic hullabaloo arranged at City Hall for the next day. He was rushed to a secluded nursing home and confined to bed. It was nine days before he was able to get up, or to be more exact, before he was permitted to get up. Meanwhile the greatest minds in the country, in solemn assembly, had arranged a secret conference of city, state, and government officials, which Smurch was to attend for the purpose of being instructed in the ethics and behavior of heroism.

On the day that the little mechanic was finally allowed to get up and dress and, for the first time in two weeks, took a great chew of tobacco, he was permitted to receive the newspapermen—this by way of testing him out. Smurch did not wait for questions. "Youse guys," he said—and the *Times* man winced—"youse guys can tell the cock-eyed world dat I put it over on Lindbergh, see? Yeh—an' made an ass o' them two frogs." The "two frogs" was a reference to a pair of gallant French fliers who, in attempting a flight only halfway round the world, had, two weeks before, unhappily been lost at sea. The *Times* man was bold enough, at this point, to sketch out for Smurch the accepted formula for interviews in cases of this kind; he explained that there should be no arrogant statements belittling the achievements of other heroes, particularly heroes of foreign nations. "Ah, the hell with that," said Smurch. "I did it, see? I did it, an' I'm talkin' about it." And he did talk about it.

None of this extraordinary interview was, of course, printed. On the contrary, the newspapers, already under the disciplined direction of a secret directorate created for the occasion and composed of statesmen and editors, gave out to a panting and restless world that "Jacky," as he had been arbitrarily nicknamed, would consent to say only that he was very happy and that anyone could have done what he did. "My achievement has been, I fear, slightly exaggerated," the *Times* man's article had him protest, with a modest smile. These newspaper stories were kept from the hero, a restriction which did not serve to abate the rising malevolence of his temper. The situation was, indeed, extremely grave, for Pal Smurch was, as he kept insisting, "rarin' to go." He could not much longer be kept from a nation clamorous to lionize him. It was the most desperate crisis the United States of America had faced since the sinking of the *Lusitania*.

On the afternoon of the twenty-seventh of July, Smurch was spirited away to a conference-room in which were gathered mayors, governors, government officials, behaviorist psychologists, and editors. He gave them each a limp, moist paw and a brief unlovely grin. "Hah ya?" he said. When Smurch was seated, the Mayor of New York arose and, with obvious pessimism, attempted to explain what he must say and how he must act when presented to the world, ending his talk with a high tribute to the hero's courage and integrity. The Mayor was followed by Governor Fanniman of New York, who, after a touching declaration of faith, introduced Cameron Spottiswood, Second Secretary of the American Embassy in Paris, the gentleman selected to coach Smurch in the amenities of public ceremonies. Sitting in a chair, with a soiled yellow tie in his hand and his shirt open at the throat, unshaved, smoking a rolled cigarette, Jack Smurch listened with a leer on his lips. "I get ya, I get ya," he cut in nastily. "Ya want me to ack like a softy, huh? Ya want me to ack like that —— baby-faced Lindbergh, huh? Well, nuts to that, see?" Everyone took in his breath sharply; it was a sigh and a hiss. "Mr. Lindbergh," began a United States Senator, purple with rage, "and Mr. Byrd—" Smurch, who was paring his nails with a jackknife, cut in again, "Byrd!" he exclaimed. "Aw fa God's sake, dat big ——" Somebody shut off his blasphemies with a sharp word. A newcomer had entered the room. Everyone stood up, except Smurch, who, still busy with his nails, did not even glance up. "Mr. Smurch," said someone sternly, "the President of the United States!" It had been thought that the presence of the Chief Executive might have a chastening effect upon the young hero, and the former had been, thanks to the remarkable co-operation of the press, secretly brought to the obscure conference-room.

A great, painful silence fell. Smurch looked up, waved a hand at the President. "How ya comin'?" he asked, and began rolling a fresh cigarette. The silence deepened. Someone coughed in a strained way. "Geez, it's hot, ain't it?" said Smurch. He loosened two more shirt buttons, revealing a hairy chest and the tattooed word "Sadie" enclosed in a stenciled heart. The great and important men in the room, faced by the most serious crisis in recent American history, exchanged worried frowns. Nobody seemed to know how to proceed. "Come awn, come awn," said Smurch. "Let's get the hell out of here!" When do I start cuttin' in on de parties, huh? And what's they goin' to be *in* it?" He rubbed a thumb and forefinger together meaningly. "Money!" exclaimed a state senator, shocked, pale. "Yeh, money," said Pal, flipping his cigarette out of a window, "an' big money." He began rolling a fresh cigarette. "Big money," he repeated, frowning over the rice paper. He tilted back in his chair, and leered at each gentleman, separately, the leer of an animal that knows its power, the leer of a leopard loose in a bird-and-dog shop. "Aw, fa God's sake, let's get some place where it's cooler," he said. "I been cooped up plenty for three weeks!"

Smurch stood up and walked over to an open window, where he stood staring down into the street, nine floors below. The faint shouting of newsboys floated up to him. He made out his name. "Hot dog!" he cried, grinning, ecstatic. He leaned out over the sill. "You tell 'em, babies!" he shouted down. "Hot diggity dog!" In the tense little knot of men standing behind him, a quick, mad impulse flared up. An unspoken word of appeal, of command, seemed to ring through the room. Yet it was deadly silent. Charles K. L. Brand, secretary to the Mayor of New York City, happened to be standing nearest Smurch; he looked inquiringly at the President of the United States. The President, pale, grim, nodded shortly. Brand, a tall, powerfully built man, once a tackle at Rutgers, stepped forward, seized the greatest man in the world by his left shoulder and the seat of his pants, and pushed him out of the window.

"My God, he's fallen out the window!" cried a quick-witted editor.

"Get me out of here!" cried the President. Several men sprang to his side and he was hurriedly escorted out of a door toward a side-entrance of the building. The editor of the Associated Press took charge, being used to such things. Crisply he ordered certain men to leave, others to stay; quickly he outlined a story which all the papers were to agree on, sent two men to the street to handle that end of the tragedy, commanded a Senator to sob and two Congressmen go to pieces nervously. In a word, he skillfully set the stage for the gigantic task that was to follow, the task of breaking to a grief-stricken world the sad story of the untimely, accidental death of its most illustrious and spectacular figure.

The funeral was, as you know, the most elaborate, the finest, the solemnest, and the saddest ever held in the United States of America. The monument in Arlington Cemetery, with its clean white shaft of marble and the simple device of a tiny plane carved on its base, is a place for pilgrims, in deep reverence, to visit. The nations of the world paid lofty tributes to little Jacky Smurch, America's greatest hero. At a given hour there were two minutes of silence throughout the nation. Even the inhabitants of the small, bewildered town of Westfield, Iowa, observed this touching ceremony; agents of the Department of Justice saw to that. One of them was especially assigned to stand grimly in the doorway of a little shack restaurant on the edge of the tourists' camping ground just outside the town. There, under his stern scrutiny, Mrs. Emma Smurch bowed her head above two hamburger steaks sizzling on her grill—bowed her head and turned away, so that the Secret Service man could not see the twisted, strangely familiar, leer on her lips.

The Man Who Lived Underground

RICHARD WRIGHT [1908–1960]

I'VE got to hide, he told himself. His chest heaved as he waited, crouching in a dark corner of the vestibule. He was tired of running and dodging. Either he had to find a place to hide, or he had to surrender. A police car swished by through the rain, its siren rising sharply. They're looking for me all over . . . He crept to the door and squinted through the fogged plate glass. He stiffened as the siren rose and died in the distance. Yes, he had to hide, but where? He gritted his teeth. Then a sudden movement in the street caught his attention. A throng of tiny columns of water snaked into the air from the perforations of a manhole cover. The columns stopped abruptly, as though the perforations had become clogged; a gray spout of sewer water jutted up from underground and lifted the circular metal cover, juggled it for a moment, then let it fall with a clang.

He hatched a tentative plan: he would wait until the siren sounded far off, then he would go out. He smoked and waited, tense. At last the siren gave him his signal; it wailed, dying, going away from him. He stepped to the sidewalk, then paused and looked curiously at the open manhole, half expecting the cover to leap up again. He went to the center of the street and stooped and peered into the hole, but could see nothing. Water rustled in the black depths.

He started with terror; the siren sounded so near that he had the idea that he had been dreaming and had awakened to find the car upon him. He dropped instinctively to his knees and his hands grasped the rim of the manhole. The siren seemed to hoot directly above him and with a wild gasp of exertion he snatched the cover far enough off to admit his body. He swung his legs over the opening and lowered himself into watery darkness. He hung for an eternal moment to the rim by his finger tips, then he felt rough metal prongs and at once he knew that sewer workmen used these ridges to lower themselves into manholes. Fist over fist, he let his body sink until he could feel no more prongs. He swayed in dank space; the siren seemed to howl at the very rim of the manhole. He dropped and was washed violently into an ocean of warm, leaping water. His head was battered against a wall and he wondered if this were death. Frenziedly his fingers clawed and sank into a crevice. He steadied himself and measured the strength of the current with his own muscular tension. He stood slowly in water that dashed past his knees with fearful velocity.

He heard a prolonged scream of brakes and the siren broke off. Oh, God! They had found him! Looming above his head in the rain a white face hovered over the hole. "How did this damn thing get off?" he heard a policeman ask. He saw the steel cover move slowly until the hole looked like a quarter moon turned black. "Give me a hand here," someone called. The cover clanged into place, muffling the sights and sounds of the upper world. Knee-deep in the pulsing current, he breathed with aching chest, filling his lungs with the hot stench of yeasty rot.

From the perforations of the manhole cover, delicate lances of hazy violet sifted down and wove a mottled pattern upon the surface of the streaking current. His lips parted as a car swept past along the wet pavement overhead, its heavy rumble soon dying out, like the hum of a plane speeding through a dense cloud. He had never thought that cars could sound like that; everything seemed strange and unreal under here. He stood in darkness for a long time, knee-deep in rustling water, musing.

The odor of rot had become so general that he no longer smelled it. He got his cigarettes, but discovered that his matches were wet. He searched and found a dry folder in the pocket of his shirt and managed to strike one; it flared weirdly in the wet gloom, glowing greenishly, turning red, orange, then yellow. He lit a crumpled cigarette; then, by the flickering light of the match, he looked for support so that he would not have to keep his muscles flexed against the pouring water. His pupils narrowed and he saw to either side of him two steaming walls that rose and curved inward some six feet above his head to form a dripping, mouse-colored dome. The bottom of the sewer was a sloping V-trough. To the left, the sewer vanished in ashen fog. To the right was a steep down-curve into which water plunged.

He saw now that had he not regained his feet in time, he would have been swept to death, or had he entered any other manhole he would have probably drowned. Above the rush of the current he heard sharper juttings of water; tiny streams were spewing into the sewer from smaller conduits. The match died; he struck another and saw a mass of debris sweep past him and clog the throat of the down-curve. At once the water begain rising rapidly. Could he climb out before he drowned? A long hiss sounded and the debris was sucked from sight; the current lowered. He understood now what had made the water toss the manhole cover; the down-curve had become temporarily obstructed and the perforations had become clogged.

He was in danger; he might slide into a down-curve; he might wander with a lighted match into a pocket of gas and blow himself up; or he might contract some horrible disease . . . Though he wanted to leave, an irrational impulse held him rooted. To the left, the convex ceiling swooped to a height of less than five feet. With cigarette slanting from pursed lips, he waded with taut muscles, his feet sloshing over the slimy bottom, his shoes sinking into spongy slop, the slate-colored water cracking in creamy foam against his knees. Pressing his flat left palm against the lowered ceiling, he struck another match and saw a metal pole nestling in a niche of the wall. Yes, some sewer workman had left it. He reached for it, then jerked his head away as a whisper of scurrying life whisked past and was still. He held the match close and saw a huge rat, wet with slime, blinking beady eyes and baring tiny fangs. The light blinded the rat and the frizzled head moved aimlessly. He grabbed the pole and let it fly against the rat's soft body; there was shrill piping and the grizzly body splashed into the dun-colored water and was snatched out of sight, spinning in the scuttling stream.

He swallowed and pushed on, following the curve of the misty cavern, sounding the water with the pole. By the faint light of another manhole cover he saw, amid loose wet brick, a hole with walls of damp earth leading into blackness. Gingerly he poked the pole into it; it was hollow and went beyond the length of the pole. He shoved the pole before him, hoisted himself upward, got to his hands and knees, and crawled. After a few yards he paused, struck to wonderment by the silence; it seemed that he had traveled a million miles away from the world. As he inched forward again he could sense the bottom of the dirt tunnel becoming dry and lowering slightly. Slowly he rose and to his astonishment he stood erect. He could not hear the rustling of the water now and he felt confoundingly alone, yet lured by the darkness and silence.

He crept a long way, then stopped, curious, afraid. He put his right foot forward and it dangled in space; he drew back in fear. He thrust the pole outward and it swung in emptiness. He trembled, imagining the earth crumbling and burying him alive. He scratched a match and saw that the dirt floor sheered away steeply and widened into a sort of cave some five feet below him. An old sewer, he muttered. He cocked his head, hearing a feathery cadence which he could not identify. The match ceased to burn.

Using the pole as a kind of ladder, he slid down and stood in darkness. The air was a little fresher and he could still hear vague noises. Where was he? He felt suddenly that someone was standing near him and he turned sharply, but there was only darkness. He poked cautiously and felt a brick wall; he followed it and the strange sounds grew louder. He ought to get out of here. This was crazy. He could not remain here for any length of time; there was no food and no place to sleep. But the faint sounds tantalized him; they were strange but familiar. Was it a motor? A baby crying? Music? A siren? He groped on, and the sounds came so clearly that he could feel the pitch and timbre of human voices. Yes, singing! That was it! He listened with open mouth. It was a church service. Enchanted, he groped toward the waves of melody.

Jesus, take me to your home above
And fold me in the bosom of Thy love . . .

The singing was on the other side of the brick wall. Excited, he wanted to watch the service without being seen. Whose church was it? He knew most of the churches in this area above ground, but the singing sounded too strange and detached for him to guess. He looked to the left, to the right, down to the black dirt, then upward and was startled to see a bright sliver of light slicing the darkness like the blade of a razor. He struck one of his two remaining matches and saw rusty pipes running along an old concrete ceiling. Photographically he located the exact position of the pipes in his mind. The match flame sank and he sprang upward; his hands clutched a pipe. He swung his legs and tossed his body onto the bed of pipes and they creaked, swaying up and down; he thought that the tier was about to crash, but nothing happened. He edged to the crevice and saw a segment of black men and women, dressed in white robes, singing, holding tattered songbooks in their black palms. His first impulse was to laugh, but he checked himself.

What was he doing? He was crushed with a sense of guilt. Would God strike him dead for that? The singing swept on and he shook his head, disagreeing in spite of himself. They oughtn't to do that, he thought. But he could think of no reason *why* they should not do it. Just singing with the air of the sewer blowing in on them . . . He felt that he was gazing upon something abysmally obscene, yet he could not bring himself to leave.

After a long time he grew numb and dropped to the dirt. Pain throbbed in his legs and a deeper pain, induced by the sight of those black people groveling and begging for something they could never get, churned in him. A vague conviction made him feel that those people should stand unrepentant and yield no quarter in singing and praying, yet *he* had run away from the police, had pleaded with them to believe in *his* innocence. He shook his head, bewildered.

How long had he been down here? He did not know. This was a new kind of living for him; the intensity of feelings he had experienced when looking at the church people sing made him certain that he had been down here a long time, but his mind told him that the time must have been short. In this darkness the only notion he had of time was when a match flared and measured time by its fleeting light. He groped back through the hole toward the sewer and the waves of song subsided and finally he could not hear them at all. He came to where the earth hole ended and he heard the noise of the current and time lived again for him, measuring the moments by the wash of the water.

The rain must have slackened, for the flow of water had lessened and came only to his ankles. Ought he to go up into the streets and take his chances on hiding somewhere else? But they would surely catch him. The mere thought of dodging and running again from the police made him tense. No, he would stay and plot how to elude them. But what could he do down here? He walked forward into the sewer and came to another manhole cover; he stood beneath it, debating. Fine pencils of gold spilled suddenly from the little circles in the manhole cover and trembled on the surface of the current. Yes, street lamps . . . It must be night . . .

He went forward for about a quarter of an hour, wading aimlessly, poking the pole carefully before him. Then he stopped, his eyes fixed and intent. What's that? A strangely familiar image attracted and repelled him. Lit by the yellow stems from another manhole cover was a tiny nude body of a baby snagged by debris and half-submerged in water. Thinking that the baby was alive, he moved impulsively to save it, but his roused feelings told him that it was dead, cold, nothing, the same nothingness he had felt while watching the men and women singing in the church. Water blossomed about the tiny legs, the tiny arms, the tiny head, and rushed onward. The eyes were closed, as though in sleep; the fists were clenched, as though in protest; and the mouth gaped black in a soundless cry.

He straightened and drew in his breath, feeling that he had been staring for all eternity at the ripples of veined water skimming impersonally over the shriveled limbs. He felt as condemned as when the policemen had accused him. Involuntarily he lifted his hand to brush the vision away, but his arm fell listlessly to his side. Then he acted; he closed his eyes and reached forward slowly with the soggy shoe of his right foot and shoved the dead baby from where it had been lodged. He kept his eyes closed, seeing the little body twisting in the current as it floated from sight. He opened his eyes, shivered, placed his knuckles in the sockets, hearing the water speed in the somber shadows.

He tramped on, sensing at times a sudden quickening in the current as he passed some conduit whose waters were swelling the stream that slid by his feet. A few minutes later he was standing under another manhole cover, listening to the faint rumble of noises above ground. Streetcars and trucks, he mused. He looked down and saw a stagnant pool of gray-green sludge; at intervals a balloon pocket rose from the scum, glistening a bluish-purple, and burst. Then another. He turned, shook his head, and tramped back to the dirt cave by the church, his lips quivering.

Back in the cave, he sat and leaned his back against a dirt wall. His body was trembling slightly. Finally his senses quieted and he slept. When he awakened he felt stiff and cold. He had to leave this foul place, but leaving meant facing those policemen who had wrongly accused him. No, he could not go back aboveground. He remembered the beating they had given him and how he had signed his name to a confession, a confession which he had not even read. He had been too tired when they had shouted at him, demanding that he sign his name; he had signed it to end his pain.

He stood and groped about in the darkness. The church singing had stopped. How long had he slept? He did not know. But he felt refreshed and hungry. He doubled his fist nervously, realizing that he could not make a decison. As he walked about he stumbled over an old rusty iron pipe. He picked it up and felt a jagged edge. Yes, there was a brick wall and he could dig into it. What would he find? Smiling, he groped to the brick wall, sat, and began digging idly into damp cement. I can't make any noise, he cautioned himself. As time passed he grew thirsty, but there was no water. He had to kill time or go aboveground. The cement came out of the wall easily; he extracted four bricks and felt a soft draft blowing into his face. He stopped, afraid. What was beyond? He waited a long time and nothing happened; then he began digging again, soundlessly, slowly; he enlarged the hole and crawled through into a dark room and collided with another wall. He felt his way to the right; the wall ended and his fingers toyed in space, like the antennae of an insect.

He fumbled on and his feet struck something hollow, like wood. What's this? He felt with his fingers. Steps . . . He stooped and pulled off his shoes and mounted the stairs and saw a yellow chink of light shining and heard a low voice speaking. He placed his eye to a keyhole and saw the nude waxen figure of a man stretched out upon a white table. The voice, low-pitched and vibrant, mumbled indistinguishable words, neither rising nor falling. He craned his neck and squinted to see the man who was talking, but he could not locate him. Above the naked figure was suspended a huge glass container filled with a blood-red liquid from which a white rubber tube dangled. He crouched closer to the door and saw the tip end of a black object lined with pink satin. A coffin, he breathed. This is an undertaker's establishment . . . A fine-spun lace of ice covered his body and he shuddered. A throaty chuckle sounded in the depths of the yellow room.

He turned to leave. Three steps down it occurred to him that a light switch should be nearby; he felt along the wall, found an electric button, pressed it, and a blinding glare smote his pupils so hard that he was sightless, defenseless. His pupils contracted and he wrinkled his nostrils at a peculiar odor. At once he knew that he had been dimly aware of this odor in the darkness, but the light had brought it sharply to his attention. Some kind of stuff they use to embalm, he thought. He went down the steps and saw piles of lumber, coffins, and a long workbench. In one corner was a tool chest. Yes, he could use tools, could tunnel through walls with them. He lifted the lid of the chest and saw nails, a hammer, a crowbar, a screwdriver, a light bulb, and a long length of electric wire. Good! He would lug these back to his cave.

He was about to hoist the chest to his shoulders when he discovered a door behind the furnace. Where did it lead? He tried to open it and found it securely bolted. Using the crowbar so as to make no sound, he pried the door open; it swung on creaking hinges, outward. Fresh air came to his face and he caught the faint roar of faraway sound. Easy now, he told himself. He widened the door and a lump of coal rattled toward him. A coalbin . . . Evidently the door led into another basement. The roaring noise was louder now, but he could not identify it. Where was he? He groped slowly over the coal pile, then ranged in darkness over a gritty floor. The roaring noise seemed to come from above him, then below. His fingers followed a wall until he touched a wooden ridge. A door, he breathed.

The noise died to a low pitch; he felt his skin prickle. It seemed that he was playing a game with an unseen person whose intelligence outstripped his. He put his ear to the flat surface of the door. Yes, voices . . . Was this a prize fight stadium? The sound of the voices came near and sharp, but he could not tell if they were joyous or despairing. He twisted the knob until he heard a soft click and felt the springy weight of the door swinging toward him. He was afraid to open it, yet captured by curiosity and wonder. He jerked the door wide and saw on the far side of the basement a furnace glowing red. Ten feet away was still another door, half ajar. He crossed and peered through the door into an empty, high-ceilinged corridor that terminated in a dark complex of shadow. The belling voices rolled about him and his eagerness mounted. He stepped into the corridor and the voices swelled louder. He crept on and came to a narrow stairway leading circularly upward; there was no question but that he was going to ascend those stairs.

Mounting the spiraled staircase, he heard the voices roll in a steady wave, then leap to crescendo, only to die away, but always remaining audible. Ahead of him glowed red letters: E—X—I—T. At the top of the steps he paused in front of a black curtain that fluttered uncertainly. He parted the folds and looked into a convex depth tha. gleamed with clusters of shimmering lights. Sprawled below him was a stretch of human faces, tilted upward, chanting, whistling, screaming, laughing. Dangling before the faces, high upon a screen of silver, were jerking shadows. A movie, he said with slow laughter breaking from his lips.

He stood in a box in the reserved section of a movie house and the impulse he had had to tell the people in the church to stop their singing seized him. These people were laughing at their lives, he thought with amazement. They were shouting and yelling at the animated shadows of themselves. His compassion fired his imagination and he stepped out of the box, walked out upon thin air, walked on down to the audience; and, hovering in the air just above them, he stretched out his hand to touch them . . . His tension snapped and he found himself back in the box, looking down into the sea of faces. No; it could not be done; he could not awaken them. He sighed. Yes, these people were children, sleeping in their living, awake in their dying.

He turned away, parted the black curtain, and looked out. He saw no one. He started down the white stone steps and when he reached the bottom he saw a man in trim blue uniform coming toward him. So used had he become to being underground that he thought that he could walk past the man, as though he were a ghost. But the man stopped. And he stopped.

"Looking for the men's room, sir?" the man asked, and, without waiting for an answer, he turned and pointed. "This way, sir. The first door to your right."

He watched the man turn and walk up the steps and go out of sight. Then he laughed. What a funny fellow! He went back to the basement and stood in the red darkness, watching the glowing embers in the furnace. He went to the sink and turned the faucet and the water flowed in a smooth silent stream that looked like a spout of blood. He brushed the mad image from his mind and began to wash his hands leisurely, looking about for the usual bar of soap. He found one and rubbed it in his palms until a rich lather bloomed in his cupped fingers, like a scarlet sponge. He scrubbed and rinsed his hands meticulously, then hunted for a towel; there was none. He shut off the water, pulled off his shirt, dried his hands on it; when he put it on again he was grateful for the cool dampness that came to his skin.

Yes, he was thirsty; he turned on the faucet again, bowled his fingers and when the water bubbled over the brim of his cupped palms, he drank in long, slow swallows. His bladder grew tight; he shut off the water, faced the wall, bent his head, and watched a red stream strike the floor. His nostrils wrinkled against acrid wisps of vapor; though he had tramped in the waters of the sewer, he stepped back from the wall so that his shoes, wet with sewer slime, would not touch his urine.

He heard footsteps and crawled quickly into the coalbin. Lumps rattled noisily. The footsteps came into the basement and stopped. Who was it? Had someone heard him and come down to investigate? He waited, crouching, sweating. For a long time there was silence, then he heard the clang of metal and a brighter glow lit the room. Somebody's tending the furnace, he thought. Footsteps came closer and he stiffened. Looming before him was a white face lined with coal dust, the face of an old man with watery blue eyes. Highlights spotted his gaunt cheekbones, and he held a huge shovel. There was a screechy scrape of metal against stone, and the old man lifted a shovelful of coal and went from sight.

The room dimmed momentarily, then a yellow glare came as coal flared at the furnace door. Six times the old man came to the bin and went to the furnace with shovels of coal, but not once did he lift his eyes. Finally he dropped the shovel, mopped his face with a dirty handkerchief, and sighed: "Wheeew!" He turned slowly and trudged out of the basement, his footsteps dying away.

He stood, and lumps of coal clattered down the pile. He stepped from the bin and was startled to see the shadowy outline of an electric bulb hanging above his head. Why had not the old man turned it on? Oh, yes . . . He understood. The old man had worked here for so long that he had no need for light; he had learned a way of seeing in his dark world, like those sightless worms that inch along underground by a sense of touch.

His eyes fell upon a lunch pail and he was afraid to hope that it was full. He picked it up; it was heavy. He opened it. *Sandwiches!* He looked guiltily around; he was alone. He searched farther and found a folder of matches and a half-empty tin of tobacco; he put them eagerly into his pocket and clicked off the light. With the lunch pail under his arm, he went through the door, groped over the pile of coal, and stood again in the lighted basement of the undertaking establishment. I've got to get those tools, he told himself. And turn off that light. He tiptoed back up the steps and switched off the light; the invisible voice still droned on behind the door. He crept down and, seeing with his fingers, opened the lunch pail and tore off a piece of paper bag and brought out the tin and spilled grains of tobacco into the makeshift concave. He rolled it and wet it with spittle, then inserted one end into his mouth and lit it: he sucked smoke that bit his lungs. The nicotine reached his brain, went out along his arms to his finger tips, down to his stomach, and over all the tired nerves of his body.

He carted the tools to the hole he had made in the wall. Would the noise of the falling chest betray him? But he would have to take a chance; he had to have those tools. He lifted the chest and shoved it; it hit the dirt on the other side of the wall with a loud clatter. He waited, listening; nothing happened. Head first, he slithered through and stood in the cave. He grinned, filled with a cunning idea. Yes, he would now go back into the basement of the undertaking establishment and crouch behind the coal pile and dig another hole. Sure! Fumbling, he opened the tool chest and extracted a crowbar, a screwdriver, and a hammer; he fastened them securely about his person.

With another lumpish cigarette in his flexed lips, he crawled back through the hole and over the coal pile and sat, facing the brick wall. He jabbed with the crowbar and the cement sheered away; quicker than he thought, a brick came loose. He worked an hour; the other bricks did not come easily. He sighed, weak from effort. I ought to rest a little, he thought. I'm hungry. He felt his way back to the cave and stumbled along the wall till he came to the tool chest. He sat upon it, opened the lunch pail, and took out two thick sandwiches. He smelled them. Pork chops . . . His mouth watered. He closed his eyes and devoured a sandwich, savoring the smooth rye bread and juicy meat. He ate rapidly, gulping down lumpy mouthfuls that made him long for water. He ate the other sandwich and found an apple and gobbled that up too, sucking the core till the last trace of flavor was drained from it. Then, like a dog, he ground the meat bones with his teeth, enjoying the salty, tangy marrow. He finished and stretched out full length on the ground and went to sleep. . . .

. . . His body was washed by cold water that gradually turned warm and he was buoyed upon a stream and swept out to sea where waves rolled gently and suddenly he found himself walking upon the water how strange and delightful to walk upon the water and he came upon a nude woman holding a nude baby in her arms and the woman was sinking into the water holding the baby above her head and screaming *help* and he ran over the water to the woman and he reached her just before she went down and he took the baby from her hands and stood watching the breaking bubbles where the woman sank and he called *lady* and still no answer yes dive down there and rescue that woman but he could not take this baby with him and he stooped and laid the baby tenderly upon the surface of the water expecting it to sink but it floated and he leaped into the water and held his breath and strained his eyes to see through the gloomy volume of water but there was no woman and he opened his mouth and called *lady* and the water bubbled and his chest ached and his arms were tired but he could not see the woman and he called again *lady lady* and his feet touched sand at the bottom of the sea and his chest felt as though it would burst and he bent his knees and propelled himself upward and water rushed past him and his head bobbed out and he breathed deeply and looked around where was the baby the baby was gone and he rushed over the water looking for the baby calling *where is it* and the empty sky and sea threw back his voice *where is it* and he began to doubt that he could stand upon the water and then he was sinking and as he struggled the water rushed him downward spinning dizzily and he opened his mouth to call for help and water surged into his lungs and he choked . . .

He groaned and leaped erect in the dark, his eyes wide. The images of terror that thronged his brain would not let him sleep. He rose, made sure that the tools were hitched to his belt, and groped his way to the coal pile and found the rectangular gap from which he had taken the bricks. He took out the crowbar and hacked. Then dread paralyzed him. How long had he slept? Was it day or night now? He had to be careful. Someone might hear him if it were day. He hewed softly for hours at the cement, working silently. Faintly quivering in the air above him was the dim sound of yelling voices. Crazy people, he muttered. They're still there in that movie . . .

Having rested, he found the digging much easier. He soon had a dozen bricks out. His spirits rose. He took out another brick and his fingers fluttered in space. Good! What lay ahead of him? Another basement? He made the hole larger, climbed through, walked over an uneven floor and felt a metal surface. He lighted a match and saw that he was standing behind a furnace in a basement; before him, on the far side of the room, was a door. He crossed and opened it; it was full of odds and ends. Daylight spilled from a window above his head.

Then he was aware of a soft, continuous tapping. What was it? A clock? No, it was louder than a clock and more irregular. He placed an old empty box beneath the window, stood upon it, and looked into an areaway. He eased the window up and crawled through; the sound of the tapping came clearly now. He glanced about; he was alone. Then he looked upward at a series of window ledges. The tapping identified itself. That's a typewriter, he said to himself. It seemed to be coming from just above. He grasped the ridges of a rain pipe and lifted himself upward; through a half-inch opening of window he saw a door-knob about three feet away. No, it was not a doorknob; it was a small circular disk made of stainless steel with many fine markings upon it. He held his breath; an eerie white hand, seemingly detached from its arm, touched the metal knob and whirled it, first to the left, then to the right. It's a safe! . . . Suddenly he could see the dial no more; a huge metal door swung slowly toward him and he was looking into a safe filled with green wads of paper money, rows of coins wrapped in brown paper, and glass jars and boxes of various sizes. His heart quickened. Good Lord! The white hand went in and out of the safe, taking wads of bills and cylinders of coins. The hand vanished and he heard the muffled click of the big door as it closed. Only the steel dial was visible now. The typewriter still tapped in his ears, but he could not see it. He blinked, wondering if what he had seen was real. There was more money in that safe than he had seen in all his life.

As he clung to the rain pipe, a daring idea came to him and he pulled the screwdriver from his belt. If the white hand twirled that dial again, he would be able to see how far to left and right it spun and he would have the combination! His blood tingled. I can scratch the numbers right here, he thought. Holding the pipe with one hand, he made the sharp edge of the screwdriver bite into the brick wall. Yes, he could do it. Now, he was set. Now, he had a reason for staying here in the underground. He waited for a long time, but the white hand did not return. Goddamn! Had he been more alert, he could have counted the twirls and he would have had the combination. He got down and stood in the areaway, sunk in reflection.

How could he get into that room? He climbed back into the basement and saw wooden steps leading upward. Was that the room where the safe stood? Fearing that the dial was now being twirled, he clambered through the window, hoisted himself up the rain pipe, and peered; he saw only the naked gleam of the steel dial. He got down and doubled his fists. Well, he would explore the basement. He returned to the basement room and mounted the steps to the door and squinted through the keyhole; all was dark, but the tapping was still somewhere near, still faint and directionless. He pushed the door in; along one wall of a room was a table piled with radios and electrical equipment. A radio shop, he muttered.

Well, he could rig up a radio in his cave. He found a sack, slid the radio into it, and slung it across his back. Closing the door, he went down the steps and stood again in the basement, disappointed. He had not solved the problem of the steel dial and he was irked. He set the radio on the floor and again hoisted himself through the window and up the rain pipe and squinted; the metal door was swinging shut. Goddamn! He's worked the combination again. If I had been patient, I'd have had it! How could he get into that room? He *had* to get into it. He could jimmy the window, but it would be much better if he could get in without any traces. To the right of him, he calculated, should be the basement of the building that held the safe; therefore, if he dug a hole right *here,* he ought to reach his goal.

He began a quiet scraping; it was hard work, for the bricks were not damp. He eventually got one out and lowered it softly to the floor. He had to be careful; perhaps people were beyond this wall. He extracted a second layer of brick and found still another. He gritted his teeth, ready to quit. I'll dig one more, he resolved. When the next brick came out he felt air blowing into his face. He waited to be challenged, but nothing happened.

He enlarged the hole and pulled himself through and stood in quiet darkness. He scratched a match to flame and saw steps; he mounted and peered through a keyhole; Darkness . . . He strained to hear the typewriter, but there was only silence. Maybe the office had closed? He twisted the knob and swung the door in; a frigid blast made him shiver. In the shadows before him were halves and quarters of hogs and lambs and steers hanging from metal hooks on the low ceiling, red meat encased in folds of cold white fat. Fronting him was frost-coated glass from behind which came indistinguishable sounds. The odor of fresh raw meat sickened him and he backed away. A meat market, he whispered.

He ducked his head, suddenly blinded by light. He narrowed his eyes; the red-white rows of meat were drenched in yellow glare. A man wearing a crimson spotted jacket came in and took down a bloody meat cleaver. He eased the door to, holding it ajar just enough to watch the man, hoping that the darkness in which he stood would keep him from being seen. The man took down a hunk of steer and placed it upon a bloody wooden block and bent forward and whacked with the cleaver. The man's face was hard, square, grim; a jet of mustache smudged his upper lip and a glistening cowlick of hair fell over his left eye. Each time he lifted the cleaver and brought it down upon the meat, he let out a short, deep-chested grunt. After he had cut the meat, he wiped blood off the wooden block with a sticky wad of gunny sack and hung the cleaver upon a hook. His face was proud as he placed the chunk of meat in the crook of his elbow and left.

The door slammed and the light went off; once more he stood in shadow. His tension ebbed. From behind the frosted glass he heard the man's voice: "Forty-eight cents a pound, ma'am." He shuddered, feeling that there was something he had to do. But what? He stared fixedly at the cleaver, then he sneezed and was terrified for fear that the man had heard him. But the door did not open. He took down the cleaver and examined the sharp edge smeared with cold blood. Behind the ice-coated glass a cash register rang with a vibrating, musical tinkle.

Absent-mindedly holding the meat cleaver, he rubbed the glass with his thumb and cleared a spot that enabled him to see into the front of the store. The shop was empty, save for the man who was now putting on his hat and coat. Beyond the front window a wan sun shone in the streets; people passed and now and then a fragment of laughter or the whir of a speeding auto came to him. He peered closer and saw on the right counter of the shop a mosquito netting covering pears, grapes, lemons, oranges, bananas, peaches, and plums. His stomach contracted.

The man clicked out the light and he gritted his teeth, muttering, Don't lock the icebox door . . . The man went through the door of the shop and locked it from the outside. Thank God! Now, he would eat some more! He waited, trembling. The sun died and its rays lingered on in the sky, turning the streets to dusk. He opened the door and stepped inside the shop. In reverse letters across the front window was: NICK'S FRUITS AND MEATS. He laughed, picked up a soft ripe yellow pear and bit into it; juice squirted; his mouth ached as his saliva glands reacted to the acid of the fruit. He ate three pears, gobbled six bananas, and made away with several oranges, taking a bite out of their tops and holding them to his lips and squeezing them as he hungrily sucked the juice.

He found a faucet, turned it on, laid the cleaver aside, pursed his lips under the stream until his stomach felt about to burst. He straightened and belched, feeling satisfied for the first time since he had been underground. He sat upon the floor, rolled and lit a cigarette, his bloodshot eyes squinting against the film of drifting smoke. He watched a patch of sky turn red, then purple; night fell and he lit another cigarette, brooding. Some part of him was trying to remember the world he had left, and another part of him did not want to remember it. Sprawling before him in his mind was his wife, Mrs. Wooten for whom he worked, the three policemen who had picked him up . . . He possessed them now more completely than he had ever possessed them when he had lived aboveground. How this had come about he could not say, but he had no desire to go back to them. He laughed, crushed the cigarette, and stood up.

He went to the front door and gazed out. Emotionally he hovered between the world aboveground and the world underground. He longed to go out, but sober judgment urged him to remain here. Then impulsively he pried the lock loose with one swift twist of the crowbar; the door swung outward. Through the twilight he saw a white man and a white woman coming toward him. He held himself tense, waiting for them to pass; but they came directly to the door and confronted him.

"I want to buy a pound of grapes," the woman said.

Terrified, he stepped back into the store. The white man stood to one side and the woman entered.

"Give me a pound of dark ones," the woman said.

The white man came slowly forward, blinking his eyes.

"Where's Nick?" the man asked.

"Were you just closing?" the woman asked.

"Yes, ma'am," he mumbled. For a second he did not breathe, then he mumbled again: "Yes, ma'am."

"I'm sorry," the woman said.

The street lamps came on, lighting the store somewhat. Ought he run? But that would raise an alarm. He moved slowly, dreamily, to a counter and lifted up a bunch of grapes and showed them to the woman.

"Fine," the woman said. "But isn't that more than a pound?"

He did not answer. The man was staring at him intently.

"Put them in a bag for me," the woman said, fumbling with her purse.

"Yes, ma'am."

He saw a pile of paper bags under a narrow ledge; he opened one and put the grapes in.

"Thanks," the woman said, taking the bag and placing a dime in his dark palm.

"Where's Nick?" the man asked again. "At supper?"

"Sir? Yes, sir," he breathed.

They left the store and he stood trembling in the doorway. When they were out of sight, he burst out laughing and crying. A trolley car rolled noisily past and he controlled himself quickly. He flung the dime to the pavement with a gesture of contempt and stepped into the warm night air. A few shy stars trembled above him. The look of things was beautiful, yet he felt a lurking threat. He went to an unattended newsstand and looked at a stack of papers. He saw a headline: HUNT NEGRO FOR MURDER.

He felt that someone had slipped up on him from behind and was stripping off his clothes; he looked about wildly, went quickly back into the store, picked up the meat cleaver where he had left it near the sink, then made his way through the icebox to the basement. He stood for a long time, breathing heavily. They know I didn't do anything, he muttered. But how could he prove it? He had signed a confession. Though innocent, he felt guilty, condemned. He struck a match and held it near the steel blade, fascinated and repelled by the dried blotches of blood. Then his fingers gripped the handle of the cleaver with all the strength of his body, he wanted to fling the cleaver from him, but he could not. The match flame wavered and fled; he struggled through the hole and put the cleaver in the sack with the radio. He was determined to keep it, for what purpose he did not know.

He was about to leave when he remembered the safe. Where was it? He wanted to give up, but felt that he ought to make one more try. Opposite the last hole he had dug, he tunneled again, plying the crowbar. Once he was so exhausted that he lay on the concrete floor and panted. Finally he made another hole. He wriggled through and his nostrils filled with the fresh smell of coal. He struck a match; yes, the usual steps led upward. He tiptoed to a door and eased it open. A fair-haired white girl stood in front of a steel cabinet, her blue eyes wide upon him. She turned chalky and gave a high-pitched scream. He bounded down the steps and raced to his hole and clambered through, replacing the bricks with nervous haste. He paused, hearing loud voices.

"What's the matter, Alice?"

"A man . . ."

"What man? Where?"

"A man was at that door . . ."

"Oh, nonsense!"

"He was looking at me through the door!"

"Aw, you're dreaming."

"I *did* see a man!"

The girl was crying now.

"There's nobody here."

Another man's voice sounded.

"What is it, Bob?"

"Alice says she saw a man in here, in that door!"

"Let's take a look."

He waited, poised for flight. Footsteps descended the stairs.

"There's nobody down here."

"The window's locked."

"And there's no door."

"You ought to fire that dame."

"Oh, I don't know. Women are that way."

"She's too hysterical."

The men laughed. Footsteps sounded again on the stairs. A door slammed. He sighed, relieved that he had escaped. But he had not done what he had set out to do; his glimpse of the room had been too brief to determine if the safe was there. He had to know. Boldly he groped through the hole once more; he reached the steps and pulled off his shoes and tip-toed up and peered through the keyhole. His head accidentally touched the door and it swung silently in a fraction of an inch; he saw the girl bent over the cabinet, her back to him. Beyond her was the safe. He crept back down the steps, thinking exultingly: I found it!

Now he had to get the combination. Even if the window in the areaway was locked and bolted, he could gain entrance when the office closed. He scoured through the holes he had dug and stood again in the basement where he had left the radio and the cleaver. Again he crawled out of the window and lifted himself up the rain pipe and peered. The steel dial showed lonely and bright, reflecting the yellow glow of an unseen light. Resigned to a long wait, he sat and leaned against the wall. From far off came the faint sounds of life aboveground; once he looked with a baffled expression at the dark sky. Frequently he rose and climbed the pipe to see the white hand spin the dial, but nothing happened. He bit his lip with impatience. It was not the money that was luring him, but the mere fact that he could get it with impunity. Was the hand now twirling the dial? He rose and looked, but the white hand was not in sight.

Perhaps it would be better to watch continuously? Yes; he clung to the pipe and watched the dial until his eyes thickened with tears. Exhausted, he stood again in the areaway. He heard a door being shut and he clawed up the pipe and looked. He jerked tense as a vague figure passed in front of him. He stared unblinkingly, hugging the pipe with one hand and holding the screwdriver with the other, ready to etch the combination upon the wall. His ears caught: *Dong . . . Dong . . . Dong . . . Dong . . . Dong . . . Dong . . . Dong . . .* Seven o'clock, he whispered. Maybe they were closing now? What kind of a store would be open as late as this? he wondered. Did anyone live in the rear? Was there a night watchman? Perhaps the safe was *already* locked for the night! Goddamn! While he had been eating in that shop, they had locked up everything . . . Then, just as he was about to give up, the white hand touched the dial and turned it once to the right and stopped at six. With quivering fingers, he etched 1—R—6 upon the brick wall with the tip of the screwdriver. The hand twisted the dial twice to the left and stopped at two, and he engraved 2—L—2 upon the wall. The dial was spun four times to the right and stopped at six again; he wrote 4—R—6. The dial rotated three times to the left and was centered straight up and down; he wrote 3—L—0. The door swung open and again he saw the piles of green money and the rows of wrapped coins. I got it, he said grimly.

Then he was stone still, astonished. There were two hands now. A right hand lifted a wad of green bills and deftly slipped it up the sleeve of the left arm. The hands trembled; again the right hand slipped a packet of bills up the left sleeve. He's stealing he said to himself. He grew indignant, as if the money belonged to him. Though *he* had planned to steal the money, he despised and pitied the man. He felt that his stealing the money and the man's stealing were two entirely different things. He wanted to steal the money merely for the sensation involved in getting it, and he had no intention whatever of spending a penny of it; but he knew that the man who was now stealing it was going to spend it, perhaps for pleasure. The huge steel door closed with a soft click.

Though angry, he was somewhat satisfied. The office would close soon. I'll clean the place out, he mused. He imagined the entire office staff cringing with fear; the police would question everyone for a crime they had not committed, just as they had questioned him. And they would have no idea of how the money had been stolen until they discovered the holes he had tunneled in the walls of the basements. He lowered himself and laughed mischievously, with the abandoned glee of an adolescent.

He flattened himself against the wall as the window above him closed with rasping sound. He looked; somebody was bolting the window securely with a metal screen. That won't help you, he snickered to himself. He clung to the rain pipe until the yellow light in the office went out. He went back into the basement, picked up the sack containing the radio and cleaver, and crawled through the two holes he had dug and groped his way into the basement of the building that held the safe. He moved in slow motion, breathing softly. Be careful now, he told himself. There might be a night watchman . . . In his memory was the combination written in bold white characters as upon a blackboard. Eel-like he squeezed through the last hole and crept up the steps and put his hand on the knob and pushed the door in about three inches. Then his courage ebbed; his imagination wove dangers for him.

Perhaps the night watchman was waiting in there, ready to shoot. He dangled his cap on a forefinger and poked it past the jamb of the door. If anyone fired, they would hit his cap; but nothing happened. He widened the door, holding the crowbar high above his head, ready to beat off an assailant. He stood like that for five minutes; the rumble of a streetcar brought him to himself. He entered the room. Moonlight floated in from a side window. He confronted the safe, then checked himself. Better take a look around first . . . He stepped about and found a closed door. Was the night watchman in there? He opened it and saw a washbowl, a faucet, and a commode. To the left was still another door that opened into a huge dark room that seemed empty; on the far side of that room he made out the shadow of still another door. Nobody's here, he told himself.

He turned back to the safe and fingered the dial; it spun with ease. He laughed and twirled it just for fun. Get to work, he told himself. He turned the dial to the figures he saw on the blackboard of his memory; it was so easy that he felt that the safe had not been locked at all. The heavy door eased loose and he caught hold of the handle and pulled hard, but the door swung open with a slow momentum of its own. Breathless, he gaped at wads of green bills, rows of wrapped coins, curious glass jars full of white pellets, and many oblong green metal boxes. He glanced guiltily over his shoulder; it seemed impossible that someone should not call to him to stop.

They'll be surprised in the morning, he thought. He opened the top of the sack and lifted a wad of compactly tied bills; the money was crisp and new. He admired the smooth, cleancut edges. The fellows in Washington sure know how to make this stuff, he mused. He rubbed the money with his fingers, as though expecting it to reveal hidden qualities. He lifted the wad to his nose and smelled the fresh odor of ink. Just like any other paper, he mumbled. He dropped the wad into the sack and picked up another. Holding the bag, he thought and laughed.

There was in him no sense of possessiveness; he was intrigued with the form and color of the money, with the manifold reactions which he knew that men aboveground held toward it. The sack was one-third full when it occurred to him to examine the denominations of the bills; without realizing it, he had put many wads of one-dollar bills into the sack. Aw, nuts, he said in disgust. Take the big ones . . . He dumped the one-dollar bills onto the floor and swept all the hundred-dollar bills he could find into the sack, then he raked in rolls of coins with crooked fingers.

He walked to a desk upon which sat a typewriter, the same machine which the blond girl had used. He was fascinated by it; never in his life had he used one of them. It was a queer instrument of business, something beyond the rim of his life. Whenever he had been in an office where a girl was typing, he had almost always spoken in whispers. Remembering vaguely what he had seen others do, he inserted a sheet of paper into the machine; it went in lopsided and he did not know how to straighten it. Spelling in a soft diffident voice, he pecked out his name on the keys: *freddaniels*. He looked at it and laughed. He would learn to type correctly one of these days.

Yes, he would take the typewriter too. He lifted the machine and placed it atop the bulk of money in the sack. He did not feel that he was stealing, for the cleaver, the radio, the money, and the typewriter were all on the same level of value, all meant the same thing to him. They were the serious toys of the men who lived in the dead world of sunshine and rain he had left, the world that had condemned him, branded him guilty.

But what kind of a place is this? He wondered. What was in that dark room to his rear? He felt for his matches and found that he had only one left. He leaned the sack against the safe and groped forward into the room, encountering smooth, metallic objects that felt like machines. Baffled, he touched a wall and tried vainly to locate an electric switch. Well, he *had* to strike his last match. He knelt and struck it, cupping the flame near the floor with his palms. The place seemed to be a factory, with benches and tables. There were bulbs with green shades spaced about the tables; he turned on a light and twisted it low so that the glare was limited. He saw a half-filled packet of cigarettes and appropriated it. There were stools at the benches and he concluded that men worked here at some trade. He wandered and found a few half-used folders of matches. If only he could find more cigarettes! But there were none.

But what kind of a place was this? On a bench he saw a pad of paper captioned: PEER'S—MANUFACTURING JEWELERS. His lips formed an "O," then he snapped off the light and ran back to the safe and lifted one of the glass jars and stared at the tiny white pellets. Gingerly he picked up one and found that it was wrapped in tissue paper. He peeled the paper and saw a glittering stone that looked like glass, glinting white and blue sparks. Diamonds, he breathed.

Roughly he tore the paper from the pellets and soon his palm quivered with precious fire. Trembling, he took all four glass jars from the safe and put them into the sack. He grabbed one of the metal boxes, shook it, and heard a tinny rattle. He pried off the lid with the screwdriver. Rings! Hundreds of them . . . Were they worth anything? He scooped up a handful and jets of fire shot fitfully from the stones. These are diamonds too, he said. He pried open another box. Watches! A chorus of soft, metallic ticking filled his ears. For a moment he could not move, then he dumped all the boxes into the sack.

He shut the safe door, then stood looking around, anxious not to overlook anything. Oh! He had seen a door in the room where the machines were. What was in there? More valuables? He re-entered the room, crossed the floor, and stood undecided before the door. He finally caught hold of the knob and pushed the door in; the room beyond was dark. He advanced cautiously inside and ran his fingers along the wall for the usual switch, then he was stark still. *Something had moved in the room!* What was it? Ought he to creep out, taking the rings and diamonds and money? Why risk what he already had? He waited and the ensuing silence gave him confidence to explore further. Dare he strike a match? Would not a match flame make him a good target? He tensed again as he heard a faint sigh; he was now convinced that there was something alive near him, something that lived and breathed. On tiptoe he felt slowly along the wall, hoping that he would not collide with anything. Luck was with him; he found the light switch.

No; don't turn the light on . . . Then suddenly he realized that he did not know in what direction the door was. Goddamn! He had to turn the light on or strike a match. He fingered the switch for a long time, then thought of an idea. He knelt upon the floor, reached his arm up to the switch and flicked the button, hoping that if anyone shot, the bullet would go above his head. The moment the light came on he narrowed his eyes to see quickly. He sucked in his breath and his body gave a violent twitch and was still. In front of him, so close that it made him want to bound up and scream, was a human face.

He was afraid to move lest he touch the man. If the man had opened his eyes at that moment, there was no telling what he might have done. The man—long and rawboned—was stretched out on his back upon a little cot, sleeping in his clothes, his head cushioned by a dirty pillow; his face, clouded by a dark stubble of beard, looked straight up to the ceiling. The man sighed, and he grew tense to defend himself; the man mumbled and turned his face away from the light. I've got to turn off that light, he thought. Just as he was about to rise, he saw a gun and cartridge belt on the floor at the man's side. Yes, he would take the gun and cartridge belt, not to use them, but just to keep them, as one takes a memento from a country fair. He picked them up and was about to click off the light when his eyes fell upon a photograph perched upon a chair near the man's head; it was the picture of a woman, smiling, shown against a background of open fields; at the woman's side were two young children, a boy and a girl. He smiled indulgently; he could send a bullet into that man's brain and time would be over for him . . .

He clicked off the light and crept silently back into the room where the safe stood; he fastened the cartridge belt about him and adjusted the holster at his right hip. He strutted about the room on tiptoe, lolling his head non-chalantly, then paused, abruptly pulled the gun, and pointed it with grim face toward an imaginary foe. "Boom!" he whispered fiercely. Then he bent forward with silent laughter. That's just like they do it in the movies, he said.

He contemplated his loot for a long time, then got a towel from the washroom and tied the sack securely. When he looked up he was momentarily frightened by his shadow looming on the wall before him. He lifted the sack, dragged it down the basement steps, lugged it across the basement, gasping for breath. After he had struggled through the hole, he clumsily replaced the bricks, then tussled with the sack until he got it to the cave. He stood in the dark, wet with sweat, brooding about the diamonds, the rings, the watches, the money; he remembered the singing in the church, the people yelling in the movie, the dead baby, the nude man stretched out upon the white table ... He saw these items hovering before his eyes and felt that some dim meaning linked them together, that some magical relationship made them kin. He stared with vacant eyes, convinced that all of these images, with their tongueless reality, were striving to tell him something . . .

Later, seeing with his fingers, he untied the sack and set each item neatly upon the dirt floor. Exploring, he took the bulb, the socket, and the wire out of the tool chest; he was elated to find a double socket at one end of the wire. He crammed the stuff into his pockets and hoisted himself upon the rusty pipes and squinted into the church; it was dim and empty. Somewhere in this wall were live electric wires; but where? He lowered himself, groped and tapped the wall with the butt of the screwdriver, listening vainly for hollow sounds. I'll just take a chance and dig, he said.

For an hour he tried to dislodge a brick, and when he struck a match, he found that he had dug a depth of only an inch! No use in digging here, he sighed. By the flickering light of a match, he looked upward, then lowered his eyes, only to glance up again, startled. Directly above his head, beyond the pipes, was a wealth of electric wiring. I'll be damned, he snickered.

He got an old dull knife from the chest and, seeing again with his fingers, separated the two strands of wire and cut away the insulation. Twice he received a slight shock. He scraped the wiring clean and managed to join the two twin ends, then screwed in the bulb. The sudden illumination blinded him and he shut his lids to kill the pain in his eyeballs. I've got that much done, he thought jubilantly.

He placed the bulb on the dirt floor and the light cast a blatant glare on the bleak clay walls. Next he plugged one end of the wire that dangled from the radio into the light socket and bent down and switched on the button; almost at once there was the harsh sound of static, but no words or music. Why won't it work? he wondered. Had he damaged the mechanism in any way? Maybe it needed grounding? Yes ... He rummaged in the tool chest and found another length of wire, fastened it to the ground of the radio, and then tied the opposite end to a pipe. Rising and growing distinct, a slow strain of music entranced him with its measured sound. He sat upon the chest, deliriously happy.

Later he searched again in the chest and found a half-gallon can of glue; he opened it and smelled a sharp odor. Then he recalled that he had not even looked at the money. He took a wad of green bills and weighed it in his palm, then broke the seal and held one of the bills up to the light and studied it closely. *The United States of America will pay to the bearer on demand one hundred dollars,* he read in slow speech; then: *This note is legal tender for all debts, public and private* . . . He broke into a musing laugh, feeling that he was reading of the doings of people who lived on some far-off planet. He turned the bill over and saw on the other side of it a delicately beautiful building gleaming with paint and set amidst green grass. He had no desire whatever to count the money; it was what it stood for—the various currents of life swirling aboveground—that captivated him. Next he opened the rolls of coins and let them slide from their paper wrappings to the ground; the bright, new gleaming pennies and nickles and dimes piled high at his feet, a glowing mound of shimmering copper and silver. He sifted them through his fingers, listening to their tinkle as they struck the conical heap.

Oh, yes! He had forgotten. He would now write his name on the typewriter. He inserted a piece of paper and poised his fingers to write. But what was his name? He stared, trying to remember. He stood and glared about the dirt cave, his name on the tip of his lips. But it would not come to him. Why was he here? Yes, he had been running away from the police. But why? His mind was blank. He bit his lips and sat again, feeling a vague terror. But why worry? He laughed, then pecked slowly: *itwasalonghotday.* He was determined to type the sentence without making any mistakes. How did one make capital letters? He experimented and luckily discovered how to lock the machine for capital letters and then shift it back to lower case. Next he discovered how to make spaces, then he wrote neatly and correctly: *It was a long hot day.* Just why he selected that sentence he did not know; it was merely the ritual of performing the thing that appealed to him. He took the sheet out of the machine and looked around with stiff neck and hard eyes and spoke to an imaginary person:

"Yes, I'll have the contracts ready tomorrow."

He laughed. That's just the way they talk, he said. He grew weary of the game and pushed the machine aside. His eyes fell upon the can of glue, and a mischievous idea bloomed in him, filling him with nervous eagerness. He leaped up and opened the can of glue, then broke the seals on all the wads of money. I'm going to have some wallpaper, he said with a luxurious, physical laugh that made him bend at the knees. He took the towel with which he had tied the sack and balled it into a swab and dipped it into the can of glue and dabbed glue onto the wall; then he pasted one green bill by the side of another. He stepped back and cocked his head. Jesus! That's funny . . . He slapped his thighs and guffawed. He had triumphed over the world aboveground! He was free! If only people could see this! He wanted to run from this cave and yell his discovery to the world.

He swabbed all the dirt walls of the cave and pasted them with green bills; when he had finished the walls blazed with a yellow-green fire. Yes, this room would be his hide-out; between him and the world that had branded him guilty would stand this mocking symbol. He had not stolen the money; he had simply picked it up, just as a man would pick up firewood in a forest. And that was how the world aboveground now seemed to him, a wild forest filled with death.

The walls of money finally palled on him and he looked about for new interests to feed his emotions. The cleaver! He drove a nail into the wall and hung the bloody cleaver upon it. Still another idea welled up. He pried open the metal boxes and lined them side by side on the dirt floor. He grinned at the gold and fire. From one box he lifted up a fistful of ticking gold watches and dangled them by their gleaming chains. He stared with an idle smile, then began to wind them up; he did not attempt to set them at any given hour, for there was no time for him now. He took a fistful of nails and drove them into the papered walls and hung the watches upon them, letting them swing down by their glittering chains, trembling and ticking busily against the backdrop of green with the lemon sheen of the electric light shining upon the metal watch casings, converting the golden disks into blobs of liquid yellow. Hardly had he hung up the last watch than the idea extended itself; he took more nails from the chest and drove them into the green paper and took the boxes of rings and went from nail to nail and hung up the golden bands. The blue and white sparks from the stones filled the cave with brittle laughter, as though enjoying his hilarious secret. People certainly can do some funny things, he said to himself.

He sat upon the tool chest, alternately laughing and shaking his head soberly. Hours later he became conscious of the gun sagging at his hip and he pulled it from the holster. He had seen men fire guns in movies, but somehow his life had never led him into contact with firearms. A desire to feel the sensation others felt in firing came over him. But someone might hear . . . Well, what if they did? They would not know where the shot had come from. Not in their wildest notions would they think that it had come from under the streets! He tightened his fingers on the trigger; there was a deafening report and it seemed that the entire underground had caved in upon his eardrums; and in the same instant there flashed an orange-blue spurt of flame that died quickly but lingered on as a vivid after-image. He smelled the acrid stench of burnt powder filling his lungs and he dropped the gun abruptly.

The intensity of his feelings died and he hung the gun and cartridge belt upon the wall. Next he lifted the jars of diamonds and turned them bottom upward, dumping the white pellets upon the ground. One by one he picked them up and peeled the tissue paper from them and piled them in a neat heap. He wiped his sweaty hands on his trousers, lit a cigarette, and commenced playing another game. He imagined that he was a rich man who lived aboveground in the obscene sunshine and he was strolling through a park of a summer morning, smiling, nodding to his neighbors, sucking an after-breakfast cigar. Many times he crossed the floor of the cave, avoiding the diamonds with his feet, yet subtly gauging his footsteps so that his shoes, wet with sewer slime, would strike the diamonds at some undetermined moment. After twenty minutes of sauntering, his right foot smashed into the heap and diamonds lay scattered in all directions, glinting with a million tiny chuckles of icy laughter. Oh, shucks, he mumbled in mock regret, intrigued by the damage he had wrought. He continued walking, ignoring the brittle fire. He felt that he had a glorious victory locked in his heart.

He stooped and flung the diamonds more evenly over the floor and they showered rich sparks, collaborating with him. He went over the floor and trampled the stones just deeply enough for them to be faintly visible, as though they were set deliberately in the prongs of a thousand rings. A ghostly light bathed the cave. He sat on the chest and frowned. Maybe *anything's* right, he mumbled. Yes, if the world as men had made it was right, then anything else was right, any act a man took to satisfy himself, murder, theft, torture.

He straightened with a start. What was happening to him? He was drawn to these crazy thoughts, yet they made him feel vaguely guilty. He would stretch out upon the ground, then get up; he would want to crawl again through the holes he had dug, but would restrain himself; he would think of going again up into the streets, but fear would hold him still. He stood in the middle of the cave, surrounded by green walls and a laughing floor, trembling. He was going to do something, but what? Yes, he was afraid of himself, afraid of doing some nameless thing.

To control himself, he turned on the radio. A melancholy piece of music rose. Brooding over the diamonds on the floor was like looking up into a sky full of restless stars; then the illusion turned into its opposite: he was high up in the air looking down at the twinkling lights of a sprawling city. The music ended and a man recited news events. In the same attitude in which he had contemplated the city, so now, as he heard the cultivated tone, he looked down upon land and sea as men fought, as cities were razed, as planes scattered death upon open towns, as long lines of trenches wavered and broke. He heard the names of generals and the names of mountains and the names of countries and the names and numbers of divisions that were in action on different battle fronts. He saw black smoke billowing from the stacks of warships as they neared each other over wastes of water and he heard their huge thunder as red-hot shells screamed across the surface of night seas. He saw hundreds of planes wheeling and droning in the sky and heard the clatter of machine guns as they fought each other and he saw planes falling in plumes of smoke and blaze of fire. He saw steel tanks rumbling across fields of ripe wheat to meet other tanks and there was a loud clang of steel as numberless tanks collided. He saw troops with fixed bayonets charging in waves against other troops who held fixed bayonets and men groaned as steel ripped into their bodies and they went down to die . . . The voice of the radio faded and he was staring at the diamonds on the floor at his feet.

He shut off the radio, fighting an irrational compulsion to act. He walked aimlessly about the cave, touching the walls with his finger tips. Suddenly he stood still. *What was the matter with him?* Yes, he knew . . . It was these walls; these crazy walls were filling him with a wild urge to climb out into the dark sunshine aboveground. Quickly he doused the light to banish the shouting walls, then sat again upon the tool chest. Yes, he was trapped. His muscles were flexed taut and sweat ran down his face. He knew now that he could not stay here and he could not go out. He lit a cigarette with shaking fingers; the match flame revealed the green-papered walls with militant distinctness; the purple on the gun barrel glinted like a threat; the meat cleaver brooded with its eloquent splotches of blood; the mound of silver and copper smoldered angrily; the diamonds winked at him from the floor, and the gold watches ticked and trembled, crowning time the king of consciousness, defining the limits of living . . . The match blaze died and he bolted from where he stood and collided brutally with the nails upon the walls. The spell was broken. He shuddered, feeling that, in spite of his fear, sooner or later he would go up into that dead sunshine and somehow say something to somebody about all this.

He sat again upon the tool chest. Fatigue weighed upon his forehead and eyes. Minutes passed and he relaxed. He dozed, but his imagination was alert. He saw himself rising, wading again in the sweeping water of the sewer; he came to a manhole and climbed out and was amazed to discover that he hoisted himself into a room filled with armed policemen who were watching him intently. He jumped awake in the dark; he had not moved. He sighed, closed his eyes, and slept again; this time his imagination designed a scheme of protection for him. His dreaming made him feel that he was standing in a room watching over his own nude body lying stiff and cold upon a white table. At the far end of the room he saw a crowd of people huddled in a corner, afraid of his body. Though lying dead upon the table, he was standing in some mysterious way at his side, warding off the people, guarding his body, and laughing to himself as he observed the situation. They're scared of me, he thought.

He awakened with a start, leaped to his feet, and stood in the center of the black cave. It was a full minute before he moved again. He hovered between sleeping and waking, unprotected, a prey of wild fears. He could neither see nor hear. One part of him was asleep; his blood coursed slowly and his flesh was numb. On the other hand he was roused to a strange, high pitch of tension. He lifted his fingers to his face, as though about to weep. Gradually his hands lowered and he struck a match, looking about, expecting to see a door through which he could walk to safety; but there was no door, only the green walls and the moving floor. The match flame died and it was dark again.

Five minutes later he was still standing when the thought came to him that he had been asleep. Yes . . . But he was not yet fully awake; he was still queerly blind and deaf. How long had he slept? Where was he? Then suddenly he recalled the green-papered walls of the cave and in the same instant he heard loud singing coming from the church beyond the wall. Yes, they woke me up, he muttered. He hoisted himself and lay atop the bed of pipes and brought his face to the narrow slit. Men and women stood here and there between pews. A song ended and a young black girl tossed back her head and closed her eyes and broke plaintively into another hymn:

> Glad, glad, glad, oh, so glad
> I got Jesus in my soul . . .

Those few words were all she sang, but what her words did not say, her emotions said as she repeated the lines, varying the mood and tempo, making her tone express meanings which her conscious mind did not know. Another woman melted her voice with the girl's, and then an old man's voice merged with that of the two women. Soon the entire congregation was singing:

> Glad, glad, glad, oh, so glad
> I got Jesus in my soul . . .

They're wrong, he whispered in the lyric darkness. He felt that their search for a happiness they could never find made them feel that they had committed some dreadful offense which they could not remember or understand. He was now in possession of the feeling that had gripped him when he had first come into the underground. It came to him in a series of questions: Why was this sense of guilt so seemingly innate, so easy to come by, to think, to feel, so verily physical? It seemed that when one felt this guilt one was retracing in one's feelings a faint pattern designed long before; it seemed that one was always trying to remember a gigantic shock that had left a haunting impression upon one's body which one could not forget or shake off, but which had been forgotten by the conscious mind, creating in one's life a state of eternal anxiety.

He had to tear himself away from this; he got down from the pipes. His nerves were so taut that he seemed to feel his brain pushing through his skull. He felt that he had to do something, but he could not figure out what it was. Yet he knew that if he stood here until he made up his mind, he would never move. He crawled through the hole he had made in the brick wall and the exertion afforded him respite from tension. When he entered the basement of the radio store, he stopped in fear, hearing loud voices.

"Come on, boy! Tell us what you did with the radio!"

"Mister, I didn't steal the radio! I swear!"

He heard a dull thumping sound and he imagined a boy being struck violently.

"Please, mister!"

"Did you take it to a pawn shop?"

"No, sir! I didn't steal the radio! I got a radio at home," the boy's voice pleaded hysterically. "Go to my home and look!"

There came to his ears the sound of another blow. It was so funny that he had to clap his hand over his mouth to keep from laughing out loud. They're beating some poor boy, he whispered to himself, shaking his head. He felt a sort of distant pity for the boy and wondered if he ought to bring back the radio and leave it in the basement. No. Perhaps it was a good thing that they were beating the boy; perhaps the beating would bring to the boy's attention, for the first time in his life, the secret of his existence, the guilt that he could never get rid of.

Smiling, he scampered over a coal pile and stood again in the basement of the building where he had stolen the money and jewelry. He lifted himself into the areaway, climbed the rain pipe, and squinted through a two-inch opening of window. The guilty familiarity of what he saw made his muscles tighten. Framed before him in a bright tableau of daylight was the night watchman sitting upon the edge of a chair, stripped to the waist, his head sagging forward, his eyes red and puffy. The watchman's face and shoulders were stippled with red and black welts. Back of the watchman stood the safe, the steel door wide open showing the empty vault. Yes, they think he did it, he mused.

Footsteps sounded in the room and a man in a blue suit passed in front of him, then another, then still another. Policemen, he breathed. Yes, they were trying to make the watchman confess, just as they had once made him confess to a crime he had not done. He stared into the room, trying to recall something. Oh . . . Those were the same policemen who had beaten him, had made him sign that paper when he had been too tired and sick to care. Now, they were doing the same thing to the watchman. His heart pounded as he saw one of the policemen shake a finger into the watchman's face.

"Why don't you admit it's an inside job, Thompson?" the policeman said.

"I've told you all I know," the watchman mumbled through swollen lips.

"But nobody was here but you!" the policeman shouted.

"I was sleeping," the watchman said. "It was wrong, but I was sleeping all that night!"

"Stop telling us that lie!"

"It's the truth!"

"When did you get the combination?"

"I don't know how to open the safe," the watchman said.

He clung to the rain pipe, tense; he wanted to laugh, but he controlled himself. He felt a great sense of power; yes, he could go back to the cave, rip the money off the walls, pick up the diamonds and rings, and bring them here and write a note, telling them where to look for their foolish toys. No . . . What good would that do? It was not worth the effort. The watchman was guilty; although he was not guilty of the crime of which he had been accused, he was guilty, had always been guilty. The only thing that worried him was that the man who had been really stealing was not being accused. But he consoled himself: they'll catch him sometime during his life.

He saw one of the policemen slap the watchman across the mouth.

"Come clean, you bastard!"

"I've told you all I know," the watchman mumbled like a child.

One of the police went to the rear of the watchman's chair and jerked it from under him; the watchman pitched forward upon his face.

"Get up!" a policeman said.

Trembling, the watchman pulled himself up and sat limply again in the chair.

"Now, are you going to talk?"

"I've told you all I know," the watchman gasped.

"Where did you hide the stuff?"

"I didn't take it!"

"Thompson, your brains are in your feet," one of the policemen said. "We're going to string you up and get them back into your skull."

He watched the policemen clamp handcuffs on the watchman's wrists and ankles; then they lifted the watchman and swung him upside-down and hoisted his feet to the edge of a door. The watchman hung, head down, his eyes bulging. They're crazy, he whispered to himself as he clung to the ridges of the pipe.

"You going to talk?" a policeman shouted into the watchman's ear.

He heard the watchman groan.

"We'll let you hang there till you talk, see?"

He saw the watchman close his eyes.

"Let's take 'im down. He passed out," a policeman said.

He grinned as he watched them take the body down and dump it carelessly upon the floor. The policeman took off the handcuffs.

"Let 'im come to. Let's get a smoke," a policeman said.

The three policemen left the scope of his vision. A door slammed. He had an impulse to yell to the watchman that he could escape through the hole in the basement and live with him in the cave. But he wouldn't understand, he told himself. After a moment he saw the watchman rise and stand, swaying from weakness. He stumbled across the room to a desk, opened a drawer, and took out a gun. He's going to kill himself, he thought, intent, eager, detached, yearning to see the end of the man's actions. As the watchman stared vaguely about he lifted the gun to his temple; he stood like that for some minutes, biting his lips until a line of blood etched its way down a corner of his chin. No, he oughtn't do that, he said to himself in a mood of pity.

"Don't!" he half whispered and half yelled.

The watchman looked wildly about; he had heard him. But it did not help; there was a loud report and the watchman's head jerked violently and he fell like a log and lay prone, the gun clattering over the floor.

The three policemen came running into the room with drawn guns. One of the policemen knelt and rolled the watchman's body over and stared at a ragged, scarlet hole in the temple.

"Our hunch was right," the kneeling policeman said. "He was guilty, all right."

"Well, this ends the case," another policeman said.

"He knew he was licked," the third one said with grim satisfaction.

He eased down the rain pipe, crawled back through the holes he had made, and went back into his cave. A fever burned in his bones. He had to act, yet he was afraid. His eyes stared in the darkness as though propped open by invisible hands, as though they had become lidless. His muscles were rigid and he stood for what seemed to him a thousand years.

W HEN he moved again his actions were informed with precision, his muscular system reinforced from a reservoir of energy. He crawled through the hole of earth, dropped into the gray sewer current, and sloshed ahead. When his right foot went forward at a street intersection, he fell backward and shot down into water. In a spasm of terror his right hand grabbed the concrete ledge of a down-curve and he felt the streaking water tugging violently at his body. The current reached his neck and for a moment he was still. He knew if he moved clumsily he would be sucked under. He held onto the ledge with both hands and slowly pulled himself up. He sighed, standing once more in the sweeping water, thankful that he had missed death.

He waded on through sludge, moving with care, until he came to a web of light sifting down from a manhole cover. He saw steel hooks running up the side of the sewer wall; he caught hold and lifted himself and put his shoulder to the cover and moved it an inch. A crash of sound came to him as he looked into a hot glare of sunshine through which blurred shapes moved. Fear scalded him and he dropped back into the pallid current and stood paralyzed in the shadows. A heavy car rumbled past overhead, jarring the pavement, warning him to stay in his world of dark light, knocking the cover back into place with an imperious clang.

He did not know how much fear he felt, for fear claimed him completely; yet it was not a fear of the police or of people, but a cold dread at the thought of the actions he knew he would perform if he went out into that cruel sunshine. His mind said no; his body said yes; and his mind could not understand his feelings. A low whine broke from him and he was in the act of uncoiling. He climbed upward and heard the faint honking of auto horns. Like a frantic cat clutching a rag, he clung to the steel prongs and heaved his shoulder against the cover and pushed it off halfway. For a split second his eyes were drowned in the terror of yellow light and he was in a deeper darkness than he had ever known in the underground.

Partly out of the hole, he blinked, regaining enough sight to make out meaningful forms. An odd thing was happening: No one was rushing forward to challenge him. He had imagined the moment of his emergence as a desperate tussle with men who wanted to cart him off to be killed; instead, life froze about him as the traffic stopped. He pushed the cover aside, stood, swaying in a world so fragile that he expected it to collapse and drop him into some deep void. But nobody seemed to pay him heed. The cars were now swerving to shun him and the gaping hole.

"Why in hell don't you put up a red light, dummy?" a raucous voice yelled.

He understood; they thought that he was a sewer workman. He walked toward the sidewalk, weaving unsteadily through the moving traffic.

"Look where you're going, nigger!"

"That's right! Stay there and get killed!"

"You blind, you bastard?"

"Go home and sleep your drunk off!"

A policeman stood at the curb, looking in the opposite direction. When he passed the policeman, he feared that he would be grabbed, but nothing happened. Where was he? Was this real? He wanted to look about to get his bearings, but felt that something awful would happen to him if he did. He wandered into a spacious doorway of a store that sold men's clothing and saw his reflection in a long mirror: his cheekbones protruded from a hairy black face; his greasy cap was perched askew upon his head and his eyes were red and glassy. His shirt and trousers were caked with mud and hung loosely. His hands were gummed with a black stickiness. He threw back his head and laughed so loudly that passers-by stopped and stared.

He ambled on down the sidewalk, not having the merest notion of where he was going. Yet, sleeping within him, was the drive to go somewhere and say something to somebody. Half an hour later his ears caught the sound of spirited singing.

> The Lamb, the Lamb, the Lamb
> I hear thy voice a-calling
> The Lamb, the Lamb, the Lamb
> I feel thy grace a-falling

A church! He exclaimed. He broke into a run and came to brick steps leading downward to a subbasement. This is it! The church into which he had peered. Yes, he was going in and tell them. What? He did not know; but, once face to face with them, he would think of what to say. Must be Sunday, he mused. He ran down the steps and jerked the door open; the church was crowded and a deluge of song swept over him.

> The Lamb, the Lamb, the Lamb
> Tell me again your story
> The Lamb, the Lamb, the Lamb
> Flood my soul with your glory

He stared at the singing faces with a trembling smile.

"Say!" he shouted.

Many turned to look at him, but the song rolled on. His arm was jerked violently.

"I'm sorry, Brother, but you can't do that in here," a man said.

"But, mister!"

"You can't act rowdy in God's house," the man said.

"He's filthy," another man said.

"But I want to tell 'em," he said loudly.

"He stinks," someone muttered.

The song had stopped, but at once another one began.

> Oh, wondrous sight upon the cross
> Vision sweet and divine
> Oh, wondrous sight upon the cross
> Full of such love sublime

He attempted to twist away, but other hands grabbed him and rushed him into the doorway.

"Let me alone!" he screamed, struggling.

"Get out!"

"He's drunk," somebody said. "He ought to be ashamed!"

"He acts crazy!"

He felt that he was failing and he grew frantic.

"But, mister, let me tell—"

"Get away from this door, or I'll call the police!"

He stared, his trembling smile fading in a sense of wonderment.

"The police," he repeated vacantly.

"Now, get!"

He was pushed toward the brick steps and the door banged shut. The waves of song came.

> Oh, wondrous sight, wondrous sight
> Lift my heavy heart above
> Oh, wondrous sight, wondrous sight
> Fill my weary soul with love

He was smiling again now. Yes, the police . . . That was it! Why had he not thought of it before? The idea had been deep down in him, and only now did it assume supreme importance. He looked up and saw a street sign: COURT STREET—HARTSDALE AVENUE. He turned and walked northward, his mind filled with the image of the police station. Yes, that was where they had beaten him, accused him, and had made him sign a confession of his guilt. He would go there and clear up everything, make a statement. What statement?

He did not know. He was the statement, and since it was all so clear to him, surely he would be able to make it clear to others.

He came to the corner of Hartsdale Avenue and turned westward. Yeah, there's the station . . . A policeman came down the steps and walked past him without a glance. He mounted the stone steps and went through the door, paused; he was in a hallway where several policemen were standing, talking, smoking. One turned to him.

"What do you want, boy?"

He looked at the policeman and laughed.

"What in hell are you laughing about?" the policeman asked.

He stopped laughing and stared. His whole being was full of what he wanted to say to them, but he could not say it.

"Are you looking for the Desk Sergeant?"

"Yes, sir," he said quickly; then: "Oh, no, sir."

"Well, make up your mind, now."

Four policemen grouped themselves around him.

"I'm looking for the men," he said.

"What men?"

Peculiarly, at that moment he could not remember the names of the policemen; he recalled their beating him, the confession he had signed, and how he had run away from them. He saw the cave next to the church, the money on the walls, the guns, the rings, the cleaver, the watches, and the diamonds on the floor.

"They brought me here," he began.

"When?"

His mind flew back over the blur of the time lived in the underground blackness. He had no idea of how much time had elapsed, but the intensity of what had happened to him told him that it could not have transpired in a short space of time, yet his mind told him that time must have been brief.

"It was a long time ago." He spoke like a child relating a dimly remembered dream. "It was a long time," he repeated, following the promptings of his emotions. "They beat me . . . I was scared . . . I ran away."

A policeman raised a finger to his temple and made a derisive circle.

"Nuts," the policeman said.

"Do you know what place this is, boy?"

"Yes, sir. The police station," he answered sturdily, almost proudly.

"Well, who do you want to see?"

"The men," he said again, feeling that surely they knew the men. "You know the men," he said in a hurt tone.

"What's your name?"

He opened his lips to answer and no words came. He had forgotten. But what did it matter if he had? It was not important.

"Where do you live?"

Where did he live? It had been so long ago since he had lived up here in this strange world that he felt it was foolish even to try to remember. Then for a moment the old mood that had dominated him in the underground surged back. He leaned forward and spoke eagerly.

"They said I killed the woman."

"What woman?" a policeman asked.

"And I signed a paper that said I was guilty," he went on, ignoring their questions. "Then I ran off . . ."

"Did you run off from an institution?"

"No, sir," he said, blinking and shaking his head. "I came from under the ground. I pushed off the manhole cover and climbed out . . ."

"All right, now," a policeman said, placing an arm about his shoulder. "We'll send you to the psycho and you'll be taken care of."

"Maybe he's a Fifth Columnist!" a policeman shouted.

There was laughter and, despite his anxiety, he joined in. But the laughter lasted so long that it irked him.

"I got to find those men," he protested mildly.

"Say, boy, what have you been drinking?"

"Water," he said. "I got some water in a basement."

"Were the men you ran away from dressed in white, boy?"

"No, sir," he said brightly. "They were men like you."

An elderly policeman caught hold of his arm.

"Try and think hard. Where did they pick you up?"

He knotted his brows in an effort to remember, but he was blank inside. The policeman stood before him demanding logical answers and he could no longer think with his mind; he thought with his feelings and no words came.

"I was guilty," he said. "Oh, no, sir. I wasn't then, I mean, mister!"

"Aw, talk sense. Now, where did they pick you up?"

He felt challenged and his mind began reconstructing events in reverse; his feelings ranged back over the long hours and he saw the cave, the sewer, the bloody room where it was said that a woman had been killed.

"Oh, yes, sir," he said, smiling. "I was coming from Mrs. Wooten's."

"Who is she?"

"I work for her."

"Where does she live?"

"Next door to Mrs. Peabody, the woman who was killed."

The policemen were very quiet now, looking at him intently.

"What do you know about Mrs. Peabody's death, boy?"

"Nothing, sir. But they said I killed her. But it doesn't make any difference, I'm guilty!"

"What are you talking about, boy?"

His smile faded and he was possessed with memories of the underground; he saw the cave next to the church and his lips moved to speak. But how could he say it? The distance between what he felt and what these men meant was vast. Something told him, as he stood there looking into their faces, that he would never be able to tell them, that they would never believe him even if he told them.

"All the people I saw was guilty," he began slowly.

"Aw, nuts," a policeman muttered.

"Say," another policeman said, "that Peabody woman was killed over on Winewood. That's Number Ten's beat."

"Where's Number Ten?" a policeman asked.

"Upstairs in the swing room," someone answered.

"Take this boy up, Sam," a policeman ordered.

"O.K. Come along, boy."

An elderly policeman caught hold of his arm and led him up a flight of wooden stairs, down a long hall, and to a door.

"Squad Ten!" the policeman called through the door.

"What?" a gruff voice answered.

"Someone to see you!"

"About what?"

The old policeman pushed the door in and then shoved him into the room.

He stared, his lips open, his heart barely beating. Before him were the three policemen who had picked him up and had beaten him to extract the confession. They were seated about a small table, playing cards. The air was blue with smoke and sunshine poured through a high window, lighting up fantastic smoke shapes. He saw one of the policemen look up; the policeman's face was tired and a cigarette drooped limply from one corner of his mouth and both of his fat, puffy eyes were squinting and his hands gripped his cards.

"Lawson!" the man exclaimed.

The moment the man's name sounded he remembered the names of all of them: Lawson, Murphy, and Johnson. How simple it was. He waited, smiling, wondering how they would react when they knew that he had come back.

"Looking for me?" the man who had been called Lawson mumbled, sorting his cards. "For what?"

So far only Murphy, the red-headed one, had recognized him.

"Don't you-all remember me?" he blurted, running to the table.

All three of the policemen were looking at him now. Lawson, who seemed the leader, jumped to his feet.

"Where in hell have you been?"

"Do you know 'im, Lawson?" the old policeman asked.

"Huh?" Lawson frowned. "Oh, yes. I'll handle 'im." The old policeman left the room and Lawson crossed to the door and turned the key in the lock. "Come here, boy," he ordered in a cold tone.

He did not move; he looked from face to face. Yes, he would tell them about his cave.

"He looks batty to me," Johnson said, the one who had not spoken before.

"Why in hell did you come back here?" Lawson said.

"I—I just didn't want to run away no more," he said. "I'm all right, now." He paused; the men's attitude puzzled him.

"You've been hiding, huh?" Lawson asked in a tone that denoted that he had not heard his previous words. "You told us you were sick, and when we left you in the room, you jumped out of the window and ran away."

Panic filled him. Yes, they were indifferent to what he would say! They were waiting for him to speak and they would laugh at him. He had to rescue himself from this bog; he had to force the reality of himself upon them.

"Mister, I took a sackful of money and pasted it on the walls . . ." he began.

"I'll be damned," Lawson said.

"Listen," said Murphy, "let me tell you something for your own good. We don't want you, see? You're free, free as air. Now go home and forget it. It was all a mistake. We caught the guy who did the Peabody job. He wasn't colored at all. He was an Eyetalian."

"Shut up!" Lawson yelled. "Have you no sense!"

"But I want to tell 'im," Murphy said.

"We can't let this crazy fool go," Lawson exploded. "He acts nuts, but this may be a stunt . . ."

"I was down in the basement," he began in a childlike tone, as though repeating a lesson learned by heart; "and I went into a movie . . ." His voice failed. He was getting ahead of his story. First, he ought to tell them about the singing in the church, but what words could he use? He looked at them appealingly. "I went into a shop and took a sackful of money and diamonds and watches and rings . . . I didn't steal 'em, I'll give 'em all back. I just took 'em to play with . . . " He paused, stunned by their disbelieving eyes.

Lawson lit a cigarette and looked at him coldly.

"What did you do with the money?" he asked in a quiet, waiting voice.

"I pasted the hundred-dollar bills on the walls."

"What walls?" Lawson asked.

"The walls of the dirt room," he said, smiling, "the room next to the church. I hung up the rings and the watches and I stamped the diamonds into the dirt . . ." He saw that they were not understanding what he was saying. He grew frantic to make them believe, his voice tumbled on eagerly. "I saw a dead baby and a dead man . . ."

"Aw, you're nuts," Lawson snarled, shoving him into a chair.

"But mister . . ."

"Johnson, where's the paper he signed?" Lawson asked.

"What paper?"

"The confession, fool!"

Johnson pulled out his billfold and extracted a crumpled piece of paper.

"Yes, sir, mister," he said, stretching forth his hand. "That's the paper I signed . . ."

Lawson slapped him and he would have toppled had his chair not struck a wall behind him. Lawson scratched a match and held the paper over the flame; the confession burned down to Lawson's finger-tips.

He stared, thunderstruck; the sun of the underground was fleeting and the terrible darkness of the day stood before him. They did not believe him, but he *had* to make them believe him!

"But mister . . ."

"It's going to be all right, boy," Lawson said with a quiet, soothing laugh. "I've burned your confession, see? You didn't sign anything." Lawson came close to him with the black ashes cupped in his palm. "You don't remember a thing about this, do you?"

"Don't you-all be scared of me," he pleaded, sensing their uneasiness. "I'll sign another paper, if you want me to. I'll show you the cave."

"What's your game, boy?" Lawson asked suddenly.

"What are you trying to find out?" Johnson asked.

"Who sent you here?" Murphy demanded.

"Nobody sent me, mister," he said. "I just want to show you the room . . ."

"Aw, he's plumb bats," Murphy said. "Let's ship 'im to the psycho."

"No," Lawson said. "He's playing a game and I wish to God I knew what it was."

There flashed through his mind a definite way to make them believe him; he rose from the chair with nervous excitement.

"Mister, I saw the night watchman blow his brains out because you accused him of stealing," he told them. "But he didn't steal the money and diamonds. I took 'em."

Tigerishly Lawson grabbed his collar and lifted him bodily.

"Who told you about that?"

"Don't get excited, Lawson," Johnson said. "He read about it in the papers."

Lawson flung him away.

"He couldn't have," Lawson said, pulling papers from his pocket. "I haven't turned in the reports yet."

"Then how *did* he find out?" Murphy asked.

"Let's get out of here," Lawson said with quick resolution. "Listen, boy, we're going to take you to a nice, quiet place, see?"

"Yes, sir," he said. "And I'll show you the underground."

"Goddamn," Lawson muttered, fastening the gun at his hip. He narrowed his eyes at Johnson and Murphy. "Listen," he spoke just above a whisper, "say nothing about this, you hear?"

"O.K.," Johnson said.

"Sure," Murphy said.

Lawson unlocked the door and Johnson and Murphy led him down the stairs. The hallway was crowded with policemen.

"What have you got there, Lawson?"

"What did he do, Lawson?"

"He's psycho, ain't he, Lawson?"

Lawson did not answer; Johnson and Murphy led him to the car parked at the curb, pushed him into the back seat. Lawson got behind the steering wheel and the car rolled forward.

"What's up, Lawson?" Murphy asked.

"Listen," Lawson began slowly, "we tell the papers that he spilled about the Peabody job, then he escapes. The Wop is caught and we tell the papers that we steered them wrong to trap the real guy, see? Now this dope shows up and acts nuts. If we let him go, he'll squeal that we framed him, see?"

"I'm all right, mister," he said, feeling Murphy's and Johnson's arms locked rigidly into his. "I'm guilty . . . I'll show you everything in the underground. I laughed and laughed . . ."

"Shut that fool up!" Lawson ordered.

Johnson tapped him across the head with a blackjack and he fell back against the seat cushion, dazed.

"Yes, sir," he mumbled. "I'm all right."

The car sped along Hartsdale Avenue, then swung onto Pine Street and rolled to State Street, then turned south. It slowed to a stop, turned in the middle of a block, and headed north again.

"You're going around in circles, Lawson," Murphy said.

Lawson did not answer; he was hunched over the steering wheel. Finally he pulled the car to a stop at a curb.

"Say, boy, tell us the truth," Lawson asked quietly. "Where did you hide?"

"I didn't hide, mister."

The three policemen were staring at him now; he felt that for the first time they were willing to understand him.

"Then what happened?"

"Mister, when I looked through all of those holes and saw how people were living, I loved 'em . . ."

"Cut out that crazy talk!" Lawson snapped. "Who sent you back here?"

"Nobody, mister."

"Maybe he's talking straight," Johnson ventured.

"All right," Lawson said. "Nobody hid you. Now, tell us *where* you hid."

"I went underground . . ."

"What goddamn underground do you keep talking about?"

"I just went . . ." He paused and looked into the street, then pointed to a manhole cover. "I went down in there and stayed."

"In the *sewer?*"

"Yes, sir."

The policemen burst into a sudden laugh and ended quickly. Lawson swung the car around and drove to Woodside Avenue; he brought the car to a stop in front of a tall apartment building.

"What're we going to do, Lawson?" Murphy asked.

"I'm taking him up to my place," Lawson said. "We've got to wait until night. There's nothing we can do now."

They took him out of the car and led him into a vestibule.

"Take the steps," Lawson muttered.

They led him up four flights of stairs and into the living room of a small apartment. Johnson and Murphy let go of his arms and he stood uncertainly in the middle of the room.

"Now, listen, boy," Lawson began, "forget those wild lies you've been telling us. Where did you hide?"

"I just went underground, like I told you."

The room rocked with laughter. Lawson went to a cabinet and got a bottle of whisky; he placed glasses for Johnson and Murphy. The three of them drank.

He felt that he could not explain himself to them. He tried to muster all the sprawling images that floated in him; the images stood out sharply in his mind, but he could not make them have the meaning for others that they had for him. He felt so helpless that he began to cry.

"He's nuts, all right," Johnson said. "All nuts cry like that."

Murphy crossed the room and slapped him.

"Stop that raving!"

A sense of excitement flooded him; he ran to Murphy and grabbed his arm.

"Let me show you the cave," he said. "Come on, and you'll see!"

Before he knew it a sharp blow had clipped him on the chin; darkness covered his eyes. He dimly felt himself being lifted and laid out on the sofa. He heard low voices and struggled to rise, but hard hands held him down. His brain was clearing now. He pulled to a sitting posture and stared with glazed eyes. It had grown dark. How long had he been out?

"Say, boy," Lawson said soothingly, "will you show us the underground?"

His eyes shone and his heart swelled with gratitude. Lawson believed him! He rose, glad; he grabbed Lawson's arm, making the policeman spill whisky from the glass to his shirt.

"Take it easy, goddammit," Lawson said.

"Yes, sir."

"O.K. We'll take you down. But you'd better be telling us the truth, you hear?"

He clapped his hands in wild joy.

"I'll show you everything!"

He had triumphed at last! He would now do what he had felt was compelling him all along. At last he would be free of his burden.

"Take 'im down," Lawson ordered.

They led him down to the vestibule; when he reached the side-walk he saw that it was night and a fine rain was falling.

"It's just like when I went down," he told them.

"What?" Lawson asked.

"The rain," he said, sweeping his arm in a wide arc. "It was raining when I went down. The rain made the water rise and lift the cover off."

"Cut it out," Lawson snapped.

They did not believe him now, but they would. A mood of high selflessness throbbed in him. He could barely contain his rising spirits. They would see what he had seen; they would feel what he had felt. He would lead them through all the holes he had dug and . . . He wanted to make a hymn, prance about in physical ecstasy, throw his arm about the policemen in fellowship.

"Get into the car," Lawson ordered.

He climbed in and Johnson and Murphy sat at either side of him; Lawson slid behind the steering wheel and started the motor.

"Now, tell us where to go," Lawson said.

"It's right around the corner from where the lady was killed," he said.

The car rolled slowly and he closed his eyes, remembering the song he had heard in the church, the song that had wrought him to such a high pitch of terror and pity. He sang softly, lolling his head:

> Glad, glad, glad, oh, so glad
> I got Jesus in my soul . . .

"Mister," he said, stopping his song, "you ought to see how funny the rings look on the wall." He giggled. "I fired a pistol, too. Just once, to see how it felt."

"What do you suppose he's suffering from?" Johnson asked.

"Delusions of grandeur, maybe," Murphy said.

"Maybe it's because he lives in a white man's world," Lawson said.

"Say, boy, what did you eat down there?" Murphy asked, prodding Johnson anticipatorily with his elbow.

"Pears, oranges, bananas, and pork chops," he said.

The car filled with laughter.

"You didn't eat any watermelon?" Lawson asked, smiling.

"No, sir," he answered calmly. "I didn't see any."

The three policemen roared harder and louder.

"Boy, you're sure some case," Murphy said, shaking his head in wonder.

The car pulled to a curb.

"All right, boy," Lawson said. "Tell us where to go."

He peered through the rain and saw where he had gone down. The streets, save for a few dim lamps glowing softly through the rain, were dark and empty.

"Right there, mister," he said, pointing.

"Come on; let's take a look," Lawson said.

"Well, suppose he did hide down there," Johnson said, "what is that supposed to prove?"

"I don't believe he hid down there," Murphy said.

"It won't hurt to look," Lawson said. "Leave things to me."

Lawson got out of the car and looked up and down the street.

He was eager to show them the cave now. If he could show them what he had seen, then they would feel what he had felt and they in turn would show it to others and those others would feel as they had felt, and soon everybody would be governed by the same impulse of pity.

"Take 'im out," Lawson ordered.

Johnson and Murphy opened the door and pushed him out; he stood trembling in the rain, smiling. Again Lawson looked up and down the street; no one was in sight. The rain came down hard, slanting like black wires across the wind-swept air.

"All right," Lawson said. "Show us."

He walked to the center of the street, stopped and inserted a finger in one of the tiny holes of the cover and tugged, but he was too weak to budge it.

"Did you really go down in there, boy?" Lawson asked; there was a doubt in his voice.

"Yes, sir. Just a minute. I'll show you."

"Help 'im get that damn thing off," Lawson said.

Johnson stepped forward and lifted the cover; it clanged against the wet pavement. The hole gaped round and black.

"I went down in there," he announced with pride.

Lawson gazed at him for a long time without speaking, then he reached his right hand to his holster and drew his gun.

"Mister, I got a gun just like that down there," he said, laughing and looking into Lawson's face. "I fired it once then hung it on the wall. I'll show you."

"Show us how you went down," Lawson said quietly.

"I'll go down first, mister, and then you-all can come after me, hear?" he spoke like a little boy playing a game.

"Sure, sure," Lawson said soothingly. "Go ahead. We'll come."

He looked brightly at the policemen; he was bursting with happiness. He bent down and placed his hands on the rim of the hole and sat on the edge, his feet dangling into watery darkness. He heard the familiar drone of the gray current. He lowered his body and hung for a moment by his fingers, then he went downward on the steel prongs, hand over hand, until he reached the last rung. He dropped and his feet hit the water and he felt the stiff current trying to suck him away. He balanced himself quickly and looked back upward at the policemen.

"Come on, you-all!" he yelled, casting his voice above the rustling at his feet.

The vague forms that towered above him in the rain did not move. He laughed, feeling that they doubted him. But, once they saw the things he had done, they would never doubt again.

"Come on! The cave isn't far!" he yelled. "But be careful when your feet hit the water, because the current's pretty rough down here!"

Lawson still held the gun. Murphy and Johnson looked at Lawson quizzically.

"What are we going to do, Lawson?" Murphy asked.

"We are not going to follow that crazy nigger down into that sewer, are we?" Johnson asked.

"Come on, you-all!" he begged in a shout.

He saw Lawson raise the gun and point it directly at him. Lawson's face twitched, as though he were hesitating.

Then there was a thunderous report and a streak of fire ripped through his chest. He was hurled into the water, flat on his back. He looked in amazement at the blurred white faces looming above him. They shot me, he said to himself. The water flowed past him, blossoming in foam about his arms, his legs, and his head. His jaw sagged and his mouth gaped soundless. A vast pain gripped his head and gradually squeezed out consciousness. As from a great distance he heard hollow voices.

"What did you shoot him for, Lawson?"

"I had to."

"Why?"

"You've got to shoot his kind. They'd wreck things."

As though in a deep dream, he heard a metallic clank; they had replaced the manhole cover, shutting out forever the sound of wind and rain. From overhead came the muffled roar of a powerful motor and the swish of a speeding car. He felt the strong tide pushing him slowly into the middle of the sewer, turning him about. For a split second there hovered before his eyes the glittering cave, the shouting walls, and the laughing floor . . . Then his mouth was full of thick, bitter water. The current spun him around. He sighed and closed his eyes, a whirling object rushing alone in the darkness, veering, tossing, lost in the heart of the earth.

Questions

1. *Fred Daniels goes underground to escape punishment for a crime he did not commit. He is a black man, and the underground is an appropriate metaphor for the position white America has accorded blacks. The underground is more than a place of escape for him, however; it is a place where he comes to understand what the society he lives in, black and white, is about. How do various episodes—the discovery of the dead baby, the funeral parlor, the meat market, the black church—contribute to this understanding?*
2. *What is the significance of Fred Daniels' pecking out his own name on the typewriter?*   3. *What significance do you see in the fact that Daniels tries to communicate his joyous feelings at a church and a police station? What is it that he wants to communicate?*   4. *The police officer who kills Daniels sees him as a dangerous rebel, as the kind who'd "wreck things." In what sense could Daniels be seen as a rebel?*

The Lottery

SHIRLEY JACKSON   [1919–1965]

THE morning of June 27th was clear and sunny, with the fresh warmth of a full-summer day; the flowers were blossoming profusely and the grass was richly green. The people of the village began to gather in the square, between the post office and the bank, around ten o'clock; in some towns there were so many people that the lottery took two days and had to be started on June 26th, but in this village, where there were only about three hundred people, the whole lottery took less than two hours, so it could begin at ten o'clock in the morning and still be through in time to allow the villagers to get home for noon dinner.

The children assembled first, of course. School was recently over for the summer, and the feeling of liberty sat uneasily on most of them; they tended to gather together quietly for a while before they broke into boisterous play, and their talk was still of the classroom and the teacher, of books and reprimands. Bobby Martin had already stuffed his pockets full of stones, and the other boys soon followed his example, selecting the smoothest and roundest stones; Bobby and Harry Jones and Dickie Delacroix—the villagers pronounced his name "Dellacroy"—eventually made a great pile of stones in one corner of the square and guarded it against the raids of the other boys. The girls stood aside, talking among themselves, looking over their shoulders at the boys, and the very small children rolled in the dust or clung to the hands of their older brothers or sisters.

Soon the men began to gather, surveying their own children, speaking of planting and rain, tractors and taxes. They stood together, away from the pile of stones in the corner, and their jokes were quiet and they smiled rather than laughed. The women, wearing faded house dresses and sweaters, came shortly after their menfolk. They greeted one another and exchanged bits of gossip as they went to join their husbands. Soon the women, standing by their husbands, began to call to their children, and the children came reluctantly, having to be called four or five times. Bobby Martin ducked under his mother's grasping hand and ran, laughing, back to the pile of stones. His father spoke up sharply, and Bobby came quickly and took his place between his father and his oldest brother.

The lottery was conducted—as were the square dances, the teen-age club, the Halloween program—by Mr. Summers, who had time and energy to devote to civic activities. He was a round-faced, jovial man and he ran the coal business, and people were sorry for him, because he had no children and his wife was a scold. When he arrived in the square, carrying the black wooden box, there was a murmur of conversation among the villagers, and he waved and called, "Little late today, folks." The postmaster, Mr. Graves, followed him, carrying a three-legged stool, and the stool was put in the center of the square and Mr. Summers set the black box down on it. The villagers kept their distance, leaving a space between themselves and the stool, and when Mr. Summers said, "Some of you fellows want to give me a hand?" there was a hesitation before two men, Mr. Martin and his oldest son, Baxter, came forward to hold the box steady on the stool while Mr. Summers stirred up the papers inside it.

The original paraphernalia for the lottery had been lost long ago, and the black box now resting on the stool had been put into use even before Old Man Warner, the oldest man in town, was born. Mr. Summers spoke frequently to the villagers about making a new box, but no one liked to upset even as much tradition as was represented by the black box. There was a story that the present box had been made with some pieces of the box that had preceded it, the one that had been constructed when the first people settled down to make a village here. Every year, after the lottery, Mr. Summers began talking again about a new box, but every year the subject was allowed to fade off without anything's being done. The black box grew shabbier each year; by now it was no longer completely black but splintered badly along one side to show the original wood color, and in some places faded or stained.

Mr. Martin and his oldest son, Baxter, held the black box securely on the stool until Mr. Summers had stirred the papers thoroughly with his hand. Because so much of the ritual had been forgotten or discarded, Mr. Summers had been successful in having slips of paper substituted for the chips of wood that had been used for generations. Chips of wood, Mr. Summers had argued, had been all very well when the village was tiny, but now that the population was more than three hundred and likely to keep on growing, it was necessary to use something that would fit more easily into the black box. The night before the lottery, Mr. Summers and Mr. Graves made up the slips of paper and put them in the box, and it was then taken to the safe of Mr. Summers' coal company and locked up until Mr. Summers was ready to take it to the square next morning. The rest of the year, the box was put away, sometimes one place, sometimes another; it had spent one year in Mr. Graves's barn and another year underfoot in the post office, and sometimes it was set on a shelf in the Martin grocery and left there.

There was a great deal of fussing to be done before Mr. Summers declared the lottery open. There were the lists to make up—of heads of families, heads of households in each family, members of each household in each family. There was the proper swearing-in of Mr. Summers by the postmaster, as the official of the lottery; at one time, some people remembered, there had been a recital of some sort, performed by the official of the lottery, a perfunctory, tuneless chant that had been rattled off duly each year; some people believed that the official of the lottery used to stand just so when he said or sang it, others believed that he was supposed to walk among the people, but years and years ago this part of the ritual had been allowed to lapse. There had been, also, a ritual salute, which the official of the lottery had had to use in addressing each person who came up to draw from the box, but this also had changed with time, until now it was felt necessary only for the official to speak to each person approaching. Mr. Summers was very good at all this; in his clean white shirt and blue jeans, with one hand resting carelessly on the black box, he seemed very proper and important as he talked interminably to Mr. Graves and the Martins.

Just as Mr. Summers finally left off talking and turned to the assembled villagers, Mrs. Hutchinson came hurriedly along the path to the square, her sweater thrown over her shoulders, and slid into place in the back of the crowd. "Clean forgot what day it was," she said to Mrs. Delacroix, who stood next to her, and they both laughed softly. "Thought my old man was out back stacking wood," Mrs. Hutchinson went on, "and then I looked out the window and the kids were gone, and then I remembered it was the twenty-seventh and came a-running." She dried her hands on her apron, and Mrs. Delacroix said, "You're in time, though. They're still talking away up there."

Mrs. Hutchinson craned her neck to see through the crowd and found her husband and children standing near the front. She tapped Mrs. Delacroix on the arm as a farewell and began to make her way through the crowd. The people separated good-humoredly to let her through; two or three people said, in voices just loud enough to be heard across the crowd, "Here comes your Missus, Hutchinson," and "Bill, she made it after all." Mrs. Hutchinson reached her husband, and Mr. Summers, who had been waiting, said cheerfully, "Thought we were going to have to get on without you, Tessie." Mrs. Hutchinson said, grinning, "Wouldn't have me leave m'dishes in the sink, now, would you, Joe?," and soft laughter ran through the crowd as the people stirred back into position after Mrs. Hutchinson's arrival.

"Well, now," Mr. Summers said soberly, "guess we better get started, get this over with, so's we can go back to work. Anybody ain't here?"

"Dunbar," several people said. "Dunbar, Dunbar."

Mr. Summers consulted his list. "Clyde Dunbar," he said. "That's right. He's broke his leg, hasn't he? Who's drawing for him?"

"Me, I guess," a woman said, and Mr. Summers turned to look at her. "Wife draws for her husband," Mr. Summers said. "Don't you have a grown boy to do it for you, Janey?" Although Mr. Summers and everyone else in the village knew the answer perfectly well, it was the business of the official of the lottery to ask such questions formally. Mr. Summers waited with an expression of polite interest while Mrs. Dunbar answered.

"Horace's not but sixteen yet," Mrs. Dunbar said regretfully. "Guess I gotta fill in for the old man this year."

"Right," Mr. Summers said. He made a note on the list he was holding. Then he asked, "Watson boy drawing this year?"

A tall boy in the crowd raised his hand. "Here," he said. "I'm drawing for m'mother and me." He blinked his eyes nervously and ducked his head as several voices in the crowd said things like "Good fellow, Jack," and "Glad to see your mother's got a man to do it."

"Well," Mr. Summers said, "guess that's everyone. Old Man Warner make it?"

"Here," a voice said, and Mr. Summers nodded.

A sudden hush fell on the crowd as Mr. Summers cleared his throat and looked at the list. "All ready?" he called. "Now, I'll read the names—heads of families first—and the men come up and take a paper out of the box. Keep the paper folded in your hand without looking at it until everyone has had a turn. Everything clear?"

The people had done it so many times that they only half listened to the directions; most of them were quiet, wetting their lips, not looking around. Then Mr. Summers raised one hand high and said, "Adams." A man disengaged himself from the crowd and came forward. "Hi, Steve," Mr. Summers said, and Mr. Adams said, 'Hi, Joe." They grinned at one another humorlessly and nervously. Then Mr. Adams reached into the black box and took out a folded paper. He held it firmly by one corner as he turned and went hastily back to his place in the crowd, where he stood a little apart from his family, not looking down at his hand.

"Allen." Mr. Summers said. "Anderson. . . . Bentham."

"Seems like there's no time at all between lotteries any more," Mrs. Delacroix said to Mrs. Graves in the back row. "Seems like we got through with the last one only last week."

"Time sure goes fast," Mrs. Graves said.

"Clark. . . . Delacroix."

"There goes my old man," Mrs. Delacroix said. She held her breath while her husband went forward.

"Dunbar," Mr. Summers said, and Mrs. Dunbar went steadily to the box while one of the women said, "Go on, Janey," and another said, "There she goes."

"We're next," Mrs. Graves said. She watched while Mr. Graves came around from the side of the box, greeted Mr. Summers gravely, and selected a slip of paper from the box. By now, all through the crowd there were men holding the small folded papers in their large hands, turning them over and over nervously. Mrs. Dunbar and her two sons stood together, Mrs. Dunbar holding the slip of paper.

"Harburt. . . . Hutchinson."

"Get up there, Bill," Mrs. Hutchinson said, and the people near her laughed.

"Jones."

"They do say," Mr. Adams said to Old Man Warner, who stood next to him, "that over in the north village they're talking of giving up the lottery."

Old Man Warner snorted. "Pack of crazy fools," he said. "Listening to the young folks, nothing's good enough for *them*. Next thing you know, they'll be wanting to go back to living in caves, nobody work any more, live *that* way for a while. Used to be a saying about 'Lottery in June, corn be heavy soon.' First thing you know, we'd all be eating stewed chickweed and acorns. There's *always* been a lottery," he added petulantly. "Bad enough to see young Joe Summers up there joking with everybody."

"Some places have already quit lotteries," Mrs. Adams said.

"Nothing but trouble in *that,*" Old Man Warner said stoutly. "Pack of young fools."

"Martin." And Bobby Martin watched his father go forward. "Overdyke. . . . Percy."

"I wish they'd hurry," Mrs. Dunbar said to her older son. "I wish they'd hurry."

"They're almost through," her son said.

"You get ready to run tell Dad," Mrs. Dunbar said.

Mr. Summers called his own name and then stepped forward precisely and selected a slip from the box. Then he called, "Warner."

"Seventy-seventh year I been in the lottery," Old Man Warner said as he went through the crowd. "Seventy-seventh time."

"Watson." The tall boy came awkwardly through the crowd. Someone said, "Don't be nervous, Jack," said Mr. Summers said, "Take your time, son."

"Zanini."

AFTER that, there was a long pause, a breathless pause, until Mr. Summers, holding his slip of paper in the air, said, "All right, fellows." For a minute, no one moved, and then all the slips of paper were opened. Suddenly, all the women began to speak at once, saying, "Who is it," "Who's got it?," "Is it the Dunbars?," "Is it the Watsons?" Then the voices began to say, "It's Hutchinson. It's Bill," "Bill Hutchinson's got it."

"Go tell your father," Mrs. Dunbar said to her older son.

People began to look around to see the Hutchinsons. Bill Hutchinson was standing quiet, staring down at the paper in his hand. Suddenly, Tessie Hutchinson shouted to Mr. Summers, "You didn't give him time enough to take any paper he wanted. I saw you. It wasn't fair!"

"Be a good sport, Tessie," Mrs. Delacroix called, and Mrs. Graves said, "All of us took the same chance."

"Shut up, Tessie," Bill Hutchinson said.

"Well, everyone," Mr. Summers said, "that was done pretty fast, and now we've got to be hurrying a little more to get it done in time." He consulted his next list. "Bill," he said, "you draw for the Hutchinson family. You got any other households in the Hutchinsons?"

"There's Don and Eva," Mrs. Hutchinson yelled. "Make *them* take their chance!"

"Daughters draw with their husbands' families, Tessie," Mr. Summers said gently. "You know that as well as anyone else."

"It wasn't *fair*," Tessie said.

"I guess not, Joe," Bill Hutchinson said regretfully. "My daughter draws with her husband's family, that's only fair. And I've got no other family except the kids."

"Then, as far as drawing for families is concerned, it's you," Mr. Summers said in explanation, "and as far as drawing for households is concerned, that's you, too. Right?"

"Right," Bill Hutchinson said.

"How many kids, Bill?" Mr. Summers asked formally.

"Three," Bill Hutchinson said. "There's Bill, Jr., and Nancy, and little Dave. And Tessie and me."

"All right, then," Mr. Summers said. "Harry, you got their tickets back?"

Mr. Graves nodded and held up the slips of paper. "Put them in the box, then," Mr. Summers directed. "Take Bill's and put it in."

"I think we ought to start over," Mrs. Hutchinson said, as quietly as she could. "I tell you it wasn't *fair*. You didn't give him time enough to choose. *E*verybody saw that."

Mr. Graves had selected the five slips and put them in the box, and he dropped all the papers but those onto the ground, where the breeze caught them and lifted them off.

"Listen, everybody," Mrs. Hutchinson was saying to the people around her.

"Ready, Bill?" Mr. Summers asked, and Bill Hutchinson, with one quick glance around at his wife and children, nodded.

"Remember," Mr. Summers said, "take the slips and keep them folded until each person has taken one. Harry, you help little Dave." Mr. Graves took the hand of the little boy, who came willingly with him up to the box. "Take a paper out of the box, Davy," Mr. Summers said. Davy put his hand into the box and laughed. "Take just *one* paper," Mr. Summers said. "Harry, you hold it for him." Mr. Graves took the child's hand and removed the folded paper from the tight fist and held it while little Dave stood next to him and looked up at him wonderingly.

"Nancy next," Mr. Summers said. Nancy was twelve, and her school friends breathed heavily as she went forward, switching her skirt, and took a slip daintily from the box. "Bill, Jr.," Mr. Summers said, and Billy, his face red and his feet over-large, nearly knocked the box over as he got a paper out. "Tessie," Mr. Summers said. She hesitated for a minute, looking around defiantly, and then set her lips and went up to the box. She snatched a paper out and held it behind her.

"Bill," Mr. Summers said, and Bill Hutchinson reached into the box and felt around, bringing his hand out at last with the slip of paper in it.

The crowd was quiet. A girl whispered, "I hope it's not Nancy," and the sound of the whisper reached the edges of the crowd.

"It's not the way it used to be," Old Man Warner said clearly. "People ain't the way they used to be."

"All right," Mr. Summers said. "Open the papers. Harry, you open little Dave's."

Mr. Graves opened the slip of paper and there was a general sigh through the crowd as he held it up and everyone could see that it was blank. Nancy and Bill, Jr., opened theirs at the same time, and both beamed and laughed, turning around to the crowd and holding their slips of paper above their heads.

"Tessie," Mr. Summers said. There was a pause, and then Mr. Summers looked at Bill Hutchinson, and Bill unfolded his paper and showed it. It was blank.

"It's Tessie," Mr. Summers said, and his voice was hushed. "Show us her paper, Bill."

Bill Hutchinson went over to his wife and forced the slip of paper out of her hand. It had a black spot on it, the black spot Mr. Summers had made the night before with the heavy pencil in the coal-company office. Bill Hutchinson held it up, and there was a stir in the crowd.

"All right, folks," Mr. Summers said. "Let's finish quickly."

Although the villagers had forgotten the ritual and lost the original black box, they still remembered to use stones. The pile of stones the boys had made earlier was ready; there were stones on the ground with the blowing scraps of paper that had come out of the box. Mrs. Delacroix selected a stone so large she had to pick it up with both hands and turned to Mrs. Dunbar. "Come on," she said. "Hurry up."

Mrs. Dunbar had small stones in both hands, and she said, gasping for breath, "I can't run at all. You'll have to go ahead and I'll catch up with you."

The children had stones already, and someone gave little Davy Hutchinson a few pebbles.

Tessie Hutchinson was in the center of a cleared space by now, and she held her hands out desperately as the villagers moved in on her. "It isn't fair," she said. A stone hit her on the side of the head.

Old Man Warner was saying, "Come on, come on, everyone." Steve Adams was in the front of the crowd of villagers, with Mrs. Graves beside him.

"It isn't fair, it isn't right," Mrs. Hutchinson screamed, and then they were upon her.

Questions

1. *What evidence in the story suggests that the lottery is a ritualistic ceremony?* 2. *What set of beliefs underlie the old saying "Lottery in June, corn be heavy soon?"* 3. *Might this story be a comment on religious orthodoxy? Explain.*

The Sandman

DONALD BARTHELME [b. 1931]

DEAR Dr. Hodder, I realize that it is probably wrong to write a letter to one's girl friend's shrink but there are several things going on here that I think ought to be pointed out to you. I thought of making a personal visit but the situation then, as I'm sure you understand, would be completely untenable—I would be *visiting a psychiatrist*. I also understand that in writing to you I am in some sense interfering with the process but you don't have to discuss with Susan what I have said. Please consider this an "eyes only" letter. Please think of it as personal and confidential.

You must be aware, first, that because Susan is my girl friend pretty much everything she discusses with you she also discusses with me. She tells me what she said and what you said. We have been seeing each other for about six months now and I am pretty familiar with her story, or stories. Similarly, with your responses, or at least the general pattern. I know, for example, that my habit of referring to you as "the sandman" annoys you but let me assure you that I mean nothing unpleasant by it. It is simply a nickname. The reference is to the old rhyme: "Sea-sand does the sandman bring/Sleep to end the day/He dusts the children's eyes with sand/ And steals their dreams away." (This is a variant; there are other versions, but this is the one I prefer.) I also understand that you are a little bit shaky because the prestige of analysis is now, as I'm sure you know far better than I, at a nadir. This must tend to make you nervous and who can blame you? One always tends to get a little bit shook when one's methodology is in question. Of course! (By the bye, let me say that I am very pleased that you are one of the ones that talk, instead of just sitting there. I think that's a good thing, an excellent thing, I congratulate you.)

To the point. I fully understand that Susan's wish to terminate with you and buy a piano instead has disturbed you. You have every right to be disturbed and to say that she is not electing the proper course, that what she says conceals something else, that she is evading reality, etc., etc. Go ahead. But there is one possibility here that you might be, just might be, missing. Which is that she means it.

Susan says: "I want to buy a piano."

You think: She wishes to terminate the analysis and escape into the piano.

Or: Yes, it is true that her father wanted her to be a concert pianist and that she studied for twelve years with Goetzmann. But she does not really want to reopen that can of maggots. She wants me to disapprove.

Or: Having failed to achieve a career as a concert pianist, she wishes to fail again. She is now too old to achieve the original objective. The spontaneous organization of defeat!

Or: She is flirting again.

Or:

Or:

Or:

Or:

The one thing you cannot consider, by the nature of your training and of the discipline itself, is that she really might want to terminate the analysis and buy a piano. That the piano might be more necessary and valuable to her than the analysis.[1]

What we really have to consider here is the locus of hope. Does hope reside in the analysis or rather in the piano? As a shrink rather than a piano salesman you would naturally tend to opt for the analysis. But there are differences. The piano salesman can stand behind his product; you, unfortunately, cannot. A Steinway is a known quantity, whereas an analysis can succeed or fail. I don't reproach you for this, I simply note it. (An interesting question: Why do laymen feel such a desire to, in plain language, fuck over shrinks? As I am doing here, in a sense? I don't mean hostility in the psychoanalytic encounter, I mean in general. This is an interesting phenomenon and should be investigated by somebody.)

It might be useful if I gave you a little taste of my own experience of analysis. I only went five or six times. Dr. Behring was a tall thin man who never said anything much. If you could get a "What comes to mind?" out of him you were doing splendidly. There was a little incident that is, perhaps, illustrative. I went for my hour one day and told him about something I was worried about. (I was then working for a newspaper down in Texas.) There was a story that four black teenagers had come across a little white boy, about ten, in a vacant lot, sodomized him repeatedly and then put him inside a refrigerator and closed the door (this was before they had that requirement that abandoned refrigerators had to have their doors removed) and he suffocated. I don't know to this day what actually happened, but the cops had picked up *some* black kids and were reportedly beating the shit out of them in an effort to make them confess. I was not on the police run at that time but one of the police reporters told me about it and I told Dr. Behring. A good liberal, he grew white with anger and said what was I doing about it? It was the first time he had talked. So I was shaken—it hadn't occurred to me that I was required to do something about it, he was right—and after I left I called my then sister-in-law, who was at that time secretary to a City Councilman. As you can imagine, such a position is a very powerful one—the councilmen are mostly off making business deals and the executive secretaries run the office—and she got on to

---

1. For an admirable discussion of this sort of communication failure and many other matters of interest see Percy, "Toward a Triadic Theory of Meaning," *Psychiatry,* Vol. 35 (February 1972), pp. 6–14 *et seq.* [Editors' note: This and all subsequent footnotes to this story are part of the text.]

the chief of police with an inquiry as to what was going on and if there was any police brutality involved and if so, how much. The case was a very sensational one, you see; *Ebony* had a writer down there trying to cover it but he couldn't get in to see the boys and the cops had roughed him up some, they couldn't understand at that time that there could be such a thing as a black reporter. They understood that they had to be a little careful with the white reporters, but a black reporter was beyond them. But my sister-in-law threw her weight (her Councilman's weight) around a bit and suggested to the chief that if there was a serious amount of brutality going on the cops had better stop it, because there was too much outside interest in the case and it would be extremely bad PR if the brutality stuff got out. I also called a guy I knew pretty high up in the sheriff's department and suggested that *he* suggest to his colleagues that they cool it. I hinted at unspeakable political urgencies and he picked it up. The sheriff's department was separate from the police department but they both operated out of the Courthouse Building and they interacted quite a bit, in the normal course. So the long and short of it was that the cops decided to show the four black kids at a press conference to demonstrate that they weren't really beat all to rags, and that took place at four in the afternoon. I went and the kids looked O.K., except for one whose teeth were out and who the cops said had fallen down the stairs. Well, we all know the falling-down-the-stairs story but the point was the *degree* of mishandling and it was clear that the kids had not been half-killed by the cops, as the rumor stated. They were walking and talking naturally, although scared to death, as who would not be? There weren't any TV pictures because the newspaper people always pulled out the plugs of the TV people, at important moments, in those days—it was a standard thing. Now while I admit it sounds callous to be talking about the degree of brutality being minimal, let me tell you that it was no small matter, in that time and place, to force the cops to show the kids to the press at all. It was an achievement, of sorts. So about eight o'clock I called Dr. Behring at home, I hope interrupting his supper, and told him that the kids were O.K., relatively, and he said that was fine, he was glad to hear it. They were later no-billed and I stopped seeing him. That was my experience of analysis and that it may have left me a little sour, I freely grant. Allow for this bias.

To continue. I take exception to your remark that Susan's "openness" is a form of voyeurism. This remark interested me for a while, until I thought about it. Voyeurism I take to be an eroticized expression of curiosity whose chief phenomenological characteristic is the distance maintained between the voyeur and the object. The tension between the desire to draw near the object and the necessity to maintain the distance becomes a libidinous energy non-discharge, which is what the voyeur seeks.[2] The tension. But your remark indicates, in my opinion, a radical misreading of the problem. Susan's "openness"—a willingness of the heart, if you will allow such a term—is not at all

---

2. See, for example, Straus, "Shame As a Historiological Problem," in *Phenomenological Psychology.* (New York: Basic Books, 1966), p. 219.

comparable to the activities of the voyeur. Susan draws near. Distance is not her thing—not by a long chalk. Frequently, as you know, she gets burned, but she always tries again. What is operating here, I suggest, is an attempt on your part to "stabilize" Susan's behavior in reference to a state-of-affairs that you feel should obtain. Susan gets married and lives happily ever after. Or: There is within Susan a certain amount of creativity which should be liberated and actualized. Susan becomes an artist and lives happily ever after.

But your norms are, I suggest, skewing your view of the problem, and very badly.

Let us take the first case. You reason: If Susan is happy or at least functioning in the present state of affairs (that is, moving from man to man as a silver dollar moves from hand to hand), then why is she seeing a shrink? Something is wrong. New behavior is indicated. Susan is to get married and live happily ever after. May I offer another view? That is, that "seeing a shrink" might be precisely a maneuver in a situation in which Susan *does not want* to get married and live happily ever after? That getting married and living happily ever after might be, for Susan, the worst of fates, and that in order to validate her nonacceptance of this norm she defines herself to herself as shrink-needing? That you are actually certifying the behavior which you seek to change? (When she says to you that she's not shrinkable, you should listen.)

Perhaps, Dr. Hodder, my logic is feeble, perhaps my intuitions are frail. It is, God knows, a complex and difficult question. Your perception that Susan is an artist of some kind *in potentia* is, I think, an acute one. But the proposition "Susan becomes an artist and lives happily ever after" is ridiculous. (I realize that I am couching the proposition in such terms—"happily ever after"—that it is ridiculous on the face of it, but there is ridiculousness piled upon ridiculousness.) Let me point out, if it has escaped your notice, that what an artist does, is fail. Any reading of the literature[3] (I mean the theory of artistic creation), however summary, will persuade you instantly that the paradigmatic artistic experience is that of failure. The actualization fails to meet, equal, the intuition. There is something "out there" which cannot be brought "here." This is standard. I don't mean bad artists, I mean good artists. There is no such thing as a "successful artist" (except, of course, in worldly terms). The proposition should read, "Susan becomes an artist and lives unhappily ever after." This is the case. Don't be deceived.

What I am saying is, that the therapy of choice is not clear. I deeply sympathize. You have a dilemma.

I ask you to note, by the way, that Susan's is not a seeking after instant gratification as dealt out by so-called encounter or sensitivity groups, nude marathons, or dope. None of this is what is going down. "Joy" is not Susan's bag. I praise her for seeking out you rather than getting involved with any of this other idiocy. Her forte, I would suggest, is mind, and if there are games

---

3. Especially, perhaps, Ehrenzweig, *The Hidden Order of Art* (University of California Press, 1966), pp. 234–9.

being played they are being conducted with taste, decorum, and some amount of intellectual rigor. Not-bad games. When I take Susan out to dinner she does not order chocolate-covered ants, even if they are on the menu. (Have you, by the way, tried Alfredo's, at the corner of Bank and Hudson streets? It's wonderful.) (Parenthetically, the problem of analysts sleeping with their patients is well known and I understand that Susan has been routinely seducing you—a reflex, she can't help it—throughout the analysis. I understand that there is a new splinter group of therapists, behaviorists of some kind, who take this to be some kind of ethic? Is this true? Does this mean that they do it only when they want to, or whether they want to or not? At a dinner party the other evening a lady analyst was saying that three cases of this kind had recently come to her attention and she seemed to think that this was rather a lot. The problem of maintaining mentorship is, as we know, not easy. I think you have done very well in this regard, and God knows it must have been difficult, given those skirts Susan wears that unbutton up to the crotch and which she routinely leaves unbuttoned to the third button.)

Am I wandering too much for you? Bear with me. The world is waiting for the sunrise.

We are left, I submit, with the problem of her depressions. They are, I agree, terrible. Your idea that I am not "supportive" enough is, I think, wrong. I have found, as a practical matter, that the best thing to do is to just do ordinary things, read the newspaper for example, or watch basketball, or wash the dishes. That seems to allow her to come out of it better than any amount of so-called "support." (About the *chasmus hystericus* or hysterical yawning I don't worry any more. It is masking behavior, of course, but after all, you must allow us our tics. The world is waiting for the sunrise.) What do you do with a patient who finds the world unsatisfactory? The world *is* unsatisfactory; only a fool would deny it. I know that your own ongoing psychic structuralization is still going on—you are thirty-seven and I am forty-one—but you must be old enough by now to realize that shit is shit. Susan's perception that America has somehow got hold of the greed ethic and that the greed ethic has turned America into a tidy little hell is not, I think, wrong. What do you do with such a perception? Apply Band-Aids, I suppose. About her depressions, I wouldn't do anything. I'd leave them alone. Put on a record.[4]

Let me tell you a story.

One night we were at her place, about three a.m., and this man called, another lover, quite a well-known musician who is very good, very fast—a good man. He asked Susan "Is he there?," meaning me, and she said "Yes," and he said "What are you doing?," and she said, "What do you think?," and he said, "When will you be finished?," and she said, "Never." Are you, Doctor dear, in a position to appreciate the beauty of this reply, in this context?

What I am saying is that Susan is wonderful. *As is.* There are not so many

---

4. For example, Harrison, "Wah Wah," Apple Records, STCH 639, Side One, Track 3.

things around to which that word can be accurately applied. Therefore I must view your efforts to improve her with, let us say, a certain amount of ambivalence. If this makes me a negative factor in the analysis, so be it. I will be a negative factor until the cows come home, and cheerfully. I can't help it, Doctor, I am voting for the piano.

With best wishes,

"Repent, Harlequin!"
Said the Ticktockman

HARLAN ELLISON   [b. 1934]

THERE are always those who ask, what is it all about? For those who need to ask, for those who need points sharply made, who need to know "where it's at," this:

"The mass of men serve the state thus, not as men mainly, but as machines, with their bodies. They are the standing army, and the militia, jailors, constables, posse comitatus, etc. In most cases there is no free exercise whatever of the judgment or of the moral sense; but they put themselves on a level with wood and earth and stones; and wooden men can perhaps be manufactured that will serve the purposes as well. Such command no more respect than men of straw or a lump of dirt. They have the same sort of worth only as horses and dogs. Yet such as these even are commonly esteemed good citizens. Others—as most legislators, politicians, lawyers, ministers, and office-holders—serve the state chiefly with their heads; and, as they rarely make any moral distinctions, they are as likely to serve the Devil, without intending it, as God. A very few, as heroes, patriots, martyrs, reformers in the great sense, and *men*, serve the state with their consciences also, and so necessarily resist it for the most part; and they are commonly treated as enemies by It."

Henry David Thoreau,
"Civil Disobedience"

That is the heart of it. Now begin in the middle, and later learn the beginning; the end will take care of itself.

BUT because it was the very world it was, the very world they had allowed it to *become*, for months his activities did not come to the alarmed attention of The Ones Who Kept The Machine Functioning Smoothly, the ones who poured the very best butter over the cams and mainsprings of the culture. Not until it had become obvious that somehow, someway, he had become a notoriety, a celebrity, perhaps even a hero for (what Officialdom inescapably tagged) "an emotionally disturbed segment of the populace," did they turn it over to the Ticktockman and his legal machinery. But by then, because it was the very world it was, and they had no way to predict he would happen—possibly a strain of disease long-defunct, now, suddenly, reborn in a system where immunity had been forgotten, had lapsed—he had been allowed to become too real. Now he had form and substance.

He had become a *personality*, something they had filtered out of the system many decades ago. But there it was, and there *he* was, a very definitely imposing personality. In certain circles—middle-class circles—it was thought disgusting. Vulgar ostentation. Anarchistic. Shameful. In others, there was only sniggering, those strata where thought is subjugated to form and ritual, niceties, proprieties. But down below, ah, down below, where the people always needed their saints and sinners, their bread and circuses, their heroes and villains, he was considered a Bolivar; a Napoleon; a Robin Hood; a Dick Bong (Ace of Aces); a Jesus; a Jomo Kenyatta.

And at the top—where, like socially-attuned Shipwreck Kellys, every tremor and vibration threatens to dislodge the wealthy, powerful and titled from their flagpoles—he was considered a menace; a heretic; a rebel; a disgrace; a peril. He was known down the line, to the very heartmeat core, but the important reactions were high above and far below. At the very top, at the very bottom.

So his file was turned over, along with his time-card and his cardioplate, to the office of the Ticktockman.

The Ticktockman: very much over six feet tall, often silent, a soft purring man when things went timewise. The Ticktockman.

Even in the cubicles of the hierarchy, where fear was generated, seldom suffered, he was called the Ticktockman. But no one called him that to his mask.

You don't call a man a hated name, not when that man, behind his mask, is capable of revoking the minutes, the hours, the days and nights, the years of your life. He was called the Master Timekeeper to his mask. It was safer that way.

"This is *what* he is," said the Ticktockman with genuine softness, "but not *who* he is? This time-card I'm holding in my left hand has a name on it, but it is the name of *what* he is, not *who* he is. This cardioplate here in my right hand is also named, but not whom named, merely what named. Before I can exercise proper revocation, I have to know who this what is."

To his staff, all the ferrets, all the loggers, all the finks, all the commex, even the mineez, he said, "Who is this Harlequin?"

He was not purring smoothly. Timewise, it was jangle.

However, it *was* the longest single speech they had ever heard him utter at one time, the staff, the ferrets, the loggers, the finks, the commex, but not the mineez, who usually weren't around to know, in any case. But even they scurried to find out.

Who is the Harlequin?

HIGH above the third level of the city, he crouched on the humming aluminum-frame platform of the air-boat (foof! air-boat, indeed! swizzleskid is what it was, with a tow-rack jerry-rigged) and stared down at the neat Mondrian arrangement of the buildings.

Somewhere nearby, he could hear the metronomic left-right-left of the

2:47 P.M. shift, entering the Timkin roller-bearing plant in their sneakers. A minute later, precisely, he heard the softer right-left-right of the 5:00 A.M. formation, going home.

An elfish grin spread across his tanned features, and his dimples appeared for a moment. Then, scratching at his thatch of auburn hair, he shrugged within his motley, as though girding himself for what came next, and threw the joystick forward, and bent into the wind as the air-boat dropped. He skimmed over a slidewalk, purposely dropping a few feet to crease the tassels of the ladies of fashion, and—inserting thumbs in large ears—he stuck out his tongue, rolled his eyes and went wugga-wugga-wugga. It was a minor diversion. One pedestrian skittered and tumbled, sending parcels everywhichway, another wet herself, a third keeled slantwise and the walk was stopped automatically by the servitors till she could be resuscitated. It was a minor diversion.

Then he swirled away on a vagrant breeze, and was gone. Hi-ho.

As he rounded the cornice of the Time-Motion Study Building, he saw the shift, just boarding the slidewalk. With practiced motion and an absolute conservation of movement, they sidestepped up onto the slowstrip and (in a chorus line reminiscent of a Busby Berkeley film of the antediluvian 1930's) advanced across the strips ostrich-walking till they were lined up on the expresstrip.

Once more, in anticipation, the elfin grin spread, and there was a tooth missing back there on the left side. He dipped, skimmed, and swooped over them; and then, scrunching about on the air-boat, he released the holding pins that fastened shut the ends of the home-made pouring troughs that kept his cargo from dumping prematurely. And as he pulled the trough-pins, the air-boat slid over the factory workers and one hundred and fifty thousand dollars worth of jelly beans cascaded down on the expresstrip.

Jelly beans! Millons and billions of purples and yellows and greens and licorice and grape and raspberry and mint and round and smooth and crunchy outside and soft-mealy inside and sugary and bouncing jouncing tumbling clittering clattering skittering fell on the heads and shoulders and hard-hats and carapaces of the Timkin workers, tinkling on the slidewalk and bouncing away and rolling about underfoot and filling the sky on their way down with all the colors of joy and childhood and holidays, coming down in a steady rain, a solid wash, a torrent of color and sweetness out of the sky from above, and entering a universe of sanity and metronomic order with quite-mad coocoo newness. Jelly beans!

The shift workers howled and laughed and were pelted, and broke ranks, and the jelly beans managed to work their way into the mechanism of the slidewalks after which there was a hideous scraping as the sound of a million fingernails rasped down a quarter of a million blackboards, followed by a coughing and a sputtering, and then the slidewalks all stopped and everyone was dumped thisawayandthataway in a jackstraw tumble, and still laughing and popping little jelly bean eggs of childish color into their mouths. It was a holiday, and a jollity, an absolute insanity, a giggle. But . . .

The shift was delayed seven minutes.

They did not get home for seven minutes.

The master schedule was thrown off by seven minutes.

Quotas were delayed by inoperative slidewalks for seven minutes.

He had tapped the first domino in the line, and one after another, like chik chik chik, the others had fallen.

The System had been seven minutes worth of disrupted. It was a tiny matter, one hardly worthy of note, but in a society where the single driving force was order and unity and promptness and clocklike precision and attention to the clock, reverence of the gods of the passage of time, it was a disaster of major importance.

So he was ordered to appear before the Ticktockman. It was broadcast across every channel of the communications web. He was ordered to be *there* at 7:00 dammit on time. And they waited, and they waited, but he didn't show up till almost ten-thirty, at which time he merely sang a little song about moonlight in a place no one had ever heard of, called Vermont, and vanished again. But they had all been waiting since seven, and it wrecked *hell* with their schedules. So the question remained: Who is the Harlequin?

But the *unasked* question (more important of the two) was: how did we get *into* this position, where a laughing, irresponsible japer of jabberwocky and jive could disrupt our entire economic and cultural life with a hundred and fifty thousand dollars worth of jelly beans . . .

Jelly for God's sake beans! This is madness! Where did he get the money to buy a hundred and fifty thousand dollars worth of jelly beans? (They knew it would have cost that much, because they had a team of Situation Analysts pulled off another assignment, and rushed to the slidewalk scene to sweep up and count the candies, and produce findings, which disrupted *their* schedules and threw their entire branch at least a day behind.) Jelly beans! Jelly . . . beans? Now wait a second—a second accounted for—no one has manufactured jelly beans for over a hundred years. Where did he get jelly beans?

That's another good question. More than likely it will never be answered to your complete satisfaction. But then, how many questions ever are?

THE middle you know. Here is the beginning. How it starts:

A desk pad. Day for day, and turn each day. 9:00—open the mail. 9:45—appointment with planning commission board. 10:30—discuss installation progress charts with J.L. 11:15—pray for rain. 12:00—lunch. *And so it goes.*

"I'm sorry, Miss Grant, but the time for interviews was set at 2:30, and it's almost five now. I'm sorry you're late, but those are the rules. You'll have to wait till next year to submit application for this college again." *And so it goes.*

The 10:00 local stops at Cresthaven, Galesville, Tonawanda Junction, Selby and Farnhurst, but not at Indiana City, Lucasville and Colton, except on Sunday. The 10:35 express stops at Galesville, Selby and Indiana City, except on Sundays & Holidays, at which time it stops at . . . *and so it goes.*

"I couldn't wait, Fred. I had to be at Pierre Cartain's by 3:00, and you said you'd meet me under the clock in the terminal at 2:45, and you weren't there, so I had to go on. You're always late, Fred. If you'd been there, we could have sewed it up together, but as it was, well, I took the order alone . . ." *And so it goes.*

Dear Mr. and Mrs. Atterley: in reference to your son Gerold's constant tardiness, I am afraid we will have to suspend him from school unless some more reliable method can be instituted guaranteeing he will arrive at his classes on time. Granted he is an exemplary student, and his marks are high, his constant flouting of the schedules of this school makes it impractical to maintain him in a system where the other children seem capable of getting where they are supposed to be on time *and so it goes.*

YOU CANNOT VOTE UNLESS YOU APPEAR AT 8:45 A.M.

"I don't care if the script is *good*, I need it Thursday!"

CHECK-OUT TIME IS 2:00 P.M.

"You got here late. The job's taken. Sorry."

YOUR SALARY HAS BEEN DOCKED FOR TWENTY MINUTES TIME LOST.

"God, what time is it, I've gotta run!"

And so it goes. And so it goes. And so it goes. And so it goes goes goes goes tick tock tick tock tick tock and one day we no longer let time serve us, we serve time and we are slaves of the schedule, worshippers of the sun's passing, bound into a life predicated on restrictions because the system will not function if we don't keep the schedule tight.

Until it becomes more than a minor inconvenience to be late. It becomes a sin. Then a crime. Then a crime punishable by this:

EFFECTIVE 15 JULY 2389, 12:00:00 midnight, the office of the Master Timekeeper will require all citizens to submit their time-cards and cardioplates for processing. In accordance with Statute 555-7-SGH-999 governing the revocation of time per capita, all cardioplates will be keyed to the individual holder and—

What they had done, was devise a method of curtailing the amount of life a person could have. If he was ten minutes late, he lost ten minutes of his life. An hour was proportionately worth more revocation. If someone was consistently tardy, he might find himself, on a Sunday night, receiving a communique from the Master Timekeeper that his time had run out, and he would be "turned off" at high noon on Monday, please straighten your affairs, sir.

And so, by this simple scientific expedient (utilizing a scientific process held dearly secret by the Ticktockman's office) the System was maintained. It was the only expedient thing to do. It was, after all, patriotic. The schedules had to be met. After all, there *was* a war on!

But, wasn't there always?

Now that is really disgusting," the Harlequin said, when pretty Alice showed him the wanted poster. "Disgusting and *highly* improbable. After all, this isn't the days of desperadoes. A *wanted* poster!"

"You know," Alice noted, "you speak with a great deal of inflection."

"I'm sorry," said the Harlequin, humbly.

"No need to be sorry. You're always saying 'I'm sorry.' You have such massive guilt, Everett, it's really very sad."

"I'm sorry," he repeated, then pursed his lips so the dimples appeared momentarily. He hadn't wanted to say that at all. "I have to go out again. I have to *do* something."

Alice slammed her coffee-bulb down on the counter. "Oh for God's *sake*, Everett, can't you stay home just *one* night! Must you always be out in that ghastly clown suit, running around annoying people?"

"I'm—" he stopped, and clapped the jester's hat onto his auburn thatch with a tiny tingling of bells. He rose, rinsed out his coffee-bulb at the tap, and put it into the drier for a moment. "I have to go."

She didn't answer. The faxbox was purring, and she pulled a sheet out, read it, threw it toward him on the counter. "It's about you. Of course. You're ridiculous."

He read it quickly. It said the Ticktockman was trying to locate him. He didn't care, he was going to be late again. At the door, dredging for an exit line, he hurled back petulantly, "Well, *you* speak with inflection, *too!*"

Alice rolled her pretty eyes heavenward. "You're ridiculous." The Harlequin stalked out, slamming the door, which sighed shut softly, and locked itself.

There was a gentle knock, and Alice got up with an exhalation of exasperated breath, and opened the door. He stood there. "I'll be back about ten-thirty, okay?"

She pulled a rueful face. "Why do you tell me that? Why? You *know* you'll be late! You *know it!* You're *always* late, so why do you tell me these dumb things?" She closed the door.

On the other side, the Harlequin nodded to himself. *She's right. She's always right. I'll be late. I'm always late. Why do I tell her these dumb things?*

He shrugged again, and went off to be late once more.

H E had fired off the firecracker rockets that said: I will attend the 115th annual International Medical Association Invocation at 8:00 P.M. precisely. I do hope you will all be able to join me.

The words had burned in the sky, and of course the authorities were there, lying in wait for him. They assumed, naturally, that he would be late. He arrived twenty minutes early, while they were setting up the spiderwebs to trap and hold him, and blowing a large bullhorn, he frightened and unnerved them so, their own moisturized encirclement webs sucked closed, and they were hauled up, kicking and shrieking, high above the amphitheatre's floor. The Harlequin laughed and laughed, and apologized profusely. The physicians, gathered in solemn conclave, roared with laughter, and accepted the Harlequin's apologies with exaggerated bowing and posturing, and a merry time was had by all, who thought the Harlequin was a regular foofaraw in fancy pants; all, that is, but the authorities, who had been sent out by the office of the Ticktockman, who hung there like so much dockside cargo, hauled up above the floor of the amphitheatre in a most unseemly fashion.

(In another part of the same city where the Harlequin carried on his "activities," totally unrelated in every way to what concerns here, save that it illustrates the Ticktockman's power and import, a man named Marshall Delahanty received his turn-off notice from the Ticktockman's office. His wife received the notification from the grey-suited minee who delivered it, with the traditional "look of sorrow" plastered hideously across his face. She knew what it was, even without unsealing it. It was a billet-doux of immediate recognition to everyone these days. She gasped, and held it as though it were a glass slide tinged with botulism, and prayed it was not for her. Let it be for Marsh, she thought, brutally, realistically, or one of the kids, but not for me, please dear God, not for me. And then she opened it, and it *was* for Marsh, and she was at one and the same time horrified and relieved. The next trooper in the line had caught the bullet. "Marshall," she screamed, "Marshall! Termination, Marshall! OhmiGod, Marshall, whattl we do, whattl we do, Marshall omigodmarshall . . ." and in their home that night was the sound of tearing paper and fear, and the stink of madness went up the flue and there was nothing, absolutely nothing they could do about it.

(But Marshall Delahanty tried to run. And early the next day, when turn-off time came, he was deep in the forest two hundred miles away, and the office of the Ticktockman blanked his cardioplate, and Marshall Delahanty keeled over, running, and his heart stopped, and the blood dried up on its way to his brain, and he was dead that's all. One light went out on his sector map in the office of the Master Timekeeper, while notification was entered for fax reproduction, and Georgette Delahanty's name was entered on the dole roles till she could re-marry. Which is the end of the footnote, and all the point that need be made, except don't laugh, because that is what would happen to the Harlequin if ever the Ticktockman found out his real name. It isn't funny.)

The shopping level of the city was thronged with the Thursday-colors of the buyers. Women in canary yellow chitons and men in pseudo-Tyrolean outfits that were jade and leather and fit very tightly, save for the balloon pants.

When the Harlequin appeared on the still-being-constructed shell of the new Efficiency Shopping Center, his bullhorn to his elfishly-laughing lips, everyone pointed and stared, and he berated them:

"Why let them order you about? Why let them tell you to hurry and scurry like ants or maggots? Take your time! Saunter a while! Enjoy the sunshine, enjoy the breeze, let life carry you at your own pace! Don't be slaves of time, it's a helluva way to die, slowly, by degrees . . . down with the Ticktockman!"

Who's the nut? most of the shoppers wanted to know. Who's the nut oh wow I'm gonna be late I gotta run . . .

And the construction gang on the Shopping Center received an urgent order from the office of the Master Timekeeper that the dangerous criminal known as the Harlequin was atop their spire, and their aid was urgently needed in apprehending him. The work crew said no, they would lose time on their construction schedule, but the Ticktockman managed to pull the proper threads of governmental webbing, and they were told to cease work and catch that nitwit up there on the spire with the bullhorn. So a dozen and more burly workers began climbing into their construction platforms, releasing the a-grav plates, and rising toward the Harlequin.

After the debacle (in which, through the Harlequin's attention to personal safety, no one was seriously injured), the workers tried to re-assemble, and assault him again, but it was too late. He had vanished. It had attracted quite a crowd, however, and the shopping cycle was thrown off by hours, simply hours. The purchasing needs of the system were therefore falling behind, and so measures were taken to accelerate the cycle for the rest of the day, but it got bogged down and speeded up and they sold too many float-valves and not nearly enough wegglers, which meant that the popli ratio was off, which made it necessary to rush cases and cases of spoiling Smash-O to stores that usually needed a case only every three or four hours. The shipments were bollixed, the trans-shipments were mis-routed, and in the end, even the swizzleskid industries felt it.

"Don't come back till you have him!" the Ticktockman said, very quietly, very sincerely, extremely dangerously.

They used dogs. They used probes. They used cardioplate crossoffs. They used feepers. They used bribery. They used stiktytes. They used intimidation. They used torment. They used torture. They used finks. They used cops. They used search&seizure. They used fallaron. They used betterment incentive. They used fingerprints. They used Bertillon. They used cunning. They used guile. They used treachery. They used Raoul Mitgong, but he didn't help much. They used applied physics. They used techniques of criminology.

And what the hell: they caught him.

After all, his name was Everett C. Marm, and he wasn't much to begin with, except a man who had no sense of time.

"REPENT, Harlequin!" said the Ticktockman.

"Get stuffed!" the Harlequin replied, sneering.

"You've been late a total of sixty-three years, five months, three weeks, two days, twelve hours, forty-one minutes, fifty-nine seconds, point oh three six one one one microseconds. You've used up everything you can, and more. I'm going to turn you off."

"Scare someone else. I'd rather be dead than live in a dumb world with a bogey man like you."

"It's my job."

"You're full of it. You're a tyrant. You have no right to order people around and kill them if they show up late."

"You can't adjust. You can't fit in."

"Unstrap me, and I'll fit my fist into your mouth."

"You're a non-conformist."

"That didn't used to be a felony."

"It is now. Live in the world around you."

"I hate it. It's a terrible world."

"Not everyone thinks so. Most people enjoy order."

"I don't, and most of the people I know don't."

"That's not true. How do you think we caught you?"

"I'm not interested."

"A girl named pretty Alice told us who you were."

"That's a lie."

"It's true. You unnerve her. She wants to belong, she wants to conform, I'm going to turn you off."

"Then do it already, and stop arguing with me."

"I'm not going to turn you off."

"You're an idiot!"

"Repent, Harlequin!" said the Ticktockman.

"Get stuffed."

So they sent him to Coventry. And in Coventry they worked him over. It was just like what they did to Winston Smith in "1984", which was a book none of them knew about, but the techniques are really quite ancient, and so they did it to Everett C. Marm, and one day quite a long time later, the Harlequin appeared on the communications web, appearing elfish and dimpled and bright-eyed, and not at all brainwashed, and he said he had been wrong, that it was a good, a very good thing indeed, to belong, and be right on time hip-ho and away we go, and everyone stared up at him on the public screens that covered an entire city block, and they said to themselves, well, you see, he was just a nut after all, and if that's the way the system is run, then let's do it that way, because it doesn't pay to fight city hall, or in this case, the Ticktockman. So Everett C. Marm was destroyed, which was a loss, because of what Thoreau said earlier, but you can't make an omelet without breaking a few eggs, and in every revolution, a few die who shouldn't, but they have to, because that's the way it happens, and if you make only a little change, then it seems to be worthwhile. Or, to make the point lucidly:

"UH, excuse me, sir, I, uh, don't know how to uh, to uh, tell you this, but you were three minutes late. The schedule is a little, uh, bit off."

He grinned sheepishly.

"That's ridiculous!" murmured the Ticktockman behind his mask. "Check your watch." And then he went into his office, going mrmee, mrmee, mrmee, mrmee.

conformity and rebellion

POETRY

from

Paradise Lost[1]

JOHN MILTON   [1608–1674]

"Is this the region, this the soil, the clime,"
Said then the lost archangel, "this the seat
That we must change for Heaven? this mournful gloom
For that celestial light? Be it so, since he
Who now is sovereign can dispose and bid
What shall be right: farthest from him is best,
Whom reason hath equaled, force hath made supreme
Above his equals. Farewell, happy fields,
Where joy forever dwells! Hail, horrors! hail,
Infernal world! and thou, profoundest Hell,   10
Receive thy new possessor, one who brings
A mind not to be changed by place or time.
The mind is its own place, and in itself
Can make a Heaven of Hell, a Hell of Heaven.
What matter where, if I be still the same,
And what I should be, all but° less than he   *only*
Whom thunder hath made greater? Here at least
We shall be free; th' Almighty hath not built
Here for his envy, will not drive us hence:
Here we may reign secure; and, in my choice,   20
To reign is worth ambition, though in Hell:
Better to reign in Hell than serve in Heaven.
But wherefore let we then our faithful friends,
Th' associates and copartners of our loss,
Lie thus astonished on th' oblivious pool,
And call them not to share with us their part
In this unhappy mansion, or once more
With rallied arms to try what may be yet
Regained in Heaven, or what more lost in Hell?"

---

1. Is the statement in line 22 a logical extension of the statement in lines 13–14? Explain.   **2.** Is the rebellious Satan heroic or ignoble? Defend your answer.   **3.** What are the political implications of Satan's analysis of power (ll. 4–8)?

---

1.   The first part of *Paradise Lost,* a poem on the expulsion of Adam and Eve from the Garden of Eden, tells the story of Satan's rebellion against God, his defeat and expulsion from heaven. In this passage, Satan surveys the infernal region to which God has banished him.

Sonnet XVII

JOHN MILTON [1608–1674]

When I consider how my light is spent,[1]
    Ere half my days, in this dark world and wide,
    And that one talent[2] which is death to hide
    Lodged with me useless, though my soul more bent
To serve therewith my maker, and present
    My true account, lest he, returning, chide.
    'Doth God exact day-labour, light denied?'
    I fondly° ask; but Patience, to prevent   *foolishly*
That murmur, soon replies: 'God doth not need
    Either man's work or his own gifts; who best   10
    Bear his mild yoke, they serve him best; his state
Is kingly—thousands at his bidding speed
    And post o'er land and ocean without rest:
    They also serve who only stand and wait.'

from

An Essay on Man

ALEXANDER POPE [1688–1744]

    Cease then, nor ORDER imperfection name:
Our proper bliss depends on what we blame.
Know thy own point: this kind, this due degree
Of blindness, weakness, Heaven bestows on thee.
Submit—In this, or any other sphere,
Secure to be as blest as thou canst bear:
Safe in the hand of one disposing Power,
Or in the natal, or the mortal hour.
All Nature is but art, unknown to thee;
All chance, direction, which thou canst not see;   10
All discord, harmony not understood;
All partial evil, universal good:
And, spite of pride, in erring reason's spite,
One truth is clear: Whatever IS, is RIGHT.

---

1. Milton was blind when he wrote this sonnet.
2. The parable of the Master who gave his servants "talents" (literally, coins of precious metal) occurs in Matthew 25:14–30.

The World Is Too Much with Us

WILLIAM WORDSWORTH [1770–1850]

The world is too much with us; late and soon,
Getting and spending, we lay waste our powers;
Little we see in Nature that is ours;
We have given our hearts away, a sordid boon!
This Sea that bares her bosom to the moon,
The winds that will be howling at all hours,
And are up-gathered now like sleeping flowers,
For this, for everything, we are out of tune;
It moves us not.—Great God! I'd rather be
A Pagan suckled in a creed outworn;   10
So might I, standing on this pleasant lea,
Have glimpses that would make me less forlorn;
Have sight of Proteus rising from the sea;
Or hear Old Triton blow his wreathèd horn.[1]

1. What does "world" mean in line 1? 2. What does Wordsworth complain of in the first four lines? 3. In lines 4–8 Wordsworth tells us what we have lost; in the concluding lines he suggests a remedy. What is that remedy? What do Proteus and Triton symbolize?

Ulysses[2]

ALFRED, LORD TENNYSON [1809–1892]

    It little profits that an idle king,
By this still hearth, among these barren crags,
Matched with an aged wife, I mete and dole
Unequal laws unto a savage race,
That hoard, and sleep, and feed, and know not me.
    I cannot rest from travel; I will drink
Life to the lees. All times I have enjoyed
Greatly, have suffered greatly, both with those
That loved me, and alone; on shore, and when

---

1. Proteus and Triton are both figures from Greek mythology. Proteus had the power to assume different forms; Triton was often represented as blowing on a conch shell.

---

2. Ulysses, according to Greek legend, was the king of Ithaca and a hero of the Trojan War. Tennyson represents him as eager to resume the life of travel and adventure.

Through scudding drifts the rainy Hyades[3]   10
Vexed the dim sea. I am become a name;
For always roaming with a hungry heart
Much have I seen and known—cities of men
And manners, climates, councils, governments,
Myself not least, but honored of them all—
And drunk delight of battle with my peers,
Far on the ringing plains of windy Troy.
I am a part of all that I have met;
Yet all experience is an arch wherethrough
Gleams that untraveled world whose margin fades   20
Forever and forever when I move.
How dull it is to pause, to make an end,
To rust unburnished, not to shine in use!
As though to breathe were life! Life piled on life
Were all too little, and of one to me
Little remains; but every hour is saved
From that eternal silence, something more,
A bringer of new things; and vile it were
For some three suns to store and hoard myself,
And this gray spirit yearning in desire   30
To follow knowledge like a sinking star,
Beyond the utmost bound of human thought.

    This is my son, mine own Telemachus,
To whom I leave the scepter and the isle—
Well-loved of me, discerning to fulfill
This labor, by slow prudence to make mild
A rugged people, and through soft degrees
Subdue them to the useful and the good.
Most blameless is he, centered in the sphere
Of common duties, decent not to fail   40
In offices of tenderness, and pay
Meet° adoration to my household gods,   *proper*
When I am gone. He works his work, I mine.

    There lies the port; the vessel puffs her sail;
There gloom the dark, broad seas. My mariners,
Souls that have toiled, and wrought, and thought with me—
That ever with a frolic welcome took
The thunder and the sunshine, and opposed
Free hearts, free foreheads—you and I are old;
Old age hath yet his honor and his toil.   50
Death closes all; but something ere the end,
Some work of noble note, may yet be done,

---

3. A group of stars in the constellation Taurus. According to Greek mythology, the rising of these
stars with the sun foretold rain.

Not unbecoming men that strove with Gods.
The lights begin to twinkle from the rocks;
The long day wanes; the slow moon climbs; the deep
Moans round with many voices. Come, my friends,
'Tis not too late to seek a newer world.
Push off, and sitting well in order smite
The sounding furrows; for my purpose holds
To sail beyond the sunset, and the baths   60
Of all the western stars, until I die.
It may be that the gulfs will wash us down;
It may be we shall touch the Happy Isles,[4]
And see the great Achilles, whom we knew.
Though much is taken, much abides; and though
We are not now that strength which in old days
Moved earth and heaven, that which we are, we are—
One equal temper of heroic hearts,
Made weak by time and fate, but strong in will
To strive, to seek, to find, and not to yield.   70

1. *Is Ulysses' desire to abdicate his duties as king irresponsible? Defend your answer.*
2. *At the conclusion of the poem Ulysses is determined not to yield. Yield to what?*
3. *Contrast Ulysses with his son Telemachus as the latter is described in lines 33–43. Is Telemachus admirable? Explain.*

Much Madness Is Divinest Sense

EMILY DICKINSON [1830–1886]

Much Madness is divinest Sense—
To a discerning Eye—
Much Sense—the starkest Madness—
'Tis the Majority
In this, as All, prevail—
Assent—and you are sane—
Demur—you're straightway dangerous—
And handled with a Chain—

4. The Islands of the Blessed (also Elysium), thought to be in the far western oceans, where those favored by the gods, such as Achilles, enjoyed life after death.

I'm Nobody! Who Are You?

EMILY DICKINSON   [1830–1886]

I'm nobody! Who are you?
Are you nobody, too?
Then there's a pair of us—don't tell!
They'd banish us, you know.

How dreary to be somebody!
How public, like a frog
To tell your name the livelong June
To an admiring bog!

Revolution Is the Pod

EMILY DICKINSON   [1830–1886]

Revolution is the Pod
Systems rattle from
When the Winds of Will are stirred
Excellent is Bloom

But except its Russet Base
Every Summer be
The Entomber of itself,
So of Liberty—

Left inactive on the Stalk
All its Purple fled
Revolution shakes it for
Test if it be dead.

10

What Soft—Cherubic Creatures

EMILY DICKINSON   [1830–1886]

What Soft—Cherubic Creatures—
These Gentlewomen are—

One would as soon assault a Plush—
Or violate a Star—

Such Dimity Convictions—
A Horror so refined
Of freckled Human Nature—
Of Deity—ashamed—

It's such a common-Glory—
A Fisherman's—Degree—   10
Redemption—Brittle Lady—
Be so—ashamed of Thee—

Thou Art Indeed Just, Lord

GERARD MANLEY HOPKINS [1844–1889]

*Justus quidem tu es, Domine, si disputem tecum: verumtamen
justa loquar ad te: Quare via impiorum prosperatur? & c.*[1]

Thou art indeed just, Lord, if I contend
With thee; but, sir, so what I plead is just.
Why do sinners' ways prosper? and why must
Disappointment all I endeavour end?
    Wert thou my enemy, O thou my friend,
How wouldst thou worse, I wonder, than thou dost
Defeat, thwart me? Oh, the sots and thralls of lust
Do in spare hours more thrive than I that spend,
Sir, life upon thy cause. See, banks and brakes
Now, leavèd how thick! lacèd they are again   10
With fretty chervil,° look, and fresh wind shakes   parsley
Them; birds build—but not I build; no, but strain,
Time's eunuch, and not breed one work that wakes.
Mine, O thou lord of life, send my roots rain.

1. *Summarize the debate in this poem. What implications about divine justice emerge
from the poet's questions in lines 3 and 4?* **2.** *How is the nature imagery used to indicate the speaker's plight?* **3.** *How would you characterize the poet's attitude toward
God?*

---

1. The first three lines of the poem translate the Latin epigraph.

Easter 1916[1]

WILLIAM BUTLER YEATS [1865–1939]

I have met them at close of day
Coming with vivid faces
From counter or desk among grey
Eighteenth-century houses.
I have passed with a nod of the head
Or polite meaningless words,
Or have lingered awhile and said
Polite meaningless words,
And thought before I had done
Of a mocking tale or a gibe   10
To please a companion
Around the fire at the club,
Being certain that they and I
But lived where motley is worn:
All changed, changed utterly:
A terrible beauty is born.

That woman's days were spent
In ignorant good-will,
Her nights in argument
Until her voice grew shrill.   20
What voice more sweet than hers
When, young and beautiful,
She rode to harriers?
This man had kept a school
And rode our wingèd horse;[2]
This other his helper and friend
Was coming into his force;
He might have won fame in the end,
So sensitive his nature seemed,
So daring and sweet his thought.   30
This other man I had dreamed
A drunken, vainglorious lout.
He had done most bitter wrong
To some who are near my heart,
Yet I number him in the song;

---

1. On Easter Sunday of 1916, a group of Irish nationalists seized key points in Ireland, including the Dublin Post Office, from which they proclaimed an independent Irish Republic. At first, most Irishmen were indifferent to the nationalists' futile and heroic gesture, but as the rebellion was crushed and the leaders executed, they became heroes in their countrymen's eyes. Some of those leaders are alluded to in the second stanza and are named in lines 75 and 76.
2. In Greek mythology, a winged horse is associated with poetic inspiration.

He, too, has resigned his part
In the casual comedy;
He, too, has been changed in his turn,
Transformed utterly:
A terrible beauty is born.   40

Hearts with one purpose alone
Through summer and winter seem
Enchanted to a stone
To trouble the living stream.
The horse that comes from the road,
The rider, the birds that range
From cloud to tumbling cloud,
Minute by minute they change;
A shadow of cloud on the stream
Changes minute by minute;   50
A horse-hoof slides on the brim,
And a horse plashes within it;
The long-legged moor-hens dive,
And hens to moor-cocks call;
Minute by minute they live:
The stone's in the midst of all.

Too long a sacrifice
Can make a stone of the heart.
O when may it suffice?
That is Heaven's part, our part   60
To murmur name upon name,
As a mother names her child
When sleep at last has come
On limbs that had run wild.
What is it but nightfall?
No, no, not night but death;
Was it needless death after all?
For England may keep faith
For all that is done and said.
We know their dream; enough   70
To know they dreamed and are dead;
And what if excess of love
Bewildered them till they died?
I write it out in a verse—
MacDonagh and MacBride
And Connolly and Pearse
Now and in time to be,
Wherever green is worn,
Are changed, changed utterly:
A terrible beauty is born.   80

1. *In the first stanza the attitude of the poet toward the people he is describing is*

indifferent, even contemptuous. How is that attitude modified in the rest of the poem? **2.** What does "they" in line 55 refer to? What does the "stone" in lines 43 and 56 symbolize? What is Yeats contrasting? **3.** How does the poet answer the question he asks in line 67? **4.** What is "changed utterly," and in what sense can beauty be "terrible"?

Miniver Cheevy

EDWIN ARLINGTON ROBINSON   [1869–1935]

Miniver Cheevy, child of scorn,
    Grew lean while he assailed the seasons;
He wept that he was ever born,
    And he had reasons.

Miniver loved the days of old
    When swords were bright and steeds were prancing;
The vision of a warrior bold
    Would set him dancing.

Miniver sighed for what was not,
    And dreamed, and rested from his labors;   10
He dreamed of Thebes and Camelot,
    And Priam's neighbors.[1]

Miniver mourned the ripe renown
    That made so many a name so fragrant;
He mourned Romance, now on the town,
    And Art, a vagrant.

Miniver loved the Medici,[2]
    Albeit he had never seen one;
He would have sinned incessantly
    Could he have been one.   20

Miniver cursed the commonplace
    And eyed a khaki suit with loathing;
He missed the medieval grace
    Of iron clothing.

---

1.   Thebes was an ancient Greek city, famous in history and legend; Camelot was the site of the legendary King Arthur's court; Priam was king of Troy during the Trojan War.
2.   A family of bankers and statesmen, notorious for their cruelty, who ruled Florence for nearly two centuries during the Italian Renaissance.

Miniver scorned the gold he sought,
    But sore annoyed was he without it;
Miniver thought, and thought, and thought,
    And thought about it.

Miniver Cheevy, born too late,
    Scratched his head and kept on thinking;   30
Miniver coughed, and called it fate,
    And kept on drinking.

We Wear the Mask

PAUL LAURENCE DUNBAR   [1872–1906]

We wear the mask that grins and lies,
It hides our cheeks and shades our eyes—
This debt we pay to human gulle;
With torn and bleeding hearts we smile,
And mouth with myriad subtleties.

Why should the world be over-wise,
In counting all our tears and sighs?
Nay, let them only see us, while
    We wear the mask.

We smile, but, O great Christ, our cries
To thee from tortured souls arise.
We sing, but oh the clay is vile   10
Beneath our feet, and long the mile;
But let the world dream otherwise,
    We wear the mask!

Patterns

AMY LOWELL   [1874–1925]

I walk down the garden-paths,
And all the daffodils

Are blowing, and the bright blue squills.
I walk down the patterned garden-paths
In my stiff, brocaded gown.
With my powdered hair and jeweled fan,
I too am a rare
Pattern. As I wander down
The garden-paths.

My dress is richly figured,   10
And the train
Makes a pink and silver stain
On the gravel, and the thrift
Of the borders.
Just a plate of current fashion,
Tripping by in high-heeled, ribboned shoes.
Not a softness anywhere about me,
Only whalebone and brocade.
And I sink on a seat in the shade
Of a lime tree. For my passion   20
Wars against the stiff brocade.
The daffodils and squills
Flutter in the breeze
As they please.
And I weep;
For the lime-tree is in blossom
And one small flower has dropped upon my bosom.

And the plashing of waterdrops
In the marble fountain
Comes down the garden-paths.   30
The dripping never stops.
Underneath my stiffened gown
Is the softness of a woman bathing in a marble basin,
A basin in the midst of hedges grown
So thick, she cannot see her lover hiding,
But she guesses he is near,
And the sliding of the water
Seems the stroking of a dear
Hand upon her.
What is Summer in a fine brocaded gown!   40
I should like to see it lying in a heap upon the ground.
All the pink and silver crumpled up on the ground.

I would be the pink and silver as I ran along the paths,
And he would stumble after,
Bewildered by my laughter.
I should see the sun flashing from his sword-hilt and the buckles on his shoes.
I would choose

To lead him in a maze along the patterned paths,
A bright and laughing maze for my heavy-booted lover.
Till he caught me in the shade, 50
And the buttons of his waistcoat bruised my body as he clasped me,
Aching, melting, unafraid.
With the shadows of the leaves and the sundrops,
All about us in the open afternoon—
I am very like to swoon
With the weight of this brocade,
For the sun sifts through the shade.

Underneath the fallen blossom
In my bosom
Is a letter I have hid. 60
It was brought to me this morning by a rider from the Duke.
"Madam, we regret to inform you that Lord Hartwell
Died in action Thursday se'nnight."
As I read it in the white, morning sunlight,
The letters squirmed like snakes.
"Any answer, Madam," said my footman.
"No," I told him.
"See that the messenger takes some refreshment.
No, no answer." 70
And I walked into the garden,
Up and down the patterned paths,
In my stiff, correct brocade.
The blue and yellow flowers stood up proudly in the sun,
Each one.
I stood upright too,
Held rigid to the pattern
By the stiffness of my gown;
Up and down I walked,
Up and down. 80

In a month he would have been my husband.
In a month, here, underneath this lime,
We would have broke the pattern;
He for me, and I for him,
He as Colonel, I as Lady,
On this shady seat.
He had a whim
That sunlight carried blessing.
And I answered, "It shall be as you have said."
Now he is dead. 90

In Summer and in Winter I shall walk
Up and down
The patterned garden-paths
In my stiff, brocaded gown.

The squills and daffodils
Will give place to pillared roses, and to asters, and to snow.
I shall go
Up and down
In my gown.
Gorgeously arrayed,   100
Boned and stayed.
And the softness of my body will be guarded from embrace
By each button, hook, and lace.
For the man who should loose me is dead,
Fighting with the Duke in Flanders,
In a pattern called a war.
Christ! What are patterns for?

Departmental

ROBERT FROST [1874–1963]

An ant on the table cloth
Ran into a dormant moth
Of many times his size.
He showed not the least surprise.
His business wasn't with such.
He gave it scarcely a touch,
And was off on his duty run.
Yet if he encountered one
Of the hive's enquiry squad
Whose work is to find out God   10
And the nature of time and space,
He would put him onto the case.
Ants are a curious race;
One crossing with hurried tread
The body of one of their dead
Isn't given a moment's arrest—
Seems not even impressed.
But he no doubt reports to any
With whom he crosses antennae,
And they no doubt report   20
To the higher up at court.
Then word goes forth in Formic:
"Death's come to Jerry McCormic,
Our selfless forager Jerry.
Will the special Janizary
Whose office it is to bury

The dead of the commissary
Go bring him home to his people.
Lay him in state on a sepal.
Wrap him for shroud in a petal.   30
Embalm him with ichor of nettle.
This is the word of your Queen."
And presently on the scene
Appears a solemn mortician;
And taking formal position
With feelers calmly atwiddle,
Seizes the dead by the middle,
And heaving him high in air,
Carries him out of there.
No one stands round to stare.   40
It is nobody else's affair.

It couldn't be called ungentle.
But how thoroughly departmental.

*1. What comment does this poem make on human society? Is ant society a good meta-
phor for human society? Explain.   2. How do the diction and rhyme help establish the
tone?   3. Does the tone of the poem indicate approval or disapproval of the society pictured? Indicate specific words that convey that tone.*

Sunday Morning

WALLACE STEVENS   [1879–1955]

I
Complacencies of the peignoir, and late
Coffee and oranges in a sunny chair,
And the green freedom of a cockatoo
Upon a rug mingle to dissipate
The holy hush of ancient sacrifice.
She dreams a little, and she feels the dark
Encroachment of that old catastrophe,
As a calm darkens among water-lights.
The pungent oranges and bright, green wings
Seem things in some procession of the dead,   10
Winding across wide water, without sound.
The day is like wide water, without sound,
Stilled for the passing of her dreaming feet
Over the seas, to silent Palestine,
Dominion of the blood and sepulchre.

II
Why should she give her bounty to the dead?
What is divinity if it can come
Only in silent shadows and in dreams?
Shall she not find in comforts of the sun,
In pungent fruit and bright, green wings, or else   20
In any balm or beauty of the earth,
Things to be cherished like the thought of heaven?
Divinity must live within herself:
Passions of rain, or moods in falling snow;
Grievings in loneliness, or unsubdued
Elations when the forest blooms; gusty
Emotions on wet roads on autumn nights;
All pleasures and all pains, remembering
The bough of summer and the winter branch.
These are the measures destined for her soul.   30

III
Jove in the clouds had his inhuman birth.
No mother suckled him, no sweet land gave
Large-mannered motions to his mythy mind
He moved among us, as a muttering king,
Magnificent, would move among his hinds,
Until our blood, commingling, virginal,
With heaven, brought such requital to desire
The very hinds discerned it, in a star.
Shall our blood fail? Or shall it come to be
The blood of paradise? And shall the earth   40
Seem all of paradise that we shall know?
The sky will be much friendlier then than now,
A part of labor and a part of pain,
And next in glory to enduring love,
Not this dividing and indifferent blue.

IV
She says, "I am content when wakened birds,
Before they fly, test the reality
Of misty fields, by their sweet questionings;
But when the birds are gone, and their warm fields
Return no more, where, then, is paradise?"   50
There is not any haunt of prophecy,
Nor any old chimera of the grave,
Neither the golden underground, nor isle
Melodious, where spirits gat them home,
Nor visionary south, nor cloudy palm
Remote on heaven's hill, that has endured
As April's green endures; or will endure
Like her remembrance of awakened birds,
Or her desire for June and evening, tipped
By the consummation of the swallow's wings.   60

V

She says, "But in contentment I still feel
The need of some imperishable bliss."
Death is the mother of beauty; hence from her,
Alone, shall come fulfilment to our dreams
And our desires. Although she strews the leaves
Of sure obliteration on our paths,
The path sick sorrow took, the many paths
Where triumph rang its brassy phrase, or love
Whispered a little out of tenderness,
She makes the willow shiver in the sun   70
For maidens who were wont to sit and gaze
Upon the grass, relinquished to their feet.
She causes boys to pile new plums and pears
On disregarded plate. The maidens taste
And stray impassioned in the littering leaves.

VI

Is there no change of death in paradise?
Does ripe fruit never fall? Or do the boughs
Hang always heavy in that perfect sky,
Unchanging, yet so like our perishing earth,
With rivers like our own that seek for seas   80
They never find, the same receding shores
That never touch with inarticulate pang?
Why set the pear upon those river-banks
Or spice the shores with odors of the plum?
Alas, that they should wear our colors there,
The silken weavings of our afternoons,
And pick the strings of our insipid lutes!
Death is the mother of beauty, mystical,
Within whose burning bosom we devise
Our earthly mothers waiting, sleeplessly.   90

VII

Supple and turbulent, a ring of men
Shall chant in orgy on a summer morn
Their boisterous devotion to the sun,
Not as a god, but as a god might be,
Naked among them, like a savage source.
Their chant shall be a chant of paradise,
Out of their blood, returning to the sky;
And in their chant shall enter, voice by voice,
The windy lake wherein their lord delights,
The trees, like serafin, and echoing hills,   100
That choir among themselves long afterward.
They shall know well the heavenly fellowship
Of men that perish and of summer morn.
And whence they came and whither they shall go
The dew upon their feet shall manifest.

VIII

She hears, upon that water without sound,
A voice that cries, "The tomb in Palestine
Is not the porch of spirits lingering.
It is the grave of Jesus, where he lay."
We live in an old chaos of the sun,   110
Or old dependency of day and night,
Or island solitude, unsponsored, free,
Of that wide water, inescapable.
Deer walk upon our mountains, and the quail
Whistle about us their spontaneous cries;
Sweet berries ripen in the wilderness;
And, in the isolation of the sky,
At evening, casual flocks of pigeons make
Ambiguous undulations as they sink,
Downward to darkness, on extended wings.   120

1. *In the opening stanza, the lady's enjoyment of a late Sunday morning breakfast in a relaxed and sensuous atmosphere is troubled by thoughts of what Sunday morning should mean to her. What are the thoughts that disturb her complacency?* **2.** *The poem is, in a sense, a commentary by the speaker on the lady's desire for truth and certainty more enduring than the physical world can provide. Is the speaker sympathetic to her quest? Explain.* **3.** *What does the speaker mean when he says, "Death is the mother of beauty" (ll. 63 and 88)?* **4.** *In stanza VI, what is the speaker's attitude toward the conventional Christian conception of paradise?* **5.** *Stanza VII presents the speaker's vision of an alternative religion. How does it differ from the paradise of stanza VI?* **6.** *In what ways does the cry in the final stanza (ll. 107–110) state the lady's dilemma? How do the lines about the pigeons at the end of the poem sum up the speaker's belief?*

If We Must Die

CLAUDE McKAY   [1890–1948]

If we must die, let it not be like hogs
Hunted and penned in an inglorious spot,
While round us bark the mad and hungry dogs,
Making their mock at our accursèd lot.
If we must die, O let us nobly die,
So that our precious blood may not be shed
In vain; then even the monsters we defy
Shall be constrained to honor us though dead!
O kinsmen! we must meet the common foe!
Though far outnumbered let us show us brave,   10
And for their thousand blows deal one deathblow!

What though before us lies the open grave?
Like men we'll face the murderous, cowardly pack,
Pressed to the wall, dying, but fighting back!

the Cambridge ladies
who live in furnished souls

E. E. CUMMINGS   [1894–1962]

the Cambridge ladies who live in furnished souls
are unbeautiful and have comfortable minds
(also, with the church's protestant blessings
daughters, unscented shapeless spirited)
they believe in Christ and Longfellow, both dead,
are invariably interested in so many things—
at the present writing one still finds
delighted fingers knitting for the is it Poles?
perhaps. While permanent faces coyly bandy
scandal of Mrs. N and Professor D   10
. . . . the Cambridge ladies do not care, above
Cambridge if sometimes in its box of
sky lavender and cornerless, the
moon rattles like a fragment of angry candy

1. What images does the poet use to describe the Cambridge ladies? What do the images suggest? 2. What is the effect of the interruption "is it" in line 8? 3. In the final lines the moon seems to protest against the superficiality of these ladies. What is the effect of comparing the moon to a fragment of candy?

next to of course god america i

E. E. CUMMINGS   [1894–1962]

"next to of course god america i
love you land of the pilgrims' and so forth oh
say can you see by the dawn's early my

country 'tis of centuries come and go
and are no more what of it we should worry
in every language even deafanddumb
thy sons acclaim your glorious name by gorry
by jingo by gee by gosh by gum
why talk of beauty what could be more beautiful than these heroic happy dead
who rushed like lions to the roaring slaughter
they did not stop to think they died instead
then shall the voice of liberty be mute?"

He spoke. And drank rapidly a glass of water

10

Harlem

LANGSTON HUGHES   [1902–1967]

What happens to a dream deferred?

    Does it dry up
    like a raisin in the sun?
    Or fester like a sore—
    And then run?
    Does it stink like rotten meat?
    Or crust and sugar over—
    like a syrupy sweet?

    Maybe it just sags
    like a heavy load.

10

    Or does it explode?

Same in Blues

LANGSTON HUGHES   [1902–1967]

I said to my baby,
Baby, take it slow.
I can't, she said, I can't!
I got to go!

There's a certain
amount of traveling
in a dream deferred.

Lulu said to Leonard,
I want a diamond ring.
Leonard said to Lulu,
You won't get a goddam thing!   10

A certain
amount of nothing
in a dream deferred.

Daddy, daddy, daddy,
All I want is you.
You can have me, baby—
but my lovin' days is through.

A certain
amount of impotence
in a dream deferred.   20

Three parties
On my party line—
But that third party,
Lord, ain't mine!

There's liable
to be confusion
in a dream deferred.

From river to river
Uptown and down,   30
There's liable to be confusion
when a dream gets kicked around.

The Unknown Citizen

(To JS/07/M/378 This Marble Monument Is Erected by the State)

W. H. AUDEN   [1907–1973]

He was found by the Bureau of Statistics to be
One against whom there was no official complaint,
And all the reports on his conduct agree

That, in the modern sense of an old-fashioned word, he was a saint,
For in everything he did he served the Greater Community.
Except for the War till the day he retired
He worked in a factory and never got fired,
But satisfied his employers, Fudge Motors Inc.
Yet he wasn't a scab or odd in his views,
For his Union reports that he paid his dues,   10
(Our report on his Union shows it was sound)
And our Social Psychology workers found
That he was popular with his mates and liked a drink.
The Press are convinced that he bought a paper every day
And that his reactions to advertisements were normal in every way.
Policies taken out in his name prove that he was fully insured,
And his Health-card shows he was once in hospital but left it cured.
Both Producers Research and High-Grade Living declare
He was fully sensible to the advantages of the Installment Plan
And had everything necessary to the Modern Man,   20
A phonograph, a radio, a car and a frigidaire.
Our researchers into Public Opinion are content
That he held the proper opinions for the time of year;
When there was peace, he was for peace; when there was war, he went.
He was married and added five children to the population,
Which our Eugenist says was the right number for a parent of his generation,
And our teachers report that he never interfered with their education.
Was he free? Was he happy? The question is absurd:
Had anything been wrong, we should certainly have heard.   30

Dolor

THEODORE ROETHKE [1908–1963]

I have known the inexorable sadness of pencils,
Neat in their boxes, dolor of pad and paper-weight,
All the misery of manilla folders and mucilage,
Desolation in immaculate public places,
Lonely reception room, lavatory, switchboard,
The unalterable pathos of basin and pitcher,
Ritual of multigraph, paper-clip, comma,
Endless duplication of lives and objects.
And I have seen dust from the walls of institutions,
Finer than flour, alive, more dangerous than silica,   10
Sift, almost invisible, through long afternoons of tedium,
Dropping a fine film on nails and delicate eyebrows,
Glazing the pale hair, the duplicate grey standard faces.

From a Correct Address in a Suburb of a Major City

HELEN SORRELLS   [b. 1908]

She wears her middle age like a cowled
gown, sleeved in it, folded high
at the breast,

charming, proper at cocktails
but the inner one raging
and how to hide her,

how to keep her leashed, contain
the heat of her, the soaring cry
never yet loosed,

demanding a chance before the years devour her,   10
before the marrow of her fine long legs
congeals and she

settles forever for this street, this house,
her face set to the world
sweet, sweet

above the shocked, astonished
hunger.

The Conscientious Objector

KARL SHAPIRO   [b. 1913]

The gates clanged and they walked you into jail
More tense than felons but relieved to find
The hostile world shut out, flags that dripped
From every mother's windowpane, obscene
The bloodlust sweating from the public heart,
The dog authority slavering at your throat.
A sense of quiet, of pulling down the blind
Possessed you. Punishment you felt was clean.

The decks, the catwalks, and the narrow light
Composed a ship. This was a mutinous crew   10
Troubling the captains for plain decencies,
A *Mayflower* brim with pilgrims headed out
To establish new theocracies to west,
A Noah's ark coasting the topmost seas
Ten miles above the sodomites and fish.
These inmates loved the only living doves.

Like all men hunted from the world you made
A good community, voyaging the storm
To no safe Plymouth or green Ararat;
Trouble or calm, the men with Bibles prayed,   20
The gaunt politicals construed our hate.
The opposite of all armies, you were best
Opposing uniformity and yourselves;
Prison and personality were your fate.

You suffered not so physically but knew
Maltreatment, hunger, ennui of the mind.
Well might the soldier kissing the hot beach
Erupting in his face damn all your kind.
Yet you who saved neither yourselves nor us
Are equally with those who shed the blood   30
The heroes of our cause. Your conscience is
What we come back to in the armistice.

1. *Who is the speaker of this poem, and what are his assumptions about "good citizenship"?*   2. *Why does the conscientious objector feel that punishment is clean (l. 8)?*   3. *The prison is compared to the Mayflower and Noah's ark. Do you find the allusive comparisons between the prisoners and the occupants of the Mayflower and the ark effective? Explain.*   4. *What, finally, are the differences between the man described here and Auden's unknown citizen? Is the conscientious objector "free"? "Happy"? Is he an unknown citizen?*

Naming of Parts

HENRY REED   [b. 1914]

Today we have naming of parts. Yesterday,
We had daily cleaning. And tomorrow morning,
We shall have what to do after firing. But today,
Today we have naming of parts. Japonica
Glistens like coral in all of the neighboring gardens,
        And today we have naming of parts.

This is the lower sling swivel. And this
Is the upper sling swivel, whose use you will see,
When you are given your slings. And this is the piling swivel,
Which in your case you have not got. The branches   10
Hold in the gardens their silent, eloquent gestures,
      Which in our case we have not got.

This is the safety-catch, which is always released
With an easy flick of the thumb. And please do not let me
See anyone using his finger. You can do it quite easy
If you have any strength in your thumb. The blossoms
Are fragile and motionless, never letting anyone see
      Any of them using their finger.

And this you can see is the bolt. The purpose of this
Is to open the breech, as you see. We can slide it   20
Rapidly backwards and forwards: we call this
Easing the spring. And rapidly backwards and forwards
The early bees are assaulting and fumbling the flowers:
      They call it easing the Spring.

They call it easing the Spring: it is perfectly easy
If you have any strength in your thumb: like the bolt,
And the breech, and the cocking-piece, and the point of balance,
Which in our case we have not got; and the almond-blossom
Silent in all of the gardens and the bees going backwards and forwards,
      For today we have naming of parts.   30

1. *The poem has two speakers. Identify their speeches, and characterize the
speakers.* **2.** *The poem incorporates a subtle underlying sexuality. Trace the language
that generates it. What function does that sexuality serve in the poem?* **3.** *The last line
of each stanza repeats a phrase from within the stanza. What is the effect of the
repetition?*

Judging Distances

HENRY REED [b. 1914]

Not only how far away, but the way that you say it
Is very important. Perhaps you may never get
The knack of judging a distance, but at least you know
How to report on a landscape: the central sector,
The right of arc and that, which we had last Tuesday,
      And at least you know

That maps are of time, not place, so far as the army
Happens to be concerned—the reason being,
Is one which need not delay us. Again, you know
There are three kinds of tree, three only, the fir and the poplar,   10
And those which have bushy tops to; and lastly
    That things only seem to be things.

A barn is not called a barn, to put it more plainly,
Or a field in the distance, where sheep may be safely grazing.
You must never be over-sure. You must say, when reporting:
At five o'clock in the central sector is a dozen
Of what appear to be animals; whatever you do,
    Don't call the bleeders *sheep*.

I am sure that's quite clear; and suppose, for the sake of example,
The one at the end, asleep, endeavors to tell us   20
What he sees over there to the west, and how far away,
After first having come to attention. There to the west,
On the fields of summer the sun and the shadows bestow
    Vestments of purple and gold.

The still white dwellings are like a mirage in the heat,
And under the swaying elms a man and a woman
Lie gently together. Which is, perhaps, only to say
That there is a row of houses to the left of arc,
And that under some poplars a pair of what appear to be humans
    Appear to be loving.   30

Well that, for an answer, is what we might rightly call
Moderately satisfactory only, the reason being,
Is that two things have been omitted, and those are important.
The human beings, now: in what direction are they,
And how far away, would you say? And do not forget
    There may be dead ground [1] in between.

There may be dead ground in between; and I may not have got
The knack of judging a distance; I will only venture
A guess that perhaps between me and the apparent lovers,
(Who, incidentally, appear by now to have finished,)   40
At seven o'clock from the houses, is roughly a distance
    Of about one year and a half.

1. *Identify and characterize the two speakers.* **2.** *Maps are of time (l. 7) because direction is indicated by such expressions as "at seven o'clock from the houses" (l. 41). What is the effect, then, of the last stanza?* **3.** *What devices are used to establish the central contrast of the poem? Why is the poet's judgment so clear to the reader?*

---

1. A military term describing space that cannot be reached by a given weapon.

from
The Children of the Poor

GWENDOLYN BROOKS [b. 1917]

4

First fight. Then fiddle. Ply the slipping string
With feathery sorcery; muzzle the note
With hurting love, the music that they wrote
Bewitch, bewilder. Qualify to sing
Threadwise. Devise no salt, no hempen thing
For the dear instrument to bear. Devote
The bow to silks and honey. Be remote
A while from malice and from murdering.
But first to arms, to armor. Carry hate
In front of you and harmony behind.   10
Be deaf to music and to beauty blind.
Win war. Rise bloody, maybe not too late
For having first to civilize a space
Wherein to play your violin with grace.

II

Life for my child is simple, and is good.
He knows his wish. Yes, but that is not all.
Because I know mine too.
And we both want joy of undeep and unabiding things,
Like kicking over a chair or throwing blocks out of a window
Or tipping over an icebox pan
Or snatching down curtains or fingering an electric outlet
Or a journey or a friend or an illegal kiss.
No. There is more to it than that.
It is that he has never been afraid.   10
Rather, he reaches out and lo the chair falls with a beautiful crash,
And the blocks fall, down on the people's heads,
And the water comes slooshing sloppily out across the floor.
And so forth.
Not that success, for him, is sure, infallible.
But never has he been afraid to reach.
His lesions are legion.
But reaching is his rule.

1. In sonnet 4, the poet advises the children: "First fight, Then fiddle." The meaning of "fight" is clear. What does "fiddle" symbolize?   **2.** Why does the poet advocate violence?   **3.** Is the child described in poem II different from the children addressed in sonnet 4?   **4.** Explain the meaning of line 4 in poem II.   **5.** What does "reaching" in the last line mean?

The Sundays of Satin-Legs Smith

GWENDOLYN BROOKS [b. 1917]

Inamoratas, with an approbation,
Bestowed his title. Blessed his inclination.
He wakes, unwinds, elaborately: a cat
Tawny, reluctant, royal. He is fat
And fine this morning. Definite. Reimbursed.

He waits a moment, he designs his reign,
That no performance may be plain or vain.
Then rises in a clear delirium.

He sheds, with his pajamas, shabby days.
And his desertedness, his intricate fear, the   10
Postponed resentments and the prim precautions.

Now, at his bath, would you deny him lavender
Or take away the power of his pine?
What smelly substitute, heady as wine,
Would you provide? life must be aromatic.
There must be scent, somehow there must be some.
Would you have flowers in his life? suggest
Asters? a Really Good geranium?
A white carnation? would you prescribe a Show
With the cold lilies, formal chrysanthemum   20
Magnificence, poinsettias, and emphatic
Red of prize roses? might his happiest
Alternative (you muse) be, after all,
A bit of gentle garden in the best
Of taste and straight tradition? Maybe so.
But you forget, or did you ever know,
His heritage of cabbage and pigtails,
Old intimacy with alleys, garbage pails,
Down in the deep (but always beautiful) South
Where roses blush their blithest (it is said)   30
And sweet magnolias put Chanel to shame.

No! He has not a flower to his name.
Except a feather one, for his lapel.
Apart from that, if he should think of flowers
It is in terms of dandelions or death.
Ah, there is little hope. You might as well—
Unless you care to set the world a-boil

And do a lot of equalizing things,
Remove a little ermine, say, from kings,
Shake hands with paupers and appoint them men,   40
For instance—certainly you might as well
Leave him his lotion, lavender and oil.

Let us proceed. Let us inspect, together
With his meticulous and serious love,
The innards of this closet. Which is a vault
Whose glory is not diamonds, not pearls,
Not silver plate with just enough dull shine.
But wonder-suits in yellow and in wine,
Sarcastic green and zebra-striped cobalt.
With shoulder padding that is wide   50
And cocky and determined as his pride;
Ballooning pants that taper off to ends
Scheduled to choke precisely.
                              Here are hats
Like bright umbrellas; and hysterical ties
Like narrow banners for some gathering war.

People are so in need, in need of help.
People want so much that they do not know.

Below the tinkling trade of little coins
The gold impulse not possible to show   60
Or spend. Promise piled over and betrayed.

These kneaded limbs receive the kiss of silk.
Then they receive the brave and beautiful
Embrace of some of that equivocal wool.
He looks into his mirror, loves himself—
The near curve here; the angularity
That is appropriate at just its place;
The technique of a variegated grace.

Here is all his sculpture and his art
And all his architectural design.   70
Perhaps you would prefer to this a fine
Value of marble, complicated stone.
Would have him think with horror of baroque,
Rococo. You forget and you forget.

He dances down the hotel steps that keep
Remnants of last night's high life and distress.
As spat-out purchased kisses and spilled beer.
He swallows sunshine with a secret yelp.
Passes to coffee and a roll or two.
Has breakfasted.   80

Out. Sounds about him smear,
Become a unit. He hears and does not hear
The alarm clock meddling in somebody's sleep;
Children's governed Sunday happiness;
The dry tone of a plane; a woman's oath;
Consumption's spiritless expectoration;
An indignant robin's resolute donation
Pinching a track through apathy and din;
Restaurant vendors weeping; and the L°   *elevated train*
That comes on like a slightly horrible thought.   90

Pictures, too, as usual, are blurred.
He sees and does not see the broken windows
Hiding their shame with newsprint; little girl
With ribbons decking wornness, little boy
Wearing the trousers with the decentest patch,
To honor Sunday; women on their way
From "service," temperate holiness arranged
Ably on asking faces; men estranged
From music and from wonder and from joy
But far familiar with the guiding awe   100
Of foodlessness.
        He loiters.
                Restaurant vendors
Weep, or out of them rolls a restless glee.
The Lonesome Blues, the Long-lost Blues, I Want A
Big Fat Mama. Down these sore avenues
Comes no Saint-Saëns, no piquant elusive Grieg,
And not Tschaikovsky's wayward eloquence
And not the shapely tender drift of Brahms.
But could he love them? Since a man must bring   110
To music what his mother spanked him for
When he was two: bits of forgotten hate,
Devotion: whether or not his mattress hurts:
The little dream his father humored: the thing
His sister did for money: what he ate
For breakfast—and for dinner twenty years
Ago last autumn: all his skipped desserts.

The pasts of his ancestors lean against
Him. Crowd him. Fog out his identity.
Hundreds of hungers mingle with his own,   120
Hundreds of voices advise so dexterously
He quite considers his reactions his,
Judges he walks most powerfully alone,
That everything is—simply what it is.

But movie-time approaches, time to boo
The hero's kiss, and boo the heroine

Whose ivory and yellow it is sin
For his eye to eat of. The Mickey Mouse,
However, is for everyone in the house.

Squires his lady to dinner at Joe's Eats.   130
His lady alters as to leg and eye,
Thickness and heights, such minor points as these,
From Sunday to Sunday. But no matter what
Her name or body positively she's
In Queen Lace stockings with ambitious heels
That strain to kiss the calves, and vivid shoes
Frontless and backless, Chinese fingernails,
Earrings, three layers of lipstick, intense hat
Dripping wIth the most voluble of veils.
Her affable extremes are like sweet bombs   140
About him, whom no middle grace or good
Could gratify. He had no education
In quiet arts of compromise. He would
Not understand your counsels on control, nor
Thank you for your late trouble.
                            At Joe's Eats
You get your fish or chicken on meat platters.
With coleslaw, macaroni, candied sweets,
Coffee and apple pie. You go out full.
(The end is—isn't it?—all that really matters.)   150

          And even and intrepid come
          The tender boots of night to home.

          Her body is like new brown bread
          Under the Woolworth mignonette.
          Her body is a honey bowl
          Whose waiting honey is deep and hot.
          Her body is like summer earth,
          Receptive, soft, and absolute . . .

---

1. *Who are the "you" of the poem? Why do they disapprove of Satin-Legs?* **2.** *What does the description of Satin-Legs' wardrobe (ll. 43–56) tell us about him?* **3.** *What is Satin-Legs' "heritage of cabbage and pigtails" (l. 27)? With what is that heritage contrasted?* **4.** *Is the poem a tribute to Satin-Legs or a criticism of him?*

In Goya's Greatest Scenes

LAWRENCE FERLINGHETTI [b. 1919]

In Goya's greatest scenes [1] we seem to see
                              the people of the world
          exactly at the moment when
                they first attained the title of
                              'suffering humanity'
            They writhe upon the page
                        in a veritable rage
                              of adversity
          Heaped up
                  groaning with babies and bayonets   10
                                  under cement skies
            in an abstract landscape of blasted trees
                bent statues bats wings and beaks
                      slippery gibbets
              cadavers and carnivorous cocks
          and all the final hollering monsters
                of the
                        'imagination of disaster'
            they are so bloody real
                              it is as if they really still existed   20

        And they do

            Only the landscape is changed

      They still are ranged along the roads
            plagued by legionaires
                          false windmills and demented roosters

    They are the same people
                      only further from home
        on freeways fifty lanes wide
                  on a concrete continent
                        spaced with bland billboards   30
                illustrating imbecile illusions of happiness

    The scene shows fewer tumbrils [2]

---

1. Francisco Jose de Goya (1764–1828), famous Spanish artist, celebrated for his representations of "suffering humanity."
2. Carts in which prisoners were conducted to the place of execution.

but more maimed citizens
                    in painted cars
and they have strange license plates
and engines
                    that devour America

1. To whom does the word "they" refer in line 26? 2. What is responsible for the "suffering" of modern American "humanity"?

Women

MAY SWENSON [b. 1919]

Women   Or they
   should be   should be
      pedestals   little horses
         moving   those wooden
            pedestals   sweet
               moving   oldfashioned
                  to the   painted
                     motions   rocking
                        of men   horses

         the gladdest things in the toyroom

               The   feelingly
               pegs   and then
               of their   unfeelingly
               ears   To be
               so familiar   joyfully
               and dear   ridden
               to the trusting   rockingly
            fists   ridden until
      To be chafed   the restored

egos dismount and the legs stride away

Immobile   willing
   sweetlipped   to be set
      sturdy   into motion
         and smiling   Women
            women   should be
               should always   pedestals
                  be waiting   to men

Poetry of Departures

PHILIP LARKIN   [b. 1922]

Sometimes you hear, fifth-hand,
As epitaph:
He chucked up everything
And just cleared off,
And always the voice will sound
Certain you approve
This audacious, purifying,
Elemental move.

And they are right, I think.
We all hate home   10
And having to be there:
I detest my room,
Its specially-chosen junk,
The good books, the good bed,
And my life, in perfect order:
So to hear it said

He walked out on the whole crowd
Leaves me flushed and stirred,
Like *Then she undid her dress*
Or *Take that you bastard;*   20
Surely I can, if he did?
And that helps me stay
Sober and industrious.
But I'd go today,

Yes, swagger the nut-strewn roads,
Crouch in the fo'c'sle
Stubbly with goodness, if
It weren't so artificial,
Such a deliberate step backwards
To create an object: 30
Books; china; a life
Reprehensibly perfect.

1. What motivates the kind of person who "chucked up everything and just cleared off"? Why might such an action be characterized as "purifying" and "elemental"?   **2.** In what sense is the simile of lines 16–20 appropriate? What function does it serve?   **3.** Why does the poet conclude that departing is "artificial" (l. 28) and that perfection is "reprehensible" (l. 32)?

Simplicity

LOUIS SIMPSON [b. 1923]

Climbing the staircase
step by step, feeling my way . . .
I seem to have some trouble with my vision.
The stairs are littered with paper,
eggshells, and other garbage.
Then she comes to the door.
Without eye-shadow or lipstick,
with her hair tied in a bun,
in a white dress, she seems ethereal.

"Peter," she says, "how nice!   10
I thought that you were Albert,
but he hardly ever comes."
She says, "I hope you like my dress.
It's simple. I made it myself.
Nowadays everyone's wearing simple things.
The thing is to be sincere,
and then, when you're tired of something,
you just throw it away."

I'll spare you the description
of all her simple objects: 20
the bed pushed in one corner;
the naked bulb that hangs
on a wire down from the ceiling
that is stamped out of metal
in squares, each square containing
a pattern of leaves and flowers;
the window with no blinds, admitting
daylight, and the wall
where a stream of yellow ice hangs down
in waves.   30

            She is saying
"I have sat in this room
all day. There is a time
when you just stare at the wall
all day, and nothing moves.
I can't go on like this any longer,
counting the cracks in the wall,
doting on my buttons."

I seem to be disconnected

from the voice that is speaking
and the sound of the voice that answers.
Things seem to be moving into a vacuum.
I put my head in my hands
and try to concentrate.
But the light shines through my hands,

and then (how shall I put it
exactly?) it's as though she begins
giving off vibrations,
waves of resentment, an aura
of hate you could cut with a knife . . . .
Squirming, looking over her shoulder. . . .
Her whole body seems
to shrink, and she speaks in hisses:

"They want to remove my personality.
They're giving me psychotherapy
and *ikebana,* the art of flower-arrangement.
Some day, I suppose, I'll be cured,
and then I'll go and live in the suburbs,
doting on dogs and small children."

I go down the stairs, feeling my way
step by step. When I come out,
the light on the snow is blinding.
My shoes crunch on ice and my head
goes floating along, and a voice
from a high, barred window cries
"Write me a poem!"

I Have Come To Claim

JUDY GRAHN [b. 1940]

I have come to claim
Marilyn Monroe's body
for the sake of my own.
dig it up, hand it over,
cram it in this paper sack.
hubba. hubba. hubba.
look at those luscious
long brown bones, that wide and crusty
pelvis. ha Ha, oh she wanted so much to be serious

but she never stops smiling now.
Has she lost her mind?

Marilyn, be serious—they're taking
your picture, and they're taking the pictures
of eight young women in New York City
who murdered themselves for being pretty
by the same method as you, the very
next day, after you!
I have claimed their bodies too,
they smile up out of my paper sack
like brainless cinderellas.

the reporters are furious, they're asking
me questions
what right does a women have
to Marilyn Monroe's body? and what
am I doing for lunch? They think I
mean to eat you. Their teeth are lurid
and they want to pose me, leaning
on the shovel, nude. Dont squint.
But when one of the reporters comes too close
I beat him, bust his camera
with your long, smooth thigh
and with your lovely knucklebone
I break his eye.

Long ago you wanted to write poems;
Be serious, Marilyn
I am going to take you in this paper sack
around the world, and
write on it:—the poems of Marilyn Monroe—
Dedicated to all princes,
the male poets who were so sorry to see you go,
before they had a crack at you.
They wept for you, and also
they wanted to stuff you
while you still had a little meat left
in useful places;
but they were too slow.

Now I shall take them my paper sack
and we shall act out a poem together:
"How would you like to see Marilyn Monroe,
in action, smiling, and without her clothes?"
We shall wait long enough to see them make familiar faces
and then I shall beat them with your skull.
hubba. hubba. hubba. hubba. hubba.
Marilyn, be serious
Today I have come to claim your body for my own.

Eleanor Rigby

JOHN LENNON [b. 1940] and PAUL McCARTNEY [b. 1942]

Ah, look at all the lonely people!
Ah, look at all the lonely people!
Eleanor Rigby picks up the rice
    in the church
Where a wedding has been.
Lives in a dream.
Waits at the window, wearing the face
    that she keeps in a jar by the door.
Who is it for?

All the lonely people,   10
    where do they all come from?
All the lonely people,
    where do they all belong?

Father McKenzie writing the words
    of a sermon that no one will hear—
No one comes near. Look at him
    working, darning his socks in the night
    when there's nobody there.
What does he care?

All the lonely people,   20
    where do they all come from?
All the lonely people.
    where do they all belong?

Ah, look at all the lonely people!
Ah, look at all the lonely people!
Eleanor Rigby died in the church and
    was buried along with her name.
Nobody came.
Father McKenzie wiping the dirt from
    his hands as he walks from the grave.   30
No one was saved.

All the lonely people,
    where do they all come from?
All the lonely people,
    where do they all belong?

1. How does the first stanza establish Eleanor Rigby's character? What is the meaning of lines 7–8? 2. What does the portrait of Father McKenzie contribute to our understanding of the theme of the lyric? 3. What signifiance has the juxtaposition of Father McKenzie's writing "a sermon that no one will hear" and "darning his socks in the night" (stanza 3)? 4. What is the significance of Eleanor Rigby's dying in the church? Why was "No one saved" (l. 31)? 5. What answers, if any, does the poem suggest to the questions in the last stanza?

Blowin' in the Wind

BOB DYLAN [b. 1941]

How many roads must a man walk down
Before you call him a man?
Yes, 'n' how many seas must a white dove sail
Before she sleeps in the sand?
Yes, 'n' how many times must the cannon balls fly
Before they're forever banned?
The answer, my friend, is blowin' in the wind,
The answer is blowin' in the wind.

How many times must a man look up
Before he can see the sky?   10
Yes, 'n' how many ears must one man have
Before he can hear people cry?
Yes, 'n' how many deaths will it take till he knows
That too many people have died?
The answer, my friend, is blowin' in the wind,
The answer is blowin' in the wind.

How many years can a mountain exist
Before it's washed to the sea?
Yes, 'n' how many years can some people exist
Before they're allowed to be free?   20
Yes, 'n' how many times can a man turn his head,
Pretending he just doesn't see?
The answer, my friend, is blowin' in the wind,
The answer is blowin' in the wind.

Dreams

NIKKI GIOVANNI [b. 1943]

i used to dream militant
dreams of taking
over america to show
these white folks how it should be
done
i used to dream radical dreams
of blowing everyone away with my perceptive powers
of correct analysis
i even used to think i'd be the one
to stop the riot and negotiate the peace   10
then i awoke and dug
that if i dreamed natural
dreams of being a natural
woman doing what a woman
does when she's natural
i would have a revolution

Do What You Want, Be What You Are

DARYL HALL [b. 1946] AND JOHN OATES [b. 1948]

Do what you want girl, but be what you are.
There ain't no right or wrong way,
Just a play from the heart.
It ain't a sign of weakness to give yourself away,
Because the strong give up and move on,
While the weak give up and stay.

Chorus:
So do what you want to do,
But be what you are.

Do you believe in hot cars, leather bars, or movie stars?
Is that what's real?   10
Payin' dues, Earth Shoes, Chicago blues,
Is that how you feel?

You can change, but you can't conceal
What's deep inside you;
It's your game, it's your deal.

Chorus:
So do what you want to do,
But be what you are.

DRAMA

Antigone*

SOPHOCLES   [496?–406 B.C.]

CHARACTERS

Antigonê	**Teiresias**
Ismenê	**A Sentry**
Eurydicê	**A Messenger**
Creon	**Chorus**
Haimon	

SCENE.   *Before the Palace of Creon, King of Thebes. A central double door, and two lateral doors. A platform extends the length of the façade, and from this platform three steps lead down into the "orchestra," or chorus-ground.*

TIME.   *Dawn of the day after the repulse of the Argive army from the assault on Thebes.*

Prologue

[*Antigonê and Ismenê enter from the central door of the Palace.*]

Antigonê.   Ismenê, dear sister,
　　You would think that we had already suffered enough
　　For the curse on Oedipus[1]:
　　I cannot imagine any grief
　　That you and I have not gone through. And now—

---

*An English version by Dudley Fitts and Robert Fitzgerald.
1.   Oedipus, a former King of Thebes, unwittingly killed his father and married his own mother, Io-castê. By her he had four children, the sisters Antigonê and Ismenê and the brothers Polyneicês and Eteoclês. When Oedipus realized what he had done, he blinded himself and left Thebes. Eteoclês drove Polyneicês out of Thebes after a quarrel, but Polyneicês returned with an army and laid siege to Thebes. In the ensuing struggle, the brothers killed each other. Creon became king and, as a punishment, decreed that Polyneicês be denied the rites of burial.

Have they told you of the new decree of our King Creon?

Ismenê. I have heard nothing: I know
That two sisters lost two brothers, a double death
In a single hour; and I know that the Argive army
Fled in the night; but beyond this, nothing.   *10*

Antigonê. I thought so. And that is why I wanted you
To come out here with me. There is something we must do.

Ismenê. Why do you speak so strangely?

Antigonê. Listen, Ismenê:
Creon buried our brother Eteoclês
With military honors, gave him a soldier's funeral,
And it was right that he should; but Polyneicês,
Who fought as bravely and died as miserably,—
They say that Creon has sworn
No one shall bury him, no one mourn for him,   *20*
But his body must lie in the fields, a sweet treasure
For carrion birds to find as they search for food.
That is what they say, and our good Creon is coming here
To announce it publicly; and the penalty—
Stoning to death in the public square!

There it is,
And now you can prove what you are:
A true sister, or a traitor to your family.

Ismenê. Antigonê, you are mad! What could I possibly do?

Antigonê. You must decide whether you will help me or not.

Ismenê. I do not understand you. Help you in what?   *30*

Antigonê. Ismenê, I am going to bury him. Will you come?

Ismenê. Bury him! You have just said the new law forbids it.

Antigonê. He is my brother. And he is your brother, too.

Ismenê. But think of the danger! Think what Creon will do!

Antigonê. Creon is not strong enough to stand in my way.

Ismenê. Ah sister!
Oedipus died, everyone hating him
For what his own search brought to light, his eyes
Ripped out by his own hand; and Iocastê died,
His mother and wife at once: she twisted the cords   *40*
That strangled her life; and our two brothers died,
Each killed by the other's sword. And we are left:
But oh, Antigonê,
Think how much more terrible than these
Our own death would be if we should go against Creon
And do what he has forbidden! We are only women,
We cannot fight with men, Antigonê!
The law is strong, we must give in to the law

In this thing, and in worse. I beg the Dead
To forgive me, but I am helpless: I must yield   50
To those in authority. And I think it is dangerous business
To be always meddling.

Antigonê.   If that is what you think,
I should not want you, even if you asked to come.
You have made your choice, you can be what you want to be.
But I will bury him; and if I must die,
I say that this crime is holy: I shall lie down
With him in death, and I shall be as dear
To him as he to me.

                    It is the dead,
Not the living, who make the longest demands:
We die for ever . . .

                    You may do as you like,   60
Since apparently the laws of the gods mean nothing to you.

Ismenê.   They mean a great deal to me; but I have no strength
To break laws that were made for the public good.

Antigonê.   That must be your excuse, I suppose. But as for me,
I will bury the brother I love.

Ismenê.   Antigonê,
I am so afraid for you!

Antigonê.   You need not be:
You have yourself to consider, after all.

Ismenê.   But no one must hear of this, you must tell no one!
I will keep it a secret, I promise!

Antigonê.   Oh tell it! Tell everyone!
Think how they'll hate you when it all comes out   70
If they learn that you knew about it all the time!

Ismenê.   So fiery! You should be cold with fear.

Antigonê.   Perhaps. But I am doing only what I must.

Ismenê.   But can you do it? I say that you cannot.

Antigonê.   Very well: when my strength gives out, I shall do no more.

Ismenê.   Impossible things should not be tried at all.

Antigonê.   Go away, Ismenê:
I shall be hating you soon, and the dead will too,
For your words are hateful. Leave me my foolish plan:
I am not afraid of the danger; if it means death,   80
It will not be the worst of deaths—death without honor.

Ismenê.   Go then, if you feel that you must.
You are unwise,
But a loyal friend indeed to those who love you.

[*Exit into the Palace. Antigonê goes off, L. Enter the Chorus.*]

Párodos[2]

Chorus.   Now the long blade of the sun, lying   [*Strophe 1*]
    Level east to west, touches with glory
    Thebes of the Seven Gates. Open, unlidded
    Eye of golden day! O marching light
    Across the eddy and rush of Dircê's stream,[3]
    Striking the white shields of the enemy
    Thrown headlong backward from the blaze of morning!

Choragos.[4]   Polyneicês their commander
    Roused them with windy phrases,
    He the wild eagle screaming   10
    Insults above our land,
    His wings their shields of snow,
    His crest their marshalled helms.

Chorus.   Against our seven gates in a yawning ring   [*Antistrophe 1*]
    The famished spears came onward in the night;
    But before his jaws were sated with our blood,
    Or pinefire took the garland of our towers,
    He was thrown back; and as he turned, great Thebes—
    No tender victim for his noisy power—
    Rose like a dragon behind him, shouting war.   20

Choragos.   For God hates utterly
    The bray of bragging tongues;
    And when he beheld their smiling,
    Their swagger of golden helms,
    The frown of his thunder blasted
    Their first man from our walls.

Chorus.   We heard his shout of triumph high in the air   [*Strophe 2*]
    Turn to a scream; far out in a flaming arc
    He fell with his windy torch, and the earth struck him.
    And others storming in fury no less than his   30
    Found shock of death in the dusty joy of battle.

Choragos.   Seven captains at seven gates
    Yielded their clanging arms to the god
    That bends the battle-line and breaks it.
    These two only, brothers in blood,

---

2.   The *Párodos* is the ode sung by the Chorus as it entered the theater and moved down the aisles to the playing area. The *strophe,* in Greek tragedy, is the unit of verse the Chorus chanted as it moved to the left in a dance rhythm. The Chorus sang the *antistrophe* as it moved to the right, and the *epode* while standing still.
3.   A stream near Thebes.
4.   Choragos is the leader of the Chorus.

Face to face in matchless rage,
Mirroring each the other's death,
Clashed in long combat.

Chorus. But now in the beautiful morning of victory   [*Antistrophe 2*]
Let Thebes of the many chariots sing for joy!   40
With hearts for dancing we'll take leave of war:
Our temples shall be sweet with hymns of praise,
And the long night shall echo with our chorus.

Scene I

Choragos. But now at last our new King is coming:
Creon of Thebes, Menoikeus' son.
In this auspicious dawn of his reign
What are the new complexities
That shifting Fate has woven for him?
What is his counsel? Why has he summoned
The old men to hear him?

[*Enter Creon from the Palace, C. He addresses the Chorus from the top step.*]

Creon. Gentlemen: I have the honor to inform you that our Ship of State, which recent storms have threatened to destroy, has come safely to harbor at last, guided by the merciful wisdom of Heaven. I have summoned you here this morning because I know that I can depend upon you: your devotion to King Laïos was absolute; you never hesitated in your duty to our late ruler Oedipus; and when Oedipus died, your loyalty was transferred to his children. Unfortunately, as you know, his two sons, the princes Eteoclês and Polyneicês, have killed each other in battle; and I, as the next in blood, have succeeded to the full power of the throne.

I am aware, of course, that no Ruler can expect complete loyalty from his subjects until he has been tested in office. Nevertheless, I say to you at the very outset that I have nothing but contempt for the kind of Governor who is afraid, for whatever reason, to follow the course that he knows is best for the State; and as for the man who sets private friendship above the public welfare,—I have no use for him, either. I call God to witness that if I saw my country headed for ruin, I should not be afraid to speak out plainly; and I need hardly remind you that I would never have any dealings with an enemy of the people. No one values friendship more highly than I; but we must remember that friends made at the risk of wrecking our Ship are not real friends at all.

These are my principles, at any rate, and that is why I have made the following decision concerning the sons of Oedipus: Eteoclês, who died as a man should die, fighting for his country, is to be buried with full military honors, with all the ceremony that is usual when the greatest heroes die; but his brother Polyneices, who broke his exile to come back with fire and sword against his native city and the shrines of his fathers' gods, whose one idea was to spill the blood of his blood and sell his own people into slavery—Polyneicês, I say, is to have no burial: no man is to touch him or say the least prayer for him; he shall lie on the plain, unburied; and the birds and the scavenging dogs can do with him whatever they like.

This is my command, and you can see the wisdom behind it. As long as I am King, no traitor is going to be honored with the loyal man. But whoever shows by word and deed that he is on the side of the State,—he shall have my respect while he is living and my reverence when he is dead.

Choragos. If that is your will, Creon son of Menoikeus,
You have the right to enforce it: we are yours.

Creon. That is my will. Take care that you do your part.

Choragos. We are old men: let the younger ones carry it out.

Creon. I do not mean that: the sentries have been appointed.

Choragos. Then what is it that you would have us do?

Creon. You will give no support to whoever breaks this law.

Choragos. Only a crazy man is in love with death!   50

Creon. And death it is; yet money talks, and the wisest
Have sometimes been known to count a few coins too many.

[*Enter Sentry from L.*]

Sentry. I'll not say that I'm out of breath from running, King, because every time I stopped to think about what I have to tell you, I felt like going back. And all the time a voice kept saying, "You fool, don't you know you're walking straight into trouble?"; and then another voice: "Yes, but if you let somebody else get the news to Creon first, it will be even worse than that for you!" But good sense won out, at least I hope it was good sense, and here I am with a story that makes no sense at all; but I'll tell it anyhow, because, as they say, what's going to happen's going to happen, and—

Creon. Come to the point. What have you to say?

Sentry. I did not do it. I did not see who did it. You must not punish me for what someone else has done.

Creon. A comprehensive defense! More effective, perhaps,
If I knew its purpose. Come: what is it?

Sentry. A dreadful thing . . . I don't know how to put it—

Creon. Out with it!

Sentry.   Well, then;
The dead man—
                    Polyneicês—

[*Pause. The Sentry is overcome, fumbles for words. Creon waits impassively.*]

                    out there—

someone,—

New dust on the slimy flesh! 70

[*Pause. No sign from Creon.*]

Someone has given it burial that way, and
Gone . . .

[*Long pause. Creon finally speaks with deadly control.*]

Creon.   And the man who dared do this?
Sentry.   I swear I
Do not know! You must believe me!
Listen:
The ground was dry, not a sign of digging, no,
Not a wheeltrack in the dust, no trace of anyone.
It was when they relieved us this morning: and one of them,
The corporal, pointed to it.
There it was,
The strangest—
Look:
The body, just mounded over with light dust: you see? 80
Not buried really, but as if they'd covered it
Just enough for the ghost's peace. And no sign
Of dogs or any wild animal that had been there.

And then what a scene there was! Every man of us
Accusing the other: we all proved the other man did it,
We all had proof that we could not have done it.
We were ready to take hot iron in our hands,
Walk through fire, swear by all the gods,
It was not I!
I do not know who it was, but it was not I! 90

[*Creon's rage has been mounting steadily, but the Sentry is too intent upon his
story to notice it.*]

And then, when this came to nothing, someone said
A thing that silenced us and made us stare
Down at the ground: you had to be told the news,
And one of us had to do it! We threw the dice,
And the bad luck fell to me. So here I am,
No happier to be here than you are to have me:
Nobody likes the man who brings bad news.
Choragos.   I have been wondering, King: can it be that the gods have done
this?
Creon [*furiously*].   Stop!
Must you doddering wrecks 100

Go out of your heads entirely? "The gods!"
Intolerable!
The gods favor this corpse? Why? How had he served them?
Tried to loot their temples, burn their images,
Yes, and the whole State, and its laws with it!
Is it your senile opinion that the gods love to honor bad men?
A pious thought!—
                    No, from the very beginning
There have been those who have whispered together,
Stiff-necked anarchists, putting their heads together,
Scheming against me in alleys. These are the men,   *110*
And they have bribed my own guard to do this thing.
[*Sententiously.*] Money!
There's nothing in the world so demoralizing as money.
Down go your cities,
Homes gone, men gone, honest hearts corrupted,
Crookedness of all kinds, and all for money!
[*To Sentry.*]   But you—!
I swear by God and by the throne of God,
The man who has done this thing shall pay for it!
Find that man, bring him here to me, or your death
Will be the least of your problems: I'll string you up   *120*
Alive, and there will be certain ways to make you
Discover your employer before you die;
And the process may teach you a lesson you seem to have missed:
The dearest profit is sometimes all too dear:
That depends on the source. Do you understand me?
A fortune won is often misfortune.

Sentry.   King, may I speak?
Creon.   Your very voice distresses me.
Sentry.   Are you sure that it is my voice, and not your conscience?
Creon.   By God, he wants to analyze me now!
Sentry.   It is not what I say, but what has been done, that hurts you.   *130*
Creon.   You talk too much.
Sentry.   Maybe; but I've done nothing.
Creon.   Sold your soul for some silver: that's all you've done.
Sentry.   How dreadful it is when the right judge judges wrong!
Creon.   Your figures of speech
May entertain you now; but unless you bring me the man,
You will get little profit from them in the end.

[*Exit Creon into the Palace.*]

Sentry.   "Bring me the man"—!
I'd like nothing better than bringing him the man!
But bring him or not, you have seen the last of me here.

At any rate, I am safe!   140

[*Exit Sentry.*]

Ode I

Chorus.   Numberless are the world's wonders, but none   [*Strophe 1*]
    More wonderful than man; the stormgray sea
    Yields to his prows, the huge crests bear him high;
    Earth, holy and inexhaustible, is graven
    With shining furrows where his plows have gone
    Year after year, the timeless labor of stallions.

    The lightboned birds and beasts that cling to cover,   [*Antistrophe 1*]
    The lithe fish lighting their reaches of dim water,
    All are taken, tamed in the net of his mind;
    The lion on the hill, the wild horse windy-maned,   10
    Resign to him; and his blunt yoke has broken
    The sultry shoulders of the mountain bull.

    Words also, and thought as rapid as air,   [*Strophe 2*]
    He fashions to his good use; statecraft is his,
    And his the skill that deflects the arrows of snow,
    The spears of winter rain: from every wind
    He has made himself secure—from all but one:
    In the late wind of death he cannot stand.

    O clear intelligence, force beyond all measure!   [*Antistrophe 2*]
    O fate of man, working both good and evil!   20
    When the laws are kept, how proudly his city stands!
    When the laws are broken, what of his city then?
    Never may the anárchic man find rest at my hearth,
    Never be it said that my thoughts are his thoughts.

Scene II

[*Re-enter Sentry leading Antigonê.*]

Choragos.   What does this mean? Surely this captive woman
    Is the Princess, Antigonê. Why should she be taken?
Sentry.   Here is the one who did it! We caught her
    In the very act of burying him.—Where is Creon?
Choragos.   Just coming from the house.

[*Enter Creon, C.*]

Creon.   What has happened?
Why have you come back so soon?
Sentry [*expansively*].   O King,
A man should never be too sure of anything:
I would have sworn
That you'd not see me here again: your anger
Frightened me so, and the things you threatened me with;   10
But how could I tell then
That I'd be able to solve the case so soon?
No dice-throwing this time: I was only too glad to come!

Here is this woman. She is the guilty one:
We found her trying to bury him.
Take her, then; question her; judge her as you will.
I am through with the whole thing now, and glád óf it.
Creon.   But this is Antigonê! Why have you brought her here?
Sentry.   She was burying him, I tell you!
Creon [*severely*].   Is this the truth?
Sentry.   I saw her with my own eyes. Can I say more?   20
Creon.   The details: come, tell me quickly!
Sentry.   It was like this:
After those terrible threats of yours, King,
We went back and brushed the dust away from the body.
The flesh was soft by now, and stinking,
So we sat on a hill to windward and kept guard.
No napping this time! We kept each other awake.
But nothing happened until the white round sun
Whirled in the center of the round sky over us:
Then, suddenly,
A storm of dust roared up from the earth, and the sky   30
Went out, the plain vanished with all its trees
In the stinging dark. We closed our eyes and endured it.
The whirlwind lasted a long time, but it passed;
And then we looked, and there was Antigonê!
I have seen
A mother bird come back to a stripped nest, heard
Her crying bitterly a broken note or two
For the young ones stolen. Just so, when this girl
Found the bare corpse, and all her love's work wasted,
She wept, and cried on heaven to damn the hands   40
That had done this thing.
                          And then she brought more dust
And sprinkled wine three times for her brother's ghost.

We ran and took her at once. She was not afraid,
Not even when we charged her with what she had done.
She denied nothing.
                          And this was a comfort to me,
And some uneasiness: for it is a good thing
To escape from death, but it is no great pleasure
To bring death to a friend.
                          Yet I always say
There is nothing so comfortable as your own safe skin!
Creon [*slowly, dangerously*].   And you, Antigonê,   50
     You with your head hanging,—do you confess this thing?
Antigonê.   I do. I deny nothing.
Creon [*to Sentry*].   You may go.

[*Exit Sentry.*]

     [*To Antigonê.*]   Tell me, tell me briefly:
     Had you heard my proclamation touching this matter?
Antigonê.   It was public. Could I help hearing it?
Creon.   And yet you dared defy the law.
Antigonê.   I dared.
     It was not God's proclamation. That final Justice
     That rules the world below makes no such laws.

     Your edict, King, was strong,
     But all your strength is weakness itself against   60
     The immortal unrecorded laws of God.
     They are not merely now: they were, and shall be,
     Operative for ever, beyond man utterly.

     I knew I must die, even without your decree:
     I am only mortal. And if I must die
     Now, before it is my time to die,
     Surely this is no hardship: can anyone
     Living, as I live, with evil all about me,
     Think Death less than a friend? This death of mine
     Is of no importance; but if I had left my brother   70
     Lying in death unburied, I should have suffered.
     Now I do not.
                     You smile at me. Ah Creon,
     Think me a fool, if you like; but it may well be
     That a fool convicts me of folly.
Choragos.   Like father, like daughter: both headstrong, deaf to reason!
     She has never learned to yield.
Creon.   She has much to learn.
     The inflexible heart breaks first, the toughest iron

Cracks first, and the wildest horses bend their necks
At the pull of the smallest curb.
                                        Pride? In a slave?
This girl is guilty of a double insolence,   80
Breaking the given laws and boasting of it.
Who is the man here,
She or I, if this crime goes unpunished?
Sister's child, or more than sister's child,
Or closer yet in blood—she and her sister
Win bitter death for this!
[To servants.]   Go, some of you,
Arrest Ismenê. I accuse her equally.
Bring her: you will find her sniffling in the house there.

Her mind's a traitor: crimes kept in the dark
Cry for light, and the guardian brain shudders;   90
But how much worse than this
Is brazen boasting of barefaced anarchy!
Antigonê.   Creon, what more do you want than my death?
Creon.   Nothing.
That gives me everything.
Antigone.   Then I beg you: kill me.
This talking is a great weariness: your words
Are distasteful to me, and I am sure that mine
Seem so to you. And yet they should not seem so:
I should have praise and honor for what I have done.
All these men here would praise me
Were their lips not frozen shut with fear of you.   100
[Bitterly.]   Ah the good fortune of kings,
Licensed to say and do whatever they please!
Creon.   You are alone here in that opinion.
Antigonê.   No, they are with me. But they keep their tongues in leash.
Creon.   Maybe. But you are guilty, and they are not.
Antigonê.   There is no guilt in reverence for the dead.
Creon.   But Eteoclês—was he not your brother too?
Antigonê.   My brother too.
Creon.   And you insult his memory?
Antigonê [softly].   The dead man would not say that I insult it.
Creon.   He would: for you honor a traitor as much as him.   110
Antigonê.   His own brother, traitor or not, and equal in blood.
Creon.   He made war on his country. Eteoclês defended it.
Antigonê.   Nevertheless, there are honors due all the dead.
Creon.   But not the same for the wicked as for the just.
Antigonê.   Ah Creon, Creon,
Which of us can say what the gods hold wicked?

Creon. An enemy is an enemy, even dead.

Antigonê. It is my nature to join in love, not hate.

Creon [*finally losing patience*].   Go join them, then; if you must have your
      love,

  Find it in hell!   120

Choragos. But see, Ismenê comes:

[*Enter Ismenê, guarded.*]

  Those tears are sisterly, the cloud

  That shadows her eyes rains down gentle sorrow.

Creon. You too, Ismenê,

  Snake in my ordered house, sucking my blood

  Stealthily—and all the time I never knew

  That these two sisters were aiming at my throne!

                                             Ismenê,

  Do you confess your share in this crime, or deny it?

  Answer me.

Ismenê. Yes, if she will let me say so. I am guilty.   130

Antigonê [*coldly*].   No, Ismenê. You have no right to say so.

  You would not help me, and I will not have you help me.

Ismenê. But now I know what you meant; and I am here

  To join you, to take my share of punishment.

Antigonê. The dead man and the gods who rule the dead

  Know whose act this was. Words are not friends.

Ismenê. Do you refuse me, Antigonê? I want to die with you:

  I too have a duty that I must discharge to the dead.

Antigonê. You shall not lessen my death by sharing it.

Ismenê. What do I care for life when you are dead?   140

Antigone. Ask Creon. You're always hanging on his opinions.

Ismenê. You are laughing at me. Why, Antigonê?

Antigonê. It's a joyless laughter, Ismenê.

Ismenê.   But can I do nothing?

Antigonê. Yes. Save yourself. I shall not envy you.

  There are those who will praise you; I shall have honor, too.

Ismenê. But we are equally guilty!

Antigonê.   No more, Ismenê.

  You are alive, but I belong to Death.

Creon [*to the Chorus*].   Gentlemen, I beg you to observe these girls:

  One has just now lost her mind; the other,

  It seems, has never had a mind at all.   150

Ismenê. Grief teaches the steadiest minds to waver, King.

Creon. Yours certainly did, when you assumed guilt with the guilty!

Ismenê. But how could I go on living without her?

Creon.   You are.

  She is already dead.

Ismenê.   But your own son's bride!

Creon.   There are places enough for him to push his plow.

   I want no wicked women for my sons!

Ismenê.   O dearest Haimon, how your father wrongs you!

Creon.   I've had enough of your childish talk of marriage!

Choragos.   Do you really intend to steal this girl from your son?

Creon.   No; Death will do that for me.

Choragos.   Then she must die?   160

Creon [*ironically*].   You dazzle me.

                     —But enough of this talk!

   [*To Guards.*]   You there, take them away and guard them well:

   For they are but women, and even brave men run

   When they see Death coming.

[*Exeunt Ismenê, Antigonê, and Guards.*]

Ode II

Chorus.   Fortunate is the man who has never tasted   [*Strophe 1*]
          God's vengeance!
   Where once the anger of heaven has struck, that house is shaken
   For ever: damnation rises behind each child
   Like a wave cresting out of the black northeast,
   When the long darkness under sea roars up
   And bursts drumming death upon the windwhipped sand.

   I have seen this gathering sorrow from time long past   [*Antistrophe 1*]
   Loom upon Oedipus' children: generation from generation
   Takes the compulsive rage of the enemy god.
   So lately this last flower of Oedipus' line   10
   Drank the sunlight! but now a passionate word
   And a handful of dust have closed up all its beauty.

          What mortal arrogance   [*Strophe 2*]
          Transcends the wrath of Zeus?
   Sleep cannot lull him, nor the effortless long months
   Of the timeless gods: but he is young for ever,
   And his house is the shining day of high Olympos.
          All that is and shall be,
          And all the past, is his.
   No pride on earth is free of the curse of heaven.   20

          The straying dreams of men   [*Antistrophe 2*]
          May bring them ghosts of joy:
   But as they drowse, the waking embers burn them;

Or they walk with fíxed éyes, as blind men walk.
But the ancient wisdom speaks for our own time:
>   Fate works most for woe
>   With Folly's fairest show.
Man's little pleasure is the spring of sorrow.

Scene III

Choragos.   But here is Haimon, King, the last of all your sons.
  Is it grief for Antigonê that brings him here,
  And bitterness at being robbed of his bride?

[Enter Haimon.]

Creon.   We shall soon see, and no need of diviners.

                                           —Son,

  You have heard my final judgment on that girl:
  Have you come here hating me, or have you come
  With deference and with love, whatever I do?
Haimon.   I am your son, father. You are my guide.
  You make things clear for me, and I obey you.
  No marriage means more to me than your continuing wisdom.   10
Creon.   Good. That is the way to behave: subordinate
  Everything else, my son, to your father's will.
  This is what a man prays for, that he may get
  Sons attentive and dutiful in his house,
  Each one hating his father's enemies,
  Honoring his father's friends. But if his sons
  Fail him, if they turn out unprofitably,
  What has he fathered but trouble for himself
  And amusement for the malicious?

                              So you are right
  Not to lose your head over this woman.   20
  Your pleasure with her would soon grow cold, Haimon,
  And then you'd have a hellcat in bed and elsewhere.
  Let her find her husband in Hell!
  Of all the people in this city, only she
  Has had contempt for my law and broken it.

  Do you want me to show myself weak before the people?
  Or to break my sworn word? No, and I will not.
  The woman dies.
  I suppose she'll plead "family ties." Well, let her.
  If I permit my own family to rebel,   30
  How shall I earn the world's obedience?

Show me the man who keeps his house in hand,
He's fit for public authority.
                              I'll have no dealings
With law-breakers, critics of the government:
Whoever is chosen to govern should be obeyed—
Must be obeyed, in all things, great and small,
Just and unjust! O Haimon,
The man who knows how to obey, and that man only,
Knows how to give commands when the time comes.
You can depend on him, no matter how fast   40
The spears come: he's a good soldier, he'll stick it out.

Anarchy, anarchy! Show me a greater evil!
This is why cities tumble and the great houses rain down,
This is what scatters armies!

No, no: good lives are made so by discipline.
We keep the laws then, and the lawmakers,
And no woman shall seduce us. If we must lose,
Let's lose to a man, at least! Is a woman stronger than we?
Choragos.   Unless time has rusted my wits,
What you say, King, is said with point and dignity.   50
Haimon [*boyishly earnest*].   Father:
Reason is God's crowning gift to man, and you are right
To warn me against losing mine. I cannot say—
I hope that I shall never want to say!—that you
Have reasoned badly. Yet there are other men
Who can reason, too; and their opinions might be helpful.
You are not in a position to know everything
That people say or do, or what they feel:
Your temper terrifies them—everyone
Will tell you only what you like to hear.   60
But I, at any rate, can listen; and I have heard them
Muttering and whispering in the dark about this girl.
They say no woman has ever, so unreasonably,
Died so shameful a death for a generous act:
"She covered her brother's body. Is this indecent?
She kept him from dogs and vultures. Is this a crime?
Death?—She should have all the honor that we can give her!"

This is the way they talk out there in the city.

You must believe me:
Nothing is closer to me than your happiness.   70
What could be closer? Must not any son

Value his father's fortune as his father does his?
I beg you, do not be unchangeable:
Do not believe that you alone can be right.
The man who thinks that,
The man who maintains that only he has the power
To reason correctly, the gift to speak, the soul—
A man like that, when you know him, turns out empty.

It is not reason never to yield to reason!

In flood time you can see how some trees bend   80
And because they bend, even their twigs are safe,
While stubborn trees are torn up, roots and all.
And the same thing happens in sailing:
Make your sheet fast, never slacken,—and over you go,
Head over heels and under: and there's your voyage.
Forget you are angry! Let yourself be moved!
I know I am young; but please let me say this:
The ideal condition
Would be, I admit, that men should be right by instinct;
But since we are all too likely to go astray,   90
The reasonable thing is to learn from those who can teach.

Choragos.   You will do well to listen to him, King,
If what he says is sensible. And you, Haimon,
Must listen to your father.—Both speak well.

Creon.   You consider it right for a man of my years and experience
To go to school to a boy?

Halmon.   It is not right
If I am wrong. But if I am young, and right,
What does my age matter?

Creon.   You think it right to stand up for an anarchist?

Haimon.   Not at all. I pay no respect to criminals.   100

Creon.   Then she is not a criminal?

Haimon.   The City would deny it, to a man.

Creon.   And the City proposes to teach me how to rule?

Haimon.   Ah. Who is it that's talking like a boy now?

Creon.   My voice is the one voice giving orders in this City!

Haimon.   It is no City if it takes orders from one voice.

Creon.   The State is the King!

Haimon.   Yes, if the State is a desert.

[*Pause.*]

Creon.   This boy, it seems, has sold out to a woman.

Haimon.   If you are a woman: my concern is only for you.

Creon.   So? Your "concern"! In a public brawl with your father!   110

Haimon. How about you, in a public brawl with justice?

Creon. With justice, when all that I do is within my rights?

Haimon. You have no right to trample on God's right.

Creon [*completely out of control*]. Fool, adolescent fool! Taken in by a
        woman!

Haimon. You'll never see me taken in by anything vile.

Creon. Every word you say is for her!

Haimon [*quietly, darkly*].   And for you.
    And for me. And for the gods under the earth.

Creon. You'll never marry her while she lives.

Haimon. Then she must die.—But her death will cause another.

Creon. Another?   120
    Have you lost your senses? It this an open threat?

Haimon. There is no threat in speaking to emptiness.

Creon. I swear you'll regret this superior tone of yours!
    You are the empty one!

Haimon.   If you were not my father,
    I'd say you were perverse.

Creon. You girlstruck fool, don't play at words with me!

Haimon. I am sorry. You prefer silence.

Creon.   Now, by God—!
    I swear, by all the gods in heaven above us,
    You'll watch, it, I swear you shall!
    [*To the servants.*]   Bring her out!
    Bring the woman out! Let her die before his eyes!   130
    Here, this instant, with her bridegroom beside her!

Haimon. Not here, no; she will not die here, King.
    And you will never see my face again.
    Go on raving as long as you've a friend to endure you.

[*Exit Haimon.*]

Choragos. Gone, gone.
    Creon, a young man in a rage is dangerous!

Creon. Let him do, or dream to do, more than a man can.
    He shall not save these girls from death.

Choragos.   These girls?
    You have sentenced them both?

Creon.   No, you are right.
    I will not kill the one whose hands are clean.   140

Choragos. But Antigonê?

Creon [*somberly*]. I will carry her far away
    Out there in the wilderness, and lock her
    Living in a vault of stone. She shall have food,
    As the custom is, to absolve the State of her death.
    And there let her pray to the gods of hell:

They are her only gods:
Perhaps they will show her an escape from death,
Or she may learn,
           though late,
That piety shown the dead is pity in vain.

[*Exit Creon.*]

Ode III

Chorus. Love, unconquerable   [*Strophe*]
    Waster of rich men, keeper
    Of warm lights and all-night vigil
    In the soft face of a girl:
    Sea-wanderer, forest-visitor!
    Even the pure Immortals cannot escape you,
    And mortal man, in his one day's dusk,
    Trembles before your glory.

    Surely you swerve upon ruin   [*Antistrophe*]
    The just man's consenting heart,   10
    As here you have made bright anger
    Strike between father and son—
    And none had conquered but Love!
    A girl's glance working the will of heaven:
    Pleasure to her alone who mocks us,
    Merciless Aphroditê.[5]

Scene IV

Choragos [*as Antigonê enters guarded*]. But I can no longer stand in awe of
        this,
    Nor, seeing what I see, keep back my tears.
    Here is Antigonê, passing to that chamber
    Where all find sleep at last.

Antigonê. Look upon me, friends, and pity me   [*Strophe 1*]
    Turning back at the night's edge to say
    Good-by to the sun that shines for me no longer;
    Now sleepy Death
    Summons me down to Acheron,[6] that cold shore:

---

5. Aphroditê is the goddess of love.
6. A river of Hades.

There is no bridesong there, nor any music.   10
Chorus.   Yet not unpraised, not without a kind of honor,
You walk at last into the underworld;
Untouched by sickness, broken by no sword.
What woman has ever found your way to death?

Antigonê.   How often I have heard the story of Niobê,[7]   *[Antistrophe 1]*
Tantalos' wretched daughter, how the stone
Clung fast about her, ivy-close: and they say
The rain falls endlessly
And sifting soft snow; her tears are never done.
I feel the loneliness of her death in mine.   20
Chorus.   But she was born of heaven, and you
Are woman, woman-born. If her death is yours,
A mortal woman's, is this not for you
Glory in our world and in the world beyond?

Antigonê.   You laugh at me. Ah, friends, friends,   *[Strophe 2]*
Can you not wait until I am dead? O Thebes,
O men many-charioted, in love with Fortune,
Dear springs of Dircê, sacred Theban grove,
Be witnesses for me, denied all pity,
Unjustly judged! and think a word of love   30
For her whose path turns
Under dark earth, where there are no more tears.
Chorus.   You have passed beyond human daring and come at last
Into a place of stone where Justice sits.
I cannot tell
What shape of your father's guilt appears in this.

Antigonê.   You have touched it at last: that bridal bed   *[Antistrophe 2]*
Unspeakable, horror of son and mother mingling:
Their crime, infection of all our family!
O Oedipus, father and brother!   40
Your marriage strikes from the grave to murder mine.
I have been a stranger here in my own land:
All my life
The blasphemy of my birth has followed me.
Chorus.   Reverence is a virtue, but strength
Lives in established law: that must prevail.

---

7. Niobê married an ancestor of Oedipus named Amphion. Her fourteen children were killed by
Apollo and Artemis after Niobê boasted to their mother, Leto, that her children were superior to
them. She wept incessantly and was finally transformed into a rock on Mt. Sipylos, whose streams are
her tears.

You have made your choice,
Your death is the doing of your conscious hand.

Antigonê.   Then let me go, since all your words are bitter,   [*Epode*]
And the very light of the sun is cold to me.   *50*
Lead me to my vigil, where I must have
Neither love nor lamentation; no song, but silence.

[*Creon interrupts impatiently.*]

Creon.   If dirges and planned lamentations could put off death,
Men would be singing for ever.
[*To the servants.*]   Take her, go!
You know your orders: take her to the vault
And leave her alone there. And if she lives or dies,
That's her affair, not ours: our hands are clean.

Antigonê.   O tomb, vaulted bride-bed in eternal rock,
Soon I shall be with my own again
Where Persephonê⁸ welcomes the thin ghosts underground: *60*
And I shall see my father again, and you, mother,
And dearest Polyneicês—
                              dearest indeed
To me, since it was my hand
That washed him clean and poured the ritual wine:
And my reward is death before my time!

And yet, as men's hearts know, I have done no wrong,
I have not sinned before God. Or if I have,
I shall know the truth in death. But if the guilt
Lies upon Creon who judged me, then, I pray,
May his punishment equal my own.
Choragos.   O passionate heart,   *70*
Unyielding, tormented still by the same winds!
Creon.   Her guards shall have good cause to regret their delaying.
Antigonê.   Ah! That voice is like the voice of death!
Creon.   I can give you no reason to think you are mistaken.
Antigonê.   Thebes, and you my fathers' gods,
And rulers of Thebes, you see me now, the last
Unhappy daughter of a line of kings,
Your kings, led away to death. You will remember
What things I suffer, and at what men's hands,
Because I would not transgress the laws of heaven.   *80*

---

8.   Queen of Hades.

[*To the guards, simply.*] Come: let us wait no longer.

[*Exit Antigonê, L., guarded.*]

Ode IV

Chorus.   All Danaê's[9] beauty was locked away   [*Strophe 1*]
    In a brazen cell where the sunlight could not come:
    A small room, still as any grave, enclosed her.
    Yet she was a princess too,
    And Zeus in a rain of gold poured love upon her.
    O child, child,
    No power in wealth or war
    Or tough sea-blackened ships
    Can prevail against untiring Destiny!

    And Dryas' son[10] also, that furious king,   [*Antistrophe 1*]
    Bore the god's prisoning anger for his pride: 11
    Sealed up by Dionysos in deaf stone,
    His madness died among echoes.
    So at the last he learned what dreadful power
    His tongue had mocked:
    For he had profaned the revels,
    And fired the wrath of the nine
    Implacable Sisters[11] that love the sound of the flute.

    And old men tell a half-remembered tale   [*Strophe 2*]
    Of horror where a dark ledge splits the sea   20
    And a double surf beats on the grày shòres:
    How a king's new woman,[12] sick
    With hatred for the queen he had imprisoned,
    Ripped out his two sons' eyes with her bloody hands
    While grinning Arês[13] watched the shuttle plunge
    Four times: four blind wounds crying for revenge,

    Crying, tears and blood mingled.—Piteously born,   [*Antistrophe 2*]
    Those sons whose mother was of heavenly birth!

---

9.   Though Danaê, a beautiful princess of Aȑgos, was confined by her father, Zeus visited her in the form of a shower of gold, and she gave birth to Perseus as a result.
10.   Lycurgus, King of Thrace, who was driven mad by Dionysos, the god of wine.
11.   The Muses.
12.   The ode alludes to a story indicating the uselessness of high birth against implacable fate. The king's new woman is Eidothea, the second wife of King Phineus. Though Cleopatra, his first wife, was the daughter of Boreas, the north wind, and Phineus was descended from kings, yet Eidothea, out of hatred for Cleopatra, blinded their two sons.
13.   The god of war.

Her father was the god of the North Wind
And she was cradled by gales,   30
She raced with young colts on the glittering hills
And walked untrammeled in the open light:
But in her marriage deathless Fate found means
To build a tomb like yours for all her joy.

Scene V

[*Enter blind Teiresias, led by a boy. The opening speeches of Teiresias should
be in singsong contrast to the realistic lines of Creon.*]

Teiresias.   This is the way the blind man comes, Princes, Princes,
    Lock-step, two heads lit by the eyes of one.
Creon.   What new thing have you to tell us, old Teiresias?
Teiresias.   I have much to tell you: listen to the prophet, Creon.
Creon.   I am not aware that I have ever failed to listen.
Teiresias.   Then you have done wisely, King, and ruled well.
Creon.   I admit my debt to you. But what have you to say?
Telresias.   This, Creon: you stand once more on the edge of fate.
Creon.   What do you mean? Your words are a kind of dread.
Teiresias.   Listen, Creon: 10
    I was sitting in my chair of augury, at the place
    Where the birds gather about me. They were all a-chatter,
    As is their habit, when suddenly I heard
    A strange note in their jangling, a scream, a
    Whirring fury; I knew that they were fighting,
    Tearing each other, dying
    In a whirlwind of wings clashing. And I was afraid.
    I began the rites of burnt-offering at the altar,
    But Hephaistos[14] failed me: instead of bright flame,
    There was only the sputtering slime of the fat thigh-flesh   20
    Melting: the entrails dissolved in gray smoke;
    The bare bone burst from the welter. And no blaze!

    This was a sign from heaven. My boy described it,
    Seeing for me as I see for others.

    I tell you, Creon, you yourself have brought
    This new calamity upon us. Our hearths and altars
    Are stained with the corruption of dogs and carrion birds
    That glut themselves on the corpse of Oedipus' son.

14.   The god of fire.

The gods are deaf when we pray to them, their fire
Recoils from our offering, their birds of omen
Have no cry of comfort, for they are gorged
With the thick blood of the dead.

                       O my son,
These are no trifles! Think: all men make mistakes,
But a good man yields when he knows his course is wrong,
And repairs the evil. The only crime is pride.

Give in to the dead man, then: do not fight with a corpse—
What glory is it to kill a man who is dead?
Think, I beg you:
It is for your own good that I speak as I do.
You should be able to yield for your own good.

Creon.   It seems that prophets have made me their especial province.
All my life long
I have been a kind of butt for the dull arrows
Of doddering fortune-tellers!

                     No, Teiresias:
If your birds—if the great eagles of God himself
Should carry him stinking bit by bit to heaven,
I would not yield. I am not afraid of pollution:
No man can defile the gods.

                 Do what you will,
Go into business, make money, speculate
In India gold or that synthetic gold from Sardis,
Get rich otherwise than by my consent to bury him.
Teiresias, it is a sorry thing when a wise man
Sells his wisdom, lets out his words for hire!

Teiresias.   Ah Creon! Is there no man left in the world—

Creon.   To do what?—Come, let's have the aphorism!

Teiresias.   No man who knows that wisdom outweighs any wealth?

Creon.   As surely as bribes are baser than any baseness.

Teiresias.   You are sick, Creon! You are deathly sick!

Creon.   As you say: it is not my place to challenge a prophet.

Teiresias.   Yet you have said my prophecy is for sale.

Creon.   The generation of prophets has always loved gold.

Teiresias.   The generation of kings has always loved brass.

Creon.   You forget yourself! You are speaking to your King.

Teiresias.   I know it. You are a king because of me.

Creon.   You have a certain skill; but you have sold out.

Teiresias.   King, you will drive me to words that—

Creon.   Say them, say them!
Only remember: I will not pay you for them.

Teiresias.   No, you will find them too costly.

Creon.   No doubt. Speak:
  Whatever you say, you will not change my will.
Teiresias.   Then take this, and take it to heart!   70
  The time is not far off when you shall pay back
  Corpse for corpse, flesh of your own flesh.
  You have thrust the child of this world into living night,
  You have kept from the gods below the child that is theirs:
  The one in a grave before her death, the other,
  Dead, denied the grave. This is your crime:
  And the Furies and the dark gods of Hell
  Are swift with terrible punishment for you.

  Do you want to buy me now, Creon?
                                            Not many days,
  And your house will be full of men and women weeping,   80
  And curses will be hurled at you from far
  Cities grieving for sons unburied, left to rot
  Before the walls of Thebes.

  These are my arrows, Creon: they are all for you.

  [*To boy.*] But come, child: lead me home.
  Let him waste his fine anger upon younger men.
  Maybe he will learn at last
  To control a wiser tongue in a better head.

[*Exit Teiresias.*]

Choragos.   The old man has gone, King, but his words
  Remain to plague us. I am old, too,   90
  But I cannot remember that he was ever false.
Creon.   That is true. . . . It troubles me.
  Oh it is hard to give in! but it is worse
  To risk everything for stubborn pride.
Choragos.   Creon: take my advice.
Creon.   What shall I do?
Choragos.   Go quickly: free Antigonê from her vault
  And build a tomb for the body of Polyneicês.
Creon.   You would have me do this?
Choragos.   Creon, yes!
  And it must be done at once: God moves
  Swiftly to cancel the folly of stubborn men.   100
Creon.   It is hard to deny the heart! But I
  Will do it: I will not fight with destiny.
Choragos.   You must go yourself, you cannot leave it to others.
Creon.   I will go.

—Bring axes, servants:
Come with me to the tomb. I buried her, I
Will set her free.
                    Oh quickly!
My mind misgives—
The laws of the gods are mighty, and a man must serve them
To the last day of his life!

[*Exit Creon.*]

Paean[15]

Choragos.   God of many names   [*Strophe 1*]
Chorus.   O Iacchos[16]
                                         son
of Kadmeian Sémelê
                    O born of the Thunder!
Guardian of the West
                    Regent
of Eleusis' plain
                    O Prince of maenad Thebes
and the Dragon Field by rippling Ismenos:[17]

Choragos.   God of many names   [*Antistrophe 1*]
Chorus.   the flame of torches
flares on our hills
                    the nymphs of Iacchos
dance at the spring of Castalia:[18]
from the vine-close mountain
                              come ah come in ivy:
Evohê evohê! sings through the streets of Thebes   10

Choragos.   God of many names   [*Strophe 2*]
Chorus.   Iacchos of Thebes
heavenly Child
                    of Sémele bride of the Thunderer!
The shadow of plague is upon us:
                              come
with clement feet

---

15. A hymn.
16. Iacchos is a name for Dionysos. His mother was Sémelê, daughter of Kadmos, the founder of Thebes. His father was Zeus. The Maenads were priestesses of Dionysos who cry "evohe evohe."
17. A river of Thebes, sacred to Apollo. Dragon Field refers to the legend that the ancestors of Thebes. His father was Zeus. The Maenads were priestesses of Dionysos who cried "evohê evohê."
18. A spring on Mt. Parnasos.

> oh come from Parnasos
> > down the long slopes
> > > across the lamenting water

Choragos. Iô Fire! Chorister of the throbbing stars!   [*Antistrophe 2*]
    O purest among the voices of the night!
    Thou son of God, blaze for us!
Chorus. Come with choric rapture of circling Maenads
    Who cry *Iô Iacche!*
> > > *God of many names!*   20

Exodos

[*Enter Messenger, L.*]

Messenger. Men of the line of Kadmos, you who live
    Near Amphion's[19] citadel:
> > I cannot say
> Of any condition of human life "This is fixed,
> This is clearly good, or bad." Fate raises up,
> And Fate casts down the happy and unhappy alike:
> No man can foretell his Fate.
> > > Take the case of Creon:
> Creon was happy once, as I count happiness:
> Victorious in battle, sole governor of the land,
> Fortunate father of children nobly born.
> And now it has all gone from him! Who can say   10
> That a man is still alive when his life's joy falls?
> He is a walking dead man. Grant him rich,
> Let him live like a king in his great house:
> If his pleasure is gone, I would not give
> So much as the shadow of smoke for all he owns.
Choragos. Your words hint at sorrow: what is your news for us?
Messenger. They are dead. The living are guilty of their death.
Choragos. Who is guilty? Who is dead? Speak!
Messenger.   Haimon.
    Haimon is dead; and the hand that killed him
    Is his own hand.
Choragos.   His father's? or his own?   20
Messenger. His own, driven mad by the murder his father had done.
Choragos. Teiresias, Teiresias, how clearly you saw it all!

---

19. A child of Zeus and Antiope. He is noted for building the walls of Thebes by charming the stones into place with a lyre.

Messenger.   This is my news: you must draw what conclusions you can from
           it.
Choragos.   But look: Eurydicê, our Queen:
      Has she overheard us?

[*Enter Eurydicê from the Palace, C.*]

Eurydice.   I have heard something, friends:
      As I was unlocking the gate of Pallas'[20] shrine,
      For I needed her help today, I heard a voice
      Telling of some new sorrow. And I fainted
      There at the temple with all my maidens about me.   30
      But speak again: whatever it is, I can bear it:
      Grief and I are no strangers.
Messenger.   Dearest Lady,
      I will tell you plainly all that I have seen.
      I shall not try to comfort you: what is the use,
      Since comfort could lie only in what is not true?
      The truth is always best.
                          I went with Creon
      To the outer plain where Polyneicês was lying,
      No friend to pity him, his body shredded by dogs.
      We made our prayers in that place to Hecatê[21]
      And Pluto,[22] that they would be merciful. And we bathed   40
      The corpse with holy water, and we brought
      Fresh-broken branches to burn what was left of it,
      And upon the urn we heaped up a towering barrow
      Of the earth of his own land.
                          When we were done, we ran
      To the vault where Antigonê lay on her couch of stone.
      One of the servants had gone ahead,
      And while he was yet far off he heard a voice
      Grieving within the chamber, and he came back
      And told Creon. And as the King went closer,
      The air was full of wailing, the words lost,   50
      And he begged us to make all haste. "Am I a prophet?"
      He said, weeping, "And must I walk this road,
      The saddest of all that I have gone before?
      My son's voice calls me on. Oh quickly, quickly!
      Look through the crevice there, and tell me
      If it is Haimon, or some deception of the gods!"

---

20. Pallas Athene, goddess of wisdom.
21. Hecatê is often identified with Persephone, a goddess of Hades; generally Hecatê is a goddess of
sorcery and witchcraft.
22. King of Hades and brother of Zeus and Poseidon.

We obeyed; and in the cavern's farthest corner
We saw her lying:
She had made a noose of her fine linen veil
And hanged herself. Haimon lay beside her,   60
His arms about her waist, lamenting her,
His love lost under ground, crying out
That his father had stolen her away from him.

When Creon saw him the tears rushed to his eyes
And he called to him: "What have you done, child? Speak to me.
What are you thinking that makes your eyes so strange?
O my son, my son, I come to you on my knees!"
But Haimon spat in his face. He said not a word,
Staring—
            And suddenly drew his sword
And lunged. Creon shrank back, the blade missed; and the boy,   70
Desperate against himself, drove it half its length
Into his own side, and fell. And as he died
He gathered Antigone close in his arms again,
Choking, his blood bright red on her white cheek.
And now he lies dead with the dead, and she is his
At last, his bride in the houses of the dead.

[Exit Eurydice into the Palace.]

Choragos.   She has left us without a word. What can this mean?
Messenger.   It troubles me, too; yet she knows what is best,
  Her grief is too great for public lamentation,
  And doubtless she has gone to her chamber to weep   80
  For her dead son, leading her maidens in his dirge.
Choragos.   It may be so: but I fear this deep silence.

[Pause.]

Messenger.   I will see what she is doing. I will go in.

[Exit Messenger into the Palace.]
[Enter Creon with attendants, bearing Haimon's body.]

Choragos.   But here is the King himself: oh look at him,
  Bearing his own damnation in his arms.
Creon.   Nothing you say can touch me any more.
  My own blind heart has brought me
  From darkness to final darkness. Here you see
  The father murdering, the murdered son—
  And all my civic wisdom!   90
  Haimon my son, so young, so young to die,

I was the fool, not you; and you died for me.

Choragos.   That is the truth; but you were late in learning it.

Creon.   This truth is hard to bear. Surely a god
Has crushed me beneath the hugest weight of heaven,
And driven me headlong a barbaric way
To trample out the thing I held most dear.

The pains that men will take to come to pain!

[*Enter Messenger from the Palace.*]

Messenger.   The burden you carry in your hands is heavy,
But it is not all: you will find more in your house.   *100*

Creon.   What burden worse than this shall I find there?

Messenger.   The Queen is dead.

Creon.   O port of death, deaf world,
Is there no pity for me? And you, Angel of evil,
I was dead, and your words are death again.
Is it true, boy? Can it be true?
Is my wife dead? Has death bred death?

Messenger.   You can see for yourself.

[*The doors are opened, and the body of Eurydicê is disclosed within.*]

Creon.   Oh pity!
All true, all true, and more than I can bear!   *110*
O my wife, my son!

Messenger.   She stood before the altar, and her heart
Welcomed the knife her own hand guided,
And a great cry burst from her lips for Megareus[23] dead,
And for Haimon dead, her sons; and her last breath
Was a curse for their father, the murderer of her sons,
And she fell, and the dark flowed in through her closing eyes.

Creon.   O God, I am sick with fear.
Are there no swords here? Has no one a blow for me?

Messenger.   Her curse is upon you for the deaths of both.   *120*

Creon.   It is right that it should be. I alone am guilty.
I know it, and I say it. Lead me in,
Quickly, friends.
I have neither life nor substance. Lead me in.

Choragos.   You are right, if there can be right in so much wrong.
The briefest way is best in a world of sorrow.

Creon.   Let it come,
Let death come quickly, and be kind to me.

---

23.   Son of Creon who was killed in the attack on Thebes.

I would not ever see the sun again.

Choragos.   All that will come when it will; but we, meanwhile,   *130*
Have much to do. Leave the future to itself.

Creon.   All my heart was in that prayer!

Choragos.   Then do not pray any more: the sky is deaf.

Creon.   Lead me away. I have been rash and foolish.
I have killed my son and my wife.
I look for comfort; my comfort lies here dead.
Whatever my hands have touched has come to nothing.
Fate has brought all my pride to a thought of dust.

[*As Creon is being led into the house, the Choragos advances and speaks
directly to the audience.*]

Choragos.   There is no happiness where there is no wisdom;
No wisdom but in submission to the gods.   *140*
Big words are always punished,
And proud men in old age learn to be wise.

Questions

1. Critics have traditionally divided over the question of whether Antigone or Creon is
the protagonist in the play. How does the answer to this question affect one's interpretation of the play?   **2.** How does the Prologue establish the mood and theme of
the play?   **3.** Does the character of Antigone change during the course of the play?   **4.**
Does the action of the play prepare us for the change in Creon—that is, for his realization that he has been wrong?   **5.** Can Antigone be read as a justification for civil disobedience? Explain.   **6.** Is there any justification for Antigone's cold refusal to allow
Ismene to share her martyrdom? Explain.   **7.** To what extent and in what ways does the
Chorus contribute to the dramatic development and tension of the play?

A Doll's House*

HENRIK IBSEN [1828–1906]

CHARACTERS

Torvald Helmer, *a lawyer*
Nora, *his wife*
Dr. Rank
Mrs. Linde
Krogstad
The Helmers' three small children
Anne-Marie, *the children's nurse*
A Housemaid
A Porter

SCENE.   *The Helmers' living room.*

Act I

A pleasant, tastefully but not expensively furnished, living room. A door on the rear wall, right, leads to the front hall, another door, left, to Helmer's study. Between the two doors a piano. A third door in the middle of the left wall; further front a window. Near the window a round table and a small couch. Towards the rear of the right wall a fourth door; further front a tile stove with a rocking chair and a couple of armchairs in front of it. Between the stove and the door a small table. Copperplate etchings on the walls. A whatnot with porcelain figurines and other small objects. A small bookcase with de luxe editions. A rug on the floor; fire in the stove. Winter day.

The doorbell rings, then the sound of the front door opening. Nora, dressed for outdoors, enters, humming cheerfully. She carries several packages, which she puts down on the table, right. She leaves the door to the front hall open; there a Porter is seen holding a Christmas tree and a basket. He gives them to the Maid who has let them in.

Nora.   Be sure to hide the Christmas tree, Helene. The children mustn't see it before tonight when we've trimmed it. *(Opens her purse; to the Porter.)* How much?

---

*A new translation by Otto Reinert.

Porter. Fifty øre.

Nora. Here's a crown. No, keep the change. *(The Porter thanks her, leaves. Nora closes the door. She keeps laughing quietly to herself as she takes off her coat, etc. She takes a bag of macaroons from her pocket and eats a couple. She walks cautiously over to the door to the study and listens.)* Yes, he's home. *(Resumes her humming, walks over to the table, right.)*

Helmer *(in his study).* Is that my little lark twittering out there?

Nora *(opening some packages).* That's right.

Helmer. My squirrel bustling about?

Nora. Yes.

Helmer. When did squirrel come home?

Nora. Just now. *(Puts the bag of macaroons back in her pocket, wipes her mouth.)* Come out here, Torvald. I want to show you what I've bought.

Helmer. I'm busy! *(After a little while he opens the door and looks in, pen in hand.)* Bought, eh? All that? So little wastrel has been throwing money around again?

Nora. Oh but Torvald, this Christmas we can be a little extravagant, can't we? It's the first Christmas we don't have to scrimp.

Helmer. I don't know about that. We certainly don't have money to waste.

Nora. Yes, Torvald, we do. A little, anyway. Just a tiny little bit? Now that you're going to get that big salary and make lots and lots of money.

Helmer. Starting at New Year's, yes. But payday isn't till the end of the quarter.

Nora. That doesn't matter. We can always borrow.

Helmer. Nora! *(Goes over to her and playfully pulls her ear.)* There you go being irresponsible again. Suppose I borrowed a thousand crowns today and you spent it all for Christmas and on New Year's Eve a tile hit me in the head and laid me out cold.

Nora *(putting her hand over his mouth).* I won't have you say such horrid things.

Helmer. But suppose it happened. Then what?

Nora. If it did, I wouldn't care whether we owed money or not.

Helmer. But what about the people I had borrowed from?

Nora. Who cares about them! They are strangers.

Helmer. Nora, Nora, you *are* a woman! No, really! You know how I feel about that. No debts! A home in debt isn't a free home, and if it isn't free it isn't beautiful. We've managed nicely so far, you and I, and that's the way we'll go on. It won't be for much longer.

Nora *(walks over toward the stove).* All right, Torvald. Whatever you say.

Helmer *(follows her).* Come, come, my little songbird mustn't droop her wings. What's this? Can't have a pouty squirrel in the house, you know. *(Takes out his wallet.)* Nora, what do you think I have here?

Nora *(turns around quickly).* Money!

Helmer. Here. *(Gives her some bills.)* Don't you think I know Christmas is expensive?

Nora *(counting).* Ten—twenty—thirty—forty. Thank you, thank you, Torvald. This helps a lot.

Helmer. I certainly hope so.

Nora. It does, it does. But I want to show you what I got. It was cheap, too. Look. New clothes for Ivar. And a sword. And a horse and trumpet for Bob. And a doll and a little bed for Emmy. It isn't any good, but it wouldn't last, anyway. And here's some dress material and scarves for the maids. I feel bad about old Anne-Marie, though. She really should be getting much more.

Helmer. And what's in here?

Nora *(cries).* Not till tonight!

Helmer. I see. But now what does my little prodigal have in mind for herself?

Nora. Oh, nothing. I really don't care.

Helmer. Of course you do. Tell me what you'd like. Within reason.

Nora. Oh, I don't know. Really, I don't. The only thing —

Helmer. Well?

Nora *(fiddling with his buttons, without looking at him).* If you really want to give me something, you might—you could—

Helmer. All right, let's have it.

Nora *(quickly).* Some money, Torvald. Just as much as you think you can spare. Then I'll buy myself something one of these days.

Helmer. No, really Nora—

Nora. Oh yes, please, Torvald. Please? I'll wrap the money in pretty gold paper and hang it on the tree. Won't that be nice?

Helmer. What's the name for little birds that are always spending money?

Nora. Wastrels, I know. But please let's do it my way, Torvald. Then I'll have time to decide what I need most. Now that's sensible, isn't it?

Helmer *(smiling).* Oh, very sensible. That is, if you really bought yourself something you could use. But it all disappears in the household expenses or you buy things you don't need. And then you come back to me for more.

Nora. Oh, but Torvald—

Helmer. That's the truth, dear little Nora, and you know it. *(Puts his arm around her.)* My wastrel is a little sweetheart, but she *does* go through an awful lot of money awfully fast. You've no idea how expensive it is for a man to keep a wastrel.

Nora. That's not fair, Torvald. I really save all I can.

Helmer *(laughs).* Oh, I believe that. All you can. Meaning, exactly nothing!

Nora *(hums, smiles mysteriously).* You don't know all the things we songbirds and squirrels need money for, Torvald.

Helmer. You know, you're funny. Just like your father. You're always looking for ways to get money, but as soon as you do it runs through your fingers and you can never say what you spent it for. Well, I guess I'll just have to take you the way you are. It's in your blood. Yes, that sort of thing is hereditary, Nora.

Nora. In that case, I wish I had inherited many of Daddy's qualities.

Helmer. And I don't want you any different from just what you are—my own sweet little songbird. Hey!—I think I just noticed something. Aren't you looking—what's the word?—a little—sly—?

Nora. I am?

Helmer. You definitely are. Look at me.

Nora *(looks at him).* Well?

Helmer *(wagging a finger).* Little sweet-tooth hasn't by any chance been on a rampage today, has she?

Nora. Of course not. Whatever makes you think that?

Helmer. A little detour by the pastryshop maybe?

Nora. No, I assure you, Torvald—

Helmer. Nibbled a little jam?

Nora. Certainly not!

Helmer. Munched a macaroon or two?

Nora. No, really, Torvald, I honestly—

Helmer. All right. Of course I was only joking.

Nora *(walks toward the table, right).* You know I wouldn't do anything to displease you.

Helmer. I know. And I have your promise. *(Over to her.)* All right, keep your little Christmas secrets to yourself, Nora darling. They'll all come out tonight, I suppose, when we light the tree.

Nora. Did you remember to invite Rank?

Helmer. No, but there's no need to. He knows he'll have dinner with us. Anyway, I'll see him later this morning. I'll ask him then. I did order some good wine. Oh Nora, you've no idea how much I'm looking forward to tonight!

Nora. Me, too. And the children, Torvald! They'll have such a good time!

Helmer. You know, it *is* nice to have a good, safe job and a comfortable income. Feels good just thinking about it. Don't you agree?

Nora. Oh, it's wonderful!

Helmer. Remember last Christmas? For three whole weeks you shut yourself up every evening till long after midnight, making ornaments for the Christmas tree and I don't know what else. Some big surprise for all of us, anyway. I'll be damned if I've ever been so bored in my whole life!

Nora. I wasn't bored at all!

Helmer *(smiling).* But you've got to admit you didn't have much to show for it in the end.

Nora. Oh, don't tease me again about that! Could I help it that the cat got in and tore up everything?

Helmer. Of course you couldn't, my poor little Nora. You just wanted to please the rest of us, and that's the important thing. But I *am* glad the hard times are behind us. Aren't you?

Nora. Oh yes. I think it's just wonderful.

Helmer. This year, I won't be bored and lonely. And you won't have to strain your dear eyes and your delicate little hands—

Nora *(claps her hands).* No I won't, will I Torvald? Oh, how wonderful, how lovely, to hear you say that! *(Puts her arm under his.)* Let me tell you how I think we should arrange things, Torvald. Soon as Christmas is over—*(The doorbell rings.)* Someone's at the door. *(Straightens things up a bit.)* A caller, I suppose. Bother!

Helmer. Remember, I'm not home for visitors.

The Maid *(in the door to the front hall).* Ma'am, there's a lady here—

Nora. All right. Ask her to come in.

The Maid *(to Helmer).* And the Doctor just arrived.

Helmer. Is he in the study?

The Maid. Yes, sir.

Helmer exits into his study. The Maid shows Mrs. Linde in and closes the door behind her as she leaves. Mrs. Linde is in travel dress.

Mrs. Linde *(timid and a little hesitant).* Good morning, Nora.

Nora *(uncertainly).* Good morning.

Mrs. Linde. I don't believe you know who I am.

Nora. No—I'm not sure—Though I know I should—Of course! Kristine! It's you!

Mrs. Linde. Yes, it's me.

Nora. And I didn't even recognize you! I had no idea! *(In a lower voice.)* You've changed, Kristine.

Mrs. Linde. I'm sure I have. It's been nine or ten long years.

Nora. Has it really been that long? Yes, you're right. I've been so happy these last eight years. And now you're here. Such a long trip in the middle of winter. How brave!

Mrs. Linde. I got in on the steamer this morning.

Nora. To have some fun over the holidays, of course. That's lovely. For we *are* going to have fun. But take off your coat! You aren't cold, are you? *(Helps her.)* There, now! Let's sit down here by the fire and just relax and talk. No, you sit there. I want the rocking chair. *(Takes her hands.)* And now you've got your old face back. It was just for a minute, right at first— Though you are a little more pale, Kristine. And maybe a little thinner.

Mrs. Linde. And much, much older, Nora.

Nora. Maybe a little older. Just a teeny-weeny bit, not much. *(Interrupts herself, serious.)* Oh, but how thoughtless of me, chatting away like this! Sweet, good Kristine, can you forgive me?

Mrs. Linde. Forgive you what, Nora?

Nora *(in a low voice).* You poor dear, you lost your husband, didn't you?

Mrs. Linde. Three years ago, yes.

Nora. I know. I saw it in the paper. Oh please believe me, Kristine. I really meant to write you, but I never got around to it. Something was always coming up.

Mrs. Linde. Of course, Nora. I understand.

Nora. No, that wasn't very nice of me. You poor thing, all you must have been through. And he didn't leave you much, either, did he?

Mrs. Linde. No.

Nora. And no children?

Mrs. Linde. No.

Nora. Nothing at all, in other words?

Mrs. Linde. Not so much as a sense of loss—a grief to live on—

Nora *(incredulous).* But Kristine, how can that *be?*

Mrs. Linde *(with a sad smile, strokes Nora's hair).* That's the way it sometimes is, Nora.

Nora. All alone. How awful for you. I have three darling children. You can't see them right now, though; they're out with their nurse. But now you must tell me everything—

Mrs. Linde. No, no; I'd rather listen to you.

Nora. No, you begin. Today I won't be selfish. Today I'll think only of you. Except there's one thing I've just got to tell you first. Something marvelous that's happened to us just these last few days. You haven't heard, have you?

Mrs. Linde. No; tell me.

Nora. Just think. My husband's been made manager of the Mutual Bank.

Mrs. Linde. Your husband—! Oh, I'm so glad!

Nora. Yes, isn't that great? You see, private law practice is so uncertain, especially when you won't have anything to do with cases that aren't—you know—quite nice. And of course Torvald won't do that and I quite agree with him. Oh, you've no idea how delighted we are! He takes over at New Year's, and he'll be getting a big salary and all sorts of extras. From now on we'll be able to live in quite a different way—exactly as we like. Oh, Kristine! I feel so carefree and happy! It's lovely to have lots and lots of money and not have to worry about a thing! Don't you agree?

Mrs. Linde. It would be nice to have enough at any rate.

Nora. No, I don't mean just enough. I mean lots and lots!

Mrs. Linde *(smiles).* Nora, Nora, when are you going to be sensible? In school you spent a great deal of money.

Nora *(quietly laughing).* Yes, and Torvald says I still do. *(Raises her finger at Mrs. Linde.)* But "Nora, Nora" isn't so crazy as you all think. Believe me, we've had nothing to be extravagant with. We've both had to work.

Mrs. Linde. You too?

Nora. Yes. Oh, it's been little things, mostly—sewing, crocheting, embroidery—that sort of thing. *(Casually.)* And other things too. You know, of course, that Torvald left government service when we got married? There was no chance of promotion in his department, and of course he had to make more money than he had been making. So for the first few years he worked altogether too hard. He had to take jobs on the side and work night and day. It turned out to be too much for him. He became seriously ill. The doctors told him he needed to go south.

Mrs. Linde.   That's right; you spent a year in Italy, didn't you?

Nora.   Yes, we did. But you won't believe how hard it was to get away. Ivar had just been born. But of course we had to go. Oh, it was a wonderful trip. And it saved Torvald's life. But it took a lot of money, Kristine.

Mrs. Linde.   I'm sure it did.

Nora.   Twelve hundred specie dollars. Four thousand eight hundred crowns. That's a lot of money.

Mrs. Linde.   Yes. So it's lucky you have it when something like that happens.

Nora.   Well, actually we got the money from Daddy.

Mrs. Linde.   I see. That was about the time your father died, I believe.

Nora.   Yes, just about then. And I couldn't even go and take care of him. I was expecting little Ivar any day. And I had poor Torvald to look after, desperately sick and all. My dear, good Daddy! I never saw him again, Kristine. That's the saddest thing that's happened to me since I got married.

Mrs. Linde.   I know you were very fond of him. But then you went to Italy?

Nora.   Yes, for now we had the money, and the doctors urged us to go. So we left about a month later.

Mrs. Linde.   And when you came back your husband was well again?

Nora.   Healthy as a horse!

Mrs. Linde.   But—the doctor?

Nora.   What do you mean?

Mrs. Linde.   I thought the maid said it was the doctor, that gentleman who came the same time I did.

Nora.   Oh, that's Dr. Rank. He doesn't come as a doctor. He's our closest friend. He looks in at least once every day. No, Torvald hasn't been sick once since then. And the children are strong and healthy, too, and so am I. *(Jumps up and claps her hands.)* Oh God, Kristine! Isn't it wonderful to be alive and happy! Isn't it just lovely!—But now I'm being mean again, talking only about myself and my things. *(Sits down on a footstool close to Mrs. Linde and puts her arms on her lap.)* Please don't be angry with me! Tell me, is it really true that you didn't care for your husband? Then why did you marry him?

Mrs. Linde.   Mother was still alive then, but she was bedridden and helpless. And I had my two younger brothers to look after. I didn't think I had the right to turn him down.

Nora.   No, I suppose not. So he had money then?

Mrs. Linde.   He was quite well off, I think. But it was an uncertain business, Nora. When he died, the whole thing collapsed and there was nothing left.

Nora.   And then—?

Mrs. Linde.   Well, I had to manage as best I could. With a little store and a little school and anything else I could think of. The last three years have been one long work day for me, Nora, without any rest. But now it's over. My poor mother doesn't need me any more. She's passed away. And the boys are on their own too. They've both got jobs and support themselves.

Nora. What a relief for you—

Mrs. Linde. No, not relief. Just a great emptiness. Nobody to live for any more. (*Gets up restlessly.*) That's why I couldn't stand it any longer in that little hole. Here in town it has to be easier to find something to keep me busy and occupy my thoughts. With a little luck I should be able to find a permanent job, something in an office—

Nora. Oh but Kristine, that's exhausting work, and you look worn out already. It would be much better for you to go to a resort.

Mrs. Linde (*walks over to the window*). I don't have a Daddy who can give me the money, Nora.

Nora (*getting up*). Oh, don't be angry with me.

Mrs. Linde (*over to her*). Dear Nora, don't *you* be angry with *me*. That's the worst thing about my kind of situation: you become so bitter. You've nobody to work for, and yet you have to look out for yourself, somehow. You've got to keep on living, and so you become selfish. Do you know—when you told me about your husband's new position I was delighted not so much for your sake as for my own.

Nora. Why was that? Oh, I see. You think maybe Torvald can give you a job?

Mrs. Linde. That's what I had in mind.

Nora. And he will too, Kristine. Just leave it to me. I'll be ever so subtle about it. I'll think of something nice to tell him, something he'll like. Oh I so much want to help you.

Mrs. Linde. That's very good of you, Nora—making an effort like that for me. Especially since you've known so little trouble and hardship in your own life.

Nora. I—?—have known so little—?

Mrs. Linde (*smiling*). Oh well, a little sewing or whatever it was. You're still a child, Nora.

Nora (*with a toss of her head, walks away*). You shouldn't sound so superior.

Mrs. Linde. I shouldn't?

Nora. You're just like all the others. None of you think I'm good for anything really serious.

Mrs. Linde. Well, now—

Nora. That I've never been through anything difficult.

Mrs. Linde. But Nora! You just told me all your troubles!

Nora. That's nothing! (*Lowers her voice.*) I haven't told you about *it*.

Mrs. Linde. It? What's that? What do you mean?

Nora. You patronize me, Kristine, and that's not fair. You're proud that you worked so long and so hard for your mother.

Mrs. Linde. I don't think I patronize anyone. But it *is* true that I'm both proud and happy that I could make mother's last years comparatively easy.

Nora. And you're proud of all you did for your brothers.

Mrs. Linde. I think I have the right to be.

Nora. And so do I. But now I want to tell you something, Kristine. I have something to be proud and happy about too.

Mrs. Linde. I don't doubt that for a moment. But what exactly do you mean?

Nora. Not so loud! Torvald mustn't hear—not for anything in the world. Nobody must know about this, Kristine. Nobody but you.

Mrs. Linde. But what is it?

Nora. Come here. (*Pulls her down on the couch beside her.*) You see, I *do* have something to be proud and happy about. I've saved Torvald's life.

Mrs. Linde. Saved—? How do you mean—"saved"?

Nora. I told you about our trip to Italy. Torvald would have died if he hadn't gone.

Mrs. Linde. I understand that. And so your father gave you the money you needed.

Nora (*smiles*). Yes, that's what Torvald and all the others think. But—

Mrs. Linde. But what?

Nora. Daddy didn't give us a penny. *I* raised that money.

Mrs. Linde. *You* did? That whole big amount?

Nora. Twelve hundred specie dollars. Four thousand eight hundred crowns. *Now* what do you say?

Mrs. Linde. But Nora, how could you? Did you win in the state lottery?

Nora (*contemptuously*). State lottery! (*Snorts.*) What is so great about that?

Mrs. Linde. Where did it come from then?

Nora (*humming and smiling, enjoying her secret*). Hmmm. Tra-la-la-la-la!

Mrs. Linde. You certainly couldn't have borrowed it.

Nora. Oh? And why not?

Mrs. Linde. A wife can't borrow money without her husband's consent.

Nora (*with a toss of her head*). Oh, I don't know—take a wife with a little bit of a head for business—a wife who knows how to manage things—

Mrs. Linde. But Nora, I don't understand at all—

Nora. You don't have to. I didn't say I borrowed the money, did I? I could have gotten it some other way. (*Leans back.*) An admirer may have given it to me. When you're as tolerably goodlooking as I am—

Mrs. Linde. Oh, you're crazy.

Nora. I think you're dying from curiosity, Kristine.

Mrs. Linde. I'm beginning to think you've done something very foolish, Nora.

Nora (*sits up*). Is it foolish to save your husband's life?

Mrs. Linde. I say it's foolish to act behind his back.

Nora. But don't you see: he couldn't be told! You're missing the whole point, Kristine. We couldn't even let him know how seriously ill he was. The doctors came to *me* and told me his life was in danger, that nothing could save him but a stay in the south. Don't you think I tried to work on him? I told him how lovely it would be if I could go abroad like other young wives. I cried and begged. I said he'd better remember what condition I was in, that he had to be nice to me and do what I wanted. I even hinted he could borrow the money. But that almost made him angry with me. He told me I was being irresponsible and that it was his duty as my husband not to give in to my moods and whims—I think that's what he called it. All right, I said to myself, you've got to be saved somehow, and so I found a way—

Mrs. Linde. And your husband never learned from your father that the money didn't come from him?

Nora. Never. Daddy died that same week. I thought of telling him all about it and ask him not to say anything. But since he was so sick—It turned out I didn't have to—

Mrs. Linde. And you've never told your husband?

Nora. Of course not! Good heavens, how could I? He, with his strict principles! Besides, you know how men are. Torvald would find it embarrassing and humiliating to learn that he owed me anything. It would upset our whole relationship. Our happy, beautiful home would no longer be what it is.

Mrs. Linde. Aren't you ever going to tell him?

Nora (reflectively, half smiling). Yes—one day, maybe. Many, many years from now, when I'm no longer young and pretty. Don't laugh! I mean when Torvald no longer feels about me the way he does now, when he no longer thinks it's fun when I dance for him and put on costumes and recite for him. Then it will be good to have something in reserve—(Interrupts herself.) Oh, I'm just being silly! That day will never come.—Well, now, Kristine, what do you think of my great secret? Don't you think I'm good for something too?—By the way, you wouldn't believe all the worry I've had because of it. It's been very hard to meet my obligations on schedule. You see, in business there's something called quarterly interest and something called installments on the principal, and those are terribly hard to come up with. I've had to save a little here and a little there, whenever I could. I couldn't use much of the housekeeping money, for Torvald has to eat well. And I couldn't use what I got for clothes for the children. They have to look nice, and I didn't think it would be right to spend less than I got—the sweet little things!

Mrs. Linde. Poor Nora! So you had to take it from your own allowance!

Nora. Yes, of course. After all, it was my affair. Every time Torvald gave me money for a new dress and things like that, I never used more than half of it. I always bought the cheapest, simplest things for myself. Thank God, everything looks good on me, so Torvald never noticed. But it was hard many times, Kristine, for it's fun to have pretty clothes. Don't you think?

Mrs. Linde. Certainly.

Nora. Anyway, I had other ways of making money too. Last winter I was lucky enough to get some copying work. So I locked the door and sat up writing every night till quite late. God! I often got so tired—! But it was great fun, too, working and making money. It was almost like being a man.

Mrs. Linde. But how much have you been able to pay off this way?

Nora. I couldn't tell you exactly. You see, it's very difficult to keep track of business like that. All I know is I have been paying off as much as I've been able to scrape together. Many times I just didn't know what to do. *(Smiles.)* Then I used to imagine a rich old gentleman had fallen in love with me—

Mrs. Linde. What! What old gentleman?

Nora. Phooey! And now he was dead and they were reading his will, and there it said in big letters, "All my money is to be paid in cash immediately to the charming Mrs. Nora Helmer."

Mrs. Linde. But dearest Nora—who *was* this old gentleman?

Nora. For heaven's sake, Kristine, don't you see? There *was* no old gentleman. He was just somebody I made up when I couldn't think of any way to raise the money. But never mind him. The old bore can be anyone he likes to for all I care. I have no use for him or his last will, for now I don't have a single worry in the world. *(Jumps up.)* Dear God, what a lovely thought this is! To be able to play and have fun with the children, to have everything nice and pretty in the house, just the way Torvald likes it! Not a care! And soon spring will be here, and the air will be blue and high. Maybe we can travel again. Maybe I'll see the ocean again! Oh, yes, yes!— it's wonderful to be alive and happy!

The doorbell rings.

Mrs. Linde *(getting up).* There's the doorbell. Maybe I better be going.

Nora. No, please stay. I'm sure it's just someone for Torvald—

The Maid *(in the hall door).* Excuse me, ma'am. There's a gentleman here who'd like to see Mr. Helmer.

Nora. You mean the bank manager.

The Maid. Sorry, ma'am; the bank manager. But I didn't know—since the Doctor is with him—

Nora. Who is the gentleman?

Krogstad *(appearing in the door).* It's just me, Mrs. Helmer.

Mrs. Linde starts, looks, turns away toward the window.

Nora *(takes a step toward him, tense, in a low voice).* You? What do you want? What do you want with my husband?

Krogstad. Bank business—in a way. I have a small job in the Mutual, and I understand your husband is going to be our new boss—

Nora. So it's just—

Krogstad. Just routine business, ma'am. Nothing else.

Nora. All right. In that case, why don't you go through the door to the office.

Dismisses him casually as she closes the door. Walks over to the stove and tends the fire.

Mrs. Linde. Nora—who was that man?

Nora. His name's Krogstad. He's a lawyer.

Mrs. Linde. So it *was* him.

Nora. Do you know him?

Mrs. Linde. I used to—many years ago. For a while he clerked in our part of the country.

Nora. Right. He did.

Mrs. Linde. He has changed a great deal.

Nora. I believe he had a very unhappy marriage.

Mrs. Linde. And now he's a widower, isn't he?

Nora. With many children. There now; it's burning nicely again. *(Closes the stove and moves the rocking chair a little to the side.)*

Mrs. Linde. They say he's into all sorts of business.

Nora. Really? Maybe so. I wouldn't know. But let's not think about business. It's such a bore.

Dr. Rank *(appears in the door to Helmer's study).* No, I don't want to be in the way. I'd rather talk to your wife a bit. *(Closes the door and notices Mrs. Linde.)* Oh, I beg your pardon. I believe I'm in the way here too.

Nora. No, not at all. *(Introduces them.)* Dr. Rank. Mrs. Linde.

Rank. Aha. A name often heard in this house. I believe I passed you on the stairs coming up.

Mrs. Linde. Yes. I'm afraid I climb stairs very slowly. They aren't good for me.

Rank. I see. A slight case of inner decay, perhaps?

Mrs. Linde. Overwork, rather.

Rank. Oh, is that all? And now you've come to town to relax at all the parties?

Mrs. Linde. I have come to look for a job.

Rank. A proven cure for overwork, I take it?

Mrs. Linde. One has to live, Doctor.

Rank. Yes, that seems to be the common opinion.

Nora. Come on, Dr. Rank—you want to live just as much as the rest of us.

Rank. Of course I do. Miserable as I am, I prefer to go on being tortured as long as possible. All my patients feel the same way. And that's true of the moral invalids too. Helmer is talking with a specimen right this minute.

Mrs. Linde *(in a low voice).* Ah!

Nora. What do you mean?

Rank. Oh, this lawyer, Krogstad. You don't know him. The roots of his character are decayed. But even he began by saying something about having *to live*—as if it were a matter of the highest importance.

Nora. Oh? What did he want with Torvald?

Rank. I don't really know. All I heard was something about the bank.

Nora. I didn't know that Krog—that this Krogstad had anything to do with the Mutual Bank.

Rank. Yes, he seems to have some kind of job there. *(To Mrs. Linde.)* I don't know if you are familiar in your part of the country with the kind of person who is always running around trying to sniff out cases of moral decrepitude and as soon as he finds one puts the individual under observation in some excellent position or other. All the healthy ones are left out in the cold.

Mrs. Linde. I should think it's the sick who need looking after the most.

Rank *(shrugs his shoulders)*. There we are. That's the attitude that turns society into a hospital.

Nora, absorbed in her own thoughts, suddenly starts giggling and clapping her hands.

Rank. What's so funny about that? Do you even know what society is?

Nora. What do I care about your stupid society! I laughed at something entirely different—something terribly amusing. Tell me, Dr. Rank—all the employees in the Mutual Bank, from now on they'll all be dependent on Torvald, right?

Rank. Is that what you find so enormously amusing?

Nora *(smiles and hums)*. That's my business, that's my business! *(Walks around.)* Yes, I do think it's fun that we—that Torvald is going to have so much influence on so many people's lives. *(Brings out the bag of macaroons.)* Have a macaroon, Dr. Rank.

Rank. Well, well—macaroons. I thought they were banned around here.

Nora. Yes, but these were some that Kristine gave me.

Mrs. Linde. What! I?

Nora. That's all right. Don't look so scared. You couldn't know that Torvald won't let me have them. He's afraid they'll ruin my teeth. But who cares! Just once in a while—! Right, Dr. Rank? Have one! *(Puts a macaroon into his mouth.)* You too, Kristine. And one for me. A very small one. Or at most two. *(Walks around again.)* Yes, I really feel very, very happy. Now there's just one thing I'm dying to do.

Rank. Oh? And what's that?

Nora. Something I'm dying to say so Torvald could hear.

Rank. And why can't you?

Nora. I don't dare to, for it's not nice.

Mrs. Linde. Not nice?

Rank. In that case, I guess you'd better not. But surely to the two of us—? What is it you'd like to say for Helmer to hear?

Nora. I want to say, "Goddammit!"

Rank. Are you out of your mind!

Mrs. Linde. For heaven's sake, Nora!

Rank. Say it. Here he comes.

Nora (*hiding the macaroons*). Shhh!

Helmer enters from his study, carrying his hat and overcoat.

Nora (*going to him*). Well, dear, did you get rid of him?

Helmer. Yes, he just left.

Nora. Torvald, I want you to meet Kristine. She's just come to town.

Helmer. Kristine—? I'm sorry; I don't think—

Nora. Mrs. Linde, Torvald dear. Mrs. Kristine Linde.

Helmer. Ah, yes. A childhood friend of my wife's, I suppose.

Mrs. Linde. Yes, we've known each other for a long time.

Nora. Just think; she has come all this way just to see you.

Helmer. I'm not sure I understand—

Mrs. Linde. Well, not really—

Nora. You see, Kristine is an absolutely fantastic secretary, and she would so much like to work for a competent executive and learn more than she knows already—

Helmer. Very sensible, I'm sure, Mrs. Linde.

Nora. So when she heard about your appointment—there was a wire—she came here as fast as she could. How about it, Torvald? Couldn't you do something for Kristine? For my sake. Please?

Helmer. Quite possibly. I take it you're a widow, Mrs. Linde?

Mrs. Linde. Yes.

Helmer. And you've had office experience?

Mrs. Linde. Some—yes.

Helmer. In that case I think it's quite likely that I'll be able to find you a position.

Nora (*claps her hands*). I knew it! I knew it!

Helmer. You've arrived at a most opportune time, Mrs. Linde.

Mrs. Linde. Oh, how can I ever thank you—

Helmer. Not at all, not at all. (*Puts his coat on.*) But today you'll have to excuse me—

Rank. Wait a minute; I'll come with you. (*Gets his fur coat from the front hall, warms it by the stove.*)

Nora. Don't be long, Torvald.

Helmer. An hour or so; no more.

Nora. Are you leaving, too, Kristine?

Mrs. Linde (*putting on her things*). Yes, I'd better go and find a place to stay.

Helmer. Good. Then we'll be going the same way.

Nora (*helping her*). I'm sorry this place is so small, but I don't think we very well could—

Mrs. Linde. Of course! Don't be silly, Nora. Goodbye, and thank you for everything.

Nora. Goodbye. We'll see you soon. You'll be back this evening, of course.

And you too, Dr. Rank; right? If you feel well enough? Of course you will. Just wrap yourself up.

General small talk as all exit into the hall. Children's voices are heard on the stairs.

Nora. There they are! There they are! *(She runs and opens the door. The nurse Anne-Marie enters with the children.)*

Nora. Come in! Come in! *(Bends over and kisses them.)* Oh, you sweet, sweet darlings! Look at them, Kristine! Aren't they beautiful?

Rank. No standing around in the draft!

Helmer. Come along, Mrs. Linde. This place isn't fit for anyone but mothers right now.

Dr. Rank, Helmer, and Mrs. Linde go down the stairs. The Nurse enters the living room with the children. Nora follows, closing the door behind her.

Nora. My, how nice you all look! Such red cheeks! Like apples and roses. *(The children all talk at the same time.)* You've had so much fun? I bet you have. Oh, isn't that nice! You pulled both Emmy and Bob on your sleigh? Both at the same time? That's very good, Ivar. Oh, let me hold her for a minute, Anne-Marie. My sweet little doll baby! *(Takes the smallest of the children from the Nurse and dances with her.)* Yes, yes, of course; Mama'll dance with you too, Bob. What? You threw snowballs? Oh, I wish I'd been there! No, no; *I* want to take their clothes off, Anne-Marie. Please let me; I think it's so much fun. You go on in. You look frozen. There's hot coffee on the stove.

The Nurse exits into the room to the left. Nora takes the children's wraps off and throws them all around. They all keep telling her things at the same time.

Nora. Oh, really? A big dog ran after you? But it didn't bite you. Of course not. Dogs don't bite sweet little doll babies. Don't peek at the packages, Ivar! What's in them? Wouldn't you like to know! No, no; that's something terrible! Play? You want to play? What do you want to play? Okay, let's play hide-and-seek. Bob hides first. You want *me* to? All right. I'll go first.

Laughing and shouting, Nora and the children play in the living room and in the adjacent room, right. Finally, Nora hides herself under the table; the children rush in, look for her, can't find her. They hear her low giggle, run to the table, lift the rug that covers it, see her. General hilarity. She crawls out, pretends to scare them. New delight. In the meantime there has been a knock on the door between the living room and the front hall, but nobody has noticed. Now the door is opened halfway; Krogstad appears. He waits a little. The play goes on.

Krogstad. Pardon me, Mrs. Helmer—

Nora *(with a muted cry turns around, jumps up).* Ah! What do you want?

Krogstad. I'm sorry. The front door was open. Somebody must have forgotten to close it—

Nora *(standing up).* My husband isn't here, Mr. Krogstad.

Krogstad. I know.

Nora. So what do you want?

Krogstad. I'd like a word with you.

Nora. With—? *(To the children.)* Go in to Anne-Marie. What? No, the strange man won't do anything bad to Mama. When he's gone we'll play some more.

She takes the children into the room to the left and closes the door.

Nora *(tense, troubled).* You want to speak with me?

Krogstad. Yes I do.

Nora. Today—? It isn't the first of the month yet.

Krogstad. No, it's Christmas Eve. It's up to you what kind of holiday you'll have.

Nora. What do you want? I can't possibly—

Krogstad. Let's not talk about that just yet. There's something else. You do have a few minutes, don't you?

Nora. Yes. Yes, of course. That is,—

Krogstad. Good. I was sitting in Olsen's restaurant when I saw your husband go by.

Nora. Yes—?

Krogstad. —with a lady.

Nora. What of it?

Krogstad. May I be so free as to ask: wasn't that lady Mrs. Linde?

Nora. Yes.

Krogstad. Just arrived in town?

Nora. Yes, today.

Krogstad. She's a good friend of yours, I understand?

Nora. Yes, she is. But I fail to see—

Krogstad. I used to know her myself.

Nora. I know that.

Krogstad. So you know about that. I thought as much. In that case, let me ask you a simple question. Is Mrs. Linde going to be employed in the bank?

Nora. What makes you think you have the right to cross-examine me like this, Mr. Krogstad—you, one of my husband's employees? But since you ask, I'll tell you. Yes, Mrs. Linde is going to be working in the bank. And it was I who recommended her, Mr. Krogstad. Now you know.

Krogstad. So I was right.

Nora *(walks up and down).* After all, one does have a little influence, you know. Just because you're a woman, it doesn't mean that—Really, Mr. Krogstad, people in a subordinate position should be careful not to offend someone who—oh well—

Krogstad. —has influence?

Nora. Exactly.

Krogstad *(changing his tone).* Mrs. Helmer, I must ask you to be good enough to use your influence on my behalf.

Nora. What do you mean?

Krogstad. I want you to make sure that I am going to keep my subordinate position in the bank.

Nora. I don't understand. Who is going to take your position away from you?

Krogstad. There's no point in playing ignorant with me, Mrs. Helmer. I can very well appreciate that your friend would find it unpleasant to run into me. So now I know who I can thank for my dismissal.

Nora. But I assure you—

Krogstad. Never mind. Just want to say you still have time. I advise you to use your influence to prevent it.

Nora. But Mr. Krogstad, I don't have any influence—none at all.

Krogstad. No? I thought you just said—

Nora. Of course I didn't mean it that way. I! Whatever makes you think that I have any influence of that kind on my husband?

Krogstad. I went to law school with your husband. I have no reason to think that the bank manager is less susceptible than other husbands.

Nora. If you're going to insult my husband, I'll ask you to leave.

Krogstad. You're brave, Mrs. Helmer.

Nora. I'm not afraid of you any more. After New Year's I'll be out of this thing with you.

Krogstad *(more controlled).* Listen, Mrs. Helmer. If necessary, I'll fight as for my life to keep my little job in the bank.

Nora. So it seems.

Krogstad. It isn't just the money; that's really the smallest part of it. There is something else—Well, I guess I might as well tell you. It's like this. I'm sure you know, like everybody else, that some years ago I committed—an impropriety.

Nora. I believe I've heard it mentioned.

Krogstad. The case never came to court, but from that moment all doors were closed to me. So I took up the kind of business you know about. I had to do something, and I think I can say about myself that I have not been among the worst. But now I want to get out of all that. My sons are growing up. For their sake I must get back as much of my good name as I can. This job in the bank was like the first rung on the ladder. And now your husband wants to kick me down and leave me back in the mud again.

Nora. But I swear to you, Mr. Krogstad; it's not at all in my power to help you.

Krogstad. That's because you don't want to. But I have the means to force you.

Nora. You don't mean you're going to tell my husband I owe you money?

Krogstad. And if I did?

Nora. That would be a mean thing to do. *(Almost crying.)* That secret, which is my joy and my pride—for him to learn about it in such a coarse and ugly manner—to learn it from *you*—! It would be terribly unpleasant for me.

Krogstad. Just unpleasant?

Nora *(heatedly).* But go ahead! Do it! It will be worse for you than for me. When my husband realizes what a bad person you are, you'll be sure to lose your job.

Krogstad. I asked you if it was just domestic unpleasantness you were afraid of?

Nora. When my husband finds out, of course he'll pay off the loan, and then we won't have anything more to do with you.

Krogstad *(stepping closer).* Listen, Mrs. Helmer—either you have a very bad memory, or you don't know much about business. I think I had better straighten you out on a few things.

Nora. What do you mean?

Krogstad. When your husband was ill, you came to me to borrow twelve hundred dollars.

Nora. I knew nobody else.

Krogstad. I promised to get you the money—

Nora. And you did.

Krogstad. I promised to get you the money on certain conditions. At the time you were so anxious about your husband's health and so set on getting him away that I doubt very much that you paid much attention to the details of our transaction. That's why I remind you of them now. Anyway, I promised to get you the money if you would sign an I.O.U., which I drafted.

Nora. And which I signed.

Krogstad. Good. But below your signature I added a few lines, making your father security for the loan. Your father was supposed to put his signature to those lines.

Nora. Supposed to—? He did.

Krogstad. I had left the date blank. That is, your father was to date his own signature. You recall that, don't you, Mrs. Helmer?

Nora. I guess so—

Krogstad. I gave the note to you. You were to mail it to your father. Am I correct?

Nora. Yes.

Krogstad. And of course you did so right away, for no more than five or six days later you brought the paper back to me, signed by your father. Then I paid you the money.

Nora. Well? And haven't I been keeping up with the payments?

Krogstad. Fairly well, yes. But to get back to what we were talking about—those were difficult days for you, weren't they, Mrs. Helmer?

Nora. Yes, they were.

Krogstad. Your father was quite ill, I believe.

Nora. He was dying.

Krogstad. And died shortly afterwards?

Nora. That's right.

Krogstad. Tell me, Mrs. Helmer; do you happen to remember the date of your father's death? I mean the exact day of the month?

Nora. Daddy died on September 29.

Krogstad. Quite correct. I have ascertained that fact. That's why there is something peculiar about this *(takes out a piece of paper)*, which I can't account for.

Nora. Peculiar? How? I don't understand—

Krogstad. It seems very peculiar, Mrs. Helmer, that your father signed this promissory note three days after his death.

Nora. How so? I don't see what—

Krogstad. Your father died on September 29. Now look. He has dated his signature October 2. Isn't that odd?

Nora remains silent.

Krogstad. Can you explain it?

Nora is still silent.

Krogstad. I also find it striking that the date and the month and the year are not in your father's handwriting but in a hand I think I recognize. Well, that might be explained. Your father may have forgotten to date his signature and somebody else may have done it here, guessing at the date before he had learned of your father's death. That's all right. It's only the signature itself that matters. And that is genuine, isn't it, Mrs. Helmer? Your father *did* put his name to this note?

Nora *(after a brief silence tosses her head back and looks defiantly at him).* No, he didn't. *I* wrote Daddy's name.

Krogstad. Mrs. Helmer—do you realize what a dangerous admission you just made?

Nora. Why? You'll get your money soon.

Krogstad. Let me ask you something. Why didn't you mail this note to your father?

Nora. Because it was impossible. Daddy was sick—you know that. If I had asked him to sign it, I would have had to tell him what the money was for. But I couldn't tell him, as sick as he was, that my husband's life was in danger. That was impossible. Surely you can see that.

Krogstad. Then it would have been better for you if you had given up your trip abroad.

Nora. No, that was impossible! That trip was to save my husband's life. I couldn't give it up.

Krogstad. But didn't you realize that what you did amounted to fraud against me?

Nora. I couldn't let that make any difference. I didn't care about you at all. I hated the way you made all those difficulties for me, even though you knew the danger my husband was in. I thought you were cold and unfeeling.

Krogstad. Mrs. Helmer, obviously you have no clear idea of what you have done. Let me tell you that what I did that time was no more and no worse. And it ruined my name and reputation.

Nora. You! Are you trying to tell me that you did something brave once in order to save your wife's life?

Krogstad. The law doesn't ask about motives.

Nora. Then it's a bad law.

Krogstad. Bad or not—if I produce this note in court you'll be judged according to the law.

Nora. I refuse to believe you. A daughter shouldn't have the right to spare her dying old father worry and anxiety? A wife shouldn't have the right to save her husband's life? I don't know the laws very well, but I'm sure that somewhere they make allowance for cases like that. And you, a lawyer, don't know that? I think you must be a bad lawyer, Mr. Krogstad.

Krogstad. That may be. But business—the kind of business you and I have with one another—don't you think I know something about that? Very well. Do what you like. But let me tell you this: if I'm going to be kicked out again, you'll keep me company. *(He bows and exits through the front hall.)*

Nora *(pauses thoughtfully; then, with a defiant toss of her head).* Oh, nonsense! Trying to scare me like that! I'm not all that silly. *(Starts picking up the children's clothes; soon stops.)* But—? No! That's impossible! I did it for love!

The Children *(in the door to the left).* Mama, the strange man just left. We saw him.

Nora. Yes, yes; I know. But don't tell anybody about the strange man. Do you hear? Not even Daddy.

The Children. We won't. But now you'll play with us again, won't you, Mama?

Nora. No, not right now.

The Children. But Mama—you promised.

Nora. I know, but I can't just now. Go to your own room. I've so much to do. Be nice now, my little darlings. Do as I say. *(She nudges them gently into the other room and closes the door. She sits down on the couch, picks up a piece of embroidery, makes a few stitches, then stops.)* No! *(Throws the embroidery down, goes to the hall door and calls out.)* Helene! Bring the Christmas tree in here, please! *(Goes to the table, left, opens the drawer, halts.)* No—that's impossible!

The Maid *(with the Christmas tree).* Where do you want it, ma'am?

Nora. There. The middle of the floor.

The Maid. You want anything else?

Nora. No, thanks. I have everything I need. *(The Maid goes out. Nora starts* *trimming the tree.)* I want candles—and flowers—That awful man! Oh, nonsense! There's nothing wrong. This will be a lovely tree. I'll do everything you want me to, Torvald. I'll sing for you—dance for you—

Helmer, a bundle of papers under his arm, enters from outside.

Nora. Ah—you're back already?

Helmer. Yes. Has anybody been here?

Nora. Here? No.

Helmer. That's funny. I saw Krogstad leaving just now.

Nora. Oh? Oh yes, that's right. Krogstad was here for just a moment.

Helmer. I can tell from your face that he came to ask you to put in a word for him.

Nora. Yes.

Helmer. And it was supposed to be your own idea, wasn't it? You were not to tell me he'd been here. He asked you that too, didn't he?

Nora. Yes, Torvald, but—

Helmer. Nora, Nora, how could you! Talk to a man like that and make him promises! And lying to me about it afterwards—!

Nora. Lying—?

Helmer. Didn't you say nobody had been here? *(Shakes his finger at her.)* My little songbird must never do that again. Songbirds are supposed to have clean beaks to chirp with—no false notes. *(Puts his arm around her waist.)* Isn't that so? Of course it is. *(Lets her go.)* And that's enough about that. *(Sits down in front of the fireplace.)* Ah, it's nice and warm in here. *(Begins to leaf through his papers.)*

Nora *(busy with the tree; after a brief pause).* Torvald.

Helmer. Yes.

Nora. I'm looking forward so much to the Stenborgs' costume party day after tomorrow.

Helmer. And I can't wait to find out what you're going to surprise me with.

Nora. Oh, that silly idea!

Helmer. Oh?

Nora. I can't think of anything. It all seems so foolish and pointless.

Helmer. Ah, my little Nora admits that?

Nora *(behind his chair, her arms on the back of the chair).* Are you very busy, Torvald?

Helmer. Well—

Nora. What are all those papers?

Helmer. Bank business.

Nora. Already?

Helmer. I've asked the board to give me the authority to make certain changes in organization and personnel. That's what I'll be doing over the holidays. I want it all settled before New Year's.

Nora. So that's why this poor Krogstad—

Helmer. Hm.

Nora *(leisurely playing with the hair on his neck).* If you weren't so busy, Torvald, I'd ask you for a great big favor.

Helmer. Let's hear it, anyway.

Nora. I don't know anyone with better taste than you, and I want so much to look nice at the party. Couldn't you sort of take charge of me, Torvald, and decide what I'll wear—Help me with my costume?

Helmer. Aha! Little Lady Obstinate is looking for someone to rescue her?

Nora. Yes, Torvald. I won't get anywhere without your help.

Helmer. All right. I'll think about it. We'll come up with something.

Nora. Oh, you *are* nice! *(Goes back to the Christmas tree. A pause.)* Those red flowers look so pretty.—Tell me, was it really all that bad what this Krogstad fellow did?

Helmer. He forged signatures. Do you have any idea what that means?

Nora. Couldn't it have been because he felt he had to?

Helmer. Yes, or like so many others he may simply have been thoughtless. I'm not so heartless as to condemn a man absolutely because of a single imprudent act.

Nora. Of course not, Torvald!

Helmer. People like him can redeem themselves morally by openly confessing their crime and taking their punishment.

Nora. Punishment—?

Helmer. But that was not the way Krogstad chose. He got out of it with tricks and evasions. That's what has corrupted him.

Nora. So you think that if—?

Helmer. Can't you imagine how a guilty person like that has to lie and fake and dissemble wherever he goes—putting on a mask before everybody he's close to, even his own wife and children. It's this thing with the children that's the worst part of it, Nora.

Nora. Why is that?

Helmer. Because when a man lives inside such a circle of stinking lies he brings infection into his own home and contaminates his whole family. With every breath of air his children inhale the germs of something ugly.

Nora *(moving closer behind him).* Are you so sure of that?

Helmer. Of course I am. I have seen enough examples of that in my work. Nearly all young criminals have had mothers who lied.

Nora. Why mothers—particularly?

Helmer. Most often mothers. But of course fathers tend to have the same influence. Every lawyer knows that. And yet, for years this Krogstad has been poisoning his own children in an atmosphere of lies and deceit. That's why I call him a lost soul morally. *(Reaches out for her hands.)* And that's why my sweet little Nora must promise me never to take his side again. Let's shake on that.—What? What's this? Give me your hand. There! Now that's settled. I assure you, I would find it impossible to work in the same room with that man. I feel literally sick when I'm around people like that.

Nora *(withdraws her hand and goes to the other side of the Christmas tree).* It's so hot in here. And I have so much to do.

Helmer *(gets up and collects his papers).* Yes, and I really should try to get some of this reading done before dinner. I must think about your costume too. And maybe just possibly I'll have something to wrap in gilt paper and hang on the Christmas tree. *(Puts his hand on her head.)* Oh my adorable little songbird! *(Enters his study and closes the door.)*

Nora *(after a pause, in a low voice).* It's all a lot of nonsense. It's not that way at all. It's impossible. It has to be impossible.

The Nurse *(in the door, left).* The little ones are asking ever so nicely if they can't come in and be with their mama.

Nora. No, no, no! Don't let them in here! You stay with them, Anne-Marie.

The Nurse. If you say so, ma'am. *(Closes the door.)*

Nora *(pale with terror).* Corrupt my little children—! Poison my home—? *(Brief pause; she lifts her head.)* That's not true. Never. Never in a million years.

Act II

The same room. The Christmas tree is in the corner by the piano, stripped shabby-looking, with burnt-down candles. Nora's outside clothes are on the couch. Nora is alone. She walks around restlessly. She stops by the couch and picks up her coat.

Nora *(drops the coat again).* There's somebody now! *(Goes to the door, listens.)* No. Nobody. Of course not—not on Christmas. And not tomorrow either.[1]—But perhaps—*(Opens the door and looks.)* No, nothing in the mailbox. All empty. *(Comes forward.)* How silly I am! Of course he isn't serious. Nothing like that could happen. After all, I have three small children.

The Nurse enters from the room, left, carrying a big carton.

The Nurse. Well, at last I found it—the box with your costume.

Nora. Thanks. Just put it on the table.

Nurse *(does so).* But it's all a big mess, I'm afraid.

Nora. Oh, I wish I could tear the whole thing to little pieces!

Nurse. Heavens! It's not as bad as all that. It can be fixed all right. All it takes is a little patience.

Nora. I'll go over and get Mrs. Linde to help me.

Nurse. Going out again? In this awful weather? You'll catch a cold.

Nora. That might not be such a bad thing. How are the children?

---

1. In Norway both December 25 and 26 are legal holidays.

Nurse. The poor little dears are playing with their presents, but—

Nora. Do they keep asking for me?

Nurse. Well, you know, they're used to being with their mamma.

Nora. I know. But Anne-Marie, from now on I can't be with them as much as before.

Nurse. Oh well. Little children get used to everything.

Nora. You think so? Do you think they'll forget their mamma if I were gone altogether?

Nurse. Goodness me—gone altogether?

Nora. Listen, Anne-Marie—something I've wondered about. How could you bring yourself to leave your child with strangers?

Nurse. But I had to, if I were to nurse you.

Nora. Yes, but how could you *want* to?

Nurse. When I could get such a nice place? When something like that happens to a poor young girl, she'd better be grateful for whatever she gets. For *he* didn't do a thing for me—the louse!

Nora. But your daughter has forgotten all about you, hasn't she?

Nurse. Oh no! Not at all! She wrote to me both when she was confirmed and when she got married.

Nora (*putting her arms around her neck*). You dear old thing—you were a good mother to me when I was little.

Nurse. Poor little Nora had no one else, you know.

Nora. And if my little ones didn't, I know you'd—oh, I'm being silly! (*Opens the carton.*) Go in to them, please. I really should—. Tomorrow you'll see how pretty I'll be.

Nurse. I know. There won't be anybody at that party half as pretty as you, ma'am. (*Goes out, left.*)

Nora (*begins to take clothes out of the carton; in a moment she throws it all down*). If only I dared to go out. If only I knew nobody would come. That nothing would happen while I was gone.—How silly! Nobody'll come. Just don't think about it. Brush the muff. Beautiful gloves. Beautiful gloves. Forget it. Forget it. One, two, three, four, five, six—(*Cries out.*) There they are! (*Moves toward the door, stops irresolutely.*)

Mrs. Linde enters from the hall. She has already taken off her coat.

Nora. Oh, it's you, Kristine. There's no one else out there, is there? I'm so glad you're here.

Mrs. Linde. They told me you'd asked for me.

Nora. I just happened to walk by. I need your help with something—badly. Let's sit here on the couch. Look. Torvald and I are going to a costume party tomorrow night—at Consul Stenborg's upstairs—and Torvald wants me to go as a Neapolitan fisher girl and dance the tarantella. I learned it when we were on Capri.

Mrs. Linde. Well, well! So you'll be putting on a whole show?

Nora.   Yes. Torvald thinks I should. Look, here's the costume. Torvald had it made for me while we were there. But it's all so torn and everything. I just don't know—

Mrs. Linde.   Oh, that can be fixed. It's not that much. The trimmings have come loose in a few places. Do you have needle and thread? Ah, here we are. All set.

Nora.   I really appreciate it, Kristine.

Mrs. Linde (*sewing*).   So you'll be in disguise tomorrow night, eh? You know—I may come by for just a moment, just to look at you.—Oh dear. I haven't even thanked you for the nice evening last night.

Nora (*gets up, moves around*).   Oh, I don't know. I don't think last night was as nice as it usually is.—You should have come to town a little earlier, Kristine.—Yes, Torvald knows how to make it nice and pretty around here.

Mrs. Linde.   You too, I should think. After all, you're your father's daughter. By the way, is Dr. Rank always as depressed as he was last night?

Nora.   No, last night was unusual. He's a very sick man, you know—very sick. Poor Rank, his spine is rotting away. Tuberculosis, I think. You see, his father was a nasty old man with mistresses and all that sort of thing. Rank has been sickly ever since he was a little boy.

Mrs. Linde (*dropping her sewing to her lap*).   But dearest Nora, where have you learned about things like that?

Nora (*still walking about*).   Oh, you know—with three children you sometimes get to talk with—other wives. Some of them know quite a bit about medicine. So you pick up a few things.

Mrs. Linde (*resumes her sewing; after a brief pause*).   Does Dr. Rank come here every day?

Nora.   Every single day. He's Torvald's oldest and best friend, after all. And my friend too, for that matter. He's part of the family, almost.

Mrs. Linde.   But tell me, is he quite sincere? I mean, isn't he the kind of man who likes to say nice things to people?

Nora.   No, not at all. Rather the opposite, in fact. What makes you say that?

Mrs. Linde.   When you introduced us yesterday, he told me he'd often heard my name mentioned in this house. But later on it was quite obvious that your husband really had no idea who I was. So how could Dr. Rank—?

Nora.   You're right, Kristine, but I can explain that. You see, Torvald loves me so very much that he wants me all to himself. That's what he says. When we were first married he got almost jealous when I as much as mentioned anybody from back home that I was fond of. So of course I soon stopped doing that. But with Dr. Rank I often talk about home. You see, he likes to listen to me.

Mrs. Linde.   Look here, Nora. In many ways you're still a child. After all, I'm quite a bit older than you and have had more experience. I want to give you a piece of advice. I think you should get out of this thing with Dr. Rank.

Nora. Get out of what thing?

Mrs. Linde. Several things in fact, if you want my opinion. Yesterday you said something about a rich admirer who was going to give you money—

Nora. One who doesn't exist, unfortunately. What of it?

Mrs. Linde. Does Dr. Rank have money?

Nora. Yes, he does.

Mrs. Linde. And no dependents?

Nora. No. But—?

Mrs. Linde. And he comes here every day?

Nora. Yes, I told you that already.

Mrs. Linde. But how can that sensitive man be so tactless?

Nora. I haven't the slightest idea what you're talking about.

Mrs. Linde. Don't play games with me, Nora. Don't you think I know who you borrowed the twelve hundred dollars from?

Nora. Are you out of your mind! The very idea—! A friend of both of us who sees us every day—! What a dreadfully uncomfortable position that would be!

Mrs. Linde. So it really isn't Dr. Rank?

Nora. Most certainly not! I would never have dreamed of asking him—not for a moment. Anyway, he didn't have any money then. He inherited it afterwards.

Mrs. Linde. Well, I still think it may have been lucky for you, Nora dear.

Nora. The idea! It would never have occurred to me to ask Dr. Rank—. Though I'm sure that if I *did* ask him—

Mrs. Linde. But of course you wouldn't.

Nora. Of course not. I can't imagine that that would ever be necessary. But I am quite sure that if I told Dr. Rank—

Mrs. Linde. Behind your husband's back?

Nora. I must get out of—this other thing. That's also behind his back. I *must* get out of it.

Mrs. Linde. That's what I told you yesterday. But—

Nora (*walking up and down*). A man manages these things so much better than a woman—

Mrs. Linde. One's husband, yes.

Nora. Silly, silly! (*Stops.*) When you've paid off all you owe, you get your I.O.U. back; right?

Mrs. Linde. Yes, of course.

Nora. And you can tear it into a hundred thousand little pieces and burn it— that dirty, filthy, paper!

Mrs. Linde (*looks hard at her, puts down her sewing, rises slowly*). Nora— you're hiding something from me.

Nora. Can you tell?

Mrs. Linde. Something's happened to you, Nora, since yesterday morning. What is it?

Nora (*going to her*).   Kristine! (*Listens.*) Shhh. Torvald just came back. Listen. Why don't you go in to the children for a while. Torvald can't stand having sewing around. Get Anne-Marie to help you.

Mrs. Linde (*gathers some of the sewing things together*).   All right, but I'm not leaving here till you and I have talked.

She goes out left, just as Helmer enters from the front hall.

Nora (*towards him*).   I have been waiting and waiting for you, Torvald.

Helmer.   Was that the dressmaker?

Nora.   No, it was Kristine. She's helping me with my costume. Oh Torvald, just wait till you see how nice I'll look!

Helmer.   I told you. Pretty good idea I had, wasn't it?

Nora.   Lovely! And wasn't it nice of me to go along with it?

Helmer (*his hand under her chin*).   Nice? To do what your husband tells you? All right, you little rascal; I know you didn't mean it that way. But don't let me interrupt you. I suppose you want to try it on.

Nora.   And you'll be working?

Helmer.   Yes. (*Shows her a pile of papers.*) Look. I've been down to the bank. (*Is about to enter his study.*)

Nora.   Torvald.

Helmer (*halts*). Yes?

Nora.   What if your little squirrel asked you ever so nicely—

Helmer.   For what?

Nora.   Would you do it?

Helmer.   Depends on what it is.

Nora.   Squirrel would run around and do all sorts of fun tricks if you'd be nice and agreeable.

Helmer.   All right. What is it?

Nora.   Lark would chirp and twitter in all the rooms, up and down—

Helmer.   So what? Lark does that anyway.

Nora.   I'll be your elfmaid and dance for you in the moonlight, Torvald.

Helmer.   Nora, don't tell me it's the same thing you mentioned this morning?

Nora (*closer to him*).   Yes, Torvald. I beg you!

Helmer.   You really have the nerve to bring that up again?

Nora.   Yes. You've just got to do as I say. You *must* let Krogstad keep his job.

Helmer.   My dear Nora. It's his job I intend to give to Mrs. Linde.

Nora.   I know. And that's ever so nice of you. But can't you just fire somebody else?

Helmer.   This is incredible! You just don't give up do you? Because you make some foolish promise, *I* am supposed to—!

Nora.   That's not the reason, Torvald. It's for your own sake. That man writes for the worst newspapers. You've said so yourself. There's no telling what he may do to you. I'm scared to death of him.

Helmer.   Ah, I understand. You're afraid because of what happened before.

Nora.   What do you mean?

Helmer. You're thinking of your father, of course.

Nora. Yes. Yes, you're right. Remember the awful things they wrote about Daddy in the newspapers. I really think they might have forced him to resign if the ministry hadn't sent you to look into the charges and if you hadn't been so helpful and understanding.

Helmer. My dear little Nora, there is a world of difference between your father and me. Your father's official conduct was not above reproach. Mine is, and I intend for it to remain that way as long as I hold my position.

Nora. Oh, but you don't know what vicious people like that may think of. Oh, Torvald! Now all of us could be so happy together here in our own home, peaceful and carefree. Such a good life, Torvald, for you and me and the children! That's why I implore you—

Helmer. And it's exactly because you plead for him that you make it impossible for me to keep him. It's already common knowledge in the bank that I intend to let Krogstad go. If it gets out that the new manager has changed his mind because of his wife—

Nora. Yes? What then?

Helmer. No, of course, that wouldn't matter at all as long as little Mrs. Pighead here got her way! Do you want me to make myself look ridiculous before my whole staff—make people think I can be swayed by just anybody—by outsiders? Believe me, I would soon enough find out what the consequences would be! Besides, there's another thing that makes it absolutely impossible for Krogstad to stay on in the bank now that I'm in charge.

Nora. What's that?

Helmer. I suppose in a pinch I could overlook his moral shortcomings—

Nora. Yes, you could; couldn't you, Torvald?

Helmer. And I understand he's quite a good worker, too. But we've known each other for a long time. It's one of those imprudent relationships you get into when you're young that embarrass you for the rest of your life. I guess I might as well be frank with you: he and I are on a first name basis. And that tactless fellow never hides the fact even when other people are around. Rather, he seems to think it entitles him to be familiar with me. Every chance he gets he comes out with his damn "Torvald, Torvald." I'm telling you, I find it most awkward. He would make my position in the bank intolerable.

Nora. You don't really mean any of this, Torvald.

Helmer. Oh? I don't? And why not?

Nora. No, for it's all so petty.

Helmer. What! Petty? You think I'm being petty!

Nora. No, I *don't* think you are petty, Torvald dear. That's exactly why I—

Helmer. Never mind. You think my reasons are petty, so it follows that I must be petty too. Petty! Indeed! By God, I'll put an end to this right now! *(Opens the door to the front hall and calls out.)* Helene!

Nora. What are you doing?

Helmer (searching among his papers).   Making a decision. (The Maid enters.) Here. Take this letter. Go out with it right away. Find somebody to deliver it. But quick. The address is on the envelope. Wait. Here's money.

The Maid.   Very good sir. (She takes the letter and goes out.)

Helmer (collecting his papers).   There now, little Mrs. Obstinate!

Nora (breathless).   Torvald—what was that letter?

Helmer.   Krogstad's dismissal.

Nora.   Call it back, Torvald! There's still time! Oh Torvald, please—call it back! For my sake, for your own sake, for the sake of the children! Listen to me, Torvald! Do it! You don't know what you're doing to all of us!

Helmer.   Too late.

Nora.   Yes. Too late.

Helmer.   Dear Nora, I forgive you this fear you're in, although it really is an insult to me. Yes, it is! It's an insult to think that I am scared of a shabby scrivener's revenge. But I forgive you, for it's such a beautiful proof how much you love me. (Takes her in his arms.) And that's the way it should be, my sweet darling. Whatever happens, you'll see that when things get really rough I have both strength and courage. You'll find out that I am man enough to shoulder the whole burden.

Nora (terrified).   What do you mean by that?

Helmer.   All of it, I tell you—

Nora (composed).   You'll never have to do that.

Helmer.   Good. Then we'll share the burden, Nora—like husband and wife, the way it ought to be. (Caresses her.) Now are you satisfied? There, there, there. Not that look in your eyes—like a frightened dove. It's all your own foolish imagination.—Why don't you practice the tarantella—and your tambourine, too. I'll be in the inner office and close both doors, so I won't hear you. You can make as much noise as you like. (Turning in the doorway.) And when Rank comes, tell him where to find me. (He nods to her, enters his study carrying his papers, and closes the door.)

Nora (transfixed by terror, whispers). He would do it. He'll do it. He'll do it in spite of the whole world.—No, this mustn't happen. Anything rather than that! There must be a way—! (The doorbell rings.) Dr. Rank! Anything rather than that! Anything—anything at all!

She passes her hand over her face, pulls herself together, and opens the door to the hall. Dr. Rank is out there, hanging up his coat. Darkness begins to fall during the following scene.

Nora.   Hello there, Dr. Rank. I recognized your ringing. Don't go in to Torvald yet. I think he's busy.

Rank.   And you?

Nora (as he enters and she closes the door behind him). You know I always have time for you.

Rank.   Thanks. I'll make use of that as long as I can.

Nora.   What do you mean by that—As long as you can?

Rank. Does that frighten you?

Nora. Well, it's a funny expression. As if something was going to happen.

Rank. Something is going to happen that I've long been expecting. But I admit I hadn't thought it would come quite so soon.

Nora *(seizes his arm).* What is it you've found out? Dr. Rank—tell me!

Rank *(sits down by the stove).* I'm going downhill fast. There's nothing to do about that.

Nora *(with audible relief).* So it's you—

Rank. Who else? No point in lying to myself. I'm in worse shape than any of my other patients, Mrs. Helmer. These last few days I've been making up my inner status. Bankrupt. Chances are that within a month I'll be rotting up in the cemetery.

Nora. Shame on you! Talking that horrid way!

Rank. The thing itself is horrid—damn horrid. The worst of it, though, is all that other horror that comes first. There is only one more test I need to make. After that I'll have a pretty good idea when I'll start coming apart. There is something I want to say to you. Helmer's refined nature can't stand anything hideous. I don't want him in my sick room.

Nora. Oh, but Dr. Rank—

Rank. I don't want him there. Under no circumstance. I'll close my door to him. As soon as I have full certainty that the worst is about to begin I'll give you my card with a black cross on it. Then you'll know the last horror of destruction has started.

Nora. Today you're really quite impossible. And I had hoped you'd be in a particularly good mood.

Rank. With death on my hands? Paying for someone else's sins? Is there justice in that? And yet there isn't a single family that isn't ruled by the same law of ruthless retribution, in one way or another.

Nora *(puts her hands over her ears).* Poppycock! Be fun! Be fun!

Rank. Well, yes. You may just as well laugh at the whole thing. My poor, innocent spine is suffering from my father's frolics as a young lieutenant.

Nora *(over by the table, left).* Right. He was addicted to asparagus and goose live paté, wasn't he?

Rank. And truffles.

Nora. Of course. Truffles. And oysters too, I think.

Rank. And oysters. Obviously.

Nora. And all the port and champagne that go with it. It's really too bad that goodies like that ruin your backbone.

Rank. Particularly an unfortunate backbone that never enjoyed any of it.

Nora. Ah yes, that's the saddest part of it all.

Rank *(looks searchingly at her).* Hm—

Nora *(after a brief pause).* Why did you smile just then?

Rank. No, it was you that laughed.

Nora. No, it was you that smiled, Dr. Rank!

Rank *(gets up).* You're more of a mischief-maker than I thought.

Nora. I feel in the mood for mischief today.

Rank. So it seems.

Nora (with both her hands on his shoulders). Dear, dear Dr. Rank, don't you go and die and leave Torvald and me.

Rank. Oh, you won't miss me for very long. Those who go away are soon forgotten.

Nora (with an anxious look). Do you believe that?

Rank. You'll make new friends, and then—

Nora. Who'll make new friends?

Rank. Both you and Helmer, once I'm gone. You yourself seem to have made a good start already. What was this Mrs. Linde doing here last night?

Nora. Aha—Don't tell me you're jealous of poor Kristine?

Rank. Yes, I am. She'll be my successor in this house. As soon as I have made my excuses, that woman is likely to—

Nora. Shh—not so loud. She's in there.

Rank. Today too? There you are!

Nora. She's mending my costume. My God, you really *are* unreasonable. (Sits down on the couch). Now be nice, Dr. Rank. Tomorrow you'll see how beautifully I'll dance, and then you are to pretend I'm dancing just for you—and for Torvald too, of course. (Takes several items out of the carton.) Sit down, Dr. Rank; I want to show you something.

Rank (sitting down). What?

Nora. Look.

Rank. Silk stockings.

Nora. Flesh-colored. Aren't they lovely? Now it's getting dark in here, but tomorrow—No, no. You only get to see the foot. Oh well, you might as well see all of it.

Rank. Hmm.

Nora. Why do you look so critical? Don't you think they'll fit?

Rank. That's something I can't possibly have a reasoned opinion about.

Nora (looks at him for a moment). Shame on you. (Slaps his ear lightly with the stocking.) That's what you get. (Puts the things back in the carton.)

Rank. And what other treasures are you going to show me?

Nora. Nothing at all, because you're naughty. (She hums a little and rummages in the carton.)

Rank (after a brief silence). When I sit here like this, talking confidently with you, I can't imagine—I can't possibly imagine what would have become of me if I had't had you and Helmer.

Nora (smiles). Well, yes—I do believe you like being with us.

Rank (in a lower voice, lost in thought). And then to have to go away from it all—

Nora. Nonsense. You are not going anywhere.

Rank (as before). —and not to leave behind as much as a poor little token of gratitude, hardly a brief memory of someone missed, nothing but a vacant place that anyone can fill.

Nora. And what if I were to ask you—? No—

Rank. Ask me what?

Nora. For a great proof of your friendship—

Rank. Yes, yes—?

Nora. No, I mean—for an enormous favor—

Rank. Would you really for once make me as happy as all that?

Nora. But you don't even know what it is.

Rank. Well, then; tell me.

Nora. Oh, but I can't, Dr. Rank. It's altogether too much to ask—It's advice and help and a favor—

Rank. So much the better. I can't even begin to guess what it is you have in mind. So for heaven's sake tell me! Don't you trust me?

Nora. Yes, I trust you more than anyone else I know. You are my best and most faithful friend. I know that. So I will tell you. All right, Dr. Rank. There is something you can help me prevent. You know how much Torvald loves me—beyond all words. Never for a moment would he hesitate to give his life for me.

Rank (leaning over to her).   Nora—do you really think he's the only one—?

Nora (with a slight start).   Who—?

Rank.   —would gladly give his life for you.

Nora (heavily).   I see.

Rank. I have sworn an oath to myself to tell you before I go. I'll never find a better occasion.—All right, Nora; now you know. And now you also know that you can confide in me more than in anyone else.

Nora (gets up; in a calm, steady voice).   Let me get by.

Rank (makes room for her but remains seated).   Nora—

Nora (in the door to the front hall).   Helene, bring the lamp in here, please. (Walks over to the stove.) Oh, dear Dr. Rank. That really wasn't very nice of you.

Rank (gets up). That I have loved you as much as anybody—was that not nice?

Nora. No; not that. But that you told me. There was no need for that.

Rank. What do you mean? Have you known—?

The Maid enters with the lamp, puts it on the table, and goes out.

Rank. Nora—Mrs. Helmer—I'm asking you: did you know?

Nora. Oh, how can I tell what I knew and didn't know! I really can't say—But that you could be so awkward, Dr. Rank! Just when everything was so comfortable.

Rank. Well, anyway, now you know that I'm at your service with my life and soul. And now you must speak.

Nora (looks at him).   After what just happened?

Rank. I beg of you—let me know what it is.

Nora. There is nothing I can tell you now.

Rank. Yes, yes. You mustn't punish me this way. Please let me do for you whatever anyone *can* do.

Nora. Now there is nothing you can do. Besides, I don't think I really need any help, anyway. It's probably just my imagination. Of course that's all it is. I'm sure of it! *(Sits down in the rocking chair, looks at him, smiles.)* Well, well, well, Dr. Rank! What a fine gentleman you turned out to be! Aren't you ashamed of yourself, now that we have light?

Rank. No, not really. But perhaps I ought to leave—and not come back?

Nora. Don't be silly; of course not! You'll come here exactly as you have been doing. You know perfectly well that Torvald can't do without you.

Rank. Yes, but what about you?

Nora. Oh, I always think it's perfectly delightful when you come.

Rank. That's the very thing that misled me. You are a riddle to me. It has often seemed to me that you'd just as soon be with me as with Helmer.

Nora. Well, you see, there are people you love, and then there are other people you'd almost rather be with.

Rank. Yes, there is something in that.

Nora. When I lived at home with Daddy, of course I loved him most. But I always thought it was so much fun to sneak off down to the maids' room, for they never gave me good advice and they always talked about such fun things.

Rank. Aha! So its *their* place I have taken.

Nora *(jumps up and goes over to him).* Oh dear, kind Dr. Rank, you know very well I didn't mean it that way. Can't you see that with Torvald it is the way it used to be with Daddy?

The Maid enters from the front hall.

The Maid. Ma'am! *(Whispers to her and gives her a caller's card.)*

Nora *(glances at the card).* Ah! *(Puts it in her pocket.)*

Rank. Anything wrong?

Nora. No, no; not at all. It's nothing—just my new costume—

Rank. But your costume is lying right there!

Nora. Oh yes, that one. But this is another one. I ordered it. Torvald mustn't know—

Rank. Aha. So that's the great secret.

Nora. That's it. Why don't you go in to him, please. He's in the inner office. And keep him there for a while—

Rank. Don't worry. He won't get away. *(Enters Helmer's study.)*

Nora *(to the Maid).* You say he's waiting in the kitchen?

The Maid. Yes. He came up the back stairs.

Nora. But didn't you tell him there was somebody with me?

The Maid. Yes, but he wouldn't listen.

Nora. He won't leave?

The Maid. No, not till he's had a word with you, ma'am.

Nora. All right. But try not to make any noise. And, Helene—don't tell anyone he's here. It's supposed to be a surprise for my husband.

The Maid. I understand, ma'am—*(She leaves.)*

Nora. The terrible is happening. It's happening, after all. No, no, no. It can't happen. It won't happen. *(She bolts the study door.)*

The Maid opens the front hall door for Krogstad and closes the door behind him. He wears a fur coat for traveling, boots, and a fur hat.

Nora *(toward him).* Keep your voice down. My husband's home.

Krogstad. That's all right.

Nora. What do you want?

Krogstad. To find out something.

Nora. Be quick, then. What is it?

Krogstad. I expect you know I've been fired.

Nora. I couldn't prevent it, Mr. Krogstad. I fought for you as long and as hard as I could but it didn't do any good.

Krogstad. Your husband doesn't love you any more than that? He knows what I can do to you, and yet he runs the risk—

Nora. Surely you didn't think I'd tell him?

Krogstad. No, I really didn't. It wouldn't be like Torvald Helmer to show that kind of guts—

Nora. Mr. Krogstad, I insist that you show respect for my husband.

Krogstad. By all means. All due respect. But since you're so anxious to keep this a secret, may I assume that you are a little better informed than yesterday about exactly what you have done?

Nora. Better than *you* could ever teach me.

Krogstad. Of course. Such a bad lawyer as I am—

Nora. What do you want of me?

Krogstad. I just wanted to find out how you are, Mrs. Helmer. I've been thinking about you all day. You see, even a bill collector, a pen pusher, a—anyway, someone like me—even he has a little of what they call a heart.

Nora. Then show it. Think of my little children.

Krogstad. Have you and your husband thought of mine? Never mind. All I want to tell you is that you don't need to take this business too seriously. I have no intention of bringing charges right away.

Nora. Oh no, you wouldn't; would you? I knew you wouldn't.

Krogstad. The whole thing can be settled quite amiably. Nobody else needs to know anything. It will be between the three of us.

Nora. My husband must never find out about this.

Krogstad. How are you going to prevent that? Maybe you can pay me the balance on the loan?

Nora. No, not right now.

Krogstad. Or do you have a way of raising the money one of these next few days?

Nora. None I intend to make use of.

Krogstad. It wouldn't do you any good, anyway. Even if you had the cash in your hand right this minute, I wouldn't give you your note back. It wouldn't make any difference *how* much money you offered me.

Nora. Then you'll have to tell me what you plan to use the note *for*.

Krogstad. Just keep it; that's all. Have it on hand, so to speak. I won't say a word to anybody else. So if you've been thinking about doing something desperate—

Nora. I have.

Krogstad. —like leaving house and home—

Nora. I have!

Krogstad. —or even something worse—

Nora. ' How did you know?

Krogstad. —then: don't.

Nora. How did you know I was thinking of *that?*

Krogstad. Most of us do, right at first. I did, too, but when it came down to it I didn't have the courage—

Nora (*tonelessly*). Nor do I.

Krogstad (*relieved*). See what I mean? I thought so. You don't either.

Nora. I don't. I don't.

Krogstad. Besides, it would be very silly of you. Once that first domestic blow-up is behind you—. Here in my pocket is a letter for your husband.

Nora. Telling him everything?

Krogstad. As delicately as possible.

Nora (*quickly*). He mustn't get that letter. Tear it up. I'll get you the money somehow.

Krogstad. Excuse me, Mrs. Helmer, I thought I just told you—

Nora. I'm not talking about the money I owe you. Just let me know how much money you want from my husband, and I'll get it for you.

Krogstad. I want no money from your husband.

Nora. Then, what *do* you want?

Krogstad. I'll tell you, Mrs. Helmer. I want to rehabilitate myself; I want to get up in the world; and your husband is going to help me. For a year and a half I haven't done anything disreputable. All that time I have been struggling with the most miserable circumstances. I was content to work my way up step by step. Now I've been kicked out, and I'm no longer satisfied just getting my old job back. I want more than that; I want to get to the top. I'm being quite serious. I want the bank to take me back but in a higher position. I want your husband to create a new job for me—

Nora. He'll never do that!

Krogstad. He will. I know him. He won't dare not to. And once I'm back inside and he and I are working together, you'll see! Within a year I'll be the manager's right hand. It will be Nils Krogstad and not Torvald Helmer who'll be running the Mutual Bank!

Nora. You'll never see that happen!

Krogstad. Are you thinking of—?

Nora. Now I *do* have the courage.

Krogstad. You can't scare me. A fine, spoiled lady like you—

Nora. You'll see, you'll see!

Krogstad. Under the ice, perhaps? Down into that cold, black water? Then spring comes, and you float up again—hideous, can't be identified, hair all gone—

Nora. You don't frighten me.

Krogstad. Nor you me. One doesn't do that sort of thing, Mrs. Helmer. Besides, what good would it do? He'd still be in my power.

Nora. Afterwards? When I'm no longer—?

Krogstad. Aren't you forgetting that your reputation would be in my hands?

Nora stares at him, speechless.

Krogstad. All right; now I've told you what to expect. So don't do anything foolish. When Helmer gets my letter I expect to hear from him. And don't you forget that it's your husband himself who forces me to use such means again. That I'll never forgive him. Goodbye, Mrs. Helmer. *(Goes out through the hall.)*

Nora *(at the door, opens it a little, listens).* He's going. And no letter. Of course not! That would be impossible! *(Opens the door more.)* What's he doing? He's still there. Doesn't go down. Having second thoughts—? Will he—?

The sound of a letter dropping into the mailbox. Then Krogstad's steps are heard going down the stairs, gradually dying away.

Nora *(with a muted cry runs forward to the table by the couch; brief pause).* In the mailbox. *(Tiptoes back to the door to the front hall.)* There it is. Torvald, Torvald—now we're lost!

Mrs. Linde *(enters from the left, carrying Nora's Capri costume).* There now. I think it's all fixed. Why don't we try it on you—

Nora *(in a low, hoarse voice).* Kristine, come here.

Mrs. Linde. What's wrong with you? You look quite beside yourself.

Nora. Come over here. Do you see that letter? There, look—through the glass in the mailbox.

Mrs. Linde. Yes, yes; I see it.

Nora. That letter is from Krogstad.

Mrs. Linde. Nora—it was Krogstad who lent you the money!

Nora. Yes, and now Torvald will find out about it.

Mrs. Linde. Oh believe me, Nora. That's the best thing for both of you.

Nora. There's more to it than you know. I forged a signature—

Mrs. Linde. Oh my God—!

Nora. I just want to tell you this, Kristine, that you must be my witness.

Mrs. Linde. Witness? How? Witness to what?

Nora. If I lose my mind—and that could very well happen—

Mrs. Linde. Nora!

Nora. —or if something were to happen to me—something that made it impossible for me to be here—

Mrs. Linde. Nora, Nora! You're not yourself!

Nora. —and if someone were to take all the blame, assume the whole responsibility—Do you understand—?

Mrs. Linde. Yes, yes; but how can you think—!

Nora. —then you are to witness that that's not so, Kristine. I am not beside myself. I am perfectly rational, and what I'm telling you is that nobody else has known about this. I've done it all by myself, the whole thing. Just remember that.

Mrs. Linde. I will. But I don't understand any of it.

Nora. Oh, how could you! For it's the wonderful that's about to happen.

Mrs. Linde. The wonderful?

Nora. Yes, the wonderful. But it's so terrible, Kristine. It mustn't happen for anything in the whole world!

Mrs. Linde. I'm going over to talk to Krogstad right now.

Nora. No, don't. Don't go to him. He'll do something bad to you.

Mrs. Linde. There was a time when he would have done anything for me.

Nora. He!

Mrs. Linde. Where does he live?

Nora. Oh, I don't know—Yes, wait a minute—*(Reaches into her pocket.)* here's his card.—But the letter, the letter—!

Helmer *(in his study, knocks on the door).* Nora!

Nora *(cries out in fear).* Oh, what is it? What do you want?

Helmer. That's all right. Nothing to be scared about. We're not coming in. For one thing, you've bolted the door, you know. Are you modeling your costume?

Nora. Yes, yes; I am. I'm going to be so pretty, Torvald.

Mrs. Linde *(having looked at the card).* He lives just around the corner.

Nora. Yes, but it's no use. Nothing can save us now. The letter is in the mailbox.

Mrs. Linde. And your husband has the key?

Nora. Yes. He always keeps it with him.

Mrs. Linde. Krogstad must ask for his letter back, unread. He's got to think up some pretext or other—

Nora. But this is just the time of day when Torvald—

Mrs. Linde. Delay him. Go in to him. I'll be back as soon as I can. *(She hurries out through the hall door.)*

Nora *(walks over to Helmer's door, opens it, and peeks in).* Torvald!

Helmer *(still offstage).* Well, well! So now one's allowed in one's own living room again. Come on, Rank. Now we'll see—*(In the doorway.)* But what's this?

Nora. What, Torvald dear?

Helmer. Rank prepared me for a splendid metamorphosis.

Rank *(in the doorway).* That's how I understood it. Evidently I was mistaken.

Nora. Nobody gets to admire me in my costume before tomorrow.

Helmer. But, dearest Nora—you look all done in. Have you been practicing too hard?

Nora. No, I haven't practiced at all.

Helmer. But you'll have to, you know.

Nora. I know it, Torvald. I simply must. But I can't do a thing unless you help me. I have forgotten everything.

Helmer. Oh it will all come back. We'll work on it.

Nora. Oh yes, please, Torvald. You just have to help me. Promise? I am so nervous. That big party—. You mustn't do anything else tonight. Not a bit of business. Don't even touch a pen. Will you promise, Torvald?

Helmer. I promise. Tonight I'll be entirely at your service—you helpless little thing.—Just a moment, though. First I want to—*(Goes to the door to the front hall.)*

Nora. What are you doing out there?

Helmer. Just looking to see if there's any mail.

Nora. No, no! Don't, Torvald!

Helmer. Why not?

Nora. Torvald, I beg you. There is no mail.

Helmer. Let me just look, anyway. *(Is about to go out.)*

Nora by the piano, plays the first bars of the tarantella dance.

Helmer *(halts at the door).* Aha!

Nora. I won't be able to dance tomorrow if I don't get to practice with you.

Helmer *(goes to her).* Are you really all that scared, Nora dear?

Nora. Yes, so terribly scared. Let's try it right now. There's still time before we eat. Oh please, sit down and play for me, Torvald. Teach me, coach me, the way you always do.

Helmer. Of course I will, my darling, if that's what you want. *(Sits down at the piano.)*

Nora takes the tambourine out of the carton, as well as a long, many-colored shawl. She quickly drapes the shawl around herself, then leaps into the middle of the floor.

Nora. Play for me! I want to dance!

Helmer plays and Nora dances. Dr. Rank stands by the piano behind Helmer and watches.

Helmer *(playing).* Slow down, slow down!

Nora. Can't!

Helmer. Not so violent, Nora!

Nora. It has to be this way.

Helmer *(stops playing).* No, no. This won't do at all.

Nora *(laughing, swinging her tambourine).* What did I tell you?

Rank.   Why don't you let me play?

Helmer (getting up).   Good idea. Then I can direct her better.

Rank sits down at the piano and starts playing. Nora dances more and more wildly. Helmer stands over by the stove, repeatedly correcting her. She doesn't seem to hear. Her hair comes loose and falls down over her shoulders. She doesn't notice but keeps on dancing. Mrs. Linde enters.

Mrs. Linde (stops by the door, dumbfounded).   Ah—!

Nora (dancing.)   We're having such fun, Kristine!

Helmer.   My dearest Nora, you're dancing as if it were a matter of life and death!

Nora.   It is! It is!

Helmer.   Rank, stop. This is sheer madness. Stop, I say!

Rank stops playing; Nora suddenly stops dancing.

Helmer (goes over to her).   If I hadn't seen it I wouldn't have believed it. You've forgotten every single thing I ever taught you.

Nora (tosses away the tambourine).   See? I told you.

Helmer.   Well! You certainly need coaching.

Nora.   Didn't I tell you I did? Now you've seen for yourself. I'll need your help till the very minute we're leaving for the party. Will you promise, Torvald?

Helmer.   You can count on it.

Nora.   You're not to think of anything except me—not tonight and not tomorrow. You're not to read any letters—not to look in the mailbox—

Helmer.   Ah, I see. You're still afraid of that man.

Nora.   Yes—yes, that too.

Helmer.   Nora, I can tell from looking at you. There's a letter from him out there.

Nora.   I don't know. I think so. But you're not to read it now. I don't want anything ugly to come between us before it's all over.

Rank (to Helmer in a low voice).   Better not argue with her.

Helmer (throws his arm around her).   The child shall have her way. But tomorrow night, when you've done your dance—

Nora.   Then you'll be free.

The Maid (in the door, right).   Dinner can be served any time, ma'am.

Nora.   We want champagne, Helene.

The Maid.   Very good, ma'am. (Goes out.)

Helmer.   Aha! Having a party, eh?

Nora.   Champagne from now till sunrise! (Calls out.) And some macaroons, Helene. Lots!—just this once.

Helmer (taking her hands). There, there—I don't like this wild—frenzy—Be my own sweet little lark again, the way you always are.

Nora.   Oh, I will. But you go on in. You too, Dr. Rank. Kristine, please help me put up my hair.

Rank (*in a low voice to Helmer as they go out*).   You don't think she is—you know—expecting—?

Helmer.   Oh no. Nothing like that. It's just this childish fear I was telling you about. (*They go out, right.*)

Nora.   Well?

Mrs. Linde.   Left town.

Nora.   I saw it in your face.

Mrs. Linde.   He'll be back tomorrow night. I left him a note.

Nora.   You shouldn't have. I don't want you to try to stop anything. You see, it's a kind of ecstasy, too, this waiting for the wonderful.

Mrs. Linde.   But what is it you're waiting *for?*

Nora. You wouldn't understand. Why don't you go in to the others. I'll be there in a minute.

Mrs. Linde enters the dining room, right.

Nora (*stands still for a little while, as if collecting herself; she looks at her watch*).   Five o'clock. Seven hours till midnight. Twenty-four more hours till next midnight. Then the tarantella is over. Twenty-four plus seven— thirty-one more hours to live.

Helmer (*in the door, right*).   What's happening to my little lark?

Nora (*to him, with open arms*).   Here's your lark!

Act III

The same room. The table by the couch and the chairs around it have been moved to the middle of the floor. A lighted lamp is on the table. The door to the front hall is open. Dance music is heard from upstairs.

Mrs. Linde is seated by the table, idly leafing through the pages of a book. She tries to read but seems unable to concentrate. Once or twice she turns her head in the direction of the door, anxiously listening.

Mrs. Linde. (*looks at her watch*).   Not yet. It's almost too late. If only he hasn't—(*Listens again.*) Ah! There he is. (*She goes to the hall and opens the front door carefully. Quiet footsteps on the stairs. She whispers.*) Come in. There's nobody here.

Krogstad (*in the door*).   I found your note when I got home. What's this all about?

Mrs. Linde.   I've got to talk to you.

Krogstad.   Oh? And it has to be here?

Mrs. Linde.   It couldn't be at my place. My room doesn't have a separate entrance. Come in. We're quite alone. The maid is asleep and the Helmers are at a party upstairs.

Krogstad (*entering*).   Really? The Helmers are dancing tonight, are they?

Mrs. Linde.   And why not?

Krogstad. You're right. Why not, indeed.

Mrs. Linde. All right, Krogstad. Let's talk, you and I.

Krogstad. I didn't know we had anything to talk about.

Mrs. Linde. We have much to talk about.

Krogstad. I didn't think so.

Mrs. Linde. No, because you've never really understood me.

Krogstad. What was there to understand? What happened was perfectly commonplace. A heartless woman jilts a man when she gets a more attractive offer.

Mrs. Linde. Do you think I'm all that heartless? And do you think it was easy for me to break with you?

Krogstad. No?

Mrs. Linde. You really thought it was?

Krogstad. If it wasn't, why did you write the way you did that time?

Mrs. Linde. What else could I do? If I had to make a break, I also had the duty to destroy whatever feelings you had for me.

Krogstad (clenching his hands). So that's the way it was. And you did—*that*—just for money!

Mrs. Linde. Don't forget I had a helpless mother and two small brothers. We couldn't wait for you, Krogstad. You know yourself how uncertain your prospects were then.

Krogstad. All right. But you still didn't have the right to throw me over for somebody else.

Mrs. Linde. I don't know. I have asked myself that question many times. Did I have that right?

Krogstad (in a lower voice). When I lost you I lost my footing. Look at me now. A shipwrecked man on a raft.

Mrs. Linde. Rescue may be near.

Krogstad. It *was* near. Then you came between.

Mrs. Linde. I didn't know that, Krogstad. Only today did I find out it's your job I'm taking over in the bank.

Krogstad. I believe you when you say so. But now that you *do* know, aren't you going to step aside?

Mrs. Linde. No, for it wouldn't do you any good.

Krogstad. Whether it would or not—*I* would do it.

Mrs. Linde. I have learned common sense. Life and hard necessity have taught me that.

Krogstad. And life has taught me not to believe in pretty speeches.

Mrs. Linde. Then life has taught you a very sensible thing. But you do believe in actions, don't you?

Krogstad. How do you mean?

Mrs. Linde. You referred to yourself just now as a shipwrecked man.

Krogstad. It seems to me I had every reason to do so.

Mrs. Linde. And I am a shipwrecked woman. No one to grieve for, no one to care for.

Krogstad. You made your choice.

Mrs. Linde. I had no other choice that time.

Krogstad. Let's say you didn't. What then?

Mrs. Linde. Krogstad, how would it be if we two shipwrecked people got together?

Krogstad. What's this!

Mrs. Linde. Two on one wreck are better off than each on his own.

Krogstad. Kristine!

Mrs. Linde. Why do you think I came to town?

Krogstad. Surely not because of me?

Mrs. Linde. If I'm going to live at all I must work. All my life, for as long as I can remember, I have worked. That's been my one and only pleasure. But now that I'm all alone in the world I feel nothing but this terrible emptiness and desolation. There is no joy in working just for yourself. Krogstad—give me someone and something to work for.

Krogstad. I don't believe this. Only hysterical females go in for that kind of high-minded self-sacrifice.

Mrs. Linde. Did you ever know me to be hysterical?

Krogstad. You really could do this? Listen—do you know about my past? All of it?

Mrs. Linde. Yes, I do.

Krogstad. Do you also know what people think of me around here?

Mrs. Linde. A little while ago you sounded as if you thought that together with me you might have become a different person.

Krogstad. I'm sure of it.

Mrs. Linde. Couldn't that still be?

Krogstad. Kristine—do you know what you are doing? Yes, I see you do. And you think you have the courage—?

Mrs. Linde. I need someone to be a mother to, and your children need a mother. You and I need one another. Nils, I believe in you—in the real you. Together with you I dare to do anything.

Krogstad (seizes her hands). Thanks, thanks, Kristine—now I know I'll raise myself in the eyes of others—Ah, but I forget—!

Mrs. Linde (listening). Shh!—There's the tarantella. You must go; hurry!

Krogstad. Why? What is it?

Mrs. Linde. Do you hear what they're playing up there? When that dance is over they'll be down.

Krogstad. All right. I'm leaving. The whole thing is pointless, anyway. Of course you don't know what I'm doing to the Helmers.

Mrs. Linde. Yes, Krogstad; I do know.

Krogstad. Still, you're brave enough—?

Mrs. Linde. I very well understand to what extremes despair can drive a man like you.

Krogstad. If only it could be undone!

Mrs. Linde. It could, for your letter is still out there in the mailbox.

Krogstad. Are you sure?

Mrs. Linde. Quite sure. But—

Krogstad *(looks searchingly at her).* Maybe I'm beginning to understand. You want to save your friend at any cost. Be honest with me. That's it, isn't it?

Mrs. Linde. Krogstad, you may sell yourself once for somebody else's sake, but you don't do it twice.

Krogstad. I'll demand my letter back.

Mrs. Linde. No, no.

Krogstad. Yes, of course. I'll wait here till Helmer comes down. Then I'll ask him for my letter. I'll tell him it's just about my dismissal—that he shouldn't read it.

Mrs. Linde. No, Krogstad. You are not to ask for that letter back.

Krogstad. But tell me—wasn't that the real reason you wanted to meet me here?

Mrs. Linde. At first it was, because I was so frightened. But that was yesterday. Since then I have seen the most incredible things going on in this house. Helmer must learn the whole truth. This miserable secret must come out in the open; those two must come to a full understanding. They simply can't continue with all this concealment and evasion.

Krogstad. All right; if you want to take that chance. But there is one thing I *can* do, and I'll do that right now.

Mrs. Linde *(listening).* But hurry! Go! The dance is over. We aren't safe another minute.

Krogstad. I'll be waiting for you downstairs.

Mrs. Linde. Yes, do. You must see me home.

Krogstad. I've never been so happy in my whole life. *(He leaves through the front door. The door between the living room and the front hall remains open.)*

Mrs. Linde *(straightens up the room a little and gets her things ready).* What a change! Oh yes!—what a change! People to work for—to live for—a home to bring happiness to. I can't wait to get to work—! If only they'd come soon—(Listens.) Ah, there they are. Get my coat on—(Puts on her coat and hat.)

Helmer's and Nora's voices are heard outside. A key is turned in the lock, and Helmer almost forces Nora into the hall. She is dressed in her Italian costume, with a big black shawl over her shoulders. He is in evening dress under an open black cloak.

Nora *(in the door, still resisting).* No, no, no! I don't want to! I want to go back upstairs. I don't want to leave so early.

Helmer. But dearest Nora—

Nora. Oh please, Torvald—please! I'm asking you as nicely as I can—just another hour!

Helmer. Not another minute, sweet. You know we agreed. There now. Get inside. You'll catch a cold out here. *(She still resists, but he guides her gently into the room.)*

Mrs. Linde.   Good evening.

Nora.   Kristine!

Helmer.   Ah, Mrs. Linde. Still here?

Mrs. Linde.   I know. I really should apologize, but I so much wanted to see Nora in her costume.

Nora.   You've been waiting up for me?

Mrs. Linde.   Yes, unfortunately I didn't get here in time. You were already upstairs, but I just didn't feel like leaving till I had seen you.

Helmer *(removing Nora's shawl).*   Yes, do take a good look at her, Mrs. Linde. I think I may say she's worth looking at. Isn't she lovely?

Mrs. Linde.   She certainly is—

Helmer.   Isn't she a miracle of loveliness, though? That was the general opinion at the party, too. But dreadfully obstinate—that she is, the sweet little thing. What can we do about that? Will you believe it—I practically had to use force to get her away.

Nora.   Oh Torvald, you're going to be sorry you didn't give me even half an hour more.

Helmer.   See what I mean, Mrs. Linde? She dances the tarantella—she is a tremendous success—quite deservedly so, though perhaps her performance was a little too natural—I mean, more than could be reconciled with the rules of art. But all right! The point is: she's a success, a tremendous success. So should I let her stay after that? Weaken the effect? Of course not. So I take my lovely little Capri girl—I might say, my capricious little Capri girl—under my arm—a quick turn around the room—a graceful bow in all directions, and—as they say in the novels—the beautiful apparition is gone. A finale should always be done for effect, Mrs. Linde, but there doesn't seem to be any way of getting that into Nora's head. Poooh—! It's hot in here. *(Throws his cloak down on a chair and opens the door to his room.)* Why, it's dark in here! Of course. Excuse me—*(Goes inside and lights a couple of candles.)*

Nora *(in a hurried, breathless whisper).*   Well?

Mrs. Linde *(in a low voice).*   I have talked to him.

Nora.   And—?

Mrs. Linde.   Nora—you've got to tell your husband everything.

Nora *(no expression in her voice).*   I knew it.

Mrs. Linde.   You have nothing to fear from Krogstad. But you must speak.

Nora.   I'll say nothing.

Mrs. Linde.   Then the letter will.

Nora.   Thank you, Kristine. Now I know what I have to do. Shh!

Helmer *(returning).*   Well, Mrs. Linde, have you looked your fill?

Mrs. Linde.   Yes. And now I'll say goodnight.

Helmer.   So soon? Is that your knitting?

Mrs. Linde *(takes it).*   Yes, thank you. I almost forgot.

Helmer. So you knit, do you?

Mrs. Linde. Oh yes.

Helmer. You know—you ought to take up embroidery instead.

Mrs. Linde. Oh? Why?

Helmer. Because it's so much more beautiful. Look. You hold the embroidery so—in your left hand. Then with your right you move the needle—like this—in an easy, elongated arc—you see?

Mrs. Linde. Maybe you're right—

Helmer. Knitting, on the other hand, can never be anything but ugly. Look here: arms pressed close to the sides—the needles going up and down—there's something Chinese about it somehow—. That really was an excellent champagne they served us tonight.

Mrs. Linde. Well, goodnight, Nora. And don't be obstinate any more.

Helmer. Well said, Mrs. Linde!

Mrs. Linde. Goodnight, sir.

Helmer *(sees her to the front door).* Goodnight, goodnight. I hope you'll get home all right? I'd be very glad to—but of course you don't have far to walk, do you? Goodnight, goodnight. *(She leaves. He closes the door behind her and returns to the living room.)* There! At last we got rid of her. She really is an incredible bore, that woman.

Nora. Aren't you very tired, Torvald?

Helmer. No, not in the least.

Nora. Not sleepy either?

Helmer. Not at all. Quite the opposite. I feel enormously—animated. How about you? Yes, you do look tired and sleepy.

Nora. Yes, I am very tired. Soon I'll be asleep.

Helmer. What did I tell you? I was right, wasn't I? Good thing I didn't let you stay any longer.

Nora. Everything you do is right.

Helmer *(kissing her forehead).* Now my little lark is talking like a human being. But did you notice what splendid spirits Rank was in tonight?

Nora. Was he? I didn't notice. I didn't get to talk with him.

Helmer. Nor did I—hardly. But I haven't seen him in such a good mood for a long time. *(Looks at her, comes closer to her.)* Ah! It does feel good to be back in our own home again, to be quite alone with you—my young, lovely, ravishing woman!

Nora. Don't look at me like that, Torvald!

Helmer. Am I not to look at my most precious possession? All that loveliness that is mine, nobody's but mine, all of it mine.

Nora *(walks to the other side of the table).* I won't have you talk to me like that tonight.

Helmer *(follows her).* The tarantella is still in your blood. I can tell. That only makes you all the more alluring. Listen! The guests are beginning to leave. *(Softly.)* Nora—soon the whole house will be quiet.

Nora. Yes, I hope so.

Helmer. Yes, don't you, my darling? Do you know—when I'm at a party with you, like tonight—do you know why I hardly ever talk to you, why I keep away from you, only look at you once in a while—a few stolen glances— do you know why I do that? It's because I pretend that you are my secret love, my young, secret bride-to-be, and nobody has the slightest suspicion that there is anything between us.

Nora. Yes, I know. All your thoughts are with me.

Helmer. Then when we're leaving and I lay your shawl around your delicate young shoulders—around that wonderful curve of your neck—then I imagine you're my young bride, that we're coming away from the wedding, that I am taking you to my home for the first time—that I am alone with you for the first time—quite alone with you, you young, trembling beauty! I have desired you all evening—there hasn't been a longing in me that hasn't been for you. When you were dancing the tarantella, chasing, inviting—my blood was on fire; I couldn't stand it any longer—that's why I brought you down so early—

Nora. Leave me now, Torvald. Please! I don't want all this.

Helmer. What do you mean? You're only playing your little teasing bird game with me; aren't you, Nora? Don't want to? I'm your husband, aren't I?

There is a knock on the front door.

Nora *(with a start).* Did you hear that—?

Helmer *(on his way to the hall).* Who is it?

Rank *(outside).* It's me. May I come in for a moment?

Helmer *(in a low voice, annoyed).* Oh, what does he want now? *(Aloud.)* Just a minute. *(Opens the door.)* Well! How good of you not to pass by our door.

Rank. I thought I heard your voice, so I felt like saying hello. *(Looks around.)* Ah yes—this dear, familiar room. What a cozy, comfortable place you have here, you two.

Helmer. Looked to me as if you were quite comfortable upstairs too.

Rank. I certainly was. Why not? Why not enjoy all you can in this world? As much as you can for as long as you can, anyway. Excellent wine.

Helmer. The champagne, particularly.

Rank. You noticed that too? Incredible how much I managed to put away.

Nora. Torvald drank a lot of champagne tonight, too.

Rank. Did he?

Nora. Yes, he did, and then he's always so much fun afterwards.

Rank. Well, why not have some fun in the evening after a well spent day?

Helmer. Well spent? I'm afraid I can't claim that.

Rank *(slapping him lightly on the shoulder).* But you see, I can!

Nora. Dr. Rank, I believe you must have been conducting a scientific test today.

Rank. Exactly.

Helmer.   What do you know—little Nora talking about scientific tests!

Nora.   May I congratulate you on the result?

Rank.   You may indeed.

Nora.   It was a good one?

Rank.   The best possible for both doctor and patient—certainty.

Nora (*a quick query*).   Certainty?

Rank.   Absolute certainty. So why shouldn't I have myself an enjoyable evening afterwards?

Nora.   I quite agree with you, Dr. Rank. You should.

Helmer.   And so do I. If only you don't pay for it tomorrow.

Rank.   Oh well—you get nothing for nothing in this world.

Nora.   Dr. Rank—you are fond of costume parties, aren't you?

Rank.   Yes, particularly when there is a reasonable number of amusing disguises.

Nora.   Listen—what are the two of us going to be the next time?

Helmer.   You frivolous little thing! Already thinking about the next party!

Rank.   You and I? That's easy. You'll be Fortune's Child.

Helmer.   Yes, but what is a fitting costume for that?

Rank.   Let your wife appear just the way she always is.

Helmer.   Beautiful. Very good indeed. But how about yourself? Don't you know what you'll go as?

Rank.   Yes, my friend. I know precisely what I'll be.

Helmer.   Yes?

Rank.   At the next masquerade I'll be invisible.

Helmer.   That's a funny idea.

Rank.   There's a certain black hat—you've heard about the hat that makes you invisible, haven't you? You put that on, and nobody can see you.

Helmer (*suppressing a smile*).   I guess that's right.

Rank.   But I'm forgetting what I came for. Helmer, give me a cigar—one of your dark Havanas.

Helmer.   With the greatest pleasure. (*Offers him his case.*)

Rank (*takes one and cuts off the tip*).   Thanks.

Nora (*striking a match*).   Let me give you a light.

Rank.   Thanks. (*She holds the match; he lights his cigar.*) And now goodbye!

Helmer.   Goodbye, goodbye, my friend.

Nora.   Sleep well, Dr. Rank.

Rank.   I thank you.

Nora.   Wish me the same.

Rank.   You? Well, if you really want me to—. Sleep well. And thanks for the light. (*He nods to both of them and goes out.*)

Helmer (*in a low voice*).   He had had quite a bit to drink.

Nora (*absently*).   Maybe so.

Helmer takes out his keys and goes out into the hall.

Nora.   Torvald—what are you doing out there?

Helmer. Emptying the mailbox. It is quite full. There wouldn't be room for the newspapers in the morning—

Nora. Are you going to work tonight?

Helmer. You know very well I won't.—Say! What's this? Somebody's been at the lock.

Nora. The lock—?

Helmer. Yes. Why, I wonder. I hate to think that any of the maids—. Here's a broken hairpin. It's one of yours. Nora.

Nora *(quickly).* Then it must be one of the children.

Helmer. You better make damn sure they stop that. Hm, hm.—There! I got it open, finally. *(Gathers up the mail, calls out to the kitchen.)* Helene?—Oh Helene—turn out the light here in the hall, will you? *(He comes back into the living room and closes the door.)* Look how it's been piling up. *(Shows her the bundle of letters. Starts leafing through it.)* What's this?

Nora *(by the window).* The letter! Oh no, no, Torvald!

Helmer. Two calling cards—from Rank.

Nora. From Dr. Rank?

Helmer *(looking at them).* "Doctor medicinae Rank." They were on top. He must have put them there when he left just now.

Nora. Anything written on them?

Helmer. A black cross above the name. What a macabre idea. Like announcing his own death.

Nora. That's what it is.

Helmer. Hm? You know about this? Has he said anything to you?

Nora. That card means he has said goodbye to us. He'll lock himself up to die.

Helmer. My poor friend. I knew of course he wouldn't be with me very long. But so soon—. And hiding himself away like a wounded animal—

Nora. When it has to be, it's better it happens without words. Don't you think so, Torvald?

Helmer *(walking up and down).* He'd grown so close to us. I find it hard to think of him as gone. With his suffering and loneliness he was like a clouded background for our happy sunshine. Well, it may be better this way. For him, at any rate. *(Stops.)* And perhaps for us, too, Nora. For now we have nobody but each other. *(Embraces her.)* Oh you—my beloved wife! I feel I just can't hold you close enough. Do you know, Nora—many times I have wished some great danger threatened you, so I could risk my life and blood and everything—everything, for your sake.

Nora *(frees herself and says in a strong and firm voice).* I think you should go and read your letters now, Torvald.

Helmer. No, no—not tonight. I want to be with you, my darling.

Nora. With the thought of your dying friend—?

Helmer. You are right. This has shaken both of us. Something not beautiful has come between us. Thoughts of death and dissolution. We must try to get over it—out of it. Till then—we'll each go to our own room.

Nora *(her arms around his neck).* Torvald—goodnight! Goodnight!

Helmer *(kisses her forehead).* Goodnight, my little songbird. Sleep well, Nora. Now I'll read my letters. *(He goes into his room, carrying the mail. Closes the door.)*

Nora *(her eyes desperate, her hands groping, finds Helmer's black cloak and throws it around her; she whispers, quickly, brokenly, hoarsely).* Never see him again. Never. Never. Never. *(Puts her shawl over her head.)* And never see the children again, either. Never; never.—The black, icy water—fathomless—this—! If only it was all over.—Now he has it. Now he's reading it. No, no; not yet. Torvald—goodbye—you—the children—

She is about to hurry through the hall, when Helmer flings open the door to his room and stands there with an open letter in his hand.

Helmer. Nora!

Nora *(cries out).* Ah—!

Helmer. What is it? You know what's in this letter?

Nora. Yes, I do! Let me go! Let me out!

Helmer *(holds her back).* Where do you think you're going?

Nora *(trying to tear herself loose from him).* I won't let you save me, Torvald!

Helmer *(tumbles back).* True! Is it true what he writes? Oh my God! No, no—this can't possibly be true.

Nora. It is true. I have loved you more than anything else in the whole world.

Helmer. Oh, don't give me any silly excuses.

Nora *(taking a step towards him).* Torvald—!

Helmer. You wretch! What have you done!

Nora. Let me go. You are not to sacrifice yourself for me. You are not to take the blame.

Helmer. No more playacting. *(Locks the door to the front hall.)* You'll stay here and answer me. Do you understand what you have done? Answer me! Do you understand?

Nora *(gazes steadily at him with an increasingly frozen expression).* Yes. Now I'm beginning to understand.

Helmer *(walking up and down).* What a dreadful awakening. All these years—all these eight years—she, my pride and my joy—a hypocrite, a liar—oh worse! worse!—a criminal! Oh, the bottomless ugliness in all this! Damn! Damn! Damn!

Nora, silent, keeps gazing at him.

Helmer *(stops in front of her).* I ought to have guessed that something like this would happen. I should have expected it. All your father's loose principles—Silence! You have inherited every one of your father's loose principles. No religion, no morals, no sense of duty—. Now I am being punished for my leniency with him. I did it for your sake, and this is how you pay me back.

Nora. Yes. This is how.

Helmer. You have ruined all my happiness. My whole future—that's what you have destroyed. Oh, it's terrible to think about. I am at the mercy of an unscrupulous man. He can do with me whatever he likes, demand anything of me, command me and dispose of me just as he pleases—I dare not say a word! To go down so miserably, to be destroyed—all because of an irresponsible woman!

Nora. When I am gone from the world, you'll be free.

Helmer. No noble gestures, please. Your father was always full of such phrases too. What good would it do me if you were gone from the world, as you put it? Not the slightest good at all. He could still make the whole thing public, and if he did, people would be likely to think I had been your accomplice. They might even think it was my idea—that it was I who urged you to do it! And for all this I have you to thank—you, whom I've borne on my hands through all the years of our marriage. *Now* do you understand what you've done to me?

Nora *(with cold calm).* Yes.

Helmer. I just can't get it into my head that this is happening; it's all so incredible. But we have to come to terms with it somehow. Take your shawl off. Take it off, I say! I have to satisfy him one way or another. The whole affair must be kept quiet at whatever cost.—And as far as you and I are concerned, nothing must seem to have changed. I'm talking about appearances, of course. You'll go on living here; that goes without saying. But I won't let you bring up the children; I dare not trust you with them.—Oh! Having to say this to one I have loved so much, and whom I still—! But all that is past. It's not a question of happiness any more but of hanging on to what can be salvaged—pieces, appearances—*(The doorbell rings.)*

Helmer *(jumps).* What's that? So late. Is the worst—? Has he—! Hide, Nora! Say you're sick.

Nora doesn't move. Helmer opens the door to the hall.

The Maid *(half dressed, out in the hall).* A letter for your wife, sir.

Helmer. Give it to me. *(Takes the letter and closes the door.)* Yes, it's from him. But I won't let you have it. I'll read it myself.

Nora. Yes—you read it.

Helmer *(by the lamp).* I hardly dare. Perhaps we're lost, both you and I. No; I've got to know. *(Tears the letter open, glances through it, looks at an enclosure; a cry of joy.)* Nora!

Nora looks at him with a question in her eyes.

Helmer. Nora!—No, I must read it again.—Yes, yes; it is so! I'm saved! Nora, I'm saved!

Nora. And I?

Helmer. You too, of course; we're both saved, both you and I. Look! He's returning your note. He writes that he's sorry, he regrets, a happy turn in his life—oh, it doesn't matter what he writes. We're saved, Nora! Nobody can do anything to you now. Oh Nora, Nora—. No, I want to get rid of this disgusting thing first. Let me see—*(Looks at the signature.)* No, I don't want to see it. I don't want it to be more than a bad dream, the whole thing. *(Tears up the note and both letters, throws the pieces in the stove, and watches them burn.)* There! Now it's gone.—He wrote that ever since Christmas Eve—. Good God, Nora, these must have been three terrible days for you.

Nora.   I have fought a hard fight these last three days.

Helmer.   And been in agony and seen no other way out than—. No, we won't think of all that ugliness. We'll just rejoice and tell ourselves it's over, it's all over! Oh, listen to me, Nora. You don't seem to understand. It's over. What *is* it? Why do you look like that—that frozen expression on your face? Oh my poor little Nora, don't you think I know what it is? You can't make yourself believe that I have forgiven you. But I have, Nora; I swear to you, I have forgiven you for everything. Of course I know that what you did was for love of me.

Nora.   That is true.

Helmer.   You have loved me the way a wife ought to love her husband. You just didn't have the wisdom to judge the means. But do you think I love you any less because you don't know how to act on your own? Of course not. Just lean on me. I'll advise you; I'll guide you. I wouldn't be a man if I didn't find you twice as attractive because of your womanly helplessness. You mustn't pay any attention to the hard words I said to you right at first. It was just that first shock when I thought everything was collapsing all around me. I have forgiven you, Nora. I swear to you—I really have forgiven you.

Nora.   I thank you for your forgiveness. *(She goes out through the door, right.)*

Helmer.   No, stay—*(Looks into the room she entered.)* What are you doing in there?

Nora *(within)*.   Getting out of my costume.

Helmer *(by the open door)*.   Good, good. Try to calm down and compose yourself, my poor little frightened songbird. Rest safely; I have broad wings to cover you with. *(Walks around near the door.)* What a nice and cozy home we have, Nora. Here's shelter for you. Here I'll keep you safe like a hunted dove I have rescued from the hawk's talons. Believe me: I'll know how to quiet your beating heart. It will happen by and by, Nora; you'll see. Why, tomorrow you'll look at all this in quite a different light. And soon everything will be just the way it was before. I won't need to keep reassuring you that I have forgiven you; you'll feel it yourself. Did you really think I could have abandoned you, or even reproached you? Oh, you don't know a real man's heart, Nora. There is something unspeakably sweet and satisfactory for a man to know deep in himself that he has forgiven his wife—forgiven her in all the fullness of his honest heart. You see, that way she becomes his very own all over again—in a double sense, you might say. He has, so to speak, given her a second birth; it is as if she had become his wife and his child, both. From now on that's what you'll be to me, you lost and helpless creature. Don't worry about a thing, Nora. Only be frank with me, and I'll be your will and your conscience.— What's this? You're not in bed? You've changed your dress—!

Nora (*in an everyday dress*). Yes, Torvald. I have changed my dress.

Helmer. But why—now—this late—?

Nora. I'm not going to sleep tonight.

Helmer. But my dear Nora—

Nora (*looks at her watch*). It isn't all that late. Sit down here with me, Torvald. You and I have much to talk about. (*Sits down at the table.*)

Helmer. Nora—what is this all about? That rigid face—

Nora. Sit down. This will take a while. I have much to say to you.

Helmer (*sits down, facing her across the table*). You worry me, Nora. I don't understand you.

Nora. No, that's just it. You don't understand me. And I have never understood you—not till tonight. No, don't interrupt me. Just listen to what I have to say.—This is a settling of accounts, Torvald.

Helmer. What do you mean by that?

Nora (*after a brief silence*). Doesn't one thing strike you, now that we are sitting together like this?

Helmer. What would that be?

Nora. We have been married for eight years. Doesn't it occur to you that this is the first time that you and I, husband and wife, are having a serious talk?

Helmer. Well—serious—. What do you mean by that?

Nora. For eight whole years—longer, in fact—ever since we first met, we have never talked seriously to each other about a single serious thing.

Helmer. You mean I should forever have been telling you about worries you couldn't have helped me with anyway?

Nora. I am not talking about worries. I'm saying we have never tried seriously to get to the bottom of anything together.

Helmer. But dearest Nora, I hardly think that would have been something *you*—

Nora. That's the whole point. You have never understood me. Great wrong has been done to me, Torvald. First by Daddy and then by you.

Helmer. What! By us two? We who have loved you more deeply than anyone else?

Nora (*shakes her head*). You never loved me—neither Daddy nor you. You only thought it was fun to be in love with me.

Helmer. But, Nora—what an expression to use!

Nora. That's the way it has been, Torvald. When I was home with Daddy, he told me all his opinions, and so they became my opinions too. If I disagreed with him I kept it to myself, for he wouldn't have liked that. He called me his little doll baby, and he played with me the way I played with my dolls. Then I came to your house—

Helmer. What a way to talk about our marriage!

Nora (*imperturbably*). I mean that I passed from Daddy's hands into yours. You arranged everything according to your taste, and so I came to share it—or I pretended to; I'm not sure which. I think it was a little of both, now one and now the other. When I look back on it now, it seems to me I've been living here like a pauper—just a hand-to-mouth kind of existence. I have earned my keep by doing tricks for you, Torvald. But that's the way you wanted it. You have great sins against me to answer for, Daddy and you. It's your fault that nothing has become of me.

Helmer. Nora, you're being both unreasonable and ungrateful. Haven't you been happy here?

Nora. No, never. I thought I was, but I wasn't.

Helmer. Not—not happy!

Nora. No; just having fun. And you have always been very good to me. But our home has never been more than a playroom. I have been your doll wife here, just the way I used to be Daddy's doll child. And the children have been my dolls. I thought it was fun when you played with me, just as they thought it was fun when I played with them. That's been our marriage, Torvald.

Helmer. There is something in what you are saying—exaggerated and hysterical though it is. But from now on things will be different. Playtime is over; it's time for growing up.

Nora. Whose growing up—mine or the children's?

Helmer. Both yours and the children's, Nora darling.

Nora. Oh Torvald, you're not the man to bring me up to be the right kind of wife for you.

Helmer. How can you say that?

Nora. And I—? What qualifications do I have for bringing up the children?

Helmer. Nora!

Nora. You said so yourself a minute ago—that you didn't dare to trust me with them.

Helmer. In the first flush of anger, yes. Surely, you're not going to count that.

Nora. But you were quite right. I am *not* qualified. Something else has to come first. Somehow I have to grow up myself. And you are not the man to help me do that. That's a job I have to do by myself. And that's why I'm leaving you.

Helmer (*jumps up*). What did you say!

Nora. I have to be by myself if I am to find out about myself and about all the other things too. So I can't stay here with you any longer.

Helmer. Nora, Nora!

Nora. I'm leaving now. I'm sure Kristine will put me up for tonight.

Helmer. You're out of your mind! I won't let you! I forbid you!

Nora. You can't forbid me anything any more; it won't do any good. I'm taking my own things with me. I won't accept anything from you, either now or later.

Helmer. But this is madness!

Nora. Tomorrow I'm going home—I mean back to my old home town. It will be easier for me to find some kind of job there.

Helmer. Oh, you blind, inexperienced creature—!

Nora. I must see to it that I get experience, Torvald.

Helmer. Leaving your home, your husband, your children! Not a thought of what people will say!

Nora. I can't worry about that. All I know is that I have to leave.

Helmer. Oh, this is shocking! Betraying your most sacred duties like this!

Nora. And what do you consider my most sacred duties?

Helmer. Do I need to tell you that? They are your duties to your husband and your children.

Nora. I have other duties equally sacred.

Helmer. You do not. What duties would they be?

Nora. My duties to myself.

Helmer. You are a wife and a mother before you are anything else.

Nora. I don't believe that any more. I believe I am first of all a human being, just as much as you—or at any rate that I must try to become one. Oh, I know very well that most people agree with you, Torvald, and that it says something like that in all the books. But what people say and what the books say is no longer enough for me. I have to think about these things myself and see if I can't find the answers.

Helmer. You mean to tell me you don't know what your proper place in your own home is? Don't you have a reliable guide in such matters? Don't you have religion?

Nora. Oh but Torvald—I don't really know what religion is.

Helmer. What are you saying!

Nora. All I know is what the Reverend Hansen told me when he prepared me for confirmation. He said that religion was *this* and it was *that*. When I get by myself, away from here, I'll have to look into that, too. I have to decide if what the Reverend Hansen said was right, or anyway if it is right for *me*.

Helmer. Oh, this is unheard of in a young woman! If religion can't guide you, let me appeal to your conscience. For surely you have moral feelings? Or—answer me—maybe you don't?

Nora. Well, you see, Torvald, I don't really know what to say. I just don't know. I am confused about these things. All I know is that my ideas are quite different from yours. I have just found out that the laws are different from what I thought they were, but in no way can I get it into my head that those laws are right. A woman shouldn't have the right to spare her dying old father or save her husband's life! I just can't believe that.

Helmer. You speak like a child. You don't understand the society you live in.

Nora. No, I don't. But I want to find out about it. I have to make up my mind who is right, society or I.

Helmer. You are sick, Nora; you have a fever. I really don't think you are in your right mind.

Nora. I have never felt so clearheaded and sure of myself as I do tonight.

Helmer. And clearheaded and sure of yourself you're leaving your husband and children?

Nora. Yes.

Helmer. Then there is only one possible explanation.

Nora. What?

Helmer. You don't love me any more.

Nora. No, that's just it.

Helmer. Nora! Can you say that?

Nora. I am sorry, Torvald, for you have always been so good to me. But I can't help it. I don't love you any more.

Helmer (with forced composure). And this too is a clear and sure conviction?

Nora. Completely clear and sure. That's why I don't want to stay here any more.

Helmer. And are you ready to explain to me how I came to forfeit your love?

Nora. Certainly I am. It was tonight, when the wonderful didn't happen. That was when I realized you were not the man I thought you were.

Helmer. You have to explain. I don't understand.

Nora. I have waited patiently for eight years, for I wasn't such a fool that I thought the wonderful is something that happens any old day. Then this—thing—came crashing in on me, and then there wasn't a doubt in my mind that now—now comes the wonderful. When Krogstad's letter was in that mailbox, never for a moment did it even occur to me that you would submit to his conditions. I was so absolutely certain that you would say to him: make the whole thing public—tell everybody. And when that had happened—

Helmer. Yes, then what? When I had surrendered my wife to shame and disgrace—!

Nora. When that had happened, I was absolutely certain that you would stand up and take the blame and say, "I'm the guilty one."

Helmer. Nora!

Nora. You mean I never would have accepted such a sacrifice from you? Of course not. But what would my protests have counted against yours? *That* was the wonderful I was hoping for in terror. And to prevent that I was going to kill myself.

Helmer. I'd gladly work nights and days for you, Nora—endure sorrow and want for your sake. But nobody sacrifices his *honor* for his love.

Nora. A hundred thousand women have done so.

Helmer. Oh, you think and talk like a silly child.

Nora. All right. But you don't think and talk like the man I can live with.

When you had gotten over your fright—not because of what threatened *me* but because of the risk to *you*—and the whole danger was past, then you acted as if nothing at all had happened. Once again I was your little songbird, your doll, just as before, only now you had to handle her even more carefully, because she was so frail and weak. *(Rises.)* Torvald—that moment I realized that I had been living here for eight years with a stranger and had borne him three children—Oh, I can't stand thinking about it! I feel like tearing myself to pieces!

Helmer *(heavily).*   I see it, I see it. An abyss has opened up between us.—Oh but Nora—surely it can be filled?

Nora.   The way I am now I am no wife for you.

Helmer.   I have it in me to change.

Nora.   Perhaps—if your doll is taken from you.

Helmer.   To part—to part from you! No, no, Nora! I can't grasp that thought!

Nora *(goes out, right).*   All the more reason why it has to be. *(She returns with her outdoor clothes and a small bag, which she sets down on the chair by the table.)*

Helmer.   Nora, Nora! Not now! Wait till tomorrow.

Nora *(putting on her coat).*   I can't spend the night in a stranger's rooms.

Helmer.   But couldn't we live here together like brother and sister—?

Nora *(tying on her hat).*   You know very well that wouldn't last long—. *(Wraps her shawl around her.)* Goodbye, Torvald. I don't want to see the children. I know I leave them in better hands than mine. The way I am now I can't be anything to them.

Helmer.   But some day, Nora—some day—?

Nora.   How can I tell? I have no idea what's going to become of me.

Helmer.   But you're still my wife, both as you are now and as you will be.

Nora.   Listen, Torvald—when a wife leaves her husband's house, the way I am doing now, I have heard he has no more legal responsibilities for her. At any rate, I now release you from all responsibility. You are not to feel yourself obliged to me for anything, and I have no obligations to you. There has to be full freedom on both sides. Here is your ring back. Now give me mine.

Helmer.   Even this?

Nora.   Even this.

Helmer.   Here it is.

Nora.   There. So now it's over. I'm putting the keys here. The maids know everything about the house—better than I. Tomorrow, after I'm gone, Kristine will come over and pack my things from home. I want them sent after me.

Helmer.   Over! It's all over! Nora, will you never think of me?

Nora.   I'm sure I'll often think of you and the children and this house.

Helmer.   May I write to you, Nora?

Nora.   No—never. I won't have that.

Helmer.   But send you things—? You must let me.

Nora. Nothing, nothing.

Helmer. —help you, when you need help—

Nora. I told you, no; I won't have it. I'll accept nothing from strangers.

Helmer. Nora—can I never again be more to you than a stranger?

Nora *(picks up her bag).* Oh Torvald—then the most wonderful of all would have to happen—

Helmer. Tell me what that would be—!

Nora. For that to happen, both you and I would have to change so that—Oh Torvald, I no longer believe in the wonderful.

Helmer. But I *will* believe. Tell me! Change, so that—?

Nora. So that our living together would become a true marriage. Goodbye. *(She goes out through the hall.)*

Helmer *(sinks down on a chair near the door and covers his face with his hands).* Nora! Nora! *(Looks around him and gets up.)* All empty. She's gone. *(With sudden hope.)* The most wonderful—?!

From downstairs comes the sound of a heavy door slamming shut.

Questions

1. *Does the fact that Nora abandons her children undermine her otherwise heroic decision to walk out on a hollow marriage? A German production of the play provided an alternate ending in which Nora, after struggling with her conscience, decides that she cannot abandon her children. Is this ending better than the original ending? Explain.* **2.** *How does the subplot involving Mrs. Linde and Krogstad add force to the main plot of* A Doll's House? **3.** *What function does Dr. Rank serve in the play?* **4.** *On a number of occasions Nora recalls her father. What relevance do these recollections have to the development of the theme?* **5.** *Is Krogstad presented as a stock villain, or are we meant to sympathize with him?* **6.** *What evidence does the play provide that* A Doll's House *is about not only Nora's marriage but the institution of marriage itself?*

CONfORMiTy ANd REbEllioN

QUESTIONS FOR FURTHER ANALYSIS

1. What answers do the works in this section provide to the question posed by Albert Camus in the following passage:

> The present interest of the problem of rebellion only springs from the fact that nowadays whole societies have wanted to discard the sacred. We live in an unsacrosanct moment in history. Insurrection is certainly not the sum total of human experience. But history today, with all its storm and strife, compels us to say that rebellion is one of the essential dimensions of man. It is our historic reality. Unless we choose to ignore reality, we must find our values in it. Is it possible to find a rule of conduct outside the realm of religion and its absolute values? That is the question raised by rebellion.

2. Examine some of the representatives of established order—Creon, Torvald Helmer, Old Man Warner in "The Lottery," the Ticktockman—and discuss what attitudes they share and how effectively they function as spokesmen for law and order.

3. What support do the works in this section offer for Emily Dickinson's assertion that "Much Madness Is Divinest Sense"?

4. Which works in this section can be criticized on the grounds that while they attack the established order they fail to provide any alternatives?

5. In a number of these works, the result of rebellion is defeat and death. Are these works therefore pessimistic and despairing? If not, then what is the purpose of the rebellions, and why do the authors choose to bring their characters to such ends?

6. Do any of the works in this section offer support to the idea that a single individual or a small minority can have a decisive effect on the larger society? Discuss.

7. Amy Lowell's "Patterns," Karl Shapiro's "The Conscientious Objector," Lawrence Ferlinghetti's "In Goya's Greatest Scenes," and Henry Reed's "Naming of Parts" and "Judging Distances" are, in different ways, antiwar poems. May one argue validly that while they condemn war, none of them examines the specific reasons that a nation may be obliged to fight—self-defense and national self-interest, for example—and consequently, they are irresponsible? Explain.

8. Most of us live out our lives in the ordinary and humdrum world that is rejected in such poems as Wordsworth's "The World Is Too Much with Us," Tennyson's "Ulysses," Auden's "The Unknown Citizen," and Lennon and McCartney's "Eleanor Rigby." Can it be said that these poems are counsels to social irresponsibility? In this respect, contrast these poems with Philip Larkin's "Poetry of Departures."

love and hate

La Vie, Pablo Picasso

Love and Hate

Love and death, it is often noted, are the two great themes of literature. Much of the literary art we have placed in the sections "Innocence and Experience" and "Conformity and Rebellion" speaks of love and death as well. But in those works other thematic interests dominate. In this section we gather a number of works in which love and hate are thematically central.

The rosy conception of love presented in many popular and sentimental stories ill prepares us for the complicated reality we will face. We know that the course of true love never runs smooth, but in those popular stories the obstacles that hinder the lovers are simple and external. If the young lover can land the high-paying job or convince his beloved's parents that he is worthy despite social differences, all will be well. But love in life is rarely that simple. The external obstacles may be insuperable, or the obstacles may lie deep within the personality. The major obstacle may very well be an individual's difficult and painful effort to understand that he has been deceived by an immature and sentimental conception of love.

In this age of psychoanalytic awareness, the claims of the flesh are well recognized. But psychoanalytic theory teaches us, as well, to recognize the aggressive aspect of the human condition. The omnipresent selfishness that civilization attempts to check may be aggressively violent as well as lustful. Remarkably, many literary treatments of love envision the lovers sometimes as victims of the chaos that seems to surround them and sometimes as serene and safe in the midst of violence. D. H. Lawrence's "The Horse Dealer's Daughter" is embroidered on a fabric of violence and chaos. William Faulkner in "Dry September" and James Baldwin in "Going to Meet the Man" both recognize the erotic sources of certain kinds of violence in stories ostensibly about hate. And Matthew Arnold in "Dover Beach" finds love the only refuge from a chaotic world in which "ignorant armies clash by night."

The cliché has it that love and hate are closely related, and much evidence supports this proposition. But why should love and hate, seeming opposites, lie so close together in the emotional lives of men and women? We are all egos, separate from each other. And as separate individuals, we develop elaborate behavior mechanisms which defend us from each other. Self-esteem is terribly important, and threats to self-esteem must somehow be neutralized. But the erotic love relationship differs from other relationships in that it may be defined as a rejection of separateness. The common metaphor speaks of two lovers as joining, as merging into one. That surrender of the "me" to join in an "us" leaves the lovers uniquely vulnerable to psychic injury. In short, the defenses are down, and the self-esteem of each of the lovers depends importantly on the behavior of the other. If the lover is betrayed by his beloved, the emotional consequences are uniquely disastrous—hence the peculiarly close relationship of passionate hatred with erotic love.

Words like *love* and *hate* are so general that poets rarely use them except as one term in a metaphor designed to project sharply some aspect of emotional life. The simple sexuality in such poems as Marvell's "To His Coy Mistress," Marlowe's "The Passionate Shepherd to His Love," and Campion's "I Care Not for These Ladies" may be juxtaposed with the hatred and violence generated in Othello by sexual jealousy or with the quick reprisal of the slighted Barbara Allen. And Shakespeare's description of lust in "Th' Expense of Spirit in a Waste of Shame" notes an aspect of love quite overlooked by Sir John Suckling and Edmund Waller in their songs. Molière's comic misanthrope, who, finally, is unwilling to let down his defenses despite his feeling for his lady, handles his jealousy quite differently from Othello.

Perhaps more than anything, the works in this section celebrate the elemental impulses of man that run counter to those rational formulations by which we govern our lives. We pursue Othello's love for Desdemona and Iago's hate for Othello and arrive at an irreducible mystery, for neither Othello's love nor Iago's hate yields satisfactorily to rational explanation. Reason does not tell us why Othello and Desdemona love one another or why Iago hates rather than honors Othello. Alceste in Molière's *The Misanthrope* comes, for seemingly plausible and rational reasons, to hate mankind, and yet he persists, paradoxically, in his love for the coquettish Célimène.

Love is an act of faith springing from man's deep-seated need to join with another human being not only in physical nakedness but emotional and spiritual nakedness as well. While hate is a denial of that faith and, therefore, a retreat into spiritual isolation, love is an attempt to break out of the isolation. And as Erich Fromm writes in *The Art of Loving*:

> The basic need to fuse with another person so as to transcend the prison of one's separateness is closely related to another specifically human desire, that to know the "secret of man." While life in its merely biological aspects is a miracle and a secret, man in his human aspects is an unfathomable secret to himself—and to his fellow man. We know ourselves, and yet even with all the efforts we may make, we do not know ourselves. We know our fellow man, and yet we do not know him, because we are not a thing, and our fellow man is not a thing. The further we reach into the depth of our being, or someone else's being, the more the goal of knowledge eludes us. Yet we cannot help desiring to penetrate into the secret of man's soul, into the innermost nucleus which is "he."
>
> There is one way, a desperate one, to know the secret: it is that of complete power over another person; the power which makes him do what we want, feel what we want, think what we want; which transforms him into a thing, our thing, our possession. The ultimate degree of this attempt to know lies in the extremes of sadism, the desire and ability to make a human being suffer; to torture him, to force him to betray his secret in his suffering. In this craving for penetrating man's secret, his and hence our own, lies an essential motivation for the depth and intensity of cruelty and destructiveness. . . .
>
> The other path to knowing "the secret" is love. Love is active penetration of the other person, in which my desire to know is stilled by union. In the act of fusion I know you, I know myself, I know everybody—and I "know" nothing. I know in the only way knowledge of that which is alive is possible for man—by experience of union—not by any knowledge our thought can give. Sadism is motivated by the wish to know the secret, yet I remain as ignorant as I was before. I have torn the other being apart limb from limb, yet all I have done is to destroy him. Love is the only way of knowledge, which in the act of union answers my quest. In the act of loving, of giving myself, in the act of penetrating the other person, I find myself, I discover myself, I discover us both, I discover man.

The Love of Jupiter and Semele, 1930 by Pablo Pic

FICTION

The Storm

KATE CHOPIN [1851–1904]

I

THE leaves were so still that even Bibi thought it was going to rain. Bobinôt, who was accustomed to converse on terms of perfect equality with his little son, called the child's attention to certain sombre clouds that were rolling with sinister intention from the west, accompanied by a sullen, threatening roar. They were at Friedheimer's store and decided to remain there till the storm had passed. They sat within the door on two empty kegs. Bibi was four years old and looked very wise.

"Mama'll be 'fraid, yes," he suggested with blinking eyes.

"She'll shut the house. Maybe she got Sylvie helpin' her this evenin'," Bobinôt responded reassuringly.

"No; she ent got Sylvie. Sylvie was helpin' her yistiday," piped Bibi.

Bobinôt arose and going across to the counter purchased a can of shrimps, of which Calixta was very fond. Then he returned to his perch on the keg and sat stolidly holding the can of shrimps while the storm burst. It shook the wooden store and seemed to be ripping great furrows in the distant field. Bibi laid his little hand on his father's knee and was not afraid.

II

CALIXTA, at home, felt no uneasiness for their safety. She sat at a side window sewing furiously on a sewing machine. She was greatly occupied and did not notice the approaching storm. But she felt very warm and often stopped to mop her face on which the perspiration gathered in beads. She unfastened her white sacque at the throat. It began to grow dark, and suddenly realizing the situation she got up hurriedly and went about closing windows and doors.

Out on the small front gallery she had hung Bobinôt's Sunday clothes to air and she hastened out to gather them before the rain fell. As she stepped outside, Alcée Laballière rode in at the gate. She had not seen him very often since her marriage, and never alone. She stood there with Bobinôt's coat in her hands, and the big rain drops began to fall. Alcée rode his horse under the shelter of a side projection where the chickens had huddled and there were plows and a harrow piled up in the corner.

"May I come and wait on your gallery till the storm is over, Calixta?" he asked.

"Come 'long in, M'sieur Alcée."

His voice and her own startled her as if from a trance, and she seized Bobinôt's vest. Alcée, mounting to the porch, grabbed the trousers and snatched Bibi's braided jacket that was about to be carried away by a sudden gust of wind. He expressed an intention to remain outside, but it was soon apparent that he might as well have been out in the open: the water beat in upon the boards in driving sheets, and he went inside, closing the door after him. It was even necessary to put something beneath the door to keep the water out.

"My! what a rain! It's good two years sence it rain' like that," exclaimed Calixta as she rolled up a piece of bagging and Alcée helped her to thrust it beneath the crack.

She was a little fuller of figure than five years before when she married; but she had lost nothing of her vivacity. Her blue eyes still retained their melting quality; and her yellow hair, dishevelled by the wind and rain, kinked more stubbornly than ever about her ears and temples.

The rain beat upon the low, shingled roof with a force and clatter that threatened to break an entrance and deluge them there. They were in the dining room—the sitting room—the general utility room. Adjoining was her bed room, with Bibi's couch along side her own. The door stood open, and the room with its white, monumental bed, its closed shutters, looked dim and mysterious.

Alcée flung himself into a rocker and Calixta nervously began to gather up from the floor the lengths of a cotton sheet which she had been sewing.

"If this keeps up, *Dieu sait*[1] if the levees goin' to stan' it!" she exclaimed.

"What have you got to do with the levees?"

"I got enough to do! An' there's Bobinôt with Bibi out in that storm—if he only didn' left Friedheimer's!"

"Let us hope, Calixta, that Bobinôt's got sense enough to come in out of a cyclone."

She went and stood at the window with a greatly disturbed look on her face. She wiped the frame that was clouded with moisture. It was stiflingly hot. Alcée got up and joined her at the window, looking over her shoulder. The rain was coming down in sheets obscuring the view of far-off cabins and enveloping the distant wood in a gray mist. The playing of the lightning was incessant. A bolt struck a tall chinaberry tree at the edge of the field. It filled all

---

1. God knows.

visible space with a blinding glare and the crash seemed to invade the very boards they stood upon.

Calixta put her hands to her eyes, and with a cry, staggered backward. Alcée's arm encircled her, and for an instant he drew her close and spasmodically to him.

"Bonte!"[2] she cried, releasing herself from his encircling arm and retreating from the window, "the house'll go next! If I only knew w'ere Bibi was!" She would not compose herself; she would not be seated. Alcée clasped her shoulders and looked into her face. The contact of her warm, palpitating body when he had unthinkingly drawn her into his arms, had aroused all the old-time infatuation and desire for her flesh.

"Calixta," he said, "don't be frightened. Nothing can happen. The house is too low to be struck, with so many tall trees standing about. There! aren't you going to be quiet? say, aren't you?" He pushed her hair back from her face that was warm and steaming. Her lips were as red and moist as pomegranate seed. Her white neck and a glimpse of her full, firm bosom disturbed him powerfully. As she glanced up at him the fear in her liquid blue eyes had given place to a drowsy gleam that unconsciously betrayed a sensuous desire. He looked down into her eyes and there was nothing for him to do but to gather her lips in a kiss. It reminded him of Assumption.[3]

"Do you remember—in Assumption, Calixta?" he asked in a low voice broken by passion. Oh! she remembered; for in Assumption he had kissed her and kissed and kissed her; until his senses would well nigh fail, and to save her he would resort to a desperate flight. If she was not an immaculate dove in those days, she was still inviolate; a passionate creature whose very defenselessness had made her defense, against which his honor forbade him to prevail. Now—well, now—her lips seemed in a manner free to be tasted, as well as her round, white throat and her whiter breasts.

They did not heed the crashing torrents, and the roar of the elements made her laugh as she lay in his arms. She was a revelation in that dim, mysterious chamber; as white as the couch she lay upon. Her firm, elastic flesh that was knowing for the first time its birthright, was like a creamy lily that the sun invites to contribute its breath and perfume to the undying life of the world.

The generous abundance of her passion, without guile or trickery, was like a white flame which penetrated and found response in depths of his own sensuous nature that had never yet been reached.

When he touched her breasts they gave themselves up in quivering ecstasy, inviting his lips. Her mouth was a fountain of delight. And when he possessed her, they seemed to swoon together at the very borderland of life's mystery.

---

2. An exclamation: Goodness!
3. A holiday commemorating the ascent of the Virgin Mary to heaven. A feast celebrating the event is held on August 15.

He stayed cushioned upon her, breathless, dazed, enervated, with his heart beating like a hammer upon her. With one hand she clasped his head, her lips lightly touching his forehead. The other hand stroked with a soothing rhythm his muscular shoulders.

The growl of the thunder was distant and passing away. The rain beat softly upon the shingles, inviting them to drowsiness and sleep. But they dared not yield.

The rain was over; and the sun was turning the glistening green world into a palace of gems. Calixta, on the gallery, watched Alcée ride away. He turned and smiled at her with a beaming face; and she lifted her pretty chin in the air and laughed aloud.

III

BOBINÔT and Bibi, trudging home, stopped without at the cistern to make themselves presentable.

"My! Bibi, w'at will yo' mama say! You ought to be ashame'. You oughtn' put on those good pants. Look at 'em! An' that mud on yo' collar! How you got that mud on yo' collar, Bibi? I never saw such a boy!" Bibi was the picture of pathetic resignation. Bobinôt was the embodiment of serious solicitude as he strove to remove from his own person and his son's the signs of their tramp over heavy roads and through wet fields. He scraped the mud off Bibi's bare legs and feet with a stick and carefully removed all traces from his heavy brogans. Then, prepared for the worst—the meeting with an over-scrupulous housewife, they entered cautiously at the back door.

Calixta was preparing supper. She had set the table and was dripping coffee at the hearth. She sprang up as they came in.

"Oh, Bobinôt! You back! My! but I was uneasy. W'ere you been during the rain? An' Bibi? he ain't wet? he ain't hurt?" She had clasped Bibi and was kissing him effusively. Bobinôt's explanations and apologies which he had been composing all along the way, died on his lips as Calixta felt him to see if he were dry, and seemed to express nothing but satisfaction at their safe return.

"I brought you some shrimps, Calixta," offered Bobinôt, hauling the can from his ample side pocket and laying it on the table.

"Shrimps! Oh, Bobinôt! you too good fo' anything! and she gave him a smacking kiss on the cheek that resounded. "*J'vous reponds,*[4] we'll have a feas' to night! umph-umph!"

Bobinôt and Bibi began to relax and enjoy themselves, and when the three seated themselves at table they laughed much and so loud that anyone might have heard them as far away as Laballière's.

---

4. I'm telling you.

IV

ALCÉE Laballière wrote to his wife, Clarisse, that night. It was a loving letter, full of tender solicitude. He told her not to hurry back, but if she and the babies liked it at Biloxi, to stay a month longer. He was getting on nicely; and though he missed them, he was willing to bear the separation a while longer—realizing that their health and pleasure were the first things to be considered.

V

AS for Clarisse, she was charmed upon receiving her husband's letter. She and the babies were doing well. The society was agreeable; many of her old friends and acquaintances were at the bay. And the first free breath since her marriage seemed to restore the pleasant liberty of her maiden days. Devoted as she was to her husband, their intimate conjugal life was something which she was more than willing to forego for a while.

So the storm passed and every one was happy.

The Horse Dealer's Daughter

D. H. LAWRENCE   [1885–1930]

"WELL, Mabel, and what are you going to do with yourself?" asked Joe, with foolish flippancy. He felt quite safe himself. Without listening for an answer, he turned aside, worked a grain of tobacco to the tip of his tongue, and spat it out. He did not care about anything, since he felt safe himself.

The three brothers and the sister sat round the desolate breakfast table, attempting some sort of desultory consultation. The morning's post had given the final tap to the family fortune, and all was over. The dreary dining-room itself, with its heavy mahogany furniture, looked as if it were waiting to be done away with.

But the consultation amounted to nothing. There was a strange air of ineffectuality about the three men, as they sprawled at table, smoking and reflecting vaguely on their own condition. The girl was alone, a rather short, sullen-looking young woman of twenty-seven. She did not share the same life as her brothers. She would have been good-looking, save for the impassive fixity of her face, "bull-dog," as her brothers called it.

There was a confused tramping of horses' feet outside. The three men all sprawled round in their chairs to watch. Beyond the dark hollybushes that separated the strip of lawn from the high-road, they could see a cavalcade of shire horses swinging out of their own yard, being taken for exercise. This was the last time. These were the last horses that would go through their hands. The young men watched with critical, callous look. They were all frightened at the collapse of their lives, and the sense of disaster in which they were involved left them no inner freedom.

Yet they were three fine, well-set fellows enough. Joe, the eldest, was a man of thirty-three, broad and handsome in a hot, flushed way. His face was red, he twisted his black moustache over a thick finger, his eyes were shallow and restless. He had a sensual way of uncovering his teeth when he laughed, and his bearing was stupid. Now he watched the horses with a glazed look of helplessness in his eyes, a certain stupor of downfall.

The great draught-horses swung past. They were tied head to tail, four of them, and they heaved along to where a lane branched off from the high-road, planting their great hoofs floutingly in the fine black mud, swinging their great rounded haunches sumptuously, and trotting a few sudden steps as they were led into the lane, round the corner. Every movement showed a massive, slumbrous strength, and a stupidity which held them in subjection. The groom at the head looked back, jerking the leading rope. And the cavalcade moved out of sight up the lane, the tail of the last horse bobbed up tight and stiff, held out taut from the swinging great haunches as they rocked behind the hedges in a motion like sleep.

Joe watched with glazed hopeless eyes. The horses were almost like his own body to him. He felt he was done for now. Luckily he was engaged to a woman as old as himself, and therefore her father, who was steward of a neighbouring estate, would provide him with a job. He would marry and go into harness. His life was over, he would be a subject animal now.

He turned uneasily aside, the retreating steps of the horses echoing in his ears. Then, with foolish restlessness, he reached for the scraps of bacon-rind from the plates, and making a faint whistling sound, flung them to the ter-rier that lay against the fender. He watched the dog swallow them, and waited till the creature looked into his eyes. Then a faint grin came on his face, and in a high, foolish voice he said:

"You won't get much more bacon, shall you, you little bitch?"

The dog faintly and dismally wagged its tail, then lowered its haunches, circled round, and lay down again.

There was another helpless silence at the table. Joe sprawled uneasily in his seat, not willing to go till the family conclave was dissolved. Fred Henry, the second brother, was erect, clean-limbed, alert. He had watched the passing of the horses with more sangfroid. If he was an animal, like Joe, he was an animal which controls, not one which is controlled. He was master of any horse, and he carried himself with a well-tempered air of mastery. But he was not master of the situations of life. He pushed his coarse brown moustache upwards, off his lip, and glanced irritably at his sister, who sat impassive and inscrutable.

"You'll go and stop with Lucy for a bit, shan't you?" he asked. The girl did not answer.

"I don't see what else you can do," persisted Fred Henry.

"Go as a skivvy," Joe interpolated laconically.

The girl did not move a muscle.

"If I was her, I should go in for training for a nurse," said Malcolm, the youngest of them all. He was the baby of the family, a young man of twenty-two, with a fresh, jaunty *museau*.[1]

But Mabel did not take any notice of him. They had talked at her and round her for so many years, that she hardly heard them at all.

The marble clock on the mantelpiece softly chimed the half-hour, the dog rose uneasily from the hearthrug and looked at the party at the breakfast table. But still they sat on in ineffectual conclave.

"Oh, all right," said Joe suddenly, apropos of nothing. "I'll get a move on."

He pushed back his chair, straddled his knees with a downward jerk, to get them free, in horsey fashion, and went to the fire. Still he did not go out of the room; he was curious to know what the others would do or say. He began

---

1. Nose.

to charge his pipe, looking down at the dog and saying, in a high, affected voice:

"Going wi' me? Going wi' me are ter? Tha'rt goin' further than tha counts on just now, dost hear?"

The dog faintly wagged its tail, the man stuck out his jaw and covered his pipe with his hands, and puffed intently, losing himself in the tobacco, looking down all the while at the dog with an absent brown eye. The dog looked up at him in mournful distrust. Joe stood with his knees stuck out, in real horsey fashion.

"Have you had a letter from Lucy?" Fred Henry asked of his sister.

"Last week," came the neutral reply.

"And what does she say?"

There was no answer.

"Does she *ask* you to go and stop there?" persisted Fred Henry.

"She says I can if I like."

"Well, then, you'd better. Tell her you'll come on Monday."

This was received in silence.

"That's what you'll do then, is it?" said Fred Henry, in some exasperation.

But she made no answer. There was a silence of futility and irritation in the room. Malcolm grinned fatuously.

"You'll have to make up your mind between now and next Wednesday," said Joe loudly, "or else find yourself lodgings on the kerbstone."

The face of the young woman darkened, but she sat on immutable.

"Here's Jack Fergusson!" exclaimed Malcolm, who was looking aimlessly out of the window.

"Where?" exclaimed Joe, loudly.

"Just gone past."

"Coming in?"

Malcolm craned his neck to see the gate.

"Yes," he said.

There was a silence. Mabel sat on like one condemned, at the head of the table. Then a whistle was heard from the kitchen. The dog got up and barked sharply. Joe opened the door and shouted:

"Come on."

After a moment a young man entered. He was muffled up in overcoat and a purple woollen scarf, and his tweed cap, which he did not remove, was pulled down on his head. He was of medium height, his face was rather long and pale, his eyes looked tired.

"Hello, Jack! Well, Jack!" exclaimed Malcolm and Joe. Fred Henry merely said, "Jack."

"What's doing?" asked the newcomer, evidently addressing Fred Henry.

"Same. We've got to be out by Wednesday. Got a cold?"

"I have—got it bad, too."

"Why don't you stop in?"

"*Me* stop in? When I can't stand on my legs, perhaps I shall have a chance." The young man spoke huskily. He had a slight Scotch accent.

"It's a knock-out, isn't it," said Joe, boisterously, "if a doctor goes round croaking with a cold. Looks bad for the patients, doesn't it?"

The young doctor looked at him slowly.

"Anything the matter with *you,* then?" he asked sarcastically.

"Not as I know of. Damn your eyes, I hope not. Why?"

"I thought you were very concerned about the patients, wondered if you might be one yourself."

"Damn it, no, I've never been patient to no flaming doctor, and hope I never shall be," returned Joe.

At this point Mabel rose from the table, and they all seemed to become aware of her existence. She began putting the dishes together. The young doctor looked at her, but did not address her. He had not greeted her. She went out of the room with the tray, her face impassive and unchanged.

"When are you off then, all of you?" asked the doctor.

"I'm catching the eleven-forty," replied Malcolm. "Are you goin' down wi' th' trap, Joe?"

"Yes, I've told you I am going down wi' th' trap, haven't I?"

"We'd better be getting her in then. So long, Jack, if I don't see you before I go," said Malcolm, shaking hands.

He went out, followed by Joe, who seemed to have his tail between his legs.

"Well, this is the devil's own," exclaimed the doctor, when he was left alone with Fred Henry. "Going before Wednesday, are you."

"That's the orders," replied the other.

"Where, to Northampton?"

"That's it."

"The devil!" exclaimed Fergusson, with quiet chagrin.

And there was silence between the two.

"All settled up, are you?" asked Fergusson.

"About."

There was another pause.

"Well, I shall miss yer, Freddy, boy," said the young doctor.

"And I shall miss thee, Jack," returned the other.

"Miss you like hell," mused the doctor.

Fred Henry turned aside. There was nothing to say. Mabel came in again, to finish clearing the table.

"What are *you* going to do, then, Miss Pervin?" asked Fergusson. "Going to your sister's, are you?"

Mabel looked at him with her steady, dangerous eyes, that always made him uncomfortable, unsettling his superficial ease.

"No," she said.

"Well, what in the name of fortune are *you* going to do? Say what you mean to do," cried Fred Henry, with futile intensity.

But she only averted her head, and continued her work. She folded the white table-cloth, and put on the chenille cloth.

"The sulkiest bitch that ever trod!" muttered her brother.

But she finished her task with perfectly impassive face, the young doctor watching her interestedly all the while. Then she went out.

Fred Henry stared after her, clenching his lips, his blue eyes fixing in sharp antagonism, as he made a grimace of sour exasperation.

"You could bray her into bits, and that's all you'd get out of her," he said in a small, narrowed tone.

The doctor smiled faintly.

"What's she *going* to do, then?" he asked.

"Strike me if I know!" returned the other.

There was a pause. Then the doctor stirred.

"I'll be seeing you to-night, shall I?" he said to his friend.

"Ay—where's it to be? Are we going over to Jessdale?"

"I don't know. I've got such a cold on me. I'll come round to the Moon and Stars, anyway."

"Let Lizzie and May miss their night for once, eh?"

"That's it—if I feel as I do now."

"All's one—"

The two young men went through the passage and down to the back door together. The house was large, but it was servantless now, and desolate. At the back was a small bricked house-yard, and beyond that a big square, gravelled fine and red, and having stables on two sides. Sloping, dank, winter-dark fields stretched away on the open sides.

But the stables were empty. Joseph Pervin, the father of the family, had been a man of no education, who had become a fairly large horse dealer. The stables had been full of horses, there was a great turmoil and come-and-go of horses and of dealers and grooms. Then the kitchen was full of servants. But of late things had declined. The old man had married a second time, to retrieve his fortunes. Now he was dead and everything was gone to the dogs, there was nothing but debt and threatening.

For months, Mabel had been servantless in the big house, keeping the home together in penury for her ineffectual brothers. She had kept house for ten years. But previously it was with unstinted means. Then, however brutal and coarse everything was, the sense of money had kept her proud, confident. The men might be foul-mouthed, the women in the kitchen might have bad reputations, her brothers might have illegitimate children. But so long as there was money, the girl felt herself established and brutally proud, reserved.

No company came to the house, save dealers and coarse men. Mabel had no associates of her own sex, after her sister went away. But she did not mind. She went regularly to church, she attended to her father. And she lived in the memory of her mother, who had died when she was fourteen, and whom she had loved. She had loved her father, too, in a different way, depending upon him, and feeling secure in him, until at the age of fifty-four he married again. And then she had set hard against him. Now he had died and left them all hopelessly in debt.

She had suffered badly during the period of poverty. Nothing, however, could shake the curious sullen, animal pride that dominated each member of the family. Now, for Mabel, the end had come. Still she would not cast about her. She would follow her own way just the same. She would always hold the keys of her own situation. Mindless and persistent, she endured from day to day. What should she think? Why should she answer anybody? It was enough that this was the end and there was no way out. She need not pass any more darkly along the main street of the small town, avoiding every eye. She need not demean herself any more, going into the shops and buying the cheapest food. This was at an end. She thought of nobody, not even of herself. Mindless and persistent, she seemed in a sort of ecstasy to be coming nearer to her fulfilment, her own glorification, approaching her dead mother, who was glorified.

In the afternoon she took a little bag, with shears and sponge and a small scrubbing brush, and went out. It was a grey, wintry day, with saddened, dark green fields and an atmosphere blackened by the smoke of foundries not far off. She went quickly, darkly along the causeway, heeding nobody, through the town to the churchyard.

There she always felt secure, as if no one could see her, although as a matter of fact she was exposed to the stare of every one who passed along under the churchyard wall. Nevertheless, once under the shadow of the great looming church, among the graves, she felt immune from the world, reserved within the thick churchyard wall as in another country.

Carefully she clipped the grass from the grave, and arranged the pinky white, small chrysanthemums in the tin cross. When this was done, she took an empty jar from a neighbouring grave, brought water, and carefully, most scrupulously sponged the marble head-stone and the coping-stone.

It gave her sincere satisfaction to do this. She felt in immediate contact with the world of her mother. She took minute pains, went through the park in a state bordering on pure happiness, as if in performing this task she came into a subtle, intimate connection with her mother. For the life she followed here in the world was far less real than the world of death she inherited from her mother.

The doctor's house was just by the church. Fergusson, being a mere hired assistant, was slave to the country-side. As he hurried now to attend to the out-patients in the surgery, glancing across the graveyard with his quick eye, he saw the girl at her task at the grave. She seemed so intent and remote, it was like looking into another world. Some mystical element was touched in him. He slowed down as he walked, watching her as if spell-bound.

She lifted her eyes, feeling him looking. Their eyes met. And each looked away again at once, each feeling, in some way, found out by the other.

He lifted his cap and passed on down the road. There remained distinct in his consciousness, like a vision, the memory of her face, lifted from the tombstone in the churchyard, and looking at him with slow, large, portentous eyes. It *was* portentous, her face. It seemed to mesmerize him. There was a heavy power in her eyes which laid hold of his whole being, as if he had drunk some powerful drug. He had been feeling weak and done before. Now the life came back into him, he felt delivered from his own fretted, daily self.

He finished his duties at the surgery as quickly as might be, hastily filling up the bottle of the waiting people with cheap drugs. Then, in perpetual haste, he set off again to visit several cases in another part of his round, before tea-time. At all times he preferred to walk if he could, but particularly when he was not well. He fancied the motion restored him.

The afternoon was falling. It was grey, deadened, and wintry, with a slow, moist, heavy coldness sinking in and deadening all the faculties. But why should he think or notice? He hastily climbed the hill and turned across the dark green fields, following the black cinder-track. In the distance, across a shallow dip in the country, the small town was clustered like smouldering ash, a tower, a spire, a heap of low, raw, extinct houses. And on the nearest fringe of the town, sloping into the dip, was Oldmeadow, the Pervins' house. He could see the stables and the outbuildings distinctly, as they lay towards him on the slope. Well, he would not go there many more times! Another resource would be lost to him, another place gone: the only company he cared for in the alien, ugly little town he was losing. Nothing but work, drudgery, constant hastening from dwelling to dwelling among the colliers and the ironworkers. It wore him out, but at the same time he had a craving for it. It was a stimulant to him to be in the homes of the working people, moving as it were through the innermost body of their life. His nerves were excited and gratified. He could come so near, into the very lives of the rough, inarticulate, powerfully emotional men and women. He grumbled, he said he hated the hellish hole. But as a matter of fact it excited him, the contact with the rough, strongly-feeling people was a stimulant applied direct to his nerves.

Below Oldmeadow, in the green, shallow, soddened hollow of fields lay a square, deep pond. Roving across the landscape, the doctor's quick eye detected a figure in black passing through the gate of the field, down towards the pond. He looked again. It would be Mabel Pervin. His mind suddenly became alive and attentive.

Why was she going down there? He pulled up on the path on the slope above, and stood staring. He could just make sure of the small black figure moving in the hollow of the failing day. He seemed to see her in the midst of such obscurity, that he was like a clairvoyant, seeing rather with the mind's eye than with ordinary sight. Yet he could see her positively enough, whilst he kept his eye attentive. He felt, if he looked away from her, in the thick, ugly falling dusk, he would lose her altogether.

He followed her minutely as she moved, direct and intent, like something transmitted rather than stirring in voluntary activity, straight down the field towards the pond. There she stood on the bank for a moment. She never raised her head. Then she waded slowly into the water.

He stood motionless as the small black figure walked slowly and deliberately towards the centre of the pond, very slowly, gradually moving deeper into the motionless water, and still moving forward as the water got up to her breast. Then he could see her no more in the dusk of the dead afternoon.

"There!" he exclaimed. "Would you believe it?"

And he hastened straight down, running over the wet, soddened fields, pushing through the hedges, down into the depression of callous wintry obscurity. It took him several minutes to come to the pond. He stood on the bank, breathing heavily. He could see nothing. His eyes seemed to penetrate the dead water. Yes, perhaps that was the dark shadow of her black clothing beneath the surface of the water.

He slowly ventured into the pond. The bottom was deep, soft clay, he sank in, and the water clasped dead cold round his legs. As he stirred he could smell the cold, rotten clay that fouled up into the water. It was objectionable in his lungs. Still, repelled and yet not heeding, he moved deeper into the pond. The cold water rose over his thighs, over his loins, upon his abdomen. The lower part of his body was all sunk in the hideous cold element. And the bottom was so deeply soft and uncertain, he was afraid of pitching with his mouth underneath. He could not swim, and was afraid.

He crouched a little, spreading his hands under the water and moving them round, trying to feel for her. The dead cold pond swayed upon his chest. He moved again, a little deeper, and again, with his hands underneath, he felt all around under the water. And he touched her clothing. But it evaded his fingers. He made a desperate effort to grasp it.

And so doing he lost his balance and went under, horribly, suffocating in the foul earthy water, struggling madly for a few moments. At last, after what seemed an eternity, he got his footing, rose again into the air and looked around. He gasped, and knew he was in the world. Then he looked at the water. She had risen near him. He grasped her clothing, and drawing her nearer, turned to take his way to land again.

He went very slowly, carefully, absorbed in the slow progress. He rose higher, climbing out of the pond. The water was now only about his legs; he was thankful, full of relief to be out of the clutches of the pond. He lifted her and staggered on to the bank, out of the horror of wet, grey clay.

He laid her down on the bank. She was quite unconscious and running with water. He made the water come from her mouth, he worked to restore her. He did not have to work very long before he could feel the breathing begin again in her; she was breathing naturally. He worked a little longer. He could feel her live beneath his hands; she was coming back. He wiped her face, wrapped her in his overcoat, looked round into the dim, dark grey world, then lifted her and staggered down the bank and across the fields.

It seemed an unthinkably long way, and his burden so heavy he felt he would never get to the house. But at last he was in the stable-yard, and then in the house-yard. He opened the door and went into the house. In the kitchen he laid her down on the hearth-rug, and called. The house was empty. But the fire was burning in the grate.

Then again he kneeled to attend to her. She was breathing regularly, her eyes were wide open and as if conscious, but there seemed something missing in her look. She was conscious in herself, but unconscious of her surroundings.

He ran upstairs, took blankets from a bed, and put them before the fire to warm. Then he removed her saturated, earthy-smelling clothing, rubbed her dry with a towel, and wrapped her naked in the blankets. Then he went into the dining-room, to look for spirits. There was a little whisky. He drank a gulp himself, and put some into her mouth.

The effect was instantaneous. She looked full into his face, as if she had been seeing him for some time, and yet had only just become conscious of him.

"Dr. Fergusson?" she said.

"What?" he answered.

He was divesting himself of his coat, intending to find some dry clothing upstairs. He could not bear the smell of the dead, clayey water, and he was mortally afraid for his own health.

"What did I do?" she asked.

"Walked into the pond," he replied. He had begun to shudder like one sick, and could hardly attend to her. Her eyes remained full on him, he seemed to be going dark in his mind, looking back at her helplessly. The shuddering became quieter in him, his life came back in him, dark and unknowing, but strong again.

"Was I out of my mind?" she asked, while her eyes were fixed on him all the time.

"Maybe, for the moment," he replied. He felt quiet, because his strength had come back. The strange fretful strain had left him.

"Am I out of my mind now?" she asked.

"Are you?" he reflected a moment. "No," he answered truthfully. "I don't see that you are." He turned his face aside. He was afraid now, because he felt dazed, and felt dimly that her power was stronger than his, in this issue. And she continued to look at him fixedly all the time. "Can you tell me where I shall find some dry things to put on?" he asked.

"Did you dive into the pond for me?" she asked.

"No," he answered. "I walked in. But I went in overhead as well."

There was silence for a moment. He hesitated. He very much wanted to go upstairs to get into dry clothing. But there was another desire in him. And she seemed to hold him. His will seemed to have gone to sleep, and left him, standing there slack before her. But he felt warm inside himself. He did not shudder at all, though his clothes were sodden on him.

"Why did you?" she asked.

"Because I didn't want you to do such a foolish thing," he said.

"It wasn't foolish," she said, still gazing at him as she lay on the floor, with a sofa cushion under her head. "It was the right thing to do. *I* knew best, then."

"I'll go and shift these wet things," he said. But still he had not the power to move out of her presence, until she sent him. It was as if she had the life of his body in her hands, and he could not extricate himself. Or perhaps he did not want to.

Suddenly she sat up. Then she became aware of her own immediate condition. She felt the blankets about her, she knew her own limbs. For a moment it seemed as if her reason were going. She looked round, with wild eye, as if seeking something. He stood still with fear. She saw her clothing lying scattered.

"Who undressed me?" she asked, her eyes resting full and inevitable on his face.

"I did," he replied, "to bring you round."

For some moments she sat and gazed at him awfully, her lips parted.

"Do you love me, then?" she asked.

He only stood and stared at her, fascinated. His soul seemed to melt.

She shuffled forward on her knees, and put her arms round him, round his legs, as he stood there, pressing her breasts against his knees and thighs, clutching him with strange, convulsive certainty, pressing his thighs against her, drawing him to her face, her throat, as she looked up at him with flaring, humble eyes of transfiguration, triumphant in first possession.

"You love me," she murmured, in strange transport, yearning and triumphant and confident. "You love me. I know you love me, I know."

And she was passionately kissing his knees, through the wet clothing, passionately and indiscriminately kissing his knees, his legs, as if unaware of everything.

He looked down at the tangled wet hair, the wild, bare, animal shoulders. He was amazed, bewildered, and afraid. He had never thought of loving her. He had never wanted to love her. When he rescued her and restored her, he was a doctor, and she was a patient. He had had no single personal thought of her. Nay, this introduction of the personal element was very distasteful to him, a violation of his professional honour. It was horrible to have her there embracing his knees. It was horrible. He revolted from it, violently. And yet—and yet—he had not the power to break away.

She looked at him again, with the same supplication of powerful love, and that same transcendent, frightening light of triumph. In view of the delicate flame which seemed to come from her face like a light, he was powerless. And yet he had never intended to love her. He had never intended. And something stubborn in him could not give way.

"You love me," she repeated, in a murmur of deep rhapsodic assurance. "You love me."

Her hands were drawing him, drawing him down to her. He was afraid, even a little horrified. For he had, really, no intention of loving her. Yet her hands were drawing him towards her. He put out his hand quickly to steady himself, and grasped her bare shoulder. A flame seemed to burn the hand that grasped her soft shoulder. He had no intention of loving her: his whole will was against his yielding. It was horrible. And yet wonderful was the touch of her shoulders, beautiful the shining of her face. Was she perhaps mad? He had a horror of yielding to her. Yet something in him ached also.

He had been staring away at the door, away from her. But his hand remained on her shoulder. She had gone suddenly very still. He looked down at her. Her eyes were now wide with fear, with doubt, the light was dying from her face, a shadow of terrible greyness was returning. He could not bear the touch of her eyes' question upon him, and the look of death behind the question.

With an inward groan he gave way, and let his heart yield towards her. A sudden gentle smile came on his face. And her eyes, which never left his face, slowly, slowly filled with tears. He watched the strange water rise in her eyes, like some slow fountain coming up. And his heart seemed to burn and melt away in his breast.

He could not bear to look at her any more. He dropped on his knees and caught her head with his arms and pressed her face against his throat. She was very still. His heart, which seemed to have broken, was burning with a kind of agony in his breast. And he felt her slow, hot tears wetting his throat. But he could not move.

He felt the hot tears wet his neck and the hollows of his neck, and he remained motionless, suspended through one of man's eternities. Only now it had become indispensable to him to have her face pressed close to him; he could never let her go again. He could never let her head go away from the close clutch of his arm. He wanted to remain like that for ever, with his heart hurting him in a pain that was also life to him. Without knowing, he was looking down on her damp, soft brown hair.

Then, as it were suddenly, he smelt the horrid stagnant smell of that water. And at the same moment she drew away from him and looked at him. Her eyes were wistful and unfathomable. He was afraid of them, and he fell to kissing her, not knowing what he was doing. He wanted her eyes not to have that terrible, wistful, unfathomable look.

When she turned her face to him again, a faint delicate flush was glowing, and there was again dawning that terrible shining of joy in her eyes, which really terrified him, and yet which he now wanted to see, because he feared the look of doubt still more.

"You love me?" she said, rather faltering.

"Yes." The word cost him a painful effort. Not because it wasn't true. But because it was too newly true, the *saying* seemed to tear open again his newly-torn heart. And he hardly wanted it to be true, even now.

She lifted her face to him, and he bent forward and kissed her on the mouth, gently, with the one kiss that is an eternal pledge. And as he kissed her his heart strained again in his breast. He never intended to love her. But now it was over. He had crossed over the gulf to her, and all that he had left behind had shrivelled and become void.

After the kiss, her eyes again slowly filled with tears. She sat still, away from him, with her face drooped aside, and her hands folded in her lap. The tears fell very slowly. There was complete silence. He too sat there motionless and silent on the hearthrug. The strange pain of his heart that was broken seemed to consume him. That he should love her? That this was love! That he should be ripped open in this way! Him, a doctor! How they would all jeer if they knew! It was agony to him to think they might know.

In the curious naked pain of the thought he looked again to her. She was sitting there drooped into a muse. He saw a tear fall, and his heart flared hot. He saw for the first time that one of her shoulders was quite uncovered, one arm bare, he could see one of her small breasts; dimly, because it had become almost dark in the room.

"Why are you crying?" he asked, in an altered voice.

She looked up at him, and behind her tears the consciousness of her situation for the first time brought a dark look of shame to her eyes.

"I'm not crying, really," she said, watching him half frightened.

He reached his hand, and softly closed it on her bare arm.

"I love you! I love you!" he said in a soft, low vibrating voice, unlike himself.

She shrank, and dropped her head. The soft, penetrating grip of his hand on her arm distressed her. She looked up at him.

"I want to go," she said. "I want to go and get you some dry things."

"Why?" he said. "I'm all right."

"But I want to go," she said. "And I want you to change your things."

He released her arm, and she wrapped herself in the blanket, looking at him rather frightened. And still she did not rise.

"Kiss me," she said wistfully.

He kissed her, but briefly, half in anger.

Then, after a second, she rose nervously, all mixed up in the blanket. He watched her in her confusion, as she tried to extricate herself and wrap herself up so that she could walk. He watched her relentlessly, as she knew. And as she went, the blanket trailing, and as he saw a glimpse of her feet and her white leg, he tried to remember her as she was when he had wrapped her in the blanket. But then he didn't want to remember, because she had been nothing to him then, and his nature revolted from remembering her as she was when she was nothing to him.

A tumbling, muffled noise from within the dark house startled him. Then he heard her voice:—"There are clothes." He rose and went to the foot of the stairs, and gathered up the garments she had thrown down. Then he came back to the fire, to rub himself down and dress. He grinned at his own appearance when he had finished.

The fire was sinking, so he put on coal. The house was now quite dark, save for the light of a street-lamp that shone in faintly from beyond the holly trees. He lit the gas with matches he found on the mantelpiece. Then he emptied the pockets of his own clothes, and threw all his wet things in a heap into the scullery. After which he gathered up her sodden clothes, gently, and put them in a separate heap on the copper-top in the scullery.

It was six o'clock on the clock. His own watch had stopped. He ought to go back to the surgery. He waited, and still she did not come down. So he went to the foot of the stairs and called:

"I shall have to go."

Almost immediately he heard her coming down. She had on her best dress of black voile, and her hair was tidy, but still damp. She looked at him—and in spite of herself, smiled.

"I don't like you in those clothes," she said.

"Do I look a sight?" he answered.

They were shy of one another.

"I'll make you some tea," she said.

"No, I must go."

"Must you?" And she looked at him again with the wide, strained, doubtful eyes. And again, from the pain of his breast, he knew how he loved her. He went and bent to kiss her, gently, passionately, with his heart's painful kiss.

"And my hair smells so horrible," she murmured in distraction. "And I'm so awful, I'm so awful! Oh, no, I'm too awful." And she broke into bitter, heart-broken sobbing. "You can't want to love me, I'm horrible."

"Don't be silly, don't be silly," he said, trying to comfort her, kissing her, holding her in his arms. "I want you, I want to marry you, we're going to be married, quickly, quickly—tomorrow if I can."

But she only sobbed terribly, and cried:

"I feel awful. I feel awful. I feel I'm horrible to you."

"No, I want you, I want you," was all he answered, blindly, with that terrible intonation which frightened her almost more than her horror lest he should *not* want her.

Questions

1. The central episode in the story is Mabel's attempted suicide. What symbolic qualities do the events at the pond have?   2. In what way does Mabel's character change? In what way does Jack Fergusson's?   3. Why does Fergusson resist the attraction he feels toward Mabel? Why does he finally yield?   4. What function is served by the presence of Mabel's brothers in the first third of the story?

Theater

JEAN TOOMER [1894–1967]

LIFE of nigger alleys, of pool rooms and restaurants and near-beer saloons soaks into the walls of Howard Theater and sets them throbbing jazz songs. Black-skinned, they dance and shout above the tick and trill of white-walled buildings. At night, they open doors to people who come in to stamp their feet and shout. At night, road-shows volley songs into the mass-heart of black people. Songs soak the walls and seep out to the nigger life of alleys and near-beer saloons, of the Poodle Dog and Black Bear cabarets. Afternoons, the house is dark, and the walls are sleeping singers until rehearsal begins. Or until John comes within them. Then they start throbbing to a subtle syncopation. And the space-dark air grows softly luminous.

John is the manager's brother. He is seated at the center of the theater, just before rehearsal. Light streaks down upon him from a window high above. One half his face is orange in it. One half his face is in shadow. The soft glow of the house rushes to, and compacts about, the shaft of light. John's mind coincides with the shaft of light. Thoughts rush to, and compact about it. Life of the house and of the slowly awakening stage swirls to the body of John, and thrills it. John's body is separate from the thoughts that pack his mind.

Stage-lights, soft, as if they shine through clear pink fingers. Beneath them, hid by the shadow of a set, Dorris. Other chorus girls drift in. John feels them in the mass. And as if his own body were the mass-heart of a black audience listening to them singing, he wants to stamp his feet and shout. His mind, contained above desires of his body, singles the girls out, and tries to trace origins and plot destinies.

A pianist slips into the pit and improvises jazz. The walls awake. Arms of the girls, and their limbs, which . . . jazz, jazz . . . by lifting up their tight street skirts they set free, jab the air and clog the floor in rhythm to the music. (Lift your skirts, Baby, and talk t papa!) Crude, individualized, and yet . . . monotonous. . . .

John: Soon the director will herd you, my full-lipped, distant beauties, and tame you, and blunt your sharp thrusts in loosely suggestive movements, appropriate to Broadway. (O dance!) Soon the audience will paint your dusk faces white, and call you beautiful. (O dance!) Soon I. . . . (O dance!) I'd like . . .

Girls laugh and shout. Sing discordant snatches of other jazz songs. Whirl with loose passion into the arms of passing show-men.

John: Too thick. Too easy. Too monotonous. Her whom I'd love I'd

leave before she knew that I was with her. Her? Which? (O dance!) I'd like to
. . .

Girls dance and sing. Men clap. The walls sing and press inward. They press the men and girls, they press John towards a center of physical ecstasy. Go to it, Baby! Fan yourself, and feed your papa! Put . . . nobody lied . . . and take . . . when they said I cried over you. No lie! The glitter and color of stacked scenes, the gilt and brass and crimson of the house, converge towards a center of physical ecstasy. John's feet and torso and his blood press in. He wills thought to rid his mind of passion.

"All right, girls. Alaska. Miss Reynolds, please."

The director wants to get the rehearsal through with.

The girls line up. John sees the front row: dancing ponies. The rest are in shadow. The leading lady fits loosely in the front. Lack-life, monotonous. "One, two, three—" Music starts. The song is somewhere where it will not strain the leading lady's throat. The dance is somewhere where it will not strain the girls. Above the staleness, one dancer throws herself into it. Dorris. John sees her. Her hair, crisp-curled, is bobbed. Bushy, black hair bobbing about her lemon-colored face. Her lips are curiously full, and very red. Her limbs in silk purple stockings are lovely. John feels them. Desires her. Holds off.

John: Stage-door johnny; chorus-girl. No, that would be all right. Dictie,[1] educated, stuck-up; show-girl. Yep. Her suspicion would be stronger than her passion. It wouldnt work. Keep her loveliness. Let her go.

Dorris sees John and knows that he is looking at her. Her own glowing is too rich a thing to let her feel the slimness of his diluted passion.

"Who's that?" she asks her dancing partner.

"Th manager's brother. Dictie. Nothin doin, hon."

Dorris tosses her head and dances for him until she feels she has him. Then, withdrawing disdainfully, she flirts with the director.

Dorris: Nothin doin? How come? Aint I as good as him? Couldnt I have got an education if I'd wanted one? Dont I know respectable folks, lots of em, in Philadelphia and New York and Chicago? Aint I had men as good as him? Better. Doctors an lawyers. Whats a manager's brother, anyhow?

Two steps back, and two steps front.

"Say, Mame, where do you get that stuff?"

"Whatshmean, Dorris?"

"If you two girls cant listen to what I'm telling you, I know where I can get some who can. Now listen."

Mame: Go to hell, you black bastard.

Dorris: Whats eatin at him, anyway?

"Now follow me in this, you girls. Its three counts to the right, three counts to the left, and then you shimmy—"

John: —and then you shimmy. I'll bet she can. Some good cabaret, with rooms upstairs. And what in hell do you think you'd get from it? Youre going

---

1. A snob.

wrong. Here's right: get her to herself—(Christ, but how she'd bore you after the first five minutes)—not if you get her right she wouldnt. Touch her, I mean. To herself—in some room perhaps. Some cheap, dingy bedroom. Hell no. Cant be done. But the point is, brother John, it can be done. Get her to herself somewhere, anywhere. Go down in yourself—and she'd be calling you all sorts of asses while you were in the process of going down. Hold em, bud. Cant be done. Let her go. (Dance and I'll love you!) And keep her loveliness.

"All right now, Chicken Chaser. Dorris and girls. Where's Dorris? I told you to stay on the stage, didnt I? Well? Now thats enough. All right. All right there, Professor?[2] All right. One, two, three—"

Dorris swings to the front. The line of girls, four deep, blurs within the shadow of suspended scenes. Dorris wants to dance. The director feels that and steps to one side. He smiles, and picks her for a leading lady, one of these days. Odd ends of stage-men emerge from the wings, and stare and clap. A crap game in the alley suddenly ends. Black faces crowd the rear stage doors. The girls, catching joy from Dorris, whip up within the footlights' glow. They forget set steps; they find their own. The director forgets to bawl them out. Dorris dances.

John: Her head bobs to Broadway. Dance from yourself. Dance! O just a little more.

Dorris' eyes burn across the space of seats to him.

Dorris: I bet he can love. Hell, he cant love. He's too skinny. His lips are too skinny. He wouldnt love me anyway, only for that. But I'd get a pair of silk stockings out of it. Red silk. I got purple. Cut it, kid. You cant win him to respect you that away. He wouldnt anyway. Maybe he would. Maybe he'd love. I've heard em say that men who look like him (what does he look like?) will marry if they love. O will you love me? And give me kids, and a home, and everything? (I'd like to make your nest, and honest, hon, I wouldnt run out on you.) You will if I make you. Just watch me.

Dorris dances. She forgets her tricks. She dances.

Glorious songs are the muscles of her limbs.

And her singing is of canebrake loves and mangrove feastings.

The walls press in, singing. Flesh of a throbbing body, they press close to John and Dorris. They close them in. John's heart beats tensely against her dancing body. Walls press his mind within his heart. And then, the shaft of light goes out the window high above him. John's mind sweeps up to follow it. Mind pulls him upward into dream. Dorris dances. . . John dreams:

Dorris is dressed in a loose black gown splashed with lemon ribbons. Her feet taper long and slim from trim ankles. She waits for him just inside the stage door. John, collar and tie colorful and flaring, walks towards the stage door. There are no trees in the alley. But his feet feel as though they step on autumn leaves whose rustle has been pressed

---

2. A piano player.

out of them by the passing of a million satin slippers. The air is sweet with roasting chestnuts, sweet with bonfires of old leaves. John's melancholy is a deep thing that seals all senses but his eyes, and makes him whole.

Dorris knows that he is coming. Just at the right moment she steps from the door, as if there were no door. Her face is tinted like the autumn alley. Of old flowers, or of a southern canefield, her perfume. "Glorious Dorris." So his eyes speak. And their sadness is too deep for sweet untruth. She barely touches his arm. They glide off with footfalls softened on the leaves, the old leaves powdered by a million satin slippers.

They are in a room. John knows nothing of it. Only, that the flesh and blood of Dorris are its walls. Singing walls. Lights, soft, as if they shine through clear pink fingers. Soft lights, and warm.

John reaches for a manuscript of his, and reads. Dorris, who has no eyes, has eyes to understand him. He comes to a dancing scene. The scene is Dorris. She dances. Dorris dances. Glorious Dorris. Dorris whirls, whirls, dances. . . .

Dorris dances. The pianist crashes a bumper chord. The whole stage claps. Dorris, flushed, looks quick at John. His whole face is in shadow. She seeks for her dance in it. She finds it a dead thing in the shadow which is his dream. She rushes from the stage. Falls down the steps into her dressing-room. Pulls her hair. Her eyes, over a floor of tears, stare at the whitewashed ceiling. (Smell of dry paste, and paint, and soiled clothing.) Her pal comes in. Dorris flings herself into the old safe arms, and cries bitterly.

"I told you nothin doing," is what Mame says to comfort her.

Questions

1. *State the nature of the conflict in John.* **2.** *How does Toomer achieve dramatic conflict between John and Dorris even though they do not speak to each other?* **3.** *How does the opening paragraph establish the mood and the values of the story?*

Dry September

WILLIAM FAULKNER [1897–1962]

I

THROUGH the bloody September twilight, aftermath of sixty-two rainless days, it had gone like a fire in dry grass—the rumor, the story, whatever it was. Something about Miss Minnie Cooper and a Negro. Attacked, insulted, frightened: none of them, gathered in the barber shop on that Saturday evening where the ceiling fan stirred, wIthout freshening it, the vitiated air, sending back upon them, in recurrent surges of stale pomade and lotion, their own stale breath and odors, knew exactly what had happened.

"Except it wasn't Will Mayes," a barber said. He was a man of middle age; a thin, sand-colored man with a mild face, who was shaving a client. "I know Will Mayes. He's a good nigger. And I know Miss Minnie Cooper, too."

"What do you know about her?" a second barber said.

"Who is she?" the client said. "A young girl?"

"No," the barber said. "She's about forty, I reckon. She aint married. That's why I dont believe—"

"Believe, hell!" a hulking youth in a sweat-stained silk shirt said. "Wont you take a white woman's word before a nigger's?"

"I dont believe Will Mayes did it," the barber said. "I know Will Mayes."

"Maybe you know who did it, then. Maybe you already got him out of town, you damn niggerlover."

"I dont believe anybody did anything. I dont believe anything happened. I leave it to you fellows if them ladies that get old without getting married dont have notions that a man cant—"

"Then you are a hell of a white man," the client said. He moved under the cloth. The youth had sprung to his feet.

"You dont?" he said. "Do you accuse a white woman of lying?"

The barber held the razor poised above the half-risen client. He did not look around.

"It's this durn weather," another said. "It's enough to make a man do anything. Even to her."

Nobody laughed. The barber said in his mild, stubborn tone: "I aint accusing nobody of nothing. I just know and you fellows know how a woman that never—"

"You damn niggerlover!" the youth said.

"Shut up, Butch," another said. "We'll get the facts in plenty of time to act."

"Who is? Who's getting them?" the youth said. "Facts, hell! I—"

"You're a fine white man," the client said. "Aint you?" In his frothy beard he looked like a desert rat in the moving pictures. "You tell them, Jack," he said to the youth. "If there aint any white men in this town, you can count on me, even if I aint only a drummer and a stranger."

"That's right, boys," the barber said. "Find out the truth first. I know Will Mayes."

"Well, by God!" the youth shouted. "To think that a white man in this town—"

"Shut up, Butch," the second speaker said. "We got plenty of time."

The client sat up. He looked at the speaker. "Do you claim that anything excuses a nigger attacking a white woman? Do you mean to tell me you are a white man and you'll stand for it? You better go back North where you came from. The South dont want your kind here."

"North what?" the second said. "I was born and raised in this town."

"Well, by God!" the youth said. He looked about with a strained, baffled gaze, as if he was trying to remember what it was he wanted to say or to do. He drew his sleeve across his sweating face. "Damn if I'm going to let a white woman—"

"You tell them, Jack," the drummer said. "By God, if they—"

The screen door crashed open. A man stood in the door, his feet apart and his heavy-set body poised easily. His white shirt was open at the throat; he wore a felt hat. His hot, bold glance swept the group. His name was McLendon. He had commanded troops at the front in France and had been decorated for valor.

"Well," he said, "are you going to sit there and let a black son rape a white woman on the streets of Jefferson?"

Butch sprang up again. The silk of his shirt clung flat to his heavy shoulders. At each armpit was a dark halfmoon. "That's what I been telling them! That's what I—"

"Did it really happen?" a third said. "This aint the first man scare she ever had, like Hawkshaw says. Wasn't there something about a man on the kitchen roof, watching her undress, about a year ago?"

"What?" the client said. "What's that?" The barber had been slowly forcing him back into the chair; he arrested himself reclining, his head lifted, the barber still pressing him down.

McLendon whirled on the third speaker. "Happen? What the hell difference does it make? Are you going to let the black sons get away with it until one really does it?"

"That's what I'm telling them!" Butch shouted. He cursed, long and steady, pointless.

"Here, here," a fourth said. "Not so loud. Dont talk so loud."

"Sure," McLendon said; "no talking necessary at all. I've done my talking. Who's with me?" He poised on the balls of his feet, roving his gaze.

The barber held the drummer's face down, the razor poised. "Find out the facts first, boys. I know Willy Mayes. It wasn't him. Let's get the sheriff and do this thing right."

McLendon whirled upon him his furious, rigid face. The barber did not look away. They looked like men of different races. The other barbers had ceased also above their prone clients. "You mean to tell me," McLendon said, "that you'd take a nigger's word before a white woman's? Why, you damn niggerloving—"

The third speaker rose and grasped McLendon's arm; he too had been a soldier, "Now, now. Let's figure this thing out. Who knows anything about what really happened?"

"Figure out hell!" McLendon jerked his arm free. "All that're with me get up from there. The ones that aint—" He roved his gaze, dragging his sleeve across his face.

Three men rose. The drummer in the chair sat up. "Here," he said, jerking at the cloth about his neck; "get this rag off me. I'm with him. I dont live here, but by God, if our mothers and wives and sisters—" He smeared the cloth over his face and flung it to the floor. McLendon stood in the floor and cursed the others. Another rose and moved toward him. The remainder sat uncomfortable, not looking at one another, then one by one they rose and joined him.

The barber picked the cloth from the floor. He began to fold it neatly. "Boys, dont do that. Will Mayes never done it. I know."

"Come on," McLendon said. He whirled. From his hip pocket protruded the butt of a heavy automatic pistol. They went out. The screen door crashed behind them reverberant in the dead air.

The barber wiped the razor carefully and swiftly, and put it away, and ran to the rear, and took his hat from the wall. "I'll be back as soon as I can," he said to the other barbers. "I cant let—" He went out, running. The two other barbers followed him to the door and caught it on the rebound, leaning out and looking up the street after him. The air was flat and dead. It had a metallic taste at the base of the tongue.

"What can he do?" the first said. The second one was saying "Jees Christ, Jees Christ" under his breath. "I'd just as lief be Will Mayes as Hawk, if he gets McLendon riled."

"Jees Christ, Jees Christ," the second whispered.

"You reckon he really done it to her?" the first said.

II

SHE was thirty-eight or thirty-nine. She lived in a small frame house with her invalid mother and a thin, sallow, unflagging aunt, where each morning between ten and eleven she would appear on the porch in a lace-trimmed boudoir cap, to sit swinging in the porch swing until noon. After dinner she lay down for a while, until the afternoon began to cool. Then, in one of the three or four new voile dresses which she had each summer, she would go downtown to spend the afternoon in the stores with the other ladies, where they would handle the goods and haggle over the prices in cold, immediate voices, without any intention of buying.

She was of comfortable people—not the best in Jefferson, but good people enough—and she was still on the slender side of ordinary looking, with a bright, faintly haggard manner and dress. When she was young she had had a slender, nervous body and a sort of hard vivacity which had enabled her for a time to ride upon the crest of the town's social life as exemplified by the high school party and church social period of her contemporaries while still children enough to be unclassconscious.

She was the last to realize that she was losing ground; that those among whom she had been a little brighter and louder flame than any other were beginning to learn the pleasure of snobbery—male—and retaliation—female. That was when her face began to wear that bright, haggard look. She still carried it to parties on shadowy porticoes and summer lawns, like a mask or a flag, with that bafflement of furious repudiation of truth in her eyes. One evening at a party she heard a boy and two girls, all schoolmates, talking. She never accepted another invitation.

She watched the girls with whom she had grown up as they married and got homes and children, but no man ever called on her steadily until the children of the other girls had been calling her "aunty" for several years, the while their mothers told them in bright voices about how popular Aunt Minnie had been as a girl. Then the town began to see her driving on Sunday afternoons with the cashier in the bank. He was a widower of about forty—a high-colored man, smelling always faintly of the barber shop or of whisky. He owned the first automobile in town, a red runabout; Minnie had the first motoring bonnet and veil the town ever saw. Then the town began to say: "Poor Minnie." "But she is old enough to take care of herself," others said. That was when she began to ask her old schoolmates that their children call her "cousin" instead of "aunty."

It was twelve years now since she had been relegated into adultery by public opinion, and eight years since the cashier had gone to a Memphis bank, returning for one day each Christmas, which he spent at an annual bachelors' party at a hunting club on the river. From behind their curtains the neighbors would see the party pass, and during the over-the-way Christmas day visiting they would tell her about him, about how well he looked, and how they heard that he was prospering in the city, watching with bright, secret eyes her haggard, bright face. Usually by that hour there would be the scent of whisky on her breath. It was supplied her by a youth, a clerk at the soda fountain: "Sure; I buy it for the old gal. I reckon she's entitled to a little fun."

Her mother kept to her room altogether now; the gaunt aunt ran the house. Against that background Minnie's bright dresses, her idle and empty days, had a quality of furious unreality. She went out in the evenings only with women now, neighbors, to the moving pictures. Each afternoon she dressed in one of the new dresses and went downtown alone, where her young "cousins" were already strolling in the late afternoons with their delicate, silken heads and thin, awkward arms and conscious hips, clinging to one another or shrieking and giggling with paired boys in the soda fountain when she passed and went on along the serried store fronts, in the doors of which the sitting and lounging men did not even follow her with their eyes any more.

III

THE barber went swiftly up the street where the sparse lights, insect-swirled, glared in rigid and violent suspension in the lifeless air. The day had died in a pall of dust; above the darkened square, shrouded by the spent dust, the sky was as clear as the inside of a brass bell. Below the east was a rumor of the twice-waxed moon.

When he overtook them McLendon and three others were getting into a car parked in an alley. McLendon stooped his thick head, peering out beneath the top. "Changed your mind, did you?" he said. "Damn good thing; by God, tomorrow when this town hears about how you talked tonight—"

"Now, now," the other ex-soldier said. "Hawkshaw's all right. Come on, Hawk; jump in."

"Will Mayes never done it, boys," the barber said. "If anybody done it. Why, you all know well as I do there aint any town where they got better niggers than us. And you know how a lady will kind of think things about men when there aint any reason to, and Miss Minnie anyway—"

"Sure, sure," the soldier said. "We're just going to talk to him a little; that's all."

"Talk hell!" Butch said. "When we're through with the—"

"Shut up, for God's sake!" the soldier said. "Do you want everybody in town—"

"Tell them, by God!" McLendon said. "Tell every one of the sons that'll let a white woman—"

"Let's go; let's go: here's the other car." The second car slid squealing out of a cloud of dust at the alley mouth. McLendon started his car and took the lead. Dust lay like fog in the street. The street lights hung nimbused as in water. They drove on out of town.

A rutted lane turned at right angles. Dust hung above it too, and above all the land. The dark bulk of the ice plant, where the Negro Mayes was night watchman, rose against the sky. "Better stop here, hadn't we?" the soldier said. McLendon did not reply. He hurled the car up and slammed to a stop, the headlights glaring on the blank wall.

"Listen here, boys," the barber said; "if he's here, dont that prove he

WILLIAM FAULKNER 565

never done it? Dont it? If it was him, he would run. Dont you see he would?" The second car came up and stopped. McLendon got down; Butch sprang down beside him. "Listen, boys," the barber said.

"Cut the lights off!" McLendon said. The breathless dark rushed down. There was no sound in it save their lungs as they sought air in the parched dust in which for two months they had lived; then the diminishing crunch of McLendon's and Butch's feet, and a moment later McLendon's voice:

"Will! . . . Will!"

Below the east the wan hemorrhage of the moon increased. It heaved above the ridge, silvering the air, the dust, so that they seemed to breathe, live, in a bowl of molten lead. There was no sound of nightbird nor insect, no sound save their breathing and a faint ticking of contracting metal about the cars. Where their bodies touched one another they seemed to sweat dryly, for no more moisture came. "Christ!" a voice said; "let's get out of here."

But they didn't move until vague noises began to grow out of the darkness ahead; then they got out and waited tensely in the breathless dark. There was another sound: a blow, a hissing expulsion of breath and McLendon cursing in undertone. They stood a moment longer, then they ran forward. They ran in a stumbling clump, as though they were fleeing something. "Kill him, kill the son," a voice whispered. McLendon flung them back.

"Not here," he said. "Get him into the car." "Kill him, kill the black son!" the voice murmured. They dragged the Negro to the car. The barber had waited beside the car. He could feel himself sweating and he knew he was going to be sick at the stomach.

"What is it, captains?" the Negro said. "I aint done nothing. 'Fore God, Mr John." Someone produced handcuffs. They worked busily about the Negro as though he were a post, quiet, intent, getting in one another's way. He submitted to the handcuffs, looking swiftly and constantly from dim face to dim face. "Who's here, captains?" he said, leaning to peer into the faces until they could feel his breath and smell his sweaty reek. He spoke a name or two. "What you all say I done, Mr John?"

McLendon jerked the car door open. "Get in!" he said.

The Negro did not move. "What you all going to do with me, Mr John? I aint done nothing. White folks, captains, I aint done nothing: I swear 'fore God." He called another name.

"Get in!" McLendon said. He struck the Negro. The others expelled their breath in a dry hissing and struck him with random blows and he whirled and cursed them, and swept his manacled hands across their faces and slashed the barber upon the mouth, and the barber struck him also. "Get him in there," McLendon said. They pushed at him. He ceased struggling and got in and sat quietly as the others took their places. He sat between the barber and the soldier, drawing his limbs in so as not to touch them, his eyes going swiftly and constantly from face to face. Butch clung to the running board. The car moved on. The barber nursed his mouth with his handkerchief.

"What's the matter, Hawk?" the soldier said.

"Nothing," the barber said. They regained the highroad and turned away from town. The second car dropped back out of the dust. They went on, gaining speed; the final fringe of houses dropped behind.

"Goddamn, he stinks!" the soldier said.

"We'll fix that," the drummer in front beside McLendon said. On the running board Butch cursed into the hot rush of air. The barber leaned suddenly forward and touched McLendon's arm.

"Let me out, John," he said.

"Jump out, niggerlover," McLendon said without turning his head. He drove swiftly. Behind them the sourceless lights of the second car glared in the dust. Presently McLendon turned into a narrow road. It was rutted with disuse. It led back to an abandoned brick kiln—a series of reddish mounds and weed- and vine-choked vats without bottom. It had been used for pasture once, until one day the owner missed one of his mules. Although he prodded carefully in the vats with a long pole, he could not even find the bottom of them.

"John," the barber said.

"Jump out, then," McLendon said, hurling the car along the ruts. Beside the barber the Negro spoke:

"Mr Henry."

The barber sat forward. The narrow tunnel of the road rushed up and past. Their motion was like an extinct furnace blast: cooler, but utterly dead. The car bounded from rut to rut.

"Mr Henry," the Negro said.

The barber began to tug furiously at the door. "Look out, there!" the soldier said, but the barber had already kicked the door open and swung onto the running board. The soldier leaned across the Negro and grasped at him, but he had already jumped. The car went on without checking speed.

The impetus hurled him crashing through dust-sheathed weeds, into the ditch. Dust puffed about him, and in a thin, vicious crackling of sapless stems he lay choking and retching until the second car passed and died away. Then he rose and limped on until he reached the highroad and turned toward town, brushing at his clothes with his hands. The moon was higher, riding high and clear of the dust at last, and after a while the town began to glare beneath the dust. He went on, limping. Presently he heard cars and the glow of them grew in the dust behind him and he left the road and crouched again in the weeds until they passed. McLendon's car came last now. There were four people in it and Butch was not on the running board.

They went on; the dust swallowed them; the glare and the sound died away. The dust of them hung for a while, but soon the eternal dust absorbed it again. The barber climbed back onto the road and limped on toward town.

IV

As she dressed for supper on that Saturday evening, her own flesh felt like fever. Her hands trembled among the hooks and eyes, and her eyes had a feverish look, and her hair swirled crisp and crackling under the comb.

While she was still dressing the friends called for her and sat while she donned her sheerest underthings and stockings and a new voile dress. "Do you feel strong enough to go out?" they said, their eyes bright too, with a dark glitter. "When you have had time to get over the shock, you must tell us what happened. What he said and did; everything."

In the leafed darkness, as they walked toward the square, she began to breathe deeply, something like a swimmer preparing to dive, until she ceased trembling, the four of them walking slowly because of the terrible heat and out of solicitude for her. But as they neared the square she began to tremble again, walking with her head up, her hands clenched at her sides, their voices about her murmurous, also with that feverish, glittering quality of their eyes.

They entered the square, she in the center of the group, fragile in her fresh dress. She was trembling worse. She walked slower and slower, as children eat ice cream, her head up and her eyes bright in the haggard banner of her face, passing the hotel and the coatless drummers in chairs along the curb looking around at her: "That's the one: see? The one in pink in the middle." "Is that her? What did they do with the nigger? Did they—?" "Sure. He's all right." "All right, is he?" "Sure. He went on a little trip." Then the drug store, where even the young men lounging in the doorway tipped their hats and followed with their eyes the motion of her hips and legs when she passed.

They went on, passing the lifted hats of the gentlemen, the suddenly ceased voices, deferent, protective. "Do you see?" the friends said. Their voices sounded like long, hovering sighs of hissing exultation. "There's not a Negro on the square. Not one."

They reached the picture show. It was like a miniature fairyland with its lighted lobby and colored lithographs of life caught in its terrible and beautiful mutations. Her lips began to tingle. In the dark, when the picture began, it would be all right; she could hold back the laughing so it would not waste away so fast and so soon. So she hurried on before the turning faces, the undertones of low astonishment, and they took their accustomed places where she could see the aisle against the silver glare and the young men and girls coming in two and two against it.

The lights flicked away; the screen glowed silver, and soon life began to unfold, beautiful and passionate and sad, while still the young men and girls entered, scented and sibilant in the half dark, their paired backs in silhouette delicate and sleek, their slim, quick bodies awkward, divinely young, while beyond them the silver dream accumulated, inevitably on and on. She began to laugh. In trying to suppress it, it made more noise than ever; heads began to turn. Still laughing, her friends raised her and led her out, and she stood at the curb, laughing on a high, sustained note, until the taxi came up and they helped her in.

They removed the pink voile and the sheer underthings and the stockings, and put her to bed, and cracked ice for her temples, and sent for the doctor. He was hard to locate, so they ministered to her with hushed ejaculations, renewing the ice and fanning her. While the ice was fresh and cold she stopped laughing and lay still for a time, moaning only a little. But soon the laughing welled again and her voice rose screaming.

"Shhhhhhhhhhh! Shhhhhhhhhhhhhh!" they said, freshening the ice-pack, smoothing her hair, examining it for gray; "poor girl!" Then to one another: "Do you suppose anything really happened?" their eyes darkly aglitter, secret and passionate. "Shhhhhhhhhh! Poor girl! Poor Minnie!"

V

IT was midnight when McLendon drove up to his neat new house. It was trim and fresh as a birdcage and almost as small, with its clean, green-and-white paint. He locked the car and mounted the porch and entered. His wife rose from a chair beside the reading lamp. McLendon stopped in the floor and stared at her until she looked down.

"Look at that clock," he said, lifting his arm, pointing. She stood before him, her face lowered, a magazine in her hands. Her face was pale, strained, and weary-looking. "Haven't I told you about sitting up like this, waiting to see when I come in?"

"John," she said. She laid the magazine down. Poised on the balls of his feet, he glared at her with his hot eyes, his sweating face.

"Didn't I tell you?" He went toward her. She looked up then. He caught her shoulder. She stood passive, looking at him.

"Don't, John. I couldn't sleep . . . The heat; something. Please, John. You're hurting me."

"Didn't I tell you?" He released her and half struck, half flung her across the chair, and she lay there and watched him quietly as he left the room.

He went on through the house, ripping off his shirt, and on the dark, screened porch at the rear he stood and mopped his head and shoulders with the shirt and flung it away. He took the pistol from his hip and laid it on the table beside the bed, and sat on the bed and removed his shoes, and rose and slipped his trousers off. He was sweating again already, and he stooped and hunted furiously for the shirt. At last he found it and wiped his body again, and, with his body pressed against the dusty screen, he stood panting. There was no movement, no sound, not even an insect. The dark world seemed to lie stricken beneath the cold moon and the lidless stars.

To Room Nineteen

DORIS LESSING   [b. 1919]

THIS is a story, I suppose, about a failure in intelligence: the Rawlings' marriage was grounded in intelligence.

They were older when they married than most of their married friends: in their well-seasoned late twenties. Both had had a number of affairs, sweet rather than bitter; and when they fell in love—for they did fall in love—had known each other for some time. They joked that they had saved each other "for the real thing." That they had waited so long (but not too long) for this real thing was to them a proof of their sensible discrimination. A good many of their friends had married young, and now (they felt) probably regretted lost opportunities; while others, still unmarried, seemed to them arid, self-doubting, and likely to make desperate or romantic marriages.

Not only they, but others, felt they were well matched: their friends' delight was an additional proof of their happiness. They had played the same roles, male and female, in this group or set, if such a wide, loosely connected, constantly changing constellation of people could be called a set. They had both become, by virtue of their moderation, their humor, and their abstinence from painful experience people to whom others came for advice. They could be, and were, relied on. It was one of those cases of a man and a woman linking themselves whom no one else had ever thought of linking, probably because of their similarities. But then everyone exclaimed: Of course! How right! How was it we never thought of it before!

And so they married amid general rejoicing, and because of their foresight and their sense for what was probable, nothing was a surprise to them.

Both had well-paid jobs. Matthew was a subeditor on a large London newspaper, and Susan worked in an advertising firm. He was not the stuff of which editors or publicised journalists are made, but he was much more than "a subeditor," being one of the essential background people who in fact steady, inspire and make possible the people in the limelight. He was content with this position. Susan had a talent for commercial drawing. She was humorous about the advertisements she was responsible for, but she did not feel strongly about them one way or the other.

Both, before they married, had had pleasant flats, but they felt it unwise to base a marriage on either flat, because it might seem like a submission of personality on the part of the one whose flat it was not. They moved into a new flat in South Kensington on the clear understanding that when their marriage had settled down (a process they knew would not take long, and was in fact more a humorous concession to popular wisdom than what was due to themselves) they would buy a house and start a family.

And this is what happened. They lived in their charming flat for two years, giving parties and going to them, being a popular young married couple, and then Susan became pregnant, she gave up her job, and they bought a house in Richmond. It was typical of this couple that they had a son first, then a daughter, then twins, son and daughter. Everything right, appropriate, and what everyone would wish for, if they could choose. But people did feel these two had chosen; this balanced and sensible family was no more than what was due to them because of their infallible sense for *choosing* right.

And so they lived with their four children in their gardened house in Richmond and were happy. They had everything they had wanted and had planned for.

And yet . . .

Well, even this was expected, that there must be a certain flatness. . . .

Yes, yes, of course, it was natural they sometimes felt like this. Like what?

Their life seemed to be like a snake biting its tail. Matthew's job for the sake of Susan, children, house, and garden—which caravanserai needed a well-paid job to maintain it. And Susan's practical intelligence for the sake of Matthew, the children, the house and the garden—which unit would have collapsed in a week without her.

But there was no point about which either could say: "For the sake of *this* is all the rest." Children? But the children can't be a centre of life and a reason for being. They can be a thousand things that are delightful, interesting, satisfying, but they can't be a wellspring to live from. Or they shouldn't be. Susan and Matthew knew that well enough.

Matthew's job? Ridiculous. It was an interesting job, but scarcely a reason for living. Matthew took pride in doing it well; but he could hardly be expected to be proud of the newspaper: the newspaper he read, *his* newspaper, was not the one he worked for.

Their love for each other? Well, that was nearest it. If this wasn't a centre, what was? Yes, it was around this point, their love, that the whole extraordinary structure revolved. For extraordinary it certainly was. Both Susan and Matthew had moments of thinking so, of looking in secret disbelief at this thing they had created: marriage, four children, big house, garden, charwomen, friends, cars . . . and this *thing,* this entity, all of it had come into existence, been blown into being out of nowhere, because Susan loved Matthew and Matthew loved Susan. Extraordinary. So that was the central point, the wellspring.

And if one felt that it simply was not strong enough, important enough, to support it all, well whose fault was that? Certainly neither Susan's nor Matthew's. It was in the nature of things. And they sensibly blamed neither themselves nor each other.

On the contrary, they used their intelligence to preserve what they had created from a painful and explosive world: they looked around them, and took lessons. All around them, marriages collapsing, or breaking, or rubbing along (even worse, they felt). They must not make the same mistakes, they must not.

They had avoided the pitfall so many of their friends had fallen into—of buying a house in the country *for the sake of the children;* so that the husband became a weekend husband, a weekend father, and the wife always careful not to ask what went on in the town flat which they called (in joke) a bachelor flat. No, Matthew was a full-time husband, a full-time father, and at nights, in the big married bed in the big married bedroom (which had an attractive view of the river) they lay beside each other talking and he told her about his day, and what he had done, and whom he had met; and she told him about her day (not as interesting, but that was not her fault) for both knew of the hidden resentments and deprivations of the woman who has lived her own life—and above all, has earned her own living—and is now dependent on a husband for outside interests and money.

Nor did Susan make the mistake of taking a job for the sake of her independence, which she might very well have done, since her old firm, missing her qualities of humour, balance, and sense, invited her often to go back. Children needed their mother to a certain age, that both parents knew and agreed on; and when these four healthy wisely brought-up children were of the right age, Susan would work again, because she knew, and so did he, what happened to women of fifty at the height of their energy and ability, with grown-up children who no longer needed their full devotion.

So here was this couple, testing their marriage, looking after it, treating it like a small boat full of helpless people in a very stormy sea. Well, of course, so it was. . . . The storms of the world were bad, but not too close—which is not to say they were selfishly felt: Susan and Matthew were both well-informed and responsible people. And the inner storms and quicksands were understood and charted. So everything was all right. Everything was in order. Yes, things were under control.

So what did it matter if they felt dry, flat? People like themselves, fed on a hundred books (psychological, anthropological, sociological) could scarcely be unprepared for the dry, controlled wistfulness which is the distinguishing mark of the intelligent marriage. Two people, endowed with education, with discrimination, with judgement, linked together voluntarily from their will to be happy together and to be of use to others—one sees them everywhere, one knows them, one even is that thing oneself: sadness because so much is after all so little. These two, unsurprised, turned towards each other with even more courtesy and gentle love: this was life, that two people, no matter how carefully chosen, could not be everything to each other. In fact, even to say so, to think in such a way, was banal, they were ashamed to do it.

It was banal, too, when one night Matthew came home late and confessed he had been to a party, taken a girl home and slept with her. Susan forgave him, of course. Except that forgiveness is hardly the word. Understanding, yes. But if you understand something, you don't forgive it, you are the thing itself: forgiveness is for what you *don't* understand. Nor had he *confessed*—what sort of word is that?

The whole thing was not important. After all, years ago they had joked: Of course I'm not going to be faithful to you, no one can be faithful to one other person for a whole lifetime. (And there was the word *faithful*—stupid, all these words, stupid, belonging to a savage old world.) But the incident left both of them irritable. Strange, but they were both bad-tempered, annoyed. There was something unassimilable about it.

Making love splendidly after he had come home that night, both had felt that the idea that Myra Jenkins, a pretty girl met at a party, could be even relevant was ridiculous. They had loved each other for over a decade, would love each other for years more. Who, then, was Myra Jenkins?

Except, thought Susan, unaccountably bad-tempered, she was (is?) the first. In ten years. So either the ten years' fidelity was not important, or she isn't. (No, no, there is something wrong with this way of thinking, there must be.) But if she isn't important, presumably it wasn't important either when Matthew and I first went to bed with each other that afternoon whose delight even now (like a very long shadow at sundown) lays a long, wandlike finger over us. (Why did I say sundown?) Well, if what we felt that afternoon was not important, nothing is important, because if it hadn't been for what we felt, we wouldn't be Mr. and Mrs. Rawlings with four children, etc., etc. The whole thing is *absurd*—for him to have come home and told me was absurd. For him not to have told me was absurd. For me to care, or for that matter not to care, is absurd . . . and who is Myra Jenkins? Why, no one at all.

There was only one thing to do, and of course these sensible people did it: they put the thing behind them, and consciously, knowing what they were doing, moved forward into a different phase of their marriage, giving thanks for past good fortune as they did so.

For it was inevitable that the handsome, blond, attractive, manly man, Matthew Rawlings, should be at times tempted (oh, what a word!) by the attractive girls at parties she could not attend because of the four children; and that sometimes he would succumb (a word even more repulsive, if possible) and that she, a good-looking woman in the big well-tended garden at Richmond, would sometimes be pierced as by an arrow from the sky with bitterness. Except that bitterness was not in order, it was out of court. Did the casual girls touch the marriage? They did not. Rather it was they who knew defeat because of the handsome Matthew Rawlings' marriage body and soul to Susan Rawlings.

In that case why did Susan feel (though luckily not for longer than a few seconds at a time) as if life had become a desert, and that nothing mattered, and that her children were not her own?

Meanwhile her intelligence continued to assert that all was well. What if her Matthew did have an occasional sweet afternoon, the odd affair? For she knew quite well, except in her moments of aridity, that they were very happy, that the affairs were not important.

Perhaps that was the trouble? It was in the nature of things that the adventures and delights could no longer be hers, because of the four children and the big house that needed so much attention. But perhaps she was secretly wishing, and even knowing that she did, that the wildness and the beauty could be his. But he was married to her. She was married to him. They were married inextricably. And therefore the gods could not strike him with the real magic, not really. Well, was it Susan's fault that after he came home from an adventure he looked harassed rather than fulfilled? (In fact, that was how she knew he had been *unfaithful,* because of his sullen air, and his glances at her, similar to hers at him: What is it that I share with this person that shields all delight from me?) But none of it by anybody's fault. (But what did they feel ought to be somebody's fault?) Nobody's fault, nothing to be at fault, no one to blame, no one to offer or to take it . . . and nothing wrong, either, except that Matthew never was really struck, as he wanted to be, by joy; and that Susan was more and more often threatened by emptiness. (It was usually in the garden that she was invaded by this feeling: she was coming to avoid the garden, unless the children or Matthew were with her.) There was no need to use the dramatic words, unfaithful, forgive, and the rest: intelligence forbade them. Intelligence barred, too, quarrelling, sulking, anger, silences of withdrawal, accusations and tears. Above all, intelligence forbids tears.

A high price has to be paid for the happy marriage with the four healthy children in the large white gardened house.

And they were paying it, willingly, knowing what they were doing. When they lay side by side or breast to breast in the big civilised bedroom overlooking the wild sullied river, they laughed, often, for no particular reason; but they knew it was really because of these two small people, Susan and Matthew, supporting such an edifice on their intelligent love. The laugh comforted them; it saved them both, from what, they did not know.

They were now both fortyish. The older children, boy and girl, were ten and eight, at school. The twins, six, were still at home. Susan did not have nurses or girls to help her: childhood is short; and she did not regret the hard work. Often enough she was bored, since small children can be boring; she was often very tired; but she regretted nothing. In another decade, she would turn herself back into being a woman with a life of her own.

Soon the twins would go to school, and they would be away from home from nine until four. These hours, so Susan saw it, would be the preparation for her own slow emancipation away from the role of hub-of-the-family into woman-with-her-own-life. She was already planning for the hours of freedom when all the children would be "off her hands." That was the phrase used by Matthew and by Susan and by their friends, for the moment when the youngest child went off to school. "They'll be off your hands, darling Susan, and you'll have time to yourself." So said Matthew, the intelligent husband, who had often enough commended and consoled Susan, standing by her in spirit during the years when her soul was not her own, as she said, but her children's.

What it amounted to was that Susan saw herself as she had been at twenty-eight, unmarried; and then again somewhere about fifty, blossoming from the root of what she had been twenty years before. As if the essential Susan were in abeyance, as if she were in cold storage. Matthew said something like this to Susan one night: and she agreed that it was true—she did feel something like that. What, then, was this essential Susan? She did not know. Put like that it sounded ridiculous, and she did not really feel it. Anyway, they had a long discussion about the whole thing before going off to sleep in each other's arms.

So the twins went off to their school, two bright affectionate children who had no problems about it, since their older brother and sister had trodden this path so successfully before them. And now Susan was going to be alone in the big house, every day of the school term, except for the daily woman who came in to clean.

It was now, for the first time in this marriage, that something happened which neither of them had foreseen.

This is what happened. She returned, at nine-thirty, from taking the twins to the school by car, looking forward to seven blissful hours of freedom. On the first morning she was simply restless, worrying about the twins "naturally enough" since this was their first day away at school. She was hardly able to contain herself until they came back. Which they did happily, excited by the world of school, looking forward to the next day. And the next day Susan took them, dropped them, came back, and found herself reluctant to enter her big and beautiful home because it was as if something was waiting for her there that she did not wish to confront. Sensibly, however, she parked the car in the garage, entered the house, spoke to Mrs. Parkes the daily woman about her duties, and went up to her bedroom. She was possessed by a fever which drove her out again, downstairs, into the kitchen, where Mrs. Parkes was making cake and did not need her, and into the garden. There she sat on a bench and tried to calm herself, looking at trees, at a brown glimpse of the river. But she was filled with tension, like a panic: as if an enemy was in the garden with her. She spoke to herself severely, thus: All this is quite natural. First, I spent twelve years of my adult life working, *living my own life*. Then I married, and from the moment I became pregnant for the first time I signed myself over, so to speak, to other people. To the children. Not for one moment in twelve years have I been alone, had time to myself. So now I have to learn to be myself again. That's all.

And she went indoors to help Mrs. Parkes cook and clean, and found some sewing to do for the children. She kept herself occupied every day. At the end of the first term she understood she felt two contrary emotions. First: secret astonishment and dismay that during those weeks when the house was empty of children she had in fact been more occupied (had been careful to keep herself occupied) than ever she had been when the children were around her needing her continual attention. Second: that now she knew the house would be full of them, and for five weeks, she resented the fact she would never be alone. She was already looking back at those hours of sewing, cooking (but by herself), as at a lost freedom which would not be hers for five long weeks. And the two months of term which would succeed the five weeks stretched alluringly open to her—freedom. But what freedom—when in fact she had been so careful *not* to be free of small duties during the last weeks? She looked at herself, Susan Rawlings, sitting in a big chair by the window in the bedroom, sewing shirts or dresses, which she might just as well have bought. She saw herself making cakes for hours at a time in the big family kitchen: yet usually she bought cakes. What she saw was a woman alone, that was true, but she had not felt alone. For instance, Mrs. Parkes was always somewhere in the house. And she did not like being in the garden at all, because of the closeness there of the enemy—irritation, restlessness, emptiness, whatever it was, which keeping her hands occupied made less dangerous for some reason.

Susan did not tell Matthew of these thoughts. They were not sensible. She did not recognize herself in them. What should she say to her dear friend and husband Matthew? "When I go into the garden, that is, if the children are not there, I feel as if there is an enemy there waiting to invade me." "What enemy, Susan darling?" "Well I don't know, really. . . ." "Perhaps you should see a doctor?"

No, clearly this conversation should not take place. The holidays began and Susan welcomed them. Four children, lively, energetic, intelligent, demanding: she was never, not for a moment of her day, alone. If she was in a room, they would be in the next room, or waiting for her to do something for them; or it would soon be time for lunch or tea, or to take one of them to the dentist. Something to do: five weeks of it, thank goodness.

On the fourth day of these so welcome holidays, she found she was storming with anger at the twins, two shrinking beautiful children who (and this is what checked her) stood hand in hand looking at her with sheer dismayed disbelief. This was their calm mother, shouting at them. And for what? They had come to her with some game, some bit of nonsense. They looked at each other, moved closer for support, and went off hand in hand, leaving Susan holding on to the windowsill of the living room, breathing deep, feeling sick. She went to lie down, telling the older children she had a headache. She heard the boy Harry telling the little ones. "It's all right, Mother's got a headache." She heard that *It's all right* with pain.

That night she said to her husband: "Today I shouted at the twins, quite unfairly." She sounded miserable, and he said gently: "Well, what of it?"

"It's more of an adjustment than I thought, their going to school."

"But Susie, Susie darling. . . ." For she was crouched weeping on the bed. He comforted her: "Susan, what is all this about? You shouted at them? What of it? If you shouted at them fifty times a day it wouldn't be more than the little devils deserve." But she wouldn't laugh. She wept. Soon he comforted her with his body. She became calm. Calm, she wondered what was wrong with her, and why she should mind so much that she might, just once, have behaved unjustly with the children. What did it matter? They had forgotten it all long ago: Mother had a headache and everything was all right.

It was a long time later that Susan understood that that night, when she had wept and Matthew had driven the misery out of her with his big solid body, was the last time, ever in their married life, that they had been—to use their mutual language—with each other. And even that was a lie, because she had not told him of her real fears at all.

The five weeks passed, and Susan was in control of herself, and good and kind, and she looked forward to the holidays with a mixture of fear and longing. She did not know what to expect. She took the twins off to school (the elder children took themselves to school) and she returned to the house determined to face the enemy wherever he was, in the house, or the garden or—where?

She was again restless, she was possessed by restlessness. She cooked and sewed and worked as before, day after day, while Mrs. Parkes remonstrated: "Mrs. Rawlings, what's the need for it? I can do that, it's what you pay me for."

And it was so irrational that she checked herself. She would put the car into the garage, go up to her bedroom, and sit, hands in her lap, forcing herself to be quiet. She listened to Mrs. Parkes moving around the house. She looked out into the garden and saw the branches shake the trees. She sat defeating the enemy, restlessness. Emptiness. She ought to be thinking about her life, about herself. But she did not. Or perhaps she could not. As soon as she forced her mind to think about Susan (for what else did she want to be alone for?) it skipped off to thoughts of butter or school clothes. Or it thought of Mrs. Parkes. She realised that she sat listening for the movements of the cleaning woman, following her every turn, bend, thought. She followed her in her mind from kitchen to bathroom, from table to oven, and it was as if the duster, the cleaning cloth, the saucepan, were in her own hand. She would hear herself saying: No, not like that, don't put that there. . . . Yet she did not give a damn what Mrs. Parkes did, or if she did it at all. Yet she could not prevent herself from being conscious of her, every minute. Yes, this was what was wrong with her: she needed, when she was alone, to be really alone, with no one near. She could not endure the knowledge that in ten minutes or in half an hour Mrs. Parkes would call up the stairs: "Mrs. Rawlings, there's no silver polish. Madam, we're out of flour."

So she left the house and went to sit in the garden where she was screened from the house by trees. She waited for the demon to appear and claim her, but he did not.

She was keeping him off, because she had not, after all, come to an end of arranging herself.

She was planning how to be somewhere where Mrs. Parkes would not come after her with a cup of tea, or a demand to be allowed to telephone (always irritating since Susan did not care who she telephoned or how often), or just a nice talk about something. Yes, she needed a place, or a state of affairs, where it would not be necessary to keep reminding herself: In ten minutes I must telephone Matthew about . . . and at half past three I must leave early for the children because the car needs cleaning. And at ten o'clock tomorrow I must remember. . . . She was possessed with resentment that the seven hours of freedom in every day (during the weekdays in the school term) were not free, that never, not for one second, ever, was she free from the pressure of time, from having to remember this or that. She could never forget herself; never really let herself go into forgetfulness.

Resentment. It was poisoning her. (She looked at this emotion and thought it was absurd. Yet she felt it.) She was a prisoner. (She looked at this thought too, and it was no good telling herself it was a ridiculous one.) She must tell Matthew—but what? She was filled with emotions that were utterly ridiculous, that she despised, yet that nevertheless she was feeling so strongly she could not shake them off.

The school holidays came round, and this time they were for nearly two months, and she behaved with a conscious controlled decency that nearly drove her crazy. She would lock herself in the bathroom, and sit on the edge of the bath, breathing deep, trying to let go into some kind of calm. Or she went up into the spare room, usually empty, where no one would expect her to be. She heard the children calling "Mother, Mother," and kept silent, feeling guilty. Or she went to the very end of the garden, by herself, and looked at the slow-moving brown river; she looked at the river and closed her eyes and breathed slow and deep, taking it into her being, into her veins.

Then she returned to the family, wife and mother, smiling and responsible, feeling as if the pressure of these people—four lively children and her husband—were a painful pressure on the surface of her skin, a hand pressing on her brain. She did not once break down into irritation during these holidays, but it was like living out a prison sentence, and when the children went back to school, she sat on a white stone seat near the flowing river, and she thought: It is not even a year since the twins went to school, since *they were off my hands* (What on earth did I think I meant when I used that stupid phrase?) and yet I'm a different person. I'm simply not myself. I don't understand it.

Yet she had to understand it. For she knew that this structure—big white house, on which the mortgage still cost four hundred a year, a husband, so good and kind and insightful, four children, all doing so nicely, and the garden where she sat, and Mrs. Parkes the cleaning woman—all this depended on her, and yet she could not understand why, or even what it was she contributed to it.

She said to Matthew in their bedroom: "I think there must be something wrong with me."

And he said: "Surely not, Susan? You look marvellous—you're as lovely as ever."

She looked at the handsome blond man, with his clear, intelligent, blue-eyed face, and thought: Why is it I can't tell him? Why not? And she said: "I need to be alone more than I am."

At which he swung his slow blue gaze at her, and she saw what she had been dreading: Incredulity. Disbelief. And fear. An incredulous blue stare from a stranger who was her husband, as close to her as her own breath.

He said: "But the children are at school and off your hands."

She said to herself: I've got to force myself to say: Yes, but do you realize that I never feel free? There's never a moment I can say to myself: There's nothing I have to remind myself about, nothing I have to do in half an hour, or an hour, or two hours. . . .

But she said: "I don't feel well."

He said: "Perhaps you need a holiday."

She said appalled: "But not without you, surely?" For she could not imagine herself going off without him. Yet that was what he meant. Seeing her face, he laughed, and opened his arms, and she went into them, thinking: Yes, yes, but why can't I say it? And what is it I have to say?

She tried to tell him, about never being free. And he listened and said: "But Susan, what sort of freedom can you possibly want—short of being dead! Am I ever free? I go to the office, and I have to be there at ten—all right, half past ten, sometimes. And I have to do this or that, don't I? Then I've got to come home at a certain time—I don't mind it, you know I don't—but if I'm not going to be back home at six I telephone you. When can I ever say to myself: I have nothing to be responsible for in the next six hours?"

Susan, hearing this, was remorseful. Because it was true. The good marriage, the house, the children, depended just as much on his voluntary bondage as it did on hers. But why did he not feel bound? Why didn't he chafe and become restless? No, there was something really wrong with her and this proved it.

And that word *bondage*—why had she used it? She had never felt marriage, or the children, as bondage. Neither had he, or surely they wouldn't be together lying in each other's arms content after twelve years of marriage.

No, her state (whatever it was) was irrelevant, nothing to do with her real good life with her family. She had to accept the fact that after all, she was an irrational person and to live with it. Some people had to live with crippled arms, or stammers, or being deaf. She would have to live knowing she was subject to a state of mind she could not own.

Nevertheless, as a result of this conversation with her husband, there was a new regime next holidays.

The spare room at the top of the house now had a cardboard sign saying: PRIVATE! DO NOT DISTURB! on it. (This sign had been drawn in coloured chalks by the children, after a discussion between the parents in which it was decided this was psychologically the right thing.) The family and Mrs. Parkes knew this was "Mother's Room" and that she was entitled to her privacy. Many serious conversations took place between Matthew and the children about not taking Mother for granted. Susan overheard the first, between father and Harry, the older boy, and was surprised at her irritation over it. Surely she could have a room somewhere in that big house and retire into it without such a fuss being made? Without it being so solemnly discussed? Why couldn't she simply have announced: "I'm going to fit out the little top room for myself, and when I'm in it I'm not to be disturbed for anything short of fire"? Just that, and finished; instead of long earnest discussions. When she heard Harry and Matthew explaining it to the twins with Mrs. Parkes coming in—"Yes, well, a family sometimes gets on top of a woman"—she had to go right away to the bottom of the garden until the devils of exasperation had finished their dance in her blood.

But now there was a room, and she could go there when she liked, she used it seldom: she felt even more caged there than in her bedroom. One day she had gone up there after a lunch for ten children she had cooked and served because Mrs. Parkes was not there, and had sat alone for a while looking into the garden. She saw the children stream out from the kitchen and stand looking up at the window where she sat behind the curtains. They were all—her children and their friends—discussing Mother's Room. A few minutes later, the chase of children in some game came pounding up the stairs, but ended as abruptly as if they had fallen over a ravine, so sudden was the silence. They had remembered she was there, and had gone silent in a great gale of "Hush! Shhhhhh! Quiet, you'll disturb her. . . ." And they went tiptoeing downstairs like criminal conspirators. When she came down to make tea for them, they all apologised. The twins put their arms around her, from front and back, making a human cage of loving limbs, and promised it would never oc-cur again. "We forgot, Mummy, we forgot all about it!"

What it amounted to was that Mother's Room, and her need for privacy, had become a valuable lesson in respect for other people's rights. Quite soon Susan was going up to the room only because it was a lesson it was a pity to drop. Then she took sewing up there, and the children and Mrs. Parkes came in and out: it had become another family room.

She sighed, and smiled, and resigned herself—she made jokes at her own expense with Matthew over the room. That is, she did from the self she liked, she respected. But at the same time, something inside her howled with impatience, with rage. . . . And she was frightened. One day she found herself kneeling by her bed and praying: "Dear God, keep it away from me, keep him away from me." She meant the devil, for she now thought of it, not caring if she were irrational, as some sort of demon. She imagined him, or it, as a youngish man, or perhaps a middle-aged man pretending to be young. Or a man young-looking from immaturity? At any rate, she saw the young-looking face which, when she drew close, had dry lines about mouth and eyes. He was thinnish, meagre in build. And he had a reddish complexion, and ginger hair. That was he—a gingery, energetic man, and he wore a reddish hairy jacket, unpleasant to the touch.

Well, one day she saw him. She was standing at the bottom of the garden, watching the river ebb past, when she raised her eyes and saw this person, or being, sitting on the white stone bench. He was looking at her, and grinning. In his hand was a long crooked stick, which he had picked off the ground, or broken off the tree above him. He was absent-mindedly, out of an absent-minded or freakish impulse of spite, using the stick to stir around in the coils of a blindworm or a grass snake (or some kind of snakelike creature: it was whitish and unhealthy to look at, unpleasant). The snake was twisting about, flinging its coils from side to side in a kind of dance of protest against the teasing prodding stick.

Susan looked at him thinking: Who is the stranger? What is he doing in our garden? Then she recognised the man around whom her terrors had crystallised. As she did so, he vanished. She made herself walk over to the bench. A shadow from a branch lay across thin emerald grass, moving jerkily over its roughness, and she could see why she had taken it for a snake, lashing and twisting. She went back to the house thinking: Right, then, so I've seen him with my own eyes, so I'm not crazy after all—there *is* a danger because I've seen him. He is lurking in the garden and sometimes even in the house, and he wants *to get into me and to take me over.*

She dreamed of having a room or a place, anywhere, where she could go and sit, by herself, no one knowing where she was.

Once, near Victoria, she found herself outside a news agent that had Rooms to Let advertised. She decided to rent a room, telling no one. Sometimes she could take the train in to Richmond and sit alone in it for an hour or two. Yet how could she? A room would cost three or four pounds a week, and she earned no money, and how could she explain to Matthew that she needed such a sum? What for? It did not occur to her that she was taking it for granted she wasn't going to tell him about the room.

Well, it was out of the question, having a room; yet she knew she must.

One day, when a school term was well established, and none of the children had measles or other ailments, and everything seemed in order, she did the shopping early, explained to Mrs. Parkes she was meeting an old school friend, took the train to Victoria, searched until she found a small quiet hotel, and asked for a room for the day. They did not let rooms by the day, the manageress said, looking doubtful, since Susan so obviously was not the kind of woman who needed a room for unrespectable reasons. Susan made a long explanation about not being well, being unable to shop without frequent rests for lying down. At last she was allowed to rent the room provided she paid a full night's price for it. She was taken up by the manageress and a maid, both concerned over the state of her health . . . which must be pretty bad if, living at Richmond (she had signed her name and address in the register), she needed a shelter at Victoria.

The room was ordinary and anonymous, and was just what Susan needed. She put a shilling in the gas fire, and sat, eyes shut, in a dingy armchair with her back to a dingy window. She was alone. She was alone. She was alone. She could feel pressures lifting off her. First the sounds of traffic came very loud; then they seemed to vanish; she might even have slept a little. A knock on the door: it was Miss Townsend the manageress, bringing her a cup of tea with her own hands, so concerned was she over Susan's long silence and possible illness.

Miss Townsend was a lonely woman of fifty, running this hotel with all the rectitude expected of her, and she sensed in Susan the possibility of understanding companionship. She stayed to talk. Susan found herself in the middle of a fantastic story about her illness, which got more and more improbable as she tried to make it tally with the large house at Richmond, well-off husband, and four children. Suppose she said instead: Miss Townsend, I'm here in your hotel because I need to be alone for a few hours, above all *alone and with no one knowing where I am.* She said it mentally, and saw, mentally, the look that would inevitably come on Miss Townsend's elderly maiden's face. "Miss Townsend, my four children and my husband are driving me insane, do you understand that? Yes, I can see from the gleam of hysteria in your eyes that comes from loneliness controlled but only just contained that I've got everything in the world you've ever longed for. Well, Miss Townsend, I don't want any of it. You can have it, Miss Townsend. I wish I was absolutely alone in the world, like you. Miss Townsend, I'm besieged by seven devils, Miss Townsend, Miss Townsend, let me stay here in your hotel where the devils can't get me. . . ." Instead of saying all this, she described her anaemia, agreed to try Miss Townsend's remedy for it, which was raw liver, minced, between whole-meal bread, and said yes, perhaps it would be better if she stayed at home and let a friend do shopping for her. She paid her bill and left the hotel, defeated.

At home Mrs. Parkes said she didn't really like it, no, not really, when Mrs. Rawlings was away from nine in the morning until five. The teacher had telephoned from school to say Joan's teeth were paining her, and she hadn't known what to say; and what was she to make for the children's tea, Mrs. Rawlings hadn't said.

All this was nonsense, of course. Mrs. Parkes's complaint was that Susan had withdrawn herself spiritually, leaving the burden of the big house on her.

Susan looked back at her day of "freedom" which had resulted in her becoming a friend to the lonely Miss Townsend, and in Mrs. Parkes's remonstrances. Yet she remembered the short blissful hour of being alone, really alone. She was determined to arrange her life, no matter what it cost, so that she could have that solitude more often. An absolute solitude, where no one knew her or cared about her.

But how? She thought of saying to her old employer: I want to back you up in a story with Matthew that I am doing part-time work for you. The truth is that . . . but she would have to tell him a lie too, and which lie? She could not say: I want to sit by myself three or four times a week in a rented room. And besides, he knew Matthew, and she could not really ask him to tell lies on her behalf, apart from his being bound to think it meant a lover.

Suppose she really took a part-time job, which she could get through fast and efficiently, leaving time for herself. What job? Addressing envelopes? Canvassing?

And there was Mrs. Parkes, working widow, who knew exactly what she was prepared to give to the house, who knew by instinct when her mistress withdrew in spirit from her responsibilities. Mrs. Parkes was one of the servers of this world, but she needed someone to serve. She had to have Mrs. Rawlings, her madam, at the top of the house or in the garden, so that she could come and get support from her: "Yes, the bread's not what it was when I was a girl. . . . Yes, Harry's got a wonderful appetite, I wonder where he puts it all. . . . Yes, it's lucky the twins are so much of a size, they can wear each other's shoes, that's a saving in these hard times. . . . Yes, the cherry jam from Switzerland is not a patch on the jam from Poland, and three times the price. . . ." And so on. That sort of talk Mrs. Parkes must have, every day, or she would leave, not knowing herself why she left.

Susan Rawlings, thinking these thoughts, found that she was prowling through the great thicketed garden like a wild cat: she was walking up the stairs, down the stairs, through the rooms, into the garden, along the brown running river, back, up through the house, down again. . . . It was a wonder Mrs. Parkes did not think it strange. But on the contrary, Mrs. Rawlings could do what she liked, she could stand on her head if she wanted, provided she was *there*. Susan Rawlings prowled and muttered through her house, hating Mrs. Parkes, hating poor Miss Townsend, dreaming of her hour of solitude in the dingy respectability of Miss Townsend's hotel bedroom, and she knew quite well she was mad. Yes, she was mad.

She said to Matthew that she must have a holiday. Matthew agreed with her. This was not as things had been once—how they had talked in each other's arms in the marriage bed. He had, she knew, diagnosed her finally as *unreasonable*. She had become someone outside himself that he had to manage. They were living side by side in this house like two tolerably friendly strangers.

Having told Mrs. Parkes, or rather, asked for her permission, she went off on a walking holiday in Wales. She chose the remotest place she knew of. Every morning the children telephoned her before they went off to school, to encourage and support her, just as they had over Mother's Room. Every evening she telephoned them, spoke to each child in turn, and then to Matthew. Mrs. Parkes, given permission to telephone for instructions or advice, did so every day at lunchtime. When, as happened three times, Mrs. Rawlings was out on the mountainside, Mrs. Parkes asked that she should ring back at such and such a time, for she would not be happy in what she was doing without Mrs. Rawlings' blessing.

Susan prowled over wild country with the telephone wire holding her to her duty like a leash. The next time she must telephone, or wait to be telephoned, nailed her to her cross. The mountains themselves seemed trammelled by her unfreedom. Everywhere on the mountains, where she met no one at all, from breakfast time to dusk, excepting sheep, or a shepherd, she came face to face with her own craziness which might attack her in the broadest valleys, so that they seemed too small; or on a mountaintop from which she could see a hundred other mountains and valleys, so that they seemed too low, too small, with the sky pressing down too close. She would stand gazing at a hillside brilliant with ferns and bracken, jewelled with running water, and see nothing but her devil, who lifted inhuman eyes at her from where he leaned negligently on a rock, switching at his ugly yellow boots with a leafy twig.

She returned to her home and family, with the Welsh emptiness at the back of her mind like a promise of freedom.

She told her husband she wanted to have an *au pair* girl.

They were in their bedroom, it was late at night, the children slept. He sat, shirted and slippered, in a chair by the window, looking out. She sat brushing her hair and watching him in the mirror. A time-hallowed scene in the connubial bedroom. He said nothing, while she heard the arguments coming into his mind, only to be rejected because every one was *reasonable*.

"It seems strange to get one now, after all, the children are in school most of the day. Surely the time for you to have help was when you were stuck with them day and night. Why don't you ask Mrs. Parkes to cook for you? She's even offered to—I can understand if you are tired of cooking for six people. But you know that an *au pair* girl means all kinds of problems, it's not like having an ordinary char in during the day. . . ."

Finally he said carefully: "Are you thinking of going back to work?"

"No," she said, "no, not really." She made herself sound vague, rather stupid. She went on brushing her black hair and peering at herself so as to be oblivious of the short uneasy glances her Matthew kept giving her. "Do you think we can't afford it?" she went on vaguely, not at all the old efficient Susan who knew exactly what they could afford.

"It's not that," he said, looking out of the window at dark trees, so as not to look at her. Meanwhile she examined a round, candid, pleasant face with clear dark brows and clear grey eyes. A sensible face. She brushed thick healthy black hair and thought: Yet that's the reflection of a madwoman. How very strange! Much more to the point if what looked back at me was the gingery green-eyed demon with his dry meagre smile. . . . Why wasn't Matthew agreeing? After all, what else could he do? She was breaking her part of the bargain and there was no way of forcing her to keep it: that her spirit, her soul, should live in this house, so that the people in it could grow like plants in water, and Mrs. Parkes remain content in their service. In return for this, he would be a good loving husband, and responsible towards the children. Well, nothing like this had been true of either of them for a long time. He did his duty, perfunctorily; she did not even pretend to do hers. And he had become like other husbands, with his real life in his work and the people he met there, and very likely a serious affair. All this was her fault.

At last he drew heavy curtains, blotting out the trees, and turned to force her attention: "Susan, are you really sure we need a girl?" But she would not meet his appeal at all: She was running the brush over her hair again and again, lifting fine black clouds in a small hiss of electricity. She was peering in and smiling as if she were amused at the clinging hissing hair that followed the brush.

"Yes, I think it would be a good idea on the whole," she said, with the cunning of a madwoman evading the real point.

In the mirror she could see her Matthew lying on his back, his hands behind his head, staring upwards, his face sad and hard. She felt her heart (the old heart of Susan Rawlings) soften and call out to him. But she set it to be indifferent.

He said: "Susan, the children?" It was an appeal that *almost* reached her. He opened his arms, lifting them from where they had lain by his sides, palms up, empty. She had only to run across and fling herself into them, onto his hard, warm chest, and melt into herself, into Susan. But she could not. She would not see his lifted arms. She said vaguely: "Well, surely it'll be even better for them? We'll get a French or a German girl and they'll learn the language."

In the dark she lay beside him, feeling frozen, a stranger. She felt as if Susan had been spirited away. She disliked very much this woman who lay here, cold and indifferent beside a suffering man, but she could not change her.

Next morning she set about getting a girl, and very soon came Sophie Traub from Hamburg, a girl of twenty, laughing, healthy, blue-eyed, intending to learn English. Indeed, she already spoke a good deal. In return for a room— "Mother's Room"—and her food, she undertook to do some light cooking, and to be with the children when Mrs. Rawlings asked. She was an intelligent girl and understood perfectly what was needed. Susan said: "I go off sometimes, for the morning or for the day—well, sometimes the children run home from school, or they ring up, or a teacher rings up. I should be here, really. And there's the daily woman. . . ." And Sophie laughed her deep fruity Fräulein's laugh, showed her fine white teeth and her dimples, and said: "You want some person to play mistress of the house sometimes, not so?"

"Yes, that is just so," said Susan, a bit dry, despite herself, thinking in secret fear how easy it was, how much nearer to the end she was than she thought. Healthy Fräulein Traub's instant understanding of their position proved this to be true.

The *au pair* girl, because of her own common sense, or (as Susan said to herself with her new inward shudder) because she had been *chosen* so well by Susan, was a success with everyone, the children liking her, Mrs. Parkes forgetting almost at once that she was German, and Matthew finding her "nice to have around the house." For he was now taking things as they came, from the surface of life, withdrawn both as a husband and a father from the household.

One day Susan saw how Sophie and Mrs. Parkes were talking and laughing in the kitchen, and she announced that she would be away until teatime. She knew exactly where to go and what she must look for. She took the District Line to South Kensington, changed to the Circle, got off at Paddington, and walked around looking at the smaller hotels until she was satisfied with one which had FRED'S HOTEL painted on windowpanes that needed cleaning. The façade was a faded shiny yellow, like unhealthy skin. A door at the end of a passage said she must knock; she did, and Fred appeared. He was not at all attractive, not in any way, being fattish, and run-down, and wearing a tasteless striped suit. He had small sharp eyes in a white creased face, and was quite prepared to let Mrs. Jones (she chose the farcical name deliberately, staring him out) have a room three days a week from ten until six. Provided of course that she paid in advance each time she came? Susan produced fifteen shillings (no price had been set by him) and held it out, still fixing him with a bold unblinking challenge she had not known until then she could use at will. Looking at her still, he took up a ten-shilling note from her palm between thumb and forefinger, fingered it; then shuffled up two half crowns, held out his own palm with these bits of money displayed thereon, and let his gaze lower broodingly at them. They were standing in the passage, a red-shaded light above, bare boards beneath, and a strong smell of floor polish rising about them. He shot his gaze up at her over the still-extended palm, and smiled as if to say: What do you take me for? "I shan't," said Susan, "be using this room for the purposes of making money." He still waited. She added another five shillings, at which he nodded and said: "You pay, and I ask no questions." "Good," said Susan. He now went past her to the stairs, and there waited a moment: the light from the street door being in her eyes, she lost sight of him momentarily. Then she saw a sober-suited, white-faced, white-balding little man trotting up the stairs like a waiter, and she went after him. They proceeded in utter silence up the stairs of this house where no questions were asked—Fred's Hotel, which could afford the freedom for its visitors that poor Miss Townsend's hotel could not. The room was hideous. It had a single window, with thin green brocade curtains, a three-quarter bed that had a cheap green satin bedspread on it, a fireplace with a gas fire and a shilling meter by it, a chest of drawers, and a green wicker armchair.

"Thank you," said Susan, knowing that Fred (if this was Fred, and not George, or Herbert or Charlie) was looking at her, not so much with curiosity, an emotion he would not own to, for professional reasons, but with a philosophical sense of what was appropriate. Having taken her money and shown her up and agreed to everything, he was clearly disapproving of her for coming here. She did not belong here at all, so his look said. (But she knew, already, how very much she did belong: the room had been waiting for her to join it.) "Would you have me called at five o'clock, please?" and he nodded and went downstairs.

It was twelve in the morning. She was free. She sat in the armchair, she simply sat, she closed her eyes and sat and let herself be alone. She was alone and no one knew where she was. When a knock came on the door she was annoyed, and prepared to show it: but it was Fred himself, it was five o'clock and he was calling her as ordered. He flicked his sharp little eyes over the room—bed, first. It was undisturbed. She might never have been in the room at all. She thanked him, said she would be returning the day after tomorrow, and left. She was back home in time to cook supper, to put the children to bed, to cook a second supper for her husband and herself later. And to welcome Sophie back from the pictures where she had gone with a friend. All these things she did cheerfully, willingly. But she was thinking all the time of the hotel room, she was longing for it with her whole being.

Three times a week. She arrived promptly at ten, looked Fred in the eyes, gave him twenty shillings, followed him up the stairs, went into the room, and shut the door on him with gentle firmness. For Fred, disapproving of her being here at all, was quite ready to let friendship, or at least acquaintanceship, follow his disapproval, if only she would let him. But he was content to go off on her dismissing nod, with the twenty shillings in his hand.

She sat in the armchair and shut her eyes.

What did she *do* in the room? Why, nothing at all. From the chair, when it had rested her, she went to the window, stretching her arms, smiling, treasuring her anonymity, to look out. She was no longer Susan Rawlings, mother of four, wife of Matthew, employer of Mrs. Parkes and of Sophie Traub, with these and those relations with friends, schoolteachers, tradesmen. She no longer was mistress of the big white house and garden, owning clothes suitable for this and that activity or occasion. She was Mrs. Jones, and she was alone, and she had no past and no future. Here I am, she thought, after all these years of being married and having children and playing those roles of responsibility—and I'm just the same. Yet there have been times I thought that nothing existed of me except the roles that went with being Mrs. Matthew Rawlings. Yes, here I am, and if I never saw any of my family again, here I would still be . . . how very strange that is! And she leaned on the sill, and looked into the street, loving the men and women who passed, because she did not know them. She looked at the downtrodden buildings over the street, and at the sky, wet and dingy, or sometimes blue, and she felt she had never seen buildings or sky before. And then she went back to the chair, empty, her mind a blank. Sometimes she talked aloud, saying nothing—an exclamation, meaningless, followed by a comment about the floral pattern on the thin rug, or a stain on the green satin coverlet. For the most part, she wool-gathered—what word is there for it?—brooded, wandered, simply went dark, feeling emptiness run deliciously through her veins like the movement of her blood.

This room had become more her own than the house she lived in. One morning she found Fred taking her a flight higher than usual. She stopped, refusing to go up, and demanded her usual room, Number 19. "Well, you'll have to wait half an hour then," he said. Willingly she descended to the dark disinfectant-smelling hall, and sat waiting until the two, man and woman, came down the stairs, giving her swift indifferent glances before they hurried out into the street, separating at the door. She went up to the room, *her* room, which they had just vacated. It was no less hers, though the windows were set wide open, and a maid was straightening the bed as she came in.

After these days of solitude, it was both easy to play her part as mother and wife, and difficult—because it was so easy: she felt an impostor. She felt as if her shell moved here, with her family, answering to Mummy, Mother, Susan, Mrs. Rawlings. She was surprised no one saw through her, that she wasn't turned out of doors, as a fake. On the contrary, it seemed the children loved her more; Matthew and she "got on" pleasantly, and Mrs. Parkes was happy in her work under (for the most part, it must be confessed) Sophie Traub. At night she lay beside her husband, and they made love again, apparently just as they used to, when they were really married. But she, Susan, or the being who answered so readily and improbably to the name of Susan, was not there: she was in Fred's Hotel, in Paddington, waiting for the easing hours of solitude to begin.

Soon she made a new arrangement with Fred and with Sophie. It was for five days a week. As for the money, five pounds, she simply asked Matthew for it. She saw that she was not even frightened he might ask what for: he would give it to her, she knew that, and yet it was terrifying it could be so, for this close couple, these partners, had once known the destination of every shilling they must spend. He agreed to give her five pounds a week. She asked for just so much, not a penny more. He sounded indifferent about it. It was as if he were paying her, she thought: *paying her off*—yes, that was it. Terror came back for a moment, when she understood this, but she stilled it: things had gone too far for that. Now, every week, on Sunday nights, he gave her five pounds, turning away from her before their eyes could meet on the transaction. As for Sophie Traub, she was to be somewhere in or near the house until six at night, after which she was free. She was not to cook, or to clean, she was simply to be there. So she gardened or sewed, and asked friends in, being a person who was bound to have a lot of friends. If the children were sick, she nursed them. If teachers telephoned, she answered them sensibly. For the five daytimes in the school week, she was altogether the mistress of the house.

One night in the bedroom, Matthew asked: "Susan, I don't want to interfere—don't think that, please—but are you sure you are well?"

She was brushing her hair at the mirror. She made two more strokes on either side of her head, before she replied: "Yes, dear, I am sure I am well."

He was again lying on his back, his big blond head on his hands, his elbows angled up and part-concealing his face. He said: "Then Susan, I have to ask you this question, though you must understand, I'm not putting any sort of pressure on you." (Susan heard the word pressure with dismay, because this was inevitable, of course she could not go on like this.) "Are things going to go on like this?"

"Well," she said, going vague and bright and idiotic again, so as to escape: "Well, I don't see why not."

He was jerking his elbows up and down, in annoyance or in pain, and, looking at him, she saw he had got thin, even gaunt; and restless angry movements were not what she remembered of him. He said: "Do you want a divorce, is that it?"

At this, Susan only with the greatest difficulty stopped herself from laughing: she could hear the bright bubbling laughter she *would* have emitted, had she let herself. He could only mean one thing: she had a lover, and that was why she spent her days in London, as lost to him as if she had vanished to another continent.

Then the small panic set in again: she understood that he hoped she did have a lover, he was begging her to say so, because otherwise it would be too terrifying.

She thought this out, as she brushed her hair, watching the fine black stuff fly up to make its little clouds of electricity, hiss, hiss, hiss. Behind her head, across the room, was a blue wall. She realised she was absorbed in watching the black hair making shapes against the blue. She should be answering him. "Do *you* want a divorce, Matthew?"

He said: "That surely isn't the point, is it?"

"You brought it up, I didn't," she said, brightly, suppressing meaningless tinkling laughter.

Next day she asked Fred: "Have enquiries been made for me?"

He hesitated, and she said: "I've been coming here a year now. I've made no trouble, and you've been paid every day. I have a right to be told."

"As a matter of fact, Mrs. Jones, a man did come asking."

"A man from a detective agency?"

"Well, he could have been, couldn't he?"

"I was asking you . . . well, what did you tell him?"

"I told him a Mrs. Jones came every weekday from ten until five or six and stayed in Number Nineteen by herself."

"Describing me?"

"Well Mrs. Jones, I had no alternative. Put yourself in my place."

"By rights I should deduct what that man gave you for the information."

He raised shocked eyes: she was not the sort of person to make jokes like this! Then he chose to laugh: a pinkish wet slit appeared across his white crinkled face: his eyes positively begged her to laugh, otherwise he might lose some money. She remained grave, looking at him.

He stopped laughing and said: "You want to go up now?"—returning to the familiarity, the comradeship, of the country where no questions are asked, on which (and he knew it) she depended completely.

She went up to sit in her wicker chair. But it was not the same. Her husband had searched her out. (The world had searched her out.) The pressures were on her. She was here with his connivance. He might walk in at any moment, here, into Room 19. She imagined the report from the detective agency: "A woman calling herself Mrs. Jones, fitting the description of your wife (etc., etc., etc.), stays alone all day in Room No. 19. She insists on this room, waits for it if it is engaged. As far as the proprietor knows, she receives no visitors there, male or female." A report something on these lines, Matthew must have received.

Well of course he was right: things couldn't go on like this. He had put an end to it all simply by sending the detective after her.

She tried to shrink herself back into the shelter of the room, a snail pecked out of its shell and trying to squirm back. But the peace of the room had gone. She was trying consciously to revive it, trying to let go into the dark creative trance (or whatever it was) that she had found there. It was no use, yet she craved for it, she was as ill as a suddenly deprived addict.

Several times she returned to the room, to look for herself there, but instead she found the unnamed spirit of restlessness, a prickling fevered hunger for movement, an irritable self-consciousness that made her brain feel as if it had coloured lights going on and off inside it. Instead of the soft dark that had been the room's air, were now waiting for her demons that made her dash blindly about, muttering words of hate; she was impelling herself from point to point like a moth dashing itself against a windowpane, sliding to the bottom, fluttering off on broken wings, then crashing into the invisible barrier again. And again and again. Soon she was exhausted, and she told Fred that for a while she would not be needing the room, she was going on holiday. Home she went, to the big white house by the river. The middle of a weekday, and she felt guilty at returning to her own home when not expected. She stood unseen, looking in at the kitchen window. Mrs. Parkes, wearing a discarded floral overall of Susan's, was stooping to slide something into the oven. Sophie, arms folded, was leaning her back against a cupboard and laughing at some joke made by a girl not seen before by Susan—a dark foreign girl, Sophie's visitor. In an armchair Molly, one of the twins, lay curled, sucking her thumb and watching the grownups. She must have some sickness, to be kept from school. The child's listless face, the dark circles under her eyes, hurt Susan: Molly was looking at the three grownups working and talking in exactly the same way Susan looked at the four through the kitchen window: she was remote, shut off from them.

But then, just as Susan imagined herself going in, picking up the little girl, and sitting in an armchair with her, stroking her probably heated forehead, Sophie did just that: she had been standing on one leg, the other knee flexed, its foot set against the wall. Now she let her foot in its ribbon-tied red shoe slide down the wall, stood solid on two feet, clapping her hands before and behind her, and sang a couple of lines in German, so that the child lifted her heavy eyes at her and began to smile. Then she walked, or rather skipped, over to the child, swung her up, and let her fall into her lap at the same moment she sat herself. She said "Hopla! Hopla! Molly . . ." and began stroking the dark untidy young head that Molly laid on her shoulder for comfort.

Well. . . . Susan blinked the tears of farewell out of her eyes, and went quietly up the house to her bedroom. There she sat looking at the river through the trees. She felt at peace, but in a way that was new to her. She had no desire to move, to talk, to do anything at all. The devils that had haunted the house, the garden, were not there; but she knew it was because her soul was in Room 19 in Fred's Hotel; she was not really here at all. It was a sensation that should have been frightening: to sit at her own bedroom window, listening to Sophie's rich young voice sing German nursery songs to her child, listening to Mrs. Parkes clatter and move below, and to know that all this had nothing to do with her: she was already out of it.

Later, she made herself go down and say she was home: it was unfair to be here unannounced. She took lunch with Mrs. Parkes, Sophie, Sophie's Italian friend Maria, and her daughter Molly, and felt like a visitor.

A few days later, at bedtime, Matthew said: "Here's your five pounds," and pushed them over at her. Yet he must have known she had not been leaving the house at all.

She shook her head, gave it back to him, and said, in explanation, not in accusation: "As soon as you knew where I was, there was no point."

He nodded, not looking at her. He was turned away from her: thinking, she knew, how best to handle this wife who terrified him.

He said: "I wasn't trying to . . . it's just that I was worried."

"Yes, I know."

"I must confess that I was beginning to wonder . . ."

"You thought I had a lover?"

"Yes, I am afraid I did."

She knew that he wished she had. She sat wondering how to say: "For a year now I've been spending all my days in a very sordid hotel room. It's the place where I'm happy. In fact, without it I don't exist." She heard herself saying this, and understood how terrified he was that she might. So instead she said: "Well, perhaps you're not far wrong."

Probably Matthew would think the hotel proprietor lied: he would want to think so.

"Well," he said, and she could hear his voice spring up, so to speak, with relief: "in that case I must confess I've got a bit of an affair on myself."

She said, detached and interested: "Really? Who is she?" and saw Matthew's startled look because of this reaction.

"It's Phil. Phil Hunt."

She had known Phil Hunt well in the old unmarried days. She was thinking: No, she won't do, she's too neurotic and difficult. She's never been happy yet. Sophie's much better: Well Matthew will see that himself, as sensible as he is.

This line of thought went on in silence, while she said aloud: "It's no point telling you about mine, because you don't know him."

Quick, quick, invent, she thought. Remember how you invented all that nonsense for Miss Townsend.

She began slowly, careful not to contradict herself: "His name is Michael"—(Michael What?)—"Michael Plant." (What a silly name!) "He's rather like you—in looks, I mean." And indeed, she could imagine herself being touched by no one but Matthew himself. "He's a publisher." (Really? Why?) "He's got a wife already and two children."

She brought out this fantasy, proud of herself.

Matthew said: "Are you two thinking of marrying?"

She said, before she could stop herself: "Good God, no!"

She realised, if Matthew wanted to marry Phil Hunt, that this was too emphatic, but apparently it was all right, for his voice sounded relieved as he said: "It is a bit impossible to imagine oneself married to anyone else, isn't it?" With which he pulled her to him, so that her head lay on his shoulder. She turned her face into the dark of his flesh, and listened to the blood pounding through her ears saying: I am alone, I am alone, I am alone.

In the morning Susan lay in bed while he dressed.

He had been thinking things out in the night, because now he said: "Susan, why don't we make a foursome?"

Of course, she said to herself, of course he would be bound to say that. If one is sensible, if one is reasonable, if one never allows oneself a base thought or an envious emotion, naturally one says: Let's make a foursome!

"Why not?" she said.

"We could all meet for lunch. I mean, it's ridiculous, you sneaking off to filthy hotels, and me staying late at the office, and all the lies everyone has to tell."

What on earth did I say his name was?—she panicked, then said: "I think it's a good idea, but Michael is away at the moment. When he comes back though—and I'm sure you two would like each other."

"He's away, is he? So that's why you've been . . ." Her husband put his hand to the knot of his tie in a gesture of male coquetry she would not before have associated with him; and he bent to kiss her cheek with the expression that goes with the words: Oh you naughty little puss! And she felt its answering look, naughty and coy, come onto her face.

Inside she was dissolving in horror at them both, at how far they had both sunk from honesty of emotion.

So now she was saddled with a lover, and he had a mistress! How ordinary, how reassuring, how jolly! And now they would make a foursome of it, and go about to theatres and restaurants. After all, the Rawlings could well afford that sort of thing, and presumably the publisher Michael Plant could afford to do himself and his mistress quite well. No, there was nothing to stop the four of them developing the most intricate relationship of civilised tolerance, all enveloped in a charming afterglow of autumnal passion. Perhaps they would all go off on holidays together? She had known people who did. Or perhaps Matthew would draw the line there? Why should he, though, if he was capable of talking about "foursomes" at all?

She lay in the empty bedroom, listening to the car drive off with Matthew in it, off to work. Then she heard the children clattering off to school to the accompaniment of Sophie's cheerfully ringing voice. She slid down into the hollow of the bed, for shelter against her own irrelevance. And she stretched out her hand to the hollow where her husband's body had lain, but found no comfort there: he was not her husband. She curled herself up in a small tight ball under the clothes: she could stay here all day, all week, indeed, all her life.

But in a few days she must produce Michael Plant, and—but how? She must presumably find some agreeable man prepared to impersonate a publisher called Michael Plant. And in return for which she would—what? Well, for one thing they would make love. The idea made her want to cry with sheer exhaustion. Oh no, she had finished with all that—the proof of it was that the words "make love," or even imagining it, trying hard to revive no more than the pleasures of sensuality, let alone affection, or love, made her want to run away and hide from the sheer effort of the thing. . . . Good Lord, why make love at all? Why make love with anyone? Or if you are going to make love, what does it matter who with? Why shouldn't she simply walk into the street, pick up a man and have a roaring sexual affair with him? Why not? Or even with Fred? What difference did it make?

But she had let herself in for it—an interminable stretch of time with a lover, called Michael, as part of a gallant civilised foursome. Well, she could not, and she would not.

She got up, dressed, went down to find Mrs. Parkes, and asked her for the loan of a pound, since Matthew, she said, had forgotten to leave her money. She exchanged with Mrs. Parkes variations on the theme that husbands are all the same, they don't think, and without saying a word to Sophie, whose voice could be heard upstairs from the telephone, walked to the underground, travelled to South Kensington, changed to the Inner Circle, got out at Paddington, and walked to Fred's Hotel. There she told Fred that she wasn't going on holiday after all, she needed the room. She would have to wait an hour, Fred said. She went to a busy tearoom-cum-restaurant around the corner, and sat watching the people flow in and out the door that kept swinging open and shut, watched them mingle and merge and separate, felt her being flow into them, into their movement. When the hour was up she left a half crown for her pot of tea, and left the place without looking back at it, just as she had left her house, the big, beautiful white house, without another look, but silently dedicating it to Sophie. She returned to Fred, received the key of No. 19, now free, and ascended the grimy stairs slowly, letting floor after floor fall away below her, keeping her eyes lifted, so that floor after floor descended jerkily to her level of vision, and fell away out of sight.

No. 19 was the same. She saw everything with an acute, narrow, checking glance: the cheap shine of the satin spread, which had been replaced carelessly after the two bodies had finished their convulsions under it; a trace of powder on the glass that topped the chest of drawers; an intense green shade in a fold of the curtain. She stood at the window, looking down, watching people pass and pass and pass until her mind went dark from the constant movement. Then she sat in the wicker chair, letting herself go slack. But she had to be careful, because she did not want, today, to be surprised by Fred's knock at five o'clock.

The demons were not here. They had gone forever, because she was buying her freedom from them. She was slipping already into the dark fructifying dream that seemed to caress her inwardly, like the movement of her blood . . . but she had to think about Matthew first. Should she write a letter for the coroner? But what should she say? She would like to leave him with the look on his face she had seen this morning—banal, admittedly, but at least confidently healthy. Well, that was impossible, one did not look like that with a wife dead from suicide. But how to leave him believing she was dying because of a man—because of the fascinating publisher Michael Plant? Oh, how ridiculous! How absurd! How humiliating! But she decided not to trouble about it, simply not to think about the living. If he wanted to believe she had a lover, he would believe it. And he *did* want to believe it. Even when he had found out that there was no publisher in London called Michael Plant, he would think: Oh poor Susan, she was afraid to give me his real name.

And what did it matter whether he married Phil Hunt or Sophie? Though it ought to be Sophie, who was already the mother of those children . . . and what hypocrisy to sit here worrying about the children, when she was going to leave them because she had not got the energy to stay.

She had about four hours. She spent them delightfully, darkly, sweetly, letting herself slide gently, gently, to the edge of the river. Then, with hardly a break in her consciousness, she got up, pushed the thin rug against the door, made sure the windows were tight shut, put two shillings in the meter, and turned on the gas. For the first time since she had been in the room she lay on the hard bed that smelled stale, that smelled of sweat and sex.

She lay on her back on the green satin cover, but her legs were chilly. She got up, found a blanket folded in the bottom of the chest of drawers, and carefully covered her legs with it. She was quite content lying there, listening to the faint soft hiss of the gas that poured into the room, into her lungs, into her brain, as she drifted off into the dark river.

Questions

1. In what sense is the Rawlings' marriage "grounded in intelligence"? **2.** Are the sources of Susan's growing discontent clear? Explain. **3.** Why does Matthew assume that Susan is having an affair? Why does Susan encourage him in this mistaken belief? **4.** In what sense is Susan's suicide a "failure in intelligence"?

Going to Meet the Man

JAMES BALDWIN [b. 1924]

WHAT'S the matter?" she asked.

"I don't know," he said, trying to laugh, "I guess I'm tired."

"You've been working too hard," she said. "I keep telling you."

"Well, goddammit, woman," he said, "it's not my fault!" He tried again; he wretchedly failed again. Then he just lay there, silent, angry, and helpless. Excitement filled him just like a toothache, but it refused to enter his flesh. He stroked her breast. This was his wife. He could not ask her to do just a little thing for him, just to help him out, just for a little while, the way he could ask a nigger girl to do it. He lay there, and he sighed. The image of a black girl caused a distant excitement in him, like a far-away light; but, again, the excitement was more like pain; instead of forcing him to act, it made action impossible.

"Go to sleep," she said, gently, "you got a hard day tomorrow."

"Yeah," he said, and rolled over on his side, facing her, one hand still on one breast. "Goddamn the niggers. The black stinking coons. You'd think they'd learn. Wouldn't you think they'd learn? I mean, *wouldn't* you?"

"They going to be out there tomorrow," she said, and took his hand away, "get some sleep."

He lay there, one hand between his legs, staring at the frail sanctuary of his wife. A faint light came from the shutters; the moon was full. Two dogs, far away, were barking at each other, back and forth, insistently, as though they were agreeing to make an appointment. He heard a car coming north on the road and he half sat up, his hand reaching for his holster, which was on a chair near the bed, on top of his pants. The lights hit the shutters and seemed to travel across the room and then went out. The sound of the car slipped away, he heard it hit gravel, then heard it no more. Some liver-lipped students, probably, heading back to that college—but coming from where? His watch said it was two in the morning. They could be coming from anywhere, from out of state most likely, and they would be at the court-house tomorrow. The niggers were getting ready. Well, they would be ready, too.

He moaned. He wanted to let whatever was in him out; but it wouldn't come out. Goddamn! he said aloud, and turned again, on his side, away from Grace, staring at the shutters. He was a big, healthy man and he had never had any trouble sleeping. And he wasn't old enough yet to have any trouble getting it up—he was only forty-two. And he was a good man, a God-fearing man, he had tried to do his duty all his life, and he had been a deputy sheriff for several years. Nothing had ever bothered him before, certainly not getting it up. Sometimes, sure, like any other man, he knew that he wanted a little more spice than Grace could give him and he would drive over yonder and pick up a black piece or arrest her, it came to the same thing, but he couldn't do that now, no more. There was no telling what might happen once your ass was in the air. And they were low enough to kill a man then, too, everyone of them, or the girl herself might do it, right while she was making believe you made her feel so good. The niggers. What had the good Lord Almighty had in mind when he made the niggers? Well. They were pretty good at that, all right. Damn. Damn. Goddamn.

This wasn't helping him to sleep. He turned again, toward Grace again, and moved close to her warm body. He felt something he had never felt before. He felt that he would like to hold her, hold her, hold her, and be buried in her like a child and never have to get up in the morning again and go downtown to face those faces, good Christ, they were ugly! and never have to enter that jail house again and smell that smell and hear that singing; never again feel that filthy, kinky, greasy hair under his hand, never again watch those black breasts leap against the leaping cattle prod, never hear those moans again or watch that blood run down or the fat lips split or the sealed eyes struggle open. They were animals, they were no better than animals, what could be done with people like that? Here they had been in a civilized country for years and they still lived like animals. Their houses were dark, with oil cloth or cardboard in the windows, the smell was enough to make you puke your guts out, and there they sat, a whole tribe, pumping out kids, it looked like, every damn five minutes, and laughing and talking and playing music like they didn't have a care in the world, and he reckoned they didn't, neither, and coming to the door, into the sunlight, just standing there, just looking foolish, not thinking of anything but just getting back to what they were doing, saying, Yes suh, Mr. Jesse. I surely will, Mr. Jesse. Fine weather, Mr. Jesse. Why, I thank you, Mr. Jesse. He had worked for a mail-order house for a while and it had been his job to collect the payments for the stuff they bought. They were too dumb to know that they were being cheated blind, but that was no skin off his ass—he was just supposed to do his job. They would be late—they didn't have the sense to put money aside; but it was easy to scare them, and he never really had any trouble. Hell, they all liked him, the kids used to smile when he came to the door. He gave them candy, sometimes, or chewing gum, and rubbed their rough bullet heads—maybe the candy should have been poisoned. Those kids were grown now. He had had trouble with one of them today.

"There was this nigger today," he said; and stopped; his voice sounded peculiar. He touched Grace. "You awake?" he asked. She mumbled something, impatiently, she was probably telling him to go to sleep. It was all right. He knew that he was not alone.

"What a funny time," he said, "to be thinking about a thing like that— you listening?" She mumbled something again. He rolled over on his back. "This nigger's one of the ringleaders. We had trouble with him before. We must have had him out there at the work farm three or four times. Well, Big Jim C. and some of the boys really had to whip that nigger's ass today." He looked over at Grace; he could not tell whether she was listening or not; and he was afraid to ask again. "They had this line you know, to register"—he laughed, but she did not—"and they wouldn't stay where Big Jim C. wanted them, no, they had to start blocking traffic all around the court house so couldn't nothing or nobody get through, and Big Jim C. told them to disperse and they wouldn't move, they just kept up that singing, and Big Jim C. figured that the others would move if this nigger would move, him being the ring-leader, but he wouldn't move and he wouldn't let the others move, so they had to beat him and a couple of the others and they threw them in the wagon —but *I* didn't see this nigger till I got to the jail. They were still singing and I was supposed to make them stop. Well, I couldn't make them stop for me but I knew he could make them stop. He was lying on the ground jerking and moaning, they had threw him in a cell by himself, and blood was coming out his ears from where Big Jim C. and his boys had whipped him. Wouldn't you think they'd learn? I put the prod to him and he jerked some more and he kind of screamed—but he didn't have much voice left. "You make them stop that singing," I said to him, "you hear me? You make them stop that singing." He acted like he didn't hear me and I put it to him again, under his arms, and he just rolled around on the floor and blood started coming from his mouth. He'd pissed his pants already." He paused. His mouth felt dry and his throat was as rough as sandpaper; as he talked, he began to hurt all over with that peculiar excitement which refused to be released. "You all are going to stop your singing, I said to him, and you are going to stop coming down to the court house and disrupting traffic and molesting the people and keeping us from our duties and keeping doctors from getting to sick white women and getting all them Northerners in this town to give our town a bad name—!" As he said this, he kept prodding the boy, sweat pouring from beneath the helmet he had not yet taken off. The boy rolled around in his own dirt and water and blood and tried to scream again as the prod hit his testicles, but the scream did not come out, only a kind of rattle and a moan. He stopped. He was not supposed to kill the nigger. The cell was filled with a terrible odor. The boy was still. "You hear me?" he called. "You had enough?" The singing went on. "You had enough?" His foot leapt out, he had not known it was going to, and caught the boy flush on the jaw. *Jesus*, he thought, *this ain't no nigger, this is a goddamn bull*, and he screamed again, "You had enough? You going to make them stop that singing now?"

But the boy was out. And now he was shaking worse than the boy had been shaking. He was glad no one could see him. At the same time, he felt very close to a very peculiar, particular joy; something deep in him and deep in his memory was stirred, but whatever was in his memory eluded him. He took off his helmet. He walked to the cell door.

"White man," said the boy, from the floor, behind him.

He stopped. For some reason, he grabbed his privates.

"You remember Old Julia?"

The boy said, from the floor, with his mouth full of blood, and one eye, barely open, glaring like the eye of a cat in the dark, "My grandmother's name was Mrs. Julia Blossom. *Mrs.* Julia Blossom. You going to call our women by their right names yet.—And those kids ain't going to stop singing. We going to keep on singing until every one of you miserable white mothers go stark raving out of your minds. Then he closed the one eye; he spat blood; his head fell back against the floor.

He looked down at the boy, whom he had been seeing, off and on, for more than a year, and suddenly remembered him: Old Julia had been one of his mail-order customers, a nice old woman. He had not seen her for years, he supposed that she must be dead.

He had walked into the yard, the boy had been sitting in a swing. He had smiled at the boy, and asked, "Old Julia home?"

The boy looked at him for a long time before he answered. "Don't no Old Julia live here."

"This is her house. I know her. She's lived here for years."

The boy shook his head. "You might know a Old Julia someplace else, white man. But don't nobody by that name live here."

He watched the boy; the boy watched him. The boy certainly wasn't more than ten. *White man.* He didn't have time to be fooling around with some crazy kid. He yelled, "Hey! Old Julia!"

But only silence answered him. The expression on the boy's face did not change. The sun beat down on them both, still and silent; he had the feeling that he had been caught up in a nightmare, a nightmare dreamed by a child; perhaps one of the nightmares he himself had dreamed as a child. It had that feeling—everything familiar, without undergoing any other change, had been subtly and hideously displaced: the trees, the sun, the patches of grass in the yard, the leaning porch and the weary porch steps and the cardboard in the windows and the black hole of the door which looked like the entrance to a cave, and the eyes of the pickaninny, all, all, were charged with malevolence. *White man.* He looked at the boy. "She's gone out?"

The boy said nothing.

"Well," he said, "tell her I passed by and I'll pass by next week." He started to go; he stopped. "You want some chewing gum?"

The boy got down from the swing and started for the house. He said, "I don't want nothing you got, white man." He walked into the house and closed the door behind him.

Now the boy looked as though he were dead. Jesse wanted to go over to him and pick him up and pistol whip him until the boy's head burst open like a melon. He began to tremble with what he believed was rage, sweat, both cold and hot, raced down his body, the singing filled him as though it were a weird, uncontrollable, monstrous howling rumbling up from the depths of his own belly, he felt an icy fear rise in him and raise him up, and he shouted, he howled, "You lucky we *pump* some white blood into you every once in a while—your women! Here's what I got for all the black bitches in the world—!" Then he was, abruptly, almost too weak to stand; to his bewilderment, his horror, beneath his own fingers, he felt himself violently stiffen—with no warning at all; he dropped his hands and he stared at the boy and he left the cell.

"All that singing they do," he said. "All that singing." He could not remember the first time he had heard it; he had been hearing it all his life. It was the sound with which he was most familiar—though it was also the sound of which he had been least conscious—and it had always contained an obscure comfort. They were singing to God. They were singing for mercy and they hoped to go to heaven, and he had even sometimes felt, when looking into the eyes of some of the old women, a few of the very old men, that they were singing for mercy for his soul, too. Of course he had never thought of their heaven or of what God was, or could be, for them; God was the same for everyone, he supposed, and heaven was where good people went—he supposed. He had never thought much about what it meant to be a good person. He tried to be a good person and treat everybody right: it wasn't his fault if the niggers had taken it into their heads to fight against God and go against the rules laid down in the Bible for everyone to read! Any preacher would tell you that. He was only doing his duty: protecting white people from the niggers and the niggers from themselves. And there were still lots of good niggers around—he had to remember that; they weren't all like that boy this afternoon; and the good niggers must be mighty sad to see what was happening to their people. They would thank him when this was over. In that way they had, the best of them, not quite looking him in the eye, in a low voice, with a little smile: We surely thanks you, Mr. Jesse. From the bottom of our hearts, we thanks you. He smiled. They hadn't all gone crazy. This trouble would pass.—He knew that the young people had changed some of the words to the songs. He had scarcely listened to the words before and he did not listen to them now; but he knew that the words were different; he could hear that much. He did not know if the faces were different, he had never, before this trouble began, watched them as they sang, but he certainly did not like what he saw now. They hated him, and this hatred was blacker than their hearts, blacker than their skins, redder than their blood, and harder, by far, then his club. Each day, each night, he felt worn out, aching, with their smell in his nostrils and filling his lungs, as though he were drowning—drowning in niggers; and it was all to be done again when he awoke. It would never end. It would never end. Perhaps this was what the singing had meant all along. They had not been singing black folks into heaven, they had been singing white folks into hell.

Everyone felt this black suspicion in many ways, but no one knew how to express it. Men much older than he, who had been responsible for law and order much longer than he, were now much quieter than they had been, and the tone of their jokes, in a way that he could not quite put his finger on, had changed. These men were his models, they had been friends to his father, and they had taught him what it meant to be a man. He looked to them for courage now. It wasn't that he didn't know that what he was doing was right—he knew that, nobody had to tell him that; it was only that he missed the ease of former years. But they didn't have much time to hang out with each other these days. They tended to stay close to their families every free minute because nobody knew what might happen next. Explosions rocked the night of their tranquil town. Each time each man wondered silently if perhaps this time the dynamite had not fallen into the wrong hands. They thought that they knew where all the guns were; but they could not possibly know every move that was made in that secret place where the darkies lived. From time to time it was suggested that they form a posse and search the home of every nigger, but they hadn't done it yet. For one thing, this might have brought the bastards from the North down on their backs; for another, although the niggers were scattered throughout the town—down in the hollow near the railroad tracks, way west near the mills, up on the hill, the well-off ones, and some out near the college—nothing seemed to happen in one part of town without the niggers immediately knowing it in the other. This meant that they could not take them by surprise. They rarely mentioned it, but they *knew* that some of the niggers had guns. It stood to reason, as they said, since, after all, some of them had been in the Army. There were niggers in the Army right now and God knows they wouldn't have had any trouble stealing this half-assed government blind—the whole world was doing it, look at the European countries and all those countries in Africa. They made jokes about it—bitter jokes; and they cursed the government in Washington, which had betrayed them; but they had not yet formed a posse. Now, if their town had been laid out like some towns in the North, where all the niggers lived together in one locality, they could have gone down and set fire to the houses and brought about peace that way. If the niggers had all lived in one place, they could have kept the fire in one place. But the way this town was laid out, the fire could hardly be controlled. It would spread all over town—and the niggers would probably be helping it to spread. Still, from time to time, they spoke of doing it, anyway; so that now there was a real fear among them that somebody might go crazy and light the match.

They rarely mentioned anything not directly related to the war that they were fighting, but this had failed to establish between them the unspoken communication of soldiers during a war. Each man, in the thrilling silence which sped outward from their exchanges, their laughter, and their anecdotes, seemed wrestling, in various degrees of darkness, with a secret which he could not articulate to himself, and which, however directly it related to the war, related yet more surely to his privacy and his past. They could no longer be sure, after all, that they had all done the same things. They had never dreamed that their privacy could contain any element of terror, could threaten, that is, to reveal itself, to the scrutiny of a judgment day, while remaining unreadable and inaccessible to themselves; nor had they dreamed that the past, while certainly refusing to be forgotten, could yet so stubbornly refuse to be remembered. They felt themselves mysteriously set at naught, as no longer entering into the real concerns of other people—while here they were, outnumbered, fighting to save the civilized world. They had thought that people would care—people didn't care; not enough, anyway, to help them. It would have been a help, really, or at least a relief, even to have been forced to surrender. Thus they had lost, probably forever, their old and easy connection with each other. They were forced to depend on each other more and, at the same time, to trust each other less. Who could tell when one of them might not betray them all, for money, or for the ease of confession? But no one dared imagine what there might be to confess. They were soldiers fighting a war, but their relationship to each other was that of accomplices in a crime. They all had to keep their mouths shut.

> I stepped in the river at Jordan.

Out of the darkness of the room, out of nowhere, the line came flying up at him, with the melody and the beat. He turned wordlessly toward his sleeping wife. *I stepped in the river at Jordan.* Where had he heard that song?

"Grace," he whispered. "You awake?"

She did not answer. If she was awake, she wanted him to sleep. Her breathing was slow and easy, her body slowly rose and fell.

> I stepped in the river at Jordan.
> The water came to my knees.

He began to sweat. He felt an overwhelming fear, which yet contained a curious and dreadful pleasure.

> I stepped in the river at Jordan.
> The water came to my waist.

It had been night, as it was now, he was in the car between his mother and his father, sleepy, his head in his mother's lap, sleepy, and yet full of excitement. The singing came from far away, across the dark fields. There were no lights anywhere. They had said good-bye to all the others and turned off on this dark dirt road. They were almost home.

> I stepped in the river at Jordan,
> The water came over my head,
> I looked way over to the other side,
> He was making up my dying bed!

"I guess they singing for him," his father said, seeming very weary and subdued now. "Even when they're sad, they sound like they just about to go and tear off a piece." He yawned and leaned across the boy and slapped his wife lightly on the shoulder, allowing his hand to rest there for a moment. "Don't they?"

"Don't talk that way," she said.

"Well, that's what we going to do," he said, "you can make up your mind to that." He started whistling. "You see? When I begin to feel it, I gets kind of musical, too."

Oh, Lord! Come on and ease my troubling mind!

He had a black friend, his age, eight, who lived nearby. His name was Otis. They wrestled together in the dirt. Now the thought of Otis made him sick. He began to shiver. His mother put her arm around him.

"He's tired," she said.

"We'll be home soon," said his father. He began to whistle again.

"We didn't see Otis this morning," Jesse said. He did not know why he said this. His voice, in the darkness of the car, sounded small and accusing.

"You haven't seen Otis for a couple of mornings," his mother said.

That was true. But he was only concerned about *this* morning.

"No," said his father, "I reckon Otis's folks was afraid to let him show himself this morning."

"But Otis didn't do nothing!" Now his voice sounded questioning.

"Otis *can't* do nothing," said his father, "he's too little." The car lights picked up their wooden house, which now solemnly approached them, the lights falling around it like yellow dust. Their dog, chained to a tree, began to bark.

"We just want to make sure Otis *don't* do nothing," said his father, and stopped the car. He looked down at Jesse. "And you tell him what your Daddy said, you hear?"

"Yes sir," he said.

His father switched off the lights. The dog moaned and pranced, but they ignored him and went inside. He could not sleep. He lay awake, hearing the night sounds, the dog yawning and moaning outside, the sawing of the crickets, the cry of the owl, dogs barking far away, then no sounds at all, just the heavy, endless buzzing of the night. The darkness pressed on his eyelids like a scratchy blanket. He turned, he turned again. He wanted to call his mother, but he knew his father would not like this. He was terribly afraid. Then he heard his father's voice in the other room, low, with a joke in it; but this did not help him, it frightened him more, he knew what was going to happen. He put his head under the blanket, then pushed his head out again, for fear, staring at the dark window. He heard his mother's moan, his father's sigh; he gritted his teeth. Then their bed began to rock. His father's breathing seemed to fill the world.

That morning, before the sun had gathered all its strength, men and women, some flushed and some pale with excitement, came with news.

Jesse's father seemed to know what the news was before the first jalopy stopped in the yard, and he ran out, crying, "They got him, then? They got him?"

The first jalopy held eight people, three men and two women and three children. The children were sitting on the laps of the grown-ups. Jesse knew two of them, the two boys; they shyly and uncomfortably greeted each other. He did not know the girl.

"Yes, they got him," said one of the women, the older one, who wore a wide hat and a fancy, faded blue dress. "They found him early this morning."

"How far had he got?" Jesse's father asked.

"He hadn't got no further than Harkness," one of the men said. "Look like he got lost up there in all them trees—or maybe he just got so scared he couldn't move." They all laughed.

"Yes, and you know it's near a graveyard, too," said the younger woman, and they laughed again.

"Is that where they got him now?" asked Jesse's father.

By this time there were three cars piled behind the first one, with everyone looking excited and shining, and Jesse noticed that they were carrying food. It was like a Fourth of July picnic.

"Yeah, that's where he is," said one of the men, "declare, Jesse, you going to keep us here all day long, answering your damn fool questions. Come on, we ain't got no time to waste."

"Don't bother putting up no food," cried a woman from one of the other cars, "we got enough. Just come on."

"Why, thank you," said Jesse's father, "we be right along, then."

"I better get a sweater for the boy," said his mother, "in case it turns cold."

Jesse watched his mother's thin legs cross the yard. He knew that she also wanted to comb her hair a little and maybe put on a better dress, the dress she wore to church. His father guessed this, too, for he yelled behind her, "Now don't you go trying to turn yourself into no movie star. You just come on." But he laughed as he said this, and winked at the men; his wife was younger and prettier than most of the other women. He clapped Jesse on the head and started pulling him toward the car. "You all go on," he said, "I'll be right behind you. Jesse, you go tie up that there dog while I get this car started."

The cars sputtered and coughed and shook; the caravan began to move; bright dust filled the air. As soon as he was tied up, the dog began to bark. Jesse's mother came out of the house, carrying a jacket for his father and a sweater for Jesse. She had put a ribbon in her hair and had an old shawl around her shoulders.

"Put these in the car, son," she said, and handed everything to him. She bent down and stroked the dog, looked to see if there was water in his bowl, then went back up the three porch steps and closed the door.

"Come on," said his father, "ain't nothing in there for nobody to steal." He was sitting in the car, which trembled and belched. The last car of the caravan had disappeared but the sound of singing floated behind them.

Jesse got into the car, sitting close to his father, loving the smell of the car, and the trembling, and the bright day, and the sense of going on a great and unexpected journey. His mother got in and closed the door and the car began to move. Not until then did he ask, "Where are we going? Are we going on a picnic?"

He had a feeling that he knew where they were going, but he was not sure.

"That's right," his father said, "we're going on a picnic. You won't ever forget *this* picnic—!"

"Are we," he asked, after a moment, "going to see the bad nigger—the one that knocked down old Miss Standish?"

"Well, I reckon," said his mother, "that we *might* see him."

He started to ask, *Will a lot of niggers be there? Will Otis be there?*— but he did not ask his question, to which, in a strange and uncomfortable way, he already knew the answer. Their friends, in the other cars, stretched up the road as far as he could see; other cars had joined them; there were cars behind them. They were singing. The sun seemed, suddenly, very hot, and he was at once very happy and a little afraid. He did not quite understand what was happening, and he did not know what to ask—he had no one to ask. He had grown accustomed, for the solution of such mysteries, to go to Otis. He felt that Otis knew everything. But he could not ask Otis about this. Anyway, he had not seen Otis for two days; he had not seen a black face anywhere for more than two days; and he now realized, as they began chugging up the long hill which eventually led to Harkness, that there were no black faces on the road this morning, no black people anywhere. From the houses in which they lived, all along the road, no smoke curled, no life stirred—maybe one or two chickens were to be seen, that was all. There was no one at the windows, no one in the yard, no one sitting on the porches, and the doors were closed. He had come this road many a time and seen women washing in the yard (there were no clothes on the clotheslines) men working in the fields, children playing in the dust; black men passed them on the road other mornings, other days, on foot, or in wagons, sometimes in cars, tipping their hats, smiling, joking, their teeth a solid white against their skin, their eyes as warm as the sun, the blackness of their skin like dull fire against the white of the blue or the grey of their torn clothes. They passed the nigger church—dead-white, desolate, locked up; and the graveyard, where no one knelt or walked, and he saw no flowers. He wanted to ask, *Where are they? Where are they all?* But he did not dare. As the hill grew steeper, the sun grew colder. He looked at his mother and his father. They looked straight ahead, seeming to be listening to the singing which echoed and echoed in this graveyard silence. They were strangers to him now. They were looking at something he could not see. His father's lips had a strange, cruel curve, he wet his lips from time to time, and swallowed. He was terribly aware of his father's tongue, it was as though he had never seen it before. And his father's body suddenly seemed immense, bigger than a mountain. His eyes, which were grey-green, looked yellow in the sunlight; or at least there was a light in them which he had never seen before. His mother patted her hair and adjusted the ribbon, leaning forward to look into the car mirror. "You look all right," said his father, and laughed. "When that nigger looks at you, he's going to swear he threw his life away for nothing. Wouldn't be surprised if he don't come back to haunt you." And he laughed again.

The singing now slowly began to cease; and he realized that they were nearing their destination. They had reached a straight, narrow, pebbly road, with trees on either side. The sunlight filtered down on them from a great height, as though they were under-water; and the branches of the trees scraped against the cars with a tearing sound. To the right of them, and beneath them, invisible now, lay the town; and to the left, miles of trees which led to the high mountain range which his ancestors had crossed in order to settle in this valley. Now, all was silent, except for the bumping of the tires against the rocky road, the sputtering of motors, and the sound of a crying child. And they seemed to move more slowly. They were beginning to climb again. He watched the cars ahead as they toiled patiently upward, disappearing into the sunlight of the clearing. Presently, he felt their vehicle also rise, heard his father's changed breathing, the sunlight hit his face, the trees moved away from them, and they were there. As their car crossed the clearing, he looked around. There seemed to be millions, there were certainly hundreds of people in the clearing, staring toward something he could not see. There was a fire. He could not see the flames, but he smelled the smoke. Then they were on the other side of the clearing, among the trees again. His father drove off the road and parked the car behind a great many other cars. He looked down at Jesse.

"You all right?" he asked.

"Yes sir," he said.

"Well, come on, then," his father said. He reached over and opened the door on his mother's side. His mother stepped out first. They followed her into the clearing. At first he was aware only of confusion, of his mother and father greeting and being greeted, himself being handled, hugged, and patted, and told how much he had grown. The wind blew the smoke from the fire across the clearing into his eyes and nose. He could not see over the backs of the people in front of him. The sounds of laughing and cursing and wrath—and something else—rolled in waves from the front of the mob to the back. Those in front expressed their delight at what they saw, and this delight rolled backward, wave upon wave, across the clearing, more acrid than the smoke. His father reached down suddenly and sat Jesse on his shoulders.

Now he saw the fire—of twigs and boxes, piled high; flames made pale orange and yellow and thin as a veil under the steadier light of the sun; grey-blue smoke rolled upward and poured over their heads. Beyond the shifting curtain of fire and smoke, he made out first only a length of gleaming chain, attached to a great limb of the tree; then he saw that this chain bound two black hands together at the wrist, dirty yellow palm facing dirty yellow palm. The smoke poured up; the hands dropped out of sight; a cry went up from the crowd. Then the hands slowly came into view again, pulled upward by the chain. This time he saw the kinky, sweating, bloody head—he had never before seen a head with so much hair on it, hair so black and so tangled that it seemed like another jungle. The head was hanging. He saw the forehead, flat and high, with a kind of arrow of hair in the center, like he had, like his father had; they called it a widow's peak; and the mangled eye brows, the wide nose, the closed eyes, and the glinting eye lashes and the hanging lips, all streaming with blood and sweat. His hands were straight above his head. All his weight pulled downward from his hands; and he was a big man, a bigger man than his father, and black as an African jungle cat, and naked. Jesse pulled upward; his father's hands held him firmly by the ankles. He wanted to say something, he did not know what, but nothing he said could have been heard, for now the crowd roared again as a man stepped forward and put more wood on the fire. The flames leapt up. He thought he heard the hanging man scream, but he was not sure. Sweat was pouring from the hair in his armpits, poured down his sides, over his chest, into his navel and his groin. He was lowered again; he was raised again. Now Jesse knew that he heard him scream. The head went back, the mouth wide open, blood bubbling from the mouth; the veins of the neck jumped out; Jesse clung to his father's neck in terror as the cry rolled over the crowd. The cry of all the people rose to answer the dying man's cry. He wanted death to come quickly. They wanted to make death wait: and it was they who held death, now, on a leash which they lengthened little by little. *What did he do?* Jesse wondered. *What did the man do? What did he do?*—but he could not ask his father. He was seated on his father's shoulders, but his father was far away. There were two older men, friends of his father's, raising and lowering the chain; everyone, indiscriminately, seemed to be responsible for the fire. There was no hair left on the nigger's privates, and the eyes, now, were wide open, as white as the eyes of a clown or a doll. The smoke now carried a terrible odor across the clearing, the odor of something burning which was both sweet and rotten.

He turned his head a little and saw the field of faces. He watched his mother's face. Her eyes were very bright, her mouth was open: she was more beautiful than he had ever seen her, and more strange. He began to feel a joy he had never felt before. He watched the hanging, gleaming body, the most beautiful and terrible object he had ever seen till then. One of his father's friends reached up and in his hands he held a knife: and Jesse wished that he had been that man. It was a long, bright knife and the sun seemed to catch it, to play with it, to caress it—it was brighter than the fire.

And a wave of laughter swept the crowd. Jesse felt his father's hands on his ankles slip and tighten. The man with the knife walked toward the crowd, smiling slightly; as though this were a signal, silence fell; he heard his mother cough. Then the man with the knife walked up to the hanging body. He turned and smiled again. Now there was a silence all over the field. The hanging head looked up. It seemed fully conscious now, as though the fire had burned out terror and pain. The man with the knife took the nigger's privates in his hand, one hand, still smiling, as though he were weighing them. In the cradle of the one white hand, the nigger's privates seemed as remote as meat being weighed in the scales; but seemed heavier, too, much heavier, and Jesse felt his scrotum tighten; and huge, huge, much bigger than his father's, flaccid, hairless, the largest thing he had ever seen till then, and the blackest. The white hand stretched them, cradled them, caressed them. Then the dying man's eyes looked straight into Jesse's eyes—it could not have been as long as a second, but it seemed longer than a year. Then Jesse screamed, and the crowd screamed as the knife flashed, first up, then down cutting the dreadful thing away, and the blood came roaring down. Then the crowd rushed forward, tearing at the body with their hands, with knives, with rocks, with stones, howling and cursing. Jesse's head, of its own weight, fell downward toward his father's head. Someone stepped forward and drenched the body with kerosene. Where the man had been, a great sheet of flame appeared. Jesse's father lowered him to the ground.

"Well, I told you," said his father, "you wasn't never going to forget *this* picnic." His father's face was full of sweat, his eyes were very peaceful. At that moment Jesse loved his father more than he had ever loved him. He felt that his father had carried him through a mighty test, had revealed to him a great secret which would be the key to his life forever.

"I reckon," he said. "I reckon."

Jesse's father took him by the hand and, with his mother a little behind them, talking and laughing with the other women, they walked through the crowd, across the clearing. The black body was on the ground, the chain which had held it was being rolled up by one of his father's friends. Whatever the fire had left undone, the hands and the knives and the stones of the people had accomplished. The head was caved in, one eye was torn out, one ear was hanging. But one had to look carefully to realize this, for it was, now, merely, a black charred object on the black, charred ground. He lay spread-eagled with what had been a wound between what had been his legs.

"They going to leave him here, then?" Jesse whispered.

"Yeah," said his father, "they'll come and get him by and by. I reckon we better get over there and get some of that food before it's all gone."

"I reckon," he muttered now to himself, "I reckon." Grace stirred and touched him on the thigh: the moonlight covered her like glory. Something bubbled up in him, his nature again returned to him. He thought of the boy in the cell; he thought of the man in the fire; he thought of the knife and grabbed himself and stroked himself and a terrible sound, something between a high laugh and a howl, came out of him and dragged his sleeping wife up on one elbow. She stared at him in a moonlight which had now grown cold as ice. He thought of the morning and grabbed her, laughing and crying, crying and laughing, and he whispered, as he stroked her, as he took her, "Come on, sugar, I'm going to do you like a nigger, just like a nigger, come on, sugar, and love me just like you'd love a nigger." He thought of the morning as he labored and she moaned, thought of morning as he labored harder than he ever had before, and before his labors had ended, he heard the first cock crow and the dogs begin to bark, and the sound of tires on the gravel road.

Questions

1. *What is Jesse's failure at the beginning of the story? How does it relate to the rest of the story?* 2. *Under what circumstances was the young leader of the black demonstrators arrested? Why was he beaten? What does Jesse experience after he beats the prisoner?* 3. *Why did the young black leader, as a ten-year-old boy, tell Jesse on one occasion, "Don't no Old Julia live here"?* 4. *Why is Jesse so determined to stop the prisoners from singing?* 5. *Is Jesse a totally evil and depraved man? Upon what details in the narrative do you base your answer?* 6. *Baldwin and Faulkner (in "Dry September") juxtapose murderous violence and sexual excitement. Is that juxtaposition justified? Explain.*

POETRY

Bonny Barbara Allan

ANONYMOUS

It was in and about the Martinmas[1] time,
    When the green leaves were a falling,
That Sir John Graeme, in the West Country,
    Fell in love with Barbara Allan.

He sent his man down through the town,
    To the place where she was dwelling:
"O haste and come to my master dear,
    Gin° ye be Barbara Allan."   *if*

O hooly,° hooly rose she up,   *slowly*
    To the place where he was lying,   10
And when she drew the curtain by:
    "Young man, I think you're dying."

"O it's I'm sick, and very, very sick,
    And 'tis a' for Barbara Allan."
"O the better for me ye s'° never be,   *ye shall*
    Though your heart's blood were a-spilling.

"O dinna° ye mind,° young man," said she,   *don't/remember*
    "When ye was in the tavern a drinking,
That ye made the healths gae° round and round,   *go*
    And slighted Barbara Allan?"   20

He turned his face unto the wall,
    And death was with him dealing:
"Adieu, adieu, my dear friends all,
    And be kind to Barbara Allan."

And slowly, slowly raise she up,
    And slowly, slowly left him,
And sighing said, she could not stay,
    Since death of life had reft him.

1. November 11.

She had not gane a mile but twa,
　　When she heard the dead-bell ringing,
And every jow° that the dead-bell geid,°
　　It cried, "Woe to Barbara Allan!"

30 stroke/gave

"O mother, mother, make my bed!
　　O make it saft and narrow!
Since my love died for me to-day,
　　I'll die for him to-morrow."

They Flee from Me

SIR THOMAS WYATT　[1503?–1542]

They flee from me, that sometime did me seek,[1]
With naked foot stalking in my chamber.
I have seen them, gentle, tame, and meek,
That now are wild, and do not remember
That sometime they put themselves in danger
To take bread at my hand; and now they range,
Busily seeking with a continual change.

Thanked be Fortune, it hath been otherwise
Twenty times better; but once in special,
In thin array, after a pleasant guise,
When her loose gown from her shoulders did fall,
And she me caught in her arms long and small,°
And therewith all sweetly did me kiss
And softly said, "Dear heart, how like you this?"

It was no dream, I lay broad waking.
But all is turned, thorough my gentleness,
Into a strange fashion of forsaking;
And I have leave to go, of her goodness,
And she also to use newfangleness.°
But since that I so kindely[2] am served,
I fain would know what she hath deserved.

10

slender

fickleness
20

1. *"They" in line 1 apparently refers to animals or birds. What creatures do you see and for what might they be a metaphor?* **2.** *What sort of relationship is described in the last stanza? How does the poet feel about it?* **3.** *How does the first stanza serve to introduce the theme of the poem?*

---

1. I.e., formerly pursued me.
2. I.e., served in kind. The pun on the modern meaning of *kindly* is intended.

Since There's No Help, Come Let Us Kiss and Part

MICHAEL DRAYTON [1563–1631]

Since there's no help, come let us kiss and part;
Nay, I have done, you get no more of me,
And I am glad, yea glad with all my heart
That thus so cleanly I myself can free;
Shake hands forever, cancel all our vows,
And when we meet at any time again,
Be it not seen in either of our brows
That we one jot of former love retain.
Now at the last gasp of love's latest breath,
When, his pulse failing, passion speechless lies,   10
When faith is kneeling by his bed of death,
And innocence is closing up his eyes,
    Now if thou wouldst, when all have given him over,
    From death to life thou mightst him yet recover.

1. *Describe the scene in lines 9-12. Why is "innocence" described as closing "love's" eyes?* **2.** *How might the lady save love from death?*

The Passionate Shepherd to His Love

CHRISTOPHER MARLOWE [1564–1593]

Come live with me and be my love,
And we will all the pleasures prove
That valleys, groves, hills, and fields,
Woods, or steepy mountain yields.

And we will sit upon the rocks,
Seeing the shepherds feed their flocks,
By shallow rivers to whose falls
Melodious birds sing madrigals.

And I will make thee beds of roses
And a thousand fragrant posies,   10
A cap of flowers, and a kirtle°   *skirt*
Embroidered all with leaves of myrtle;

A gown made of the finest wool
Which from our pretty lambs we pull;
Fair lined slippers for the cold,
With buckles of the purest gold;

A belt of straw and ivy buds,
With coral clasps and amber studs:
And if these pleasures may thee move,
Come live with me, and be my love.   20

The shepherds' swains shall dance and sing
For thy delight each May morning:
If these delights thy mind may move,
Then live with me and be my love.

The Nymph's Reply to the Shepherd

SIR WALTER RALEGH   [1552?–1618]

If all the world and love were young,
And truth in every shepherd's tongue,
These pretty pleasures might me move
To live with thee and be thy love.

Time drives the flocks from field to fold
When rivers rage and rocks grow cold,
And Philomel° becometh dumb;   *the nightingale*
The rest complains of cares to come.

The flowers do fade, and wanton fields
To wayward winter reckoning yields;   10
A honey tongue, a heart of gall,
Is fancy's spring, but sorrow's fall.

Thy gowns, thy shoes, thy beds of roses,
Thy cap, thy kirtle, and thy posies
Soon break, soon wither, soon forgotten—
In folly ripe, in reason rotten.

Thy belt of straw and ivy buds,
Thy coral clasps and amber studs,
All these in me no means can move
To come to thee and be thy love.   *20*

But could youth last and love still breed,
Had joys no date° nor age no need,   *end*
Then these delights my mind might move
To live with thee and be thy love.

Sonnets

WILLIAM SHAKESPEARE   [1564–1616]

18

Shall I compare thee to a summer's day?
Thou art more lovely and more temperate:
Rough winds do shake the darling buds of May,
And summer's lease hath all too short a date:
Sometime too hot the eye of heaven shines,
And often is his gold complexion dimmed;
And every fair from fair sometimes declines,
By chance or nature's changing course untrimmed;
But thy eternal summer shall not fade,
Nor lose possession of that fair thou ow'st;°   *ownest 10*
Nor shall death brag thou wander'st In hls shade,
When in eternal lines to time thou grow'st:
    So long as men can breathe, or eyes can see,
    So long lives this, and this gives life to thee.

1. *Why does the poet argue that "a summer's day" is an inappropriate metaphor for his beloved?*   2. *What is "this" in line 14?*

29

When, in disgrace with fortune and men's eyes,
I all alone beweep my outcast state
And trouble deaf heaven with my bootless cries
And look upon myself and curse my fate,
Wishing me like to one more rich in hope,
Featured like him, like him with friends possessed,
Desiring this man's art and that man's scope,
With what I most enjoy contented least;
Yet in these thoughts myself almost despising,

Haply I think on thee, and then my state,   10
Like to the lark at break of day arising
From sullen earth, sings hymns at heaven's gate;
    For thy sweet love remembered such wealth brings
    That then I scorn to change my state with kings.

116

Let me not to the marriage of true minds
Admit impediments:¹ love is not love
Which alters when it alteration finds,
Or bends with the remover to remove.²
Oh no! it is an ever-fixed mark
That looks on tempests and is never shaken;
It is the star to every wandering bark,
Whose worth's unknown although his height be taken.³
Love's not Time's fool, though rosy lips and cheeks
Within his bending sickle's compass come;   10
Love alters not with his brief hours and weeks,
But bears it out⁴ even to the edge of doom.
    If this be error and upon me proved,
    I never writ, nor no man ever loved.

129

Th' expense of spirit in a waste of shame
Is lust in action; and till action, lust
Is perjured, murderous, bloody, full of blame,
Savage, extreme, rude, cruel, not to trust;
Enjoyed no sooner but despisèd straight;
Past reason hunted; and no sooner had,
Past reason hated, as a swallowed bait,
On purpose laid to make the taker mad:
Mad in pursuit, and in possession so;
Had, having, and in quest to have, extreme;   10
A bliss in proof,° and proved, a very woe;   *experience*
Before, a joy proposed; behind, a dream.
    All this the world well knows; yet none knows well
    To shun the heaven that leads men to this hell.

---

1. *Paraphrase "Th' expense of spirit in a waste of shame / Is lust in action."* **2.** *Describe the sound patterns and metrical variations in lines 3 and 4. What do they contribute to the "sense" of the lines?* **3.** *Explain the paradox in the final couplet.*

---

1.   An echo of the marriage service: "If any of you know cause or just impediments why these persons should not be joined together . . ."
2.   I.e., love does not change when a rival attempts to remove its object.
3.   The star serves the navigator who measures its height above the horizon but does not understand its value.
4.   Endures.

130

My mistress' eyes are nothing like the sun;
Coral is far more red than her lips' red;
If snow be white, why then her breasts are dun;
If hairs be wires, black wires grow on her head.
I have seen roses damasked,° red and white,   *variegated*
But no such roses see I in her cheeks;
And in some perfumes is there more delight
Than in the breath that from my mistress reeks.
I love to hear her speak, yet well I know
That music hath a far more pleasing sound;   10
I grant I never saw a goddess go;
My mistress, when she walks, treads on the ground.
        And yet, by heaven, I think my love as rare
        As any she belied with false compare.[1]

138

When my love swears that she is made of truth
I do believe her, though I know she lies,
That she might think me some untutored youth
Unlearnèd in the world's false subtleties.
Thus vainly thinking that she thinks me young,
Although she knows my days are past the best,
Simply I credit her false-speaking tongue:
On both sides thus is simple truth suppressed.
But wherefore says she not she is unjust?
And wherefore say not I that I am old?   10
Oh, love's best habit[2] is in seeming trust,
And age, in love, loves not to have years told.
        Therefore I lie with her, and she with me,
        And in our faults by lies we flattered be.

I Care Not for These Ladies

THOMAS CAMPION   [1567–1620]

I care not for these ladies,
That must be wooed and prayed:

---

1. I.e., as any woman misrepresented with false comparisons.

---

2. Clothing, with a pun suggesting behavior.

Give me kind Amaryllis,[1]
The wanton country maid.
Nature art disdaineth,
Her beauty is her own.
     Her when we court and kiss,
     She cries, "Forsooth, let go!"
     But when we come where comfort is,
     She never will say no.   10

If I love Amaryllis,
She gives me fruit and flowers:
But if we love these ladies,
We must give golden showers.
Give them gold, that sell love,
Give me the nut-brown lass,
     Who, when we court and kiss,
     She cries, "Forsooth, let go!"
     But when we come where comfort is,
     She never will say no.   20

These ladies must have pillows,
And beds by strangers wrought;
Give me a bower of willows,
Of moss and leaves unbought,
And fresh Amaryllis,
With milk and honey fed;
     Who, when we court and kiss,
     She cries, "Forsooth, let go!"
     But when we come where comfort is,
     She never will say no.   30

The Flea

JOHN DONNE [1572–1631]

Mark but this flea, and mark in this,
How little that which thou deniest me is;
It sucked me first, and now sucks thee,
And in this flea our two bloods mingled be;
Thou know'st that this cannot be said
A sin, nor shame, nor loss of maidenhead,
     Yet this enjoys before it woo,
     And pampered swells with one blood made of two,

---

1. A conventional name for a country girl in pastoral poetry.

And this, alas, is more than we would do.

Oh stay, three lives in one flea spare,   10
Where we almost, yea more than married, are.
This flea is you and I, and this
Our marriage bed and marriage temple is;
Though parents grudge, and you, we are met,
And cloistered in these living walls of jet,
    Though use° make you apt to kill me   *custom*
    Let not to that, self-murder added be,
    And sacrilege, three sins in killing three.

Cruel and sudden, hast thou since
Purpled thy nail, in blood of innocence?   20
Wherein could this flea guilty be,
Except in that drop which it sucked from thee?
Yet thou triumph'st, and say'st that thou
Find'st not thy self nor me the weaker now;
    'Tis true, then learn how false fears be;
    Just so much honor, when thou yield'st to me,
    Will waste, as this flea's death took life from thee.

A Valediction:
Forbidding Mourning

JOHN DONNE [1572–1631]

As virtuous men pass mildly away,
    And whisper to their souls to go,
Whilst some of their sad friends do say
    The breath goes now, and some say, No;

So let us melt, and make no noise,
    No tear-floods, nor sigh-tempests move,
'Twere profanation of our joys
    To tell the laity our love.

Moving of th' earth° brings harms and fears,   *earthquake*
    Men reckon what it did and meant;   10
But trepidation of the spheres,
    Though greater far, is innocent.[1]

---

1.   The movement of the heavenly spheres is harmless.

Dull sublunary° lovers' love   under the moon
    (Whose soul is sense) cannot admit
Absence, because it doth remove
    Those things which elemented it.

But we by a love so much refined
    That our selves know not what it is,
Inter-assurèd of the mind,
    Care less, eyes, lips, and hands to miss.   20

Our two souls therefore, which are one,
    Though I must go, endure not yet
A breach, but an expansion,
    Like gold to airy thinness beat.

If they be two, they are two so
    As stiff twin compasses are two;
Thy soul, the fixed foot, makes no show
    To move, but doth, if th' other do.

And though it in the center sit,
    Yet when the other far doth roam,   30
It leans and harkens after it,
    And grows erect, as that comes home.

Such wilt thou be to me, who must
    Like th' other foot, obliquely run;
Thy firmness makes my circle just,
    And makes me end where I begun.

1. *Two kinds of love are described in this poem—spiritual and physical. How does the simile drawn in the first two stanzas help define the differences between them?* 2. *How does the contrast between earthquakes and the movement of the spheres in stanza three further develop the contrast between the two types of lovers?* 3. *Explain the comparison between a drawing compass and the lovers in the last three stanzas.*

Corinna's Going A-Maying

ROBERT HERRICK [1591–1674]

Get up! get up for shame! the blooming morn
Upon her wings presents the god unshorn.
    See how Aurora¹ throws her fair

---

1. Aurora is the goddess of the morning. The god unshorn is Apollo, god of the sun.

Fresh-quilted colors through the air:
Get up, sweet slug-a-bed, and see
The dew bespangling herb and tree.
Each flower has wept and bowed toward the east
Above an hour since, yet you not dressed;
    Nay, not so much as out of bed?
    When all the birds have matins said,   10
    And sung their thankful hymns, 'tis sin,
    Nay, profanation to keep in,
Whenas a thousand virgins on this day
Spring, sooner than the lark, to fetch in May.

Rise, and put on your foliage, and be seen
To come forth, like the springtime, fresh and green,
    And sweet as Flora.² Take no care
    For jewels for your gown or hair;
    Fear not; the leaves will strew
    Gems in abundance upon you;   20
Besides, the childhood of the day has kept,
Against you come, some orient pearls unwept;
    Come and receive them while the light
    Hangs on the dew-locks of the night,
    And Titan° on the eastern hill   *the sun*
    Retires himself, or else stands still
Till you come forth. Wash, dress, be brief in praying:
Few beads° are best when once we go a-Maying.   *prayers*

Come, my Corinna, come; and, coming mark
How each field turns a street, each street a park   30
    Made green and trimmed with trees; see how
    Devotion gives each house a bough
    Or branch: each porch, each door ere this,
    An ark, a tabernacle is,
Made up of whitethorn neatly interwove,
As if here were those cooler shades of love.
    Can such delights be in the street
    And open fields, and we not see 't?
    Come, we'll abroad; and let's obey
    The proclamation made for May,   40
And sin no more, as we have done, by staying;
But, my Corinna, come, let's go a-Maying.

There's not a budding boy or girl this day
But is got up and gone to bring in May;
    A deal of youth, ere this, is come
    Back, and with whitethorn laden home.

---

2. Flora is the goddess of flowers.

Some have dispatched their cakes and cream
    Before that we have left to dream;
And some have wept, and wooed, and plighted troth,
And chose their priest, ere we can cast off sloth.   50
    Many a green-gown° has been given,   grass-stained gown
    Many a kiss, both odd and even,
    Many a glance, too, has been sent
    From out the eye, love's firmament;
Many a jest told of the keys betraying
This night, and locks picked; yet we're not a-Maying.

Come, let us go while we are in our prime,
And take the harmless folly of the time.
    We shall grow old apace, and die
    Before we know our liberty.   60
    Our life is short, and our days run
    As fast away as does the sun;
And, as a vapor or a drop of rain
Once lost, can ne'er be found again;
    So when or you or I are made
    A fable, song, or fleeting shade,
    All love, all liking, all delight
    Lies drowned with us in endless night.
Then while time serves, and we are but decaying,
Come, my Corinna, come, let's go a-Maying.   70

1. *Note that the poem alludes to pagan and to Christian elements, especially in the first three stanzas. How are these religious allusions used? Does the language introduce an ironic reversal of common Christian attitudes?* **2.** *Mayday celebrations reflect pagan spring fertility rites designed to ensure increase in crops, herds, and population. Trace the sexual aspects of the Mayday celebration in the poem. Is the poem a frank invitation to sexual union (like Marlowe's "The Passionate Shepherd to His Love"), or does the language of the last stanza raise some questions, by implication, about the claims of the flesh?*

Go, Lovely Rose!

EDMUND WALLER [1606–1687]

    Go, lovely rose!
Tell her that wastes her time and me
    That now she knows,
When I resemble° her to thee,   compare
How sweet and fair she seems to be.

Tell her that's young,
And shuns to have her graces spied,
    That hadst thou sprung
In deserts, where no men abide,
Thou must have uncommended died.

    Small is the worth
Of beauty from the light retired;
    Bid her come forth,
Suffer herself to be desired,
And not blush so to be admired.

    Then die! that she
The common fate of all things rare
    May read in thee;
How small a part of time they share
That are so wondrous sweet and fair!   20

Why So Pale and Wan, Fond Lover?

SIR JOHN SUCKLING [1609–1642]

Why so pale and wan, fond lover?
    Prithee, why so pale?
Will, when looking well can't move her,
    Looking ill prevail?
    Prithee, why so pale?

Why so dull and mute, young sinner?
    Prithee, why so mute?
Will, when speaking well can't win her,
    Saying nothing do 't?
    Prithee, why so mute?   10

Quit, quit, for shame; this will not move,
    This cannot take her.
If of herself she will not love,
    Nothing can make her:
    The devil take her!

Out upon It!

SIR JOHN SUCKLING [1609–1642]

Out upon it! I have loved
    Three whole days together;
And am like to love three more,
    If it prove fair weather.

Time shall molt away his wings,
    Ere he shall discover
In the whole wide world again
    Such a constant lover.

But the spite on 't is, no praise
    Is due at all to me: 10
Love with me had made no stays
    Had it any been but she.

Had it any been but she,
    And that very face,
There had been at least ere this
    A dozen dozen in her place.

1. *State the central irony in the poem.* **2.** *Is this poem a compliment to the speaker's beloved? Explain.*

To His Coy Mistress

ANDREW MARVELL [1621–1678]

    Had we but world enough, and time,
This coyness, lady, were no crime.
We would sit down, and think which way
To walk, and pass our long love's day.
Thou by the Indian Ganges' side
Shouldst rubies find; I by the tide
Of Humber would complain. I would
Love you ten years before the flood,
And you should, if you please, refuse
Till the conversion of the Jews.   10
My vegetable love should grow
Vaster than empires and more slow;

An hundred years should go to praise
Thine eyes, and on thy forehead gaze;
Two hundred to adore each breast,
But thirty thousand to the rest;
An age at least to every part,
And the last age should show your heart.
For, lady, you deserve this state,
Nor would I love at lower rate.   20
     But at my back I always hear
Time's wingèd chariot hurrying near;
And yonder all before us lie
Deserts of vast eternity.
Thy beauty shall no more be found,
Nor, in thy marble vault, shall sound
My echoing song; then worms shall try
That long-preserved virginity,
And your quaint honor turn to dust,
And into ashes all my lust: 30
The grave's a fine and private place,
But none, I think, do there embrace.
     Now therefore, while the youthful hue
Sits on thy skin like morning dew,
And while thy willing soul transpires
At every pore with instant fires,
Now let us sport us while we may,
And now, like amorous birds of prey,
Rather at once our time devour   39
Than languish in his slow-chapped° power.   slow-jawed
Let us roll all our strength and all
Our sweetness up into one ball,
And tear our pleasures with rough strife
Thorough the iron gates of life:
Thus, though we cannot make our sun
Stand still, yet we will make him run.

1. State the argument of the poem (see ll. 1–2, 21–22, 33–34). **2.** Compare the figures of speech in the first verse paragraph with those in the last. How do they differ? **3.** Characterize the attitude toward life recommended by the poet.

The Definition of Love

ANDREW MARVELL [1621–1678]

My love is of a birth as rare
As 'tis, for object, strange and high;

It was begotten by Despair
Upon Impossibility.

Magnanimous Despair alone
Could show me so divine a thing,
Where feeble Hope could ne'er have flown,
But vainly flapped its tinsel wing.

And yet I quickly might arrive
Where my extended soul is fixed;   10
But Fate does iron wedges drive,
And always crowds itself betwixt.

For Fate with jealous eyes does see
Two perfect loves, nor lets them close;°   unite
Their union would her ruin be,
And her tyrannic power depose.

And therefore her decrees of steel
Us as the distant poles have placed
(Though Love's whole world on us doth wheel),
Not by themselves to be embraced;   20

Unless the giddy heaven fall,
And earth some new convulsion tear,
And, us to join, the world should all
Be cramped into a planisphere.[1]

As lines, so loves, oblique may well
Themselves in every angle greet;
But ours, so truly parallel,
Though infinite, can never meet.

Therefore the love which us doth bind,
But Fate so enviously debars,   30
Is the conjunction of the mind,
And opposition of the stars.[2]

1. *How does the poet characterize his love at the outset? In what sense is such love "rare"?* **2.** *What role does "Fate" play in his relationship with his beloved?* **3.** *What kind of images does the poet use to describe the hopelessness of his ever being joined with his beloved?* **4.** *In view of Fate's opposition to a physical union, how does the speaker characterize his love at the end of the poem?*

---

1. A map of the globe projected on a plane.
2. In astronomical terms, conjunction is a configuration in which two celestial bodies have their least apparent separation; opposition is a configuration in which two celestial bodies are opposite (i.e., separated by 180°) from each other in the sky.

A Poison Tree

WILLIAM BLAKE [1757–1827]

I was angry with my friend:
I told my wrath, my wrath did end.
I was angry with my foe:
I told it not, my wrath did grow.

And I watered it in fears,
Night & morning with my tears;
And I sunnéd it with smiles,
And with soft deceitful wiles.

And it grew both day and night,
Till it bore an apple bright.   *10*
And my foe beheld it shine,
And he knew that it was mine,

And into my garden stole,
When the night had veil'd the pole;
In the morning glad I see
My foe outstretched beneath the tree.

1. *Is anything gained from the parallel readers might draw between this tree and the tree
in the Garden of Eden? Explain.* **2.** *Can you articulate what the "poison" is?* **3.** *Does
your own experience verify the first stanza of the poem?*

A Red, Red Rose

ROBERT BURNS [1759–1796]

O My Luve's like a red, red rose,
    That's newly sprung in June;
O My Luve's like the melodie
    That's sweetly played in tune.

As fair art thou, my bonnie lass,
    So deep in luve am I;
And I will luve thee still, my dear,
    Till a' the seas gang dry.

Till a' the seas gang dry, my dear,

And the rocks melt wi' the sun: 10
O I will love thee still, my dear,
    While the sands o' life shall run.

And fare thee weel, my only luve,
    And fare thee weel awhile!
And I will come again, my luve,
    Though it were ten thousand mile.

Soliloquy of the Spanish Cloister

ROBERT BROWNING   [1812–1889]

1
Gr-r-r—there go, my heart's abhorrence!
    Water your damned flower-pots, do!
If hate killed men, Brother Lawrence,
    God's blood, would not mine kill you!
What? your myrtle-bush wants trimming?
    Oh, that rose has prior claims—
Needs its leaden vase filled brimming?
    Hell dry you up with its flames!

2
At the meal we sit together: 9
    Salve tibi!° I must hear   *Hail to thee!*
Wise talk of the kind of weather,
    Sort of season, time of year:
Not a plenteous cork-crop: scarcely
    Dare we hope oak-galls, [1] *I doubt:*
What's the Latin name for "parsley"?
    What's the Greek name for Swine's Snout?

3
Whew! We'll have our platter burnished,
    Laid with care on our own shelf!
With a fire-new spoon we're furnished,
    And a goblet for ourself,   20
Rinsed like something sacrificial
    Ere 'tis fit to touch our chaps—
Marked with L for our initial!
    (He-he! There his lily snaps!)

---

1.   Abnormal outgrowths on oak trees, used in the tanning process.

4

Saint, forsooth! While brown Dolores
    Squats outside the Convent bank
With Sanchicha, telling stories,
    Steeping tresses in the tank,
Blue-black, lustrous, thick like horsehairs,
    —Can't I see his dead eye glow,   *30*
Bright as 'twere a Barbary corsair's? [2]
    (That is, if he'd let it show!)

5

When he finishes refection,°   *dinner*
    Knife and fork he never lays
Cross-wise, to my recollection,
    As do I, in Jesu's praise.
I the Trinity illustrate,
    Drinking watered orange-pulp—
In three sips the Arian [3] frustrate;
    While he drains his at one gulp.   *40*

6

Oh, those melons? If he's able
    We're to have a feast! so nice!
One goes to the Abbot's table,
    All of us get each a slice.
How go on your flowers? None double?
    Not one fruit-sort can you spy?
Strange! And I, too, at such trouble,
    Keep them close-nipped on the sly!

7

There's a great text in Galatians, [4]
    Once you trip on it, entails   *50*
Twenty-nine distinct damnations,
    One sure, if another fails:
If I trip him just a-dying,
    Sure of heaven as sure can be,
Spin him around and send him flying
    Off to hell, a Manichee? [5]

8

Or, my scrofulous French novel
    On grey paper with blunt type!

---

2. North African pirates, renowned for ferocity and lust.
3. Followers of the heretic Arius (256–336) who denied the doctrine of the Trinity.
4. This probably refers to Galatians 5:15–23 where St. Paul lists a number of "works of the flesh" that lead to damnation.
5. A believer in the Manichean heresy, which held that the world was ruled by two equally strong forces—one good, one evil.

Simply glance at it, you grovel
    Hand and foot in Belial's[6] gripe: 60
If I double down its pages
    At the woeful sixteenth print,
When he gathers his greengages,
    Ope a sieve and slip it in't?

9

Or, there's Satan! one might venture
    Pledge one's soul to him, yet leave
Such a flaw in the indenture
    As he'd miss till, past retrieve,
Blasted lay that rose-acacia
    We're so proud of! *Hy, Zy, Hine* [7] . . .   70
'St, there's vespers! *Plena gratiâ*
    Ave, Virgo! [8] Gr-r-r—you swine!

1. *Characterize the speaker of this dramatic monologue.* **2.** *Is it possible to characterize Brother Lawrence as well? Can you suggest reasons for the speaker's hatred?* **3.** *Show how the speaker, in his own imprecations and actions, specifically violates each part of the threefold monastic vow of poverty, chastity, and obedience. (See stanzas 3, 4, and 6.)*

Dover Beach*

MATTHEW ARNOLD [1822–1888]

The sea is calm tonight.
The tide is full, the moon lies fair
Upon the straits; on the French coast the light
Gleams and is gone; the cliffs of England stand,
Glimmering and vast, out in the tranquil bay.
Come to the window, sweet is the night-air!
Only, from the long line of spray
Where the sea meets the moon-blanched land,
Listen! you hear the grating roar
Of pebbles which the waves draw back, and fling,   10
At their return, up the high strand,

---

6. One of the names of the devil.
7. Possibly the beginning of a conjuration of the devil; possibly a response to the ringing of the bells that signal vespers.
8. Hail Virgin, full of grace.

---

*This poem is considered in detail in the essay "Three Critical Approaches: Formalist, Sociological, Psychoanalytic" at the end of the book.

Begin, and cease, and then again begin,
With tremulous cadence slow, and bring
The eternal note of sadness in.

Sophocles long ago
Heard it on the Aegean, and it brought
Into his mind the turbid ebb and flow
Of human misery; we
Find also in the sound a thought,
Hearing it by this distant northern sea.   20
The Sea of Faith
Was once, too, at the full, and round earth's shore
Lay like the folds of a bright girdle furled.
But now I only hear
Its melancholy, long, withdrawing roar,
Retreating, to the breath
Of the night-wind, down the vast edges drear
And naked shingles° of the world.   *pebble beaches*

Ah, love, let us be true
To one another! for the world, which seems   30
To lie before us like a land of dreams,
So various, so beautiful, so new,
Hath really neither joy, nor love, nor light,
Nor certitude, nor peace, nor help for pain;
And we are here as on a darkling plain
Swept with confused alarms of struggle and flight,
Where ignorant armies clash by night.

from

Modern Love

GEORGE MEREDITH   [1828–1909]

17
At dinner, she is hostess, I am host.
Went the feast ever cheerfuller? She keeps
The Topic over intellectual deeps
In buoyancy afloat. They see no ghost.
With sparkling surface-eyes we ply the ball:
It is in truth a most contagious game:
HIDING THE SKELETON, shall be its name.
Such play as this the devils might appall!
But here's the greater wonder: in that we,

Enamored of an acting naught can tire,   *10*
Each other, like true hypocrites, admire;
Warm-lighted looks, Love's ephemeridae,°   *short-lived insects*
Shoot gayly o'er the dishes and the wine.
We waken envy of our happy lot.
Fast, sweet, and golden, shows the marriage knot.
Dear guests, you now have seen Love's corpse-light¹ shine.

1. What, precisely, is "Love's corpse-light" (l. 16) a metaphor for in this poem? **2.** *Is the "marriage knot" really "fast, sweet, and golden" (l. 15)? Explain.*

Mine Enemy Is Growing Old

EMILY DICKINSON [1830–1886]

Mine Enemy is growing old—
I have at last Revenge—
The Palate of the Hate departs—
If any would avenge

Let him be quick—the Viand flits—
It is a faded Meat—
Anger as soon as fed is dead—
'Tis starving makes it fat—

1. Explain the paradox contained in the last two lines.

To Phoebe

W. S. GILBERT [1836–1911]

"Gentle, modest little flower
    Sweet epitome of May
Love me but for half-an-hour,
    Love me, love me, little fay."

---

1.   I.e., corpse-candle, a soft light which, when seen in churchyards, portends a funeral.

Sentences so fiercely flaming
    In your tiny shell-like ear,
I should always be exclaiming
    If I loved you, PHOEBE dear!

"Smiles that thrill from any distance
    Shed upon me while I sing!   10
Please ecstaticize existence,
    Love me, oh, thou fairy thing!"
Words like these, outpouring sadly,
    You'd perpetually hear,
If I loved you, fondly, madly;—
    But I do not, PHOEBE dear!

The Windhover[1]

TO CHRIST OUR LORD

GERARD MANLEY HOPKINS [1844–1889]

I caught this morning morning's minion,° king-   *favorite*
    dom of daylight's dauphin,[2] dapple-dawn-drawn Falcon, in his riding
    Of the rolling level underneath him steady air, and striding
High there, how he rung upon the rein of a wimpling° wing   *rippling*
In his ecstasy! then off, off forth on swing,
    As a skate's heel sweeps smooth on a bow-bend: the hurl and gliding
    Rebuffed the big wind. My heart in hiding
Stirred for a bird,—the achieve of, the mastery of the thing!

Brute beauty and valour and act, oh, air, pride, plume, here
    Buckle! AND the fire that breaks from thee then, a billion   10
Times told lovelier, more dangerous, O my chevalier!

    No wonder of it: shéer plód makes plough down sillion[3]
Shine, and blue-bleak embers, ah my dear,
    Fall, gall themselves, and gash gold-vermilion.

1. *Although the metrical quality of this poem is unique to Hopkins, it is structured as a sonnet. Describe the function of each of its parts—that is, the octave and each of the three-line divisions of the sestet.*   **2.** *The poem expresses a love of God. On what is that*

---

1.   A small hawk, so called because it is able to hover in the wind.
2.   Heir to kingly splendor.
3.   The ridge between ploughed furrows.

love, or awe, of God based? **3.** *Do the sound patterns of the poem convey emotional intensity? Explain.* **4.** *The word Buckle in line 10 may mean "collapse" or "join." How do you read it? Explain.*

Pied Beauty

GERARD MANLEY HOPKINS [1844–1889]

Glory be to God for dappled things—
    For skies of couple-colour as a brinded° cow;   *brindled*
        For rose-moles all in stipple upon trout that swim;
Fresh-firecoal chestnut-falls,[1] finches' wings;
    Landscape plotted and pieced[2]—fold, fallow, and plough
        And all trades, their gear and tackle, and trim.°   *equipment*
All things counter,° original, spare, strange;   *contrasted*
    Whatever is fickle, freckled (who knows how?)
        With swift, slow; sweet, sour; adazzle, dim;
He fathers-forth whose beauty is past change: *10*
        Praise him.

The Harlot's House

OSCAR WILDE [1854–1900]

We caught the tread of dancing feet,
We loitered down the moonlit street,
And stopped beneath the harlot's house.

Inside, above the din and fray,
We heard the loud musicians play
The "Treues Liebes Herz" of Strauss.[3]

Like strange mechanical grotesques,
Making fantastic arabesques,
The shadows raced across the blind.

---

1. Fallen chestnuts, with the outer husks removed, colored like fresh fire coal.
2. Reference to the variegated pattern of land put to different uses.

---

3. "True Love's Heart," a waltz by Strauss.

We watched the ghostly dancers spin   10
To sound of horn and violin,
Like black leaves wheeling in the wind.

Like wire-pulled automatons,
Slim silhouetted skeletons
Went sidling through the slow quadrille.

They took each other by the hand,
And danced a stately saraband;
Their laughter echoed thin and shrill.

Sometimes a clockwork puppet pressed
A phantom lover to her breast,   20
Sometimes they seemed to try to sing.

Sometimes a horrible marionette
Came out, and smoked its cigarette
Upon the steps like a live thing.

Then, turning to my love, I said,
"The dead are dancing with the dead,
The dust is whirling with the dust."

But she—she heard the violin,
And left my side, and entered in:
Love passed into the house of lust.   30

Then suddenly the tune went false,
The dancers wearied of the waltz,
The shadows ceased to wheel and whirl.

And down the long and silent street,
The dawn, with silver-sandaled feet,
Crept like a frightened girl.

The Silken Tent

ROBERT FROST [1874–1963]

She is as in a field a silken tent
At midday when a sunny summer breeze
Has dried the dew and all its ropes relent,
So that in guys it gently sways at ease,

And its supporting central cedar pole,
That is its pinnacle to heavenward
And signifies the sureness of the soul,
Seems to owe naught to any single cord,
But strictly held by none, is loosely bound   10
By countless silken ties of love and thought
To everything on earth the compass round,
And only by one's going slightly taut
In the capriciousness of summer air
Is of the slightest bondage made aware.

Fire and Ice

ROBERT FROST [1874–1963]

Some say the world will end in fire,
Some say in ice,
From what I've tasted of desire
I hold with those who favor fire.
But if it had to perish twice,
I think I know enough of hate
To say that for destruction ice
Is also great
And would suffice.

A Virginal

EZRA POUND [1885–1972]

No, no! Go from me. I have left her lately.
I will not spoil my sheath with lesser brightness,
For my surrounding air has a new lightness;
Slight are her arms, yet they have bound me straitly
And left me cloaked as with a gauze of æther;
As with sweet leaves; as with a subtle clearness.
Oh, I have picked up magic in her nearness
To sheathe me half in half the things that sheathe her.
No, no! Go from me. I have still the flavor,
Soft as spring wind that's come from birchen bowers.   10

Green come the shoots, aye April in the branches,
As winter's wound with her sleight hand she staunches,
Hath of the trees a likeness of the savor:
As white their bark, so white this lady's hours.

The Love Song of J. Alfred Prufrock

T. S. ELIOT   [1888–1965]

> *S'io credesse che mia risposta fosse*
> *A persona che mai tornasse al mondo,*
> *Questa fiamma staria senza piu scosse.*
> *Ma perciocche giammai di questo fondo*
> *Non torno vivo alcun, s'i'odo il vero,*
> *Senza tema d' infamia ti rispondo.*[1]

Let us go then, you and I,
When the evening is spread out against the sky
Like a patient etherized upon a table;
Let us go, through certain half-deserted streets,
The muttering retreats
Of restless nights in one-night cheap hotels
And sawdust restaurants with oyster shells:
Streets that follow like a tedious argument
Of insidious intent
To lead you to an overwhelming question . . .   10
Oh, do not ask, "What is it?"
Let us go and make our visit.

In the room the women come and go
Talking of Michelangelo.

The yellow fog that rubs its back upon the windowpanes,
The yellow smoke that rubs its muzzle on the windowpanes
Licked its tongue into the corners of the evening,
Lingered upon the pools that stand in drains,
Let fall upon its back the soot that falls from chimneys,
Slipped by the terrace, made a sudden leap,   20
And seeing that it was a soft October night,
Curled once about the house, and fell asleep.

---

1. From Dante, *Inferno*, XXVII, 61–66. The speaker is Guido de Montefeltro, who is imprisoned in a flame in the level of Hell reserved for false counselors. He tells Dante and Virgil, "If I thought my answer were given to one who might return to the world, this flame would stay without further movement. But since from this depth none has ever returned alive, if what I hear is true, I answer you without fear of infamy."

And indeed there will be time
For the yellow smoke that slides along the street,
Rubbing its back upon the windowpanes;
There will be time, there will be time
To prepare a face to meet the faces that you meet;
There will be time to murder and create,
And time for all the works and days of hands
That lift and drop a question on your plate;   30
Time for you and time for me,
And time yet for a hundred indecisions,
And for a hundred visions and revisions,
Before the taking of a toast and tea.

In the room the women come and go
Talking of Michelangelo.

And indeed there will be time
To wonder, "Do I dare?" and, "Do I dare?"
Time to turn back and descend the stair,
With a bald spot in the middle of my hair—   40
(They will say: "How his hair is growing thin!")
My morning coat, my collar mounting firmly to the chin,
My necktie rich and modest, but asserted by a simple pin—
(They will say: "But how his arms and legs are thin!")
Do I dare
Disturb the universe?
In a minute there is time
For decisions and revisions which a minute will reverse.

For I have known them all already, known them all—
Have known the evenings, mornings, afternoons,   50
I have measured out my life with coffee spoons;
I know the voices dying with a dying fall
Beneath the music from a farther room.
      So how should I presume?

And I have known the eyes already, known them all—
The eyes that fix you in a formulated phrase,
And when I am formulated, sprawling on a pin,
When I am pinned and wriggling on the wall,
Then how should I begin
To spit out all the butt-ends of my days and ways?   60
      And how should I presume?

And I have known the arms already, known them all—
Arms that are braceleted and white and bare
(But in the lamplight, downed with light brown hair!)
Is it perfume from a dress
That makes me so digress?

Arms that lie along a table, or wrap about a shawl.
    And should I then presume?
    And how should I begin?

                  .   .   .   .   .

Shall I say, I have gone at dusk through narrow streets   70
And watched the smoke that rises from the pipes
Of lonely men in shirt-sleeves, leaning out of windows? . . .

I should have been a pair of ragged claws
Scuttling across the floors of silent seas.

                  .   .   .   .   .

And the afternoon, the evening, sleeps so peacefully!
Smoothed by long fingers,
Asleep . . . tired . . . or it malingers,
Stretched on the floor, here beside you and me.
Should I, after tea and cakes and ices,
Have the strength to force the moment to its crisis?   80
But though I have wept and fasted, wept and prayed,
Though I have seen my head (grown slightly bald) brought in upon a platter,[2]
I am no prophet—and here's no great matter;
I have seen the moment of my greatness flicker,
And I have seen the eternal Footman hold my coat, and snicker,
And in short, I was afraid.

And would it have been worth it, after all,
After the cups, the marmalade, the tea,
Among the porcelain, among some talk of you and me,
Would it have been worth while,   90
To have bitten off the matter with a smile,
To have squeezed the universe into a ball
To roll it toward some overwhelming question,
To say: "I am Lazarus,[3] come from the dead,
Come back to tell you all, I shall tell you all"—
If one, settling a pillow by her head,
    Should say: "That is not what I meant at all.
    That is not it, at all."

And would it have been worth it, after all,
Would it have been worth while,   100
After the sunsets and the dooryards and the sprinkled streets,
After the novels, after the teacups, after the skirts that trail along the floor—
And this, and so much more?—

---

2. Like the head of John the Baptist. See Matthew 14:3–12.
3. See John 11:1–14 and Luke 16:19–26.

It is impossible to say just what I mean!
But as if a magic lantern threw the nerves in patterns on a screen:
Would it have been worth while
If one, settling a pillow or throwing off a shawl,
And turning toward the window, should say:
    "That is not it at all,
    That is not what I meant, at all."   110

                   . . . . . .

No! I am not Prince Hamlet, nor was meant to be;
Am an attendant lord, one that will do
To swell a progress,° start a scene or two,   *state journey*
Advise the prince; no doubt, an easy tool,
Deferential, glad to be of use,
Politic, cautious, and meticulous;
Full of high sentence,° but a bit obtuse;   *sententiousness*
At times, indeed, almost ridiculous—
Almost, at times, the Fool.

I grow old . . . I grow old . . .   120
I shall wear the bottoms of my trousers rolled.°   *cuffed*

Shall I part my hair behind? Do I dare to eat a peach?
I shall wear white flannel trousers, and walk upon the beach.
I have heard the mermaids singing, each to each.

I do not think that they will sing to me.

I have seen them riding seaward on the waves
Combing the white hair of the waves blown back
When the wind blows the water white and black.

We have lingered in the chambers of the sea
By sea-girls wreathed with seaweed red and brown   130
Till human voices wake us, and we drown.

1. This poem may be understood as a stream of consciousness passing through the mind of Prufrock. The "you and I" of line 1 may be different aspects of his personality. Or perhaps the "you and I" is parallel to Guido who speaks the epigraph and Dante to whom he tells the story that resulted in his damnation—hence, "you" is the reader and "I" is Prufrock. Apparently Prufrock is on his way to a tea and is pondering his relationship with a certain lady. The poem is disjointed because it proceeds by psychological rather than logical stages. To what social class does Prufrock belong? How does Prufrock respond to the attitudes and values of his class?   **2.** Line 92 provides a good example of literary allusion (see the last stanza of Marvell, "To His Coy Mistress," especially ll. 41–42). How does an awareness of the allusion contribute to the reader's response to the stanza here?   **3.** What might the song of the mermaids (l. 124) signify, and why does Prufrock think they will not sing to him (l. 125)?   **4.** T. S. Eliot once said that some poetry "can communicate without being understood." Is this such a poem?

if everything happens
that can't be done

E. E. CUMMINGS   [1894–1962]

if everything happens that can't be done
(and anything's righter
than books
could plan)
the stupidest teacher will almost guess
(with a run
skip
around we go yes)
there's nothing as something as one

one hasn't a why or because or although   10
(and buds know better
than books
don't grow)
one's anything old being everything new
(with a what
which
around we come who)
one's everyanything so

so world is a leaf so tree is a bough
(and birds sing sweeter   20
than books
tell how)
so here is away and so your is a my
(with a down
up
around again fly)
forever was never till now

now i love you and you love me
(and books are shuter
than books   30
can be)
and deep in the high that does nothing but fall
(with a shout
each
around we go all)
there's somebody calling who's we

we're anything brighter than even the sun

(we're everything greater
than books
might mean)   40
we're everyanything more than believe
(with a spin
leap
alive we're alive)
we're wonderful one times one

1. What fundamental contrast is stated by the poem?   **2.** Lines 2–4 and 6–8 of each stanza could be printed as single lines. Why do you think Cummings decided to print them as he does?   **3.** What common attitude toward lovers is expressed by the last lines of the stanzas?   **4.** Is the poem free verse or formal verse?

from
Five Songs

W. H. AUDEN [1907–1973]

That night when joy began
Our narrowest veins to flush,
We waited for the flash
Of morning's levelled gun.

But morning let us pass,
And day by day relief
Outgrew his nervous laugh,
Grows credulous of peace.

As mile by mile is seen
No trespasser's reproach,   10
And love's best glasses reach
No fields but are his own.

1. Describe the sound relationships among the last words in the lines of each stanza.   **2.** What is the controlling metaphor in the poem? Is it appropriate for a love poem?   **3.** If it were suggested that the poem describes a homosexual relationship, would your response to the poem's figurative language change?

To a Child Born in Time of Small War

HELEN SORRELLS [b. 1908]

Child, you were conceived in my upstairs room,
my girlhood all around. Later I spent
nights there alone imploring the traitor moon
to keep me childless still. I never meant
to bear you in this year of discontent.
Yet you were there in your appointed place,
remnant of leaving, of a sacrament.
Child, if I loved you then, it was to trace
on a cold sheet your likeness to his absent face.

In May we were still alone. That month your life   10
stirred in my dark, as if my body's core
grew quick with wings. I turned away, more wife
than mother still, unwilling to explore
the fact of you. There was an orient shore,
a tide of hurt, that held my heart and mind.
It was as if you lived behind a door
I was afraid to open, lest you bind
my breaking. Lost in loss, I was not yours to find.

I swelled with summer. You were hard and strong,
making me know you were there. When the mail   20
brought me no letter, and the time was long
between the war's slow gains, and love seemed frail,
I fought you. You were error, judgment, jail.
Without you, there were ways I, too, could fight
a war. Trapped in your growing, I would rail
against your grotesque carriage, swollen, tight.
I would have left you, and I did in dreams of flight.

Discipline of the seasons brought me round.
Earth comes to term and so, in time, did we.
You are a living thing of sight and sound.   30
Nothing of you is his, you are all of me:
your sex, gray eye, the struggle to be free
that made your birth like death, but I awake
for that caught air, your cry. I try to see,
but cannot, the same lift his eyebrows take.
Child, if I love you now, it is for your own sake.

The Dover Bitch

A CRITICISM OF LIFE

ANTHONY HECHT [b. 1922]

So there stood Matthew Arnold and this girl
With the cliffs of England crumbling away behind them,
And he said to her, "Try to be true to me,
And I'll do the same for you, for things are bad
All over, etc., etc."
Well now, I knew this girl. It's true she had read
Sophocles in a fairly good translation
And caught that bitter allusion to the sea,
But all the time he was talking she had in mind
The notion of what his whiskers would feel like   10
On the back of her neck. She told me later on
That after a while she got to looking out
At the lights across the channel, and really felt sad,
Thinking of all the wine and enormous beds
And blandishments in French and the perfumes.
And then she got really angry. To have been brought
All the way down from London, and then be addressed
As sort of a mournful cosmic last resort
Is really tough on a girl, and she was pretty.
Anyway, she watched him pace the room   20
And finger his watch-chain and seem to sweat a bit,
And then she said one or two unprintable things.
But you mustn't judge her by that. What I mean to say is,
She's really all right. I still see her once in a while
And she always treats me right. We have a drink
And I give her a good time, and perhaps it's a year
Before I see her again, but there she is,
Running to fat, but dependable as they come,
And sometimes I bring her a bottle of *Nuit d'Amour.*

1. *This poem is a response to Matthew Arnold's "Dover Beach," which appears earlier in this section. What is the fundamental difference between the speaker's conception of love in Arnold's poem and the girl's conception of love as reported in this poem?* **2.** *Arnold's poem is often read as a pained response to the breakdown of religious tradition and social and political order in the mid-nineteenth century. Is this poem, in contrast, optimistic? Is the relationship between the speaker and the girl at the end of the poem admirable? Explain.* **3.** *Do you suppose Hecht was moved to write this poem out of admiration for "Dover Beach"? Explain.*

The Ache of Marriage

DENISE LEVERTOV [b. 1923]

The ache of marriage:

thigh and tongue, beloved,
are heavy with it,
it throbs in the teeth

We look for communion
and are turned away, beloved,
each and each

It is leviathan and we
in its belly
looking for joy, some joy   10
not to be known outside it

two by two in the ark of
the ache of it.

Love Song: I and Thou

ALAN DUGAN [b. 1923]

Nothing is plumb, level or square:
    the studs are bowed, the joists
are shaky by nature, no piece fits
    any other piece without a gap
or pinch, and bent nails
    dance all over the surfacing
like maggots. By Christ
    I am no carpenter. I built
the roof for myself, the walls
    for myself, the floors   10
for myself, and got
    hung up in it myself. I
danced with a purple thumb
    at this house-warming, drunk
with my prime whiskey: rage.
    Oh I spat rage's nails

into the frame-up of my work:
    it held. It settled plumb,
level, solid, square and true
    for that great moment. Then   20
it screamed and went on through,
    skewing as wrong the other way.
God damned it. This is hell,
    but I planned it, I sawed it,
I nailed it, and I
    will live in it until it kills me.
I can nail my left palm
    to the left-hand cross-piece but
I can't do everything myself.
    I need a hand to nail the right,   30
a help, a love, a you, a wife.

Unwanted

EDWARD FIELD [b. 1924]

The poster with my picture on it
Is hanging on the bulletin board in the Post Office.

I stand by it hoping to be recognized
Posing first full face and then profile

But everybody passes by and I have to admit
The photograph was taken some years ago.

I was unwanted then and I'm unwanted now
Ah guess ah'll go up echo mountain and crah.

I wish someone would find my fingerprints somewhere
Maybe on a corpse and say, You're it.   10

Description: Male, or reasonably so
White, but not lily-white and usually deep-red

Thirty-fivish, and looks it lately
Five-feet-nine and one-hundred-thirty pounds: no physique

Black hair going gray, hairline receding fast
What used to be curly, now fuzzy

Brown eyes starey under beetling brow
Mole on chin, probably will become a wen

It is perfectly obvious that he was not popular at school
No good at baseball, and wet his bed.   *20*

His aliases tell his history: Dumbell, Good-for-nothing,
Jewboy, Fieldinsky, Skinny, Fierce Face, Greaseball, Sissy.

Warning: This man is not dangerous, answers to any name
Responds to love, don't call him or he will come.

Regret

VASSAR MILLER [b. 1924]

Had you come to me
as I to you once
with naked asking,
I should have let you.
We should have slept,
two arrows bound together
wounding no one.
Instead, you chose to lie
set to the bow of your own darkness.

A Marriage

ROBERT CREELEY   [b. 1926]

The first retainer
he gave to her
was a golden
wedding ring.

The second—late at night
he woke up,
leaned over on an elbow,
and kissed her.

The third and the last—
he died with
and gave up loving
and lived with her.

10

The Farmer's Wife

ANNE SEXTON [b. 1928]

From the hodge porridge
of their country lust,
their local life in Illinois,
where all their acres look
like a sprouting broom factory,
they name just ten years now
that she has been his habit;
as again tonight he'll say
honey bunch let's go
and she will not say how there   10
must be more to living
than this brief bright bridge
of the raucous bed or even
the slow braille touch of him
like a heavy god grown light,
that old pantomime of love
that she wants although
it leaves her still alone,
built back again at last,
mind's apart from him, living   20
her own self in her own words
and hating the sweat of the house
they keep when they finally lie
each in separate dreams
and then how she watches him,
still strong in the blowzy bag
of his usual sleep while
her young years bungle past
their same marriage bed
and she wishes him cripple, or poet,   30
or even lonely, or sometimes,
better, my lover, dead.

Living in Sin

ADRIENNE RICH [b. 1929]

She had thought the studio would keep itself;
no dust upon the furniture of love.
Half heresy, to wish the taps less vocal,
the panes relieved of grime. A plate of pears,
a piano with a Persian shawl, a cat
stalking the picturesque amusing mouse
had risen at his urging.
Not that at five each separate stair would writhe
under the milkman's tramp; that morning light
so coldly would delineate the scraps   10
of last night's cheese and three sepulchral bottles;
that on the kitchen shelf among the saucers
a pair of beetle-eyes would fix her own—
Envoy from some village in the moldings . . .
Meanwhile, he, with a yawn,
sounded a dozen notes upon the keyboard,
declared it out of tune, shrugged at the mirror,
rubbed at his beard, went out for cigarettes;
while she, jeered by the minor demons,
pulled back the sheets and made the bed and found   20
a towel to dust the table-top,
and let the coffee-pot boil over on the stove.
By evening she was back in love again,
though not so wholly but throughout the night
she woke sometimes to feel the daylight coming
like a relentless milkman up the stairs.

Daddy

SYLVIA PLATH [1932–1963]

You do not do, you do not do
Any more, black shoe
In which I have lived like a foot
For thirty years, poor and white,
Barely daring to breathe or Achoo.

Daddy, I have had to kill you,
You died before I had time——

Marble-heavy, a bag full of God,
Ghastly statue with one grey toe
Big as a Frisco seal

                                                 10

And a head in the freakish Atlantic
Where it pours bean green over blue
In the waters off beautiful Nauset.
I used to pray to recover you.
Ach, du.[1]

In the German tongue, in the Polish town
Scraped flat by the roller
Of wars, wars, wars.
But the name of the town is common.
My Polack friend   20

Says there are a dozen or two.
So I never could tell where you
Put your foot, your root,
I never could talk to you.
The tongue stuck in my jaw.

It stuck in a barb wire snare.
Ich, ich, ich, ich,[2]
I could hardly speak.
I thought every German was you.
And the language obscene   30

An engine, an engine
Chuffing me off like a Jew.
A Jew to Dachau, Auschwitz, Belsen.
I began to talk like a Jew.
I think I may well be a Jew.

The snows of the Tyrol, the clear beer of Vienna
Are not very pure or true.
With my gypsy ancestress and my weird luck
And my Taroc pack and my Taroc pack
I may be a bit of a Jew.   40

I have always been scared of *you,*
With your Luftwaffe,[3] your gobbledygoo.
And your neat moustache
And your Aryan eye, bright blue.
Panzer-man,[4] panzer-man, O You——

---

1. German for "Ah, you."
2. German for "I, I, I, I."
3. Name of the German air force during World War II.
4. Panzer refers to German armored divisions during World War II.

Not God but a swastika
So black no sky could squeak through.
Every woman adores a Fascist,
The boot in the face, the brute
Brute heart of a brute like you.   50

You stand at the blackboard, daddy,
In the picture I have of you,
A cleft in your chin instead of your foot
But no less a devil for that, no not
Any less the black man who

Bit my pretty red heart in two.
I was ten when they buried you.
At twenty I tried to die
And get back, back, back to you.   60
I thought even the bones would do.

But they pulled me out of the sack,
And they stuck me together with glue.
And then I knew what to do.
I made a model of you,
A man in black with a Meinkampf⁵ look

And a love of the rack and the screw.
And I said I do, I do.
So daddy, I'm finally through.
The black telephone's off at the root,
The voices just can't worm through.   70

If I've killed one man, I've killed two——
The vampire who said he was you
And drank my blood for a year,
Seven years, if you want to know.
Daddy, you can lie back now.

There's a stake in your fat black heart
And the villagers never liked you.
They are dancing and stamping on you.
They always *knew* it was you.
Daddy, daddy, you bastard, I'm through.   80

1. *What sort of verse is suggested by the peculiar structure, idiosyncratic rhyme, unusual words (such as achoo, gobbledygoo), and repetitions in the poem? What emotional associations does the title "Daddy" possess? Are those associations reinforced or contradicted by the poem?* **2.** *How do the allusions to Nazism function in the poem?* **3.** *Does the poem exhibit the speaker's love for her father or her hatred for*

5.   My Battle, the title of Adolf Hitler's political autobiography.

him? Explain.   **4.** *What sort of man does the speaker marry (see stanzas 13 and 14)?*   **5.** *How does the speaker characterize her husband and her father in the last two stanzas? Might the "Daddy" of the last line of the poem refer to something more than the speaker's father? Explain.*

The Accident Has Occurred

MARGARET ATWOOD [b. 1939]

The accident has occurred,
the ship has broken, the motor
of the car has failed, we have been
separated from the others,
we are alone in the sand, the ocean,
the frozen snow

I remember what I have to do
in order to stay alive,
I take stock of our belongings
most of them useless   10

I know I should be digging shelters,
killing seabirds and making
clothes from their feathers,
cutting the rinds from cacti, chewing
roots for water, scraping through
the ice for treebark, for moss

but I rest here without power
to save myself, tasting
salt in my mouth, the fact that
you won't save me   20

watching the mirage of us
hands locked, smiling,
as it fades into the white desert.

I touch you, straighten the sheet, you turn over
in the bed, tender
sun comes through the curtains

Which of us will survive
which of us will survive the other

The Cinema Show

GENESIS [1]

Home from work our Juliet
Clears her morning meal.
She dabs her skin with pretty smells
Concealing to appeal.
I will make my bed,
She said, but turned to go.
Can she be late for her cinema show?

Romeo locks his basement flat,
And scurries up the stair.
With head held high and floral tie,   10
A weekend millionaire.
I will make my bed
With her tonight, he cries.
Can he fail, armed with his chocolate surprise?

Take a little trip back with father Tiresias,[2]
Listen to the old one speak of all he has lived through.
I have crossed between the poles, for me there's no mystery.
Once a man, like the sea I raged,
Once a woman, like the earth I gave.
There is in fact more earth than sea.   20

---

1. A musical group comprised of Mike Rutherford, Tony Banks, Phil Collins, Steve Hackett, and Peter Gabriel (the last is no longer a member of the group).
2. In Greek myth, a blind seer who had been both a man and a woman and who was able to foresee the future.

love and hate

Young Couple, 1917 by Emil Nolde

DRAMA

Othello

WILLIAM SHAKESPEARE [1564–1616]

CHARACTERS

Duke of Venice
Brabantio, *a Senator*
Senators
Gratiano, *Brother to Brabantio*
Lodovico, *Kinsman to Brabantio*
Othello, *a noble Moor; in the service of the Venetian State*
Cassio, *his Lieutenant*
Iago, *his Ancient*
Roderigo, *a Venetian Gentleman*
Montano, *Othello's predecessor in the Government of Cyprus*
Clown, *Servant to Othello*
Desdemona, *Daughter to Brabantio, and Wife to Othello*
Emilia, *Wife to Iago*
Bianca, *Mistress to Cassio*
Sailor, Officers, Gentlemen, Messengers, Musicians, Heralds, Attendants

SCENE. *For the first Act, in Venice; during the rest of the Play, at a Sea-port in Cyprus*

Act I

SCENE 1. *Venice. A Street.*

(*Enter Roderigo and Iago.*)

Roderigo. Tush! Never tell me; I take it much unkindly
That thou, Iago, who hast had my purse

As if the strings were thine, shouldst know of this.[1]

Iago. 'Sblood,[2] but you will not hear me:
If ever I did dream of such a matter,
Abhor me.

Roderigo. Thou told'st me thou didst hold him[3] in thy hate.

Iago. Despise me if I do not. Three great ones of the city,
In personal suit to make me his lieutenant,
Off-capp'd[4] to him; and, by the faith of man,   10
I know my price, I am worth no worse a place;
But he, as loving his own pride and purposes,
Evades them, with a bombast circumstance[5]
Horribly stuff'd with epithets of war;
And, in conclusion,
Nonsuits[6] my mediators;[7] for, 'Certes,'[8] says he,
'I have already chosen my officer.'
And what was he?
Forsooth, a great arithmetician,
One Michael Cassio, A Florentine,   20
A fellow almost damn'd in a fair wife;[9]
That never set a squadron in the field,
Nor the division of a battle knows
More than a spinster; unless[10] the bookish theoric,[11]
Wherein the toged consuls can propose
As masterly as he: mere prattle, without practice,
Is all his soldiership. But he, sir, had the election;
And I—of whom his eyes had seen the proof
At Rhodes, at Cyprus, and on other grounds
Christian and heathen—must be be-lee'd[12] and calm'd   30
By debitor and creditor; this counter-caster,[13]
He, in good time, must his lieutenant be,
And I—God bless the mark!—his Moorship's ancient.[14]

Roderigo. By heaven, I rather would have been his hangman.

Iago. Why, there's no remedy: 'tis the curse of the service,
Preferment goes by letter and affection,
Not by the old gradation,[15] where each second
Stood heir to the first. Now, sir, be judge yourself,
Whe'r[16] I in any just term am affin'd[17]
To love the Moor.

---

1. *I.e.,* Othello's successful courtship of Desdemona.   2. By God's blood.   3. *I.e.,* Othello.   4. Took off their caps.   5. Pompous wordiness, circumlocution. 6. Turns down.   7. Spokesmen.   8. In truth.   9. A much debated phrase. In the Italian source the Captain (*i.e.,* Cassio) was married, and it may be that Shakespeare originally intended Bianca to be Cassio's wife but later changed his mind and failed to alter the phrase here accordingly. Or perhaps Iago simply sneers at Cassio as a notorious ladies' man.   10. Except. 11. Theory.   12. Left without wind for my sails.   13. Bookkeeper (*cf.* "arithmetician" above).   14. Ensign (but Iago's position in the play seems to be that of Othello's aide-de-camp).   15. Seniority.   16. Whether.   17. Obliged.

Roderigo.   I would not follow him then.   40

Iago.   O! sir, content you;
    I follow him to serve my turn upon him;
    We cannot all be masters, nor all masters
    Cannot be truly follow'd. You shall mark
    Many a duteous and knee-crooking knave,
    That, doting on his own obsequious bondage,
    Wears out his time, much like his master's ass,
    For nought but provender, and when he's old, cashier'd;
    Whip me such honest knaves. Others there are
    Who, trimm'd in forms and visages of duty,   50
    Keep yet their hearts attending on themselves,
    And, throwing but shows of service on their lords,
    Do well thrive by them, and when they have lin'd their coats
    Do themselves homage: these fellows have some soul;
    And such a one do I profess myself. For, sir,
    It is as sure as you are Roderigo,
    Were I the Moor, I would not be Iago:
    In following him, I follow but myself;
    Heaven is my judge, not I for love and duty,
    But seeming so, for my peculiar end: 60
    For when my outward action doth demonstrate
    The native act and figure of my heart
    In compliment extern,[18] 'tis not long after
    But I will wear my heart upon my sleeve
    For daws to peck at: I am not what I am.

Roderigo.   What a full fortune does the thick-lips owe,[19]
    If he can carry 't thus!

Iago.   Call up her father;
    Rouse him, make after him, poison his delight,
    Proclaim him in the streets, incense her kinsmen,
    And, though he in a fertile climate dwell,[20]   70
    Plague him with flies; though that his joy be joy,
    Yet throw such changes of vexation on 't
    As it may lose some colour.

Roderigo.   Here is her father's house; I'll call aloud.

Iago.   Do; with like timorous[21] accent and dire yell
    As when, by night and negligence, the fire
    Is spied in populous cities.

Roderigo.   What, ho! Brabantio: Signior Brabantio, ho!

Iago.   Awake! what, ho! Brabantio! thieves! thieves! thieves!
    Look to your house, your daughter, and your bags!   80
    Thieves! thieves!

---

18. External show.   19. Own.   20. *I.e.*, is fortunate.   21. Frightening.

(*Enter Brabantio, above, at a window.*)

Brabantio.   What is the reason of this terrible summons?
   What is the matter there?
Roderigo.   Signior, is all your family within?
Iago.   Are your doors lock'd?
Brabantio.   Why? wherefore ask you this?
Iago.   'Zounds![22] sir, you're robb'd; for shame, put on your gown;
   Your heart is burst, you have lost half your soul;
   Even now, now, very now, an old black ram
   Is tupping[23] your white ewe. Arise, arise!
   Awake the snorting[24] citizens with the bell,   90
   Or else the devil will make a grandsire of you.
   Arise, I say.
Brabantio.   What! have you lost your wits?
Roderigo.   Most reverend signior, do you know my voice?
Brabantio.   Not I, what are you?
Roderigo.   My name is Roderigo.
Brabantio.   The worser welcome:
   I have charg'd thee not to haunt about my doors:
   In honest plainness thou hast heard me say
   My daughter is not for thee; and now, in madness,
   Being full of supper and distempering draughts,
   Upon malicious knavery dost thou come   100
   To start my quiet.
Roderigo.   Sir, sir, sir!
Brabantio.   But thou must needs be sure
   My spirit and my place[25] have in them power
   To make this bitter to thee.
Roderigo.   Patience, good sir.
Brabantio.   What tell'st thou me of robbing? this is Venice;
   My house is not a grange.[26]
Roderigo.   Most grave Brabantio,
   In simple and pure soul I come to you.
Iago.   'Zounds! sir; you are one of those that will not serve God if the devil bid
   you. Because we come to do you service and you think we are ruffians,
   you'll have your daughter covered with a Barbary horse; you'll have your
   nephews neigh to you; you'll have coursers for cousins and gennets[27] for
   germans.[28]
Brabantio.   What profane wretch art thou?
Iago.   I am one, sir, that comes to tell you, your daughter and the Moor are
   now making the beast with two backs.

---

22. By God's wounds.   23. Copulating.   24. Snoring.   25. Position.
26. Isolated farm house.   27. Spanish horses.   28. Blood relations.

Brabantio.   Thou art a villain.

Iago.   You are—a senator.

Brabantio.   This thou shalt answer; I know thee, Roderigo.

Roderigo.   Sir, I will answer any thing. But, I beseech you,
    If 't be your pleasure and most wise consent,—
    As partly, I find, it is,—that your fair daughter,   *120*
    At this odd-even[29] and dull watch o' the night,
    Transported with no worse nor better guard
    But with a knave of common hire, a gondolier,
    To the gross clasps of a lascivious Moor,—
    If this be known to you, and your allowance,[30]
    We then have done you bold and saucy wrongs;
    But if you know not this, my manners tell me
    We have your wrong rebuke. Do not believe
    That, from[31] the sense of all civility,
    I thus would play and trifle with your reverence: *130*
    Your daughter, if you have not given her leave,
    I say again, hath made a gross revolt;
    Tying her duty, beauty, wit and fortunes
    In[32] an extravagant[33] and wheeling stranger
    Of here and every where. Straight satisfy yourself:
    If she be in her chamber or your house,
    Let loose on me the justice of the state
    For thus deluding you.

Brabantio: Strike on the tinder, ho!
    Give me a taper! call up all my people!
    This accident[34] is not unlike my dream;   *140*
    Belief of it oppresses me already.
    Light, I say! light!   (*Exit, from above.*)

Iago.   Farewell, for I must leave you:
    It seems not meet nor wholesome to my place
    To be produc'd,[35] as, if I stay, I shall,
    Against the Moor; for I do know the state,
    However this may gall him with some check,[36]
    Cannot with safety cast him; for he's embark'd
    With such loud reason to the Cyprus wars,—
    Which even now stand in act,—that, for their souls,
    Another of his fathom[37] they have none,   *150*
    To lead their business; in which regard,
    Though I do hate him as I do hell-pains,
    Yet, for necessity of present life,

---

29. Between night and morning.   30. By your approval.   31. Away from.
32. To.   33. Expatriate.   34. Happening.   35. *I.e.*, as a witness.   36. Restraining adversity.   37. Caliber, ability.

I must show out a flag and sign of love,
Which is indeed but sign. That you shall surely find him,
Lead to the Sagittary³⁸ the raised search;
And there will I be with him. So, farewell.   (*Exit.*)

(*Enter below, Brabantio, and servants with torches.*)

Brabantio.   It is too true an evil: gone she is,
And what 's to come of my despised time
Is nought but bitterness. Now, Roderigo,   160
Where didst thou see her? O, unhappy girl!
With the Moor, sayst thou? Who would be a father!
How didst thou know 'twas she? O, she deceives me
Past thought. What said she to you? Get more tapers!
Raise all my kindred! Are they married, think you?
Roderigo.   Truly, I think they are.
Brabantio.   O heaven! How got she out? O treason of the blood:
Fathers, from hence trust not your daughters' minds
By what you see them act. Are there not charms
By which the property of youth and maidhood   170
May be abus'd? Have you not read, Roderigo,
Of some such thing?
Roderigo.   Yes, sir, I have indeed.
Brabantio.   Call up my brother. O! that you had had her.
Some one way, some another! Do you know
Where we may apprehend her and the Moor?
Roderigo.   I think I can discover him, if you please
To get good guard and go along with me.
Brabantio.   Pray you, lead on. At every house I'll call;
I may command at most. Get weapons, ho!
And raise some special officers of night.   180
On, good Roderigo; I'll deserve³⁹ your pains.   (*Exeunt.*)

SCENE 2.   *Another street.*

(*Enter Othello, Iago, and Attendants, with torches.*)

Iago.   Though in the trade of war I have slain men,
Yet do I hold it very stuff o' the conscience
To do no contriv'd murder: I lack iniquity
Sometimes to do me service. Nine or ten times
I had thought to have yerk'd⁴⁰ him here under the ribs.

---

38.   The name of an inn (?).   39.   *I.e.,* reward.   40.   Stabbed.

Othello. 'Tis better as it is.

Iago.   Nay, but he prated,
And spoke such scurvy and provoking terms
Against your honour
That, with the little godliness I have,
I did full hard forbear him. But, I pray, sir,   10
Are you fast married? Be assur'd of this,
That the magnifico[41] is much belov'd,
And hath in his effect a voice potential
As double[42] as the duke's; he will divorce you,
Or put upon you what restraint and grievance
The law—with all his might to enforce it on—
Will give him cable.[43]

Othello.   Let him do his spite:
My services which I have done the signiory[44]
Shall out-tongue his complaints. 'Tis yet to know,[45]
Which when I know that boasting is an honour   20
I shall promulgate, I fetch my life and being
From men of royal siege, and my demerits[46]
May speak unbonneted[47] to as proud a fortune
As this[48] that I have reach'd; for know, Iago,
But that I love the gentle Desdemona,
I would not my unhoused[49] free condition
Put into circumscription and confine
For the sea's worth. But, look! what lights come yond?

Iago.   Those are the raised[50] father and his friends:
You were best[51] go in.

Othello.   Not I; I must be found: 30
My parts, my title, and my perfect[52] soul
Shall manifest me rightly. Is it they?

Iago.   By Janus,[53] I think no.

(Enter Cassio and certain Officers, with torches.)

Othello.   The servants of the duke, and my lieutenant.
The goodness of the night upon you, friends!
What is the news?

Cassio.   The duke does greet you, general,
And he requires your haste-post-haste appearance,
Even on the instant.

---

41. One of the grandees, or rulers, of Venice; here, Brabantio.   42. Iago means that Brabantio's influence equals that of the Doge's, with his double vote.   43. *I.e.,* scope.
44. The Venetian government.   45. *I.e.,* the signiory does not as yet know.
46. Merits.   47. *I.e.,* as equals.   48. *I.e.,* that of Desdemona's family.   49. Unconfined.   50. Aroused.   51. Had better.   52. Untroubled by a bad conscience.
53. The two-faced Roman god of portals and doors and (hence) of beginnings and ends.

Othello.   What is the matter, think you?
Cassio.   Something from Cyprus, as I may divine.
   It is a business of some heat;⁵⁴ the galleys   40
   Have sent a dozen sequent⁵⁵ messengers
   This very night at one another's heels,
   And many of the consuls,⁵⁶ rais'd and met,
   Are at the duke's already. You have been hotly call'd for;
   When, being not at your lodging to be found,
   The senate hath sent about three several⁵⁷ quests
   To search you out.
Othello.   'Tis well I am found by you.
   I will but spend a word here in the house,
   And go with you.   *(Exit.)*
Cassio.   Ancient, what makes he here?
Iago.   Faith, he to-night hath boarded a land carrack;⁵⁸   50
   If it prove lawful prize, he's made for ever.
Cassio.   I do not understand.
Iago.   He's married.
Cassio.   To who?

(Re-enter Othello.)

Iago.   Marry,⁵⁹ to—Come, captain, will you go?
Othello.   Have with you.
Cassio.   Here comes another troop to seek for you.
Iago.   It is Brabantio. General, be advis'd;
   He comes to bad intent.

(Enter Brabantio, Roderigo, and Officers, with torches and weapons.)

Othello.   Holla! stand there!
Roderigo.   Signior, it is the Moor.
Brabantio.   Down with him, thief!

(They draw on both sides.)

Iago.   You, Roderigo! Come, sir, I am for you.⁶⁰
Othello.   Keep up your bright swords, for the dew will rust them.
   Good signior, you shall more command with years   60
   Than with your weapons.
Brabantio.   O thou foul thief! where hast thou stow'd my daughter?
   Damn'd as thou art, thou hast enchanted her;

---

54. Urgency.   55. Following one another.   56. *I.e.*, senators.   57. Separate.
58. Treasure ship.   59. By the Virgin Mary.   60. Let you and me fight.

For I'll refer me to all things of sense,
If she in chains of magic were not bound,
Whether a maid so tender, fair, and happy,
So opposite to marriage that she shunn'd
The wealthy curled darlings of our nation,
Would ever have, to incur a general mock,
Run from her guardage to the sooty bosom   70
Of such a thing as thou; to fear, not to delight.
Judge me the world, if 'tis not gross in sense[61]
That thou hast practis'd on her with foul charms,
Abus'd her delicate youth with drugs or minerals
That weaken motion:[62] I'll have 't disputed on;
'Tis probable, and palpable to thinking.
I therefore apprehend and do attach[63] thee
For an abuser of the world, a practiser
Of arts inhibited and out of warrant.[64]
Lay hold upon him: if he do resist,   80
Subdue him at his peril.

Othello.   Hold your hands,
Both you of my inclining,[65] and the rest:
Were it my cue to fight, I should have known it
Without a prompter. Where will you that I go
To answer this your charge?

Brabantio.   To prison; till fit time
Of law and course of direct session[66]
Call thee to answer.

Othello.   What if I do obey?
How may the duke be therewith satisfied,
Whose messengers are here about my side,
Upon some present[67] business of the state   90
To bring me to him?

Officer.   'Tis true, most worthy signior;
The duke's in council, and your noble self,
I am sure, is sent for.

Brabantio.   How! the duke in council!
In this time of the night! Bring him away.
Mine's not an idle cause: the duke himself,
Or any of my brothers of the state,[68]
Cannot but feel this wrong as 'twere their own;
For if such actions may have passage free,
Bond-slaves and pagans shall our statesmen be.   (*Exeunt.*)

---

61. Obvious.   62. Normal reactions.   63. Arrest.   64. Prohibited and illegal.
65. Party.   66. Normal process of law.   67. Immediate, pressing.   68. Fellow senators.

SCENE 3. *A Council Chamber.*

(The Duke and Senators sitting at a table. Officers attending.)

Duke.   There is no composition[69] in these news
That gives them credit.
First Senator.   Indeed, they are disproportion'd;
My letters say a hundred and seven galleys.
Duke.   And mine, a hundred and forty.
Second Senator.   And mine, two hundred:
But though they jump[70] not on a just[71] account,—
As in these cases, where the aim[72] reports,
'Tis oft with difference,—yet do they all confirm
A Turkish fleet, and bearing up to Cyprus.
Duke.   Nay, it is possible enough to judgment:
I do not so secure me in[73] the error,   10
But the main article[74] I do approve[75]
In fearful sense.
Sailor *(within)*.   What, ho! what, ho! what, ho!
Officer.   A messenger from the galleys.

(Enter a Sailor.)

Duke.   Now, what's the business?
Sailor.   The Turkish preparation makes for Rhodes;
So was I bid report here to the state
By Signior Angelo.
Duke.   How say you by this change?
First Senator.   This cannot be
By no[76] assay[77] of reason; 'tis a pageant[78]
To keep us in false gaze.[79] When we consider
The importancy of Cyprus to the Turk,   20
And let ourselves again but understand,
That as it more concerns the Turk than Rhodes,
So may he with more facile question bear[80] it,
For that it stands not in such warlike brace,[81]
But altogether lacks the abilities
That Rhodes is dress'd in: if we make thought of this,
We must not think the Turk is so unskilful
To leave that latest which concerns him first,

---

69. Consistency, agreement.   70. Coincide.   71. Exact.   72. Conjecture.
73. Draw comfort from.   74. Substance.   75. Believe.   76. Any.   77. Test.
78. (Deceptive) show.   79. Looking in the wrong direction.   80. More easily capture.
81. State of defense.

Neglecting an attempt of ease and gain,
To wake and wage a danger profitless.   30
Duke. Nay, in all confidence, he's not for Rhodes.
Officer. Here is more news.

(*Enter a Messenger.*)

Messenger. The Ottomites,[82] reverend and gracious,
Steering with due course toward the isle of Rhodes,
Have there injointed[83] them with an after fleet.[84]
First Senator. Ay, so I thought. How many, as you guess?
Messenger. Of thirty sail; and now they do re-stem[85]
Their backward course, bearing with frank appearance
Their purposes toward Cyprus. Signior Montano,
Your trusty and most valiant servitor,   40
With his free duty[86] recommends[87] you thus,
And prays you to believe him.
Duke. 'Tis certain then, for Cyprus.
Marcus Luccicos, is not he in town?
First Senator. He's now in Florence.
Duke. Write from us to him; post-post-haste dispatch.
First Senator. Here comes Brabantio and the valiant Moor.

(*Enter Brabantio, Othello, Iago, Roderigo, and Officers.*)

Duke. Valiant Othello, we must straight employ you
Against the general enemy Ottoman.
(*To Brabantio*) I did not see you; welcome, gentle signior;   50
We lack'd your counsel and your help to-night.
Brabantio. So did I yours. Good your Grace, pardon me;
Neither my place nor aught I heard of business
Hath rais'd me from my bed, nor doth the general care
Take hold of me, for my particular grief
Is of so flood-gate[88] and o'erbearing nature
That it engluts and swallows other sorrows
And it is still itself.
Duke.   Why, what's the matter?
Brabantio. My daughter! O! my daughter.
Duke.
Senators.   Dead?
Brabantio.   Ay, to me;
She is abus'd, stol'n from me, and corrupted   60
By spells and medicines bought of mountebanks;

---

82. Turks.   83. Joined.   84. Fleet that followed after.   85. Steer again.
86. Unqualified expressions of respect.   87. Informs.   88. Torrential.

For nature so preposterously to err,
Being not deficient, blind, or lame of sense,
Sans[89] witchcraft could not.

Duke. Whoe'er he be that in this foul proceeding
Hath thus beguil'd your daughter of herself
And you of her, the bloody book of law
You shall yourself read in the bitter letter
After your own sense; yea, though our proper[90] son
Stood[91] in your action.[92]

Brabantio.   Humbly I thank your Grace.   70
Here is the man, this Moor; whom now, it seems,
Your special mandate for the state affairs
Hath hither brought.

Duke. }
Senators. }   We are very sorry for it.

Duke (to Othello). What, in your own part, can you say to this?

Brabantio. Nothing, but this is so.

Othello. Most potent, grave, and reverend signiors,
My very noble and approv'd[93] good masters,
That I have ta'en away this old man's daughter,
It is most true; true, I have married her:
The very head and front of my offending   80
Hath this extent, no more. Rude am I in my speech,
And little bless'd with the soft phrase of peace;
For since these arms of mine had seven years' pith,[94]
Till now some nine moons wasted,[95] they have us'd
Their dearest action in the tented field;
And little of this great world can I speak,
More than pertains to feats of broil and battle;
And therefore little shall I grace my cause
In speaking for myself. Yet, by your gracious patience,
I will a round[96] unvarnish'd tale deliver   90
Of my whole course of love; what drugs, what charms,
What conjuration, and what mighty magic,
For such proceeding I am charg'd withal,
I won his daughter.

Brabantio.   A maiden never bold;
Of spirit so still and quiet, that her motion
Blush'd at herself;[97] and she, in spite of nature,
Of years, of country, credit, every thing,

---

89. Without.   90. Own.   91. Were accused.   92. Suit.   93. Tested (by past experience).   94. Strength.   95. Past.   96. Blunt.   97. *I.e.*, (her modesty was such that) she blushed at her own emotions; or: could not move without blushing.

To fall in love with what she fear'd to look on!
It is a judgment maim'd and most imperfect
That will confess[98] perfection so could err   *100*
Against all rules of nature, and must be driven
To find out practices of cunning hell,
Why this should be. I therefore vouch again
That with some mixtures powerful o'er the blood,
Or with some dram conjur'd to this effect,.
He wrought upon her.
Duke.   To vouch this, is no proof,
Without more certain and more overt test
Than these thin habits[99] and poor likelihoods
Of modern[100] seeming do prefer against him.
First Senator. But, Othello, speak: *110*
Did you by indirect and forced courses
Subdue and poison this young maid's affections;
Or came it by request and such fair question[101]
As soul to soul affordeth?
Othello.   I do beseech you;
Send for the lady to the Sagittary,
And let her speak of me before her father:
If you do find me foul in her report,
The trust, the office I do hold of you,
Not only take away, but let your sentence
Even fall upon my life.
Duke.   Fetch Desdemona hither.   *120*
Othello. Ancient, conduct them; you best know the place.

                              (*Exeunt Iago and Attendants.*)

And, till she come, as truly as to heaven
I do confess the vices of my blood,
So justly to your grave ears I'll present
How I did thrive in this fair lady's love,
And she in mine.
Duke. Say it, Othello.
Othello. Her father lov'd me; oft invited me;
Still[102] question'd me the story of my life
From year to year, the battles, sieges, fortunes   *130*
That I have pass'd.
I ran it through, even from my boyish days
To the very moment that he bade me tell it;

---

98. Assert.   99. Weak appearances.   100. Commonplace.   101. Conversation.
102. Always, regularly.

Wherein I spake of most disastrous chances,
Of moving accidents by flood and field,
Of hair-breadth 'scapes i' the imminent deadly breach,
Of being taken by the insolent foe
And sold to slavery, of my redemption thence
And portance[103] in my travel's history;
Wherein of antres[104] vast and deserts idle,[105]   140
Rough quarries, rocks, and hills whose heads touch heaven,
It was my hint[106] to speak, such was the process;
And of the Cannibals that each other eat,
The Anthropophagi,[107] and men whose heads
Do grow beneath their shoulders. This to hear
Would Desdemona seriously incline;
But still the house-affairs would draw her thence;
Which ever as she could with haste dispatch,
She'd come again, and with a greedy ear
Devour up my discourse. Which I observing,   150
Took once a pliant[108] hour, and found good means
To draw from her a prayer of earnest heart
That I would all my pilgrimage dilate,[109]
Whereof by parcels[110] she had something heard,
But not intentively:[111] I did consent;
And often did beguile her of her tears,
When I did speak of some distressful stroke
That my youth suffer'd. My story being done,
She gave me for my pains a world of sighs:
She swore, in faith, 'twas strange, 'twas passing[112] strange;   160
'Twas pitiful, 'twas wondrous pitiful:
She wish'd she had not heard it, yet she wish'd
That heaven had made her[113] such a man; she thank'd me,
And bade me, if I had a friend that lov'd her,
I should but teach him how to tell my story,
And that would woo her. Upon this hint I spake.
She lov'd me for the dangers I had pass'd,
And I lov'd her that she did pity them.
This only is the witchcraft I have us'd:
Here comes the lady; let her witness it.   170

(Enter Desdemona, Iago, and Attendants.) /

Duke.   I think this tale would win my daughter too.
Good Brabantio,

---

103. Behavior.   104. Caves.   105. Empty, sterile.   106. Opportunity.
107. Man-eaters.   108. Suitable.   109. Relate in full.   110. Piecemeal.
111. In sequence.   112. Surpassing.   113. Direct object; not "for her."

Take up this mangled matter at the best;
Men do their broken weapons rather use
Than their bare hands.

Brabantio.   I pray you, hear her speak:
If she confess that she was half the wooer,
Destruction on my head, if my bad blame
Light on the man! Come hither, gentle mistress:
Do you perceive in all this noble company
Where most you owe obedience?

Desdemona.   My noble father,   180
I do perceive here a divided duty:
To you I am bound for life and education;
My life and education both do learn[114] me
How to respect you; you are the lord of duty,
I am hitherto your daughter: but here's my husband;
And so much duty as my mother show'd
To you, preferring you before her father,
So much I challenge[115] that I may profess
Due to the Moor my lord.

Brabantio.   God be with you! I have done.
Please it your Grace, on to the state affairs: 190
I had rather to adopt a child than get it.
Come hither, Moor:
I here do give thee that with all my heart
Which, but thou hast[116] already, with all my heart
I would keep from thee. For your sake,[117] jewel,
I am glad at soul I have no other child;
For thy escape would teach me tyranny,
To hang clogs on them. I have done, my lord.

Duke.   Let me speak like yourself and lay a sentence,[118]
Which as a grize[119] or step, may help these lovers   200
Into your favour.
When remedies are past, the griefs are ended
By seeing the worst, which[120] late on hopes depended.
To mourn a mischief that is past and gone
Is the next way to draw new mischief on.
What cannot be preserv'd when Fortune takes,
Patience her injury a mockery makes.[121]
The robb'd that smiles steals something from the thief;
He robs himself that spends a bootless grief.

---

114. Teach.   115. Claim as right.   116. Didn't you have it.   117. Because of
you.   118. Provide a maxim.   119. Step.   120. The antecedent is "griefs."
121. To suffer an irreparable loss patiently is to make light of injury (*i.e.*, to triumph over adversity).

Brabantio.   So let the Turk of Cyprus us beguile;   *210*
      We lose it not so long as we can smile.
      He bears the sentence[122] well that nothing bears
      But the free comfort which from thence he hears;
      But he bears both the sentence and the sorrow
      That, to pay grief, must of poor patience borrow.
      These sentences, to sugar, or to gall,
      Being strong on both sides, are equivocal:[123]
      But words are words: I never yet did hear
      That the bruis'd heart was pierced[124] through the ear.
      I humbly beseech you, proceed to the affairs of state.   *220*

Duke.   The Turk with a most mighty preparation makes for Cyprus. Othello, the fortitude[125] of the place is best known to you; and though we have there a substitute of most allowed sufficiency,[126] yet opinion, a sovereign mistress of effects, throws a more safer voice on you:[127] you must therefore be content to slubber[128] the gloss of your new fortunes with this more stubborn[129] and boisterous expedition.

Othello.   The tyrant custom, most grave senators,
      Hath made the flinty and steel couch of war
      My thrice-driven[130] bed of down: I do agnize[131]
      A natural and prompt alacrity   *230*
      I find in hardness, and do undertake
      These present wars against the Ottomites.
      Most humbly therefore bending to your state,[132]
      I crave fit disposition[133] for my wife,
      Due reference of place and exhibition,[134]
      With such accommodation and besort[135]
      As levels with[136] her breeding.

Duke.   If you please,
      Be 't at her father's.

Brabantio.   I'll not have it so.

Othello.   Nor I.

Desdemona.   Nor I; I would not there reside,
      To put my father in impatient thoughts   *240*
      By being in his eye. Most gracious duke,
      To my unfolding[137] lend your gracious ear;
      And let me find a charter[138] in your voice
      To assist my simpleness.

---

122. (1) Verdict, (2) Maxim.   123. Sententious comfort (like the Duke's trite maxims) can hurt as well as soothe.   124. (1) Lanced (*i.e.*, cured), (2) Wounded.   125. Strength. 126. Admitted competence.   127. General opinion, which mainly determines action, thinks Cyprus safer with you in command.   128. Besmear.   129. Rough.   130. Made as soft as possible.   131. Recognize.   132. Submitting to your authority. 133. Disposal.   134. Provision.   135. Fitness.   136. Is proper to. 137. Explanation.   138. Permission.

Duke.   What would you, Desdemona?

Desdemona.   That I did love the Moor to live with him,
My downright violence and storm of fortunes
May trumpet to the world; my heart's subdu'd
Even to the very quality of my lord;[139]
I saw Othello's visage in his mind,   250
And to his honours and his valiant parts
Did I my soul and fortunes consecrate.
So that, dear lords, if I be left behind,
A moth of peace, and he go to the war,
The rites[140] for which I love him are bereft me,
And I a heavy interim shall support[141]
By his dear[142] absence. Let me go with him.

Othello.   Let her have your voices.
Vouch with me, heaven, I therefore beg it not
To please the palate of my appetite,   260
Nor to comply with heat,—the young affects[143]
In me defunct,—and proper satisfaction,
But to be free and bounteous to her mind;
And heaven defend[144] your good souls that you think
I will your serious and great business scant
For[145] she is with me. No, when light-wing'd toys
Of feather'd Cupid seel[146] with wanton dulness
My speculative and offic'd instruments,[147]
That[148] my disports corrupt and taint my business,
Let housewives make a skillet of my helm,   270
And all indign[149] and base adversities
Make head against my estimation![150]

Duke.   Be it as you shall privately determine,
Either for her stay or going. The affair cries haste,
And speed must answer it.

First Senator.   You must away to-night.

Othello.   With all my heart.

Duke.   At nine i' the morning here we'll meet again.
Othello, leave some officer behind,
And he shall our commission bring to you;
With such things else of quality and respect   280
As doth import you.[151]

---

139. *I.e.*, I have become a soldier, like Othello.   140. *I.e.*, of marriage, or of war, or of both.
141. Endure.   142. Closely concerning (*i.e.*, Desdemona).   143. The passions of
youth (hence, here, *immoderate* sexual passion).   144. Forbid.   145. Because.
146. Blind (v.) by sewing up the eyelids (a term from falconry).   147. Reflective and executive faculties and organs.   148. So that.   149. Shameful.   150. Reputation.
151. Concern.

Othello.   So please your Grace, my ancient;
     A man he is of honesty and trust:
     To his conveyance I assign my wife,
     With what else needful your good grace shall think
     To be sent after me.
Duke.   Let it be so.
     Good-night to every one. (*To Brabantio*) And, noble signior,
     If virtue no delighted[152] beauty lack,
     Your son-in-law is far more fair than black.
First Senator.   Adieu, brave Moor! use Desdemona well.
Brabantio.   Look to her, Moor, if thou hast eyes to see: 290
     She has deceiv'd her father, and may thee.

                              (*Exeunt Duke, Senators, Officers, &c.*)

Othello.   My life upon her faith! Honest Iago,
     My Desdemona must I leave to thee:
     I prithee, let thy wife attend on her;
     And bring them after in the best advantage.[153]
     Come, Desdemona; I have but an hour
     Of love, of worldly matters and direction,
     To spend with thee: we must obey the time.

                              (*Exeunt Othello and Desdemona.*)

Roderigo.   Iago!
Iago.   What sayst thou, noble heart?   300
Roderigo.   What will I do, think'st thou?
Iago.   Why, go to bed, and sleep.
Roderigo.   I will incontinently[154] drown myself.
Iago.   Well, if thou dost, I shall never love thee after.
     Why, thou silly gentleman!
Roderigo.   It is silliness to live when to live is torment; and then have we a
     prescription to die when death is our physician.
Iago.   O! villanous; I have looked upon the world for four times seven years,
     and since I could distinguish betwixt a benefit and an injury, I never found
     man that knew how to love himself. Ere I would say, I would drown myself
     for the love of a guinea-hen, I would change my humanity with a baboon.
Roderigo.   What should I do? I confess it is my shame to be so fond;[155] but it is
     not in my virtue[156] to amend it.
Iago.   Virtue! a fig! 'tis in ourselves that we are thus, or thus. Our bodies are
     our gardens, to the which our wills are gardeners; so that if we will plant
     nettles or sow lettuce, set hyssop and weed up thyme, supply it with one

---

152. Delightful.   153. Opportunity.   154. Forthwith.   155. Infatuated.
156. Strength.

gender[157] of herbs or distract it with many, either to have it sterile with idleness or manured with industry, why, the power and corrigible[158] authority of this lies in our wills. If the balance of our lives had not one scale of reason to poise another of sensuality, the blood and baseness of our natures would conduct us to most preposterous conclusions; but we have reason to cool our raging motions, our carnal stings, our unbitted[159] lusts, whereof I take this that you call love to be a sect or scion.[160]

Roderigo. It cannot be.

Iago. It is merely a lust of the blood and a permission of the will. Come, be a man. Drown thyself! drown cats and blind puppies. I have professed me thy friend, and I confess me knit to thy deserving with cables of perdurable toughness; I could never better stead thee than now. Put money in thy purse; follow these wars; defeat thy favour[161] with a usurped[162] beard; I say, put money in thy purse. It cannot be that Desdemona should long continue her love to the Moor,—put money in thy purse,—nor he his to her. It was a violent commencement in her, and thou shalt see an answerable sequestration;[163] put but money in thy purse. These Moors are changeable in their wills;—fill thy purse with money:—the food that to him now is as luscious as locusts,[164] shall be to him shortly as bitter as coloquintida.[165] She must change for youth: when she is sated with his body, she will find the error of her choice. She must have change, she must: therefore put money in thy purse. If thou wilt needs damn thyself, do it a more delicate way than drowning. Make all the money thou canst. If sanctimony and a frail vow betwixt an erring[166] barbarian and a supersubtle[167] Venetian be not too hard for my wits and all the tribe of hell, thou shalt enjoy her; therefore make money. A pox of drowning thyself! it is clean out of the way: seek thou rather to be hanged in compassing thy joy than to be drowned and go without her.

Roderigo. Wilt thou be fast to my hopes, if I depend on the issue?[168]

Iago. Thou art sure of me: go, make money. I have told thee often, and I retell thee again and again, I hate the Moor; my cause is hearted; thine hath no less reason. Let us be conjunctive[169] in our revenge against him; if thou canst cuckold him, thou dost thyself a pleasure, me a sport. There are many events in the womb of time which will be delivered. Traverse;[170] go: provide thy money. We will have more of this to-morrow. Adieu.

Roderigo. Where shall we meet i' the morning?

Iago. At my lodging.

Roderigo. I'll be with thee betimes.

---

157. Kind.   158. Corrective.   159. *I.e.,* uncontrolled.   160. Offshoot.
161. Change thy appearance (for the worse?).   162. Assumed.   163. Estrangement.
164. Sweet-tasting fruits (perhaps the carob, the edible seed-pod of an evergreen tree in the Mediterranean area).   165. Purgative derived from a bitter apple.   166. Vagabond.
167. Exceedingly refined.   168. Rely on the outcome.   169. Allied.   170. March.

Iago. Go to: farewell. Do you hear, Roderigo?

Roderigo. What say you?

Iago. No more of drowning, do you hear?

Roderigo. I am changed. I'll sell all my land

Iago. Go to; farewell! put money enough in your purse.   *(Exit Roderigo.)*

    Thus do I ever make my fool my purse;   360

    For I mine own gain'd knowledge should profane,

    If I would time expend with such a snipe[171]

    But for my sport and profit. I hate the Moor,

    And it is thought abroad[172] that 'twixt my sheets

    He has done my office: I know not if 't be true,

    But I, for mere suspicion in that kind,

    Will do as if for surety.[173] He holds me well;[174]

    The better shall my purpose work on him.

    Cassio's a proper[175] man; let me see now:

    To get his place; and to plume up[176] my will   370

    In double knavery; how, how? Let's see:

    After some time to abuse Othello's ear

    That he[177] is too familiar with his wife:

    He hath a person and a smooth dispose[178]

    To be suspected; framed[179] to make women false,

    The Moor is of a free and open nature,

    That thinks men honest that but seem to be so,

    And will as tenderly be led by the nose

    As asses are.

    I have't; it is engender'd: hell and night   380

    Must bring this monstrous birth to the world's light.   *(Exit.)*

Act II

SCENE 1. *A Sea-port Town in Cyprus. An open place near the Quay.*

(Enter Montano and two Gentlemen.)

Montano. What from the cape can you discern at sea?

First Gentleman. Nothing at all: it is a high-wrought flood;

    I cannot 'twixt the heaven and the main[180]

    Descry a sail.

Montano. Methinks the wind hath spoke aloud at land;

---

171. Dupe.   172. People think.   173. As if it were certain.   174. In high regard.
175. Handsome.   176. Make ready.   177. *I.e.,* Cassio.   178. Bearing.
179. Designed, apt.   180. Ocean.

A fuller blast ne'er shook our battlements;
If it hath ruffian'd so upon the sea,
What ribs of oak, when mountains melt on them,
Can hold the mortise?[181] what shall we hear of this?

Second Gentleman. A segregation[182] of the Turkish fleet;   *10*
For do but stand upon the foaming shore,
The chidden billow seems to pelt the clouds;
The wind-shak'd surge, with high and monstrous mane,
Seems to cast water on the burning bear[183]
And quench the guards of the ever-fixed pole:[184]
I never did like[185] molestation view
On the enchafed[186] flood.

Montano.   If that[187] the Turkish fleet
Be not enshelter'd and embay'd, they are drown'd;
It is impossible they bear it out.

(*Enter a Third Gentleman.*)

Third Gentleman. News, lad! our wars are done.   *20*
The desperate tempest hath so bang'd the Turks
That their designment halts;[188] a noble ship of Venice
Hath seen a grievous wrack and suffrance[189]
On most part of their fleet.

Montano. How! is this true?

Third Gentleman.   The ship is here put in,
A Veronesa;[190] Michael Cassio,
Lieutenant to the warlike Moor Othello,
Is come on shore: the Moor himself's at sea,
And is in full commission here for Cyprus.

Montano. I am glad on 't; 'tis a worthy governor.   *30*

Third Gentleman. But this same Cassio, though he speak of comfort
Touching the Turkish loss, yet he looks sadly
And prays the Moor be safe; for they were parted
With foul and violent tempest.

Montano.   Pray heaven he be;
For I have serv'd him, and the man commands
Like a full soldier. Let's to the sea-side, ho!
As well to see the vessel that's come in
As to throw out our eyes for brave Othello,

---

181. Hold the joints together.   182. Scattering.   183. Ursa Minor (the Little Dipper).
184. Polaris, the North Star, almost directly above the Earth's axis, is part of the constellation of
the Little Bear, or Dipper.   185. Similar.   186. Agitated.   187. If.   188. Plan
is stopped.   189. Damage.   190. Probably a *type* of ship, rather than a ship from Verona
—not only because Verona is an inland city but also because of "a noble ship of Venice" above.

Even till we make the main and the aerial blue
An indistinct regard.[191]

Third Gentleman.   Come, let's do so;   40
For every minute is expectancy
Of more arrivance.

(*Enter Cassio.*)

Cassio. Thanks, you the valiant of this warlike isle,
That so approve the Moor. O! let the heavens
Give him defence against the elements,
For I have lost him on a dangerous sea.
Montano. Is he well shipp'd?
Cassio. His bark is stoutly timber'd, and his pilot
Of very expert and approv'd allowance;[192]
Therefore my hopes, not surfeited to death,[193]   50
Stand in bold cure.[194]

(*Within,* 'A sail!—a sail!—a sail!' *Enter a Messenger.*)

Cassio. What noise?
Messenger. The town is empty; on the brow o' the sea
Stand ranks of people, and they cry 'A sail!'
Cassio. My hopes do shape him for the governor.

(*Guns heard.*)

Second Gentleman. They do discharge their shot of courtesy;
Our friends at least.
Cassio.   I pray you, sir, go forth.
And give us truth who 'tis that is arriv'd.
Second Gentleman. I shall.   (*Exit.*)
Montano. But, good lieutenant, is your general wiv'd?   60
Cassio. Most fortunately: he hath achiev'd a maid
That paragons[195] description and wild fame;
One that excels the quirks[196] of blazoning pens,
And in th' essential vesture of creation[197]
Does tire the ingener.[198]

(*Re-enter Second Gentleman.*)

How now! who has put in?
Second Gentleman. 'Tis one Iago, ancient to the general.

---

191. Till our (straining) eyes can no longer distinguish sea and sky.   192. Admitted and proven to be expert.   193. Over indulged.   194. With good chance of being fulfilled. 195. Exceeds, surpasses.   196. Ingenuities.   197. *I.e.,* just as God made her; or: (even in) the (mere) essence of human nature.   198. Inventor (*i.e.,* of her praises?).

Cassio.   He has had most favourable and happy speed:
Tempests themselves, high seas, and howling winds,
The gutter'd[199] rocks, and congregated sands,
Traitors ensteep'd[200] to clog the guiltless keel,   70
As having sense of beauty, do omit
Their mortal[201] natures, letting go safely by
The divine Desdemona.
Montano.   What is she?
Cassio.   She that I spake of, our great captain's captain,
Left in the conduct of the bold Iago,
Whose footing[202] here anticipates our thoughts
A se'nnight's[203] speed. Great Jove, Othello guard,
And swell his sail with thine own powerful breath,
That he may bless this bay with his tall[204] ship,
Make love's quick pants in Desdemona's arms,   80
Give renew'd fire to our extincted spirits,
And bring all Cyprus comfort!

(Enter Desdemona, Emilia, Iago, Roderigo, and Attendants.)

                            O! behold,
The riches of the ship is come on shore.
Ye men of Cyprus, let her have your knees.
Hail to thee, lady! and the grace of heaven,
Before, behind thee, and on every hand,
Enwheel thee round!
Desdemona.   I thank you, valiant Cassio
What tidings can you tell me of my lord?
Cassio.   He is not yet arriv'd; nor know I aught
But that he's well, and will be shortly here.   90
Desdemona.   O! but I fear—How lost you company?
Cassio.   The great contention of the sea and skies
Parted our fellowship. But hark! a sail.

(Cry within, 'A sail—a sail!' Guns heard.)

Second Gentleman.   They give their greeting to the citadel:
This likewise is a friend.
Cassio.   See for the news!   *(Exit Gentleman.)*
Good ancient, you are welcome:—*(To Emilia)* welcome, mistress.
Let it not gall your patience, good Iago,
That I extend my manners; 'tis my breeding
That gives me this bold show of courtesy.   *(Kissing her.)*

---

199. Jagged; or: submerged.   200. Submerged.   201. Deadly.   202. Landing.
203. Week's.   204. Brave.

Iago.   Sir, would she give you so much of her lips   100
       As of her tongue she oft bestows on me,
       You'd have enough.
Desdemona.   Alas! she has no speech.
Iago.   In faith, too much;
       I find it still when I have list[205] to sleep:
       Marry, before your ladyship, I grant,
       She puts her tongue a little in her heart,
       And chides with thinking.[206]
Emilia.   You have little cause to say so.
Iago.   Come on, come on; you are pictures[207] out of doors,
       Bells[208] in your parlours, wild cats in your kitchens,   110
       Saints in your injuries, devils being offended,
       Players[209] in your housewifery,[210] and housewives[211] in your beds.
Desdemona.   O! fie upon thee, slanderer.
Iago.   Nay, it is true, or else I am a Turk:
       You rise to play and go to bed to work.
Emilia.   You shall not write my praise.
Iago.   No, let me not.
Desdemona.   What wouldst thou write of me, if thou shouldst praise me?
Iago.   O gentle lady, do not put me to 't,
       For I am nothing if not critical,
Desdemona.   Come on; assay. There's one gone to the harbour?   120
Iago.   Ay, madam.
Desdemona (aside).   I am not merry, but I do beguile
       The thing I am by seeming otherwise.
       (To Iago.) Come, how wouldst thou praise me?
Iago.   I am about it; but indeed my invention
       Comes from my pate[212] as birdlime does from frize;[213]
       It plucks out brains and all: but my muse labours
       And thus she is deliver'd.
       If she be fair and wise, fairness and wit,
       The one's for use, the other useth it.   130
Desdemona.   Well prais'd! How if she be black and witty?
Iago.   If she be black,[214] and thereto have a wit,
       She'll find a white that shall her blackness fit.
Desdemona.   Worse and worse.
Emilia.   How if fair and foolish?
Iago.   She never yet was foolish that was fair,
       For even her folly[215] help'd to an heir.

---

205. Wish.   206. *I.e.*, without words.   207. *I.e.*, made up, "painted."   208. *I.e.*,
jangly.   209. Triflers, wastrels.   210. Housekeeping.   211. (1) Hussies, (2) (unduly)
frugal with their sexual favors, (3) businesslike, serious.   212. Head.   213. Coarse
cloth.   214. Brunette, dark haired.   215. Here also, wantonness.

Desdemona. These are old fond[216] paradoxes to make fools laugh i' the alehouse. What miserable praise hast thou for her that's foul and foolish?

Iago. There's none so foul and foolish thereunto,   *140*
But does foul pranks which fair and wise ones do.

Desdemona. O heavy ignorance! thou praisest the worst best. But what praise couldst thou bestow on a deserving woman indeed, one that, in the authority of her merit, did justly put on the vouch[217] of very malice itself?

Iago. She that was ever fair and never proud,
Had tongue at will and yet was never loud,
Never lack'd gold and yet went never gay,
Fled from her wish and yet said 'Now I may,'
She that being anger'd, her revenge being nigh,
Bade her wrong stay and her displeasure fly,   *150*
She that in wisdom never was so frail
To change the cod's head for the salmon's tail,[218]
She that could think and ne'er disclose her mind,
See suitors following and not look behind,
She was a wight, if ever such wight were,—

Desdemona. To do what?

Iago. To suckle fools and chronicle small beer.[219]

Desdemona. O most lame and impotent conclusion! Do not learn of him, Emilia, though he be thy husband. How say you, Cassio? Is he not a most profane and liberal[220] counsellor?   *160*

Cassio. He speaks home,[221] madam; you may relish him more in the soldier than in[222] the scholar.

Iago (*aside*). He takes her by the palm: ay, well said, whisper; with as little a web as this will I ensnare as great a fly as Cassio. Ay, smile upon her, do; I wlll gyve[223] thee in thine own courtship. You say true, 'tis so, indeed. If such tricks as these strip you out of your lieutenantry, it had been better you had not kissed your three fingers so oft, which now again you are most apt to play the sir[224] in. Very good; well kissed! an excellent courtesy! 'tis so, indeed. Yet again your fingers to your lips? would they were clyster-pipes[225] for your sake! (*A trumpet heard.*) The Moor! I know his trumpet.[226]

Cassio. 'Tis truly so.

Desdemona. Let's meet him and receive him.

Cassio. Lo! where he comes.

(*Enter Othello and Attendants.*)

---

216. Foolish.   217. Compel the approval.   218. To make a foolish exchange (a bawdy secondary meaning is probable).   219. *I.e.,* keep petty household accounts. 220. Free-spoken, licentious.   221. To the mark, aptly.   222. As . . . as.   223. Entangle.   224. Gentleman.   225. Syringes, enema pipes.   226. *I.e.,* Othello's distinctive trumpet call.

Othello.   O my fair warrior!

Desdemona.   My dear Othello!

Othello.   It gives me wonder great as my content
   To see you here before me. O my soul's joy!
   If after every tempest come such calms,
   May the winds blow till they have waken'd death!
   And let the labouring bark climb hills of seas   180
   Olympus-high, and duck again as low
   As hell's from heaven! If it were now to die,
   'Twere now to be most happy, for I fear
   My soul hath her content so absolute
   That not another comfort like to this
   Succeeds in unknown fate.

Desdemona.   The heavens forbid
   But that our loves and comforts should increase
   Even as our days do grow!

Othello.   Amen to that, sweet powers!
   I cannot speak enough of this content;   190
   It stops me here; it is too much of joy:
   And this, and this, the greatest discords be   (*Kissing her.*)
   That e'er our hearts shall make!

Iago (*aside*).   O! you are well tun'd now,
   But I'll set down[227] the pegs that make this music,
   As honest as I am.

Othello.   Come, let us to the castle.
   News, friends; our wars are done, the Turks are drown'd.
   How does my old acquaintance of this isle?
   Honey, you shall be well desir'd[228] in Cyprus;
   I have found great love amongst them. O my sweet,
   I prattle out of fashion, and I dote   200
   In mine own comforts. I prithee, good Iago,
   Go to the bay and disembark my coffers.
   Bring thou the master to the citadel;
   He is a good one, and his worthiness
   Does challenge much respect. Come, Desdemona,
   Once more well met at Cyprus.

                    (*Exeunt all except Iago and Roderigo.*)

Iago.   Do thou meet me presently at the harbour. Come hither. If thou be'st
valiant, as they say base men being in love have then a nobility in their natures more than is native to them, list[229] me. The lieutenant to-night
watches on the court of guard:[230] first, I must tell thee this, Desdemona is
directly in love with him.

---

227. Loosen.   228. Welcomed.   229. Listen to.   230. Guardhouse.

Roderigo. With him! Why, 'tis not possible.

Iago. Lay thy finger thus, and let thy soul be instructed. Mark me with what violence she first loved the Moor but for bragging and telling her fantastical lies; and will she love him still for prating? let not thy discreet heart think it. Her eye must be fed; and what delight shall she have to look on the devil? When the blood is made dull with the act of sport, there should be, again to inflame it, and to give satiety a fresh appetite, loveliness in favour, sympathy in years, manners, and beauties; all which the Moor is defective in. Now, for want of these required conveniences, her delicate tenderness will find itself abused, begin to heave the gorge,[231] disrelish and abhor the Moor; very nature will instruct her in it, and compel her to some second choice. Now, sir, this granted, as it is a most pregnant[232] and unforced position, who stands so eminently in the degree of this fortune as Cassio does? a knave very voluble, no further conscionable[233] than in putting on the mere form of civil and humane seeming, for the better compassing of his salt[234] and most hidden loose affection? why, none; why, none: a slipper[235] and subtle knave, a finder-out of occasions, that has an eye can stamp and counterfeit advantages, though true advantage never present itself; a devilish knave! Besides, the knave is handsome, young, and hath all those requisites in him that folly and green minds look after; a pestilent complete knave! and the woman hath found him already.

Roderigo. I cannot believe that in her; she is full of most blessed condition.

Iago. Blessed fig's end! the wine she drinks is made of grapes;[236] if she had been blessed she would never have loved the Moor; blessed pudding! Didst thou not see her paddle with the palm of his hand? didst not mark that?

Roderlgo. Yes, that I did; but that was but courtesy.

Iago. Lechery, by this hand! an index[237] and obscure prologue to the history of lust and foul thoughts. They met so near with their lips, that their breaths embraced together. Villanous thoughts, Roderigo! when these mutualities so marshal the way, hard at hand comes the master and main exercise, the incorporate[238] conclusion. Pish![239] But, sir, be you ruled by me: I have brought you from Venice. Watch you to-night; for the command, I'll lay 't upon you: Cassio knows you not. I'll not be far from you: do you find some occasion to anger Cassio, either by speaking too loud, or tainting[240] his discipline; or from what other course you please, which the time shall more favourably minister.

Roderigo. Well.   250

Iago. Sir, he is rash and very sudden in choler, and haply may strike at you: provoke him, that he may; for even out of that will I cause these of Cyprus

---

231. Vomit.   232. Obvious.   233. Conscientious.   234. Lecherous.
235. Slippery.   236. *I.e.*, she is only flesh and blood.   237. Pointer.   238. Carnal.   239. Exclamation of disgust.   240. Disparaging.

to mutiny, whose qualification[241] shall come into no true taste again but by the displanting of Cassio. So shall you have a shorter journey to your desires by the means I shall then have to prefer[242] them; and the impediment most profitably removed, without the which there were no expectation of our prosperity.

Roderigo. I will do this, if I can bring it to any opportunity.

Iago. I warrant thee. Meet me by and by at the citadel: I must fetch his necessaries ashore. Farewell.   260

Roderigo. Adieu.   (*Exit.*)

Iago. That Cassio loves her, I do well believe it;
That she loves him, 'tis apt,[243] and of great credit:[244]
The Moor, howbeit that I endure him not,
Is of a constant, loving, noble nature;
And I dare think he'll prove to Desdemona
A most dear[245] husband. Now, I do love her too;
Not out of absolute lust,—though peradventure[246]
I stand accountant[247] for as great a sin,—
But partly led to diet my revenge,   270
For that I do suspect the lusty Moor
Hath leap'd into my seat; the thought whereof
Doth like a poisonous mineral gnaw my inwards;
And nothing can or shall content my soul
Till I am even'd with him, wife for wife;
Or failing so, yet that I put the Moor
At least into a jealousy so strong
That judgment cannot cure. Which thing to do,
If this poor trash[248] of Venice, whom I trash[249]
For his quick hunting, stand the putting-on,[250]   280
I'll have our Michael Cassio on the hip;
Abuse him to the Moor in the rank garb,[251]
For I fear Cassio with my night-cap too,
Make the Moor thank me, love me, and reward me
For making him egregiously an ass
And practising upon his peace and quiet
Even to madness. 'Tis here, but yet confus'd:
Knavery's plain face is never seen till us'd.   (*Exit.*)

---

241. Appeasement.   242. Advance.   243. Natural, probable.   244. Easily believable.   245. A pun on the word in the sense of: expensive.   246. Perchance, perhaps.   247. Accountable.   248. *I.e.,* Roderigo.   249. Check, control.
250. Inciting.   251. Gross manner.

SCENE 2. *A Street.*

(*Enter a Herald with a proclamation; people following.*)

Herald. It is Othello's pleasure, our noble and valiant general, that, upon certain tidings now arrived, importing the mere[252] perdition of the Turkish fleet, every man put himself into triumph; some to dance, some to make bonfires, each man to what sport and revels his addiction leads him; for, besides these beneficial news, it is the celebration of his nuptial. So much was his pleasure should be proclaimed. All offices[253] are open, and there is full liberty of feasting from this present hour of five till the bell have told eleven. Heaven bless the isle of Cyprus and our noble general Othello!   (*Exeunt.*)

SCENE 3. *A Hall in the Castle.*

(*Enter Othello, Desdemona, Cassio, and Attendants.*)

Othello.   Good Michael, look you to the guard to-night:
Let's teach ourselves that honourable stop,[254]
Not to outsport discretion.
Cassio.   Iago hath direction what to do:
But, notwithstanding, with my personal[255] eye
Will I look to 't.
Othello.   Iago is most honest.
Michael, good-night; to-morrow with your earliest
Let me have speech with you. (*To Desdemona.*) Come, my dear love,
The purchase made, the fruits are to ensue;
That profit's yet to come 'twixt me and you.   10
Good-night.

                    (*Exeunt Othello, Desdemona, and Attendants.*)

(*Enter Iago.*)

Cassio. Welcome, Iago; we must to the watch.
Iago.   Not this hour, lieutenant; 'tis not yet ten o' the clock. Our general casts us thus early for the love of his Desdemona, who let us not therefore blame; he hath not yet made wanton the night with her, and she is sport for Jove.
Cassio. She's a most exquisite lady.
Iago. And, I'll warrant her, full of game.

---

252. Utter.   253. Kitchens and storehouses.   254. Discipline.   255. Own.

Cassio. Indeed, she is a most fresh and delicate creature.

Iago. What an eye she has! methinks it sounds a parley[256] of provocation.   20

Cassio. An inviting eye: and yet methinks right modest.

Iago. And when she speaks, is it not an alarum[257] to love?

Cassio. She is indeed perfection.

Iago. Well, happiness to their sheets! Come, lieutenant, I have a stoup of wine, and here without are a brace[258] of Cyprus gallants that would fain have a measure to the health of black Othello.

Cassio. Not to-night, good Iago: I have very poor and unhappy brains for drinking: I could well wish courtesy would invent some other custom of entertainment.

Iago. O! they are our friends; but one cup: I'll drink for you.   30

Cassio. I have drunk but one cup to-night, and that was craftily qualified[259] too, and, behold, what innovation[260] it makes here: I am unfortunate in the infirmity, and dare not task my weakness with any more.

Iago. What, man! 'tis a night of revels; the gallants desire it.

Cassio. Where are they?

Iago. Here at the door; I pray you, call them in.

Cassio. I'll do 't; but it dislikes me.   (*Exit.*)

Iago.   If I can fasten but one cup upon him,
With that which he hath drunk to-night already,
He'll be as full of quarrel and offence   40
As my young mistress' dog. Now, my sick fool Roderigo,
Whom love has turn'd almost the wrong side out,
To Desdemona hath to-night carous'd
Potations pottle-deep;[261] and he's to watch.
Three lads of Cyprus, noble swelling spirits,
That hold their honours in a wary distance,[262]
The very elements[263] of this warlike isle,
Have I to-night fluster'd with flowing cups,
And they watch too. Now, 'mongst this flock of drunkards,
Am I to put our Cassio in some action   50
That may offend the isle. But here they come.
If consequence[264] do but approve my dream,
My boat sails freely, both with wind and stream.

(*Re-enter Cassio, with him Montano, and Gentlemen. Servant following with wine.*)

Cassio. 'Fore God, they have given me a rouse[265] already.

Montano. Good faith, a little one; not past a pint, as I am a soldier.

Iago. Some wine, ho!

---

256. Conference.   257. Call-to-arms.   258. Pair.   259. Diluted.
260. Change, revolution.   261. Bottoms-up.   262. Take offense easily.
263. Types.   264. Succeeding events.   265. Drink.

(*Sings*)   And let me the canakin[266] clink, clink;
             And let me the canakin clink:
             A soldier's a man;
             A life's but a span;   60
             Why then let a soldier drink.
        Some wine, boys!
Cassio.   'Fore God, an excellent song.
Iago.   I learned it in England, where indeed they are most potent in potting;
        your Dane, your German, and your swag-bellied[267] Hollander,—drink,
        ho!—are nothing to your English.
Cassio.   Is your Englishman so expert in his drinking?
Iago.   Why, he drinks you[268] with facility your Dane dead drunk; he sweats
        not to overthrow your Almain;[269] he gives your Hollander a vomit ere the
        next pottle can be filled.   70
Cassio.   To the health of our general!
Montano. I am for it, lieutenant; and I'll do you justice.
Iago.   O sweet England!
(*Sings*)   King Stephen was a worthy peer,
                His breeches cost him but a crown;
             He held them sixpence all too dear,
                With that he call'd the tailor lown.[270]
             He was a wight of high renown,
                And thou art but of low degree:
             'Tis pride that pulls the country down,   80
                Then take thine auld cloak about thee.
        Some wine, ho!
Cassio.   Why, this is a more exquisite song than the other.
Iago.   Will you hear 't again?
Cassio.   No; for I hold him to be unworthy of his place that does those things.
        Well, God's above all; and there be souls must be saved, and there be
        souls must not be saved.
Iago.   It's true, good lieutenant.
Cassio.   For mine own part,—no offence to the general, nor any man of
        quality,—I hope to be saved.   90
Iago.   And so do I too, lieutenant.
Cassio.   Ay; but, by your leave, not before me; the lieutenant is to be saved
        before the ancient. Let's have no more of this; let's to our affairs. God for-
        give us our sins! Gentlemen, let's look to our business. Do not think,
        gentlemen, I am drunk: this is my ancient; this is my right hand, and this is
        my left hand. I am not drunk now; I can stand well enough, and speak well
        enough.
All.   Excellent well.

---

266. Small cup.   267. With a pendulous belly.   268. The "ethical" dative, *i.e.*, you'll
see that he drinks.   269. German.   270. Lout, rascal.

Cassio. Why, very well, then; you must not think then that I am drunk. (*Exit.*)

Montano. To the platform, masters; come, let's set the watch.   100

Iago. You see this fellow that is gone before;
    He is a soldier fit to stand by Caesar
    And give direction; and do but see his vice;
    'Tis to his virtue a just equinox,[271]
    The one as long as the other; 'tis pity of him.
    I fear the trust Othello puts him in,
    On some odd time of his infirmity,
    Will shake this island.

Montano.   But is he often thus?

Iago. 'Tis evermore the prologue to his sleep;
    He'll watch the horologe a double set,[272]   110
    If drink rock not his cradle.

Montano.   It were well
    The general were put in mind of it.
    Perhaps he sees it not; or his good nature
    Prizes the virtue that appears in Cassio,
    And looks not on his evils. Is not this true?

(*Enter Roderigo.*)

Iago (*aside to him*).   How now, Roderigo!
I pray you, after the lieutenant; go.   (*Exit Roderigo*)

Montano. And 'tis great pity that the noble Moor
    Should hazard such a place as his own second
    With one of an ingraft[273] infirmity;   120
    It were an honest action to say
    So to the Moor.

Iago.   Not I, for this fair island:
    I do love Cassio well, and would do much
    To cure him of this evil. But hark! what noise?

(*Cry within, 'Help! Help!' Re-enter Cassio, driving in Roderigo.*)

Cassio. You rogue! you rascal!

Montano.   What's the matter, lieutenant?

Cassio. A knave teach me my duty!
    I'll beat the knave into a twiggen[274] bottle.

Roderigo. Beat me!

Cassio.   Dost thou prate, rogue?

(*Striking Roderigo.*)

---

271. Equivalent.   272. Stand watch twice twelve hours.   273. Ingrained.
274. Wicker.

Montano (*staying him*).   Nay, good lieutenant;
  I pray you, sir, hold your hand.
Cassio.   Let me go, sir,   130
  Or I'll knock you o'er the mazzard.[275]
Montano.   Come, come; you're drunk.
Cassio.   Drunk!

(*They fight.*)

Iago (*aside to Roderigo*).   Away, I say! go out, and cry a mutiny.

                                              (*Exit Roderigo.*)

  Nay, good lieutenant! God's will, gentlemen!
  Help, ho! Lieutenant! sir! Montano! sir!
  Help, masters! Here's a goodly watch indeed!

(*Bell rings.*)

  Who's that that rings the bell? Diablo, ho!
  The town will rise: God's will! lieutenant, hold!
  You will be sham'd for ever.

(*Re-enter Othello and Attendants.*)

Othello.   What is the matter here?
Montano.   'Zounds! I bleed still; I am hurt to the death.   140

(*He faints.*)

Othello.   Hold, for your lives!
Iago.   Hold, ho, lieutenant! Sir! Montano! gentlemen!
  Have you forgot all sense of place and duty?
  Hold! the general speaks to you; hold for shame!
Othello.   Why, how now, ho! from whence ariseth this?
  Are we turn'd Turks, and to ourselves do that
  Which heaven hath forbid the Ottomites?
  For Christian shame put by this barbarous brawl;
  He that stirs next to carve for his own rage
  Holds his soul light; he dies upon his motion.   150
  Silence that dreadful bell! it frights the isle
  From her propriety. What is the matter, masters?
  Honest Iago, that look'st dead with grieving,
  Speak, who began this? On thy love, I charge thee.
Iago.   I do not know; friends all but now, even now,
  In quarter[276] and in terms like bride and groom
  Devesting[277] them for bed; and then, but now,—
  As if some planet had unwitted men,—

---

275. Head.   276. On duty.   277. Undressing.

Swords out, and tilting one at other's breast,
In opposition bloody. I cannot speak   160
Any beginning to this peevish odds,[278]
And would in action glorious I had lost
Those legs that brought me to a part of it!

Othello.   How comes it, Michael, you are thus forgot?

Cassio.   I pray you, pardon me; I cannot speak.

Othello.   Worthy Montano, you were wont be civil;
The gravity and stillness of your youth
The world hath noted, and your name is great
In mouths of wisest censure:[279] what's the matter,
That you unlace[280] your reputation thus   170
And spend your rich opinion[281] for the name
Of a night-brawler? give me answer to it.

Montano.   Worthy Othello, I am hurt to danger;
Your officer, Iago, can inform you,
While I spare speech, which something now offends[282] me,
Of all that I do know; nor know I aught
By me that 's said or done amiss this night,
Unless self-charity be sometimes a vice,
And to defend ourselves it be a sin
When violence assails us.

Othello.   Now, by heaven,   180
My blood begins my safer guides to rule,
And passion, having my best judgment collied,[283]
Assays to lead the way. If I once stir,
Or do but lift this arm, the best of you
Shall sink in my rebuke. Give me to know
How this foul rout began, who set it on;
And he that is approv'd[284] in this offence,
Though he had twinn'd with me—both at a birth—
Shall lose me. What! in a town of war,
Yet wild, the people's hearts brimful of fear,   190
To manage private and domestic quarrel,
In night, and on the court and guard of safety!
'Tis monstrous. Iago, who began 't?

Montano.   If partially affin'd,[285] or leagu'd in office,
Thou dost deliver more or less than truth,
Thou art no soldier.

Iago.   Touch me not so near;
I had rather[286] have this tongue cut from my mouth

---

278. Silly quarrel.   279. Judgment.   280. Undo.   281. High reputation.
282. Pains, harms.   283. Clouded.   284. Proved (*i.e.*, guilty).   285. Favorably
biased (by ties of friendship, or as Cassio's fellow officer).   286. More quickly.

Than it should do offence to Michael Cassio;
Yet, I persuade myself, to speak the truth
Shall nothing wrong him. Thus it is, general.   200
Montano and myself being in speech,
There comes a fellow crying out for help,
And Cassio following with determin'd sword
To execute upon him. Sir, this gentleman
Steps in to Cassio, and entreats his pause;
Myself the crying fellow did pursue,
Lest by his clamour, as it so fell out,
The town might fall in fright; he, swift of foot,
Outran my purpose, and I return'd the rather
For that I heard the clink and fall of swords,   210
And Cassio high in oath, which till to-night
I ne'er might say before. When I came back,—
For this was brief,—I found them close together,
At blow and thrust, even as again they were
When you yourself did part them.
More of this matter can I not report:
But men are men; the best sometimes forget:
Though Cassio did some little wrong to him,
As men in rage strike those that wish them best,
Yet, surely Cassio, I believe, receiv'd   220
From him that fled some strange indignity,
Which patience could not pass.
Othello.   I know, Iago.
Thy honesty and love doth mince[287] this matter,
Making it light to Cassio. Cassio, I love thee;
But never more be officer of mine.

(*Enter Desdemona, attended.*)

Look! if my gentle love be not rais'd up;
(*To Cassio.*)   I'll make thee an example.
Desdemona.   What's the matter?
Othello.   All's well now, sweeting; come away to bed.
Sir, for your hurts, myself will be your surgeon.
Lead him off.   (*Montano is led off.*)
Iago, look with care about the town,   231
And silence those whom this vile brawl distracted.
Come, Desdemona; 'tis the soldier's life,
To have their balmy slumbers wak'd with strife.

(*Exeunt all but Iago and Cassio.*)

---

287.   Tone down.

Iago. What! are you hurt, lieutenant?

Cassio. Ay; past all surgery.

Iago. Marry, heaven forbid!

Cassio. Reputation, reputation, reputation! O! I have lost my reputation. I have lost the immortal part of myself, and what remains is bestial. My reputation, Iago, my reputation!   240

Iago. As I am an honest man, I thought you had received some bodily wound; there is more offence in that than in reputation. Reputation is an idle and most false imposition;[288] oft got without merit, and lost without deserving: you have lost no reputation at all, unless you repute yourself such a loser. What! man; there are ways to recover the general again; you are but now cast in his mood,[289] a punishment more in policy[290] than in malice; even so as one would beat his offenceless dog to affright an imperious lion. Sue to him again, and he is yours.

Cassio. I will rather sue to be despised than to deceive so good a commander with so slight, so drunken and so indiscreet an officer. Drunk! and speak parrot![291] and squabble, swagger, swear, and discourse fustian[292] with one's own shadow! O thou invisible spirit of wine! if thou hast no name to be known by, let us call thee devil!

Iago. What was he that you followed with your sword? What hath he done to you?

Cassio. I know not.

Iago. Is 't possible?

Cassio. I remember a mass of things, but nothing distinctly; a quarrel, but nothing wherefore. O God! that men should put an enemy in their mouths to steal away their brains; that we should, with joy, pleasance,[293] revel, and applause, transform ourselves into beasts.

Iago. Why, but you are now well enough; how came you thus recovered?

Cassio. It hath pleased the devil drunkenness to give place to the devil wrath; one unperfectness shows me another, to make me frankly despise myself.

Iago. Come, you are too severe a moraler. As the time, the place, and the condition of this country stands, I could heartily wish this had not befallen, but since it is as it is, mend it for your own good.

Cassio. I will ask him for my place again; he shall tell me I am a drunkard! Had I as many mouths as Hydra,[294] such an answer would stop them all. To be now a sensible man, by and by a fool, and presently a beast! O strange! Every inordinate cup is unblessed and the ingredient[295] is a devil.

Iago. Come, come; good wine is a good familiar creature if it be well used; exclaim no more against it. And, good lieutenant, I think you think I love you.

---

288. Something external.   289. Dismissed because he is angry.   290. *I.e.,* more for the sake of the example, or to show his fairness.   291. *I.e.,* without thinking.   292. *I.e.,* nonsense.   293. Pleasure.   294. Many-headed snake in Greek mythology.   295. Contents.

Cassio. I have well approved it, sir. I drunk!

Iago. You or any man living may be drunk at some time, man. I'll tell you what you shall do. Our general's wife is now the general; I may say so in this respect, for that he hath devoted and given up himself to the contemplation, mark, and denotement of her parts and graces: confess yourself freely to her; importune her; she'll help to put you in your place again. She is of so free, so kind, so apt, so blessed a disposition, that she holds it a vice in her goodness not to do more than she is requested. This broken joint between you and her husband entreat her to splinter;[296] and, my fortunes against any lay[297] worth naming, this crack of your love shall grow stronger than it was before.

Cassio. You advise me well.

Iago. I protest, in the sincerity of love and honest kindness.

Cassio. I think it freely; and betimes in the morning I will beseech the virtuous Desdemona to undertake for me. I am desperate of my fortunes if they check me here.   290

Iago. You are in the right. Good-night, lieutenant; I must to the watch.

Cassio. Good-night, honest Iago!   (*Exit.*)

Iago. And what's he then that says I play the villain?
When this advice is free I give and honest,
Probal[298] to thinking and indeed the course
To win the Moor again? For 'tis most easy
The inclining Desdemona to subdue
In any honest suit; she's fram'd as fruitful[299]
As the free elements. And then for her
To win the Moor, were 't to renounce his baptism,   300
All seals and symbols of redeemed sin,
His soul is so enfetter'd to her love,
That she may make, unmake, do what she list,
Even as her appetite shall play the god
With his weak function.[300] How am I then a villain
To counsel Cassio to this parallel[301] course,
Directly to his good? Divinity of hell!
When devils will the blackest sins put on,
They do suggest at first with heavenly shows,
As I do now; for while this honest fool   310
Plies Desdemona to repair his fortunes,
And she for him pleads strongly to the Moor,
I'll pour this pestilence into his ear
That she repeals[302] him for her body's lust;
And, by how much she strives to do him good,
She shall undo her credit with the Moor.

---

296. Bind up with splints.   297. Wager.   298. Provable.   299. Generous.
300. Faculties.   301. Purposeful.   302. I.e., seeks to recall.

So will I turn her virtue into pitch,
And out of her own goodness make the net
That shall enmesh them all.

(Re-enter Roderigo.)

How now, Roderigo!

Roderigo.   I do follow here in the chase, not like a hound that hunts, but one
that fills up the cry.[303] My money is almost spent; I have been to-night exceedingly well cudgelled; and I think the issue will be, I shall have so
much experience for my pains; and so, with no money at all and a little
more wit, return again to Venice.

Iago.   How poor are they that have not patience!
What wound did ever heal but by degrees?
Thou know'st we work by wit and not by witchcraft,
And wit depends on dilatory time.
Does 't not go well? Cassio hath beaten thee,
And thou by that small hurt hast cashiered Cassio.   330
Though other things grow fair against the sun,
Yet fruits that blossom first will first be ripe:
Content thyself awhile. By the mass, 'tis morning;
Pleasure and action make the hours seem short.
Retire thee; go where thou art billeted:
Away, I say; thou shalt know more hereafter:
Nay, get thee gone. *(Exit Roderigo.)* Two things are to be done,
My wife must move for Cassio to her mistress;
I'll set her on;
Myself the while to draw the Moor apart,   340
And bring him jump[304] when he may Cassio find
Soliciting his wife: ay, that's the way:
Dull not device by coldness and delay.   *(Exit.)*

Act III

SCENE 1.   *Cyprus. Before the Castle.*

(Enter Cassio, and some Musicians.)

Cassio.   Masters, play here, I will content your pains;[305]
Something that's brief; and bid 'Good-morrow, general.'   *(Music.)*

(Enter Clown.)

Clown.   Why, masters, have your instruments been in Naples, that they speak
i' the nose[306] thus?

---

303.   Pack (hunting term).   304.   At the exact moment.   305.   Reward your efforts.
306.   Naples was notorious for venereal disease, and syphilis was believed to affect the nose.

First Musician. How, sir, how?

Clown. Are these, I pray you, wind-instruments?

First Musician. Ay, marry, are they, sir.

Clown. O! thereby hangs a tail.

First Musician. Whereby hangs a tale, sir?

Clown. Marry, sir, by many a wind-instrument that I know. But, masters, here's money for you; and the general so likes your music, that he desires you, for love's sake, to make no more noise with it.

First Musician. Well, sir, we will not.

Clown. If you have any music that may not be heard, to 't again; but, as they say, to hear music the general does not greatly care.

First Musician. We have none such, sir.

Clown. Then put up your pipes in your bag, for I'll away.
Go; vanish into air; away! *(Exeunt Musicians.)*

Cassio. Dost thou hear, mine honest friend?

Clown. No, I hear not your honest friend; I hear you.   20

Cassio. Prithee, keep up thy quillets.[307] There's a poor piece of gold for thee. If the gentlewoman that attends the general's wife be stirring, tell her there's one Cassio entreats her a little favour of speech: wilt thou do this?

Clown. She is stirring, sir: if she will stir hither, I shall seem to notify unto her.

Cassio. Do, good my friend.   *(Exit Clown.)*

(Enter Iago.)

In happy time, Iago.

Iago. You have not been a-bed, then?

Cassio. Why, no; the day had broke
Before we parted. I have made bold, Iago,
To send in to your wife; my suit to her
Is, that she will to virtuous Desdemona   30
Procure me some access.

Iago.   I'll send her to you presently;
And I'll devise a mean to draw the Moor
Out of the way, that your converse and business
May be more free.

Cassio. I humbly thank you for 't.   *(Exit Iago.)*
                    I never knew
A Florentine more kind and honest.[308]

(Enter Emilia.)

Emilia. Good-morrow, good lieutenant: I am sorry
For your displeasure,[309] but all will soon be well.

---

307. Quibbles.   308. Cassio means that not even a fellow Florentine could behave to him in a friendlier fashion than does Iago.   309. Disgrace.

The general and his wife are talking of it,
And she speaks for you stoutly: the Moor replies   40
That he you hurt is of great fame in Cyprus
And great affinity,[310] and that in wholesome wisdom
He might not but refuse you; but he protests he loves you,
And needs no other suitor but his likings
To take the safest occasion by the front[311]
To bring you in again.[312]

Cassio.   Yet, I beseech you,
If you think fit, or that it may be done,
Give me advantage of some brief discourse
With Desdemona alone.

Emilia.   Pray you, come in:
I will bestow you where you shall have time   50
To speak your bosom[313] freely.

Cassio.   I am much bound to you.   (*Exeunt.*)

SCENE 2.   *A Room in the Castle.*

(*Enter Othello, Iago, and Gentlemen.*)

Othello.   These letters give, Iago, to the pilot,
And by him do my duties to the senate;
That done, I will be walking on the works;
Repair there to me.

Iago.   Well, my good lord, I'll do 't.

Othello.   This fortification, gentlemen, shall we see 't?

Gentlemen.   We'll wait upon your lordship.   (*Exeunt.*)

SCENE 3.   *Before the Castle.*

(*Enter Desdemona, Cassio, and Emilia.*)

Desdemona.   Be thou assur'd, good Cassio, I will do
All my abilities in thy behalf.

Emilia.   Good madam, do: I warrant it grieves my husband,
As if the case were his.

Desdemona.   O! that's an honest fellow. Do not doubt, Cassio,

---

310. Family connection.   311. Forelock.   312. Restore you (to Othello's favor).
313. Heart, inmost thoughts.

But I will have my lord and you again
As friendly as you were.

Cassio.   Bounteous madam,
Whatever shall become of Michael Cassio,
He's never any thing but your true servant.

Desdemona.   I know 't; I thank you. You do love my lord;   10
You have known him long; and be you well assur'd
He shall in strange ness[314] stand no further off
Than in a politic[315] distance.

Cassio.   Ay, but, lady,
That policy may either last so long,
Or feed upon such nice[316] and waterish diet,
Or breed itself so out of circumstance,
That, I being absent and my place supplied,
My general will forget my love and service.

Desdemona.   Do not doubt[317] that; before Emilia here
I give thee warrant of thy place. Assure thee,   20
If I do vow a friendship, I'll perform it
To the last article; my lord shall never rest;
I'll watch him tame,[318] and talk him out of patience;
His bed shall seem a school, his board a shrift;[319]
I'll intermingle every thing he does
With Cassio's suit. Therefore be merry, Cassio;
For thy solicitor shall rather die
Than give thy cause away.[320]

(*Enter Othello, and Iago at a distance.*)

Emilia.   Madam, here comes my lord.

Cassio.   Madam, I'll take my leave.   30

Desdemona.   Why, stay, and hear me speak.

Cassio.   Madam, not now; I am very ill at ease,
Unfit for mine own purposes.

Desdemona.   Well, do your discretion.   (*Exit Cassio.*)

Iago.   Ha! I like not that.

Othello.   What dost thou say?

Iago.   Nothing, my lord: or if—I know not what.

Othello.   Was not that Cassio parted from my wife?

Iago.   Cassio, my lord? No, sure, I cannot think it,
That he would steal away so guilty-like,
Seeing you coming.

Othello.   I do believe 'twas he.   40

---

314. Aloofness.   315. *I.e.,* dictated by policy.   316. Slight, trivial.   317. Fear.
318. Outwatch him (*i.e.,* keep him awake) till he submits.   319. Confessional.
320. Abandon your cause.

Desdemona. How now, my lord!
  I have been talking with a suitor here,
  A man that languishes in your displeasure.
Othello.   Who is 't you mean?
Desdemona.   Why, your lieutenant, Cassio. Good my lord,
  If I have any grace or power to move you,
  His present[321] reconciliation take;
  For if he be not one that truly loves you,
  That errs in ignorance and not in cunning,
  I have no judgment in an honest face.   50
  I prithee[322] call him back.
Othello.   Went he hence now?
Desdemona.   Ay, sooth; so humbled,
  That he hath left part of his grief with me,
  To suffer with him. Good love, call him back.
Othello.   Not now, sweet Desdemona; some other time.
Desdemona.   But shall 't be shortly?
Othello.   The sooner, sweet, for you.
Desdemona.   Shall 't be to-night at supper?
Othello.   No, not to-night.
Desdemona.   To-morrow dinner, then?
Othello.   I shall not dine at home;
  I meet the captains at the citadel.
Desdemona.   Why, then, to-morrow night; or Tuesday morn;
  Or Tuesday noon, or night; or Wednesday morn: 60
  I prithee name the time, but let it not
  Exceed three days: in faith, he's penitent;
  And yet his trespass, in our common reason,—
  Save that they say, the wars must make examples
  Out of their best,—is not almost[323] a fault
  To incur a private check.[324] When shall he come?
  Tell me, Othello: I wonder in my soul,
  What you could ask me, that I should deny,
  Or stand so mammering[325] on. What! Michael Cassio,   70
  That came a wooing with you, and so many a time,
  When I have spoke of you dispraisingly,
  Hath ta'en your part; to have so much to do
  To bring him in! Trust me, I could do much,—
Othello.   Prithee, no more; let him come when he will;
  I deny thee nothing.
Desdemona.   Why, this is not a boon;
  'Tis as I should entreat you wear your gloves,

---

321. Immediate.   322. Pray thee.   323. Hardly.   324. (Even) a private repri-
mand.   325. Shilly-shallying.

Or feed on nourishing dishes, or keep you warm,
Or sue to you to do a peculiar profit
To your own person: nay, when I have a suit   *80*
Wherein I mean to touch your love indeed,
It shall be full of poise[326] and difficult weight,
And fearful to be granted.

Othello.   I will deny thee nothing:
Whereon, I do beseech thee, grant me this,
To leave me but a little to myself.

Desdemona.   Shall I deny you? no: farewell, my lord.

Othello.   Farewell, my Desdemona: I'll come to thee straight.

Desdemona.   Emilia, come. Be as your fancies teach you;
Whate'er you be, I am obedient.   (*Exit, with Emilia.*)

Othello.   Excellent wretch![327] Perdition catch my soul,   *90*
But I do love thee! and when I love thee not,
Chaos is[328] come again.

Iago.   My noble lord,—

Othello.   What dost thou say, Iago?

Iago.   Did Michael Cassio, when you woo'd my lady,
Know of your love?

Othello.   He did, from first to last: why dost thou ask?

Iago.   But for a satisfaction of my thought;
No further harm.

Othello.   Why of thy thought, Iago?

Iago.   I did not think he had been acquainted with her.

Othello.   O! yes; and went between us very oft.   *100*

Iago.   Indeed!

Othello.   Indeed! ay, indeed; discern'st thou aught in that?
Is he not honest?

Iago.   Honest, my lord?

Othello.   Honest! ay, honest.

Iago.   My lord, for aught I know.

Othello.   What dost thou think?

Iago.   Think, my lord!

Othello.   Think, my lord!
By heaven, he echoes me,
As if there were some monster in his thought
Too hideous to be shown. Thou dost mean something:
I heard thee say but now, thou lik'dst not that,
When Cassio left my wife; what didst not like?   *110*
And when I told thee he was of my counsel
In my whole course of wooing, thou criedst, 'Indeed!'

---

326. Weight.   327. Here, a term of endearment.   328. Will have.

And didst contract and purse thy brow together,
As if thou then hadst shut up in thy brain
Some horrible conceit.[329] If thou dost love me,
Show me thy thought.

Iago.   My lord, you know I love you.

Othello.   I think thou dost;
And, for[330] I know thou art full of love and honesty,
And weigh'st thy words before thou givest them breath,
Therefore these stops[331] of thine fright me the more;   120
For such things in a false disloyal knave
Are tricks of custom, but in a man that's just
They are close dilations,[332] working from the heart
That passion cannot rule.

Iago.   For Michael Cassio,
I dare be sworn I think that he is honest.

Othello.   I think so too.

Iago.   Men should be what they seem;
Or those that be not, would they might seem none!

Othello.   Certain, men should be what they seem.

Iago.   Why then, I think Cassio's an honest man.

Othello.   Nay, yet there's more in this.   130
I pray thee, speak to me as to thy thinkings,
As thou dost ruminate, and give thy worst of thoughts
The worst of words.

Iago.   Good my lord, pardon me;
Though I am bound to every act of duty,
I am not bound to[333] that all slaves are free to.
Utter my thoughts? Why, say they are vile and false;
As where's that palace whereinto foul things
Sometimes intrude not? who has a breast so pure
But some uncleanly apprehensions[334]
Keep leets and law-days,[335] and in session sit   140
With meditations lawful?

Othello.   Thou dost conspire against thy friend, Iago,
If thou but think'st him wrong'd, and mak'st his ear
A stranger to thy thoughts.

Iago.   I do beseech you,
Though I perchance am vicious in my guess,—
As, I confess, it is my nature's plague
To spy into abuses, and oft my jealousy[336]
Shapes faults that are not,—that your wisdom yet,

---

329. Fancy.   330. Because.   . 331. Interruptions, hesitations.   332. Secret (i.e.,
involuntary, unconscious) revelations.   333. Bound with regard to.   334. Conceptions.   335. Sittings of the local courts.   336. Suspicion.

From one that so imperfectly conceits,
Would take no notice, nor build yourself a trouble   150
Out of his scattering and unsure observance.
It were not for your quiet nor your good,
Nor for my manhood, honesty, or wisdom,
To let you know my thoughts.

Othello.   What dost thou mean?

Iago.   Good name in man and woman, dear my lord,
Is the immediate jewel of[337] their souls:
Who steals my purse steals trash; 'tis something, nothing;
'Twas mine, 'tis his, and has been slave to thousands;
But he that filches from me my good name
Robs me of that which not enriches him,   160
And makes me poor indeed.

Othello.   By heaven, I'll know thy thoughts.

Iago.   You cannot, if my heart were in your hand;
Nor shall not, whilst 'tis in my custody.

Othello.   Ha!

Iago.   O! beware, my lord, of jealousy;
It is the green-ey'd monster which doth mock
The meat it feeds on: that cuckold[338] lives in bliss
Who, certain of his fate, loves not his wronger;
But, O! what damned minutes tells[339] he o'er
Who dotes, yet doubts; suspects, yet soundly loves!   170

Othello.   O misery!

Iago.   Poor and content is rich, and rich enough,
But riches fineless[340] is as poor as winter
To him that ever fears he shall be poor.
Good heaven, the souls of all my tribe defend
From jealousy!

Othello.   Why, why is this?
Think'st thou I'd make a life of jealousy,
To follow still the changes of the moon
With fresh suspicions? No; to be once in doubt
Is once to be resolved. Exchange me for a goat   180
When I shall turn the business of my soul
To such exsufflicate[341] and blown[342] surmises,
Matching thy inference. 'Tis not to make me jealous
To say my wife is fair, feeds well, loves company,
Is free of speech, sings, plays, and dances well;
Where virtue is, these are more virtuous:
Nor from mine own weak merits will I draw

---

337. Jewel closest to.   338. Husband of an adulterous woman.   339. Counts.
340. Boundless.   341. Spat out (?).   342. Fly-blown.

The smallest fear, or doubt of her revolt;
For she had eyes, and chose me. No, Iago;
I'll see before I doubt; when I doubt, prove;   190
And, on the proof, there is no more but this,
Away at once with love or jealousy!

Iago.   I am glad of it; for now I shall have reason
To show the love and duty that I bear you
With franker spirit; therefore, as I am bound,
Receive it from me; I speak not yet of proof.
Look to your wife; observe her well with Cassio;
Wear your eye thus, not jealous nor secure:
I would not have your free and noble nature
Out of self-bounty³⁴³ be abus'd; look to 't: 200
I know our country disposition³⁴⁴ well;
In Venice they do let heaven see the pranks
They dare not show their husbands; their best conscience
Is not to leave 't undone, but keep 't unknown.

Othello.   Dost thou say so?

Iago.   She did deceive her father, marrying you;
And when she seem'd to shake and fear your looks,
She lov'd them most.

Othello.   And so she did.

Iago.   Why, go to,³⁴⁵ then;
She that so young could give out such a seeming,
To seel her father's eyes up close as oak,   210
He thought 'twas witchcraft; but I am much to blame;
I humbly do beseech you of your pardon
For too much loving you.

Othello.   I am bound to thee for ever.

Iago.   I see, this hath a little dash'd your spirits.

Othello.   Not a jot, not a jot.

Iago.   I' faith, I fear it has.
I hope you will consider what is spoke
Comes from my love. But I do see you're mov'd;
I am to pray you not to strain my speech
To grosser issues nor to larger reach
Than to suspicion.   220

Othello.   I will not.

Iago.   Should you do so, my lord,
My speech should fall into such vile success
As my thoughts aim not at. Cassio's my worthy friend—
My lord, I see you're mov'd.

---

343. Innate generosity.   344. *I.e.*, that of Venice.   345. Colloquialism; here, something like "all right."

Othello.   No, not much mov'd:
    I do not think but Desdemona's honest.[346]
Iago.   Long live she so! and long live you to think so!
Othello.   And yet, how nature erring from itself,—
Iago.   Ay, there's the point: as, to be bold with you,
    Not to affect many proposed matches
    Of her own clime,[347] complexion, and degree,[348]   230
    Whereto, we see, in all things nature tends;
    Foh! one may smell in such, a will most rank,
    Foul disproportion, thoughts unnatural.
    But pardon me; I do not in position[349]
    Distinctly[350] speak of her, though I may fear
    Her will, recoiling[351] to her better judgment,
    May fall to match you with her country forms
    And happily[352] repent.
Othello.   Farewell, farewell:
    If more thou dost perceive, let me know more;
    Set on thy wife to observe. Leave me, Iago.   240
Iago.   My lord, I take my leave.   (*Going.*)
Othello.   Why did I marry? This honest creature, doubtless,
    Sees and knows more, much more, than he unfolds.
Iago (*returning*).   My lord, I would I might entreat your honour
    To scan this thing no further; leave it to time.
    Although 'tis fit that Cassio have his place,
    For, sure he fills it up with great ability,
    Yet, if you please to hold him off awhile,
    You shall by that perceive him and his means:
    Note if your lady strain his entertainment[353]   250
    With any strong or vehement importunity;
    Much will be seen in that. In the mean time,
    Let me be thought too busy[354] in my fears,
    As worthy cause I have to fear I am,
    And hold her free, I do beseech your honour.
Othello.   Fear not my government.
Iago.   I once more take my leave.   (*Exit.*)
Othello.   This fellow's of exceeding honesty,
    And knows all qualities, with a learned spirit,
    Of human dealings; if I do prove her haggard,[355]   260
    Though that her jesses[356] were my dear heart-strings,
    I'd whistle her off and let her down the wind,[357]

---

346. Chaste.   347. Country.   348. Social rank.   349. In definite assertion.
350. Specifically.   351. Reverting.   352. Perhaps.   353. Urge his re-welcome
(*i.e.*, to Othello's trust and favor).   354. Meddlesome.   355. Wild hawk.
356. Leather thongs by which the hawk's legs were strapped to the trainer's wrist.   357. I'd
let her go and take care of herself.

To prey at fortune. Haply, for I am black,
And have not those soft parts of conversation
That chamberers[358] have, or, for I am declin'd
Into the vale of years—yet that's not much—
She's gone, I am abus'd;[359] and my relief
Must be to loathe her. O curse of marriage!
That we can call these delicate creatures ours,
And not their appetites. I had rather be a toad,   270
And live upon the vapour of a dungeon,
Than keep a corner in the thing I love
For others' uses. Yet, 'tis the plague of great ones;
Prerogativ'd[360] are they less than the base;
'Tis destiny unshunnable, like death:
Even then this forked plague[361] is fated to us
When we do quicken.[362]
                    Look! where she comes.
If she be false, O! then heaven mocks itself.
I'll not believe it.

(Re-enter Desdemona and Emilia.)

Desdemona.   How now, my dear Othello!
  Your dinner and the generous[363] islanders   280
  By you invited, do attend your presence.
Othello.   I am to blame.
Desdemona.   Why do you speak so faintly?
  Are you not well?
Othello.   I have a pain upon my forehead here.[364]
Desdemona.   Faith, that's with watching; 'twill away again:
  Let me but bind it hard, within this hour
  It will be well.
Othello.   Your napkin[365] is too little:

(She drops her handkerchief.)

  Let it alone. Come, I'll go in with you.
Desdemona.   I am very sorry that you are not well.

                              (Exeunt Othello and Desdemona.)

Emilia.   I am glad I have found this napkin;   290
  This was her first remembrance from the Moor;
  My wayward husband hath a hundred times
  Woo'd me to steal it, but she so loves the token,

---

358. Courtiers; or (more specifically): gallants, frequenters of bed chambers.   359. Deceived.   360. Privileged.   361. *I.e.,* the cuckold's proverbial horns.   362. Are
conceived, come alive.   363. Noble.   364. Othello again refers to his cuckoldom.
365. Handkerchief.

For he conjur'd her she should ever keep it,
That she reserves it evermore about her
To kiss and talk to. I'll have the work ta'en out,[366]
And giv 't Iago:
What he will do with it heaven knows, not I;
I nothing but[367] to please his fantasy.[368]

(*Enter Iago.*)

Iago.   How now! what do you here alone?   300
Emilia.   Do not you chide; I have a thing for you.
Iago.   A thing for me? It is a common thing—
Emilia.   Ha!
Iago.   To have a foolish wife.
Emilia.   O! is that all? What will you give me now
        For that same handkerchief?
Iago.   What handkerchief?
Emilia.   What handkerchief!
        Why, that the Moor first gave to Desdemona:
        That which so often you did bid me steal.
Iago.   Hath stol'n it from her?   310
Emilia.   No, faith; she let it drop by negligence,
        And, to the advantage, I, being there, took 't up.
        Look, here it is.
Iago.   A good wench; give it me.
Emilia.   What will you do with 't, that you have been so earnest
        To have me filch it?
Iago.   Why, what's that to you? (*Snatches it.*)
Emilia.   If it be not for some purpose of import
        Give 't me again; poor lady! she'll run mad
        When she shall lack it.
Iago.   Be not acknown on 't;[369] I have use for it.
        Go, leave me.   (*Exit Emilia.*)
        I will in Cassio's lodging lose this napkin,   321
        And let him find it; trifles light as air
        Are to the jealous confirmations strong
        As proofs of holy writ; this may do something.
        The Moor already changes with my poison:
        Dangerous conceits are in their natures poisons,
        Which at the first are scarce found to distaste,[370]
        But with a little act upon the blood,
        Burn like the mines of sulphur. I did say so:
        Look! where he comes!

---

366. Pattern copied.   367. *I.e.*, only want.   368. Whim.   369. You know nothing
about it.   370. Scarce can be tasted.

(*Enter Othello.*)

Not poppy,[371] nor mandragora,[372]   *330*
Nor all the drowsy syrups[373] of the world,
Shall ever medicine thee to that sweet sleep
Which thou owedst yesterday.

Othello.   Ha! ha! false to me?

Iago.   Why, how now, general! no more of that.

Othello.   Avaunt! be gone! thou hast set me on the rack;
I swear 'tis better to be much abus'd
Than but to know 't a little.

Iago.   How now, my lord!

Othello.   What sense had I of her stol'n hours of lust?
I saw 't not, thought it not, it harm'd not me;
I slept the next night well, was free and merry;   *340*
I found not Cassio's kisses on her lips;
He that is robb'd, not wanting what is stol'n,
Let him not know 't, and he's not robb'd at all.

Iago.   I am sorry to hear this.

Othello.   I had been happy, if the general camp,[374]
Pioners[375] and all, had tasted her sweet body,
So[376] I had nothing known. O! now, for ever
Farewell the tranquil mind; farewell content!
Farewell the plumed troop and the big wars
That make ambition virtue! O, farewell!   *350*
Farewell the neighing steed, and the shrill trump,
The spirit-stirring drum, the ear-piercing fife,
The royal banner, and all quality,
Pride, pomp, and circumstance[377] of glorious war!
And, O you mortal engines,[378] whose rude throats
The immortal Jove's dread clamours counterfeit,
Farewell! Othello's occupation's gone!

Iago.   Is it possible, my lord?

Othello.   Villain, be sure thou prove my love a whore,
Be sure of it; give me the ocular proof;   *360*
Or, by the worth of mine eternal soul,
Thou hadst been better have been born a dog
Than answer my wak'd wrath.

Iago.   Is 't come to this?

Othello.   Make me to see 't; or, at the least, so prove it,
That the probation[379] bear no hinge nor loop
To hang a doubt on; or woe upon thy life!

---

371. Opium.   372. A soporific.   373. *I.e.,* soporifics.   374. Whole army.
375. Lowest rank of manual laborers in the army.   376. As long as.   377. Pageantry.
378. Deadly artillery.   379. Proof.

Iago. My noble lord,—

Othello. If thou dost slander her and torture me,
    Never pray more; abandon all remorse;
    On horror's head horrors accumulate;   *370*
    Do deeds to make heaven weep, all earth amaz'd;
    For nothing canst thou to damnation add
    Greater than that.

Iago.   O grace! O heaven forgive me!
    Are you a man! have you a soul or sense?
    God be wi' you; take mine office. O wretched fool!
    That liv'st to make thine honesty a vice.
    O monstrous world! Take note, take note, O world!
    To be direct and honest is not safe.
    I thank you for this profit,[380] and, from hence
    I'll love no friend, sith[381] love breeds such offence.   *380*

Othello. Nay, stay; thou shouldst be honest.

Iago. I should be wise; for honesty's a fool,
    And loses that it works for.

Othello.   By the world,
    I think my wife be honest and think she is not;
    I think that thou art just and think thou art not.
    I'll have some proof. Her name, that was as fresh
    As Dian's[382] visage, is now begrim'd and black
    As mine own face. If there be cords or knives,
    Poison or fire or suffocating streams,
    I'll not endure it. Would I were satisfied!   *390*

Iago. I see, sir, you are eaten up with passion.
    I do repent me that I put it to you.
    You would be satisfied?

Othello.   Would! nay, I will.

Iago. And may; but how? how satisfied, my lord?
    Would you, the supervisor,[383] grossly gape on;
    Behold her tupp'd?

Othello.   Death and damnation! O!

Iago. It were a tedious[384] difficulty, I think,
    To bring them to that prospect; damn them then,
    If ever mortal eyes do see them bolster[385]
    More[386] than their own! What then? how then?   *400*
    What shall I say? Where's satisfaction?
    It is impossible you should see this,
    Were they as prime[387] as goats, as hot as monkeys,

---

380. Lesson.   381. Since.   382. Diana's, the goddess of the moon.   383. Observer.   384. Laborious.   385. Lie together.   386. Other.   387. Lustful.

As salt as wolves in pride,[388] and fools as gross
As ignorance made drunk; but yet, I say,
If imputation, and strong circumstances,
Which lead directly to the door of truth,
Will give you satisfaction, you may have it.

Othello.   Give me a living reason she's disloyal.

Iago.   I do not like the office;   410
But, sith I am enter'd in this cause so far,
Prick'd to 't by foolish honesty and love,
I will go on. I lay with Cassio lately;
And, being troubled with a raging tooth,
I could not sleep.
There are a kind of men so loose of soul
That in their sleeps will mutter their affairs;
One of this kind is Cassio.
In sleep I heard him say, 'Sweet Desdemona,
Let us be wary, let us hide our loves!'   420
And then, sir, would he gripe[389] and wring my hand,
Cry, 'O, sweet creature!' and then kiss me hard,
As if he pluck'd up kisses by the roots,
That grew upon my lips; then laid his leg
Over my thigh, and sigh'd, and kiss'd; and then
Cried, 'Cursed fate, that gave thee to the Moor!'

Othello.   O monstrous! monstrous!

Iago.   Nay, this was but his dream.

Othello.   But this denoted a foregone conclusion:[390]
'Tis a shrewd doubt,[391] though it be but a dream.

Iago.   And this may help to thicken other proofs   430
That do demonstrate thinly.

Othello.   I'll tear her all to pieces.

Iago.   Nay, but be wise; yet we see nothing done;
She may be honest yet. Tell me but this:
Have you not sometimes seen a handkerchief
Spotted with strawberries in your wife's hand?

Othello.   I gave her such a one; 'twas my first gift.

Iago.   I know not that; but such a handkerchief—
I am sure it was your wife's—did I to-day
See Cassio wipe his beard with.

Othello.   If it be that,—

Iago.   If it be that, or any that was hers,   440
It speaks against her with the other proofs.

---

388. Heat.   389. Seize.   390. Previous consummation.   391. (1) Cursed, (2) Acute, suspicion.

Othello.   O! that the slave had forty thousand lives;
      One is too poor, too weak for my revenge.
      Now do I see 'tis true. Look here, Iago;
      All my fond love thus do I blow to heaven:
      'Tis gone.
      Arise, black vengeance, from the hollow hell!
      Yield up, O love! thy crown and hearted throne
      To tyrannous hate. Swell, bosom, with thy fraught,[392]
      For 'tis of aspics'[393] tongues!
Iago.   Yet be content.[394]   450
Othello.   O! blood, blood, blood!
Iago.   Patience, I say; your mind, perhaps, may change.
Othello.   Never, Iago. Like to the Pontic sea,[395]
      Whose icy current and compulsive course
      Ne'er feels retiring ebb, but keeps due on
      To the Propontic and the Hellespont,[396]
      Even so my bloody thoughts, with violent pace,
      Shall ne'er look back, ne'er ebb to humble love,
      Till that a capable[397] and wide revenge
      Swallow them up.   (*Kneels.*)
                  Now, by yond marble heaven,   460
      In the due reverence of a sacred vow
      I here engage my words.
Iago.   Do not rise yet.   (*Kneels.*)
      Witness, you ever-burning lights above!
      You elements that clip[398] us round about!
      Witness, that here Iago doth give up
      The execution of his wit, hands, heart,
      To wrong'd Othello's service! Let him command,
      And to obey shall be in me remorse,[399]
      What bloody business ever.[400]   (*They rise.*)
Othello.   I greet thy love,
      Not with vain thanks, but with acceptance bounteous,   470
      And will upon the instant put thee to 't:
      Within these three days let me hear thee say
      That Cassio 's not alive.
Iago.   My friend is dead; 'tis done at your request:
      But let her live.
Othello.   Damn her, lewd minx! O, damn her!
      Come, go with me apart; I will withdraw.

---

392. Burden.   393. Poisonous snakes.   394. Patient.   395. The Black Sea.
396. The Sea of Marmara, The Dardanelles.   397. Comprehensive.   398. Encompass.
399. Probably a corrupt line; the meaning appears to be: "to obey shall be my solemn obligation."
400. Soever.

To furnish me with some swift means of death
For the fair devil. Now art thou my lieutenant.
Iago.   I am your own for ever.   (*Exeunt.*)

SCENE 4.   *Before the Castle.*

(*Enter Desdemona, Emilia, and Clown.*)

Desdemona.   Do you know, sirrah,[401] where Lieutenant Cassio lies?[402]
Clown.   I dare not say he lies any where.
Desdemona.   Why, man?
Clown.   He is a soldier; and for one to say a soldier lies, is stabbing.[403]
Desdemona.   Go to;[404] where lodges he?
Clown.   To tell you where he lodges is to tell you where I lie.
Desdemona.   Can anything be made of this?
Clown.   I know not where he lodges, and for me to devise[405] a lodging, and say he lies here or he lies there, were to lie in mine own throat.
Desdemona.   Can you inquire him out, and be edified by report?   10
Clown.   I will catechize the world for him; that is, make questions, and by them answer.
Desdemona.   Seek him, bid him come hither; tell him I have moved my lord in his behalf, and hope all will be well.
Clown.   To do this is within the compass of man's wit, and therefore I will attempt the doing it.   (*Exit.*)
Desdemona.   Where should I lose that handkerchief, Emilia?
Emilia.   I know not, madam.
Desdemona.   Believe me, I had rather have lost my purse
Full of cruzadoes;[406] and, but my noble Moor   20
Is true of mind, and made of no such baseness
As jealous creatures are, it were enough
To put him to ill thinking.
Emilia.   Is he not jealous?
Desdemona.   Who! he? I think the sun where he was born
Drew all such humours from him.
Emilia.   Look! where he comes.
Desdemona.   I will not leave him now till Cassio
Be call'd to him.

(*Enter Othello.*)

How is 't with you, my lord?

---

401. Common form of address to inferiors.   402. Lives.   403. *I.e.,* is cause for stabbing.   404. Here apparently: "Come on!"   405. Invent.   406. Portuguese gold coins.

Othello. Well, my good lady. (*Aside*) O! hardness to dissemble.
How do you, Desdemona?

Desdemona. Well, my good lord.

Othello. Give me your hand. This hand is moist,[107] my lady.   30

Desdemona. It yet has felt no age nor known no sorrow.

Othello. This argues fruitfulness and liberal[108] heart;
Hot, hot, and moist; this hand of yours requires
A sequester[109] from liberty, fasting and prayer,
Much castigation, exercise devout;
For here 's a young and sweating devil here,
That commonly rebels. 'Tis a good hand,
A frank one.

Desdemona. You may, indeed, say so;
For 'twas that hand that gave away my heart.

Othello. A liberal hand; the hearts of old gave hands,   40
But our new heraldry[110] is hands not hearts.

Desdemona. I cannot speak of this. Come now, your promise.

Othello. What promise, chuck?[111]

Desdemona. I have sent to bid Cassio come speak with you.

Othello. I have a salt and sorry rheum offends me.
Lend me thy handkerchief.

Desdemona. Here, my lord.

Othello. That which I gave you.

Desdemona. I have it not about me.

Othello. Not?

Desdemona. No, indeed, my lord.

Othello. That is a fault.
That handkerchief
Did an Egyptian[112] to my mother give;   50
She was a charmer,[413] and could almost read
The thoughts of people; she told her, while she kept it,
'Twould make her amiable[114] and subdue my father
Entirely to her love, but if she lost it
Or made a gift of it, my father's eye
Should hold her loathed, and his spirits should hunt
After new fancies.[415] She dying gave it me;
And bid me, when my fate would have me wive,
To give it her. I did so; and take heed on 't;
Make it a darling like your precious eye;   60

---

407. A supposed symptom of a lustful nature.   408. With overtones of: too free, loose.
409. Separation.   410. *I.e.*, new heraldic symbolism (Othello means that the new way is not
to give the heart together with the hand.)   411. Common term of endearment.
412. Gypsy.   413. Sorceress.   414. Lovable, desirable.   415. Loves.

To lose 't or give 't away, were such perdition
As nothing else could match.

Desdemona.   Is 't possible?

Othello.   'Tis true; there 's magic in the web of it;
A sibyl,[416] that had number'd in the world
The sun to course two hundred compasses,
In her prophetic fury sew'd the work;
The worms were hallow'd that did breed the silk,
And it was dy'd in mummy[417] which the skilful
Conserv'd of maidens' hearts.

Desdemona.   Indeed! is 't true?

Othello.   Most veritable; therefore look to 't well.   70

Desdemona.   Then would to heaven that I had never seen it!

Othello.   Ha! wherefore?

Desdemona.   Why do you speak so startingly and rash?

Othello.   Is 't lost? is 't gone? speak, is it out o' the way?

Desdemona.   Heaven bless us!

Othello.   Say you?

Desdemona.   It is not lost: but what an if[418] it were?

Othello.   How!

Desdemona.   I say, it is not lost.

Othello.   Fetch 't, let me see 't!

Desdemona.   Why, so I can, sir, but I will not now.   80
This is a trick to put me from my suit:
Pray you let Cassio be receiv'd again.

Othello.   Fetch me the handkerchief; my mind misgives.

Desdemona.   Come, come;
You'll never meet a more sufficient[419] man.

Othello.   The handkerchief!

Desdemona.   I pray, talk[420] me of Cassio.

Othello.   The handkerchief!

Desdemona.   A man that all his time
Hath founded his good fortunes on your love,
Shar'd dangers with you,—

Othello.   The handkerchief!   90

Desdemona.   In sooth, you are to blame.

Othello.   Away!   (*Exit.*)

Emilia.   Is not this man jealous?

Desdemona.   I ne'er saw this before.
Sure, there 's some wonder in this handkerchief;
I am most unhappy in the loss of it.

---

416. Prophetess.   417. Drug (medicinal or magic) derived from embalmed bodies.
418. If.   419. Adequate.   420. Talk to.

Emilia.   'Tis not a year or two shows us a man;
   They are all but[421] stomachs, and we all but[421] food;
   They eat us hungerly, and when they are full
   They belch us. Look you! Cassio and my husband.   *100*

(*Enter Iago and Cassio.*)

Iago.   There is no other way; 'tis she must do 't:
   And, lo! the happiness;[422] go and importune her.
Desdemona.   How now, good Cassio! what 's the news with you?
Cassio.   Madam, my former suit: I do beseech you
   That by your virtuous means I may again
   Exist, and be a member of his love
   Whom I with all the office[423] of my heart
   Entirely honour; I would not be delay'd.
   If my offence be of such mortal kind
   That nor my service past, nor present sorrows,   *110*
   Nor purpos'd merit in futurity,
   Can ransom me into his love again,
   But to know so must be my benefit;
   So shall I clothe me in a forc'd content,
   And shut myself up in some other course
   To fortune's alms.
Desdemona.   Alas! thrice-gentle Cassio!
   My advocation is not now in tune;
   My lord is not my lord, nor should I know him,
   Were he in favour[424] as in humour alter'd.
   So help me every spirit sanctified,   *120*
   As I have spoken for you all my best
   And stood within the blank of[425] his displeasure
   For my free speech. You must awhile be patient;
   What I can do I will, and more I will
   Than for myself I dare: let that suffice you.
Iago.   Is my lord angry?
Emilia.   He went hence but now,
   And certainly in strange unquietness.
Iago.   Can he be angry? I have seen the cannon,
   When it hath blown his ranks[426] into the air,
   And, like the devil, from his very arm   *130*
   Puff'd his own brother; and can he be angry?
   Something of moment[427] then; I will go meet him;
   There's matter in 't indeed, if he be angry.
Desdemona.   I prithee, do so. (*Exit Iago.*) Something, sure, of state,[428]

---

421. Only ... only.   422. "What luck!"   423. Duty.   424. Appearance.
425. As the target for.   426. *I.e.*, his soldiers.   427. Important.   428. Public
affairs.

Either from Venice, or some unhatch'd[129] practice
Made demonstrable here in Cyprus to him,
Hath puddled[430] his clear spirit; and, in such cases
Men's natures wrangle with inferior things,
Though great ones are their object. 'Tis even so;
For let our finger ache, and it indues[131]   140
Our other healthful members even to that sense
Of pain. Nay, we must think men are not gods,
Nor of them look for such observancy[132]
As fits the bridal.[133] Beshrew me much, Emilia,
I was—unhandsome warrior as I am—
Arraigning his unkindness with[134] my soul;
But now I find I had suborn'd the witness,[135]
And he 's indicted falsely.

Emilia.   Pray heaven it be state matters, as you think,
And no conception,[136] nor no jealous toy[137]   150
Concerning you.

Desdemona.   Alas the day! I never gave him cause.

Emilia.   But jealous souls will not be answer'd so;
They are not ever jealous for the cause,
But jealous for they are jealous; 'tis a monster
Begot upon itself, born on itself.

Desdemona.   Heaven keep that monster from Othello's mind!

Emilia.   Lady, amen.

Desdemona.   I will go seek him. Cassio, walk hereabout;
If I do find him fit, I'll move your suit   160
And seek to effect it to my uttermost.

Cassio.   I humbly thank your ladyship.   (*Exeunt Desdemona and Emilia.*)

(*Enter Bianca.*)

Bianca.   Save you, friend Cassio!

Cassio.   What make you from home?
How is it with you, my most fair Bianca?
I' faith, sweet love, I was coming to your house.

Bianca.   And I was going to your lodging, Cassio.
What! keep a week away? seven days and nights?
Eight score eight hours? and lovers' absent hours,
More tedious than the dial eight score times?
O weary reckoning!

Cassio.   Pardon me, Bianca,   170
I have this while with leaden thoughts been press'd;

---

429. Abortive or budding plot.   430. Muddied.   431. Brings, leads.   432. Attention.   433. Wedding.   434. To.   435. *I.e.*, caused my soul to bring in wrong
charges.   436. Fancy, supposition.   437. Fancy.

But I shall, in a more continuate[138] time,
Strike off[139] this score of absence. Sweet Bianca,

(*Giving her Desdemona's handkerchief.*)

Take me this work out.
Bianca.   O Cassio! whence came this?
This is some token from a newer friend;
To the felt absence now I feel a cause;
Is 't come to this? Well, well.
Cassio.   Go to, woman!
Throw your vile guesses in the devil's teeth,
From whence you have them. You are jealous now
That this is from some mistress, some remembrance: 180
No, in good troth, Bianca.
Bianca.   Why, whose is it?
Cassio. I know not, sweet; I found it in my chamber.
I like the work well; ere it be demanded,—[440]
As like enough it will,—I'd have it copied;
Take it and do 't; and leave me for this time.
Bianca. Leave you! wherefore?
Cassio. I do attend here on[441] the general,
And think it no addition,[442] nor my wish,
To have him see me woman'd.
Bianca.   Why, I pray you?
Cassio. Not that I love you not.
Bianca.   But that you do not love me.   190
I pray you, bring me on the way a little
And say if I shall see you soon at night.
Cassio. 'Tis but a little way that I can bring you,
For I attend here; but I 'll see you soon.
Bianca. 'Tis very good; I must be circumstanc'd.[443]   (*Exeunt.*)

Act IV

SCENE 1. *Cyprus. Before the Castle.*

(*Enter Othello and Iago.*)

Iago. Will you think so?
Othello.   Think so, Iago!

---

438. Uninterrupted.   439. Cancel (i.e., make up for).   440. Asked for.
441. Wait for.   442. Advantage, credit.   443. Governed by circumstances.

Iago.   What!
    To kiss in private?

Othello.   An unauthoriz'd kiss.

Iago.   Or to be naked with her friend a-bed
    An hour or more, not meaning any harm?

Othello.   Naked a-bed, Iago, and not mean harm?
    It is hypocrisy against the devil:[444]
    They that mean virtuously, and yet do so,
    The devil their virtue tempts, and they tempt heaven.

Iago.   If they do nothing, 'tis a venial slip;
    But if I give my wife a handkerchief,—   10

Othello.   What then?

Iago.   Why, then, 'tis hers, my lord; and, being hers,
    She may, I think, bestow 't on any man.

Othello.   She is protectress of her honour too;
    May she give that?

Iago.   Her honour is an essence that 's not seen;
    They have it very oft that have it not:[445]
    But for the handkerchief,—

Othello.   By heaven, I would most gladly have forgot it:—
    Thou said'st,—O! it comes o'er my memory,   20
    As doth the raven[446] o'er the infected house,
    Boding to all,—he had my handkerchief.

Iago.   Ay, what of that?

Othello.   That's not so good now.

Iago.   What,
    If I had said I had seen him do you wrong?
    Or heard him say, as knaves be such abroad,[447]
    Who having, by their own importunate suit,
    Or voluntary dotage[448] of some mistress,
    Convinced or supplied them,[449] cannot choose
    But they must blab.

Othello.   Hath he said any thing?

Iago.   He hath, my lord; but be you well assur'd,   30
    No more than he 'll unswear.

Othello.   What hath he said?

Iago.   Faith, that he did—I know not what he did.

Othello.   What? what?

Iago.   Lie—

Othello.   With her?

---

444. *I.e.*, by not committing the sin which the situation invites.   445. *I.e.*, some unchaste women are thought chaste.   446. (1) A bad omen, (2) A carrier of the plague.   447. As there are some such in the world.   448. Foolish affection.   449. Overcome (their reluctance) or satisfied (their desires).

Iago.   With her, on her; what you will.

Othello.   Lie with her; lie on her! We say, lie on her, when they belie her. Lie
with her! that's fulsome. Handkerchief,—confessions,—handkerchief! To
confess, and be hanged for his labour. First, to be hanged, and then to
confess: I tremble at it. Nature would not invest herself in such shadowing
passion without some instruction.[450] It is not words that shake me thus.
Pish! Noses, ears, and lips. Is it possible?—Confess!—Handkerchief!—O
devil!

(Falls in a trance.)

Iago.   Work on,
    My medicine, work! Thus credulous fools are caught;
    And many worthy and chaste dames even thus,
    All guiltless, meet reproach. What, ho! my lord!
    My lord, I say! Othello!

(Enter Cassio.)

                        How now, Cassio!

Cassio.   What's the matter?

Iago.   My lord is fallen into an epilepsy;[451]
    This is his second fit; he had one yesterday.   50

Cassio.   Rub him about the temples.

Iago.   No, forbear;
    The lethargy[452] must have his quiet course,
    If not, he foams at mouth, and by and by
    Breaks out to savage madness. Look! he stirs;
    Do you withdraw yourself a little while,
    He will recover straight; when he is gone,
    I would on great occasion[453] speak with you.   *(Exit Cassio.)*
    How is it, general? have you not hurt your head?

Othello.   Dost thou mock me?[454]

Iago.   I mock you! no, by heaven.
    Would you would bear your fortune like a man!   60

Othello.   A horned man's a monster and a beast.

Iago.   There 's many a beast then, in a populous city,
    And many a civil[455] monster.

Othello.   Did he confess it?

Iago.   Good sir, be a man;
    Think every bearded fellow that's but yok'd
    May draw[456] with you; there 's millions now alive
    That nightly lie in those unproper[457] beds

---

450. I would not fall into such passion unless there were some real grounds for it.
451. Seizure, fit.   452. Coma.   453. Important matter.   454. Another allusion
to the cuckold's horns.   455. Citizen.   456. *I.e.*, pull the burden of cuckolddom.
457. Not exclusively their own.

WILLIAM SHAKESPEARE   715

Which they dare swear peculiar;[458] your case is better.
O! 'tis the spite of hell, the fiend's arch-mock,
To lip[459] a wanton in a secure[460] couch,   70
And to suppose her chaste. No, let me know;
And knowing what I am, I know what she shall be.

Othello.   O! thou art wise; 'tis certain.

Iago.   Stand you awhile apart;
Confine yourself but in a patient list.[461]
Whilst you were here o'erwhelmed with your grief,—
A passion most unsuiting such a man,—
Cassio came hither; I shifted him away,
And laid good 'scuse upon your ecstasy;[462]
Bade him anon return and here speak with me;
The which he promis'd. Do but encave yourself,   80
And mark the fleers, the gibes, and notable scorns,
That dwell in every region of his face;
For I will make him tell the tale anew,
Where, how, how oft, how long ago, and when
He hath, and is again to cope[463] your wife:
I say, but mark his gesture. Marry, patience;
Or I shall say you are all in all in spleen,[464]
And nothing of a man.

Othello.   Dost thou hear, Iago?
I will be found most cunning in my patience;
But—dost thou hear?—most bloody.

Iago.   That's not amiss: 90
But yet keep time[465] in all. Will you withdraw?   *(Othello goes apart.)*
Now will I question Cassio of Bianca,
A housewife[466] that by selling her desires
Buys herself bread and clothes; it is a creature
That dotes on Cassio; as 'tis the strumpet's plague
To beguile many and be beguil'd by one.
He, when he hears of her, cannot refrain
From the excess of laughter. Here he comes:

(Re-enter Cassio.)

As he shall smile, Othello shall go mad;
And his unbookish[467] jealousy must construe   100
Poor Cassio's smiles, gestures, and light behaviour
Quite in the wrong. How do you now, lieutenant?

Cassio.   The worser that you give me the addition[468]
Whose want[469] even kills me.

---

458. Exclusively their own.   459. Kiss.   460. *I.e.,* without suspicion of having a rival.
461. Bounds of patience.   462. Derangement, trance.   463. Close with.
464. Completely overcome by passion.   465. Maintain control.   466. Hussy.
467. Unpracticed, naive.   468. Title.   469. The want of which.

Iago. Ply Desdemona well, and you are sure on 't.
(*Speaking lower*) Now, if this suit lay in Bianca's power,
How quickly should you speed!

Cassio.   Alas! poor caitiff![470]

Othello. Look! how he laughs already!

Iago. I never knew woman love man so.

Cassio. Alas! poor rogue, I think, i' faith, she loves me.   110

Othello. Now he denies it faintly, and laughs it out.

Iago. Do you hear, Cassio?

Othello.   Now he importunes him
To tell it o'er: go to; well said, well said.

Iago. She gives it out that you shall marry her;
Do you intend it?

Cassio. Ha, ha, ha!

Othello. Do you triumph, Roman?[471] do you triumph?

Cassio. I marry her! what? a customer?[472] I prithee, bear some charity to my
wit;[473] do not think it so unwholesome. Ha, ha, ha!

Othello. So, so, so, so. They laugh that win.[474]   120

Iago. Faith, the cry goes that you shall marry her.

Cassio. Prithee, say true.

Iago. I am a very villain else.

Othello. Have you scored me?[475] Well.

Cassio. This is the monkey's own giving out: she is persuaded I will marry
her, out of her own love and flattery, not out of my promise.

Othello. Iago beckons me;[476] now he begins the story.

Cassio. She was here even now; she haunts me in every place. I was the other
day talking on the sea-bank with certain Venetians, and thither comes this
bauble,[477] and, by this hand, she falls me thus about my neck;—   130

Othello. Crying, 'O dear Cassio!' as it were; his gesture imports it.

Cassio. So hangs and lolls and weeps upon me; so hales[478] and pulls me; ha,
ha, ha!

Othello. Now he tells how she plucked him to my chamber. O! I see that
nose of yours, but not the dog I shall throw it to.

Cassio. Well, I must leave her company.

Iago. Before me![479] look, where she comes.

Cassio. 'Tis such another fitchew![480] marry, a perfumed one.

(*Enter Bianca.*)

What do you mean by this haunting of me?

Bianca. Let the devil and his dam haunt you! What did you mean by that

---

470. Wretch.   471. *I.e.*, one who triumphs(?).   472. Courtesan, prostitute.
473. Give me credit for some sense.   474. "He who laughs last laughs longest"(?).
475. Wounded, defaced(?); or: settled my account(?).   476. Signals.   477. Plaything.
478. Hauls.   479. An exclamation of surprise.   480. Polecat, noted both for its strong smell
and for its lechery.

same handkerchief you gave me even now? I was a fine fool to take it. I must take out the work! A likely piece of work, that you should find it in your chamber, and not know who left it there! This is some minx's token, and I must take out the work! There, give it your hobby-horse;[481] wheresoever you had it I'll take out no work on 't.

Cassio.   How now, my sweet Bianca! how now, how now!

Othello.   By heaven, that should be[482] my handkerchief!

Bianca.   An you'll come to supper to-night, you may; an you will not, come when you are next prepared[483] for.   (*Exit.*)

Iago.   After her, after her.   150

Cassio.   Faith, I must; she 'll rail in the street else.

Iago.   Will you sup there?

Cassio.   Faith, I intend so.

Iago.   Well, I may chance to see you, for I would very fain[484] speak with you.

Cassio.   Prithee come; will you?

Iago.   Go to; say no more.   (*Exit Cassio.*)

Othello (*advancing*):   How shall I murder him, Iago?

Iago.   Did you perceive how he laughed at his vice?

Othello.   O! Iago!

Iago.   And did you see the handkerchief?   160

Othello.   Was that mine?

Iago.   Yours, by this hand; and to see how he prizes the foolish woman your wife! she gave it him, and he hath given it his whore.

Othello.   I would have him nine years a-killing. A fine woman! a fair woman! a sweet woman!

Iago.   Nay, you must forget that.

Othello.   Ay, let her rot, and perish, and be damned to-night; for she shall not live. No, my heart is turned to stone; I strike it, and it hurts my hand. O! the world hath not a sweeter creature; she might lie by an emperor's side and command him tasks.   170

Iago.   Nay, that's not your way.[485]

Othello.   Hang her! I do but say what she is. So delicate with her needle! An admirable musician! O, she will sing the savageness out of a bear. Of so high and plenteous wit and invention!

Iago.   She 's the worse for all this.

Othello.   O! a thousand, a thousand times. And then, of so gentle a condition![486]

Iago.   Ay, too gentle.[487]

Othello.   Nay, that 's certain;—but yet the pity of it, Iago! O! Iago, the pity of it, Iago!   180

Iago.   If you are so fond over her iniquity, give her patent to offend; for, if it touch not you, it comes near nobody.

---

481.   Harlot.   482.   *I.e.*, I think that is.   483.   Expected (Bianca means that if he does not come that night, she will never want to see him again).   484.   Gladly.   485.   Proper course.   486.   So much the high-born lady.   487.   *I.e.*, yielding.

Othello. I will chop her into messes.[488] Cuckold me!

Iago. O! 'tis foul in her.

Othello. With mine officer!

Iago. That's fouler.

Othello. Get me some poison, Iago; this night: I'll not expostulate with her, lest her body and beauty unprovide my mind again.[489] This night, Iago.

Iago. Do it not with poison, strangle her in her bed, even the bed she hath contaminated.   *190*

Othello. Good, good; the justice of it pleases; very good.

Iago. And for Cassio, let me be his undertaker;[490] you shall hear more by midnight.

Othello. Excellent good. (*A trumpet within.*) What trumpet is that same?

Iago. Something from Venice, sure. 'Tis Lodovico,
Come from the duke; and see, your wife is with him.

(*Enter Lodovico, Desdemona, and Attendants.*)

Lodovico. God save you, worthy general!

Othello.   With all my heart, sir.

Lodovico. The duke and senators of Venice greet you.

(*Gives him a packet.*)

Othello. I kiss the instrument of their pleasures.

(*Opens the packet, and reads.*)

Desdemona. And what's the news, good cousin Lodovico?   *200*

Iago. I am very glad to see you, signior;
Welcome to Cyprus.

Lodovico. I thank you. How does Lieutenant Cassio?

Iago. Lives, sir.

Desdemona. Cousin, there's fall'n between him and my lord
An unkind[491] breach; but you shall make all well.

Othello. Are you sure of that?

Desdemona. My lord?

Othello (*reads*). 'This fail you not to do, as you will'—

Lodovico. He did not call; he's busy in the paper.   *210*
Is there division[492] twixt my lord and Cassio?

Desdemona. A most unhappy one; I would do much
To atone[493] them, for the love I bear to Cassio.

Othello. Fire and brimstone!

Desdemona.   My lord?

Othello.   Are you wise?

Desdemona. What! is he angry?

---

488. Bits.   489. Unsettle my intention.   490. Dispatcher.   491. Unnatural.
492. Estrangement.   493. Reconcile.

Lodovico.   May be the letter mov'd him;
    For, as I think, they do command him home,
    Deputing Cassio in his government.
Desdemona. Trust me, I am glad on 't.
Othello.   Indeed!
Desdemona.   My lord?
Othello. I am glad to see you mad.
Desdemona.   Why, sweet Othello?
Othello. Devil!   (*Strikes her.*)
Desdemona. I have not deserved this.   220
Lodovico. My lord, this would not be believ'd in Venice,
    Though I should swear I saw 't; 'tis very much;
    Make her amends, she weeps.
Othello.   O devil, devil!
    If that the earth could teem with woman's tears,
    Each drop she falls[494] would prove a crocodile.[495]
    Out of my sight!
Desdemona.   I will not stay to offend you.   (*Going.*)
Lodovico. Truly, an obedient lady;
    I do beseech your lordship, call her back.
Othello. Mistress!
Desdemona.   My lord?
Othello.   What would you with her, sir?
Lodovico. Why, I, my lord?   230
Othello. Ay; you did wish that I would make her turn:
    Sir, she can turn, and turn, and yet go on,
    And turn again; and she can weep, sir, weep;
    And she 's obedient, as you say, obedient,
    Very obedient. Proceed you in your tears.
    Concerning this, sir,—O well-painted passion!—
    I am commanded home. Get you away;
    I 'll send for you anon. Sir, I obey the mandate,
    And will return to Venice. Hence! avaunt![496]   (*Exit Desdemona.*)
    Cassio shall have my place. And, sir, to-night,   240
    I do entreat that we may sup together;
    You are welcome, sir, to Cyprus. Goats and monkeys!   (*Exit.*)
Lodovico. Is this the noble Moor whom our full senate
    Call all-in-all sufficient? is this the noble nature
    Whom passion could not shake? whose solid virtue
    The shot of accident nor dart of chance
    Could neither graze nor pierce?
Iago.   He is much chang'd.
Lodovico. Are his wits safe? is he not light of brain?

---

494. Lets fall.   495. The crocodile's tears were supposed to be hypocritical.   496. Begone!

Iago.   He 's that he is; I may not breathe my censure.   250
  What he might be, if, what he might, he is not,
  I would to heaven he were![497]
Lodovico.   What! strike his wife!
Iago.   Faith, that was not so well; yet would I knew
  That stroke would prove the worst!
Lodovico.   Is it his use?
  Or did the letters work upon his blood,
  And new-create this fault?
Iago.   Alas, alas!
  It is not honesty in me to speak
  What I have seen and known. You shall observe him,
  And his own courses[498] will denote him so
  That I may save my speech. Do but go after
  And mark how he continues.   260
Lodovico.   I am sorry that I am deceiv'd in him.   (*Exeunt.*)

SCENE 2.   *A Room in the Castle.*

(*Enter Othello and Emilia.*)

Othello.   You have seen nothing, then?
Emilia.   Nor ever heard, nor ever did suspect.
Othello.   Yes, you have seen Cassio and her together.
Emilia.   But then I saw no harm, and then I heard
  Each syllable that breath made up between them.
Othello.   What! did they never whisper?
Emilia.   Never, my lord.
Othello.   Nor send you out o' the way?
Emilia.   Never.
Othello.   To fetch her fan, her gloves, her mask, nor nothing?[499]
Emilia.   Never, my lord.   10
Othello.   That's strange.
Emilia.   I durst, my lord, to wager she is honest,
  Lay down my soul at stake: if you think other,
  Remove your thought; it doth abuse your bosom.
  If any wretch have put this in your head,
  Let heaven requite it with the serpent's curse!
  For, if she be not honest, chaste, and true,
  There 's no man happy; the purest of their wives
  Is foul as slander.

---

497. Another of Iago's gnomic speeches; perhaps approximately: "If now he is not himself, I wish
he would be what he could be!"   498. Actions.   499. Anything.

Othello. Bid her come hither; go. *(Exit Emilia.)*
She says enough; yet she 's a simple⁵⁰⁰ bawd   20
That cannot say as much. This is a subtle whore,
A closet lock and key of villanous secrets;
And yet she 'll kneel and pray; I have seen her do 't.

(Re-enter Emilia with Desdemona.)

Desdemona. My lord, what is your will?
Othello.   Pray, chuck, come hither.
Desdemona. What is your pleasure?
Othello.   Let me see your eyes;
Look in my face.
Desdemona.   What horrible fancy 's this?
Othello *(to Emilia).* Some of your function,⁵⁰¹ mistress;
Leave procreants alone and shut the door;
Cough or cry 'hem' if any body come;
Your mystery,⁵⁰² your mystery; nay, dispatch.   *(Exit Emilia.)*
Desdemona. Upon my knees, what doth your speech import?   31
I understand a fury in your words.
But not the words.
Othello. Why, what art thou?
Desdemona.   Your wife, my lord; your true
And loyal wife.
Othello.   Come, swear it, damn thyself;
Lest, being like one of heaven, the devils themselves
Should fear to seize thee; therefore be double-damn'd;
Swear thou art honest.
Desdemona.   Heaven doth truly know it.
Othello. Heaven truly knows that thou art false as hell.
Desdemona. To whom, my lord? with whom? how am I false?   40
Othello. Ah! Desdemona; away, away, away!
Desdemona. Alas, the heavy day!—Why do you weep?
Am I the motive of these tears, my lord?
If haply you my father do suspect
An instrument of this your calling back,
Lay not your blame on me; if you have lost him,
Why, I have lost him too.
Othello.   Had it pleas'd heaven
To try me with affliction, had he rain'd
All kinds of sores and shames on my bare head,
Steep'd me in poverty to the very lips,   50
Given to captivity me and my utmost hopes,

---

500. Simpleminded.   501. To your duty, business.   502. Trade.

I should have found in some part of my soul
A drop of patience; but, alas! to make me
The fixed figure for the time of scorn[503]
To point his slow and moving finger at;
Yet could I bear that too; well, very well:
But there, where I have garner'd[504] up my heart,
Where either I must live or bear no life,
The fountain from the which my current runs
Or else dries up; to be discarded thence!   60
Or keep it as a cistern for foul toads
To knot and gender in![505] Turn thy complexion there,[506]
Patience, thou young and rose-lipp'd cherubin;
Ay, there, look grim as hell!

Desdemona.   I hope my noble lord esteems me honest.

Othello.   O! ay; as summer flies are in the shambles,[507]
That quicken even with blowing. O thou weed!
Who art so lovely fair and smell'st so sweet
That the sense aches at thee, would thou hadst ne'er been born.

Desdemona.   Alas! what ignorant sin have I committed?   70

Othello.   Was this fair paper, this most goodly book,
Made to write 'whore' upon? What committed!
Committed! O thou public commoner![508]
I should make very forges of my cheeks,
That would to cinders burn up modesty,
Did I but speak thy deeds. What committed!
Heaven stops the nose at it and the moon winks,[509]
The bawdy wind that kisses all it meets
Is hush'd within the hollow mine of earth,
And will not hear it. What committed!   80
Impudent strumpet!

Desdemona.   By heaven, you do me wrong.

Othello.   Are not you a strumpet?

Desdemona.   No, as I am a Christian.
If to preserve this vessel for my lord
From any other foul unlawful touch
Be not to be a strumpet, I am none.

Othello.   What! not a whore?

Desdemona.   No, as I shall be sav'd.

Othello.   Is it possible?

Desdemona.   O! heaven forgive us.

Othello.   I cry you mercy,[510] then;

---

503. *I.e.,* the scornful world.   504. Stored.   505. Bunch up and procreate.
506. *I.e.,* change your color to suit the "cistern for foul toads."   507. Slaughterhouse.
508. Harlot.   509. Closes her eyes.   510. Beg your pardon.

I took you for that cunning whore of Venice
That married with Othello. You, mistress,   90
That have the office opposite to Saint Peter,
And keep the gate of hell!

(*Re-enter Emilia.*)

                    You, you, ay, you!
We have done our course; there's money for your pains.
I pray you, turn the key and keep our counsel.   (*Exit.*)
Emilia.   Alas! what does this gentleman conceive?[511]
How do you, madam? how do you, my good lady?
Desdemona.   Faith, half asleep.
Emilia.   Good madam, what's the matter with my lord?
Desdemona.   With who?
Emilia.   Why, with my lord, madam.   100
Desdemona.   Who is thy lord?
Emilia.   He that is yours, sweet lady.
Desdemona.   I have none; do not talk to me, Emilia;
I cannot weep, nor answer have I none,
But what should go by water.[512] Prithee, to-night
Lay on my bed my wedding sheets: remember:
And call thy husband hither.
Emilia.   Here is a change indeed!   (*Exit.*)
Desdemona.   'Tis meet I should be us'd so, very meet.
How have I been behav'd, that he might stick
The small'st opinion on my least misuse?[513]

(*Re-enter Emilia, with Iago.*)

Iago.   What is your pleasure, madam? How is it with you?   110
Desdemona.   I cannot tell. Those that do teach young babes
Do it with gentle means and easy tasks;
He might have chid me so; for, in good faith,
I am a child to chiding.
Iago.   What's the matter, lady?
Emilia.   Alas, Iago, my lord hath so bewhor'd her,
Thrown such despite[514] and heavy terms upon her,
As true hearts cannot bear.
Desdemona.   Am I that name, Iago?
Iago.   What name, fair lady?
Desdemona.   Such as she says my lord did say I was.
Emilia.   He call'd her whore; a beggar in his drink   120
Could not have laid such terms upon his callat.[515]

---

511. Imagine.   512. Be conveyed by means of tears.   513. The least suspicion on my
slightest misconduct.   514. Abuse.   515. Slut.

Iago.   Why did he so?

Desdemona.   I do not know; I am sure I am none such.

Iago.   Do not weep, do not weep. Alas the day!

Emilia.   Has she forsook so many noble matches,
Her father and her country and her friends,
To be call'd whore? would it not make one weep?

Desdemona.   It is my wretched fortune.

Iago.   Beshrew [516] him for it!
How comes this trick upon him?

Desdemona.   Nay, heaven doth know.

Emilia.   I will be hang'd, if some eternal villain,   *130*
Some busy and insinuating rogue,
Some cogging [517] cozening slave, to get some office,
Have not devis'd this slander; I 'll be hang'd else.

Iago.   Fie! there is no such man; it is impossible.

Desdemona.   If any such there be, heaven pardon him!

Emilia.   A halter pardon him, and hell gnaw his bones!
Why should he call her whore? who keeps her company?
What place? what time? what form? what likelihood?
The Moor 's abus'd by some most villanous knave,
Some base notorious knave, some scurvy fellow.   *140*
O heaven! that such companions [518] thou'dst unfold,
And put in every honest hand a whip
To lash the rascals naked through the world,
Even from the east to the west!

Iago.   Speak within door.

Emilia.   O! fie upon them. Some such squire he was
That turn'd your wit the seamy side without, [519]
And made you to suspect me with the Moor.

Iago.   You are a fool; go to.

Desdemona.   O good Iago,
What shall I do to win my lord again?
Good friend, go to him; for, by this light of heaven,   *150*
I know not how I lost him. Here I kneel:
If e'er my will did trespass 'gainst his love,
Either in discourse of thought or actual deed,
Or that mine eyes, mine ears, or any sense,
Delighted them [520] in any other form;
Or that I do not yet, [521] and ever did,
And ever will, though he do shake me off
To beggarly divorcement, love him dearly,
Comfort forswear me! Unkindness may do much;

---

516. Curse.   517. Cheating.   518. Fellows (derogatory).   519. Outward.
520. Found delight.   521. Still.

And his unkindness may defeat[522] my life,   *160*
But never taint my love. I cannot say 'whore':
It does abhor me now I speak the word;
To do the act that might the addition earn
Not the world's mass of vanity could make me.

Iago.   I pray you be content, 'tis but his humour;
The business of the state does him offence,
And he does chide with you.

Desdemona.   If 'twere no other,—

Iago.   'Tis but so, I warrant.   (*Trumpets.*)
Hark! how these instruments summon to supper;
The messengers of Venice stay the meat: *170*
Go in, and weep not; all things shall be well.

                              (*Exeunt Desdemona and Emilia.*)

(*Enter Roderigo.*)

How now, Roderigo!

Roderigo.   I do not find that thou dealest justly with me.

Iago.   What in the contrary?[523]

Roderigo.   Every day thou daffest me[524] with some device, Iago; and rather, as it seems to me now, keepest from me all conveniency,[525] than suppliest me with the least advantage of hope. I will indeed no longer endure it, nor am I yet persuaded to put up[526] in peace what already I have foolishly suffered.

Iago.   Will you hear me, Roderigo?   *180*

Roderigo.   Faith, I have heard too much, for your words and performances are no kin together.

Iago.   You charge me most unjustly.

Roderigo.   With nought but truth. I have wasted myself out of my means. The jewels you have had from me to deliver to Desdemona would half have corrupted a votarist;[527] you have told me she has received them, and returned me expectations and comforts of sudden respect[528] and acquaintance, but I find none.

Iago.   Well; go to; very well.

Roderigo.   Very well! go to! I cannot go to, man; nor 'tis not very well: by this hand, I say, it is very scurvy, and begin to find myself fobbed[529] in it.

Iago.   Very well.

Roderigo.   I tell you 'tis not very well. I will make myself known to Desdemona; if she will return me my jewels, I will give over my suit and repent my unlawful solicitation; if not, assure yourself I will seek satisfaction of you.

Iago.   You have said now.[530]

---

522. Destroy.   523. *I.e.,* what reason do you have for saying that.   524. You put me off.   525. Favorable circumstances.   526. Put up with.   527. Nun.   528. Immediate consideration.   529. Cheated.   530. *I.e.,* "I suppose you're through?" (?); or: "Now you're talking" (?).

Roderigo. Ay, and said nothing, but what I protest intendment of doing.

Iago. Why, now I see there's mettle in thee, and even from this instant do build on thee a better opinion than ever before. Give me thy hand, Roderigo; thou hast taken against me a most just exception; but yet, I protest, I have dealt most directly in thy affair.

Roderigo. It hath not appeared.

Iago. I grant indeed it hath not appeared, and your suspicion is not without wit and judgment. But, Roderigo, if thou hast that in thee indeed, which I have greater reason to believe now than ever, I mean purpose, courage, and valour, this night show it: if thou the next night following enjoy not Desdemona, take me from this world with treachery and devise engines for[531] my life.

Roderigo. Well, what is it? is it within reason and compass?   *210*

Iago. Sir, there is especial commission come from Venice to depute Cassio in Othello's place.

Roderigo. Is that true? why, then Othello and Desdemona return again to Venice.

Iago. O, no! he goes into Mauritania, and takes away with him the fair Desdemona, unless his abode be lingered here by some accident; wherein none can be so determinate[532] as the removing of Cassio.

Roderigo. How do you mean, removing of him?

Iago. Why, by making him uncapable of Othello's place; knocking out his brains.   *220*

Roderigo. And that you would have me do?

Iago. Ay; if you dare do yourself a profit and a right. He sups to-night with a harlotry,[533] and thither will I go to him; he knows not yet of his honourable fortune. If you will watch his going thence,—which I will fashion to fall out between twelve and one,—you may take him at your pleasure; I will be near to second your attempt, and he shall fall between us. Come, stand not amazed at it, but go along with me; I will show you such a necessity in his death that you shall think yourself bound to put it on him. It is now high supper-time, and the night grows to waste; about it.

Roderigo. I will hear further reason for this.   *230*

Iago. And you shall be satisfied.   (*Exeunt.*)

SCENE 3.   *Another Room in the Castle.*

(*Enter Othello, Lodovico, Desdemona, Emilia, and Attendants.*)

Lodovico.   I do beseech you, sir, trouble yourself no further.

Othello.   O! pardon me; 'twill do me good to walk.

---

531.   Devices against.   532.   Effective.   533.   Harlot.

Lodovico. Madam, good–night; I humbly thank your ladyship.

Desdemona. Your honour is most welcome.

Othello. Will you walk, sir?

O! Desdemona,—

Desdemona. My lord?

Othello. Get you to bed on the instant; I will be returned forthwith; dismiss your attendant there; look it be done.

Desdemona. I will, my lord. *(Exeunt Othello, Lodovico, and Attendants.)*

Emilia. How goes it now? He looks gentler than he did. 10

Desdemona. He says he will return incontinent;[534]

He hath commanded me to go to bed,

And bade me to dismiss you.

Emilia. Dismiss me!

Desdemona. It was his bidding; therefore, good Emilia,

Give me my nightly wearing, and adieu:

We must not now displease him.

Emilia. I would you had never seen him.

Desdemona. So would not I; my love doth so approve him,

That even his stubbornness,[535] his checks[536] and frowns,—

Prithee, unpin me,—have grace and favour in them. 20

Emilia. I have laid those sheets you bade me on the bed.

Desdemona. All 's one.[537] Good faith! how foolish are our minds!

If I do die before thee, prithee, shroud me

In one of those same sheets.

Emilia. Come, come, you talk.

Desdemona. My mother had a maid call'd Barbara;

She was in love, and he she lov'd prov'd mad[538]

And did forsake her; she had a song of 'willow';

An old thing 'twas, but it express'd her fortune,

And she died singing it; that song to-night

Will not go from my mind; I have much to do 30

But to go hang my head all at one side,

And sing it like poor Barbara. Prithee, dispatch.

Emilia. Shall I go fetch your night-gown?

Desdemona. No, unpin me here.

This Lodovico is a proper man.

Emilia. A very handsome man.

Desdemona. He speaks well.

Emilia. I know a lady in Venice would have walked barefoot to Palestine for a touch of his nether lip.

Desdemona (*sings*).

The poor soul sat sighing by a sycamore tree,

---

534. At once. 535. Roughness. 536. Rebukes 537. *I.e.*, it doesn't matter.
538. Wild.

Sing all a green willow;   40
Her hand on her bosom, her head on her knee,
    Sing willow, willow, willow:
The fresh streams ran by her, and murmur'd her moans;
    Sing willow, willow, willow:
Her salt tears fell from her, and soften'd the stones;—

Lay by these:—
    Sing willow, willow, willow:

Prithee, hie thee;[539] he 'll come anon.—

    Sing all a green willow must be my garland.
    Let nobody blame him, his scorn I approve,—   50
Nay, that's not next. Hark! who is it that knocks?
Emilia.   It is the wind.
Desdemona.
    I call'd my love false love; but what said he then?
        Sing willow, willow, willow:
    If I court moe[540] women, you 'll couch with moe men.

    So, get thee gone; good-night. Mine eyes do itch;
    Doth that bode weeping?
Emilia.   'Tis neither here nor there.
Desdemona.   I have heard it said so. O! these men, these men!
    Dost thou in conscience think, tell me, Emilia,
    That there be women do abuse their husbands   60
    In such gross kind?
Emilia.   There be some such, no question.
Desdemona.   Wouldst thou do such a deed for all the world?
Emilia.   Why, would not you?
Desdemona.   No, by this heavenly light!
Emilia.   Nor I neither by this heavenly light;
    I might do 't as well i' the dark.
Desdemona.   Wouldst thou do such a deed for all the world?
Emilia.   The world is a huge thing; 'tis a great price
    For a small vice.
Desdemona.   In troth, I think thou wouldst not.
Emilia.   In troth, I think I should, and undo 't when I had done. Marry, I would·
not do such a thing for a joint-ring,[541] nor measures of lawn,[542] nor for
gowns, petticoats, nor caps, nor any petty exhibition;[543] but for the whole
world, who would not make her husband a cuckold to make him a
monarch? I should venture purgatory for 't.

---

539. Hurry.   540. More.   541. Ring made in separable halves.   542. Fine
linen.   543. Offer, gift.

Desdemona. Beshrew me, if I would do such a wrong
    For the whole world.

Emilia. Why, the wrong is but a wrong i' the world; and having the world for
    your labour, 'tis a wrong in your own world, and you might quickly make
    it right.

Desdemona. I do not think there is any such woman.

Emilia. Yes, a dozen; and as many to the vantage,[544] as   80
    Would store[545] the world they played for.
    But I do think it is their husbands' faults
    If wives do fall. Say that they slack their duties,
    And pour our treasures into foreign laps,
    Or else break out in peevish jealousies,
    Throwing restraint upon us; or say they strike us,
    Or scant[546] our former having[547] in despite;
    Why, we have galls,[548] and though we have some grace,
    Yet have we some revenge. Let husbands know
    Their wives have sense like them; they see and smell,   90
    And have their palates both for sweet and sour,
    As husbands have. What is it that they do
    When they change us for others? Is it sport?[549]
    I think it is; and doth affection breed it?
    I think it doth; is 't frailty that thus errs?
    It is so too; and have not we affections,
    Desires for sport, and frailty, as men have?
    Then, let them use us well; else let them know,
    The ills we do, their ills instruct us so.

Desdemona. Good-night, good-night; heaven me such usage[550] send,   100
    Not to pick bad from bad, but by bad mend!   (*Exeunt.*)

Act V

SCENE 1. *Cyprus. A Street.*

(*Enter Iago and Roderigo.*)

Iago. Here, stand behind this bulk;[551] straight will he come:
    Wear thy good rapier bare, and put it home.
    Quick, quick; fear nothing; I 'll be at thy elbow.
    It makes us, or it mars us; think on that,
    And fix most firm thy resolution.

Roderigo. Be near at hand; I may miscarry in 't.

---

544. Over and above.   545. Populate.   546. Reduce.   547. Allowance.
548. Spirits, temper.   549. Lust, sexual enjoyment.   550. Habits (?), treatment (?).
551. Jutting part of a wall.

Iago. Here, at thy hand: be bold, and take thy stand. (*Retires.*)

Roderigo. I have no great devotion to the deed;
And yet he has given me satisfying reasons:
'Tis but a man gone: forth, my sword; he dies. 10

Iago. I have rubb'd this young quat[552] almost to the sense,[553]
And he grows angry. Now, whether he kill Cassio,
Or Cassio him, or each do kill the other,
Every way makes my gain: live Roderigo,
He calls me to a restitution large
Of gold and jewels that I bobb'd[554] from him,
As gifts to Desdemona;
It must not be: if Cassio do remain,
He hath a dally beauty in his life
That makes me ugly: and, besides, the Moor 20
May unfold me to him; there stand I in much peril.
No, he must die. But so;[555] I hear him coming.

(*Enter Cassio.*)

Roderigo. I know his gait; 'tis he. Villain, thou diest!

(*Makes a pass at Cassio.*)

Cassio. That thrust had been mine enemy indeed
But that my coat is better than thou know'st;
I will make proof of thine.

(*Draws, and wounds Roderigo.*)

Roderigo. O! I am slain.

(*Iago from behind wounds Cassio in the leg, and exit.*)

Cassio. I am maim'd for ever. Help, ho! murder! murder! (*Falls.*)

(*Enter Othello, at a distance.*)

Othello. The voice of Cassio: Iago keeps his word.
Roderigo. O! villain that I am!
Othello. It is e'en so.
Cassio. O, help, ho! light! a surgeon! 30
Othello. 'Tis he: O brave Iago, honest and just!
That hast such noble sense of thy friend's wrong;
Thou teachest me. Minion,[556] your dear lies dead,
And your unblest fate hies; strumpet, I come!
Forth of my heart those charms, thine eyes, are blotted;
Thy bed lust-stain'd shall with lust's blood be spotted. (*Exit.*)

---

552. Pimple.   553. To the quick.   554. Swindled.   555. *I.e.*, that's the only way.
556. (Cassio's) darling, *i.e.*, Desdemona.

(Enter Lodovico and Gratiano, at a distance.)

Cassio. What ho! no watch? no passage?[557] murder! murder!

Gratiano. 'Tis some mischance; the cry is very direful.

Cassio. O, help!

Lodovico. Hark!   40

Roderigo. O wretched villain!

Lodovico. Two or three groans: it is a heavy[558] night;

    These may be counterfeits; let 's think 't unsafe

    To come in to the cry[559] without more help.

Roderigo. Nobody come? then shall I bleed to death.

Lodovico. Hark!

(Re-enter Iago, with a light.)

Gratiano. Here 's one comes in his shirt, with light and weapons.

Iago. Who 's there? whose noise is this that cries on murder?

Lodovico. We do not know.

Iago.   Did not you hear a cry?

Cassio. Here, here! for heaven's sake, help me.

Iago.   What 's the matter?   50

Gratiano. This is Othello's ancient, as I take it.

Lodovico. The same indeed; a very valiant fellow.

Iago. What are you here that cry so grievously?

Cassio. Iago? O! I am spoil'd, undone by villains!

    Give me some help.

Iago. O me, lieutenant! what villains have done this?

Cassio. I think that one of them is hereabout,

    And cannot make away.

Iago.   O treacherous villains!

    (To Lodovico and Gratiano.) What are you there? come in, and

    give some help.

Roderigo. O! help me here.   60

Cassio. That 's one of them.

Iago.   O murderous slave! O villain!

(Stabs Roderigo.)

Roderigo. O damn'd Iago! O inhuman dog!

Iago. Kill men i' the dark! Where be these bloody thieves?

    How silent is this town! Ho! murder! murder!

    What may you be? are you of good or evil?

Lodovico. As you shall prove us, praise us.

Iago. Signior Lodovico?

Lodovico. He, sir.

---

557. Passer-by.   558. Dark.   559. Where the cry comes from.

Iago.   I cry you mercy. Here 's Cassio hurt by villains.

Gratiano.   Cassio!   70

Iago.   How is it, brother?

Cassio.   My leg is cut in two.

Iago.   Marry, heaven forbid.
Light, gentlemen; I 'll bind it with my shirt.

(*Enter Bianca.*)

Bianca.   What is the matter, ho? who is 't that cried?

Iago.   Who is 't that cried!

Bianca.   O my dear Cassio! my sweet Cassio!
O Cassio, Cassio, Cassio!

Iago.   O notable strumpet! Cassio, may you suspect
Who they should be that have thus mangled you?

Cassio.   No.   80

Gratiano.   I am sorry to find you thus; I have been to seek you.

Iago.   Lend me a garter. So. O! for a chair,
To bear him easily hence!

Bianca.   Alas; he faints! O Cassio, Cassio, Cassio!

Iago.   Gentlemen all, I do suspect this trash[560]
To be a party in this injury.
Patience awhile, good Cassio. Come, come.
Lend me a light. Know we this face, or no?
Alas! my friend and my dear countryman,
Roderigo? no: yes, sure, O heaven! Roderigo.   90

Gratiano.   What! of Venice?

Iago.   Even he, sir: did you know him?

Gratiano.   Know him! ay.

Iago.   Signior Gratiano? I cry you gentle pardon;
These bloody accidents must excuse my manners,
That so neglected you.

Gratiano.   I am glad to see you.

Iago.   How do you, Cassio? O! a chair, a chair!

Gratiano.   Roderigo!

(*A chair brought in.*)

Iago.   He, he, 'tis he,—O! that 's well said; the chair:
Some good men bear him carefully from hence;
I 'll fetch the general's surgeon. (*To Bianca.*) For you, mistress,   100
Save you your labour. He that lies slain here, Cassio,
Was my dear friend. What malice was between you?

Cassio.   None in the world; nor do I know that man.

Iago (*to Bianca*).   What! look you pale? O! bear him out o' the air—

---

560.   *I.e.*, Bianca.

(Cassio and Roderigo are borne off.)

Stay you, good gentlemen. Look you pale, mistress?—
Do you preceive the gastness[561] of her eye?
Nay, if you stare, we shall hear more anon.
Behold her well; I pray you, look upon her.
Do you see, gentlemen? nay, guiltiness will speak
Though tongues were out of use.   110

(Enter Emilia.)

Emilia. 'Las! what 's the matter? what 's the matter, husband?
Iago. Cassio hath here been set on in the dark
By Roderigo and fellows that are 'scaped:
He 's almost slain, and Roderigo dead.
Emilia. Alas! good gentleman; alas! good Cassio!
Iago. This is the fruit of whoring. Prithee, Emilia,
Go know of Cassio where he supp'd to-night.
(To Bianca.) What! do you shake at that?
Bianca. He supp'd at my house; but I therefore shake not.
Iago. O! did he so? I charge you, go with me.   120
Emilia. Fie, fie, upon thee, strumpet!
Bianca. I am no strumpet, but of life as honest
As you that thus abuse me.
Emilia.   As I! foh! fie upon thee!
Iago. Kind gentlemen, let 's go see poor Cassio dress'd.[562]
Come, mistress, you must tell 's another tale.
Emilia, run you to the citadel,
And tell my lord and lady what hath happ'd.
Will you go on afore? *(Aside.)* This is the night
That either makes me or fordoes[563] me quite.   *(Exeunt.)*

SCENE 2. *A Bedchamber in the Castle. Desdemona in bed asleep. A light burning.*

(Enter Othello.)

Othello. It is the cause,[564] it is the cause, my soul;
Let me not name it to you, you chaste stars!
It is the cause. Yet I 'll not shed her blood,
Nor scar that whiter skin of hers than snow,
And smooth as monumental alabaster.

---

561. Terror.   562. Bandaged.   563. Ruins.   564. *I.e.,* Desdemona's unchastity
(Othello means that the severity of the punishment is required by the nature of her sin.)

Yet she must die, else she 'll betray more men.
Put out the light, and then put out the light:
If I quench thee, thou flaming minister,[565]
I can again thy former light restore,
Should I repent me; but once put out thy light,   10
Thou cunning'st[566] pattern of excelling nature,
I know not where is that Promethean[567] heat
That can thy light relume.[568] When I have pluck'd the rose,
I cannot give it vital growth again,
It needs must wither: I 'll smell it on the tree. (*Kisses her.*)
O balmy breath, that dost almost persuade
Justice to break her sword! One more, one more.
Be thus when thou art dead, and I will kill thee,
And love thee after. One more, and this the last:
So sweet was ne'er so fatal. I must weep,   20
But they are cruel tears; this sorrow 's heavenly,
It strikes where it doth love. She wakes.

Desdemona.   Who 's there? Othello?
Othello.   Ay, Desdemona.
Desdemona.   Will you come to bed, my lord?
Othello.   Have you pray'd to-night, Desdemona?
Desdemona.   Ay, my lord.
Othello.   If you bethink yourself of any crime
Unreconcil'd as yet to heaven and grace,
Solicit for it straight.
Desdemona.   Alas! my lord, what may you mean by that?
Othello.   Well, do it, and be brief; I will walk by:[569]   30
I would not kill thy unprepared spirit;
No; heaven forfend![570] I would not kill thy soul.
Desdemona.   Talk you of killing?
Othello.   Ay, I do.
Desdemona.   Then heaven
Have mercy on me!
Othello.   Amen! with all my heart.
Desdemona.   If you say so, I hope you will not kill me.
Othello.   Hum!
Desdemona.   And yet I fear you; for you are fatal then
When your eyes roll so. Why I should fear I know not,
Since guiltiness I know not; but yet I feel I fear.
Othello.   Think on thy sins.
Desdemona.   They are loves I bear to you.   40

---

565. *I.e.*, the candle.   566. Most intricately wrought.   567. In Greek mythology the demi-god Prometheus stole fire from the gods and gave it to man.   568. Relight.
569. Nearby.   570. Forbid.

Othello. Ay, and for that thou diest.

Desdemona. That death 's unnatural that kills for loving.
Alas! why gnaw you so your nether lip?
Some bloody passion shakes your very frame;
These are portents,[571] but yet, I hope, I hope
They do not point on me.

Othello.   Peace, and be still!

Desdemona. I will so. What 's the matter?

Othello. That handkerchief which I so lov'd and gave thee
Thou gav'st to Cassio.

Desdemona.   No, by my life and soul!
Send for the man and ask him.

Othello.   Sweet soul, take heed,   50
Take heed of perjury; thou 'rt on thy death-bed.

Desdemona. Ay, but not yet to die.

Othello.   Yes, presently;[572]
Therefore confess thee freely of thy sin;
For to deny each article with oath
Cannot remove nor choke the strong conception[573]
That I do groan withal. Thou art to die.

Desdemona. Then Lord have mercy on me!

Othello.   I say, amen.

Desdemona. And have you mercy too! I never did
Offend you in my life; never lov'd Cassio
But with such general warranty[574] of heaven   60
As I might love; I never gave him token.

Othello. By heaven, I saw my handkerchief in 's hand.
O perjur'd woman! thou dost stone[575] my heart,
And mak'st me call what I intend to do
A murder, which I thought a sacrifice:
I saw the handkerchief.

Desdemona.   He found it then;
I never gave it him. Send for him hither;
Let him confess a truth.

Othello.   He hath confessed.

Desdemona. What, my lord?

Othello. That he hath us'd thee.

Desdemona.   How? Unlawfully?

Othello.   Ay.   70

Desdemona. He will not say so.

Othello.   No; his mouth is stopp'd:
Honest Iago hath ta'en order for 't.[576]

---

571. Omens.   572. At once.   573. Belief.   574. Permission.   575. Turn to
stone.   576. Taken steps.

Desdemona. O! my fear interprets. What! is he dead?

Othello. Had all his hairs been lives, my great revenge
Had stomach[577] for them all.

Desdemona. Alas! he is betray'd and I undone.

Othello. Out, strumpet! Weep'st thou for him to my face?

Desdemona. O! banish me, my lord, but kill me not!

Othello. Down, strumpet!

Desdemona. Kill me to-morrow; let me live to-night!   80

Othello. Nay, if you strive,—

Desdemona. But half an hour!

Othello.   Being done, there is no pause.

Desdemona. But while I say one prayer!

Othello.   It is too late.   (*He smothers her*)

Emilia (*within*). My lord, my lord! what, ho! my lord, my lord!

Othello. What noise is this? Not dead? not yet quite dead?
I that am cruel am yet merciful;
I would not have thee linger in thy pain.
So, so.

Emilia (*within*). What, ho! my lord, my lord!

Othello.   Who's there?

Emilia (*within*). O! good my lord, I would speak a word with you!   90

Othello. Yes; 'tis Emilia: by and by.[578] She 's dead.
'Tis like[579] she comes to speak of Cassio's death;
The noise was high. Ha! no more moving?
Still as the grave. Shall she come in? Were 't good?[580]
I think she stirs again: no. What 's best to do?
If she come in she'll sure speak to my wife:
My wife! my wife! what wife? I have no wife;
O, insupportable! O heavy hour!
Methinks it should be now a huge eclipse
Of sun and moon, and that the affrighted globe   100
Should yawn[581] at alteration.

Emilia (*within*).   I do beseech you
That I may speak with you, O! good my lord.

Othello. I had forgot thee: O! come in, Emilia:
Soft, by and by: let me the curtains draw.
Where art thou?   (*Unlocks the door.*)

(*Enter Emilia.*)

                              What 's the matter with thee now?

Emilia. O! my good lord, yonder 's foul murder done.

Othello. What! now?

---

577 Appetite.   578. *I.e.,* "just a moment."   579. Likely.   580. Would that be wise.   581. Open up (as in an earthquake).

Emilia.   But now, my lord.

Othello.   It is the very error[582] of the moon;
    She comes more near the earth than she was wont,   *110*
    And makes men mad.

Emilia.   Cassio, my lord, has kill'd a young Venetian
    Call'd Roderigo.

Othello.   Roderigo kill'd!
    And Cassio kill'd?

Emilia.   No, Cassio is not kill'd.

Othello.   Not Cassio kill'd! then murder 's out of tune,
    And sweet revenge grows harsh.

Desdemona.   O! falsely, falsely murder'd.

Emilia.   Alas! what cry is that?

Othello.   That! what?

Emilia.   Out, and alas! that was my lady's voice:
    Help! Help, ho! help! O lady, speak again!   *120*
    Sweet Desdemona! O! sweet mistress, speak.

Desdemona.   A guiltless death I die.

Emilia.   O! who hath done this deed?

Desdemona.   Nobody; I myself; farewell:
    Commend me to my kind lord. O! farewell!   (*Dies.*)

Othello.   Why, how should she be murder'd?

Emilia.   Alas! who knows?

Othello.   You heard her say herself it was not I.

Emilia.   She said so; I must needs report the truth.

Othello.   She 's like a liar gone to burning hell;
    'Twas I that kill'd her.

Emilia.   O! the more angel she,   *130*
    And you the blacker devil.

Othello.   She turn'd to folly, and she was a whore.

Emilia.   Thou dost belie her, and thou art a devil.

Othello.   She was false as water.

Emilia.   Thou art rash as fire to say
    That she was false! O! she was heavenly true.

Othello.   Cassio did tup her; ask thy husband else.
    O! I were damn'd beneath all depth in hell
    But that I did proceed[583] upon just grounds
    To this extremity. Thy husband knew it all.

Emilia.   My husband!   *140*

Othello.   Thy husband.

Emilia.   That she was false to wedlock?

Othello.   Ay, with Cassio. Nay, had she been true,
    If heaven would make me such another world

---

582. Straying.   583. Had I not proceeded.

Of one entire and perfect chrysolite,[584]
I'd not have sold her for it.

Emilia.   My husband!

Othello.   Ay, 'twas he that told me first:
An honest man he is, and hates the slime
That sticks on filthy deeds.

Emilia.   My husband!

Othello.   What needs this iterance,[585] woman? I say thy husband.   150

Emilia.   O mistress! villany hath made mocks with love.
My husband say that she was false!

Othello.   He, woman;
I say, thy husband: dost understand the word?
My friend, thy husband, honest, honest Iago.

Emilia.   If he say so, may his pernicious soul
Rot half a grain a day! he lies to the heart:
She was too fond of her most filthy bargain.[586]

Othello.   Ha!

Emilia.   Do thy worst:
This deed of thine is no more worthy heaven   160
Than thou wast worthy her.

Othello.   Peace! you were best.[587]

Emilia.   Thou hast not half the power to do me harm
As I have to be hurt. O gull! O dolt!
As ignorant as dirt! thou hast done a deed,—
I care not for thy sword; I'll make thee known,
Though I lost twenty lives. Help! help, ho! help!
The Moor has kill'd my mistress! murder! murder!

(*Enter Montano, Gratiano, Iago, and others.*)

Montano.   What is the matter? How now, general!

Emilia.   O! are you come, Iago? you have done well,
That men must lay their murders on your neck.   170

Gratiano.   What is the matter?

Emilia.   Disprove this villain if thou be'st a man:
He says thou told'st him that his wife was false.
I know thou didst not, thou 'rt not such a villain.
Speak, for my heart is full.

Iago.   I told him what I thought, and told no more
Than what he found himself was apt and true.

Emilia.   But did you ever tell him she was false?

Iago.   I did.

Emilia.   You told a lie, an odious damned lie;   180

---

584. Topaz.   585. Repetition.   586. *I.e.,* Othello.   587. You'd better be quiet.

Upon my soul, a lie, a wicked lie;
She false with Cassio! Did you say with Cassio?

Iago. With Cassio, mistress. Go to, charm[588] your tongue.

Emilia. I will not charm my tongue; I am bound to speak.
My mistress here lies murder'd in her bed.

All. O heavens forfend!

Emilia. And your reports have set the murder on.

Othello. Nay, stare not, masters; it is true, indeed.

Gratiano. 'Tis a strange truth.

Montano. O monstrous act!

Emilia.   Villany! villany! villany!   190
I think upon 't, I think, I smell 't; O villany!
I thought so then;[589] I'll kill myself for grief.
O! villany, villany!

Iago. What! are you mad? I charge you, get you home.

Emilia. Good gentlemen, let me have leave to speak:
'Tis proper I obey him, but not now.
Perchance, Iago, I will ne'er go home.

Othello. O! O! O!   *(Falls on the bed.)*

Emilia.   Nay, lay thee down and roar,
For thou hast kill'd the sweetest innocent
That e'er did lift up eye.

Othello.   O! she was foul.   *(Rises.)*
I scarce did know you, uncle. There lies your niece,   201
Whose breath, indeed, these hands have newly stopp'd:
I know this act shows terrible and grim.

Gratiano. Poor Desdemona! I am glad thy father 's dead.
Thy match was mortal to him, and pure grief
Shore[590] his old thread in twain: did he live now,
This sight would make him do a desperate turn,
Yea, curse his better angel from his side,
And fall to reprobation.[591]

Othello. 'Tis pitiful; but yet Iago knows   210
That she with Cassio hath the act of shame
A thousand times committed; Cassio confess'd it:
And she did gratify[592] his amorous works
With that recognizance and pledge of love
Which I first gave her. I saw it in his hand:
It was a handkerchief, an antique token
My father gave my mother.

---

588. *I.e.,* into silence.   589. *Cf.* "I will be hang'd, if some eternal villain,/Some busy and insinuating rogue,/Some cogging cozening slave, to get some office,/Have not devis'd this
slander; . . ." (IV, ii, p. 609). Emilia means, not that she guessed Iago's guilt, but that she rightly
guessed the slanderer's motive.   590. Cut.   591. Damnation.   592. Reward.

Emilia.   O heaven! O heavenly powers!

Iago.   Come, hold your peace.

Emilia.   'Twill out, 'twill out; I hold my peace, sir? no;
No, I will speak as liberal as the north;[593]   220
Let heaven and men and devils, let them all,
All, all, cry shame against me, yet I'll speak.

Iago.   Be wise, and get you home.

Emilia.   I will not.

(Iago threatens to stab Emilia.)

Gratiano.   Fie!
Your sword upon a woman!

Emilia.   O thou dull Moor! that handkerchief thou speak'st of
I found by fortune and did give my husband;
For often, with a solemn earnestness,
More than, indeed, belong'd to such a trifle,
He begg'd of me to steal it.

Iago.   Villainous whore!

Emilia.   She give it Cassio! no, alas! I found it,   230
And I did give 't my husband.

Iago.   Filth, thou liest!

Emilia.   By heaven, I do not, I do not, gentlemen.
O murderous coxcomb![594] what should such a fool
Do with so good a wife?

Othello.   Are there no stones[595] in heaven
But what serve for the thunder? Precious villain!

(He runs at Iago. Iago stabs Emilia.)

Gratiano.   The woman falls; sure, he has kill'd his wife.   *(Exit Iago.)*

Emilia.   Ay, ay; O! lay me by my mistress' side.

Gratiano.   He 's gone; but his wife 's kill'd.

Montano.   'Tis a notorious[596] villain. Take you this weapon,
Which I have here recover'd from the Moor.   240
Come, guard the door without; let him not pass,
But kill him rather. I'll after that same villain,
For 'tis a damned slave.   *(Exeunt Montano and Gratiano.)*

Othello.   I am not valiant neither,
But every puny whipster[597] gets my sword.
But why should honour outlive honesty?
Let it go all.

Emilia.   What did thy song bode, lady?
Hark, canst thou hear me? I will play the swan,

---

593. *I.e.,* the north wind (?), the supposedly free-spoken people of north England (?).
594. Idiot.   595. *I.e.,* thunderbolts (to strike Iago down).   596. Notable.
597. *I.e.,* a small boy whipping a top.

And die in music:—

(*Sings.*)   Willow, willow, willow.

Moor, she was chaste; she lov'd thee, cruel Moor;

So come my soul to bliss as I speak true;   250

So speaking as I think, I die, I die.   (*Dies.*)

Othello.   I have another weapon in this chamber;

It is a sword of Spain, the ice-brook's temper.[598]

O! here it is. Uncle, I must come forth.

Gratiano (*within*).   If thou attempt it, it will cost thee dear:

Thou hast no weapon, and perforce must suffer.

Othello.   Look in upon me then, and speak with me,

Or, naked[599] as I am, I will assault thee.

(*Re-enter Gratiano.*)

Gratiano.   What is the matter?

Othello.   Behold! I have a weapon;

A better never did itself sustain   260

Upon a soldier's thigh: I have seen the day,

That with this little arm, and this good sword,

I have made my way through more impediments

Than twenty times your stop: but, O vain boast!

Who can control his fate? 'tis not so now.

Be not afraid, though you do see me weapon'd;

Here is my journey's end, here is my butt,[600]

And very sea-mark of my utmost sail.[601]

Do you go back dismay'd? 'tis a lost fear;

Man but a rush[602] against Othello's breast,   270

And he retires. Where should Othello go?

Now how dost thou look now? O ill-starr'd wench!

Pale as thy smock! when we shall meet at compt,[603]

This look of thine will hurl my soul from heaven,

And fiends will snatch at it. Cold, cold, my girl!

Even like thy chastity.

O! cursed, cursed slave. Whip me, ye devils,

From the possession of this heavenly sight!

Blow me about in winds! roast me in sulphur!

Wash me in steep-down gulfs of liquid fire!   280

O Desdemona! Desdemona! dead!

Oh! Oh! Oh!

(*Enter Lodovico, Montano, Cassio carried in a chair, and Officers with Iago, prisoner.*)

---

598. Tempered in icy water (or the reference may be to Innsbruck, famed for the quality of its steel, but this hardly fits "a sword of Spain").   599. Unarmed.   600. Goal, end, limit. 601. Destination of my farthest journey.   602. Wield but a reed.   603. On the day of judgment.

Lodovico.   Where is this rash and most unfortunate man?

Othello.   That's he that was Othello; here I am.

Lodovico.   Where is that viper? bring the villain forth.

Othello.   I look down towards his feet;[604] but that 's a fable.
    If that thou be'st a devil, I cannot kill thee.   *(Wounds Iago.)*

Lodovico.   Wrench his sword from him.   *(Othello is disarmed.)*

Iago.   I bleed, sir; but not kill'd.

Othello.   I am not sorry neither; I'd have thee live;
    For, in my sense,[605] 'tis happiness to die.   290

Lodovico.   O thou Othello! that wert once so good,
    Fall'n in the practice[606] of a damned slave,[607]
    What shall be said to thee?

Othello.   Why, any thing:
    An honourable murderer, if you will;
    For nought did I in hate, but all in honour.

Lodovico.   This wretch hath part confess'd his villany:
    Did you and he consent in Cassio's death?

Othello.   Ay.

Cassio.   Dear general, I never gave you cause.

Othello.   I do believe it, and I ask your pardon.   300
    Will you, I pray, demand that demi-devil
    Why he hath thus ensnar'd my soul and body?

Iago.   Demand me nothing: what you know, you know:
    From this time forth I never will speak word.

Lodovico.   What! not to pray?

Gratiano.   Torments will ope[608] your lips.

Othello.   Well, thou dost best.

Lodovico.   Sir, you shall understand what hath befall'n,
    Which, as I think, you know not. Here is a letter
    Found in the pocket of the slain Roderigo,
    And here another; the one of them imports   310
    The death of Cassio to be undertook
    By Roderigo.

Othello.   O villain!

Cassio.   Most heathenish and most gross!

Lodovico.   Now here's another discontented paper,
    Found in his pocket too; and this, it seems,
    Roderigo meant to have sent this damned villain,
    But that, belike,[609] Iago in the interim[610]
    Came in and satisfied him.

Othello.   O the pernicious caitiff!

---

604. *I.e.*, for the Devil's cloven hoof.   605. The way I feel.   606. Plot, machination.
607. *I.e.*, Iago.   608. Open.   609. Most likely.   610. In the meantime.

How came you, Cassio, by that handkerchief
That was my wife's?

Cassio.   I found it in my chamber;   *320*
And he himself confess'd but even now
That there he dropp'd it for a special purpose
Which wrought to his desire.

Othello.   O fool! fool! fool!

Cassio.   There is besides in Roderigo's letter
How he upbraids Iago that he made him
Brave me upon the watch; whereon it came
That I was cast:[611] and even but now he spake,
After long seeming dead, Iago hurt him,
Iago set him on.

Lodovico.   You must forsake this room and go with us;   *330*
Your power and your command is taken off,
And Cassio rules in Cyprus. For this slave,
If there be any cunning cruelty
That can torment him much and hold him long,
It shall be his. You shall close prisoner rest,
Till that the nature of your fault be known
To the Venetian state. Come, bring him away.

Othello.   Soft you; a word or two before you go.
I have done the state some service, and they know 't;
No more of that. I pray you, in your letters,   *340*
When you shall these unlucky deeds relate,
Speak of me as I am; nothing extenuate,
Nor set down aught[612] in malice: then, must you speak
Of one that lov'd not wisely but too well;
Of one not easily jealous, but, being wrought,
Perplex'd[613] in the extreme; of one whose hand
Like the base Indian,[614] threw a pearl away
Richer than all his tribe; of one whose subdu'd[615] eyes
Albeit unused to the melting mood,
Drop tears as fast as the Arabian trees   *350*
Their med'cinable gum. Set you down this;
And say besides, that in Aleppo once,
Where a malignant and a turban'd Turk
Beat a Venetian and traduc'd the state,
I took by the throat the circumcised dog,
And smote him, thus.   *(Stabs himself.)*

Lodovico.   O bloody period![616]

---

611. Dismissed.   612. Anything.   613. Distracted.   614. The Folio reads "Iudean." Both readings denote the foolish infidel who fails to appreciate the treasure he possesses.   615. Overcome (by grief).   616. Ending.

Gratiano.   All that's spoke is marr'd.

Othello.   I kiss'd thee ere I killed thee; no way but this,

(Falling upon Desdemona.)

    Killing myself to die upon a kiss.   *(Dies.)*

Cassio.   This did I fear, but thought he had no weapon;   360

    For he was great of heart.

Lodovico *(to Iago).*   O Spartan dog!

    More fell[617] than anguish, hunger, or the sea.

    Look on the tragic loading of this bed;

    This is thy work; the object poisons sight;

    Let it be hid. Gratiano, keep the house,

    And seize upon the fortunes of the Moor,

    For they succeed on you. To you, lord governor,

    Remains the censure of this hellish villain,

    The time, the place, the torture; O! enforce it.

    Myself will straight aboard, and to the state   370

    This heavy act with heavy heart relate.   *(Exeunt.)*

Questions

1. *What motivates Iago to seek vengeance? Do you find his motives a convincing basis for his acts? Explain.* **2.** *What function does Roderigo serve in the play? Bianca? Emilia?* **3.** *Compare the speeches of Cassio and Iago in Act II, Scene 1. What does the difference in language and style reveal about their characters?* **4.** *Othello crumbles in Act III, Scene 3, as Iago creates the jealousy that destroys Othello's self-confidence and peace of mind. Is the rapidity of Othello's emotional collapse justified? Does his being black have anything to do with his emotional turmoil? Explain.* **5.** *Carefully determine how much time elapses between the arrival at Cyprus and the end of the action. Can you find narrated events that could not possibly have occurred within that time? Do the chronological inconsistencies disturb you? Explain.* **6.** *The first part of Act IV, Scene 2 (until Othello exists), is sometimes called the "brothel" scene. What features of Othello's language and behavior justify that designation?* **7.** *Discuss the relationship between love and hate in this play.*

---

617.   Grim, cruel.

The Misanthrope*

MOLIÈRE [1622–1673]

CHARACTERS

Alceste, *in love with Célimène*
Philinte, *Alceste's friend*
Oronte, *in love with Célimène*
Célimène, *Alceste's beloved*
Éliante, *Célimène's cousin*
Arsinoé, *a friend of Célimène's*
Acaste
Clitandre } *Marquesses*
Basque, *Célimène's servant*
A Guard *of the Marshalsea*
Dubois, *Alceste's valet*

The Scene throughout is in Célimène's house at Paris.

Act I

SCENE 1. *Philinte, Alceste*

Philinte. Now, what's got into you?
Alceste (*seated*). Kindly leave me alone.
Philinte. Come, come, what is it? This lugubrious tone . . .
Alceste. Leave me, I said; you spoil my solitude.

Philinte. Oh, listen to me, now, and don't be rude.
Alceste. I choose to be rude, Sir, and to be hard of hearing.
Philinte. These ugly moods of yours are not endearing;
Friends though we are, I really must insist . . .
Alceste (*abruptly rising*). Friends? Friends, you say? Well, cross me off your list.
I've been your friend till now, as you well know;
But after what I saw a moment ago

---

*English version by Richard Wilbur.

I tell you flatly that our ways must part.
I wish no place in a dishonest heart.

Philinte. Why, what have I done, Alceste? Is this quite just?

Alceste. My God, you ought to die of self-disgust.
I call your conduct inexcusable, Sir,
And every man of honor will concur.
I see you almost hug a man to death,
Exclaim for joy until you're out of breath,
And supplement these loving demonstrations
With endless offers, vows, and protestations;
Then when I ask you "Who was that?" I find
That you can barely bring his name to mind!
Once the man's back is turned, you cease to love him,
And speak with absolute indifference of him!
By God, I say it's base and scandalous
To falsify the heart's affections thus;
If I caught myself behaving in such a way,
I'd hang myself for shame, without delay.

Philinte. It hardly seems a hanging matter to me;
I hope that you will take it graciously
If I extend myself a slight reprieve,
And live a little longer, by your leave.

Alceste. How dare you joke about a crime so grave?

Philinte. What crime? How else are people to behave?

Alceste. I'd have them be sincere, and never part
With any word that isn't from the heart.

Philinte. When someone greets us with a show of pleasure,
It's but polite to give him equal measure,
Return his love the best that we know how,
And trade him offer for offer, vow for vow.

Alceste. No, no, this formula you'd have me follow,
However fashionable, is false and hollow,
And I despise the frenzied operations
Of all these barterers of protestations,
These lavishers of meaningless embraces,
These utterers of obliging commonplaces,
Who court and flatter everyone on earth
And praise the fool no less than the man of worth.
Should you rejoice that someone fondles you,
Offers his love and service, swears to be true,
And fills your ears with praises of your name,
When to the first damned fop he'll say the same?
No, no: no self-respecting heart would dream
Of prizing so promiscuous an esteem;
However high the praise, there's nothing worse

Than sharing honors with the universe.
Esteem is founded on comparison:
To honor all men is to honor none.
Since you embrace this indiscriminate vice,
Your friendship comes at far too cheap a price;
I spurn the easy tribute of a heart
Which will not set the worthy man apart:
I choose, Sir, to be chosen; and in fine,
The friend of mankind is no friend of mine.

Philinte. But in polite society, custom decrees
That we show certain outward courtesies. . . .

Alceste. Ah, no! we should condemn with all our force
Such false and artificial intercourse.
Let men behave like men; let them display
Their inmost hearts in everything they say;
Let the heart speak, and let our sentiments
Not mask themselves in silly compliments.

Philinte. In certain cases it would be uncouth
And most absurd to speak the naked truth;
With all respect for your exalted notions,
It's often best to veil one's true emotions.
Wouldn't the social fabric come undone
If we were wholly frank with everyone?
Suppose you met with someone you couldn't bear;
Would you inform him of it then and there?

Alceste. Yes.

Philinte. Then you'd tell old Emilie it's pathetic
The way she daubs her features with cosmetic
And plays the gay coquette at sixty-four?

Alceste. I would.

Philinte. And you'd call Dorilas a bore,
And tell him every ear at court is lame
From hearing him brag about his noble name?

Alceste. Precisely.

Philinte. Ah, you're joking.

Alceste. Au contraire:
In this regard there's none I'd choose to spare.
All are corrupt; there's nothing to be seen
In court or town but aggravates my spleen.
I fall into deep gloom and melancholy
When I survey the scene of human folly,
Finding on every hand base flattery,
Injustice, fraud, self-interest, treachery. . . .
Ah, it's too much; mankind has grown so base,
I mean to break with the whole human race.

Philinte. This philosophic rage is a bit extreme;
        You've no idea how comical you seem;
        Indeed, we're like those brothers in the play
        Called *School for Husbands*, one of whom was prey . . .
Alceste. Enough, now! None of your stupid similes.
Philinte. Then let's have no more tirades, if you please.
        The world won't change, whatever you say or do;
        And since plain speaking means so much to you,
        I'll tell you plainly that by being frank
        You've earned the reputation of a crank,
        And that you're thought ridiculous when you rage
        And rant against the manners of the age.
Alceste. So much the better; just what I wish to hear.
        No news could be more grateful to my ear.
        All men are so detestable in my eyes,
        I should be sorry if they thought me wise.
Philinte. Your hatred's very sweeping, is it not?
Alceste. Quite right: I hate the whole degraded lot.
Philinte. Must all poor human creatures be embraced,
        Without distinction, by your vast distaste?
        Even in these bad times, there are surely a few . . .
Alceste. No, I include all men in one dim view:
        Some men I hate for being rogues; the others
        I hate because they treat the rogues like brothers,
        And, lacking a virtuous scorn for what is vile,
        Receive the villain with a complaisant smile.
        Notice how tolerant people choose to be
        Toward that bold rascal who's at law with me.
        His social polish can't conceal his nature;
        One sees at once that he's a treacherous creature;
        No one could possibly be taken in
        By those soft speeches and that sugary grin.
        The whole world knows the shady means by which
        The low-brow's grown so powerful and rich,
        And risen to a rank so bright and high
        That virtue can but blush, and merit sigh.
        Whenever his name comes up in conversation,
        None will defend his wretched reputation;
        Call him knave, liar, scoundrel, and all the rest,
        Each head will nod, and no one will protest.
        And yet his smirk is seen in every house,
        He's greeted everywhere with smiles and bows,
        And when there's any honor that can be got
        By pulling strings, he'll get it, like as not.
        My God! It chills my heart to see the ways

Men come to terms with evil nowadays;
Sometimes, I swear, I'm moved to flee and find
Some desert land unfouled by humankind.
Philinte. Come, let's forget the follies of the times
And pardon mankind for its petty crimes;
Let's have an end of rantings and of railings,
And show some leniency toward human failings.
This world requires a pliant rectitude;
Too stern a virtue makes one stiff and rude;
Good sense views all extremes with detestation,
And bids us to be noble in moderation.
The rigid virtues of the ancient days
Are not for us; they jar with all our ways
And ask of us too lofty a perfection.
Wise men accept their times without objection,
And there's no greater folly, if you ask me,
Than trying to reform society.
Like you, I see each day a hundred and one
Unhandsome deeds that might be better done,
But still, for all the faults that meet my view,
I'm never known to storm and rave like you.
I take men as they are, or let them be,
And teach my soul to bear their frailty;
And whether in court or town, whatever the scene,
My phlegm's as philosophic as your spleen.
Alceste. This phlegm which you so eloquently commend,
Does nothing ever rile it up, my friend?
Suppose some man you trust should treacherously
Conspire to rob you of your property,
And do his best to wreck your reputation?
Wouldn't you feel a certain indignation?
Philinte. Why, no. These faults of which you so complain
Are part of human nature, I maintain,
And it's no more a matter for disgust
That men are knavish, selfish and unjust,
Than that the vulture dines upon the dead,
And wolves are furious, and apes ill-bred.
Alceste. Shall I see myself betrayed, robbed, torn to bits,
And not . . . Oh, let's be still and rest our wits.
Enough of reasoning, now. I've had my fill.
Philinte. Indeed, you would do well, Sir, to be still.
Rage less at your opponent, and give some thought
To how you'll win this lawsuit that he's brought.
Alceste. I assure you I'll do nothing of the sort.
Philinte. Then who will plead your case before the court?

Alceste. Reason and right and justice will plead for me.
Philinte. Oh, Lord. What judges do you plan to see?
Alceste. Why, none. The justice of my cause is clear.
Philinte. Of course, man; but there's politics to fear. . . .
Alceste. No, I refuse to lift a hand. That's flat.
　I'm either right, or wrong.
Philinte. 　　　　　　　　Don't count on that.
Alceste. No, I'll do nothing.
Philinte. 　　　　　　　Your enemy's influence
　Is great, you know . . .
Alceste. 　　　　　　　That makes no difference.
Philinte. It will; you'll see.
Alceste. 　　　　　　Must honor bow to guile?
　If so, I shall be proud to lose the trial.
Philinte. Oh, really . . .
Alceste. 　　　　　　I'll discover by this case
　Whether or not men are sufficiently base
　And impudent and villainous and perverse
　To do me wrong before the universe.
Philinte. What a man!
Alceste. 　　　　　Oh, I could wish, whatever the cost,
　Just for the beauty of it, that my trial were lost.
Philinte. If people heard you talking so, Alceste,
　They'd split their sides. Your name would be a jest.
Alceste. So much the worse for jesters.
Philinte. 　　　　　　　　　May I enquire
　Whether this rectitude you so admire,
　And these hard virtues you're enamored of
　Are qualities of the lady whom you love?
　It much surprises me that you, who seem
　To view mankind with furious disesteem,
　Have yet found something to enchant your eyes
　Amidst a species which you so despise.
　And what is more amazing, I'm afraid,
　Is the most curious choice your heart has made.
　The honest Éliante is fond of you,
　Arsinoé, the prude, admires you too;
　And yet your spirit's been perversely led
　To choose the flighty Célimène instead,
　Whose brittle malice and coquettish ways
　So typify the manners of our days.
　How is it that the traits you most abhor
　Are bearable in this lady you adore?
　Are you so blind with love that you can't find them?
　Or do you contrive, in her case, not to mind them?

Alceste.   My love for that young widow's not the kind
  That can't perceive defects; no, I'm not blind.
  I see her faults, despite my ardent love,
  And all I see I fervently reprove.
  And yet I'm weak; for all her falsity,
  That woman knows the art of pleasing me,
  And though I never cease complaining of her,
  I swear I cannot manage not to love her.
  Her charm outweighs her faults; I can but aim
  To cleanse her spirit in my love's pure flame.
Philinte.   That's no small task; I wish you all success.
  You think then that she loves you?
Alceste.   Heavens, yes!
  I wouldn't love her did she not love me.
Philinte.   Well, if her taste for you is plain to see,
  Why do these rivals cause you such despair?
Alceste.   True love, Sir, is possessive, and cannot bear
  To share with all the world. I'm here today
  To tell her she must send that mob away.
Philinte.   If I were you, and had your choice to make,
  Éliante, her cousin, would be the one I'd take;
  That honest heart, which cares for you alone,
  Would harmonize far better with your own.
Alceste.   True, true: each day my reason tells me so;
  But reason doesn't rule in love, you know.
Philinte.   I fear some bitter sorrow is in store;
  This love . . .

SCENE 2.   *Oronte, Alceste, Philinte*

Oronte (*to Alceste*).   The servants told me at the door
  That Éliante and Célimène were out,
  But when I heard, dear Sir, that you were about,
  I came to say, without exaggeration,
  That I hold you in the vastest admiration,
  And that it's always been my dearest desire
  To be the friend of one I so admire.
  I hope to see my love of merit requited,
  And you and I in friendship's bond united.
  I'm sure you won't refuse—if I may be frank—
  A friend of my devotedness—and rank.

  (*During this speech of Oronte's, Alceste is abstracted, and seems un-*

aware that he is being spoken to. He only breaks off his reverie when Oronte says:)

It was for you, if you please, that my words were intended.

Alceste. For me, Sir?

Oronte. Yes, for you. You're not offended?

Alceste. By no means. But this much surprises me. . . .
The honor comes most unexpectedly. . . .

Oronte. My high regard should not astonish you;
The whole world feels the same. It is your due.

Alceste. Sir . . .

Oronte. Why, in all the State there isn't one
Can match your merits; they shine, Sir, like the sun.

Alceste. Sir . . .

Oronte. You are higher in my estimation
Than all that's most illustrious in the nation.

Alceste. Sir . . .

Oronte. If I lie, may heaven strike me dead!
To show you that I mean what I have said,
Permit me, Sir, to embrace you most sincerely,
And swear that I will prize our friendship dearly.
Give me your hand. And now, Sir, if you choose,
We'll make our vows.

Alceste. Sir . . .

Oronte. What! You refuse?

Alceste. Sir, it's a very great honor you extend:
But friendship is a sacred thing, my friend;
It would be profanation to bestow
The name of friend on one you hardly know.
All parts are better played when well-rehearsed;
Let's put off friendship, and get acquainted first.
We may discover it would be unwise
To try to make our natures harmonize.

Oronte. By heaven! You're sagacious to the core;
This speech has made me admire you even more.
Let time, then, bring us closer day by day;
Meanwhile, I shall be yours in every way.
If, for example, there should be anything
You wish at court, I'll mention it to the King.
I have his ear, of course; it's quite well known
That I am much in favor with the throne.
In short, I am your servant. And now, dear friend,
Since you have such fine judgment, I intend
To please you, if I can, with a small sonnet

I wrote not long ago. Please comment on it,
And tell me whether I ought to publish it.
Alceste.   You must excuse me, Sir; I'm hardly fit
To judge such matters.
Oronte.   Why not?
Alceste.   I am, I fear,
Inclined to be unfashionably sincere.
Oronte.   Just what I ask; I'd take no satisfaction
In anything but your sincere reaction.
I beg you not to dream of being kind.
Alceste.   Since you desire it, Sir, I'll speak my mind.
Oronte.   *Sonnet.* It's a sonnet. . . . *Hope* . . . The poem's addressed
To a lady who wakened hopes within my breast.
Hope . . . this is not the pompous sort of thing,
Just modest little verses, with a tender ring.
Alceste.   Well, we shall see.
Oronte.   *Hope* . . . I'm anxious to hear
Whether the style seems properly smooth and clear,
And whether the choice of words is good or bad.
Alceste.   We'll see, we'll see.
Oronte.   Perhaps I ought to add
That it took me only a quarter-hour to write it.
Alceste.   The time's irrelevant, Sir: kindly recite it.
Oronte (*reading*).

> *Hope comforts us awhile, 'tis true,*
> *Lulling our cares with careless laughter,*
> *And yet such joy is full of rue,*
> *My Phyllis, if nothing follows after.*

Philinte.   I'm charmed by this already; the style's delightful.
Alceste (*sotto voce, to Philinte*).   How can you say that? Why, the thing is frightful.
Oronte.   *Your fair face smiled on me awhile,*
> *But was it kindness so to enchant me?*
> *'Twould have been fairer not to smile,*
> *If hope was all you meant to grant me.*

Philinte.   What a clever thought! How handsomely you phrase it!
Alceste (*sotto voce, to Philinte*).   You know the thing is trash. How dare you praise it?
Oronte.   *If it's to be my passion's fate*
> *Thus everlastingly to wait,*
> *Then death will come to set me free:*
> *For death is fairer than the fair;*
> *Phyllis, to hope is to despair*
> *When one must hope eternally.*

Philinte.   The close is exquisite—full of feeling and grace.

Alceste (*sotto voce, aside*).   Oh, blast the close; you'd better close your face
    Before you send your lying soul to hell.

Philinte.   I can't remember a poem I've liked so well.

Alceste (*sotto voce, aside*).   Good Lord!

Oronte (*to Philinte*).   I fear you're flattering me a bit.

Philinte.   Oh, no!

Alceste (*sotto voce, aside*).   What else d'you call it, you hypocrite?

Oronte (*to Alceste*).   But you, Sir, keep your promise now: don't shrink
    From telling me sincerely what you think.

Alceste.   Sir, these are delicate matters; we all desire
    To be told that we've the true poetic fire.
    But once, to one whose name I shall not mention,
    I said, regarding some verse of his invention,
    That gentlemen should rigorously control
    That itch to write which often afflicts the soul;
    That one should curb the heady inclination
    To publicize one's little avocation;
    And that in showing off one's works of art
    One often plays a very clownish part.

Oronte.   Are you suggesting in a devious way
    That I ought not . . .

Alceste.   Oh, that I do not say.
    Further, I told him that no fault is worse
    Than that of writing frigid, lifeless verse,
    And that the merest whisper of such a shame
    Suffices to destroy a man's good name.

Oronte.   D'you mean to say my sonnet's dull and trite?

Alceste.   I don't say that. But I went on to cite
    Numerous cases of once-respected men
    Who came to grief by taking up the pen.

Oronte.   And am I like them? Do I write so poorly?

Alceste.   I don't say that. But I told this person, "Surely
    You're under no necessity to compose;
    Why you should wish to publish, heaven knows.
    There's no excuse for printing tedious rot
    Unless one writes for bread, as you do not.
    Resist temptation, then, I beg of you;
    Conceal your pastimes from the public view;
    And don't give up, on any provocation,
    Your present high and courtly reputation,
    To purchase at a greedy printer's shop
    The name of silly author and scribbling fop."
    These were the points I tried to make him see.

Oronte.   I sense that they are also aimed at me;
But now—about my sonnet—I'd like to be told . . .
Alceste.   Frankly, that sonnet should be pigeonholed.
You've chosen the worst models to imitate.
The style's unnatural. Let me illustrate:

> For example, *Your fair face smiled on me awhile,*
> Followed by, *'Twould have been fairer not to smile!*
> Or this: *such joy is full of rue;*
> Or this: *For death is fairer than the fair;*
> Or, *Phyllis, to hope is to despair*
>> *When one must hope eternally!*

This artificial style, that's all the fashion,
Has neither taste, nor honesty, nor passion;
It's nothing but a sort of wordy play,
And nature never spoke in such a way.
What, in this shallow age, is not debased?
Our fathers, though less refined, had better taste;
I'd barter all that men admire today
For one old love song I shall try to say:

> *If the King had given me for my own*
> *Paris, his citadel,*
> *And I for that must leave alone*
> *Her whom I love so well,*
> *I'd say then to the Crown,*
> *Take back your glittering town;*
> *My darling is more fair, I swear,*
> *My darling is more fair.*

The rhyme's not rich, the style is rough and old,
But don't you see that it's the purest gold
Beside the tinsel nonsense now preferred,
And that there's passion in its every word?

> *If the King had given me for my own*
> *Paris, his citadel,*
> *And I for that must leave alone*
> *Her whom I love so well,*
> *I'd say then to the Crown,*
> *Take back your glittering town;*
> *My darling is more fair, I swear,*
> *My darling is more fair.*

There speaks a loving heart. (*To Philinte.*) You're laughing, eh?
Laugh on, my precious wit. Whatever you say,
I hold that song's worth all the bibelots
That people hail today with ah's and oh's.
Oronte.   And I maintain my sonnet's very good.
Alceste.   It's not at all surprising that you should.

You have your reasons; permit me to have mine
For thinking that you cannot write a line.

Oronte. Others have praised my sonnet to the skies.

Alceste. I lack their art of telling pleasant lies.

Oronte. You seem to think you've got no end of wit.

Alceste. To praise your verse, I'd need still more of it.

Oronte. I'm not in need of your approval, Sir.

Alceste. That's good; you couldn't have it if you were.

Oronte. Come now, I'll lend you the subject of my sonnet;
I'd like to see you try to improve upon it.

Alceste. I might, by chance, write something just as shoddy;
But then I wouldn't show it to everybody.

Oronte. You're most opinionated and conceited.

Alceste. Go find your flatterers, and be better treated.

Oronte. Look here, my little fellow, pray watch your tone.

Alceste. My great big fellow, you'd better watch your own.

Philinte (*stepping between them*).   Oh, please, please, gentlemen!
This will never do.

Oronte. The fault is mine, and I leave the field to you.
I am your servant, Sir, in every way.

Alceste. And I, Sir, am your most abject valet.

SCENE 3.   *Philinte, Alceste*

Philinte. Well, as you see, sincerity in excess
Can get you into a very pretty mess;
Oronte was hungry for appreciation. . . .

Alceste. Don't speak to me.

Philinte.   What?

Alceste.   No more conversation.

Philinte. Really, now . . .

Alceste.   Leave me alone.

Philinte.   If I . . .

Alceste.   Out of my sight!

Philinte. But what . . .

Alceste.   I won't listen.

Philinte.   But . . .

Alceste.   Silence!

Philinte.   Now, is it polite . . .

Alceste. By heaven, I've had enough. Don't follow me.

Philinte. Ah, you're just joking. I'll keep you company.

Act II

Alceste. Shall I speak plainly, Madam? I confess
Your conduct gives me infinite distress,
And my resentment's grown too hot to smother.
Soon, I foresee, we'll break with one another.
If I said otherwise, I should deceive you;
Sooner or later, I shall be forced to leave you,
And if I swore that we shall never part,
I should misread the omens of my heart.
Célimène. You kindly saw me home, it would appear,
So as to pour invectives in my ear.
Alceste. I've no desire to quarrel. But I deplore
Your inability to shut the door
On all these suitors who beset you so.
There's what annoys me, if you care to know.
Célimène. Is it my fault that all these men pursue me?
Am I to blame if they're attracted to me?
And when they gently beg an audience,
Ought I to take a stick and drive them hence?
Alceste. Madam, there's no necessity for a stick;
A less responsive heart would do the trick.
Of your attractiveness I don't complain;
But those your charms attract, you then detain
By a most melting and receptive manner,
And so enlist their hearts beneath your banner.
It's the agreeable hopes which you excite
That keep these lovers round you day and night;
Were they less liberally smiled upon,
That sighing troop would very soon be gone.
But tell me, Madam, why it is that lately
This man Clitandre interests you so greatly?
Because of what high merits do you deem
Him worthy of the honor of your esteem?
Is it that your admiring glances linger
On the splendidly long nail of his little finger?
Or do you share the general deep respect
For the blond wig he chooses to affect?
Are you in love with his embroidered hose?
Do you adore his ribbons and his bows?
Or is it that this paragon bewitches
Your tasteful eye with his vast German breeches?

Perhaps his giggle, or his falsetto voice,
Makes him the latest gallant of your choice?

Célimène. You're much mistaken to resent him so.
Why I put up with him you surely know:
My lawsuit's very shortly to be tried,
And I must have his influence on my side.

Alceste. Then lose your lawsuit, Madam, or let it drop;
Don't torture me by humoring such a fop.

Célimène. You're jealous of the whole world, Sir.

Alceste.   That's true,
Since the whole world is well-received by you.

Célimène. That my good nature is so unconfined
Should serve to pacify your jealous mind;
Were I to smile on one, and scorn the rest,
Then you might have some cause to be distressed.

Alceste. Well, if I mustn't be jealous, tell me, then,
Just how I'm better treated than other men.

Célimène. You know you have my love. Will that not do?

Alceste. What proof have I that what you say is true?

Célimène. I would expect, Sir, that my having said it
Might give the statement a sufficient credit.

Alceste. But how can I be sure that you don't tell
The selfsame thing to other men as well?

Célimène. What a gallant speech! How flattering to me!
What a sweet creature you make me out to be!
Well then, to save you from the pangs of doubt,
All that I've said I hereby cancel out;
Now, none but yourself shall make a monkey of you:
Are you content?

Alceste.   Why, why am I doomed to love you?
I swear that I shall bless the blissful hour
When this poor heart's no longer in your power!
I make no secret of it: I've done my best
To exorcise this passion from my breast;
But thus far all in vain; it will not go;
It's for my sins that I must love you so.

Célimène. Your love for me is matchless, Sir; that's clear.

Alceste. Indeed, in all the world it has no peer;
Words can't describe the nature of my passion,
And no man ever loved in such a fashion.

Célimène. Yes, it's a brand-new fashion, I agree:
You show your love by castigating me,
And all your speeches are enraged and rude.
I've never been so furiously wooed.

Alceste. Yet you could calm that fury, if you chose.

Come, shall we bring our quarrels to a close?
Let's speak with open hearts, then, and begin . . .

SCENE 2.   *Célimène, Alceste, Basque*

Célimène.   What is it?
Basque.   Acaste is here.
Célimène.   Well, send him in.

SCENE 3.   *Célimène, Alceste*

Alceste.   What! Shall we never be alone at all?
    You're always ready to receive a call,
    And you can't bear, for ten ticks of the clock,
    Not to keep open house for all who knock.
Célimène.   I couldn't refuse him: he'd be most put out.
Alceste.   Surely that's not worth worrying about.
Célimène.   Acaste would never forgive me if he guessed
    That I consider him a dreadful pest.
Alceste.   If he's a pest, why bother with him then?
Célimène.   Heavens! One can't antagonize such men;
    Why, they're the chartered gossips of the court,
    And have a say in things of every sort.
    One must receive them, and be full of charm;
    They're no great help, but they can do you harm,
    And though your influence be ever so great,
    They're hardly the best people to alienate.
Alceste.   I see, dear lady, that you could make a case
    For putting up with the whole human race;
    These friendships that you calculate so nicely . . .

SCENE 4.   *Alceste, Célimène, Basque*

Basque.   Madam, Clitandre is here as well.
Alceste.   Precisely.
Célimène.   Where are you going?
Alceste.   Elsewhere.
Célimène.   Stay.
Alceste.   No, no.

Célimène.   Stay, Sir.

Alceste.   I can't.

Célimène.   I wish it.

Alceste.   No, I must go.
I beg you, Madam, not to press the matter;
You know I have no taste for idle chatter.

Célimène.   Stay: I command you.

Alceste.   No, I cannot stay.

Célimène.   Very well; you have my leave to go away.

     SCENE 5.   *Éliante, Philinte, Acaste, Clitandre, Alceste, Célimène,*
                Basque

Éliante (*to Célimène*).   The Marquesses have kindly come to call.
Were they announced?

Célimène.   Yes. Basque, bring chairs for all.

(*Basque provides the chairs, and exits.*)

(*To Alceste.*) You haven't gone?

Alceste.   No; and I shan't depart
Till you decide who's foremost in your heart.

Célimène.   Oh, hush.

Alceste.   It's time to choose; take them, or me.

Célimène.   You're mad.

Alceste.   I'm not, as you shall shortly see.

Célimène.   Oh?

Alceste.   You'll decide.

Célimène.   You're joking now, dear friend.

Alceste.   No, no; you'll choose; my patience is at an end.

Clitandre.   Madam, I come from court, where poor Cléonte
Behaved like a perfect fool, as is his wont.
Has he no friend to counsel him, I wonder,
And teach him less unerringly to blunder?

Célimène.   It's true, the man's a most accomplished dunce;
His gauche behavior charms the eye at once;
And every time one sees him, on my word,
His manner's grown a trifle more absurd.

Acaste.   Speaking of dunces, I've just now conversed
With old Damon, who's one of the very worst;
I stood a lifetime in the broiling sun
Before his dreary monologue was done.

Célimène.   Oh, he's a wondrous talker, and has the power
To tell you nothing hour after hour:

If, by mistake, he ever came to the point,
The shock would put his jawbone out of joint.

Éliante (*to Philinte*).   The conversation takes its usual turn,
And all our dear friends' ears will shortly burn.

Clitandre.   Timante's a character, Madam.

Célimène.   Isn't he, though?
A man of mystery from top to toe,
Who moves about in a romantic mist
On secret missions which do not exist.
His talk is full of eyebrows and grimaces;
How tired one gets of his momentous faces;
He's always whispering something confidential
Which turns out to be quite inconsequential;
Nothing's too slight for him to mystify;
He even whispers when he says "good-by."

Acaste.   Tell us about Géralde.

Célimène.   That tiresome ass.
He mixes only with the titled class,
And fawns on dukes and princes, and is bored
With anyone who's not at least a lord.
The man's obsessed with rank, and his discourses
Are all of hounds and carriages and horses;
He uses Christian names with all the great,
And the word Milord, with him, is out of date.

Clitandre.   He's very taken with Bélise, I hear.

Célimène.   She is the dreariest company, poor dear.
Whenever she comes to call, I grope about
To find some topic which will draw her out,
But, owing to her dry and faint replies,
The conversation wilts, and droops, and dies.
In vain one hopes to animate her face
By mentioning the ultimate commonplace;
But sun or shower, even hail or frost
Are matters she can instantly exhaust.
Meanwhile her visit, painful though it is,
Drags on and on through mute eternities,
And though you ask the time, and yawn, and yawn,
She sits there like a stone and won't be gone.

Acaste.   Now for Adraste.

Célimène.   Oh, that conceited elf
Has a gigantic passion for himself;
He rails against the court, and cannot bear it
That none will recognize his hidden merit;
All honors given to others give offense
To his imaginary excellence.

Clitandre.   What about young Cléon? His house, they say,
   Is full of the best society, night and day.
Célimène.   His cook has made him popular, not he:
   It's Cléon's table that people come to see.
Éliante.   He gives a splendid dinner, you must admit.
Célimène.   But must he serve himself along with it?
   For my taste, he's a most insipid dish
   Whose presence sours the wine and spoils the fish.
Philinte.   Damis, his uncle, is admired no end.
   What's your opinion, Madam?
Célimène.   Why, he's my friend.
Philinte.   He seems a decent fellow, and rather clever.
Célimène.   He works too hard at cleverness, however.
   I hate to see him sweat and struggle so
   To fill his conversation with bons mots.
   Since he's decided to become a wit
   His taste's so pure that nothing pleases it;
   He scolds at all the latest books and plays,
   Thinking that wit must never stoop to praise,
   That finding fault's a sign of intellect,
   That all appreciation is abject,
   And that by damning everything in sight
   One shows oneself in a distinguished light.
   He's scornful even of our conversations:
   Their trivial nature sorely tries his patience;
   He folds his arms, and stands above the battle,
   And listens sadly to our childish prattle.
Acaste.   Wonderful, Madam! You've hit him off precisely.
Clitandre.   No one can sketch a character so nicely.
Alceste.   How bravely, Sirs, you cut and thrust at all
   These absent fools, till one by one they fall:
   But let one come in sight, and you'll at once
   Embrace the man you lately called a dunce,
   Telling him in a tone sincere and fervent
   How proud you are to be his humble servant.
Clitandre.   Why pick on us? *Madame's* been speaking, Sir,
   And you should quarrel, if you must, with her.
Alceste.   No, no, by God, the fault is yours, because
   You lead her on with laughter and applause,
   And make her think that she's the more delightful
   The more her talk is scandalous and spiteful.
   Oh, she would stoop to malice far, far less
   If no such claque approved her cleverness.
   It's flatterers like you whose foolish praise
   Nourishes all the vices of these days.

Philinte. But why protest when someone ridicules
    Those you'd condemn, yourself, as knaves or fools?
Célimène. Why, Sir? Because he loves to make a fuss.
    You don't expect him to agree with us,
    When there's an opportunity to express
    His heaven-sent spirit of contrariness?
    What other people think, he can't abide;
    Whatever they say, he's on the other side;
    He lives in deadly terror of agreeing;
    'Twould make him seem an ordinary being.
    Indeed, he's so in love with contradiction,
    He'll turn against his most profound conviction
    And with a furious eloquence deplore it,
    If only someone else is speaking for it.
Alceste. Go on, dear lady, mock me as you please;
    You have your audience in ecstasies.
Philinte. But what she says is true: you have a way
    Of bridling at whatever people say;
    Whether they praise or blame, your angry spirit
    Is equally unsatisfied to hear it.
Alceste. Men, Sir, are always wrong, and that's the reason
    That righteous anger's never out of season;
    All that I hear in all their conversation
    Is flattering praise or reckless condemnation.
Célimène. But . . .
Alceste.   No, no, Madam, I am forced to state
    That you have pleasures which I deprecate,
    And that these others, here, are much to blame
    For nourishing the faults which are your shame.
Clitandre. I shan't defend myself, Sir; but I vow
    I'd thought this lady faultless until now.
Acaste. I see her charms and graces, which are many;
    But as for faults, I've never noticed any.
Alceste. I see them, Sir; and rather than ignore them,
    I strenuously criticize her for them.
    The more one loves, the more one should object
    To every blemish, every least defect.
    Were I this lady, I would soon get rid
    Of lovers who approved of all I did,
    And by their slack indulgence and applause
    Endorsed my follies and excused my flaws.
Célimène. If all hearts beat according to your measure,
    The dawn of love would be the end of pleasure;
    And love would find its perfect consummation
    In ecstasies of rage and reprobation.

Éliante.   Love, as a rule, affects men otherwise,
       And lovers rarely love to criticize.
       They see their lady as a charming blur,
       And find all things commendable in her.
       If she has any blemish, fault, or shame,
       They will redeem it by a pleasing name.
       The pale-faced lady's lily-white, perforce;
       The swarthy one's a sweet brunette, of course;
       The spindly lady has a slender grace;
       The fat one has a most majestic pace;
       The plain one, with her dress in disarray,
       They classify as *beauté négligée*;
       The hulking one's a goddess in their eyes,
       The dwarf, a concentrate of Paradise;
       The haughty lady has a noble mind;
       The mean one's witty, and the dull one's kind;
       The chatterbox has liveliness and verve,
       The mute one has a virtuous reserve.
       So lovers manage, in their passion's cause,
       To love their ladies even for their flaws.
Alceste.   But I still say . . .
Célimène.   I think it would be nice
       To stroll around the gallery once or twice.
       What! You're not going, Sirs?
Clitandre and Acaste.   No, Madam, no.
Alceste.   You seem to be in terror lest they go.
       Do what you will, Sirs; leave, or linger on,
       But I shan't go till after you are gone.
Acaste.   I'm free to linger, unless I should perceive
       Madame is tired, and wishes me to leave.
Clitandre.   And as for me, I needn't go today
       Until the hour of the King's *coucher.*
Célimène (*to Alceste*).   You're joking, surely?
Alceste.   Not in the least; we'll see
       Whether you'd rather part with them, or me.

       SCENE 6.   *Alceste, Célimène, Éliante, Acaste, Philinte, Clitandre,*
              Basque

Basque (*to Alceste*).   Sir, there's a fellow here who bids me state
       That he must see you, and that it can't wait.
Alceste.   Tell him that I have no such pressing affairs.

Basque.   It's a long tailcoat that this fellow wears,
  With gold all over.
Célimène (*to Alceste*).   You'd best go down and see.
  Or—have him enter.

  SCENE 7.   *Alceste, Célimène, Éliante, Acaste, Philinte, Clitandre,
  Guard*

Alceste (*confronting the Guard*).   Well, what do you want with me?
  Come in, Sir.
Guard.   I've a word, Sir, for your ear.
Alceste.   Speak it aloud, Sir; I shall strive to hear.
Guard.   The Marshals have instructed me to say
  You must report to them without delay.
Alceste.   Who? Me, Sir?
Guard.   Yes, Sir; you.
Alceste.   But what do they want?
Philinte (*to Alceste*).   To scotch your silly quarrel with Oronte.
Celimene (*to Philinte*).   What quarrel?
Philinte.   Oronte and he have fallen out
  Over some verse he spoke his mind about;
  The Marshals wish to arbitrate the matter.
Alceste.   Never shall I equivocate or flatter!
Philinte.   You'd best obey their summons; come, let's go.
Alceste.   How can they mend our quarrel, I'd like to know?
  Am I to make a cowardly retraction,
  And praise those jingles to his satisfaction?
  I'll not recant; I've judged that sonnet rightly.
  It's bad.
Philinte.   But you might say so more politely. . . .
Alceste.   I'll not back down; his verses make me sick.
Philinte.   If only you could be more politic!
  But come, let's go.
Alceste.   I'll go, but I won't unsay
  A single word.
Philinte.   Well, let's be on our way.
Alceste.   Till I am ordered by my lord the King
  To praise that poem, I shall say the thing
  Is scandalous, by God, and that the poet
  Ought to be hanged for having the nerve to show it.

(*To Clitandre and Acaste, who are laughing.*)

By heaven, Sirs, I really didn't know
That I was being humorous.

Célimène. Go, Sir, go;
Settle your business.

Alceste. I shall, and when I'm through,
I shall return to settle things with you.

Act III

SCENE 1. *Clitandre, Acaste*

Clitandre. Dear Marquess, how contented you appear;
All things delight you, nothing mars your cheer.
Can you, in perfect honesty, declare
That you've a right to be so debonair?

Acaste. By Jove, when I survey myself, I find
No cause whatever for distress of mind.
I'm young and rich; I can in modesty
Lay claim to an exalted pedigree;
And owing to my name and my condition
I shall not want for honors and position.
Then as to courage, that most precious trait,
I seem to have it, as was proved of late
Upon the field of honor, where my bearing,
They say, was very cool and rather daring.
I've wit, of course; and taste in such perfection
That I can judge without the least reflection,
And at the theater, which is my delight,
Can make or break a play on opening night,
And lead the crowd in hisses or bravos,
And generally be known as one who knows.
I'm clever, handsome, gracefully polite;
My waist is small, my teeth are strong and white;
As for my dress, the world's astonished eyes
Assure me that I bear away the prize.
I find myself in favor everywhere,
Honored by men, and worshiped by the fair;
And since these things are so, it seems to me
I'm justified in my complacency.

Clitandre. Well, if so many ladies hold you dear,
Why do you press a hopeless courtship here?

Acaste.   Hopeless, you say? I'm not the sort of fool
That likes his ladies difficult and cool.
Men who are awkward, shy, and peasantish
May pine for heartless beauties, if they wish,
Grovel before them, bear their cruelties,
Woo them with tears and sighs and bended knees,
And hope by dogged faithfulness to gain
What their poor merits never could obtain.
For men like me, however, it makes no sense
To love on trust, and foot the whole expense.
Whatever any lady's merits be,
I think, thank God, that I'm as choice as she;
That if my heart is kind enough to burn
For her, she owes me something in return;
And that in any proper love affair
The partners must invest an equal share.

Clitandre.   You think, then, that our hostess favors you?

Acaste.   I've reason to believe that that is true.

Clitandre.   How did you come to such a mad conclusion?
You're blind, dear fellow. This is sheer delusion.

Acaste.   All right, then: I'm deluded and I'm blind.

Clitandre.   Whatever put the notion in your mind?

Acaste.   Delusion.

Clitandre.   What persuades you that you're right?

Acaste.   I'm blind.

Clitandre.   But have you any proofs to cite?

Acaste.   I tell you I'm deluded.

Clitandre.   Have you, then,
Received some secret pledge from Célimène?

Acaste.   Oh, no: she scorns me.

Clitandre.   Tell me the truth, I beg.

Acaste.   She·just can't bear me.

Clitandre.   Ah, don't pull my leg.
Tell me what hope she's given you, I pray.

Acaste.   I'm hopeless, and it's you who win the day.
She hates me thoroughly, and I'm so vexed
I mean to hang myself on Tuesday next.

Clitandre.   Dear Marquess, let us have an armistice
And make a treaty. What do you say to this?
If ever one of us can plainly prove
That Célimène encourages his love,
The other must abandon hope, and yield,
And leave him in possession of the field.

Acaste.   Now, there's a bargain that appeals to me;
With all my heart, dear Marquess, I agree.
But hush.

SCENE 2.   *Célimène, Acaste, Clitandre*

Célimène.   Still here?
Clitandre.   'Twas love that stayed our feet.
Célimène.   I think I heard a carriage in the street.
Whose is it? D'you know?

SCENE 3.   *Célimène, Acaste, Clitandre, Basque*

Basque.   Arsinoé is here,
Madame.
Célimène.   Arsinoé, you say? Oh, dear.
Basque.   Éliante is entertaining her below.
Célimène.   What brings the creature here, I'd like to know?
Alcaste.   They say she's dreadfully prudish, but in fact
I think her piety . . .
Célimène.   It's all an act.
At heart she's worldly, and her poor success
In snaring men explains her prudishness.
It breaks her heart to see the beaux and gallants
Engrossed by other women's charms and talents,
And so she's always in a jealous rage
Against the faulty standards of the age.
She lets the world believe that she's a prude
To justify her loveless solitude,
And strives to put a brand of moral shame
On all the graces that she cannot claim.
But still she'd love a lover; and Alceste
Appears to be the one she'd love the best.
His visits here are poison to her pride;
She seems to think I've lured him from her side;
And everywhere, at court or in the town,
The spiteful, envious woman runs me down.
In short, she's just as stupid as can be,
Vicious and arrogant in the last degree,
And . . .

SCENE 4. *Arsinoé, Célimène, Clitandre, Acaste*

Célimène.   Ah! What happy chance has brought you here?
  I've thought about you ever so much, my dear.
Arsinoé.   I've come to tell you something you should know.
Célimène.   How good of you to think of doing so!

  (Clitandre and Acaste go out, laughing.)

SCENE 5. *Arsinoé, Célimène*

Arsinoé.   It's just as well those gentlemen didn't tarry.
Célimène.   Shall we sit down?
Arsinoé.   That won't be necessary.
  Madam, the flame of friendship ought to burn
  Brightest in matters of the most concern,
  And as there's nothing which concerns us more
  Than honor, I have hastened to your door
  To bring you, as your friend, some information
  About the status of your reputation.
  I visited, last night, some virtuous folk,
  And, quite by chance, it was of you they spoke;
  There was, I fear, no tendency to praise
  Your light behavior and your dashing ways.
  The quantity of gentlemen you see
  And your by now notorious coquetry
  Were both so vehemently criticized
  By everyone, that I was much surprised.
  Of course, I needn't tell you where I stood;
  I came to your defense as best I could,
  Assured them you were harmless, and declared
  Your soul was absolutely unimpaired.
  But there are some things, you must realize,
  One can't excuse, however hard one tries,
  And I was forced at last into conceding
  That your behavior, Madam, is misleading,
  That it makes a bad impression, giving rise
  To ugly gossip and obscene surmise,
  And that if you were more *overtly* good,
  You wouldn't be so much misunderstood.
  Not that I think you've been unchaste—no! no!
  The saints preserve me from a thought so low!

But mere good conscience never did suffice:
One must avoid the outward show of vice.
Madam, you're too intelligent, I'm sure,
To think my motives anything but pure
In offering you this counsel—which I do
Out of a zealous interest in you.

Célimène.   Madam, I haven't taken you amiss;
I'm very much obliged to you for this;
And I'll at once discharge the obligation
By telling you about *your* reputation.
You've been so friendly as to let me know
What certain people say of me, and so
I mean to follow your benign example
By offering you a somewhat similar sample.
The other day, I went to an affair
And found some most distinguished people there
Discussing piety, both false and true.
The conversation soon came round to you.
Alas! Your prudery and bustling zeal
Appeared to have a very slight appeal.
Your affectation of a grave demeanor,
Your endless talk of virtue and of honor,
The aptitude of your suspicious mind
For finding sin where there is none to find,
Your towering self-esteem, that pitying face
With which you contemplate the human race,
Your sermonizings and your sharp aspersions
On people's pure and innocent diversions—
All these were mentioned, Madam, and, in fact,
Were roundly and concertedly attacked.
"What good," they said, "are all these outward shows,
When everything belies her pious pose?
She prays incessantly; but then, they say,
She beats her maids and cheats them of their pay;
She shows her zeal in every holy place,
But still she's vain enough to paint her face;
She holds that naked statues are immoral,
But with a naked *man* she'd have no quarrel."
Of course, I said to everybody there
That they were being viciously unfair;
But still they were disposed to criticize you,
And all agreed that someone should advise you
To leave the morals of the world alone,
And worry rather more about your own.

They felt that one's self-knowledge should be great
Before one thinks of setting others straight;
That one should learn the art of living well
Before one threatens other men with hell,
And that the Church is best equipped, no doubt,
To guide our souls and root our vices out.
Madam, you're too intelligent, I'm sure,
To think my motives anything but pure
In offering you this counsel—which I do
Out of a zealous interest in you.

Arsinoé.   I dared not hope for gratitude, but I
Did not expect so acid a reply;
I judge, since you've been so extremely tart,
That my good counsel pierced you to the heart.

Célimène.   Far from it, Madam. Indeed, it seems to me
We ought to trade advice more frequently.
One's vision of oneself is so defective
That it would be an excellent corrective.
If you are willing, Madam, let's arrange
Shortly to have another frank exchange
In which we'll tell each other, *entre nous,*
What you've heard tell of me, and I of you.

Arsinoé.   Oh, people never censure you, my dear;
It's me they criticize. Or so I hear.

Célimène.   Madam, I think we either blame or praise
According to our taste and length of days.
There is a time of life for coquetry,
And there's a season, too, for prudery.
When all one's charms are gone, it is, I'm sure,
Good strategy to be devout and pure:
It makes one seem a little less forsaken.
Some day, perhaps, I'll take the road you've taken:
Time brings all things. But I have time aplenty,
And see no cause to be a prude at twenty.

Arsinoé.   You give your age in such a gloating tone
That one would think I was an ancient crone;
We're not so far apart, in sober truth,
That you can mock me with a boast of youth!
Madam, you baffle me. I wish I knew
What moves you to provoke me as you do.

Célimène.   For my part, Madam, I should like to know
Why you abuse me everywhere you go.
Is it my fault, dear lady, that your hand
Is not, alas, in very great demand?

If men admire me, if they pay me court
And daily make me offers of the sort
You'd dearly love to have them make to you,
How can I help it? What would you have me do?
If what you want is lovers, please feel free
To take as many as you can from me.

Arsinoé. Oh, come. D'you think the world is losing sleep
Over that flock of lovers which you keep,
Or that we find it difficult to guess
What price you pay for their devotedness?
Surely you don't expect us to suppose
Mere merit could attract so many beaux?
It's not your virtue that they're dazzled by;
Nor is it virtuous love for which they sigh.
You're fooling no one, Madam; the world's not blind;
There's many a lady heaven has designed
To call men's noblest, tenderest feelings out,
Who has no lovers dogging her about;
From which it's plain that lovers nowadays
Must be acquired in bold and shameless ways,
And only pay one court for such reward
As modesty and virtue can't afford.
Then don't be quite so puffed up, if you please,
About your tawdry little victories;
Try, if you can, to be a shade less vain,
And treat the world with somewhat less disdain.
If one were envious of your amours,
One soon could have a following like yours;
Lovers are no great trouble to collect
If one prefers them to one's self-respect.

Célimène. Collect them then, my dear; I'd love to see
You demonstrate that charming theory;
Who knows, you might . . .

Arsinoé. Now, Madam, that will do;
It's time to end this trying interview,
My coach is late in coming to your door,
Or I'd have taken leave of you before.

Célimène. Oh, please don't feel that you must rush away;
I'd be delighted, Madam, if you'd stay.
However, lest my conversation bore you,
Let me provide some better company for you;
This gentleman, who comes most apropos,
Will please you more than I could do, I know.

SCENE 6. *Alceste, Célimène, Arsinoé*

Célimène. Alceste, I have a little note to write
Which simply must go out before tonight;
Please entertain *Madame;* I'm sure that she
Will overlook my incivility.

SCENE 7. *Alceste, Arsinoé*

Arsinoé. Well, Sir, our hostess graciously contrives
For us to chat until my coach arrives;
And I shall be forever in her debt
For granting me this little tête-a-tête.
We women very rightly give our hearts
To men of noble character and parts,
And your especial merits, dear Alceste,
Have roused the deepest sympathy in my breast.
Oh, how I wish they had sufficient sense
At court, to recognize your excellence!
They wrong you greatly, Sir. How it must hurt you
Never to be rewarded for your virtue!
Alceste. Why, Madam, what cause have I to feel aggrieved?
What great and brilliant thing have I achieved?
What service have I rendered to the King
That I should look to him for anything?
Arsinoé. Not everyone who's honored by the State
Has done great services. A man must wait
Till time and fortune offer him the chance.
Your merit, Sir, is obvious at a glance,
And . . .
Alceste. Ah, forget my merit; I am not neglected.
The court, I think, can hardly be expected
To mine men's souls for merit, and unearth
Our hidden virtues and our secret worth.
Arsinoé. *Some* virtues, though, are far too bright to hide;
Yours are acknowledged, Sir, on every side.
Indeed, I've heard you warmly praised of late
By persons of considerable weight.
Alceste. This fawning age has praise for everyone,
And all distinctions, Madam, are undone.
All things have equal honor nowadays,

And no one should be gratified by praise.
To be admired, one only need exist,
And every lackey's on the honors list.
Arsinoé. I only wish, Sir, that you had your eye
On some position at court, however high;
You'd only have to hint at such a notion
For me to set the proper wheels in motion;
I've certain friendships I'd be glad to use
To get you any office you might choose.
Alceste. Madam, I fear that any such ambition
Is wholly foreign to my disposition.
The soul God gave me isn't of the sort
That prospers in the weather of a court.
It's all too obvious that I don't possess
The virtues necessary for success.
My one great talent is for speaking plain;
I've never learned to flatter or to feign;
And anyone so stupidly sincere
Had best not seek a courtier's career.
Outside the court, I know, one must dispense
With honors, privilege, and influence;
But still one gains the right, foregoing these,
Not to be tortured by the wish to please.
One needn't live in dread of snubs and slights,
Nor praise the verse that every idiot writes,
Nor humor silly Marquesses, nor bestow
Politic sighs on Madam So-and-So.
Arsinoé. Forget the court, then; let the matter rest.
But I've another cause to be distressed
About your present situation, Sir.
It's to your love affair that I refer.
She whom you love, and who pretends to love you,
Is, I regret to say, unworthy of you.
Alceste. Why, Madam? Can you seriously intend
To make so grave a charge against your friend?
Arsinoé. Alas, I must. I've stood aside too long
And let that lady do you grievous wrong;
But now my debt to conscience shall be paid:
I tell you that your love has been betrayed.
Alceste. I thank you, Madam; you're extremely kind.
Such words are soothing to a lover's mind.
Arsinoé. Yes, though she *is* my friend, I say again
You're very much too good for Célimène.
She's wantonly misled you from the start.

Alceste.   You may be right; who knows another's heart?
  But ask yourself if it's the part of charity
  To shake my soul with doubts of her sincerity.
Arsinoé.   Well, if you'd rather be a dupe than doubt her,
  That's your affair. I'll say no more about her.
Alceste.   Madam, you know that doubt and vague suspicion
  Are painful to a man in my position;
  It's most unkind to worry me this way
  Unless you've some real proof of what you say.
Arsinoé.   Sir, say no more: all doubts shall be removed,
  And all that I've been saying shall be proved.
  You've only to escort me home, and there
  We'll look into the heart of this affair.
  I've ocular evidence which will persuade you
  Beyond a doubt, that Célimène's betrayed you.
  Then, if you're saddened by that revelation,
  Perhaps I can provide some consolation.

Act IV

SCENE 1.   *Éliante, Philinte*

Philinte.   Madam, he acted like a stubborn child;
  I thought they never would be reconciled;
  In vain we reasoned, threatened, and appealed;
  He stood his ground and simply would not yield.
  The Marshals, I feel sure, have never heard
  An argument so splendidly absurd.
  "No, gentlemen," said he, "I'll not retract.
  His verse is bad: extremely bad, in fact.
  Surely it does the man no harm to know it.
  Does it disgrace him, not to be a poet?
  A gentleman may be respected still,
  Whether he writes a sonnet well or ill.
  That I dislike his verse should not offend him;
  In all that touches honor, I commend him;
  He's noble, brave, and virtuous—but I fear
  He can't in truth be called a sonneteer.
  I'll gladly praise his wardrobe; I'll endorse
  His dancing, or the way he sits a horse;
  But, gentlemen, I cannot praise his rhyme.
  In fact, it ought to be a capital crime
  For anyone so sadly unendowed

To write a sonnet, and read the thing aloud."
At length he fell into a gentler mood
And, striking a concessive attitude,
He paid Oronte the following courtesies:
"Sir, I regret that I'm so hard to please,
And I'm profoundly sorry that your lyric
Failed to provoke me to a panegyric."
After these curious words, the two embraced,
And then the hearing was adjourned—in haste.

Éliante. His conduct has been very singular lately;
Still, I confess that I respect him greatly.
The honesty in which he takes such pride
Has—to my mind—its noble, heroic side.
In this false age, such candor seems outrageous;
But I could wish that it were more contagious.

Philinte. What most intrigues me in our friend Alceste
Is the grand passion that rages in his breast.
The sullen humors he's compounded of
Should not, I think, dispose his heart to love;
But since they do, it puzzles me still more
That he should choose your cousin to adore.

Éliante. It does, indeed, belie the theory
That love is born of gentle sympathy,
And that the tender passion must be based
On sweet accords of temper and of taste.

Philinte. Does she return his love, do you suppose?

Éliante. Ah, that's a difficult question, Sir. Who knows?
How can we judge the truth of her devotion?
Her heart's a stranger to its own emotion.
Sometimes it thinks it loves, when no love's there;
At other times it loves quite unaware.

Philinte. I rather think Alceste is in for more
Distress and sorrow than he's bargained for;
Were he of my mind, Madam, his affection
Would turn in quite a different direction,
And we would see him more responsive to
The kind regard which he receives from you.

Éliante. Sir, I believe in frankness, and I'm inclined,
In matters of the heart, to speak my mind.
I don't oppose his love for her; indeed,
I hope with all my heart that he'll succeed,
And were it in my power, I'd rejoice
In giving him the lady of his choice.
But if, as happens frequently enough
In love affairs, he meets with a rebuff—

If Célimène should grant some rival's suit—
I'd gladly play the role of substitute;
Nor would his tender speeches please me less
Because they'd once been made without success.

Philinte. Well, Madam, as for me, I don't oppose
Your hopes in this affair; and heaven knows
That in my conversations with the man
I plead your cause as often as I can.
But if those two should marry, and so remove
All chance that he will offer you his love,
Then I'll declare my own, and hope to see
Your gracious favor pass from him to me.
In short, should you be cheated of Alceste,
I'd be most happy to be second best.

Éliante. Philinte, you're teasing.

Philinte. Ah, Madam, never fear;
No words of mine were ever so sincere,
And I shall live in fretful expectation
Till I can make a fuller declaration.

SCENE 2. *Alceste, Éliante, Philinte*

Alceste. Avenge me, Madam! I must have satisfaction,
Or this great wrong will drive me to distraction!

Éliante. Why, what's the matter? What's upset you so?

Alceste. Madam, I've had a mortal, mortal blow.
If Chaos repossessed the universe,
I swear I'd not be shaken any worse,
I'm ruined. . . . I can say no more. . . . My soul . . .

Éliante. Do try, Sir, to regain your self-control.

Alceste. Just heaven! Why were so much beauty and grace
Bestowed on one so vicious and so base?

Éliante. Once more, Sir, tell us. . . .

Alceste. My world has gone to wrack;
I'm—I'm betrayed; she's stabbed me in the back:
Yes, Célimène (who would have thought it of her?)
Is false to me, and has another lover.

Éliante. Are you quite certain? Can you prove these things?

Philinte. Lovers are prey to wild imaginings
And jealous fancies. No doubt there's some mistake. . . .

Alceste. Mind your own business, Sir, for heaven's sake.

(To Éliante.)

Madam, I have the proof that you demand
Here in my pocket, penned by her own hand.
Yes, all the shameful evidence one could want
Lies in this letter written to Oronte—
Oronte! whom I felt sure she couldn't love,
And hardly bothered to be jealous of.

Philinte.   Still, in a letter, appearances may deceive;
This may not be so bad as you believe.

Alceste.   Once more I beg you, Sir, to let me be;
Tend to your own affairs; leave mine to me.

Éliante.   Compose yourself; this anguish that you feel . . .

Alceste.   Is something, Madam, you alone can heal.
My outraged heart, beside itself with grief,
Appeals to you for comfort and relief.
Avenge me on your cousin, whose unjust
And faithless nature has deceived my trust;
Avenge a crime your pure soul must detest.

Éliante.   But how, Sir?

Alceste.   Madam, this heart within my breast
Is yours; pray take it; redeem my heart from her,
And so avenge me on my torturer.
Let her be punished by the fond emotion,
The ardent love, the bottomless devotion,
The faithful worship which this heart of mine
Will offer up to yours as to a shrine.

Éliante.   You have my sympathy, Sir, in all you suffer;
Nor do I scorn the noble heart you offer;
But I suspect you'll soon be mollified,
And this desire for vengeance will subside.
When some belovèd hand has done us wrong
We thirst for retribution—but not for long;
However dark the deed that she's committed,
A lovely culprit's very soon acquitted.
Nothing's so stormy as an injured lover,
And yet no storm so quickly passes over.

Alceste.   No, Madam, no—this is no lovers' spat;
I'll not forgive her; it's gone too far for that;
My mind's made up; I'll kill myself before
I waste my hopes upon her any more.
Ah, here she is. My wrath intensifies.
I shall confront her with her tricks and lies,
And crush her utterly, and bring you then
A heart no longer slave to Célimène.

SCENE 3. *Célimène, Alceste*

Alceste (*aside*).   Sweet heaven, help me to control my passion.
Célimène (*aside*).   Oh, Lord.

(*To Alceste*)

                Why stand there staring in that fashion?
And what d'you mean by those dramatic sighs,
And that malignant glitter in your eyes?
Alceste.   I mean that sins which cause the blood to freeze
Look innocent beside your treacheries;
That nothing Hell's or Heaven's wrath could do
Ever produced so bad a thing as you.
Célimène.   Your compliments were always sweet and pretty.
Alceste.   Madam, it's not the moment to be witty.
No, blush and hang your head; you've ample reason,
Since I've the fullest evidence of your treason.
Ah, this is what my sad heart prophesied;
Now all my anxious fears are verified;
My dark suspicion and my gloomy doubt
Divined the truth, and now the truth is out.
For all your trickery, I was not deceived;
It was my bitter stars that I believed.
But don't imagine that you'll go scot-free;
You shan't misuse me with impunity.
I know that love's irrational and blind;
I know the heart's not subject to the mind,
And can't be reasoned into beating faster;
I know each soul is free to choose its master;
Therefore had you but spoken from the heart,
Rejecting my attentions from the start,
I'd have no grievance, or at any rate
I could complain of nothing but my fate.
Ah, but so falsely to encourage me—
That was a treason and a treachery
For which you cannot suffer too severely,
And you shall pay for that behavior dearly.
Yes, now I have no pity, not a shred;
My temper's out of hand; I've lost my head;
Shocked by the knowledge of your double-dealings,
My reason can't restrain my savage feelings;
A righteous wrath deprives me of my senses,
And I won't answer for the consequences.

Célimène. What does this outburst mean? Will you please explain?
Have you, by any chance, gone quite insane?
Alceste. Yes, yes, I went insane the day I fell
A victim to your black and fatal spell,
Thinking to meet with some sincerity
Among the treacherous charms that beckoned me.
Célimène. Pooh. Of what treachery can you complain?
Alceste. How sly you are, how cleverly you feign!
But you'll not victimize me any more.
Look: here's a document you've seen before.
This evidence, which I acquired today,
Leaves you, I think, without a thing to say.
Célimène. Is this what sent you into such a fit?
Alceste. You should be blushing at the sight of it.
Célimène. Ought I to blush? I truly don't see why.
Alceste. Ah, now you're being bold as well as sly;
Since there's no signature, perhaps you'll claim . . .
Célimène. I wrote it, whether or not it bears my name.
Alceste. And you can view with equanimity
This proof of your disloyalty to me!
Célimène. Oh, don't be so outrageous and extreme.
Alceste. You take this matter lightly, it would seem.
Was it no wrong to me, no shame to you,
That you should send Oronte this billet-doux?
Célimène. Oronte! Who said it was for him?
Alceste. 					Why, those
Who brought me this example of your prose.
But what's the difference? If you wrote the letter
To someone else, it pleases me no better.
My grievance and your guilt remain the same.

Célimène. But need you rage, and need I blush for shame,
If this was written to a *woman* friend?

Alceste. Ah! Most ingenious. I'm impressed no end;
And after that incredible evasion
Your guilt is clear. I need no more persuasion.
How dare you try so clumsy a deception?
D'you think I'm wholly wanting in perception?
Come, come, let's see how brazenly you'll try
To bolster up so palpable a lie:
Kindly construe this ardent closing section
As nothing more than sisterly affection!
Here, let me read it. Tell me, if you dare to,
That this is for a woman . . .

Célimène.   I don't care to.
What right have you to badger and berate me,
And so highhandedly interrogate me?

Alceste.   Now, don't be angry; all I ask of you
Is that you justify a phrase or two . . .

Célimène.   No, I shall not. I utterly refuse,
And you may take those phrases as you choose.

Alceste.   Just show me how this letter could be meant
For a woman's eyes, and I shall be content.

Célimène.   No, no, it's for Oronte; you're perfectly right.
I welcome his attentions with delight,
I prize his character and his intellect,
And everything is just as you suspect.
Come, do your worst now; give your rage free rein;
But kindly cease to bicker and complain.

Alceste (*aside*).   Good God! Could anything be more inhuman?
Was ever a heart so mangled by a woman?
When I complain of how she has betrayed me,
She bridles, and commences to upbraid me!
She tries my tortured patience to the limit;
She won't deny her guilt; she glories in it!
And yet my heart's too faint and cowardly
To break these chains of passion, and be free,
To scorn her as it should, and rise above
This unrewarded, mad, and bitter love.

(*To Célimène.*)

Ah, traitress, in how confident a fashion
You take advantage of my helpless passion,
And use my weakness for your faithless charms
To make me once again throw down my arms!
But do at least deny this black transgression;
Take back that mocking and perverse confession;
Defend this letter and your innocence,
And I, poor fool, will aid in your defense.
Pretend, pretend, that you are just and true,
And I shall make myself believe in you.

Célimène.   Oh, stop it. Don't be such a jealous dunce,
Or I shall leave off loving you at once.
Just why should I *pretend*? What could impel me
To stoop so low as that? And kindly tell me
Why, if I loved another, I shouldn't merely
Inform you of it, simply and sincerely!
I've told you where you stand, and that admission
Should altogether clear me of suspicion;

After so generous a guarantee,
What right have you to harbor doubts of me?
Since women are (from natural reticence)
Reluctant to declare their sentiments,
And since the honor of our sex requires
That we conceal our amorous desires,
Ought any man for whom such laws are broken
To question what the oracle has spoken?
Should he not rather feel an obligation
To trust that most obliging declaration?
Enough, now. Your suspicions quite disgust me;
Why should I love a man who doesn't trust me?
I cannot understand why I continue,
Fool that I am, to take an interest in you.
I ought to choose a man less prone to doubt,
And give you something to be vexed about.

Alceste.   Ah, what a poor enchanted fool I am;
These gentle words, no doubt, were all a sham,
But destiny requires me to entrust
My happiness to you, and so I must.
I'll love you to the bitter end, and see
How false and treacherous you dare to be.

Célimène.   No, you don't really love me as you ought.

Alceste.   I love you more than can be said or thought;
Indeed, I wish you were in such distress
That I might show my deep devotedness.
Yes, I could wish that you were wretchedly poor,
Unloved, uncherished, utterly obscure;
That fate had set you down upon the earth
Without possessions, rank, or gentle birth;
Then, by the offer of my heart, I might
Repair the great injustice of your plight;
I'd raise you from the dust, and proudly prove
The purity and vastness of my love.

Célimène.   This is a strange benevolence indeed!
God grant that I may never be in need. . . .
Ah, here's Monsieur Dubois, in quaint disguise.

SCENE 4.   *Célimène, Alceste, Dubois*

Alceste.   Well, why this costume? Why those frightened eyes?
What ails you?

Dubois.   Well, Sir, things are most mysterious.

Alceste. What do you mean?

Dubois.   I fear they're very serious.

Alceste. What?

Dubois.   Shall I speak more loudly?

Alceste.   Yes; speak out.

Dubois. Isn't there someone here, Sir?

Alceste.   Speak, you lout!
Stop wasting time.

Dubois.   Sir, we must slip away.

Alceste. How's that?

Dubois.   We must decamp without delay.

Alceste. Explain yourself.

Dubois.   I tell you we must fly.

Alceste. What for?

Dubois.   We mustn't pause to say good-by.

Alceste. Now what d'you mean by all of this, you clown?

Dubois. I mean, Sir, that we've got to leave this town.

Alceste. I'll tear you limb from limb and joint from joint
If you don't come more quickly to the point.

Dubois. Well, Sir, today a man in a black suit,
Who wore a black and ugly scowl to boot,
Left us a document scrawled in such a hand
As even Satan couldn't understand.
It bears upon your lawsuit, I don't doubt;
But all hell's devils couldn't make it out.

Alceste. Well, well, go on. What then? I fail to see
How this event obliges us to flee.

Dubois. Well, Sir: an hour later, hardly more,
A gentleman who's often called before
Came looking for you in an anxious way.
Not finding you, he asked me to convey
(Knowing I could be trusted with the same)
The following message. . . . Now, what *was* his name?

Alceste. Forget his name, you idiot. What did he say?

Dubois. Well, it was one of your friends, Sir, anyway.
He warned you to begone, and he suggested
That if you stay, you may well be arrested.

Alceste. What? Nothing more specific? Think, man, think!

Dubois. No, Sir. He had me bring him pen and ink,
And dashed you off a letter which, I'm sure,
Will render things distinctly less obscure.

Alceste. Well—let me have it!

Célimène.   What *is* this all about?

Alceste. God knows; but I have hopes of finding out.
How long am I to wait, you blitherer?

Dubois (*after a protracted search for the letter*). I must have left it on your
  table, Sir.
Alceste. I ought to . . .
Célimène. No, no, keep your self-control;
  Go find out what's behind his rigmarole.
Alceste. It seems that fate, no matter what I do,
  Has sworn that I may not converse with you;
  But, Madam, pray permit your faithful lover
  To try once more before the day is over.

Act V

SCENE 1. *Alceste, Philinte*

Alceste. No, it's too much. My mind's made up, I tell you.
Philinte. Why should this blow, however hard, compel you . . .
Alceste. No, no, don't waste your breath in argument;
  Nothing you say will alter my intent;
  This age is vile, and I've made up my mind
  To have no further commerce with mankind.
  Did not truth, honor, decency, and the laws
  Oppose my enemy and approve my cause?
  My claims were justified in all men's sight;
  I put my trust in equity and right;
  Yet, to my horror and the world's disgrace,
  Justice is mocked, and I have lost my case!
  A scoundrel whose dishonesty is notorious
  Emerges from another lie victorious!
  Honor and right condone his brazen fraud,
  While rectitude and decency applaud!
  Before his smirking face, the truth stands charmed,
  And virtue conquered, and the law disarmed!
  His crime is sanctioned by a court decree!
  And not content with what he's done to me,
  The dog now seeks to ruin me by stating
  That I composed a book now circulating,
  A book so wholly criminal and vicious
  That even to speak its title is seditious!
  Meanwhile Oronte, my rival, lends his credit
  To the same libelous tale, and helps to spread it!
  Oronte! a man of honor and of rank,
  With whom I've been entirely fair and frank;
  Who sought me out and forced me, willy-nilly,

To judge some verse I found extremely silly;
And who, because I properly refused
To flatter him, or see the truth abused,
Abets my enemy in a rotten slander!
There's the reward of honesty and candor!
The man will hate me to the end of time
For failing to commend his wretched rhyme!
And not this man alone, but all humanity
Do what they do from interest and vanity;
They prate of honor, truth, and righteousness,
But lie, betray, and swindle nonetheless.
Come then: man's villainy is too much to bear;
Let's leave this jungle and this jackal's lair.
Yes! treacherous and savage race of men,
You shall not look upon my face again.

Philinte.   Oh, don't rush into exile prematurely;
Things aren't as dreadful as you make them, surely.
It's rather obvious, since you're still at large,
That people don't believe your enemy's charge.
Indeed, his tale's so patently untrue
That it may do more harm to him than you.

Alceste.   Nothing could do that scoundrel any harm:
His frank corruption is his greatest charm,
And, far from hurting him, a further shame
Would only serve to magnify his name.

Philinte.   In any case, his bald prevarication
Has done no injury to your reputation,
And you may feel secure in that regard.
As for your lawsuit, it should not be hard
To have the case reopened, and contest
This judgment . . .

Alceste.   No, no, let the verdict rest.
Whatever cruel penalty it may bring,
I wouldn't have it changed for anything.
It shows the times' injustice with such clarity
That I shall pass it down to our posterity
As a great proof and signal demonstration
Of the black wickedness of this generation.
It may cost twenty thousand francs; but I
Shall pay their twenty thousand, and gain thereby
The right to storm and rage at human evil,
And send the race of mankind to the devil.

Philinte.   Listen to me. . . .

Alceste.   Why? What can you possibly say?
Don't argue, Sir; your labor's thrown away.

Do you propose to offer lame excuses
For men's behavior and the times' abuses?
Philinte.   No, all you say I'll readily concede:
This is a low, conniving age indeed;
Nothing but trickery prospers nowadays,
And people ought to mend their shabby ways.
Yes, man's a beastly creature; but must we then
Abandon the society of men?
Here in the world, each human frailty
Provides occasion for philosophy,
And that is virtue's noblest exercise;
If honesty shone forth from all men's eyes,
If every heart were frank and kind and just,
What could our virtues do but gather dust
(Since their employment is to help us bear
The villainies of men without despair)?
A heart well-armed with virtue can endure. . . .
Alceste.   Sir, you're a matchless reasoner, to be sure;
Your words are fine and full of cogency;
But don't waste time and eloquence on me.
My reason bids me go, for my own good.
My tongue won't lie and flatter as it should;
God knows what frankness it might next commit,
And what I'd suffer on account of it.
Pray let me wait for Célimène's return
In peace and quiet. I shall shortly learn,
By her response to what I have in view,
Whether her love for me is feigned or true.
Philinte.   Till then, let's visit Éliante upstairs.
Alceste.   No, I am too weighed down with somber cares.
Go to her, do; and leave me with my gloom
Here in the darkened corner of this room.
Philinte.   Why, that's no sort of company, my friend;
I'll see if Éliante will not descend.

SCENE 2.   *Célimène, Oronte, Alceste*

Oronte.   Yes, Madam, if you wish me to remain
Your true and ardent lover, you must deign
To give me some more positive assurance.
All this suspense is quite beyond endurance.
If your heart shares the sweet desires of mine,
Show me as much by some convincing sign;

And here's the sign I urgently suggest:
That you no longer tolerate Alceste,
But sacrifice him to my love, and sever
All your relations with the man forever.

Célimène.   Why do you suddenly dislike him so?
You praised him to the skies not long ago.

Oronte.   Madam, that's not the point. I'm here to find
Which way your tender feelings are inclined.
Choose, if you please, between Alceste and me,
And I shall stay or go accordingly.

Alceste *(emerging from the corner)*.   Yes, Madam, choose; this gentleman's demand
Is wholly just, and I support his stand.
I too am true and ardent; I too am here
To ask you that you make your feelings clear.
No more delays, now; no equivocation;
The time has come to make your declaration.

Oronte.   Sir, I've no wish in any way to be
An obstacle to your felicity.

Alceste.   Sir, I've no wish to share her heart with you;
That may sound jealous, but at least it's true.

Oronte.   If, weighing us, she leans in your direction . . .

Alceste.   If she regards you with the least affection . . .

Oronte.   I swear I'll yield her to you there and then.

Alceste.   I swear I'll never see her face again.

Oronte.   Now Madam, tell us what we've come to hear.

Alceste.   Madam, speak openly and have no fear.

Oronte.   Just say which one is to remain your lover.

Alceste.   Just name one name, and it will all be over.

Oronte.   What! Is it possible that you're undecided?

Alceste.   What! Can your feelings possibly be divided?

Célimène.   Enough: this inquisition's gone too far:
How utterly unreasonable you are!
Not that I couldn't make the choice with ease;
My heart has no conflicting sympathies;
I know full well which one of you I favor,
And you'd not see me hesitate or waver.
But how can you expect me to reveal
So cruelly and bluntly what I feel?
I think it altogether too unpleasant
To choose between two men when both are present;
One's heart has means more subtle and more kind
Of letting its affections be divined,
Nor need one be uncharitably plain
To let a lover know he loves in vain.

Oronte. No, no, speak plainly; I for one can stand it.
  I beg you to be frank.
Alceste.   And I demand it.
  The simple truth is what I wish to know,
  And there's no need for softening the blow.
  You've made an art of pleasing everyone,
  But now your days of coquetry are done:
  You have no choice now, Madam, but to choose,
  For I'll know what to think if you refuse;
  I'll take your silence for a clear admission
  That I'm entitled to my worst suspicion.
Oronte. I thank you for this ultimatum, Sir,
  And I may say I heartily concur.
Célimène. Really, this foolishness is very wearing:
  Must you be so unjust and overbearing?
  Haven't I told you why I must demur?
  Ah, here's Éliante; I'll put the case to her.

SCENE 3. *Éliante, Philinte, Célimène, Oronte, Alceste*

Célimène. Cousin, I'm being persecuted here
  By these two persons, who, it would appear,
  Will not be satisfied till I confess
  Which one I love the more, and which the less,
  And tell the latter to his face that he
  Is henceforth banished from my company.
  Tell me, has ever such a thing been done?
Éliante. You'd best not turn to me; I'm not the one
  To back you in a matter of this kind:
  I'm all for those who frankly speak their mind.
Oronte. Madam, you'll search in vain for a defender.
Alceste. You're beaten, Madam, and may as well surrender.
Oronte. Speak, speak, you must; and end this awful strain.
Alceste. Or don't, and your position will be plain.
Oronte. A single word will close this painful scene.
Alceste. But if you're silent, I'll know what you mean.

SCENE 4. *Arsinoé, Célimène, Éliante, Alceste, Philinte, Acaste,
          Clitandre, Oronte*

Acaste (to Célimène). Madam, with all due deference, we two
  Have come to pick a little bone with you.

Clitandre (*to Oronte and Alceste*).   I'm glad you're present, Sirs; as you'll
   soon learn,
   Our business here is also your concern.
Arsinoé (*to Célimène*).   Madam, I visit you so soon again
   Only because of these two gentlemen,
   Who came to me indignant and aggrieved
   About a crime too base to be believed.
   Knowing your virtue, having such confidence in it,
   I couldn't think you guilty for a minute,
   In spite of all their telling evidence;
   And, rising above our little difference,
   I've hastened here in friendship's name to see
   You clear yourself of this great calumny.
Acaste.   Yes, Madam, let us see with what composure
   You'll manage to respond to this disclosure.
   You lately sent Clitandre this tender note.
Clitandre.   And this one, for Acaste, you also wrote.
Acaste (*to Oronte and Alceste*).   You'll recognize this writing, Sirs, I think;
   The lady is so free with pen and ink
   That you must know it all too well, I fear.
   But listen: this is something you should hear.

"How absurd you are to condemn my lightheartedness in society, and
to accuse me of being happiest in the company of others. Nothing could
be more unjust; and if you do not come to me instantly and beg pardon
for saying such a thing, I shall never forgive you as long as I live. Our big
bumbling friend the Viscount . . ."

What a shame that he's not here.

"Our big bumbling friend the Viscount, whose name stands first in
your complaint, is hardly a man to my taste; and ever since the day I
watched him spend three-quarters of an hour spitting into a well, so as
to make circles in the water, I have been unable to think highly of him.
As for the little Marquess . . ."

In all modesty, gentlemen, that is I.

"As for the little Marquess, who sat squeezing my hand for such a long
while yesterday, I find him in all respects the most trifling creature alive;
and the only things of value about him are his cape and his sword. As for
the man with the green ribbons . . ."

(*To Alceste.*) It's your turn now, Sir.

"As for the man with the green ribbons, he amuses me now and then
with his bluntness and his bearish ill-humor; but there are many times

indeed when I think him the greatest bore in the world. And as for the sonneteer..."

(*To Oronte.*) Here's your helping.

"And as for the sonneteer, who has taken it into his head to be witty, and insists on being an author in the teeth of opinion, I simply cannot be bothered to listen to him, and his prose wearies me quite as much as his poetry. Be assured that I am not always so well-entertained as you suppose; that I long for your company, more than I dare to say, at all these entertainments to which people drag me, and that the presence of those one loves is the true and perfect seasoning to all one's pleasures."

Clitandre.   And now for me.

"Clitandre, whom you mention, and who so pesters me with his saccharine speeches, is the last man on earth for whom I could feel any affection. He is quite mad to suppose that I love him, and so are you, to doubt that you are loved. Do come to your senses; exchange your suppositions for his; and visit me as often as possible, to help me bear the annoyance of his unwelcome attentions."

It's a sweet character that these letters show,
And what to call it, Madam, you well know.
Enough. We're off to make the world acquainted
With this sublime self-portrait that you've painted.
Acaste.   Madam, I'll make you no farewell oration;
No, you're not worthy of my indignation.
Far choicer hearts than yours, as you'll discover,
Would like this little Marquess for a lover.

SCENE 5.   *Célimène, Éliante, Arsinoé, Alceste, Oronte, Philinte*

Oronte.   So! After all those loving letters you wrote,
You turn on me like this, and cut my throat!
And your dissembling, faithless heart, I find,
Has pledged itself by turns to all mankind!
How blind I've been! But now I clearly see;
I thank you, Madam, for enlightening me.
My heart is mine once more, and I'm content;
The loss of it shall be your punishment.

(*To Alceste.*)

Sir, she is yours; I'll seek no more to stand
Between your wishes and this lady's hand.

SCENE 6. *Célimène, Éliante, Arsinoé, Alceste, Philinte*

Arsinoé (*to Célimène*).   Madam, I'm forced to speak. I'm far too stirred
    To keep my counsel, after what I've heard.
    I'm shocked and staggered by your want of morals.
    It's not my way to mix in others' quarrels;
    But really, when this fine and noble spirit,
    This man of honor and surpassing merit,
    Laid down the offering of his heart before you,
    How *could* you . . .
Alceste.   Madam, permit me, I implore you,
    To represent myself in this debate.
    Don't bother, please, to be my advocate.
    My heart, in any case, could not afford
    To give your services their due reward;
    And if I chose, for consolation's sake,
    Some other lady, 'twould not be you I'd take.
Arsinoé.   What makes you think you could, Sir? And how dare you
    Imply that I've been trying to ensnare you?
    If you can for a moment entertain
    Such flattering fancies, you're extremely vain.
    I'm not so interested as you suppose
    In Célimène's discarded gigolos.
    Get rid of that absurd illusion, do.
    Women like me are not for such as you.
    Stay with this creature, to whom you're so attached;
    I've never seen two people better matched.

SCENE 7. *Célimène, Éliante, Alceste, Philinte*

Alceste (*to Célimène*).   Well, I've been still throughout this exposé,
    Till everyone but me has said his say.
    Come, have I shown sufficient self-restraint?
    And may I now . . .
Célimène.   Yes, make your just complaint.
    Reproach me freely, call me what you will;
    You've every right to say I've used you ill.
    I've wronged you, I confess it; and in my shame
    I'll make no effort to escape the blame.

The anger of those others I could despise;
My guilt toward you I sadly recognize.
Your wrath is wholly justified, I fear;
I know how culpable I must appear,
I know all things bespeak my treachery,
And that, in short, you've grounds for hating me.
Do so; I give you leave.

Alceste.   Ah, traitress—how,
How should I cease to love you, even now?
Though mind and will were passionately bent
On hating you, my heart would not consent.

(To Éliante and Philinte.)

Be witness to my madness, both of you;
See what infatuation drives one to;
But wait; my folly's only just begun,
And I shall prove to you before I'm done
How strange the human heart is, and how far
From rational we sorry creatures are.

(To Célimène.)

Woman, I'm willing to forget your shame,
And clothe your treacheries in a sweeter name;
I'll call them youthful errors, instead of crimes,
And lay the blame on these corrupting times.
My one condition is that you agree
To share my chosen fate, and fly with me
To that wild, trackless, solitary place
In which I shall forget the human race.
Only by such a course can you atone
For those atrocious letters; by that alone
Can you remove my present horror of you,
And make it possible for me to love you.

Célimène.   What! *I* renounce the world at my young age,
And die of boredom in some hermitage?

Alceste.   Ah, if you really loved me as you ought,
You wouldn't give the world a moment's thought;
Must you have me, and all the world beside?

Célimène.   Alas, at twenty one is terrified
Of solitude. I fear I lack the force
And depth of soul to take so stern a course.

But if my hand in marriage will content you,
Why, there's a plan which I might well consent to,
And . . .
Alceste.　　　No, I detest you now. I could excuse
Everything else, but since you thus refuse
To love me wholly, as a wife should do,
And see the world in me, as I in you,
Go! I reject your hand, and disenthrall
My heart from your enchantments, once for all.

　　　SCENE 8.　*Éliante, Alceste, Philinte*

Alceste (*to Éliante*).　　Madam, your virtuous beauty has no peer;
Of all this world, you only are sincere;
I've long esteemed you highly, as you know;
Permit me ever to esteem you so,
And if I do not now request your hand,
Forgive me, Madam, and try to understand.
I feel unworthy of it; I sense that fate
Does not intend me for the married state,
That I should do you wrong by offering you
My shattered heart's unhappy residue,
And that in short . . .
Éliante.　　　　　　　Your argument's well taken:
Nor need you fear that I shall feel forsaken.
Were I to offer him this hand of mine,
Your friend Philinte, I think, would not decline.
Philinte.　Ah, Madam, that's my heart's most cherished goal,
For which I'd gladly give my life and soul.
Alceste (*to Éliante and Philinte*).　May you be true to all you now profess,
And so deserve unending happiness.
Meanwhile, betrayed and wronged in everything,
I'll flee this bitter world where vice is king,
And seek some spot unpeopled and apart
Where I'll be free to have an honest heart.
Philinte.　Come, Madam, let's do everything we can
To change the mind of this unhappy man.

Questions

1. *Is the reader meant to admire Alceste for his principled refusal to abide by the rules of a complacent and superficial aristocratic society, or does Molière want us to laugh* at Alceste's rigidity, his insistence on turning everything into a challenge? Explain. **2.** Contrast Philinte's attitudes with those of Alceste. Why, despite their differences, does Philinte remain loyal to Alceste? **3.** What bearing does the exchange between Célimène and Arsinoé at the end of Act III have on the theme of the play? **4.** What does Alceste's jealous love for Célimène tell us about his character and principles? **5.** Considering Alceste's own attitudes and the kind of society he is a part of, what explanation is there for his assertion (in Act I, Scene 1), regarding his lawsuit, that "Reason and right and justice will plead for me"? **6.** What is Eliante's function in the play? **7.** Does the final scene of the play present a clear resolution of the issues? Explain.

Desire Under the Elms

EUGENE O'NEILL   [1888–1953]

CHARACTERS

Ephraim Cabot
Simeon ⎫
Peter   ⎬ *His sons*
Eben   ⎭
Abbie Putnam
Young Girl, Two Farmers, The Fiddler, A Sheriff, and **other folk** from the
neighboring farms.

*The action of the entire play takes place in, and immediately outside of, the
Cabot farmhouse in New England, in the year 1850. The south end of the house
faces front to a stone wall with a wooden gate at center opening on a country
road. The house is in good condition but in need of paint. Its walls are a sickly
grayish, the green of the shutters faded. Two enormous elms are on each side
of the house. They bend their trailing branches down over the roof. They appear to protect and at the same time subdue. There is a sinister maternity in
their aspect, a crushing, jealous absorption. They have developed from their
intimate contact with the life of man in the house an appalling humanness.
They brood oppressively over the house. They are like exhausted women
resting their sagging breasts and hands and hair on its roof, and when it rains
their tears trickle down monotonously and rot on the shingles.*

*There is a path running from the gate around the right corner of the house
to the front door. A narrow porch is on this side. The end wall facing us has
two windows in its upper story, two larger ones on the floor below. The two
upper are those of the father's bedroom and that of the brothers. On the left,
ground floor, is the kitchen—on the right, the parlor, the shades of which are
always drawn down.*

Part One

SCENE 1.   *Exterior of the farmhouse. It is sunset of a day at the beginning of
summer in the year 1850. There is no wind and everything is still. The sky above
the roof is suffused with deep colors, the green of the elms glows, but the
house is in shadow, seeming pale and washed out by contrast.*

*A door opens and Eben Cabot comes to the end of the porch and stands
looking down the road to the right. He has a large bell in his hand and this he*

swings mechanically, awakening a deafening clangor. Then he puts his hands on his hips and stares up at the sky. He sighs with a puzzled awe and blurts out with halting appreciation.

Eben. God, Purty! (*His eyes fall and he stares about him frowningly. He is twenty-five, tall and sinewy. His face is well-formed, good-looking, but its expression is resentful and defensive. His defiant, dark eyes remind one of a wild animal's in captivity. Each day is a cage in which he finds himself trapped but inwardly unsubdued. There is a fierce repressed vitality about him. He has black hair, mustache, a thin curly trace of beard. He is dressed in rough farm clothes.*

He spits on the ground with intense disgust, turns and goes back into the house.

Simeon and Peter come in from their work in the fields. They are tall men, much older than their half-brother [Simeon is thirty-nine and Peter thirty-seven], built on a squarer, simpler model, fleshier in body, more bovine and homelier in face, shrewder and more practical. Their shoulders stoop a bit from years of farm work. They clump heavily along in their clumsy thick-soled boots caked with earth. Their clothes, their faces, hands, bare arms and throats are earth-stained. They smell of earth. They stand together for a moment in front of the house and, as if with the one impulse, stare dumbly up at the sky, leaning on their hoes. Their faces have a compressed, unresigned expression. As they look upward, this softens.)

Simeon (*grudgingly*). Purty.

Peter. Ay-eh.

Simeon (*suddenly*). Eighteen years ago.

Peter. What?

Simeon. Jenn. My woman. She died.

Peter. I'd fergot.

Simeon. I rec'lect—now an' agin. Makes it lonesome. She'd hair long's a hoss' tail—an' yaller like gold!

Peter. Waal—she's gone. (*This with indifferent finality—then after a pause*) They's gold in the West, Sim.

Simeon (*still under the influence of sunset—vaguely*). In the sky!

Peter. Waal—in a manner o'speakin'—thar's the promise. (*Growing excited*) Gold in the sky—in the West—Golden Gate—Californi-a!—Goldest West!—field o'gold!

Simeon (*excited in his turn*). Fortunes layin' just atop o' the ground waitin' t' be picked! Solomon's mines they says! (*For a moment they continue looking up at the sky—then their eyes drop*).

Peter (*with sardonic bitterness*). Here—it's stones atop o' the ground—stones atop o' stones—makin' stone walls—year atop o' year—him 'n' yew 'n' me 'n' then Eben—makin' stone walls fur him to fence us in!

Simeon. We've wuked. Give our strength. Give our years. Plowed 'em under in the ground,—(*he stamps rebelliously*)—rottin'—makin' soil for his crops! (*A pause*) Waal—the farm pays good for hereabouts.

Peter. If we plowed in Californi-a, they'd be lumps o'gold in the furrow!

Simeon. Californi-a's t'other side o' earth, a'most. We got t' calc'late—

Peter (*after a pause*). 'Twould be hard fur me, too, to give up what we've 'arned here by our sweat. (*A pause.* Eben *sticks his head out of the dining-room window, listening.*)

Simeon. Ay-eh. (*A pause*) Mebbe—he'll die soon.

Peter (*doubtfully*). Mebbe.

Simeon. Mebbe—fur all we knows—he's dead now.

Peter. Ye'd need proof.

Simeon. He's been gone two months—with no word.

Peter. Left us in the fields an evenin' like this. Hitched up an' druv off into the West. That's plum onnateral. He hain't never been off this farm 'ceptin' t' the village in thirty year or more, not since he married Eben's maw. (*A pause. Shrewdly*) I calc'late we might git him declared crazy by the court.

Simeon. He skinned 'em too slick. He got the best o'all on 'em. They'd never b'lieve him crazy. (*A pause*) We got t' wait—till he's under ground.

Eben (*with a sardonic chuckle*). Honor thy father! (*They turn, startled, and stare at him. He grins, then scowls*) I pray he's died. (*They stare at him. He continues matter-of-factly*) Supper's ready.

Simeon and **Peter** (*together*). Ay-eh.

Eben (*gazing up at the sky*). Sun's downin' purty.

Simeon and **Peter** (*together*). Ay-eh. They's gold in the West.

Eben. Ay-eh. (*Pointing*) Yonder atop o' the hill pasture, ye mean?

Simeon and **Peter** (*together*). In Californi-a!

Eben. Hunh? (*Stares at them indifferently for a second, then drawls*) Waal—supper's gittin' cold. (*He turns back into kitchen.*)

Simeon (*startled—smacks his lips*). I air hungry!

Peter (*sniffing*). I smells bacon!

Simeon (*with hungry appreciation*). Bacon's good!

Peter (*in same tone*). Bacon's bacon! (*They turn, shouldering each other, their bodies bumping and rubbing together as they hurry clumsily to their food, like two friendly oxen toward their evening meal. They disappear around the right corner of house and can be heard entering the door.*)

SCENE 2. *The color fades from the sky. Twilight begins. The interior of the kitchen is now visible. A pine table is at center, a cookstove in the right rear corner, four rough wooden chairs, a tallow candle on the table. In the middle of the rear wall is fastened a big advertising poster with a ship in full sail and the world "California" in big letters. Kitchen utensils hang from nails. Everything is neat and in order but the atmosphere is of a men's camp kitchen rather than that of a home.*

Places for three are laid. Eben takes boiled potatoes and bacon from the stove and puts them on the table, also a loaf of bread and a crock of water. Simeon and Peter shoulder in, slump down in their chairs without a word. Eben joins them. The three eat in silence for a moment, the two elder as naturally unrestrained as beasts of the field, Eben picking at his food without appetite, glancing at them with a tolerant dislike.

Simeon (*suddenly turns to Eben*). Looky here! Ye'd oughtn't t' said that, Eben.

Peter. 'Twa'n't righteous.

Eben. What?

Simeon. Ye prayed he'd died.

Eben. Waal—don't yew pray it? (*A pause.*)

Peter. He's our Paw.

Eben (*violently*). Not mine!

Simeon (*dryly*). Ye'd not let no one else say that about yer Maw! Ha! (*He gives one abrupt sardonic guffaw. Peter grins.*)

Eben (*very pale*). I meant—I hain't his'n—I hain't like him—he hain't me!

Peter (*dryly*). Wait till ye've growed his age!

Eben (*intensely*). I'm Maw—every drop o' blood! (*A pause. They stare at him with indifferent curiosity.*)

Peter (*reminiscently*). She was good t' Sim 'n' me. A good step-maw's scurse.

Simeon. She was good t' everyone.

Eben (*greatly moved, gets to his feet and makes an awkward bow to each of them—stammering*). I be thankful t' ye. I'm her—her heir. (*He sits down in confusion.*)

Peter (*after a pause—judicially*). She was good even t' him.

Eben (*fiercely*). An' fur thanks he killed her!

Simeon (*after a pause*). No one never kills nobody. It's allus somethin'. That's the murderer.

Eben. Didn't he slave Maw t' death?

Peter. He's slaved himself t' death. He's slaved Sim 'n' me 'n' yew t' death— on'y none o' us hain't died—yit.

Simeon. It's somethin'—drivin' him—t' drive us!

Eben (*vengefully*). Waal—I hold him t' jedgment! (*Then scornfully*) Somethin'! What's somethin'?

Simeon. Dunno.

Eben (*sardonically*). What's drivin' yew to Californi-a, mebbe? (*They look at him in surprise*) Oh, I've heerd ye! (*Then, after a pause*) But ye'll never go t' the gold fields!

Peter (*assertively*). Mebbe!

Eben. Whar'll ye git the money?

Peter. We kin walk. It's an a'mighty ways—Californi-a—but if yew was t' put all the steps we've walked on this farm end t' end we'd be in the moon!

Eben. The Injuns'll skulp ye on the plains.

Simeon (*with grim humor*). We'll mebbe make 'em pay a hair fur a hair!

Eben (*decisively*). But t'aint that. Ye won't never go because ye'll wait here fur yer share o' the farm, thinkin' allus he'll die soon.

Simeon (*after a pause*). We've a right.

Peter. Two-thirds belong t' us.

Eben (*jumping to his feet*). Ye've no right! She wa'n't yewr Maw! It was her farm! Didn't he steal it from her? She's dead. It's my farm.

Simeon (*sardonically*). Tell that t' Paw—when he comes! I'll bet ye a dollar he'll laugh—fur once in his life. Ha! (*He laughs himself in one single mirthless bark.*)

Peter (*amused in turn, echoes his brother*). Ha!

Simeon (*after a pause*). What've ye got held agin us, Eben? Year arter year it's skulked in yer eye—somethin'.

Peter. Ay-eh.

Eben. Ay-eh. They's somethin'. (*Suddenly exploding*) Why didn't ye never stand between him 'n' my Maw when he was slavin' her to her grave—t' pay her back fur the kindness she done t' yew? (*There is a long pause. They stare at him in surprise.*)

Simeon. Waal—the stock's got t' be watered.

Peter. 'R they was woodin' t' do.

Simeon. 'R plowin'.

Peter. 'R hayin'.

Simeon. 'R spreadin' manure.

Peter. 'R weedin'.

Simeon. 'R prunin'.

Peter. 'R milkin'.

Eben (*breaking in harshly*). An' makin' walls—stone atop o' stone—makin' walls till yer heart's a stone ye heft up out o' the way o' growth onto a stone wall t' wall in yer heart!

Simeon (*matter-of-factly*). We never had no time t' meddle.

Peter (*to Eben*). Yew was fifteen afore yer Maw died—an' big fur yer age. Why didn't ye never do nothin'?

Eben (*harshly*). They was chores t' do, wa'n't they? (*A pause—then slowly*) It was on'y arter she died I come to think o' it. Me cookin—doin' her work—that made me know her, suffer her sufferin'—she'd come back t' help—come back t' bile potatoes—come back t' fry bacon—come back t' bake biscuits—come back all cramped up t' shake the fire, an' carry ashes, her eyes weepin' an' bloody with smoke an' cinders same's they used t' be. She still comes back—stands by the stove thar in the evein'—she can't find it nateral sleepin' an' restin' in peace. She can't git used t' bein free—even in her grave.

Simeon. She never complained none.

Eben. She'd got too tired. She'd got too used t' bein' too tired. That was what he done. (*With vengeful passion*) An' sooner'r later, I'll meddle. I'll say the thin's I didn't say then t' him! I'll yell 'em at the top o' my lungs. I'll see t' it my Maw gits some rest an' sleep in her grave! (*He sits down again, relapsing into a brooding silence. They look at him with a queer indifferent curiosity.*)

Peter (*after a pause*).　Whar in tarnation d'ye s'pose he went, Sim?

Simeon.　Dunno. He druv off in the buggy, all spick an' span, with the mare all breshed an' shiny, druv off clackin' his tongue an' wavin' his whip. I remember it right well. I was finishin' plowin', it was spring an' May an' sunset, an' gold in the West, an' he druv off into it. I yells "Whar ye goin', Paw?" an' he hauls up by the stone wall a jiffy. His old snake's eyes was glitterin' in the sun like he's been drinkin' a jugful an' he says with a mule's grin: "Don't ye run away till I come back!"

Peter.　Wonder if he knowed we was wantin' fur Californi-a?

Simeon.　Mebbe. I didn't say nothin' and he says, lookin' kinder queer an' sick: "I been hearin' the hens cluckin' an' the roosters crowin' all the durn day. I been listenin' t' the cows lowin' an' everythin' else kickin' up till I can't stand it no more. It's spring an' I'm feelin' damned," he says. "Damned like an old bare hickory tree fit on'y fur burnin'," he says. An' then I calc'late I must've looked a mite hopeful, fur he adds real spry and vicious: "But don't git no fool idee I'm dead. I've sworn t' live a hundred an' I'll do it, if on'y t' spite yer sinful greed! An' now I'm ridin' out t' learn God's message t' me in the spring, like the prophets done. An' yew git back t' yer plowin'," he says. An' he druv off singin' a hymn. I thought he was drunk—'r I'd stopped him goin'.

Eben (*scornfully*).　No, ye wouldn't! Ye're scared o' him. He's stronger—inside—than both o' ye put together!

Peter (*sardonically*).　An' yew—be yew Samson?

Eben.　I'm gittin' stronger. I kin feel it growin' in me—growin' an' growin'—till it'll bust out—! (*He gets up and puts on his coat and a hat. They watch him, gradually breaking into grins. Eben avoids their eyes sheepishly*) I'm goin' out fur a spell—up the road.

Peter.　T' the village?

Simeon.　T' see Minnie?

Eben (*defiantly*).　Ay-eh?

Peter (*jeeringly*).　The Scarlet Woman!

Simeon.　Lust—that's what's growin' in ye!

Eben.　Waal—she's purty!

Peter.　She's been purty fur twenty year!

Simeon.　A new coat o' paint'll make a heifer out of forty.

Eben.　She hain't forty!

Peter.　If she hain't, she's teeterin' on the edge.

Eben (*desperately*).　What d'yew know—

Peter.　All they is . . . Sim knew her—an' then me arter—

Simeon.　An' Paw kin tell yew somethin' too! He was fust!

Eben.   D'ye mean t' say he . . .?

Simeon (*with a grin*).   Ay-eh! We air his heirs in everythin'!

Eben (*intensely*).   That's more to it! That grows on it! It'll bust soon! (*Then violently*) I'll go smash my fist in her face! (*He pulls open the door in rear violently.*)

Simeon (*with a wink at* Peter—*drawlingly*).   Mebbe—but the night's wa'm—purty—by the time ye git thar mebbe ye'll kiss her instead!

Peter.   Sart'n he will! (*They both roar with coarse laughter.* Eben *rushes out and slams the door—then the outside front door—comes around the corner of the house and stands still by the gate, staring up at the sky.*)

Simeon (*looking after him*).   Like his Paw.

Peter.   Dead spit an' image!

Simeon.   Dog'll eat dog!

Peter.   Ay-eh. (*Pause. With yearning*) Mebbe a year from now we'll be in Californi-a.

Simeon.   Ay-eh. (*A pause. Both yawn*) Let's git t' bed. (*He blows out the candle. They go out door in rear.* Eben *stretches his arms up to the sky—rebelliously.*)

Eben.   Waal—thar's a star, an' somewhar's they's him, an' here's me, an' thar's Min up the road—in the same night. What if I does kiss her? She's like t'night, she's soft 'n' wa'm, her eyes kin wink like a star, her mouth's wa'm, her arms're wa'm, she smells like a wa'm plowed field, she's purty . . . Ay-eh! By God A'mighty she's purty, an' I don't give a damn how many sins she's sinned afore mine or who she's sinned 'em with, my sin's as purty as any one of 'em! (*He strides off down the road to the left.*)

SCENE 3.   *It is the pitch darkness just before dawn.* Eben *comes in from the left and goes around to the porch, feeling his way, chuckling bitterly and cursing half-aloud to himself.*

Eben.   The cussed old miser! (*He can be heard going in the front door. There is a pause as he goes upstairs, then a loud knock on the bedroom door of the brothers*) Wake up!

Simeon (*startledly*).   Who's thar?

Eben (*pushing open the door and coming in, a lighted candle in his hand. The bedroom of the brothers is revealed. Its ceiling is the sloping roof. They can stand upright only close to the center dividing wall of the upstairs.* Simeon *and* Peter *are in a double bed, front.* Eben's *cot is to the rear.* Eben *has a mixture of a silly grin and vicious scowl on his face*).   I be!

Peter (*angrily*).   What in hell's-fire . . . ?

Eben.   I got news fur ye! Ha! (*He gives one abrupt sardonic guffaw.*)

Simeon (*angrily*).   Couldn't ye hold it 'til we'd got our sleep?

Eben.   It's nigh sunup. (*Then explosively*) He's gone an' married agen!

Simeon and **Peter** (*explosively*).   Paw?

Eben. Got himself hitched to a female 'bout thirty-five—an' purty, they says . . .

Simeon (*aghast*). It's a durn lie!

Peter. Who says?

Simeon. They been stringin' ye!

Eben. Think I'm a dunce, do ye? The hull village says. The preacher from New Dover, he brung the news—told it t' our preacher—New Dover, that's whar the old loon got himself hitched—that's whar the woman lived—

Peter (*no longer doubting—stunned*). Waal . . . !

Simeon (*the same*). Waal . . . !

Eben (*sitting down on a bed—with vicious hatred*). Ain't he a devil out o' hell? It's jest t' spite us—the damned old mule!

Peter (*after a pause*). Everythin'll go t' her now.

Simeon. Ay-eh. (*A pause—dully*) Waal—if it's done—

Peter. It's done us. (*Pause—then persuasively*) They's gold in the fields o' Californi-a, Sim. No good a-stayin' here now.

Simeon. Jest what I was a-thinkin'. (*Then with decision*) S'well fust's last! Let's light out and git this mornin'.

Peter. Suits me.

Eben. Ye must like walkin'.

Simeon (*sardonically*). If ye'd grow wings on us we'd fly thar!

Eben. Ye'd like ridin' better—on a boat, wouldn't ye? (*Fumbles in his pocket and takes out a crumpled sheet of foolscap*) Waal, if ye sign this ye kin ride on a boat. I've had it writ out an' ready in case ye'd ever go. It says fur three hundred dollars t' each ye agree yewr shares o' the farm is sold t' me. (*They look suspiciously at the paper. A pause.*)

Simeon (*wonderingly*). But if he's hitched agen—

Peter. An' whar'd yew git that sum o' money, anyways?

Eben (*cunningly*). I know whar it's hid. I been waitin'—Maw told me. She knew whar it lay fur years, but she was waitin' . . . It's her'n—the money he hoarded from her farm an' hid from Maw. It's my money by rights now.

Peter. Whar's it hid?

Eben (*cunningly*). Whar yew won't never find it without me. Maw spied on him—'r she'd never knowed. (*A pause. They look at him suspiciously, and he at them*) Waal, is it fa'r trade?

Simeon. Dunno.

Peter. Dunno.

Simeon (*looking at window*). Sky's grayin'.

Peter. Ye better start the fire, Eben.

Simeon. An' fix some vittles.

Eben. Ay-eh. (*Then with a forced jocular heartiness*) I'll git ye a good one. If ye're startin' t' hoof it t' Californi-a ye'll need somethin' that'll stick t' yer ribs. (*He turns to the door, adding meaningly*) But ye kin ride on a boat if ye'll swap. (*He stops at the door and pauses. They stare at him.*)

Simeon (*suspiciously*).   Whar was ye all night?

Eben (*defiantly*).   Up t' Min's. (*Then slowly*) Walkin' thar, fust I felt's if I'd kiss
her; then I got a-thinkin' o' what ye'd said o' him an' her an' I says, I'll bust
her nose fur that! Then I got t' the village an' heerd the news an' I got
madder'n hell an' run all the way t' Min's not knowin' what I'd do—(*He
pauses—then sheepishly but more defiantly*) Waal—when I seen her, I
didn't hit her—nor I didn't kiss her nuther—I begun t' beller like a calf an'
cuss at the same time, I was so durn mad—an' she got scared—an' I jest
grabbed holt an' tuk her! (*Proudly*) Yes, sirree! I tuk her. She may've been
his'n—an' your'n, too—but she's mine now!

Simeon (*dryly*).   In love, air yew?

Eben (*with lofty scorn*).   Love! I don't take no stock in sech slop!

Peter (*winking at* Simeon).   Mebbe Eben's aimin' t' marry, too.

Simeon.   Min'd make a true faithful he'pmeet! (*They snicker.*)

Eben.   What do I care fur her—'ceptin' she's round an' wa'm? The p'int is she
was his'n—an' now she b'longs t' me! (*He goes to the door—then turns—
rebelliously*) An' Min hain't sech a bad un. They's worse'n Min in the
world, I'll bet ye! Wait'll we see this cow the Old Man's hitched t'! She'll
beat Min, I got a notion! (*He starts to go out.*)

Simeon (*suddenly*).   Mebbe ye'll try t' make her your'n, too?

Peter.   Ha! (*He gives a sardonic laugh of relish at this idea.*)

Eben (*spitting with disgust*).   Her—here—sleepin' with him—stealin' my
Maw's farm! I'd as soon pet a skunk 'r kiss a snake! (*He goes out. The two
stare after him suspiciously. A pause. They listen to his steps receding.*)

Peter.   He's startin' the fire.

Simeon.   I'd like t' ride t' Californi-a—but—

Peter.   Min might o' put some scheme in his head.

Simeon.   Mebbe it's all a lie 'bout Paw marryin'. We'd best wait an' see the
bride.

Peter.   An' don't sign nothin' till we does!

Simeon.   Nor till we've tested it's good money! (*Then with a grin*) But if Paw's
hitched we'd be sellin' Eben somethin' we'd never git nohow!

Peter.   We'll wait an' see. (*Then with sudden vindictive anger*) An' till he
comes, let's yew 'n' me not wuk a lick, let Eben tend to thin's if he's a mind
t', let's us jest sleep an' eat an' drink likker an' let the hull damned farm go
t' blazes!

Simeon (*excitedly*).   By God, we've 'arned a rest! We'll play rich fur a change.
I hain't a-going to stir outa bed till breakfast's ready.

Peter.   An' on the table!

Simeon (*after a pause—thoughtfully*).   What d'ye calc'late she'll be like—our
new Maw? Like Eben thinks?

Peter.   More'n' likely.

Simeon (*vindictively*).   Waal—I hope she's a she-devil that'll make him wish
he was dead an' livin' in the pit o' hell fur comfort!

Peter (*fervently*).   Amen!

Simeon (*imitating his father's voice*).   "I'm ridin' out t' learn God's message t' me in the spring like the prophets done," he says. I'll bet right then an' thar he knew plumb well he was goin' whorin', the stinkin' old hypocrite!

SCENE 4. *Same as Scene Two—shows the interior of the kitchen with a lighted candle on table. It is gray dawn outside. Simeon and Peter are just finishing their breakfast. Eben sits before his plate of untouched food, brooding frowningly.*

Peter (*glancing at him rather irritably*).   Lookin' glum don't help none.

Simeon (*sarcastically*).   Sorrowin' over his lust o' the flesh!

Peter (*with a grin*).   Was she yer fust?

Eben (*angrily*).   None o' yer business. (*A pause*) I was thinkin' o' him. I got a notion he's gittin' near—I kin feel him comin' on like yew kin feel malaria chill afore it takes ye.

Peter.   It's too early yet.

Simeon.   Dunno. He'd like t' catch us nappin'—jest t' have somethin' t' hoss us 'round over.

Peter (*mechanically gets to his feet. Simeon does the same*).   Waal—let's git t' wuk. (*They both plod mechanically toward the door before they realize. Then they stop short.*)

Simeon (*grinning*).   Ye're a cussed fool, Pete—and I be wuss! Let him see we hain't wukin'! We don't give a durn!

Peter (*as they go back to the table*).   Not a damned durn! It'll serve t' show him we're done with him. (*They sit down again. Eben stares from one to the other with surprise.*)

Simeon (*grins at him*).   We're aimin' t' start bein' lilies o' the field.

Peter.   Nary a toil 'r spin 'r lick o' wuk do we put in!

Simeon.   Ye're sole owner—till he comes—that's what ye wanted. Waal, ye got t' be sole hand, too.

Peter.   The cows air bellerin'. Ye better hustle at the milkin'.

Eben (*with excited joy*).   Ye mean ye'll sign the paper?

Simeon (*dryly*).   Mebbe.

Peter.   Mebbe.

Simeon.   We're considerin'. (*Peremptorily*) Ye better git t' wuk.

Eben (*with queer excitement*).   It's Maw's farm agen! It's my farm! Them's my cows! I'll milk my durn fingers off fur cows o' mine! (*He goes out door in rear, they stare after him indifferently.*)

Simeon.   Like his Paw.

Peter.   Dead spit 'n' image!

Simeon.   Waal—let dog eat dog! (*Eben comes out of front door and around the corner of the house. The sky is beginning to grow flushed with sunrise. Eben stops by the gate and stares around him with glowing, possessive eyes. He takes in the whole farm with his embracing glance of desire.*)

Eben.   It's purty! It's damned purty! It's mine! (*He suddenly throws his head* back boldly and glares with hard, defiant eyes at the sky) Mine, d'ye hear? Mine! (*He turns and walks quickly off left, rear, toward the barn. The two brothers light their pipes.*)

Simeon (*putting his muddy boots up on the table, tilting back his chair, and puffing defiantly*).   Waal—this air solid comfort—fur once.

Peter.   Ay-eh. (*He follows suit. A pause. Unconsciously they both sigh.*)

Simeon (*suddenly*).   He never was much o' a hand at milkin', Eben wa'n't.

Peter (*with a snort*).   His hands air like hoofs! (*A pause.*)

Simeon.   Reach down the jug thar! Let's take a swaller. I'm feelin' kind o' low.

Peter.   Good idee! (*He does so—gets two glasses—they pour out drinks of whisky*) Here's t' the gold in Californi-a!

Simeon.   An' luck t' find it! (*They drink—puff resolutely—sigh—take their feet down from the table.*)

Peter.   Likker don't 'pear t' sot right.

Simeon.   We hain't used t' it this early. (*A pause. They become very restless.*)

Peter.   Gittin' close in this kitchen.

Simeon (*with immense relief*).   Let's git a breath o' air. (*They arise briskly and go out rear—appear around house and stop by the gate. They stare up at the sky with a numbed appreciation.*)

Peter.   Purty!

Simeon.   Ay-eh. Gold's t' the East now.

Peter.   Sun's startin' with us fur the Golden West.

Simeon (*staring around the farm, his compressed face tightened, unable to conceal his emotion*).   Waal—it's our last mornin'—mebbe.

Peter (*the same*).   Ay-eh.

Simeon (*stamps his foot on the earth and addresses it desperately*).   Waal— ye've thirty year o' me buried in ye—spread out over ye—blood an' bone an' sweat—rotted away—fertilizin' ye—richin' yer soul—prime manure, by God, that's what I been t' ye!

Peter.   Ay-eh! An' me!

Simeon.   An' yew, Peter. (*He sighs—then spits*) Waal—no use'n cryin' over spilt milk.

Peter.   They's gold in the West—an' freedom, mebbe. We been slaves t' stone walls here.

Simeon (*defiantly*).   We hain't nobody's slaves from this out—nor no thin's slaves nuther. (*A pause—restlessly*) Speakin' o' milk, wonder how Eben's managin'?

Peter.   I s'pose he's managin'.

Simeon.   Mebbe we'd ought t' help—this once.

Peter.   Mebbe. The cows know us.

Simeon.   An' likes us. They don't know him much.

Peter.   An' the hosses, an' pigs, an' chickens. They don't know him much.

Simeon.   They knows us like brothers—an' likes us! (*Proudly*) Hain't we raised 'em t' be fust-rate, number one prize stock?

Peter.   We hain't—not no more.

Simeon (*dully*).   I was fergittin'. (*Then resignedly*) Waal, let's go help Eben a spell an' git waked up.

Peter.   Suits me. (*They are starting off down left, rear, for the barn when* Eben *appears from there hurrying toward them, his face excited.*)

Eben (*breathlessly*).   Waal—thar they be! The old mule an' the bride! I seen 'em from the barn down below at the turnin'.

Peter.   How could ye tell that far?

Eben.   Hain't I as far-sight as he's near-sight? Don't I know the mare 'n' buggy, an' two people settin' in it? Who else . . . ? An' I tell ye I kin feel 'em a - comin', too! (*He squirms as if he had the itch.*)

Peter (*beginning to be angry*).   Waal—let him do his own unhitchin'!

Simeon (*angry in his turn*).   Let's hustle in an' git our bundles an' be a-goin' as he's a-comin'. I don't want never t' step inside the door agen arter he's back. (*The both start back around the corner of the house.* Eben *follows them.*)

Eben (*anxiously*).   Will ye sign it afore ye go?

Peter.   Let's see the color o' the old skinflint's money an' we'll sign. (*They disappear left. The two brothers clump upstairs to get their bundles.* Eben *appears in the kitchen, runs to window, peers out, comes back and pulls up a strip of flooring in under stove, takes out a canvas bag and puts it on table, then sets the floorboard back in place. The two brothers appear a moment after. They carry old carpetbags.*)

Eben (*puts his hand on bag guardingly*).   Have ye signed?

Simeon (*shows paper in his hand*).   Ay-eh. (*Greedily*) Be that the money?

Eben (*opens bag and pours out pile of twenty-dollar gold pieces*): Twenty-dollar pieces—thirty of 'em. Count 'em. (*Peter does so, arranging them in stacks of five, biting one or two to test them.*)

Peter.   Six hundred. (*He puts them in bag and puts it inside his shirt carefully.*)

Simeon (*handing paper to* Eben).   Har ye be.

Eben (*after a glance, folds it carefully and hides it under his shirt—gratefully*).   Thank yew.

Peter.   Thank yew fur the ride.

Simeon.   We'll send ye a lump o' gold fur Christmas. (*A pause.* Eben *stares at them and they at him.*)

Peter (*awkwardly*).   Waal— we're a-goin'.

Simeon.   Comin' out t' the yard?

Eben.   No. I'm waitin' in here a spell. (*Another silence. The brothers edge awkwardly to door in rear—then turn and stand.*)

Simeon.   Waal—good-by.

Peter.   Good-by.

Eben.   Good-by. (*They go out. He sits down at the table, faces the stove and pulls out the paper. He looks from it to the stove. His face, lighted up by the shaft of sunlight from the window, has an expression of trance. His lips move. The two brothers come out to the gate.*)

Peter (*looking off toward barn*).   Thar he be—unhitchin'.

Simeon (*with a chuckle*).   I'll bet ye he's riled!

Peter.   An' thar she be.

Simeon.   Let's wait 'n' see what our new Maw looks like.

Peter (*with a grin*).   An' give him our partin' cuss!

Simeon (*grinning*).   I feel like raisin' fun. I feel light in my head an' feet.

Peter.   Me, too. I feel like laffin' till I'd split up the middle.

Simeon.   Reckon it's the likker?

Peter.   No. My feet feel itchin' t' walk an' walk—an' jump high over thin's—an'. . . .

Simeon.   Dance? (*A pause*).

Peter (*puzzled*).   It's plumb onnateral.

Simeon (*a light coming over his face*).   I calc'late it's 'cause school's out. It's holiday. Fur once we're free!

Peter (*dazedly*).   Free?

Simeon.   The halter's broke—the harness is busted—the fence bars is down—the stone walls air crumblin' an' tumblin'! We'll be kickin' up an' tearin' away down the road!

Peter (*drawing a deep breath—oratorically*).   Anybody that wants this stinkin' old rock-pile of a farm kin hev it. T'ain't our'n, no sirree!

Simeon (*takes the gate off its hinges and puts it under his arm*).   We harby 'bolishes shet gates, an' open gates, an' all gates, by thunder!

Peter.   We'll take it with us fur luck an' let 'er sail free down some river.

Simeon (*as a sound of voices comes from left, rear*).   Har they comes! (*The two brothers congeal into two stiff, grim-visaged statues,* Ephraim Cabot *and* Abbie Putnam *come in.* Cabot *is seventy-five, tall and gaunt, with great, wiry, concentrated power, but stoop-shouldered from toil. His face is as hard as if it were hewn out of a boulder, yet there is a weakness in it, a petty pride in its own narrow strength. His eyes are small, close together, and extremely near-sighted, blinking continually in the effort to focus on objects, their stare having a straining, ingrowing quality. He is dressed in his dismal black Sunday suit.* Abbie *is thirty-five, buxom, full of vitality. Her round face is pretty but marred by its rather gross sensuality. There is strength and obstinacy in her jaw, a hard determination in her eyes, and about her whole personality the same unsettled, untamed, desperate quality which is so apparent in* Eben.*)*

Cabot (*as they enter—a queer strangled emotion in his dry cracking voice*).   Har we be t' hum, Abbie.

Abbie (*with lust for the word*).   Hum! (*Her eyes gloating on the house without seeming to see the two stiff figures at the gate*) It's purty—purty! I can't b'lieve it's r'ally mine.

Cabot (*sharply*).   Yewr'n? Mine! (*He stares at her penetratingly, she stares back. He adds relentingly*) Our'n—mebbe! It was lonesome too long. I was growin' old in the spring. A hum's got t' hev a woman.

Abbie (*her voice taking possession*).   A woman's got t' hev a hum!

Cabot (*nodding uncertainly*).   Ay-eh. (*Then irritably*) Whar be they? Ain't thar nobody about—'r wukin'—'r nothin'?

Abbie (*sees the brothers. She returns their stare of cold appraising contempt with interest—slowly*).   Thar's two men loafin' at the gate an' starin' at me like a couple o' strayed hogs.

Cabot (*straining his eyes*).   I kin see 'em—but I can't make out. . . .

Simeon.   It's Simeon.

Peter.   It's Peter.

Cabot (*exploding*).   Why hain't ye wukin'?

Simeon (*dryly*).   We're waitin' t' welcome ye hum—yew an' the bride!

Cabot (*confusedly*).   Huh? Waal—this be yer new Maw, boys. (*She stares at them and they at her.*)

Simeon (*turns away and spits contemptuously*).   I see her!

Peter (*spits also*).   An' I see her!

Abbie (*with the conqueror's conscious superiority*).   I'll go in an' look at *my* house. (*She goes slowly around to porch.*)

Simeon (*with a snort*).   Her house!

Peter (*calls after her*).   Ye'll find Eben inside. Ye better not tell him its *yewr* house.

Abbie (*mouthing the name*).   Eben. (*Then quietly*) I'll tell Eben.

Cabot (*with a contemptuous sneer*).   Ye needn't heed Eben. Eben's a dumb fool—like his Maw—soft an' simple!

Simeon (*with his sardonic burst of laughter*).   Ha! Eben's a chip o' yew—spit 'n' image—hard 'n' bitter's a hickory tree! Dog'll eat dog. He'll eat ye yet, old man!

Cabot (*commandingly*).   Ye git t' wuk!

Simeon (*as Abbie disappears in house—winks at Peter and says tauntingly*).   So that thar's our new Maw, be it? Whar in hell did ye dig her up? (*He and Peter laugh.*)

Peter.   Ha! Ye'd better turn her in the pen with the other sows. (*They laugh uproariously, slapping their thighs.*)

Cabot (*so amazed at their effrontery that he stutters in confusion*).   Simeon! Peter! What's come over ye? Air ye drunk?

Simeon.   We're free, old man—free o' yew an' the hull damned farm! (*They grow more and more hilarious and excited.*)

Peter.   An' we're startin' out fur the gold fields o' Californi-a!

Simeon.   Ye kin take this place an' burn it!

Peter.   An' bury it—fur all we cares!

Simeon.   We're free, old man! (*He cuts a caper.*)

Peter.   Free! (*He gives a kick in the air.*)

Simeon (*in a frenzy*).   Whoop!

Peter.   Whoop! (*They do an absurd Indian war dance about the old man who is petrified between rage and the fear that they are insane.*)

Simeon.   We're free as Injuns! Lucky we don't skulp ye!

Peter. An' burn yer barn an' kill the stock!

Simeon. An' rape yer new woman! Whoop! (*He and* Peter *stop their dance, holding their sides, rocking with wild laughter.*)

Cabot (*edging away*). Lust fur gold—fur the sinful, easy gold o' Californi-a! It's made ye mad!

Simeon (*tauntingly*). Wouldn't ye like us to send ye back some sinful gold, ye old sinner?

Peter. They's gold besides what's in Californi-a! (*He retreats back beyond the vision of the old man and takes the bag of money and flaunts it in the air above his head, laughing.*)

Simeon. And sinfuller, too!

Peter. We'll be voyagin' on the sea! Whoop! (*He leaps up and down.*)

Simeon. Livin' free! Whoop! (*He leaps in turn.*)

Cabot (*suddenly roaring with rage*). My cuss on ye!

Simeon. Take our'n in trade fur it! Whoop!

Cabot. I'll hev ye both chained up in the asylum!

Peter. Ye old skinflint! Good-by!

Simeon. Ye old blood sucker! Good-by!

Cabot. Go afore I . . . !

Peter. Whoop! (*He picks a stone from the road.* Simeon *does the same.*)

Simeon. Maw'll be in the parlor.

Peter. Ay-eh! One! Two!

Cabot (*frightened*). What air ye . . . ?

Peter. Three! (*They both throw, the stones hitting the parlor window with a crash of glass, tearing the shade.*)

Simeon. Whoop!

Peter. Whoop!

Cabot (*in a fury now, rushing toward them*). If I kin lay hands on ye—I'll break yer bones fur ye! (*But they beat a capering retreat before him,* Simeon *with the gate still under his arm.* Cabot *comes back, panting with impotent rage. Their voices as they go off take up the song of the gold-seekers to the old tune of "Oh, Susannah!"*)

"I jumped aboard the Liza ship,
And traveled on the sea.
And every time I thought of home
I wished it wasn't me!
Oh! Californi-a,
That's the land fur me!
I'm off to Californi-a!
With my wash bowl on my knee."

(*In the meantime, the window of the upper bedroom on right is raised and* Abbie *sticks her head out. She looks down at* Cabot—*with a sigh of relief*).

Abbie. Waal—that's the last o' them two, hain't it? (*He doesn't answer. Then in possessive tones*) This here's a nice bedroom, Ephraim. It's a r'al nice bed. Is it my room, Ephraim?

Cabot (*grimly—without looking up*). Our'n! (*She cannot control a grimace of aversion and pulls back her head slowly and shuts the window. A sudden horrible thought seems to enter* Cabot's *head*) They been up to somethin'! Mebbe—mebbe they've pizened the stock—'r somethin'! (*He almost runs off down toward the barn. A moment later the kitchen door is slowly pushed open and Abbie enters. For a moment she stands looking at Eben. He does not notice her at first. Her eyes take him in penetratingly with a calculating appraisal of his strength as against hers. But under this her desire is dimly awakened by his youth and good looks. Suddenly he becomes conscious of her presence and looks up. Their eyes meet. He leaps to his feet, glowering at her speechlessly.*)

Abbie (*in her most seductive tones which she uses all through this scene*). Be you—Eben? I'm Abbie—(*she laughs*) I mean, I'm yer new Maw.

Eben (*viciously*). No, damn ye!

Abbie (*as if she hadn't heard—with a queer smile*). Yer Paw's spoke a lot o' yew. . . .

Eben. Ha!

Abbie. Ye mustn't mind him. He's an old man. (*A long pause. They stare at each other*) I don't want t' pretend playin' Maw t' ye, Eben. (*Admiringly*) Ye're too big an' too strong fur that. I want t' be frens with ye. Mebbe with me fur a fren ye'd find ye'd like livin' here better. I kin make it easy fur ye with him, mebbe. (*With a scornful sense of power*) I calc'late I kin git him t' do most anythin' fur me.

Eben (*with bitter scorn*). Ha! (*They stare again,* Eben *obscurely moved, physically attracted to her—in forced stilted tones*) Yew kin go t' the devil!

Abbie (*calmly*). If cussin' me does ye good, cuss all ye've a mind t'. I'm all prepared t' have ye agin me—at fust. I don't blame ye nuther. I'd feel the same at any stranger comin' t' take my Maw's place. (*He shudders. She is watching him carefully*) Yew must've cared a lot fur yewr Maw, didn't ye? My Maw died afore I'd growed. I don't remember her none. (*A pause*) But yew won't hate me long, Eben. I'm not the wust in the world—an' yew an' me've got a lot in common. I kin tell that by lookin' at ye. Waal—I've had a hard life, too—oceans o' trouble an' nuthin' but wuk fur reward. I was a orphan early an' had t' wuk fur others in other folks' hums. Then I married an' he turned out a drunken spreer an' so he had to wuk fur others' an' me too agen in other folks' hums, an' the baby died, an' my husband got sick an' died too, an' I was glad sayin' now I'm free fur once, on'y I diskivered right away all I was free fur was t' wuk agen in other folks' hums, doin' other folks' wuk till I'd most give up hope o' ever doin' my own wuk in my own hum, an' then your Paw come. . . . (Cabot *appears returning from the barn. He comes to the gate and looks down the road* the brothers have gone. A faint strain of their retreating voices is heard: "Oh, Californi-a! That's the place for me." He stands glowering, his fist clenched, his face grim with rage.)

Eben (*fighting against his growing attraction and sympathy—harshly*). An' bought yew—like a harlot! (*She is stung and flushes angrily. She has been sincerely moved by the recital of her troubles. He adds furiously*) An' the price he's payin' ye—this farm—was my Maw's, damn ye!—an' mine now!

Abbie (*with a cool laugh of confidence*). Yewr'n? We'll see 'bout that! (*Then strongly*) Waal—what if I did need a hum? What else'd I marry an old man like him fur?

Eben (*maliciously*). I'll tell him ye said that!

Abbie (*smiling*). I'll say ye're lyin' a-purpose—an' he'll drive ye off the place!

Eben. Ye devil!

Abbie (*defying him*). This be my farm—this be my hum—this be my kitchen—!

Eben (*furiously, as if he were going to attack her*). Shut up, damn ye!

Abbie (*walks up to him—a queer coarse expression of desire in her face and body—slowly*). An' upstairs—that be my bedroom—an' my bed! (*He stares into her eyes, terribly confused and torn. She adds softly*) I hain't bad nor mean—'ceptin' fur an enemy—but I got t' fight fur what's due me out o' life, if I ever 'spect t' git it. (*Then putting her hand on his arm—seductively*) Let's yew 'n' me be frens, Eben.

Eben (*stupidly—as if hypnotized*). Ay-eh. (*Then furiously flinging off her arm*) No, ye durned old witch! I hate ye! (*He rushes out the door.*)

Abbie (*looks after him smiling satisfiedly—then half to herself, mouthing the word*). Eben's nice. (*She looks at the table, proudly*) I'll wash up my dishes now. (*Eben appears outside, slamming the door behind him. He comes around corner, stops on seeing his father, and stands staring at him with hate.*)

Cabot (*raising his arms to heaven in the fury he can no longer control*). Lord God o' Hosts, smite the undutiful sons with Thy wust cuss!

Eben (*breaking in violently*). Yew 'n' yewr God! Allus cussin' folks—allus naggin' em!

Cabot (*oblivious to him—summoningly*). God o' the old! God o' the lonesome!

Eben (*mockingly*). Naggin' His sheep t' sin! T' hell with yewr God! (*Cabot turns. He and Eben glower at each other.*)

Cabot (*harshly*). So it's yew. I might've knowed it. (*Shaking his finger threateningly at him*) Blasphemin' fool! (*Then quickly*) Why hain't ye t' wuk?

Eben. Why hain't yew? They've went. I can't wuk it all alone.

Cabot (*contemptuously*). Nor noways! I'm wuth ten o' ye yit, old's I be! Ye'll never be more'n half a man! (*Then, matter-of-factly*) Waal—let's git t' the barn. (*They go. A last faint note of the "Californi-a song is heard from the distance. Abbie is washing her dishes.*)

Part Two

SCENE 1. *The exterior of the farmhouse, as in Part One—a hot Sunday afternoon two months later. Abbie, dressed in her best, is discovered sitting in a rocker at the end of the porch. She rocks listlessly, enervated by the heat, staring in front of her with bored, half-closed eyes.*

Eben sticks his head out of his bedroom window. He looks around furtively and tries to see—or hear—if anyone is on the porch, but although he has been careful to make no noise, Abbie has sensed his movement. She stops rocking, her face grows animated and eager, she waits attentively. Eben seems to feel her presence, he scowls back his thoughts of her and spits with exaggerated disdain—then withdraws back into the room. Abbie waits, holding her breath as she listens with passionate eagerness for every sound within the house.

Eben comes out. Their eyes meet. His falter, he is confused, he turns away and slams the door resentfully. At this gesture, Abbie laughs tantalizingly, amused but at the same time piqued and irritated. He scowls, strides off the porch to the path and starts to walk past her to the road with a grand swagger of ignoring her existence. He is dressed in his store suit, spruced up, his face shines from soap and water. Abbie leans forward on her chair, her eyes hard and angry now, and, as he passes her, gives a sneering, taunting chuckle.

Eben (*stung—turns on her furiously*). What air yew cacklin' 'bout?
Abbie (*triumphant*). Yew!
Eben. What about me?
Abbie. Ye look all slicked up like a prize bull.
Eben (*with a sneer*). Waal—ye hain't so durned purty yerself, be ye? (*They stare into each other's eyes, his held by hers in spite of himself, hers glowingly possessive. Their physical attraction becomes a palpable force quivering in the hot air.*)
Abbie (*softly*). Ye don't mean that, Eben. Ye may think ye mean it, mebbe, but ye don't. Ye can't. It's agin nature, Eben. Ye been fightin' yer nature ever since the day I come—tryin' t' tell yerself I hain't purty t'ye. (*She laughs a low humid laugh without taking her eyes from his. A pause—her body squirms desirously—she murmurs languorously*) Hain't the sun strong an' hot? Ye kin feel it burnin' into the earth—Nature—makin' thin's grow—bigger 'n' bigger—burnin' inside ye—makin' ye want t' grow—into somethin' else—till ye're jined with it—an' it's your'n—but it owns ye, too—an' makes ye grow bigger—like a tree—like them elums—(*She laughs again softly, holding his eyes. He takes a step toward her, compelled against his will*) Nature'll beat ye, Eben. Ye might's well own up t' it fust's last.
Eben (*trying to break from her spell—confusedly*). If Paw'd hear ye goin' on. . . . (*Resentfully*) But ye've made such a damned idjit out o' the old devil . . . ! (*Abbie laughs.*)

Abbie. Waal—hain't it easier fur yew with him changed softer?

Eben (*defiantly*). No. I'm fightin' him—fightin' yew—fightin' fur Maw's rights t' her hum! (*This breaks her spell for him. He glowers at her*) An' I'm onto ye. Ye hain't foolin' me a mite. Ye're aimin' t' swaller up everthin' an' make it your'n. Waal, you'll find I'm a heap sight bigger hunk nor yew kin chew! (*He turns from her with a sneer.*)

Abbie (*trying to regain her ascendancy—seductively*). Eben!

Eben. Leave me be! (*He starts to walk away.*)

Abbie (*more commandingly*). Eben!

Eben (*stops—resentfully*). What d'ye want?

Abbie (*trying to conceal a growing excitement*). Whar air ye goin'?

Eben (*with malicious nonchalance*). Oh—up the road a spell.

Abbie. T' the village?

Eben (*airily*). Mebbe.

Abbie (*excitedly*). T' see that Min, I s'pose?

Eben. Mebbe.

Abbie (*weakly*). What d'ye want t' waste time on her fur?

Eben (*revenging himself now—grinning at her*). Ye can't beat Nature, didn't ye say? (*He laughs and again starts to walk away.*)

Abbie (*bursting out*). An ugly old hake!

Eben (*with a tantalizing sneer*). She's purtier'n yew be!

Abbie. That every wuthless drunk in the country has. . . .

Eben (*tauntingly*). Mebbe—but she's better'n yew. She owns up fa'r 'n' squar' t' her doin's.

Abbie (*furiously*). Don't ye dare compare. . . .

Eben. She don't go sneakin' an' stealin'—what's mine.

Abbie (*savagely seizing on his weak point*). Your'n? Yew mean—my farm?

Eben. I mean the farm yew sold yerself fur like any other old whore—my farm!

Abbie (*stung—fiercely*). Ye'll never live t' see the day when even a stinkin' weed on it 'll belong t' ye! (*Then in a scream*) Git out o' my sight! Go on t' yer slut—disgracin' yer Paw 'n' me! I'll get yer Paw t' horsewhip ye off the place if I want t'! Ye're only livin' here 'cause I tolerate ye! Git along! I hate the sight o' ye! (*She stops panting and glaring at him.*)

Eben (*returning her glance in kind*). An' I hate the sight o' yew! (*He turns and strides off up the road. She follows his retreating figure with concentrated hate. Old* Cabot *appears coming up from the barn. The hard, grim expression of his face has changed. He seems in some queer way softened, mellowed. His eyes have taken on a strange, incongruous dreamy quality. Yet there is not a hint of physical weakness about him—rather he looks more robust and younger.* Abbie *sees him and turns away quickly with unconcealed aversion. He comes slowly up to her.*)

Cabot (*mildly*). War yew an' Eben quarrelin' agen?

Abbie (*shortly*). No.

Cabot. Ye was talkin' a'mighty loud. (*He sits down on the edge of the porch.*)

Abbie (*snappishly*).   If ye heerd us they hain't no need askin' questions.

Cabot. I didn't hear what ye said.

Abbie (*relieved*).   Waal—it wa'n't nothin' t' speak on.

Cabot (*after a pause*). Eben's queer.

Abbie (*bitterly*).   He's the dead spit 'n' image o' yew!

Cabot (*queerly interested*).   D'ye think so, Abbie? (*After a pause, ruminatingly*) Me 'n' Eben's allus fit 'n' fit. I never could b'ar him noways. He's so thunderin' soft—like his Maw.

Abbie (*scornfully*).   Ay-eh! 'Bout as soft as yew be!

Cabot (*as if he hadn't heard*).   Mebbe I been too hard on him.

Abbie (*jeeringly*).   Waal—ye're gittin' soft now—soft as slop! That's what Eben was sayin'.

Cabot (*his face instantly grim and ominous*).   Eben was sayin'? Waal, he'd best not do nothin' t' try me 'r he'll soon diskiver. . . . (*A pause. She keeps her face turned away. His gradually softens. He stares up at the sky*) Purty, hain't it?

Abbie (*crossly*).   I don't see nothin' purty.

Cabot. The sky. Feels like a wa'm field up thar.

Abbie (*sarcastically*). Air yew aimin' t' buy up over the farm too? (*She snickers contemptuously.*)

Cabot (*strangely*).   I'd like t' own my place up thar. (*A pause*) I'm gittin' old, Abbie. I'm gittin' ripe on the bough. (*A pause. She stares at him mystified. He goes on*) It's allus lonesome cold in the house—even when it's bilin' hot outside. Hain't yew noticed?

Abbie. No.

Cabot. It's wa'm down t' the barn—nice smellin' an' warm—with the cows. (*A pause*) Cows is queer.

Abbie. Like yew?

Cabot. Like Eben. (*A pause*) I'm gittin' t' feel resigned t' Eben—jest as I got t' feel 'bout his Maw. I'm gittin' t' learn to b'ar his softness—jest like her'n. I calc'late I c'd a'most take t' him—if he wa'n't sech a dumb fool! (*A pause*) I s'pose it's old age a'creepin' in my bones.

Abbie (*indifferently*).   Waal—ye hain't dead yet.

Cabot (*roused*).   No, I hain't, yew bet—not by a hell of a sight—I'm sound 'n' tough as hickory! (*Then moodily*) But arter three score and ten the Lord warns ye t' prepare. (*A pause*) That's why Eben's come in my head. Now that his cussed sinful brothers is gone their path t' hell, they's no one left but Eben.

Abbie (*resentfully*).   They's me, hain't they? (*Agitatedly*) What's all this sudden likin' ye've tuk to Eben? Why don't ye say nothin' 'bout me? Hain't I yer lawful wife?

Cabot (*simply*). Ay-eh. Ye be. (*A pause—he stares at her desirously—his eyes grow avid—then with a sudden movement he seizes her hands and*

squeezes them, declaiming in a queer camp-meeting preacher's tempo)
Yew air my Rose o' Sharon! Behold, yew air fair; yer eyes air doves; yer
lips air like scarlet; yer two breasts air like two fawns; yer navel be like a
round goblet; yer belly be like a heap o' wheat. . . . *(He covers her hand
with kisses. She does not seem to notice. She stares before her with hard
angry eyes.)*

Abbie *(jerking her hands away—harshly).*   So ye're plannin' t' leave the farm
t' Eben, air ye?

Cabot *(dazedly).*   Leave . . . ? *(Then with resentful obstinacy)* I hain't a-givin' it
t' no one!

Abbie *(remorselessly).*   Ye can't take it with ye.

Cabot *(thinks a moment—then reluctantly).*   No, I calc'late not. *(After a
pause—with a strange passion)* But if I could, I would, by the Etarnal! 'R if I
could, in my dyin' hour, I'd set it afire an' watch it burn—this house an'
every ear o' corn an' every tree down t' the last blade o' hay! I'd sit an'
know it was all a-dying with me an' no one else'd ever own what was
mine, what I'd made out o' nothin' with my own sweat 'n' blood! *(A
pause—then he adds with a queer affection)* 'Ceptin' the cows. Them I'd
turn free.

Abbie *(harshly).*   An' me?

Cabot *(with a queer smile).*   Ye'd be turned free, too.

Abbie *(furiously).*   So that's the thanks I git fur marryin' ye—t' have ye change
kind to Eben who hates ye, an' talk o' turnin' me out in the road.

Cabot *(hastily).*   Abbie! Ye know I wa'n't. . . .

Abbie *(vengefully).*   Just let me tell ye a thing or two 'bout Eben! Whar's he
gone? T' see that harlot, Min! I tried fur t' stop him. Disgracin' yew an'
me—on the Sabbath, too!

Cabot *(rather guiltily).*   He's a sinner—nateral-born. It's lust eatin' his heart.

Abbie *(enraged beyond endurance—wildly vindictive).*   An' his lust fur me!
Kin ye find excuses fur that?

Cabot *(stares at her—after a dead pause).*   Lust—fur yew?

Abbie *(defiantly).*   He was tryin' t' make love t' me—when ye heerd us quarrelin'.

Cabot *(stares at her—then a terrible expression of rage comes over his face—
he springs to his feet shaking all over).*   By the A'mighty God—I'll end
him!

Abbie *(frightened now for Eben).*   No! Don't ye!

Cabot *(violently).*   I'll git the shotgun an' blow his soft brains t' the top o'
them elums!

Abbie *(throwing her arms around him).*   No, Ephraim!

Cabot *(pushing her away violently).*   I will, by God!

Abbie *(in a quieting tone).*   Listen, Ephraim. 'Twa'n't nothin' bad—on'y a
boy's foolin'—'twa'n't meant serious—jest jokin' an' teasin'. . . .

Cabot.   Then why did ye say—lust?

Abbie. It must hev sounded wusser'n I meant. An' I was mad at thinkin' ye'd leave him the farm.

Cabot (*quieter but still grim and cruel*).   Waal then, I'll horsewhip him off the place if that much'll content ye.

Abbie (*reaching out and taking his hand*).   No. Don't think o' me! Ye mustn't drive him off. 'Tain't sensible. Who'll ye get to help ye on the farm? They's no one hereabouts.

Cabot (*considers this—then nodding his appreciation*).   Ye got a head on ye. (*Then irritably*) Waal, let him stay. (*He sits down on the edge of the porch. She sits beside him. He murmurs contemptuously*) I oughtn't t' git riled so—at that 'ere fool calf. (*A pause*) But har's the p'int. What son o' mine'll keep on here t' the farm—when the Lord does call me? Simeon an' Peter air gone t' hell—an' Eben's follerin' 'em.

Abbie.   They's me.

Cabot.   Ye're on'y a woman.

Abbie.   I'm yewr wife.

Cabot.   That hain't me. A son is me—my blood—mine. Mine ought t' git mine. An' then it's still mine—even though I be six foot under. D'ye see?

Abbie (*giving him a look of hatred*).   Ay-eh. I see. (*She becomes very thoughtful, her face growing shrewd, her eyes studying* Cabot *craftily.*)

Cabot.   I'm gittin' old—ripe on the bough. (*Then with a sudden forced reassurance*) Not but what I hain't a hard nut t' crack even yet—an' fur many a year t' come! By the Etarnal, I kin break most o' the young fellers' backs at any kind o' work any day o' the year!

Abbie (*suddenly*).   Mebbe the Lord'll give *us* a son.

Cabot (*turns and stares at her eagerly*).   Ye mean—a son—t' me 'n' yew?

Abbie (*with a cajoling smile*).   Ye're a strong man yet, hain't ye? 'Tain't no-ways impossible, be it? We know that. Why d'ye stare so? Hain't ye never thought o' that afore? I been thinkin' o' it all along. Ay-eh—an' I been prayin' it'd happen, too.

Cabot (*his face growing full of joyous pride and a sort of religious ecstasy*).   Ye been prayin', Abbie?—fur a son?—t' us?

Abbie.   Ay-eh. (*With a grim resolution*) I want a son now.

Cabot (*excitedly clutching both of her hands in his*).   It'd be the blessin' o' God, Abbie—the blessin' o' God A'mighty on me—in my old age—in my lonesomeness! They hain't nothin' I wouldn't do fur ye then, Abbie. Ye'd hev on'y t' ask it—anythin' ye'd a mind t'!

Abbie (*interrupting*).   Would ye will the farm t' me then—t' me an' it . . . ?

Cabot (*vehemently*).   I'd do anythin' ye axed, I tell ye! I swar it! May I be ever-lastin' damned t' hell if I wouldn't (*He sinks to his knees pulling her down with him. He trembles all over with the fervor of his hopes*) Pray t' the Lord agen, Abbie. It's the Sabbath! I'll jine ye'! Two prayers air better nor one. "An' God hearkened unto Rachel"! An' God hearkened unto Abbie! Pray, Abbie! Pray fur him to hearken! (*He bows his head, mumbling. She* *pretends to do likewise but gives him a side glance of scorn and triumph.)*

SCENE 2. *About eight in the evening. The interior of the two bedrooms on the top floor is shown. Eben is sitting on the side of his bed in the room on the left. On account of the heat he has taken off everything but his undershirt and pants. His feet are bare. He faces front, brooding moodily, his chin propped on his hands, a desperate expression on his face.*

In the other room Cabot and Abbie are sitting side by side on the edge of their bed, an old four-poster with feather mattress. He is in his night shirt, she in her nightdress. He is still in the queer, excited mood into which the notion of a son has thrown him. Both rooms are lighted dimly and flickeringly by tallow candles.

Cabot. The farm needs a son.

Abbie. I need a son.

Cabot. Ay-eh. Sometimes ye air the farm an' sometimes the farm be yew. That's why I clove t' ye in my lonesomeness. (*A pause. He pounds his knee with his fist*) Me an' the farm has got t' beget a son!

Abbie. Ye'd best go t' sleep. Ye're gittin' thin's all mixed.

Cabot (*with an impatient gesture*). No, I hain't. My mind's clear's a well. Ye don't know me, that's it. (*He stares hopelessly at the floor.*)

Abbie (*indifferently*). Mebbe. (*In the next room Eben gets up and paces up and down distractedly. Abbie hears him. Her eyes fasten on the intervening wall with concentrated attention. Eben stops and stares. Their hot glances seem to meet through the wall. Unconsciously he stretches out his arms for her and she half rises. Then aware, he mutters a curse at himself and flings himself face downward on the bed, his clenched fists above his head, his face buried in the pillow. Abbie relaxes with a faint sigh but her eyes remain fixed on the wall; she listens with all her attention for some movement from Eben.*)

Cabot (*suddenly raises his head and looks at her—scornfully*). Will ye ever know me—'r will any man 'r woman? (*Shaking his head*) No. I calc'late 't wa'n't t' be. (*He turns away. Abbie looks at the wall. Then, evidently unable to keep silent about his thoughts without looking at his wife, he puts out his hand and clutches her knee. She starts violently, looks at him, sees he is not watching her, concentrates again on the wall and pays no attention to what he says*) Listen, Abbie. When I come here fifty odd year ago—I was jest twenty an' the strongest an' hardest ye ever seen—ten times as strong an' fifty times as hard as Eben. Waal—this place was nothing' but fields o' stones. Folks laughed when I tuk it. They couldn't know what I knowed. When ye kin make corn sprout out o' stones, God's livin' in yew! They wa'n't strong enuf fur that! They reckoned God was easy. They laughed. They don't laugh no more. Some died hereabouts. Some went West an' died. They're all under ground—fur follerin' arter an easy God. God hain't easy. (*He shakes his head slowly*) An' I growed hard. Folks kept allus sayin' he's a hard man like 'twas sinful t' be hard, so's at last I said back at 'em: Waal then, by thunder, ye'll git me hard an' see how ye like it! (*Then suddenly*) But I give in t' weakness once. 'Twas arter I'd been here two year. I got weak—despairful—they was so many stones. They was a party leavin', givin' up, going' West. I jined 'em. We tracked on 'n' on. We come t' broad medders, plains, whar the soil was black an' rich as gold. Nary a stone. Easy. Ye'd on'y to plow an' sow an' then set an' smoke yer pipe an' watch thin's grow. I could o' been a rich man—but somethin' in me fit me an' fit me—the voice o' God sayin': "This hain't wuth nothin' t' Me. Git ye back t' hum!" I got afeered o' that voice an' I lit out back t' hum here, leavin' my claim an' crops t' whoever'd a mind t' take 'em. Ay-eh. I actooly give up what was rightful mine! God's hard, not easy! God's in the stones! Build my church on a rock—out o' stones an' I'll be in them! That's what He meant t' Peter! (*He sighs heavily—a pause*) Stones. I picked 'em up an' piled 'em into walls. Ye kin read the years o' my life in them walls, every day a hefted stone, climbin' over the hills up and down, fencin' in the fields that was mine, whar I'd made thin's grow out o' nothin'—like the will o' God, like the servant o' His hand. It wa'n't easy. It was hard an' He made me hard fur it. (*He pauses*) All the time I kept gittin' lonesomer. I tuk a wife. She bore Simeon an' Peter. She was a good woman. She wuked hard. We was married twenty year. She never knowed me. She helped but she never knowed what she was helpin'. I was allus lonesome. She died. After that it wa'n't so lonesome fur a spell. (*A pause*) I lost count o' the years. I had no time t' fool away countin' 'em. Sim an' Peter helped. The farm growed. It was all mine! When I thought o' that I didn't feel lonesome. (*A pause*) But ye can't hitch yer mind t' one thin' day an' night. I tuk another wife—Eben's Maw. Her folks was contestin' me at law over my deeds t' the farm—my farm! That's why Eben keeps a-talkin' his fool talk o' this bein' his Maw's farm. She bore Eben. She was purty—but soft. She tried t' be hard. She couldn't. She never knowed me nor nothin'. It was lonesomer 'n hell with her. After a matter o' sixteen odd years, she died. (*A pause*) I lived with the boys. They hated me 'cause I was hard. I hated them 'cause they was soft. They coveted the farm without knowin' what it meant. It made me bitter 'n wormwood. It aged me—them coveting what I'd made fur mine. Then this spring the call come—the voice o' God cryin' in my wilderness, in my lonesomeness—t' go out an' seek an' find! (*Turning to her with strange passion*) I sought ye an' I found ye! Yew air my Rose o' Sharon! Yer eyes air like. . . . (*She has turned a blank face, resentful eyes to his. He stares at her for a moment—then harshly*) Air ye any the wiser fur all I've told ye?

Abbie (*confusedly*).   Mebbe.

Cabot (*pushing her away from him—angrily*).   Ye don't know nothin'—nor never will. If ye don't hev a son t' redeem ye. . . . (*This in a tone of cold threat.*)

Abbie (*resentfully*).   I've prayed, hain't I?

Cabot (*bitterly*).   Pray agen—fur understandin'!

Abbie (*a veiled threat in her tone*).   Ye'll have a son out o' me, I promise ye.

Cabot.   How kin ye promise?

Abbie.   I got second-sight mebbe. I kin foretell. (*She gives a queer smile.*)

Cabot.   I believe ye have. Ye give me the chills sometimes. (*He shivers*) It's cold in this house. It's oneasy. They's thin's pokin' about in the dark—in the corners. (*He pulls on his trousers, tucking in his night shirt, and pulls on his boots.*)

Abbie (*surprised*).   Whar air ye goin'?

Cabot (*queerly*).   Down whar it's restful—whar it's warm down t' the barn. (*Bitterly*) I kin talk t' the cows. They know. They know the farm an' me. They'll give me peace. (*He turns to go out the door.*)

Abbie (*a bit frightenedly*).   Air ye ailin' tonight, Ephraim?

Cabot.   Growin'. Growin' ripe on the bough. (*He turns and goes, his boots clumping down the stairs.* Eben *sits up with a start, listening.* Abbie *is conscious of his movement and stares at the wall.* Cabot *comes out of the house around the corner and stands by the gate, blinking at the sky. He stretches up his hands in a tortured gesture*) God A'mighty, call from the dark! (*He listens as if expecting an answer. Then his arms drop, he shakes his head and plods off toward the barn.* Eben *and* Abbie *stare at each other through the wall.* Eben *sighs heavily and* Abbie *echoes it. Both become terribly nervous, uneasy. Finally* Abbie *gets up and listens, her ear to the wall. He acts as if he saw every move she was making, he becomes resolutely still. She seems driven into a decision—goes out the door in rear determinedly. His eyes follow her. Then as the door of his room is opened softly, he turns away, waits in an attitude of strained fixity.* Abbie *stands for a second staring at him, her eyes burning with desire. Then with a little cry she runs over and throws her arms about his neck, she pulls his head back and covers his mouth with kisses. At first, he submits dumbly; then he puts his arms about her neck and returns her kisses, but finally, suddenly aware of his hatred, he hurls her away from him, springing to his feet. They stand speechless and breathless, panting like two animals.*)

Abbie (*at last—painfully*).   Ye shouldn't, Eben—ye shouldn't—I'd make ye happy!

Eben (*harshly*).   I don't want t' be happy—from yew!

Abbie (*helplessly*).   Ye do, Eben! Ye do! Why d'ye lie?

Eben (*viciously*).   I don't take t'ye, I tell ye! I hate the sight o' ye!

Abbie (*with an uncertain troubled laugh*).   Waal, I kissed ye anyways—an' ye kissed back—yer lips was burnin'—ye can't lie 'bout that! (*Intensely*) If ye don't care, why did ye kiss me back—why was yer lips burnin'?

Eben (*wiping his mouth*).   It was like pizen on 'em. (*Then tauntingly*) When I kissed ye back, mebbe I thought 'twas someone else.

Abbie (*wildly*).   Min?

Eben.   Mebbe.

Abbie (*torturedly*).   Did ye go t' see her? Did ye r'ally go? I thought ye mightn't. Is that why ye throwed me off jest now?

Eben (*sneeringly*).   What if it be?

Abbie (*raging*).   Then ye're a dog, Eben Cabot!

Eben (*threateningly*).   Ye can't talk that way t' me!

Abbie (*with a shrill laugh*).   Can't I? Did ye think I was in love with ye—a weak thin' like yew? Not much! I on'y wanted ye fur a purpose o' my own—an' I'll hev ye fur it yet 'cause I'm stronger'n yew be!

Eben (*resentfully*).   I knowed well it was on'y part o' yer plan t' swaller every-thin'!

Abbie (*tauntingly*).   Mebbe!

Eben (*furious*).   Git out o' my room!

Abbie.   This air my room an' ye're on'y hired help!

Eben (*threateningly*).   Git out afore I murder ye!

Abbie (*quite confident now*).   I hain't a mite afeerd. Ye want me, don't ye? Yes, ye do! An' yer Paw's son'll never kill what he wants! Look at yer eyes! They's lust fur me in 'em, burnin' 'em up! Look at yer lips now! They're tremblin' an' longin' t' kiss me, an' yer teeth t' bite! (*He is watching her now with a horrible fascination. She laughs a crazy triumphant laugh*) I'm a-goin' t' make all o' this hum my hum! They's one room hain't mine yet, but it's a-goin' t' be tonight. I'm a-goin' down now an' light up! (*She makes him a mocking bow*) Won't ye come courtin' me in the best parlor, Mister Cabot?

Eben (*staring at her—horribly confused—dully*).   Don't ye dare! It hain't been opened since Maw died an' was laid out thar! Don't ye . . . ! (*But her eyes are fixed on his so burningly that his will seems to wither before hers. He stands swaying toward her helplessly*).

Abbie (*holding his eyes and putting all her will into her words as she backs out the door*).   I'll expect ye afore long, Eben.

Eben (*stares after her for a while, walking toward the door. A light appears in the parlor window. He murmurs*).   In the parlor? (*This seems to arouse connotations for he comes back and puts on his white shirt, collar, half ties the tie mechanically, puts on coat, takes his hat, stands barefooted looking about him in bewilderment, mutters wonderingly*) Maw! Whar air yew? (*Then goes slowly toward the door in rear.*)

SCENE 3.   *A few minutes later. The interior of the parlor is shown. A grim, repressed room like a tomb in which the family has been interred alive. Abbie sits on the edge of the horsehair sofa. She has lighted all the candles and the room is revealed in all its preserved ugliness. A change has come over the woman. She looks awed and frightened now, ready to run away.*

The door is opened and Eben appears. His face wears an expression of obsessed confusion. He stands staring at her, his arms hanging disjointedly from his shoulders, his feet bare, his hat in his hand.

Abbie (*after a pause—with a nervous, formal politeness*).   Won't ye set?

Eben (*dully*).   Ay-eh. (*Mechanically he places his hat carefully on the floor near the door and sits stiffly beside her on the edge of the sofa. A pause. They both remain rigid, looking straight ahead with eyes full of fear.*)

Abbie.   When I fust come in—in the dark—they seemed somethin' here.

Eben (*simply*).   Maw.

Abbie.   I kin still feel—somethin'. . . .

Eben.   It's Maw.

Abbie.   At fust I was feered o' it. I wanted t' yell an' run. Now—since yew come—seems like it's growin' soft an' kind t' me. (*Addressing the air—queerly*) Thank yew.

Eben.   Maw allus loved me.

Abbie.   Mebbe it knows I love yew, too. Mebbe that makes it kind t' me.

Eben (*dully*).   I dunno. I should think she'd hate ye.

Abbie (*with certainty*).   No. I kin feel it don't—not no more.

Eben.   Hate ye fur stealin' her place—here in her hum—settin' in her parlor whar she was laid—(*He suddenly stops, staring stupidly before him.*)

Abbie.   What is it, Eben?

Eben (*in a whisper*).   Seems like Maw didn't want me t' remind ye.

Abbie (*excitedly*).   I knowed, Eben! It's kind t' me! It don't b'ar me no grudges fur what I never knowed an' couldn't help!

Eben.   Maw b'ars him a grudge.

Abbie.   Waal, so does all o' us.

Eben.   Ay-eh. (*With passion*) I does, by God!

Abbie (*taking one of his hands in hers and patting it*).   Thar! Don't git riled thinkin' o' him. Think o' yer Maw who's kind t' us. Tell me about yer Maw, Eben.

Eben.   They hain't nothin' much. She was kind. She was good.

Abbie (*putting one arm over his shoulder. He does not seem to notice—passionately*).   I'll be kind an' good t' ye!

Eben.   Sometimes she used t' sing fur me.

Abbie.   I'll sing fur ye!

Eben.   This was her hum. This was her farm.

Abbie.   This is my hum! This is my farm!

Eben.   He married her t' steal 'em. She was soft an' easy. He couldn't 'preciate her.

Abbie.   He can't 'preciate me!

Eben.   He murdered her with his hardness.

Abbie.   He's murderin' me!

Eben.   She died. (*A pause*) Sometimes she used to sing fur me. (*He bursts into a fit of sobbing.*)

Abbie (*both her arms around him—with wild passion*).   I'll sing fur ye! I'll die fur ye! (*In spite of her overwhelming desire for him, there is a sincere maternal love in her manner and voice—a horribly frank mixture of lust and mother love*) Don't cry, Eben! I'll take yer Maw's place! I'll be everythin' she was t' ye! Let me kiss ye, Eben! (*She pulls his head around. He makes a bewildered pretense of resistance. She is tender*) Don't be afeered! I'll kiss ye pure, Eben—same 's if I was a Maw t' ye—an' ye kin kiss me back 's if yew was my son—my boy—sayin' good-night t' me! Kiss me, Eben. (*They kiss in restrained fashion. Then suddenly wild passion overcomes her. She kisses him lustfully again and again and he flings his arms about her and returns her kisses. Suddenly, as in the bedroom, he frees himself from her violently and springs to his feet. He is trembling all over, in a strange state of terror. Abbie strains her arms toward him with fierce pleading*) Don't ye leave me, Eben! Can't ye see it hain't enuf—lovin' ye like a Maw—can't ye see it's got t' be that an' more—much more—a hundred times more—fur me t' be happy—fur yew t' be happy?

Eben (*to the presence he feels in the room*).   Maw! Maw! What d'ye want? What air ye tellin' me?

Abbie.   She's tellin' ye t' love me. She knows I love ye an' I'll be good t' ye. Can't ye feel it? Don't ye know? She's tellin' ye t' love me, Eben!

Eben.   Ay-eh. I feel—mebbe she—but—I can't figger out—why—when ye've stole her place—here in her hum—in the parlor whar she was—

Abbie (*fiercely*).   She knows I love ye!

Eben (*his face suddenly lighting up with a fierce, triumphant grin*).   I see it! I see why. It's her vengeance on him—so's she kin rest quiet in her grave!

Abbie (*wildly*).   Vengeance o' God on the hull o' us! What d'we give a durn? I love ye, Eben! God knows I love ye! (*She stretches out her arms for him.*)

Eben (*throws himself on his knees beside the sofa and grabs her in his arms— releasing all his pent-up passion*).   An' I love yew, Abbie—now I kin say it! I been dyin' fur want o' ye—every hour since ye come! I love ye! (*Their lips meet in a fierce, bruising kiss.*)

SCENE 4.   *Exterior of the farmhouse. It is just dawn. The front door at right is opened and Eben comes out and walks around to the gate. He is dressed in his working clothes. He seems changed. His face wears a bold and confident expression, he is grinning to himself with evident satisfaction. As he gets near the gate, the window of the parlor is heard opening and the shutters are flung back and Abbie sticks her head out. Her hair tumbles over her shoulders in disarray, her face is flushed, she looks at Eben with tender, languorous eyes and calls softly.*

Abbie.   Eben. (*As he turns—playfully*) Jest one more kiss afore ye go. I'm goin' to miss ye fearful all day.

Eben.   An' me yew, ye kin bet! (*He goes to her. They kiss several times. He draws away, laughingly*) Thar. That's enuf, hain't it? Ye won't hev none left fur next time.

Abbie.   I got a million o' 'em left fur yew! (*Then a bit anxiously*) D'ye r'ally love me, Eben?

Eben (*emphatically*).   I like ye better'n any gal I ever knowed! That's gospel!

Abbie.   Likin' hain't lovin'.

Eben.   Waal then—I love ye. Now air yew satisfied?

Abbie.   Ay-eh, I be. (*She smiles at him adoringly.*)

Eben.   I better git t' the barn. The old critter's liable t' suspicion an' come sneakin' up.

Abbie (*with a confident laugh*).   Let him! I kin allus pull the wool over his eyes. I'm goin' t' leave the shutters open and let in the sun 'n' air. This room's been dead long enuf. Now it's goin' t' be my room!

Eben (*frowning*).   Ay-eh.

Abbie (*hastily*).   I meant—our room.

Eben.   Ay-eh.

Abbie.   We made it our'n last night, didn't we? We give it life—our lovin' did. (*A pause.*)

Eben (*with a strange look*).   Maw's gone back t' her grave. She kin sleep now.

Abbie.   May she rest in peace! (*Then tenderly rebuking*) Ye oughtn't t' talk o' sad thin's—this mornin'.

Eben.   It jest come up in my mind o' itself.

Abbie.   Don't let it. (*He doesn't answer. She yawns*) Waal, I'm a-goin' t' steal a wink o' sleep. I'll tell the Old Man I hain't feelin' pert. Let him git his own vittles.

Eben.   I see him comin' from the barn. Ye better look smart an' git upstairs.

Abbie.   Ay-eh. Good-by. Don't ferget me. (*She throws him a kiss. He grins— then squares his shoulders and awaits his father confidently. Cabot walks slowly up from the left, staring up at the sky with a vague face.*)

Eben (*jovially*).   Mornin', Paw. Star-gazin' in daylight?

Cabot.   Purty, hain't it?

Eben (*looking around him possessively*).   It's a durned purty farm.

Cabot.   I mean the sky.

Eben (*grinning*).   How d'ye know? Them eyes o' your'n can't see that fur. (*This tickles his humor and he slaps his thigh and laughs*) Ho-ho! That's a good un!

Cabot (*grimly sarcastic*).   Ye're feelin' right chipper, hain't ye? Whar'd ye steal the likker?

Eben (*good-naturedly*).   'Tain't likker. Jest life. (*Suddenly holding out his hand—soberly*) Yew 'n' me is quits. Let's shake hands.

Cabot (*suspiciously*).   What's come over ye?

Eben.   Then don't. Mebbe it's jest as well. (*A moment's pause*) What's come over me? (*Queerly*) Didn't ye feel her passin'—goin' back t' her grave?

Cabot (*dully*).   Who?

Eben.   Maw. She kin rest now an' sleep content. She's quit with ye.

Cabot (*confusedly*).   I rested. I slept good—down with the cows. They know how t' sleep. They're teachin' me.

Eben (*suddenly jovial again*).   Good fur the cows! Waal—ye better git t' work.

Cabot (*grimly amused*).   Air ye bossin' me, ye calf?

Eben (*beginning to laugh*).   Ay-eh! I'm bossin' yew! Ha-ha-ha! See how ye like it! Ha-ha-ha! I'm the prize rooster o' this roost. Ha-ha-ha! (*He goes off toward the barn laughing.*)

Cabot (*looks after him with scornful pity*).   Soft-headed. Like his Maw. Dead spit 'n' image. No hope in him! (*He spits with contemptuous disgust*) A born fool! (*Then matter-of-factly*) Waal—I'm gittin' peckish. (*He goes toward door.*)

Part Three

SCENE 1.   *A night in late spring the following year. The kitchen and the two bedrooms upstairs are shown. The two bedrooms are dimly lighted by a tallow candle in each. Eben is sitting on the side of the bed in his room, his chin propped on his fists, his face a study of the struggle he is making to understand his conflicting emotions. The noisy laughter and music from below where a kitchen dance is in progress annoy and distract him. He scowls at the floor.*

In the next room a cradle stands beside the double bed.

In the kitchen all is festivity. The stove has been taken down to give more room to the dancers. The chairs, with wooden benches added, have been pushed back against the walls. On these are seated, squeezed in tight against one another, farmers and their wives and their young folks of both sexes from the neighboring farms. They are all chattering and laughing loudly. They evidently have some secret joke in common. There is no end of winking, of nudging, of meaning nods of the head toward Cabot who, in a state of extreme hilarious excitement increased by the amount he has drunk, is standing near the rear door where there is a small keg of whisky and serving drinks to all the men. In the left corner, front, dividing the attention with her husband, Abbie Is sitting in a rocking chair, a shawl wrapped around her shoulders. She is very pale, her face is thin and drawn, her eyes are fixed anxiously on the open door in rear as if waiting for someone.

The musician is tuning up his fiddle, seated in the far right corner. He is a lanky young fellow with a long, weak face. His pale eyes blink incessantly and he grins about him slyly with a greedy malice.

Abbie (*suddenly turning to a young girl on her right*).   Whar's Eben?

Young Girl (*eying her scornfully*).   I dunno, Mrs. Cabot. I hain't seen Eben in ages. (*Meaningly*) Seems like he's spent most o' his time t' hum since yew come.

Abbie (*vaguely*).   I tuk his Maw's place.

Young Girl.   Ay-eh. So I've heerd. (*She turns away to retail this bit of gossip to her mother sitting next to her. Abbie turns to her left to a big stoutish middle-aged man whose flushed face and starting eyes show the amount of "likker" he has consumed.*)

Abbie.   Ye hain't seen Eben, hev ye?

Man.   No, I hain't. (*Then he adds with a wink*) If yew hain't, who would?

Abbie. He's the best dancer in the county. He'd ought t' come an' dance.

Man (*with a wink*). Mebbe he's doin' the dutiful an' walkin' the kid t' sleep. It's a boy, hain't it?

Abbie (*nodding vaguely*). Ay-eh—born two weeks back—purty's a picter.

Man. They all is—t' their Maws. (*Then in a whisper, with a nudge and a leer*) Listen, Abbie—if ye ever git tired o' Eben, remember me! Don't fergit now! (*He looks at her uncomprehending face for a second—then grunts disgustedly*) Waal—guess I'll likker agin. (*He goes over and joins* Cabot *who is arguing noisily with an old farmer over cows. They all drink.*)

Abbie (*this time appealing to nobody in particular*). Wonder what Eben's a-doin'? (*Her remark is repeated down the line with many a guffaw and titter until it reaches the fiddler. He fastens his blinking eyes on Abbie.*)

Fiddler (*raising his voice*). Bet I kin tell ye, Abbie, what Eben's doin'! He's down t' the church offerin' up prayers o' thanksgivin'. (*They all titter expectantly.*)

A Man. What fur? (*Another titter.*)

Fiddler. 'Cause unto him a—(*He hesitates just long enough*) brother is born! (*A roar of laughter. They all look from* Abbie *to* Cabot. *She is oblivious, staring at the door.* Cabot, *although he hasn't heard the words, is irritated by the laughter and steps forward, glaring about him. There is an immediate silence.*)

Cabot. What're ye all bleatin' about—like a flock o' goats? Why don't ye dance, damn ye? I axed ye here t' dance—t' eat, drink an' be merry—an' thar ye set cacklin' like a lot o' wet hens with the pip! Ye've swilled my likker an' guzzled my vittles like hogs, hain't ye? Then dance fur me, can't ye? That's fa'r an' squar', hain't it? (*A grumble of resentment goes around but they are all evidently in too much awe of him to express it openly.*)

Fiddler (*slyly*). We're waitin' fur Eben. (*A suppressed laugh.*)

Cabot (*with a fierce exultation*). T'hell with Eben! Eben's done fur now! I got a new son! (*His mood switching with drunken suddenness*) But ye needn't t' laugh at Eben, none o' ye! He's my blood, if he be a dumb fool. He's better nor any o' yew! He kin do a day's work a'most up t' what I kin—an' that'd put any o' yew pore critters t' shame!

Fiddler. An' he kin do a good night's work too! (*A roar of laughter.*)

Cabot. Laugh, ye damn fools! Ye're right jist the same, Fiddler. He kin work day an' night too, like I kin, if need be!

Old Farmer (*from behind the keg where he is weaving drunkenly back and forth—with great simplicity*). They hain't many t' touch ye, Ephraim—a son at seventy-six. That's a hard man fur ye! I be on'y sixty-eight an' I couldn't do it. (*A roar of laughter in which* Cabot *joins uproariously.*)

Cabot (*slapping him on the back*). I'm sorry fur ye, Hi. I'd never suspicion sech weakness from a boy like yew!

Old Farmer. An' I never reckoned yew had it in ye nuther, Ephraim. (*There is another laugh.*)

Cabot (*suddenly grim*). I got a lot in me—a hell of a lot—folks don't know on.

(*Turning to the fiddler*) Fiddle 'er up, durn ye! Give 'em somthin' t' dance t'! What air ye, an ornament? Hain't this a celebration? Then grease yer elbow an' go it!

Fiddler (*seizes a drink which the* Old Farmer *holds out to him and downs it*).   Here goes! (*He starts to fiddle "Lady of the Lake." Four young fellows and four girls form in two lines and dance a square dance. The* Fiddler *shouts directions for the different movements, keeping his words in the rhythm of the music and interspersing them with jocular personal remarks to the dancers themselves. The people seated along the walls stamp their feet and clap their hands in unison.* Cabot *is especially active in this respect. Only* Abbie *remains apathetic, staring at the door as if she were alone in a silent room.*)

Fiddler.   Swing your partner t' the right! That's it, Jim! Give her a b'ar hug! Her Maw hain't lookin'. (*Laughter*) Change partners! That suits ye, don't it, Essie, now ye got Reub afore ye? Look at her redden up, will ye? Waal, life is short an' so's love, as the feller says. (*Laughter.*)

Cabot (*excitedly, stamping his foot*).   Go it, boys! Go it, gals!

Fiddler (*with a wink at the others*).   Ye're the spryest seventy-six ever I sees, Ephraim! Now if ye'd on'y good eye-sight . . . ! (*Suppressed laughter. He gives* Cabot *no chance to retort but roars*) Promenade! Ye're walkin' like a bride down the aisle, Sarah! Waal, while they's life they's allus hope, I've heerd tell. Swing your partner to the left! Gosh A'mighty, look at Johnny Cook high-steppin'! They hain't goin' t'be much strength left fur howin' in the corn lot t'morrow. (*Laughter.*)

Cabot.   Go it! Go it! (*Then suddenly, unable to restrain himself any longer, he prances into the midst of the dancers, scattering them, waving his arms about wildly*) Ye're all hoofs! Git out o' my road! Give me room! I'll show ye dancin'. Ye're all too soft! (*He pushes them roughly away. They crowd back toward the walls, muttering, looking at him resentfully.*)

Fiddler (*jeeringly*).   Go it, Ephraim! Go it! (*He starts "Pop Goes the Weasel," increasing the tempo with every verse until at the end he is fiddling crazily as fast as he can go.*)

Cabot (*starts to dance, which he does very well and with tremendous vigor. Then he begins to improvise, cuts incredibly grotesque capers, leaping up and cracking his heels together, prancing around in a circle with body bent in an Indian war dance, then suddenly straightening up and kicking as high as he can with both legs. He is like a monkey on a string. And all the while he intersperses his antics with shouts and derisive comments*).   Whoop! Here's dancin' fur ye! Whoop! See that! Seventy-six, if I'm a day! Hard as iron yet! Beatin' the young 'uns like I allus done! Look at me! I'd invite ye t' dance on my hundredth birthday on'y ye'll all be dead by then. Ye're a sickly generation! Yer hearts air pink, not red! Yer veins is full o' mud an' water! I be the on'y man in the county! Whoop! See that! I'm a Injun! I've killed Injuns in the West afore ye was born—an' skulped 'em too! They's a arrer wound on my backside I c'd show ye! The hull tribe chased me. I outrun 'em all—with the arrer stuck in me! An' I tuk vengeance on 'em. Ten eyes fur an eye, that was my motter! Whoop! Look at me! I kin kick the ceilin' off the room! Whoop!

Fidder (*stops playing—exhaustedly*). God A'mighty, I got enuf. Ye got the devil's strength in ye.

Cabot (*delightedly*). Did I beat yew, too? Wa'al, ye played smart. Hev a swig. (*He pours whisky for himself and* Fiddler. *They drink. The others watch* Cabot *silently with cold, hostile eyes. There is a dead pause. The* Fiddler *rests.* Cabot *leans against the keg, panting, glaring around him confusedly. In the room above,* Eben *gets to his feet and tiptoes out the door in rear, appearing a moment later in the other bedroom. He moves silently, even frightenedly, toward the cradle and stands there looking down at the baby. His face is as vague as his reactions are confused, but there is a trace of tenderness, of interested discovery. At the same moment that he reaches the cradle,* Abbie *seems to sense something. She gets up weakly and goes to* Cabot.)

Abbie. I'm goin' up t' the baby.

Cabot (*with real solicitation*). Air ye able fur the stairs? D'ye want me t' help ye, Abbie?

Abbie. No. I'm able. I'll be down agen soon.

Cabot. Don't ye git wore out! He needs ye, remember—our son does! (*He grins affectionately, patting her on the back. She shrinks from his touch.*)

Abbie (*dully*). Don't—tech me. I'm goin'—up. (*She goes.* Cabot *looks after her. A whisper goes around the room.* Cabot *turns. It ceases. He wipes his forehead streaming with sweat. He is breathing pantingly.*)

Cabot. I'm a-goin' out t' git fresh air. I'm feelin' a mite dizzy. Fiddle up thar! Dance, all o' ye! Here's likker fur them as wants it. Enjoy yerselves. I'll be back. (*He goes, closing the door behind him.*)

Fiddler (*sarcastically*). Don't hurry none on our account! (*A suppressed laugh. He imitates* Abbie) Whar's Eben? (*More laughter.*)

A Woman (*loudly*). What's happened in this house is plain as the nose on yer face! (Abbie *appears in the doorway upstairs and stands looking in surprise and adoration at* Eben *who does not see her.*)

A Man. Ssshh! He's li-ble t' be listenin' at the door. That'd be like him. (*Their voices die to an intensive whispering. Their faces are concentrated on this gossip. A noise as of dead leaves in the wind comes from the room.* Cabot *has come out from the porch and stands by the gate, leaning on it, staring at the sky blinkingly.* Abbie *comes across the room silently.* Eben *does not notice her until quite near.*)

Eben (*starting*). Abbie!

Abbie. Ssshh! (*She throws her arms around him. They kiss—then bend over the cradle together*) Ain't he purty?—dead spit 'n' image o' yew!

Eben (*pleased*). Air he? I can't tell none.

Abbie. E-zactly like!

Eben (*frowningly*).   I don't like this. I don't like lettin' on what's mine's his'n. I been doin' that all my life. I'm gittin' t' the end o' b'arin' it!

Abbie (*putting her fingers on his lips*).   We're doin' the best we kin. We got t' wait. Somethin's bound t' happen. (*She puts her arms around him*) I got t' go back.

Eben.   I'm goin' out. I can't b'ar it with the fiddle playin' an' the laughin'.

Abbie.   Don't git feelin' low. I love ye, Eben. Kiss me. (*He kisses her. They remain in each other's arms.*)

Cabot (*at the gate, confusedly*).   Even the music can't drive it out—somethin'. Ye kin feel it droppin' off the elums, climbin' up the roof, sneakin' down the chimney, pokin' in the corners! They's no peace in houses, they's no rest livin' with folks. Somethin's always livin' with ye. (*With a deep sigh*) I'll go t' the barn an' rest a spell. (*He goes wearily toward the barn.*)

Fiddler (*tuning up*).   Let's celebrate the old skunk gittin' fooled! We kin have some fun now he's went. (*He starts to fiddle "Turkey in the Straw." There is real merriment now. The young folks get up to dance.*)

SCENE 2.   *A half-hour later—Exterior—Eben is standing by the gate looking up at the sky, an expression of dumb pain bewildered by itself on his face. Cabot appears, returning from the barn, walking wearily, his eyes on the ground. He sees Eben and his whole mood immediately changes. He becomes excited, a cruel, triumphant grin comes to his lips, he strides up and slaps Eben on the back. From within comes the whining of the fiddle and the noise of stamping feet and laughing voices.*

Cabot.   So har ye be!

Eben (*startled, stares at him with hatred for a moment—then dully*).   Ay-eh.

Cabot (*surveying him jeeringly*).   Why hain't ye been in t' dance? They was all axin' fur ye.

Eben.   Let 'em ax!

Cabot.   They's a hull passel o' purty gals.

Eben.   T' hell with 'em!

Cabot.   Ye'd ought t' be marryin' one o' 'em soon.

Eben.   I hain't marryin' no one.

Cabot.   Ye might 'arn a share o' a farm that way.

Eben (*with a sneer*).   Like yew did, ye mean? I hain't that kind.

Cabot (*stung*).   Ye lie! 'Twas yer Maw's folks aimed t' steal my farm from me.

Eben.   Other folks don't say so. (*After a pause—defiantly*) An' I got a farm, anyways!

Cabot (*derisively*).   Whar?

Eben (*stamps a foot on the ground*).   Har!

Cabot (*throws his head back and laughs coarsely*).   Ho-ho! Ye hev, hev ye! Waal, that's a good un!

Eben (*controlling himself—grimly*).   Ye'll see!

Cabot (*stares at him suspiciously, trying to make him out—a pause—then with scornful confidence*). Ay-eh. I'll see. So'll ye. It's ye that's blind—blind as a mole underground. (Eben *suddenly laughs, one short sardonic bark: "Ha." A pause.* Cabot *peers at him with renewed suspicion*) Whar air ye hawin' 'bout? (Eben *turns away without answering.* Cabot *grows angry*) God A'mighty, yew air a dumb dunce! They's nothin' in that thick skull o' your'n but noise—like a empty keg it be! (Eben *doesn't seem to hear.* Cabot's *rage grows*) Yewr farm! God A'mighty! If ye wa'n't a born donkey ye'd know ye'll never own stick nor stone on it, specially now arter him bein' born. It's his'n, I tell ye—his'n arter I die—but I'll live a hundred jest t' fool ye all—an' he'll be growed then—yewr age a'most! (Eben *laughs again his sardonic "Ha." This drives* Cabot *into a fury*) Ha? Ye think ye kin git 'round that someways, do ye? Waal, it'll be her'n, too—Abbie's—ye won't git 'round her—she knows yer tricks—she'll be too much fur ye— she wants the farm her'n—she was afeerd o' ye—she told me ye was sneakin' 'round tryin' t' make love t' her t' git her on yer side . . . ye . . . ye mad fool, ye! (*He raises his clenched fists threateningly.*)

Eben (*is confronting him choking with rage*). Ye lie, ye old skunk! Abbie never said no sech thing!

Cabot (*suddenly triumphant when he sees how shaken* Eben *is*). She did. An' I says, I'll blow his brains t' the top o' them elums—an' she says no, that hain't sense, who'll ye git t'help ye on the farm in his place—an' then she says yew'n me ought t' have a son—I know we kin, she says—an' I says, if we do, ye kin have anythin' I've got ye've a mind t'. An' she says, I wants Eben cut off so's this farm'll be mine when ye die! (*With terrible gloating*) An that's what's happened, hain't it? An' the farm's her'n! An' the dust o' the road—that's you'rn! Ha! Now who's hawin'?

Eben (*has been listening, petrified with grief and rage—suddenly laughs wildly and brokenly*). Ha-ha-ha! So that's her sneakin' game—all along!—like I suspicioned at fust—t' swaller it all—an' me, too . . . ! (*Madly*) I'll murder her! (*He springs toward the porch but* Cabot *is quicker and gets in between.*)

Cabot. No, ye don't!

Eben. Git out o' my road! (*He tries to throw* Cabot *aside. They grapple in what becomes immediately a murderous struggle. The old man's concentrated strength is too much for* Eben. Cabot *gets one hand on his throat and presses him back across the stone well. At the same moment,* Abbie *comes out on the porch. With a stifled cry she runs toward them.*)

Abbie. Eben! Ephraim! (*She tugs at the hand on* Eben's *throat*) Let go, Ephraim! Ye're chokin' him!

Cabot (*removes his hand and flings* Eben *sideways full length on the grass, gasping and choking. With a cry,* Abbie *kneels beside him, trying to take his head on her lap, but he pushes her away.* Cabot *stands looking down with fierce triumph*). Ye needn't t've fret, Abbie, I wa'n't aimin' t' kill him. He hain't wuth hangin' fur—not by a hell of a sight! (*More and more* *triumphantly*) Seventy-six an' him not thirty yit—an' look whar he be fur thinkin' his Paw was easy! No, by God, I hain't easy! An' him upstairs, I'll raise him t' be like me! (*He turns to leave them*) I'm goin' in an' dance!— sing an' celebrate! (*He walks to the porch—then turns with a great grin*) I don't calc'late it's left in him, but if he gits pesky, Abbie, ye jest sing out. I'll come a-runnin' an' by the Etarnal, I'll put him across my knee an' birch him! Ha-ha-ha! (*He goes into the house laughing. A moment later his loud "whoop" is heard.*)

Abbie (*tenderly*). Eben. Air ye hurt? (*She tries to kiss him but he pushes her violently away and struggles to a sitting position.*)

Eben (*gaspingly*). T' hell—with ye!

Abbie (*not believing her ears*). It's me, Eben—Abbie—don't ye know me?

Eben (*glowering at her with hatred*). Ay-eh—I know ye—now! (*He suddenly breaks down, sobbing weakly.*)

Abbie (*fearfully*). Eben—what's happened t' ye—why did ye look at me 's if ye hated me?

Eben (*violently, between sobs and gasps*). I do hate ye! Ye're a whore—a damn trickin' whore!

Abbie (*shrinking back horrified*). Eben! Ye don't know what ye're sayin'!

Eben (*scrambling to his feet and following her—accusingly*). Ye're nothin' but a stinkin' passel o' lies! Ye've been lyin' t' me every word ye spoke, day an' night, since we fust—done it. Ye've kept sayin' ye loved me. . . .

Abbie (*frantically*). I do love ye! (*She takes his hand but he flings hers away.*)

Eben (*unheeding*). Ye've made a fool o' me—a sick, dumb fool—a-purpose! Ye've been on'y playin' yer sneakin', stealin' game all along—gittin' me t' lie with ye so's ye'd hev a son he'd think was his'n, an' makin' him promise he'd give ye the farm and let me eat dust, if ye did git him a son! (*Staring at her with anguished, bewildered eyes*) They must be a devil livin' in ye! T'ain't human t' be as bad as that be!

Abbie (*stunned—dully*). He told yew . . . ?

Eben. Hain't it true? It hain't no good in yew lyin'.

Abbie (*pleadingly*). Eben, listen—ye must listen—it was long ago—afore we done nothin'—yew was scornin' me—goin' t' see Min—when I was lovin' ye—an' I said it t' him t' git vengeance on ye!

Eben (*unheedingly. With tortured passion*). I wish he was dead! I wish I was dead along with ye afore this come! (*Ragingly*) But I'll git my vengeance too! I'll pray Maw t' come back t' help me—t' put her cuss on yew an' him!

Abbie (*brokenly*). Don't ye, Eben! Don't ye! (*She throws herself on her knees before him, weeping*) I didn't mean t' do bad t' ye! Fergive me, won't ye?

Eben (*not seeming to hear her—fiercely*). I'll git squar' with the old skunk— an' yew! I'll tell him the truth 'bout the son he's so proud o'! Then I'll leave ye here t' pizen each other—with Maw comin' out o' her grave at nights—an' I'll go t' the gold fields o' Californi-a whar Sim an' Peter be!

Abbie (*terrified*). Ye won't—leave me? Ye can't!

Eben (*with fierce determination*). I'm a-goin', I tell ye! I'll git rich thar an' come back an' fight him fur the farm he stole—an' I'll kick ye both out in the road—t' beg an' sleep in the woods—an' yer son along with ye—t' starve an' die! (*He is hysterical at the end.*)

Abbie (*with a shudder—humbly*).   He's yewr son, too, Eben.

Eben (*torturedly*).   I wish he never was born! I wish he'd die this minit! I wish I'd never sot eyes on him! It's him—yew havin' him—a-purpose t' steal— that's changed everythin'!

Abbie (*gently*).   Did ye believe I loved ye—afore he come?

Eben.   Ay-eh—like a dumb ox!

Abbie.   An' ye don't believe no more?

Eben.   B'lieve a lyin' thief! Ha!

Abbie (*shudders—then humbly*).   An' did ye r'ally love me afore?

Eben (*brokenly*).   Ay-eh—an' ye was trickin' me!

Abbie.   An' ye don't love me now!

Eben (*violently*).   I hate ye, I tell ye!

Abbie.   An' ye're truly goin' West—goin' t' leave me—all account o' him being born?

Eben.   I'm a-goin' in the mornin'—or may God strike me t' hell!

Abbie (*after a pause—with a dreadful cold intensity—slowly*).   If that's what his comin 's done t' me—killin' yewr love—takin' yew away—my on'y joy—the on'y joy I ever knowed—like heaven t' me—purtier'n heaven— then I hate him, too, even if I be his Maw!

Eben (*bitterly*).   Lies! Ye love him! He'll steal the farm fur ye! (*Brokenly*) But t'ain't the farm so much—not no more—it's yew foolin' me—gittin' me t' love ye—lyin' yew loved me—jest t' git a son t' steal!

Abbie (*distractedly*).   He won't steal! I'd kill him fust! I do love ye! I'll prove t' ye . . . !

Eben (*harshly*).   T'ain't no use lyin' no more. I'm deaf t' ye! (*He turns away*) I hain't seein' ye agen. Good-by!

Abbie (*pale with anguish*).   Hain't ye even goin' t' kiss me—not once—arter all we loved?

Eben (*in a hard voice*).   I hain't wantin' t' kiss ye never agen! I'm wantin' t' forgit I ever sot eyes on ye!

Abbie.   Eben!—ye mustn't—wait a spell—I want t' tell ye. . . .

Eben.   I'm a-goin' in t' git drunk. I'm a-goin' t' dance.

Abbie (*clinging to his arm—with passionate earnestness*).   If I could make it— 's if he'd never come up between us—if I could prove t' ye I wa'n't schemin' t' steal from ye—so's everythin' could be jest the same with us, lovin' each other jest the same, kissin' an' happy the same's we've been happy afore he come—if I could do it—ye'd love me agen, wouldn't ye? Ye'd kiss me agen? Ye wouldn't never leave me, would ye?

Eben (*moved*).   I calc'late not. (*Then shaking her hand off his arm—with a bitter smile*) But ye hain't God, be ye?

Abbie (*exultantly*).   Remember ye've promised! (*Then with strange intensity*) Mebbe I kin take back one thin' God does!

Eben (*peering at her*).   Ye're gittin' cracked, hain't ye? (*Then going towards door*) I'm a-goin t' dance.

Abbie (*calls after him intensely*).   I'll prove t' ye! I'll prove I love ye better'n. . . . (*He goes in the door, not seeming to hear. She remains standing where she is, looking after him—then she finishes desperately*) Better'n everythin' else in the world!

SCENE 3.   *Just before dawn in the morning—shows the kitchen and* Cabot's *bedroom. In the kitchen, by the light of a tallow candle on the table,* Eben *is sitting, his chin propped on his hands, his drawn face blank and expressionless. His carpetbag is on the floor beside him. In the bedroom, dimly lighted by a small whale-oil lamp,* Cabot *lies asleep.* Abbie *is bending over the cradle, listening, her face full of terror yet with an undercurrent of desperate triumph. Suddenly, she breaks down and sobs, appears about to throw herself on her knees beside the cradle; but the old man turns restlessly, groaning in his sleep, and she controls herself, and shrinking away from the cradle with a gesture of horror, backs swiftly toward the door in rear and goes out. A moment later she comes into the kitchen and, running to* Eben, *flings her arms about his neck and kisses him wildly. He hardens himself, he remains unmoved and cold, he keeps his eyes straight ahead.*

Abbie (*hysterically*).   I done it, Eben! I told ye I'd do it! I've proved I love ye— better'n everythin'—so's ye can't never doubt me no more!

Eben (*dully*).   Whatever ye done, it hain't no good now.

Abbie (*wildly*).   Don't ye say that! Kiss me, Eben, won't ye? I need ye t' kiss me arter what I done! I need ye t' say ye love me!

Eben (*kisses her without emotion—dully*).   That's fur good-by. I'm a-goin' soon.

Abbie.   No! No! Ye won't go—not now!

Eben (*going on with his own thoughts*).   I been a-thinkin'—an' I hain't goin' t' tell Paw nothin'. I'll leave Maw t' take vengeance on ye. If I told him, the old skunk'd jest be stinkin' mean enuf to take it out on that baby. (*His voice showing emotion in spite of him*) An' I don't want nothin' bad t' happen t' him. He hain't t' blame fur yew. (*He adds with a certain queer pride*) An' he looks like me! An' by God, he's mine! An' some day I'll be a-comin' back an' . . . !

Abbie (*too absorbed in her own thoughts to listen to him—pleadingly*).   They's no cause fur ye t' go now—they's no sense—it's all the same's it was—they's nothing' come b'tween us now—arter what I done!

Eben (*something in her voice arouses him. He stares at her a bit frightenedly*).   Ye look mad, Abbie. What did ye do?

Abbie.   I—I killed him, Eben.

Eben (*amazed*).   Ye killed him?

Abbie (*dully*).   Ay-eh.

Eben (*recovering from his astonishment—savagely*).   An' serves him right! But we got t' do somethin' quick 't make it look 's if the old skunk'd killed himself when he was drunk. We kin prove by 'em all how drunk he got.

Abbie (*wildly*). No! No! Not him! (*Laughing distractedly*) But that's what I ought t' done, hain't it? I oughter killed him instead! Why didn't ye tell me?

Eben (*appalled*). Instead? What d'ye mean?

Abbie. Not him.

Eben (*his face grown ghastly*). Not—not that baby!

Abbie (*dully*). Ay-eh.

Eben (*falls to his knees as if he'd been struck—his voice trembling with horror*). Oh, God A'mighty! A'mighty God! Maw, whar was ye, why didn't ye stop her?

Abbie (*simply*). She went back t' her grave that night we fust done it, remember? I hain't felt her about since. (*A pause. Eben hides his head in his hands, trembling all over as if he had the ague. She goes on dully*) I left the piller over his little face. Then he killed himself. He stopped breathin'. (*She begins to weep softly.*)

Eben (*rage beginning to mingle with grief*). He looked like me. He was mine, damn ye!

Abbie (*slowly and brokenly*). I didn't want t' do it. I hated myself fur doin' it. I loved him. He was so purty—dead spit 'n' image o' yew. But I loved yew more—an' yew was goin' away—far off whar I'd never see ye agen, never kiss ye, never feel ye pressed agin me agen—an' ye said ye hated me fur havin' him—ye said ye hated him an' wished he was dead—ye said if it hadn't been fur him comin' it'd be the same's afore between us.

Eben (*unable to endure this, springs to his feet in a fury, threatening her, his twitching fingers seeming to reach out for her throat*). Ye lie! I never said—I never dreamed ye'd—I'd cut off my head afore I'd hurt his finger!

Abbie (*piteously, sinking on her knees*). Eben, don't ye look at me like that—hatin' me—not after what I done fur ye—fur us—so's we could be happy agen—

Eben (*furiously now*). Shut up, or I'll kill ye! I see yer game now—the same old sneakin' trick—ye're aimin' t' blame me fur the murder ye done!

Abbie (*moaning—putting her hands over her ears*). Don't ye, Eben! Don't ye! (*She grasps his legs.*)

Eben (*his mood suddenly changing to horror, shrinks away from her*). Don't ye tech me! Ye're pizen! How could ye—t' murder a pore little critter—Ye must've swapped yer soul t' hell! (*Suddenly raging*) Ha! I kin see why ye done it! Not the lies ye jest told—but 'cause ye wanted t' steal agen—steal the last thin' ye'd left me—my part o' him—no, the hull o' him—ye saw he looked like me—ye knowed he was all mine—an' ye couldn't b'ar it—I know ye! Ye killed him fur bein' mine! (*All this has driven him almost insane. He makes a rush past her for the door—then turns—shaking both fists at her, violently*) But I'll take vengeance now! I'll git the Sheriff! I'll tell him everythin'! Then I'll sing "I'm off to Californi-a" an' go—gold—

Golden Gate—gold sun—fields o' gold in the West! (*This last he half shouts, half croons incoherently, suddenly breaking off passionately*) I'm a-goin' fur the Sheriff t' come an' git ye! I want ye tuk away, locked up from me! I can't stand t' luk at ye! Murderer an' thief 'r not, ye still tempt me! I'll give ye up t' the Sheriff. (*He turns and runs out, around the corner of house, panting and sobbing, and breaks into a swerving sprint down the road.*)

Abbie (*struggling to her feet, runs to the door, calling after him*). I love ye, Eben! I love ye! (*She stops at the door weakly, swaying, about to fall*) I don't care what ye do—if ye'll on'y love me agen—(*She falls limply to the floor in a faint.*)

SCENE 4. *About an hour later. Same as Scene Three. Shows the kitchen and Cabot's bedroom. It is after dawn. The sky is brilliant with the sunrise. In the kitchen, Abbie sits at the table, her body limp and exhausted, her head bowed down over her arms, her face hidden. Upstairs, Cabot is still asleep but awakens with a start. He looks toward the window and gives a snort of surprise and irritation—throws back the covers and begins hurriedly pulling on his clothes. Without looking behind him, he begins talking to Abbie whom he supposes beside him.*

Cabot. Thunder 'n' lightin', Abbie! I hain't slept this late in fifty year! Looks 's if the sun was full riz a'most. Must've been the dancin' an' likker. Must be gittin' old. I hope Eben's t' wuk. Ye might've tuk the trouble t' rouse me, Abbie. (*He turns—sees no one there—surprised*) Waal—whar air she? Gittin' vittles, I calc'late. (*He tiptoes to the cradle and peers down—proudly*) Mornin', sonny. Purty's a picture! Sleepin sound. He don't beller all night like most o' 'em. (*He goes quietly out the door in rear—a few moments later enters kitchen—sees Abbie—with satisfaction*) So thar ye be. Ye got any vittles cooked?

Abbie (*without moving*). No.

Cabot (*coming to her, almost sympathetically*). Ye feelin' sick?

Abbie. No.

Cabot (*pats her on shoulder. She shudders*). Ye'd best lie down a spell. (*Half jocularly*) Yer son'll be needin' ye soon. He'd ought t' wake up with a gnashin' appetite, the sound way he's sleepin'.

Abbie (*shudders—then in a dead voice*). He hain't never goin' t' wake up.

Cabot (*jokingly*). Takes after me this mornin'. I hain't slept so late in . . .

Abbie. He's dead.

Cabot (*stares at her—bewilderedly*). What. . . .

Abbie. I killed him.

Cabot (*stepping back from her—aghast*). Air ye drunk—'r crazy—'r . . . !

Abbie (*suddenly lifts her head and turns on him—wildly*). I killed him, I tell ye! I smothered him. Go up an' see if ye don't b'lieve me! (*Cabot stares at her a second, then bolts out the rear door—can be heard bounding up the* stairs—and rushes into the bedroom and over to the cradle. Abbie has sunk back lifelessly into her former position. Cabot puts his hand down on the body in the crib. An expression of fear and horror comes over his face.)

Cabot (shrinking away—tremblingly). God A'mighty! God A'mighty. (He stumbles out the door—in a short while returns to the kitchen—comes to Abbie, the stunned expression still on his face—hoarsely) Why did ye do it? Why? (As she doesn't answer, he grabs her violently by the shoulder and shakes her) I ax ye why ye done it! Ye'd better tell me 'r . . . !

Abbie (gives him a furious push which sends him staggering back and springs to her feet—with wild rage and hatred). Don't ye dare tech me! What right hev ye t' question me 'bout him? He wa'n't yewr son! Think I'd have a son by yew? I'd die fust! I hate the sight o' ye an' allus did! It's yew I should've murdered, if I'd had good sense! I hate ye! I love Eben. I did from the fust. An' he was Eben's son—mine an' Eben's—not your'n!

Cabot (stands looking at her dazedly—a pause—finding his words with an effort—dully). That was it—what I felt—pokin' round the corners—while ye lied—holdin' yerself from me—sayin' ye'd a'ready conceived—(He lapses into a crushed silence—then with a strange emotion) He's dead, sart'n. I felt his heart. Pore little critter! (He blinks back one tear, wiping his sleeve across his nose.)

Abbie (hysterically). Don't ye! Don't ye! (She sobs unrestrainedly.)

Cabot (with a concentrated effort that stiffens his body into a rigid line and hardens his face into a stony mask—through his teeth to himself). I got t' be—like a stone—a rock o' jedgment! (A pause. He gets complete control over himself—harshly) If he was Eben's, I be glad he air gone! An' mebbe I suspicioned it all along. I felt they was somethin' onnateral—somewhars— the house got so lonesome—an' cold—drivin' me down t' the barn—t' the beasts o' the field. . . . Ay-eh. I must've suspicioned—somethin'. Ye didn't fool me—not altogether, leastways—I'm too old a bird—growin' ripe on the bough. . . . (He becomes aware he is wandering, straightens again, looks at Abbie with a cruel grin) So ye'd like t' hev murdered me 'stead o' him, would ye? Waal, I'll live to a hundred! I'll live t' see ye hung! I'll de- liver ye up t' the jedgment o' God an' the law! I'll git the Sheriff now. (Starts for the door.)

Abbie (dully). Ye needn't. Eben's gone fur him.

Cabot (amazed). Eben—gone fur the sheriff?

Abbie. Ay-eh.

Cabot. T' inform agen ye?

Abbie. Ay-eh.

Cabot (considers this—a pause—then in a hard voice). Waal, I'm thankful for him savin' me the trouble. I'll git t' wuk. (He goes to the door—then turns—in a voice full of strange emotion) He'd ought t' been my son, Ab- bie. Ye'd ought t' loved me. I'm a man. If ye'd loved me, I'd never told no

Sheriff on ye no matter what ye did, if they was t' brile me alive!

Abbie (*defensively*).   They's more to it nor yew know, makes him tell.

Cabot (*dryly*).   Fur yewr sake, I hope they be. (*He goes out—comes around to the gate—stares up at the sky. His control relaxes. For a moment he is old and weary. He murmurs despairingly*) God A'mighty, I be lonesomer'n ever! (*He hears running footsteps from the left, immediately is himself again. Eben runs in, panting exhaustedly, wild-eyed and mad looking. He lurches through the gate. Cabot grabs him by the shoulder. Eben stares at him dumbly*) Did ye tell the Sheriff?

Eben (*nodding stupidly*).   Ay-eh.

Cabot (*gives him a push away that sends him sprawling—laughing with withering contempt*).   Good fur ye! A prime chip o' yer Maw ye be! (*He goes toward the barn, laughing harshly. Eben scrambles to his feet. Suddenly Cabot turns—grimly threatening*) Git off this farm when the Sheriff takes her—or, by God, he'll have t' come back an' git me fur murder, too! (*He stalks off. Eben does not appear to have heard him. He runs to the door and comes into the kitchen. Abbie looks up with a cry of anguished joy. Eben stumbles over and throws himself on his knees beside her—sobbing brokenly.*)

Eben.   Fergive me!

Abbie (*happily*).   Eben! (*She kisses him and pulls his head over against her breast.*)

Eben.   I love ye! Fergive me!

Abbie (*ecstatically*).   I'd fergive ye all the sins in hell fur sayin' that! (*She kisses his head, pressing it to her with a fierce passion of possession.*)

Eben (*brokenly*).   But I told the Sheriff. He's comin' fur ye!

Abbie.   I kin b'ar what happens t' me—now!

Eben.   I woke him up. I told him. He says, wait 'til I get dressed. I was waiting. I got to thinkin' o' yew. I got to thinkin' how I'd loved ye. It hurt like somethin' was bustin' in my chest an' head. I got t' cryin'. I knowed sudden I loved ye yet, an' allus would love ye!

Abbie (*caressing his hair—tenderly*).   My boy, hain't ye?

Eben.   I begun t' run back. I cut across the fields an' through the woods. I thought ye might have time t' run away—with me—an' . . .

Abbie (*shaking her head*).   I got t' take my punishment—t' pay fur my sin.

Eben.   Then I want t' share it with ye.

Abbie.   Ye didn't do nothin'.

Eben.   I put it in yer head. I wisht he was dead! I as much as urged ye t' do it!

Abbie.   No. It was me alone!

Eben.   I'm as guilty as yew be! He was the child o' our sin.

Abbie (*lifting her head as if defying God*).   I don't repent that sin! I hain't askin' God t' fergive that!

Eben.   Nor me—but it led up t' the other—an' the murder ye did, ye did 'count o' me—an' it's my murder, too. I'll tell the Sheriff—an' if ye deny it,

I'll say we planned it t'gether—an' they'll all b'lieve me, fur they suspicion everythin' we've done, an' it'll seem likely an' true to 'em. An' it is true—way down. I did help ye—somehow.

Abbie (*laying her head on his—sobbing*).   No! I don't want yew t' suffer!

Eben.   I got t' pay fur my part o' the sin! An' I'd suffer wust leavin' ye, goin' West, thinkin' o' ye day an' night, bein' out when yew was in—(*Lowering his voice*) 'r bein' alive when yew was dead. (*A pause*) I want t' share with ye, Abbie—prison 'r death 'r hell 'r anythin'! (*He looks into her eyes and forces a trembling smile*) If I'm sharin' with ye, I won't feel lonesome, leastways.

Abbie (*weakly*).   Eben! I won't let ye! I can't let ye!

Eben (*kissing her—tenderly*).   Ye can't he'p yerself. I got ye beat fur once!

Abbie (*forcing a smile—adoringly*).   I hain't beat—s'long's I got ye!

Eben (*hears the sound of feet outside*).   Ssshh! Listen! They've come t' take us!

Abbie.   No, it's him. Don't give him no chance to fight ye, Eben. Don't say no-thin'—no matter what he says. An' I won't neither. (*It is Cabot. He comes up from the barn in a great state of excitement and strides into the house and then into the kitchen. Eben is kneeling beside Abbie, his arm around her, hers around him. They stare straight ahead.*)

Cabot (*stares at them, his face hard. A long pause—vindictively*).   Ye make a slick pair o' murderin' turtle doves! Ye'd ought t' be both hung on the same limb an' left thar t' swing in the breeze an' rot—a warnin' t' old fools like me t' b'ar their lonesomeness alone—an' fur young fools like ye t' hobble their lust. (*A pause. The excitement returns to his face, his eyes snap, he looks a bit crazy*) I couldn't work today. I couldn't take no inter-est. T' hell with the farm! I'm leavin' it! I've turned the cows an' other stock loose! I've druv 'em into the woods whar they kin be free! By freein' 'em, I'm freein' myself! I'm quittin' here today! I'll set fire t' house an' barn an' watch 'em burn, an' I'll leave yer Maw t' haunt the ashes, an' I'll will the fields back t' God, so that nothin' human kin never touch 'em! I'll be a-goin' to Californi-a—t' jine Simeon an' Peter—true sons o' mine if they be dumb fools—an' the Cabots'll find Solomon's Mines t'gether! (*He suddenly cuts a mad caper*) Whoop! What was the song they sung? "Oh, Californi-a! That's the land fur me." (*He sings this—then gets on his knees by the floor-board under which the money was hid*) An' I'll sail thar on one o' the finest clippers I kin find! I've got the money! Pity ye didn't know whar this was hidden so's ye could steal. . . . (*He has pulled up the board. He stares—feels—stares again. A pause of dead silence. He slowly turns, slumping into a sitting position on the floor, his eyes like those of a dead fish, his face the sickly green of an attack of nausea. He swallows painfully several times—forces a weak smile at last*) So—ye did steal it!

Eben (*emotionlessly*).   I swapped it t' Sim an' Peter fur their share o' the farm—t' pay their passage t' Californi-a.

Cabot (*with one sardonic*).   Ha! (*He begins to recover. Gets slowly to his* *feet—strangely*) I calc'late God give it to 'em—not yew! God's hard, not easy! Mebbe they's easy gold in the West but it hain't God's gold. It hain't fur me. I kin hear His voice warnin' me agen t' be hard an' stay on my farm. I kin see his hand usin' Eben t' steal t' keep me from weakness. I kin feel I be in the palm o' His hand. His fingers guidin me. (*A pause—then he mutters sadly*) It's a-goin' t' be lonesomer now than ever it war afore—an' I'm gittin' old, Lord—ripe on the bough. . . . (*Then stiffening*) Waal—what d'ye want? God's lonesome, hain't He? God's hard an' lonesome! (*A pause. The Sheriff with two men comes up the road from the left. They move cautiously to the door. The Sheriff knocks on it with the butt of his pistol.*)

Sheriff. Open in the name o' the law! (*They start.*)

Cabot. They've come fur ye. (*He goes to the rear door*) Come in, Jim! (*The three men enter. Cabot meets them in doorway*) Jest a minit, Jim. I got 'em safe here. (*The Sheriff nods. He and his companions remain in the doorway.*)

Eben (*suddenly calls*). I lied this mornin', Jim. I helped her do it. Ye kin take me, too.

Abbie (*brokenly*). No!

Cabot. Take 'em both. (*He comes forward—stares at Eben with a trace of grudging admiration*) Purty good—fur yew! Waal, I got t' round up the stock. Good-by.

Eben. Good-by.

Abbie. Good-by. (*Cabot turns and strides past the men—comes out and around the corner of the house, his shoulders squared, his face stony, and stalks grimly toward the barn. In the meantime the Sheriff and men have come into the room.*)

Sheriff (*embarrassedly*). Waal—we'd best start.

Abbie. Wait. (*Turns to Eben*) I love ye, Eben.

Eben. I love ye, Abbie. (*They kiss. The three men grin and shuffle embarrassedly. Eben takes Abbie's hand. They go out the door in rear, the men following, and come from the house, walking hand in hand to the gate. Eben stops there and points to the sunrise sky*) Sun's a-rizin'. Purty, hain't it?

Abbie. Ay-eh. (*They both stand for a moment looking up raptly in attitudes strangely aloof and devout.*)

Sheriff (*looking around at the farm enviously—to his companion*). It's a jim-dandy farm, no denyin'. Wished I owned it!

Questions

1. The struggle for possession of the Cabot farm is the central conflict in this drama. Yet, at its conclusion, another force dominates the action. Is the shift convincing? Explain. **2.** Throughout the play, Eben claims that he is nothing like his father. Others see him as the spitting image of this father. Which view is justified? Explain. **3.** Many of the *stage directions are embodied in language that goes beyond instructions to the set de-signer. What function does such novelistic writing serve in the drama?* **4.** *What function do the allusions to Minnie serve in the play?* **5.** *Identify the overtones of pat-ricide and incest present in the play. What conventional psychoanalytic complex is sug-gested by those overtones? Are the suggestions weakened or reinforced by the infan-ticide? Explain.*

love and hate

QUESTIONS FOR FURTHER ANALYSIS

1. Every story in this section incorporates some sexual element. Distinguish among the functions served by the sexual aspects of the stories.

2. Shakespeare's *Othello* and Molière's *The Misanthrope* both deal with hate as well as love. What differences in the definitions of love and hate emerge from the two plays? What changed plot elements would result in a comic *Othello* and a tragic *Misanthrope*? What do such speculative plot changes reveal concerning cultural attitudes about love and hate?

3. It has been argued that the events in O'Neill's *Desire Under the Elms* unfold with all the inevitability of a Greek tragedy. Is this a valid critical judgment? Explain.

4. Faulkner's "Dry September" and Baldwin's "Going to Meet the Man" are both based on a lynching. What differences in treatment emerge? Is there evidence in the stories that enables a reader to determine the race of each writer?

5. Blake's "A Poison Tree," Browning's "Soliloquy of a Spanish Cloister," Dickinson's "Mine Enemy Is Growing Old," and Dugan's "Love Song: I and Thou" all seem to descrlbe some aspects of hate. Are there clues to the origins of the hatred? What images predominate? Are the hatreds of different varieties?

6. Chopin's "The Storm" and Lessing's "To Room Nineteen" deal with infidelity. Distinguish between the attitudes toward infidelity developed by these stories.

7. An eighteenth-century dramatist wrote: "Love, like death, [is] a universal leveller of mankind." What does this mean? Which works, if any, in this section support the proposition?

8. Examine the works in this section in terms of the support they provide for the contention that love and hate are closely related emotions.

9. What images are characteristically associated with love in the prose and poetry of this section? What images are associated with hate? What insight, if any, does this use of figurative language provide into our cultural evaluations of nature?

10. Which works in this section treat love or hate in a way that corresponds most closely with your own experience or conception of those emotional states? Which contradict your experience? Isolate, in each case, the elements in the work responsible for your response and discuss them in terms of their "truth" or "falsity."

THE PRESENCE OF dEATH

THE PRESENCE OF dEATH
The inevitability of death is not implied in the Biblical story of creation; it required an act of disobedience before an angry God passed sentence of hard labor and mortality on mankind: "In the sweat of your face you shall eat bread till you return to the ground, for out of it you were taken; you are dust and to dust you shall return." These words, written down some 2,800 years ago, preserve an ancient explanation for a condition of life which yet remains persistently enigmatic—the dissolution of the flesh and the personality as accident or age culminates in death, the "undiscovered country, from whose bourn / No traveller returns." Though we cannot know what death is like, from earliest times men and women have attempted to characterize death, to cultivate beliefs about it. The mystery of it and the certainty of it make death, in every age, an important theme for literary art.

Beliefs about the nature of death vary widely. The ancient Jews of the Pentateuch reveal no conception of immortality. Ancient Buddhist writings describe death as a mere translation from one painful life to another in an ongoing expiation which only the purest can avoid. The Christians came to conceive of a soul, separate from the body, which at the body's death is freed for a better (or worse) disembodied eternal life. More recently in the western world, the history of the attitudes about death reflect the great ideological revolutions that affected all thought—the Copernican revolution, which displaced the earth from the center of the solar system; the Darwinian revolution, which exchanged for man, the greatest glory of God's creation, an upright primate with an opposable thumb whose days, like the dinosaur's, are likely to be numbered by the flux between the fire and ice of geological history; and the Freudian revolution, which robbed man of his proudest certainty, the conviction that he possessed a dependable and controlling rational mind. All these ideological changes serve to diminish man, to mock his self-importance, and, inevitably, to alter his conception of death.

But despite the impact of intellectual history, death remains invested with a special awe—perhaps because it infallibly mediates between all human differences. For the churchly, death, like birth and marriage, is the occasion for solemn ritual that reaffirms for the congregation its own communal life and the promise of a better life hereafter—though the belief in immortality does not eliminate sadness and regret. For those for whom there is no immortality, death is nonetheless a ceremonial affair, full of awe, for nothing human is so purely defined, so utterly important, as a life ended. Further, both the religious and the secular see death in moral terms. For both, the killer is hateful. For both, there are some deaths that are deserved, some deaths that human weakness makes inevitable, some deaths that are outrageously unfair. For both, there are courageous deaths, which exalt the community, and cowardly deaths too embarrassing to recognize.

Everyman and *The Seventh Seal,* though separated by almost six hundred years, both confront death from a Christian standpoint that distrusts, even condemns, this-worldliness. But whereas for Everyman, death represents a perilous consummation for a life too thoughtlessly pleasurable, for the Knight of the *The Seventh Seal* and his strange band of followers, death comes, one feels, as a release from a dark and menacing world. And this conception of *release* from the prison of life animates much of the essentially optimistic religious poetry of death—John Donne's sonnet "Death, Be Not Proud" is an outstanding example. Another view that establishes death as the great leveler, bringing kings and emperors to that selfsame dust, reassures the impoverished when they contrast their misery with the wealth of the mighty.

That leveling aspect of death, apparent in such poems as Nashe's "A Litany in Time of Plague" and Shakespeare's "Fear No More the Heat of the Sun," leads easily and logically to the tradition wherein life itself is made absurd by the fact of death. You may remember that Macbeth finally declares that life is "a tale / Told by an idiot, full of sound and fury, / Signifying nothing." And the contemplation of suicide, which the pain and absurdity of life would seem to commend, provokes such diverse responses as Mishima's macabre story "Patriotism," Ignatow's poem "For John Berryman," and Maxine Kumin's suggestive sonnet "Will." Some rage against death—Dylan Thomas in "Do Not Go Gentle into That Good Night"; others caution a quiet resignation—Frost in "After Apple-Picking" and Catherine Davis in her answer to Thomas, "After a Time." Much fine poetry on death is elegiac; it speaks the melancholy response of the living to the fact of death in such poems as Gray's "Elegy Written in a Country Churchyard," Housman's "To an Athlete Dying Young," Ransom's "Bells for John Whiteside's Daughter," Roethke's "Elegy for Jane."

In short, literary treatments of death display immense diversity. In Tolstoy's *The Death of Ivan Ilych,* dying leads to a redemptive awareness. In Pinter's *The Dumb Waiter,* the awe of death is drowned in a sea of banal trivia. In Malamud's tragicomic "Idiots First," the protagonist insists upon and wins fair treatment from death, and in Cummings' "nobody loses all the time," the comic lightens the weight of death. The circumstances of death and the way one confronts it paradoxically lend to life its meaning and its value.

FICTION

The Masque of the Red Death

EDGAR ALLAN POE [1809–1849]

THE "Red Death" had long devastated the country. No pestilence had ever been so fatal, or so hideous. Blood was its Avatar[1] and its seal—the redness and the horror of blood. There were sharp pains, and sudden dizziness, and then profuse bleeding at the pores, with dissolution. The scarlet stains upon the body and especially upon the face of the victim, were the pest ban which shut him out from the aid and from the sympathy of his fellow-men. And the whole seizure, progress and termination of the disease, were the incidents of half an hour.

But the Prince Prospero was happy and dauntless and sagacious. When his dominions were half depopulated, he summoned to his presence a thousand hale and light-hearted friends from among the knights and dames of his court, and with these retired to the deep seclusion of one of his castellated abbeys. This was an extensive and magnificent structure, the creation of the prince's own eccentric yet august taste. A strong and loftly wall girdled it in. This wall had gates of iron. The courtiers, having entered, brought furnaces and massy hammers and welded the bolts. They resolved to leave means neither of ingress or egress to the sudden impulses of despair or of frenzy from within. The abbey was amply provisioned. With such precautions the courtiers might bid defiance to contagion. The external world could take care of itself. In the meantime it was folly to grieve, or to think. The prince had provided all the appliances of pleasure. There were buffoons, there were improvisatori,[2] there were ballet-dancers, there were musicians, there was Beauty, there was wine. All these and security were within. Without was the "Red Death."

It was toward the close of the fifth or sixth month of his seclusion, and while the pestilence raged most furiously abroad, that the Prince Prospero entertained his thousand friends at a masked ball of the most unusual magnificence.

1. Manifestation.
2. Musicians who improvise.

It was a voluptuous scene, that masquerade. But first let me tell of the rooms in which it was held. There were seven—an imperial suite. In many palaces, however, such suites form a long and straight vista, while the folding doors slide back nearly to the walls on either hand, so that the view of the whole extent is scarcely impeded. Here the case was very different; as might have been expected from the duke's love of the *bizarre*. The apartments were so irregularly disposed that the vision embraced but little more than one at a time. There was a sharp turn at every twenty or thirty yards, and at each turn a novel effect. To the right and left, in the middle of each wall, a tall and narrow Gothic window looked out upon a closed corridor which pursued the windings of the suite. These windows were of stained glass whose color varied in accordance with the prevailing hue of the decorations of the chamber into which it opened. That at the eastern extremity was hung, for example, in blue—and vividly blue were its windows. The second chamber was purple in its ornaments and tapestries, and here the panes were purple. The third was green throughout, and so were the casements. The fourth was furnished and lighted with orange—the fifth with white—the sixth with violet. The seventh apartment was closely shrouded in black velvet tapestries that hung all over the ceiling and down the walls, falling in heavy folds upon a carpet of the same material and hue. But in this chamber only, the color of the windows failed to correspond with the decorations. The panes here were scarlet—a deep blood color. Now in no one of the seven apartments was there any lamp or candelabrum, amid the profusion of golden ornaments that lay scattered to and fro or depended from the roof. There was no light of any kind emanating from lamp or candle within the suite of chambers. But in the corridors that followed the suite, there stood, opposite to each window, a heavy tripod, bearing a brazier of fire that projected its rays through the tinted glass and so glaringly illumined the room. And thus were produced a multitude of gaudy and fantastic appearances. But in the western or black chamber the effect of the fire-light that streamed upon the dark hangings through the blood-tinted panes, was ghastly in the extreme, and produced so wild a look upon the countenances of those who entered, that there were few of the company bold enough to set foot within its precincts at all.

It was in this apartment, also, that there stood against the western wall, a gigantic clock of ebony. Its pendulum swung to and fro with a dull, heavy, monotonous clang; and when the minute-hand made the circuit of the face, and the hour was to be stricken, there came from the brazen lungs of the clock a sound which was clear and loud and deep and exceedingly musical, but of so peculiar a note and emphasis that, at each lapse of an hour, the musicians of the orchestra were constrained to pause, momentarily, in their performance, to hearken to the sound; and thus the waltzers perforce ceased their evolutions; and there was a brief disconcert of the whole gay company; and, while the chimes of the clock yet rang, it was observed that the giddiest grew pale, and the more aged and sedate passed their hands over their brows as if in confused reverie or meditation. But when the echoes had fully ceased, a light laughter at once pervaded the assembly; the musicians looked at each other and smiled as if at their own nervousness and folly, and made whispering vows, each to the other, that the next chiming of the clock should produce in them no similar emotion; and then, after the lapse of sixty minutes, (which embrace three thousand and six hundred seconds of the Time that flies,) there came yet another chiming of the clock, and then were the same disconcert and tremulousness and meditation as before.

But, in spite of these things, it was a gay and magnificent revel. The tastes of the duke were peculiar. He had a fine eye for colors and effects. He disregarded the *decora*[3] of mere fashion. His plans were bold and fiery, and his conceptions glowed with barbaric lustre. There are some who would have thought him mad. His followers felt that he was not. It was necessary to hear and see and touch him to be *sure* that he was not.

He had directed, in great part, the moveable embellishments of the seven chambers, upon occasion of this great *fête;* and it was his own guiding taste which had given character to the masqueraders. Be sure they were grotesque. There were much glare and glitter and piquancy and phantasm—much of what has been since seen in "Hernani."[4] There were arabesque figures with unsuited limbs and appointments. There were delirious fancies such as the madman fashions. There was much of the beautiful, much of the wanton, much of the *bizarre,* something of the terrible, and not a little of that which might have excited disgust. To and fro in the seven chambers there stalked, in fact, a multitude of dreams. And these—the dreams—writhed in and about, taking hue from the rooms, and causing the wild music of the orchestra to seem as the echo of their steps. And, anon, there strikes the ebony clock which stands in the hall of the velvet. And then, for a moment, all is still, and all is silent save the voice of the clock. The dreams are stiff-frozen as they stand. But the echoes of the chime die away—they have endured but an instant—and a light, half-subdued laughter floats after them as they depart. And now again the music swells, and the dreams live, and writhe to and fro more merrily than ever, taking hue from the many-tinted windows through which stream the rays from the tripods. But to the chamber which lies most westwardly of the seven, there are now none of the maskers who venture; for the night is waning away; and there flows a ruddier light through the blood-colored panes; and the blackness of the sable drapery appals; and to him whose foot falls upon the sable carpet, there comes from the near clock of ebony a muffled peal more solemnly emphatic than any which reaches *their* ears who indulge in the more remote gaieties of the other apartments.

But these other apartments were densely crowded, and in them beat feverishly the heart of life. And the revel went whirlingly on, until at length there commenced the sounding of midnight upon the clock. And then the music ceased, as I have told; and the evolutions of the waltzers were quieted;

---

3. Dictates.
4. A play by Victor Hugo (1802–1885).

and there was an uneasy cessation of all things as before. But now there were twelve strokes to be sounded by the bell of the clock; and thus it happened, perhaps, that more of thought crept, with more of time, into the meditations of the thoughtful among those who revelled. And thus, too, it happened, perhaps, that before the last echoes of the last chime had utterly sunk into silence, there were many individuals in the crowd who had found leisure to become aware of the presence of a masked figure which had arrested the attention of no single individual before. And the rumor of this new presence having spread itself whisperingly around, there arose at length from the whole company a buzz, or murmur, expressive of disapprobation and surprise—then, finally, of terror, of horror, and of disgust.

In an assembly of phantasms such as I have painted, it may well be supposed that no ordinary appearance could have excited such sensation. In truth the masquerade license of the night was nearly unlimited; but the figure in question had out-Heroded Herod,[5] and gone beyond the bounds of even the prince's indefinite decorum. There are chords in the hearts of the most reckless which cannot be touched without emotion. Even with the utterly lost, to whom life and death are equally jests, there are matters of which no jest can be made. The whole company, indeed, seemed now deeply to feel that in the costume and bearing of the stranger neither wit nor propriety existed. The figure was tall and gaunt, and shrouded from head to foot in the habiliments of the grave. The mask which concealed the visage was made so nearly to resemble the countenance of a stiffened corpse that the closest scrutiny must have had difficulty in detecting the cheat. And yet all this might have been endured, if not approved, by the mad revellers around. But the mummer had gone so far as to assume the type of the Red Death. His vesture was dabbled in *blood*—and his broad brow, with all the features of the face, was besprinkled with the scarlet horror.

When the eyes of Prince Prospero fell upon this spectral image (which with a slow and solemn movement, as if more fully to sustain its *rôle,* stalked to and fro among the waltzers) he was seen to be convulsed, in the first moment with a strong shudder either of terror or distaste; but, in the next, his brow reddened with rage.

"Who dares?" he demanded hoarsely of the courtiers who stood near him—"who dares insult us with this blasphemous mockery? Seize him and unmask him—that we may know whom we have to hang at sunrise, from the battlements!"

It was in the eastern or blue chamber in which stood the Prince Prospero as he uttered these words. They rang throughout the seven rooms loudly and clearly—for the prince was a bold and robust man, and the music had become hushed at the waving of his hand.

It was in the blue room where stood the prince, with a group of pale

---

5. I.e., ranted and raved (see Matthew 2).

courtiers by his side. At first, as he spoke, there was a slight rushing movement of this group in the direction of the intruder, who at the moment was also near at hand, and now, with deliberate and stately step, made closer approach to the speaker. But from a certain nameless awe with which the mad assumptions of the mummer had inspired the whole party, there were found none who put forth hand to seize him; so that, unimpeded, he passed within a yard of the prince's person; and, while the vast assembly, as if with one impulse, shrank from the centres of the rooms to the walls, he made his way uninterruptedly, but with the same solemn and measured step which had distinguished him from the first, through the blue chamber to the purple—through the purple to the green—through the green to the orange—through this again to the white—and even thence to the violet, ere a decided movement had been made to arrest him. It was then, however, that the Prince Prospero, maddening with rage and the shame of his own momentary cowardice, rushed hurriedly through the six chambers, while none followed him on account of a deadly terror that had seized upon all. He bore aloft a drawn dagger, and had approached, in rapid impetuosity, to within three or four feet of the retreating figure, when the latter, having attained the extremity of the velvet apartment, turned suddenly and confronted his pursuer. There was a sharp cry—and the dagger dropped gleaming upon the sable carpet, upon which, instantly afterwards, fell prostrate in death the Prince Prospero. Then, summoning the wild courage of despair, a throng of the revellers at once threw themselves into the black apartment, and, seizing the mummer, whose tall figure stood erect and motionless within the shadow of the ebony clock, gasped in unutterable horror at finding the grave-cerements and corpse-like mask which they handled with so violent a rudeness, untenanted by any tangible form.

And now was acknowledged the presence of the Red Death. He had come like a thief in the night. And one by one dropped the revellers in the blood-bedewed halls of their revel, and died each in the despairing posture of his fall. And the life of the ebony clock went out with that of the last of the gay. And the flames of the tripods expired. And Darkness and Decay and the Red Death held illimitable dominion over all.

The Death of Iván Ilých*

LEO TOLSTOY   [1828–1910]

CHAPTER I

During an interval in the Melvínski trial in the large building of the Law Courts the members and public prosecutor met in Ivan Egorovich Shébek's private room, where the conversation turned on the celebrated Krasóvski case. Fëdor Vasílievich warmly maintained that it was not subject to their jurisdiction, Iván Egórovich maintained the contrary, while Peter Ivánovich, not having entered into the discussion at the start, took no part in it but looked through the *Gazette* which had just been handed in.

"Gentlemen," he said, "Iván Ilých has died!"

"You don't say so!"

"Here, read it yourself," replied Peter Ivánovich, handing Fëdor Vasílievich the paper still damp from the press. Surrounded by a black border were the words: "Praskóvya Fëdorovna Golovíná, with profound sorrow, informs relatives and friends of the demise of her beloved husband Iván Ilých Golovín, Member of the Court of Justice, which occurred on February the 4th of this year 1882. The funeral will take place on Friday at one o'clock in the afternoon."

Iván Ilých had been a colleague of the gentlemen present and was liked by them all. He had been ill for some weeks with an illness said to be incurable. His post had been kept open for him, but there had been conjectures that in case of his death Alexéev might receive his appointment, and that either Vínnikov or Shtábel would succeed Alexéev. So on receiving the news of Iván Ilých's death the first thought of each of the gentlemen in that private room was of the changes and promotions it might occasion among themselves or their acquaintances.

"I shall be sure to get Shtábel's place or Vínnikov's," thought Fëdor Vasílievich. "I was promised that long ago, and the promotion means an extra eight hundred rubles a year for me besides the allowance."

"Now I must apply for my brother-in-law's transfer from Kalúga," thought Peter Ivánovich. "My wife will be very glad, and then she won't be able to say that I never do anything for her relations."

"I thought he would never leave his bed again," said Peter Ivánovich aloud. "It's very sad."

"But what really was the matter with him?"

"The doctors couldn't say—at least they could, but each of them said something different. When last I saw him I thought he was getting better."

---

*Translated by Aylmer Maude.

"And I haven't been to see him since the holidays. I always meant to go."

"Had he any property?"

"I think his wife had a little—but something quite trifling."

"We shall have to go to see her, but they live so terribly far away."

"Far away from you, you mean. Everything's far away from your place."

"You see, he never can forgive my living on the other side of the river," said Peter Ivánovich, smiling at Shébek. Then, still talking of the distances between different parts of the city, they returned to the Court.

Besides considerations as to the possible transfers and promotions likely to result from Iván Ilých's death, the mere fact of the death of a near acquaintance aroused, as usual, in all who heard of it the complacent feeling that "it is he who is dead and not I."

Each one thought or felt, "Well, he's dead but I'm alive!" But the more intimate of Iván Ilých's acquaintances, his so-called friends, could not help thinking also that they would now have to fulfill the very tiresome demands of propriety by attending the funeral service and paying a visit of condolence to the widow.

Fëdor Vasílievich and Peter Ivánovich had been his nearest acquaintances. Peter Ivánovich had studied law with Iván Ilých and had considered himself to be under obligations to him.

Having told his wife at dinner-time of Iván Ilých's death, and of his conjecture that it might be possible to get her brother transferred to their circuit, Peter Ivánovich sacrificed his usual nap, put on his evening clothes, and drove to Ivan Ilých's house.

At the entrance stood a carriage and two cabs. Leaning against the wall in the hall downstairs near the cloak-stand was a coffin-lid covered with cloth of gold, ornamented with gold cord and tassels, that had been polished up with metal powder. Two ladies in black were taking off their fur cloaks. Peter Ivanovich recognized one of them as Iván Ilých's sister, but the other was a stranger to him. His colleague Schwartz was just coming downstairs, but on seeing Peter Ivánovich enter he stopped and winked at him, as if to say: "Iván Ilých has made a mess of things—not like you and me."

Schwartz's face with his Piccadilly whiskers, and his slim figure in evening dress, had as usual an air of elegant solemnity which contrasted with the playfulness of his character and had a special piquancy here; or so it seemed to Peter Ivánovich.

Peter Ivánovich allowed the ladies to precede him and slowly followed them upstairs. Schwartz did not come down but remained where he was, and Peter Ivánovich understood that he wanted to arrange where they should play bridge that evening. The ladies went upstairs to the widow's room, and Schwartz with seriously compressed lips but a playful look in his eyes, indicated by a twist of his eye-brows the room to the right where the body lay.

Peter Ivánovich, like everyone else on such occasions, entered feeling uncertain what he would have to do. All he knew was that at such times it is always safe to cross oneself. But he was not quite sure whether one should make obeisances while doing so. He therefore adopted a middle course. On entering the room he began crossing himself and made a slight movement resembling a bow. At the same time, as far as the motion of his head and arm allowed, he surveyed the room. Two young men—apparently nephews, one of whom was a high-school pupil—were leaving the room, crossing themselves as they did so. An old woman was standing motionless, and a lady with strangely arched eyebrows was saying something to her in a whisper. A vigorous, resolute Church Reader, in a frock-coat, was reading something in a loud voice with an expression that precluded any contradiction. The butler's assistant, Gerásim, stepping lightly in front of Peter Ivánovich, was strewing something on the floor. Noticing this, Peter Ivánovich was immediately aware of a faint odour of a decomposing body.

The last time he had called on Iván Ilych, Peter Ivánovich had seen Gerásim in the study. Iván Ilých had been particularly fond of him and he was performing the duty of a sick nurse.

Peter Ivánovich continued to make the sign of the cross slightly inclining his head in an intermediate direction between the coffin, the Reader, and the icons on the table in a corner of the room. Afterwards, when it seemed to him that this movement of his arm in crossing himself had gone on too long, he stopped and began to look at the corpse.

The dead man lay, as dead men always lie, in a specially heavy way, his rigid limbs sunk in the soft cushions of the coffin, with the head forever bowed on the pillow. His yellow waxen brow with bald patches over his sunken temples was thrust up in the way peculiar to the dead, the protruding nose seeming to press on the upper lip. He was much changed and had grown even thinner since Peter Ivánovich had last seen him, but, as is always the case with the dead, his face was handsomer and above all more dignified than when he was alive. The expression on the face said that what was necessary had been accomplished, and accomplished rightly. Besides this there was in that expression a reproach and a warning to the living. This warning seemed to Peter Ivánovich out of place, or at least not applicable to him. He felt a certain discomfort and so he hurriedly crossed himself once more and turned and went out of the door—too hurriedly and too regardless of propriety, as he himself was aware.

Schwartz was waiting for him in the adjoining room with legs spread wide apart and both hands toying with his top-hat behind his back. The mere sight of that playful, well-groomed, and elegant figure refreshed Peter Ivánovich. He felt that Schwartz was above all these happenings and would not surrender to any depressing influences. His very look said that this incident of a church service for Iván Ilých could not be a sufficient reason for infringing the order of the session—in other words, that it would certainly not prevent his unwrapping a new pack of cards and shuffling them that evening while a footman placed four fresh candles on the table: in fact, there was no reason for supposing that this incident would hinder their spending the evening agreeably. Indeed he said this in a whisper as Peter Ivánovich passed him, proposing that they should meet for a game at Fëdor Vasílievich's. But apparently Peter Ivánovich was not destined to play bridge that evening. Praskóvya Fëdorovna (a short, fat woman who despite all efforts to the contrary had continued to broaden steadily from her shoulders downwards and who had the same extraordinarily arched eyebrows as the lady who had been standing by the coffin), dressed all in black, her head covered with lace, came out of her own room with some other ladies, conducted them to the room where the dead body lay, and said: "The service will begin immediately. Please go in."

Schwartz, making an indefinite bow, stood still, evidently neither accepting nor declining this invitation. Praskóvya Fëdorovna recognizing Peter Ivánovich, sighed, went close up to him, took his hand, and said: "I know you were a true friend to Iván Ilých . . ." and looked at him awaiting some suitable response. And Peter Ivánovich knew that, just as it had been the right thing to cross himself in that room, so what he had to do here was to press her hand, sigh, and say, "Believe me . . ." So he did all this and as he did it felt that the desired result had been achieved: that both he and she were touched.

"Come with me. I want to speak to you before it begins," said the widow. "Give me your arm."

Peter Ivánovich gave her his arm and they went to the inner rooms, passing Schwartz who winked at Peter Ivánovich compassionately.

"That does for our bridge! Don't object if we find another player. Perhaps you can cut in when you do escape," said his playful look.

Peter Ivánovich sighed still more deeply and despondently, and Praskóvya Fëdorovna pressed his arm gratefully. When they reached the drawing-room, upholstered in pink cretonne and lighted by a dim lamp, they sat down at the table—she on a sofa and Peter Ivánovich on a low pouffe, the springs of which yielded spasmodically under his weight. Praskóvya Fëdorovna had been on the point of warning him to take another seat, but felt that such a warning was out of keeping with her present condition and so changed her mind. As he sat down on the pouffe Peter Ivánovich recalled how Iván Ilých had arranged this room and had consulted him regarding this pink cretonne with green leaves. The whole room was full of furniture and knick-knacks, and on her way to the sofa the lace of the widow's black shawl caught on the carved edge of the table. Peter Ivánovich rose to detach it, and the springs of the pouffe, relieved of his weight, rose also and gave him a push. The widow began detaching her shawl herself, and Peter Ivánovich again sat down, suppressing the rebellious springs of the pouffe under him. But the widow had not quite freed herself and Peter Ivánovich got up again, and again the pouffe rebelled and even creaked. When this was all over she took out a clean cambric handkerchief and began to weep. The episode with the shawl and the struggle with the pouffe had cooled Peter Ivánovich's emotions and he sat there with a sullen look on his face. This awkward situation was interrupted by Sokolóv, Iván Ilých's butler, who came to report that the plot in the cemetery that Praskóvya Fëdorovna had chosen would cost two hundred rubles. She stopped weeping and, looking at Peter Ivánovich with the air of a victim, remarked in French that it was very hard for her. Peter Ivánovich made a silent gesture signifying his full conviction that it must indeed be so.

"Please smoke," she said in a magnanimous yet crushed voice, and turned to discuss with Sokolóv the price of the plot for the grave.

Peter Ivánovich while lighting his cigarette heard her inquiring very circumstantially into the price of different plots in the cemetery and finally decide which she would take. When that was done she gave instructions about engaging the choir. Sokólov then left the room.

"I look after everything myself," she told Peter Ivánovich, shifting the albums that lay on the table; and noticing that the table was endangered by his cigarette-ash, she immediately passed him an ashtray, saying as she did so: "I consider it an affectation to say that my grief prevents my attending to practical affairs. On the contrary, if anything can—I won't say console me, but—distract me, it is seeing to everything concerning him." She again took out her handkerchief as if preparing to cry, but suddenly, as if mastering her feeling, she shook herself and began to speak calmly. "But there is something I want to talk to you about."

Peter Ivánovich bowed, keeping control of the springs of the pouffe, which immediately began quivering under him.

"He suffered terribly the last few days."

"Did he?" said Peter Ivánovich.

"Oh, terribly! He screamed unceasingly, not for minutes but for hours. For the last three days he screamed incessantly. It was unendurable. I cannot understand how I bore it; you could hear him three rooms off. Oh, what I have suffered!"

"Is it possible that he was conscious all that time?" asked Peter Ivánovich.

"Yes," she whispered. "To the last moment. He took leave of us a quarter of an hour before he died, and asked us to take Volódya away."

The thought of the sufferings of this man he had known so intimately, first as a merry little boy, then as a school-mate, and later as a grown-up colleague, suddenly struck Peter Ivánovich with horror, despite an unpleasant consciousness of his own and this woman's dissimulation. He again saw that brow, and that nose pressing down on the lip, and felt afraid for himself.

"Three days of frightful suffering and then death! Why, that might suddenly, at any time, happen to me," he thought, and for a moment felt terrified. But—he did not himself know how—the customary reflection at once occurred to him that this had happened to Iván Ilých and not to him, and that it should not and could not happen to him, and that to think that it could would be yielding to depression which he ought not to do, as Schwartz's expression plainly showed. After which reflection Peter Ivánovich felt reassured, and began to ask with interest about the details of Iván Ilých's death, as though death was an accident natural to Iván Ilých but certainly not to himself.

After many details of the really dreadful physical sufferings Iván Ilých had endured (which details he learnt only from the effect those sufferings had produced on Praskóvya Fëdorovna's nerves) the widow apparently found it necessary to get to business.

"Oh, Peter Ivánovich, how hard it is! How terribly, terribly hard!" and she again began to weep.

Peter Ivánovich sighed and waited for her to finish blowing her nose. When she had done so he said, "Believe me . . ." and she again began talking and brought out what was evidently her chief concern with him—namely, to question him as to how she could obtain a grant of money from the government on the occasion of her husband's death. She made it appear that she was asking Peter Ivánovich's advice about her pension, but he soon saw that she already knew about that to the minutest detail, more even than he did himself. She knew how much could be got out of the government in consequence of her husband's death, but wanted to find out whether she could not possibly extract something more. Peter Ivánovich tried to think of some means of doing so, but after reflecting for a while and, out of propriety, condemning the government for its niggardliness, he said he thought that nothing more could be got. Then she sighed and evidently began to devise means of getting rid of her visitor. Noticing this, he put out his cigarette, rose, pressed her hand, and went out into the anteroom.

In the dining-room where the clock stood that Iván Ilých had liked so much and had bought at an antique shop, Peter Ivánovich met a priest and a few acquaintances who had come to attend the service, and he recognized Iván Ilých's daughter, a handsome young woman. She was in black and her slim figure appeared slimmer than ever. She had a gloomy, determined, almost angry expression, and bowed to Peter Ivánovich as though he were in some way to blame. Behind her, with the same offended look, stood a wealthy young man, an examining magistrate, whom Peter Ivánovich also knew and who was her fiancé, as he had heard. He bowed mournfully to them and was about to pass into the death-chamber, when from under the stairs appeared the figure of Iván Ilých's schoolboy son, who was extremely like his father. He seemed a little Iván Ilých, such as Peter Ivánovich remembered when they studied law together. His tear-stained eyes had in them the look that is seen in the eyes of boys of thirteen or fourteen who are not pure-minded. When he saw Peter Ivánovich he scowled morosely and shame-facedly. Peter Ivánovich nodded to him and entered the death-chamber. The service began: candles, groans, incense, tears, and sobs. Peter Ivánovich stood looking gloomily down at his feet. He did not look once at the dead man, did not yield to any depressing influence, and was one of the first to leave the room. There was no one in the anteroom, but Gerásim darted out of the dead man's room, rummaged with his strong hands among the fur coats to find Peter Ivánovich's and helped him on with it.

"Well, friend Gerásim," said Peter Ivánovich, so as to say something. "It's a sad affair, isn't it?"

"It's God's will. We shall all come to it some day," said Gerásim, displaying his teeth—the even, white teeth of a healthy peasant—and, like a man in the thick of urgent work, he briskly opened the front door, called the coachman, helped Peter Ivánovich into the sledge, and sprang back to the porch as if in readiness for what he had to do next.

Peter Ivánovich found the fresh air particularly pleasant after the smell of incense, the dead body, and carbolic acid.

"Where to, sir?" asked the coachman.

"It's not too late even now. . . . I'll call around on Fëdor Vasilievich."

He accordingly drove there and found them just finishing the first rubber, so that it was quite convenient for him to cut in.

CHAPTER II

IVÁN Ilých's life had been most simple and most ordinary and therefore most terrible.

He had been a member of the Court of Justice, and died at the age of forty-five. His father had been an official who after serving in various ministries and departments of Petersburg had made the sort of career which brings men to positions from which by reason of their long service they cannot be dismissed, though they are obviously unfit to hold any responsible position, and for whom therefore posts are specially created, which though fictitious carry salaries of from six to ten thousand rubles that are not fictitious, and in receipt of which they live on to a great age.

Such was the Privy Councillor and superfluous member of various superfluous institutions, Ilyá Epímovich Golovín.

He had three sons, of whom Iván Ilých was the second. The eldest son was following in his father's footsteps only in another department, and was already approaching that stage in the service at which a similar sinecure would be reached. The third son was a failure. He had ruined his prospects in a number of positions and was now serving in the railway department. His father and brothers, and still more their wives, not merely disliked meeting him, but avoided remembering his existence unless compelled to do so. His sister had married Baron Greff, a Petersburg official of her father's type. Iván Ilých was *le phénix de la famille*[1] as people said. He was neither as cold and formal as his elder brother nor as wild as the younger, but was a happy mean between them—an intelligent, polished, lively and agreeable man. He had studied with his younger brother at the School of Law, but the latter had failed to complete the course and was expelled when he was in the fifth class. Iván Ilých finished the course well. Even when he was at the School of Law he was just what he remained for the rest of his life: a capable, cheerful, good-natured, and sociable man, though strict in the fulfilment of what he considered to be his duty: and

---

1. The phoenix of the family, here meaning "rare bird" or "prodigy."

he considered his duty to be what was so considered by those in authority. Neither as a boy nor as a man was he a toady, but from early youth was by nature attracted to people of high station as a fly is drawn to the light, assimilating their ways and views of life and establishing friendly relations with them. All the enthusiasms of childhood and youth passed without leaving much trace on him; he succumbed to sensuality, to vanity, and latterly among the highest classes to liberalism, but always within limits which his instinct unfailingly indicated to him as correct.

At school he had done things which had formerly seemed to him very horrid and made him feel disgusted with himself when he did them; but when later on he saw that such actions were done by people of good position and that they did not regard them as wrong, he was able not exactly to regard them as right, but to forget about them entirely or not be at all troubled at remembering them.

Having graduated from the School of Law and qualified for the tenth rank of the civil service, and having received money from his father for his equipment, Iván Ilých ordered himself clothes at Scharmer's, the fashionable tailor, hung a medallion inscribed *respice finen*[2] on his watch-chain, took leave of his professor and the prince who was patron of the school, had a farewell dinner with his comrades at Donon's first-class restaurant, and with his new and fashionable portmanteau, linen, clothes, shaving and other toilet appliances, and a travelling rug, all purchased at the best shops, he set off for one of the provinces where, through his father's influence, he had been attached to the Governor as an official for special service.

In the province Iván Ilých soon arranged as easy and agreeable a position for himself as he had had at the School of Law. He performed his official tasks, made his career, and at the same time amused himself pleasantly and decorously. Occasionally he paid official visits to country districts, where he behaved with dignity both to his superiors and inferiors, and performed the duties entrusted to him, which related chiefly to the sectarians,[3] with an exactness and incorruptible honesty of which he could not but feel proud.

In official matters, despite his youth and taste for frivolous gaiety, he was exceedingly reserved, punctilious, and even severe; but in society he was often amusing and witty, and always good-natured, correct in his manner, and *bon enfant*, as the governor and his wife—with whom he was like one of the family—used to say of him.

In the provinces he had an affair with a lady who made advances to the elegant young lawyer, and there was also a milliner; and there were carousals with aides-de-camp who visited the district, and after-supper visits to a certain outlying street of doubtful reputation; and there was too some obsequiousness to his chief and even to his chief's wife, but all this was done with

2. Regard the end.
3. A large sect, whose members were placed under many legal restrictions, which broke away from the Orthodox Church in the seventeenth century.

such a tone of good breeding that no hard names could be applied to it. It all came under the heading of the French saying: *"Il faut que jeunesse se passe."*[4] It was all done with clean hands, in clean linen, with French phrases, and above all among people of the best society and consequently with the approval of people of rank.

So Iván Ilých served for five years and then came a change in his official life. The new and reformed judicial institutions were introduced, and new men were needed. Iván Ilých became such a new man. He was offered the post of Examining Magistrate, and he accepted it though the post was in another province and obliged him to give up the connexions he had formed and to make new ones. His friends met to give him a send-off; they had a group-photograph taken and presented him with a silver cigarette-case, and he set off to his new post.

As examining magistrate Iván Ilých was just as *comme il faut*[5] and decorous a man, inspiring general respect and capable of separating his official duties from his private life, as he had been when acting as an official on special service. His duties now as examining magistrate were far more interesting and attractive than before. In his former position it had been pleasant to wear an undress uniform made by Scharmer, and to pass through the crowd of petitioners and officials who were timorously awaiting an audience with the governor, and who envied him as with free and easy gait he went straight into his chief's private room to have a cup of tea and a cigarette with him. But not many people had then been directly dependent on him—only police officials and the sectarians when he went on special missions—and he liked to treat them politely, almost as comrades, as if he were letting them feel that he who had the power to crush them was treating them in this simple, friendly way. There were then but few such people. But now, as an examining magistrate, Iván Ilých felt that everyone without exception, even the most important and self-satisfied, was in his power, and that he need only write a few words on a sheet of paper with a certain heading, and this or that important, self-satisfied person would be brought before him in the role of an accused person or a witness, and if he did not choose to allow him to sit down, would have to stand before him and answer his questions. Iván Ilých never abused his power; he tried on the contrary to soften its expression, but the consciousness of it and of the possibility of softening its effect, supplied the chief interest and attraction of his office. In his work itself, especially in his examinations, he very soon acquired a method of eliminating all considerations irrelevant to the legal aspect of the case, and reducing even the most complicated case to a form in which it would be presented on paper only in its externals, completely excluding his personal opinion of the matter, while above all observing every prescribed

---

4. Youth must have its fling.
5. Proper.

formality. The work was new and Iván Ilých was one of the first men to apply the new Code of 1864.[6]

On taking up the post of examining magistrate in a new town, he made new acquaintances and connexions, placed himself on a new footing, and assumed a somewhat different tone. He took up an attitude of rather dignified aloofness towards the provincial authorities, but picked out the best circle of legal gentlemen and wealthy gentry living in the town and assumed a tone of slight dissatisfaction with the government, of moderate liberalism, and of enlightened citizenship. At the same time, without at all altering the elegance of his toilet, he ceased shaving his chin and allowed his beard to grow as it pleased.

Iván Ilých settled down very pleasantly in this new town. The society there, which inclined towards opposition to the Governor, was friendly, his salary was larger, and he began to play *vint*,[7] which he found added not a little to the pleasure of life, for he had a capacity for cards, played good-humouredly, and calculated rapidly and astutely, so that he usually won.

After living there for two years he met his future wife, Praskóvya Fëdorovna Míkhel, who was the most attractive, clever, and brilliant girl of the set in which he moved, and among other amusements and relaxations from his labours as examining magistrate, Iván Ilých established light and playful relations with her.

While he had been an official on special service he had been accustomed to dance, but now as an examining magistrate it was exceptional for him to do so. If he danced now, he did it as if to show that though he served under the reformed order of things, and had reached the fifth official rank, yet when it came to dancing he could do it better than most people. So at the end of an evening he sometimes danced with Praskóvya Fëdorovna, and it was chiefly during these dances that he captivated her. She fell in love with him. Iván Ilých had at first no definite intention of marrying, but when the girl fell in love with him he said to himself: "Really, why shouldn't I marry?"

Praskóvya Fëdorovna came of a good family, was not bad looking, and had some little property. Iván Ilých might have aspired to a more brilliant match, but even this was good. He had his salary, and she, he hoped, would have an equal income. She was well connected, and was a sweet, pretty, and thoroughly correct young woman. To say that Ivan Ilých married because he fell in love with Praskóvya Fëdorovna and found that she sympathized with his views of life would be as incorrect as to say that he married because his social circle approved of the match. He was swayed by both these considerations: the marriage gave him personal satisfaction, and at the same time it was considered the right thing by the most highly placed of his associates.

So Iván Ilých got married.

---

6. Judicial procedures were thoroughly reformed after the emancipation of the serfs in 1861.
7. A card game similar to bridge.

The preparations for marriage and the beginning of married life, with its conjugal caresses, the new furniture, new crockery, and new linen, were very pleasant until his wife became pregnant—so that Iván Ilých had begun to think that marriage would not impair the easy, agreeable, gay and always decorous character of his life, approved of by society and regarded by himself as natural, but would even improve it. But from the first months of his wife's pregnancy, something new, unpleasant, depressing, and unseemly, and from which there was no way of escape, unexpectedly showed itself.

His wife, without any reason—*de gaieté de coeur* as Iván Ilých expressed it to himself—began to disturb the pleasure and propriety of their life. She began to be jealous without any cause, expected him to devote his whole attention to her, found fault with everything, and made coarse and ill-mannered scenes.

At first Iván Ilých hoped to escape from the unpleasantness of this state of affairs by the same easy and decorous relation to life that had served him heretofore: he tried to ignore his wife's disagreeable moods, continued to live in his usual easy and pleasant way, invited friends to his house for a game of cards, and also tried going out to his club or spending his evenings with friends. But one day his wife began upbraiding him so vigorously, using such coarse words, and continued to abuse him every time he did not fulfil her demands, so resolutely and with such evident determination not to give way till he submitted—that is, till he stayed at home and was bored just as she was—that he became alarmed. He now realized that matrimony—at any rate with Praskóvya Fëdorovna—was not always conducive to the pleasures and amenities of life but on the contrary often infringed both comfort and propriety, and that he must therefore entrench himself against such infringement. And Iván Ilých began to seek for means of doing so. His official duties were the one thing that imposed upon Praskóvya Fëdorovna, and by means of his official work and the duties attached to it he began struggling with his wife to secure his own independence.

With the birth of their child, the attempts to feed it and the various failures in doing so, and with the real and imaginary illnesses of mother and child, in which Iván Ilých's sympathy was demanded but about which he understood nothing, the need of securing for himself an existence outside his family life became still more imperative.

As his wife grew more irritable and exacting and Iván Ilých transferred the centre of gravity of his life more and more to his official work, so did he grow to like his work better and became more ambitious than before.

Very soon, within a year of his wedding, Iván Ilých had realized that marriage, though it may add some comforts to life, is in fact a very intricate and difficult affair towards which in order to perform one's duty, that is, to lead a decorous life approved of by society, one must adopt a definite attitude just as towards one's official duties.

And Iván Ilých evolved such an attitude towards married life. He only required of it those conveniences—dinner at home, housewife, and bed—

which it could give him, and above all that propriety of external forms required by public opinion. For the rest he looked for light-hearted pleasure and propriety, and was very thankful when he found them, but if he met with antagonism and querulousness he at once retired into his separate fenced-off world of official duties, where he found satisfaction.

Iván Ilých was esteemed a good official, and after three years was made Assistant Public Prosecutor. His new duties, their importance, the possibility of indicting and imprisoning anyone he chose, the publicity his speeches received, and the success he had in all these things, made his work still more attractive.

More children came. His wife became more and more querulous and ill-tempered, but the attitude Iván Ilých had adopted towards his home life rendered him almost impervious to her grumbling.

After seven years' service in that town he was transferred to another province as Public Prosecutor. They moved, but were short of money and his wife did not like the place they moved to. Though the salary was higher the cost of living was greater, besides which two of their children died and family life became still more unpleasant for him.

Praskóvya Fëdorovna blamed her husband for every inconvenience they encountered in their new home. Most of the conversations between husband and wife, especially as to the the children's education, led to topics which recalled former disputes, and those disputes were apt to flare up again at any moment. There remained only those rare periods of amorousness which still came to them at times but did not last long. These were islets at which they anchored for a while and then again set out upon that ocean of veiled hostility which showed itself in their aloofness from one another. This aloofness might have grieved Iván Ilých had he considered that it ought not to exist, but he now regarded the position as normal, and even made it the goal at which he aimed in family life. His aim was to free himself more and more from those unpleasantnesses and to give them a semblance of harmlessness and propriety. He attained this by spending less and less time with his family, and when obliged to be at home he tried to safeguard his position by the presence of outsiders. The chief thing however was that he had his official duties. The whole interest of his life now centered in the official world and that interest absorbed him. The consciousness of his power, being able to ruin anybody he wished to ruin, the importance, even the external dignity of his entry into court, or meetings with his subordinates, his success with superiors and inferiors, and above all his masterly handling of cases, of which he was conscious— all this gave him pleasure and filled his life, together with chats with his colleagues, dinners, and bridge. So that on the whole Iván Ilých's life continued to flow as he considered it should do—pleasantly and properly.

So things continued for another seven years. His eldest daughter was already sixteen, another child had died, and only one son was left, a schoolboy and a subject of dissension. Iván Ilých wanted to put him in the School of Law, but to spite him Praskóvya Fëdorovna entered him at the High School. The daughter had been educated at home and had turned out well: the boy did not learn badly either.

CHAPTER III

So Iván Ilých lived for seventeen years after his marriage. He was already a Public Prosecutor of long standing, and had declined several proposed transfers while awaiting a more desirable post, when an unanticipated and unpleasant occurrence quite upset the peaceful course of his life. He was expecting to be offered the post of presiding judge in a University town, but Happe somehow came to the front and obtained the appointment instead. Iván Ilých became irritable, reproached Happe, and quarrelled both with him and with his immediate superiors—who became colder to him and again passed him over when other appointments were made.

This was in 1880, the hardest year of Iván Ilých's life. It was then that it became evident on the one hand that his salary was insufficient for them to live on, and on the other that he had been forgotten, and not only this, but that what was for him the greatest and most cruel injustice appeared to others a quite ordinary occurrence. Even his father did not consider it his duty to help him. Iván Ilých felt himself abandoned by everyone, and that they regarded his position with a salary of 3,500 rubles as quite normal and even fortunate. He alone knew that with the consciousness of the injustices done him, with his wife's incessant nagging, and with the debts he had contracted by living beyond his means, his position was far from normal.

In order to save money that summer he obtained leave of absence and went with his wife to live in the country at her brother's place.

In the country, without his work, he experienced *ennui* for the first time in his life, and not only *ennui* but intolerable depression, and he decided that it was impossible to go on living like that, and that it was necessary to take energetic measures.

Having passed a sleepless night pacing up and down the veranda, he decided to go to Petersburg and bestir himself, in order to punish those who had failed to appreciate him and to get transferred to another ministry.

Next day, despite many protests from his wife and her brother, he started for Petersburg with the sole object of obtaining a post with a salary of five thousand rubles a year. He was no longer bent on any particular department, or tendency, or kind of activity. All he now wanted was an appointment to another post with a salary of five thousand rubles, either in the administration, in the banks, with the railways, in one of the Empress Márya's Institutions,[8] or even in the customs—but it had to carry with it a salary of five thousand rubles and be in a ministry other than that in which they had failed to appreciate him.

---

8. A charitable organization founded in the late eighteenth century by the Empress Márya.

And this quest of Iván Ilých's was crowned with remarkable and unexpected success. At Kursk an acquaintance of his, F. I. Ilyín, got into the first-class carriage, sat down beside Iván Ilých, and told him of a telegram just received by the Governor of Kursk announcing that a change was about to take place in the ministry: Peter Ivánovich was to be superseded by Iván Semënovich.

The proposed change, apart from its significance for Russia, had a special significance for Iván Ilých, because by bringing forward a new man, Peter Petróvich, and consequently his friend Zachár Ivánovich, it was highly favourable for Iván Ilých, since Zachár Ivánovich was a friend and colleague of his.

In Moscow this news was confirmed, and on reaching Petersburg Iván Ilých found Zachár Ivánovich and received a definite promise of an appointment in his former Department of Justice.

A week later he telegraphed to his wife: "Zachár in Miller's place. I shall receive appointment on presentation of report."

Thanks to this change of personnel, Iván Ilých had unexpectedly obtained an appointment in his former ministry which placed him two stages above his former colleagues besides giving him five thousand rubles salary and three thousand five hundred rubles for expenses connected with his removal. All his ill humour towards his former enemies and the whole department vanished, and Iván Ilých was completely happy.

He returned to the country more cheerful and contented than he had been for a long time. Praskóvya Fëdorovna also cheered up and a truce was arranged between them. Iván Ilých told of how he had been fêted by everybody in Petersburg, how all those who had been his enemies were put to shame and now fawned on him, how envious they were of his appointment, and how much everybody in Petersburg had liked him.

Praskóvya Fëdorovna listened to all this and appeared to believe it. She did not contradict anything, but only made plans for their life in the town to which they were going. Iván Ilých saw with delight that these plans were his plans, that he and his wife agreed, and that, after a stumble, his life was regaining its due and natural character of pleasant lightheartedness and decorum.

Iván Ilých had come back for a short time only, for he had to take up his new duties on the 10th of September. Moreover, he needed time to settle into the new place, to move all his belongings from the province, and to buy and order many additional things: in a word, to make such arrangements as he had resolved on, which were almost exactly what Praskóvya Fëdorovna too had decided on.

Now that everything had happened so fortunately, and that he and his wife were at one in their aims and moreover saw so little of one another, they got on together better than they had done since the first years of marriage. Iván Ilých had thought of taking his family away with him at once, but the insistence of his wife's brother and her sister-in-law, who had suddenly become particularly amiable and friendly to him and his family, induced him to depart alone.

So he departed, and the cheerful state of mind induced by his success and by the harmony between his wife and himself, the one intensifying the other, did not leave him. He found a delightful house, just the thing both he and his wife had dreamt of. Spacious, lofty reception rooms in the old style, a convenient and dignified study, rooms for his wife and daughter, a study for his son—it might have been specially built for them. Iván Ilých himself superintended the arrangements, chose the wall-papers, supplemented the furniture (preferably with antiques which he considered particularly *comme il faut*), and supervised the upholstering. Everything progressed and progressed and approached the ideal he had set himself: even when things were only half completed they exceeded his expectations. He saw what a refined and elegant character, free from vulgarity, it would all have when it was ready. On falling asleep he pictured to himself how the reception-room would look. Looking at the yet unfinished drawing-room he could see the fireplace, the screen, the what-not, the little chairs dotted here and there, the dishes and plates on the walls, and the bronzes, as they would be when everything was in place. He was pleased by the thought of how his wife and daughter, who shared his taste in this matter, would be impressed by it. They were certainly not expecting as much. He had been particularly successful in finding, and buying cheaply, antiques which gave a particularly aristocratic character to the whole place. But in his letters he intentionally understated everything in order to be able to surprise them. All this so absorbed him that his new duties—though he liked his official work—interested him less than he had expected. Sometimes he even had moments of absent-mindedness during the Court Sessions, and would consider whether he should have straight or curved cornices for his curtains. He was so interested in it all that he often did things himself, rearranging the furniture, or rehanging the curtains. Once when mounting a step-ladder to show the upholsterer, who did not understand, how he wanted the hangings draped, he made a false step and slipped, but being a strong and agile man he clung on and only knocked his side against the knob of the window frame. The bruised place was painful but the pain soon passed, and he felt particularly bright and well just then. He wrote: "I feel fifteen years younger." He thought he would have everything ready by September, but it dragged on till mid-October. But the result was charming not only in his eyes but to everyone who saw it.

In reality it was just what is usually seen in the houses of people of moderate means who want to appear rich, and therefore succeed only in resembling others like themselves: there were damasks, dark wood, plants, rugs, and dull and polished bronzes—all the things people of a certain class have in order to resemble other people of that class. His house was so like the others that it would never have been noticed, but to him it all seemed to be quite exceptional. He was very happy when he met his family at the station and brought them to the newly furnished house all lit up, where a footman in a white tie opened the door into the hall decorated with plants, and when they went on into the drawing-room and the study uttering exclamations of delight. He conducted them everywhere, drank in their praises eagerly, and beamed with pleasure. At tea that evening, when Praskóvya Fëdorovna among other things asked him about his fall, he laughed, and showed them how he had gone flying and had frightened the upholsterer.

"It's a good thing I'm a bit of an athlete. Another man might have been killed, but I merely knocked myself, just here; it hurts when it's touched, but it's passing off already—it's only a bruise."

So they began living in their new home—in which, as always happens, when they got thoroughly settled in they found they were just one room short—and with the increased income, which as always was just a little (some five hundred rubles) too little, but it was all very nice.

Things went particularly well at first, before everything was finally arranged and while something had still to be done: this thing bought, that thing ordered, another thing moved, and something else adjusted. Though there were some disputes between husband and wife, they were both so well satisfied and had so much to do that it all passed off without any serious quarrels. When nothing was left to arrange it became rather dull and something seemed to be lacking, but they were then making acquaintances, forming habits, and life was growing fuller.

Iván Ilých spent his mornings at the law court and came home to dinner, and at first he was generally in a good humour, though he occasionally became irritable just on account of his house. (Every spot on the tablecloth or the upholstery, and every broken window-blind string, irritated him. He had devoted so much trouble to arranging it all that every disturbance of it distressed him.) But on the whole his life ran its course as he believed life should do: easily, pleasantly, and decorously.

He got up at nine, drank his coffee, read the paper, and then put on his undress uniform and went to the law courts. There the harness in which he worked had already been stretched to fit him and he donned it without a hitch: petitioners, inquiries at the chancery, the chancery itself, and the sittings public and administrative. In all this the thing was to exclude everything fresh and vital, which always disturbs the regular course of official business, and to admit only official relations with people, and then only on official grounds. A man would come, for instance, wanting some information. Iván Ilých, as one in whose sphere the matter did not lie, would have nothing to do with him: but if the man had some business with him in his official capacity, something that could be expressed on officially stamped paper, he would do everything, positively everything he could within the limits of such relations, and in doing so would maintain the semblance of friendly human relations, that is, would observe the courtesies of life. As soon as the official relations ended, so did everything else. Iván Ilých possessed this capacity to separate his real life from the official side of affairs and not mix the two, in the highest degree, and by long practice and natural aptitude had brought it to such a pitch that sometimes, in the manner of a virtuoso, he would even allow himself to let the human and official relations mingle. He let himself do this just because he felt that he could at any time he chose resume the strictly official attitude again and drop the human relation. And he did it all easily, pleasantly, correctly, and even artistically. In the intervals between the sessions he smoked, drank tea, chatted a little about politics, a little about general topics, a little about cards, but most of all about official appointments. Tired, but with the feelings of a virtuoso—one of the first violins who has played his part in an orchestra with precision—he would return home to find that his wife and daughter had been out paying calls, or had a visitor, and that his son had been to school, had done his homework with his tutor, and was duly learning what is taught at High Schools. Everything was as it should be. After dinner, if they had no visitors, Iván Ilých sometimes read a book that was being much discussed at the time, and in the evening settled down to work, that is, read official papers, compared the depositions of witnesses, and noted paragraphs of the Code applying to them. This was neither dull nor amusing. It was dull when he might have been playing bridge, but if no bridge was available it was at any rate better than doing nothing or sitting with his wife. Iván Ilých's chief pleasure was giving little dinners to which he invited men and women of good social position, and just as his drawing-room resembled all other drawing-rooms so did his enjoyable little parties resemble all other such parties.

Once they even gave a dance. Iván Ilých enjoyed it and everything went off well, except that it led to a violent quarrel with his wife about the cakes and sweets. Praskóvya Fëdorovna had made her own plans, but Iván Ilých insisted on getting everything from an expensive confectioner and ordered too many cakes, and the quarrel occurred because some of those cakes were left over and the confectioner's bill came to forty-five rubles. It was a great and disagreeable quarrel. Praskóvya Fëdorovna called him "a fool and an imbecile," and he clutched at his head and made angry allusions to divorce.

But the dance itself had been enjoyable. The best people were there, and Iván Ilých had danced with Princess Trúfonova, a sister of the distinguished founder of the Society "Bear my Burden."

The pleasures connected with his work were pleasures of ambition; his social pleasures were those of vanity; but Iván Ilých's greatest pleasure was playing bridge. He acknowledged that whatever disagreeable incident happened in his life, the pleasure that beamed like a ray of light above everything else was to sit down to bridge with good players, not noisy partners, and of course to four-handed bridge (with five players it was annoying to have to stand out, though one pretended not to mind), to play a clever and serious game (when the cards allowed it) and then to have supper and drink a glass of wine. After a game of bridge, especially if he had won a little (to win a large sum was unpleasant), Iván Ilých went to bed in specially good humour.

So they lived. They formed a circle of acquaintances among the best people and were visited by people of importance and by young folk. In their views as to their acquaintances, husband, wife and daughter were entirely agreed, and tacitly and unanimously kept at arm's length and shook off the various shabby friends and relations who, with much show of affection, gushed into the drawing-room with its Japanese plates on the walls. Soon these shabby friends ceased to obtrude themselves and only the best people remained in the Golovíns' set.

Young men made up to Lisa, and Petríshchev, an examining magistrate and Dmítri Ivanovich Petríshchev's son and sole heir, began to be so attentive to her that Iván Ilých had already spoken to Praskóvya Fëdorovna about it, and considered whether they should not arrange a party for them or get up some private theatricals.

So they lived, and all went well, without change, and life flowed pleasantly.

CHAPTER IV

THEY were all in good health. It could not be called ill health if Iván Ilých sometimes said that he had a queer taste in his mouth and felt some discomfort in his left side.

But this discomfort increased and, though not exactly painful, grew into a sense of pressure in his side accompanied by ill humour. And his irritability became worse and worse and began to mar the agreeable, easy, and correct life that had established itself in the Golovín family. Quarrels between husband and wife became more and more frequent, and soon the ease and amenity disappeared and even the decorum was barely maintained. Scenes again became frequent, and very few of those islets remained on which husband and wife could meet without an explosion. Praskóvya Fëdorovna now had good reason to say that her husband's temper was trying. With characteristic exaggeration she said he had always had a dreadful temper, and that it had needed all her good nature to put up with it for twenty years. It was true that now the quarrels were started by him. His bursts of temper always came just before dinner, often just as he began to eat his soup. Sometimes he noticed that a plate or dish was chipped, or the food was not right, or his son put his elbow on the table, or his daughter's hair was not done as he liked it, and for all this he blamed Praskóvya Fëdorovna. At first she retorted and said disagreeable things to him, but once or twice he fell into such a rage at the beginning of dinner that she realized it was due to some physical derangement brought on by taking food, and so she restrained herself and did not answer, but only hurried to get the dinner over. She regarded this self-restraint as highly praiseworthy. Having come to the conclusion that her husband had a dreadful temper and made her life miserable, she began to feel sorry for herself, and the more she pitied herself the more she hated her husband. She began to wish he would die; yet she did not want him to die because then his salary would cease. And this irritated her against him still more. She considered herself dreadfully unhappy just because not even his death could save her, and though she concealed her exasperation, that hidden exasperation of hers increased his irritation also.

After one scene in which Iván Ilých had been particularly unfair and after which he had said in explanation that he certainly was irritable but that it was due to his not being well, she said that if he was ill it should be attended to, and insisted on his going to see a celebrated doctor.

He went. Everything took place as he had expected and as it always does. There was the usual waiting and the important air assumed by the doctor, with which he was so familiar (resembling that which he himself assumed in court), and the sounding and listening, and the questions which called for answers that were forgone conclusions and were evidently unnecessary, and the look of importance which implied that "if only you put yourself in our hands we will arrange everything—we know indubitably how it has to be done, always in the same way for everybody alike." It was all just as it was in the law courts. The doctor put on just the same air towards him as he himself put on towards an accused person.

The doctor said that so-and-so indicated that there was so-and-so inside the patient, but if the investigation of so-and-so did not confirm this, then he must assume that and that. If he assumed that and that, then . . . and so on. To Iván Ilých only one question was important: was his case serious or not? But the doctor ignored that inappropriate question. From his point of view it was not the one under consideration, the real question was to decide between a floating kidney, chronic catarrh, or appendicitis. It was not a question of Iván Ilých's life or death, but one between a floating kidney and appendicitis. And that question the doctor solved brilliantly, as it seemed to Iván Ilých, in favour of the appendix, with the reservation that should an examination of the urine give fresh indications the matter would be reconsidered. All this was just what Iván Ilých had himself brilliantly accomplished a thousand times in dealing with men on trial. The doctor summed up just as brilliantly, looking over his spectacles triumphantly and even gaily at the accused. From the doctor's summing up Iván Ilých concluded that things were bad, but that for the doctor, and perhaps for everybody else, it was a matter of indifference, though for him it was bad. And this conclusion struck him painfully, arousing in him a great feeling of pity for himself and of bitterness towards the doctor's indifference to a matter of such importance.

He said nothing of this, but rose, placed the doctor's fee on the table, and remarked with a sigh: "We sick people probably often put inappropriate questions. But tell me, in general, is this complaint dangerous, or not? . . ."

The doctor looked at him sternly over his spectacles with one eye, as if to say: "Prisoner, if you will not keep to the questions put to you, I shall be obliged to have you removed from the court."

"I have already told you what I consider necessary and proper. The analysis may show something more." And the doctor bowed.

Iván Ilých went out slowly, seated himself disconsolately in his sledge, and drove home. All the way home he was going over what the doctor had said, trying to translate those complicated, obscure, scientific phrases into plain language and find in them an answer to the question: "Is my condition bad? Is it very bad? Or is there as yet nothing much wrong?" And it seemed to him that the meaning of what the doctor had said was that it was very bad. Everything in the streets seemed depressing. The cabmen, the houses, the passers-by, and the shops, were dismal. His ache, this dull gnawing ache that never ceased for a moment, seemed to have acquired a new and more serious significance from the doctor's dubious remarks. Iván Ilých now watched it with a new and oppressive feeling.

He reached home and began to tell his wife about it. She listened, but in the middle of his account his daughter came in with her hat on, ready to go out with her mother. She sat down reluctantly to listen to this tedious story, but could not stand it long, and her mother too did not hear him to the end.

"Well, I am very glad," she said. "Mind now to take your medicine regularly. Give me the prescription and I'll send Gerásim to the chemist's." And she went to get ready to go out.

While she was in the room Iván Ilých had hardly taken time to breathe, but he sighed deeply when she left it.

"Well," he thought, "perhaps it isn't so bad after all."

He began taking his medicine and following the doctor's directions, which had been altered after the examination of the urine. But then it happened that there was a contradiction between the indications drawn from the examination of the urine and the symptoms that showed themselves. It turned out that what was happening differed from what the doctor had told him, and that he had either forgotten, or blundered, or hidden something from him. He could not, however, be blamed for that, and Iván Ilých still obeyed his orders implicitly and at first derived some comfort from doing so.

From the time of his visit to the doctor, Iván Ilých's chief occupation was the exact fulfilment of the doctor's instructions regarding hygiene and the taking of medicine, and the observation of his pain and his excretions. His chief interests came to be people's ailments and people's health. When sickness, deaths, or recoveries, were mentioned in his presence, especially when the illness resembled his own, he listened with agitation which he tried to hide, asked questions, and applied what he heard to his own case.

The pain did not grow less, but Iván Ilých made efforts to force himself to think that he was better. And he could do this so long as nothing agitated him. But as soon as he had any unpleasantness with his wife, any lack of success in his official work, or held bad cards at bridge, he was at once acutely sensible of his disease. He had formerly borne such mischances, hoping soon to adjust what was wrong, to master it and attain success, or make a grand slam. But now every mischance upset him and plunged him into despair. He would say to himself: "There now, just as I was beginning to get better and the medicine had begun to take effect, comes this accursed misfortune, or unpleasantness . . ." And he was furious with the mishap, or with the people who were causing the unpleasantness and killing him, for he felt that this fury was killing him but could not restrain it. One would have thought that it should have been clear to him that this exasperation with circumstances and people aggravated his illness, and that he ought therefore to ignore unpleasant occurrences. But he drew the very opposite conclusion: he said that he needed peace, and he watched for everything that might disturb it and became irritable at the slightest infringement of it. His condition was rendered worse by the fact that he read medical books and consulted doctors. The progress of his disease was so gradual that he could deceive himself when comparing one day with another—the difference was so slight. But when he consulted the doctors it seemed to him that he was getting worse, and even very rapidly. Yet despite this he was continually consulting them.

That month he went to see another celebrity, who told him almost the same as the first had done but put his questions rather differently, and the interview with this celebrity only increased Iván Ilých's doubts and fears. A friend of a friend of his, a very good doctor, diagnosed his illness again quite differently from the others, and though he predicted recovery, his questions and suppositions bewildered Iván Ilých still more and increased his doubts. A homoeopathist diagnosed the disease in yet another way, and prescribed medicine which Iván Ilých took secretly for a week. But after a week, not feeling any improvement and having lost confidence both in the former doctor's treatment and in this one's, he became still more despondent. One day a lady acquaintance mentioned a cure effected by a wonder-working icon. Iván Ilých caught himself listening attentively and beginning to believe that it had occurred. This incident alarmed him. "Has my mind really weakened to such an extent?" he asked himself. "Nonsense! It's all rubbish. I mustn't give way to nervous fears but having chosen a doctor must keep strictly to his treatment. That is what I will do. Now it's all settled. I won't think about it, but will follow the treatment seriously till summer, and then we shall see. From now there must be no more of this wavering!" This was easy to say but impossible to carry out. The pain in his side oppressed him and seemed to grow worse and more incessant, while the taste in his mouth grew stranger and stranger. It seemed to him that his breath had a disgusting smell, and he was conscious of a loss of appetite and strength. There was no deceiving himself: something terrible, new, and more important than anything before in his life, was taking place within him of which he alone was aware. Those about him did not understand or would not understand it, but thought everything in the world was going on as usual. That tormented Iván Ilých more than anything. He saw that his household, especially his wife and daughter who were in a perfect whirl of visiting, did not understand anything of it and were annoyed that he was so depressed and so exacting, as if he were to blame for it. Though they tried to disguise it he saw that he was an obstacle in their path, and that his wife had adopted a definite line in regard to his illness and kept to it regardless of anything he said or did. Her attitude was this: "You know," she would say to her friends, "Iván Ilých can't do as other people do, and keep to the treatment prescribed for him. One day he'll take his drops and keep strictly to his diet and go to bed in good time, but the next day unless I watch him he'll suddenly forget his medicine, eat sturgeon—which is forbidden—and sit up playing cards till one o'clock in the morning."

"Oh, come, when was that?" Iván Ilých would ask in vexation. "Only once at Peter Ivánovich's."

"And yesterday with Shébek."

"Well, even if I hadn't stayed up, this pain would have kept me awake."

"Be that as it may you'll never get well like that, but will always make us wretched."

Praskóvya Fëdorovna's attitude to Iván Ilých's illness, as she expressed it both to others and to him, was that it was his own fault and was another of the annoyances he caused her. Iván Ilých felt that this opinion escaped her involuntarily—but that did not make it easier for him.

At the law courts too, Iván Ilých noticed, or thought he noticed, a strange attitude towards himself. It sometimes seemed to him that people were watching him inquisitively as a man whose place might soon be vacant. Then again, his friends would suddenly begin to chaff him in a friendly way about his low spirits, as if the awful, horrible, and unheard-of thing that was going on within him, incessantly gnawing at him and irresistibly drawing him away, was a very agreeable subject for jests. Schwartz in particular irritated him by his jocularity, vivacity, and *savoir-faire*, which reminded him of what he himself had been ten years ago.

Friends came to make up a set and they sat down to cards. They dealt, bending the new cards to soften them, and he sorted the diamonds in his hand and found he had seven. His partner said "No trumps" and supported him with two diamonds. What more could be wished for? It ought to be jolly and lively. They would make a grand slam. But suddenly Iván Ilých was conscious of that gnawing pain, that taste in his mouth, and it seemed ridiculous that in such circumstances he should be pleased to make a grand slam.

He looked at his partner Mikháil Mikháylovich, who rapped the table with his strong hand and instead of snatching up the tricks pushed the cards courteously and indulgently towards Iván Ilých that he might have the pleasure of gathering them up without the trouble of stretching out his hand for them. "Does he think I am too weak to stretch out my arm?" thought Iván Ilých, and forgetting what he was doing he over-trumped his partner, missing the grand slam by three tricks. And what was most awful of all was that he saw how upset Mikháil Mikháylovich was about it but did not himself care. And it was dreadful to realize why he did not care.

They all saw that he was suffering, and said: "We can stop if you are tired. Take a rest." Lie down? No, he was not at all tired, and he finished the rubber. All were gloomy and silent. Iván Ilých felt that he had diffused this gloom over them and could not dispel it. They had supper and went away, and Iván Ilých was left alone with the consciousness that his life was poisoned and was poisoning the lives of others, and that this poison did not weaken but penetrated more and more deeply into his whole being.

With this consciousness, and with physical pain besides the terror, he must go to bed, often to lie awake the greater part of the night. Next morning he had to get up again, dress, go to the law courts, speak, and write; or if he did not go out, spend at home those twenty-four hours a day each of which was a torture. And he had to live thus all alone on the brink of an abyss, with no one who understood or pitied him.

CHAPTER V

So one month passed and then another. Just before the New Year his brother-in-law came to town and stayed at their house. Iván Ilých was at the law courts and Praskóvya Fëdorovna had gone shopping. When Iván Ilých came home and entered his study he found his brother-in-law there—a healthy, florid man—unpacking his portmanteau himself. He raised his head on hearing Iván Ilých's footsteps and looked up at him for a moment without a word. That stare told Iván Ilých everything. His brother-in-law opened his mouth to utter an exclamation of surprise but checked himself, and that action confirmed it all.

"I have changed, eh?"

"Yes, there is a change."

And after that, try as he would to get his brother-in-law to return to the subject of his looks, the latter would say nothing about it. Praskóvya Fëdorovna came home and her brother went out to her. Iván Ilých locked the door and began to examine himself in the glass, first full face, then in profile. He took up a portrait of himself taken with his wife, and compared it with what he saw in the glass. The change in him was immense. Then he bared his arms to the elbow, looked at them, drew the sleeves down again, sat down on an ottoman, and grew blacker than night.

"No, no, this won't do!" he said to himself, and jumped up, went to the table, took up some law papers and began to read them, but could not continue. He unlocked the door and went into the reception-room. The door leading to the drawing-room was shut. He approached it on tiptoe and listened.

"No, you are exaggerating!" Praskóvya Fëdorovna was saying.

"Exaggerating! Don't you see it? Why, he's a dead man! Look at his eyes—there's no light in them. But what is it that is wrong with him?"

"No one knows. Nikoláevich (that was another doctor) said something, but I don't know what. And Leshchetítsky (this was the celebrated specialist) said quite the contrary . . ."

Iván Ilých walked away, went to his own room, lay down, and began musing: "The kidney, a floating kidney." He recalled all the doctors had told him of how it detached itself and swayed about. And by an effort of imagination he tried to catch that kidney and arrest it and support it. So little was needed for this, it seemed to him. "No, I'll go to see Peter Ivánovich again." (That was the friend whose friend was a doctor.) He rang, ordered the carriage, and got ready to go.

"Where are you going, Jean?" asked his wife, with a specially sad and exceptionally kind look.

This exceptionally kind look irritated him. He looked morosely at her.

"I must go to see Peter Ivánovich."

He went to see Peter Ivánovich, and together they went to see his friend, the doctor. He was in, and Iván Ilých had a long talk with him.

Reviewing the anatomical and physiological details of what in the doctor's opinion was going on inside him, he understood it all.

There was something, a small thing, in the vermiform appendix. It might all come right. Only stimulate the energy of one organ and check the activity of another, then absorption would take place and everything would come right. He got home rather late for dinner, ate his dinner, and conversed cheerfully, but could not for a long time bring himself to go back to work in his room. At last, however, he went to his study and did what was necessary, but the consciousness that he had put something aside—an important, intimate matter which he would revert to when his work was done—never left him. When he had finished his work he remembered that this intimate matter was the thought of his vermiform appendix. But he did not give himself up to it, and went to the drawing-room for tea. There were callers there, including the examining magistrate who was a desirable match for his daughter, and they were conversing, playing the piano and singing. Iván Ilých, as Praskóvya Fëdorovna remarked, spent that evening more cheerfully than usual, but he never for a moment forgot that he had postponed the important matter of the appendix. At eleven o'clock he said good-night and went to his bedroom. Since his illness he had slept alone in a small room next to his study. He undressed and took up a novel by Zola, but instead of reading it he fell into thought, and in his imagination that desired improvement in the vermiform appendix occurred. There was the absorption and evacuation and the re-establishment of normal activity. "Yes, that's it!" he said to himself. "One need only assist nature, that's all." He remembered his medicine, rose, took it, and lay down on his back watching for the beneficent action of the medicine and for it to lessen the pain. "I need only take it regularly and avoid all injurious influences. I am already feeling better, much better." He began touching his side: it was not painful to the touch. "There, I really don't feel it. It's much better already." He put out the light and turned on his side . . . "The appendix is getting better, absorption is occurring." Suddenly he felt the old, familiar, dull, gnawing pain, stubborn and serious. There was the same familiar loathsome taste in his mouth. His heart sank and he felt dazed. "My God! My God!" he muttered. "Again, again! And it will never cease." And suddenly the matter presented itself in a quite different aspect. "Vermiform appendix! Kidney!" he said to himself. "It's not a question of appendix or kidney, but of life and . . . death. Yes, life was there and now it is going, going and I cannot stop it. Yes. Why deceive myself? Isn't it obvious to everyone but me that I'm dying, and that it's only a question of weeks, days . . . it may happen this moment. There was light and now there is darkness. I was here and now I'm going there! Where?" A chill came over him, his breathing ceased, and he felt only the throbbing of his heart.

"When I am not, what will there be? There will be nothing. Then where shall I be when I am no more? Can this be dying? No, I don't want to!" He jumped up and tried to light the candle, felt for it with trembling hands, dropped candle and candlestick on the floor, and fell back on his pillow.

"What's the use? It makes no difference," he said to himself, staring with wide-open eyes into the darkness. "Death. Yes, death. And none of them know or wish to know it, and they have no pity for me. Now they are playing." (He heard through the door the distant sound of a song and its accompaniment.) "It's all the same to them, but they will die too! Fools! I first, and they later, but it will be the same for them. And now they are merry . . . the beasts!"

Anger choked him and he was agonizingly, unbearably miserable. "It is impossible that all men have been doomed to suffer this awful horror!" He raised himself.

"Something must be wrong. I must calm myself—must think it all over from the beginning." And he again began thinking. "Yes, the beginning of my illness: I knocked my side, but I was still quite well that day and the next. It hurt a little, then rather more. I saw the doctors, then followed despondency and anguish, more doctors, and I drew nearer to the abyss. My strength grew less and I kept coming nearer and nearer, and now I have wasted away and there is no light in my eyes. I think of the appendix—but this is death! I think of mending the appendix, and all the while here is death! Can it really be death?" Again terror seized him and he gasped for breath. He leant down and began feeling for the matches, pressing with his elbow on the stand beside the bed. It was in his way and hurt him, he grew furious with it, pressed on it still harder, and upset it. Breathless and in despair he fell on his back, expecting death to come immediately.

Meanwhile the visitors were leaving. Praskóvya Fëdorovna was seeing them off. She heard something fall and came in.

"What has happened?"

"Nothing. I knocked it over accidentally."

She went out and returned with a candle. He lay there panting heavily, like a man who has run a thousand yards, and stared upwards at her with a fixed look.

"What is it, Jean?"

"No . . . o . . . thing. I upset it." ("Why speak of it? She won't understand," he thought.)

And in truth she did not understand. She picked up the stand, lit his candle, and hurried away to see another visitor off. When she came back he still lay on his back, looking upwards.

"What is it? Do you feel worse?"

"Yes."

She shook her head and sat down.

"Do you know, Jean, I think we must ask Leshchetítsky to come and see you here."

This meant calling in the famous specialist, regardless of expense. He smiled malignantly and said "No." She remained a little longer and then went up to him and kissed his forehead.

While she was kissing him he hated her from the bottom of his soul and with difficulty refrained from pushing her away.

"Good-night. Please God you'll sleep."

"Yes."

CHAPTER VI

IVÁN Ilých saw that he was dying, and he was in continual despair.

In the depth of his heart he knew he was dying, but not only was he not accustomed to the thought, he simply did not and could not grasp it.

The syllogism he had learnt from Kiezewetter's Logic:[9] "Caius is a man, men are mortal, therefore Caius is mortal," had always seemed to him correct as applied to Caius, but certainly not as applied to himself. That Caius—man in the abstract—was mortal, was perfectly correct, but he was not Caius, not an abstract man, but a creature quite, quite separate from all others. He had been little Ványa, with a mamma and a papa; with Mitya and Volódya, and the toys, a coachman and a nurse, afterwards with Kátenka and with all the joys, griefs, and delights of childhood, boyhood, and youth. What did Caius know of the smell of that striped leather ball Ványa had been so fond of? Had Caius kissed his mother's hand like that, and did the silk of her dress rustle so for Caius? Had he rioted like that at school when the pastry was bad? Had Caius been in love like that? Could Caius preside at a session as he did? "Caius really was mortal, and it was right for him to die; but for me, little Ványa, Iván Ilých, with all my thoughts and emotions, it's altogether a different matter. It cannot be that I ought to die. That would be too terrible."

Such was his feeling.

"If I had to die like Caius I should have known it was so. An inner voice would have told me so, but there was nothing of the sort in me and I and all my friends felt that our case was quite different from that of Caius. And now here it is!" he said to himself. "It can't be. It's impossible! But here it is. How is this? How is one to understand it?"

He could not understand it, and tried to drive this false, incorrect, morbid thought away and to replace it by other proper and healthy thoughts. But that thought, and not the thought only but the reality itself, seemed to come and confront him.

---

9. Karl Kiezewetter (1766–1819), author of an outline of logic widely used in Russian schools at the time.

And to replace that thought he called up a succession of others, hoping to find in them some support. He tried to get back into the former current of thoughts that had once screened the thought of death from him. But strange to say, all that had formerly shut off, hidden, and destroyed, his consciousness of death, no longer had that effect. Iván Ilých now spent most of his time in attempting to re-establish that old current. He would say to himself: "I will take up my duties again—after all I used to live by them." And banishing all doubts he would go to the law courts, enter into conversation with his colleagues, and sit carelessly as was his wont, scanning the crowd with a thoughtful look and leaning both his emaciated arms on the arms of his oak chair; bending over as usual to a colleague and drawing his papers nearer he would interchange whispers with him, and then suddenly raising his eyes and sitting erect would pronounce certain words and open the proceedings. But suddenly in the midst of those proceedings the pain in his side, regardless of the stage the proceedings had reached, would begin its own gnawing work. Iván Ilých would turn his attention to it and try to drive the thought of it away, but without success. *It* would come and stand before him and look at him, and he would be petrified and the light would die out of his eyes, and he would again begin asking himself whether *It* alone was true. And his colleagues and subordinates would see with surprise and distress that he, the brilliant and subtle judge, was becoming confused and making mistakes. He would shake himself, try to pull himself together, manage somehow to bring the sitting to a close, and return home with the sorrowful consciousness that his judicial labours could not as formerly hide from him what he wanted them to hide, and could not deliver him from *It*. And what was worst of all was that *It* drew his attention to itself not in order to make him take some action but only that he should look at *It*, look it straight in the face: look at it and without doing anything, suffer inexpressibly.

And to save himself from this condition Iván Ilých looked for consolations—new screens—and new screens were found and for a while seemed to save him, but then they immediately fell to pieces or rather became transparent, as if *It* penetrated them and nothing could veil *It*.

In these latter days he would go into the drawing-room he had arranged—that drawing-room where he had fallen and for the sake of which (how bitterly ridiculous it seemed) he had sacrificed his life—for he knew that his illness originated with that knock. He would enter and see that something had scratched the polished table. He would look for the cause of this and find that it was the bronze ornamentation of an album, that had got bent. He would take up the expensive album which he had lovingly arranged, and feel vexed with his daughter and her friends for their untidiness—for the album was torn here and there and some of the photographs turned upside down. He would put it carefully in order and bend the ornamentation back into position. Then it would occur to him to place all those things in another corner of the room, near the plants. He would call the footman, but his daughter or wife would come to help him. They would not agree, and his wife would contradict him, and he would dispute and grow angry. But that was all right, for then he did not think about *It*. *It* was invisible.

But then, when he was moving something himself, his wife would say: "Let the servants do it. You will hurt yourself again." And suddenly *It* would flash through the screen and he would see it. It was just a flash, and he hoped it would disappear, but he would involuntarily pay attention to his side. "It sits there as before, gnawing just the same!" And he could no longer forget *It*, but could distinctly see it looking at him from behind the flowers. "What is it all for?"

"It really is so I lost my life over that curtain as I might have done when storming a fort. Is that possible? How terrible and how stupid. It can't be true! It can't, but it is!"

He would go to his study, lie down, and again be alone with *It*: face to face with *It*. And nothing could be done with *It* except to look at it and shudder.

CHAPTER VII

How it happened it is impossible to say because it came about step by step, unnoticed, but in the third month of Iván Ilých's illness, his wife, his daughter, his son, his acquaintances, the doctors, the servants, and above all he himself, were aware that the whole interest he had for other people was whether he would soon vacate his place, and at last release the living from the discomfort caused by his presence and be himself released from his sufferings.

He slept less and less. He was given opium and hypodermic injections of morphine, but this did not relieve him. The dull depression he experienced in a somnolent condition at first gave him a little relief, but only as something new, afterwards it became as distressing as the pain itself or even more so.

Special foods were prepared for him by the doctors' orders, but all those foods became increasingly distasteful and disgusting to him.

For his excretions also special arrangements had to be made, and this was a torment to him every time—a torment from the uncleanliness, the unseemliness, and the smell, and from knowing that another person had to take part in it.

But just through this most unpleasant matter Iván Ilých obtained comfort. Gerásim, the butler's young assistant, always came in to carry the things out. Gerásim was a clean, fresh peasant lad, grown stout on town food and always cheerful and bright. At first the sight of him, in his clean Russian peasant costume, engaged on that disgusting task embarrassed Iván Ilých.

Once when he got up from the commode too weak to draw up his trousers, he dropped into a soft armchair and looked with horror at his bare, enfeebled thighs with the muscles so sharply marked on them.

Gerásim with a firm light tread, his heavy boots emitting a pleasant smell of tar and fresh winter air, came in wearing a clean Hessian apron, the sleeves of his print shirt tucked up over his strong bare young arms; and refraining from looking at his sick master out of consideration for his feelings, and restraining the joy of life that beamed from his face, went up to the commode.

"Gerásim!" said Ivan Ilých in a weak voice.

Gerásim started, evidently afraid he might have committed some blunder, and with a rapid movement turned his fresh, kind, simple young face which just showed the first downy signs of a beard.

"Yes, sir?"

"That must be very unpleasant for you. You must forgive me. I am helpless."

"Oh, why, sir," and Gerásim's eyes beamed and he showed his glistening white teeth, "what's a little trouble? It's a case of illness with you, sir."

And his deft strong hands did their accustomed task, and he went out of the room stepping lightly. Five minutes later he as lightly returned.

Iván Ilých was still sitting in the same position in the armchair.

"Gerásim," he said when the latter had replaced the freshly-washed utensil. "Please come here and help me." Gerásim went up to him. "Lift me up. It is hard for me to get up, and I have sent Dmítri away."

Gerásim went up to him, grasped his master with his strong arms deftly but gently, in the same way that he stepped—lifted him, supported him with one hand, and with the other drew up his trousers and would have set him down again, but Iván Ilých asked to be led to the sofa. Gerásim, without an effort and without apparent pressure, led him, almost lifting him, to the sofa and placed him on it.

"Thank you. How easily and well you do it all!"

Gerásim smiled again and turned to leave the room. But Iván Ilých felt his presence such a comfort that he did not want to let him go.

"One thing more, please move up that chair. No, the other one—under my feet. It is easier for me when my feet are raised."

Gerásim brought the chair, set it down gently in place, and raised Iván Ilých's legs on to it. It seemed to Iván Ilých that he felt better while Gerásim was holding up his legs.

"It's better when my legs are higher," he said. "Place that cushion under them."

Gerásim did so. He again lifted the legs and placed them, and again Iván Ilých felt better while Gerásim held his legs. When he set them down Iván Ilých fancied he felt worse.

"Gerásim," he said. "Are you busy now?"

"Not at all, sir," said Gerásim, who had learnt from the townsfolk how to speak to gentlefolk.

"What have you still to do?"

"What have I to do? I've done everything except chopping the logs for to-morrow."

"Then hold my legs up a bit higher, can you?"

"Of course I can. Why not?" And Gerásim raised his master's legs higher and Iván Ilých thought that in that position he did not feel any pain at all.

"And how about the logs?"

"Don't trouble about that, sir. There's plenty of time."

Iván Ilých told Gerásim to sit down and hold his legs, and began to talk to him. And strange to say it seemed to him that he felt better while Gerásim held his legs up.

After that Iván Ilých would sometimes call Gerásim and get him to hold his legs on his shoulders, and he liked talking to him. Gerásim did it all easily, willingly, simply, and with a good nature that touched Iván Ilých. Health, strength, and vitality in other people were offensive to him, but Gerásim's strength and vitality did not mortify but soothed him.

What tormented Iván Ilých most was the deception, the lie, which for some reason they all accepted, that he was not dying but was simply ill, and that he only need keep quiet and undergo a treatment and then something very good would result. He however knew that do what they would nothing would come of it, only still more agonizing suffering and death. This deception tortured him—their not wishing to admit what they all knew and what he knew, but wanting to lie to him concerning his terrible condition, and wishing and forcing him to participate in that lie. Those lies—lies enacted over him on the eve of his death and destined to degrade this awful, solemn act to the level of their visitings, their curtains, their sturgeon for dinner—were a terrible agony for Iván Ilých. And strangely enough, many times when they were going through their antics over him he had been within a hairbreadth of calling out to them: "Stop lying! You know and I know that I am dying. Then at least stop lying about it!" But he had never had the spirit to do it. The awful, terrible act of his dying was, he could see, reduced by those about him to the level of a casual, unpleasant, and almost indecorous incident (as if someone entered a drawing-room diffusing an unpleasant odour) and this was done by that very decorum which he had served all his life long. He saw that no one felt for him, because no one even wished to grasp his position. Only Gerásim recognized it and pitied him. And so Iván Ilých felt at ease only with him. He felt comforted when Gerásim supported his legs (sometimes all night long) and refused to go to bed, saying: "Don't you worry, Iván Ilých. I'll get sleep enough later on," or when he suddenly became familiar and exclaimed: "If you weren't sick it would be another matter, but as it is, why should I grudge a little trouble?" Gerásim alone did not lie; everything showed that he alone understood the facts of the case and did not consider it necessary to disguise them, but simply felt sorry for his emaciated and enfeebled master. Once when Iván Ilých was sending him away he even said straight out: "We shall all of us die, so why should I grudge a little trouble?"—expressing the fact that he did not think his work burdensome, because he was doing it for a dying man and hoped someone would do the same for him when his time came.

Apart from this lying, or because of it, what most tormented Iván Ilých was that no one pitied him as he wished to be pitied. At certain moments after prolonged suffering he wished most of all (though he would have been ashamed to confess it) for someone to pity him as a sick child is pitied. He longed to be petted and comforted. He knew he was an important functionary, that he had a beard turning grey, and that therefore what he longed for was impossible, but still he longed for it. And in Gerásim's attitude towards him there was something akin to what he wished for, and so that attitude comforted him. Iván Ilých wanted to weep, wanted to be petted and cried over, and then his colleague Shébek would come, and instead of weeping and being petted, Iván Ilých would assume a serious, severe, and profound air, and by force of habit would express his opinion on a decision of the Court of Cassation and would stubbornly insist on that view. This falsity around him and within him did more than anything else to poison his last days.

CHAPTER VIII

IT was morning. He knew it was morning because Gerásim had gone, and Peter the footman had come and put out the candles, drawn back one of the curtains, and begun quietly to tidy up. Whether it was morning or evening, Friday or Sunday, made no difference, it was all just the same: the gnawing, unmitigated, agonizing pain, never ceasing for an instant, the consciousness of life inexorably waning but not yet extinguished, that approach of that ever dreaded and hateful Death which was the only reality, and always the same falsity. What were days, weeks, hours, in such a case?

"Will you have some tea, sir?"

"He wants things to be regular, and wishes the gentlefolk to drink tea in the morning," thought Iván Ilých, and only said "No".

"Wouldn't you like to move onto the sofa, sir?"

"He wants to tidy up the room, and I'm in the way. I am uncleanliness and disorder," he thought, and said only:

"No, leave me alone."

The man went on bustling about. Iván Ilých stretched out his hand. Peter came up, ready to help.

"What is it, sir?"

"My watch."

Peter took the watch which was close at hand and gave it to his master.

"Half-past eight. Are they up?"

"No sir, except Vladímir Ivánich" (the son) "who has gone to school. Praskóvya Fëdorovna ordered me to wake her if you asked for her. Shall I do so?"

"No, there's no need to." "Perhaps I'd better have some tea," he thought, and added aloud: "Yes, bring me some tea."

Peter went to the door but Iván Ilých dreaded being left alone. "How can I keep him here? Oh yes, my medicine." "Peter, give me my medicine."

"Why not? Perhaps it may still do me some good." He took a spoonful and swallowed it. "No, it won't help. It's all tomfoolery, all deception," he decided as soon as he became aware of the familiar, sickly, hopeless taste. "No, I can't believe in it any longer. But the pain, why this pain? If it would only cease just for a moment!" And he moaned. Peter turned towards him. "It's all right. Go and fetch me some tea."

Peter went out. Left alone Iván Ilých groaned not so much with pain, terrible though that was, as from mental anguish. Always and for ever the same, always these endless days and nights. If only it would come quicker! If only *what* would come quicker? Death, darkness? . . . No, no! Anything rather than death!

When Peter returned with the tea on a tray, Iván Ilých stared at him for a time in perplexity, not realizing who and what he was. Peter was disconcerted by that look and his embarrassment brought Iván Ilých to himself.

"Oh, tea! All right, put it down. Only help me to wash and put on a clean shirt."

And Iván Ilých began to wash. With pauses for rest, he washed his hands and then his face, cleaned his teeth, brushed his hair, and looked in the glass. He was terrified by what he saw, especially by the limp way in which his hair clung to his pallid forehead.

While his shirt was being changed he knew that he would be still more frightened at the sight of his body, so he avoided looking at it. Finally he was ready. He drew on a dressing-gown, wrapped himself in a plaid, and sat down in the armchair to take his tea. For a moment he felt refreshed, but as soon as he began to drink the tea he was again aware of the same taste, and the pain also returned. He finished it with an effort, and then lay down stretching out his legs, and dismissed Peter.

Always the same. Now a spark of hope flashes up, then a sea of despair rages, and always pain; always pain, always despair, and always the same. When alone he had a dreadful and distressing desire to call someone, but he knew beforehand that with others present it would be still worse. "Another dose of morphine—to lose consciousness. I will tell him, the doctor, that he must think of something else. It's impossible, impossible, to go on like this."

An hour and another pass like that. But now there is a ring at the door bell. Perhaps it's the doctor? It is. He comes in fresh, hearty, plump, and cheerful, with that look on his face that seems to say: "There now, you're in a panic about something, but we'll arrange it all for you directly!" The doctor knows this expression is out of place here, but he has put it on once for all and can't take it off—like a man who has put on a frock-coat in the morning to pay a round of calls.

The doctor rubs his hands vigorously and reassuringly.

"Brr! How cold it is! There's such a sharp frost; just let me warm myself!" he says, as if it were only a matter of waiting till he was warm, and then he would put everything right.

"Well now, how are you?"

Iván Ilých feels that the doctor would like to say: "Well, how are our affairs?" but that even he feels that this would not do, and says instead: "What sort of a night have you had?"

Iván Ilých looks at him as much as to say: "Are you really never ashamed of lying?" But the doctor does not wish to understand this question, and Iván Ilých says: "Just as terrible as ever. The pain never leaves me and never subsides. If only something . . ."

"Yes, you sick people are always like that. . . . There, now I think I am warm enough. Even Praskóvya Fëdorovna, who is so particular, could find no fault with my temperature. Well, now I can say good-morning," and the doctor presses his patient's hand.

Then, dropping his former playfulness, he begins with a most serious face to examine the patient, feeling his pulse and taking his temperature, and then begins the sounding and auscultation.

Iván Ilých knows quite well and definitely that all this is nonsense and pure deception, but when the doctor, getting down on his knee, leans over him, putting his ear first higher then lower, and performs various gymnastic movements over him with a significant expression on his face, Iván Ilých submits to it all as he used to submit to the speeches of the lawyers, though he knew very well that they were all lying and why they were lying.

The doctor, kneeling on the sofa, is still sounding him when Praskóvya Fëdorovna's silk dress rustles at the door and she is heard scolding Peter for not having let her know of the doctor's arrival.

She comes in, kisses her husband, and at once proceeds to prove that she has been up a long time already, and only owing to a misunderstanding failed to be there when the doctor arrived.

Iván Ilých looks at her, scans her all over, sets against her the whiteness and plumpness and cleanness of her hands and neck, the gloss of her hair, and the sparkle of her vivacious eyes. He hates her with his whole soul. And the thrill of hatred he feels for her makes him suffer from her touch.

Her attitude towards him and his disease is still the same. Just as the doctor had adopted a certain relation to his patient which he could not abandon, so had she formed one towards him—that he was not doing something he ought to do and was himself to blame, and that she reproached him lovingly for this—and she could not now change that attitude.

"You see he doesn't listen to me and doesn't take his medicine at the proper time. And above all he lies in a position that is no doubt bad for him—with his legs up."

She described how he made Gerásim hold his legs up.

The doctor smiled with a contemptuous affability that said: "What's to be done? These sick people do have foolish fancies of that kind, but we must forgive them."

When the examination was over the doctor looked at his watch, and then Praskóvya Fëdorovna announced to Iván Ilých that it was of course as he pleased, but she had sent to-day for a celebrated specialist who would examine him and have a consultation with Michael Danílovich (their regular doctor).

"Please don't raise any objections. I am doing this for my own sake," she said ironically, letting it be felt that she was doing it all for his sake and only said this to leave him no right to refuse. He remained silent, knitting his brows. He felt that he was so surrounded and involved in a mesh of falsity that it was hard to unravel anything.

Everything she did for him was entirely for her own sake, and she told him she was doing for herself what she actually was doing for herself, as if that was so incredible that he must understand the opposite.

At half-past eleven the celebrated specialist arrived. Again the sounding began and the significant conversations in his presence and in another room, about the kidneys and the appendix, and the questions and answers, with such an air of importance that again, instead of the real question of life and death which now alone confronted him, the question arose of the kidney and appendix which were not behaving as they ought to and would now be attacked by Michael Danílovich and the specialist and forced to amend their ways.

The celebrated specialist took leave of him with a serious though not hopeless look, and in reply to the timid question Iván Ilých, with eyes glistening with fear and hope, put to him as to whether there was a chance of recovery, said that he could not vouch for it but there was a possibility. The look of hope with which Iván Ilých watched the doctor out was so pathetic that Praskóvya Fëdorovna, seeing it, even wept as she left the room to hand the doctor his fee.

The gleam of hope kindled by the doctor's encouragement did not last long. The same room, the same pictures, curtains, wall-paper, medicine bottles, were all there, and the same aching suffering body, and Iván Ilých began to moan. They gave him a subcutaneous injection and he sank into oblivion.

It was twilight when he came to. They brought him his dinner and he swallowed some beef tea with difficulty, and then everything was the same again and night was coming on.

After dinner, at seven o'clock, Praskóvya Fëdorovna came into the room in evening dress, her full bosom pushed up by her corset, and with traces of powder on her face. She had reminded him in the morning that they were going to the theatre. Sarah Bernhardt was visiting the town and they had a box, which he had insisted on their taking. Now he had forgotten about it and her toilet offended him, but he concealed his vexation when he remembered that he had himself insisted on their securing a box and going because it would be an instructive and aesthetic pleasure for the children.

Praskóvya Fëdorovna came in, self-satisfied but yet with a rather guilty air. She sat down and asked how he was but, as he saw, only for the sake of asking and not in order to learn about it, knowing that there was nothing to learn—and then went on to what she really wanted to say: that she would not on any account have gone but that the box had been taken and Helen and their daughter were going, as well as Petríshchev (the examining magistrate, their daughter's fiancé) and that it was out of the question to let them go alone; but that she would have much preferred to sit with him for a while; and he must be sure to follow the doctor's orders while she was away.

"Oh, and Fëdor Petróvich" (the fiancé) "would like to come in. May he? And Lisa?"

"All right."

Their daughter came in in full evening dress, her fresh young flesh exposed (making a show of that very flesh which in his own case caused so much suffering), strong, healthy, evidently in love, and impatient with illness, suffering, and death, because they interfered with her happiness.

Fëdor Petróvich came in too, in evening dress, his hair curled à la Capoul, a tight stiff collar round his long sinewy neck, an enormous white shirt-front and narrow black trousers tightly stretched over his strong thighs. He had one white glove tightly drawn on, and was holding his opera hat in his hand.

Following him the schoolboy crept in unnoticed, in a new uniform, poor little fellow, and wearing gloves. Terribly dark shadows showed under his eyes, the meaning of which Iván Ilých knew well.

His son had always seemed pathetic to him, and now it was dreadful to see the boy's frightened look of pity. It seemed to Iván Ilých that Vásya was the only one besides Gerásim who understood and pitied him.

They all sat down and again asked how he was. A silence followed. Lisa asked her mother about the opera-glasses, and there was an altercation between mother and daughter as to who had taken them and where they had been put. This occasioned some unpleasantness.

Fëdor Petróvich inquired of Iván Ilých whether he had ever seen Sarah Bernhardt. Iván Ilých did not at first catch the question, but then replied: "No, have you seen her before?"

"Yes, in *Adrienne Lecouvreur*."[10]

Praskóvya Fëdorovna mentioned some roles in which Sarah Bernhardt was particularly good. Her daughter disagreed. Conversation sprang up as to the elegance and realism of her acting—the sort of conversation that is always repeated and is always the same.

In the midst of the conversation Fëdor Petróvich glanced at Iván Ilých and became silent. The others also looked at him and grew silent. Iván Ilých was staring with glittering eyes straight before him, evidently indignant with them. This had to be rectified, but it was impossible to do so. The silence had to be broken, but for a time no one dared to break it and they all became afraid that the conventional deception would suddenly become obvious and the truth become plain to all. Lisa was the first to pluck up courage and break that silence, but by trying to hide what everybody was feeling, she betrayed it.

"Well, if we are going it's time to start," she said, looking at her watch, a present from her father, and with a faint and significant smile at Fëdor Petró-

---

10. A play by the French dramatist Eugène Scribe (1791–1861).

vich relating to something known only to them. She got up with a rustle of her dress.

They all rose, said good-night, and went away.

When they had gone it seemed to Iván Ilých that he felt better; the falsity had gone with them. But the pain remained—that same pain and that same fear that made everything monotonously alike, nothing harder and nothing easier. Everything was worse.

Again minute followed minute and hour followed hour. Everything remained the same and there was no cessation. And the inevitable end of it all became more and more terrible.

"Yes, send Gerasim here," he replied to a question Peter asked.

CHAPTER IX

HIS wife returned late at night. She came in on tiptoe, but he heard her, opened his eyes, and made haste to close them again. She wished to send Gerásim away and to sit with him herself, but he opened his eyes and said: "No, go away."

"Are you in great pain?"

"Always the same."

"Take some opium."

He agreed and took some. She went away.

Till about three in the morning he was in a state of stupefied misery. It seemed to him that he and his pain were being thrust into a narrow, deep black sack, but though they were pushed further and further in they could not be pushed to the bottom. And this, terrible enough in itself, was accompanied by suffering. He was frightened yet wanted to fall through the sack, he struggled but yet co-operated. And suddenly he broke through, fell, and regained consciousness. Gerásim was sitting at the foot of the bed dozing quietly and patiently, while he himself lay with his emaciated stockinged legs resting on Gerásim's shoulders; the same shaded candle was there and the same unceasing pain.

"Go away, Gerásim," he whispered.

"It's all right, sir. I'll stay a while."

"No. Go away."

He removed his legs from Gerásim's shoulders, turned sideways onto his arm, and felt sorry for himself. He only waited till Gerásim had gone into the next room and then restrained himself no longer but wept like a child. He wept on account of his helplessness, his terrible loneliness, the cruelty of man, the cruelty of God, and the absence of God.

"Why hast Thou done all this? Why hast Thou brought me here? Why, why dost Thou torment me so terribly?"

He did not expect an answer and yet wept because there was no answer and could be none. The pain again grew more acute, but he did not stir and did not call. He said to himself: "Go on! Strike me! But what is it for? What have I done to Thee? What is it for?"

Then he grew quiet and not only ceased weeping but even held his breath and became all attention. It was as though he were listening not to an audible voice but to the voice of his soul, to the current of thoughts arising within him.

"What is it you want?" was the first clear conception capable of expression in words, that he heard.

"What do you want? What do you want?" he repeated to himself.

"What do I want? To live and not to suffer," he answered.

And again he listened with such concentrated attention that even his pain did not distract him.

"To live? How?" asked his inner voice.

"Why, to live as I used to—well and pleasantly."

"As you lived before, well and pleasantly?" the voice repeated.

And in imagination he began to recall the best moments of his pleasant life. But strange to say none of these best moments of his pleasant life now seemed at all what they had then seemed—none of them except the first recollections of childhood. There, in childhood, there had been something really pleasant with which it would be possible to live if it could return. But the child who had experienced that happiness existed no longer, it was like a reminiscence of somebody else.

As soon as the period began which had produced the present Iván Ilých, all that had then seemed joys now melted before his sight and turned into something trivial and often nasty.

And the further he departed from childhood and the nearer he came to the present the more worthless and doubtful were the joys. This began with the School of Law. A little that was really good was still found there—there was light-heartedness, friendship, and hope. But in the upper classes there had already been fewer of such good moments. Then during the first years of his official career, when he was in the service of the Governor, some pleasant moments again occurred: they were the memories of love for a woman. Then all became confused and there was still less of what was good; later on again there was still less that was good, and the further he went the less there was. His marriage, a mere accident, then the disenchantment that followed it, his wife's bad breath and the sensuality and hypocrisy: then that deadly official life and those preoccupations about money, a year of it, and two, and ten, and twenty, and always the same thing. And the longer it lasted the more deadly it became. "It is as if I had been going downhill while I imagined I was going up. And that is really what it was. I was going up in public opinion, but to the same extent life was ebbing away from me. And now it is all done and there is only death."

"Then what does it mean? Why? It can't be that life is so senseless and horrible. But if it really has been so horrible and senseless, why must I die and die in agony? There is something wrong!"

"Maybe I did not live as I ought to have done," it suddenly occurred to him. "But how could that be, when I did everything properly?" he replied, and immediately dismissed from his mind this, the sole solution of all the riddles of life and death, as something quite impossible.

"Then what do you want now? To live? Live how? Live as you lived in the law courts when the usher proclaimed "The judge is coming!" "The judge is coming, the judge!" he repeated to himself. "Here he is, the judge. But I am not guilty!" he exclaimed angrily. "What is it for?" And he ceased crying, but turning his face to the wall continued to ponder on the same question: Why, and for what purpose, is there all this horror? But however much he pondered he found no answer. And whenever the thought occurred to him, as it often did, that it all resulted from his not having lived as he ought to have done, he at once recalled the correctness of his whole life and dismissed so strange an idea.

CHAPTER X

ANOTHER fortnight passed. Iván Ilých now no longer left his sofa. He would not lie in bed but lay on the sofa, facing the wall nearly all the time. He suffered ever the same unceasing agonies and in his loneliness pondered always on the same insoluble question: "What is this? Can it be that it is Death?" And the inner voice answered: "Yes, it is Death."

"Why these sufferings?" And the voice answered, "For no reason—they just are so." Beyond and besides this there was nothing.

From the very beginning of his illness, ever since he had first been to see the doctor, Iván Ilých's life had been divided between two contrary and alternating moods: now it was despair and the expectation of this uncomprehended and terrible death, and now hope and an intently interested observation of the functioning of his organs. Now before his eyes there was only a kidney or an intestine that temporarily evaded its duty, and now only that incomprehensible and dreadful death from which it was impossible to escape.

These two states of mind had alternated from the very beginning of his illness, but the further it progressed the more doubtful and fantastic became the conception of the kidney, and the more real the sense of impending death.

He had but to call to mind what he had been three months before and what he was now, to call to mind with what regularity he had been going downhill, for every possibility of hope to be shattered.

Latterly during that loneliness in which he found himself as he lay facing the back of the sofa, a loneliness in the midst of a populous town and surrounded by numerous acquaintances and relations but that yet could not have been more complete anywhere—either at the bottom of the sea or under the earth—during that terrible loneliness Iván Ilých had lived only in memories of the past. Pictures of his past rose before him one after another. They always began with what was nearest in time and then went back to what was most remote—to his childhood—and rested there. If he thought of the stewed prunes that had been offered him that day, his mind went back to the raw shrivelled French plums of his childhood, their peculiar flavour and the flow of saliva when he sucked their stones, and along with the memory of that taste came a whole series of memories of those days: his nurse, his brother, and their toys. "No, I mustn't think of that. . . . It is too painful," Iván Ilých said to himself, and brought himself back to the present—to the button on the back of the sofa and the creases in its morocco. "Morocco is expensive, but it does not wear well: there had been a quarrel about it. It was a different kind of quarrel and a different kind of morocco that time when we tore father's portfolio and were punished, and mamma brought us some tarts. . . ." And again his thoughts dwelt on his childhood, and again it was painful and he tried to banish them and fix his mind on something else.

Then again together with that chain of memories another series passed through his mind—of how his illness had progressed and grown worse. There also the further back he looked the more life there had been. There had been more of what was good in life and more of life itself. The two merged together. "Just as the pain went on getting worse and worse so my life grew worse and worse," he thought. "There is one bright spot there at the back, at the beginning of life, and afterwards all becomes blacker and blacker and proceeds more and more rapidly—in inverse ratio to the square of the distance from death," thought Iván Ilých. And the example of a stone falling downwards with increasing velocity entered his mind. Life, a series of increasing sufferings, flies, further and further towards its end—the most terrible suffering. "I am flying. . . ." He shuddered, shifted himself, and tried to resist, but was already aware that resistance was impossible, and again with eyes weary of gazing but unable to cease seeing what was before them, he stared at the back of the sofa and waited—awaiting that dreadful fall and shock and destruction.

"Resistance is impossible!" he said to himself. "If I could only understand what it is all for! But that too is impossible. An explanation would be possible if it could be said that I have not lived as I ought to. But it is impossible to say that," and he remembered all the legality, correctitude, and propriety of his life. "That at any rate can certainly not be admitted," he thought, and his lips smiled ironically as if someone could see that smile and be taken in by it. "There is no explanation! Agony, death. . . . What for?"

CHAPTER XI

ANOTHER two weeks went by in this way and during that fortnight an event occurred that Iván Ilých and his wife had desired. Petríshchev formally proposed. It happened in the evening. The next day Praskóvya Fëdorovna came into her husband's room considering how best to inform him of it, but that very night there had been a fresh change for the worse in his condition. She found him still lying on the sofa but in a different position. He lay on his back, groaning and staring fixedly straight in front of him.

She began to remind him of his medicines, but he turned his eyes towards her with such a look that she did not finish what she was saying; so great an animosity, to her in particular, did that look express.

"For Christ's sake, let me die in peace!" he said.

She would have gone away, but just then their daughter came in and went up to say good morning. He looked at her as he had done at his wife, and in reply to her inquiry about his health said dryly that he would soon free them all of himself. They were both silent and after sitting with him for a while went away.

"Is it our fault?" Lisa said to her mother. "It's as if we were to blame! I am sorry for papa, but why should we be tortured?"

The doctor came at his usual time. Iván Ilých answered "Yes" and "No", never taking his angry eyes from him, and at last said: "You know you can do nothing for me, so leave me alone."

"We can ease your sufferings."

"You can't even do that. Let me be."

The doctor went into the drawing-room and told Praskóvya Fëdorovna that the case was very serious and that the only resource left was opium to allay her husband's sufferings, which must be terrible.

It was true, as the doctor said, that Iván Ilých's physical sufferings were terrible, but worse than the physical sufferings were his mental sufferings which were his chief torture.

His mental sufferings were due to the fact that that night, as he looked at Gerásim's sleepy, good-natured face with its prominent cheek-bones, the question suddenly occurred to him: "What if my whole life has really been wrong?"

It occurred to him that what had appeared perfectly impossible before, namely that he had not spent his life as he should have done, might after all be true. It occurred to him that his scarcely perceptible attempts to struggle against what was considered good by the most highly placed people, those scarcely noticeable impulses which he had immediately suppressed, might have been the real thing, and all the rest false. And his professional duties and the whole arrangement of his life and of his family, and all his social and official interests, might all have been false. He tried to defend all those things to himself and suddenly felt the weakness of what he was defending. There was nothing to defend.

"But if that is so," he said to himself, "and I am leaving this life with the consciousness that I have lost all that was given me and it is impossible to rectify it—what then?"

He lay on his back and began to pass his life in review in quite a new way. In the morning when he saw first his footman, then his wife, then his daughter, and then the doctor, their every word and movement confirmed to him the awful truth that had been revealed to him during the night. In them he saw himself—all that for which he had lived—and saw clearly that it was not real at all, but a terrible and huge deception which had hidden both life and death. This consciousness intensified his physical suffering tenfold. He groaned and tossed about, and pulled at his clothing which choked and stifled him. And he hated them on that account.

He was given a large dose of opium and became unconscious, but at noon his sufferings began again. He drove everybody away and tossed from side to side.

His wife came to him and said:

"Jean, my dear, do this for me. It can't do any harm and often helps. Healthy people often do it."

He opened his eyes wide.

"What? Take communion? Why? It's unnecessary! However. . . ."

She began to cry.

"Yes, do, my dear. I'll send for our priest. He is such a nice man."

"All right. Very well," he muttered.

When the priest came and heard his confession, Iván Ilých was softened and seemed to feel a relief from his doubts and consequently from his sufferings, and for a moment there came a ray of hope. He again began to think of the vermiform appendix and the possibility of correcting it. He received the sacrament with tears in his eyes.

When they laid him down again afterwards he felt a moment's ease, and the hope that he might live awoke in him again. He began to think of the operation that had been suggested to him. "To live! I want to live!" he said to himself.

His wife came in to congratulate him after his communion, and when uttering the usual conventional words she added:

"You feel better, don't you?"

Without looking at her he said "Yes".

Her dress, her figure, the expression of her face, the tone of her voice, all revealed the same thing. "This is wrong, it is not as it should be. All you have lived for and still live for is falsehood and deception, hiding life and death from you." And as soon as he admitted that thought, his hatred and his agonizing physical suffering again sprang up, and with that suffering a consciousness of the unavoidable, approaching end. And to this was added a new sensation of grinding shooting pain and a feeling of suffocation.

The expression of his face when he uttered that "yes" was dreadful. Having uttered it, he looked her straight in the eyes, turned on his face with a rapidity extraordinary in his weak state and shouted:

"Go away! Go away and leave me alone!"

CHAPTER XII

FROM that moment the screaming began that continued for three days, and was so terrible that one could not hear it through two closed doors without horror. At the moment he answered his wife he realized that he was lost, that there was no return, that the end had come, the very end, and his doubts were still unsolved and remained doubts.

"Oh! Oh! Oh!" he cried in various intonations. He had begun by screaming "I won't!" and continued screaming on the letter "o"

For three whole days, during which time did not exist for him, he struggled in that black sack into which he was being thrust by an invisible, resistless force. He struggled as a man condemned to death struggles in the hands of the executioner, knowing that he cannot save himself. And every moment he felt that despite all his efforts he was drawing nearer and nearer to what terrified him. He felt that his agony was due to his being thrust into that black hole and still more to his not being able to get right into it. He was hindered from getting into it by his conviction that his life had been a good one. That very justification of his life held him fast and prevented his moving forward, and it caused him most torment of all.

Suddenly some force struck him in the chest and side, making it still harder to breathe, and he fell through the hole and there at the bottom was a light. What had happened to him was like the sensation one sometimes experiences in a railway carriage when one thinks one is going backwards while one is really going forwards and suddenly becomes aware of the real direction.

"Yes, it was all not the right thing," he said to himself, "but that's no matter. It can be done. But what *is* the right thing?" he asked himself, and suddenly grew quiet.

This occurred at the end of the third day, two hours before his death. Just then his schoolboy son had crept softly in and gone up to the bedside. The dying man was still screaming desperately and waving his arms. His hand fell on the boy's head, and the boy caught it, pressed it to his lips, and began to cry.

At that very moment Iván Ilých fell through and caught sight of the light, and it was revealed to him that though his life had not been what it should have been, this could still be rectified. He asked himself, "What *is* the right thing?" and grew still, listening. Then he felt that someone was kissing his hand. He opened his eyes, looked at his son, and felt sorry for him. His wife came up to him and he glanced at her. She was gazing at him open-mouthed, with undried tears on her nose and cheek and a despairing look on her face. He felt sorry for her too.

"Yes, I am making them wretched," he thought. "They are sorry, but it will be better for them when I die." He wished to say this but had not the strength to utter it. "Besides, why speak? I must act," he thought. With a look at his wife he indicated his son and said: "Take him away . . . sorry for him . . . sorry for you too. . . ." He tried to add, "forgive me," but said "forego" and waved his hand, knowing that He whose understanding mattered would understand.

And suddenly it grew clear to him that what had been oppressing him and would not leave him was all dropping away at once from two sides, from ten sides, and from all sides. He was sorry for them, he must act so as not to hurt them: release them and free himself from these sufferings. "How good and how simple!" he thought. "And the pain?" he asked himself. "What has become of it? Where are you, pain?"

He turned his attention to it.

"Yes, here it is. Well, what of it? Let the pain be."

"And death . . . where is it?"

He sought his former accustomed fear of death and did not find it. "Where is it? What death?" There was no fear because there was no death.

In place of death there was light.

"So that's what it is!" he suddenly exclaimed aloud. "What joy!"

To him all this happened in a single instant, and the meaning of that instant did not change. For those present his agony continued for another two hours. Something rattled in his throat, his emaciated body twitched, then the gasping and rattle became less and less frequent.

"It is finished!" said someone near him.

He heard these words and repeated them in his soul.

"Death is finished," he said to himself. "It is no more!"

He drew in a breath, stopped in the midst of a sigh, stretched out, and died.

Questions

1. *Why does Tolstoy begin the story immediately after Ilých's death and then move back to recount his life?*   2. *Is there any evidence that Ilých's death is a moral judgment—that is, a punishment for his life? Explain.*   3. *Why is Gerásim, Ilých's peasant servant, most sympathetic to his plight?*   4. *At the very end, Ilých achieves peace and understanding, and the questions that have been torturing him are resolved. He realizes that "though his life had not been what it should have been, this could still be rectified." What does this mean?*

An Occurrence
at Owl Creek Bridge

AMBROSE BIERCE [1842–1914?]

I

A man stood upon a railroad bridge in northern Alabama, looking down into the swift water twenty feet below. The man's hands were behind his back, the wrists bound with a cord. A rope closely encircled his neck. It was attached to a stout cross-timber above his head and the slack fell to the level of his knees. Some loose boards laid upon the sleepers supporting the metals of the railway supplied a footing for him and his executioners—two private soldiers of the Federal army, directed by a sergeant who in civil life may have been a deputy sheriff. At a short remove upon the same temporary platform was an officer in the uniform of his rank, armed. He was a captain. A sentinel at each end of the bridge stood with his rifle in the position known as "support," that is to say, vertical in front of the left shoulder, the hammer resting on the forearm thrown straight across the chest—a formal and unnatural position, enforcing an erect carriage of the body. It did not appear to be the duty of these two men to know what was occurring at the centre of the bridge; they merely blockaded the two ends of the foot planking that traversed it.

Beyond one of the sentinels nobody was in sight; the railroad ran straight away into a forest for a hundred yards, then, curving, was lost to view. Doubtless there was an outpost farther along. The other bank of the stream was open ground—a gentle acclivity topped with a stockade of vertical tree trunks, loopholed for rifles, with a single embrasure through which protruded the muzzle of a brass cannon commanding the bridge. Midway of the slope between bridge and fort were the spectators—a single company of infantry in line, at "parade rest," the butts of the rifles on the ground, the barrels inclining slightly backward against the right shoulder, the hands crossed upon the stock. A lieutenant stood at the right of the line, the point of his sword upon the ground, his left hand resting upon his right. Excepting the group of four at the centre of the bridge, not a man moved. The company faced the bridge, staring stonily, motionless. The sentinels, facing the banks of the stream, might have been statues to adorn the bridge. The captain stood with folded arms, silent, observing the work of his subordinates, but making no sign. Death is a dignitary who when he comes announced is to be received with formal manifestations of respect, even by those most familiar with him. In the code of military etiquette silence and fixity are forms of deference.

The man who was engaged in being hanged was apparently about thirty-five years of age. He was a civilian, if one might judge from his habit, which was that of a planter. His features were good—a straight nose, firm mouth, broad forehead, from which his long, dark hair was combed straight back, falling behind his ears to the collar of his well-fitting frock-coat. He wore a mustache and pointed beard, but no whiskers; his eyes were large and dark gray, and had a kindly expression which one would hardly have expected in one whose neck was in the hemp. Evidently this was no vulgar assassin. The liberal military code makes provision for hanging many kinds of persons, and gentlemen are not excluded.

The preparations being complete, the two private soldiers stepped aside and each drew away the plank upon which he had been standing. The sergeant turned to the captain, saluted and placed himself immediately behind that officer, who in turn moved apart one pace. These movements left the condemned man and the sergeant standing on the two ends of the same plank, which spanned three of the cross-ties of the bridge. The end upon which the civilian stood almost, but not quite, reached a fourth. This plank had been held in place by the weight of the captain; it was now held by that of the sergeant. At a signal from the former the latter would step aside, the plank would tilt and the condemned man go down between two ties. The arrangement commended itself to his judgment as simple and effective. His face had not been covered nor his eyes bandaged. He looked a moment at his "unsteadfast footing," then let his gaze wander to the swirling water of the stream racing madly beneath his feet. A piece of dancing driftwood caught his attention and his eyes followed it down the current. How slowly it appeared to move! What a sluggish stream!

He closed his eyes in order to fix his last thoughts upon his wife and children. The water, touched to gold by the early sun, the brooding mists under the banks at some distance down the stream, the fort, the soldiers, the piece of drift—all had distracted him. And now he became conscious of a new disturbance. Striking through the thought of his dear ones was a sound which he could neither ignore nor understand, a sharp, distinct, metallic percussion like the stroke of a blacksmith's hammer upon the anvil; it had the same ringing quality. He wondered what it was, and whether immeasurably distant or near by—it seemed both. Its recurrence was regular, but as slow as the tolling of a death knell. He awaited each stroke with impatience and—he knew not why—apprehension. The intervals of silence grew progressively longer; the delays became maddening. With their greater infrequency the sounds increased in strength and sharpness. They hurt his ear like the thrust of a knife; he feared he would shriek. What he heard was the ticking of his watch.

He unclosed his eyes and saw again the water below him. "If I could free my hands," he thought, "I might throw off the noose and spring into the stream. By diving I could evade the bullets and, swimming vigorously, reach the bank, take to the woods and get away home. My home, thank God, is as yet outside their lines; my wife and little ones are still beyond the invader's farthest advance."

As these thoughts, which have here to be set down in words, were flashed into the doomed man's brain rather than evolved from it the captain nodded to the sergeant. The sergeant stepped aside.

II

PEYTON Farquhar was a well-to-do planter, of an old and highly respected Alabama family. Being a slave owner and like other slave owners a politician he was naturally an original secessionist and ardently devoted to the Southern cause. Circumstances of an imperious nature, which it is unnecessary to relate here, had prevented him from taking service with the gallant army that had fought the disastrous campaigns ending with the fall of Corinth, and he chafed under the inglorious restraint, longing for the release of his energies, the larger life of the soldier, the opportunity for distinction. That opportunity, he felt, would come, as it comes to all in war time. Meanwhile he did what he could. No service was too humble for him to perform in aid of the South, no adventure too perilous for him to undertake if consistent with the character of a civilian who was at heart a soldier, and who in good faith and without too much qualification assented to at least a part of the frankly villainous dictum that all is fair in love and war.

One evening while Farquhar and his wife were sitting on a rustic bench near the entrance to his grounds, a gray-clad soldier rode up to the gate and asked for a drink of water. Mrs. Farquhar was only too happy to serve him with her own white hands. While she was fetching the water her husband approached the dusty horseman and inquired eagerly for news from the front.

"The Yanks are repairing the railroads," said the man, "and are getting ready for another advance. They have reached the Owl Creek bridge, put it in order and built a stockade on the north bank. The commandant has issued an order, which is posted everywhere, declaring that any civilian caught interfering with the railroad, its bridges, tunnels or trains will be summarily hanged. I saw the order."

"How far is it to the Owl Creek bridge?" Farquhar asked.

"About thirty miles."

"Is there no force on this side the creek?"

"Only a picket post half a mile out, on the railroad, and a single sentinel at this end of the bridge."

"Suppose a man—a civilian and student of hanging—should elude the picket post and perhaps get the better of the sentinel," said Farquhar, smiling, "what could he accomplish?"

The soldier reflected. "I was there a month ago," he replied. "I observed that the flood of last winter had lodged a great quantity of driftwood against the wooden pier at this end of the bridge. It is now dry and would burn like tow."

The lady had now brought the water, which the soldier drank. He thanked her ceremoniously, bowed to her husband and rode away. An hour later, after nightfall, he repassed the plantation, going northward in the direction from which he had come. He was a Federal scout.

III

As Peyton Farquhar fell straight downward through the bridge he lost consciousness and was as one already dead. From this state he was awakened—ages later, it seemed to him—by the pain of a sharp pressure upon his throat, followed by a sense of suffocation. Keen, poignant agonies seemed to shoot from his neck downward through every fibre of his body and limbs. These pains appeared to flash along well-defined lines of ramification and to beat with an inconceivably rapid periodicity. They seemed like streams of pulsating fire heating him to an intolerable temperature. As to his head, he was conscious of nothing but a feeling of fulness—of congestion. These sensations were unaccompanied by thought. The intellectual part of his nature was already effaced; he had power only to feel, and feeling was torment. He was conscious of motion. Encompassed in a luminous cloud, of which he was now merely the fiery heart, without material substance, he swung through unthinkable arcs of oscillation, like a vast pendulum. Then all at once, with terrible suddenness, the light about him shot upward with the noise of a loud plash; a frightful roaring was in his ears, and all was cold and dark. The power of thought was restored; he knew that the rope had broken and he had fallen into the stream. There was no additional strangulation; the noose about his neck was already suffocating him and kept the water from his lungs. To die of hanging at the bottom of a river!—the idea seemed to him ludicrous. He opened his eyes in the darkness and saw above him a gleam of light, but how distant, how inaccessible! He was still sinking, for the light became fainter and fainter until it was a mere glimmer. Then it began to grow and brighten, and he knew that he was rising toward the surface—knew it with reluctance, for he was now very comfortable. "To be hanged and drowned," he thought, "that is not so bad; but I do not wish to be shot. No; I will not be shot; that is not fair."

He was not conscious of an effort, but a sharp pain in his wrist apprised him that he was trying to free his hands. He gave the struggle his attention, as an idler might observe the feat of a juggler, without interest in the outcome. What splendid effort!—what magnificent, what superhuman strength! Ah, that was a fine endeavor! Bravo! The cord fell away; his arms parted and floated upward, the hands dimly seen on each side in the growing light. He watched them with a new interest as first one and then the other pounced upon the noose at his neck. They tore it away and thrust it fiercely aside, its undulations resembling those of a water-snake. "Put it back, put it back!" He thought he shouted these words to his hands, for the undoing of the noose had been succeeded by the direst pang that he had yet experienced. His neck ached horribly, his brain was on fire; his heart, which had been fluttering faintly, gave a great leap, trying to force itself out at his mouth. His whole body was racked and wrenched with an insupportable anguish! But his disobedient hands gave no heed to the command. They beat the water vigorously with quick, downward strokes, forcing him to the surface. He felt his head emerge; his eyes were blinded by the sunlight; his chest expanded convulsively, and with a supreme and crowning agony his lungs engulfed a great draught of air, which instantly he expelled in a shriek!

He was now in full possession of his physical senses. They were, indeed, preternaturally keen and alert. Something in the awful disturbance of his organic system had so exalted and refined them that they made record of things never before perceived. He felt the ripples upon his face and heard their separate sounds as they struck. He looked at the forest on the bank of the stream, saw the individual trees, the leaves and the veining of each leaf—saw the very insects upon them: the locusts, the brilliant-bodied flies, the gray spiders stretching their webs from twig to twig. He noted the prismatic colors in all the dewdrops upon a million blades of grass. The humming of the gnats that danced above the eddies of the stream, the beating of the dragon-flies' wings, the strokes of the water-spiders' legs, like oars which had lifted their boat—all these made audible music. A fish slid along beneath his eyes and he heard the rush of its body parting the water.

He had come to the surface facing down the stream; in a moment the visible world seemed to wheel slowly round, himself the pivotal point, and he saw the bridge, the fort, the soldiers upon the bridge, the captain, the sergeant, the two privates, his executioners. They were in silhouette against the blue sky. They shouted and gesticulated, pointing at him. The captain had drawn his pistol, but did not fire; the others were unarmed. Their movements were grotesque and horrible, their forms gigantic.

Suddenly he heard a sharp report and something struck the water smartly within a few inches of his head, spattering his face with spray. He heard a second report, and saw one of the sentinels with his rifle at his shoulder, a light cloud of blue smoke rising from the muzzle. The man in the water saw the eye of the man on the bridge gazing into his own through the sights of the rifle. He observed that it was a gray eye and remembered having read that gray eyes were keenest, and that all famous marksmen had them. Nevertheless, this one had missed.

A counter-swirl had caught Farquhar and turned him half round; he was again looking into the forest on the bank opposite the fort. The sound of a clear, high voice in a monotonous singsong now rang out behind him and came across the water with a distinctness that pierced and subdued all other sounds, even the beating of the ripples in his ears. Although no soldier, he had frequented camps enough to know the dread significance of that deliberate, drawling, aspirated chant; the lieutenant on shore was taking a part in the morning's work. How coldly and pitilessly—with what an even, calm intonation, presaging, and enforcing tranquillity in the men—with what accurately measured intervals fell those cruel words:

"Attention, company! . . . Shoulder arms! . . . Ready! . . . Aim! . . . Fire!"

Farquhar dived—dived as deeply as he could. The water roared in his ears like the voice of Niagara, yet he heard the dulled thunder of the volley and, rising again toward the surface, met shining bits of metal, singularly flattened, oscillating slowly downward. Some of them touched him on the face and hands, then fell away, continuing their descent. One lodged between his collar and neck; it was uncomfortably warm and he snatched it out.

As he rose to the surface, gasping for breath, he saw that he had been a long time under water; he was perceptibly farther down stream—nearer to safety. The soldiers had almost finished reloading; the metal ramrods flashed all at once in the sunshine as they were drawn from the barrels, turned in the air, and thrust into their sockets. The two sentinels fired again, independently and ineffectually.

The hunted man saw all this over his shoulder; he was now swimming vigorously with the current. His brain was as energetic as his arms and legs; he thought with the rapidity of lightning.

"The officer," he reasoned, "will not make that martinet's error a second time. It is as easy to dodge a volley as a single shot. He has probably already given the command to fire at will. God help me, I cannot dodge them all!"

An appalling plash within two yards of him was followed by a loud, rushing sound, *diminuendo,* which seemed to travel back through the air to the fort and died in an explosion which stirred the very river to its deeps! A rising sheet of water curved over him, fell down upon him, blinded him, strangled him! The cannon had taken a hand in the game. As he shook his head free from the commotion of the smitten water he heard the deflected shot humming through the air ahead, and in an instant it was cracking and smashing the branches in the forest beyond.

"They will not do that again," he thought; "the next time they will use a charge of grape. I must keep my eye upon the gun; the smoke will apprise me—the report arrives too late; it lags behind the missile. That is a good gun."

Suddenly he felt himself whirled round and round—spinning like a top. The water, the banks, the forests, the now distant bridge, fort and men—all were commingled and blurred. Objects were represented by their colors only; circular horizontal streaks of color—that was all he saw. He had been caught in a vortex and was being whirled on with a velocity of advance and gyration that made him giddy and sick. In a few moments he was flung upon the gravel at the foot of the left bank of the stream—the southern bank—and behind a projecting point which concealed him from his enemies. The sudden arrest of his motion, the abrasion of one of his hands on the gravel, restored him, and he wept with delight. He dug his fingers into the sand, threw it over himself in handfuls and audibly blessed it. It looked like diamonds, rubies, emeralds; he could think of nothing beautiful which it did not resemble. The trees upon the bank were giant garden plants; he noted a definite order in their arrangement, inhaled the fragrance of their blooms. A strange, roseate light shone through the spaces among their trunks and the wind made in their branches the music of aeolian harps. He had no wish to perfect his escape—was content to remain in that enchanting spot until retaken.

A whiz and rattle of grapeshot among the branches high above his head roused him from his dream. The baffled cannoneer had fired him a random farewell. He sprang to his feet, rushed up the sloping bank, and plunged into the forest.

All that day he traveled, laying his course by the rounding sun. The forest seemed interminable; nowhere did he discover a break in it, not even a woodman's road. He had not known that he lived in so wild a region. There was something uncanny in the revelation.

By night fall he was fatigued, footsore, famishing. The thought of his wife and children urged him on. At last he found a road which led him in what he knew to be the right direction. It was as wide and straight as a city street, yet it seemed untraveled. No fields bordered it, no dwelling anywhere. Not so much as the barking of a dog suggested human habitation. The black bodies of the trees formed a straight wall on both sides, terminating on the horizon in a point, like a diagram in a lesson in perspective. Overhead, as he looked up through this rift in the wood, shone great golden stars looking unfamiliar and grouped in strange constellations. He was sure they were arranged in some order which had a secret and malign significance. The wood on either side was full of singular noises, among which—once, twice, and again, he distinctly heard whispers in an unknown tongue.

His neck was in pain and lifting his hand to it he found it horribly swollen. He knew that it had a circle of black where the rope had bruised it. His eyes felt congested; he could no longer close them. His tongue was swollen with thirst; he relieved its fever by thrusting it forward from between his teeth into the cold air. How softly the turf had carpeted the untraveled avenue—he could no longer feel the roadway beneath his feet!

Doubtless, despite his suffering, he had fallen asleep while walking, for now he sees another scene—perhaps he has merely recovered from a delirium. He stands at the gate of his own home. All is as he left it, and all bright and beautiful in the morning sunshine. He must have traveled the entire night. As he pushes open the gate and passes up the wide white walk, he sees a flutter of female garments; his wife, looking fresh and cool and sweet, steps down from the veranda to meet him. At the bottom of the steps she stands waiting, with a smile of ineffable joy, an attitude of matchless grace and dignity. Ah, how beautiful she is! He springs forward with extended arms. As he is about to clasp her he feels a stunning blow upon the back of the neck; a blinding white light blazes all about him with a sound like the shock of a cannon—then all is darkness and silence!

Peyton Farquhar was dead; his body, with a broken neck, swung gently from side to side beneath the timbers of the Owl Creek bridge.

The Jilting of Granny Weatherall

KATHERINE ANNE PORTER [b. 1890]

SHE flicked her wrist neatly out of Doctor Harry's pudgy careful fingers and pulled the sheet up to her chin. The brat ought to be in knee breeches. Doctoring around the country with spectacles on his nose! "Get along now, take your schoolbooks and go. There's nothing wrong with me."

Doctor Harry spread a warm paw like a cushion on her forehead where the forked green vein danced and made her eyelids twitch. "Now, now, be a good girl, and we'll have you up in no time."

"That's no way to speak to a woman nearly eighty years old just because she's down. I'd have you respect your elders, young man."

"Well, Missy, excuse me." Doctor Harry patted her cheek. "But I've got to warn you, haven't I? You're a marvel, but you must be careful or you're going to be good and sorry."

"Don't tell me what I'm going to be. I'm on my feet now, morally speaking. It's Cornelia. I had to go to bed to get rid of her."

Her bones felt loose, and floated around in her skin, and Doctor Harry floated like a balloon around the foot of the bed. He floated and pulled down his waistcoat and swung his glasses on a cord. "Well, stay where you are, it certainly can't hurt you."

"Get along and doctor your sick," said Granny Weatherall. "Leave a well woman alone. I'll call for you when I want you. . . . Where were you forty years ago when I pulled through milk-leg and double pneumonia? You weren't even born. Don't let Cornelia lead you on," she shouted, because Doctor Harry appeared to float up to the ceiling and out. "I pay my own bills, and I don't throw my money away on nonsense!"

She meant to wave good-by, but it was too much trouble. Her eyes closed of themselves, it was like a dark curtain drawn around the bed. The pillow rose and floated under her, pleasant as a hammock in a light wind. She listened to the leaves rustling outside the window. No, somebody was swishing newspapers: no, Cornelia and Doctor Harry were whispering together. She leaped broad awake, thinking they whispered in her ear.

"She was never like this, *never* like this!" "Well, what can we expect?" "Yes, eighty years old. . . ."

Well, and what if she was? She still had ears. It was like Cornelia to whisper around doors. She always kept things secret in such a public way. She was always being tactful and kind. Cornelia was dutiful; that was the trouble with her. Dutiful and good: "So good and dutiful," said Granny, "that I'd like to spank her." She saw herself spanking Cornelia and making a fine job of it.

"What'd you say, Mother?"

Granny felt her face tying up in hard knots.

"Can't a body think, I'd like to know?"

"I thought you might want something."

"I do. I want a lot of things. First off, go away and don't whisper."

She lay and drowsed, hoping in her sleep that the children would keep out and let her rest a minute. It had been a long day. Not that she was tired. It was always pleasant to snatch a minute now and then. There was always so much to be done, let me see: tomorrow.

Tomorrow was far away and there was nothing to trouble about. Things were finished somehow when the time came; thank God there was always a little margin over for peace: then a person could spread out the plan of life and tuck in the edges orderly. It was good to have everything clean and folded away, with the hair brushes and tonic bottles sitting straight on the white embroidered linen: the day started without fuss and the pantry shelves laid out with rows of jelly glasses and brown jugs and white stone-china jars with blue whirligigs and words painted on them: coffee, tea, sugar, ginger, cinnamon, allspice: and the bronze clock with the lion on top nicely dusted off. The dust that lion could collect in twenty-four hours! The box in the attic with all those letters tied up, well she'd have to go through that tomorrow. All those letters—George's letters and John's letters and her letters to them both—lying around for the children to find afterwards made her uneasy. Yes, that would be tomorrow's business. No use to let them know how silly she had been once.

While she was rummaging around she found death in her mind and it felt clammy and unfamiliar. She had spent so much time preparing for death there was no need for bringing it up again. Let it take care of itself now. When she was sixty she had felt very old, finished, and went around making farewell trips to see her children and grandchildren, with a secret in her mind: This is the very last of your mother, children! Then she made her will and came down with a long fever. That was all just a notion like a lot of other things, but it was lucky too, for she had once for all got over the idea of dying for a long time. Now she couldn't be worried. She hoped she had better sense now. Her father had lived to be one hundred and two years old and had drunk a noggin of strong hot toddy on his last birthday. He told the reporters it was his daily habit, and he owed his long life to that. He had made quite a scandal and was very pleased about it. She believed she'd just plague Cornelia a little.

"Cornelia! Cornelia!" No footsteps, but a sudden hand on her cheek. "Bless you, where have you been?"

"Here, mother."

"Well, Cornelia, I want a noggin of hot toddy."

"Are you cold, darling?"

"I'm chilly, Cornelia. Lying in bed stops the circulation. I must have told you that a thousand times."

Well, she could just hear Cornelia telling her husband that Mother was getting childish and they'd have to humor her. The thing that most annoyed her was that Cornelia thought she was deaf, dumb, and blind. Little hasty glances and tiny gestures tossed around her and over her head saying. "Don't cross her, let her have her way, she's eighty years old," and she sitting there as if she lived in a thin glass cage. Sometimes Granny almost made up her mind to pack up and move back to her own house where nobody could remind her every minute that she was old. Wait, wait, Cornelia, till your own children whisper behind your back!

In her day she had kept a better house and had got more work done. She wasn't too old yet for Lydia to be driving eighty miles for advice when one of the children jumped the track, and Jimmy still dropped in and talked things over: "Now, Mammy, you've a good business head, I want to know what you think of this? . . ." Old Cornelia couldn't change the furniture around without asking. Little things, little things! They had been so sweet when they were little. Granny wished the old days were back again with the children young and everything to be done over. It had been a hard pull, but not too much for her. When she thought of all the food she had cooked, and all the clothes she had cut and sewed, and all the gardens she had made—well, the children showed it. There they were, made out of her, and they couldn't get away from that. Sometimes she wanted to see John again and point to them and say, Well, I didn't do so badly, did I? But that would have to wait. That was for tomorrow. She used to think of him as a man, but now all the children were older than their father, and he would be a child beside her if she saw him now. It seemed strange and there was something wrong in the idea. Why, he couldn't possibly recognize her. She had fenced in a hundred acres once, digging the post holes herself and clamping the wires with just a negro boy to help. That changed a woman. John would be looking for a young woman with the peaked Spanish comb in her hair and the painted fan. Digging post holes changed a woman. Riding country roads in the winter when women had their babies was another thing: sitting up nights with sick horses and sick negroes and sick children and hardly ever losing one. John, I hardly ever lost one of them! John would see that in a minute, that would be something he could understand, she wouldn't have to explain anything!

It made her feel like rolling up her sleeves and putting the whole place to rights again. No matter if Cornelia was determined to be everywhere at once, there were a great many things left undone on this place. She would start tomorrow and do them. It was good to be strong enough for everything, even if all you made melted and changed and slipped under your hands, so that by the time you finished you almost forgot what you were working for. What was it I set out to do? she asked herself intently, but she could not remember. A fog rose over the valley, she saw it marching across the creek swallowing the trees and moving up hill like an army of ghosts. Soon it would be at the near edge of the orchard, and then it was time to go in and light the lamps. Come in, children, don't stay out in the night air.

Lighting the lamps had been beautiful. The children huddled up to her and breathed like little calves waiting at the bars in the twilight. Their eyes followed the match and watched the flame rise and settle in a blue curve, then they moved away from her. The lamp was lit, they didn't have to be scared and hang on to mother any more. Never, never, never more. God, for all my life I thank Thee. Without Thee, my God, I could never have done it. Hail, Mary, full of grace.

I want you to pick all the fruit this year and see that nothing is wasted. There's always someone who can use it. Don't let good things rot for want of using. You waste life when you waste good food. Don't let things get lost. It's bitter to lose things. Now, don't let me get to thinking, not when I am tired and taking a little nap before supper. . . .

The pillow rose about her shoulders and pressed against her heart and the memory was being squeezed out of it: oh, push down the pillow, some-body: it would smother her if she tried to hold it. Such a fresh breeze blowing and such a green day with no threats in it. But he had not come, just the same. What does a woman do when she has put on the white veil and set out the white cake for a man and he doesn't come? She tried to remember. No, I swear he never harmed me but in that. He never harmed me but in that . . . and what if he did? There was the day, the day, but a whirl of dark smoke rose and covered it, crept up and over into the bright field where everything was planted so carefully in orderly rows. That was hell, she knew hell when she saw it. For sixty years she had prayed against remembering him and against losing her soul in the deep pit of hell, and now the two things were mingled in one and the thought of him was a smoky cloud from hell that moved and crept in her head when she had just got rid of Doctor Harry and was trying to rest a minute. Wounded vanity, Ellen, said a sharp voice in the top of her mind. Don't let your wounded vanity get the upper hand of you. Plenty of girls get jilted. You were jilted, weren't you? Then stand up to it. Her eyelids wavered and let in streamers of blue-gray light like tissue paper over her eyes. She must get up and pull the shades down or she'd never sleep. She was in bed again and the shades were not down. How could that happen? Better turn over, hide from the light, sleeping in the light gave you nightmares. "Mother, how do you feel now?" and a stinging wetness on her forehead. But I don't like having my face washed in cold water!

Hapsy? George? Lydia? Jimmy? No, Cornelia, and her features were swollen and full of little puddles. "They're coming, darling, they'll all be here soon." Go wash your face, child, you look funny.

Instead of obeying, Cornelia knelt down and put her head on the pillow. She seemed to be talking but there was no sound. "Well, are you tongue-tied? Whose birthday is it? Are you going to give a party?"

Cornelia's mouth moved urgently in strange shapes. "Don't do that, you bother me, daughter."

"Oh, no, Mother, Oh, no. . . ."

Nonsense. It was strange about children. They disputed your every word. "No what, Cornelia?"

"Here's Doctor Harry."

"I won't see that boy again. He just left five minutes ago."

"That was this morning, Mother. It's night now. Here's the nurse."

"This is Doctor Harry, Mrs. Weatherall. I never saw you look so young and happy!"

"Ah, I'll never be young again—but I'd be happy if they'd let me lie in peace and get rested."

She thought she spoke up loudly, but no one answered. A warm weight on her forehead, a warm bracelet on her wrist, and a breeze went on whispering, trying to tell her something. A shuffle of leaves in the everlasting hand of God. He blew on them and they danced and rattled. "Mother, don't mind, we're going to give you a little hypodermic." "Look here, daughter, how do ants get in this bed? I saw sugar ants yesterday." Did you send for Hapsy too?

It was Hapsy she really wanted. She had to go a long way back through a great many rooms to find Hapsy standing with a baby on her arm. She seemed to herself to be Hapsy also, and the baby on Hapsy's arm was Hapsy and himself and herself, all at once, and there was no surprise in the meeting. Then Hapsy melted from within and turned flimsy as gray gauze and the baby was a gauzy shadow, and Hapsy came up close and said, "I thought you'd never come," and looked at her very searchingly and said, "You haven't changed a bit!" They leaned forward to kiss, when Cornelia began whispering from a long way off, "Oh, is there anything you want to tell me? Is there anything I can do for you?"

Yes, she had changed her mind after sixty years and she would like to see George. I want you to find George. Find him and be sure to tell him I forgot him. I want him to know I had my husband just the same and my children and my house like any other woman. A good house too and a good husband that I loved and fine children out of him. Better than I hoped for even. Tell him I was given back everything he took away and more. Oh, no, oh, God, no, there was something else besides the house and the man and the children. Oh, surely they were not all? What was it? Something not given back. . . . Her breath crowded down under her ribs and grew into a monstrous frightening shape with cutting edges; it bored up into her head, and the agony was unbelievable: Yes, John, get the doctor now, no more talk, my time has come.

When this one was born it should be the last. The last. It should have been born first, for it was the one she had truly wanted. Everything came in good time. Nothing left out, left over. She was strong, in three days she would be as well as ever. Better. A woman needed milk in her to have her full health.

"Mother, do you hear me?"

"I've been telling you—"

"Mother, Father Connolly's here."

"I went to Holy Communion only last week. Tell him I'm not so sinful as all that."

"Father just wants to speak to you."

He could speak as much as he pleased. It was like him to drop in and inquire about her soul as if it were a teething baby, and then stay on for a cup of tea and a round of cards and gossip. He always had a funny story of some sort, usually about an Irishman who made his little mistakes and confessed them, and the point lay in some absurd thing he would blurt out in the confessional showing his struggles between native piety and original sin. Granny felt easy about her soul. Cornelia, where are your manners? Give Father Connolly a chair. She had her secret comfortable understanding with a few favorite saints who cleared a straight road to God for her. All as surely signed and sealed as the papers for the new Forty Acres. Forever . . . heirs and assigns forever. Since the day the wedding cake was not cut, but thrown out and wasted. The whole bottom dropped out of the world, and there she was blind and sweating with nothing under her feet and the walls falling away. His hand had caught her under the breast, she had not fallen, there was the freshly polished floor with the green rug on it, just as before. He had cursed like a sailor's parrot and said, "I'll kill him for you." Don't lay a hand on him, for my sake leave something to God. "Now, Ellen, you must believe what I tell you. . . ."

So there was nothing, nothing to worry about any more, except sometimes in the night one of the children screamed in a nightmare, and they both hustled out shaking and hunting for the matches and calling, "There, wait a minute, here we are!" John, get the doctor now, Hapsy's time has come. But there was Hapsy standing by the bed in a white cap. "Cornelia, tell Hapsy to take off her cap. I can't see her plain."

Her eyes opened very wide and the room stood out like a picture she had seen somewhere. Dark colors with the shadows rising towards the ceiling in long angles. The tall black dresser gleamed with nothing on it but John's picture, enlarged from a little one, with John's eyes very black when they should have been blue. You never saw him, so how do you know how he looked? But the man insisted the copy was perfect, it was very rich and handsome. For a picture, yes, but it's not my husband. The table by the bed had a linen cover and a candle and a crucifix. The light was blue from Cornelia's silk lampshades. No sort of light at all, just frippery. You had to live forty years with kerosene lamps to appreciate honest electricity. She felt very strong and she saw Doctor Harry with a rosy nimbus around him.

"You look like a saint, Doctor Harry, and I vow that's as near as you'll ever come to it."

"She's saying something."

"I heard you, Cornelia. What's all this carrying-on?"

"Father Connolly's saying—"

Cornelia's voice staggered and bumped like a cart in a bad road. It rounded corners and turned back again and arrived nowhere. Granny stepped up in the cart very lightly and reached for the reins, but a man sat beside her and she knew him by his hands, driving the cart. She did not look in his face, for she knew without seeing, but looked instead down the road where the trees leaned over and bowed to each other and a thousand birds were singing a Mass. She felt like singing too, but she put her hand in the bosom of her dress and pulled out a rosary, and Father Connolly murmured Latin in a very solemn voice and tickled her feet. My God, will you stop that nonsense? I'm a married woman. What if he did run away and leave me to face the priest by myself? I found another a whole world better. I wouldn't have exchanged my husband for anybody except St. Michael himself, and you may tell him that for me with a thank you in the bargain.

Light flashed on her closed eyelids, and a deep roaring shook her. Cornelia, is that lightning? I hear thunder. There's going to be a storm. Close all the windows. Call the children in. . . . "Mother, here we are, all of us." "Is that you, Hapsy?" "Oh, no, I'm Lydia. We drove as fast as we could." Their faces drifted above her, drifted away. The rosary fell out of her hands and Lydia put it back. Jimmy tried to help, their hands fumbled together, and Granny closed two fingers around Jimmy's thumb. Beads wouldn't do, it must be something alive. She was so amazed her thoughts ran round and round. So, my dear Lord, this is my death and I wasn't even thinking about it. My children have come to see me die. But I can't, it's not time. Oh, I always hated surprises. I wanted to give Cornelia the amethyst set—Cornelia, you're to have the amethyst set, but Hapsy's to wear it when she wants, and, Doctor Harry, do shut up. Nobody sent for you. Oh, my dear Lord, do wait a minute. I meant to do something about the Forty Acres, Jimmy doesn't need it and Lydia will later on, with that worthless husband of hers. I meant to finish the altar cloth and send six bottles of wine to Sister Borgia for her dyspepsia. I want to send six bottles of wine to Sister Borgia, Father Connolly, now don't let me forget.

Cornelia's voice made short turns and tilted over and crashed. "Oh, Mother, oh, Mother, oh, Mother. . . ."

"I'm not going, Cornelia. I'm taken by surprise. I can't go."

You'll see Hapsy again. What about her? "I thought you'd never come." Granny made a long journey outward, looking for Hapsy. What if I don't find her? What then? Her heart sank down and down, there was no bottom to death, she couldn't come to the end of it. The blue light from Cornelia's lampshade drew into a tiny point in the center of her brain, it flickered and winked like an eye, quietly it fluttered and dwindled. Granny lay curled down within herself, amazed and watchful, staring at the point of light that was herself; her body was now only a deeper mass of shadow in an endless darkness and this darkness would curl around the light and swallow it up. God, give a sign!

For the second time there was no sign. Again no bridegroom and the priest in the house. She could not remember any other sorrow because this grief wiped them all away. Oh, no, there's nothing more cruel than this—I'll never forgive it. She stretched herself with a deep breath and blew out the light.

Questions

1. *Characterize Granny. What facts do we know about her life?* 2. *Why, after sixty full years, does the jilting by George loom so large in Granny's mind? Are we to accept her own strong statements that the pain of the jilting was more than compensated for by the happiness she ultimately found with her husband John, her children, and her grandchildren? Explain.* 3. *Why does the author not present us with Granny's final thoughts in an orderly and sequential pattern?* 4. *Granny is revealed to us not only through her direct thoughts but also through the many images that float through her mind—the fog (p. 904), the blowing breeze (pp. 905 and 906), "a whirl of dark smoke" (p. 905), and others. What do these images reveal about Granny?* 5. *The final paragraph echoes Christ's parable of the bridegroom (Matthew 25:1–13). Why does Granny connect this final, deep religious grief with the grief she felt when George jilted her?*

Idiots First

BERNARD MALAMUD [b. 1914]

THE thick ticking of the tin clock stopped. Mendel, dozing in the dark, awoke in fright. The pain returned as he listened. He drew on his cold embittered clothing, and wasted minutes sitting at the edge of the bed.

"Isaac," he ultimately sighed.

In the kitchen, Isaac, his astonished mouth open, held six peanuts in his palm. He placed each on the table. "One . . . two . . . nine."

He gathered each peanut and appeared in the doorway. Mendel, in loose hat and long overcoat, still sat on the bed. Isaac watched with small eyes and ears, thick hair graying the sides of his head.

"Schlaf," he nasally said.

"No," muttered Mendel. As if stifling he rose. "Come, Isaac."

He wound his old watch though the sight of the stopped clock nauseated him.

Isaac wanted to hold it to his ear.

"No, it's late." Mendel put the watch carefully away. In the drawer he found the little paper bag of crumpled ones and fives and slipped it into his overcoat pocket. He helped Isaac on with his coat.

Isaac looked at one dark window, then at the other. Mendel stared at both blank windows.

They went slowly down the darkly lit stairs, Mendel first, Isaac watching the moving shadows on the wall. To one long shadow he offered a peanut.

"Hungrig."

In the vestibule the old man gazed through the thin glass. The November night was cold and bleak. Opening the door he cautiously thrust his head out. Though he saw nothing he quickly shut the door.

"Ginzburg, that he came to see me yesterday," he whispered in Isaac's ear.

Isaac sucked air.

"You know who I mean?"

Isaac combed his chin with his fingers.

"That's the one, with the black whiskers. Don't talk to him or go with him if he asks you."

Isaac moaned.

"Young people he don't bother so much," Mendel said in afterthought.

It was suppertime and the street was empty but the store windows dimly lit their way to the corner. They crossed the deserted street and went on. Isaac, with a happy cry, pointed to the three golden balls. Mendel smiled but was exhausted when they got to the pawnshop.

The pawnbroker, a red-bearded man with black horn-rimmed glasses, was eating a whitefish at the rear of the store. He craned his head, saw them, and settled back to sip his tea.

In five minutes he came forward, patting his shapeless lips with a large white handkerchief.

Mendel, breathing heavily, handed him the worn gold watch. The pawnbroker, raising his glasses, screwed in his eyepiece. He turned the watch over once. "Eight dollars."

The dying man wet his cracked lips. "I must have thirty-five."

"So go to Rothschild."

"Cost me myself sixty."

"In 1905." The pawnbroker handed back the watch. It had stopped ticking. Mendel wound it slowly. It ticked hollowly.

"Isaac must go to my uncle that he lives in California."

"It's a free country," said the pawnbroker.

Isaac, watching a banjo, snickered.

"What's the matter with him?" the pawnbroker asked.

"So let be eight dollars," muttered Mendel, "but where will I get the rest till tonight?"

"How much for my hat and coat?" he asked.

"No sale." The pawnbroker went behind the cage and wrote out a ticket. He locked the watch in a small drawer but Mendel still heard it ticking.

In the street he slipped the eight dollars into the paper bag, then searched in his pockets for a scrap of writing. Finding it, he strained to read the address by the light of the street lamp.

As they trudged to the subway, Mendel pointed to the sprinkled sky.

"Isaac, look how many stars are tonight."

"Eggs," said Isaac.

"First we will go to Mr. Fishbein, after we will eat."

They got off the train in upper Manhattan and had to walk several blocks before they located Fishbein's house.

"A regular palace," Mendel murmured, looking forward to a moment's warmth.

Isaac stared uneasily at the heavy door of the house.

Mendel rang. The servant, a man with long sideburns, came to the door and said Mr. and Mrs. Fishbein were dining and could see no one.

"He should eat in peace but we will wait till he finishes."

"Come back tomorrow morning. Tomorrow morning Mr. Fishbein will talk to you. He don't do business or charity at this time of the night."

"Charity I am not interested—"

"Come back tomorrow."

"Tell him it's life or death—"

"Whose life or death?"

"So if not his, then mine."

"Don't be such a big smart aleck."

"Look me in my face," said Mendel, "and tell me if I got time till tomorrow morning?"

The servant stared at him, then at Isaac, and reluctantly let them in.

The foyer was a vast high-ceilinged room with many oil paintings on the walls, voluminous silken draperies, a thick flowered rug at foot, and a marble staircase.

Mr. Fishbein, a paunchy bald-headed man with hairy nostrils and small patent leather feet, ran lightly down the stairs, a large napkin tucked under a tuxedo coat button. He stopped on the fifth step from the bottom and examined his visitors.

"Who comes on Friday night to a man that he has guests, to spoil him his supper?"

"Excuse me that I bother you, Mr. Fishbein," Mendel said. "If I didn't come now I couldn't come tomorrow."

"Without more preliminaries, please state your business. I'm a hungry man."

"Hungrig," wailed Isaac.

Fishbein adjusted his pince-nez. "What's the matter with him?"

"This is my son Isaac. He is like this all his life."

Isaac mewled.

"I am sending him to California."

"Mr. Fishbein don't contribute to personal pleasure trips."

"I am a sick man and he must go tonight on the train to my Uncle Leo."

"I never give to unorganized charity," Fishbein said, "but if you are hungry I will invite you downstairs in my kitchen. We having tonight chicken with stuffed derma."

"All I ask is thirty-five dollars for the train ticket to my uncle in California. I have already the rest."

"Who is your uncle? How old a man?"

"Eighty-one years, a long life to him."

Fishbein burst into laughter. "Eighty-one years and you are sending him this halfwit."

Mendel, flailing both arms, cried, "Please, without names."

Fishbein politely conceded.

"Where is open the door there we go in the house," the sick man said. "If you will kindly give me thirty-five dollars, God will bless you. What is thirty-five dollars to Mr. Fishbein? Nothing. To me, for my boy, is everything."

Fishbein drew himself up to his tallest height.

"Private contributions I don't make—only to institutions. This is my fixed policy."

Mendel sank to his creaking knees on the rug.

"Please, Mr. Fishbein, if not thirty-five, give maybe twenty."

"Levinson!" Fishbein angrily called.

The servant with the long sideburns appeared at the top of the stairs.

"Show this party where is the door—unless he wishes to partake food before leaving the premises."

"For what I got chicken won't cure it," Mendel said.

"This way if you please," said Levinson, descending.

Isaac assisted his father up.

"Take him to an institution," Fishbein advised over the marble balustrade. He ran quickly up the stairs and they were at once outside, buffeted by winds.

The walk to the subway was tedious. The wind blew mournfully. Mendel, breathless, glanced furtively at shadows. Isaac, clutching his peanuts in his frozen fist, clung to his father's side. They entered a small park to rest for a minute on a stone bench under a leafless two-branched tree. The thick right branch was raised, the thin left one hung down. A very pale moon rose slowly. So did a stranger as they approached the bench.

"Gut yuntif" [Happy holiday], he said hoarsely.

Mendel, drained of blood, waved his wasted arms. Isaac yowled sickly. Then a bell chimed and it was only ten. Mendel let out a piercing anguished cry as the bearded stranger disappeared into the bushes. A policeman came running, and though he beat the bushes with his nightstick, could turn up nothing. Mendel and Isaac hurried out of the little park. When Mendel glanced back the dead tree had its thin arm raised, the thick one down. He moaned.

They boarded a trolley, stopping at the home of a former friend, but he had died years ago. On the same block they went into a cafeteria and ordered two fried eggs for Isaac. The tables were crowded except where a heavy-set man sat eating soup with kasha. After one look at him they left in haste, although Isaac wept.

Mendel had another address on a slip of paper but the house was too far away, in Queens, so they stood in a doorway shivering.

What can I do, he frantically thought, in one short hour?

He remembered the furniture in the house. It was junk but might bring a few dollars. "Come, Isaac." They went once more to the pawnbroker's to talk to him, but the shop was dark and an iron gate—rings and gold watches glinting through it—was drawn tight across his place of business.

They huddled behind a telephone pole, both freezing. Isaac whimpered.

"See the big moon, Isaac. The whole sky is white."

He pointed but Isaac wouldn't look.

Mendel dreamed for a minute of the sky lit up, long sheets of light in all directions. Under the sky, in California, sat Uncle Leo drinking tea with lemon. Mendel felt warm but woke up cold.

Across the street stood an ancient brick synagogue.

He pounded on the huge door but no one appeared. He waited till he had breath and desperately knocked again. At last there were footsteps within, and the synagogue door creaked open on its massive brass hinges.

A darkly dressed sexton, holding a dripping candle, glared at them.

"Who knocks this time of night with so much noise on the synagogue door?"

Mendel told the sexton his troubles. "Please, I would like to speak to the rabbi."

"The rabbi is an old man. He sleeps now. His wife won't let you see him. Go home and come back tomorrow."

"To tomorrow I said goodbye already. I am a dying man."

Though the sexton seemed doubtful he pointed to an old wooden house next door. "In there he lives." He disappeared into the synagogue with his lit candle casting shadows around him.

Mendel, with Isaac clutching his sleeve, went up the wooden steps and rang the bell. After five minutes a big-faced, gray-haired bulky woman came out on the porch with a torn robe thrown over her nightdress. She emphatically said the rabbi was sleeping and could not be waked.

But as she was insisting, the rabbi himself tottered to the door. He listened a minute and said, "Who wants to see me let them come in."

They entered a cluttered room. The rabbi was an old skinny man with bent shoulders and a wisp of white beard. He wore a flannel nightgown and black skullcap; his feet were bare.

"Vey is mir" [Woe is me], his wife muttered. "Put on shoes or tomorrow comes sure pneumonia." She was a woman with a big belly, years younger than her husband. Staring at Isaac, she turned away.

Mendel apologetically related his errand. "All I need more is thirty-five dollars."

"Thirty-five?" said the rabbi's wife. "Why not thirty-five thousand? Who has so much money? My husband is a poor rabbi. The doctors take away every penny."

"Dear friend," said the rabbi, "if I had I would give you."

"I got already seventy," Mendal said, heavy-hearted. "All I need more is thirty-five."

"God will give you," said the rabbi.

"In the grave," said Mendel. "I need tonight. Come, Isaac."

"Wait," called the rabbi.

He hurried inside, came out with a fur-lined caftan, and handed it to Mendel.

"Yascha," shrieked his wife, "not your new coat!"

"I got my old one. Who needs two coats for one body?"

"Yascha, I am screaming—"

"Who can go among poor people, tell me, in a new coat?"

"Yascha," she cried, "what can this man do with your coat? He needs tonight the money. The pawnbrokers are asleep."

"So let him wake them up."

"No." She grabbed the coat from Mendel.

He held on to a sleeve, wrestling her for the coat. Her I know, Mendel thought. "Shylock," he muttered. Her eyes glittered.

The rabbi groaned and tottered dizzily. His wife cried out as Mendel yanked the coat from her hands.

"Run," cried the rabbi.

"Run, Isaac."

They ran out of the house and down the steps.

"Stop, you thief," called the rabbi's wife.

The rabbi pressed both hands to his temples and fell to the floor.

"Help!" his wife wept. "Heart attack! Help!"

But Mendel and Isaac ran through the streets with the rabbi's new fur-lined caftan. After them noiselessly ran Ginzburg.

It was very late when Mendel bought the train ticket in the only booth open.

There was no time to stop for a sandwich so Isaac ate his peanuts and they hurried to the train in the vast deserted station.

"So in the morning," Mendel gasped as they ran, "there comes a man that he sells sandwiches and coffee. Eat but get change. When reaches California the train, will be waiting for you on the station Uncle Leo. If you don't recognize him he will recognize you. Tell him I send best regards."

But when they arrived at the gate to the platform it was shut, the light out.

Mendel, groaning, beat on the gate with his fists.

"Too late," said the uniformed ticket collector, a bulky, bearded man with hairy nostrils and a fishy smell.

He pointed to the station clock. "Already past twelve."

"But I see standing there still the train," Mendel said, hopping in his grief.

"It just left—in one more minute."

"A minute is enough. Just open the gate."

"Too late I told you."

Mendel socked his bony chest with both hands. "With my whole heart I beg you this little favor."

"Favors you had enough already. For you the train is gone. You shoulda been dead already at midnight. I told you that yesterday. This is the best I can do."

"Ginzburg!" Mendel shrank from him.

"Who else?" The voice was metallic, eyes glittered, the expression amused.

"For myself," the old man begged, "I don't ask a thing. But what will happen to my boy?"

Ginzburg shrugged slightly. "What will happen happens. This isn't my responsibility. I got enough to think about without worrying about somebody on one cylinder."

"What then is your responsibility?"

"To create conditions. To make happen what happens. I ain't in the anthropomorphic business."

"Whatever business you in, where is your pity?"

"This ain't my commodity. The law is the law."

"Which law is this?"

"The cosmic universal law, goddamit, the one I got to follow myself."

"What kind of a law is it?" cried Mendel. "For God's sake, don't you understand what I went through in my life with this poor boy? Look at him. For thirty-nine years, since the day he was born, I wait for him to grow up, but he don't. Do you understand what this means in a father's heart? Why don't you let him go to his uncle?" His voice had risen and he was shouting.

Isaac mewled loudly.

"Better calm down or you'll hurt somebody's feelings," Ginzburg said with a wink toward Isaac.

"All my life," Mendel cried, his body trembling, "what did I have? I was poor. I suffered from my health. When I worked I worked too hard. When I didn't work was worse. My wife died a young woman. But I didn't ask from anybody nothing. Now I ask a small favor. Be so kind, Mr. Ginzburg."

The ticket collector was picking his teeth with a match stick.

"You ain't the only one, my friend, some got it worse than you. That's how it goes in this country."

"You dog you." Mendel lunged at Ginzburg's throat and began to choke. "You bastard, don't you understand what it means human?"

They struggled nose to nose, Ginzburg, though his astonished eyes bulged, began to laugh. "You pipsqueak nothing. I'll freeze you to pieces."

His eyes lit in rage and Mendel felt an unbearable cold like an icy dagger invading his body, all of his parts shriveling.

Now I die without helping Isaac.

A crowd gathered. Isaac yelped in fright.

Clinging to Ginzburg in his last agony, Mendel saw reflected in the ticket collector's eyes the depth of his terror. But he saw that Ginzburg, staring at himself in Mendel's eyes, saw mirrored in them the extent of his own awful wrath. He beheld a shimmering, starry, blinding light that produced darkness.

Ginzburg looked astounded. "Who me?"

His grip on the squirming old man slowly loosened, and Mendel, his heart barely beating, slumped to the ground.

"Go." Ginzburg muttered, "take him to the train."

"Let pass," he commanded a guard.

The crowd parted. Isaac helped his father up and they tottered down the steps to the platform where the train waited, lit and ready to go.

Mendel found Isaac a coach seat and hastily embraced him. "Help Uncle Leo, Isaakil. Also remember your father and mother."

"Be nice to him," he said to the conductor. "Show him where everything is."

He waited on the platform until the train began slowly to move. Isaac sat at the edge of his seat, his face strained in the direction of his journey. When the train was gone, Mendel ascended the stairs to see what had become of Ginzburg.

Questions

1. *Can this story be read as a religious drama? In this connection, consider the rabbi, the only person who helps Mendel. His compassion and his indifference to material things reveal him as a man of God. What does the supernatural Ginzburg represent?* 2. *What is the significance of the fact that Isaac, for whom Mendel is determined to provide before death claims him, is an idiot?* 3. *How do the various episodes in this story establish Mendel's character and prepare the reader for the final, climactic confrontation between Mendel and Ginzburg?* 4. *Mendel wins his battle with Ginzburg. What does that victory signify?*

Patriotism*

YUKIO MISHIMA   [1925–1970]

IN the twenty-eighth of February, 1936 (on the third day, that is, of the February Incident[1]), Lieutenant Shinji Takeyama of the Konoe Transport Battalion—profoundly disturbed by the knowledge that his closest colleagues had been with the mutineers from the beginning, and indignant at the imminent prospect of Imperial troops attacking Imperial troops—took his officer's sword and ceremonially disemboweled himself in the eight-mat room of his private residence in the sixth block of Aoba-chō, in Yotsuya Ward. His wife, Reiko, followed him, stabbing herself to death. The lieutenant's farewell note consisted of one sentence: "Long live the Imperial Forces." His wife's, after apologies for her unfilial conduct in thus preceding her parents to the grave, concluded: "The day which, for a soldier's wife, had to come, has come. . . ." The last moments of this heroic and dedicated couple were such as to make the gods themselves weep. The lieutenant's age, it should be noted, was thirty-one, his wife's twenty-three; and it was not half a year since the celebration of their marriage.

2

THOSE who saw the bride and bridegroom in the commemorative photograph—perhaps no less than those actually present at the lieutenant's wedding—had exclaimed in wonder at the bearing of this handsome couple. The lieutenant, majestic in military uniform, stood protectively beside his bride, his right hand resting upon his sword, his officer's cap held at his left side. His expression was severe, and his dark brows and wide-gazing eyes well conveyed the clear integrity of youth. For the beauty of the bride in her white over-robe no comparisons were adequate. In the eyes, round beneath soft brows, in the slender, finely shaped nose, and in the full lips, there was both sensuousness and refinement. One hand, emerging shyly from a sleeve of the over-robe, held a fan, and the tips of the fingers, clustering delicately, were like the bud of a moonflower.

After the suicide, people would take out this photograph and examine it, and sadly reflect that too often there was a curse on these seemingly flawless unions. Perhaps it was no more than imagination, but looking at the picture

---

*Translated by Geoffrey W. Sargeant.
1.   On February 26, 1936, a long period of political turmoil culminated in an attempted coup led by young officers. Units commanded by the rebels seized and held central Tokyo for a number of days, and numerous high-ranking government officials, including Lord Privy Seal Saitō, were assassinated. The mutiny was crushed by loyal troops, and the leaders were executed.

after the tragedy it almost seemed as if the two young people before the gold-lacquered screen were gazing, each with equal clarity, at the deaths which lay before them.

Thanks to the good offices of their go-between, Lieutenant General Ozeki, they had been able to set themselves up in a new home at Aoba-chō in Yotsuya. "New home" is perhaps misleading. It was an old three-room rented house backing onto a small garden. As neither the six- nor the four-and-a-half mat room downstairs was favored by the sun, they used the upstairs eight-mat room as both bedroom and guest room. There was no maid, so Reiko was left alone to guard the house in her husband's absence.

The honeymoon trip was dispensed with on the grounds that these were times of national emergency. The two of them had spent the first night of their marriage at this house. Before going to bed, Shinji, sitting erect on the floor with his sword laid before him, had bestowed upon his wife a soldierly lecture. A woman who had become the wife of a soldier should know and resolutely accept that her husband's death might come at any moment. It could be tomorrow. It could be the day after. But, no matter when it came—he asked—was she steadfast in her resolve to accept it? Reiko rose to her feet, pulled open a drawer of the cabinet, and took out what was the most prized of her new possessions, the dagger her mother had given her. Returning to her place, she laid the dagger without a word on the mat before her, just as her husband had laid his sword. A silent understanding was achieved at once and the lieutenant never again sought to test his wife's resolve.

In the first few months of her marriage Reiko's beauty grew daily more radiant, shining serene like the moon after rain.

As both were possessed of young, vigorous bodies, their relationship was passionate. Nor was this merely a matter of the night. On more than one occasion, returning home straight from maneuvers, and begrudging even the time it took to remove his mud-splashed uniform, the lieutenant had pushed his wife to the floor almost as soon as he had entered the house. Reiko was equally ardent in her response. For a little more or a little less than a month, from the first night of their marriage Reiko knew happiness, and the lieutenant, seeing this, was happy too.

Reiko's body was white and pure, and her swelling breasts conveyed a firm and chaste refusal; but, upon consent, those breasts were lavish with their intimate, welcoming warmth. Even in bed these two were frighteningly and awesomely serious. In the very midst of wild, intoxicating passions, their hearts were sober and serious.

By day the lieutenant would think of his wife in the brief rest periods between training; and all day long, at home, Reiko would recall the image of her husband. Even when apart, however, they had only to look at the wedding photograph for their happiness to be once more confirmed. Reiko felt not the slightest surprise that a man who had been a complete stranger until a few months ago should now have become the sun about which her whole world revolved.

All these things had a moral basis, and were in accordance with the Education Rescript's[2] injunction that "husband and wife should be harmonious." Not once did Reiko contradict her husband, nor did the lieutenant ever find reason to scold his wife. On the god shelf below the stairway, alongside the tablet from the Great Ise Shrine,[3] were set photographs of their Imperial Majesties, and regularly every morning, before leaving for duty, the lieutenant would stand with his wife at this hallowed place and together they would bow their heads low. The offering water was renewed each morning, and the sacred sprig of sasaki was always green and fresh. Their lives were lived beneath the solemn protection of the gods and were filled with an intense happiness which set every fiber in their bodies trembling.

3

ALTHOUGH Lord Privy Seal Saitō's house was in their neighborhood, neither of them heard any noise of gunfire on the morning of February 26. It was a bugle, sounding muster in the dim, snowy dawn, when the ten-minute tragedy had already ended, which first disrupted the lieutenant's slumbers. Leaping at once from his bed, and without speaking a word, the lieutenant donned his uniform, buckled on the sword held ready for him by his wife, and hurried swiftly out into the snow-covered streets of the still darkened morning. He did not return until the evening of the twenty-eighth.

Later, from the radio news, Reiko learned the full extent of this sudden eruption of violence. Her life throughout the subsequent two days was lived alone, in complete tranquillity, and behind locked doors.

In the lieutenant's face, as he hurried silently out into the snowy morning, Reiko had read the determination to die. If her husband did not return, her own decision was made: she too would die. Quietly she attended to the disposition of her personal possessions. She chose her sets of visiting kimonos as keepsakes for friends of her schooldays, and she wrote a name and address on the stiff paper wrapping in which each was folded. Constantly admonished by her husband never to think of the morrow, Reiko had not even kept a diary and was now denied the pleasure of assiduously rereading her record of the happiness of the past few months and consigning each page to the fire as she did so. Ranged across the top of the radio were a small china dog, a rabbit, a squirrel, a bear, and a fox. There were also a small vase and a water pitcher. These comprised Reiko's one and only collection. But it would hardly do, she imagined, to give such things as keepsakes. Nor again would it be quite proper to ask specifically for them to be included in the coffin. It seemed to Reiko, as these thoughts passed through her mind, that the expressions on the small animals' faces grew even more lost and forlorn.

---

2. The Education Rescript was a code promulgated during the Meiji, the reign of Emperor Mutsuhito which lasted from 1867 to 1912. The period is regarded as an historic era in the development of modern Japan.
3. The Great Ise Shrine is the highest ranking shrine in Japan. The emperor's ancestors were buried there.

Reiko took the squirrel in her hand and looked at it. And then, her thoughts turning to a realm far beyond these childlike affections, she gazed up into the distance at the great sunlike principle which her husband embodied. She was ready, and happy, to be hurtled along to her destruction in that gleaming sun chariot—but now, for these few moments of solitude, she allowed herself to luxuriate in this innocent attachment to trifles. The time when she had genuinely loved these things, however, was long past. Now she merely loved the memory of having once loved them, and their place in her heart had been filled by more intense passions, by a more frenzied happiness. . . . For Reiko had never, even to herself, thought of those soaring joys of the flesh as a mere pleasure. The February cold, and the icy touch of the china squirrel, had numbed Reiko's slender fingers; yet, even so, in her lower limbs, beneath the ordered repetition of the pattern which crossed the skirt of her trim *meisen* kimono, she could feel now, as she thought of the lieutenant's powerful arms reaching out toward her, a hot moistness of the flesh which defied the snows.

She was not in the least afraid of the death hovering in her mind. Waiting alone at home, Reiko firmly believed that everything her husband was feeling or thinking now, his anguish and distress, was leading her—just as surely as the power in his flesh—to a welcome death. She felt as if her body could melt away with ease and be transformed to the merest fraction of her husband's thought.

Listening to the frequent announcements on the radio, she heard the names of several of her husband's colleagues mentioned among those of the insurgents. This was news of death. She followed the developments closely, wondering anxiously, as the situation became daily more irrevocable, why no Imperial ordinance was sent down, and watching what had at first been taken as a movement to restore the nation's honor come gradually to be branded with the infamous name of mutiny. There was no communication from the regiment. At any moment, it seemed, fighting might commence in the city streets where the remains of the snow still lay.

Toward sundown on the twenty-eighth Reiko was startled by a furious pounding on the front door. She hurried downstairs. As she pulled with fumbling fingers at the bolt, the shape dimly outlined beyond the frosted-glass panel made no sound, but she knew it was her husband. Reiko had never known the bolt on the sliding door to be so stiff. Still it resisted. The door just would not open.

In a moment, almost before she knew she had succeeded, the lieutenant was standing before her on the cement floor inside the porch, muffled in a khaki greatcoat, his top boots heavy with slush from the street. Closing the door behind him, he returned the bolt once more to its socket. With what significance, Reiko did not understand.

"Welcome home."

Reiko bowed deeply, but her husband made no response. As he had already unfastened his sword and was about to remove his greatcoat, Reiko moved around behind to assist. The coat, which was cold and damp and had lost the odor of horse dung it normally exuded when exposed to the sun, weighed heavily upon her arm. Draping it across a hanger, and cradling the sword and leather belt in her sleeves, she waited while her husband removed his top boots and then followed behind him into the "living room." This was the six-mat room downstairs.

Seen in the clear light from the lamp, her husband's face, covered with a heavy growth of bristle, was almost unrecognizably wasted and thin. The cheeks were hollow, their luster and resilience gone. In his normal good spirits he would have changed into old clothes as soon as he was home and have pressed her to get supper at once, but now he sat before the table still in his uniform, his head drooping dejectedly. Reiko refrained from asking whether she should prepare the supper.

After an interval the lieutenant spoke.

"I knew nothing. They hadn't asked me to join. Perhaps out of consideration, because I was newly married. Kanō, and Homma too, and Yamaguchi."

Reiko recalled momentarily the faces of high-spirited young officers, friends of her husband, who had come to the house occasionally as guests.

"There may be an Imperial ordinance sent down tomorrow. They'll be posted as rebels, I imagine. I shall be in command of a unit with orders to attack them. . . . I can't do it. It's impossible to do a thing like that."

He spoke again.

"They've taken me off guard duty, and I have permission to return home for one night. Tomorrow morning, without question, I must leave to join the attack. I can't do it, Reiko."

Reiko sat erect with lowered eyes. She understood clearly that her husband had spoken of his death. The lieutenant was resolved. Each word, being rooted in death, emerged sharply and with powerful significance against this dark, unmovable background. Although the lieutenant was speaking of his dilemma, already there was no room in his mind for vacillation.

However, there was a clarity, like the clarity of a stream fed from melting snows, in the silence which rested between them. Sitting in his own home after the long two-day ordeal, and looking across at the face of his beautiful wife, the lieutenant was for the first time experiencing true peace of mind. For he had at once known, though she said nothing, that his wife divined the resolve which lay beneath his words.

"Well, then . . ." The lieutenant's eyes opened wide. Despite his exhaustion they were strong and clear, and now for the first time they looked straight into the eyes of his wife. "Tonight I shall cut my stomach."

Reiko did not flinch.

Her round eyes showed tension, as taut as the clang of a bell.

"I am ready," she said. "I ask permission to accompany you."

The lieutenant felt almost mesmerized by the strength in those eyes. His words flowed swiftly and easily, like the utterances of a man in delirium, and it was beyond his understanding how permission in a matter of such weight could be expressed so casually.

"Good. We'll go together. But I want you as a witness, first, for my own suicide. Agreed?"

When this was said a sudden release of abundant happiness welled up in both their hearts. Reiko was deeply affected by the greatness of her husband's trust in her. It was vital for the lieutenant, whatever else might happen, that there should be no irregularity in his death. For that reason there had to be a witness. The fact that he had chosen his wife for this was the first mark of his trust. The second, and even greater mark, was that though he had pledged that they should die together he did not intend to kill his wife first—he had deferred her death to a time when he would no longer be there to verify it. If the lieutenant had been a suspicious husband, he would doubtless, as in the usual suicide pact, have chosen to kill his wife first.

When Reiko said, "I ask permission to accompany you," the lieutenant felt these words to be the final fruit of the education which he had himself given his wife, starting on the first night of their marriage, and which had schooled her, when the moment came, to say what had to be said without a shadow of hesitation. This flattered the lieutenant's opinion of himself as a self-reliant man. He was not so romantic or conceited as to imagine that the words were spoken spontaneously, out of love for her husband.

With happiness welling almost too abundantly in their hearts, they could not help smiling at each other. Reiko felt as if she had returned to her wedding night.

Before her eyes was neither pain nor death. She seemed to see only a free and limitless expanse opening out into vast distances.

"The water is hot. Will you take your bath now?"

"Ah yes, of course."

"And supper . . . ?"

The words were delivered in such level, domestic tones that the lieutenant came near to thinking, for the fraction of a second, that everything had been a hallucination.

"I don't think we'll need supper. But perhaps you could warm some sake?"

"As you wish."

As Reiko rose and took a *tanzen* gown from the cabinet for after the bath, she purposely directed her husband's attention to the opened drawer. The lieutenant rose, crossed to the cabinet, and looked inside. From the ordered array of paper wrappings he read, one by one, the addresses of the keepsakes. There was no grief in the lieutenant's response to this demonstration of heroic resolve. His heart was filled with tenderness. Like a husband who is proudly shown the childish purchases of a young wife, the lieutenant, overwhelmed by affection, lovingly embraced his wife from behind and implanted a kiss upon her neck.

Reiko felt the roughness of the lieutenant's unshaven skin against her neck. This sensation, more than being just a thing of this world, was for Reiko almost the world itself, but now—with the feeling that it was soon to be lost forever—it had freshness beyond all her experience. Each moment had its own vital strength, and the senses in every corner of her body were reawakened. Accepting her husband's caresses from behind, Reiko raised herself on the tips of her toes, letting the vitality seep through her entire body.

"First the bath, and then, after some sake . . . lay out the bedding upstairs, will you?"

The lieutenant whispered the words into his wife's ear. Reiko silently nodded.

Flinging off his uniform, the lieutenant went to the bath. To faint background noises of slopping water Reiko tended the charcoal brazier in the living room and began the preparations for warming the sake.

Taking the *tanzen*, a sash, and some underclothes, she went to the bathroom to ask how the water was. In the midst of a coiling cloud of steam the lieutenant was sitting cross-legged on the floor, shaving, and she could dimly discern the rippling movements of the muscles on his damp, powerful back as they responded to the movement of his arms.

There was nothing to suggest a time of any special significance. Reiko, going busily about her tasks, was preparing side dishes from odds and ends in stock. Her hands did not tremble. If anything, she managed even more efficiently and smoothly than usual. From time to time, it is true, there was a strange throbbing deep within her breast. Like distant lightning, it had a moment of sharp intensity and then vanished without trace. Apart from that, nothing was in any way out of the ordinary.

The lieutenant, shaving in the bathroom, felt his warmed body miraculously healed at last of the desperate tiredness of the days of indecision and filled—in spite of the death which lay ahead—with pleasurable anticipation. The sound of his wife going about her work came to him faintly. A healthy physical craving, submerged for two days, reasserted itself.

The lieutenant was confident there had been no impurity in that joy they had experienced when resolving upon death. They had both sensed at that moment—though not, of course, in any clear and conscious way—that those permissible pleasures which they shared in private were once more beneath the protection of Righteousness and Divine Power, and of a complete and unassailable morality. On looking into each other's eyes and discovering there an honorable death, they had felt themselves safe once more behind steel walls which none could destroy, encased in an impenetrable armor of Beauty and Truth. Thus, so far from seeing any inconsistency or conflict between the urges of his flesh and the sincerity of his patriotism, the lieutenant was even able to regard the two as parts of the same thing.

Thrusting his face close to the dark, cracked, misted wall mirror, the lieutenant shaved himself with great care. This would be his death face. There must be no unsightly blemishes. The clean-shaven face gleamed once more with a youthful luster, seeming to brighten the darkness of the mirror. There was a certain elegance, he even felt, in the association of death with this radiantly healthy face.

Just as it looked now, this would become his death face! Already, in fact, it had half departed from the lieutenant's personal possession and had become the bust above a dead soldier's memorial. As an experiment he closed his eyes tight. Everything was wrapped in blackness, and he was no longer a living, seeing creature.

Returning from the bath, the traces of the shave glowing faintly blue beneath his smooth cheeks, he seated himself beside the now well-kindled charcoal brazier. Busy though Reiko was, he noticed, she had found time lightly to touch up her face. Her cheeks were gay and her lips moist. There was no shadow of sadness to be seen. Truly, the lieutenant felt, as he saw this mark of his young wife's passionate nature, he had chosen the wife he ought to have chosen.

As soon as the lieutenant had drained his sake cup he offered it to Reiko. Reiko had never before tasted sake, but she accepted without hesitation and sipped timidly.

"Come here," the lieutenant said.

Reiko moved to her husband's side and was embraced as she leaned backward across his lap. Her breast was in violent commotion, as if sadness, joy, and the potent sake were mingling and reacting within her. The lieutenant looked down into his wife's face. It was the last face he would see in this world, the last face he would see of his wife. The lieutenant scrutinized the face minutely, with the eyes of a traveler bidding farewell to splendid vistas which he will never revisit. It was a face he could not tire of looking at—the features regular yet not cold, the lips lightly closed with a soft strength. The lieutenant kissed those lips, unthinkingly. And suddenly, though there was not the slightest distortion of the face into the unsightliness of sobbing, he noticed that tears were welling slowly from beneath the long lashes of the closed eyes and brimming over into a glistening stream.

When, a little later, the lieutenant urged that they should move to the upstairs bedroom, his wife replied that she would follow after taking a bath. Climbing the stairs alone to the bedroom, where the air was already warmed by the gas heater, the lieutenant lay down on the bedding with arms outstretched and legs apart. Even the time at which he lay waiting for his wife to join him was no later and no earlier than usual.

He folded his hands beneath his head and gazed at the dark boards of the ceiling in the dimness beyond the range of the standard lamp. Was it death he was now waiting for? Or a wild ecstasy of the senses? The two seemed to overlap, almost as if the object of this bodily desire was death itself. But, however that might be, it was certain that never before had the lieutenant tasted such total freedom.

There was the sound of a car outside the window. He could hear the screech of its tires skidding in the snow piled at the side of the street. The sound of its horn re-echoed from near-by walls. . . . Listening to these noises he had the feeling that this house rose like a solitary island in the ocean of a society going as restlessly about its business as ever. All around, vastly and untidily, stretched the country for which he grieved. He was to give his life for it. But would that great country, with which he was prepared to remonstrate to the extent of destroying himself, take the slightest heed of his death? He did not know; and it did not matter. His was a battlefield without glory, a battlefield where none could display deeds of valor: it was the front line of the spirit.

Reiko's footsteps sounded on the stairway. The steep stairs in this old house creaked badly. There were fond memories in that creaking, and many a time, while waiting in bed, the lieutenant had listened to its welcome sound. At the thought that he would hear it no more he listened with intense concentration, striving for every corner of every moment of this precious time to be filled with the sound of those soft footfalls on the creaking stairway. The moments seemed transformed to jewels, sparkling with inner light.

Reiko wore a Nagoya sash about the waist of her *yukata*, but as the lieutenant reached toward it, its redness sobered by the dimness of the light, Reiko's hand moved to his assistance and the sash fell away, slithering swiftly to the floor. As she stood before him, still in her *yukata*, the lieutenant inserted his hands through the side slits beneath each sleeve, intending to embrace her as she was; but at the touch of his finger tips upon the warm naked flesh, and as the armpits closed gently about his hands, his whole body was suddenly aflame.

In a few moments the two lay naked before the glowing gas heater.

Neither spoke the thought, but their hearts, their bodies, and their pounding breasts blazed with the knowledge that this was the very last time. It was as if the words "The Last Time" were spelled out, in invisible brushstrokes, across every inch of their bodies.

The lieutenant drew his wife close and kissed her vehemently. As their tongues explored each other's mouths, reaching out into the smooth, moist interior, they felt as if the still unknown agonies of death had tempered their senses to the keenness of red-hot steel. The agonies they could not yet feel, the distant pains of death, had refined their awareness of pleasure.

"This is the last time I shall see your body," said the lieutenant. "Let me look at it closely." And, tilting the shade on the lampstand to one side, he directed the rays along the full length of Reiko's outstretched form.

Reiko lay still with her eyes closed. The light from the low lamp clearly revealed the majestic sweep of her white flesh. The lieutenant, not without a touch of egocentricity, rejoiced that he would never see this beauty crumble in death.

At his leisure, the lieutenant allowed the unforgettable spectacle to engrave itself upon his mind. With one hand he fondled the hair, with the other he softly stroked the magnificent face, implanting kisses here and there where his eyes lingered. The quiet coldness of the high, tapering forehead, the closed eyes with their long lashes beneath faintly etched brows, the set of the finely shaped nose, the gleam of teeth glimpsed between full, regular lips, the soft cheeks and the small, wise chin . . . these things conjured up in the lieutenant's mind the vision of a truly radiant death face, and again and again he pressed his lips tight against the white throat—where Reiko's own hand was soon to strike—and the throat reddened faintly beneath his kisses. Returning to the mouth he laid his lips against it with the gentlest of pressures, and moved them rhythmically over Reiko's with the light rolling motion of a small boat. If he closed his eyes, the world became a rocking cradle.

Wherever the lieutenant's eyes moved his lips faithfully followed. The high, swelling breasts, surmounted by nipples like the buds of a wild cherry, hardened as the lieutenant's lips closed about them. The arms flowed smoothly downward from each side of the breast, tapering toward the wrists, yet losing nothing of their roundness or symmetry, and at their tips were those delicate fingers which had held the fan at the wedding ceremony. One by one, as the lieutenant kissed them, the fingers withdrew behind their neighbor as if in shame. . . . The natural hollow curving between the bosom and the stomach carried in its lines a suggestion not only of softness but of resilient strength, and while it gave forewarning of the rich curves spreading outward from here to the hips it had, in itself, an appearance only of restraint and proper discipline. The whiteness and richness of the stomach and hips was like milk brimming in a great bowl, and the sharply shadowed dip of the navel could have been the fresh impress of a raindrop, fallen there that very moment. Where the shadows gathered more thickly, hair clustered, gentle and sensitive, and as the agitation mounted in the now no longer passive body there hung over this region a scent like the smoldering of fragrant blossoms, growing steadily more pervasive.

At length, in a tremulous voice, Reiko spoke.

"Show me. . . . Let me look too, for the last time."

Never before had he heard from his wife's lips so strong and unequivocal a request. It was as if something which her modesty had wished to keep hidden to the end had suddenly burst its bonds of constraint. The lieutenant obediently lay back and surrendered himself to his wife. Lithely she raised her white, trembling body, and—burning with an innocent desire to return to her husband what he had done for her—placed two white fingers on the lieutenant's eyes, which gazed fixedly up at her, and gently stroked them shut.

Suddenly overwhelmed by tenderness, her cheeks flushed by a dizzying uprush of emotion, Reiko threw her arms about the lieutenant's close-cropped head. The bristly hairs rubbed painfully against her breast, the prominent nose was cold as it dug into her flesh, and his breath was hot. Relaxing her embrace, she gazed down at her husband's masculine face. The severe brows, the closed eyes, the splendid bridge of the nose, the shapely lips drawn firmly together . . . the blue, cleanshaven cheeks reflecting the light and gleaming smoothly. Reiko kissed each of these. She kissed the broad nape of the neck, the strong, erect shoulders, the powerful chest with its twin circles like shields and its russet nipples. In the armpits, deeply shadowed by the ample flesh of the shoulders and chest, a sweet and melancholy odor emanated from the growth of hair, and in the sweetness of this odor was contained, somehow, the essence of young death. The lieutenant's naked skin glowed like a field of barley, and everywhere the muscles showed in sharp relief, converging on the lower abdomen about the small, unassuming navel. Gazing at the youthful, firm stomach, modestly covered by a vigorous growth of hair, Reiko thought of it as it was soon to be, cruelly cut by the sword, and she laid her head upon it, sobbing in pity, and bathed it with kisses.

At the touch of his wife's tears upon his stomach the lieutenant felt ready to endure with courage the cruelest agonies of his suicide.

What ecstasies they experienced after these tender exchanges may well be imagined. The lieutenant raised himself and enfolded his wife in a powerful embrace, her body now limp with exhaustion after her grief and tears. Passionately they held their faces close, rubbing cheek against cheek. Reiko's body was trembling. Their breasts, moist with sweat, were tightly joined, and every inch of the young and beautiful bodies had become so much one with the other that it seemed impossible there should ever again be a separation. Reiko cried out. From the heights they plunged into the abyss, and from the abyss they took wing and soared once more to dizzying heights. The lieutenant panted like the regimental standard-bearer on a route march. . . . As one cycle ended, almost immediately a new wave of passion would be generated, and together—with no trace of fatigue—they would climb again in a single breathless movement to the very summit.

4

WHEN the lieutenant at last turned away, it was not from weariness. For one thing, he was anxious not to undermine the considerable strength he would need in carrying out his suicide. For another, he would have been sorry to mar the sweetness of these last memories by overindulgence.

Since the lieutenant had clearly desisted, Reiko too, with her usual compliance, followed his example. The two lay naked on their backs, with fingers interlaced, staring fixedly at the dark ceiling. The room was warm from the heater, and even when the sweat had ceased to pour from their bodies they felt no cold. Outside, in the hushed night, the sounds of passing traffic had ceased. Even the noises of the trains and streetcars around Yotsuya station did not penetrate this far. After echoing through the region bounded by the moat, they were lost in the heavily wooded park fronting the broad driveway before Akasaka Palace. It was hard to believe in the tension gripping this whole quarter, where the two factions of the bitterly divided Imperial Army now confronted each other, poised for battle.

Savoring the warmth glowing within themselves, they lay still and recalled the ecstasies they had just known. Each moment of the experience was relived. They remembered the taste of kisses which had never wearied, the touch of naked flesh, episode after episode of dizzying bliss. But already, from the dark boards of the ceiling, the face of death was peering down. These joys had been final, and their bodies would never know them again. Not that joy of this intensity—and the same thought had occurred to them both—was ever likely to be reexperienced, even if they should live on to old age.

The feel of their fingers intertwined—this too would soon be lost. Even the wood-grain patterns they now gazed at on the dark ceiling boards would be taken from them. They could feel death edging in, nearer and nearer.

There could be no hesitation now. They must have the courage to reach out to death themselves, and to seize it.

"Well, let's make our preparations," said the lieutenant. The note of determination in the words was unmistakable, but at the same time Reiko had never heard her husband's voice so warm and tender.

After they had risen, a variety of tasks awaited them.

The lieutenant, who had never once before helped with the bedding, now cheerfully slid back the door of the closet, lifted the mattress across the room by himself, and stowed it away inside.

Reiko turned off the gas heater and put away the lamp standard. During the lieutenant's absence she had arranged this room carefully, sweeping and dusting it to a fresh cleanness, and now—if one overlooked the rosewood table drawn into one corner—the eight-mat room gave all the appearance of a reception room ready to welcome an important guest.

"We've seen some drinking here, haven't we? With Kanō and Homma and Noguchi . . ."

"Yes, they were great drinkers, all of them."

"We'll be meeting them before long, in the other world. They'll tease us, I imagine, when they find I've brought you with me."

Descending the stairs, the lieutenant turned to look back into this calm clean room, now brightly illuminated by the ceiling lamp. There floated across his mind the faces of the young officers who had drunk there, and laughed, and innocently bragged. He had never dreamed then that he would one day cut open his stomach in this room.

In the two rooms downstairs husband and wife busied themselves smoothly and serenely with their respective preparations. The lieutenant went to the toilet, and then to the bathroom to wash. Meanwhile Reiko folded away her husband's padded robe, placed his uniform tunic, his trousers, and a newly cut bleached loincloth in the bathroom, and set out sheets of paper on the living-room table for the farewell notes. Then she removed the lid from the writing box and began rubbing ink from the ink tablet. She had already decided upon the wording of her own note.

Reiko's fingers pressed hard upon the cold gilt letters of the ink tablet, and the water in the shallow well at once darkened, as if a black cloud had spread across it. She stopped thinking that this repeated action, this pressure from her fingers, this rise and fall of faint sound, was all and solely for death. It was a routine domestic task, a simple paring away of time until death should finally stand before her. But somehow, in the increasingly smooth motion of the tablet rubbing on the stone, and in the scent from the thickening ink, there was unspeakable darkness.

Neat in his uniform, which he now wore next to his skin, the lieutenant emerged from the bathroom. Without a word he seated himself at the table, bolt upright, took a brush in his hand, and stared undecidedly at the paper before him.

Reiko took a white silk kimono with her and entered the bathroom. When she reappeared in the living room, clad in the white kimono and with her face lightly made up, the farewell note lay completed on the table beneath the lamp. The thick black brushstrokes said simply:

"Long Live the Imperial Forces—Army Lieutenant Takeyama Shinji."

While Reiko sat opposite him writing her own note, the lieutenant gazed in silence, intensely serious, at the controlled movement of his wife's pale fingers as they manipulated the brush.

With their respective notes in their hands—the lieutenant's sword strapped to his side, Reiko's small dagger thrust into the sash of her white kimono—the two of them stood before the god shelf and silently prayed. Then they put out all the downstairs lights. As he mounted the stairs the lieutenant turned his head and gazed back at the striking, white-clad figure of his wife, climbing behind him, with lowered eyes, from the darkness beneath.

The farewell notes were laid side by side in the alcove of the upstairs room. They wondered whether they ought not to remove the hanging scroll, but since it had been written by their go-between, Lieutenant General Ozeki, and consisted, moreover, of two Chinese characters signifying "Sincerity," they left it where it was. Even if it were to become stained with splashes of blood, they felt that the lieutenant general would understand.

The lieutenant sitting erect with his back to the alcove, laid his sword on the floor before him.

Reiko sat facing him, a mat's width away. With the rest of her so severely white the touch of rouge on her lips seemed remarkably seductive.

Across the dividing mat they gazed intently into each other's eyes. The lieutenant's sword lay before his knees. Seeing it, Reiko recalled their first night and was overwhelmed with sadness. The lieutenant spoke, in a hoarse voice:

"As I have no second to help me I shall cut deep. It may look unpleasant, but please do not panic. Death of any sort is a fearful thing to watch. You must not be discouraged by what you see. Is that all right?"

"Yes."

Reiko nodded deeply.

Looking at the slender white figure of his wife the lieutenant experienced a bizarre excitement. What he was about to perform was an act in his public capacity as a soldier, something he had never previously shown his wife. It called for a resolution equal to the courage to enter battle; it was a death of no less degree and quality than death in the front line. It was his conduct on the battlefield that he was now to display.

Momentarily the thought led the lieutenant to a strange fantasy. A lonely death on the battlefield, a death beneath the eyes of his beautiful wife . . . in the sensation that he was now to die in these two dimensions, realizing an impossible union of them both, there was sweetness beyond words. This must be the very pinnacle of good fortune, he thought. To have every moment of his death observed by those beautiful eyes—it was like being borne to death on a gentle, fragrant breeze. There was some special favor here. He did not understand precisely what it was, but it was a domain unknown to others: a dispensation granted to no one else had been permitted to himself. In the radiant, bridelike figure of his white-robed wife the lieutenant seemed to see a vision of all those things he had loved and for which he was to lay down his life—the Imperial Household, the Nation, the Army Flag. All these, no less than the wife who sat before him, were presences observing him closely with clear and never-faltering eyes.

Reiko too was gazing intently at her husband, so soon to die, and she thought that never in this world had she seen anything so beautiful. The lieutenant always looked well in uniform, but now, as he contemplated death with severe brows and firmly closed lips, he revealed what was perhaps masculine beauty at its most superb.

"It's time to go," the lieutenant said at last.

Reiko bent her body low to the mat in a deep bow. She could not raise her face. She did not wish to spoil her make-up with tears, but the tears could not be held back.

When at length she looked up she saw hazily through the tears that her husband had wound a white bandage around the blade of his now unsheathed sword, leaving five or six inches of naked steel showing at the point.

Resting the sword in its cloth wrapping on the mat before him, the lieutenant rose from his knees, resettled himself cross-legged, and unfastened the hooks of his uniform collar. His eyes no longer saw his wife. Slowly, one by one, he undid the flat brass buttons. The dusky brown chest was revealed, and then the stomach. He unclasped his belt and undid the buttons of his trousers. The pure whiteness of the thickly coiled loincloth showed itself. The lieutenant pushed the cloth down with both hands, further to ease his stomach, and then reached for the white-bandaged blade of his sword. With his left hand he massaged his abdomen, glancing downward as he did so.

To reassure himself on the sharpness of his sword's cutting edge the lieutenant folded back the left trouser flap, exposing a little of his thigh, and lightly drew the blade across the skin. Blood welled up in the wound at once, and several streaks of red trickled downward, glistening in the strong light.

It was the first time Reiko had ever seen her husband's blood, and she felt a violent throbbing in her chest. She looked at her husband's face. The lieutenant was looking at the blood with calm appraisal. For a moment—though thinking at the same time that it was hollow comfort—Reiko experienced a sense of relief.

The lieutenant's eyes fixed his wife with an intense, hawk-like stare. Moving the sword around to his front, he raised himself slightly on his hips and let the upper half of his body lean over the sword point. That he was mustering his whole strength was apparent from the angry tension of the uniform at his shoulders. The lieutenant aimed to strike deep into the left of his stomach. His sharp cry pierced the silence of the room.

Despite the effort he had himself put into the blow, the lieutenant had the impression that someone else had struck the side of his stomach agonizingly with a thick rod of iron. For a second or so his head reeled and he had no idea what had happened. The five or six inches of naked point had vanished completely into his flesh, and the white bandage, gripped in his clenched fist, pressed directly against his stomach.

He returned to consciousness. The blade had certainly pierced the wall of the stomach, he thought. His breathing was difficult, his chest thumped violently, and in some far deep region, which he could hardly believe was a part of himself, a fearful and excruciating pain came welling up as if the ground had split open to disgorge a boiling stream of molten rock. The pain came suddenly nearer, with terrifying speed. The lieutenant bit his lower lip and stifled an instinctive moan.

Was this *seppuku*?—he was thinking. It was a sensation of utter chaos, as if the sky had fallen on his head and the world was reeling drunkenly. His will power and courage, which had seemed so robust before he made the incision, had now dwindled to something like a single hairlike thread of steel, and he was assailed by the uneasy feeling that he must advance along this thread, clinging to it with desperation. His clenched fist had grown moist. Looking down, he saw that both his hand and the cloth were drenched in blood. His loincloth too was dyed a deep red. It struck him as incredible that, amidst this terrible agony, things which could be seen could still be seen, and existing things existed still.

The moment the lieutenant thrust the sword into his left side and she saw the deathly pallor fall across his face, like an abruptly lowered curtain, Reiko had to struggle to prevent herself from rushing to his side. Whatever happened, she must watch. She must be a witness. That was the duty her husband had lain upon her. Opposite her, a mat's space away, she could clearly see her husband biting his lip to stifle the pain. The pain was there, with absolute certainty, before her eyes. And Reiko had no means of rescuing him from it.

The sweat glistened on her husband's forehead. The lieutenant closed his eyes, and then opened them again, as if experimenting. The eyes had lost their luster, and seemed innocent and empty like the eyes of a small animal.

The agony before Reiko's eyes burned as strong as the summer sun, utterly remote from the grief which seemed to be tearing herself apart within. The pain grew steadily in stature, stretching upward. Reiko felt that her husband had already become a man in a separate world, a man whose whole being had been resolved into pain, a prisoner in a cage of pain where no hand could reach out to him. But Reiko felt no pain at all. Her grief was not pain. As she thought about this, Reiko began to feel as if someone had raised a cruel wall of glass high between herself and her husband.

Ever since her marriage her husband's existence had been her own existence, and every breath of his had been a breath drawn by herself. But now, while her husband's existence in pain was a vivid reality, Reiko could find in this grief of hers no certain proof at all of her own existence.

With only his right hand on the sword the lieutenant began to cut sideways across his stomach. But as the blade became entangled with the entrails it was pushed constantly outward by their soft resilience; and the lieutenant realized that it would be necessary, as he cut, to use both hands to keep the point pressed deep into his stomach. He pulled the blade across. It did not cut as easily as he had expected. He directed the strength of his whole body into his right hand and pulled again. There was a cut of three or four inches.

The pain spread slowly outward from the inner depths until the whole stomach reverberated. It was like the wild clanging of a bell. Or like a thousand bells which jangled simultaneously at every breath he breathed and every throb of his pulse, rocking his whole being. The lieutenant could no longer stop himself from moaning. But by now the blade had cut its way through to below the navel, and when he noticed this he felt a sense of satisfaction, and a renewal of courage.

The volume of blood had steadily increased, and now it spurted from the wound as if propelled by the beat of the pulse. The mat before the lieutenant was drenched red with splattered blood, and more blood overflowed onto it from pools which gathered in folds of the lieutenant's khaki trousers. A spot, like a bird, came flying across to Reiko and settled on the lap of her white silk kimono.

By the time the lieutenant had at last drawn the sword across to the right side of his stomach, the blade was already cutting shallow and had revealed its naked tip, slippery with blood and grease. But, suddenly stricken by a fit of vomiting, the lieutenant cried out hoarsely. The vomiting made the fierce pain fiercer still, and the stomach, which had thus far remained firm and compact, now abruptly heaved, opening wide its wound, and the entrails burst through, as if the wound too were vomiting. Seemingly ignorant of their master's suffering, the entrails gave an impression of robust health and almost disagreeable vitality as they slipped smoothly out and spilled over into the crotch. The lieutenant's head drooped, his shoulders heaved, his eyes opened to narrow slits, and a thin trickle of saliva dribbled from his mouth. The gold markings on his epaulettes caught the light and glinted.

Blood was scattered everywhere. The lieutenant was soaked in it to his knees, and he sat now in a crumpled and listless posture, one hand on the floor. A raw smell filled the room. The lieutenant, his head drooping, retched repeatedly, and the movement showed vividly in his shoulders. The blade of the sword, now pushed back by the entrails and exposed to its tip, was still in the lieutenant's right hand.

It would be difficult to imagine a more heroic sight than that of the lieutenant at this moment, as he mustered his strength and flung back his head. The movement was performed with sudden violence, and the back of his head struck with a sharp crack against the alcove pillar. Reiko had been sitting until now with her face lowered, gazing in fascination at the tide of blood advancing toward her knees, but the sound took her by surprise and she looked up.

The lieutenant's face was not the face of a living man. The eyes were hollow, the skin parched, the once so lustrous cheeks and lips the color of dried mud. The right hand alone was moving. Laboriously gripping the sword, it hovered shakily in the air like the hand of a marionette and strove to direct the point at the base of the lieutenant's throat. Reiko watched her husband make this last, most heart-rending, futile exertion. Glistening with blood and grease, the point was thrust at the throat again and again. And each time it missed its aim. The strength to guide it was no longer there. The straying point struck the collar and the collar badges. Although its hooks had been unfastened, the stiff military collar had closed together again and was protecting the throat.

Reiko could bear the sight no longer. She tried to go to her husband's help, but she could not stand. She moved through the blood on her knees, and her white skirts grew deep red. Moving to the rear of her husband, she helped no more than by loosening the collar. The quivering blade at last contacted the naked flesh of the throat. At that moment Reiko's impression was that she herself had propelled her husband forward; but that was not the case. It was a movement planned by the lieutenant himself, his last exertion of strength. Abruptly he threw his body at the blade, and the blade pierced his neck, emerging at the nape. There was a tremendous spurt of blood and the lieutenant lay still, cold blue-tinged steel protruding from his neck at the back.

5

SLOWLY, her socks slippery with blood, Reiko descended the stairway. The upstairs room was now completely still.

Switching on the ground-floor lights, she checked the gas jet and the main gas plug and poured water over the smoldering, half-buried charcoal in the brazier. She stood before the upright mirror in the four-and-a-half-mat room and held up her skirts. The bloodstains made it seem as if a bold, vivid pattern was printed across the lower half of her white kimono. When she sat down before the mirror, she was conscious of the dampness and coldness of her husband's blood in the region of her thighs, and she shivered. Then, for a long while, she lingered over her toilet preparations. She applied the rouge generously to her cheeks, and her lips too she painted heavily. This was no longer make-up to please her husband. It was make-up for the world which she would leave behind, and there was a touch of the magnificent and the spectacular in her brushwork. When she rose, the mat before the mirror was wet with blood. Reiko was not concerned about this.

Returning from the toilet, Reiko stood finally on the cement floor of the porchway. When her husband had bolted the door here last night it had been in preparation for death. For a while she stood immersed in the consideration of a simple problem. Should she now leave the bolt drawn? If she were to lock the door, it could be that the neighbors might not notice their suicide for several days. Reiko did not relish the thought of their two corpses putrifying before discovery. After all, it seemed, it would be best to leave it open. . . . She released the bolt, and also drew open the frosted-glass door a fraction. . . . At once a chill wind blew in. There was no sign of anyone in the midnight streets and stars glittered ice-cold through the trees in the large house opposite.

Leaving the door as it was, Reiko mounted the stairs. She had walked here and there for some time and her socks were no longer slippery. About halfway up, her nostrils were already assailed by a peculiar smell.

The lieutenant was lying on his face in a sea of blood. The point protruding from his neck seemed to have grown even more prominent than before. Reiko walked heedlessly across the blood. Sitting beside the lieutenant's corpse, she stared intently at the face, which lay on one cheek on the mat. The eyes were opened wide, as if the lieutenant's attention had been attracted by something. She raised the head, folding it in her sleeve, wiped the blood from the lips, and bestowed a last kiss.

Then she rose and took from the closet a new white blanket and a waist cord. To prevent any derangement of her skirts, she wrapped the blanket about her waist and bound it there firmly with the cord.

Reiko sat herself on a spot about one foot distant from the lieutenant's body. Drawing the dagger from her sash, she examined its dully gleaming blade intently, and held it to her tongue. The taste of the polished steel was slightly sweet.

Reiko did not linger. When she thought how the pain which had previously opened such a gulf between herself and her dying husband was now to become a part of her own experience, she saw before her only the joy of herself entering a realm her husband had already made his own. In her husband's agonized face there had been something inexplicable which she was seeing for the first time. Now she would solve that riddle. Reiko sensed that at last she too would be able to taste the true bitterness and sweetness of that great moral principle in which her husband believed. What had until now been tasted only faintly through her husband's example she was about to savor directly with her own tongue.

Reiko rested the point of the blade against the base of her throat. She thrust hard. The wound was only shallow. Her head blazed, and her hands shook uncontrollably. She gave the blade a strong pull sideways. A warm substance flooded into her mouth, and everything before her eyes reddened, in a vision of spouting blood. She gathered her strength and plunged the point of the blade deep into her throat.

Questions

1. *Despite the title and the political event that sets the plot in motion, this story focuses almost exclusively on the relationship between the hero and heroine, their lovemaking, and their ritual suicides. In what ways do the intensely psychological explorations of the story define and clarify the meaning of patriotism for Lieutenant Takeyama?* 2. *In the West, we tend to view the family—the relationship between husband and wife—as a private and personal matter that has little to do with public, political life. How do Lieutenant Takeyama and his wife view their relationship?* 3. *Lieutenant Takeyama views "the urges of his flesh and the sincerity of his patriotism" as "two parts of the same thing." What does he mean by this?* 4. *What does Mishima achieve by the opening paragraph? Why does he sacrifice suspense by recounting at the outset the major events and the story's outcome?* 5. *What connections does the story establish between love and death?* 6. *What is the significance of Reiko's deliberations as to whether or not she should leave the door bolt drawn?*

the presence of death

Girl Held in the Lap of Death, 1934 by Käthe Kollwitz

POETRY

Edward

ANONYMOUS

1

"Why does your brand° sae° drap wi' bluid,   *sword/so*
         Edward, Edward,
Why does your brand sae drap wi' bluid,
    And why sae sad gang° ye, O?"   *go*
"O I ha'e killed my hawk sae guid,
         Mither, mither,
O I ha'e killed my hawk sae guid,
    And I had nae mair but he, O."

2

"Your hawke's bluid was never sae reid,°   *red*
         Edward, Edward,   10
Your hawke's bluid was never sae reid,
    My dear son I tell thee, O."
"O I ha'e killed my reid-roan steed,
         Mither, mither,
O I ha'e killed my reid-roan steed,
    That erst was sae fair and free, O."

3

"Your steed was auld, and ye ha'e gat mair,
         Edward, Edward,
Your steed was auld, and ye ha'e gat mair,
    Some other dule° ye drie,° O."   *grief/suffer*
"O I ha'e killed my fader dear,   21
         Mither, mither,
O I ha'e killed my fader dear,
    Alas, and wae° is me, O!"   *woe*

4

"And whatten penance wul ye drie for that,
   Edward, Edward?
And whatten penance wul ye drie for that,
  My dear son, now tell me O?"
"I'll set my feet in yonder boat,
   Mither, mither,   30
I'll set my feet in yonder boat,
  And I'll fare over the sea, O."

5

"And what wul ye do wi' your towers and your ha',
   Edward, Edward?
And what wul ye do wi' your towers and your ha',
  That were sae fair to see, O?"
"I'll let them stand tul they down fa',
   Mither, mither,
I'll let them stand tul they down fa',   39
  For here never mair maun° I be, O."   *must*

6

"And what wul ye leave to your bairns° and your wife, *children*
   Edward, Edward?
And what wul ye leave to your bairns and your wife,
  Whan ye gang over the sea, O?"
"The warlde's° room, let them beg thrae° life, *world's/through*
   Mither, mither,
The warlde's room, let them beg thrae life,
  For them never mair wul I see, O."

7

"And what wul ye leave to your ain mither dear,
   Edward, Edward?
And what wul ye leave to your ain mither dear,   50
  My dear son, now tell me, O?"
"The curse of hell frae° me sall° ye bear,   *from/shall*
   Mither, mither,
The curse of hell frae me sall ye bear,
  Sic° counsels ye gave to me, O."   *such*

1. Why does the mother reject Edward's answers to her first two questions? **2.** Does the poem provide any clues as to the motive of the murder? **3.** What effects are achieved through the question-and-answer technique? **4.** Edward has murdered his father and then bitterly turns away from his mother, wife, and children. What basis is there in the poem for nevertheless sympathizing with Edward?

Sonnet

WILLIAM SHAKESPEARE [1564–1616]

73

That time of year thou mayst in me behold
When yellow leaves, or none, or few, do hang
Upon those boughs which shake against the cold,
Bare ruined choirs, where late the sweet birds sang.
In me thou see'st the twilight of such day
As after sunset fadeth in the west;
Which by and by black night doth take away,
Death's second self, that seals up all in rest.
In me thou see'st the glowing of such fire,
That on the ashes of his youth doth lie,   10
As the deathbed whereon it must expire,
Consumed with that which it was nourished by.
This thou perceiv'st, which makes thy love more strong,
To love that well which thou must leave ere long.

Fear No More
the Heat o' the Sun[1]

WILLIAM SHAKESPEARE [1564–1616]

Fear no more the heat o' the sun,
    Nor the furious winter's rages;
Thou thy worldly task hast done,
    Home art gone, and ta'en thy wages:
Golden lads and girls all must,
As chimney-sweepers, come to dust.

Fear no more the frown o' the great;
    Thou art past the tyrant's stroke;
Care no more to clothe and eat;
    To thee the reed is as the oak: 10
The scepter, learning, physic°, must[2]   *medicine*
All follow this, and come to dust.

---

1. From *Cymbeline,* Act IV, Scene 2.
2. I.e., kings, scholars, and physicians.

Fear no more the lightning flash,
    Nor the all-dreaded thunder stone;[3]
Fear not slander, censure rash;
    Thou hast finished joy and moan:
All lovers young, all lovers must
Consign to° thee, and come to dust.   *agree with*

No exorciser harm thee!
Nor no witchcraft charm thee!   20
Ghost unlaid forbear thee!
Nothing ill come near thee!
Quiet consummation have;
And renownéd be thy grave!

A Litany in Time of Plague

THOMAS NASHE [1567–1601]

Adieu, farewell, earth's bliss;
This world uncertain is;
Fond° are life's lustful joys;   *foolish*
Death proves them all but toys;
None from his darts can fly;
I am sick, I must die.
    Lord, have mercy on us!

Rich men, trust not in wealth,
Gold cannot buy you health;
Physic himself must fade.   10
All things to end are made,
The plague full swift goes by;
I am sick, I must die.
    Lord, have mercy on us!

Beauty is but a flower
Which wrinkles will devour;
Brightness falls from the air;
Queens have died young and fair;
Dust hath closed Helen's[4] eye.
I am sick, I must die.   20
    Lord, have mercy on us!

---

3. It was believed that thunder was caused by falling meteorites.

---

4. Helen of Troy, a fabled beauty.

Strength stoops unto the grave,
Worms feed on Hector[5] brave;
Swords may not fight with fate,
Earth still holds ope her gate.
"Come, come!" the bells do cry.
I am sick, I must die.
    Lord, have mercy on us.

Wit with his wantonness
Tasteth death's bitterness;   30
Hell's executioner
Hath no ears for to hear
What vain art can reply.
I am sick, I must die.
    Lord, have mercy on us.

Haste, therefore, each degree,
To welcome destiny;
Heaven is our heritage,
Earth but a player's stage;
Mount we unto the sky.   40
I am sick, I must die.
    Lord, have mercy on us.

Death, Be Not Proud

JOHN DONNE   [1572–1631]

Death, be not proud, though some have callèd thee
Mighty and dreadful, for thou art not so;
For those whom thou think'st thou dost overthrow
Die not, poor Death, nor yet canst thou kill me.
From rest and sleep, which but thy pictures be,
Much pleasure; then from thee much more must flow,
And soonest our best men with thee do go,
Rest of their bones, and soul's delivery.
Thou art slave to fate, chance, kings, and desperate men,
And dost with poison, war, and sickness dwell,   10
And poppy or charms can make us sleep as well
And better than thy stroke; why swell'st thou then?
One short sleep past, we wake eternally
And death shall be no more; Death, thou shalt die.

---

5. Commander of the Trojan forces in the Trojan War.

Elegy Written in a Country Churchyard

THOMAS GRAY [1716–1771]

The curfew tolls the knell of parting day,
    The lowing herd wind slowly o'er the lea,
The plowman homeward plods his weary way,
    And leaves the world to darkness and to me.

Now fades the glimmering landscape on the sight,
    And all the air a solemn stillness holds,
Save where the beetle wheels his droning flight,
    And drowsy tinklings lull the distant folds;

Save that from yonder ivy-mantled tower
    The moping owl does to the moon complain   10
Of such, as wandering near her secret bower,
    Molest her ancient solitary reign.

Beneath those rugged elms, that yew tree's shade,
    Where heaves the turf in many a moldering heap,
Each in his narrow cell forever laid,
    The rude° forefathers of the hamlet sleep.   *untaught*

The breezy call of incense-breathing Morn,
    The swallow twittering from the straw-built shed,
The cock's shrill clarion, or the echoing horn,°   *hunter's horn*
    No more shall rouse them from their lowly bed.   20

For them no more the blazing hearth shall burn,
    Or busy housewife ply her evening care;
No children run to lisp their sire's return,
    Or climb his knees the envied kiss to share.

Oft did the harvest to their sickle yield,
    Their furrow oft the stubborn glebe° has broke;   *field*
How jocund did they drive their team afield!
    How bowed the woods beneath their sturdy stroke!

Let not Ambition mock their useful toil,
    Their homely joys, and destiny obscure;   30
Nor Grandeur hear with a disdainful smile
    The short and simple annals of the poor.

The boast of heraldry,° the pomp of power,   *noble birth*
    And all that beauty, all that wealth e'er gave,
Awaits alike the inevitable hour.
    The paths of glory lead but to the grave.

Nor you, ye proud, impute to these the fault,
    If Memory o'er their tomb no trophies° raise,   *memorial*
Where through the long-drawn aisle and fretted° vault   *decorated*
    The pealing anthem swells the note of praise.   40

Can storied° urn or animated bust   *inscribed*
    Back to its mansion call the fleeting breath?
Can Honor's voice provoke the silent dust,
    Or Flattery soothe the dull cold ear of Death?

Perhaps in this neglected spot is laid
    Some heart once pregnant with celestial fire;
Hands that the rod of empire might have swayed,
    Or waked to ecstasy the living lyre.

But Knowledge to their eyes her ample page
    Rich with the spoils of time did ne'er unroll;   50
Chill Penury repressed their noble rage,
    And froze the genial current of the soul.

Full many a gem of purest ray serene,
    The dark unfathomed caves of ocean bear:
Full many a flower is born to blush unseen,
    And waste its sweetness on the desert air.

Some village Hampden,[1] that with dauntless breast
    The little tyrant of his fields withstood;
Some mute inglorious Milton here may rest,
    Some Cromwell guiltless of his country's blood.   60

The applause of listening senates to command,
    The threats of pain and ruin to despise,
To scatter plenty o'er a smiling land,
    And read their history in a nation's eyes,

Their lot forbade: nor circumscribed alone
    Their growing virtues, but their crimes confined;
Forbade to wade through slaughter to a throne,
    And shut the gates of mercy on mankind,

---

1. John Hampden (1594–1643) championed the people against the autocratic policies of Charles I.

The struggling pangs of conscious truth to hide,
    To quench the blushes of ingenuous shame,   70
Or heap the shrine of Luxury and Pride
    With incense kindled at the Muse's flame.

Far from the madding crowd's ignoble strife,
    Their sober wishes never learned to stray;
Along the cool sequestered vale of life
    They kept the noiseless tenor of their way.

Yet even these bones from insult to protect
    Some frail memorial still erected nigh,
With uncouth rhymes and shapeless sculpture decked,
    Implores the passing tribute of a sigh.   80

Their name, their years, spelt by the unlettered Muse,
    The place of fame and elegy supply:
And many a holy text around she strews,
    That teach the rustic moralist to die.

For who to dumb Forgetfulness a prey,
    This pleasing anxious being e'er resigned,
Left the warm precincts of the cheerful day,
    Nor cast one longing lingering look behind?

On some fond breast the parting soul relies,
    Some pious drops the closing eye requires;   90
Even from the tomb the voice of Nature cries,
    Even in our ashes live their wonted fires.

For thee, who mindful of the unhonored dead
    Dost in these lines their artless tale relate;
If chance, by lonely contemplation led,
    Some kindred spirit shall inquire thy fate,

Haply some hoary-headed swain may say,
    "Oft have we seen him at the peep of dawn
Brushing with hasty steps the dews away
    To meet the sun upon the upland lawn.   100

"There at the foot of yonder nodding beech
    That wreathes its old fantastic roots so high,
His listless length at noontide would he stretch,
    And pore upon the brook that babbles by.

"Hard by yon wood, now smiling as in scorn,
    Muttering his wayward fancies he would rove,
Now drooping, woeful wan, like one forlorn,
    Or crazed with care, or crossed in hopeless love.

"One morn I missed him on the customed hill,
    Along the heath and near his favorite tree;   110
Another came; nor yet beside the rill,
    Nor up the lawn, nor at the wood was he;

"The next with dirges due in sad array
    Slow through the churchway path we saw him borne.
Approach and read (for thou canst read) the lay,
    Graved on the stone beneath yon aged thorn."

THE EPITAPH

Here rests his head upon the lap of Earth
    A youth to Fortune and to Fame unknown
Fair Science° frowned not on his humble birth,   learning
    And Melancholy marked him for her own.   120

Large was his bounty, and his soul sincere,
    Heaven did a recompense as largely send:
He gave to Misery all he had, a tear,
    He gained from Heaven ('twas all he wished) a friend.

No farther seek his merits to disclose,
    Or draw his frailties from their dread abode
(There they alike in trembling hope repose),
    The bosom of his Father and his God.

1. Does this poem celebrate the advantages of obscurity and ignorance over fame, wealth, and knowledge? Explain. 2. Why have the people Gray honors in this poem lived and died in obscurity? Does the poet offer any suggestions for change? Explain. 3. Why would "Ambition mock their useful toil" (l. 29)?

Ozymandias[1]

PERCY BYSSHE SHELLEY [1792–1822]

I met a traveller from an antique land
Who said: Two vast and trunkless legs of stone
Stand in the desert . . . Near them, on the sand,
Half sunk, a shattered visage lies, whose frown,
And wrinkled lip, and sneer of cold command,
Tell that its sculptor well those passions read

---

1. Egyptian monarch of the thirteenth century B.C., said to have erected a huge statue of himself.

Which yet survive, stamped on these lifeless things,
The hand that mocked them, and the heart that fed:
And on the pedestal these words appear:
"My name is Ozymandias, king of kings: 10
Look on my works, ye Mighty, and despair!"
Nothing beside remains. Round the decay
Of that colossal wreck, boundless and bare
The lone and level sands stretch far away.

When I Have Fears

JOHN KEATS [1795–1821]

When I have fears that I may cease to be
    Before my pen has gleaned my teeming brain,
Before high-piléd books, in charact'ry,°   *written symbols*
    Hold like rich garners the full-ripened grain;
When I behold, upon the night's starred face,
    Huge cloudy symbols of a high romance,
And think that I may never live to trace
    Their shadows, with the magic hand of chance;
And when I feel, fair creature of an hour,
    That I shall never look upon thee more,   10
Never have relish in the faery° power   *magical*
    Of unreflecting love!—then on the shore
Of the wide world I stand alone, and think
Till Love and Fame to nothingness do sink.

1. *What consequences of death does the poet fear in each of the three quatrains?* **2.** *What value have "Love and Fame" in the face of death?*

Ode to a Nightingale

JOHN KEATS [1795–1821]

1
My heart aches, and a drowsy numbness pains
    My sense, as though of hemlock I had drunk,
Or emptied some dull opiate to the drains

One minute past, and Lethe-wards[1] had sunk:
'Tis not through envy of thy happy lot,
    But being too happy in thine happiness—
        That thou, light-wingéd Dryad of the trees,
           In some melodious plot
    Of beechen green, and shadows numberless,
        Singest of summer in full-throated ease.   10

2

O, for a draught of vintage! that hath been
    Cooled a long age in the deep-delvéd earth,
Tasting of Flora[2] and the country green,
    Dance, and Provencal song,[3] and sunburnt mirth!
O for a beaker full of the warm South,
        Full of the true, the blushful Hippocrene,[4]
           With beaded bubbles winking at the brim,
              And purple-stainéd mouth;
    That I might drink, and leave the world unseen,
        And with thee fade away into the forest dim: 20

3

Fade far away, dissolve, and quite forget
    What thou among the leaves hast never known,
The weariness, the fever, and the fret
    Here, where men sit and hear each other groan;
Where palsy shakes a few, sad, last gray hairs,
        Where youth grows pale, and specter-thin, and dies;
           Where but to think is to be full of sorrow
              And leaden-eyed despairs,
    Where Beauty cannot keep her lustrous eyes,
        Or new Love pine at them beyond tomorrow.   30

4

Away! away! for I will fly to thee,
    Not charioted by Bacchus[5] and his pards,
But on the viewless wings of Poesy,
    Though the dull brain perplexes and retards:
Already with thee! tender is the night,
        And haply the Queen-Moon is on her throne,
           Clustered around by all her starry Fays;°   _fairies_
              But here there is no light,
    Save what from heaven is with the breezes blown
        Through verdurous glooms and winding mossy ways.   40

---

1.   Towards Lethe, in Greek mythology the river in Hades which caused forgetfulness.
2.   Roman goddess of flowers.
3.   Provence, in southern France, renowned for its medieval troubadors.
4.   In Greek mythology, the fountain of the Muses whose waters gave poetic inspiration.
5.   The god of wine, often represented in a chariot drawn by leopards ("pards").

5

I cannot see what flowers are at my feet,
    Nor what soft incense hangs upon the boughs,
But, in embalmèd darkness, guess each sweet
    Wherewith the seasonable month endows
The grass, the thicket, and the fruit tree wild;
      White hawthorn, and the pastoral eglantine;
        Fast fading violets covered up in leaves;
          And mid-May's eldest child,
      The coming musk-rose, full of dewy wine,
        The murmurous haunt of flies on summer eves.   50

6

Darkling° I listen; and for many a time   *in darkness*
    I have been half in love with easeful Death,
Called him soft names in many a musèd rhyme,
    To take into the air my quiet breath;
Now more than ever seems it rich to die,
      To cease upon the midnight with no pain,
        While thou art pouring forth thy soul abroad
          In such an ecstasy!
      Still wouldst thou sing, and I have ears in vain—
        To thy high requiem become a sod.   60

7

Thou wast not born for death, immortal Bird!
    No hungry generations tread thee down;
The voice I hear this passing night was heard
    In ancient days by emperor and clown:
Perhaps the selfsame song that found a path
      Through the sad heart of Ruth,[6] when, sick for home,
        She stood in tears amid the alien corn;
          The same that ofttimes hath
      Charmed magic casements, opening on the foam
        Of perilous seas, in faery lands forlorn.   70

8

Forlorn! the very word is like a bell
    To toll me back from thee to my sole self!
Adieu! the fancy cannot cheat so well
    As she is famed to do, deceiving elf.
Adieu! adieu! thy plaintive anthem fades
      Past the near meadows, over the still stream,
        Up the hill side; and now 'tis buried deep
          In the next valley-glades:
      Was it a vision, or a waking dream?
        Fled is that music:—Do I wake or sleep?   80

---

6. The young widow in the Old Testament (Ruth, 2) who left her own people to live in a strange land, where she gleaned in the barley fields ("alien corn").

1. *What does the nightingale represent?* **2.** *In stanza 6, Keats declares that the very moment at which the nightingale's song is most ecstatic would be the right moment to die; yet the realization that the nightingale's song would continue after his death jars him. Why?* **3.** *In what sense is the nightingale "not born for death" (l. 61)? Does this line imply that all men are born for death? Explain.* **4.** *In stanza 4, Keats says that he will reach the nightingale "on the viewless wings of Poesy." Why are the wings of poetry "viewless," and what is the connection between the nightingale and poetry?*

Ode on a Grecian Urn

JOHN KEATS [1795–1821]

1

Thou still unravished bride of quietness,
    Thou foster child of silence and slow time,
Sylvan historian, who canst thus express
    A flowery tale more sweetly than our rhyme:
What leaf-fringed legend haunts about thy shape
    Of deities or mortals, or of both,
        In Tempe or the dales of Arcady?[1]
    What men or gods are these? What maidens loath?
What mad pursuit? What struggle to escape?
        What pipes and timbrels? What wild ecstasy?   10

2

Heard melodies are sweet, but those unheard
    Are sweeter; therefore, ye soft pipes, play on;
Not to the sensual ear, but, more endeared,
    Pipe to the spirit ditties of no tone:
Fair youth, beneath the trees, thou canst not leave
    Thy song, nor ever can those trees be bare;
        Bold Lover, never, never canst thou kiss,
Though winning near the goal—yet, do not grieve;
        She cannot fade, though thou hast not thy bliss,
    Forever wilt thou love, and she be fair!   20

3

Ah, happy, happy boughs! that cannot shed
    Your leaves, nor ever bid the Spring adieu;
And, happy melodist, unweariéd,
    Forever piping songs forever new;
More happy love! more happy, happy love!

---

1.   Tempe and Arcady are valleys in Greece famous for their beauty. In ancient times, Tempe was regarded as sacred to Apollo.

Forever warm and still to be enjoyed,
    Forever panting, and forever young;
All breathing human passion far above,[2]
    That leaves a heart high-sorrowful and cloyed,
        A burning forehead, and a parching tongue.   30

4

Who are these coming to the sacrifice?
    To what green altar, O mysterious priest,
Lead'st thou that heifer lowing at the skies,
    And all her silken flanks with garlands dressed?
What little town by river or sea shore,
    Or mountain-built with peaceful citadel,
        Is emptied of this folk, this pious morn?
And, little town, thy streets forevermore
    Will silent be; and not a soul to tell
        Why thou art desolate, can e'er return.   40

5

O Attic[3] shape! Fair attitude! with brede
    Of marble men and maidens overwrought,
With forest branches and the trodden weed;
    Thou, silent form, dost tease us out of thought
As doth eternity: Cold Pastoral!
    When old age shall this generation waste,
        Thou shalt remain, in midst of other woe
Than ours, a friend to man, to whom thou say'st,
    "Beauty is truth, truth beauty,—that is all
        Ye know on earth, and all ye need to know."   50

1. *Describe the scene the poet sees depicted on the urn. Describe the scene the poet imagines as a consequence of the scene on the urn.* 2. *Why are the boughs, the piper, and the lovers happy in stanza 3?* 3. *Explain the assertion of stanza 2 that "Heard melodies are sweet, but those unheard / Are sweeter."* 4. *Does the poem support the assertion of the last two lines? What does that assertion mean?* 5. *In what sense might it be argued that this poem is about mortality and immortality?*

---

2. I.e., far above all breathing human passion.
3. Athenian, thus simple and graceful.

The Emperor Worm

EDGAR ALLAN POE [1809–1849]

Lo! 'tis a gala night
    Within the lonesome latter years!
An angel throng, bewinged, bedight
    In veils, and drowned in tears,
Sit in a theatre, to see
    A play of hopes and fears,
While the orchestra breathes fitfully
    The music of the spheres.

Mimes, in the form of God on high,
    Mutter and mumble low,   10
And hither and thither fly—
    Mere puppets they, who come and go
At bidding of vast formless things
    That shift the scenery to and fro,
Flapping from out their Condor wings
    Invisible Woe!

That motley drama!—oh, be sure
    It shall not be forgot!
With its Phantom chased forever more,
    By a crowd that seize it not,   20
Through a circle that ever returneth in
    To the self-same spot,
And much of Madness and more of Sin
    And Horror the soul of the plot.

But see, amid the mimic rout,
    A crawling shape intrude!
A blood-red thing that writhes from out
    The scenic solitude!
It writhes!—it writhes!—with mortal pangs
    The mimes become its food,   30
And the seraphs sob at vermin fangs
    In human gore imbued.

Out—out are the lights—out all!
    And over each quivering form,
The curtain, a funeral pall,
    Comes down with the rush of a storm,
And the angels, all pallid and wan,
    Uprising, unveiling, affirm
That the play is the tragedy, "Man,"
    And its hero the Conqueror Worm.   40

Growing Old

MATTHEW ARNOLD   [1822–1888]

What is it to grow old?
Is it to lose the glory of the form,
The luster of the eye?
Is it for beauty to forego her wreath?
—Yes, but not this alone.

Is it to feel our strength—
Not our bloom only, but our strength—decay?
Is it to feel each limb
Grow stiffer, every function less exact,
Each nerve more loosely strung?   10

Yes, this, and more; but not
Ah, 'tis not what in youth we dreamed 'twould be!
'Tis not to have our life
Mellowed and softened as with sunset glow,
A golden day's decline.

'Tis not to see the world
As from a height, with rapt prophetic eyes,
And heart profoundly stirred;
And weep, and feel the fullness of the past,
The years that are no more.   20

It is to spend long days
And not once feel that we were ever young;
It is to add, immured
In the hot prison of the present, month
To month with weary pain.

It is to suffer this,
And feel but half, and feebly, what we feel.
Deep in our hidden heart
Festers the dull remembrance of a change,
But no emotion—none.   30

It is—last stage of all—
When we are frozen up within, and quite
The phantom of ourselves,
To hear the world applaud the hollow ghost
Which blamed the living man.

After Great Pain,
a Formal Feeling Comes

EMILY DICKINSON [1830–1886]

After great pain, a formal feeling comes—
The Nerves sit ceremonious, like Tombs—
The stiff Heart questions was it He, that bore,
And Yesterday, or Centuries before?

The Feet, mechanical, go round—
Of Ground, or Air, or Ought—
A Wooden way
Regardless grown,
A Quartz contentment, like a stone—

This is the Hour of Lead—   10
Remembered, if outlived,
As Freezing persons, recollect the Snow–
First—Chill—then Stupor—then the letting go—

1. *Is this poem about physical or psychic pain? Explain.* **2.** *What is the meaning of "stiff Heart" (l. 3) and "Quartz contentment" (l. 9)? Are they part of a larger pattern of images? Explain.*

I Heard a Fly Buzz—When I Died

EMILY DICKINSON [1830–1886]

I heard a Fly buzz—when I died—
The Stillness in the Room
Was like the Stillness in the Air—
Between the Heaves of Storm—

The Eyes around—had wrung them dry—
And Breaths were gathering firm
For that last Onset—when the King
Be witnessed—in the Room—

I willed my Keepsakes—Signed away
What portion of me be   10
Assignable—and then it was
There interposed a Fly—

With Blue—uncertain stumbling Buzz—
Between the light—and me—
And then the Windows failed—and then
I could not see to see—

How the Waters Closed Above Him

EMILY DICKINSON [1830–1886]

How the Waters closed above Him
We shall never know—
How He stretched His Anguish to us
That—is covered too—

Spreads the Pond Her Base of Lilies
Bold above the Boy
Whose unclaimed Hat and Jacket
Sum the History—

Apparently with No Surprise

EMILY DICKINSON [1830–1886]

Apparently with no surprise
To any happy flower,
The frost beheads it at its play
In accidental power.
The blond assassin passes on,
The sun proceeds unmoved
To measure off another day
For an approving God.

Rest

CHRISTINA ROSSETTI   [1830–1894]

O Earth, lie heavily upon her eyes;
Seal her sweet eyes weary of watching, Earth;
Lie close around her: leave no room for mirth
With its harsh laughter, nor for sound of sighs.

She hath no questions, she hath no replies,
Hushed in and curtained with a blessèd dearth
Of all that irked her from the hour of birth;
With stillness that is almost Paradise.

Darkness more clear than noonday holdeth her,
Silence more musical than any song;   10
Even her very heart has ceased to stir.
Until the morning of Eternity
Her rest shall not begin nor end, but be;
And when she wakes she will not think it long.

1. Does the speaker see the death of the girl as tragic? Explain.   2. What has been the girl's experience of life?   3. Explain the paradoxes of lines 9 and 10.

To an Athlete Dying Young

A. E. HOUSMAN   [1859–1936]

The time you won your town the race
We chaired you through the market place;
Man and boy stood cheering by,
And home we brought you shoulder-high.

Today, the road all runners come,
Shoulder-high we bring you home,
And set you at your threshold down,
Townsman of a stiller town.

Smart lad, to slip betimes away
From fields where glory does not stay   10
And early though the laurel grows
It withers quicker than the rose.

Eyes the shady night has shut
Cannot see the record cut,

And silence sounds no worse than cheers
After earth has stopped the ears:

Now you will not swell the rout
Of lads that wore their honors out,
Runners whom renown outran
And the name died before the man.   20

So set, before its echoes fade,
The fleet foot on the sill of shade,
And hold to the low lintel up
The still defended challenge cup.

And round that early laureled head
Will flock to gaze the strengthless dead
And find unwithered on its curls
The garland briefer than a girl's.

Sailing to Byzantium[1]

WILLIAM BUTLER YEATS   [1865–1939]

1
That is no country for old men. The young
In one another's arms, birds in the trees
—Those dying generations—at their song,
The salmon-falls, the mackerel-crowded seas,
Fish, flesh, or fowl, commend all summer long
Whatever is begotten, born, and dies.
Caught in that sensual music all neglect
Monuments of unaging intellect.

2
An aged man is but a paltry thing,
A tattered coat upon a stick, unless   10
Soul clap its hands and sing, and louder sing
For every tatter in its mortal dress,
Nor is there singing school but studying
Monuments of its own magnificence;
And therefore I have sailed the seas and come
To the holy city of Byzantium.

---

1. Capital of the ancient Eastern Roman Empire, Byzantium (modern Istanbul) is celebrated for its great art, including mosaics (in ll. 17–18, Yeats addresses the figures in one of these mosaics). In *A Vision*, Yeats cites Byzantium as possibly the only civilization which had achieved what he called "Unity of Being," a state where "religious, aesthetic and practical life were one. . . ."

3

O sages standing in God's holy fire
As in the gold mosaic of a wall,
Come from the holy fire, perne in a gyre,[2]
And be the singing-masters of my soul.   20
Consume my heart away; sick with desire
And fastened to a dying animal
It knows not what it is; and gather me
Into the artifice of eternity.

4

Once out of nature I shall never take
My bodily form from any natural thing,
But such a form as Grecian goldsmiths make
Of hammered gold and gold enameling
To keep a drowsy Emperor awake;[3]
Or set upon a golden bough to sing   30
To lords and ladies of Byzantium
Of what is past, or passing, or to come.

---

1. *Examine the ways in which the imagery of bird and song are used throughout this poem.* 2. *This poem incorporates a series of contrasts, among them "That" country and Byzantium, the real birds of the first stanza and the artificial bird of the final stanza. What others do you find?* 3. *What are the meanings of "generations" (l. 3)?* 4. *For what is the poet "sick with desire" (l. 21)?* 5. *In what sense is eternity an "artifice" (l. 24)?*

Richard Cory

EDWIN ARLINGTON ROBINSON [1869–1935]

Whenever Richard Cory went down town,
We people on the pavement looked at him:
He was a gentleman from sole to crown,
Clean favored, and imperially slim.

And he was always quietly arrayed,
And he was always human when he talked;
But still he fluttered pulses when he said,
"Good-morning," and he glittered when he walked.

---

2. I.e., whirl in a spiral motion. Yeats associated this motion with the cycles of history and the fate of the individual. Here he entreats the sages represented in the mosaic to take him out of the natural world described in the first stanza and into the eternal world of art.
3. "I have read somewhere," Yeats wrote, "that in the Emperor's palace at Byzantium was a tree made of gold and silver, and artificial birds that sang." The poet wishes to become an artificial bird (a work of art) in contrast to the real birds of the first stanza.

And he was rich—yes, richer than a king—
And admirably schooled in every grace:
In fine, we thought that he was everything
To make us wish that we were in his place.

So on we worked, and waited for the light,
And went without the meat, and cursed the bread;
And Richard Cory, one calm summer night,
Went home and put a bullet through his head.

The Poor Relation

EDWIN ARLINGTON ROBINSON [1869–1935]

No longer torn by what she knows
And sees within the eyes of others,
Her doubts are when the daylight goes,
Her fears are for the few she bothers.
She tells them it is wholly wrong
Of her to stay alive so long;
And when she smiles her forehead shows
A crinkle that had been her mother's.

Beneath her beauty, blanched with pain,
And wistful yet for being cheated,   10
A child would seem to ask again
A question many times repeated;
But no rebellion has betrayed
Her wonder at what she has paid
For memories that have to stain,
For triumph born to be defeated.

To those who come for what she was—
The few left who know where to find her—
She clings, for they are all she has;
And she may smile when they remind her,   20
As heretofore, of what they know
Of roses that are still to blow
By ways where not so much as grass
Remains of what she sees behind her.

They stay a while, and having done
What penance or the past requires,
They go, and leave her there alone
To count her chimneys and her spires.

Her lip shakes when they go away,
And yet she would not have them stay;
She knows as well as anyone
That Pity, having played, soon tires.

But one friend always reappears.
A good ghost, not to be forsaken;
Whereat she laughs and has no fears
Of what a ghost may reawaken,
But welcomes, while she wears and mends
The poor relation's odds and ends,
Her truant from a tomb of years—
Her power of youth so early taken.

Poor laugh, more slender than her song
It seems; and there are none to hear it
With even the stopped ears of the strong
For breaking heart or broken spirit.
The friends who clamored for her place,
And would have scratched her for her face,
Have lost her laughter for so long
That none would care enough to fear it.

None live who need fear anything
From her, whose losses are their pleasure;
The plover with a wounded wing
Stays not the flight that others measure;
So there she waits, and while she lives,
And death forgets, and faith forgives,
Her memories go foraging
For bits of childhood song they treasure.

And like a giant harp that hums
On always, and is always blending
The coming of what never comes
With what has past and had an ending,
The City trembles, throbs, and pounds
Outside, and through a thousand sounds
The small intolerable drums
Of Time are like slow drops descending.

Bereft enough to shame a sage
And given little to long sighing,
With no illusion to assuage
The lonely changelessness of dying,—
Unsought, unthought-of, and unheard,
She sings and watches like a bird,
Safe in a comfortable cage
From which there will be no more flying.

1. *Is the woman described in the poem really poor (i.e., in the economic sense of the word)? Where does she live? What may the reader infer about her youthful years?* **2.** *Examine the meter and the rhyme scheme carefully. Note that in some stanzas the second, fourth, and last lines end with an extra unstressed syllable. Characterize the emotional effect of that metrical variation.* **3.** *Who is the "good ghost" of stanza five?*

Mr. Flood's Party

EDWIN ARLINGTON ROBINSON [1869–1935]

Old Eben Flood, climbing alone one night
Over the hill between the town below
And the forsaken upland hermitage
That held as much as he should ever know
On earth again of home, paused warily.
The road was his with not a native near;
And Eben, having leisure, said aloud,
For no man else in Tilbury Town to hear:

"Well, Mr. Flood, we have the harvest moon
Again, and we may not have many more;   10
The bird is on the wing, the poet says,
And you and I have said it here before.
Drink to the bird." He raised up to the light
The jug that he had gone so far to fill,
And answered huskily: "Well, Mr. Flood,
Since you propose it, I believe I will."

Alone, as if enduring to the end
A valiant armor of scarred hopes outworn,
He stood there in the middle of the road
Like Roland's ghost winding a silent horn.   20
Below him, in the town among the trees,
Where friends of other days had honored him,
A phantom salutation of the dead
Rang thinly till old Eben's eyes were dim.

Then, as a mother lays her sleeping child
Down tenderly, fearing it may awake,
He set the jug down slowly at his feet
With trembling care, knowing that most things break;
And only when assured that on firm earth
It stood, as the uncertain lives of men   30
Assuredly did not, he paced away,
And with his hand extended paused again:

"Well, Mr. Flood, we have not met like this
In a long time; and many a change has come
To both of us, I fear, since last it was
We had a drop together. Welcome home!"
Convivially returning with himself,
Again he raised the jug up to the light;
And with an acquiescent quaver said:
"Well, Mr. Flood, if you insist, I might.   40

"Only a very little, Mr. Flood—
For auld lang syne. No more, sir; that will do."
So, for the time, apparently it did,
And Eben evidently thought so too;
For soon amid the silver loneliness
Of night he lifted up his voice and sang,
Secure, with only two moons listening,
Until the whole harmonious landscape rang—

"For auld lang syne." The weary throat gave out,
The last word wavered; and the song being done,   50
He raised again the jug regretfully
And shook his head, and was again alone.
There was not much that was ahead of him,
And there was nothing in the town below—
Where strangers would have shut the many doors
That many friends had opened long ago.

After Apple-Picking

ROBERT FROST   [1874–1963]

My long two-pointed ladder's sticking through a tree
Toward heaven still,
And there's a barrel that I didn't fill
Beside it, and there may be two or three
Apples I didn't pick upon some bough.
But I am done with apple-picking now.
Essence of winter sleep is on the night,
The scent of apples: I am drowsing off.
I cannot rub the strangeness from my sight
I got from looking through a pane of glass   10
I skimmed this morning from the drinking trough
And held against the world of hoary grass.
It melted, and I let it fall and break.

But I was well
Upon my way to sleep before it fell,
And I could tell
What form my dreaming was about to take.
Magnified apples appear and disappear,
Stem end and blossom end,
And every fleck of russet showing clear.
My instep arch not only keeps the ache,   20
It keeps the pressure of a ladder-round.
I feel the ladder sway as the boughs bend.
And I keep hearing from the cellar bin
The rumbling sound
Of load on load of apples coming in.
For I have had too much
Of apple-picking: I am overtired
Of the great harvest I myself desired.
There were ten thousand thousand fruit to touch,   30
Cherish in hand, lift down, and not let fall.
For all
That struck the earth,
No matter if not bruised or spiked with stubble,
Went surely to the cider-apple heap
As of no worth.
One can see what will trouble
This sleep of mine, whatever sleep it is.
Were he not gone,
The woodchuck could say whether it's like his   40
Long sleep, as I describe its coming on,
Or just some human sleep.

1. *What does apple-picking symbolize?* **2.** *Why is the speaker uncertain, at the end, what kind of sleep is coming on him?*

'Out, Out-'[1]

ROBERT FROST [1874–1963]

The buzz-saw snarled and rattled in the yard
And made dust and dropped stove-length sticks of wood,
Sweet-scented stuff when the breeze drew across it.
And from there those that lifted eyes could count
Five mountain ranges one behind the other

---

1. The title is taken from the famous speech of Macbeth upon hearing that his wife has died (*Macbeth*, Act V, Scene 6).

Under the sunset far into Vermont.
And the saw snarled and rattled, snarled and rattled,
As it ran light, or had to bear a load.
And nothing happened: day was all but done.
Call it a day, I wish they might have said   10
To please the boy by giving him the half hour
That a boy counts so much when saved from work.
His sister stood beside them in her apron
To tell them 'Supper.' At the word, the saw,
As if to prove saws knew what supper meant,
Leaped out at the boy's hand, or seemed to leap—
He must have given the hand. However it was,
Neither refused the meeting. But the hand!
The boy's first outcry was a rueful laugh,
As he swung toward them holding up the hand   20
Half in appeal, but half as if to keep
The life from spilling. Then the boy saw all—
Since he was old enough to know, big boy
Doing a man's work, though a child at heart—
He saw all spoiled. 'Don't let him cut my hand off—
The doctor, when he comes. Don't let him, sister!'
So. But the hand was gone already.
The doctor put him in the dark of ether.
He lay and puffed his lips out with his breath.
And then—the watcher at his pulse took fright.   30
No one believed. They listened at his heart.
Little—less—nothing!—and that ended it.
No more to build on there. And they, since they
Were not the one dead, turned to their affairs.

Design

ROBERT FROST [1874–1963]

I found a dimpled spider, fat and white,
On a white heal-all, holding up a moth
Like a white piece of rigid satin cloth—
Assorted characters of death and blight
Mixed ready to begin the morning right,
Like the ingredients of a witches' broth—
A snow-drop spider, a flower like a froth,
And dead wings carried like a paper kite.

What had that flower to do with being white,
The wayside blue and innocent heal-all?   10
What brought the kindred spider to that height,

Then steered the white moth thither in the night?
What but design of darkness to appall?—
If design govern in a thing so small.

Last Lines—1916[1]
(WRITTEN THE NIGHT BEFORE HIS EXECUTION)

PADRAIC PEARSE [1879–1916]

The beauty of the world hath made me sad,
This beauty that will pass;
Sometimes my heart hath shaken with great joy
To see a leaping squirrel in a tree,
Or a red lady-bird upon a stalk,
Or little rabbits in a field at evening,
Lit by a slanting sun,
Or some green hill where shadows drifted by,
Some quiet hill where mountainy man hath sown
And soon would reap, near to the gate of Heaven;   10
Or children with bare feet upon the sands
Of some ebbed sea, or playing on the streets
Of little towns in Connacht,
Things young and happy.
And then my heart hath told me:
These will pass,
Will pass and change, will die and be no more,
Things bright and green, things young and happy;
And I have gone upon my way
Sorrowful.   20

Tract

WILLIAM CARLOS WILLIAMS   [1883–1963]

I will teach you my townspeople
how to perform a funeral—
for you have it over a troop
of artists—
unless one should scour the world—
you have the ground sense necessary.

---

1. Padraic Pearse was one of the Irish revolutionaries executed for his role in the Easter 1916 uprising. See note to W. B. Yeats' "Easter 1916," p. 408.

See! the hearse leads.
I begin with a design for a hearse.
For Christ's sake not black—
nor white either—and not polished!   10
Let it be weathered—like a farm wagon—
with gilt wheels (this could be
applied fresh at small expense)
or no wheels at all:
a rough dray to drag over the ground.

Knock the glass out!
My God—glass, my townspeople!
For what purpose? Is it for the dead
to look out or for us to see
how well he is housed or to see   20
the flowers or the lack of them—
or what?
To keep the rain and snow from him?
He will have a heavier rain soon:
pebbles and dirt and what not.
Let there be no glass—
and no upholstery! phew!
and no little brass rollers
and small easy wheels on the bottom—
my townspeople what are you thinking of!   30

A rough plain hearse then
with gilt wheels and no top at all.
On this the coffin lies
by its own weight.

        No wreaths please—
especially no hot-house flowers.
Some common memento is better,
something he prized and is known by:
his old clothes—a few books perhaps—
God knows what! You realize   40
how we are about these things,
my townspeople—
something will be found—anything—
even flowers if he had come to that.
So much for the hearse.

For heaven's sake though see to the driver!
Take off the silk hat! In fact
that's no place at all for him
up there unceremoniously
dragging our friend out of his own dignity!   50
Bring him down—bring him down!
Low and inconspicuous! I'd not have him ride

on the wagon at all—damn him—
the undertaker's understrapper!
Let him hold the reins
and walk at the side
and inconspicuously too!

Then briefly as to yourselves:
Walk behind—as they do in France,
seventh class, or if you ride   60
Hell take curtains! Go with some show
of inconvenience; sit openly—
to the weather as to grief.
Or do you think you can shut grief in?
What—from us? We who have perhaps
nothing to lose? Share with us
share with us—it will be money
in your pockets.

            Go now
I think you are ready.

Hurt Hawks

ROBINSON JEFFERS [1887–1962]

1
The broken pillar of the wing jags from the clotted shoulder,
The wing trails like a banner in defeat,
No more to use the sky forever but live with famine
And pain a few days: cat nor coyote
Will shorten the week of waiting for death, there is game without talons.
He stands under the oak-bush and waits
The lame feet of salvation; at night he remembers freedom
And flies in a dream, the dawns ruin it.
He is strong and pain is worse to the strong, incapacity is worse.
The curs of the day come and torment him   10
At distance, no one but death the redeemer will humble that head,
The intrepid readiness, the terrible eyes.
The wild God of the world is sometimes merciful to those
That ask mercy, not often to the arrogant.
You do not know him, you communal people, or you have forgotten him;
Intemperate and savage, the hawk remembers him;
Beautiful and wild, the hawks, and men that are dying, remember him.

2

I'd sooner, except the penalties, kill a man than a hawk; but the great redtail[1]
Had nothing left but unable misery
From the bone too shattered for mending, the wing that trailed under his
    talons when he moved.   20
We had fed him six weeks, I gave him freedom,
He wandered over the foreland hill and returned in the evening, asking for
    death,
Not like a beggar, still eyed with the old
Implacable arrogance. I gave him the lead gift in the twilight. What fell was re-
    laxed,
Owl-downy, soft feminine feathers; but what
Soared: the fierce rush: the night-herons by the flooded river cried fear at its
    rising
Before it was quite unsheathed from reality.

Bells for John Whiteside's Daughter

JOHN CROWE RANSOM [b. 1888]

There was such speed in her little body,
And such lightness in her footfall,
It is no wonder that her brown study°   *reverie*
Astonishes us all.

Her wars were bruited in our high window.
We looked among orchard trees and beyond,
Where she took arms against her shadow,
Or harried unto the pond

The lazy geese, like a snow cloud
Dripping their snow on the green grass,   10
Tricking and stopping, sleepy and proud,
Who cried in goose, Alas,

For the tireless heart within the little
Lady with rod that made them rise
From their noon apple-dreams, and scuttle
Goose-fashion under the skies!

But now go the bells, and we are ready;
In one house we are sternly stopped
To say we are vexed at her brown study,
Lying so primly propped.   20

---

1. I.e., red-tailed hawk.

Dulce et Decorum Est

WILFRED OWEN   [1893–1918]

Bent double, like old beggars under sacks,
Knock-kneed, coughing like hags, we cursed through sludge,
Till on the haunting flares we turned our backs,
And towards our distant rest began to trudge.
Men marched asleep. Many had lost their boots,
But limped on, blood-shod. All went lame, all blind;
Drunk with fatigue; deaf even to the hoots
Of gas-shells dropping softly behind.

Gas! GAS! Quick, boys!—An ecstasy of fumbling,
Fitting the clumsy helmets just in time,   10
But someone still was yelling out and stumbling
And flound'ring like a man in fire or lime.—
Dim through the misty panes and thick green light,
As under a green sea, I saw him drowning.
In all my dreams before my helpless sight
He plunges at me, guttering, choking, drowning.

If in some smothering dreams, you too could pace
Behind the wagon that we flung him in,
And watch the white eyes writhing in his face,
His hanging face, like a devil's sick of sin,   20
If you could hear, at every jolt, the blood
Come gargling from the froth-corrupted lungs
Bitter as the cud
Of vile, incurable sores on innocent tongues,—
My friend, you would not tell with such high zest
To children ardent for some desperate glory,
The old lie: *Dulce et decorum est
Pro patria mori.*[1]

nobody loses all the time

E. E. CUMMINGS   [1894–1962]

nobody loses all the time

i had an uncle named

---

1.   A quotation from the Latin poet Horace, "It is sweet and fitting to die for one's country."

Sol who was a born failure and
nearly everybody said he should have gone
into vaudeville perhaps because my Uncle Sol could
sing McCann He Was A Diver on Xmas Eve like Hell Itself which
may or may not account for the fact that my Uncle

Sol indulged in that possibly most inexcusable
of all to use a highfalootin phrase
luxuries that is or to   10
wit farming and be
it needlessly
added

my Uncle Sol's farm
failed because the chickens
ate the vegetables so
my Uncle Sol had a
chicken farm till the
skunks ate the chickens when

my Uncle Sol   20
had a skunk farm but
the skunks caught cold and
died and so
my Uncle Sol imitated the
skunks in a subtle manner

or by drowning himself in the watertank
but somebody who'd given my Uncle Sol a Victor
Victrola and records while he lived presented to
him upon the auspicious occasion of his decease a
scrumptious not to mention splendiferous funeral with   30
tall boys in black gloves and flowers and everything and

i remember we all cried like the Missouri
when my Uncle Sol's coffin lurched because
somebody pressed a button
(and down went
my Uncle
Sol

and started a worm farm)

1. *Explain the title.*   2. *What is the speaker's attitude toward Uncle Sol?*

On a Squirrel Crossing the Road in Autumn, in New England

RICHARD EBERHART [b. 1904]

It is what he does not know,
Crossing the road under the elm trees,
About the mechanism of my car,
About the Commonwealth of Massachusetts,
About Mozart, India, Arcturus,

That wins my praise. I engage
At once in whirling squirrel-praise.

He obeys the orders of nature
Without knowing them.
It is what he does not know   10
That makes him beautiful.
Such a knot of little purposeful nature!

I who can see him as he cannot see himself
Repose in the ignorance that is his blessing.

It is what man does not know of God
Composes the visible poem of the world.
                              . . . Just missed him!

In Memory of W. B. Yeats

(D. JAN. 1939)

W. H. AUDEN [1907–1973]

1
He disappeared in the dead of winter:
The brooks were frozen, the airports almost deserted,
And snow disfigured the public statues;
The mercury sank in the mouth of the dying day.
O all the instruments agree
The day of his death was a dark cold day.

Far from his illness
The wolves ran on through the evergreen forests,

The peasant river was untempted by the fashionable quays;
By mourning tongues   10
The death of the poet was kept from his poems.

But for him it was his last afternoon as himself,
An afternoon of nurses and rumors;
The provinces of his body revolted,
The squares of his mind were empty,
Silence invaded the suburbs,
The current of his feeling failed: he became his admirers.

Now he is scattered among a hundred cities
And wholly given over to unfamiliar affections;
To find his happiness in another kind of wood   20
And be punished under a foreign code of conscience.
The words of a dead man
Are modified in the guts of the living.

But in the importance and noise of tomorrow
When the brokers are roaring like beasts on the floor of the
        Bourse,°   *stock exchange*
And the poor have the sufferings to which they are fairly accustomed,
And each in the cell of himself is almost convinced of his freedom;
A few thousand will think of this day
As one thinks of a day when one did something slightly unusual.
O all the instruments agree   30
The day of his death was a dark cold day.

> 2
> You were silly like us: your gift survived it all;
> The parish of rich women, physical decay,
> Yourself; mad Ireland hurt you into poetry.
> Now Ireland has her madness and her weather still,
> For poetry makes nothing happen: it survives
> In the valley of its saying where executives
> Would never want to tamper; it flows south
> From ranches of isolation and the busy griefs,
> Raw towns that we believe and die in; it survives,   40
> A way of happening, a mouth.

> 3
> Earth, receive an honored guest;
> William Yeats is laid to rest:
> Let the Irish vessel lie
> Emptied of its poetry.
>
> In the nightmare of the dark
> All the dogs of Europe bark,
> And the living nations wait,
> Each sequestered in its hate;

Intellectual disgrace   50
Stares from every human face,
And the seas of pity lie
Locked and frozen in each eye.

Follow, poet, follow right
To the bottom of the night,
With your unconstraining voice
Still persuade us to rejoice;

With the farming of a verse
Make a vineyard of the curse,
Sing of human unsuccess   60
In a rapture of distress;

In the deserts of the heart
Let the healing fountain start,
In the prison of his days
Teach the free man how to praise.

1. *In what sense does a dead poet become "his admirers" (l. 17)?* **2.** *Why does Auden view the death of Yeats as a significant event?* **3.** *Is Auden's statement that "poetry makes nothing happen" (l. 36) consistent with the attitudes expressed in the final three stanzas?*

Musée des Beaux Arts

W. H. AUDEN [1907–1973]

About suffering they were never wrong,
The Old Masters: how well they understood
Its human position; how it takes place
While someone else is eating or opening a window or just walking dully along;
How, when the aged are reverently, passionately waiting
For the miraculous birth, there always must be
Children who did not specially want it to happen, skating
On a pond at the edge of the wood:
They never forgot
That even the dreadful martyrdom must run its course   10
Anyhow in a corner, some untidy spot
Where the dogs go on with their doggy life and the torturer's horse
Scratches its innocent behind on a tree.

In Brueghel's *Icarus*,[1] for instance: how everything turns away
Quite leisurely from the disaster; the ploughman may
Have heard the splash, the forsaken cry,
But for him it was not an important failure; the sun shone
As it had to on the white legs disappearing into the green
Water; and the expensive delicate ship that must have seen
Something amazing, a boy falling out of the sky,   20
Had somewhere to get to and sailed calmly on.

Elegy for Jane

MY STUDENT, THROWN BY A HORSE

THEODORE ROETHKE   [1908–1963]

I remember the neckcurls, limp and damp as tendrils;
And her quick look, a sidelong pickerel smile;
And how, once startled into talk, the light syllables leaped for her,
And she balanced in the delight of her thought,
A wren, happy, tail into the wind,
Her song trembling the twigs and small branches.
The shade sang with her;
The leaves, their whispers turned to kissing;
And the mold sang in the bleached valleys under the rose.

Oh, when she was sad, she cast herself down into such a pure depth,   10
Even a father could not find her:
Scraping her cheek against straw;
Stirring the clearest water.

My sparrow, you are not here,
Waiting like a fern, making a spiny shadow.
The sides of wet stones cannot console me,
Nor the moss, wound with the last light.

If only I could nudge you from this sleep,
My maimed darling, my skittery pigeon.
Over this damp grave I speak the words of my love: 20
I, with no rights in this matter,
Neither father nor lover.

---

1. "Landscape with the Fall of Icarus" by Peter Brueghel the elder. According to Greek myth, Icarus, escaping from Crete by using artificial wings, flew so high that the sun melted the wax that fastened the wings, and he fell into the sea and drowned.

Between the World and Me

RICHARD WRIGHT [1908–1960]

And one morning while in the woods I stumbled suddenly upon the thing,
Stumbled upon it in a grassy clearing guarded by scaly oaks and elms.
And the sooty details of the scene rose, thrusting themselves between the
    world and me. . . .
There was a design of white bones slumbering forgottenly upon a cushion of
    ashes.
There was a charred stump of a sapling pointing a blunt finger accusingly at the
    sky.
There were torn tree limbs, tiny veins of burnt leaves, and a scorched coil of
    greasy hemp;
A vacant shoe, an empty tie, a ripped shirt, a lonely hat, and a pair of trousers
    stiff with black blood.
And upon the trampled grass were buttons, dead matches, butt-ends of cigars
    and cigarettes, peanut shells, a drained gin-flask, and a whore's lipstick;
Scattered traces of tar, restless arrays of feathers, and the lingering smell of
    gasoline.
And through the morning air the sun poured yellow surprise into the eye
    sockets of a stony skull. . . .   10
And while I stood my mind was frozen with a cold pity for the life that was
    gone.
The ground gripped my feet and my heart was circled by icy walls of fear—
The sun died in the sky; a night wind muttered in the grass and fumbled the
    leaves in the trees; the woods poured forth the hungry yelping of hounds;
    the darkness screamed with thirsty voices; and the witnesses rose and
    lived:
The dry bones stirred, rattled, lifted, melting themselves into my bones.
The grey ashes formed flesh firm and black, entering into my flesh.
The gin-flask passed from mouth to mouth; cigars and cigarettes glowed, the
    whore smeared the lipstick red upon her lips,
And a thousand faces swirled around me, clamoring that my life be
    burned. . . .

And then they had me, stripped me, battering my teeth into my throat till I
    swallowed my own blood.
My voice was drowned in the roar of their voices, and my black wet body
    slipped and rolled in their hands as they bound me to the sapling.
And my skin clung to the bubbling hot tar, falling from me in limp patches.   20
And the down and quills of the white feathers sank into my raw flesh, and I
    moaned in my agony.
Then my blood was cooled mercifully, cooled by a baptism of gasoline.

And in a blaze of red I leaped to the sky as pain rose like water, boiling my
    limbs.
Panting, begging I clutched childlike, clutched to the hot sides of death.
Now I am dry bones and my face a stony skull staring in yellow surprise at the
    sun. . . .

The Bull Calf

IRVING LAYTON [b. 1912]

The thing could barely stand. Yet taken
from his mother and the barn smells
he still impressed with his pride,
with the promise of sovereignty in the way
his head moved to take us in.
The fierce sunlight tugging the maize from the ground
licked at his shapely flanks.
He was too young for all that pride.
I thought of the deposed Richard II.[1]

"No money in bull calves," Freeman had said.   10
The visiting clergyman rubbed the nostrils
now snuffing pathetically at the windless day.
"A pity," he sighed.
My gaze slipped off his hat toward the empty sky
that circled over the black knot of men,
over us and the calf waiting for the first blow.

Struck,
the bull calf drew in his thin forelegs
as if gathering strength for a mad rush. . .
tottered . . . raised his darkening eyes to us,   20
and I saw we were at the far end
of his frightened look, growing smaller and smaller
till we were only the ponderous mallet
that flicked his bleeding ear
and pushed him over on his side, stiffly,
like a block of wood.

Below the hill's crest

---

1. Richard II (1367–1400) was overthrown by Henry IV and deposed by Parliament in 1399.

the river snuffled on the improvised beach.
We dug a deep pit and threw the dead calf into it.
It made a wet sound, a sepulchral gurgle,   30
as the warm sides bulged and flattened.
Settled, the bull calf lay as if asleep,
one foreleg over the other,
bereft of pride and so beautiful now,
without movement, perfectly still in the cool pit,
I turned away and wept.

Do Not Go Gentle into That Good Night

DYLAN THOMAS   [1914–1953]

Do not go gentle into that good night,
Old age should burn and rave at close of day;
Rage, rage against the dying of the light.

Though wise men at their end know dark is right,
Because their words had forked no lightning they
Do not go gentle into that good night.

Good men, the last wave by, crying how bright
Their frail deeds might have danced in a green bay,
Rage, rage against the dying of the light.

Wild men who caught and sang the sun in flight,   10
And learn, too late, they grieved it on its way,
Do not go gentle into that good night.

Grave men, near death, who see with blinding sight
Blind eyes could blaze like meteors and be gay,
Rage, rage against the dying of the light.

And you, my father, there on the sad height,
Curse, bless, me now with your fierce tears, I pray.
Do not go gentle into that good night.
Rage, rage against the dying of the light.

1. What do wise, good, wild, and grave men have in common? 2. Why does the poet use the adjective "gentle" rather than the adverb "gently"? 3. What is the "sad height" (l. 16)?

The Death of the Ball Turret Gunner

RANDALL JARRELL [1914–1965]

From my mother's sleep I fell into the State,
And I hunched in its belly till my wet fur froze.
Six miles from earth, loosed from its dream of life,
I woke to black flak and the nightmare fighters.
When I died they washed me out of the turret with a hose.

1. To what do "its" (ll. 2 and 3) and "they" (l.5) refer? 2. Why is the mother described as asleep?

Losses

RANDALL JARRELL [1914–1965]

It was not dying: everybody died.
It was not dying: we had died before
In the routine crashes—and our fields
Called up the papers, wrote home to our folks,
And the rates rose, all because of us.
We died on the wrong page of the almanac,
Scattered on mountains fifty miles away;
Diving on haystacks, fighting with a friend,
We blazed up on the lines we never saw.
We died like aunts or pets or foreigners.   10
(When we left high school nothing else had died
For us to figure we had died like.)

In our new planes, with our new crews, we bombed
The ranges by the desert or the shore,
Fired at towed targets, waited for our scores—

And turned into replacements and woke up
One morning, over England, operational.
It wasn't different: but if we died
It was not an accident but a mistake
(But an easy one for anyone to make).   20
We read our mail and counted up our missions—
In bombers named for girls, we burned
The cities we had learned about in school—
Till our lives wore out; our bodies lay among
The people we had killed and never seen.
When we lasted long enough they gave us medals;
When we died they said, "Our casualties were low."
They said, "Here are the maps"; we burned the cities.

It was not dying—no, not ever dying;
But the night I died I dreamed that I was dead,
And the cities said to me: "Why are you dying?   30
We are satisfied, if you are; but why did I die?"

1. *Who is the speaker in this poem?* 2. *Why are the deaths described as "not an accident but a mistake" (l. 19)?* 3. *Explain the final stanza.*

For John Berryman[1]

DAVID IGNATOW [b. 1914]

You're dead, what can I do for you?
I am not unsympathetic;
I thought about you often enough
though we never spoke together
but once when I shied away,
feeling something that I fought
in me too—and came out with this
manner of living, by living.

It is depressing to live

---

1. A poet and biographer who committed suicide in 1972.

but to kill myself in protest   10
is to assume there is something
to life withheld from me, yet
who withholds it? Think about it.
What is the answer?

But suicide is not so wrong
for one who thought and prayed
his way toward it. I wish, though,
I had known sooner, to have
helped you go on living,
as I do, half a suicide,   20
the need defended by the other half
that thinks to live in that knowledge
is praiseworthy.

Five Ways to Kill a Man

EDWIN BROCK   [b. 1917]

There are many cumbersome ways to kill a man:
you can make him carry a plank of wood
to the top of a hill and nail him to it. To do this
properly you require a crowd of people
wearing sandals, a cock that crows, a cloak
to dissect, a sponge, some vinegar and one
man to hammer the nails home.

Or you can take a length of steel,
shaped and chased° in a traditional way,   *ornamented*
and attempt to pierce the metal cage he wears.   10
But for this you need white horses,
English trees, men with bows and arrows,
at least two flags, a prince and a
castle to hold your banquet in.

Dispensing with nobility, you may, if the wind
allows, blow gas at him. But then you need
a mile of mud sliced through with ditches,
not to mention black boots, bomb craters,
more mud, a plague of rats, a dozen songs

and some round hats made of steel.   20

In an age of aeroplanes, you may fly
miles above your victim and dispose of him by
pressing one small switch. All you then
require is an ocean to separate you, two
systems of government, a nation's scientists,
several factories, a psychopath and
land that no one needs for several years.

These are, as I began, cumbersome ways
to kill a man. Simpler, direct, and much more neat
is to see that he is living somewhere in the middle   30
of the twentieth century, and leave him there.

The Pardon

RICHARD WILBUR [b. 1921]

My dog lay dead five days without a grave
In the thick of summer, hid in a clump of pine
And a jungle of grass and honeysuckle-vine.
I who had loved him while he kept alive

Went only close enough to where he was
To sniff the heavy honeysuckle-smell
Twined with another odor heavier still
And hear the flies' intolerable buzz.

Well, I was ten and very much afraid.
In my kind world the dead were out of range   10
And I could not forgive the sad or strange
In beast or man. My father took the spade

And buried him. Last night I saw the grass
Slowly divide (it was the same scene
But now it glowed a fierce and mortal green)
And saw the dog emerging. I confess

I felt afraid again, but still he came
In the carnal sun, clothed in a hymn of flies,

And death was breeding in his lively eyes.
I started in to cry and call his name,   20

Asking forgiveness of his tongueless head.
. . . I dreamt the past was never past redeeming:
But whether this was false or honest dreaming
I beg death's pardon now. And mourn the dead.

After a Time

CATHERINE DAVIS [b. 1924]

After a time, all losses are the same.
One more thing lost is one thing less to lose;
And we go stripped at last the way we came.

Though we shall probe, time and again, our shame,
Who lack the wit to keep or to refuse,
After a time, all losses are the same.

No wit, no luck can beat a losing game;
Good fortune is a reassuring ruse:
And we go stripped at last the way we came.

Rage as we will for what we think to claim,   10
Nothing so much as this bare thought subdues:
After a time, all losses are the same.

The sense of treachery—the want, the blame—
Goes in the end, whether or not we choose,
And we go stripped at last the way we came.

So we, who would go raging, will go tame
When what we have we can no longer use:
After a time, all losses are the same;
And we go stripped at last the way we came.

1. What difference in effect would occur if the refrain "After a time" were changed to "When life is done"?   2. What are the various meanings of "stripped" in line 3 and line 19?   3. Explain the meaning of "The sense of treachery" (l. 13).   4. Does this poem say that life is meaningless? Explain.   5. Compare this poem with Dylan Thomas' "Do Not Go Gentle into That Good Night."

Will

MAXINE KUMIN [b. 1925]

For love, for money, for reasons less than plain
one swims the Channel or the Hellespont,
masters mountains, in drought prays down the rain,
burns barns or bridges and hurries to the front.
God serves the choosy. They know what to want
and how to bear hope out to the edge of pain.
Nothing drops from them by accident.
But one, in a warm bath opening his vein
and leaning back to watch his act of will,
knows even the chestiest Leanders ¹ drown,   10
the Alps have avalanches they can spill,
nor does the front line always shoot to kill;
and also knows, as the watered pulse runs down,
that would-be suicides are sometimes found.

1. Explain the meaning of "God serves the choosy" (l. 5). 2. Does the poem provide any clues as to why the would-be suicide opens his veins? If so, why, as the last line seems to suggest, does he wish to be rescued before he dies?

Relic

TED HUGHES [b. 1930]

I found this jawbone at the sea's edge:
There, crabs, dogfish, broken by the breakers or tossed
To flap for half an hour and turn to a crust
Continue the beginning. The deeps are cold:
In that darkness camaraderie does not hold:
Nothing touches but, clutching, devours. And the jaws,
Before they are satisfied or their stretched purpose
Slacken, go down jaws; go gnawn bare. Jaws
Eat and are finished and the jawbone comes to the beach:
This is the sea's achievement; with shells,   10

---

1. According to legend Leander nightly swam the Hellespont (now called the Dardenelles) from Abydos to Sestos in Greece in order to visit his beloved Hero. On one occasion a storm came up and Leander drowned.

Vertebrae, claws, carapaces, skulls.

Time in the sea eats its tail, thrives, casts these
Indigestibles, the spars of purposes
That failed far from the surface. None grow rich
In the sea. This curved jawbone did not laugh
But gripped, gripped and is now a cenotaph.°   empty tomb

1. What is the "relic" of the title? What characteristic of nature does it symbolize?   2. What does "Continue the beginning" (l. 4) signify?   3. This poem is metrically quite irregular and thus difficult to scan. Further, there are only two pair of perfect rhymes (ll. 4–5 and 15–16). Yet the poem is richly musical. Identify the poetic devices that generate the music.

People

YEVGENY YEVTUSHENKO   [b. 1933]

No people are uninteresting.
Their fate is like the chronicle of planets.

Nothing in them is not particular,
and planet is dissimilar from planet.

And if a man lived in obscurity
making his friends in that obscurity
obscurity is not uninteresting.

To each his world is private,
and in that world one excellent minute.

And in that world one tragic minute.   10
These are private.

In any man who dies there dies with him
his first snow and kiss and fight.
It goes with him.

They are left books and bridges
and painted canvas and machinery.

Whose fate is to survive.
But what has gone is also not nothing:

by the rule of the game something has gone.
Not people die but worlds die in them.   20

Whom we knew as faulty, the earth's creatures.
Of whom, essentially, what did we know?

Brother of a brother? Friend of friends?
Lover of lover?

We who knew our fathers
in everything, in nothing.

They perish. They cannot be brought back.
The secret worlds are not regenerated.

And every time again and again
I make my lament against destruction.   30

After the Rain

STANLEY CROUCH [b. 1945]

John's[1] words were the words
Bird[2] and the other winged creatures
sang:
    How the darkness could
    and would someday
    sink behind the sun,
    how we, when we grew
    to ourselves, past what we were,
    how we would dance outside
    bucking the eyes of all stars and all light   10
    how we would be as gentle
    as the rebuilt wings of a broken sparrow,
    how we would lick back the rain
    and wash ourselves with light
    and our eyes would meet His
    our God, our Om,[3] our Allah, our Brahman.

---

1. John Coltrane (1926–1967) was one of the great tenor sax players of modern jazz.
2. Charlie Parker (1920–1955), alto sax player, known as Bird, was one of the great creative geniuses of modern jazz.
3. In various Eastern religions, a sacred word used in mystical contemplation of ultimate reality.

And we, like all oceans,
would know
and love each other.
Salaam.[4]   20

---

4.   An Arabic salutation meaning "peace."

the presence of death

DRAMA

Everyman

ANONYMOUS

CHARACTERS

God	Cousin	Strength
Messenger	Goods	Discretion
Death	Good Deeds	Five Wits
Everyman	Knowledge	Angel
Fellowship	Confession	Doctor
Kindred	Beauty	

Here Beginneth a Treatise how the High Father of Heaven Sendeth Death to Summon Every Creature to Come and Give Account of their Lives in this World, and is in Manner of a Moral Play.

Messenger.   I pray you all give your audience,
    And hear this matter with reverence,
    By figure[1] a moral play:
    The *Summoning of Everyman* called it is,
    That of our lives and ending shows
    How transitory we be all day.
    This matter is wondrous precious,
    But the intent of it is more gracious,
    And sweet to bear away.
    The story saith: Man, in the beginning
    Look well, and take good heed to the ending,
    Be you never so gay!
    Ye think sin in the beginning full sweet,

---

1.   form

Which in the end causeth the soul to weep,
When the body lieth in clay.
Here shall you see how Fellowship and Jollity,
Both Strength, Pleasure, and Beauty,
Will fade from thee as flower in May;
For ye shall hear how our Heaven King
Calleth Everyman to a general reckoning:
Give audience, and hear what he doth say. *(Exit.)*

(God speaketh:)

God. I perceive, here in my majesty,
How that all creatures be to me unkind,
Living without dread in worldly prosperity:
Of ghostly² sight the people be so blind,
Drowned in sin, they know me not for their God;
In worldly riches is all their mind,
They fear not my righteousness, the sharp rod.
My law that I showed, when I for them died,
They forget clean,³ and shedding of my blood red;
I hanged between two, it cannot be denied;
To get them life I suffered¹ to be dead;
I healed their feet, with thorns hurt was my head.
I could do no more than I did, truly;
And now I see the people do clean forsake me:
They use the seven deadly sins damnable,
As pride, covetise, wrath, and lechery
Now in the world be made commendable;
And thus they leave of angels the heavenly company.
Every man liveth so after his own pleasure,
And yet of their life they be nothing⁵ sure:
I see the more that I them forbear
The worse they be from year to year.
All that liveth appaireth⁶ fast;
Therefore I will, in all the haste,
Have a reckoning of every man's person;
For, and⁷ I leave the people thus alone
In their life and wicked tempests,
Verily they will become much worse than beasts;
For now one would by envy another up eat;

---

2. spiritual
3. completely, altogether
4. allowed myself
5. not at all
6. becomes worse
7. if

Charity they do all clean forget.
I hoped well that every man
In my glory should make his mansion,
And thereto I had them all elect;
But now I see, like traitors deject,
They thank me not for the pleasure that I to them meant,
Nor yet for their being I them have lent.
I proffered the people great multitude of mercy,
And few there be that asketh it heartily.
They be so cumbered with worldly riches
That needs on them I must do justice,
On every man living without fear.
Where art thou, Death, thou mighty messenger?

(Enter Death.)

Death.   Almighty God, I am here at your will,
Your commandment to fulfil.
God.   Go thou to Everyman,
And show him, in my name,
A pilgrimage he must on him take,
Which he in no wise[8] may escape;
And that he bring with him a sure reckoning
Without delay or any tarrying.   *(God withdraws.)*
Death.   Lord, I will in the world go run overall,[9]
And cruelly outsearch both great and small;
Every man will I beset that liveth beastly
Out of God's laws, and dreadeth not folly.
He that loveth riches I will strike with my dart,
His sight to blind, and from heaven to depart[10]—
Except that alms be his good friend—
In hell for to dwell, world without end.
Lo, yonder I see Everyman walking.
Full little he thinketh on my coming;
His mind is on fleshly lusts and his treasure,
And great pain it shall cause him to endure
Before the Lord, Heaven King.

(Enter Everyman.)

Everyman, stand still! Wither art thou going
Thus gaily? Hast thou thy Maker forgot?

---

8.   manner
9.   everywhere
10.   separate

Everyman. Why askest thou?
   Wouldest thou wit?[11]
Death. Yea, sir; I will show you:
   In great haste I am sent to thee
   From God out of his majesty.
Everyman. What, sent to me?
Death. Yea, certainly.
   Though thou hast forgot him here,
   He thinketh on thee in the heavenly sphere,
   As, ere we depart, thou shalt know.
Everyman. What desireth God of me?
Death. That shall I show thee:
   A reckoning he will needs have
   Without any longer respite.
Everyman. To give a reckoning longer leisure I crave;
   This blind[12] matter troubleth my wit.
Death. On thee thou must take a long journey;
   Therefore thy book of count[13] with thee thou bring,
   For turn again thou cannot by no way.
   And look thou be sure of thy reckoning,
   For before God thou shalt answer, and show
   Thy many bad deeds, and good but a few;
   How thou hast spent thy life, and in what wise,
   Before the chief Lord of paradise.
   Have ado[14] that we were in that way,[15]
   For, wit thou well, thou shalt make none[16] attorney.
Everyman. Full unready I am such reckoning to give.
   I know thee not. What messenger art thou?
Death. I am Death, that no man dreadeth,[17]
   For every man I rest,[18] and no man spareth;
   For it is God's commandment
   That all to me shall be obedient.
Everyman. O Death, thou comest when I had thee least in mind!
   In thy power it lieth me to save;
   Yet of my good will I give thee, if thou wilt be kind:
   Yea, a thousand pound shalt thou have,
   And defer this matter till another day.

---

11. know
12. obscure
13. account
14. see to it
15. on that journey
16. have no
17. dreads no man
18. arrest

Death. Everyman, it may not be, by no way.

    I set not by[19] gold, silver, nor riches.

    Ne by pope, emperor, king, duke, ne princes;

    For, and I would receive gifts great,

    All the world I might get;

    But my custom is clean contrary.

    I give thee no respite. Come hence, and not tarry.

Everyman. Alas, shall I have no longer respite?

    I may say Death giveth no warning!

    To think on thee, it maketh my heart sick,

    For all unready is my book of reckoning.

    But twelve year and I might have abiding,

    My counting-book I would make so clear

    That my reckoning I should not need to fear.

    Wherefore, Death, I pray thee, for God's mercy,

    Spare me till I be provided of remedy.

Death. Thee availeth not to cry, weep, and pray;

    But haste thee lightly[20] that thou were gone that journey,

    And prove thy friends if thou can;

    For, wit thou well, the tide abideth no man,

    And in the world each living creature

    For Adam's sin must die of nature.[21]

Everyman. Death, if I should this pilgrimage take,

    And my reckoning surely make,

    Show me, for[22] saint charity,

    Should I not come again shortly?

Death. No, Everyman; and thou be once there,

    Thou mayst never more come here,

    Trust me verily.

Everyman. O gracious God in the high seat celestial,

    Have mercy on me in this most need!

    Shall I have no company from this vale terrestrial

    Of mine acquaintance, that way me to lead?

Death. Yea, if any be so hardy

    That would go with thee and bear thee company.

    Hie[23] thee that thou were gone to God's magnificence,

    Thy reckoning to give before his presence.

    What, weenest[24] thou thy life is given thee,

    And thy worldly goods also?

---

19. do not care for
20. quickly
21. as a natural thing
22. in the name of
23. hurry
24. think

Everyman.   I had wend[25] so, verily.
Death.   Nay, nay; it was but lent thee;
    For as soon as thou art go,
    Another a while shall have it, and then go therefro,[26]
    Even as thou hast done.
    Everyman, thou art mad! Thou hast thy wits five,
    And here on earth will not amend thy life;
    For suddenly I do come.
Everyman.   O wretched caitiff, whither shall I flee,
    That I might scape this endless sorrow?
    Now, gentle Death, spare me till to-morrow,
    That I may amend me
    With good advisement.[27]
Death.   Nay, thereto I will not consent,
    Nor no man will I respite;
    But to the heart suddenly I shall smite
    Without any advisement.
    And now out of thy sight I will me hie;
    See thou make thee ready shortly,
    For thou mayst say this is the day
    That no man living may scape away.   *(Exit Death.)*
Everyman.   Alas, I may well weep with sighs deep!
    Now have I no manner of company
    To help me in my journey, and me to keep;
    And also my writing is full unready.
    How shall I do now for to excuse me?
    I would to God I had never be get![28]
    To my soul a full great profit it had be;
    For now I fear pains huge and great.
    The time passeth. Lord, help, that all wrought!
    For though I mourn it availeth nought.
    The day passeth, and is almost ago;[29]
    I wot not well what for to do.
    To whom were I best my complaint to make?
    What and I to Fellowship thereof spake,
    And showed him of this sudden chance?
    For in him is all mine affiance;[30]
    We have in the world so many a day
    Been good friends in sport and play.

---

25. thought
26. from it
27. reflection
28. been born
29. gone
30. trust

I see him yonder, certainly.
I trust that he will bear me company;
Therefore to him will I speak to ease my sorrow.
Well met, good Fellowship, and good morrow!

(Fellowship speaketh:)

Fellowship. Everyman, good morrow, by this day!
Sir, why lookest thou so piteously?
If any thing be amiss, I pray thee me say,
That I may help to remedy.
Everyman. Yea, good Fellowship, yea;
I am in great jeopardy.
Fellowship. My true friend, show to me your mind;
I will not forsake thee to my life's end,
In the way of good company.
Everyman. That was well spoken, and lovingly.
Fellowship. Sir, I must needs know your heaviness;[31]
I have pity to see you in any distress.
If any have you wronged, ye shall revenged be,
Though I on the ground be slain for thee—
Though that I know before that I should die.
Everyman. Verily, Fellowship, gramercy.
Fellowship. Tush! by thy thanks I set not a straw.
Show me your grief, and say no more.
Everyman. If I my heart should to you break,[32]
And then you to turn your mind from me,
And would not me comfort when ye hear me speak,
Then should I ten times sorrier be.
Fellowship. Sir, I say as I will do indeed.
Everyman. Then be you a good friend at need:
I have found you true herebefore.
Fellowship. And so ye shall evermore;
For, in faith, and thou go to hell,
I will not forsake thee by the way.
Everyman. Ye speak like a good friend; I believe you well.
I shall deserve it, and I may.
Fellowship. I speak of no deserving, by this day!
For he that will say, and nothing do,
Is not worthy with good company to go;
Therefore show me the grief of your mind,
As to your friend most loving and kind.

---

31. sorrow
32. open

Everyman.   I shall show you how it is:
    Commanded I am to go a journey,
    A long way, hard and dangerous,
    And give a strait count, without delay,
    Before the high Judge, Adonai.[33]
    Wherefore, I pray you, bear me company,
    As ye have promised, in this journey.
Fellowship.   That is matter indeed. Promise is duty;
    But, and I should take such a voyage on me,
    I know it well, it should be to my pain;
    Also it maketh me afeard, certain.
    But let us take counsel here as well as we can,
    For your words would fear[34] a strong man.
Everyman.   Why, ye said if I had need
    Ye would me never forsake, quick[35] ne dead,
    Though it were to hell, truly.
Fellowship.   So I said, certainly,
    But such pleasures be set aside, the sooth to say;
    And also, if we took such a journey,
    When should we come again?
Everyman.   Nay, never again, till the day of doom.
Fellowship.   In faith, then will not I come there!
    Who hath you these tidings brought?
Everyman.   Indeed, Death was with me here.
Fellowship.   Now, by God that all hath bought,
    If Death were the messenger,
    For no man that is living to-day
    I will not go that loath journey—
    Not for the father that begat me!
Everyman.   Ye promised otherwise, pardie.[36]
Fellowship.   I wot well I said so, truly;
    And yet if thou wilt eat, and drink, and make good cheer,
    Or haunt to women the lusty company,[37]
    I would not forsake you while the day is clear,[38]
    Trust me verily.
Everyman.   Yea, thereto ye would be ready!
    To go to mirth, solace, and play,
    Your mind will sooner apply,
    Than to bear me company in my long journey.

---

33. Hebrew name for God
34. frighten
35. alive
36. by God
37. frequent the pleasant company of women
38. until daybreak

Fellowship.   Now, in good faith, I will not that way.
   But and thou will murder, or any man kill,
   In that I will help thee with a good will.
Everyman.   O, that is a simple advice indeed.
   Gentle fellow, help me in my necessity!
   We have loved long, and now I need;
   And now, gentle Fellowship, remember me.
Fellowship.   Whether ye have loved me or no,
   By Saint John, I will not with thee go.
Everyman.   Yet, I pray thee, take the labour, and do so much for me
   To bring me forward,[39] for saint charity,
   And comfort me till I come without the town.
Fellowship.   Nay, and thou would give me a new gown,
   I will not a foot with thee go;
   But, and thou had tarried, I would not have left thee so.
   And as now God speed thee in thy journey,
   For from thee I will depart as fast as I may.
Everyman.   Whither away, Fellowship? Will thou forsake me?
Fellowship.   Yea, by my fay![40] To God I betake[41] thee.
Everyman.   Farewell, good Fellowship; for thee my heart is sore.
   Adieu for ever! I shall see thee no more.
Fellowship.   In faith, Everyman, farewell now at the ending;
   For you I will remember that parting is mourning.

                                    (Exit Fellowship.)

Everyman.   Alack! shall we thus depart indeed—
   Ah, Lady, help!—without any more comfort?
   Lo, Fellowship forsaketh me in my most need.
   For help in this world whither shall I resort?
   Fellowship herebefore with me would merry make,
   And now little sorrow for me doth he take.
   It is said, 'In prosperity men friends may find,
   Which in adversity be full unkind.'
   Now whither for succour shall I flee,
   Sith that[42] Fellowship hath forsaken me?
   To my kinsmen I will, truly,
   Praying them to help me in my necessity;
   I believe that they will do so,
   For kind[43] will creep where it may not go.
   I will go say, for yonder I see them.
   Where be ye now, my friends and kinsmen?

---

39. escort me
40. faith
41. commend
42. since
43. kinship, family

(Enter Kindred and Cousin.)

Kindred. Here be we now at your commandment.
Cousin, I pray you show us your intent
In any wise, and do not spare.[44]
Cousin. Yea, Everyman, and to us declare
If ye be disposed to go anywhither;
For, wit you well, we will live and die together.
Kindred. In wealth and woe we will with you hold,
For over his kin a man may be bold.[45]
Everyman. Gramercy, my friends and kinsmen kind.
Now shall I show you the grief of my mind:
I was commanded by a messenger,
That is a high king's chief officer;
He bade me go a pilgrimage, to my pain,
And I know well I shall never come again;
Also I must give a reckoning strait,
For I have a great enemy[46] that hath me in wait,
Which intendeth me for to hinder.
Kindred. What account is that which ye must render?
That would I know.
Everyman. Of all my works I must show
How I have lived and my days spent;
Also of ill deeds that I have used[47]
In my time, sith life was me lent;
And of all virtues that I have refused.
Therefore, I pray you, go thither with me
To help to make mine account, for saint charity.
Cousin. What, to go thither? Is that the matter?
Nay, Everyman, I had liefer[48] fast[49] bread and water
All this five year and more.
Everyman. Alas, that ever I was bore![50]
For now shall I never be merry,
If that you forsake me.
Kindred. Ah, sir, what ye be a merry man!
Take good heart to you, and make no moan.
But one thing I warn you, by Saint Anne—
As for me, ye shall go alone.
Everyman. My Cousin, will you not with me go?

---

44.   hold back
45.   a man may freely command the services of his family
46.   i.e., the Devil
47.   practiced
48.   rather
49.   have nothing but
50.   born

Cousin.   No, by our Lady! I have the cramp in my toe.
Trust not to me, for, so God me speed,
I will deceive you in your most need.
Kindred.   It availeth not us to tice.[51]
Ye shall have my maid with all my heart;
She loveth to go to feasts, there to be nice,[52]
And to dance, and abroad to start:[53]
I will give her leave to help you in that journey,
If that you and she may agree.
Everyman.   Now show me the very effect of your mind:
Will you go with me, or abide behind?
Kindred.   Abide behind? Yea, that will I, and I may!
Therefore farewell till another day.   *(Exit Kindred.)*
Everyman.   How should I be merry or glad?
For fair promises men to me make,
But when I have most need they me forsake.
I am deceived; that maketh me sad.
Cousin.   Cousin Everyman, farewell now,
For verily I will not go with you.
Also of mine own an unready reckoning
I have to account; therefore I make tarrying.
Now God keep thee, for now I go.   *(Exit Cousin.)*
Everyman.   Ah, Jesus, is all come hereto?
Lo, fair words maketh fools fain,[54]
They promise, and nothing will do, certain.
My kinsmen promised me faithfully
For to abide with me steadfastly,
And now fast away do they flee:
Even so Fellowship promised me.
What friend were best me of to provide?[55]
I lose my time here longer to abide.
Yet in my mind a thing there is:
All my life I have loved riches;
If that my Good[56] now help me might,
He would make my heart full light.
I will speak to him in this distress—
Where art thou, my Goods and riches?

(Goods speaks from a corner:)

---

51. entice
52. wanton
53. rush
54. glad
55. to provide me with
56. goods, possessions

Goods. Who calleth me? Everyman? What! hast thou haste?
    I lie here in corners, trussed and piled so high,
    And in chests I am locked so fast,
    Also sacked in bags. Thou mayst see with thine eye
    I cannot stir; in packs low I lie.
    What would ye have? Lightly me say.
Everyman. Come hither, Good, in all the haste thou may,
    For of counsel I must desire thee.
Goods. Sir, and ye in the world have sorrow or adversity,
    That can I help you to remedy shortly.
Everyman. It is another disease that grieveth me;
    In this world it is not, I tell thee so.
    I am sent for, another way to go,
    To give a strait count general
    Before the highest Jupiter of all;
    And all my life I have had joy and pleasure in thee,
    Therefore, I pray thee, go with me;
    For, peradventure, thou mayst before God Almighty
    My reckoning help to clean and purify;
    For it is said ever among[57]
    That money maketh all right that is wrong.
Goods. Nay, Everyman, I sing another song.
    I follow no man in such voyages;
    For, and I went with thee,
    Thou shouldst fare much the worse for me;
    For because on me thou did set thy mind,
    Thy reckoning I have made blotted and blind,
    That thine account thou cannot make truly;
    And that hast thou for the love of me.
Everyman. That would grieve me full sore,
    When I should come to that fearful answer.
    Up, let us go thither together.
Goods. Nay, not so! I am too brittle, I may not endure;
    I will follow no man one foot, be ye sure.
Everyman. Alas, I have thee loved, and had great pleasure
    All my life-days on good and treasure.
Goods. That is to thy damnation, without leasing,
    For my love is contrary to the love everlasting;
    But if thou had me loved moderately during,
    As to the poor to give part of me,
    Then shouldst thou not in this dolour be,
    Nor in this great sorrow and care.

---

57. at times

Everyman.   Lo, now was I deceived ere I was ware,
   And all I may wite[58] misspending of time.
Goods.   What, weenest thou that I am thine?
Everyman.   I had wend so.
Goods.   Nay, Everyman, I say no.
   As for a while I was lent thee;
   A season thou hast had me in prosperity.
   My condition is man's soul to kill;
   If I save one, a thousand I do spill.
   Weenest thou that I will follow thee?
   Nay, not from this world, verily.
Everyman.   I had wend otherwise.
Goods.   Therefore to thy soul Good is a thief;
   For when thou art dead, this is my guise[59]—
   Another to deceive in this same wise
   As I have done thee, and all to his soul's reprief.[60]
Everyman.   O false Good, cursed may thou be,
   Thou traitor to God, that hast deceived me
   And caught me in thy snare!
Goods.   Marry, thou brought thyself in care,
   Whereof I am glad;
   I must needs laugh, I cannot be sad.
Everyman.   Ah, Good, thou hast had long my heartly love;
   I gave thee that which should be the Lord's above.
   But wilt thou not go with me indeed?
   I pray thee truth to say.
Goods.   No, so God me speed!
   Therefore farewell, and have good day.   (*Exit Goods.*)
Everyman.   O, to whom shall I make my moan
   For to go with me in that heavy journey?
   First Fellowship said he would with me gone;
   His words were very pleasant and gay,
   But afterward he left me alone.
   Then spake I to my kinsmen, all in despair,
   And also they gave me words fair;
   They lacked no fair speaking,
   But all forsook me in the ending.
   Then went I to my Goods, that I loved best,
   In hope to have comfort, but there had I least;
   For my Goods sharply did me tell
   That he bringeth many into hell.

---

58. blame on
59. practice
60. shame

Then of myself I was ashamed,
And so I am worthy to be blamed;
Thus may I well myself hate.
Of whom shall I now counsel take?
I think that I shall never speed
Till that I go to my Good Deed.
But, alas, she is so weak
That she can neither go nor speak;
Yet will I venture on her now.
My Good Deeds, where be you?

(*Good Deeds speaks from the ground*:)

Good Deeds.   Here I lie, cold in the ground;
Thy sins hath me sore bound,
That I cannot stir.
Everyman.   O Good Deeds, I stand in fear!
I must you pray of counsel,
For help now should come right well.
Good Deeds.   Everyman, I have understanding
That ye be summoned account to make
Before Messias, of Jerusalem King;
And you do by me,[61] that journey with you will I take.
Everyman.   Therefore I come to you, my moan to make;
I pray you that ye will go with me.
Good Deeds.   I would full fain, but I cannot stand, verily.
Everyman.   Why, is there anything on you fall?
Good Deeds.   Yea, sir, I may thank you of[62] all;
If ye had perfectly cheered me,
Your book of count full ready had be.
Look, the books of your works and deeds eke![63]
Behold how they lie under the feet,
To your soul's heaviness.
Everyman.   Our Lord Jesus help me!
For one letter here I cannot see.
Good Deeds.   There is a blind reckoning in time of distress.
Everyman.   Good Deeds, I pray you help me in this need,
Or else I am for ever damned indeed;
Therefore help me to make reckoning
Before the Redeemer of all thing,
That King is, and was, and ever shall.
Good Deeds.   Everyman, I am sorry of your fall,
And fain would I help you, and I were able.

---

61.   as I advise
62.   for
63.   also

Everyman.   Good Deeds, your counsel I pray you give me.
Good Deeds.   That shall I do verily;
  Though that on my feet I may not go,
  I have a sister that shall with you also,
  Called Knowledge, which shall with you abide,
  To help you to make that dreadful reckoning.

  (*Enter Knowledge.*)

Knowledge.   Everyman, I will go with thee, and be thy guide,
  In thy most need to go by thy side.
Everyman.   In good condition I am now in every thing,
  And am wholly content with this good thing,
  Thanked be God my creator.
Good Deeds.   And when she hath brought you there
  Where thou shalt heal thee of thy smart,[64]
  Then go you with your reckoning and your Good Deeds together,
  For to make you joyful at heart
  Before the blessed Trinity.
Everyman.   My Good Deeds, gramercy!
  I am well content, certainly,
  With your words sweet.
Knowledge.   Now go we together lovingly
  To Confession, that cleansing river.
Everyman.   For joy I weep; I would we were there!
  But, I pray you, give me cognition
  Where dwelleth that holy man, Confession.
Knowledge.   In the house of salvation:
  We shall find him in that place,
  That shall us comfort, by God's grace.

  (*Knowledge takes Everyman to Confession.*)

  Lo, this is Confession. Kneel down and ask mercy,
  For he is in good conceit[65] with God Almighty.
Everyman.   O glorious fountain, that all uncleanness doth clarify,
  Wash from me the spots of vice unclean,
  That on me no sin may be seen.
  I come with Knowledge for my redemption,
  Redempt with heart and full contrition;
  For I am commanded a pilgrimage to take,
  And great accounts before God to make.
  Now I pray you, Shrift,[66] mother of salvation,
  Help my Good Deeds for my piteous exclamation.

---

64. pain
65. esteem
66. confession

Confession.   I know your sorrow well, Everyman.
Because with Knowledge ye come to me,
I will you comfort as well as I can,
And a precious jewel I will give thee,
Called penance, voider of adversity;
Therewith shall your body chastised be,
With abstinence and perseverance in God's service.
Here shall you receive that scourge of me,
Which is penance strong that ye must endure,
To remember thy Saviour was scourged for thee
With sharp scourges, and suffered it patiently;
So must thou, ere thou scape that painful pilgrimage.
Knowledge, keep him in this voyage,
And by that time Good Deeds will be with thee.
But in any wise be siker[67] of mercy,
For your time draweth fast; and ye will saved be,
Ask God mercy, and he will grant truly.
When with the scourge of penance man doth him[68] bind,
The oil of forgiveness then shall he find.
Everyman.   Thanked be God for his gracious work!
For now I will my penance begin;
This hath rejoiced and lighted my heart,
Though the knots be painful and hard within.
Knowledge.   Everyman, look your penance that ye fulfil,
What pain that ever it to you be;
And Knowledge shall give you counsel at will
How your account ye shall make clearly.
Everyman.   O eternal God, O heavenly figure,
O way of righteousness, O goodly vision,
Which descended down in a virgin pure
Because he would every man redeem,
Which Adam forfeited by his disobedience:
O blessed Godhead, elect and high divine,
Forgive my grievous offence;
Here I cry thee mercy in this presence.
O ghostly treasure, O ransomer and redeemer,
Of all the world hope and conductor,[69]
Mirror of joy, and founder of mercy,
Which enlumineth heaven and earth thereby,[70]
Hear my clamourous complaint, though it late be;

---

67. sure
68. himself
69. guide
70. besides

Receive my prayers, of thy benignity;
Though I be a sinner most abominable,
Yet let my name be written in Moses' table.
O Mary, pray to the Maker of all thing,
Me for to help at my ending;
And save me from the power of my enemy,
For Death assaileth me strongly.
And, Lady, that I may by mean of thy prayer
Of your Son's glory to be[71] partner,
By the means of his passion, I it crave;
I beseech you help my soul to save.
Knowledge, give me the scourge of penance;
My flesh therewith shall give acquittance:[72]
I will now begin, if God give me grace.

Knowledge. Everyman, God give you time and space!
Thus I bequeath you in the hands of our Saviour;
Now may you make your reckoning sure.

Everyman. In the name of the Holy Trinity,
My body sore punished shall be:
Take this, body, for the sin of the flesh!

(Scourges himself.)

Also thou delightest to go gay and fresh,
And in the way of damnation thou did me bring,
Therefore suffer now strokes and punishing.
Now of penance I will wade the water clear,
To save me from purgatory, that sharp fire.

(Good Deeds rises from the ground.)

Good Deeds. I thank God, now I can walk and go,
And am delivered of my sickness and woe.
Therefore with Everyman I will go, and not spare;
His good works I will help him to declare.

Knowledge. Now, Everyman, be merry and glad!
Your Good Deeds cometh now; ye may not be sad.
Now is your Good Deeds whole and sound,
Going upright upon the ground.

Everyman. My heart is light, and shall be evermore;
Now will I smite faster than I did before.

Good Deeds. Everyman, pilgrim, my special friend,
Blessed be thou without end;
For thee is preparate the eternal glory.

---

71. be
72. atonement

Ye have me made whole and sound,
Therefore I will bide by thee in every stound.[73]

Everyman.   Welcome, my Good Deeds; now I hear thy voice,
I weep for very sweetness of love.

Knowledge.   Be no more sad, but ever rejoice;
God seeth thy living in his throne above.
Put on this garment to thy behoof,[74]
Which is wet with your tears,
Or else before God you may it miss,
When ye to your journey's end come shall.

Everyman.   Gentle Knowledge, what do ye it call?

Knowledge.   It is a garment of sorrow:
From pain it will you borrow;[75]
Contrition it is,
That geteth forgiveness;
It pleaseth God passing well.

Good Deeds.   Everyman, will you wear it for your heal?

Everyman.   Now blessed be Jesu, Mary's Son,
For now have I on true contrition.
And let us go now without tarrying;
Good Deeds, have we clear our reckoning?

Good Deeds.   Yea, indeed, I have it here.

Everyman.   Then I trust we need not fear;
Now, friends, let us not part in twain.

Knowledge.   Nay, Everyman, that will we not, certain.

Good Deeds.   Yet must thou lead with thee
Three persons of great might.

Everyman.   Who should they be?

Good Deeds.   Discretion and Strength they hight,[76]
And thy Beauty may not abide behind.

Knowledge.   Also ye must call to mind
Your Five Wits as for your counsellors.

Good Deeds.   You must have them ready at all hours.

Everyman.   How shall I get them hither?

Knowledge.   You must call them all together,
And they will hear you incontinent.[77]

Everyman.   My friends, come hither and be present,
Discretion, Strength, my Five Wits,[78] and Beauty.

(*Enter Beauty, Strength, Discretion, and Five Wits.*)

---

73. always (or: in every attack)
74. advantage
75. take
76. are called
77. immediately
78. senses

Beauty. Here at your will we be all ready.
What will ye that we should do?
Good Deeds. That ye would with Everyman go,
And help him in his pilgrimage.
Advise you, will ye with him or not in that voyage?
Strength. We will bring him all thither,
To his help and comfort, ye may believe me.
Discretion. So will we go with him all together.
Everyman. Almighty God, lofed[79] may thou be!
I give thee laud that I have hither brought
Strength, Discretion, Beauty, and Five Wits. Lack I nought.
And my Good Deeds, with Knowledge clear,
All be in my company at my will here;
I desire no more to[80] my business.
Strength. And I, Strength, will by you stand in distress,
Though thou would in battle fight on the ground.
Five Wits. And though it were through the world round,
We will not depart for sweet ne sour.
Beauty. No more will I unto death's hour,
Whatsoever thereof befall.
Discretion. Everyman, advise you first of all;
Go with a good advisement and deliberation.
We all give you virtuous monition
That all shall be well.
Everyman. My friends, harken what I will tell:
I pray God reward you in his heavenly sphere.
Now harken, all that be here,
For I will make my testament
Here before you all present:
In alms half my good I will give with my hands twain
In the way of charity, with good intent,
And the other half still shall remain
In queth,[81] to be returned there[82] it ought to be.
This I do in despite of the fiend of hell,
To go quit out of his peril
Ever after and this day.
Knowledge. Everyman, harken what I say:
Go to priesthood, I you advise,
And receive of him in any wise
The holy sacrament and ointment together.

---

79. praised
80. for
81. bequest
82. where

Then shortly see ye turn again hither;
We will all abide you here.

Five Wits.   Yea, Everyman, hie you that ye ready were.
There is no emperor, king, duke, ne baron,
That of God hath commission
As hath the least priest in the world being;
For of the blessed sacraments pure and benign
He beareth the keys, and thereof hath the cure[83]
For man's redemption—it is ever sure—
Which God for our soul's medicine
Gave us out of his heart with great pine.
Here in this transitory life, for thee and me,
The blessed sacraments seven there be:
Baptism, confirmation, with priesthood good,
And the sacrament of God's precious flesh and blood,
Marriage, the holy extreme unction, and penance;
These seven be good to have in remembrance,
Gracious sacraments of high divinity.

Everyman.   Fain would I receive that holy body,
And meekly to my ghostly father I will go.

Five Wits.   Everyman, that is the best that ye can do.
God will you to salvation bring,
For priesthood exceedeth all other thing:
To us Holy Scripture they do teach,
And converteth man from sin heaven to reach;
God hath to them more power given
Than to any angel that is in heaven.
With five words[84] he may consecrate,
God's body in flesh and blood to make,
And handleth his Maker between his hands.
The priest bindeth and unbindeth all bands,
Both in earth and in heaven.
Thou ministers[85] all the sacraments seven;
Though we kissed thy feet, thou were worthy;
Thou art surgeon that cureth sin deadly:
No remedy we find under God
But all only[86] priesthood.
Everyman, God gave priests that dignity,
And setteth them in his stead among us to be;
Thus be they above angels in degree.

---

83. charge
84. i.e., *Hoc est enim corpus meum* (Lat. "For this is my body"; from the sacrament of the Eucharist)
85. administer
86. except

(*Everyman goes to the priest to receive the last sacraments.*)

Knowledge. If priests be good, it is so,[87] surely.
But when Jesus hanged on the cross with great smart,
There he gave out of his blessed heart
The same sacrament in great torment:
He sold them not to us, that Lord omnipotent.
Therefore Saint Peter the apostle doth say
That Jesu's curse hath all they
Which God their Saviour do buy or sell,
Or they for any money do take or tell.[88]
Sinful priests giveth the sinners example bad;
Their children sitteth by other men's fires, I have heard;
And some haunteth women's company
With unclean life, as lusts of lechery:
These be with sin made blind.
Five Wits. I trust to God no such may we find;
Therefore let us priesthood honour,
And follow their doctrine for our souls' succour.
We be their sheep, and they shepherds be
By whom we all be kept in surety.
Peace, for yonder I see Everyman come,
Which hath made true satisfaction.
Good Deeds. Methink it is he indeed.

(*Re-enter Everyman.*)

Everyman. Now Jesu be your alder speed![89]
I have received the sacrament for my redemption,
And then mine extreme unction:
Blessed be all they that counselled me to take it!
And now, friends, let us go without longer respite;
I thank God that ye have tarried so long.
Now set each of you on this rood[90] your hand,
And shortly follow me:
I go before there I would be; God be our guide!
Strength. Everyman, we will not from you go
Till ye have done this voyage long.
Discretion. I, Discretion, will bide by you also.
Knowledge. And though this pilgrimage be never so strong,[91]
I will never part you fro.

---

87. i.e., "above angels in degree"
88. count
89. help to all of you
90. cross
91. hard, difficult

Strength. Everyman, I will be as sure by thee
As ever I did by Judas Maccabee.[92]

(*Everyman comes to his grave.*)

Everyman. Alas, I am so faint I may not stand;
My limbs under me doth fold.
Friends, let us not turn again to this land,
Not for all the world's gold;
For into this cave must I creep
And turn to earth, and there to sleep.
Beauty. What, into this grave? Alas!
Everyman. Yea, there shall ye consume, more and less.[93]
Beauty. And what, should I smother here?
Everyman. Yea, by my faith, and never more appear.
In this world live no more we shall,
But in heaven before the highest Lord of all.
Beauty. I cross out all this; adieu, by Saint John!
I take my cap in my lap, and am gone.
Everyman. What, Beauty, whither will ye?
Beauty. Peace, I am deaf; I look not behind me,
Not and thou wouldest give me all the gold in thy chest.   (*Exit Beauty.*)
Everyman. Alas, whereto may I trust?
Beauty goeth fast away from me;
She promised with me to live and die.
Strength. Everyman, I will thee also forsake and deny;
Thy game liketh me not at all.
Everyman. Why, then, ye will forsake me all?
Sweet Strength, tarry a little space.
Strength. Nay, sir, by the rood of grace!
I will hie me from thee fast,
Though thou weep till thy heart to-brast.[94]
Everyman. Ye would ever bide by me, ye said.
Strength. Yea, I have you far enough conveyed.
Ye be old enough, I understand,
Your pilgrimage to take on hand;
I repent me that I hither came.
Everyman. Strength, you to displease I am to blame;
Yet promise is debt, this ye well wot.
Strength. In faith, I care not.
Thou art but a fool to complain;

---

92. Jewish religious and national leader against Syria in the 2nd century B.C. He told his men that "the success of war is not in the multitude: but strength cometh from heaven" (Apocrypha, I Maccabees, 3:19)
93. high and low
94. broke to pieces

You spend your speech and waste your brain.
Go thrust thee into the ground!   *(Exit Strength.)*

Everyman. I had wend surer I should you have found.
He that trusteth in his Strength
She him deceiveth at the length.
Both Strength and Beauty forsaketh me;
Yet they promised me fair and lovingly.

Discretion. Everyman, I will after Strength be gone;
As for me, I will leave you alone.

Everyman. Why, Discretion, will ye forsake me?

Discretion. Yea, in faith, I will go from thee,
For when Strength goeth before
I follow after evermore.

Everyman. Yet, I pray thee, for the love of the Trinity,
Look in my grave once piteously.

Discretion. Nay, so nigh will I not come;
Farewell, every one!   *(Exit Discretion.)*

Everyman. O, all things faileth, save God alone—
Beauty, Strength, and Discretion;
For when Death bloweth his blast,
They all run from me full fast.

Five Wits. Everyman, my leave now of thee I take;
I will follow the other, for here I thee forsake.

Everyman. Alas, then may I wail and weep,
For I took you for my best friend.

Five Wits. I will no longer thee keep;
Now farewell, and there an end.   *(Exit Five Wits.)*

Everyman. O Jesu, help! All hath forsaken me.

Good Deeds. Nay, Everyman; I will bide with thee.
I will not forsake thee indeed;
Thou shalt find me a good friend at need.

Everyman. Gramercy, Good Deeds! Now may I true friends see.
They have forsaken me, every one;
I loved them better than my Good Deeds alone.
Knowledge, will ye forsake me also?

Knowledge. Yea, Everyman, when ye to Death shall go;
But not yet, for no manner of danger.

Everyman. Gramercy, Knowledge, with all my heart.

Knowledge. Nay, yet I will not from hence depart
Till I see where ye shall become.

Everyman. Methink, alas, that I must be gone
To make my reckoning and my debts pay,
For I see my time is nigh spent away.
Take example, all ye that this do hear or see,
How they that I loved best do forsake me,
Except my Good Deeds that bideth truly.

Good Deeds.   All earthly things is but vanity:
      Beauty, Strength, and Discretion do man forsake,
      Foolish friends, and kinsmen, that fair spake—
      All fleeth save Good Deeds, and that am I.
Everyman.   Have mercy on me, God most mighty;
      And stand by me, thou mother and maid, holy Mary.
Good Deeds.   Fear not; I will speak for thee.
Everyman.   Here I cry God mercy.
Good Deeds.   Short[95] our end, and minish our pain;
      Let us go and never come again.
Everyman.   Into thy hands, Lord, my soul I commend;
      Receive it, Lord, that it be not lost.
      As thou me boughtest, so me defend,
      And save me from the fiend's boast,
      That I may appear with that blessed host
      That shall be saved at the day of doom.
      In manus tuas, of mights most
      For ever, *commendo spiritum meum.*[96]   *(He sinks into his grave.)*
Knowledge.   Now hath he suffered that we all shall endure;
      The Good Deeds shall make all sure.
      Now hath he made ending;
      Methinketh that I hear angels sing,
      And make great joy and melody
      Where Everyman's soul received shall be.
Angel.   Come, excellent elect spouse, to Jesu!
      Hereabove thou shalt go
      Because of thy singular virtue.
      Now the soul is taken the body fro,
      Thy reckoning is crystal-clear.
      Now shalt thou into the heavenly sphere,
      Unto the which all ye shall come
      That liveth well before the day of doom.

      (Enter Doctor.)

Doctor.   This moral men may have in mind.
      Ye hearers, take it of worth,[97] old and young,
      And forsake Pride, for he deceiveth you in the end;
      And remember Beauty, Five Wits, Strength, and Discretion,
      They all at the last do every man forsake,
      Save[98] his Good Deeds there doth he take.

---

95.   shorten
96.   into thy hands I commend my spirit (Luke, 23:46)
97.   value it
98.   unless

But beware, for and they be small
Before God, he hath no help at all;
None excuse may be there for every man.
Alas, how shall he do then?
For after death amends may no man make,
For then mercy and pity doth him forsake.
If his reckoning be not clear when he doth come,
God will say: 'Ite, maledicti, in ignem eternum.'[99]
And he that hath his account whole and sound,
High in heaven he shall be crowned;
Unto which place God bring us all thither,
That we may live body and soul together.
Thereto help the Trinity!
Amen, say ye, for saint charity.

Thus Endeth this Moral Play of Everyman.

Questions

1. What does the dramatist's utilization of the allegorical mode within a timeless setting contribute to the meaning of the play? **2.** What difference, if any, would there be if God appeared at the end of the play rather than at the beginning? **3.** What thematic reasons are there for the order in which Everyman meets his various friends? **4.** Some commentators have seen **Everyman** as a psychological drama of great tension and suspense. Do you agree? Explain.

---

99. depart, ye cursed, into everlasting fire (Matthew, 25:41)

The Dumb Waiter

HAROLD PINTER   [b. 1930]

SCENE.   *A basement room. Two beds, flat against the back wall. A serving hatch, closed, between the beds. A door to the kitchen and lavatory, left. A door to a passage, right.*

Ben is lying on a bed, left, reading a paper. Gus is sitting on a bed, right, tying his shoelaces, with difficulty. Both are dressed in shirts, trousers and braces.
   Silence.
   Gus ties his laces, rises, yawns and begins to walk slowly to the door, left. He stops, looks down, and shakes his foot.
   Ben lowers his paper and watches him. Gus kneels and unties his shoelace and slowly takes off the shoe. He looks inside it and brings out a flattened matchbox. He shakes it and examines it. Their eyes meet. Ben rattles his paper and reads. Gus puts the matchbox in his pocket and bends down to put on his shoe. He ties his lace, with difficulty. Ben lowers his paper and watches him. Gus walks to the door, left, stops, and shakes the other foot. He kneels, unties his shoelace, and slowly takes off the shoe. He looks inside it and brings out a flattened cigarette packet. He shakes it and examines it. Their eyes meet. Ben rattles his paper and reads. Gus puts the packet in his pocket, bends down, puts on his shoe and ties the lace.
   He wanders off, left.
   Ben slams the paper down on the bed and glares after him. He picks up the paper and lies on his back, reading.
   Silence.
   A lavatory chain is pulled twice off, left, but the lavatory does not flush.
   Silence.
   Gus re-enters, left, and halts at the door, scratching his head.
   Ben slams down the paper.

Ben.   Kaw!

He picks up the paper.

   What about this? Listen to this!

He refers to the paper.

   A man of eighty-seven wanted to cross the road. But there was a lot of traffic, see? He couldn't see how he was going to squeeze through. So he crawled under a lorry.
Gus.   He what?
Ben.   He crawled under a lorry. A stationary lorry.

Gus. No?

Ben. The lorry started and ran over him.

Gus. Go on!

Ben. That's what it says here.

Gus. Get away.

Ben. It's enough to make you want to puke, isn't it?

Gus. Who advised him to do a thing like that?

Ben. A man of eighty-seven crawling under a lorry!

Gus. It's unbelievable.

Ben. It's down here in black and white.

Gus. Incredible.

Silence. Gus shakes his head and exits. Ben lies back and reads. The lavatory chain is pulled once off left, but the lavatory does not flush. Ben whistles at an item in the paper. Gus re-enters.

I want to ask you something.

Ben. What are you doing out there?

Gus. Well, I was just—

Ben. What about the tea?

Gus. I'm just going to make it.

Ben. Well, go on, make it.

Gus. Yes, I will. *(He sits in a chair. Ruminatively.)* He's laid on some very nice crockery this time, I'll say that. It's sort of striped. There's a white stripe.

Ben reads.

It's very nice. I'll say that.

Ben turns the page.

You know, sort of round the cup. Round the rim. All the rest of it's black, you see. Then the saucer's black, except for right in the middle, where the cup goes, where it's white.

Ben reads.

Then the plates are the same, you see. Only they've got a black stripe—the plates—right across the middle. Yes, I'm quite taken with the crockery.

Ben *(still reading).* What do you want plates for? You're not going to eat.

Gus. I've brought a few biscuits.

Ben. Well, you'd better eat them quick.

Gus. I always bring a few biscuits. Or a pie. You know I can't drink tea without anything to eat.

Ben. Well, make the tea then, will you? Time's getting on.

Gus brings out the flattened cigarette packet and examines it.

Gus. You got any cigarettes? I think I've run out.

He throws the packet high up and leans forward to catch it.

I hope it won't be a long job, this one.

Aiming carefully, he flips the packet under his bed.

Oh, I wanted to ask you something.
Ben *(slamming his paper down).*   Kaw!
Gus.   What's that?
Ben.   A child of eight killed a cat!
Gus.   Get away.
Ben.   It's a fact. What about that, eh? A child of eight killing a cat!
Gus.   How did he do it?
Ben.   It was a girl.
Gus.   How did she do it?
Ben.   She—

He picks up the paper and studies it.

It doesn't say.
Gus.   Why not?
Ben.   Wait a minute. It just says—Her brother, aged eleven, viewed the incident from the toolshed.
Gus.   Go on!
Ben.   That's bloody ridiculous.

Pause.

Gus.   I bet he did it.
Ben.   Who?
Gus.   The brother.
Ben.   I think you're right.

Pause.

(Slamming down the paper.) What about that, eh? A kid of eleven killing a cat and blaming it on his little sister of eight! It's enough to—

He breaks off in disgust and seizes the paper. Gus rises.

Gus.   What time is he getting in touch?

Ben reads.

What time is he getting in touch?
Ben.   What's the matter with you? It could be any time. Any time.
Gus *(moves to the foot of Ben's bed).*   Well, I was going to ask you something.
Ben.   What?
Gus.   Have you noticed the time that tank takes to fill?
Ben.   What tank?
Gus.   In the lavatory.

Ben. No. Does it?

Gus. Terrible.

Ben. Well, what about it?

Gus. What do you think's the matter with it?

Ben. Nothing.

Gus. Nothing?

Ben. It's got a deficient ballcock, that's all.

Gus. A deficient what?

Ben. Ballcock.

Gus. No? Really?

Ben. That's what I should say.

Gus. Go on! That didn't occur to me.

Gus wanders to his bed and presses the mattress.

> I didn't have a very restful sleep today, did you? It's not much of a bed. I could have done with another blanket too. *(He catches sight of a picture on the wall.)* Hello, what's this? *(Peering at it.)* "The First Eleven." Cricketers. You seen this, Ben?

Ben *(reading).* What?

Gus. The first eleven.

Ben. What?

Gus. There's a photo here of the first eleven.

Ben. What first eleven?

Gus *(studying the photo).* It doesn't say.

Ben. What about that tea?

Gus. They all look a bit old to me.

Gus wanders downstage, looks out front, then all about the room.

> I wouldn't like to live in this dump. I wouldn't mind if you had a window, you could see what it looked like outside.

Ben. What do you want a window for?

Gus. Well, I like to have a bit of a view, Ben. It whiles away the time.

He walks about the room.

> I mean, you come into a place when it's still dark, you come into a room you've never seen before, you sleep all day, you do your job, and then you go away in the night again.

Pause.

> I like to get a look at the scenery. You never get the chance in this job.

Ben. You get your holidays, don't you?

Gus. Only a fortnight.

Ben *(lowering the paper).* You kill me. Anyone would think you're working every day. How often do we do a job? Once a week? What are you complaining about?

Gus. Yes, but we've got to be on tap though, haven't we? You can't move out of the house in case a call comes.

Ben. You know what your trouble is?

Gus. What?

Ben. You haven't got any interests.

Gus. I've got interests.

Ben. What? Tell me one of your interests.

Pause.

Gus. I've got interests.

Ben. Look at me. What have I got?

Gus. I don't know. What?

Ben. I've got my woodwork. I've got my model boats. Have you ever seen me idle? I'm never idle. I know how to occupy my time, to its best advantage. Then when a call comes, I'm ready.

Gus. Don't you ever get a bit fed up?

Ben. Fed up? What with?

Silence.

Ben reads, Gus feels in the pocket of his jacket, which hangs on the bed.

Gus. You got any cigarettes? I've run out.

The lavatory flushes off left.

There she goes.

Gus sits on his bed.

No, I mean, I say the crockery's good. It is. It's very nice. But that's about all I can say for this place. It's worse than the last one. Remember that last place we were in? Last time, where was it? At least there was a wireless there. No, honest. He doesn't seem to bother much about our comfort these days.

Ben. When are you going to stop jabbering?

Gus. You'd get rheumatism in a place like this, if you stay long.

Ben. We're not staying long. Make the tea, will you? We'll be on the job in a minute.

Gus picks up a small bag by his bed and brings out a packet of tea. He examines it and looks up.

Gus. Eh, I've been meaning to ask you.

Ben. What the hell is it now?

Gus. Why did you stop the car this morning, in the middle of that road?

Ben *(lowering the paper).* I thought you were asleep.

Gus. I was, but I woke up when you stopped. You did stop, didn't you?

Pause.

In the middle of that road. It was still dark, don't you remember? I looked out. It was all misty. I thought perhaps you wanted to kip, but you were sitting up dead straight, like you were waiting for something.

Ben. I wasn't waiting for anything.

Gus. I must have fallen asleep again. What was all that about then? Why did you stop?

Ben *(picking up the paper).* We were too early.

Gus. Early? *(He rises.)* What do you mean? We got the call, didn't we, saying we were to start right away. We did. We shoved out on the dot. So how could we be too early?

Ben *(quietly).* Who took the call, me or you?

Gus. You.

Ben. We were too early.

Gus. Too early for what?

Pause.

You mean someone had to get out before we got in?

He examines the bedclothes.

I thought these sheets didn't look too bright. I thought they ponged a bit. I was too tired to notice when I got in this morning. Eh, that's taking a bit of a liberty, isn't it? I don't want to share my bed-sheets. I told you things were going down the drain. I mean, we've always had clean sheets laid on up till now. I've noticed it.

Ben. How do you know those sheets weren't clean?

Gus. What do you mean?

Ben. How do you know they weren't clean? You've spent the whole day in them, haven't you?

Gus. What, you mean it might be my pong? *(He sniffs sheets.)* Yes. *(He sits slowly on bed.)* It could be my pong, I suppose. It's difficult to tell. I don't really know what I pong like, that's the trouble.

Ben *(referring to the paper).* Kaw!

Gus. Eh, Ben.

Ben. Kaw!

Gus. Ben.

Ben. What?

Gus. What town are we in? I've forgotten.

Ben. I've told you. Birmingham.

Gus. Go on!

He looks with interest about the room.

> That's in the Midlands. The second biggest city in Great Britain. I'd never have guessed.

He snaps his fingers.

> Eh, it's Friday today, isn't it? It'll be Saturday tomorrow.

Ben. What about it?

Gus *(excited).* We could go and watch the Villa.

Ben. They're playing away.

Gus. No, are they? Caarr! What a pity.

Ben. Anyway, there's no time. We've got to get straight back.

Gus. Well, we have done in the past, haven't we? Stayed over and watched a game, haven't we? For a bit of relaxation.

Ben. Things have tightened up, mate. They've tightened up.

Gus chuckles to himself.

Gus. I saw the Villa get beat in a cup tie once. Who was it against now? White shirts. It was one-all at half-time. I'll never forget it. Their opponents won by a penalty. Talk about drama. Yes, it was a disputed penalty. Disputed. They got beat two–one, anyway, because of it. You were there yourself.

Ben. Not me.

Gus. Yes, you were there. Don't you remember that disputed penalty?

Ben. No.

Gus. He went down just inside the area. Then they said he was just acting. I didn't think the other bloke touched him myself. But the referee had the ball on the spot.

Ben. Didn't touch him! What are you talking about? He laid him out flat!

Gus. Not the Villa. The Villa don't play that sort of game.

Ben. Get out of it.

Pause.

Gus. Eh, that must have been here, in Birmingham.

Ben. What must?

Gus. The Villa. That must have been here.

Ben. They were playing away.

Gus. Because you know who the other team was? It was the Spurs. It was Tottenham Hotspur.

Ben. Well, what about it?

Gus. We've never done a job in Tottenham.

Ben. How do you know?

Gus. I'd remember Tottenham.

Ben turns on his bed to look at him.

Ben. Don't make me laugh, will you?

Ben turns back and reads. Gus yawns and speaks through his yawn.

Gus. When's he going to get in touch?

Pause.

> Yes, I'd like to see another football match. I've always been an ardent football fan. Here, what about coming to see the Spurs tomorrow?

Ben *(tonelessly).*   They're playing away.

Gus. Who are?

Ben. The Spurs.

Gus. Then they might be playing here.

Ben. Don't be silly.

Gus. If they're playing away they might be playing here. They might be playing the Villa.

Ben *(tonelessly).*   But the Villa are playing away.

Pause. An envelope slides under the door, right. Gus sees it. He stands, looking at it.

Gus. Ben.

Ben. Away. They're all playing away.

Gus. Ben, look here.

Ben. What?

Gus. Look.

Ben turns his head and sees the envelope. He stands.

Ben. What's that?

Gus. I don't know.

Ben. Where did it come from?

Gus. Under the door.

Ben. Well, what is it?

Gus. I don't know.

They stare at it.

Ben. Pick it up.

Gus. What do you mean?

Ben. Pick it up!

Gus slowly moves towards it, bends and picks it up.

> What is it?

Gus. An envelope.

Ben. Is there anything on it?

Gus. No.

Ben. Is it sealed?

Gus. Yes.

Ben. Open it.
Gus. What?
Ben. Open it!

Gus opens it and looks inside.

What's in it?

Gus empties twelve matches into his hand.

Gus. Matches.
Ben. Matches?
Gus. Yes.
Ben. Show it to me.

Gus passes the envelope. Ben examines it.

Nothing on it. Not a word
Gus. That's funny, isn't it?
Ben. It came under the door?
Gus. Must have done.
Ben. Well, go on.
Gus. Go on where?
Ben. Open the door and see if you can catch anyone outside.
Gus. Who, me?
Ben. Go on!

Gus stares at him, puts the matches in his pocket, goes to his bed and brings a revolver from under the pillow. He goes to the door, opens it, looks out and shuts it.

Gus. No one.

He replaces the revolver.

Ben. What did you see?
Gus. Nothing.
Ben. They must have been pretty quick.

Gus takes the matches from his pocket and looks at them.

Gus. Well, they'll come in handy.
Ben. Yes.
Gus. Won't they?
Ben. Yes, you're always running out, aren't you?
Gus. All the time.
Ben. Well, they'll come in handy then.
Gus. Yes.
Ben. Won't they?
Gus. Yes, I could do with them. I could do with them too.

Ben. You could, eh?

Gus. Yes.

Ben. Why?

Gus. We haven't got any.

Ben. Well, you've got some now, haven't you?

Gus. I can light the kettle now.

Ben. Yes, you're always cadging matches. How many have you got there?

Gus. About a dozen.

Ben. Well, don't lose them. Red too. You don't even need a box.

Gus probes his ear with a match.

(*Slapping his hand*). Don't waste them! Go on, go and light it.

Gus. Eh?

Ben. Go and light it.

Gus. Light what?

Ben. The kettle.

Gus. You mean the gas.

Ben. Who does?

Gus. You do.

Ben (*his eyes narrowing*). What do you mean, I mean the gas?

Gus. Well, that's what you mean, don't you? The gas.

Ben (*powerfully*). If I say go and light the kettle I mean go and light the kettle.

Gus. How can you light a kettle?

Ben. It's a figure of speech! Light the kettle. It's a figure of speech!

Gus. I've never heard it.

Ben. Light the kettle! It's common usage!

Gus. I think you've got it wrong.

Ben (*menacing*). What do you mean?

Gus. They say put on the kettle.

Ben (*taut*). Who says?

They stare at each other, breathing hard.

(*Deliberately.*) I have never in all my life heard anyone say put on the kettle.

Gus. I bet my mother used to say it.

Ben. Your mother? When did you last see your mother?

Gus. I don't know, about—

Ben. Well, what are you talking about your mother for?

They stare.

Gus, I'm not trying to be unreasonable. I'm just trying to point out something to you.

Gus. Yes, but—

Ben. Who's the senior partner here, me or you?

Gus. You.

Ben. I'm only looking after your interests, Gus. You've got to learn, mate.

Gus. Yes, but I've never heard—

Ben. (*vehemently*).   Nobody says light the gas! What does the gas light?

Gus. What does the gas—?

Ben (*grabbing him with two hands by the throat, at arm's length*).
     THE KETTLE, YOU FOOL!

Gus takes the hands from his throat.

Gus. All right. All right.

Pause.

Ben. Well, what are you waiting for?

Gus. I want to see if they light.

Ben. What?

Gus. The matches.

He takes out the flattened box and tries to strike.

     No.

He throws the box under the bed. Ben stares at him. Gus raises his foot.

     Shall I try it on here?

Ben stares. Gus strikes a match on his shoe. It lights.

     Here we are.

Ben (*wearily*).   Put on the bloody kettle, for Christ's sake.

Ben goes to his bed, but, realising what he has said, stops and half turns. They look at each other. Gus slowly exits, left. Ben slams his paper down on the bed and sits on it, head in hands.

Gus (*entering*).   It's going.

Ben. What?

Gus. The stove.

Gus goes to his bed and sits.

     I wonder who it'll be tonight.

Silence.

Eh, I've been wanting to ask you something.

Ben (*putting his legs on the bed*).   Oh, for Christ's sake.

Gus. No. I was going to ask you something.

He rises and sits on Ben's bed.

Ben. What are you sitting on my bed for?

Gus sits.

What's the matter with you? You're always asking me questions. What's the matter with you?

Gus. Nothing.

Ben. You never used to ask me so many damn questions. What's come over you?

Gus. No, I was just wondering.

Ben. Stop wondering. You've got a job to do. Why don't you just do it and shut up?

Gus. That's what I was wondering about.

Ben. What?

Gus. The job.

Ben. What job?

Gus (*tentatively*). I thought perhaps you might know something.

Ben looks at him.

I thought perhaps you—I mean—have you got any idea—who it's going to be tonight?

Ben. Who what's going to be?

They look at each other.

Gus (*at length*). Who it's going to be.

Silence.

Ben. Are you feeling all right?

Gus. Sure.

Ben. Go and make the tea.

Gus. Yes, sure.

Gus exits, left, Ben looks after him. He then takes his revolver from under the pillow and checks it for ammunition. Gus re-enters.

The gas has gone out.

Ben. Well, what about it?

Gus. There's a meter.

Ben. I haven't got any money.

Gus. Nor have I.

Ben. You'll have to wait.

Gus. What for?

Ben. For Wilson.

Gus. He might not come. He might just send a message. He doesn't always come.

Ben. Well, you'll have to do without it, won't you?

Gus. Blimey.

Ben. You'll have a cup of tea afterwards. What's the matter with you?

Gus. I like to have one before.

Ben holds the revolver up to the light and polishes it.

Ben. You'd better get ready anyway.

Gus. Well, I don't know, that's a bit much, you know, for my money.

He picks up a packet of tea from the bed and throws it into the bag.

I hope he's got a shilling, anyway, if he comes. He's entitled to have. After all, it's his place, he could have seen there was enough gas for a cup of tea.

Ben. What do you mean, it's his place?

Gus. Well, isn't it?

Ben. He's probably only rented it. It doesn't have to be his place.

Gus. I know it's his place. I bet the whole house is. He's not even laying on any gas now either.

Gus sits on his bed.

It his place all right. Look at all the other places. You go to this address, there's a key there, there's a teapot, there's never a soul in sight—(*He pauses.*) Eh, nobody ever hears a thing, have you ever thought of that? We never get any complaints, do we, too much noise or anything like that? You never see a soul, do you?—except the bloke who comes. You ever noticed that? I wonder if the walls are sound-proof. (*He touches the wall above his bed.*) Can't tell. All you do is wait, eh? Half the time he doesn't even bother to put in an appearance, Wilson.

Ben. Why should he? He's a busy man.

Gus (*thoughtfully*). I find him hard to talk to, Wilson. Do you know that, Ben?

Ben. Scrub round it, will you?

Pause.

Gus. There are a number of things I want to ask him. But I can never get round to it, when I see him.

Pause.

I've been thinking about the last one.

Ben. What last one?

Gus. That girl.

Ben grabs the paper, which he reads.

(*Rising, looking down at Ben*). How many times have you read that paper?

Ben slams the paper down and rises.

Ben (*angrily*). What do you mean?

Gus. I was just wondering how many times you'd—

Ben. What are you doing, criticising me?

Gus. No, I was just—

Ben. You'll get a swipe round your earhole if you don't watch your step.

Gus. Now look here, Ben—

Ben. I'm not looking anywhere! (*He addresses the room.*) How many times have I—! A bloody liberty!

Gus. I didn't mean that.

Ben. You just get on with it, mate. Get on with it, that's all.

Ben gets back on the bed.

Gus. I was just thinking about that girl, that's all.

Gus sits on his bed.

She wasn't much to look at, I know, but still. It was a mess though, wasn't it? What a mess. Honest, I can't remember a mess like that one. They don't seem to hold together like men, women. A loose texture, like. Didn't she spread, eh? She didn't half spread. Kaw! But I've been meaning to ask.

Ben sits up and clenches his eyes.

Who clears up after we've gone? I'm curious about that. Who does the clearing up? Maybe they don't clear up. Maybe they just leave them there, eh? What do you think? How many jobs have we done? Blimey, I can't count them. What if they never clear anything up after we've gone.

Ben (*pityingly*). You mutt. Do you think we're the only branch of this organisation? Have a bit of common. They got departments for everything.

Gus. What cleaners and all?

Ben. You birk!

Gus. No, it was that girl made me start to think—

There is a loud clatter and racket in the bulge of wall between the beds, of something descending. They grab their revolvers, jump up and face the wall. The noise comes to a stop. Silence. They look at each other. Ben gestures sharply towards the wall. Gus approaches the wall slowly. He bangs it with his revolver. It is hollow. Ben moves to the head of his bed, his revolver cocked. Gus puts his revolver on his bed and pats along the bottom of the centre panel. He finds a rim. He lifts the panel. Disclosed is a serving-hatch, a "dumb waiter." A wide box is held by pulleys. Gus peers into the box. He brings out a piece of paper.

Ben. What is it?

Gus. You have a look at it.

Ben. Read it.

Gus (*reading*). Two braised steak and chips. Two sago puddings. Two teas without sugar.

Ben. Let me see that. (*He takes the paper.*)

Gus (*to himself*).   Two teas without sugar.

Ben. Mmnn.

Gus. What do you think of that?

Ben. Well—

The box goes up. Ben levels his revolver.

Gus. Give us a chance! They're in a hurry, aren't they?

Ben re-reads the note. Gus looks over his shoulder.

That's a bit—that's a bit funny, isn't it?

Ben (*quickly*).   No. It's not funny. It probably used to be a café here, that's all. Upstairs. These places change hands very quickly.

Gus. A café?

Ben. Yes.

Gus. What, you mean this was the kitchen, down here?

Ben. Yes, they change hands overnight, these places. Go into liquidation. The people who run it, you know, they don't find it a going concern, they move out.

Gus. You mean the people who ran this place didn't find it a going concern and moved out?

Ben. Sure.

Gus. WELL, WHO'S GOT IT NOW?

Silence.

Ben. What do you mean, who's got it now?

Gus. Who's got it now? If they moved out, who moved in?

Ben. Well, that all depends—

The box descends with a clatter and bang. Ben levels his revolver. Gus goes to the box and brings out a piece of paper.

Gus (*reading*).   Soup of the day. Liver and onions. Jam tart.

A pause. Gus looks at Ben. Ben takes the note and reads it. He walks slowly to the hatch. Gus follows. Ben looks into the hatch but not up it. Gus puts his hand on Ben's shoulder. Ben throws it off. Gus puts his finger to his mouth. He leans on the hatch and swiftly looks up it. Ben flings him away in alarm. Ben looks at the note. He throws his revolver on the bed and speaks with decision.

Ben. We'd better send something up.

Gus. Eh?

Ben. We'd better send something up.

Gus. Oh! Yes. Yes. Maybe you're right.

They are both relieved at the decision.

Ben (*purposefully*). Quick! What have you got in that bag?
Gus. Not much.

Gus goes to the hatch and shouts up it.

Wait a minute!
Ben. Don't do that!

Gus examines the contents of the bag and brings them out, one by one.

Gus. Biscuits. A bar of chocolate. Half a pint of milk.
Ben. That all?
Gus. Packet of tea.
Ben. Good.
Gus. We can't send the tea. That's all the tea we've got.
Ben. Well, there's no gas. You can't do anything with it, can you?
Gus. Maybe they can send us down a bob.
Ben. What else is there?
Gus (*reaching into bag*). One Eccles cake.
Ben. One Eccles cake?
Gus. Yes.
Ben. You never told me you had an Eccles cake.
Gus. Didn't I?
Ben. Why only one? Didn't you bring one for me?
Gus. I didn't think you'd be keen.
Ben. Well, you can't send up one Eccles cake, anyway.
Gus. Why not?
Ben. Fetch one of those plates.
Gus. All right.

Gus goes towards the door, left, and stops.

Do you mean I can keep the Eccles cake then?
Ben. Keep it?
Gus. Well, they don't know we've got it, do they?
Ben. That's not the point.
Gus. Can't I keep it?
Ben. No, you can't. Get the plate.

Gus exits, left. Ben looks in the bag. He brings out a packet of crisps. Enter Gus with a plate.

(*Accusingly, holding up the crisps*). Where did these come from?
Gus. What?
Ben. Where did these crisps come from?
Gus. Where did you find them?

Ben (*hitting him on the shoulder*).   You're playing a dirty game, my lad!

Gus.   I only eat those with beer!

Ben.   Well, where were you going to get the beer?

Gus.   I was saving them till I did.

Ben.   I'll remember this. Put everything on the plate.

They pile everything on to the plate. The box goes up without the plate.

Wait a minute!

They stand.

Gus.   It's gone up.

Ben.   It's all your stupid fault, playing about!

Gus.   What do we do now?

Ben.   We'll have to wait till it comes down.

Ben puts the plate on the bed, puts on his shoulder holster, and starts to put on his tie.

You'd better get ready.

Gus goes to his bed, puts on his tie, and starts to fix his holster.

Gus.   Hey, Ben.

Ben.   What?

Gus.   What's going on here?

Pause.

Ben.   What do you mean?

Gus.   How can this be a café?

Ben.   It used to be a café.

Gus.   Have you seen the gas stove?

Ben.   What about it?

Gus.   It's only got three rings.

Ben.   So what?

Gus.   Well you couldn't cook much on three rings, not for a busy place like this.

Ben (*irritably*).   That's why the service is slow!

Ben puts on his waistcoat.

Gus.   Yes, but what happens when we're not here? What do they do then? All those menus coming down and nothing going up. It might have been going on like this for years.

Ben brushes his jacket.

What happens when we go?

Ben puts on his jacket.

They can't do much business.

The box descends. They turn about. Gus goes to the hatch and brings out a note.

Gus *(reading).*   Macaroni Pastitsio. Ormitha Macarounada.
Ben.   What was that?
Gus.   Macaroni Pastitsio. Ormitha Macarounada.
Ben.   Greek dishes.
Gus.   No.
Ben.   That's right.
Gus.   That's pretty high class.
Ben.   Quick before it goes up.

Gus puts the plate in the box.

Gus *(calling up the hatch).*   Three McVitie and Price! One Lyons Red Label!
   One Smith's Crisps! One Eccles cake! One Fruit and Nut!
Ben.   Cadbury's.
Gus *(up the hatch).*   Cadbury's!
Ben *(handing the milk).*   One bottle of milk.
Gus *(up the hatch).*   One bottle of milk! Half a pint! *(He looks at the label.)*
   Express Dairy! *(He puts the bottle in the box.)*

The box goes up.

Just did it.
Ben.   You shouldn't shout like that.
Gus.   Why not?
Ben.   It isn't done.

Ben goes to his bed.

Well, that should be all right, anyway, for the time being.
Gus.   You think so, eh?
Ben.   Get dressed, will you? It'll be any minute now.

Gus puts on his waistcoat. Ben lies down and looks up at the ceiling.

Gus.   This is some place. No tea and no biscuits.
Ben.   Eating makes you lazy, mate. You're getting lazy, you know that? You
   don't want to get slack on your job.
Gus.   Who me?
Ben.   Slack, mate, slack.
Gus.   Who me? Slack?
Gus.   Have you checked your gun? You haven't even checked your gun. It
   looks disgraceful, anyway. Why don't you ever polish it?

Gus rubs his revolver on the sheet. Ben takes out a pocket mirror and straightens his tie.

Gus. I wonder where the cook is. They must have had a few, to cope with that. Maybe they had a few more gas stoves. Eh! Maybe there's another kitchen along the passage.

Ben. Of course there is! Do you know what it takes to make an Ormitha Macarounada?

Gus. No, what?

Ben. An Ormitha—! Buck your ideas up, will you?

Gus. Takes a few cooks, eh?

Gus puts his revolver in its holster.

The sooner we're out of this place the better.

He puts on his jacket.

Why doesn't he get in touch? I feel like I've been here years. (*He takes his revolver out of its holster to check the ammunition.*) We've never let him down though, have we? We've never let him down. I was thinking only the other day, Ben. We're reliable, aren't we?

He puts his revolver back in its holster.

Still, I'll be glad when it's over tonight.

He brushes his jacket.

I hope the bloke's not going to get excited tonight, or anything. I'm feeling a bit off. I've got a splitting headache.

Silence.

The box descends. Ben jumps up. Gus collects the note.

(*Reading.*) One Bamboo Shoots, Water Chestnuts and Chicken. One Char Siu and Beansprouts.

Ben. Beansprouts?

Gus. Yes.

Ben. Blimey.

Gus. I wouldn't know where to begin.

He looks back at the box. The packet of tea is inside it. He picks it up.

They've sent back the tea.

Ben (*anxious*).   What'd they do that for?

Gus. Maybe it isn't tea-time.

The box goes up. Silence.

Ben (*throwing the tea on the bed, and speaking urgently*).   Look here. We'd better tell them.

Gus. Tell them what?

Ben. That we can't do it, we haven't got it.

Gus. All right then.

Ben. Lend us your pencil. We'll write a note.

Gus, turning for a pencil, suddenly discovers the speaking-tube, which hangs on the right wall of the hatch facing his bed.

Gus. What's this?

Ben. What?

Gus. This.

Ben (*examining it*).   This? It's a speaking tube.

Gus. How long has that been there?

Ben. Just the job. We should have used it before, instead of shouting up there.

Gus. Funny I never noticed it before.

Ben. Well, come on.

Gus. What do you do?

Ben. See that? That's a whistle.

Gus. What, this?

Ben. Yes, take it out. Pull it out.

Gus does so.

That's it.

Gus. What do we do now?

Ben. Blow into it.

Gus. Blow?

Ben. It whistles up there if you blow. Then they know you want to speak. Blow.

Gus blows. Silence.

Gus (*tube at mouth*).   I can't hear a thing.

Ben. Now you speak! Speak into it!

Gus looks at Ben, then speaks into the tube.

Gus. The larder's bare!

Ben. Give me that!

He grabs the tube and puts it to his mouth.

(*Speaking with great deference.*) Good evening. I'm sorry to—bother you, but we just thought we'd better let you know that we haven't got anything left. We sent up all we had. There's no more food down here.

He brings tube slowly to his ear.

What?

To mouth.

What?

To ear. He listens. To mouth.

No, all we had we sent up.

To ear. He listens. To mouth.

Oh, I'm very sorry to hear that.

To ear. He listens. To Gus.

The Eccles cake was stale.

He listens. To Gus.

The chocolate was melted.

He listens. To Gus.

The milk was sour.

Gus.   What about the crisps?

Ben (*listening*).   The biscuits were mouldy.

He glares at Gus. Tube to mouth.

Well, we're very sorry about that.

Tube to ear.

What?

To mouth.

What?

To ear.

Yes. Yes.

To mouth.

Yes certainly. Certainly. Right away.

To ear. The voice has ceased. He hangs up the tube.

(*Excitedly*).   Did you hear that?

Gus.   What?

Ben.   You know what he said? Light the kettle! Not put on the kettle! Not light the gas! But light the kettle!

Gus.   How can we light the kettle?

Ben.   What do you mean?

Gus.   There's no gas.

Ben (*clapping hand to head*).   Now what do we do?

Gus. What did he want us to light the kettle for?

Ben. For tea. He wanted a cup of tea.

Gus. *He* wanted a cup of tea! What about me? I've been wanting a cup of tea all night!

Ben (*despairingly*).   What do we do now?

Gus. What are we supposed to drink?

Ben sits on his bed, staring.

What about us?

Ben sits.

I'm thirsty too. I'm starving. And he wants a cup of tea. That beats the band, that does.

Ben lets his head sink on to his chest.

I could do with a bit of sustenance myself. What about you? You look as if you could do with something too.

Gus sits on his bed.

We send him up all we've got and he's not satisfied. No, honest, it's enough to make the cat laugh. Why did you send him up all that stuff? (*Thoughtfully.*) Why did I send it up?

Pause.

Who knows what he's got upstairs? He's probably got a salad bowl. They must have something up there. They won't get much from down here. You notice they didn't ask for any salads? They've probably got a salad bowl up there. Cold meat, radishes, cucumbers. Watercress. Roll mops.

Pause.

Hardboiled eggs.

Pause.

The lot. They've probably got a crate of beer too. Probably eating my crisps with a pint of beer now. Didn't have anything to say about those crisps, did he? They do all right, don't worry about that. You don't think they're just going to sit there and wait for stuff to come up from down here, do you? That'll get them nowhere.

Pause.

They do all right.

Pause.

And he wants a cup of tea.

Pause.

That's past a joke, in my opinion.

He looks over at Ben, rises, and goes to him.

What's the matter with you? You don't look too bright. I feel like an Alka-Seltzer myself.

Ben sits up.

Ben (*in a low voice*).   Time's getting on.
Gus.   I know. I don't like doing a job on an empty stomach.
Ben (*wearily*).   Be quiet a minute. Let me give you your instructions.
Gus.   What for? We always do it the same way, don't we?
Ben.   Let me give you your instructions.

Gus sighs and sits next to Ben on the bed. The instructions are stated and repeated automatically.

When we get the call, you go over and stand behind the door.
Gus.   Stand behind the door.
Ben.   If there's a knock on the door you don't answer it.
Gus.   If there's a knock on the door I don't answer it.
Ben.   But there won't be a knock on the door.
Gus.   So I won't answer it.
Ben.   When the bloke comes in—
Gus.   When the bloke comes in—
Ben.   Shut the door behind him.
Gus.   Shut the door behind him.
Ben.   Without divulging your presence.
Gus.   Without divulging my presence.
Ben.   He'll see me and come towards me.
Gus.   He'll see you and come towards you.
Ben.   He won't see you.
Gus (*absently*).   Eh?
Ben.   He won't see you.
Gus.   He won't see me.
Ben.   But he'll see me.
Gus.   He'll see you.
Ben.   He won't know you're there.
Gus.   He won't know you're there.
Ben.   He won't know *you're* there.
Gus.   He won't know I'm there.
Ben.   I take out my gun.
Gus.   You take out your gun.
Ben.   He stops in his tracks.

Gus. He stops in his tracks.
Ben. If he turns round—
Gus. If he turns round—
Ben. You're there.
Gus. I'm here.

Ben frowns and presses his forehead.

You've missed something out.
Ben. I know. What?
Gus. I haven't taken my gun out, according to you.
Ben. You take your gun out—
Gus. After I've closed the door.
Ben. After you've closed the door.
Gus. You've never missed that out before, you know that?
Ben. When he sees you behind him—
Gus. Me behind him—
Ben. And me in front of him—
Gus. And you in front of him—
Ben. He'll feel uncertain—
Gus. Uneasy.
Ben. He won't know what to do.
Gus. So what will he do?
Ben. He'll look at me and he'll look at you.
Gus. We won't say a word.
Ben. We'll look at him.
Gus. He won't say a word.
Ben. He'll look at us.
Gus. And we'll look at him.
Ben. Nobody says a word.

Pause.

Gus. What do we do if it's a girl?
Ben. We do the same.
Gus. Exactly the same?
Ben. Exactly.

Pause.

Gus. We don't do anything different?
Ben. We do exactly the same.
Gus. Oh.

Gus rises, and shivers.

Excuse me.

He exits through the door on the left. Ben remains sitting on the bed, still.

The lavatory chain is pulled once off left, but the lavatory does not flush. Silence.

Gus re-enters and stops inside the door, deep in thought. He looks at Ben, then walks slowly across to his own bed. He is troubled. He stands, thinking. He turns and looks at Ben. He moves a few paces towards him.

(*Slowly in a low, tense voice.*) Why did he send us matches if he knew there was no gas?

Silence.

Ben stares in front of him. Gus crosses to the left side of Ben, to the foot of his bed, to get to his other ear.

Ben. Why did he send us matches if he knew there was no gas?

Ben looks up.

Why did he do that?

Ben. Who?

Gus. Who sent us those matches?

Ben. What are you talking about?

Gus stares down at him.

Gus (*thickly*).   Who is it upstairs?

Ben (*nervously*).   What's one thing to do with another?

Gus.   Who is it, though?

Ben.   What's one thing to do with another?

Ben fumbles for his paper on the bed.

Gus.   I asked you a question.

Ben.   Enough!

Gus (*with growing agitation*).   I asked you before. Who moved in? I asked you. You said the people who had it before moved out. Well, who moved in?

Ben (*hunched*).   Shut up.

Gus.   I told you, didn't I?

Ben (*standing*).   Shut up!

Gus (*feverishly*).   I told you before who owned this place, didn't I? I told you.

Ben hits him viciously on the shoulder.

I told you who ran this place, didn't I?

Ben hits him viciously on the shoulder.

(*Violently.*) Well, what's he playing all these games for? That's what I want to know. What's he doing it for?

Ben.   What games?

Gus (*passionately, advancing*).   What's he doing it for? We've been through our tests, haven't we? We got right through our tests, years ago, didn't we? We took them together, don't you remember, didn't we? We've proved ourselves before now, haven't we? We've always done our job. What's he doing all this for? What's the idea? What's he playing these games for?

The box in the shaft comes down behind them. The noise is this time accompanied by a shrill whistle, as it falls. Gus rushes to the hatch and seizes the note.

(*Reading.*) Scampi!

He crumples the note, picks up the tube, takes out the whistle, blows and speaks.

WE'VE GOT NOTHING LEFT! NOTHING! DO YOU UNDERSTAND?

Ben seizes the tube and flings Gus away. He follows Gus and slaps him hard, back-handed, across the chest.

Ben.   Stop it! You maniac!

Gus.   But you heard!

Ben (*savagely*).   That's enough! I'm warning you!

Silence.
   Ben hangs the tube. He goes to his bed and lies down. He picks up his paper and reads.
   Silence.
   The box goes up.
   They turn quickly, their eyes meet. Ben turns to his paper.
   Slowly Gus goes back to his bed, and sits.
   Silence.
   The hatch falls back into place.
   They turn quickly, their eyes meet. Ben turns back to his paper.
   Silence.
   Ben throws his paper down.

Ben.   Kaw!

He picks up the paper and looks at it.

Listen to this!

Pause.

What about that, eh?

Pause.

    Kaw!

Pause.

    Have you ever heard such a thing?

Gus (*dully*).   Go on!

Ben.   It's true.

Gus.   Get away.

Ben.   It's down here in black and white.

Gus (*very low*).   Is that a fact?

Ben.   Can you imagine it.

Gus.   It's unbelievable.

Ben.   It's enough to make you want to puke, isn't it?

Gus (*almost inaudible*).   Incredible.

Ben shakes his head. He puts the paper down and rises. He fixes the revolver in his holster.

    Gus stands up. He goes towards the door on the left.

Ben.   Where are you going?

Gus.   I'm going to have a glass of water.

He exits. Ben brushes dust off his clothes and shoes. The whistle in the speaking-tube blows. He goes to it, takes the whistle out and puts the tube to his ear. He listens. He puts it to his mouth.

Ben.   Yes.

To ear. He listens. To mouth.

    Straight away. Right.

To ear. He listens. To mouth.

    Sure we're ready.

To ear. He listens. To mouth.

    Understood. Repeat. He has arrived and will be coming in straight away. The normal method to be employed. Understood.

To ear. He listens. To mouth.

    Sure we're ready.

To ear. He listens. To mouth.

    Right.

He hangs the tube up.

Gus!

He takes out a comb and combs his hair, adjusts his jacket to diminish the bulge of the revolver. The lavatory flushes off left. Ben goes quickly to the door, left.

Gus!

The door right opens sharply. Ben turns, his revolver levelled at the door.
    Gus stumbles in.
    He is stripped of his jacket, waistcoat, tie, holster and revolver.
    He stops, body stooping, his arms at his sides.
    He raises his head and looks at Ben.
    A long silence.
    They stare at each other.

Curtain

Questions

1. On one level, this play is a parody of the well-established subgenre of hard-boiled gangster stories. Yet both characters, despite their profession, constantly exhibit moral outrage. What outrages them? What does your answer suggest about the relationship between moral principles and actual behavior? **2.** Are Ben and Gus essentially interchangeable, or do they differ? Explain. **3.** Might the title of the play be a pun? Explain. **4.** What effect is conveyed by the peculiar toilet-flush business in the play? What effect is conveyed by the discussion of the newspaper stories and the characters' reaction to them? **5.** The food orders that arrive on the dumb waiter provide, at first, a comic note. What is the nature of the progression of those food orders, and what significance can be attached to both the changing quality of the orders and Gus's reaction to the last order?

The Seventh Seal*

INGMAR BERGMAN [b. 1918]

THE CAST

The squire	The witch	The church painter
Death	The knight's wife	Skat
Jof	The girl	The merchant
The knight	Raval	Woman at the inn
Mia	The monk	Leader of the soldiers
Lisa	The smith	The young monk

THE night had brought little relief from the heat, and at dawn a hot gust of wind blows across the colorless sea.

The knight, Antonius Block, lies prostrate on some spruce branches spread over the fine sand. His eyes are wide-open and bloodshot from lack of sleep.

Nearby his squire Jöns is snoring loudly. He has fallen asleep where he collapsed, at the edge of the forest among the wind-gnarled fir trees. His open mouth gapes toward the dawn, and unearthly sounds come from his throat.

At the sudden gust of wind the horses stir, stretching their parched muzzles toward the sea. They are as thin and worn as their masters.

The knight has risen and waded into the shallow water, where he rinses his sunburned face and blistered lips.

Jöns rolls over to face the forest and the darkness. He moans in his sleep and vigorously scratches the stubbled hair on his head. A scar stretches diagonally across his scalp, as white as lightning against the grime.

The knight returns to the beach and falls on his knees. With his eyes closed and brow furrowed, he says his morning prayers. His hands are clenched together and his lips form the words silently. His face is sad and bitter. He opens his eyes and stares directly into the morning sun which wallows up from the misty sea like some bloated, dying fish. The sky is gray and immobile, a dome of lead. A cloud hangs mute and dark over the western horizon. High up, barely visible, a sea gull floats on motionless wings. Its cry is weird and restless.

The knight's large gray horse lifts its head and whinnies. Antonius Block turns around.

---

*Translated by Lars Malmstrom and David Kushner.

Behind him stands a man in black. His face is very pale and he keeps his hands hidden in the wide folds of his cloak.

Knight.   Who are you?
Death.   I am Death.
Knight.   Have you come for me?
Death.   I have been walking by your side for a long time.
Knight.   That I know.
Death.   Are you prepared?
Knight.   My body is frightened, but I am not.
Death.   Well, there is no shame in that.

The knight has risen to his feet. He shivers. Death opens his cloak to place it around the knight's shoulders.

Knight.   Wait a moment.
Death.   That's what they all say. I grant no reprieves.
Knight.   You play chess, don't you?

A gleam of interest kindles in Death's eyes.

Death.   How did you know that?
Knight.   I have seen it in paintings and heard it sung in ballads.
Death.   Yes, in fact I'm quite a good chess player.
Knight.   But you can't be better than I am.

The knight rummages in the big black bag which he keeps beside him and takes out a small chessboard. He places it carefully on the ground and begins setting up the pieces.

Death.   Why do you want to play chess with me?
Knight.   I have my reasons.
Death.   That is your privilege.
Knight.   The condition is that I may live as long as I hold out against you. If I win, you will release me. Is it agreed?

The knight holds out his two fists to Death, who smiles at him suddenly. Death points to one of the knight's hands; it contains a black pawn.

Knight.   You drew black!
Death.   Very appropriate. Don't you think so?

The knight and Death bend over the chessboard. After a moment of hesitation, Antonius Block opens with his king's pawn. Death moves, also using his king's pawn.

THE morning breeze has died down. The restless movement of the sea has ceased, the water is silent. The sun rises from the haze and its glow whitens. The sea gull floats under the dark cloud, frozen in space. The day is already scorchingly hot.

The squire Jöns is awakened by a kick in the rear. Opening his eyes, he grunts like a pig and yawns broadly. He scrambles to his feet, saddles his horse and picks up the heavy pack.

The knight slowly rides away from the sea, into the forest near the beach and up toward the road. He pretends not to hear the morning prayers of his squire. Jöns soon overtakes him.

Jöns *(sings).*   Between a strumpet's legs to lie
                  Is the life for which I sigh.

He stops and looks at his master, but the knight hasn't heard Jöns' song, or he pretends that he hasn't. To give further vent to his irritation, the squire sings even louder.

Jöns *(sings).*   Up above is God Almighty
                  So very far away,
                  But your brother the Devil
                  You will meet on every level.

Jöns finally gets the knight's attention. He stops singing. The knight, his horse, Jöns' own horse and Jöns himself know all the songs by heart. The long, dusty journey from the Holy Land hasn't made them any cleaner.

They ride across a mossy heath which stretches toward the horizon. Beyond it, the sea lies shimmering in the white glitter of the sun.

Jöns. In Farjestad everyone was talking about evil omens and other horrible things. Two horses had eaten each other in the night, and, in the churchyard, graves had been opened and the remains of corpses scattered all over the place. Yesterday afternoon there were as many as four suns in the heavens.

The knight doesn't answer. Close by a scrawny dog is whining, crawling toward its master, who is sleeping in a sitting position in the blazing hot sun. A black cloud of flies clusters around his head and shoulders. The miserable-looking dog whines incessantly as it lies flat on its stomach, wagging its tail.

Jöns dismounts and approaches the sleeping man. Jöns addresses him politely. When he doesn't receive an answer, he walks up to the man in order to shake him awake. He bends over the sleeping man's shoulder, but quickly pulls back his hand. The man falls backward on the heath, his face turned toward Jöns. It is a corpse, staring at Jöns with empty eye sockets and white teeth.

The squire remounts and overtakes his master. He takes a drink from his waterskin and hands the bag to the knight.

Knight. Well, did he show you the way?
Jöns. Not exactly.
Knight. What did he say?
Jöns. Nothing.
Knight. Was he a mute?

Jöns. No, sir, I wouldn't say that. As a matter of fact, he was quite eloquent.

Knight. Oh?

Jöns. He was eloquent, all right. The trouble is that what he had to say was most depressing. (*Sings*)

> One moment you're bright and lively,
> The next you're crawling with worms.
> Fate is a terrible villain
> And you, my friend, its poor victim.

Knight. Must you sing?

Jöns. No.

The knight hands his squire a piece of bread, which keeps him quiet for a while. The sun burns down on them cruelly, and beads of perspiration trickle down their faces. There is a cloud of dust around the horses' hoofs.

They ride past an inlet and along verdant groves. In the shade of some large trees stands a bulging wagon covered with a mottled canvas. A horse whinnies nearby and is answered by the knight's horse. The two travelers do not stop to rest under the shade of the trees but continue riding until they disappear at the bend of the road.

IN his sleep, Jof the juggler hears the neighing of his horse and the answer from a distance. He tries to go on sleeping, but it is stifling inside the wagon. The rays of the sun filtering through the canvas cast streaks of light across the face of Jof's wife, Mia, and their one-year-old son, Mikael, who are sleeping deeply and peacefully. Near them, Jonas Skat, an older man, snores loudly.

Jof crawls out of the wagon. There is still a spot of shade under the big trees. He takes a drink of water, gargles, stretches and talks to his scrawny old horse.

Jof. Good morning. Have you had breakfast? I can't eat grass, worse luck. Can't you teach me how? We're a little hard up. People aren't very interested in juggling in this part of the country.

He has picked up the juggling balls and slowly begins to toss them. Then he stands on his head and cackles like a hen. Suddenly he stops and sits down with a look of utter astonishment on his face. The wind causes the trees to sway slightly. The leaves stir and there is a soft murmur. The flowers and the grass bend gracefully, and somewhere a bird raises its voice in a long warble.

Jof's face breaks into a smile and his eyes fill with tears. With a dazed expression he sits flat on his behind while the grass rustles softly, and bees and butterflies hum around his head. The unseen bird continues to sing.

Suddenly the breeze stops blowing, the bird stops singing, Jof's smile fades, the flowers and grass wilt in the heat. The old horse is still walking around grazing and swishing its tail to ward off the flies.

Jof comes to life. He rushes into the wagon and shakes Mia awake.

Jof. Mia, wake up, Wake up! Mia, I've just seen something. I've got to tell you about it!

Mia *(sits up, terrified)*. What is it? What's happened?

Jof. Listen, I've had a vision. No, it wasn't a vision. It was real, absolutely real.

Mia. Oh, so you've had a vision again!

Mia's voice is filled with gentle irony. Jof shakes his head and grabs her by the shoulders.

Jof. But I did see her!

Mia. Whom did you see?

Jof. The Virgin Mary.

Mia can't help being impressed by her husband's fervor. She lowers her voice.

Mia. Did you really see her?

Jof. She was so close to me that I could have touched her. She had a golden crown on her head and wore a blue gown with flowers of gold. She was barefoot and had small brown hands with which she was holding the Child and teaching Him to walk. And then she saw me watching her and she smiled at me. My eyes filled with tears and when I wiped them away, she had disappeared. And everything became so still in the sky and on the earth. Can you understand . . .

Mia. What an imagination you have.

Jof. You don't believe me! But it was real, I tell you, not the kind of reality you see everyday, but a different kind.

Mia. Perhaps it was the kind of reality you told us about when you saw the Devil paint your wagon wheels red, using his tail as a brush.

Jof *(embarrassed)*. Why must you keep bringing that up?

Mia. And then you discovered that you had red paint under your nails.

Jof. Well, perhaps that time I made it up. *(Eagerly)* I did it just so that you would believe in my other visions. The real ones. The ones that I didn't make up.

Mia. *(severely)*. You have to keep your visions under control. Otherwise people will think that you're a half-wit, which you're not. At least not yet —as far as I know. But, come to think of it, I'm not so sure about that.

Jof *(angry)*. I didn't ask to have visions. I can't help it if voices speak to me, if the Holy Virgin appears before me and angels and devils like my company.

Skat *(sits up)*. Haven't I told you once and for all that I need my morning's sleep! I have asked you politely, pleaded with you, but nothing works. So now I'm telling you to *shut up!*

His eyes are popping with rage. He turns over and continues snoring where he left off. Mia and Jof decide that it would be wisest to leave the wagon. They sit down on a crate. Mia has Mikael on her knees. He is naked and squirms vigorously. Jof sits close to his wife. Slumped over, he still looks dazed and astonished. A dry, hot wind blows from the sea.

Mia. If we would only get some rain. Everything is burned to cinders. We won't have anything to eat this winter.

Jof *(yawning).* We'll get by.

He says this smilingly, with a casual air. He stretches and laughs contentedly.

Mia. I want Mikael to have a better life than ours.

Jof. Mikael will grow up to be a great acrobat—or a juggler who can do the one impossible trick.

Mia. What's that?

Jof. To make one of the balls stand absolutely still in the air.

Mia. But that's impossible.

Jof. Impossible for us—but not for him.

Mia. You're dreaming again.

She yawns. The sun has made her a bit drowsy and she lies down on the grass. Jof does likewise and puts one arm around his wife's shoulders.

Jof. I've composed a song. I made it up during the night when I couldn't sleep. Do you want to hear it?

Mia. Sing it. I'm very curious.

Jof. I have to sit up first.

He sits with his legs crossed, makes a dramatic gesture with his arms and sings in a loud voice.

Jof.   On a lily branch a dove is perched
              Against the summer sky,
              She sings a wondrous song of Christ
              And there's great joy on high.

He interrupts his singing in order to be complimented by his wife.

Jof. Mia! Are you asleep?

Mia. It's a lovely song.

Jof. I haven't finished yet.

Mia. I heard it, but I think I'll sleep a little longer. You can sing the rest to me afterward.

Jof. All you do is sleep.

Jof is a bit offended and glances over at his son, Mikael, but he is also sleeping soundly in the high grass. Jonas Skat comes out from the wagon. He yawns; he is very tired and in a bad humor. In his hands he holds a crudely made death mask.

Skat. Is this supposed to be a mask for an actor? If the priests didn't pay us so well, I'd say no thank you.

Jof. Are you going to play Death?

Skat. Just think, scaring decent folk out of their wits with this kind of nonsense.

Jof. When are we supposed to do this play?

Skat. At the saints' feast in Elsinore. We're going to perform right on the church steps, believe it or not.

Jof. Wouldn't it be better to play something bawdy? People like it better, and, besides, it's more fun.

Skat. Idiot. There's a rumor going around that there's a terrible pestilence in the land, and now the priests are prophesying sudden death and all sorts of spiritual agonies.

Mia is awake now and lies contentedly on her back, sucking on a blade of grass and looking smilingly at her husband.

Jof. And what part am I to play?

Skat. You're such a damn fool, so you're going to be the Soul of Man.

Jof. That's a bad part, of course.

Skat. Who makes the decisions around here? Who is the director of this company anyhow?

Skat, grinning, holds the mask in front of his face and recites dramatically.

Skat. Bear this in mind, you fool. Your life hangs by a thread. Your time is short. (*In his usual voice*) Are the women going to like me in this getup? Will I make a hit? No! I feel as if I were dead already.

He stumbles into the wagon muttering furiously. Jof sits, leaning forward. Mia lies beside him on the grass.

Mia. Jof!

Jof. What is it?

Mia. Sit still. Don't move.

Jof. What do you mean?

Mia. Don't say anything.

Jof. I'm as silent as a grave.

Mia. Shh! I love you.

Waves of heat envelop the gray stone church in a strange white mist. The knight dismounts and enters. After tying up the horses, Jöns slowly follows him in. When he comes onto the church porch he stops in surprise. To the right of the entrance there is a large fresco on the wall, not quite finished. Perched on a crude scaffolding is a painter wearing a red cap and paint-stained clothes. He has one brush in his mouth, while with another in his hand he outlines a small, terrified human face amidst a sea of other faces.

Jöns. What is this supposed to represent?

Painter. The Dance of Death.

Jöns. And that one is Death?

Painter. Yes, he dances off with all of them.

Jöns. Why do you paint such nonsense?

Painter. I thought it would serve to remind people that they must die.

Jöns. Well, it's not going to make them feel any happier.

Painter. Why should one always make people happy? It might not be a bad idea to scare them a little once in a while.

Jöns. Then they'll close their eyes and refuse to look at your painting.

Painter. Oh, they'll look. A skull is almost more interesting than a naked woman.

Jöns. If you do scare them . . .

Painter. They'll think.

Jöns. And if they think . . .

Painter. They'll become still more scared.

Jöns. And then they'll run right into the arms of the priests.

Painter. That's not my business.

Jöns. You're only painting your Dance of Death.

Painter. I'm only painting things as they are. Everyone else can do as he likes.

Jöns. Just think how some people will curse you.

Painter. Maybe. But then I'll paint something amusing for them to look at. I have to make a living—at least until the plague takes me.

Jöns. The plague. That sounds horrible.

Painter. You should see the boils on a diseased man's throat. You should see how his body shrivels up so that his legs look like knotted strings—like the man I've painted over there.

The painter points with his brush. Jöns sees a small human form writhing in the grass, its eyes turned upward in a frenzied look of horror and pain.

Jöns. That looks terrible.

Painter. It certainly does. He tries to rip out the boil, he bites his hands, tears his veins open with his fingernails and his screams can be heard everywhere. Does that scare you?

Jöns. Scare? Me? You don't know me. What are the horrors you've painted over there?

Painter. The remarkable thing is that the poor creatures think the pestilence is the Lord's punishment. Mobs of people who call themselves Slaves of Sin are swarming over the country, flagellating themselves and others, all for the glory of God.

Jöns. Do they really whip themselves?

Painter. Yes, it's a terrible sight. I crawl into a ditch and hide when they pass by.

Jöns. Do you have any brandy? I've been drinking water all day and it's made me as thirsty as a camel in the desert.

Painter. I think I frightened you after all.

Jöns sits down with the painter, who produces a jug of brandy.

THE knight is kneeling before a small altar. It is dark and quiet around him. The air is cool and musty. Pictures of saints look down on him with stony eyes. Christ's face is turned upward, His mouth open as if in a cry of anguish.

On the ceiling beam there is a representation of a hideous devil spying on a miserable human being. The knight hears a sound from the confession booth and approaches it. The face of Death appears behind the grill for an instant, but the knight doesn't see him.

Knight. I want to talk to you as openly as I can, but my heart is empty.

Death doesn't answer.

Knight. The emptiness is a mirror turned toward my own face. I see myself in it, and I am filled with fear and disgust.

Death doesn't answer.

Knight. Through my indifference to my fellow men, I have isolated myself from their company. Now I live in a world of phantoms. I am imprisoned in my dreams and fantasies.
Death. And yet you don't want to die.
Knight. Yes, I do.
Death. What are you waiting for?
Knight. I want knowledge.
Death. You want guarantees?
Knight. Call it whatever you like. Is it so cruelly inconceivable to grasp God with the senses? Why should he hide himself in a mist of half-spoken promises and unseen miracles?

Death doesn't answer.

Knight. How can we have faith in those who believe when we can't have faith in ourselves? What is going to happen to those of us who want to believe but aren't able to? And what is to become of those who neither want to nor are capable of believing?

The knight stops and waits for a reply, but no one speaks or answers him. There is complete silence.

Knight. Why can't I kill God within me? Why does he live on in this painful and humiliating way even though I curse Him and want to tear Him out of my heart? Why, in spite of everything, is He a baffling reality that I can't shake off? Do you hear me?
Death. Yes, I hear you.
Knight. I want knowledge, not faith, not suppositions, but knowledge. I want God to stretch out his hand toward me, reveal Himself and speak to me.
Death. But he remains silent.
Knight. I call out to him in the dark but no one seems to be there.
Death. Perhaps no one is there.
Knight. Then life is an outrageous horror. No one can live in the face of death, knowing that all is nothingness.
Death. Most people never reflect about either death or the futility of life.

Knight. But one day they will have to stand at that last moment of life and look toward the darkness.

Death. When *that* day comes . . .

Knight. In our fear, we make an image, and that image we call God.

Death. You are worrying . . .

Knight. Death visited me this morning. We are playing chess together. This reprieve gives me the chance to arrange an urgent matter.

Death. What matter is that?

Knight. My life has been a futile pursuit, a wandering, a great deal of talk without meaning. I feel no bitterness or self-reproach because the lives of most people are very much like this. But I will use my reprieve for one meaningful deed.

Death. Is that why you are playing chess with Death?

Knight. He is a clever opponent, but up to now I haven't lost a single man.

Death. How will you outwit Death in your game?

Knight. I use a combination of the bishop and the knight which he hasn't yet discovered. In the next move I'll shatter one of his flanks.

Death. I'll remember that.

Death shows his face at the grill of the confession booth for a moment but disappears instantly.

Knight. You've tricked and cheated me! But we'll meet again, and I'll find a way.

Death (*invisible*). We'll meet at the inn, and there we'll continue playing.

The knight raises his hand and looks at it in the sunlight which comes through the tiny window.

Knight. This is my hand. I can move it, feel the blood pulsing through it. The sun is still high in the sky and I, Antonius Block, am playing chess with Death.

He makes a fist of his hand and lifts it to his temple.

Meanwhile, Jöns and the painter have gotten drunk and are talking animatedly together.

Jöns. Me and my master have been abroad and have just come home. Do you understand, you little pictor?

Painter. The Crusade.

Jöns (*drunk*). Precisely. For ten years we sat in the Holy Land and let snakes bite us, flies sting us, wild animals eat us, heathens butcher us, the wine poison us, the women give us lice, the lice devour us, the fevers rot us, all for the Glory of God. Our crusade was such madness that only a real idealist could have thought it up. But what you said about the plague was horrible.

Painter. It's worse than that.

Jöns. Ah me. No matter which way you turn, you have your rump behind you. That's the truth.

Painter. The rump behind you, the rump behind you—there's a profound truth.

Jöns paints a small figure which is supposed to represent himself.

Jöns. This is squire Jöns. He grins at Death, mocks the Lord, laughs at himself and leers at the girls. His world is a Jöns-world, believable only to himself, ridiculous to all including himself, meaningless to Heaven and of no interest to Hell.

The knight walks by, calls to his squire and goes out into the bright sunshine. Jöns manages to get himself down from the scaffolding.

Outside the church, four soldiers and a monk are in the process of putting a woman in the stocks. Her face is pale and child-like, her head has been shaved, and her knuckles are bloody and broken. Her eyes are wide open, yet she doesn't appear to be fully conscious.

Jöns and the knight stop and watch in silence. The soldiers are working quickly and skillfully, but they seem frightened and dejected. The monk mumbles from a small book. One of the soldiers picks up a wooden bucket and with his hand begins to smear a bloody paste on the wall of the church and around the woman. Jöns holds his nose.

Jöns. That soup of yours has a hell of a stink. What is it good for?

Soldier. She has had carnal intercourse with the Evil One.

He whispers this with a horrified face and continues to splash the sticky mess on the wall.

Jöns. And now she's in the stocks.

Soldier. She will be burned tomorrow morning at the parish boundary. But we have to keep the Devil away from the rest of us.

Jöns (*holding his nose*). And you do that with this stinking mess?

Soldier. It's the best remedy: blood mixed with the bile of a big black dog. The Devil can't stand the smell.

Jöns. Neither can I.

Jöns walks over toward the horses. The knight stands for a few moments looking at the young girl. She is almost a child. Slowly she turns her eyes toward him.

Knight. Have you seen the Devil?

The monk stops reading and raises his head.

Monk. You must not talk to her.

Knight. Can that be so dangerous?

Monk. I don't know, but she is believed to have caused the pestilence with which we are afflicted.

Knight. I understand.

He nods resignedly and walks away. The young woman starts to moan as though she were having a horrible nightmare. The sound of her cries follows the two riders for a considerable distance down the road.

THE sun stands high in the sky, like a red ball of fire. The waterskin is empty and Jöns looks for a well where he can fill it.

They approach a group of peasant cottages at the edge of the forest. Jöns ties up the horses, slings the skin over his shoulder and walks along the path toward the nearest cottage. As always, his movements are light and almost soundless. The door to the cottage is open. He stops outside, but when no one appears he enters. It is very dark inside and his foot touches a soft object. He looks down. Beside the whitewashed fireplace, a woman is lying with her face to the ground.

At the sound of approaching steps, Jöns quickly hides behind the door. A man comes down a ladder from the loft. He is broad and thick-set. His eyes are black and his face is pale and puffy. His clothes are well cut but dirty and in rags. He carries a cloth sack. Looking around, he goes into the inner room, bends over the bed, tucks something into the bag, slinks along the walls, looking on the shelves, finds something else which he tucks in his bag.

Slowly he re-enters the outer room, bends over the dead woman and carefully slips a ring from her finger. At that moment a young woman comes through the door. She stops and stares at the stranger.

Raval. Why do you look so surprised? I steal from the dead. These days it's quite a lucrative enterprise.

The girl makes a movement as if to run away.

Raval. You're thinking of running to the village and telling. That wouldn't serve any purpose. Each of us has to save his own skin. It's as simple as that.

Girl. Don't touch me.

Raval. Don't try to scream. There's no one around to hear you, neither God nor man.

Slowly he closes the door behind the girl. The stuffy room is now in almost total darkness. But Jons becomes clearly visible.

Jöns. I recognize you, although it's a long time since we met. Your name is Raval, from the theological college at Roskilde. You are Dr. Mirabilis, Coelestis et Diabilis.

Raval smiles uneasily and looks around.

Jöns. Am I not right?

The girl stands immobile.

Jöns. You were the one who, ten years ago, convinced my master of the necessity to join a better-class crusade to the Holy Land.

Raval looks around.

Jöns. You look uncomfortable. Do you have a stomach-ache?

Raval smiles anxiously.

Jöns. When I see you, I suddenly understand the meaning of these ten years, which previously seemed to me such a waste. Our life was too good and we were too satisfied with ourselves. The Lord wanted to punish us for our complacency. That is why He sent you to spew out your holy venom and poison the knight.

Raval. I acted in good faith.

Jöns. But now you know better, don't you? Because now you have turned into a thief. A more fitting and rewarding occupation for scoundrels. Isn't that so?

With a quick movement he knocks the knife out of Raval's hand, gives him a kick so that he falls on the floor and is about to finish him off. Suddenly the girl screams. Jöns stops and makes a gesture of generosity with his hand.

Jöns. By all means. I'm not bloodthirsty. (*He bends over Raval*)

Raval. Don't beat me.

Jöns. I don't have the heart to touch you, Doctor. But remember this: The next time we meet, I'll brand your face the way one does with thieves. (*He rises*) What I really came for is to get my waterskin filled.

Girl. We have a deep well with cool, fresh water. Come, I'll show you.

They walk out of the house. Raval lies still for a few moments, then he rises slowly and looks around. When no one is in sight, he takes his bag and steals away.

Jöns quenches his thirst and fills his bag with water. The girl helps him.

Jöns. Jöns is my name. I am a pleasant and talkative young man who has never had anything but kind thoughts and has only done beautiful and noble deeds. I'm kindest of all to young women. With them, there is no limit to my kindness.

He embraces her and tries to kiss her, but she holds herself back. Almost immediately he loses interest, hoists the waterbag on his shoulder and pats the girl on the cheek.

Jöns. Goodbye, my girl. I could very well have raped you, but between you and me, I'm tired of that kind of love. It runs a little dry in the end.

He laughs kindly and walks away from her. When he has walked a short distance he turns; the girl is still there.

Jöns.   Now that I think of it, I will need a housekeeper. Can you prepare good food? (*The girl nods*) As far as I know, I'm still a married man, but I have high hopes that my wife is dead by now. That's why I need a housekeeper. (*The girl doesn't answer but gets up*) The devil with it! Come along and don't stand there staring. I've saved your life, so you owe me a great deal.

She begins walking toward him, her head bent. He doesn't wait for her but walks toward the knight, who patiently awaits his squire.

THE Embarrassment Inn lies in the eastern section of the province. The plague has not yet reached this area on its way along the coast.

The actors have placed their wagon under a tree in the yard of the inn. Dressed in colorful costumes, they perform a farce.

The spectators watch the performance, commenting on it noisily. There are merchants with fat, beer-sweaty faces, apprentices and journeymen, farmhands and milkmaids. A whole flock of children perch in the trees around the wagon.

The knight and his squire have sat down in the shadow of a wall. They drink beer and doze in the midday heat. The girl from the deserted village sleeps at Jons' side.

Skat beats the drums, Jof blows the flute, Mia performs a gay and lively dance. They perspire under the hot white sun. When they have finished Skat comes forward and bows.

Skat.   Noble ladies and gentlemen, I thank you for your interest. Please remain standing a little longer, or sit on the ground, because we are now going to perform a tragedia about an unfaithful wife, her jealous husband, and the handsome lover—that's me.

Mia and Jof have quickly changed costumes and again step out on the stage. They bow to the public.

Skat.   Here is the husband. Here is the wife. If you'll shut up over there, you'll see something splendid. As I said, I play the lover and I haven't entered yet. That's why I'm going to hide behind the curtain for the time being. (*He wipes the sweat from his forehead*) It's damned hot. I think we'll have a thunderstorm.

He places his leg in front of Jof as if to trip him, raises Mia's skirt, makes a face as if he could see all the wonders of the world underneath it, and disappears behind the gaudily patched curtains.

Skat is very handsome, now that he can see himself in the reflection of a tin washbowl. His hair is tightly curled, his eyebrows are beautifully bushy, glittering earrings vie for equal attention with his teeth, and his cheeks are flushed rose red.

He sits out in back on the tailboard of the wagon, dangling his legs and whistling to himself.

In the meantime Jof and Mia play their tragedy; it is not, however, received with great acclaim.

Skat suddenly discovers that someone is watching him as he gazes contentedly into the tin bowl. A woman stands there, stately in both height and volume.

Skat frowns, toys with his small dagger and occasionally throws a roguish but fiery glance at the beautiful visitor.

She suddenly discovers that one of her shoes doesn't quite fit. She leans down to fix it and in doing so allows her generous bosom to burst out of its prison—no more than honor and chastity allow, but still enough so that the actor with his experienced eye immediately sees that there are ample rewards to be had here.

Now she comes a little closer, kneels down and opens a bundle containing several dainty morsels and a skin filled with red wine. Jonas Skat manages not to fall off the wagon in his excitement. Standing on the steps of the wagon, he supports himself against a nearby tree, crosses his legs and bows.

The woman quietly bites into a chicken leg dripping with fat. At this moment the actor is stricken by a radiant glance full of lustful appetites.

When he sees this look, Skat makes an instantaneous decision, jumps down from the wagon and kneels in front of the blushing damsel.

She becomes weak and faint from his nearness, looks at him with a glassy glance and breathes heavily. Skat doesn't neglect to press kisses on her small, chubby hands. The sun shines brightly and small birds make noises in the bushes.

Now she is forced to sit back; her legs seem unwilling to support her any longer. Bewildered, she singles out another chicken leg from the large sack of food and holds it up in front of Skat with an appealing and triumphant expression, as if it were her maidenhood being offered as a prize.

Skat hesitates momentarily, but he is still the strategist. He lets the chicken leg fall to the grass, and murmurs in the woman's rosy ear.

His words seem to please her. She puts her arms around the actor's neck and pulls him to her with such fierceness that both of them lose their balance and tumble down on the soft grass. The small birds take to their wings with frightened shrieks.

Jof stands in the hot sun with a flickering lantern in his hand. Mia pretends to be asleep on a bench which has been pulled forward on the stage.

Jof.   Night and moonlight now prevail
              Here sleeps my wife so frail . . .
Voice from the Public.   Does she snore?

Jof.   May I point out that this is a tragedy, and in tragedies one doesn't snore.
Voice from the Public.   I think she should snore anyhow.

This opinion causes mirth in the audience. Jof becomes slightly confused and goes out of character, but Mia keeps her head and begins snoring.

Jof.   Night and moonlight now prevail.
                 There snores—I mean sleeps—my wife so frail.
                 Jealous I am, as never before,
                 I hide myself behind this door.
                 Faithful is she
                 To her lover—not me.
                 He soon comes a-stealing
                 To awaken her lusty feeling.
                 I shall now kill him dead
                 For cuckolding me in my bed.
                 There he comes in the moonlight,
                 His white legs shining bright.
                 Quiet as a mouse, here I'll lie,
                 Tell him not that he's about to die.

Jof hides himself. Mia immediately ends her snoring and sits up, looking to the left.

Mia.   Look, there he comes in the night
                 My lover, my heart's delight.

She becomes silent and looks wide-eyed in front of her.

The mood in the yard in front of the inn has, up to now, been rather lighthearted despite the heat.

Now a rapid change occurs. People who had been laughing and chattering fall silent. Their faces seem to pale under their sunbrowned skins, the children stop their games and stand with gaping mouths and frightened eyes. Jof steps out in front of the curtain. His painted face bears an expression of horror. Mia has risen with Mikael in her arms. Some of the women in the yard have fallen on their knees, others hide their faces, many begin to mutter half-forgotten prayers.

All have turned their faces toward the white road. Now a shrill song is heard. It is frenzied, almost a scream.

A crucified Christ sways above the hilltop.

The cross-bearers soon come into sight. They are Dominican monks, their hoods pulled down over their faces. More and more of them follow, carrying litters with heavy coffins or clutching holy relics, their hands stretched out spasmodically. The dust wells up around their black hoods; the censers sway and emit a thick, ashen smoke which smells of rancid herbs.

After the line of monks comes another procession. It is a column of men, boys, old men, women, girls, children. All of them have steel-edged scourges in their hands with which they whip themselves and each other, howling ecstatically. They twist in pain; their eyes bulge wildly; their lips are gnawed to shreds and dripping with foam. They have been seized by madness. They bite their own hands and arms, whip each other in violent, almost rhythmic outbursts. Throughout it all the shrill song howls from their bursting throats. Many sway and fall, lift themselves up again, support each other and help each other to intensify the scourging.

Now the procession pauses at the crossroads in front of the inn. The monks fall on their knees, hiding their faces with clenched hands, arms pressed tightly together. Their song never stops. The Christ figure on its timbered cross is raised above the heads of the crowd. It is not Christ triumphant, but the suffering Jesus with the sores, the blood, the hammered nails and the face in convulsive pain. The Son of God, nailed on the wood of the cross, suffering scorn and shame.

The penitents have now sunk down in the dirt of the road. They collapse where they stood like slaughtered cattle. Their screams rise with the song of the monks, through misty clouds of incense, toward the white fire of the sun.

A large square monk rises from his knees and reveals his face, which is red-brown from the sun. His eyes glitter; his voice is thick with impotent scorn.

Monk.   God has sentenced us to punishment. We shall all perish in the black death. You, standing there like gaping cattle, you who sit there in your glutted complacency, do you know that this may be your last hour? Death stands right behind you. I can see how his crown gleams in the sun. His scythe flashes as he raises it above your heads. Which one of you shall he strike first? You there, who stand staring like a goat, will your mouth be twisted into the last unfinished gasp before nightfall? And you, woman, who bloom with life and self-satisfaction, will you pale and become extinguished before the morning dawns? You back there, with your swollen nose and stupid grin, do you have another year left to dirty the earth with your refuse? Do you know, you insensible fools, that you shall die today or tomorrow, or the next day, because all of you have been sentenced? Do you hear what I say? Do you hear the word? You have been sentenced, sentenced!

The monk falls silent, looking around with a bitter face and a cold scornful glance. Now he clenches his hands, straddles the ground and turns his face upward.

Monk.   Lord have mercy on us in our humiliation! Don't turn your face from us in loathing and contempt, but be merciful to us for the sake of your son, Jesus Christ.

He makes the sign of the cross over the crowd and then begins a new song in a strong voice. The monks rise and join in the song. As if driven by some superhuman force, the penitents begin to whip themselves again, still wailing and moaning.

The procession continues. New members have joined the rear of the column; others who were unable to go on lie weeping in the dust of the road.

Jöns the squire drinks his beer.

Jöns. This damned ranting about doom. Is that food for the minds of modern people? Do they really expect us to take them seriously?

The knight grins tiredly.

Jöns. Yes, now you grin at me, my lord. But allow me to point out that I've either read, heard or experienced most of the tales which we people tell each other.

Knight (*yawns*). Yes, yes.

Jöns. Even the ghost stories about God the Father, the angels, Jesus Christ and the Holy Ghost—all these I've accepted without too much emotion.

He leans down over the girl as she crouches at his feet and pats her on the head. The knight drinks his beer silently.

Jöns (*contentedly*). My little stomach is my world, my head is my eternity, and my hands, two wonderful suns. My legs are time's damned pendulums, and my dirty feet are two splendid starting points for my philosophy. Everything is worth precisely as much as a belch, the only difference being that a belch is more satisfying.

The beer mug is empty. Sighing, Jöns gets to his feet. The girl follows him like a shadow.

In the yard he meets a large man with a sooty face and a dark expression. He stops Jöns with a roar.

Jöns. What are you screaming about?

Plog. I am Plog, the smith, and you are the squire Jöns.

Jöns. That's possible.

Plog. Have you seen my wife?

Jöns. No, I haven't. But if I had seen her and she looked like you, I'd quickly forget that I'd seen her.

Plog. Well, in that case you haven't seen her.

Jöns. Maybe she's run off.

Plog. Do you know anything?

Jöns. I know quite a lot, but not about your wife. Go to the inn. Maybe they can help you.

The smith sighs sadly and goes inside.

THE inn is very small and full of people eating and drinking to forget their newly aroused fear of eternity. In the open fireplace a roasting pig turns on an iron spit. The sun shines outside the casement window, its sharp rays piercing the darkness of the room, which is thick with fumes and perspiration.

Merchant.   Yes, it's true! The plague is spreading along the west coast. People are dying like flies. Usually business would be good at this time of year, but, damn it, I've still got my whole stock unsold.

Woman.   They speak of the judgment day. And all these omens are terrible. Worms, chopped-off hands and other monstrosities began pouring out of an old woman, and down in the village another woman gave birth to a calf's head.

Old Man.   The day of judgment. Imagine.

Farmer.   It hasn't rained here for a month. We'll surely lose our crops.

Merchant.   And people are acting crazy, I'd say. They flee the country and carry the plague with them wherever they go.

Old Man.   The day of judgment. Just think, just think!

Farmer.   If it's as they say, I suppose a person should look after his house and try to enjoy life as long as he can.

Woman.   But there have been other things too, such things that can't even be spoken of. (*Whispers*) Things that mustn't be named—but the priests say that the woman carries it between her legs and that's why she must cleanse herself.

Old Man.   Judgment day. And the Riders of the Apocalypse stand at the bend in the village road. I imagine they'll come on judgment night, at sundown.

Woman.   There are many who have purged themselves with fire and died from it, but the priests say that it's better to die pure than to live for hell.

Merchant.   This is the end, yes, it is. No one says it out loud, but all of us know that it's the end. And people are going mad from fear.

Farmer.   So you're afraid too.

Merchant.   Of course I'm afraid.

Old Man.   The judgment day becomes night, and the angels descend and the graves open. It will be terrible to see.

They whisper in low tones and sit close to each other. Plog, the smith, shoves his way into a place next to Jof, who is still dressed in his costume. Opposite him sits Raval, leaning slightly forward, his face perspiring heavily. Raval rolls an armlet out on the table.

Raval.   Do you want this armlet? You can have it cheap.

Jof.   I can't afford it.

Raval.   It's real silver.

Jof.   It's nice. But it's surely too expensive for me.

Plog.   Excuse me, but has anyone here seen my wife?

Jof.   Has she disappeared?

Plog.   They say she's run away.

Jof.   Has she deserted you?

Plog.   With an actor.

Jof.   An actor! If she's got such bad taste, then I think you should let her go.

Plog. You're right. My first thought, of course, was to kill her.

Jof. Oh. But to murder her, that's a terrible thing to do.

Plog. I'm also going to kill the actor.

Jof. The actor?

Plog. Of course, the one she eloped with.

Jof. What has he done to deserve that?

Plog. Are you stupid?

Jof. The actor! Now I understand. There are too many of them, so even if he hasn't done anything in particular you ought to kill him merely because he's an actor.

Plog. You see, my wife has always been interested in the tricks of the theater.

Jof. And that turned out to be her misfortune.

Plog. Her misfortune, but not mine, because a person who's born unfortunate can hardly suffer from any further misfortune. Isn't that true?

Now Raval enters the discussion. He is slightly drunk and his voice is shrill and evil.

Raval. Listen, you! You sit there and lie to the smith.

Jof. I! A liar!

Raval. You're an actor too and it's probably your partner who's run off with Plog's old lady.

Plog. Are you an actor too?

Jof. An actor! Me! I wouldn't quite call myself that!

Raval. We ought to kill you; it's only logical.

Jof (*laughs*). You're really funny.

Raval. How strange—you've turned pale. Have you anything on your conscience?

Jof. You're funny. Don't you think he's funny? (*To Plog*) Oh, you don't.

Raval. Maybe we should mark you up a little with a knife, like they do petty scoundrels of your kind.

Plog bangs his hands down on the table so that the dishes jump. He gets up.

Plog (*shouting*). What have you done with my wife?

The room becomes silent. Jof looks around, but there is no exit, no way to escape. He puts his hands on the table. Suddenly a knife flashes through the air and sinks into the table top between his fingers.

Jof snatches away his hands and raises his head. He looks half surprised, as if the truth had just become apparent to him.

Jof. Do you want to hurt me? Why? Have I provoked someone, or got in the way? I'll leave right now and never come back.

Jof looks from one face to another, but no one seems ready to help him or come to his defense.

Raval. Get up so everyone can hear you. Talk louder.

Trembling, Jof rises. He opens his mouth as if to say something, but not a word comes out.

Raval. Stand on your head so that we can see how good an actor you are.

Jof gets up on the table and stands on his head. A hand pushes him forward so that he collapses on the floor. Plog rises, pulls him to his feet with one hand.

Plog (*shouts*). What have you done with my wife?

The smith beats him so furiously that Jof flies across the table. Raval leans over him.

Raval. Don't lie there moaning. Get up and dance.
Jof. I don't want to. I can't.
Raval. Show us how you imitate a bear.
Jof. I can't play a bear.
Raval. Let's see if you can't after all.

Raval prods Jof lightly with the knife point. Jof gets up with cold sweat on his cheeks and forehead, frightened half to death. He begins to jump and hop on top of the tables, swinging his arms and legs and making grotesque faces. Some laugh, but most of the people sit silently. Jof gasps as if his lungs were about to burst. He sinks to his knees, and someone pours beer over him.

Raval. Up again! Be a good bear.
Jof. I haven't done any harm. I haven't got the strength to play a bear any more.

At that moment the door opens and Jöns enters. Jof sees his chance and steals out. Raval intends to follow him, but suddenly stops. Jöns and Raval look at each other.

Jöns. Do you remember what I was going to do to you if we met again?

Raval steps back without speaking.

Jöns. I'm a man who keeps his word.

Jöns raises his knife and cuts Raval from forehead to cheek. Raval staggers toward the wall.

THE hot day has become night. Singing and howling can be heard from the inn. In a hollow near the forest, the light still lingers. Hidden in the grass and the shrubbery, nightingales sing and their voices echo through the stillness.

The players' wagon stands in a small ravine, and not far away the horse grazes on the dry grass. Mia has sat down in front of the wagon with her son in her arms. They play together and laugh happily.

Now a soft gleam of light strokes the hilltops, a last reflection from the red clouds over the sea.

Not far from the wagon, the knight sits crouched over his chess game. He lifts his head.

The evening light moves across the heavy wagon wheels, across the woman and the child.

The knight gets up.

Mia sees him and smiles. She holds up her struggling son, as if to amuse the knight.

Knight. What's his name?
Mia. Mikael.
Knight. How old is he?
Mia. Oh, he'll soon be two.
Knight. He's big for his age.
Mia. Do you think so? Yes, I guess he's rather big.

She puts the child down on the ground and half rises to shake out her red skirt. When she sits down again, the knight steps closer.

Knight. You played some kind of show this afternoon.
Mia. Did you think it was bad?
Knight. You are more beautiful now without your face painted, and this gown is more becoming.
Mia. You see, Jonas Skat has run off and left us, so we're in real trouble now.
Knight. Is that your husband?
Mia (*laughs*). Jonas! The other man is my husband. His name is Jof.
Knight. Oh, that one.
Mia. And now there's only him and me. We'll have to start doing tricks again and that's more trouble than it's worth.
Knight. Do you do tricks also?
Mia. We certainly do. And Jof is a very skillful juggler.
Knight. Is Mikael going to be an acrobat?
Mia. Jof wants him to be.
Knight. But you don't.
Mia. I don't know. (*Smiling*) Perhaps he'll become a knight.
Knight. Let me assure you, that's no pleasure either.
Mia. No, you don't look so happy.
Knight. No.
Mia. Are you tired?
Knight. Yes.
Mia. Why?
Knight. I have dull company.
Mia. Do you mean your squire?
Knight. No, not him.
Mia. Who do you mean, then?
Knight. Myself.
Mia. I understand.

Knight. Do you, really?

Mia. Yes, I understand rather well. I have often wondered why people torture themselves as often as they can. Isn't that so?

She nods energetically and the knight smiles seriously.

Now the shrieks and the noise from the inn become louder. Black figures flicker across the grass mound. Someone collapses, gets up and runs. It is Jof. Mia stretches out her arms and receives him. He holds his hands in front of his face, moaning like a child, and his body sways. He kneels. Mia holds him close to her and sprinkles him with small, anxious questions: What have you done? How are you? What is it? Does it hurt? What can I do? Have they been cruel to you? She runs for a rag, which she dips in water, and carefully bathes her husband's dirty, bloody face.

Eventually a rather sorrowful visage emerges. Blood runs from a bruise on his forehead and his nose, and a tooth has been loosened, but otherwise Jof seems unhurt.

Jof. Ouch, it hurts.

Mia. Why did you have to go there? And of course you drank.

Mia's anxiety has been replaced by a mild anger. She pats him a little harder than necessary.

Jof. Ouch! I didn't drink anything.

Mia. Then I suppose you were boasting about the angels and devils you consort with. People don't like someone who has too many ideas and fantasies.

Jof. I swear to you that I didn't say a word about angels.

Mia. You were, of course, busy singing and dancing. You can never stop being an actor. People also become angry at that, and you know it.

Jof doesn't answer but searches for the armlet. He holds it up in front of Mia with an injured expression.

Jof. Look what I bought for you.

Mia. You couldn't afford it.

Jof (*angry*). But I got it anyhow.

The armlet glitters faintly in the twilight. Mia now pulls it across her wrist. They look at it in silence, and their faces soften. They look at each other, touch each other's hands. Jof puts his head against Mia's shoulder and sighs.

Jof. Oh, how they beat me.

Mia. Why didn't you beat them back?

Jof. I only become frightened and angry. I never get a chance to hit back. I can get angry, you know that. I roared like a lion.

Mia. Were they frightened?

Jof. No, they just laughed.

Their son Mikael crawls over to them. Jof lies down on the ground and pulls his son on top of him. Mia gets down on her hands and knees and playfully sniffs at Mikael.

Mia.   Do you notice how good he smells?
Jof.   And he is so compact to hold. You're a sturdy one. A real acrobat's body.

He lifts Mikael up and holds him by the legs. Mia looks up suddenly, remembering the knight's presence.

Mia.   Yes, this is my husband, Jof.
Jof.   Good evening.
Knight.   Good evening.

Jof becomes a little embarrassed and rises. All three of them look at one another silently.

Knight.   I have just told your wife that you have a splendid son. He'll bring great joy to you.
Jof.   Yes, he's fine.

They become silent again.

Jof.   Have we nothing to offer the knight, Mia?
Knight.   Thank you, I don't want anything.
Mia (*housewifely*).   I picked a basket of wild strawberries this afternoon. And we have a drop of milk fresh from a cow . . .
Jof. . . . that we were *allowed* to milk. So, if you would like to partake of this humble fare, it would be a great honor.
Mia.   Please be seated and I'll bring the food.

They sit down. Mia disappears with Mikael.

Knight.   Where are you going next?
Jof.   Up to the saints' feast at Elsinore.
Knight.   I wouldn't advise you to go there.
Jof.   Why not, if I may ask?
Knight.   The plague has spread in that direction, following the coast line south. It's said that people are dying by the tens of thousands.
Jof.   Really! Well, sometimes life is a little hard.
Knight.   May I suggest . . . (*Jof looks at him, surprised*) . . . that you follow me through the forest tonight and stay at my home if you like. Or go along the east coast. You'll probably be safer there.

Mia has returned with a bowl of wild strawberries and the milk, places it between them and gives each of them a spoon.

Jof.   I wish you good appetite.
Knight.   I humbly thank you.
Mia.   These are wild strawberries from the forest. I have never seen such large ones. They grow up there on the hillside. Notice how they smell!

She points with a spoon and smiles. The knight nods, as if he were pondering some profound thought. Jof eats heartily.

Jof. Your suggestion is good, but I must think it over.

Mia. It might be wise to have company going through the forest. It's said to be full of trolls and ghosts and bandits. That's what I've heard.

Jof (*staunchly*). Yes, I'd say that it's not a bad idea, but I have to think about it. Now that Skat has left, I am responsible for the troupe. After all, I have become director of the whole company.

Mia (*mimics*). After all, I have become director of the whole company.

Jöns comes walking slowly down the hill, closely followed by the girl. Mia points with her spoon.

Mia. Do you want some strawberries?

Jof. This man saved my life. Sit down, my friend, and let us be together.

Mia (*stretches herself*). Oh, how nice this is.

Knight. For a short while.

Mia. Nearly always. One day is like another. There is nothing strange about that. The summer, of course, is better than the winter, because in summer you don't have to be cold. But spring is best of all.

Jof. I have written a poem about the spring. Perhaps you'd like to hear it. I'll run and get my lyre. (*He sprints toward the wagon*)

Mia. Not now, Jof. Our guests may not be amused by your songs.

Jöns (*politely*). By all means. I write little songs myself. For example, I know a very funny song about a wanton fish which I doubt that you've heard yet.

The knight looks at him.

Jöns. You'll not get to hear it either. There are persons here who don't appreciate my art and I don't want to upset anyone. I'm a sensitive soul.

Jof has come out with his lyre, sits on a small, gaudy box and plucks at the instrument, humming quietly, searching for his melody. Jöns yawns and lies down.

Knight. People are troubled by so much.

Mia. It's always better when one is two. Have you no one of your own?

Knight. Yes, I think I had someone.

Mia. And what is she doing now?

Knight. I don't know.

Mia. You look so solemn. Was she your beloved?

Knight. We were newly married and we played together. We laughed a great deal. I wrote songs to her eyes, to her nose, to her beautiful little ears. We went hunting together and at night we danced. The house was full of life . . .

Mia. Do you want some more strawberries?

Knight (*shakes his head*). Faith is a torment, did you know that? It is like loving someone who is out there in the darkness but never appears, no matter how loudly you call.

Mia. I don't understand what you mean.

Knight. Everything I've said seems meaningless and unreal while I sit here with you and your husband. How unimportant it all becomes suddenly.

He takes the bowl of milk in his hand and drinks deeply from it several times. Then he carefully puts it down and looks up, smiling.

Mia. Now you don't look so solemn.

Knight. I shall remember this moment. The silence, the twilight, the bowls of strawberries and milk, your faces in the evening light. Mikael sleeping, Jof with his lyre. I'll try to remember what we have talked about. I'll carry this memory between my hands as carefully as if it were a bowl filled to the brim with fresh milk. (*He turns his face away and looks out toward the sea and the colorless gray sky*) And it will be an adequate sign—it will be enough for me.

He rises, nods to the others and walks down toward the forest. Jof continues to play on his lyre. Mia stretches out on the grass.

The knight picks up his chess game and carries it toward the beach. It is quiet and deserted; the sea is still.

Death. I have been waiting for you.

Knight. Pardon me. I was detained for a few moments. Because I revealed my tactics to you, I'm in retreat. It's your move.

Death. Why do you look so satisfied?

Knight. That's my secret.

Death. Of course. Now I take your knight.

Knight. You did the right thing.

Death. Have you tricked me?

Knight. Of course. You fell right in the trap. Check!

Death. What are you laughing at?

Knight. Don't worry about my laughter; save your king instead.

Death. You're rather arrogant.

Knight. Our game amuses me.

Death. It's your move. Hurry up. I'm a little pressed for time.

Knight. I understand that you've a lot to do, but you can't get out of our game. It takes time.

Death is about to answer him but stops and leans over the board. The knight smiles.

Death. Are you going to escort the juggler and his wife through the forest? Those whose names are Jof and Mia and who have a small son.

Knight. Why do you ask?
Death. Oh, no reason at all.

The knight suddenly stops smiling. Death looks at him scornfully.

IMMEDIATELY after sundown, the little company gathers in the yard of the inn. There is the knight, Jöns and the girl, Jof and Mia in their wagon. Their son, Mikael, is already asleep. Jonas Skat is still missing.

Jöns goes into the inn to get provisions for the night journey and to have a last mug of beer. The inn is now empty and quiet except for a few farmhands and maidens who are eating their evening meal in a corner.

At one of the small windows sits a lonely, hunched-over fellow, with a jug of brandy in his hands. His expression is very sad. Once in a while he is shaken by a gigantic sob. It is Plog, the smith, who sits there and whimpers.

Jöns. God in heaven, isn't this Plog, the smith?
Plog. Good evening.
Jöns. Are you sitting here sniveling in loneliness?
Plog. Yes, yes, look at the smith. He moans like a rabbit.
Jöns. If I were in your boots, I'd be happy to get rid of a wife in such an easy way.

Jöns pats the smith on the back, quenches his thirst with beer, and sits down by his side.

Plog. Are *you* married?
Jöns. *I!* A hundred times and more. I can't keep count of all my wives any longer. But it's often that way when you're a traveling man.
Plog. I can assure you that *one* wife is worse than a hundred, or else I've had worse luck than any poor wretch in this miserable world, which isn't impossible.
Jöns. Yes, it's hell *with* women and hell *without* them. So, however you look at it, it's still best to kill them off while it's most amusing.
Plog. Women's nagging, the shrieking of children and wet diapers, sharp nails and sharp words, blows and pokes, and the devil's aunt for a mother-in-law. And then, when one wants to sleep after a long day, there's a new song—tears, whining and moans loud enough to wake the dead.

Jöns nods delightedly. He has drunk deeply and talks with an old woman's voice.

Jöns. Why don't you kiss me good night?
Plog (*in the same way*).   Why don't you sing a song for me?
Jöns. Why don't you love me the way you did when we first met?
Plog. Why don't you look at my new shift?
Jöns. You only turn your back and snore.
Plog. Oh hell!

Jöns. Oh hell. And now she's gone. Rejoice!

Plog (*furious*). I'll snip their noses with pliers, I'll bash in their chests with a small hammer, I'll tap their heads ever so lightly with a sledge.

Plog begins to cry loudly and his whole body sways in an enormous attack of sorrow. Jöns looks at him with interest.

Jöns. Look how he howls again.

Plog. Maybe I love her.

Jöns. So, maybe you love her! Then, you poor misguided ham shank, I'll tell you that love is another word for lust, plus lust, plus lust and a damn lot of cheating, falseness, lies and all kinds of other fooling around.

Plog. Yes, but it hurts anyway.

Jöns. Of course. Love is the blackest of all plagues, and if one could die of it, there would be some pleasure in love. But you almost always get over it.

Plog. No, no, not me.

Jöns. Yes, you too. There are only a couple of poor wretches who die of love once in a while. Love is as contagious as a cold in the nose. It eats away at your strength, your independence, your morale, if you have any. If everything is imperfect in this imperfect world, love is most perfect in its perfect imperfection.

Plog. You're happy, you with your oily words, and, besides, you believe your own drivel.

Jöns. Believe! Who said that I believed it? But I love to give good advice. If you ask me for advice you'll get two pieces for the price of one, because after all I really am an educated man.

Jöns gets up from the table and strokes his face with his hands. The smith becomes very unhappy and grabs his belt.

Plog. Listen, Jöns. May I go with you through the forest? I'm so lonely and don't want to go home because everyone will laugh at me.

Jöns. Only if you don't whimper all the time, because in that case we'll all have to avoid you.

The smith gets up and embraces Jöns. Slightly drunk, the two new friends walk toward the door.

When they come out in the yard, Jof immediately catches sight of them, becomes angry and yells a warning to Jöns.

Jof. Jöns! Watch out. That one wants to fight all the time. He's not quite sane.

Jöns. Yes, but now he's just sniveling.

The smith steps up to Jof, who blanches with fear. Plog offers his hand.

Plog. I'm really sorry if I hurt you. But I have such a hell of a temper, you know. Shake hands.

Jof gingerly proffers a frightened hand and gets it thoroughly shaken and squeezed. While Jof tries to straighten out his fingers, Plog is seized by great good will and opens his arms.

Plog. Come in my arms, little brother.
Jof. Thank you, thank you, perhaps later. But now we're really in a hurry.

JOF climbs up on the wagon seat quickly and clucks at the horse.
The small company is on its way toward the forest and the night.
It is dark in the forest.

First comes the knight on his large horse. Then Jof and Mia follow, sitting close to each other in the juggler's wagon. Mia holds her son in her arms. Jöns follows them with his heavily laden horse. He has the smith in tow. The girl sits on top of the load on the horse's back, hunched over as if asleep.

The footsteps, the horses' heavy tramp on the soft path, the human breathing—yet it is quiet.

Then the moon sails out of the clouds. The forest suddenly becomes alive with the night's unreality. The dazzling light pours through the thick foliage of the beech trees, a moving, quivering world of light and shadow.

The wanderers stop. Their eyes are dark with anxiety and foreboding. Their faces are pale and unreal in the floating light. It is very quiet.

Plog. Now the moon has come out of the clouds.
Jöns. That's good. Now we can see the road better.
Mia. I don't like the moon tonight.
Jof. The trees stand so still.
Jöns. That's because there's no wind.
Plog. I guess he means that they stand *very* still.
Jof. It's completely quiet.
Jöns. If one could hear a fox at least.
Jof. Or an owl.
Jöns. Or a human voice besides one's own.
Girl. They say it's dangerous to remain standing in moonlight.

Suddenly, out of the silence and the dim light falling across the forest road, a ghostlike cart emerges.

It is the witch being taken to the place where she will be burned. Next to her eight soldiers shuffle along tiredly, carrying their lances on their backs. The girl sits in the cart, bound with iron chains around her throat and arms. She stares fixedly into the moonlight.

A black figure sits next to her, a monk with his hood pulled down over his head.

Jöns. Where are you going?
Soldier. To the place of execution.

Jöns. Yes, now I can see. It's the girl who has done it with the Black One. The witch?

The soldier nods sourly. Hesitantly, the travelers follow. The knight guides his horse over to the side of the cart. The witch seems to be half conscious, but her eyes are wide open.

Knight. I see that they have hurt your hands.

The witch's pale, childish face turns toward the knight and she shakes her head.

Knight. I have a potion that will stop your pain.

She shakes her head again.

Jöns. Why do you burn her at this time of night? People have so few diversions these days.

Soldier. Saints preserve us, be quiet! It's said that she brings the Devil with her wherever she goes.

Jöns. You are eight brave men, then.

Soldier. Well, we've been paid. And this is a volunteer job.

The soldier speaks in whispers while glancing anxiously at the witch.

Knight (*to witch*). What's your name?

Tyan. My name is Tyan, my lord.

Knight. How old are you?

Tyan. Fourteen, my lord.

Knight. And is it true that you have been in league with the Devil?

Tyan nods quietly and looks away. Now they arrive at the parish border. At the foot of the nearby hills lies a crossroads. The pyre has already been stacked in the center of the forest clearing. The travelers remain there, hesitant and curious.

The soldiers have tied up the cart horse and bring out two long wooden beams. They nail rungs across the beams so that it looks like a ladder. Tyan will be bound to this like an eelskin stretched out to dry.

The sound of the hammering echoes through the forest. The knight has dismounted and walks closer to the cart. Again he tries to catch Tyan's eyes, touches her very lightly as if to waken her.

Slowly she turns her face toward him.

Knight. They say that you have been in league with the Devil.

Tyan. Why do you ask?

Knight. Not out of curiosity, but for very personal reasons. I too want to meet him.

Tyan. Why?

Knight. I want to ask him about God. He, if anyone, must know.

Tyan. You can see him anytime.

Knight. How?
Tyan. You must do as I tell you.

The knight grips the wooden rail of the cart so tightly that his knuckles whiten. Tyan leans forward and joins her gaze with his.

Tyan. Look into my eyes.

The knight meets her gaze. They stare at each other for a long time.

Tyan. What do you see? Do you see *him*?
Knight. I see fear in your eyes, an empty, numb fear. But nothing else.

He falls silent. The soldiers work at the stacks; their hammering echoes in the forest.

Tyan. No one, nothing, no one?
Knight (*shakes his head*). No.
Tyan. Can't you see him behind your back?
Knight (*looks around*). No, there is no one there.
Tyan. But he is with me everywhere. I only have to stretch out my hand and I can feel his hand. He is with me now too. The fire won't hurt me. He will protect me from everything evil.
Knight. Has he told you this?
Tyan. I know it.
Knight. Has he said it?
Tyan. I know it, I know it. You must see him somewhere, you must. The priests had no difficulty seeing him, nor did the soldiers. They are so afraid of him that they don't even dare touch me.

The sound of the hammers stops. The soldiers stand like black shadows rooted in the moss. They fumble with the chains and pull at the neck iron. Tyan moans weakly, as if she were far away.

Knight. Why have you crushed her hands?
Soldier (*surly*). We didn't do it.
Knight. Who did?
Soldier. Ask the monk.

The soldiers pull the iron and chains. Tyan's shaven head sways, gleaming in the moonlight. Her blackened mouth opens as if to scream, but no sound emerges.

They take her down from the cart and lead her toward the ladder and the stake. The knight turns to the monk, who remains seated in the cart.

Knight. What have you done with the child?

Death turns around and looks at him.

Death. Don't you ever stop asking questions?
Knight. No, I'll never stop.

The soldiers chain Tyan to the rungs of the ladder. She submits resignedly, moans weakly like an animal and tries to ease her body into position.

When they have fastened her, they walk over to light the pyre. The knight steps up and leans over her.

Jöns. For a moment I thought of killing the soldiers, but it would do no good. She's nearly dead already.

One of the soldiers approaches. Thick smoke wells down from the pyre and sweeps over the quiet shadows near the crossroads and the hill.

Soldier. I've told you to be careful. Don't go too close to her.

The knight doesn't heed this warning. He cups his hand, fills it with water from the skin and gives it to Tyan. Then he gives her a potion.

Knight. Take this and it will stop the pain.

Smoke billows down over them and they begin to cough. The soldiers step forward and raise the ladder against a nearby fir tree. Tyan hangs there motionlessly, her eyes wide open.

The knight straightens up and stands immobile. Jöns is behind him, his voice nearly choked with rage.

Jöns. What does she see? Can you tell me?
Knight (*shakes his head*). She feels no more pain.
Jöns. You don't answer my question. Who watches over that child? Is it the angels, or God, or the Devil, or only the emptiness? Emptiness, my lord!
Knight. This cannot be.
Jöns. Look at her eyes, my lord. Her poor brain has just made a discovery. Emptiness under the moon.
Knight. No.
Jöns. We stand powerless, our arms hanging at our sides, because we see what she sees, and our terror and hers are the same. (*An outburst*) That poor little child. I can't stand it, I can't stand it . . .

His voice sticks in his throat and he suddenly walks away. The knight mounts his horse. The travelers depart from the crossroads. Tyan finally closes her eyes.

THE forest is now very dark. The road winds between the trees. The wagon squeaks and rattles over stones and roots. A bird suddenly shrieks.

Jof lifts his head and wakes up. He has been asleep with his arms around Mia's shoulders. The knight is sharply silhouetted against the tree trunks.

His silence makes him seem almost unreal.

Jöns and the smith are slightly drunk and support each other. Suddenly Plog has to sit down. He puts his hands over his face and howls piteously.

Plog. Oh, now it came over me again!

Jöns. Don't scream. What came over you?

Plog. My wife, damn it. She is so beautiful. She is so beautiful that she can't be described without the accompaniment of a lyre.

Jöns. Now it starts again.

Plog. Her smile is like brandy. Her eyes like blackberries . . .

Plog searches for beautiful words. He gestures gropingly with his large hands.

Jöns (*sighs*). Get up, you tear-drenched pig. We'll lose the others.

Plog. Yes, of course, of course. Her nose is like a little pink potato; her behind is like a juicy pear—yes, the whole woman is like a strawberry patch. I can see her in front of me, with arms like wonderful cucumbers.

Jöns. Saints almighty, stop! You're a very bad poet, despite the fact that you're drunk. And your vegetable garden bores me.

They walk across an open meadow. Here it is a little brighter and the moon shimmers behind a thin sky. Suddenly the smith points a large finger toward the edge of the forest.

Plog. Look there.

Jöns. Do you see something?

Plog. There, over there!

Jöns. I don't see anything.

Plog. Hang on to something, my friends. The hour is near! Who is that at the edge of the forest if not my own dearly beloved, with actor attached?

The two lovers discover the smith and it's too late. They cannot retreat. Skat immediately takes to his heels. Plog chases him, swinging his sledge and bellowing like a wild boar.

For a few confusing moments the two rivals stumble among the stones and bushes in the gray gloom of the forest. The duel begins to look senseless, because both of them are equally frightened.

The travelers silently observe this confused performance. Lisa screams once in a while, more out of duty than out of impulse.

Skat (*panting*). You miserable stubbleheaded bastard of seven scurvy bitches, if I were in your lousy rags I would be stricken with such eternal shame about my breath, my voice, my arms and legs—in short, about my whole body—that I would immediately rid nature of my own embarrassing self.

Plog (*angry*). Watch out, you perfumed slob, that I don't fart on you and immediately blow you down to the actor's own red-hot hell, where you can sit and recite monologues to each other until the dust comes out of the Devil's ears.

Then Lisa throws herself around her husband's neck.

Lisa. Forgive me, dear little husband. I'll never do it again. I am so sorry and you can't imagine how terribly that man over there betrayed me.

Plog. I'll kill him anyway.

Lisa. Yes, do that, just kill him. He isn't even a human being.

Jöns. Hell, he's an actor.

Lisa. He is only a false beard, false teeth, false smiles, rehearsed lines, and he's as empty as a jug. Just kill him.

Lisa sobs with excitement and sorrow. The smith looks around, a little confused. The actor uses this opportunity. He pulls out a dagger and places the point against his breast.

Skat. She's right. Just kill me. If you thought that I was going to apologize for being what I am, you are mistaken.

Lisa. Look how sickening he is. How he makes a fool of himself, how he puts on an act. Dear Plog, kill him!

Skat. My friends, you have only to push, and my unreality will soon be transformed into a new solid reality. An absolutely tangible corpse.

Lisa. Do something then. Kill him.

Plog (*embarrassed*). He has to fight me, otherwise I can't kill him.

Skat. Your life's thread now hangs by a very ragged shred. Idiot, your day is short.

Plog. You'll have to irritate me a little more to get me as angry as before.

Skat looks at the travelers with a pained expression and then lifts his eyes toward the night sky.

Skat. I forgive all of you. Pray for me sometimes.

Skat sinks the dagger into his breast and slowly falls to the ground. The travelers stand confused. The smith rushes forward and begins to pull at the actor's hands.

Plog. Oh dear, dear, I didn't mean it that way! Look, there's no life left in him. I was beginning to like him, and in my opinion Lisa was much too spiteful.

Jof leans over his colleague.

Jof. He's dead, totally, enormously dead. In fact, I've never seen such a dead actor.

Lisa. Come on, let's go. This is nothing to mourn over. He has only himself to blame.

Plog. And I have to be married to *her*.

Jöns. We must go on.

Skat lies in the grass and keeps the dagger pressed tightly to his breast. The travelers depart and soon they have disappeared into the dark forest on the other side of the meadow. When Skat is sure that no one can see him, he sits up and lifts the dagger from his breast. It is a stage dagger with a blade that pushes into the handle. Skat laughs to himself.

Skat. Now that was a good scene. I'm really a good actor. After all, why shouldn't I be a little pleased with myself? But where shall I go? I'll wait until it becomes light and then I'll find the easiest way out of the forest. I'll climb up a tree for the time being so that no bears, wolves or ghosts can get at me.

He soon finds a likely tree and climbs up into its thick foliage. He sits down as comfortably as possible and reaches for his food pouch.

Skat (*yawns*). Tomorrow I'll find Jof and Mia and then we'll go to the saints' feast in Elsinore. We'll make lots of money there. (Yawns) Now, I'll sing a little song to myself:

I am a little bird
Who sings whate'er he will,
And when I am in danger
I fling out a pissing trill
As in the carnal thrill.

(*Speaks*) It's boring to be alone in the forest tonight. (*Sings*) The terrible night doesn't frighten me . . .

He interrupts himself and listens. The sound of industrious sawing is heard through the silence.

Skat. Workmen in the forest. Oh, well! (*Sings*) The terrible night doesn't frighten me . . . Hey, what the devil . . . it's *my* tree they're cutting down.

He peers through the foliage. Below him stands a dark figure diligently sawing away at the base of the tree. Skat becomes frightened and angry.

Skat. Hey, you! Do you hear me, you tricky bastard? What are you doing with my tree?

The sawing continues without a pause. Skat becomes more frightened.

Skat. Can't you at least answer me? Politeness costs so little. Who are you?

Death straightens his back and squints up at him. Skat cries out in terror.

Death. I'm sawing down your tree because your time is up.
Skat. It won't do. I haven't got time.
Death. So you haven't got time.
Skat. No, I have my performance.
Death. Then it's been canceled because of death.
Skat. My contract.
Death. Your contract is terminated.
Skat. My children, my family.
Death. Shame on you, Skat!
Skat. Yes, I'm ashamed.

Death begins to saw again. The tree creaks.

Skat. Isn't there any way to get off? Aren't there any special rules for actors?
Death. No, not in this case.
Skat. No loopholes, no exceptions?

Death saws.

Skat. Perhaps you'll take a bribe.

Death saws.

Skat. Help!

Death saws.

Skat. Help! Help!

The tree falls. The forest becomes silent again.

NIGHT and then dawn.
The travelers have come to a sort of clearing and have collapsed on the moss. They lie quietly and listen to their own breathing, their heartbeats, and the wind in the tree tops. Here the forest is wild and impenetrable. Huge boulders stick up out of the ground like the heads of black giants. A fallen tree lies like a mighty barrier between light and shadow.
Mia, Jof and their child have sat down apart from the others. They look at the light of the moon, which is no longer full and dead but mysterious and unstable.
The knight sits bent over his chess game. Lisa cries quietly behind the smith's back. Jöns lies on the ground and looks up at the heavens.

Jöns. Soon dawn will come, but the heat continues to hang over us like a smothering blanket.
Lisa. I'm so frightened.
Plog. We feel that something is going to happen to us, but we don't know what.
Jöns. Maybe it's the day of judgment.
Plog. The day of judgment . . .

Now something moves behind the fallen tree. There is a rustling sound and a moaning cry that seems to come from a wounded animal. Everyone listens intently, all faces turned toward the sound.
A voice comes out of the darkness.

Raval. Do you have some water?

Raval's perspiring face soon becomes visible. He disappears in the darkness, but his voice is heard again.

Raval. Can't you give me a little water? (*Pause*) I have the plague.
Jöns. Don't come here. If you do I'll slit your throat. Keep to the other side of the tree.
Raval. I'm afraid of death.

No one answers. There is complete silence. Raval gasps heavily for air. The dry leaves rustle with his movements.

Raval. I don't want to die! I don't want to!

No one answers. Raval's face appears suddenly at the base of the tree. His eyes bulge wildly and his mouth is ringed with foam.

Raval. Can't you have pity on me? Help me! At least talk to me.

No one answers. The trees sigh. Raval begins to cry.

Raval. I am going to die. I. I. *I!* What will happen to me! Can no one console me! Haven't you any compassion? Can't you see that I . . .

His words are choked off by a gurgling sound. He disappears in the darkness behind the fallen tree. It becomes quiet for a few moments.

Raval (*Whispers*). Can't anyone . . . only a little water.

Suddenly the girl gets up with a quick movement, snatches Jöns' water bag and runs a few steps. Jöns grabs her and holds her fast.

Jöns. It's no use. It's no use. I know that it's no use. It's meaningless. It's totally meaningless. I tell you that it's meaningless. Can't you hear that I'm consoling you?

Raval. Help me, help me!

No one answers, no one moves. Raval's sobs are dry and convulsive, like a frightened child's. His sudden scream is cut off in the middle.

Then it becomes quiet.

The girl sinks down and hides her face in her hands. Jöns places his hand on her shoulder.

THE knight is no longer alone. Death has come to him and he raises his hand.

Death. Shall we play our game to the end?
Knight. Your move!

Death raises his hand and strikes the knight's queen. Antonius Block looks at Death.

Death. Now I take your queen.
Knight. I didn't notice that.

The knight leans over the game. The moonlight moves over the chess pieces, which seem to have a life of their own.

Jof has dozed off for a few moments, but suddenly he wakens. Then he sees the knight and Death together.

He becomes very frightened and awakens Mia.

Jof. Mia!

Mia. Yes, what is it?

Jof. I see something terrible. Something I almost can't talk about.

Mia. What do you see?

Jof. The knight is sitting over there playing chess.

Mia. Yes, I can see that too and I don't think it's so terrible.

Jof. But do you see who he's playing with?

Mia. He is alone. You *mustn't* frighten me this way.

Jof. No, no, he isn't alone.

Mia. Who is it, then?

Jof. Death. He is sitting there playing chess with Death himself.

Mia. You mustn't say that.

Jof. We must try to escape.

Mia. One can't do that.

Jof. We must try. They are so occupied with their game that if we move very quietly, they won't notice us.

Jof gets up carefully and disappears into the darkness behind the trees. Mia remains standing, as if paralyzed by fear. She stares fixedly at the knight and the chess game. She holds her son in her arms.

Now Jof returns.

Jof. I have harnessed the horse. The wagon is standing near the big tree. You go first and I'll follow you with the packs. See that Mikael doesn't wake up.

Mia does what Jof has told her. At the same moment, the knight looks up from his game.

Death. It is your move, Antonius Block.

The knight remains silent. He sees Mia go through the moonlight toward the wagon. Jof bends down to pick up the pack and follows at a distance.

Death. Have you lost interest in our game?

The knight's eyes become alarmed. Death looks at him intently.

Knight. Lost interest? On the contrary.

Death. You seem anxious. Are you hiding anything?

Knight. Nothing escapes you—or does it?

Death. Nothing escapes me. No one escapes from me.

Knight. It's true that I'm worried.

He pretends to be clumsy and knocks the chess pieces over with the hem of his coat. He looks up at Death.

Knight. I've forgotten how the pieces stood.

Death (laughs contentedly). But I have not forgotten. You can't get away that easily.

Death leans over the board and rearranges the pieces. The knight looks past him toward the road. Mia has just climbed up on the wagon. Jof takes the horse by the bridle and leads it down to the road. Death notices nothing; he is completely occupied with reconstructing the game.

Death.   Now I see something interesting.
Knight.   What do you see?
Death.   You are mated on the next move, Antonius Block.
Knight.   That's true.
Death.   Did you enjoy your reprieve?
Knight.   Yes, I did.
Death.   I'm happy to hear that. Now I'll be leaving you. When we meet again, you and your companions' time will be up.
Knight.   And you will divulge your secrets.
Death.   I have no secrets.
Knight.   So you know nothing.
Death.   I have nothing to tell.

The knight wants to answer, but Death is already gone.

A murmur is heard in the tree tops. Dawn comes, a flickering light without life, making the forest seem threatening and evil. Jof drives over the twisting road. Mia sits beside him.

Mia.   What a strange light.
Jof.   I guess it's the thunderstorm which comes with dawn.
Mia.   No, it's something else. Something terrible. Do you hear the roar in the forest?
Jof.   It's probably rain.
Mia.   No, it isn't rain. He has seen us and he's following us. He has overtaken us; he's coming toward us.
Jof.   Not yet, Mia. In any case, not yet.
Mia.   I'm so afraid. I'm so afraid.

The wagon rattles over roots and stones; it sways and creaks. Now the horse stops with his ears flat against his head. The forest sighs and stirs ponderously.

Jof.   Get into the wagon, Mia. Crawl in quickly. We'll lie down, Mia, with Mikael between us.

They crawl into the wagon and crouch around the sleeping child.

Jof.   It is the Angel of Death that's passing over us, Mia. It's the Angel of Death. *The Angel of Death, and he's very big.*
Mia.   Do you feel how cold it is? I'm freezing. I'm terribly cold.

She shivers as if she had a fever. They pull the blankets over them and lie closely together. The wagon canvas flutters and beats in the wind. The roar outside is like a giant bellowing.

THE castle is silhouetted like a black boulder against the heavy dawn. Now the storm moves there, throwing itself powerfully against walls and abutments. The sky darkens; it is almost like night.

Antonius Block has brought his companions with him to the castle. But it seems deserted. They walk from room to room. There is only emptiness and quiet echoes. Outside, the rain is heard roaring noisily.

Suddenly the knight stands face to face with his wife. They look at each other quietly.

Karin. I heard from people who came from the crusade that you were on your way home. I've been waiting for you here. All the others have fled from the plague.

The knight is silent. He looks at her.

Karin. Don't you recognize me any more?

The knight nods, silent.

Karin. You also have changed.

She walks closer and looks searchingly into his face. The smile lingers in her eyes and she touches his hand lightly.

Karin. Now I can see that it's you. Somewhere in your eyes, somewhere in your face, but hidden and frightened, is that boy who went away so many years ago.
Knight. It's over now and I'm a little tired.
Karin. I see that you're tired.
Knight. Over there stand my friends.
Karin. Ask them in. They will break the fast with us.

They all sit down at the table in the room, which is lit by torches on the walls. Silently they eat the hard bread and the salt-darkened meat. Karin sits at the head of the table and reads aloud from a thick book.

Karin. "And when the Lamb broke the seventh seal, there was silence in heaven for about the space of half an hour. And I saw the seven angels which stood before God; and to them were given seven trumpets. And another . . ."

Three mighty knocks sound on the large portal. Karin interrupts her reading and looks up from the book. Jöns rises quickly and goes to open the door.

Karin. "The first angel sounded, and there followed hail and fire mingled with blood, and they were cast upon the earth; and the third part of the trees was burnt up and all the green grass was burnt up."

Now the rain becomes quiet. There is suddenly an immense, frightening silence in the large, murky room where the burning torches throw uneasy shadows over the ceiling and the walls. Everyone listens tensely to the stillness.

Karin. "And the second angel sounded, and as it were a great mountain burning with fire was cast into the sea; and a third part of the sea became blood..."

Steps are heard on the stairs. Jöns returns and sits down silently at his place but does not continue to eat.

Knight. Was someone there?
Jöns. No, my lord. I saw no one.

Karin lifts her head for a moment but once again leans over the large book.

Karin. "And the third angel sounded, and there fell a great star from heaven, burning as it were a torch, and it fell upon the third part of the rivers and upon the fountains of waters; and the name of the star is called Wormwood..."

They all lift their heads, and when they see who is coming toward them through the twilight of the large room, they rise from the table and stand close together.

Knight. Good morning, noble lord.
Karin. I am Karin, the knight's wife, and welcome you courteously to my house.
Plog. I am a smith by profession and rather good at my trade, if I say so myself. My wife Lisa—curtsy for the great lord, Lisa. She's a little difficult to handle once in a while and we had a little spat, so to say, but no worse than most people.

The knight hides his face in his hands.

Knight. From our darkness, we call out to Thee, Lord. Have mercy on us because we are small and frightened and ignorant.
Jöns. (*bitterly*): In the darkness where You are supposed to be, where all of us probably are ... In the darkness You will find no one to listen to Your cries or be touched by Your sufferings. Wash Your tears and mirror Yourself in Your indifference.
Knight. God, You who are somewhere, who *must* be somewhere, have mercy upon us.
Jöns. I could have given you an herb to purge you of your worries about eternity. Now it seems to be too late. But in any case, feel the immense triumph of this last minute when you can still roll your eyes and move your toes.
Karin. Quiet, quiet.
Jöns. I shall be silent, but under protest.
Girl (*on her knees*). It is the end.

JOF and Mia lie close together and listen to the rain tapping lightly on the wagon canvas, a sound which diminishes until finally there are only single drops.

They crawl out of their hiding place. The wagon stands on a height above a slope, protected by an enormous tree. They look across ridges, forests, the wide plains, and the sea, which glistens in the sunlight breaking through the clouds.

Jof stretches his arms and legs. Mia dries the wagon seat and sits down next to her husband. Mikael crawls between Jof's knees.

A lone bird tests its voice after the storm. The trees and bushes drip. From the sea comes a strong and fragrant wind.

Jof points to the dark, retreating sky where summer lightning glitters like silver needles over the horizon.

Jof. I see them, Mia! I see them! Over there against the dark, stormy sky. They are all there. The smith and Lisa and the knight and Raval and Jöns and Skat. And Death, the severe master, invites them to dance. He tells them to hold each other's hands and then they must tread the dance in a long row. And first goes the master with his scythe and hourglass, but Skat dangles at the end with his lyre. They dance away from the dawn and it's a solemn dance toward the dark lands, while the rain washes their faces and cleans the salt of the tears from their cheeks.

He is silent. He lowers his hand.

His son, Mikael, has listened to his words. Now he crawls up to Mia and sits down in her lap.

Mia (*smiling*).   You with your visions and dreams.

Questions

1. *What is the nature of the knight's quest? Do you admire him for the seriousness and single-mindedness of his quest? What is the knight's own judgment on the result of his lifelong pursuit?*   2. *In contrast to the knight, his squire Jöns is an agnostic and hedonist who believes that the meaning of life is to be found in living. Does a comparison of the actions of the two men suggest which one is more humane?*   3. *How does the milk and wild strawberries scene help define the theme?*   4. *How does the comic subplot of Skat, Plog the blacksmith, and his faithless wife relate to the theme?*   5. *Why do Jof, Mia, and their child survive? Has Bergman prepared us for this ending, or does it come as a surprise?*   6. *Can you suggest why Bergman, a twentieth-century artist concerned with modern man, set his drama in the Middle Ages?*

tHE pRESENCE Of dEATH

QUESTIONS FOR FURTHER ANALYSIS

1. In *Everyman,* Tolstoy's "The Death of Iván Ilých," Bergman's *The Seventh Seal,* and Donne's sonnet, "Death, Be Not Proud," death and dying are considered from a religious viewpoint. Do these works develop a similar attitude toward death, or do the attitudes they develop differ crucially?

2. State the argument against resignation to death made in Thomas' "Do Not Go Gentle into That Good Night." State the argument of Catherine Davis' reply, "After a Time." What other works in this section support each position?

3. Read chapters 8–10 in The Revelation of St. John the Divine in the New Testament. The opening of the "seventh seal" is described there, along with the consequences of that event. Does the allusive title of Bergman's screenplay enhance or detract from the story line? Are the knight and his friends "saved" or "damned" at the end? Does the religious conception of a man facing death developed in *Everyman* differ from or support the conception developed in *The Seventh Seal*?

4. Although Gray's "Elegy Written in a Country Churchyard," Housman's "To an Athlete Dying Young," Ransom's "Bells for John Whiteside's Daughter," Auden's "In Memory of W. B. Yeats," and Roethke's "Elegy for Jane" employ different poetic forms, they all embody a poetic mode called *elegy*. Define *elegy* in terms of the characteristic tone of these poems. Compare the elegiac tone with the tone of such poems as Poe's "The Emperor Worm" and Thomas' "Do Not Go Gentle into That Good Night." How do they differ?

5. What figurative language in the prose and poetry of this section is commonly associated with death itself? With dying? Contrast the characteristic imagery of this section with the characteristic imagery of love poetry. What might the differences indicate about the way we perceive man in nature?

6. Yevtushenko, in his poem "People," writes, "Not people die but worlds die in them." Illustrate the meaning of this line with a discussion of Bierce's "An Occurrence at Owl Creek Bridge," Katherine Anne Porter's "The Jilting of Granny Weatherall," and Robinson's poem "The Poor Relation."

7. Are there works in this section that illustrate the first four of Edwin Brock's "Five Ways to Kill a Man"? Explain the fifth way. What works lend support to that method?

8. Discuss the attitude toward death developed in Mishima's "Patriotism" in terms of its contrast with other attitudes toward death developed in such stories as Bierce's "An Occurrence at Owl Creek Bridge" and Malamud's "Idiots First."

9. Which works in this section treat death and dying in a way that corresponds most closely with your own attitudes toward morality? Which contradict your attitudes? Isolate, in each case, the elements in the work responsible for your response and discuss them in terms of their "truth" or "falsity."

appendices

Pastoral, 1945 by Pablo Picasso

APPENDICES

The Poet and His Craft

One of the discoveries a student of poetry quickly makes is that a good poem grows in richness and subtlety with rereading and close scrutiny. We grasp the theme of the poem perhaps on first reading, but on further reading and analysis, we discover that a particular word is charged with more meaning than we had thought or that an image relates to other parts of the poem in ways the first reading did not reveal. The excitement that comes from discovering something new and enriching in a poem is one of the great pleasures of studying poetry. Soon, however, the excitement is dampened for many readers as they inevitably begin to ask themselves: Did the poet really intend to put this or that into the poem, or are we just demonstrating a cleverness and super-subtlety that would surprise the poet as much as it disquiets us?

The question cannot be answered with direct evidence because most poets do not give us statements about their intentions in writing a particular poem. But many poets have left records, in the form of notebooks and journals, of early versions of their poems. An examination of these early versions shows very clearly that most finished poems are the result of painstaking and often protracted revision as the poet searches for the right word, the right phrase, the right sequence of image and idea to embody his theme. That poets work with such care and calculation suggests a general answer to our question: What we find in a good poem is more likely than not the result of the poet's skill, assuming that we are attending to the whole poem and not just free associating from some part of it.

A comparison of the draft versions with the final versions of the three poems below provides a fascinating glimpse into the process of poetic creation. A careful consideration of why particular changes were made will probably make for a fuller understanding of the final version. But more important for our purposes here, your analysis will be an exercise in close and subtle reading firmly grounded in different versions. While the reasons you offer for changes will be speculative and not subject to any kind of definitive proof, the poet did make these changes for *some* reason. Thus, although we can rarely, if ever, know what the poet intended, our detailed knowledge of how poems are written makes equally clear that what we find in a poem is probably the result of the poet's skill, not chance or our clever imaginings.

In the draft versions, variants and deletions are indicated by brackets. Line numbers in the questions refer to the final version.

LONDON   (WILLIAM BLAKE, 1757–1827)

I wander through each chartered[1] street,
Near where the chartered Thames does flow
And mark in every face I meet
Marks of weakness, marks of woe.

In every cry of every man,
In every infant's cry of fear,
In every voice; in every ban,
The mind-forged manacles I hear:

How the chimney-sweeper's cry
Every blackening church appalls,   10
And the hapless soldier's sigh
Runs in blood down palace-walls.

But most, through midnight streets I hear
How the youthful harlot's curse
Blasts the new-born infant's tear,
And blights with plagues the marriage-hearse.

LONDON   (NOTEBOOK VERSION, 1793)

I wander thro' each dirty street,
Near where the dirty Thames does flow,
And [see] mark in every face I meet
Marks of weakness, marks of woe.

In every cry of every man
In [every voice of every child]
      every infant's cry of fear
In every voice, in every ban
The [german] mind forg'd [links I hear] manacles I hear.

[But most] How the chimney sweeper's cry
[Blackens o'er the churches' walls]   10
Every black'ning church appalls,
And the hapless soldier's sigh
Runs in blood down palace walls.

[But most the midnight harlot's curse
From every dismal street I hear,
Weaves around the marriage hearse
And blasts the new born infant's tear.]

But most [from every] thro' wintry streets I hear
How the midnight harlot's curse   20

---

1. Preempted by the state and leased out under royal patent.

Blasts the new born infant's tear,
And [hangs] smites with plagues the marriage hearse.

But most the shrieks of youth I hear
But most thro' midnight & . . . .
How the youthful . . .

1. *How does the change from "dirty" to "chartered" (ll. 1–2) help establish the theme of the poem?* **2.** *Suggest why Blake changed "see" to "mark" in line 3.* **3.** *Would it have made any significant difference if Blake had retained "In every voice of every child" as line 6? Explain.* **4.** *Look up the meaning and derivation of "appalls" and then consider what Blake achieves by the revision of line 10.*

THE LAST LAUGH   (WILFRED OWEN, 1893–1918)

'O Jesus Christ! I'm hit,' he said; and died.
Whether he vainly cursed, or prayed indeed,
The Bullets chirped—In vain! vain! vain!
Machine-guns chuckled,—Tut-tut! Tut-tut!
And the Big Gun guffawed.

Another sighed,—'O Mother, mother! Dad!'
Then smiled, at nothing, childlike, being dead.
      And the lofty Shrapnel-cloud
      Leisurely gestured,—Fool!
      And the falling splinters tittered.   10

'My Love!' one moaned. Love-languid seemed his mood,
Till, slowly lowered, his whole face kissed the mud.
      And the Bayonets' long teeth grinned;
      Rabbles of Shells hooted and groaned;
      And the Gas hissed.

LAST WORDS   (EARLY VERSION)

"O Jesus Christ!" one fellow sighed.
And kneeled, and bowed, tho' not in prayer, and died.
      And the Bullets sang "In Vain,"
      Machine Guns chuckled "Vain,"
      Big Guns guffawed "In Vain."

"Father and mother!" one boy said.
Then smiled—at nothing, like a small child; being dead.
      And the Shrapnel Cloud
      Slowly gestured "Vain,"
      The falling splinters muttered "Vain."   10

"My love!" another cried, "My love, my bud!"
Then, gently lowered, his whole face kissed the mud.
      And the Flares gesticulated, "Vain."

The Shells hooted, "In Vain,"
And the Gas hissed, "In Vain."

1. *What does Owen achieve in dramatic effect by the revision of the first two lines?* **2.** *How does Owen's changing the exact rhymes of the first version to the off rhymes of the final version affect the meaning of the poem?* **3.** *What insights into the revision of line 7 are provided by scanning the poem?* **4.** *Suggest why Owen abandoned the "In Vain" motif in the final version.* **5.** *Examine the changes in verbs. What effect do the changes have on the tone of the poem?*

THE SECOND COMING   (WILLIAM BUTLER YEATS, 1865–1939)

Turning and turning in the widening gyre°   spiral
The falcon cannot hear the falconer;
Things fall apart; the center cannot hold;
Mere anarchy is loosed upon the world,
The blood-dimmed tide is loosed, and everywhere
The ceremony of innocence is drowned;
The best lack all conviction, while the worst
Are full of passionate intensity.

Surely some revelation is at hand;
Surely the Second Coming is at hand;   10
The Second Coming! Hardly are those words out
When a vast image out of *Spiritus Mundi²*
Troubles my sight: somewhere in sands of the desert
A shape with lion body and the head of a man,
A gaze blank and pitiless as the sun,
Is moving its slow thighs, while all about it
Reel shadows of the indignant desert birds.
The darkness drops again; but now I know
That twenty centuries of stony sleep
Were vexed to nightmare by a rocking cradle,   20
And what rough beast, its hour come round at last,
Slouches towards Bethlehem to be born?

THE SECOND COMING (FIRST FULL DRAFT)

Turning and turning in the wide gyre [widening gyre]
The falcon cannot hear the falconer
[Things fall apart, the centre has lost]
Things fall apart—the centre cannot hold
[Vile] Mere anarchy is loose there on the world
The blood stained flood [dim tide] is loose and anarchy
[The good are wavering and intensity]
The best [lose] lack all conviction while the worst
Are full of passionate intensity.

---

2.   The Soul or Spirit of the Universe, which Yeats believed constituted a fund of racial images and memories.

Surely some revelation is at hand
[The cradle at Bethlehem has rocked must leap anew]
[Surely the great falcon must come]
[Surely the hour of the second birth is here]
[Surely the hour of the second birth has struck]
[The second Birth! Scarce have those] words been spoken
The second [Birth] coming. [Scarce have the words been spoken]
[Before the dark was cut as with a knife]
And new intensity rent as it were cloth
And a [stark] lost image out of spiritus mundi
Troubles my sight. [A waste of sand]—A waste of desert sand
A shape with lion's body & with and the head [breast and head] of a man
[An eye] A gaze blank and pitiless as the sun
[Move with a slow slouching step]
Moves its slow [feet] thighs while all about its head
[An angry crowd of desert]
[Fall] [Run] shadows of the [desert birds they] indignant desert birds
The darkness drops again but now I know
[For] That twenty centuries of [its] stony sleep
[Were vexed & all but broken by the second]
Were vexed to nightmare by a rocking cradle
[And now at last]
[And now at last knowing its hour come round]
And what [at last] [wild thing] rough beast its hour come round at last
      knowing the hour [come round]
[It slouches towards Bethlehem to be born]
It has set out for Bethlehem to be born
It has set out for Bethlehem to be born
[Is slouching] towards Bethlehem to be born
Slouches towards Bethlehem to be born

1. Can you suggest why "Reel" (l. 17) is a better word than "Fall" or "Run?"   **2.** After many trials, Yeats decided on "The Second Coming" rather than "The Second Birth" for line 10. Can you suggest why (aside from number of syllables) Yeats decided as he did?   **3.** Examine the changes Yeats made in the description of the sphinx (ll. 14–16). Does the description in the final version represent an improvement over that of the draft version? Why?   **4.** In the draft version of line 19, Yeats used the pronoun "its" to modify "stony sleep," making clear that these words refer to the sphinx. Does the deletion of the pronoun in the final version weaken the poem by making "stony sleep" ambiguous? Explain.

Reading Fiction

An author is a god, creator of the world he describes. That world has a limited and very special landscape. It is peopled with men and women of a particular complexion, of particular gifts and failings. Its history, almost always, is determined by the tight interaction of its people within its narrow geography. Everything that occurs in a work of fiction—every figure, every tree, every furnished room and crescent moon and dreary fog—has been *purposely* put there by its creator. When a story pleases, when it moves its reader, he has responded to that carefully created world. The pleasure, the emotional commitment, the human response are not results of analysis. The reader has not registered in some mental adding machine the several details that establish character, the particular appropriateness of the weather to the events in the story, the marvelous rightness of the furnishings, the manipulation of the point of view, the plot, the theme, the style. He has recognized and accepted the world of the author and has been delighted (or saddened or made angry) by what happens in it.

But how does it come about that readers recognize the artificial worlds, often quite different from their own, that authors create? And why is it that readers who recognize some fictional worlds effortlessly are bewildered and lost in other fictional worlds? Is it possible to extend the boundaries of readers' recognition? Can more and more of the landscapes and societies of fiction be made available to that onlooking audience?

The answer to the first of these questions is easy. Readers are comfortable in literary worlds that, however exotic the landscapes and the personalities that people them, incorporate moral imperatives which reflect the value system in the readers' world. Put another way, much fiction ends with its virtuous characters rewarded and its villains punished. This we speak of as poetic justice. Comedies, and most motion pictures of the recent past, end this way. But such endings are illustrations of poetic justice, and *poetic* seems to suggest that somehow such endings are ideal rather than "real." Not much experience of life is required to recognize that injustice, pain, frustration, and downright villainy often prevail, that the beautiful young girl and the strong, handsome hero do not always overcome all obstacles, marry, and live happily ever after, that not every man is strong and handsome nor every woman beautiful. But readers, knowing that, respond to tragic fiction as well—where virtue is defeated, where obstacles prove too much for the men and women, where ponderous forces result in defeat, even death. Unhappy outcomes are painful to contemplate, but it is not difficult to recognize the world in which they occur. That world is much like our own. And unhappy outcomes serve to emphasize the very ideals which we have established in this world as the aims and goals of human activity. Consequently, both the "romantic" comedies that gladden with justice and success and the "realistic" stories that end in defeat provide readers with recognizable and available emotional worlds, however exotic the settings and the characters in those stories might be.

If we look at fiction this way, the answer to the question "Why is it that some readers are bewildered and lost in some fictional worlds?" is clearly implied. Some fictional worlds *seem* to incorporate a strange set of moral imperatives. Readers are not altogether certain who are the virtuous characters and who are the villains or even what constitutes virtue and evil. Sometimes tragic oppositions in a fictional world that brooks no compromise puzzle readers who live in a world where compromise has become almost a virtue. Sometimes, particularly in more recent fiction that reflects the ever widening influence of psychoanalytic theory, the landscape and the behavior of characters is designed to represent deep interiors, the less-than-rational hearts and minds of characters. Those weird interiors are not part of the common awareness of readers; the moral questions raised there are not the same moral questions that occupy most of our waking hours. Such fictional worlds (those of Franz Kafka, for example) are difficult to map, and bewildered readers may well reject these underworlds for the sunshine of the surfaces they know more immediately.

Studying Literature

It might be useful to distinguish between three different kinds of discussion that take literature for a subject. Literary *history* attends to the consequences for literature of the passing of time. Certain forms that were popular in medieval times—the religious allegory, for instance—have waned in popularity and importance. Certain authors have been measurably influenced by their predecessors. Certain features of Elizabethan culture and belief illuminate passages in Shakespeare's plays. Most of the footnotes in this book provide readers with historical information (the meaning of an archaic word, perhaps, the characteristics of some half-forgotten Greek god, or an allusion to an earlier literary work). Sometimes such information liberates the enduring life of old stories for new readers. Literary *criticism*, on the other hand, attends to the *value* of a work. It is good? Bad? Minor? Major? Criticism itself has a history: taste changes over the years; standards of judgment change; cultural forces contribute to critical judgments. But, though information about the history of criticism may help you understand why an author did what he did, it will not significantly help you make your own critical judgment. The story must finally speak for itself to you—no amount of historical justification can really enliven a dead work for a new reader. Unconcerned with both history and criticism, literary *theory* attends to the *craft* of literature. How does the author manipulate language (the substance of all literature—and the only substance) in order to create a world which affects his readers? Over many years of incessant examination of literature, observers have noted that certain techniques, certain characteristic uses of language, occur again and again—so frequently that it is useful to name them. Literary theory makes particular use of these observations in its discussion of *form* and the features on which form depends. Note that theoretical discussions frequently trespass on the discipline of psychology. Theoreticians and critics frequently speak of the *effect* on readers of an author's craft—his images, his clever symbols, his vision of mortality, his colors and shapes. But it is a dangerous business to assert that certain combinations of words will generate, invariably, the same complex emotional response. What are we to make of the spectacle of two critics, or two teachers, testifying that the same story affects them quite differently? Is one of them wrong? Are both of them wrong, perhaps? Perhaps! But we do the best we can, and we use all the varieties of human experience that authors and critics and theoreticians share in an attempt to respond significantly to significant fiction.

Fiction and Reality

Why do people read fiction (or go to movies)? The question is not so easy to answer as one might suppose. The first response is likely to have something to do with "amusement" or "entertainment." But you have doubtless read stories and novels (or seen movies) that end tragically. Is it accurate to say that they were amusing or entertaining? Is it entertaining to be made sad or to be made angry by the defeat of "good" people? Or does the emotional impact of such stories somehow enlarge our own humanity? Fiction teaches its readers by providing them a vast range of experience that they could not acquire otherwise. Especially for the relatively young, conceptions of love, of success in life, of war, of malignant evil and cleansing virtue are learned from fiction—not from life. And herein lies a great danger, for literary artists are notorious liars, and their lies frequently become the source of people's convictions about human nature and human society.

To illustrate, a huge number of television series based on the exploits of the FBI, or the Hawaiian police force, or the dedicated surgeons at the general hospital, or the young lawyers always end with a capture, with a successful (though dangerous) operation, with justice triumphant. But, in the real world, police are able to resolve only about 10 percent of reported crime, disease ravages, and economic and political power often extends into the courtroom. The very existence of such television drama bespeaks a yearning that things should be different; their heroes are heroic in that they regularly overcome those obstacles that we all experience but that, alas, we do not overcome.

Some writers, beginning about the middle of the nineteenth century, were particularly incensed at the real damage which a lying literature promotes, and they devoted their energies to exposing and counteracting the lies of the novelists, particularly those lies that formed attitudes about what constituted human success and happiness. Yet that popular fiction, loosely called *escapist,* is still most widely read for reasons that would probably fill several studies in social psychology. It needs no advocate. The fiction in this book, on the other hand, has been chosen largely because it does not lie about life—at least it does not lie about life in the ordinary way. And the various authors employ a large variety of literary methods and modes in an effort to illuminate the deepest wells of human experience. Consequently, many of these stories do not retail high adventure (though some do), since an adventurous inner life does not depend on an incident-filled outer life. Some stories, like Toomer's "Theater" and Porter's "The Jilting of Granny Weatherall," might almost be said to be about what does *not* happen rather than what does—not-happening being as much incident, after all, as happening.

All fiction attempts to be interesting, to involve the reader in situations, to force some aesthetic response from him—most simply put, in the widest sense of the word, to entertain. Some fiction aspires to nothing more. Other fiction seeks, as well, to establish some truth about the nature of man—Kafka's "Metamorphosis" and Hemingway's "The Short Happy Life of Francis Macomber" ask the reader to perceive the inner life of central figures. Some fiction seeks to explore the relationships among men—Faulkner's "Dry September," Toomer's "Theater," and Lawrence's "The Horse Dealer's Daughter" depend for their force on the powerful interaction of one character with another. Still other fiction seeks to explore the connection between men and society—Ellison's "'Repent, Harlequin!' Said the Ticktockman" and Wright's "The Man Who Lived Underground" acquire their force from the implied struggle between men seeking a free and rich emotional life and the tyrannically ordering society that would sacrifice their humanity to some ideal of social efficiency.

We have been talking about that aspect of fiction which literary theorists identify as *theme*. Theorists also talk about plot, characterization, setting, point of view, and conflict—all terms naming aspects of fiction that generally have to do with the author's technique. Let us here deal with one story—James Joyce's "Araby." Read it. Then compare your private responses to the story with what we hope will be helpful and suggestive remarks about the methods of fiction.

The Methods of Fiction

One can perceive only a few things simultaneously and can hardly respond to everything contained in a well-wrought story all at once. When he has finished the story, the reader likely thinks back, makes readjustments, and reflects on the significance of things before he reaches that set of emotional and intellectual experiences that we have been calling *response*. Most readers of short stories respond first to what may be called the *tone* of the opening lines. Now tone is an aspect of literature about which it is particularly difficult to talk, because it is an aura—a shimmering and shifting atmosphere that depends for its substance on rather delicate emotional responses to language and situation. Surely, before the reader knows anything at all about the plot of "Araby," he has experienced a tone.

> North Richmond Street, being blind, was a quiet street except at the hour when the Christian Brothers' School set the boys free. An uninhabited house of two storeys stood at the blind end, detached from its neighbors in a square ground. The other houses of the street, conscious of decent lives within them, gazed at one another with brown imperturbable faces.

Is the scene gay? Vital and active? Is this opening appropriate for a story that goes on to celebrate joyous affirmations about life and living? You should answer these questions negatively. Why? Because the dead end street is described as "blind," because the Christian Brothers' School sounds much like a prison (it sets the boys free), because a vacant house fronts the dead end, because the other houses, personified, are conscious of decent lives within (a mildly ironic description—*decent* suggesting ordinary, thin-lipped respectability rather than passion or heroism), because those houses gaze at one another with "brown imperturbable faces"—*brown* being nondescript, as opposed, say, to scarlet, gold, bright blue, and *imperturbable faces* reinforcing the priggish decency within.

Compare this opening from Faulkner's "Dry September":

> Through the bloody September twilight, aftermath of sixty-two rainless days, it had gone like fire in a dry grass—the rumor, the story, whatever it was. Something about Miss Minnie Cooper and a Negro.

The tone generated by "bloody twilight," "rainless days," "fire in a dry grass" is quite different from the blind, brown apathy of "Araby." And unsurprisingly, Faulkner's story involves movement to a horrifying violence. "Araby," on the other hand, is a story about the dawning of awareness in the mind and heart of the child of one of those decent families in brown and blind North Richmond Street. Tone, of course, permeates all fiction, and it may change as the narrative develops. Since short stories generally reveal change, the manipulation of tone is just one more tool used in the working of design.

Short stories, of course, are short, but this fact implies some serious considerations. In some ways, a large class of good short fiction deals with events that may be compared to the tip of the proverbial iceberg. The events animating the story represent only a tiny fraction of the characters' lives and experiences; yet, that fraction is terribly important and provides the basis for wide understanding both to the characters within the story and to its readers. In "Araby," the plot, the connected sequence of events, may be simply stated. A young boy who lives in a rather drab, respectable neighborhood develops a crush on the sister of one of his playmates. She asks him if he intends to go to a charity fair that she cannot attend. He resolves to go and purchase a gift for her. He is tormented by the late and drunken arrival of his uncle who has promised him the money he needs. When the boy finally arrives at the bazaar, he is disappointed by the difference between his expectation and the actuality of the almost deserted fair. He perceives some minor events, overhears some minor conversation, and finally sees himself "as a creature driven and derided by vanity." Yet this tiny stretch of experience out of the life of the boy introduces him to an awareness about the differences between imagination and reality, between his romantic infatuation and the vulgar reality all about him. We are talking now about what is called the *theme* of the story. Emerging from the workaday events that constitute its plot is a general statement about intensely idealized childish "love," the shattering recognition of the false sentimentality that occasions it, and the enveloping vulgarity of adult life. The few pages of the story, by detailing a few events out of a short period of the protagonist's life, illuminate one aspect of the loss of innocence that we all endure and that is always painful. In much of the literature in the section on innocence and experience, the protagonists learn painfully the moral complexities of a world that had once seemed uncomplicated and predictable. That education does not always occur, as in "Araby," at an early age, either in literature or life.

Certainly theme is a centrally important aspect of prose fiction, but "good" themes do not neccessarily ensure good stories. One may write a wretched story with the same theme as "Araby." What, then, independent of theme, is the difference between good stories and bad stories? Instinctively you know how to answer this question. Good stories, to begin with, are interesting; they present characters you care about; however fantastic, they are yet somehow plausible; they project a moral world you recognize. One of the obvious differences between short stories and novels requires that story writers develop character rapidly and limit the number of developed characters. Many stories have only one fleshed character; the other characters are frequently two-dimensional projections or even stereotypes. We see their surface only, not their souls. Rarely does a short story have more than three developed characters. Again, unlike novels, short stories usually work themselves out in restricted geographical setting, in a single place, and within a rather short period of time.

We often speak of character, setting, plot, theme, and style as separate aspects of a story in order to break down a complex narrative into more manageable parts. But it is important to understand that this analytic process of separating various elements is something we have done to the story—the story (if it is a good one) is an integrated whole. The closer we examine the separate elements, the clearer it becomes that each is integrally related to the others.

It is part of the boy's character that he lives in a brown imperturbable house in North Richmond Street, that he does the things he does (which is, after all, the plot), that he learns what he does (which is the theme), and that all of this characterization emerges from Joyce's rich and suggestive style. Consider this paragraph:

> Her image accompanied me even in places the most hostile to romance. On Saturday evenings when my aunt went marketing I had to go to carry some of the parcels. We walked through the flaring streets, jostled by drunken men and bargaining women, amid the curses of labourers, the shrill litanies of shop-boys who stood on guard by the barrels of pigs' cheeks, the nasal chanting of street-singers, who sang a *come-all-you* about O'Donovan Rossa, or a ballad about the troubles in our native land. These noises converged in a single sensation of life for me: I imagined that I bore my chalice safely through a throng of foes. Her name sprang to my lips at moments in strange prayers and praises which I myself did not understand. My eyes were often full of tears (I could not tell why) and at times a flood from my heart seemed to pour itself out into my bosom. I thought little of the future. I did not know whether I would ever speak to her or not or, if I spoke to her, how I could tell her of my confused adoration. But my body was like a harp and her words and gestures were like fingers running upon the wires.

This paragraph furthers the plot. But it suggests much more. The boy thinks of his friend's sister even when he carries parcels for his aunt during the shopping trips through a crowded and coarse part of town. In those coarse market streets the shop-boys cry shrill "litanies," the girl's name springs to his lips in strange "prayers and praises," and the boy confesses a confused "adoration." Further, he bears "his chalice safely through a throng of foes." Now the words *litanies, prayers, praises, adoration* all come from a special vocabulary that is easy to identify. It is the vocabulary of the church. The *chalice* and the *throng of foes* come from the vocabulary of chivalric romance, which is alluded to in the first line of the quoted paragraph. Joyce's diction evokes a sort of holy chivalry that characterizes the boy on this otherwise altogether ordinary shopping trip. This paragraph suggests to the careful reader that the boy has cast his awakening sexuality in a mold that mixes the disparate shapes of the heroic knight, winning his lady by force of arms, and the ascetic penitent, adoring the holy virgin, mother of god.

Playing the word game, of course, can be dangerous. But from the beginning of this story to its end, a certain religious quality shimmers. That now-dead priest of the story's second paragraph had three books (at least). One is a romantic chivalric novel by Sir Walter Scott; one is a sensational account of the adventures of a famous rogue; one is what a priest might be expected to have at hand—an Easter week devotional guide. That priest who read Scott novels might have understood the boy's response—that mixture of religious devotion and romance. Shortly after the shopping trip, the boy finally speaks to the girl, and it is instructive to see her as he does. He stands at the *railings* and looks up (presumably) at her, she bowing her head towards him. "The light from the lamp opposite our door caught the white curve of her neck, lit up her hair that rested there and, falling, lit up the hand upon the railing. It fell over one side of her dress and caught the white border of a petticoat, just visible as she stood at ease." Skip the petticoat, for a moment. Might the description of Mangan's sister remind the careful reader of quite common sculptured representations of the Virgin Mary? But the petticoat! And the white curve of her neck! This erotic overlay characterizes the boy's response. The sexuality is his own; the chivalry, the religious adoration, comes from the culture in which he is immersed—comes from Scott, the ballads sung in the market place, the "Arab's Farewell to his Steed" sung by the boy's uncle. And it is the culture that so romanticizes and elevates the boy's yearning.

He finally gets to Araby—"the word called to him through the silence in which his soul luxuriated and cast an Eastern enchantment over him." His purpose is to serve his lady—to bring her something from that exotic place. What he finds is a weary-looking man guarding a turnstile, the silence that pervades a church after a service, and two men counting money on a salver (that tray is called a *salver* by design). And in this setting he overhears the courtship of a young lady by two gentlemen:

> "O, I never said such a thing!"
> "O, but you did!"
> "O, but I didn't!"
> "Didn't she say that?"
> "Yes, I heard her."
> "O, there's a . . . fib!"

This is Araby, this is love in a darkened hall where money is counted. Is it any wonder that the boy, in the moment of personal illumination that Joyce calls an epiphany, sees himself as a creature driven and derided by vanity?

"Araby" is a careful, even a delicate story. Nothing much happens— what does occur largely in the boy's perception and imagination. The story focuses on the boy's confusion of sexual attraction with the lofty sentiments of chivalry and religion. The climax occurs when he confronts the darkened, money-grubbing fair and the utterly banal expression of the sexual attraction between the gentlemen and the young lady. The result is a sudden deflation of the boy's ego, his sense of self, as he recognizes his own delusions about the nature of love and the relationship between men, women, heroism, god, and money.

We would like to conclude with a discussion of one feature of fiction that sometimes proves troublesome to developing readers. Often the events of a story, upon which much depends, puzzle or annoy readers. Why does that fool do that? Why doesn't X simply tell Y the way he feels and then the tragedy would be averted? In a sense, such responses reflect the intrusion of a reader into the world of the story. The reader, a sensible and sensitive person, understands some things about life after all and is oppressed by the characters' inability to understand at least as much. Characters choose to die when they might with a slight adjustment live. They risk danger when with a slight adjustment they might proceed safely. They suffer the pain of an unfortunate marriage when with a little trouble they might be free to live joyously. If the "whys" issuing from the reader are too insistent, too sensible, then the story must fail, at least for that reader. But many "whys" are not legitimate. Many are intrusions of the reader's hindsight, the reader's altogether different cultural and emotional fix. Henry James urged that the author must be allowed his *donnée*, his "given." He creates the society and the rules by which it operates within his own fictional world. Sometimes his creation is so close to the reader's own world that it is hardly possible to object. Black readers will recognize the inner life of Wright's man who lived underground even if the events are bizarre. Those who have grown up in a small southern town will recognize the atmosphere of Faulkner's "Dry September" and Baldwin's "Going to Meet the Man." But few readers of this book know 1895 Dublin and Irish middle-class society, which plays a brooding role in "Araby" (as it does in almost all of Joyce's work). None know the futuristic world of Harlan Ellison's Harlequin. In every case, we must finally imagine those worlds. If we cannot, the events that take place in them will be of no consequence. If those worlds are unimaginable, then the stories must fail. If they too much strain belief or remain too foreign to the reader's heart, they must likewise fail. But all response to fiction depends on the reader's acquiescence to the world of the author and his perceptions of the moral consequences of acts and attitudes in that world. At best, that acquiescence will provide much pleasure as well as emotional insight into his own existence.

Reading Poetry

For many people, the question "What is poetry?" is irrelevant if not irreverent. The attempt to answer such a question leads to abstract intellectual analysis, the very opposite of the emotional pleasure one seeks in a good poem. Why does it matter what poetry is so long as readers enjoy poems? Doesn't the attempt to define the nature of poetry lead to technical analysis of poetic devices so that study, finally, destroys pleasure?

These are valid issues that touch on very real dangers. If the study of poetry bogs down in theoretical or historical issues and the study of a poem becomes a mere exercise in the identification and discussion of poetic devices, the reader may well find that reading a poem is more effort than pleasure. He may begin to feel like the many nineteenth-century poets who complained that science, in laying bare the laws of nature, robbed the universe of its ancient awe and mystery. Walt Whitman, for example, describes such a feeling in his poem "When I Heard the Learn'd Astronomer."

> When I heard the learn'd astronomer,
> When the proofs, the figures, were ranged in columns before me,
> When I was shown the charts and diagrams, to add, divide,
>   and measure them,
> When I sitting heard the astronomer where he lectured with
>   much applause in the lecture-room,
> How soon unaccountable I became tired and sick,
> Till rising and gliding out I wander'd off by myself,
> In the mystical moist night-air, and from time to time,
> Look'd up in perfect silence at the stars.

The distinction implicit in Whitman's poem between the mind (intellectual knowledge) and the heart (emotion and feeling) is very old, but still a useful one. All of us have no doubt felt at some time that the overexercise of the mind interfered with our capacity to feel. Compelled to analyze, dissect, categorize, and classify, we finally yearn for the simple and "mindless" pleasure of unanalytical enjoyment, the pleasure of sensuous experience. But man derives pleasure in a variety of ways, and while we needn't assert a *necessary* connection between understanding and pleasure, understanding can enhance pleasure. The distinction between the mind and the heart is, after all, a fiction or metaphor that cannot be pushed too far before it breaks down. Readers may very well enjoy Dylan Thomas' "Fern Hill" without understanding Thomas' use of symbolism or color or religious imagery. But understanding that symbolism and imagery will certainly deepen the pleasure derived from the poem.

We don't mean to suggest by all this that every poem needs to be studied in detail or that it is possible to say in the abstract what kind and amount of study will be rewarding. Some poems are straightforward, requiring little by way of analysis; others, dense and complex, seem to yield little without some study. But study of even the simplest poems can be rewarding. (Consider the effect of the special vocabulary implied by such words as "arrayed," "imperially," "crown," and "glittered" in Edwin Arlington Robinson's "Richard Cory.") On the other hand, it is possible to be moved on first reading by the tone and quality of such complex poems as Leonard Cohen's "Suzanne" and T. S. Eliot's "The Love Song of J. Alfred Prufrock" even though they are difficult to understand immediately.

As to our original question—What is poetry?—we cannot offer anything like a definitive and comprehensive answer. Poetry is a form of writing that often employs rhyme, a regular rhythm, unusual word order, and an intense or heightened language. This formal definition will serve about as well as any although it is by no means comprehensive, as any collection of poems will readily demonstrate. Up to about a century ago, poetry was governed by rather precise and often elaborate rules and conventions; if a poem did not use rhyme, it certainly was characterized by rhythmic regularity, or meter. Further, there existed a long tradition of poetic types (epic, elegaic, tragic, satiric, etc.), each with quite specific rules and characteristics. While these traditions still retain some force, the old notion that these forms are part of the natural scheme of things has been largely abandoned. No one nowadays equates painting with photographic realism or music with the diatonic scale, and no one insists that the form of writing we call poetry must exhibit a combination of fixed characteristics.

Consider poetry from a different angle and ask not what poetry is but rather what functions it serves. Poetry fulfills some deep and abiding need of man, for no culture we know of has been without it. We know also that in ancient societies, before the advent of science and technology in the modern sense, the arts were not divided by types or differentiated from science. In ancient tribal societies, poetry, dance, sculpture, and painting might all be parts of a tribal ceremony designed to propitiate the gods and thereby ensure a full harvest or a successful hunt. Poetry, then, was part of a primitive (we would now label it "superstitious") science that defined and helped control the external world. Though one can only guess in these matters, it is probably safe to assume that in such a primitive society the inner emotional world of the individual was not sharply distinguished from the outer world of nature. Nature and the gods who controlled it might be harsh and unpredictible, and the function of ritual was to control and appease these gods (to ensure rain, for example). But ritual also nurtured and strengthened the individual's communal spirit and conditioned his feelings about the arduous work that the life of the tribe required.

The conditions of our lives are, of course, vastly different. We operate within an enormous industrialized society that developed over the centuries because men abandoned primitive explanations of the universe and sought others. One result of that development was a continuing differentiation and specialization of human endeavors, as science broke away from art and both divided into separate if related disciplines. Science became astronomy, biology, physics, and the like, while art became poetry, drama, painting, and sculpture. And it was modern science, not poetry or the other arts, that produced profound and measurable changes in man's life. Poetry might movingly and memorably remind us of the sorrow of unrequited love or the ravages of growing old, but science created a technology that produced undreamed of material wealth and power.

Is the very persistence of poetry evidence that it serves some important function, however obscure? On the other hand, maybe poetry is merely a vestigial organ of evolution that, like the appendix, continues to exist even though it has outlived its usefulness. Certainly, the historical process we have sketched here seems to involve a gradual diminution in the importance men attach to poetry.

It would be misleading, of course, to suggest that the scientist and the poet exist in separate worlds. But the differences between them are important. The truth that science seeks is the truth of physical reality. Social sciences such as psychology, sociology, and economics have attempted to demonstrate that human behavior can be understood in terms of a set of definite and quantifiable mechanisms. And, though no one would assert that science has achieved final answers, it is clear that the spectacular discoveries of science have left many, Walt Whitman among them, with the feeling that man's importance in the universe has diminished. Further, modern physical science has uncovered a disturbing indeterminateness and asymmetry in the universe that have far-reaching philosophical implications not only for science but for society as a whole. As the old scientific verities crumble, so, too, do the old social verities.

Science may describe and educate us about the outer world and its inexorable laws with as rigorous an objectivity and neutrality as it can achieve. It may explain to us that in a naturalistic world death comes to all living creatures or that sunsets result from certain physical phenomena; but it is silent on the terror of death and its human or emotional meaning or on the beauty of a sunset. To understand those emotions, to give them form and meaning, we turn to poetry—we read it and, perhaps, even write it. For poetry, so to speak, educates our emotions and our feelings, allows us to learn who we are and to articulate what we feel.

We might wonder whether such an assertion makes sense. What we feel, we feel. We don't need a poem to tell us that. Not so. Often we don't know what we feel except in a vague and inarticulate way. A powerful poem articulates and thereby clarifies. Further, a poem may even deepen feelings. Andrew Marvell's poem "To His Coy Mistress" may well help the reader understand his own feelings about physical love and mortality. The outrageous absurdity of a young person cut down by death when his life has barely begun is objectified by Robert Frost's "Out, Out—" and John Crowe Ransom's "Bells for John Whiteside's Daughter." The confusion that often attends the powerful emotion generated by love and death is arrested by the poet who provides order.

Poetry at its highest and most general level is a form of communication, a means of defining, affirming, and deepening its reader's humanity. This is not to say that one should approach poetry solemnly, expecting always to be loftily enlightened. Poetry is a complex form of communication that provides pleasure in various ways. One may, for instance, look upon a poem as a kind of game in which the poet skillfully works within a set of self-imposed rules—rhyme, meter, and stanzaic pattern—and delights in clever rhymes, as when Lord Byron rhymes "intellectual" with "henpecked you all" or "maxim" with "tax 'em." Anyone familiar with Plato's theory that everything in our world is an imperfect replica of an ideal heavenly form will appreciate the beauty and condensed brilliance of William Butler Yeats' lines from "Among School Children":

> Plato thought nature but a spume that plays
> Upon a ghostly paradigm of things.

Some will discover in poetry, as children often do in nursery rhymes, the pleasure of rhythm, meter, and sound—the musical aspects of poetry. The pleasures of poetry range from the loftiest insights and discoveries to memorable lines and clever rhymes.

A discussion of the major techniques and devices of poetry will provide some suggestions about how to approach poems and also furnish tools and a vocabulary for analyzing and discussing them. Keep in mind that a tool is not an end in itself but the means to an end. The end is fuller understanding and, thereby, deeper enjoyment of poetry.

The Words of Poetry

It is not unusual to hear some great and original philosopher, sociologist, or economist referred to as a mediocre writer. Yet, while one may judge the writing poor, he may at the same time recognize and honor the originality and significance of the idea conveyed. Such a distinction cannot be made in poetry. If a poem is written poorly, it is a poor poem. "In reading prose," Ralph Waldo Emerson said, "I am sensitive as soon as a sentence drags; but in poetry, as soon as one word drags." *Where* a poem arrives is inseparable from *how* it arrives. Everything must be right in a poem, every word. "The correction of prose," said Yeats, "is endless, a poem comes right with a click like a closing box."

"Poetry is heightened language" means, among other things, that the poet strives for precision and richness in the words he uses, and "precision" and "richness" are not contradictory for the poet. Words have dictionary or denotative meanings as well as associative or connotative meanings; they also have histories and relationships with other words. The English language is rich in synonyms, groups of words whose denotative meanings are roughly the same but whose connotations vary widely (portly, stout, fat; horse, steed, courser; official, statesman, politician). Many words are identical in sound and often in spelling but different in meaning (forepaws, four paws; lie down! you lie!). The meanings of words have changed in the course of time, and the poet may consciously select a word whose older meaning adds a dimension to his poem (astonished = turned to stone). There are, of course, no rules that can be given to a reader for judging a poet's effectiveness and skill in the handling of words (or anything else, for that matter). All we can do is look at particular works for examples of how a good poet manipulates words.

In a moving and passionate poem on his dying father, "Do Not Go Gentle into That Good Night," Dylan Thomas pleads with his father not to accept death passively but rather to "Rage, rage against the dying of the light." He then declares in the following stanzas that neither "wise men" nor "good men" nor "wild men" accept death quietly. And neither, Thomas says, do "grave men," punning on *grave* in its meaning of both "serious" and "burial place." William Blake's poem about the inhumane jobs children were forced into in eighteenth-century England, "The Chimney Sweeper" begins:

> When my mother died I was very young,
> And my Father sold me while yet my tongue
> Could scarcely cry "'weep! 'weep! 'weep!"
> So your chimneys I sweep, and in soot I sleep.

" 'Weep," a clipped form of "sweep," is what the boy cries as he walks a street looking for work, but *weep* clearly evokes the tears and sorrow of the mother's death and the sadness of the small boy's cruel life. And this is only part of Blake's skillful handling of words. "Cry" is also an effective pun, the precise word to describe how the boy seeks work while simultaneously reinforcing the emotional meaning of *weep*.

Henry Reed's "Naming of Parts" develops a contrast between the instructions a group of soldiers are receiving on how to operate a rifle (in order to cause death) and the lovely world of nature (which represents life and beauty). In the fourth stanza, bees are described as "assaulting and fumbling the flowers." "Fumbling," with its meaning of awkwardness and nervous uncertainty, may strike us as an arresting and perhaps puzzling word at first. Yet anyone who has watched a bee pollinating a flower will find the word extremely effective. In addition, of course, *fumbling* is a word often used to describe the actions of human beings caught up in sexual passion—a connotation precisely appropriate to the poet's purposes, since pollination is, in a sense, a sexual process. Furthermore, these various interpretations of *fumbling* contrast powerfully with the cold, mechanical precision of the death-dealing instruments the recruits are learning how to use. The next line of Reed's poem exhibits yet another resource of words: "They call it easing the Spring." The line is an exact repetition of a phrase used two lines earlier except *Spring* is now capitalized. While *Spring* retains its first meaning as part of the bolt action of the rifle, the capitalization makes it the season of the year when flowers are pollinated and the world of nature is reborn. With a mere typographical device, Reed has charged a single word with the theme of his poem. These few illustrations will suggest how sensitive the poet is to words and how much more pleasure the reader will find in poems if he develops the same sensitivity.

Sometimes meanings are not inherent in the isolated words but created in the poet's use of the word. A tree is a tree and a rose is a rose. A tree is also the apple tree in Frost's "After Apple-Picking" and something quite different in William Blake's "A Poison Tree"; a rose is specially defined in Robert Burns' "A Red, Red Rose" and Edmund Waller's "Go, Lovely Rose!" In these poems, because *tree* and *rose* are given such rich and varied meaning and are so central to the poems' development and meaning, they exceed mere connotation and become images that, finally, are symbolic.

Imagery

The world is revealed to us through our senses—sight, sound, taste, touch, and smell. And while some philosophers and psychologists might challenge the statement, it seems pretty clear that much, if not all, of our knowledge is linked to sensory experience. *Imagery* is the representation in poetry of sensory experience, one of the means by which the poet creates a world that we all know and share. Or, put another way, imagery allows the poet to create a recognizable world by drawing upon a fund of common experiences. Bad poetry is often bad because the imagery is stale ("golden sunset," "the smiling sun," "the rolling sea") or so skimpy that the poem dissolves into vague and shadowy and meaningless abstractions.

A good poet never loses touch with the sensory world. The invisible, the intangible, the abstract are anchored to the visible, the tangible, the concrete. Andrew Marvell begins his poem "To His Coy Mistress" with an elaborate statement of how he would court his beloved if their lives were measured in centuries rather than years. In the second stanza, he describes the reality:

> But at my back I always hear
> Time's wingéd chariot hurrying near;
> And yonder all before us lie
> Deserts of vast eternity.
> Thy beauty shall no more be found,
> Nor, in thy marble vault, shall sound
> My echoing song; then worms shall try
> That long-preserved virginity,
> And your quaint honor turn to dust,
> And into ashes all my lust:
> The grave's a fine and private place,
> But none, I think, do there embrace.

Time, eternity, honor, and *lust* are all vague abstractions. But Marvell joins each to a sensuous image that gives to the abstraction an extraordinary sharpness and power: Time is a winged *chariot,* eternity a sequence of *deserts,* honor turns to *dust* and lust to *ashes.*

Any analysis of the imagery of a poem will soon reveal that our definition of imagery as the representation of sensory experience needs to be qualified. One of the primary functions of language is to bring meaning and order into our lives, and poetry is the most intense use of language. We will find, therefore, that the images in poetry tend to be charged with meanings. A rose may be only a rose, but it becomes much more in Burns' and Waller's poems. Imagery, then, is closely related to, perhaps inseparable from, *figurative* language, the language which *says* one thing and *means* another.

The difference between good and bad poetry often turns on the skill with which imagery (or figurative language) is used. Marvell's images are striking, fresh, and powerful, nicely suited to his purposes. When Robert Frost in his poem "Birches" compares life to "a pathless wood," the image strikes us as natural and appropriate (the comparison of life to a path or road is a common one, as is a wood or forest to a state of moral bewilderment). We are accustomed to the imagery of birds, flowers, and sunsets in love poems, but when John Donne in "A Valediction: Forbidding Mourning" describes the relationship between himself and his beloved in terms of a drawing compass, the image may seem jarring or even ludicrous. Such a bold and daring comparison is a kind of challenge. The poet intends not only to surmount the reader's feeling that the image is strange but to develop it with such skill that the reader will accept it as natural and appropriate. And as Donne elaborates the comparison through various stages and concludes it (and the poem) with the brilliantly appropriate image of the completed circle, we recognize that he has successfully met the challenge.

Figurative Language

Figurative language is the general phrase we use to describe the many devices of language that allow us to speak nonliterally, to say one thing and mean another. Any attempt to communicate an emotion will very quickly utilize figurative language. When Robert Burns compares his love to a red rose, he does so not because he is unable to find the literal language he needs but because what he wants to say can only be expressed in figurative language. (Literal language might be used by a scientist to describe the physiological state of someone in love, but that is not what interests Burns.) The world of emotions, feelings, attitudes remains shadowy and insubstantial until figurative language gives it form and substance.

Consider, for example, these familiar old sayings: "The grass is always greener on the other side of the fence"; "A rolling stone gathers no moss"; "A bird in the hand is worth two in a bush"; "The early bird catches the worm." While these sayings unquestionably make sense in literal terms (the grass you see from a distance looks greener than the grass under your feet), the meaning of these phrases to a native speaker of English is clearly nonliteral. When we use them we are not speaking about grass or rolling stones or birds; we are making general and highly abstract observations about human attitudes and behavior. Yet strangely these generalizations and abstractions are embodied in concrete and sensuous imagery. Try to explain what any one of these expressions means and you will quickly discover that you are using many more words and much vaguer language than the expression itself. Indeed, this is precisely what happens when you attempt to paraphrase—that is, put into your own words—the meaning of a poem. Like poetry, these sayings rely on the figurative use of language.

Since poetry is an intense and heightened use of language that explores the world of feeling, it uses more varied figurative devices than does ordinary language. One of the most common figurative devices, *metaphor*, where one thing is called something else, occurs frequently in ordinary speech. "School is a rat race," we say, or "She's a bundle of nerves," and the meaning is perfectly clear—too clear, perhaps, because these metaphors are by now so common and unoriginal they have lost whatever vividness they may once have had. But when Thomas Nashe declares that "Beauty is but a flower which wrinkles will devour" or W. H. Auden, commenting on the death of William Butler Yeats, says, "let the Irish vessel lie/Emptied of its poetry," we have metaphors that compel readers to confront certain painful aspects of life.

Simile is closely related to metaphor. But where metaphor says that one thing *is* another, simile says that one thing is *like* another, as in Burns' "O My luve's like a red, red rose" and Frost's "life is too much like a pathless wood." The distinction between simile and metaphor, while easy enough to make technically, is often difficult to distinguish in terms of effects. Frost establishes a comparison between life and a pathless wood and keeps the two even more fully separated by adding the qualifiers "too much." Burns' simile maintains the same separation and, in addition, since it occurs in the opening line of the poem, eliminates any possible confusion the reader might momentarily experience about the subject of the poem if the line read, "O My love is a red, red rose." The reader can test the difference in effect between simile and metaphor by changing a metaphor into a simile or a simile into a metaphor to see if the meaning of the poem is thereby altered.

The critical vocabulary useful in discussions of poetry includes several additional terms, all of which name particular figures of speech: *metonymy, synecdoche, personification, hyperbole, understatement, paradox.* These terms are defined and illustrated in the Glossary of Literary Terms. But, though there may be a certain academic pleasure in recognizing the figures a poet uses, naming a figure of speech will never explain its effectiveness. The reader must, finally, perceive the usefulness of figures and respond emotionally to the construction of language that the poet creates in order to touch his reader's nerves.

Symbol

A *symbol* is anything that stands for or suggests something else. In this sense, most words are symbolic: the word *tree* stands for an object in the real world. When we speak of a symbol in poetry, however, we usually mean something more precise. In poetry, a symbol is an object or event that suggests more than itself. It is one of the most common and most powerful devices available to the poet, for it allows him to convey economically and simply a wide range of meanings.

It is useful to distinguish between two kinds of symbols, *public symbols* and *contextual symbols.* Public symbols are those objects or events that history has invested with rich meanings and associations. In a sense, then, a public symbol is a ready-made symbol. Yeats utilizes such a symbol in his poem "Leda and the Swan," assuming that his readers will be familiar with the myths that tell of the erotic affairs of Zeus and the consequences of those affairs—in this case, the birth of Clytemnestra, the wife of Agamemnon, and Helen, the most beautiful woman of antiquity, whose abduction precipitated the Trojan War. In "The Conscientious Objector," Karl Shapiro uses Noah's Ark and the Mayflower as symbols of a political prison whose inmates refuse to conform.

When a poet uses a public symbol, he is drawing from what he assumes is a common and shared fund of knowledge and tradition. If Yeats' reader is unaware of the symbolic meaning with which history has invested the Trojan War, it is doubtful that the poem will have much meaning for him. Nor will Shapiro's poem be clear unless we understand that Noah's Ark and the Mayflower evoke daring and heroic nonconformity.

In contrast to public symbols, contextual symbols are objects or events that are symbolic by virtue of the poet's handling of them in a particular poem —that is, by virtue of the context. Consider, for example, the opening lines of Robert Frost's "After Apple-Picking":

My long two-pointed ladder's sticking through a tree
Toward heaven still,
And there's a barrel that I didn't fill
Beside it, and there may be two or three
Apples I didn't pick upon some bough.

The apple tree is a literal tree, but as one reads through the poem, it becomes clear that the apple tree also symbolizes the speaker's life with a wide range of possible meanings (do the few apples he hasn't picked symbolize the hopes, dreams, aspirations that even the fullest life cannot satisfy?).

Amy Lowell's "Patterns" is rich in symbols. The speaker is an aristocratic lady whose life and most vital emotions are kept in rigid control by a series of patterns that the society she lives in has imposed on her. She describes herself as walking in her elegant gown down the garden paths laid out in precise patterns. Her gown is real; the path is a real path. But it very quickly becomes apparent that the patterned paths and her elegant gown are symbolic of the narrowly restricted and oppressive life her deepest feelings are at war with. They are the visible manifestation, the symbols, of the trap in which she is caught. She weeps when she notices "The daffodils and squills / Flutter in the breeze / As they please" because the flowers symbolize a freedom she knows she will never have.

The paths and flowers in Amy Lowell's poem are clear and easily recognizable examples of contextual symbols. However, contextual symbols by their very nature tend to present more difficulties than public symbols, because recognizing them depends on a sensitivity to everything else in the poem. In T. S. Eliot's dense and difficult poem "The Love Song of J. Alfred Prufrock," the speaker twice says, "In the room the women come and go / Talking of Michelangelo," a couplet that is baffling at first because it seems to have no clear relationship to what precedes and follows it. But as one reads through the poem, he begins to see that Prufrock is a man, like the young woman in Amy Lowell's poem, trapped in a life of upper-class superficialities and meaninglessness. The women discussing Michelangelo symbolize this dilettantish and arid life from which Prufrock desperately wishes to escape. Prufrock reminds himself that he will have time "To prepare a face to meet the faces that you meet," and Eleanor Rigby, in John Lennon and Paul McCartney's song, is described as "wearing the face that she keeps in a jar by the door." In both poems, that face is a symbol of a lonely existence in a society where people play elaborate games in order to conceal from others their real emotions and feelings.

A final word on symbols. If a reader fails to recognize a symbol, he has missed an important part of the poem's meaning. On the other hand, one of the pitfalls of reading poetry is that some readers become so intent on finding symbols they tend to forget that an object must first have a literal meaning before it can function as a symbol. Or, put in terms of our earlier definition, an object or event is itself before it is something else.

The setting of "After Apple-Picking" is an orchard, and the setting of "Patterns" the paths of a manorial garden. As we begin to understand the theme of each poem, we come to recognize the symbolic meanings these objects gradually take on. But there are no rules that will allow a reader to identify symbols. If you do not know what Troy symbolizes and have never heard of Helen of Troy, you will not discover the meanings of these public symbols by repeated and intensive readings of the poem; like unfamiliar words, you must look up (or be told of) their significance. On the other hand, the recognition of contextual symbols often depends on careful and sensitive reading. Readers may very well disagree on whether or not something should be taken as a symbol. When this occurs, one can only consider whether the symbolic reading adds meanings that are consistent with other elements in the poem. Is the fly in Emily Dickinson's "I Heard a Fly Buzz—When I Died" a symbol or merely an insect? Your answer will depend on what you see as the theme of the poem.

Archibald MacLeish renders the modern critical attitude toward symbolism in poetry and, at the same time, argues for the view that poems do not "mean" in the ordinary sense of that word. The various elements of a poem—imagery, figurative language, symbol—coalesce to form an *object,* something characterized not by its truth but by its objective correlation to some human experience. And most remarkably, MacLeish renders these rather complex critical positions in a poem rich in contextual symbols:

ARS POETICA

A poem should be palpable and mute
As a globed fruit,

Dumb
As old medallions to the thumb,

Silent as the sleeve-worn stone
Of casement ledges where the moss has grown—

A poem should be wordless
As the flight of birds.

A poem should be motionless in time
As the moon climbs,

Leaving, as the moon releases
Twig by twig the night-entangled trees,

Leaving, as the moon behind the winter leaves,
Memory by memory the mind—

A poem should be motionless in time
As the moon climbs.

A poem should be equal to:
Not true.

For all the history of grief
An empty doorway and a maple leaf.

For love
The leaning grasses and two lights above the sea—

A poem should not mean
But be.

Music

The *music* of poetry, by which we mean the poetic use of all the devices of
sound and rhythm inherent in language, is at once central to the poetic effect
and yet the most difficult to account for. We can discuss the ways in which
figurative language works with some clarity because we are using words to explain words. Anyone who has ever tried to explain the effect a piece of music
had on him (or who has read music criticism) will be familiar with the problem
of describing a nonverbal medium with words.

The possible musical effects of language are complex. The terms we
have to describe various musical devices deal only with the most obvious and
easily recognizable patterns. *Alliteration, assonance, consonance, caesura,
meter, onomatopoeia; rhythm,* and *rhyme* (all of them defined in the Glossary) are the key traditional terms for discussing the music of poetry. Along
with the other terms already introduced, they are an indispensable part of the
vocabulary one needs to discuss poetry. But the relationship between sound
and sense can be perceived nicely in a celebrated passage from Alexander
Pope's poem "An Essay on Criticism," in which the meaning of each line, first a
condemnation of mechanical bad verse, then an illustration of well-managed
verse, is ingeniously supported by the musical devices:

These[1] equal syllables alone require,
Though oft the ear the open vowels tire;
While expletives their feeble aid do join;
And ten low words oft creep in one dull line:
While they ring round the same unvaried chimes,
With sure returns of still expected rhymes;
Where 'er you find "the cooling western breeze,"

---

1. Bad poets.

In the next line, it "whispers through the trees";
If crystal streams "with pleasing murmurs creep,"
The reader's threatened (not in vain) with "sleep";
Then, at the last and only couplet fraught
With some unmeaning thing they call a thought,
A needless Alexandrine[2] ends the song
That, like a wounded snake, drags its slow length along.
· ·
True ease in writing comes from art, not chance,
As those move easiest who have learned to dance.
'Tis not enough no harshness gives offense,
The sound must seem an echo to the sense:
Soft is the strain when Zephyr gently blows,
And the smooth stream in smoother numbers flows;
But when loud surges lash the sounding shore,
The hoarse, rough verse should like the torrent roar:
When Ajax[3] strives some rock's vast weight to throw,
The line too labors, and the words move slow;
Not so, when swift Camilla[4] scours the plain,
Flies o'er the unbending corn, and skims along the main.

When Pope speaks of open vowels, the line is loaded with open vowels.
When Pope condemns the use of ten monosyllables, the line contains ten
monosyllables. When Pope urges that the sound should echo the sense and
speaks of the wind, the line is rich in sibilants that hiss, like the wind. When
he speaks of Ajax striving, the combination of final consonants and initial
sounds slow the line; when he speaks of Camilla's swiftness, the final consonants and initial sounds form liaisons that are swiftly pronounceable.

Or, consider the opening lines of Wilfred Owen's poem "Dulce et
Decorum Est," describing a company of battle-weary soldiers trudging toward their camp and rest:

Bent double, like old beggars under sacks,
Knock-kneed, coughing like hags, we cursed through sludge.

These lines are dominated by a series of harsh, explosive consonant sounds
(b, d, k, g) that reinforce the meaning of the lines (a description of tired
World War I soldiers). More specifically, the first two syllables of each line
are heavily stressed, which serves to slow the reading. And, finally, while the
poem ultimately develops a prevailing meter, the meter is only faintly suggested in these opening lines, through the irregular rhythms used to describe
a weary stumbling march.

Let us remember, then, that analysis of musical (or for that matter any
other) devices can illuminate and enrich our understanding of poetry. But let

---

2. Twelve-syllable line.
3. A Greek warrior celebrated for his strength.
4. A swift-footed queen in Virgil's *Aeneid.*

us also remember that analysis has its limitations. Dylan Thomas once remarked:

> You can tear a poem apart to see what makes it technically tick and say
> to yourself when the works are laid out before you—the vowels, the
> consonants, the rhymes, and rhythms—"Yes, this is it. This is why the
> poem moves me so. It is because of the craftsmanship." But you're back
> where you began. The best craftsmanship always leaves holes and gaps
> in the works of the poem so that something that is not in the poem can
> creep, crawl, flash, or thunder in.

Another writer, X. J. Kennedy, doubtless with MacLeish's poetic critical
observations in mind, puts the same idea with less reverence:

ARS POETICA

The goose that laid the golden egg
Died looking up its crotch
To find out how its sphincter worked.
Would you lay well? Don't watch.

Reading Drama

Plays are fundamentally different from other literary forms. Unlike stories and poems, almost all plays are designed to be performed, not to be read. Consequently, the aural and the visual aspects of the drama, which should be at least as important as its dialogue, are left altogether to the imagination of the reader (with the aid of some meager stage directions). Great effort is invested in such matters as costuming, set design, lighting effects, and stage movement by the director and his staff; all of that effort is lost to the reader who must somehow contrive to supply imaginatively some of those dramatic features not contained on the printed page.

As much as possible, the way to read a play is to imagine that you are its director. Hence you will concern yourself with creating the set and the lighting. You will see people dressed so that their clothes give support to their words. You will think about timing—how long between events and speeches—and blocking—how the characters move as they interact on stage. Perhaps the best way to confront the literature of the stage, to respond most fully to what is there, is to attempt to produce some scenes in class or after class. If possible, attend the rehearsals of plays in production on the campus. Nothing will provide better insight into the complexities of the theater than attending a rehearsal where the problems are encountered and solved.

As an exercise, read the opening speeches of any of the plays here and make decisions. How should the lines be spoken (quietly, angrily, haltingly)? What should the characters do as they speak (remain stationary, look in some direction, traverse the stage)? How should the stage be lit (partially, brightly, in some color that contributes to the mood of the dialogue and action)? What should the characters who are not speaking do? What possibilities exist for conveying appropriate signals solely through gesture and facial expression—signals not contained in the words you read?

Staging

Since plays are written to be staged, the particular kind of theater available to the dramatist is often crucial to the structure of the play. The Greek theater of Dionysius in Athens, for which Sophocles wrote, was an open-air amphitheater seating about 14,000 people. The skene, or stage house, from which actors entered, was fixed, though it might have had painted panels to suggest the scene. Consequently, there is no scene shifting in *Antigone*. All the dialogue and action take place in the same location before the skene building, which represents the Palace of Creon. Important things happen elsewhere, but the audience is informed of these events by messenger. Three deaths occur, but none in sight of the audience, partly as a matter of taste and partly because the conditions of the Greek stage prevented the playwright from moving the action inside the palace or to that terrifying mausoleum where both Antigone and her betrothed chose death before submission. Later dramatists, writing for a more flexible stage and a more intimate theater, were able to profit from the intensely dramatic nature of murder and suicide, but the Greeks, almost invariably, chose to tell, rather than show, the most gripping physical events in their stories.

Further, an outdoor theater of vast dimensions implies obvious restrictions on acting style. Facial expression can play no important role in such a theater, and, in fact, the actors of Sophoclean tragedy wore masks, larger than life and probably equipped with some sort of megaphone device to aid in voice projection. Those voices were denied the possibility of subtle variety in tone and expression, and the speeches were probably delivered in rather formal declamatory style. The characters wore special built-up footwear which made them larger than life. In addition to these limitations, Sophocles had as well to write within the formal limitations imposed by the Athenian government, which made available only three principal actors, all male, as the cast (exclusive of the chorus) for each play. Consequently, there are never more than three players on stage at once, and the roles are designed so that each actor takes several parts—signified by different masks. Yet, despite the austerity of production values, the unavoidable clumsiness of fortuitous messengers appearing at all the right moments, and the sharply restricted dramatis personae, among the few Greek plays that have survived are some still universally regarded as superlatively fine dramatic representations of tragic humanity.

Until recently we thought we had a clear conception of what Shakespeare's stage looked like. Scholarship has raised some doubts about this conception, but though we no longer accept the accuracy of the reconstruction shown here, we still have a good enough understanding of the shape of the playing area to re-create roughly the staging of a Shakespearean play. That staging was altogether different from the Greek. Though both theaters were open air, the enclosure around the Elizabethan stage was much smaller, and the audience capacity limited to something between 2,000 and 3,000. As in classical drama, men played all the roles, but they no longer wore masks, and the jutting stage made for great intimacy. Hence the actors' art expanded to matters of facial expression, and the style of speech and movement was certainly closer than was Greek style to what we might loosely call realism. Shakespeare has Hamlet caution the actors: "Suit the action to the word, the word to the action, with this special observance, that you o'erstep not the modesty of nature: for anything so overdone is from the purpose of playing, whose end, both at first and now, was and is, to hold as 't were, the mirror up to nature. . . ." But the characteristic matter of Shakespearean tragedy certainly did not lend itself to a modern realistic style. Those great speeches are written in verse; they frequently are meant to augment the rather meager set design by providing verbal pictures to set the stage; they are much denser in texture, image, and import than is ordinary speech.

Interior of the Swan Theatre, London, 1596

The Globe Theatre

Interior of the Globe Theatre in the days of Shakespeare

A French theater during Molière's management

The Greek theater at Epidaurus

These characteristics all serve to distinguish the Shakespearean stage from the familiar realism of most recent theater and film.

The Elizabethan stage made possible a tremendous versatility for the dramatist and the acting company. Most of the important action was played out on the uncurtained main platform, jutting into the audience and surrounded on three sides by spectators. The swiftly moving scenes followed each other without interruption, doubtless using different areas of the stage to signify different locations. There was some sort of terrace or balcony one story above the main stage, and there was an area at the back of the main protruding stage that could be curtained off when not in use. Although Shakespeare's plays are usually divided into five separate acts in printed versions, they were played straight through, without intermission, much like a modern motion picture.

Though more versatile and intimate than the Greek stage, the Elizabethan stage had limitations which clearly influenced the playwright. Those critical imperatives of time, place, and action (i.e., the time represented should not exceed one day, the location should be fixed in one place, and the action should be limited to one cohesive story line—one plot), the so-called unities that Aristotle discovered in the drama of Sophocles, may well reflect the physical conditions of the Greek theater. Elizabethan dramatists largely ignored them, and in *Othello* we move from Venice to Crete, from the fortifications of the island to the city streets to Desdemona's bedchamber. Certainly some props were used to suggest these locations, but nothing comparable to the furniture of Ibsen's stage. Instead, the playwright often wove a sort of literary scenery into the speeches of the characters. For example, in *Othello*, Roderigo has occasion to say to Iago, "Here is her father's house; I'll call aloud." The second act of *Othello* opens with some gentlemen at "an open place near the quay." Notice the dialogue:

> **Montano.**   What from the cape can you discern at sea?
> **First Gentleman.**   Nothing at all: it is a high-wrought flood;
>   I cannot, 'twixt the heaven and the main,
>   Descry a sail.
> **Montano.**   Methinks the wind hath spoke aloud at land;
>   A fuller blast n'er shook our battlements.
>   If it hath ruffian'd so upon the sea,
>   What ribs of oak, when mountains melt on them,
>   Can hold the mortise?

There is no sea, of course, and Elizabethan technology was not up to a wind machine. The men are, doubtless, looking off stage and creating the stormy setting through language. An open-air theater which played in daylight had few techniques for controlling lighting, and speeches had to be written to supply the effect:

> But look, the morn, in russet mantle clad,
> Walks o'er the dew of yon high eastern hill.

Further, the company had not the resources to place armies on the stage;

hence, a speaker in *King Henry V* boldly invites the audience to profit from imagination:

> Piece out our imperfections with your thoughts;
> Into a thousand parts divide one man,
> And make imaginary puissance;
> Think, when we talk of horses, that you see them
> Printing their proud hoofs i' the receiving earth.
> For 'tis your thoughts that now must deck our kings.

Molière's theater in the Petit-Bourbon Palace, built about twenty-five years after Shakespeare's death, was a forerunner of the common "box stage" on which so much recent drama is acted. Essentially, this stage is a box with one wall removed so that the audience can see into the playing area. Such a stage lends itself to realistic settings. Since the stage is essentially a room, it can easily be furnished to look like one. If street scenes are required, painted backdrops provide perspective and an accompanying sense of distance. Sets at an angle to the edge of the stage might be constructed. The possibilities for scenic design allowed by such a stage soon produced great set designers, and the structure of such a stage led to the development of increasingly sophisticated stage machinery, which in turn freed the dramatist from the physical limitations imposed by earlier stages. Although Molière preferred, generally, to use a single set (*The Misanthrope* is set at the home of Célimène), by Ibsen's time the versatility of the box stage enabled the father of modern drama to write elaborately detailed stage settings for the various locations in which the drama unfolds. Further, the furnishing of the stage in Ibsen's plays sometimes functions symbolically to convey visually the choking quality of certain bourgeois life-styles.

None of the historical stages has passed into mere history. The modern theater, in its vitality, still uses the Greek theater at Epidaurus, insists upon constructing approximations of the Elizabethan stage for its Shakespeare festivals, still employs with ever increasing inventiveness the box stage of Molière and Ibsen. Early in the twentieth century, some plays were produced in the "round," the action taking place on a stage in the center of the theater with the audience on all sides. A number of theaters were built that incorporated a permanent in-the-round arrangement. But versatility has become so important to the modern production designer that some feel the very best theater is simply a large empty room (with provisions for technical flexibility in the matter of lighting) that can be rearranged to suit the requirements of specific productions. This ideal of a "theater space" that can be freely manipulated has become increasingly attractive—some have been constructed—since it frees the dramatist and the performance from limitations built into permanent stage design.

Drama and Society

The history of dramatic literature (like the history of literature in general) provides evidence for another kind of history as well—the history of changing attitudes, changing values, and even changing taste. In ancient Greece, in Elizabethan England when Shakespeare wrote his enduring tragedies, right up to the end of the eighteenth century, certain expectations controlled the nature of tragedy. Those expectations were discussed by Aristotle as early as 335 B.C.; they involved the fall of a noble figure from a high place. Such tragedy reflects important cultural attitudes. It flourished in conjunction with a certain sort of politics and certain notions about human nature. The largest part of an audience of several thousand Athenians in the fifth century B.C. was certainly not itself noble. Neither was Shakespeare's audience at the Globe Theatre in London. That audience, much as a modern audience, was composed of tradesmen, artisans, petty officials, and, in Greece, even slaves. Why then were there no tragedies in which the central figure was a store-keeper, a baker or butcher, a traveling salesman?

There have been many attempts to answer this difficult question, and those answers tend to make assumptions about the way individuals see them-selves and their society. If the butcher down the street dies, well, that is sad, but after all rather unimportant to the society. If the king falls, however, the society itself is touched, and a general grief prevails that makes possible sweeping observations about the chancy conditions of life. A culture always elevates some of its members to the status of culture heroes—often by virtue of the office they hold. Even now, societies are collectively moved, and moved profoundly, by the death of a president, a prime minister—a Kennedy, a de Gaulle, a Churchill—when they are not nearly so moved by immense disasters such as killing storms or earthquakes or civil wars. But things have changed, and most rapidly within the last 150 years or so.

Simply stated, new cultural values, new attitudes about human nature have developed, especially since the advent of industrialism and since Freud began publishing his systematic observations about the way men's minds interact with their bodies. The result has been an increasing humanization of those who used to be heroes and an increasing realization of the capacity for heroism in those who are merely bakers and butchers. Thus Henrik Ibsen, frequently referred to as the father of modern drama, can compel a serious emotional response from his audience over the tribulations of a middle-class lawyer's wife in *A Doll's House*. And Arthur Miller can write an immensely suc-cessful tragedy on the life and death of a loud-mouthed traveling salesman named Willie Loman (and that last name may not be altogether accidental). These plays succeed in spite of their commonplace heroes because, as a so-ciety, we can now accept the experiences of ordinary people as emblems of our own. Perhaps we can because political institutions in the modern republics and in the socialist countries have, at least theoretically, exalted the common man and rejected political aristocracy. Certainly the reasons for the change are complex. But it remains true that neither Sophocles nor Shakespeare could have written *A Doll's House*.

Dramatic Irony

Dramatic irony allows the audience to know more than the characters do about their own circumstances. Consequently, that audience *hears more* (the ironic component) than do the characters who speak. Shakespeare's *Othello* provides an excellent illustration of the uses of dramatic irony. At the end of Act II, Cassio, who has lost his position as Othello's lieutenant, asks Iago for advice on how to regain favor. Iago, who, unknown to Cassio, had engineered Cassio's disgrace, advises him to ask Desdemona, Othello's adored wife, to intervene. Actually this is good advice; ordinarily the tactic would succeed, so much does Othello love his wife and wish to please her. But Iago explains, in a soliloquy to the audience, that he is laying groundwork for the ruin of all the objects of his envy and hatred—Cassio, Desdemona, and Othello:

> . . . for while this honest fool
> Plies Desdemona to repair his fortunes,
> And she for him pleads strongly to the Moor,
> I'll pour this pestilence into his ear
> That she repeals him for her body's lust;
> And, by how much she strives to do him good,
> She shall undo her credit with the Moor.
> So will I turn her virtue into pitch,
> And out of her own goodness make the net
> That shall enmesh them all.

Of course Desdemona, Cassio, and Othello are ignorant of Iago's enmity. Worse, all of them consider Iago a loyal friend. But the audience knows Iago's design, and that knowledge provides the chilling dramatic irony of Act III, scene 3.

When Cassio asks for Desdemona's help, she immediately consents, declaring, "I'll intermingle everything he does with Cassio's suit." At this, the audience, knowing what it does, grows a little uneasy—that audience, after all, rather likes Desdemona and doesn't want her injured. As Iago and Othello come on stage, Cassio, understandably ill at ease, leaves at the approach of the commander who has stripped him of his rank, thus providing Iago with a magnificent tactical advantage. And as Cassio leaves, Iago utters an exclamation and four simple words that may rank among the most electrifying in all of English drama:

> Ha! I like not that.

They are certainly not very poetic words; they do not conjure up any telling images; they do not mean much either to Othello or Desdemona. But they are for the audience the intensely anticipated first drop of poison. Othello hasn't heard clearly:

> What dost thou say?

Maybe it all will pass, and Iago's clever design will fail. But what a hiss of held breath the audience expels when Iago replies:

> Nothing, my lord: or if—I know not what.

And Othello is hooked:

> Was not that Cassio parted from my wife?

The bait taken, Iago beings to play his line:

> Cassio, my lord? No, sure, I cannot think it,
> That he would steal away so guilty-like,
> Seeing you coming.

And from this point on in the scene, Iago cleverly and cautiously leads Othello. He assumes the role of Cassio's great friend—reluctant to say anything that might cast suspicion on him. But he is also the "friend" of Othello and cannot keep silent his suspicions. So honest Iago (he is often called *honest* by the others in the play), apparently full of sympathy and kindness, skillfully brings the trusting Othello to emotional chaos. And every word they exchange is doubly meaningful to the audience, which perceives Othello led on the descent into a horrible jealousy by his "friend." The scene ends with Othello visibly shaken and convinced of Desdemona's faithlessness and Cassio's perfidy:

> Damn her, lewd minx! O, damn her!
> Come, go with me apart; I will withdraw,
> To furnish me with some swift means of death
> For the fair devil. Now art thou my lieutenant.

To which Iago replies:

> I am your own for ever.

Now, all of Iago's speeches in this scene operate on the audience through dramatic irony. The tension, the horror, the urge to cry out, to save Cassio, Desdemona, and Othello from the devilish Iago—all the emotional tautness in the audience results from irony, from knowing what the victims do not know. The play would have much less force if the audience did not know Iago's intentions from the outset and did not anticipate as he bends so many innocent events to his own increasingly evil ends. Note that dramatic irony is not limited to the drama; poetry, sometimes (as in William Blake's "The Chimney Sweeper"), and fiction, often (as in Joseph Conrad's "The Secret Sharer"), make use of this technique. But dramatic irony is the special tool of the dramatist, well suited to produce an electric tension in a live audience that overhears the interaction of people on stage.

Drama and Belief

Scholarly ordering that identifies the parts of drama and discusses the perceptive distinctions made by Aristotle among its parts can help you confront a play and understand how your responses were triggered by the playwright, the designers of the play, and the performers. But such analysis cannot substitute for the emotional experience produced by successful drama—your deepest responses have to do with states of mind, not with the three dramatic unities. Plays, no less than other art forms, address themselves to that incredibly complex melange of belief, attitude, intellect, and awareness that comprises a human psyche. As in *Antigone*, sometimes the play torments its audience by imposing on a courageous central character a duty that must be performed and must end in tragic death. Sometimes, as in Eugène Ionesco's *The Lesson,* the play mocks widely held cultural values—the virtue of scholars and the value of scholarship—and compels the audience to reexamine some of its fundamental values. If, as humans, we did not share the capacity for possessive love as well as jealousy, with all its terror, all its threat to self-esteem, then the tragedy of *Othello* would be incomprehensible.

While plays operate from within elaborate social and cultural constructions, response to dramatic art depends to a large extent on the condition of the responder's psyche, the state of mind he brings to the performance (or the reading). And that state of mind almost certainly changes with experience and, perhaps, with mood or preoccupation. A confirmed atheist may be indifferent to the religious dogma of *Everyman* but still be moved by the anonymous medieval dramatist's powerful vision of death. For a number of reasons, that same atheist may find himself engrossed by the powerful dramatic values in Ingmar Bergman's modern morality play *The Seventh Seal.* Though atheist, our hypothetical viewer is steeped in the tradition emanating from the Book of Revelations in the New Testament. He has frequently seen or read of death personified—that grim reaper. He discovers in Bergman's squire a character who puts forward his own skeptical view with wit and vigor. If he sees the film, he must be struck with the effect of what Aristotle called spectacle—those lowering leaden skies, the black and whiteness of things, the flagellants attempting to scourge themselves free of some God-sent plague, the burning of a beautiful young witch in the name of God, the relentless pursuit by Death, a figure of some strength, understanding, and wit himself. So, despite disbelief in God, in personifications of death, or in the validity of the Christian experience, the audience is nonetheless moved by the drama that is believable within its own well-known context.

Film

For all the versatility modern technology has given the modern dramatist in lighting, sound effects, scenery, and the like, a play, finally, is fundamentally static—locked in place upon a narrow stage, seen from a vantage point that never changes, dependent on dialogue and stage business for all its effects. If motion pictures were made by filming a performance with a stationary camera, then films would be no more than plays permanently recorded. But films are not made that way. While the film bears some obvious relationships to plays, the differences in technique and range are so significant that one must recognize that film is truly an art form itself, as distinguishable from plays as plays are from novels.

Consider some of the distinctive features of the film. It can take its audience anywhere and provide constantly changing vantage points (thus sharing something of the omniscient point of view available to the novelist). It can look up or look down. It can move close in, focus on a single sinister eye, or move out to watch the whole earth circle slowly below. It will, characteristically, in the time consumed by a typical scene in a play, combine scores of different shots lasting from one to fifteen seconds—long shots of characters in a room, middle shots of one character listening to another talk, close-ups of a head alone grimacing expressively. Through the use of fade technique, the film can change time and place instantly. Perhaps most significantly, the film can, somewhat like the novel, provide with comparative ease a great deal of descriptive material—a long shot of the whole village in which the hero's house lies or a raging, ominous sea. The dramatist most often cannot. Again, through the use of close-up, the film can comment, like the novelist. But the effect of a single watching, malevolent eye occupying almost the entire screen has no counterpart in the dramatist's or novelist's art.

These distinguishing techniques of the film point to the unique and crucial characteristic that distinguishes it from novel and play: the film is overwhelmingly and flexibly visual. For this reason film scripts are almost always very difficult to read. Not only is a shooting script distractingly cluttered with camera directions, but, more significantly, the narrative development and meaning conveyed through visual imagery is lost in print. While we would not want to suggest that there are not important differences between reading a play and seeing it performed (plays *are* written to be produced), it is nonetheless true that plays have always enjoyed wide success as literary pieces for reading, because they can be understood and enjoyed as a purely verbal art form. If the dramatist feels that the printed version of his play loses significant meanings or coherence, he can make up for the loss by adding or expanding stage directions (note the elaborate and novelistic stage directions of O'Neill's *Desire Under the Elms*).

This is the remedy employed by Ingmar Bergman for his screenplay *The Seventh Seal*. The very first clause, "The night had brought very little relief from the heat," establishes a fact novelistically. Indeed, much of the power of *The Seventh Seal* as a literary document is attributable to Bergman's skill as a writer. The entire opening passage is a skillful evocation in words of the scene evoked visually in the film with equal power. But Bergman clearly knows that the writer's art differs from the filmmaker's, and so he tells us, as he cannot in the film, that "the morning sun . . . wallows up from the misty sea like some bloated, dying fish." Bergman employs this kind of purely verbal technique throughout the descriptive prose passages, but only sparingly. For the most part, the prose passages *describe* what the film *shows*.

As successful as the printed screenplay is in describing what the film shows, we must recognize that we are ultimately dealing with a translation, with all the loss of power that translations usually involve. The dialogue, set down on paper and strung together and fleshed out by descriptive passages, captures everything except the overwhelmingly visual quality that is unique to the film, with its almost infinite possibilities for varying movement, point of view, clarity, time, and place. While the screenplay of *The Seventh Seal*, then, is a powerful work in its own right, the film is even more powerful. And comparison of the two will teach the reader much about the film as art.

Three Critical Approaches: Formalist, Sociological, Psychoanalytic

Literary criticism has to do with the *value* of literature, its goodness or badness, not with the history of literature or the theory of literature. Because value judgments tend to be highly subjective, lively, and sometimes even acrimonious, debates among literary critics accompany their diverse responses to and judgments of the same work. The judgment a literary critic makes about a story or poem is bound to reflect his own cherished values. The truth of a work of art is, obviously, very different from the truth of a mathematical formula. Certainly one's attitudes toward war, religion, sex, and politics are irrelevant to the truth of a formula but quite relevant to his judgment of a literary work.

Yet, any examination of the broad range of literary criticism reveals that groups of critics (and all readers, ultimately, are critics) share certain assumptions about literature. These shared assumptions govern the way the critic approaches a work, the elements he tends to look for and emphasize, the details he finds significant or insignificant, and, finally, his overall judgment of the value of the work. In order to illustrate diverse critical methodologies, we have examined two of the works in this anthology—Matthew Arnold's poem, "Dover Beach," and Nathaniel Hawthorne's short story, "My Kinsman, Major Molineux"—from three different critical positions: the formalist, the sociological, and the psychoanalytic. We have selected these three critical positions not because they are the only ones (there are others), but because they represent three major and distinctive approaches of literary criticism that may help readers formulate their own responses to a work of literature.

We do not suggest that one approach is more valid than the others or that the lines dividing the approaches are always clear and distinct. Readers will, perhaps, discover one approach more congenial to their temperament, more "true" to their sense of the world, than another. Again, they may find that some works seem to lend themselves to one approach, other works to a different approach. More likely, they will find themselves utilizing more than one approach in dealing with a single work. What the reader will discover in reading the three analyses of the Arnold poem and the Hawthorne story is not that they contradict one another, but that, taken together, they complement and enrich his understanding and enjoyment of these works.

Formalist Criticism

While the formalist critic would not deny the relevance of sociological, bio-graphical, and historical information to a work of art, he insists that the func-tion of criticism is to focus on the work itself as a verbal structure and to dis-cover the ways in which the work achieves (or does not achieve) unity. The job of criticism is to show how the various parts of the work are wedded to-gether into an organic whole. That is to say, we must examine the *form* of the work, for it is the form that is its meaning. Put somewhat oversimply, the for-malist critic views a work as a timeless aesthetic object; we may find what-ever we wish in the work as long as what we find is demonstrably in the work itself.

Dover Beach

FROM the perspective of the formalist critic, the fact that Matthew Arnold was deeply concerned with how man could live a civilized and enjoy-able life under the pressures of modern industrialization or that Arnold ap-pears to have suffered in his youth an intense conflict between sexual and spiritual love may be interesting but ought not to be the focal point in an analysis of his poetry. After all, the historian is best equipped to reconstruct and illuminate Matthew Arnold's Victorian England, and it is the biographer's and psychologist's job to tell us about his personal life. A critic of "Dover Beach" who speculates on these matters is doing many things, perhaps quite interesting things, but he is not giving us a description of the work itself.

"Dover Beach" (p. 630) is a dramatic monologue, a poem in which a speaker addresses another person at a particular time and place. In the opening lines, Arnold skillfully sets the scene, introduces the image of the sea that is to dominate the poem, and establishes a moment of tranquility and moon-bathed loveliness appropriate to a poem in which a man addresses his beloved. The beauty of the scene is established through visual images that give way, beginning with line 9, to a series of auditory images that undermine or bring into serious question the atmosphere established by the opening eight lines. In this contrast between visual and auditory imagery, a contrast that is developed through the entire poem, Arnold embodies one of the poem's major themes: appearance differs from reality.

In the second stanza, the "eternal note of sadness" struck in the final line of the first stanza is given an historical dimension and universalized by the allusion to Sophocles, the great Greek tragedian of fifth-century B.C. Athens. We become aware that the sadness and misery the speaker refers to are not the consequences of some momentary despair or particular historical event but are rather perennial, universal conditions of man's mortal life. Indeed, the allusion to Sophocles and the Aegean extends the feeling not only over centuries of time but over an immense geographical area, from the southern Aegean to the northern Atlantic.

The third stanza develops further the dominant sea imagery. But the real, literal seas of the earlier stanzas now become a metaphor for faith, per-haps religious faith, which once gave unity and meaning to man's life but now has ebbed away and left man stranded, helpless, bereft of virtually any defenses against sadness and misery. The "bright girdle furled," suggesting a happy and universal state, turns into a "roar" down the "naked shingles [i.e., pebble beaches] of the world."

The poet, therefore, turns, in the final stanza, to his beloved, to their love for each other as the only possible hope, meaning, and happiness in such a world. And his words to her echo the imagery of the opening lines with the important difference that the controlling verb *is* of the opening lines, denoting the actual and the real, is now replaced by the verb *seems*. The beautiful world is an illusion that conceals the bleak truth that the world provides no relief for man's misery. This grim realization leads to the powerful final image which compares man's life to a battle of armies at night. We have moved from the calm, serene, moon-bathed loveliness of the opening scene to an image of violence in a dark world where it is impossible to distinguish friend from foe or indeed even to understand what is happening.

"Dover Beach," then, is a meditation upon the irremediable pain and anguish of human existence, in the face of which the only possibility for joy and love and beauty is to be found in an intimate relationship between two human beings. The depth of the speaker's sadness is emphasized by his powerful evocation in the opening lines of the beauty of the scene. The first eight lines move with a quiet ease and flow with liquids and nasals, a movement enhanced by the balancing effect of the caesuras. In lines 9 to 14, the sounds also echo the sense, for now the sounds are much harsher and most of the lines are broken irregularly by more than one caesura. The dominant *l, m, n* sounds of the first eight lines give way to a pattern of hard *g*'s, plosive *t*'s and *b*'s.

We have already noted that the dominant image of the poem, the key to the poem's structure, is the sea. It is the real sea the speaker describes in the opening stanza, but when it sounds the "eternal note of sadness," the sea becomes symbolic. In the second stanza, the speaker is reminded of another real sea, the Aegean, which he associates with Sophocles, and the developing unity is achieved, not only at the literal level (Sophocles listening to the Aegean parallels the speaker's listening to the northern sea) but at the symbolic level (Sophocles perceived the ebb and flow of human misery as the speaker perceives the eternal note of sadness). The third stanza further develops the sea image but presents something of a problem, for it is not altogether clear what the speaker means by "Faith." If he means religious faith, and that seems most likely, we face the problem of determining what period of history Arnold is alluding to. "Dover Beach" establishes two reference points in time—the present and fifth-century B.C. Athens—that are related to each other by negative auditory images. Since the function of the lines about the Sea of Faith is to provide a sharp contrast to the present and fifth-century Athens (the visual image of "a bright girdle furled" associates the Sea of Faith with the opening eight lines), the time when the Sea of Faith was full must lie somewhere between these two points or earlier than the fifth century. Since a formalist critic deals only with the work *itself* and since there appears to be nothing elsewhere in the poem that will allow us to make a choice, we might conclude that these lines weaken the poem.

For the formalist critic, however, the final stanza presents the most serious problem. Most critics of whatever persuasion agree that they are moving and memorable lines, poignant in the speaker's desperate turning to his beloved in the face of a world whose beauty is a deception, and powerful in their description of that world, especially in the final image of ignorant armies clashing by night. But what, the formalist critic will ask, has become of the sea image? Is it not strange that the image which had dominated the poem throughout, has given it its unity, is in the climactic stanza simply dropped? On the face of it, at least, we, as formalist critics, would have to conclude that the abandonment of the unifying image in the concluding stanza is a serious structural weakness, lessened perhaps by the power of the images that replace it, but a structural weakness nonetheless. On the other hand, a formalist critic might commend the poet for his effective alternation of visual and auditory imagery throughout the poem. The first four lines of the final stanza return to visual images of an illusory "good" world (controlled by *seems*, as we have already noted) and concludes with a simile that fuses a sombre vision of darkness and night, with the harsh auditory images of *alarms* and *clashes*.

My Kinsman, Major Molineux

THIS rather strange story by Hawthorne may be summarized easily. After an opening paragraph in which Hawthorne comments on the harsh treatment of colonial governors appointed by the British crown at the hands of the people of the Massachusetts Bay Colony, we meet an eighteen-year-old boy named Robin who crosses the ferry one night into an unnamed town. He is the second son of a country minister and has been sent to town to seek out his powerful kinsman, Major Molineux, who, presumably, will use his influence to help the boy make his way in the world. Strangely, the boy is unsuccessful in locating the residence of his kinsman. Worse, he is mocked and threatened by the several people he accosts and is almost seduced by a pretty harlot. Finally, he is told to wait in a certain spot, and shortly a boisterous procession, led by a man with a face painted half red and half black, passes. The procession conducts an open cart in which his kinsman, Major Molineux, tarred and feathered, is being led out of the town and into exile. The boy joins in the laughter at the plight of his once powerful relative but soon decides (his prospects blasted) to return home. A kindly bystander urges him to stay and make his way in the world without the help of his kinsman.

The formalist critic would note that the story is about a young man's initiation into the rude adult world where he must make his own way unprotected by a sheltering family. That world is at best morally ambiguous and at worst menacingly hostile. The transformation in Robin from a self-confident but ignorant grown child to a self-doubting but aware young adult is conveyed through a series of events culminating in a violent climax. Those events, and the atmosphere surrounding them, make for a story that creates, through irony, a mounting suspense released for Robin and the reader with explosive suddenness. Hawthorne's considerable skill in creating that suspense and his method for releasing it are fundamental to the successful embodiment of the *theme*. Naive Robin, a "good child," becomes experienced Robin, more sober and more aware of the evil aspect of the human condition.

The story opens with an apparently superfluous preface in which Hawthorne tells his readers that royal governors in Massachusetts Bay (that is, governors appointed by the English crown rather than elected by the people) were treated roughly, even if they were fair and lenient. The discussion is to serve as "a preface to the following adventures, which chanced upon a summer night, not far from a hundred years ago [approximately 1732]." Hawthorne concludes that opening paragraph: "The reader, in order to avoid a long and dry detail of colonial affairs, is requested to dispense with an account of the train of circumstances that had caused much temporary inflammation of the popular mind." Now it is an article of faith for the formalist critic that no part of a literary work is superfluous. Art is *organic*. All its parts are essential to the whole. The reader may remain ignorant of some particular events that caused some particular social inflammation, but he cannot go on to the adventures of that summer night without some expectation that they will have something to do with the politics of colonial Massachusetts. If this prefatory paragraph is really superfluous, then it constitutes a flaw in the work. If it is not, we shall have, finally, to understand its function in the story.

The narrative begins with an account of the arrival of an eighteen-year-old country-bred youth on his first visit to town, at nine o'clock of a moonlit evening. All of the details provided in this second paragraph are significant and repay close reading. A young man from the country on his first visit to town, dressed humbly but serviceably, with brown curly hair, well-shaped features, and bright cheerful eyes describes an agreeable character. His physical description is pleasing. He is doubtless rather innocent (being country-bred and on his first visit to town). But he arrives at night and remains hidden in darkness until illuminated by some light-giving source. The moonlight alone doesn't suffice, and we require the help of the boatman's lantern to see him.

The manipulation of the light and the darkness in the story is crucial. As Robin walks about the town looking for the lodging of his kinsman, Major Molineux, he encounters six different people. The first, a rather dignified old man, is stopped by Robin "just when the light from the open door and windows of a barber's shop fell upon both their figures." The second encounter is within the inn, where there is light. The third encounter is with the harlot who is discerned by Robin as "a strip of scarlet petticoat, and the occasional sparkle of an eye, as if the moonbeams were trembling on some bright thing." We will see those moonbeams trembling on something altogether different later on. The fourth encounter, like the first two, ends with a threat from the sleepy watchman who carried a lantern. The fifth encounter is with the demonic man with the parti-colored face who "stepped back into the moonlight" when he unmuffled to Robin.

Now for all the local illumination that surrounds the threats, the temptation, and the final promise to Robin that his kinsman would soon be by, Robin remains in the dark. He does not understand why his questions generate such fierce threats from the elderly gentleman, the innkeeper, the watchman, and the demonic man. He sees the harlot in her parlor but doubts (quite rightly) her words and, finally, frightened a bit by the watchman, resists her seduction. The sixth encounter differs from the rest. The kindly stranger dimly sees Robin in the darkness—a literal and metaphorical darkness—and joins him. What of all this?

When the climactic moment occurs, when the procession arrives, it is lit by a dense multitude of torches "concealing, by their glare, whatever object they illuminated." This is rather a strange statement. When there is at last adequate light, the very glare conceals—and conceals what Robin must discover. Yet again, when the demonic leader of the procession fixes his eyes on Robin, "the unsteady brightness of the [torches] formed a veil which he could not penetrate." Finally, as the cart stops before Robin, "the torches blazed the brightest, there the moon shone out like day, and there, in tar-and-feathery dignity, sat his kinsman, Major Molineux!"

The orchestration of the light and darkness in the story becomes a metaphor for Robin's condition. Throughout, he is blind, despite the light. Rebuffs and laughter repeatedly greet his reiterated simple question, and in every case Robin—being, as he says, a "shrewd" youth—rationalizes the responses so that he can accept them without loss of self-esteem. The old man who threatens him is a "country representative" who simply doesn't know how powerful his kinsman is. The innkeeper who expels him is responding to Robin's poverty. The grinning demonic man with face painted half red, half black generates the ejaculation "Strange things we travellers see!" And Robin engages in some philosophical speculations upon the weird sight, which "settled this point shrewdly, rationally, and satisfactorily." In every case, however, Robin's rationalizations are wrong. As "shrewd" as he is, he constantly misunderstands because he is optimistic and self-confident. The reality would shatter both his optimism and his confidence. Despite the lighted places in the darkness, the places where the fate of his kinsman is hinted, he remains in the dark. At the climax, as the light becomes brighter and brighter, it does not illuminate but rather conceals by glare, forming an impenetrable veil through which he cannot see. Finally, when the torches blaze the brightest and the moon shines out like day, Robin sees! Presumably, now, he understands correctly the events of that long night.

But what is it that Robin understands? The question might be put another way. What is it that from the outset Robin doesn't understand? A good-looking, "shrewd" lad with a powerful relative, he expects the people he meets to behave with kindness and civility. A country youth, a minister's son, his experience of the world is limited. As the night wears on, the reader perceives Robin doggedly refusing to recognize that some sinister, evil action is afoot. Robin doesn't accept the existence of evil—everything can be explained in some rational way. With the temptation by the lovely harlot, Robin discovers within himself a sinfulness he might indignantly deny—and he does, after all, resist the temptation. But his weakness might be the beginning of wisdom, because Robin must discover that the human condition is not simple—it is complex. As he waits by the church, he peers into the window and notices the "awful radiance" within; he notices that a solitary ray of moonlight dares to rest upon the open page of the Bible. He wonders whether "that heavenly light" was "visible because no earthly and impure feet were within the walls?" And the thought makes him shiver with a strong loneliness. The implication that humans are inevitably impure grows strong.

This notion is driven home by the cryptic exchange between Robin and the kindly stranger when a great shout comes up from the still distant crowd. Robin is astonished by the numerous voices which comprise that one shout, and the stranger replies, "May not a man have several voices, Robin, as well as two complexions?" The notion that a man may have several voices has never occurred to Robin. In his attempt to deal with the strange sight of the man with two complexions, Robin rationalizes. But he does not learn from the evidence of his senses that man is complex, has different, even conflicting aspects. The stranger tries to teach him this truth—a man has many voices. Robin responds rather fatuously, thinking of the pretty harlot, "Perhaps a man may; but Heaven forbid that a woman should!" What does he mean? Doubtless he wishes to believe that the harlot was indeed the major's housekeeper, that she told the truth, spoke with one voice, and was not the embodiment of a sort of satanic evil attempting to entrap him. All in all, Robin's view of the world from the outset is simplistic. And that view encourages him in his optimistic confidence. The stranger tells him that the world is not simple—that each man speaks with many voices, that many aspects comprise the human condition. The heavenly radiance enters only into an empty church, unsoiled by impure human feet. But Robin still does not understand.

The procession approaches. Grotesque sounds—"tuneless bray," the "antipodes of music," "din"—announce the rout. Laughter dominates, and the light grows brighter and brighter. But still Robin does not understand. There sits his kinsman in tar-and-feathery dignity. Their eyes meet in an anguished and humiliating recognition. And Robin laughs.

That laughter is the outward symbol of his understanding. He has learned of human complexity. He has learned that he too contains a satanic aspect. His innocent optimism, based on an unreal conception of man, is altered to experienced doubt based on a new understanding of the complexity and the universality of that evil aspect of humanity symbolized by the behavior of the mob and the wild abiding laughter that infects even Robin.

The story is based on colonial history. The opening paragraph serves to remind us of the literal level on which the story operates. Mobs did roam the streets of Boston, did disguise themselves as Indians, did tar and feather and expel crown officers. But our attention is directed to a young, inexperienced boy. Finally, we must ask what has happened. How is Robin changed by his experiences? The images of darkness and light, the temptation scene, the moonlit church, the mob, and Robin's response to it all weave together into a single cord, the strands of which guide him to a new awareness both of himself and of his world.

Sociological Criticism

In contrast to the formalistic critic, who maintains that the proper job of criticism is to approach each work of art as a self-contained aesthetic object and to attempt to illuminate its inherent structure and unity, the sociological critic asserts that since all men are the products of a particular time and place, we can never fully understand a work without some understanding of the social forces that molded the author and all that he did and thought. The sociological critic feels that the formalistic critic's attempt to view a work as timeless denies the fundamental and self-evident fact that authors do not (and cannot) divest themselves of all the shaping forces of their history and environment. Consequently, the critic must look to those forces if he is to understand a man's works.

Dover Beach

To understand "Dover Beach," we must, according to the sociological critic, know something about the major intellectual and social currents of Victorian England and the way in which Arnold responded to them. By the time Arnold was born in 1822, the rapid advances in technology that had begun with the Industrial Revolution of the eighteenth century were producing severe strains on the social and intellectual fabric. The ancient rural, agrarian economy was giving way to the new urban, industrial economy, and the transition was long and painful. The new economy was creating a new merchant middle class whose growing wealth and power made it increasingly difficult for the upper classes to maintain exclusive political power. The passage of the celebrated Reform Bill of 1832, extending suffrage to any man who owned property worth at least ten pounds in annual rent, shifted political power to the middle class. It was not until 1867 that the franchise was extended to the lower classes. The intervening years were marked by severe social crises: depression, unemployment, rioting. Indeed, during these critical years when England was attempting to cope with the new problems of urban industrialism, the agitation and rioting of the lower classes created genuine fears of revolution (Englishmen remembered very clearly the French Revolution of 1789).

The ferment was no less intense and disruptive in the more rarified world of intellectual and theoretical debate. While it would be erroneous to assume that pre-industrial England was a world of idyllic stability, there can be little doubt that it was comparatively more settled and that the pace of change was much slower than during the nineteenth century. Perhaps the greatest stabilizing force in preindustrial England was religion. It offered men answers to the ultimate questions of human existence and, on the basis of those answers, justification and authority for the temporal order—kingship (or political control by a small aristocracy), sharp class distinctions, and the like. The technology that made industrialism possible grew out of the scientific discoveries and methodologies that challenged some of man's fundamental assumptions and faith. Specific scientific discoveries seemed to undermine the old religious faith (for example, Darwin's *The Origin of Species*, published in 1859); the scientific approach of skepticism and empirical investigation led to numerous studies of the Bible not as a sacred text of infallible truth but as an historical text that arose out of a particular time and place in the history of man. Close examination of the Bible itself resulted in discoveries of inconsistencies and contradictions as well as demonstrable evidence of its temporal rather than supernatural origin.

Matthew Arnold, born into a substantial middle-class family and educated at England's finest schools, established himself early as an important poet and as one of the leading social critics of the period. In much of his poetry and his voluminous prose writings, Arnold addressed himself to the critical questions of his time. The old values, particularly religious, were crumbling under the onslaught of new ideas; Arnold recognized that a simple reactionary defense of the old values was not possible (even if one still believed in them). Unless some new system of values could be formulated, society was likely to, at worst, fall into anarchy or, at best, offer the prospect of an arid and narrow life to individual men. And since the destiny of the nation was clearly devolving into the hands of the middle class, Arnold spent much of his career attempting to show the middle class the way to a richer and fuller life.

For an understanding of "Dover Beach," however, Arnold's attempt to define and advance cultural values is less important than his confrontation with the pain and dilemma of his age. Caught in what he called in one of his poems "this strange disease of modern life," Arnold found that modern discoveries made religious faith impossible, and yet he yearned for the security and certainty of his childhood faith. In his darker and more despairing moments, it seemed to him that with the destruction of old values the world was dissolving into chaos and meaninglessness. In these moments, he saw himself as "wandering between two worlds, one dead, / The other powerless to be born."

"Dover Beach" expresses one of those dark moments in Arnold's life— a moment shared by many of Arnold's contemporaries and modern readers as well, who, in many ways, instinctively understand the mood and meaning of the poem because the realities to which it responds are still very much with us. Simply stated, it is a poem in which the speaker declares that even in a setting of the utmost loveliness and tranquility (a sociological critic might very well here discuss the opening lines in much the same way a formalistic critic does) the uncertainty and chaos of modern life cannot for long be forgotten or ignored. For uncertainty and chaos so permeate the life and consciousness of the speaker that everything he sees, everything he meditates upon, is infected. The scene of silent loveliness described in the opening lines turns into a grating roar that sounds the eternal note of sadness.

In the second stanza, the speaker turns to ancient Greece and its greatest tragic playwright in an effort to generalize and thereby lessen and defend against the overwhelming despair he feels. If the confusion and chaos of modern life are part of the eternal human condition, then perhaps it can be borne with resignation. Yet the third stanza seems to deny this possibility, for it suggests that at some other time in man's history Christian faith gave meaning and direction to life but now that faith is no longer available.

Trapped in a world where faith is no longer possible, the speaker turns in the final stanza—turns with a kind of desperation because no other possibilities seem to exist—to his beloved and their relationship as the only chance of securing from a meaningless and grim life some fragment of meaning and joy. Everything else, he tells her, everything positive in which man might place his faith, is a mere "seeming." The real world, he concludes, in a powerful and strikingly modern image, is like two armies battling in darkness. Whether or not the final image is an allusion to a particular historical battle (as many critics have suggested), it is a graphic image to describe what modern life seemed to a sensitive Victorian who could see no way out of the dilemma.

For the sociological critic, then, an understanding of "Dover Beach" requires some knowledge of the major stresses and intellectual issues of Victorian England, because the poem is a response to and comment upon those issues by one of the great Victorian poets and social critics. Our description of those issues and Arnold's ideas is extremely sketchy and selective; it merely illustrates the approach a sociological critic might take in dealing with the poem. Nevertheless, the sketchiness of the presentation raises important questions about sociological criticism: Where does the sociological critic stop? How deep and detailed an understanding of the times and the writer's relationship to the period is necessary to understand the work? The formalistic critic might charge that the sociological critic is in constant danger of becoming so immersed in sociological matters (and even biography) that he loses sight of the work he set out to investigate. The danger, of course, is a real one, and the sociological critic must be mindful, always, that his primary focus is art, not sociology, history, or biography; the extent of his sociological investigations will be controlled and limited by the work he is attempting to illuminate. To this charge, the sociological critic might very well respond (perhaps in pique) that the formalistic critic becomes so preoccupied with matters of structure and unity that his criticism becomes arid and apparently divorced from all the human concerns that make people want to read poems in the first place. The sociological critic would agree with the comment made by Leon Trotsky, the Russian Marxist revolutionary, in his book *Literature and Revolution:*

> The methods of formal analysis are necessary, but insufficient. You may count up the alliterations in popular proverbs, classify metaphors, count up the number of vowels and consonants in a wedding song. It will undoubtedly enrich our knowledge of folk art, in one way or another; but if you don't know the peasant system of sowing, and the life that is based on it, if you don't know the part the scythe plays, and if you have not mastered the meaning of the church calendar to the peasant, of the time when the peasant marries, or when the peasant women give birth, you will have only understood the outer shell of folk art, but the kernel will not have been reached.

As a final note, a few remarks need to be made on a special form of sociological criticism, namely, ideological (i.e., Marxist, Christian, etc.) criticism. While the sociological critic differs from the formalistic critic in his approach to literature, the sociological critic tends to share with the formalistic critic the view that works of art are important in their own right and do not need to be justified in terms of any other human activity or interest. The Marxist critic, on the other hand, while sharing many of the assumptions and the approaches of the sociological critic, carries the approach an important step further. The Marxist critic sees literature as one activity among many that are to be studied and judged in terms of a larger and all-encompassing ideology. He holds that one cannot understand the literature of the past unless he understands how it reflects the relationship between economic production and social class. And since the Marxist sees his duty—indeed, the duty of all responsible and humane people—as not merely to describe the world but to change it in such a way as to free the oppressed masses of the world, he will not be content merely to illuminate a work, as does the sociological critic, or to demonstrate its aesthetic unity and beauty, as does the formalist critic. The Marxist critic will judge contemporary literature by the contribution it makes to bringing about revolution or in some way making the masses of workers (the proletariat) more conscious of their oppression and, therefore, more equipped to struggle against the oppressors.

The Marxist critic might describe "Dover Beach" very much as the sociological critic, but he would go on to point out that the emotion Arnold expresses in the poem is predictable, the inevitable end product of a dehumanizing, capitalistic economy in which a small class of oligarchs is willing, at whatever cost, to protect and increase its wealth and power. Moreover, the Marxist critic, as a materialist who believes that man makes his own history, would find Arnold's reference to "the eternal note of sadness" a mystic evasion of the real sources of his alienation and pain; Arnold's misery can be clearly and unmystically explained by the socioeconomic conditions of his time. It is Arnold's refusal to face this fact which leads him to the conclusion typical of a bourgeois artist-intellectual who refuses to face the truth; the cure for Arnold's pain cannot be found in a love relationship, because relationships between people, like everything else, are determined by socioeconomic conditions. The cure for the pain which he describes so well will be found in the world of action, in the struggle to create a socioeconomic system that is just and humane. "Dover Beach," then, is both a brilliant evocation of the alienation and misery caused by a capitalistic economy and a testimony to the inability of a bourgeois intellectual to understand what is responsible for his feelings.

My Kinsman, Major Molineux

"My Kinsman, Major Molineux" presents a nocturnal world, viewed largely from the point of view of its young hero, where nothing makes sense to him. It appears to be an allegoric or symbolic world, a dreamlike world where everything seems to mean something else. Robin searches for the meaning to the strange behavior of townsmen he accosts, for some key which will unlock the mystery. The sociological critic also searches for the key, and he finds it in the opening paragraph of the story, the paragraph that in any short story is crucial in setting the stage for the action about to unfold.

That paragraph, the sociological critic would note, is not a part of the narrative itself but is rather a straightforward summary of the historical situation in the American colonies prior to the Revolutionary War. We are given this summary, Hawthorne tells us, "as a preface to the following adventures." No critic, of whatever persuasion, can ignore that paragraph. In contrast to the actual story, the opening paragraph is clear and straightforward: on the eve of the Revolution, the bitterness and hostility of the colonists toward the mother country had become so intense that no colonial administrators, even those who were kindest in exercising their power, were safe from the wrath of the people. It is in the context of this moment of American history, when there occurred a "temporary inflammation of the popular mind," that the story of Robin's search for his kinsman must be read and interpreted. For "My Kinsman, Major Molineux" is an examination of and comment upon the American colonies as they prepared to achieve, by violence if necessary, independence from the increasingly intolerable domination of England.

We are introduced to Robin as he arrives in town, an energetic, likable, and innocent young man who has left the secure comfort of his rural family to commence a career. He is on the verge of manhood and independence, filled with anticipation and promise, as well as apprehension, as he confronts an uncertain future. But Robin, unlike most young men in his position, has the advantage of a wealthy cousin who has offered to help the young man establish himself. The story narrates Robin's polite and reasonable inquiries as to where Major Molineux resides and the bafflingly rude and hostile responses of the townspeople.

The mystery is Major Molineux, or, rather, the hostility his name evokes. For the reader, at least, the mystery begins to dispel when he learns that the major, an aristocratic and commanding figure, represents inherited wealth and civil and military rank—in short, the authority and values of the mother country. To Robin, fresh from the simple and nonpolitical world of his pastoral home, Major Molineux is a real person, his cousin, whose aid he seeks. To the townsman, on the other hand, Molineux is a symbol of the hated mother country in a political struggle that is turning increasingly ugly.

This difference between what Major Molineux means to Robin and what he means to the townspeople is prepared for at the very outset of the narrative. Robin has left the morally simplistic and nonpolitical world of his country home and come to a town that is seething with revolutionary fervor. The country is the past, America's past; the town is the present, the place where America's future will be decided. As Robin wends his way through the metropolis vainly searching for his kinsman, Hawthorn skillfully weaves into the narrative details suggestive of the political theme. Robin, we are told, enters the town "with as eager an eye as if he were entering London city." Before entering the tavern, "he beheld the broad countenance of a British hero swinging before the door." Once in the tavern, he observes a group of men who look like sailors drinking punch, which, Hawthorne tells us, "the West India trade had long since made a familiar drink in the colony." More significantly, this episode ends when the innkeeper, in response to Robin's inquiry about his cousin, merely points to a poster offering a reward for a runaway "bounden servant" and ominously advises Robin to leave. The suggestion is clear—anyone seeking Major Molineux must be a willing bond servant (bond servitude being a form of limited slavery used by England to help populate the American colonies) and, therefore, an enemy of the revolutionaries.

Robin continues his wanderings, his confusion deepening, until a stranger he accosts tells him that Major Molineux will soon pass by the very spot where they are standing. As Robin waits, his thoughts drift to his country home and family. In a dreamlike state, he dwells upon the warmth and security of the life he has left, the sturdy simplicity of a happy family bound together by a gentle and loving clergyman father. The dream ends abruptly, however, when Robin, attempting to follow his family into their home, finds the door locked. After an evening of "ambiguity and weariness," it is natural that Robin's thoughts should turn back to his home. It is just as natural that his dream should end as it does, for Robin has begun the journey to manhood and independence from which there is no turning back. Although he is not fully aware of the fact, he shares a good deal with the townsmen who have so baffled and angered him. The world of manhood and independence is the complex and ambiguous world where political battles are fought out, and Robin, like America itself, is set upon a course of action from which there is no turning back. The simplicities of an older, rural America, where authority is vested in a gentle father and the Scriptures or figures of authority like Major Molineux, must inevitably yield to the ambiguities of the metropolis, where the future will be decided.

That future, Robin's and the nation's, is dramatically embodied in the climactic episode, when Robin finally finds his kinsman. Tarred and feathered, Major Molineux sits in the midst of a garish and riotous procession, led by a man whose face is half red and half black. This man, Hawthorne tells us, is the personification of war and its consequences:

> The single horseman, clad in a military dress, and bearing a drawn sword, rode onward as the leader, and, by his fierce and variegated countenance, appeared like war personified; the red of one cheek an emblem of fire and sword; the blackness of the other betokened the mourning that attends them.

The strange Indian masquerade of those in the procession is a clear allusion to the disguise of the rebellious participants in the Boston tea party. The incomprehensible words addressed to Robin earlier by various townspeople are clearly passwords arranged to identify the conspirators against established authority.

The meaning of the night's events begins to dawn on Robin as he joins in the laughter of the throng as it wildly celebrates the demise of Major Molineux, whom Hawthorne compares to "some dead potentate, mighty no more, but majestic still in his agony." The entire scene, the entire story which this scene brings to a climax, gives Robin's laughter a crucial meaning. In joining in the the laughter of the throng, Robin identifies himself with the political goals of the revolutionaries. But more than that, in so doing he begins, finally, to see that his personal relationship, to both his home and his uncle, is parallel with and inseparable from the relationship of the colonies to its past and the mother country. Robin's joy in seeing his dignified and powerful uncle a scorned captive of the townsmen is intensely personal, the joy a young man feels, ambivalent though it may be, when he is released from the bonds of an authority figure. But the meaning of that authority figure, as the story makes clear, cannot be separated from the political theme, as Robin himself now recognizes.

Such a reading is not meant to imply that "My Kinsman, Major Molineux" is a simple story, a kind of allegory, which embodies in dramatic action a straightforward set of abstract ideas. It is, rather, a story revealing how complex a particular historical event is. That Hawthorne himself had equivocal feelings about the event is made clear by his description of the major, whose dignity and majestic bearing the utmost humiliation cannot altogether extinguish. This fact, together with the unflattering way the townspeople are presented throughout, suggests that Hawthorne viewed the event itself, at least in part, as the victory of mob rule over dignified and settled authority.

At any rate, the procession past, the tension released, Robin turns to the friendly citizen and asks directions back to the ferry. Defeated in his purpose, shaken by and perhaps not yet fully comprehending the extraordinary events of the evening, he decides to return to his family. But the kindly stranger urges Robin to stay. "Perhaps," he says, "as you are a shrewd youth, you may rise in the world without the help of your kinsman, Major Molineux." The stranger's comment is an appropriate conclusion to the story, for it appeals to Robin as a man, as an American man who must achieve independence through his own efforts, however difficult and ambiguous the struggle. Robin must make his way without the aid of his wealthy and powerful kinsman, just as America must make its way without the aid of the mother country. However problematical that freedom is, however dangerous and frightening, it is the inescapable price that real independence exacts.

Psychoanalytic Criticism

Psychoanalytic criticism always proceeds from a set of principles which describe the inner life of *all* men and women. Though there is now a great diversity of conviction about the nature of inner life and how to deal with it, certainly all analysts, and all psychoanalytic critics, assume that the development of the psyche in humans is analogous to the development of physique. Doctors can provide charts indicating physical growth stages, and analysts can supply similar charts, based on generations of case history, indicating stages in the growth of the psyche. Obviously the best psychoanalytic critic is a trained analyst, but few analysts engage in literary criticism. Most of that criticism is performed by more or less knowledgeable amateurs, and much of that criticism is based on a relatively few universal principles set down by Sigmund Freud which describe the dominating human drives and the confusions they produce. We must examine those principles.

First among them is the universality of the Oedipus complex. Freud contends that everyone moves through a psychic history which at one point, in early childhood, involves an erotic attachment to the parent of the opposite sex and an accompanying hostility and aggression against the parent of the same sex, who is seen as a rival in the jealous struggle. Such feelings, part of the natural biography of the psyche, pass or are effectively controlled in most cases. But sometimes, the child grown to adulthood is still strongly gripped by that Oedipal mode, which then may result in neurotic or even psychotic behavior. A famous lengthy analysis of Shakespeare's *Hamlet* argues that Hamlet is best understood as gripped by Oedipal feelings which account for his difficulties and his inability to act decisively, and the Laurence Olivier film of *Hamlet* presents such an interpretation. But how could Shakespeare create an Oedipal Hamlet when Freud was not to be born for some two and half centuries? Freud did not invent the Oedipus complex—he simply described it. It was always there, especially noticeable in the work of great literary artists who in every era demonstrate a special insight into the human condition. At one point in Sophocles' *Oedipus Rex*, written about 430 B.C., Jocasta the queen says to her son-husband, "Have no more fear of sleeping with your mother: / How many men, in dreams have lain with their mothers / No reasonable man is troubled by such things." And the situation of Oedipus, and the awareness of Jocasta, provide for Freud the very name for the psychic phase he detects.

Paralleling the Oedipal phase in the natural history of the psyche is the aggressive phase. This psychic feature urges physical and destructive attacks on those who exercise authority, that is, those in a position to control and to deny the primal desires of each of us. For the young, the authority figure is frequently the father. For the more mature, that authority figure may be the policeman, the government official, the office manager. As far back as the Hebrew Bible story of the Tower of Babel and the old Greek myths in which the giant Titans attack their father Zeus (much as Zeus himself attacked his father Chronos), there appears evidence of the rebellion against the father-authority figure. Freud views that aggressive hostility as another ever present component of the developing psyche. But, in the interest of civilization and the advantages which organized society provides, that aggressiveness must be controlled. The mechanisms of control are various. Early on comes the command to honor one's father and mother. The culture demands of its members that they love and revere their parents. What, then, of the frequent hostility which children feel toward those parents who punish them and deny them the freedom they seek? That hostility is often the occasion of guilt—one is supposed to love not hate his parents—and the guilt can be severe as the child (or adult) detects the variance between his desires and his "duty." Such guilt feelings sometimes generate behavior that effectively punishes. The punishment may be internal—may take the form of psychotic withdrawal or psychosomatic illness. Or the guilt may generate external behavior that requires punishment at the hands of society. In any case, the psychoanalytic critic is constantly aware that the author and/or his characters suffer and resuffer a primal tension that results from the conflict of his psychic aggressions with his social obligations.

Dover Beach

"DOVER Beach" is richly suggestive of the fundamental psychic dilemma of man in civilization. And since man in civilization is, by definition, discontent because his social duties require him to repress his primal urges, it is not surprising that the opening visual images of the poem which create a lovely and tranquil scene—calm sea, glimmering cliffs, a tranquil bay, sweet night air—are quickly modified by the ominous "only" that begins the seventh line of the poem. That *only*, in the sense of "in contrast," is addressed to a lady who has been called to the window to see the quiet and reassuring scene. No reassurance, finally, remains, as the images shift to an auditory mode:

> Listen! you hear the grating roar
> Of pebbles which the waves draw back, and fling,

Further, the land is "moon-blanched," a color with an emotional tone quite different from the earlier glimmering cliffs and fair moon. The tone is strangely changed, the emotional impact of "roar" and "blanched" suggesting something quite different from the serenity of the opening image, and the second stanza closes with the sounds of the surf bringing "the eternal note of sadness in."

Why should sadness be an *eternal* note? And why is the visual imagery largely pleasing while the auditory imagery is largely ominous? The answers to these two questions provide the focus for a psychoanalytic reading of the poem.

The "eternal note of sadness" (an auditory image) represents Arnold's recognition that, however sweet the night air and calm the sea, the central human experience is sadness. At the point in the poem where that sadness is recognized, the poet recalls the great Greek tragedian Sophocles who heard that same note of sadness over 2,000 years ago. (It is, after all, an eternal sadness.) For Sophocles, the sadness brings to mind the "turbid ebb and flow of human misery." Now Sophocles' greatest and best known tragedy, *Oedipus Rex*, ends with the chorus pointing out that no man should count himself happy until at the moment of his death he can look back over a life without pain. Fate, as it afflicted Oedipus, afflicts us all. And the fate of Oedipus provided Freud with the name of that psychic mode through which we all pass. We would all be guilty of parental murder and incest were it not for the necessity to repress those urges in order to construct a viable society. The unacceptable passions are controlled by guilt. We may not commit murder or incest on pain of punishment. We may not even desire to commit murder or incest on pain of possible psychic punishment. The dilemma, the guarantee of guilt or the guarantee of discontent, defines that eternal note of sadness which the poet hears.

We might go further. There is agreement that in infancy and very early childhood the tactile and the visual senses are most important. Somewhat later the auditory sense increases in importance. Consequently, the child recognizes security—certitude, peace, help for pain—tactily and visually, in the warmth and the form of the omnipresent and succoring mother. Later, through his ears comes the angry "no!" When discipline and painful interaction with others begin, he experiences the auditory admonition which frustrates his desires. It is immensely interesting to the psychoanalytic critic that in "Dover Beach" the tranquilities are visual but the ominous sadness is auditory—the "roar" which brings in the "note" of sadness, the "roar" of the retreating sea of faith, the "night-wind," the "alarms," the "clash by night."

We need to look at the opening lines of the final stanza. Certainly the principal agency developed by society to enforce the morality it required was religion. Ancient religious teaching recognized those very primal urges that Freud systematically described and made them offenses against God. Faith, then, became the condition that made society possible; religious injunction and religious duty served as a sort of cultural superego, a mass conscience, that not only controlled human aggression but substituted for it a set of ideal behavior patterns that could guarantee a set of gratifying rewards for humanity. Hence the poet recalls:

The Sea of Faith
Was once, too, at the full, and round earth's shore
Lay like the folds of a bright girdle furled.

This is a strange image. Surely the emotional tone of "the folds of a bright girdle furled" is positive—that bright girdle is a "good" thing, not an ominous thing. Yet, that girdle (i.e., a sash or belt worn round the waist) is restrictive. It is furled (i.e., rolled up, bound) around the land. In short, the Sea of Faith contains, limits, strictly controls the land. In the context of the poem, that containment is a good thing, for without the restricting Sea of Faith the world, despite appearances,

> Hath really neither joy, nor love, nor light,
> Nor certitude, nor peace, nor help for pain.

Without strong religious faith, acting as a cultural superego, the primal aspects of men are released—aggression and lust come to dominate human activity:

> And we are here as on a darkling plain
> Swept with confused alarms of struggle and flight,
> Where ignorant armies clash by night.

A certain confusion persists. On the one hand, the Sea of Faith serves a useful function as an emblem of the superego (loosely, the conscience), the name Freud gives to the guilt-inducing mechanism that incessantly "watches" the ego to punish it for certain kinds of behavior. When it is at the full, ignorant armies, presumably, do not clash by night. On the other hand, the superego as associated with auditory imagery is ominous. It reverberates with the painful experience of frustration. Finally, however, the usefulness of the Sea of Faith is illusory. The note of sadness is eternal. Sophocles, long before the foundation of Christianity, heard it. What emerges from the poem's images, understood psychoanalytically, is a progression from a mild note of sadness (frustrated desires) to alarms and clashes (threatening uncontrolled aggressive desires). The calm sea, the fair moon, the world is like a land of dreams—illusory and without substance. Sadness, struggle, and flight are real.

We need to deal with the girl to whom the poet speaks; we need to understand his relationship to her. The quest for that understanding involves another psychoanalytic principle, another set of images, and a reconsideration of the image of the Sea of Faith.

In earliest infancy, the ego, the sense of self, is not yet formed. The infant child considers the mother, particularly the mother's breast, as part of himself. A gradual and a painful recognition must occur in which the child is dissociated from the mother. The process begins with the birth trauma. In the womb, the child is utterly safe, never hungry, never cold. After birth, there are discomforts. But for a time the mother and her nourishing breast are so much present that the infant does not distinguish where he ends and the other, the mother, begins. But this state of affairs does not continue, and the infant becomes increasingly dissociated. Slowly he learns what is "him" and what is not, what he can control by will (moving his arm, say) and what he cannot (his mother's availability). In short, he learns the borders of his being, the edges of his existence.

Images of borders and edges constantly recur in the poem. Such images may be taken as emblems of dissociation—that is, symbols of the separation between the warm, nourishing mother and the child. Consequently, they are symbols of painful dissatisfaction. The Sea of Faith that

> . . . round earth's shore
> Lay like the folds of a bright girdle furled

seems, on the other hand, much like that warm, encompassing mother who, to the infant, was a part of himself. But dissociation occurs, and the distressed poet perceives that comforting entity withdrawing, retreating "down the vast edges drear / And naked shingles of the world." He has an edge and can no longer reside safely in close association with the source of comfort and security.

Instantly the poet turns to the girl and says

> Ah, love, let us be true
> To one another!

He perceives his companion not erotically as a love object but as the source of security, as a replacement for the withdrawing emblematic mother. He offers his "love" a mutual fidelity not to reassure her of his commitment but to assure himself of hers. He wishes to dissolve the edges of his ego and associate, as in infancy, with his "mother." Such an association will protect him from a world in which "ignorant armies clash by night."

My Kinsman, Major Molineux

THE story opens with the crossing of a river into an unnamed town after dark. If one takes a psychoanalytic stance, the mysterious opening nicely symbolizes a sort of spiritual journey into mysterious realms. More specifically, the opening suggests an inward journey into the dark recesses of the human spirit. Robin has to confront the psychic confusion resulting from the conflict between the civilized and the psychological response to paternal authority. Robin takes his journey to discover and deal with the paternal figure that is identified in his mind with safety and security, his powerful kinsman, Major Molineux. From a psychoanalytic point of view, it is reasonable to point out that Robin has at least two fathers, since his kinsman, if Robin ever finds him, will serve a paternal function. Some critics suggest that every male Robin encounters serves as a surrogate father. Note that the men Robin meets, with one exception, all act threateningly, all offer to punish him, all assume a position of authority, and, hence, all in some respect are paternalistic. The one exception, the kindly stranger who joins Robin in his watch and who urges him to make his own way without the aid of a paternalistic power is in some ways himself a kind of unreal, idealized father figure, who, though kindly and helpful, requires no price for his help.

From the psychoanalytic point of view, the story is precisely about the price required of young men by their fathers. The price, of course, is not coin. It is behavior. Robin must behave as authority wishes, not as Robin wishes. In return, he will be secure—but almost certainly discontent. Perhaps, deeper than consciousness, Robin feels the pinch of such an economy and unwittingly seeks to avoid payment. After all, the story runs its course as Robin seeks directions to the house of his kinsman. But a kind of haunting inefficiency constantly disrupts his search. Early he realizes that he should have asked the ferryman to take him to Major Molineux. But he didn't. He stops an old gentleman by seizing hold of his coat—rather curious behavior to an elderly stranger. And the stranger's response to the youth's behavior is an angry threat. That threat provokes the first round of recurrent laughter from the loungers in the barber shop. And the threat frightens Robin. Next he becomes "entangled in a succession of crooked and narrow streets," a set of literal streets near the waterfront (but also a lovely metaphor for the human psyche), where he is attracted to an inn. There he receives his second rebuff from the innkeeper, another threat, and is followed out into the street by more laughter.

Robin responds to this rebuff with considerable anger, thinks violent thoughts, but continues to pursue his quest in a most curious way. He walks up and down the main street of the town hoping to run into his kinsman. Actually he is thrilled by the rich and exotic shopwindows and strollers. It is reasonable to assert that at this point, regardless of his rationalization, Robin is not at all seeking his kinsman. He is, for once, doing what he wishes to do. He is enjoying himself, free from any paternal interference. Remarkably, as he gawks along the exotic street, he hears the distinctive cough of the old gentleman he first encountered, the gentleman who threatened him with the stocks, the gentleman who proclaimed, "I have—hem, hem—authority." Robin responds by declaring "Mercy on us!" and ducking around a corner to avoid meeting him. Strange, this, passing strange. Stranger still that just around that corner which provides the escape from authority, Robin chances upon a half-opened door through which he could discern "a strip of scarlet petticoat, and the occasional sparkle of an eye."

This encounter is quite different from the others which occur both before and after. That red petticoat and sparkling eye belong to a vivacious and devastatingly attractive lady. A harlot, to be sure, but awfully attractive. She tells Robin, in response to his standard question, that Major Molineux is asleep within (an outrageous lie which Robin can't help but doubt), and she takes him by the hand "and the touch was light, and the force was gentleness, and though Robin read in her eyes what he did not hear in her words, yet the slender-waisted woman in the scarlet petticoat proved stronger than the athletic country youth. She had drawn his half-willing footsteps nearly to the threshold" when the watchman appeared. The girl hastily withdraws, and Robin is once again warned by authority of punishment for bad behavior.

The frightened youth does not realize until the watchman has turned the corner that *he* would certainly know the whereabouts of his kinsman, Major Molineux, but his tardy shouted request to the vanished watchman is answered only by more vague laughter. Why didn't Robin ask for directions immediately? Well, he was about to sin against the paternal authority which generally represses and most particularly represses the sexual instincts of sons. The psychoanalytic critic might go even further here in explaining the sources of Robin's guilty demeanor before the watchman whose appearance is fantastically coincidental. (Is he the ever present psychic "watchman" who cries "guilty" at even our ego-gratifying *thoughts* when they violate the "law"?) The desirable girl in the scarlet petticoat says that Major Molineux cohabits with her. Her eyes and her behavior invite Robin to a sexual encounter which he, however nervously, welcomes. If Major Molineux is a surrogate father for Robin, is not the lovely scarlet lady a surrogate mother? And is not an Oedipal situation developed? For students not familiar with principles of pscyhoanalytic criticism, this will seem a rather wild reading. But reserve judgment. Consider how the story ends. Then, perhaps, the Oedipal feature will not seem bizarre.

Now events move rapidly. Robin, brought to his "senses" by the intrusion of the watchman, remembers that he is a "good" boy and rejects the lovely beckoning arm. But he is upset and feeling violent. He intends to succeed in his quest, even if it means clubbing someone with his stout oak cudgel. The next man he meets, mysteriously muffled, is forced to answer— and answer he does. The muffling, dropped, reveals a hideous, satanic face painted half red and half black. Certainly that painting is a disguise. But this man, we later discover, is the leader of the mob which destroys Major Molineux's power and dignity and, as such, represents a certain aspect first of the community but also of each man in it, particularly of Robin. An old-fashioned Freudian would have no trouble identifying him as Robin's embodied *id,* the name given by Freud to the insistent selfish, lustful, and aggressive aspect of man's psyche, just as he would have no trouble earlier identifying the intrusive watchman as Robin's *superego.* Our awful demonic parti-colored citizen tells Robin to wait where he is and within an hour he will surely meet his kinsman, Major Molineux.

Robin waits and experiences some dreams which are almost hallucinations. He is standing by a church and notices the graves. Perhaps the major is already dead and will appear to haunt him. Wouldn't it be nice to be at home, safe in his family circle? And he is there, but when he seeks to follow his family into the house, the door is closed and locked in his face. It is a normal dream for a frightened young man the first time away from home. But in the context of the story, this dream acts as a metaphor for Robin's expulsion from the safety of home. Even if he would submit again to the "father" in return for security, the opportunity is denied. One father only remains for him—his kinsman, Major Molineux (who may be dead). It is his home that Robin must seek for shelter from all the perils of independence. But the price is the same —submission and repression. The rioters draw near, the tumult grows loud, the torches cast a great light into the darkness—some revelation is at hand. And the light reveals the demonic man on horseback with a drawn sword leading a riotous procession around a cart in which the powerful, gray, dignified, upright, fatherly Major Molineux sits trembling and humiliated. All the figures Robin encountered during the story return—old "hem-hem," the laughing innkeeper, the saucy harlot. And all laugh. But Robin's laugh is louder than all the rest! For the psychoanalytic critic, that laugh cannot be interpreted other than as the laugh of exultant release from the tyranny of the father, of established authority, and the prospect of independent activity free of stifling inner guilt.

The psychoanalytic critic might go further. He might call attention to the drawn sword held by the embodied id and remark on the relationship between that phallic symbol and the thwarted desire of Robin in the encounter with the harlot. Certain figures which recur throughout the history of literature (and in dreams and psychiatric case histories) are accepted by Freudian critics as symbols of the sexual and aggressive aspects of the human condition. Such deep reading, like all deep reading, is perilous. Yet to the reader well versed in the premises of psychoanalysis and the universal symbols behind which the mind conceals its primal nature, the bold analysis enriches the literary art.

Did Hawthorne deliberately design the psychoanalytic structure of "My Kinsman, Major Molineux"? A difficult question. He certainly did not incorporate an embodied superego and id. He never heard of those psychic abstractions. He certainly did not incorporate by design a phallic sword suggesting that Robin's sexual freedom is obtained through Major Molineux's exile. But, the psychoanalytic critic responds, Hawthorne, as a sensitive artist, perceives the deep struggle between desire and duty, between primal urge and social restraint. And that struggle he incorporates. As for the drawn sword, he had no idea of its psychic significance. He would be appalled by the modern psychoanalytic response. But, for the analyst, that does not in the least contradict the modern conviction that universal symbols, however unconscious, struggle to the surface in all art. That psychoanalytic critic would admire Hawthorne's "My Kinsman, Major Molineux" for effectively and accurately portraying the rite of passage of young Robin from innocence to experience, from repressed childhood to independent manhood.

Writing About Literature*

Writing about literature is an act that compels the student to discover and come to terms with an author's work and his own often complex response to it. Every element in a literary work has been deliberately incorporated by the author—the description of the setting, the events that constitute the plot, the particular speeches of characters, the imagery. A rather mysterious intellectual and emotional event occurs within the reader as a result of the writer's purposeful manipulation of language. An essay about literature inevitably attempts some description of the author's purposes and techniques and some discussion of the reader's response. Essays of the analytical sort will emphasize the author's methods. Essays of the appreciative sort will emphasize the reader's response. But discussions of literature will always deal with both the author's purpose and the reader's response.

To illustrate the relationship between author's purpose and reader's response, consider these opening lines of a poem by W. H. Auden (the poem appears on p. 642):

> That night when joy began
> Our narrowest veins to flush,
> We waited for the flash
> Of morning's levelled gun.

The stanza tells of a new joy, probably erotic, that the speaker and his companion experience one night. But the reader must see that the speaker is apprehensive about that joy. The writer has created that mood of apprehension by using a hunting image—the flash of morning's gun—to characterize the speaker's feelings. The images in the subsequent stanzas of the poem reinforce the hunting image of the first stanza. Thus the reader responds to the poem with an awareness of the special nature of the joy.

Though the equation "writer's purpose → reader's response" is by no means exact, any attempt to write about literature is, in one way or another, an attempt to discover and describe that equation. In other words, whatever the assignment, the student's fundamental task is to provide the answers to two questions: How do I respond to this piece? How has the author brought about my response?

---

*See, as well, the appendices "Reading Fiction," "Reading Poetry," "Reading Drama," and "Three Critical Approaches." Those discussions may well suggest useful approaches to writing assignments.

Subject and Thesis

Some instructors may assign a well-defined thesis as the topic for a student essay. However, it is more likely that your instructor will provide a broad, generally stated subject: characterization in *Othello* or imagery in love poetry or innocence and experience in Joyce's "Araby." Your first crucial problem is to discover and state your *thesis*. That thesis will be the end result of the thinking and analyzing that began when you confronted the assigned subject. The thesis will immediately announce to your reader that your essay will focus on and argue for a specific position, attitude, or point of view. It might be helpful, as you attempt to formulate your thesis, to see it as a position that you intend to *argue* for with a reader who is not easy to persuade. You might, for instance, limit your essay on characterization in *Othello* to a discussion of Othello's gullibility (in which you argue that Othello is too credulous for a man in his position), or to a discussion of the hollowness of Iago's self-justification (in which you dispute Iago's explanation of his hatred for Othello). Note that both these propositions are *argumentative;* "characterization in Othello" is not. Further, you can write a well-documented essay of 1000 words supporting your view for either proposition; you cannot write a well-documented 1000 word essay on the general subject of characterization in *Othello* without being hopelessly superficial.

You may be one among the many students who find it difficult to discover a thesis. Blocks occur, and you stare desperately at the blank page, unable to begin. The technique of free writing might help to overcome such blocks. You have read and reread the work you intend to write about. Start writing about it without organizing your ideas, without trying to reach a point. Write down what you like about the work, what you dislike about it, what sort of person one or another of the characters is, what impressions the setting gave you, what images or passages seemed striking to you—write anything at all about the work. If you do this for some minutes, you will probably discover several possible theses from which to choose—that is, several views or opinions for which you could argue. Pick the one that interests you the most or seems the most promising to explore. Now go back over the work and seek to discover the specific things the author has put there that produced the response you set down in your rambling notes.

Essay Writing

If you have thought about the assignment sufficiently and reread the work you intend to write about with enough care to formulate a thesis from the general subject, then you have already accomplished a major part of the task. You have, however loosely, constructed an argument and marshalled some of the evidence to support it. Now you must begin to be rigorous! Take notes. The most efficient method is to use 3″ × 5″ index cards. Take one note per card. Assign a short descriptive heading to each note card. This procedure allows you to manipulate the notes physically, to arrange them in the most workable order when you are drafting your paper.

As you take your notes and then arrange the cards, you will begin to get some sense of the number of paragraphs you will need to support the thesis you have announced in the opening paragraph. Generally, each paragraph will focus on one major point (perhaps with its own mini-thesis), and bring together the evidence necessary to support that point.

As you write (or perhaps rewrite), you should make sure that the logical progression of ideas from paragraph to paragraph is made clear to your reader. One way to accomplish this is to link each paragraph to the preceding one by a transitional word or phrase. Even the most carefully organized essay may seem abrupt or disjointed to the reader if you have neglected to provide bridges between the paragraphs. A simple "However," "Nevertheless," "Furthermore," or "On the other hand" will often be adequate. Sometimes the entire opening sentence of a paragraph may provide the transition (and avoid the monotony of the standard words and phrases). Let us assume, for example, that you are writing an essay in which you argue that in Dylan Thomas' poem "Fern Hill" the mature speaker, now keenly aware of mortality, perceives the innocence of his childhood as a state of religious grace. In one or more paragraphs, you have analyzed the religious imagery of the poem, and you now begin a new paragraph with the sentence, "While the religious imagery dominates the poem, it is supported by a well-developed pattern of color imagery." Such a transitional sentence signals the reader that you will now consider another pattern of imagery that provides further evidence to support the thesis, since, as you will show, the color imagery is in fact a subpattern of the religious imagery.

Simply stated, in a tightly organized essay there ought to be a reason why one paragraph in the body of your essay follows rather than precedes another. In fact, you may test the organization of your essay by asking yourself whether the paragraphs can be rearranged without significant effect. If they can be, chances are good that your organization is weak, your ideas unclarified.

Having worked out an opening paragraph with a thesis and worked through the body of your essay to support the thesis, you now must confront the problem of how to conclude. Your conclusion should be brief, rarely more than three or four sentences. Ideally, it should leave the reader with a sense of both completeness and significance. For a short paper, it is unnecessary to restate or summarize your main points, since your reader will not have trouble remembering them. If your essay has been primarily analytical and objective, you might conclude with an opinion on the success or failure of the work. If you have focused on a particular aspect of the work (a pattern of imagery, the point of view), you might end with an observation on how such a close examination reveals the kind of care an author takes in creating a unified work. If your essay has been primarily appreciative and impressionistic, a general statement about the value of the work to you might bring the essay nicely to rest. Or you might conclude with a statement about the relevance of the work to the world we live in. When you have said all you have to say, you have finished. Avoid the common error of turning the conclusion into a beginning by taking up new evidence or ideas in the final paragraph.

Writing About Fiction

Let us turn to a more concrete consideration of the problem you will face in writing about a short story. Suppose, for example, that your instructor has made the following assignment: Discuss the theme of Harlan Ellison's story " 'Repent, Harlequin!' Said the Ticktockman," focusing on character and setting. Now consider the following opening (taken from a student paper):

> "'Repent Harlequin!' Said the Ticktockman" is a story depicting a society in which time governs one's life. The setting is America, the time approximately A.D. 2400 somewhere in the heart of the country. Business deals, work shifts, and school lessons are started and finished with exacting precision. Tardiness is intolerable as this would hinder the system. In a society of order, precision, and punctuality, there is no room for likes, dislikes, scruples, or morals. Thus personalities in people no longer exist. As these "person-less" people know no good or bad, they very happily follow in the course of activities which their society has dictated.

At the outset, can you locate a thesis statement? The only sentences that would seem to qualify as such a statement are the last three in the paragraph. But notice that, although those sentences are not unreasonable responses to the story, they do not establish a thesis that is *responsive to the assignment*. Since the assignment calls for a discussion of theme in terms of character and setting, there should be a thesis statement about the way in which character and setting embody the theme. Here is another opening paragraph on the same assignment (also taken from a student paper):

> Harlan Ellison's "'Repent Harlequin!' Said the Ticktockman" opens with a quotation from Thoreau's essay "Civil Disobedience" which rather clearly establishes the story's theme. Thoreau's observations about three varieties of men, those who serve the state as machines, those who serve it with their heads, and those who serve it with their consciences, are dramatized in Ellison's story, which takes

place about 400 years in the future in a setting characterized by machinelike order. The interaction among
the three characters, each of whom represents one of
Thoreau's defined types, results in a telling restatement
of his observation that "heroes, patriots, martyrs,
reformers in the great sense, and men . . . necessarily
resist [the state] and . . . are commonly treated as enemies
by it."

Compare the two openings sentence by sentence for their responsiveness to the assignment. The first sentence of the first opening does not refer to the theme of the story (or to its setting or characterization). In the second sentence, the discussion of the setting misses the most important aspect, namely, that the story is set in a machine- and time-dominated future. The last three sentences deal rather obliquely with character, but they are imprecise and do not establish a thesis for the paper. The second opening, on the other hand, immediately alludes to the theme of the story. It goes on to emphasize the relevant aspects of the futuristic setting and then moves to a discussion of the three characters that animate the story in terms of their reactions to the setting. Those reactions comprise the theme. The last sentence addresses the assignment directly and also serves as a thesis statement for the paper. It states the proposition or argument that will be supported by the information and evidence in the rest of the paper. The reader of the second opening will expect the next paragraph of the paper to discuss the setting of the story and subsequent paragraphs to discuss the response to the setting of the three principal characters.

The middles of essays are largely determined by their opening paragraphs. However long the middle of an essay may be, each of its paragraphs ought to be responsive to some explicit or implicit statement made at the beginning of the essay. Note that it is practically impossible to predict what the paragraph following the first opening will deal with. Here is the first half of that next paragraph as the student wrote it:

The Harlequin is a man in the society with no sense of
time. His having a personality enables him to have a sense
of moral values and a mind of his own. The Harlequin thinks
that it is obscene and wrong to let time totally govern the
lives of people. So he sets out to disrupt the time schedule
with ridiculous antics such as showering people with jelly
beans in order to try to break up the military fashion in
which they are so used to doing things. [The paragraph then

goes on to discuss the Ticktockman, the capture and brain-
washing of the Harlequin, and the resulting lateness of the
Ticktockman.]

Note that nothing in the opening of this student's paper prepared for the introduction of the Harlequin. In fact, the opening concluded rather inaccurately that the people within the story "happily follow in the course of activities which their society has dictated." Hence, the introduction of the Harlequin in the second paragraph represents a wholly new and unanticipated element of the story. Further, since the student has not dealt with the theme of the story (remember the assignment explicitly asked for a discussion of *theme* in terms of character and setting), his comments about the Harlequin's antics remain disconnected from any clear purpose and are thus ineffective. They are essentially devoted to what teachers constantly warn against: a mere plot summary. The student has obviously begun to write before he has analyzed the story sufficiently to understand its theme. Had he thought further he would have perceived that the central thematic issue is resistance to an oppressive state—the issue stated in the excerpt from Thoreau that opens the story. The second opening, on the other hand, makes that thematic point clearly and ought to be followed by a discussion of the environment (i.e., the setting) in which the action occurs. Here is such a paragraph taken from the second student's paper:

Ellison creates a society that reflects one possible
future development of the modern American passion for
productivity and efficiency. The setting is in perfect
keeping with the time-conscious people who inhabit the city.
It is pictured as a neat, colorless, and mechanized city
lacking in warmth. No mention is made of nature, no grass,
flowers, trees, or birds. The buildings are in a "Mondrian
arrangement," stark and geometrical. Everything moves with
precision, the cold steel slidewalks, slowstrips, and express
trips. The people move like a chorus line in unison to
board the movers with not a wasted motion. Doors close
silently and automatically lock themselves. An ideal
efficiency so dominates the social system that any "wasted
time" is deducted from the life of an inefficient citizen.

Once the setting has been established, as in the paragraph just quoted, writers attentive to the assignment will turn to the characters. But they will insistently link those characters to thematic considerations. It might be well to proceed with a short transitional paragraph that shapes the remainder of the middle of the essay:

Into this smoothly functioning but coldly mechanized society, Ellison introduces three characters: pretty Alice, one of Thoreau's machinelike creatures; the Ticktockman, one of those who "serve the state chiefly with their heads, and, as they rarely make any moral distinctions, they are as likely to serve the Devil without intending it, as God"; and Everett C. Marm, the Harlequin, whose conscience compels him to resist the oppressive state.

The reader will now expect a paragraph devoted to each of the three characters:

Pretty Alice is, doubtless, very pretty. She must be in order to have attracted Everett, because obviously she is neither very bright nor very imaginative. In the brief section in which we meet her, we find her hopelessly ordinary in her attitudes. She is upset that her husband finds it necessary to go about "annoying people." She finds him ridiculous and wishes only that he would stay home, as other people do. Clearly, she has no understanding of what Everett is struggling against. Though her exasperation finally leads her to betray him, Everett himself finds it impossible to believe that she has done so. His own loyal and com-passionate nature colors his view of her so thoroughly that he cannot imagine the treachery that must have been so simple and satisfying for Alice, whose only desire is to be like everybody else.

The Ticktockman is a more complex character. Clearly,

he sees himself as a servant of the state, and he performs his duties with resolution and competence. He skillfully supports a system he has never questioned. The system exists; it must be good. His conscience is simply not involved in the resolute performance of his duty as he sees it. He is one of those who follows orders and expects others to follow orders. As a result, the behavior of the Harlequin is more than just an irritant or a rebellion against authority. It is unnerving. The Ticktockman wishes to understand that behavior, and with Everett's time-card in his hand, he muses that he has the name of "what he is . . . not who he is. . . . Before I can exercise proper revocation, I have to know who this what is." And when he confronts Everett, he does not simply liquidate him. He insists that Everett repent. He attempts to convince Everett that the system is sound, and when he cannot with argument, he dutifully reconditions Everett, since he is, after all, more interested in justifying the system than in simply destroying its enemies. It is easy to see this man as a competent and thoughtful servant of the Devil who thinks he is serving God.

But only Everett C. Marm truly serves the state because his conscience, appalled by the herd mentality that dominates his society, requires him to resist that society. He is certainly not physically heroic. His very name suggests weak conformity. Though he loves his pretty wife, he cannot resign from the rebellious campaign his conscience insists upon. So, without violence, and mainly with the weapon of laughter, he attacks the mechanical precision of the system and succeeds in breaking it down simply by making people late. He is himself, as Alice points out, always late, and the delays that his antics produce seriously threaten the well-being of the smooth but mindless system he hates. He is, of course, captured. He refuses, even then, to submit and has his personality destroyed by the authorities that fear him. The Ticktockman is too strong for him.

An appropriate ending emerges naturally from this student's treatment of the assignment. Having established that the story presents characters who deal in different ways with the oppressive quality of life in a time- and machine-obsessed society, he concludes with his own view of the author's explicit and implicit criticisms of such a society:

Harlequin is defeated, but Ellison, finally, leaves us with an optimistic note. The idea of rebellion against the system will ferment in the minds of others. There will be more Harlequins and more disruption of the oppressive system. Doubtless many rebels will be defeated, but any system that suppresses individualism will give birth to resistance. And Harlequin's defeat is by no means a total defeat. The Ticktockman is already three minutes late.

Writing About Drama

The central problem remains the same regardless of the literary genre you are asked to discuss. You still must find an arguable thesis that deals with the literary sources of your response to the work. Hence, it may be that your essay on a play will be similar in approach to your essay on a story. One can write thematic analyses of both; one can deal with the image patterns in both; one can deal with characterization in both.

Yet playwrights must solve problems that are unique to drama as a literary form that is meant to be acted on a stage before an audience. For example, the mechanics of staging a play limit the extent to which the playwright can shift the locations and times of the action, whereas the writer of fiction can make such shifts very readily with a few words of narration. Similarly, the writer of fiction can, if he wishes, tell the story through a narrator who not only can comment on the meaning of events but can describe the thoughts and motives of some or even all of the characters. In a play, on the other hand, the curtain rises and the characters must convey information through their own words or behavior. The audience does not know what the characters think unless they speak their thoughts aloud. Though as *readers* of a play we may read the stage directions and any other information the author has provided for the director and actors (and perhaps for readers), we must bear in mind that the audience viewing the play cannot know such things as the time of year, the location of the setting, the relationships among characters, or the events that have led up to the action with which the play begins unless someone or something on the stage conveys that information.

Playwrights have developed many techniques for solving their special problems, and you may wish to focus on one of these in your essay about a play. For example, you might explain the role of the Chorus in Sophocles' *Oedipus Rex* or *Antigone* or the dramatic function of messengers in those plays. Or you might explain Tennessee Williams' use of screens in *The Glass Menagerie*, perhaps contrasting this device with the methods a writer of fiction would use to accomplish the same purpose. Or you might argue that the passage of time is distorted for dramatic purposes in Shakespeare's *Othello*. All of these subjects would involve the consideration of problems that are peculiar to the drama as a literary form that is meant to be acted on a stage.

When you confront the assignment to write about a play, put some probing questions about the play to yourself. For instance, what sort of person is Othello? Is he admirable? If so, in what respects? Generous? Wise? Courageous? Fair-minded? What evidence do you find to support your judgment? Does it come from Othello's own speeches and behavior or from what other characters say about him? If the latter, are we meant to take the opinions of those characters as the truth? Is the catastrophic conclusion of the play brought about by some flaw or weakness in Othello or merely by the malice of others?

Of course these questions, which happen to focus on the characterization of Othello, represent only a very few of those you might ask as you think about a play and search for a thesis. If you do choose to deal with some aspect of characterization, you may well find that a minor character interests you more as a subject than a major one. And, as we have suggested, you can also ask questions about imagery, about theme, or about various formal or structural aspects of a play. The point is that if you ask yourself enough questions, you will come up with a thesis that will interest you and that you can argue for and support with evidence in a paper. If you have a thesis that genuinely interests you, and if you take your notes carefully, you will find that everything tends to fall neatly into place as you write.

Writing About Poetry

As with essays about other literary forms, there are many possible approaches to writing about poetry. It is useful, however, to distinguish between two basic types of papers. The first is an *explication,* in which you examine a poem in as much detail as possible, line by line and stanza by stanza, and explain as fully as you can what the poem contains and how it works (how the author's techniques produce the reader's response). An explication is essentially a demonstration of your thorough understanding of the whole poem.

The other type of paper is an *analysis* focusing on a particular aspect or element of a poem or viewing the poem from some particular perspective. For instance, such an analysis might show how a particular pattern of imagery contributes to the meaning of the poem. Or it might argue, from clues within the poem, that the speaker of the poem is a certain kind of character. Or it might demonstrate how the connotations of certain words the poet has chosen to use help to create a particular mood. An analysis may also go outside the poem to throw light on it (see the discussion of sociological criticism, page 1126). For instance, a poem might be analyzed as an embodiment of (or departure from) a particular religious, social, political, or scientific doctrine; as an example of a traditional poetic form such as the ballad or the pastoral elegy; or as a new expression of an ancient myth. These are but a few examples; the possibilities are almost limitless.

You may well be asked to write an explication of a poem (or part of a poem). But even if your assignment is to write an analysis focusing on a particular aspect of a poem, you will first need to explicate the poem for yourself—that is, to engage in that careful response to each word and line of the poem that results in understanding of the whole work—as a basis for further discussion.

Here, then, is a sample essay that explicates a relatively difficult poem, Dylan Thomas' "Do Not Go Gentle into That Good Night." (The poem appears on p. 974.)

Dylan Thomas' villanelle "Do Not Go Gentle into That
Good Night" is addressed to his aged father. The poem
is remarkable in a number of ways, most notably in that
contrary to the most common poetic treatments of the inevitability of death which argue for serenity or celebrate
the peace that death provides, this poem urges resistance
and rage in the face of death. It justifies that unusual
attitude by describing the rage and resistance to death of
four kinds of men, all of whom can summon up the image of a
complete and satisfying life that is denied to them by
death.

The first tercet of the intricately rhymed villanelle
opens with an arresting line. The adjective "gentle"
appears where we would expect the adverb "gently." The
strange diction suggests that "gentle" may describe both
the going (i.e., gently dying) and the person (i.e.,

gentleman) who confronts death. Further, the speaker characterizes "night," here clearly a figure for death, as "good." Yet in the next line, the speaker urges that the aged should violently resist death, characterized as the "close of day" and "the dying of the light." In effect, the first three lines argue that however good death may be, the aged should refuse to die gently, should passionately rave and rage against death.

In the second tercet, the speaker turns to a description of the way the first of four types of men confronts inevitable death (which is figuratively defined throughout the poem as "that good night" and "the dying of the light"). These are the "wise men," the scholars, the philosophers, those who understand the nature and even the necessity of death, men who "know dark is right." But they do not acquiesce in death "because their words had forked no lightning," because their published wisdom failed to bring them to that sense of completeness and fulfillment that can accept death. Therefore, wise as they are, they reject the theoretical "rightness" of death and refuse to "go gentle."

The second sort of men--"good men," the moralists, the social reformers, those who attempt to better the world through action as the wise men attempt to better it through "words"--also rage against death. Their deeds are, after all, "frail." With sea imagery, the speaker suggests that these men might have accomplished fine and fertile things-- their deeds "might have danced in a green bay." But, with the "last wave" gone, they see only the frailty, the impermanence of their acts, and so they, too, rage against the death that deprives them of the opportunity to leave a meaningful legacy.

So, too, the "wild men," the poets who "sang" the loveliness and vitality of nature, learn, as they approach death, that the sensuous joys of human existence wane. As the life-giving sun moves toward dusk, as death approaches, their singing turns to grieving, and they refuse to surrender gently, to leave willingly the warmth and pleasure and beauty that life may entail.

And finally, with a pun suggestive of death, the "grave men," those who go through life with such high seriousness as to never experience gaiety and pleasure, see, as death approaches, all the joyous possibilities that they were blind to in life. And they, too, rage against the dying of a light that they had never properly seen before.

The speaker then calls upon his aged father to join these men in raging against death. It is only in this final stanza that we discover that the entire poem is addressed to the speaker's father and that, despite the generalized statements about old age and the focus upon types of men, the poem is a personal lyric. The edge of death becomes a "sad height," that summit of wisdom and experience old age attains that includes the sad knowledge of life's failure to satisfy the vision we all pursue. The depth and complexity of the speaker's sadness is startlingly given in the second line when he calls upon his father to both curse and bless him. These opposites richly suggest several related possibilities. Curse me for not living up to your expectations. Curse me for remaining alive as you die. Bless me with forgiveness for my failings. Bless me for teaching you to rage against death. And the curses and blessings are contained in the "fierce tears"--fierce because you will burn and rave and rage against death. As the poem closes by bringing together the two powerful refrains, we may reasonably feel that the speaker himself, while not facing imminent death, rages because his father's death will cut off a relationship that is incomplete.

Now let us turn to a paper focusing on a particular aspect of a poem. Suppose, for example, that your assignment is to identify and analyze a significant pattern of imagery in W. B. Yeats' "Sailing to Byzantium" (p. 954). As we noted before, you would have to explicate the poem first. You would have to understand that the speaker is an old man who no longer has any place in the world of nature, the world of the young and the transitory. That is the world of the body, and his body is decaying. He therefore looks to a world beyond time, that world of eternity symbolized by great works of art. He calls upon the "sages" of a Byzantine mosaic (itself one of those enduring works of art) to take him out of the natural world into "the artifice of eternity," where he hopes to become himself an immortal work of art, an exquisitely constructed bird who will sing forever.

Having come to this preliminary understanding of the poem through explication, you might decide that you will write your paper on Yeats' use of bird imagery. You might begin your analysis with an opening paragraph that states the general theme of the poem (along the lines indicated in the previous paragraph) and note that it turns upon a series of contrasts: body/soul, art/life, age/youth, that country/Byzantium. The final sentence of your opening paragraph might focus on the contrast between the real birds (and trees) of line two and the artificial bird of the final stanza. As you plan the details of your analysis of bird imagery (and the related imagery of singing), you quickly discover that most of your attention will be given to stanzas 1, 2, and 4. Stanza 1 powerfully creates the natural world, including real birds that sing in real trees. Stanza 2 extends the bird imagery, this time by implication, as the speaker declares that an aged man who does not rejoice in the decay of his body becomes a scarecrow scaring away birds (who now represent the soul and great works of art). The soul must therefore sing the body's death, and it can only learn such singing by studying the soul's own creations, the great works of art that are "Monuments of its own magnificence." You might mention but not dwell on the reference to "singing-masters" in stanza 3, since it is clearly a part of the pattern of imagery you are analyzing. In the final stanza, the poet, now "out of nature," imagines himself fashioned into an artificial bird (in contrast to the real birds of stanza 1) perched upon an artificial tree, an artist-singer whose songs, whose very form, are "Monuments of unaging intellect" beyond the reach of time's ravages.

Approaching Poetry—Some Questions

If you are asked to write about poetry, you may find that the following questions provide a useful entry into the assignment. Many of the questions will help you to approach writing assignments on drama and fiction as well.

1. Who is the speaker? What does the poem reveal about the speaker's character? In some poems the speaker may be nothing more than a voice meditating on a theme, while in others the speaker takes on specific personality. For example, the speaker in Shelley's "Ozymandias" is a voice meditating on the transitoriness of all things; except for the views he expresses in the poem, we know nothing about his character. The same might be said of the speaker in Hopkins' "Spring and Fall" but with this important exception: we know that he is older than Margaret and therefore has a wisdom she does not.

2. Is the speaker addressing a particular person? If so, who is that person, and why is the speaker interested in him? Many poems, like "Ozymandias," are addressed to no one in particular and therefore to anyone, any reader. Others, such as Donne's "A Valediction: Forbidding Mourning," while addressed to a specific person reveal nothing about that person because the focus of the poem is on the speaker's feelings and attitudes. In a dramatic monologue (see "Glossary of Literary Terms"), there is always at least one auditor whose character will be important to the poem.

3. Does the poem have a setting? Is the poem occasioned by a particular event? The answer to these questions will often be no for lyric poems, such as Frost's "Fire and Ice." It will always be yes if the poem is a dramatic monologue or a poem that tells or implies a story, such as Tennyson's "Ulysses" and Lowell's "Patterns."

4. Is the theme of the poem stated directly or indirectly? Some poems, such as Frost's "Provide, Provide" and Owen's "Dulce Et Decorum Est," use language in a fairly straightforward and literal way and state the theme, often in the final lines. Others, relying more heavily on figurative language and symbolism, may conclude with a statement of the theme that is more difficult to apprehend because it is made with figurative language and symbols. This difference will be readily apparent if you compare the final lines of the Frost and Owen poems mentioned above with, say, the final stanzas of Stevens' "Sunday Morning."

5. If the speaker is describing specific events, from what perspective (roughly similar to point of view in fiction) is he doing so? Is he recounting events of the past or events that are occurring in the present? If he is recalling past events, what present meaning do they have for him? These questions are particularly appropriate to the works in the section "Innocence and Experience," many of which contrast an early innocence with adult experience.

6. Does a close examination of the figurative language (see "Glossary of Literary Terms") of the poem reveal any patterns? This can be an especially useful approach with difficult and highly symbolic poems. Yeats' "Sailing to Byzantium" may begin to open up to you once you recognize the pattern of bird imagery. Likewise, Thomas' attitude toward his childhood in "Fern Hill" will be clearer if you detect the pattern of Biblical imagery that associates childhood with Adam and Eve before the fall.

7. What is the structure of the poem? A poem that tells or implies a story, such as a ballad like "Bonny Barbara Allan" or Brooks' "The Sundays of Satin-Legs Smith," will have a beginning, middle, and end. Since any narrative involves a high degree of selectivity, it is useful to ask why the poet has focused on particular details and left out others. Analyzing the structure of a nonnarrative or lyric poem can be more difficult because it does not contain an obvious series of chronologically related events. The structure of Thomas' "Fern Hill," for example, is based in part on a description of perhaps a day and a half in the speaker's life as a child. But more significant in terms of its structure is the speaker's present realization that the immortality he felt as a child was merely a stage in the inexorable movement of life toward death. The structure of the poem, therefore, will be revealed through an analysis of patterns of images (Biblical, color, day and night, dark and light) that embody the theme. To take another example, Marvell's "To His Coy Mistress" is divided into three verse paragraphs, the opening words of each ("Had we . . . ," "But . . . ," "Now therefore . . .") suggesting a logically constructed argument.

8. What do sound and meter (see "Glossary of Literary Terms") contribute to the poem? Alexander Pope said that in good poetry "the sound must seem an echo to the sense," a statement that is sometimes easier to agree with than to demonstrate. For sample analyses of the music of poetry, see the section on music in the appendix "Reading Poetry" (p. 1106) and the discussion of "Dover Beach" under formalist criticism (p. 1121) in "Three Critical Approaches."

9. What was your response to the poem on first reading? Did your response change after rereadings and study of the poem?

A Final Word

Many questions may be asked about literature. Your assignment may require you to compare and contrast literary works, to analyze the language of a work, to discuss the interaction of parts of a work, to discuss the theme of a work. Sometimes the instructor may give you free choice and ask simply that you write an essay on one of the pieces you read. This liberty will require that you create your own feasible boundaries—you will have to find a specific focus that suits the piece you choose and is manageable within a paper of the assigned length. But be sure that you do create boundaries—that, as we urged at the outset, you have a clear thesis.

Give yourself time. If you attempt to write your paper the night before it is due, you are unlikely to write a paper that is worth the time to read it. Even professional writers rarely accomplish serious and thoughtful writing overnight. You must give yourself time to think before you write a draft. Let the draft age a bit before rewriting a final draft. If you do not allow yourself a reasonable time period, you will convert an assignment that has the potential to enlarge your understanding and to produce real pleasure into an obstacle that you will surely trip over.

Consider also that finally *you* have to feel something, know something, bring something of yourself to the assignment. We can discuss formal methods for dealing with the problem of writing essays—but if you bring neither awareness, nor information, nor genuine interest to the task, the essay will remain an empty form.

Some Matters of Form

Titles

The first word and all main words of titles are capitalized. Ordinarily (unless, of course, they are the first or last word), articles (*a, an,* and *the*), prepositions (*in, on, of, with, about,* etc.), and conjunctions (*and, but, or,* etc.) are not capitalized.

The titles of parts of a larger collection, such as short stories and poems (as well as articles, essays, and songs) are enclosed in quotation marks.

The titles of plays, books, movies, and periodicals (as well as of operas, paintings, and newspapers) are italicized. In typed and handwritten manuscripts, italics are represented by underlining.

The title you give your own essay is neither placed in quotation marks nor underlined. However, a quotation used as a part of your title would be enclosed in quotation marks (see the following section on quotations). Similarly, the title of a literary work used as a part of your title would be either placed in quotation marks or underlined (see the two paragraphs just above).

Quotations

Quotation marks indicate you are transcribing someone else's words; those words must, therefore, be reproduced *exactly* as they appear in your source.

As a general rule, quotations of not more than four lines of prose or two lines of poetry are placed between quotation marks and incorporated in your own text:

```
At the climactic moment, Robin observes "an uncovered

cart.  There the torches blazed the brightest, there

the moon shone out like day, and there, in tar-and-

feathery dignity, sat his kinsman, Major Molineux!"
```

If you are quoting two lines of verse in your text, indicate the division between lines with a slash:

```
Prufrock hears the dilletantish talk in a room where

"the women come and go / Talking of Michelangelo."
```

Longer quotations are indented and single spaced. They are not enclosed in quotation marks, since the indentation signals a quotation.

As noted above, anything enclosed in quotation marks must be reproduced exactly. If you insert anything—even a word—the inserted material must be in square brackets. If you wish to omit some material from a passage in quotation marks, the omission (ellipsis) must be indicated by three . . . spaced periods (an ellipsis mark). If the words preceding the ellipsis form a complete sentence (whether or not it was a complete sentence in the original), place a period at the end of the sentence and follow the period with the ellipsis mark—that is, you'll have four periods with no space before the first, which is simply the period at the end of the sentence.

Original:

"Richard Wright, like Dostoevsky before him, sends his

hero underground to discover the truth about the upper

world, a world that has forced him to confess to a

crime he has not committed."

With insertion and omissions:

"Richard Wright . . . sends his hero [Fred Daniels]

underground to discover the truth about the upper

world. . . ."

Use a full line of spaced periods to indicate the omission of a line or more of poetry (or of a whole paragraph or more of prose):

For I have known them all already, known them all--

Have known the evenings, mornings, afternoons,

I have measured out my life with coffee spoons;

. . . .

And I have known the eyes already, known them all--

The eyes that fix you in a formulated phrase,

Periods and commas are placed *inside* quotation marks:

In "My Oedipus Complex," the narrator says, "The war

was the most peaceful period of my life."

Other punctuation marks go outside the quotation marks unless they are part of the material being quoted.

Always provide the line numbers for poetry quotations and page references for prose (see the following section on footnotes). Line and page references for short quotations incorporated into your text are given in parentheses immediately following the quotation:

```
With ironic detachment, Prufrock declares that he is

"no prophet" (l. 83).
```

For a long quotation set off from your text, the line or page reference may be placed in a footnote or, preferably, in parentheses at the end of the sentence in your text that introduces the quotation:

```
Prufrock's attitude toward the society he moves in is

made powerfully clear when he says (ll. 49-60):
```

Page references are given to the page numbers of your source, which should be identified so that your reader may follow up the reference if he wishes (see the following section on footnotes). If you are using the text of a story in this anthology, you will cite the appropriate page number of this anthology.

Footnotes

A footnote is a way of acknowledging the source of ideas you paraphrase and material you quote. Such acknowledgements (citations) are extremely important, for even an unintentional failure to give formal credit to others for their words or ideas can leave you open to an accusation of plagiarism—the presentation of someone else's idea as your own.

However, footnotes are not the only way of making such acknowledgements. Often citations can more smoothly be worked directly into the text of your paper. Or part of the citation may be given in the text, in which case only the remaining part need be in a footnote. For example, if you were to quote from James Joyce's "Araby" in this anthology, and you identified the author and title in introducing the quotation, your footnote could omit the author and title and would look like this:

```
    1 Reprinted in Richard Abcarian and Marvin Klotz,
Literature: The Human Experience, 2nd ed. (New York:
St. Martin's Press, 1978), p. 68.
```

If your paper makes repeated reference to the same story, you need not repeat the footnote each time. Instead, simply add a line to this first footnote stating that all references to "Araby" are to pages in this anthology:

> ¹ Reprinted in Richard Abcarian and Marvin Klotz, <u>Literature: The Human Experience</u>, 2nd ed. (New York: St. Martin's Press, 1978), p. 68. All further page references to this work are to this anthology.

Thereafter, you need give only parenthetical page references (or, for poetry, line references) within the text. You can assume that your reader has read the footnote.

Of course, if you do not identify the author and title of a work within the text of your essay, you will need to include that information in the footnote:

> ¹ James Joyce, "Araby," reprinted in [and so forth].

You will have noticed that a footnote for a book includes the following information: author, title, city of publication, publisher, date of publication, and page number of the material you have used. There are various footnote forms, but the following is standard:

> ² Philip Wheelwright, <u>The Burning Fountain</u> (Bloomington: Indiana University Press, 1954), pp. 30-32.

A reference to an article from a periodical should include author, title of the article, title of the journal, volume number, year, and page reference (but, as a matter of convention, without the abbreviation for page):

> ³ A. M. Tibbets, "Stephen Crane's 'The Bride Comes Comes to Yellow Sky,'" <u>English Journal</u>, 54 (April 1965), 314-316.

Note that the title of the article is in quotation marks and the title of the journal is underlined.

It is possible in a brief discussion like this to cover only the essentials of footnoting. Chances are that the information provided here will be sufficient for your purposes. If, however, you require additional information or merely want to explore the fine points, your instructor can guide you to publications in your college library that explain and give examples of footnote forms for almost every imaginable situation. The main thing to remember about footnoting, and about citations in general, is that the object is to give credit to others wherever it is due and to enable your reader to go directly to your sources, if he wishes to do so, as quickly and easily as possible.

Summing Up: A Checklist

1. Start early. You're going to need time for thinking, time for reading and taking notes, time for writing, and (very important) time for breaks between steps.

2. Read the literary work carefully, and more than once.

3. If you are allowed to choose a topic, choose one that interests you and that you can explore in some depth in a paper of the assigned length. If you have trouble finding a topic, ask yourself as many questions as you can about the work: *What* is it about? *Who* is it about? *Why* do I respond to it as I do? And so forth. Many kinds of questions have been suggested in the preceding pages, and there are more following the selections, and at the ends of the four main sections, in this anthology.

4. Convert your topic into a clearly defined thesis: a proposition you intend to argue for and support with evidence from the work. If you have trouble shaping a thesis, try the technique of free writing—forget about form and just scribble down all your thoughts and opinions: what you like, what you don't like, anything at all. Then ask yourself what made you think or feel as you do.

5. Once you have a thesis, reread the work and take careful notes on 3″ × 5″ cards, one note to a card, with a page (or, for poetry, line) reference and a short descriptive heading to remind you of the note's significance. Then arrange the cards in the order that seems appropriate to follow in your essay.

6. Start writing, and keep going. This is a rough draft—essentially a blueprint—and is for your eyes only, so don't worry much about formalities and polishing. The point is to get your ideas down on paper in approximately the right order. If making a rough outline first will help you, do it. If spontaneous writing works better, do that. But do get a clear statement of your thesis into your first paragraph; it will guide you as you write, since everything you write will (or should) be related to it.

7. Take a break. Let the rough draft cool for at least a few hours, preferably overnight. When you come back to it you'll be refreshed and you'll think more clearly. You may find that you want to do some reorganizing or add or delete material. You may also want to go back and reread or at least take another look at the literary work you're writing about.

8. Now, more carefully, working from your rough draft, write a second draft. This will be fuller, clearer, more polished. You'll have a chance to revise (assuming you followed step 1, above), so don't get unnecessarily bogged down; but do write this version *as if* it were the version your reader would see. This version, when finished, should be logically and clearly organized. The point of each paragraph should be clear—well expressed and well supported by details or examples—and its relationship to the thesis should be apparent. Transitions between paragraphs should be supplied wherever necessary to make the argument progress smoothly. Quotations should be in place, accurately transcribed.

9. Take a break. This time let the draft age for two or three days. At the moment, you're too close to the draft to read it objectively.

10. Pick up the draft as if you were the reader and had never seen it before. Now you will make your final revisions. More than polishing is involved

here. This is the time to cut out, mercilessly, things that are not pertinent to your discussion, no matter how interesting or well written they may be. Putting yourself in your reader's place, clarify anything that is vague or ambiguous. Make sure each word is the most precise one you could have chosen for your purpose. Watch, too, for overkill—points that are driven into the ground by too much discussion or detail. Finally, no matter how careful you think you have been, check all your quotations and citations for accuracy. Instructors—rightly—take these things seriously.

11. Type or neatly write out in ink the final copy for submission to your instructor, taking care to follow any special instructions about format that you have been given. Don't rush; be meticulous. When you have finished, proofread the final copy very carefully, keeping an eye out for errors in spelling or punctuation, omitted words, disagreement between subjects and verbs or between pronouns and antecedents, and other flaws (such as typographical errors) that will detract from what you have worked so hard to write.

Glossary of Literary Terms

Alexandrine See Meter.

Allegory A form of symbolism in which ideas or abstract qualities are represented as characters in a narrative and dramatic situation, resulting in a moral or philosophic statement.

> *Everyman,* p. 985
> Ingmar Bergman, *The Seventh Seal,* p. 1038

Alliteration The repetition within a line or phrase of the same initial consonant sound.

> Death, thou shalt die.—John Donne, "Death, Be Not Proud," l. 14, p. 939
> And mouth with myriad subtleties—Paul Laurence Dunbar, "We Wear the Mask," l. 5, p. 411

Allusion A reference, explicit or indirect, to something outside the work itself. The reference is usually to some famous person, event, or other literary work.

> No! I am not Prince Hamlet, nor was meant to be—T. S. Eliot, "The Love Song of J. Alfred Prufrock," l. 111, p. 640
> W. H. Auden, title of "The Unknown Citizen," p. 421

Ambiguity A phrase, statement, or situation that may be understood in two or more ways. As a literary device, it is used to enrich meaning or achieve irony.

> my Uncle Sol imitated the
> skunks in a subtle manner
>
> or by drowning himself in the watertank—E. E. Cummings, "nobody loses all the time," ll. 24–26, p. 967

Anapest See Meter.

Antistrophe See Strophe.

Apostrophe A direct address to a person who is absent or to an abstract or inanimate entity.

> How oft, in spirit, have I turned thee,
> O sylvan Wye! thou wanderer through the woods—William Wordsworth, "Lines Composed a Few Miles Above Tintern Abbey," ll. 55–56, p. 128
> Christina Rosetti, "Rest," p. 953
> John Donne, "Death, Be Not Proud," p. 939

Archetype Themes, images, and narrative patterns that are universal and thus embody some enduring aspects of man's experience. Some of these themes are the death and rebirth of the hero, the underground journey, and the search for the father.

Assonance The repetition of vowel sounds in a line, stanza, or sentence.

> His lesions are legion—Gwendolyn Brooks, "The Children of the Poor," Stanza II, l. 17, p. 427
> W. H. Auden, *from* "Five Songs," p. 642

Ballad A narrative poem, originally of folk origin, usually focusing upon a climactic episode and told without comment. The most common form is a quatrain of alternating four- and three-stress iambic lines, with the second and fourth lines rhyming. Typically the ballad will employ a *refrain*—that is, the last line of each stanza will be identical (or virtually identical), but each repetition somehow advances the story.

> "Edward," p. 935
> "Bonny Barbara Allan," p. 611

Blank Verse Lines of unrhymed iambic pentameter.

> William Wordsworth, "Lines Composed a Few Miles Above Tintern Abbey," p. 127

Cacophony The use of harsh and discordant language. *Compare* Euphony.

> Is perjured, murderous, bloody, full of blame,
> Savage, extreme, rude, cruel, not to trust—William Shakespeare, Sonnet 129, ll. 3–4, p. 616

Caesura A strong phrasal pause within a line of verse.

> There is a loveliness exists.
> Preserves us.//Not for specialists.—W. D. Snodgrass, "April Inventory," ll. 59–60, p. 157

Carpe Diem Latin, meaning "seize the day." A work, generally a lyric poem, in which the speaker calls the attention of his auditor (often a young girl) to the shortness of life and youth and then urges her to enjoy life while there is time.

> Andrew Marvell, "To His Coy Mistress," p. 624
> Robert Herrick, "Corinna's Going A-Maying," p. 620

Catharsis One of the key concepts in *The Poetics* of Aristotle by which he attempts to account for the fact that representations of suffering and death in drama paradoxically leave the audience feeling relieved rather than depressed. According to Aristotle, a tragic hero arouses in the viewer feelings of "pity and fear," pity because he is a man of great moral worth and fear because the viewer sees himself in the hero.

Central Intelligence *See* Point of View.

Comedy In drama, situations that are designed to delight and amuse rather than concern or sadden. Comic heroes rise in the course of the action from a low to a higher position. Comedy is usually concerned with social values. *Compare* Tragedy.

Conceit A figure of speech that establishes an elaborate parallel between unlike things.

> John Donne, "A Valediction: Forbidding Mourning," ll. 25–36, p. 620

Conflict The struggle of a protagonist, or main character, with forces that must be subdued. The struggle creates suspense and is usually resolved at the end of the story. The force opposing the main character may be either another person—the antagonist—(as in O'Connor's "My Oedipus Conflict"), or society (as in Ellison's "'Repent, Harlequin!' Said the Ticktockman"), or natural forces (as in Malamud's "Idiots First"), or an internal conflict within the main character (as in Conrad's "The Secret Sharer").

Connotation The associative and suggestive meanings of a word in contrast to its literal meaning. *Compare* Denotation.

Consonance Repetition of the final consonant sounds in stressed syllables.

> That night when joy began
> Our narrowest veins to flush,
> We waited for the flash
> Of morning's levelled gun—W. H. Auden, *from* "Five Songs," ll. 1–4, p. 642

Couplet A pair of rhymed lines.

> Cease then, nor ORDER imperfection name:
> Our proper bliss depends on what we blame.—Alexander Pope, *from* "An Essay on Man," ll. 1–2, p. 402

Dactyl *See* Meter.

Denotation The literal, dictionary definition of a word. *Compare* Connotation.

Denouement The final outcome or unraveling of the main conflict of a story; literally, "untying."

Diction   The choice of words in a work of literature, generally applied to indicate such distinctions as abstrct or concrete, formal or colloquial, literal or figurative.

Didactic   A work whose primary and avowed purpose is to teach or to persuade the reader of the truth of some philosophical, religious, or moral statement or doctrine.

Dimeter   *See* Meter.

Dramatic Distance   In fiction, the point of view which enables the reader to know more than the narrator of the story.

Dramatic Irony   *See* Irony.

Dramatic Monologue   A type of poem in which the speaker, who is not the poet, addresses another person (or persons) whose presence is known only from the speaker's words. Such poems are dramatic because the speaker interacts with another character at a specific time and place; they are monologues because the entire poem is uttered by the speaker.

> Robert Browning, "My Last Duchess," p. 131
> Matthew Arnold, "Dover Beach," p. 630
> T. S. Eliot, "The Love Song of J. Alfred Prufrock," p. 637

Elegy   Usually a poem lamenting the death of a particular person, but often used to describe meditative poems on the subject of man's mortality.

> W. H. Auden, "In Memory of W. B. Yeats," p. 968
> Thomas Gray, "Elegy Written in a Country Churchyard," p. 940

End-rhyme   *See* Rhyme.

End-stopped Line   A line of verse that constitutes a complete logical and grammatical unit. A line of verse that does not constitute a complete syntactic unit is designated *run-on*. Thus in the opening lines of Browning's "My Last Duchess"·

> That's my last Duchess painted on the wall,
> Looking as if she were alive. I call
> That piece a wonder, now: . . .

The opening line is end-stopped, while the second line is run-on, because the direct object of *call* "runs on" to the third line.

English Sonnet   *See* Sonnet.

Epode   *See* Strophe.

Euphony   Sounds that are pleasing to the ear. *Compare* Cacophony.

> Wallace Stevens, "Peter Quince at the Clavier," ll. 1–9, p. 148

Figurative Language   A general term covering the many ways in which language is used nonliterally. *See* Hyperbole, Irony, Metaphor, Metonymy, Paradox, Simile, Symbol, Synecdoche, Understatement.

First-person Narrator   *See* Point of View.

Foot   *See* Meter.

Free Verse   Poetry that does not adhere to the metric regularity of traditional verse and that is usually unrhymed.

> Walt Whitman, "Out of the Cradle Endlessly Rocking," p. 133

Hexameter   *See* Meter.

Hubris   In Greek tragedy, overweening pride usually exhibited in a character's defiance of the gods. Oedipus, in Sophocles' *Oedipus Rex,* is guilty of hubris.

Hyperbole   Exaggeration; overstatement. *Compare* Understatement.

> on freeways fifty lanes wide—Lawrence Ferlinghetti, "In Goya's Greatest Scenes," l. 28, p. 432
> Robert Burns, "A Red, Red Rose," p. 627

Iamb   *See* Meter.

Imagery   Language that embodies an appeal to the senses: sight, sound, smell, taste, or touch.

> Thom Gunn, "Innocence," last two stanzas, p. 158
> William Shakespeare, Sonnet 18, p. 615
> William Shakespeare, Sonnet 130, p. 617
> Robert Frost, "Birches," p. 146
> Wallace Stevens, "Peter Quince at the Clavier," p. 148

Internal Rhyme   *See* Rhyme.

Irony   Language in which the intended meaning is different from or opposite to the literal meaning. Verbal irony includes overstatement (hyperbole), understatement, and opposite statement.

> Had it any been but she,
>   And that very face,
> There had been at least ere this
>   A dozen dozen in her place.—Sir John Suckling, "Out upon It!" p. 624
> The grave's a fine and private place,
> But none, I think, do there embrace.—Andrew Marvell, "To His Coy Mistress," ll. 31–32, p. 625
> Was he free? Was he happy? The question is absurd:
> Had anything been wrong, we should certainly have heard.—W. H. Auden, "The Unknown Citizen," ll. 28–29, p. 422

Dramatic irony occurs when a reader knows things a character is ignorant of or when the speech and action of a character reveal him to be different from what he himself believes to be.

> William Blake, "The Chimney Sweeper," p. 123
> Robert Browning, "My Last Duchess," p. 131
> William Shakespeare, *Othello,* Act III, Scene 3, p. 694

Italian Sonnet   *See* Sonnet.

Lyric   Originally, a song accompanied by lyre music. Now, a relatively short poem expressing the thought or feeling of a single speaker.

> Joni Mitchell, "The Circle Game," p. 166

Metaphor   A figurative expression consisting of two elements in which one element is provided with special attributes by being equated with a second unlike element.

> If only I could nudge you from this sleep,
> My maimed darling, my skittery pigeon—Theodore Roethke, "Elegy for Jane," ll. 18–19, p. 971

Meter   Refers to recurrent patterns of accented and unaccented syllables in verse. A metrical unit is called a *foot,* and there are four basic accented patterns. An *iamb,* or *iambic foot,* consists of an unaccented syllable followed by an accented syllable (bĕfóre, tŏdáy). A *trochee,* or *trochaic foot,* consists of an accented syllable followed by an unaccented syllable (fúnnў, phántŏm). An *anapest,* or *anapestic foot,* consists of two unaccented syllables followed by an accented syllable (in the line "Ĭf ĕv́| ĕrўthĭng háp| pĕns thăt cán't | bĕ dóne," the second and third metrical feet are anapests). A *dactyl,* or *dactyllic foot,* consists of a stressed syllable followed by two unstressed syllables (sýllăblĕ, métrĭcăl). One common variant, consisting of two stressed syllables, is called a *spondee,* or *spondaic foot* (dáybŕeak, moónshíne).

> Lines are named by virtue of the number of metrical feet they contain.

one foot	monometer
two feet	dimeter

three feet	trimeter
four feet	tetrameter
five feet	pentameter
six feet	hexameter (An iambic hexameter line is an *Alexandrine.*)

Here are some examples of various metrical patterns:

Tŏ eách | hiš súff| erĭngs: áll | aře mén,   iambic tetrameter
Cŏndemíned | ălikè | tŏ grŏán;   iambic trimeter
Ońce ŭp| ón ă | mídnĭght | dréaŕy, | whíle Ī | póndeřed | wéak ănd |
   wéaŕy,   trochaic octameter (with a spondee in the third foot)
Iš thís | thĕ rég| iŏn, thís | thĕ soíl, | thĕ clíme,   iambic pentameter
Fóllŏw ĭt | uttĕrlỹ,   dactyllic dimeter
Hópe bĕ| yond hopé: dimeter line—trochee and spondee

Metonymy A figure of speech in which a word stands for a closely related idea. In the expression "the pen is mightier than the sword," *pen* and *sword* are metonymies for written ideas and military force respectively.

> Free hearts, free foreheads—you and I are old—Alfred, Lord Tennyson, "Ulysses," l. 49, p. 404
> They are sick of the palette and fiddle-bow—William Butler Yeats, "Lapis Lazuli," l. 2, p. 144

Monometer *See* Meter.

Near Rhyme *See* Rhyme

Octave *See* Sonnet.

Ode Usually a long, serious poem on exalted subjects, often in the form of an address.
> John Keats, "Ode to a Nightingale," p. 944

Off Rhyme *See* Rhyme.

Omniscient Narrator *See* Point of View.

Onomatopoeia Language that sounds like what it means. Words like *buzz, bark,* and *hiss* are onomatopoetic. Also, sound patterns that reinforce the meaning over one or more lines may be designated onomatopoetic.

> Is lust in action; and till action, lust
> Is perjured, murderous, bloody, full of blame—William Shakespeare, Sonnet 129, ll. 2–4, p. 616
> Wallace Stevens, "Peter Quince at the Clavier," stanza one, p. 148

Opposite Statement *See* Irony.

Overstatement *See* Hyperbole.

Paradox A statement that seems self-contradictory or absurd but is, somehow, valid.
> And death shall be no more; Death, thou shalt die—John Donne, "Death, Be Not Proud," l. 14, p. 939
> William Butler Yeats, "Lapis Lazuli," p. 144

Pentameter *See* Meter.

Persona Literally "mask." The term is used to describe a narrator in fiction (Sherwood Anderson's "I Want to Know Why") or the speaker in a poem (Robert Browning's "My Last Duchess"). The persona's views are different from the author's views.

Personification The attribution of human qualities to nature, animals, or things.
> Edmund Waller, "Go, Lovely Rose!" p. 622
> John Donne, "Death, Be Not Proud," p. 939

Petrarchan Sonnet *See* Sonnet.

Plot A series of actions in a story or a drama which bear a significant relationship to each other. E. M. Forster illuminates the definition: " 'The King died, and then the Queen died,' is a story. 'The King died and then the Queen died of grief,' is a plot."

Point of View The person or intelligence a writer of fiction creates to tell the story to the reader. The major techniques are:

First person, where the story is told by someone, often, though not necessarily, the principal character, who identifies himself as "I."

Sherwood Anderson, "I Want to Know Why," p. 61

Third person, where the story is told by someone (not identified as "I") who is not a participant in the action and who refers to the characters by name or as "he," "she," and "they."

Harlan Ellison, " 'Repent, Harlequin!' said the Ticktockman," p. 391

Omniscient, a variation on the third person, where the narrator knows everything about the characters and events, can move about in time and place as well as from character to character at will, and can, whenever he wishes, enter the mind of any character.

Leo Tolstoy, "The Death of Iván Ilých," p. 852

Central intelligence, another variation on the third person, where narrative elements are limited to what a single character sees, thinks, and hears.

Richard Wright, "The Man Who Lived Underground," p. 339

Quatrain A four-line stanza that may incorporate various metrical patterns.

"Bonny Barbara Allan," p. 611

Thomas Gray, "Elegy Written in a Country Churchyard," p. 940

Refrain *See* Ballad.

Rhyme The repetition of the final stressed vowel sound and any sounds following (debate, relate; pelican, belly can) produces perfect rhyme. When rhyming words appear at the end of lines, the poem is *end-rhymed.* When rhyming words appear within one line, the line contains *internal rhyme.* When the correspondence in sounds is imperfect (heaven, given; began, gun), *off rhyme,* or *near rhyme,* is produced.

Off rhyme: W. H. Auden, *from* "Five Songs," p. 642

Rhythm The alternation of accented and unaccented syllables in language. A regular pattern of alternation produces *meter.* Irregular alternation of stressed and unstressed syllables produces *free verse.*

Run-on Line *See* End-stopped Line.

Satire Writing in a comic mode that holds a subject up to scorn and ridicule, often with the purpose of correcting human vice and folly.

E. E. Cummings, "the Cambridge ladies who live in furnished souls," p. 419

W. H. Auden, "The Unknown Citizen," p. 421

Robert Frost, "Departmental," p. 414

Harlan Ellison, " 'Repent, Harlequin!' Said the Ticktockman," p. 391

Scansion The process of analyzing the metrical or rhythmical pattern of a poem.

Th' ĕxpénse| ŏf spír| ĭt ĭn| ă wáste| ŏf sháme

Ĭs lúst| ĭn ác| tiŏn,|| ănd tĭll ác| tiŏn, lúst

Ĭs pér| jurĕd, múr| derŏus, bloŏd| y̆, fúll| ŏf bláme,

Sávăge,| ĕxtréme,| rúde, crú| ĕl, nót| tŏ trúst:

In this excerpt from one of Shakespeare's sonnets, the dominant meter is iambic pentameter, but variations occur in every line. A strong caesura occurs in the middle of the second line.

Sestet   *See* Sonnet.

Setting   The place where the story occurs. Often the setting contributes significantly to the total impact of the story; for example, the dank world of the sewers that Fred Daniels inhabits in "The Man Who Lived Underground" enables him to understand his relationship with the upper world.

Shakespearean Sonnet   *See* Sonnet.

Simile   A figurative expression in which an element is provided with special attributes through a comparison with something quite different. The words *like* or *as* create the comparison, e.g. "My love is like a red, red rose," "As virtuous men pass mildly away . . . so let us melt, and make no noise."

> John Donne, "A Valediction: Forbidding Mourning," p. 619
> Robert Burns, "A Red, Red Rose," p. 627

Soliloquy   A dramatic convention in which an actor, alone on the stage, speaks his thoughts aloud.

> William Shakespeare, *Othello,* Iago's speech, Act I, Scene 3, p. 664

Sonnet   A lyric poem of fourteen lines, usually of iambic pentameter. The two major types are the Petrarchan (or Italian) and Shakespearean (or English). The *Petrarchan sonnet* is divided into an octave (the first eight lines, rhymed abbaabba) and a sestet (the final six lines, usually rhymed cdecde or cdcdcd). The *Shakespearean sonnet* consists of three quatrains and a concluding couplet, rhymed abab cdcd efef gg.

> William Shakespeare, Sonnets, pp. 615–617
> Christina Rossetti, "Rest," p. 953

Spondee   *See* Meter.

Stanza   The grouping of the lines of a poem In a recurring pattern of meter, rhyme, and number of lines. Among the most common are the *couplet* and the *quatrain.*

Stream of Consciousness   The narrative technique of some modern fiction which attempts to reproduce the full and uninterrupted flow of a character's mental process, in which ideas, memories, and sense impressions may intermingle without logical transitions. A characteristic of this technique is the abandonment of conventional rules of syntax and punctuation.

> Katherine Anne Porter, "The Jilting of Granny Weatherall," p. 902

Strophe   In Greek tragedy, the unit of verse the chorus chanted as it moved to the left in a dance rhythm. The chorus sang the *antistrophe* as it moved to the right and the *epode* while standing still.

Symbol   A thing or an action that embodies more than its literal, concrete meaning.

> Alastair Reid, "Curiosity," p. 155
> J. Peter Meinke, "Advice to My Son," p. 160

Synecdoche   A figure of speech in which a part is used to signify the whole.

> Perhaps in this neglected spot is laid
>   Some heart once pregnant with celestial fire;
> Hands that the rod of empire might have swayed,
>   Or waked to ecstacy the living lyre.—Thomas Gray, "Elegy Written in a
>   Country Churchyard," ll. 45–48, p. 941

Synesthesia   In literature, the description of one kind of sensory experience in terms of another. Taste might be described as a color or a song.

> John Keats, "Ode to a Nightingale," stanza two, p. 945

Tetrameter   *See* Meter.

Theme   The moral proposition that a literary work is designed to advance. The theme of Milton's *Paradise Lost* is to "justify the ways of God to men." The theme of Joseph

Conrad's "The Secret Sharer" might be briefly stated: The recognition of complex moral ambiguities is essential to maturity.

Third-person Narrator   *See* Point of View

Tone   The attitude embodied in the language a writer chooses. The tone of a work might be sad, joyful, ironic, solemn, playful.

> Compare: Matthew Arnold, "Dover Beach," p. 630, with Anthony Hecht, "The Dover Bitch," p. 644.

Tragedy   The dramatic representation of serious and important actions which bring misfortune to the chief character. Aristotle saw tragedy as the fall of a noble figure from a high position as the result of a flaw in his character. *Compare* Comedy.

Trimeter   *See* Meter.

Trochee   *See* Meter.

Understatement   A figure of speech that represents something as less important than it really is. *Compare* Hyperbole.

> . . . This grew; I gave commands;
> Then all smiles stopped together. . . .—Robert Browning, "My Last Duchess," ll. 45–46, p. 132

Villanelle   A French verse form of nineteen lines (of any length) divided into six stanzas—five triplets and a final quatrain—employing two rhymes and two refrains. The refrains consist of lines one (repeated as lines six, twelve, and eighteen) and three (repeated as lines nine, fifteen, and nineteen).

> Dylan Thomas "Do Not Go Gentle into That Good Night," p. 974
> Catherine Davis, "After a Time," p. 979

Recordings and Films

The catalogs of the following companies and agencies list a surprisingly comprehensive set of recordings (on records, tapes, and cassettes) of early poetry read by performers and recent poetry read by poets. Several of the plays included in this anthology have also been recorded.

Caedmon Records, 505 Eighth Ave., New York, N.Y. 10018: offers recordings of *A Doll's House, The Misanthrope, Othello, Antigone,* and *Oedipus Rex.*
The Library of Congress, Music Division, Recording Laboratory, Washington, D.C. 20540: features modern poetry.
Superintendent of Documents, U.S. Government Printing Office, Washington, D.C. 20402: Write for the catalog of the Library of Congress Tapes Archives (there is a small charge). The catalog lists a great number of taped poetry readings.
Spoken Arts, Inc., 59 Locust Ave., New Rochelle, N.Y. 10801

Catalogs listing films that bear on the teaching of poetry may be obtained from: NET Film Service, Indiana University, Audio Visual Center, Bloomington, Ind. 47401; Encyclopaedia Britannica Educational Corp., 425 N. Michigan Ave., Chicago, Ill. 60611; McGraw-Hill/Contemporary Films, 1221 Ave. of the Americas, New York, N.Y. 10020.

A comprehensive catalog of educational films is published by the National Information Center for Educational Media (NICEM), University of Southern California, University Park, Los Angeles, Calif. 90007.

Sixteen mm. films of works in this anthology available for rental:

The Lesson, from Grove Press Cinema 16 Film Library, 196 W. Houston St., New York, N.Y. 10014
Oedipus Rex (four 30-minute lessons), from Encyclopaedia Britannica Educational Corp., 425 N. Michigan Ave., Chicago, Ill. 60611
A Doll's House, from Learning Corp. of America, 1350 Ave. of the Americas, New York, N.Y. 10019
Othello (Russian version, English dialogue), from Audio/Brandon, 1619 North Cherokee, Los Angeles, Calif. 90028.
Othello (Olivier version), from Warner Bros. Film Rental, 4000 Warner Blvd., Burbank, Calif. 91522

The Lottery, from Encyclopaedia Britannica Educational Corp., 425 N. Michigan Ave., Chicago, Ill. 60611

An Occurrence at Owl Creek Bridge, from Contemporary Films/McGraw-Hill, 1221 Ave. of the Americas, New York, N.Y. 10020

Face to Face ("The Secret Sharer" and "The Bride Comes to Yellow Sky"), from Willoughby-Peerless Film Library, 415 Lexington Ave., New York, N.Y. 10017

Good Country People, from Jeff Jackson, 29023 Viewdrive, Agoura, Calif. 91301

The Masque of the Red Death, from Macmillan Films, Inc.—CCM Films, 34 MacQuesten Parkway S., Mt. Vernon, N.Y. 10550

The Seventh Seal, from Janus Films, 745 Fifth Ave., New York, N.Y. 10022

Index of Authors and Titles

ACKNOWLEDGMENTS (CONTINUED FROM PAGE X)

VANDERBILT UNIVERSITY PRESS: "To a Child Born in Time of Small War," © 1966, and "From a Correct Address in a Suburb of a Major City," © 1971, from *Seeds As They Fall* by Helen Sorrells. Copyright in the name of Helen Sorrells, 1971. Published by Vanderbilt University Press, Nashville, Tennessee.

THE VIKING PRESS INC.: "Araby" from *Dubliners* by James Joyce. Originally published by B. W. Huebsch, Inc. in 1916. Copyright © 1967 by the Estate of James Joyce. All rights reserved. Reprinted by permission of The Viking Press.

"The Horse-Dealer's Daughter" by D. H. Lawrence. From *The Complete Short Stories of D. H. Lawrence,* Vol. II. Copyright 1922 by Thomas B. Seltzer Inc., 1950 by Frieda Lawrence. Reprinted by permission of The Viking Press.

WARNER BROS. MUSIC: "Blowin' In the Wind" by Bob Dylan. Copyright © 1962 Warner Bros. Inc. All Rights Reserved. Used by Permission.

A. P. WATT & SON: "Leda and the Swan," "Lapis Lazuli," "Easter 1916," "Sailing to Byzantium," "The Second Coming," and the first full draft of "The Second Coming" from *The Collected Poems of W. B. Yeats.* Reprinted by permission of M. B. Yeats, Miss Anne Yeats, and The Macmillan Co. of London & Basingstoke.

WESLEYAN UNIVERSITY PRESS: "Regret" by Vassar Miller. Copyright © 1963 by Vassar Miller. Reprinted from *My Bones Being Wiser* by permission of Wesleyan University Press.

YELLOW DOG MUSIC, INC.: "The Cinema Show" by Peter Gabriel, Phil Collins, Tony Banks, Mike Rutherford, and Steve Hackett (Genesis). Copyright © 1973 Notebest Ltd. and Carlin Music Corp. All Rights for The USA and Canada administered by Yellow Dog Music, Inc. All Rights Reserved. Used by permission.

PICTURE CREDITS

Innocence and Experience

Color opening, p. 2: Snake Charmer, 1853 by Henri Rousseau. Oil on canvas. Transparency courtesy of Giraudon, Paris.

Fiction, p. 6: The Mystery and Melancholy of a Street, 1914 by Giorgio de Chirico. Oil on canvas, 34¼ × 28⅛". Private Collection.

Poetry, p. 122: Adam and Eve by Hans Baldung Grien. Courtesy of The Metropolitan Museum of Art, Harris Brisbane Dick Fund, 1927.

Drama, p. 168: Seated Woman, 1884–85 by Georges-Pierre Seurat. Conte crayon, 18⅞ × 12⅜". Collection, The Museum of Modern Art, New York. Abby Aldrich Rockefeller Bequest.

Conformity and Rebellion

Color opening, p. 292: Quadrille at the Moulin Rouge, 1885 by Henri de Toulouse-Lautrec. Courtesy of the National Gallery of Art, Washington; Chester Dale Collection.

Fiction, p. 296: The Shriek (Geschrei), 1896 by Edvard Munch. Lithograph, printed in black, 13¹⁵/₁₆ × 10". Collection, The Museum of Modern Art, New York. Matthew T. Mellon Fund.

Poetry, p. 400: New York, 1953 by Franz Kline. Oil on canvas. Courtesy of the Albright-Knox Art Gallery, Buffalo, New York. Gift of Seymour H. Knox.

Drama, p. 442: El Grito (The Cry), 1967 by Juan Genoves. Oil on canvas. Collection Joseph Bernstein, Louisiana. Photograph courtesy of Marlborough Gallery, New York.

Love and Hate

Color opening, p. 532: La Vie, 1881 by Pablo Picasso. Oil on canvas. Courtesy of the Cleveland Museum of Art, Gift of Hanna Fund, 1945.

Fiction, p. 538: The Love of Jupiter and Semele, 1930 by Pablo Picasso. From Les Metamorphoses of Ovid. Albert Skira, Lausanne, 1931. Etching, Sheet: 12⅞ × 10⅛". Collection, The Museum of Modern Art, New York. Gift of James Thrall Soby.

Poetry, p. 610: The Return of the Prodigal Son, c. 1642 by Rembrandt van Rijn. Pen and wash in bistre with white gouache. Courtesy of Teylers Museum, Haarlem, Holland.

Drama, p. 654: Young Couple (Junges Paar), 1917 by Emil Nolde. Woodcut, printed in black, 12⅝ × 9¹/₁₆". Collection, The Museum of Modern Art, New York. Purchase.

The Presence of Death

Color opening, p. 842: Masks Confronting Death (Masques devant la Mort), 1888 by James Ensor, Oil on canvas, 32 × 39½". Collection, The Museum of Modern Art, New York. Mrs. Simon Guggenheim Fund.

Fiction, p. 846: Liberation of the Peon, 1931 by Diego Rivera. Fresco. Courtesy of the Philadelphia Museum of Art. Given by Mr. and Mrs. Herbert Cameron Morris.

Poetry, p. 934: Girl Held in the Lap of Death (Tod mit Mädchen im Schoss), 1934 by Käthe Kollwitz. Lithograph, printed in black, 14⅞ × 16¾". Collection, The Museum of Modern Art, New York. Purchase.

Drama, p. 984: "The Dance of Death" from The Seventh Seal, directed by Ingmar Bergman. Film Still, courtesy of The Museum of Modern Art/Film Stills Archive, New York.

Appendices:

Opening picture, p. 1082: Pastoral, 1945 by Pablo Picasso. Etching, Sheet 13 ¹/₁₆ × 18 ⁵/₁₆ ". Collection, The Museum of Modern Art, New York. Acquired through the Lillie P. Bliss Bequest.

pp. 1111–1112: The Globe Theatre, 1953; Interior of the Globe Theatre in the days of Shakespeare; and a French theater during Moliére's management: Courtesy of The Bettman Archive, Inc. Interior of the Swan Theatre, London, 1596: Courtesy of Culver Pictures. The Greek theater at Epidaurus: Courtesy of the Greek National Tourist Office.

Cover: The False Mirror (Le Faux Miroir), 1928 by René Magritte. Oil on canvas, 21¼ × 31⅞". Collection, The Museum of Modern Art, New York. Purchase.